# BRIGADES OF ANTIETAM

\*\*\*

## The Union and Confederate Brigades during the 1862 Maryland Campaign

Bradley M. Gottfried, editor

The Press of the

Antietam
INSTITUTE
18 62

# Contributors

Claire Affinito
Brian S. Baracz
Matthew Borders
Mac Bryan
James M. Buchanan
Lucas I. Cade
Jason Campbell
Thomas G. Clemens
Bradley M. Gottfried
Robert Gottschalk
Laura Marfut
Sharon A. Murray
Kevin R. Pawlak
Martin Pritchett
Gary W. Rohrer
James A Rosebrock
William Sagle
J. O. Smith
Joseph Stahl
Steven R. Stotelmyer

# CONTENTS

## Union Brigades

### I Corps (Hooker) 26

### II Corps (Sumner) 69

## Cavalry Division (Pleasonton) 211

# Confederate Brigades

## Longstreet's Wing 216

## Jackson's Wing 305

# PREFACE

This book actually began with the publication of my *Brigades of Gettysburg* book, which followed the activities of each infantry brigade from June 28 through the time it left the battlefield. The book was well-received, even though it added yet another title to the thousands already written on the topic.

After retirement, I became a Certified Antietam Battlefield Guide and my interest shifted to the Maryland Campaign. The idea of writing a sequel to the *Brigades of Gettysburg* book took shape soon after. One of the best things about being a guide is being surrounded by talented guides and rangers who know so much about the campaign. Why not ask them to contribute sections, I thought? Not only did it expedite completion of the book, it also provided an outlet for those who had never published before, but had a vast knowledge to share. Hence, the idea of the *Brigades of Antietam* was born.

It has truly been a joy working with such creative colleagues, although my constant questions to better clarify material may have become burdensome at times. In the end, I hope the reader finds this book informative and a worth-while reference.

This book avoided a pitfall of my original *Brigades of Gettysburg* book as it contains both infantry and cavalry units. James Rosebrock, who contributed to this volume, is preparing a subsequent volume (*Artillery Units of Antietam*) covering the artillery units during the Maryland Campaign.

I have added twenty maps from my *Maps of Antietam* book to help the reader get a better sense of the action.

I want to especially thank Christopher Vincent, President of the Antietam Institute for his support and encouragement. Eminent scholar, Thomas Clemens, not only contributed to this work, but also readily shared Ezra Carman's and John Gould's letters with all who requested them. Antietam Ranger, Stephanie Gray, also provided access to the park's library, which contains a rich repository of materials.

Kevin Pawlak, Civil War scholar and chair of the Antietam Institute's Publications Committee, provided encouragement and did a great job of preparing the manuscript for publication. My wife, Linda, did yeoman's service in formatting the book and creating its cover. Many reviewed sections of the manuscript, but I would be remiss if I did not mention those guides who went well above the call of duty: James Buchanan, Laura Marfut and J.O. Smith. A special thanks to Ed Marfut, who read the manuscript over several times and pointed out many errors I thought I had caught.

Finally, this is the first publication of the new Antietam Institute, which was formed in 2021 to encourage greater scholarship and interest in the Maryland Campaign. Please take some time to read more about the Institute on the back cover of this book.

Bradley M. Gottfried, editor
August, 2021

## A Note About Strengths and Losses

The strength listed for each brigade at the beginning of its entry is at the start of the campaign (September 2, 1862), and is based on Scott Hartwig's analysis in his *To Antietam Creek* (Appendix B). Losses at the beginning of each brigade entry are those sustained at the Battle of Antietam. Any exceptions will be noted.

# MAP 1: SEPTEMBER 4 – 5, 1862

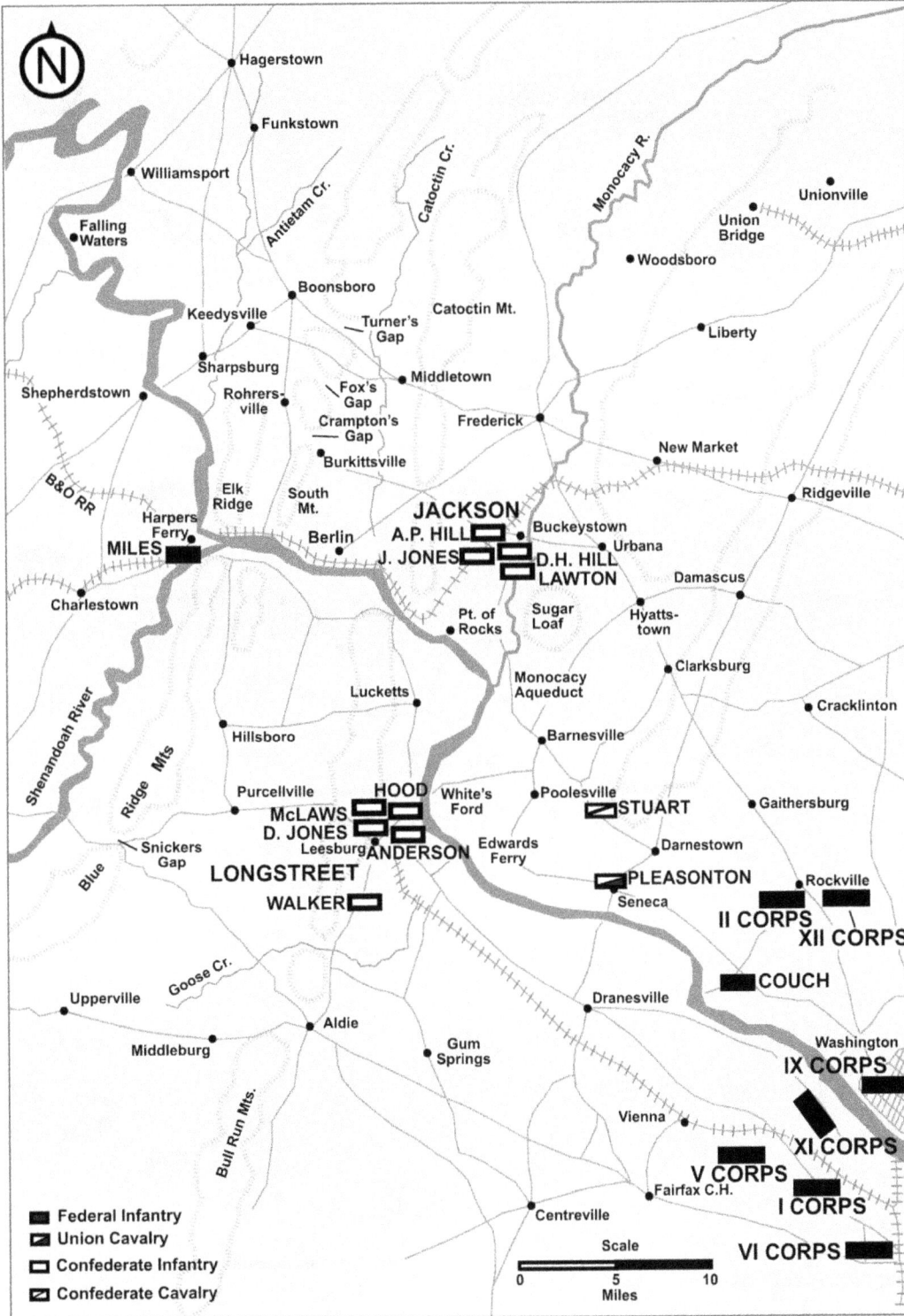

Hagerstown

Funkstown

Williamsport

Falling
Waters

Antietam Cr.

Catoctin Cr.

Monocacy R.

Unionville

Union
Bridge

Woodsboro

Boonsboro

Keedysville

Catoctin Mt.

Turner's
Gap

Liberty

Sharpsburg

Middletown

Shepherdstown

Rohrers-
ville

Fox's
Gap

Crampton's
Gap

Frederick

New Market

Burkittsville

B&O RR

Elk
Ridge

South
Mt.

JACKSON

Ridgeville

Harpers
Ferry

Berlin

A.P. HILL

J. JONES

Buckeystown

Urbana

D.H. HILL

LAWTON

MILES

Damascus

Charlestown

Pt. of
Rocks

Sugar
Loaf

Hyatts-
town

Clarksburg

Shenandoah River

Lucketts

Monocacy
Aqueduct

Cracklinton

Hillsboro

Barnesville

Ridge Mts

Purcellville

HOOD

White's
Ford

Poolesville

STUART

Gaithersburg

McLAWS

D. JONES

ANDERSON

Edwards
Ferry

Darnestown

Snickers
Gap

LONGSTREET

Leesburg

PLEASONTON

Rockville

WALKER

Seneca

II CORPS

Blue

XII CORPS

COUCH

Goose Cr.

Dranesville

Upperville

Washington

Middleburg

Aldie

Gum
Springs

IX CORPS

Bull Run Mts.

Vienna

XI CORPS

V CORPS

Fairfax C.H.

I CORPS

■ Federal Infantry

Centreville

Scale

◪ Union Cavalry

VI CORPS

□ Confederate Infantry

0          5          10

▨ Confederate Cavalry

Miles

6

# MAP 2: SEPTEMBER 11, 1862

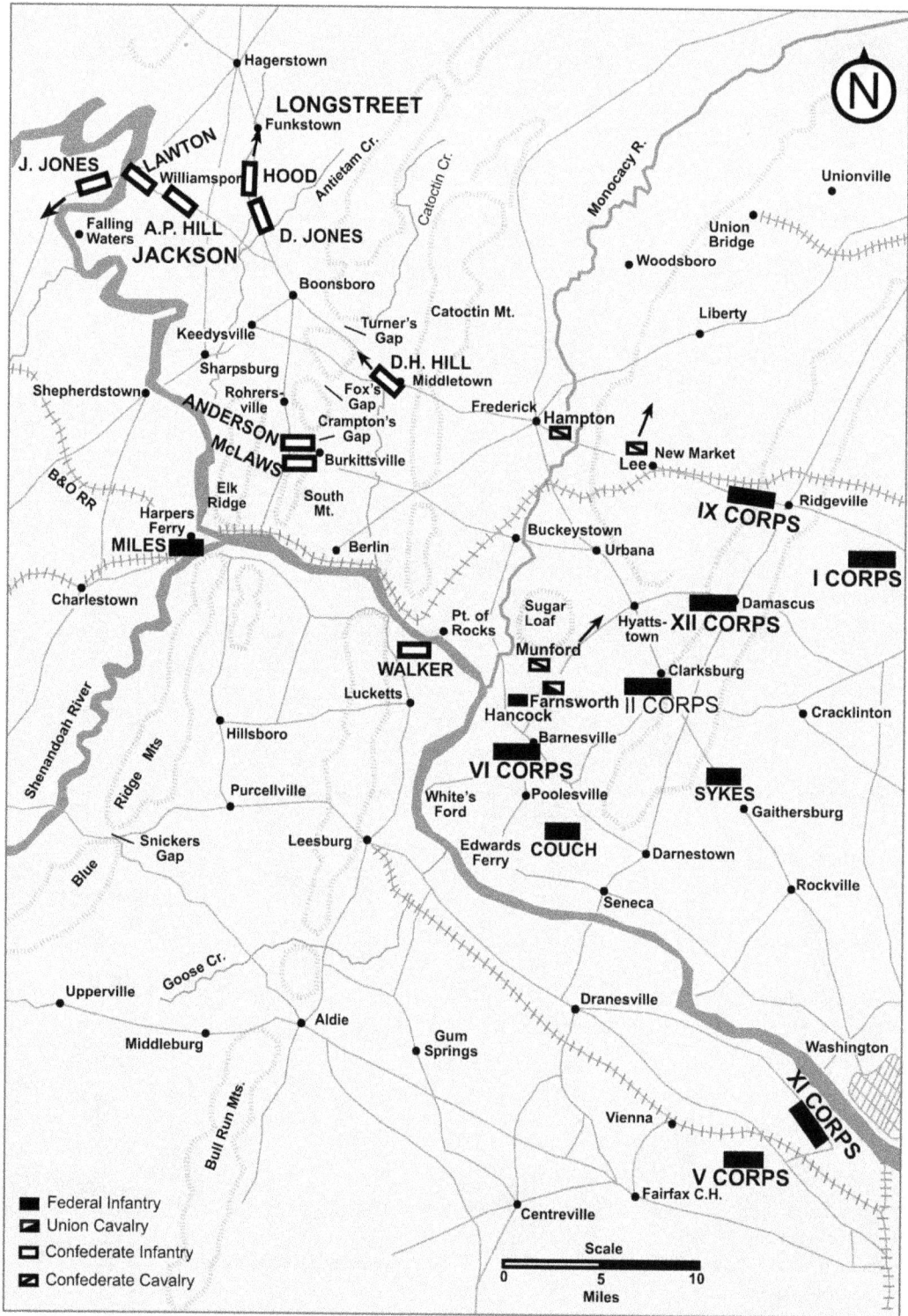

# MAP 3: SEPTEMBER 14, 1862 (MORNING)

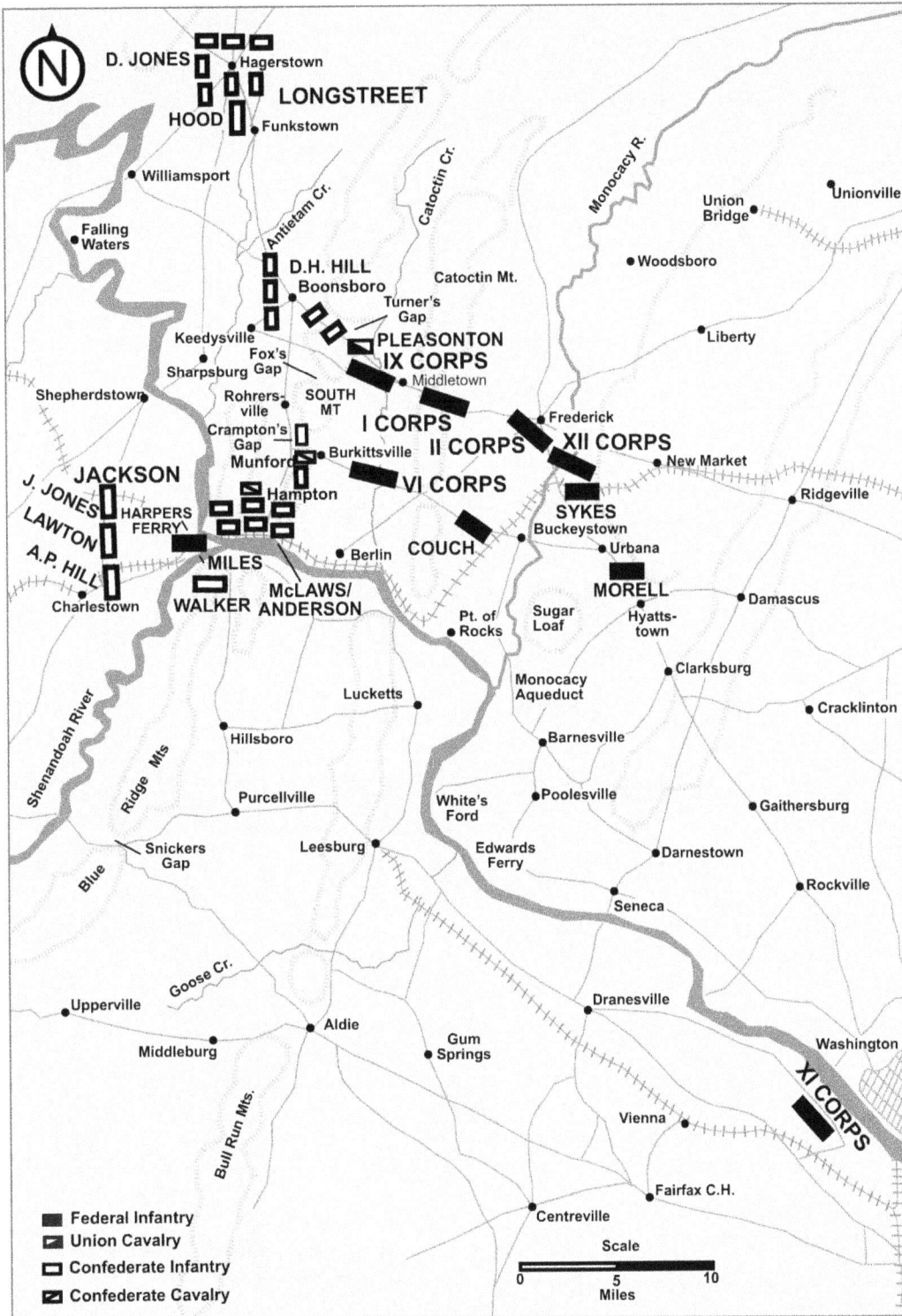

D. JONES
Hagerstown
LONGSTREET
HOOD
Funkstown

Williamsport

Falling
Waters

Antietam Cr.

Catoctin Cr.

Catoctin Mt.

Monocacy R.

Union
Bridge

Unionville

Woodsboro

Liberty

D.H. HILL
Boonsboro

Turner's
Gap

Keedysville
Fox's
Gap
Sharpsburg
Rohrers-
ville

Shepherdstown

SOUTH
MT

PLEASONTON
IX CORPS
Middletown

I CORPS
II CORPS

Frederick

XII CORPS

New Market

Ridgeville

Crampton's
Gap
Munford
Burkittsville

VI CORPS

SYKES
Buckeystown

JACKSON

J. JONES
LAWTON
HARPERS
FERRY
A.P. HILL
MILES
Charlestown
WALKER
McLAWS/
ANDERSON

Hampton

Berlin

COUCH

Urbana

MORELL

Damascus

Hyatts-
town

Pt. of
Rocks

Sugar
Loaf

Clarksburg

Cracklinton

Shenandoah River

Lucketts

Monocacy
Aqueduct

Barnesville

Hillsboro

Ridge Mts

Purcellville

White's
Ford

Poolesville

Gaithersburg

Snickers
Gap

Leesburg

Edwards
Ferry

Darnestown

Rockville

Blue

Seneca

Goose Cr.

Upperville

Aldie

Dranesville

Washington

Middleburg

Gum
Springs

Bull Run Mts.

Vienna

XI CORPS

Fairfax C.H.

Centreville

Scale

■ Federal Infantry
◣ Union Cavalry
□ Confederate Infantry
◩ Confederate Cavalry

0        5        10
Miles

8

# MAP 4: FOX'S GAP (SEPTEMBER 14, 1862): 11:00 -11:30 a.m.

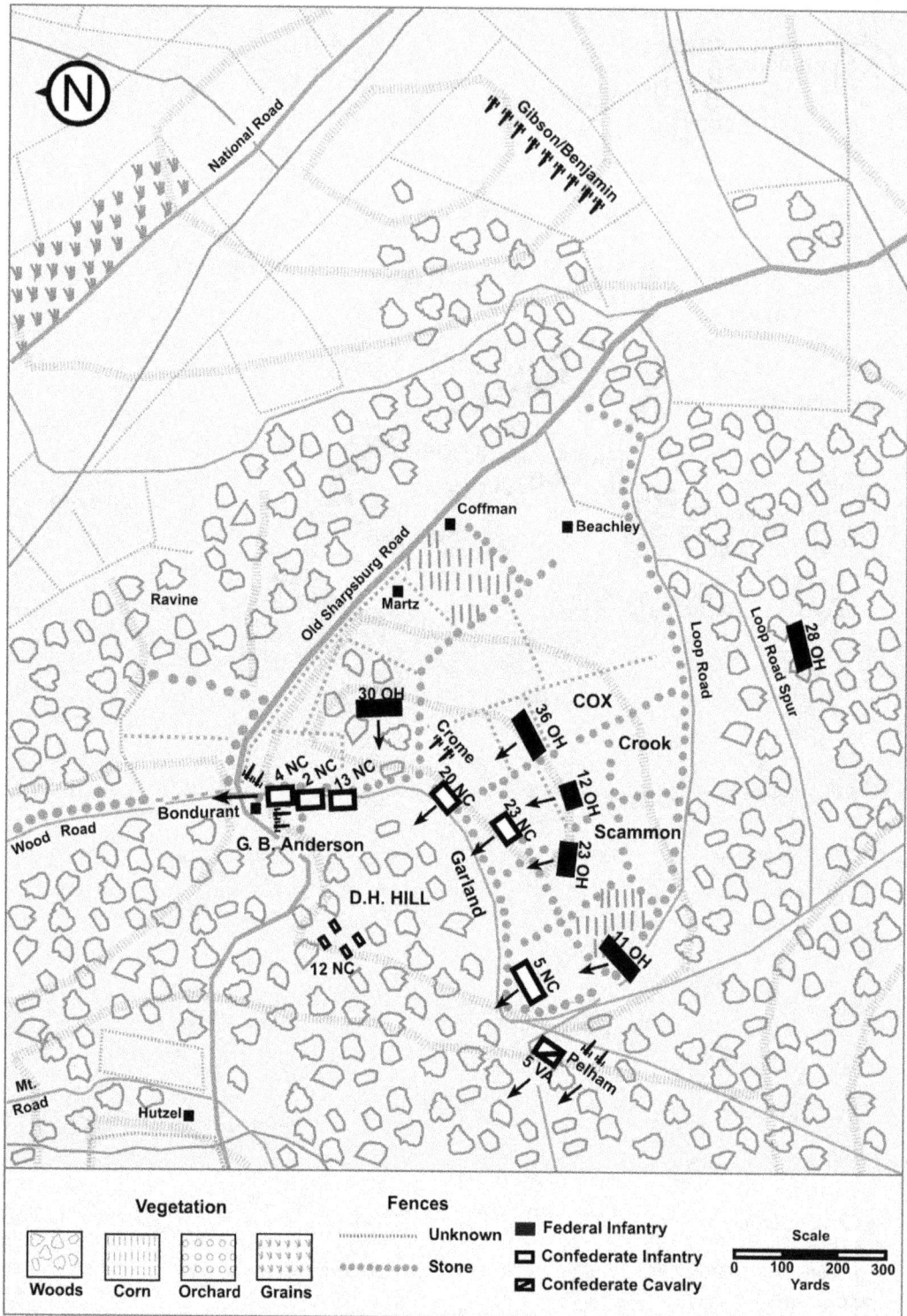

National Road

Gibson/Benjamin

Coffman

Beachley

Ravine

Old Sharpsburg Road

Martz

28 OH

Loop Road

Loop Road Spur

30 OH

COX

36 OH

Crook

Crome

4 NC  2 NC  13 NC

20 NC

12 OH

Bondurant

23 NC

Scammon

Wood  Road

23 OH

G. B. Anderson

Garland

D.H. HILL

12 NC

11 OH

5 NC

Mt.
Road

Pelham

5 VA

Hutzel

## Vegetation

| Woods | Corn | Orchard | Grains |

## Fences

............... Unknown

●●●●●●●● Stone

■ Federal Infantry

□ Confederate Infantry

▨ Confederate Cavalry

Scale

0    100    200    300
Yards

# MAP 5: FOX'S GAP (SEPTEMBER 14, 1862): 6:30 – 7:15 p.m.

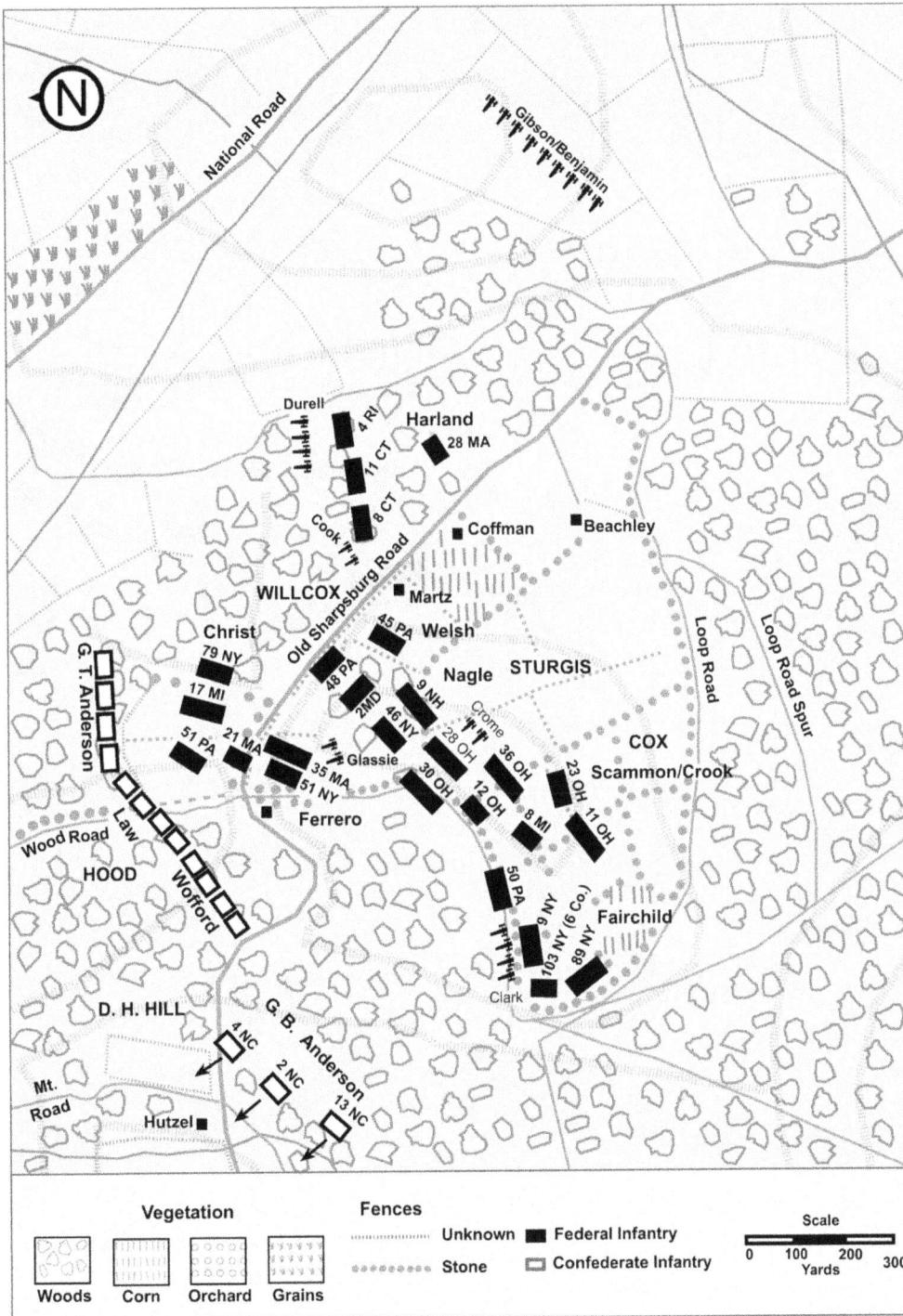

Gibson/Benjamin

National Road

N

Durell

4 RI

Harland

28 MA

11 CT

8 CT

Coffman

Beachley

Cook

WILLCOX

Martz

Old Sharpsburg Road

Christ

45 PA

Welsh

79 NY

48 PA

Nagle

STURGIS

17 MI

2 MD

9 NH

Crome

G. T. Anderson

51 PA

21 MA

46 NY

28 OH

36 OH

COX

35 MA

Glassie

30 OH

12 OH

23 OH

Scammon/Crook

51 NY

8 MI

11 OH

Ferrero

Wood Road

Law

Wofford

50 PA

Loop Road

Loop Road Spur

HOOD

103 NY

69 NY (6 Co.)

Fairchild

Clark

D. H. HILL

G. B. Anderson

4 NC

Mt.

Road

2 NC

Hutzel

13 NC

| Vegetation | | | | Fences | | |
|---|---|---|---|---|---|---|
| Woods | Corn | Orchard | Grains | Unknown | ■ Federal Infantry | |
| | | | | Stone | ☐ Confederate Infantry | |

Scale

0   100   200   300

Yards

10

# MAP 6: FROSTTOWN PLATEAU (SEPTEMBER 14, 1862): 7:00 -9:00 p.m.

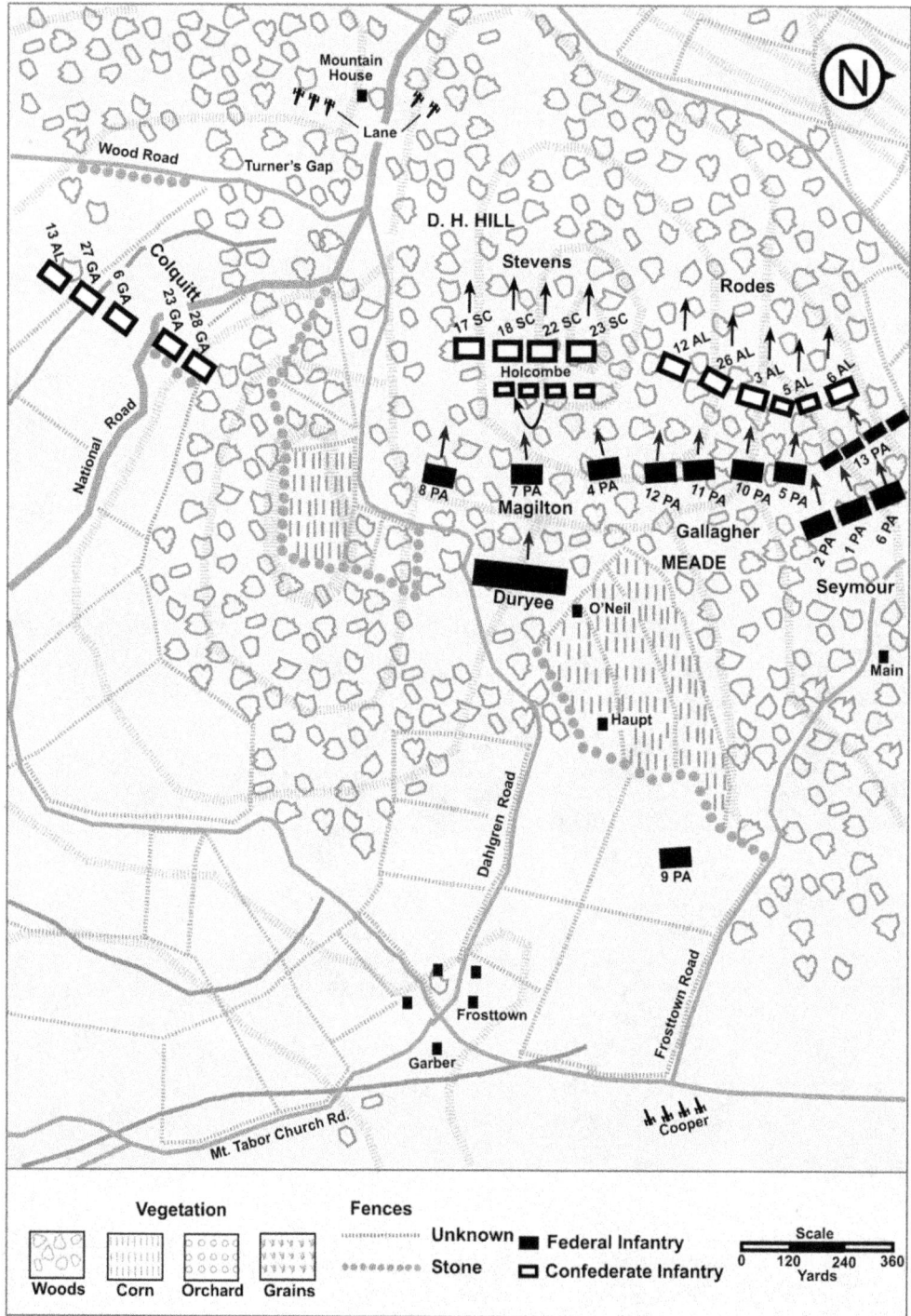

# MAP 7: CRAMPTON'S GAP (SEPTEMBER 14, 1862): 5:30 - 5:45 p.m.

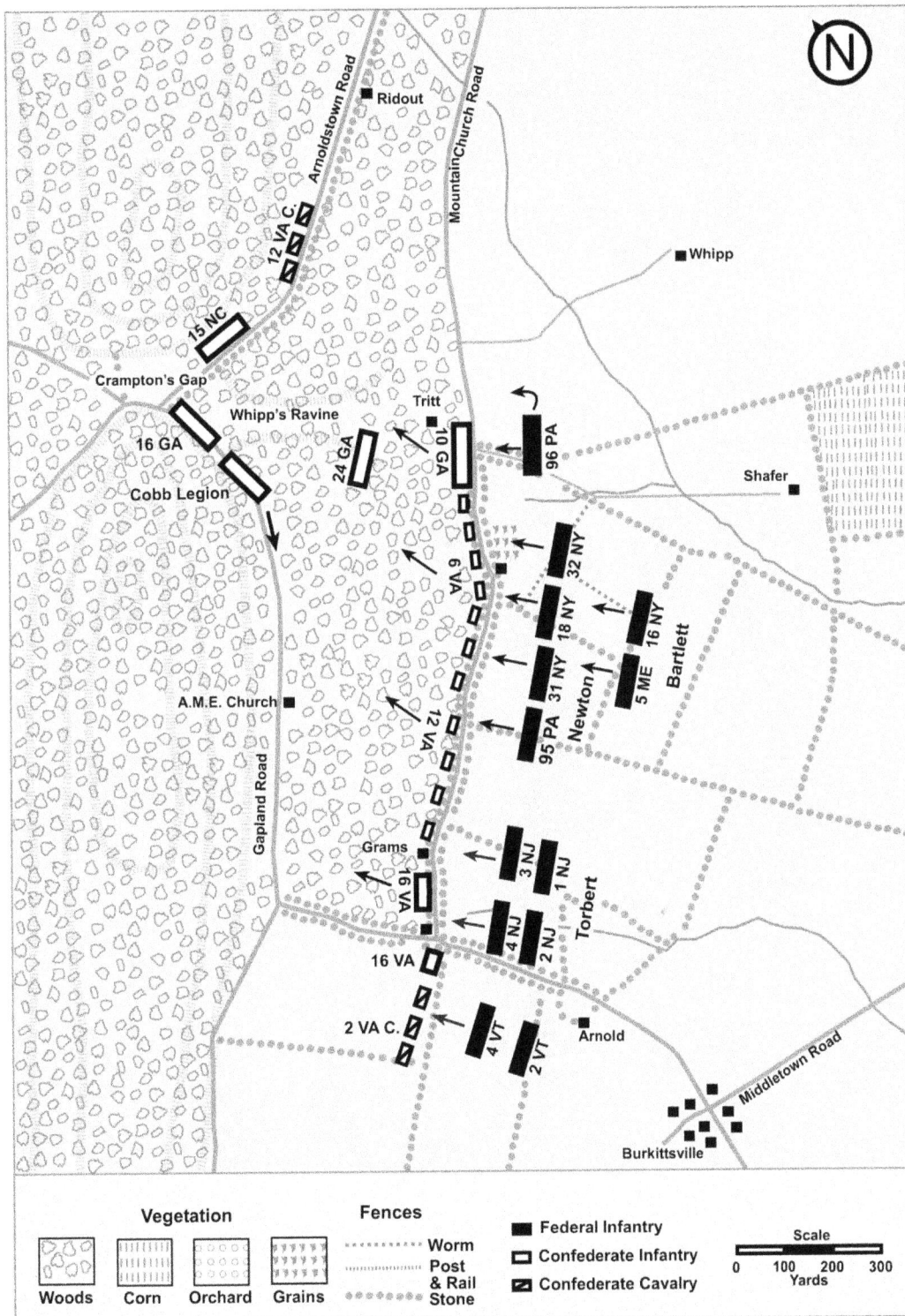

Arnoldstown Road

Mountain Church Road

Ridout

Whipp

N

12 VA C.

15 NC

Crampton's Gap

Whipp's Ravine

Tritt

96 PA

10 GA

16 GA

24 GA

Shafer

Cobb Legion

6 VA

32 NY

18 NY

16 NY

Bartlett

Gapland Road

31 NY

5 ME

Newton

95 PA

A.M.E. Church

12 VA

Grams

3 NJ

1 NJ

16 VA

Torbert

4 NJ

2 NJ

16 VA

Arnold

2 VA C.

4 VT

2 VT

Middletown Road

Burkittsville

### Vegetation

Woods    Corn    Orchard    Grains

### Fences

· · · · · Worm
Post
& Rail
Stone

■ Federal Infantry
□ Confederate Infantry
▨ Confederate Cavalry

### Scale

0    100    200    300
Yards

12

# MAP 8: CRAMPTON'S GAP (SEPTEMBER 14, 1862): 6:00 p.m.

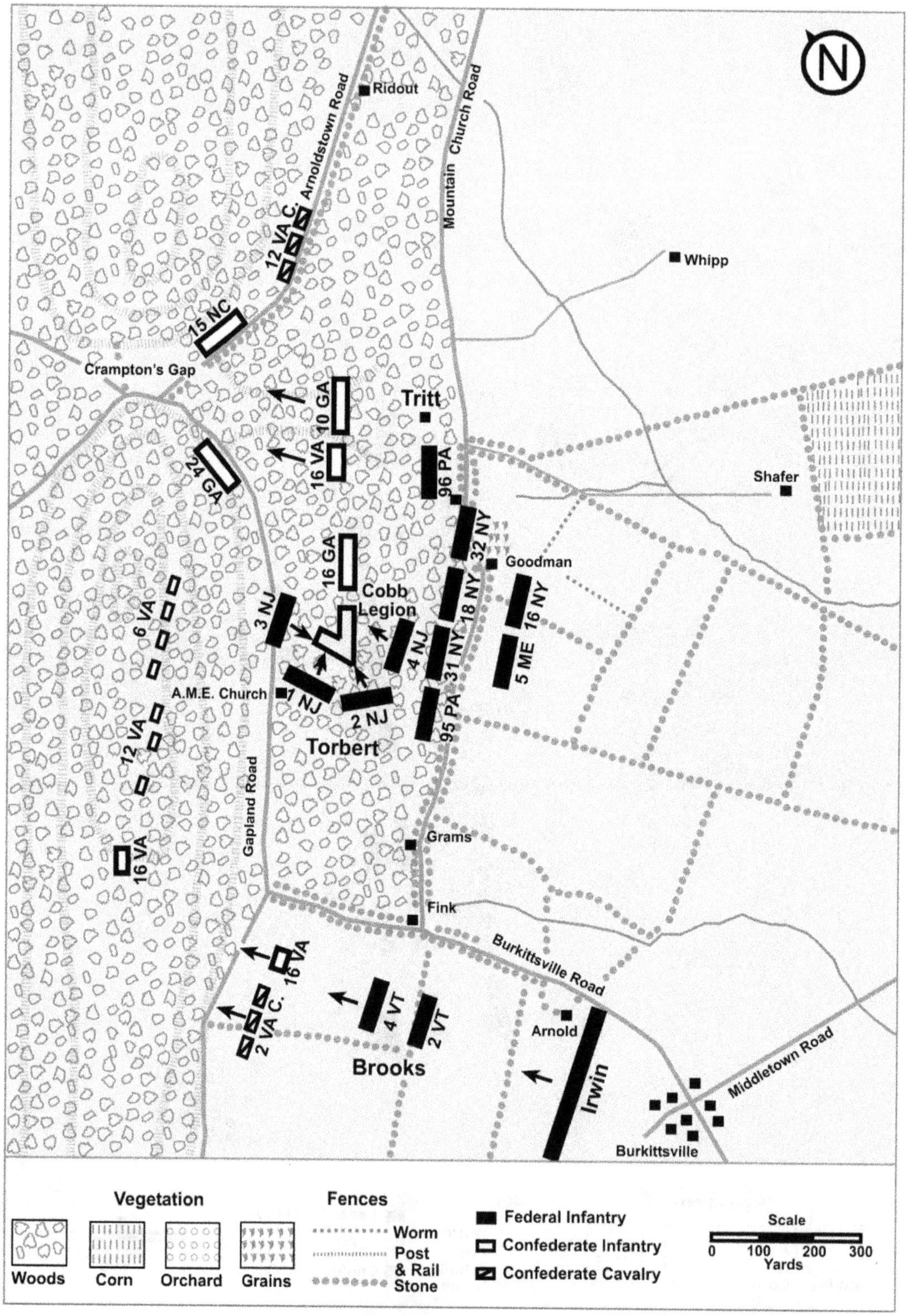

Ridout

Whipp

Arnoldstown Road

Mountain Church Road

12 VA C.

15 NC

Crampton's Gap

16 VA 10 GA

Tritt

96 PA

24 GA

16 GA

32 NY

Goodman

Shafer

6 VA

3 NJ

Cobb Legion

18 NY

16 NY

A.M.E. Church

4 NJ

31 NY

5 ME

12 VA

1 NJ

2 NJ

95 PA

Torbert

Gapland Road

Grams

16 VA

Fink

Burkittsville Road

2 VA C. 16 VA

4 VT

2 VT

Arnold

Middletown Road

Brooks

Irwin

Burkittsville

| Vegetation | | | | Fences | Federal Infantry | Scale |
|---|---|---|---|---|---|---|
| Woods | Corn | Orchard | Grains | Worm ·········· | Confederate Infantry | 0  100  200  300 |
| | | | | Post & Rail ········· | Confederate Cavalry | Yards |
| | | | | Stone ●●●●●●●● | | |

13

# MAP 9: HARPERS FERRY (SEPTEMBER 15, 1862)

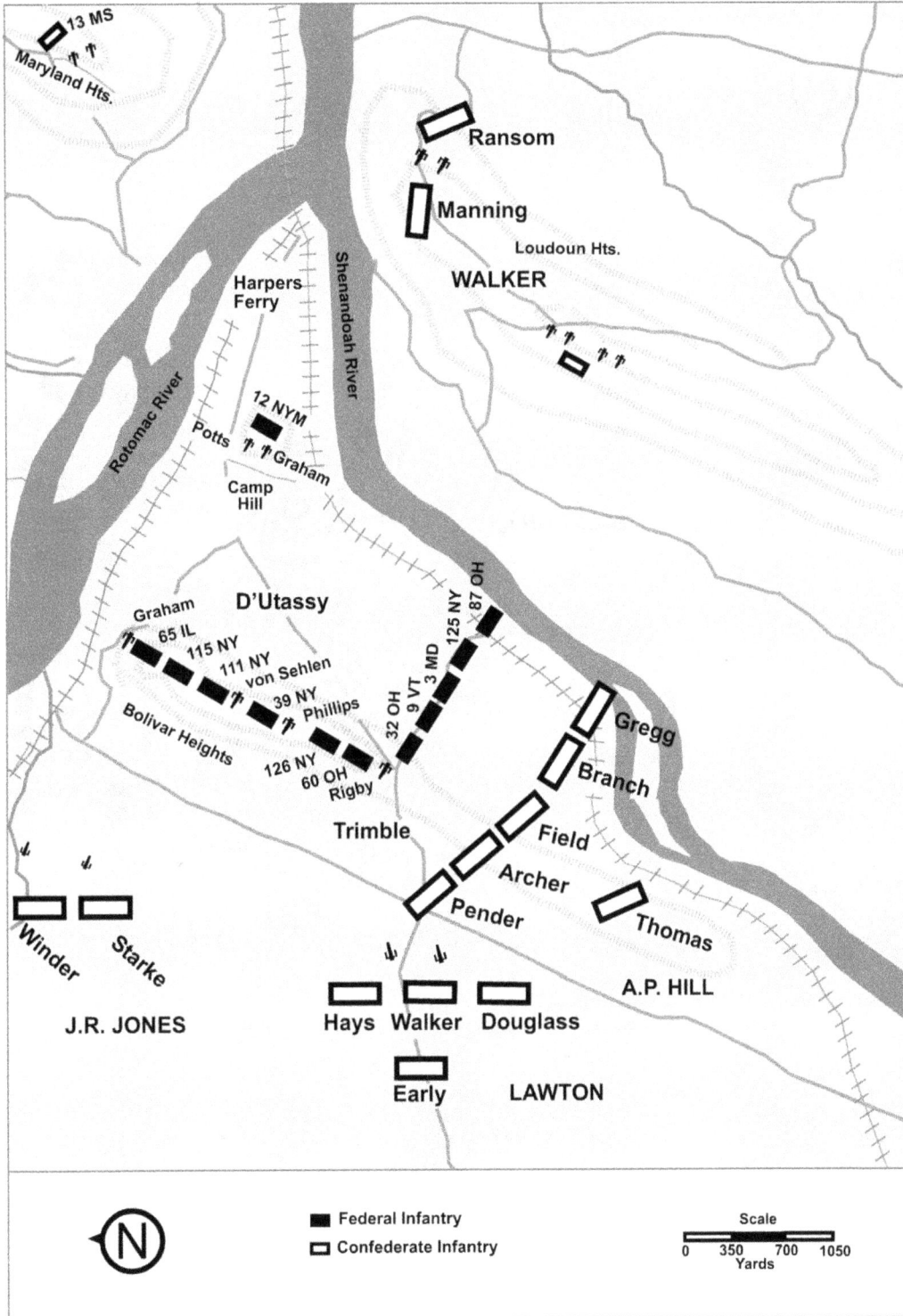

13 MS

Maryland Hts.

Ransom

Manning

Loudoun Hts.

WALKER

Potomac River

Shenandoah River

Harpers Ferry

12 NYM

Potts Graham

Camp Hill

D'Utassy

87 OH

125 NY

Graham

65 IL

115 NY

111 NY von Sehlen

3 MD

39 NY Phillips

9 VT

32 OH

Bolivar Heights

126 NY

60 OH Rigby

Gregg

Branch

Field

Archer

Pender

Thomas

A.P. HILL

Trimble

Winder Starke

J.R. JONES

Hays Walker Douglass

Early LAWTON

N

■ Federal Infantry
□ Confederate Infantry

Scale

0    350    700    1050
Yards

14

# MAP 10: ANTIETAM (SEPTEMBER 16, 1862): Noon – 4:00 p.m.

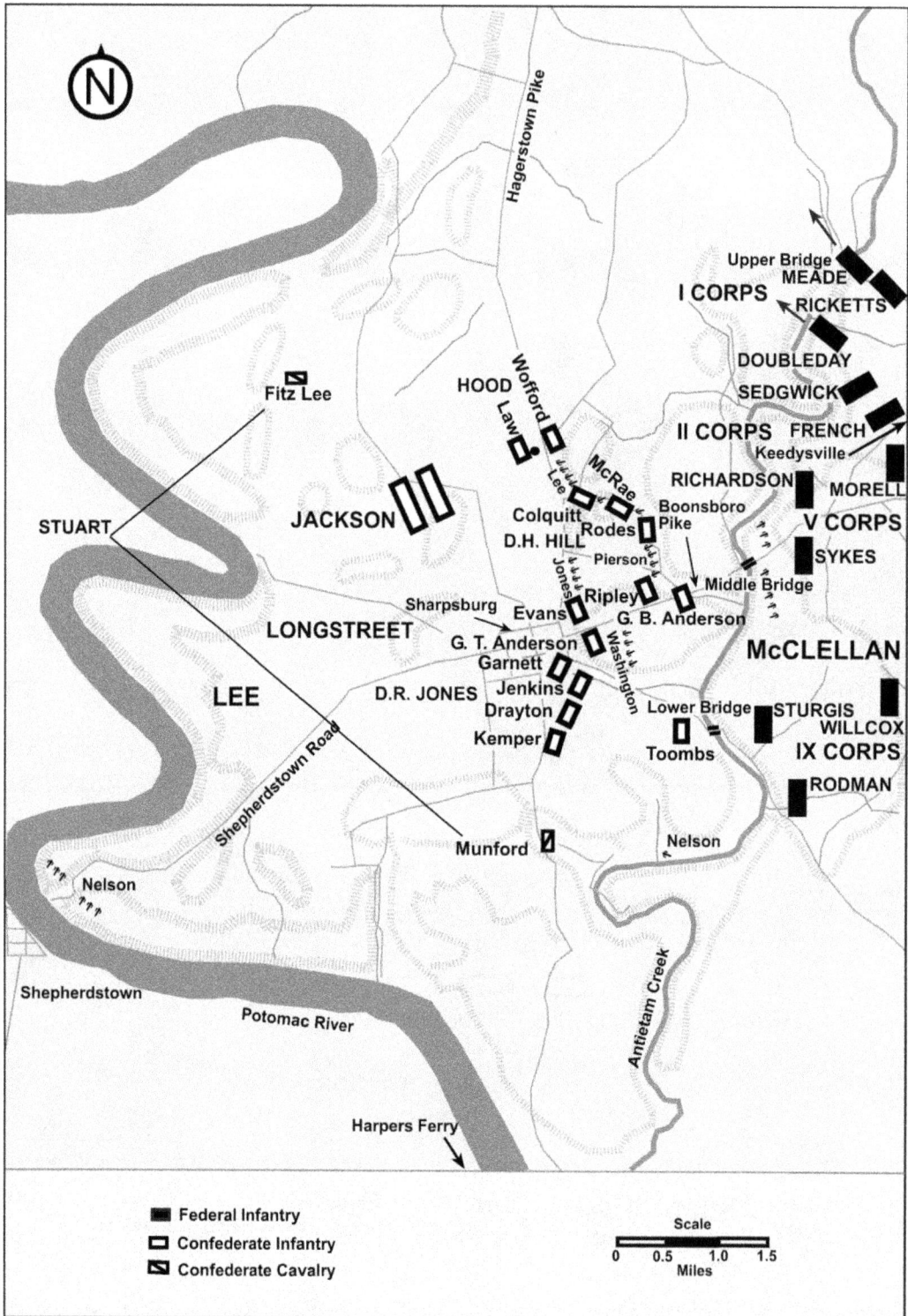

N

Hagerstown Pike

Upper Bridge
MEADE
I CORPS
RICKETTS

DOUBLEDAY
SEDGWICK
II CORPS
FRENCH
Keedysville

Fitz Lee

Wofford
HOOD
Law

Lee
McRae
RICHARDSON
MORELL

JACKSON
Colquitt
Rodes
D.H. HILL
Boonsboro
Pike
V CORPS
SYKES

Jones
Pierson
Middle Bridge

STUART
Sharpsburg
Evans
Ripley
G. B. Anderson

LONGSTREET
G. T. Anderson
Garnett
Washington
McCLELLAN

LEE
D.R. JONES
Jenkins
Drayton
Lower Bridge
STURGIS
WILLCOX

Kemper
Toombs
IX CORPS

Shepherdstown Road
Munford
Nelson
RODMAN

Nelson

Shepherdstown

Potomac River

Antietam Creek

Harpers Ferry

■ Federal Infantry
□ Confederate Infantry
◩ Confederate Cavalry

Scale
0    0.5    1.0    1.5
Miles

15

# MAP 11: ANTIETAM (SEPTEMBER 17, 1862): 6:15 – 7:00 a.m.

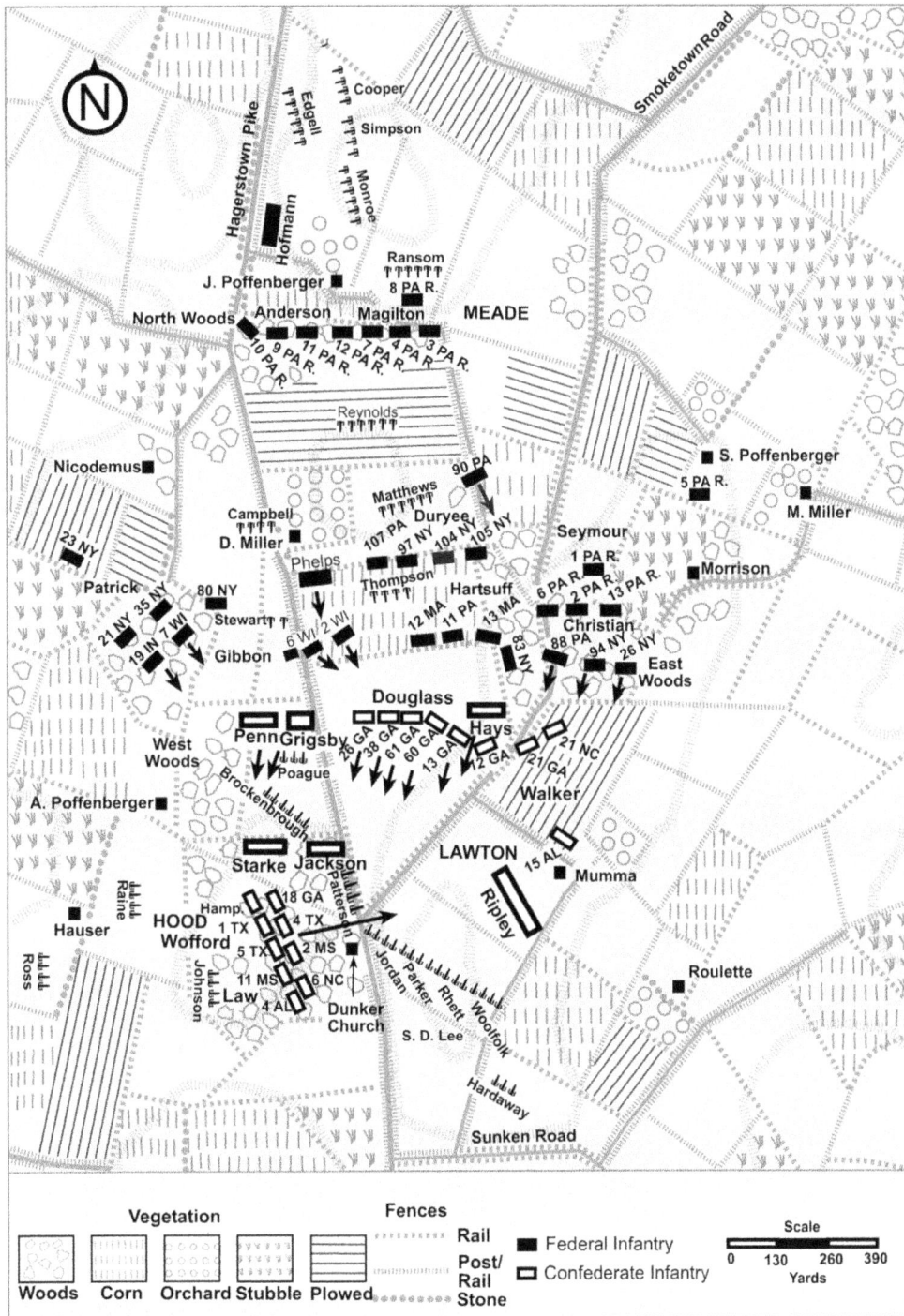

Vegetation: Woods, Corn, Orchard, Stubble, Plowed

Fences: Rail, Post/Rail, Stone

■ Federal Infantry
□ Confederate Infantry

Scale
0    130    260    390
Yards

# MAP 12: ANTIETAM (SEPTEMBER 17, 1862): 6:45 – 7:15 a.m.

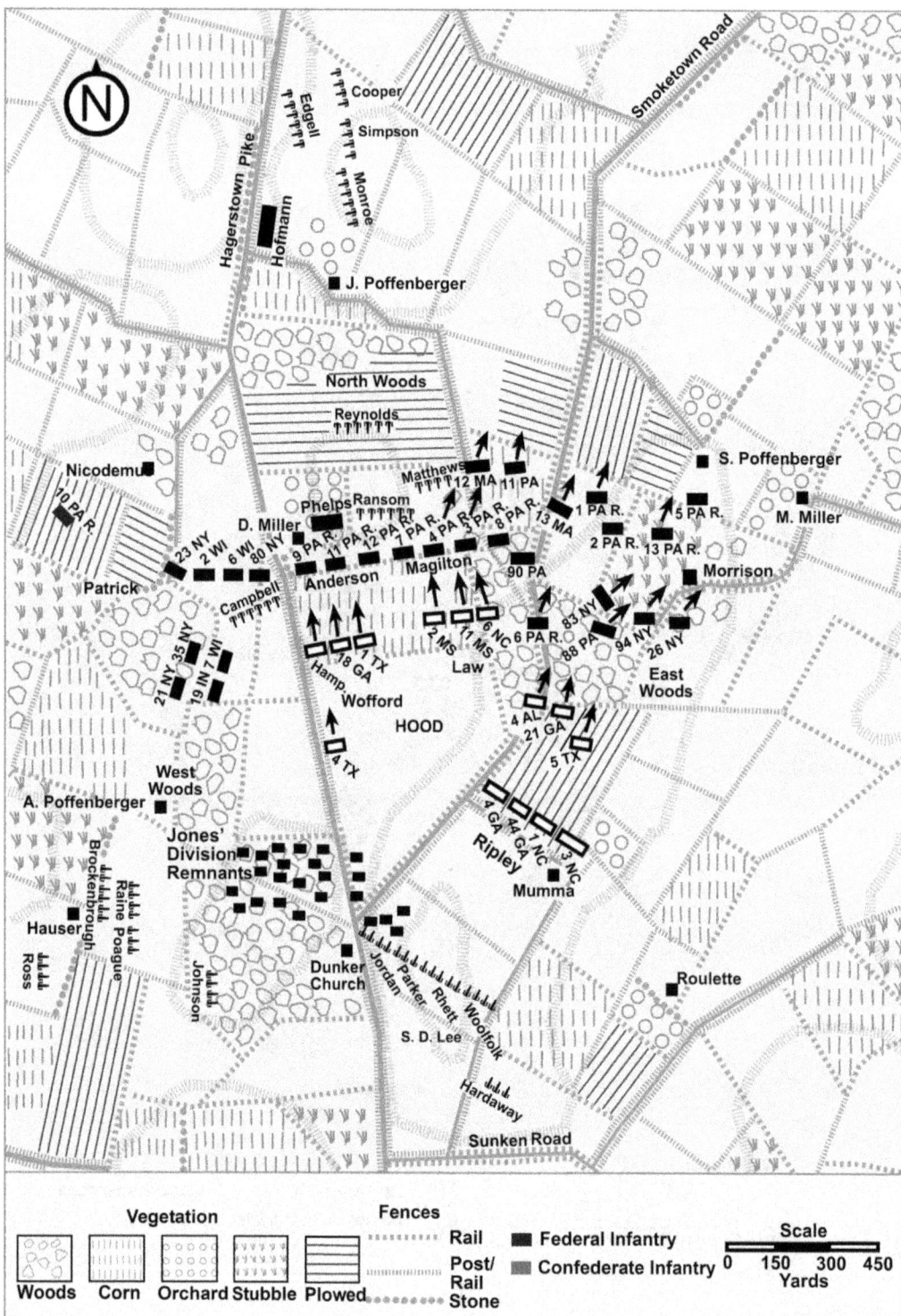

Vegetation

Woods  Corn  Orchard  Stubble  Plowed

Fences
Rail
Post/Rail
Stone

Federal Infantry
Confederate Infantry

Scale
0  150  300  450
Yards

# MAP 13: ANTIETAM (SEPTEMBER 17, 1862): 7:15 – 7:45 a.m.

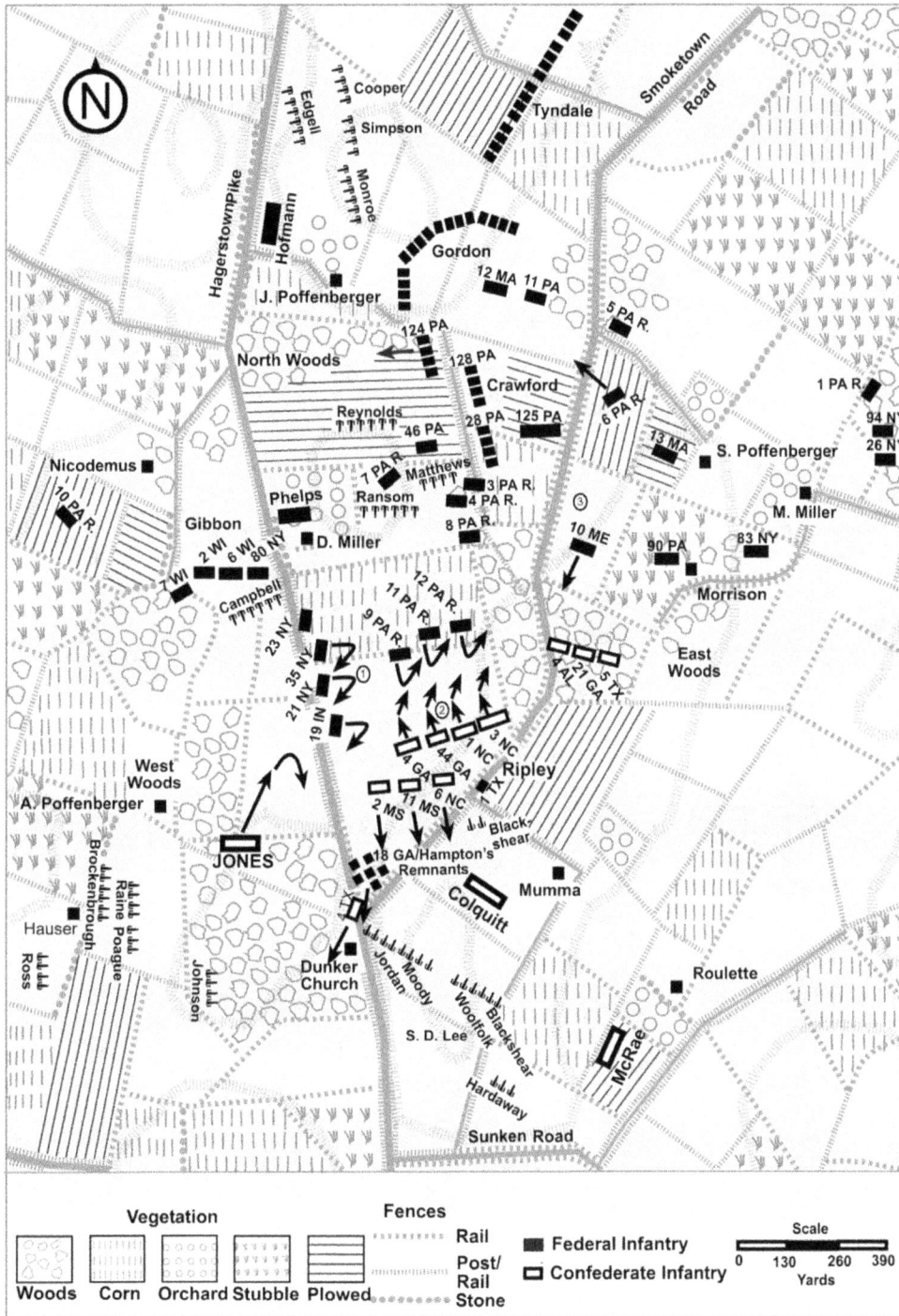

Cooper
Edgell
Simpson
Monroe
Tyndale
Smoketown Road

Hofmann
Gordon
12 MA  11 PA
J. Poffenberger
5 PA R.

124 PA
North Woods
128 PA
Crawford
1 PA R
Reynolds
46 PA
28 PA  125 PA
6 PA R
13 MA
94 NY
S. Poffenberger
26 NY

Nicodemus
7 PA R
Matthews
3 PA R.
4 PA R.
M. Miller
Phelps
Ransom
8 PA R.
10 ME
Gibbon
10 PA R.
2 WI  6 WI  80 NY
D. Miller
90 PA
83 NY
7 WI
Campbell
Morrison
23 NY
12 PA R.
11 PA R.
9 PA R.
5 TX
21 GA
35 NY
21 IN
19 IN
East Woods
3 NC
West Woods
4 GA  44 GA
1 NC  6 NC
Ripley
A. Poffenberger
2 MS  11 MS
1 TX
Black-shear
JONES
18 GA/Hampton's Remnants
Colquitt
Mumma
Hauser
Ross
Johnson
Raine Poague
Brockenbrough
Dunker Church
Jordan  Moody  Wooffolk
Blackshear
Roulette
S. D. Lee
McRae
Hardaway
Sunken Road

## Vegetation

| Woods | Corn | Orchard | Stubble | Plowed |

## Fences
Rail
Post/Rail
Stone

■ Federal Infantry
□ Confederate Infantry

## Scale
0   130   260   390
Yards

# MAP 14: ANTIETAM (SEPTEMBER 17, 1862): 8:15 – 8:45 a.m.

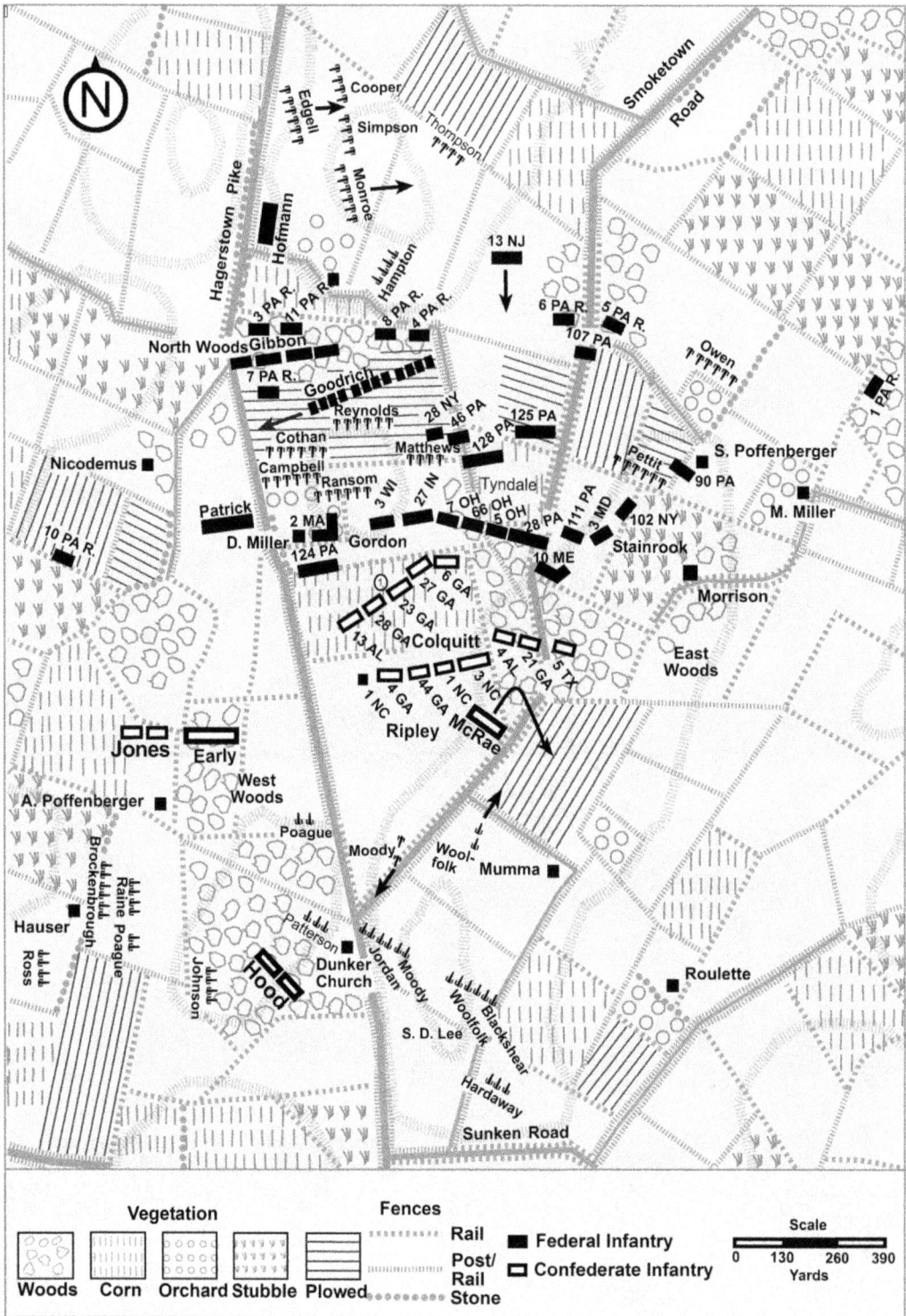

Edgell
Cooper
Simpson
Monroe
Thompson
Smoketown Road
Hofmann
13 NJ
Hampton
Hagerstown Pike
3 PA R.
11 PA R.
8 PA R.
4 PA R.
6 PA R.
5 PA R.
107 PA
Owen
North Woods
Gibbon
1 PA R.
7 PA R.
Goodrich
Reynolds
28 NY
46 PA
125 PA
Pettit
S. Poffenberger
Cothan
90 PA
Nicodemus
Matthews
128 PA
Campbell
Ransom
3 WI
27 IN
Tyndale
111 PA
3 MD
M. Miller
Patrick
7 OH
66 OH
5 OH
28 PA
102 NY
Stainrook
2 MA
D. Miller
124 PA
Gordon
10 ME
10 PA R.
6 GA
27 GA
Morrison
23 GA
28 GA
Colquitt
East Woods
13 AL
4 AL
21 GA
5 TX
4 GA
44 GA
1 NC
3 NC
1 NC
Ripley
McRae
Jones
Early
A. Poffenberger
West Woods
Poague
Moody
Wool-folk
Mumma
Hauser
Raine Poague
Brockenbrough
Patterson
Jordan
Moody
Roulette
Ross
Johnson
Hood
Dunker Church
Woolfolk
Blackshear
S. D. Lee
Hardaway
Sunken Road

| Vegetation | | | | | Fences | | Federal Infantry |
|---|---|---|---|---|---|---|---|
| Woods | Corn | Orchard | Stubble | Plowed | Rail | Post/Rail | Confederate Infantry |
| | | | | | | Stone | |

Scale
0   130   260   390
Yards

19

# MAP 15: ANTIETAM (SEPTEMBER 17, 1862): 8:45 – 9:15 a.m.

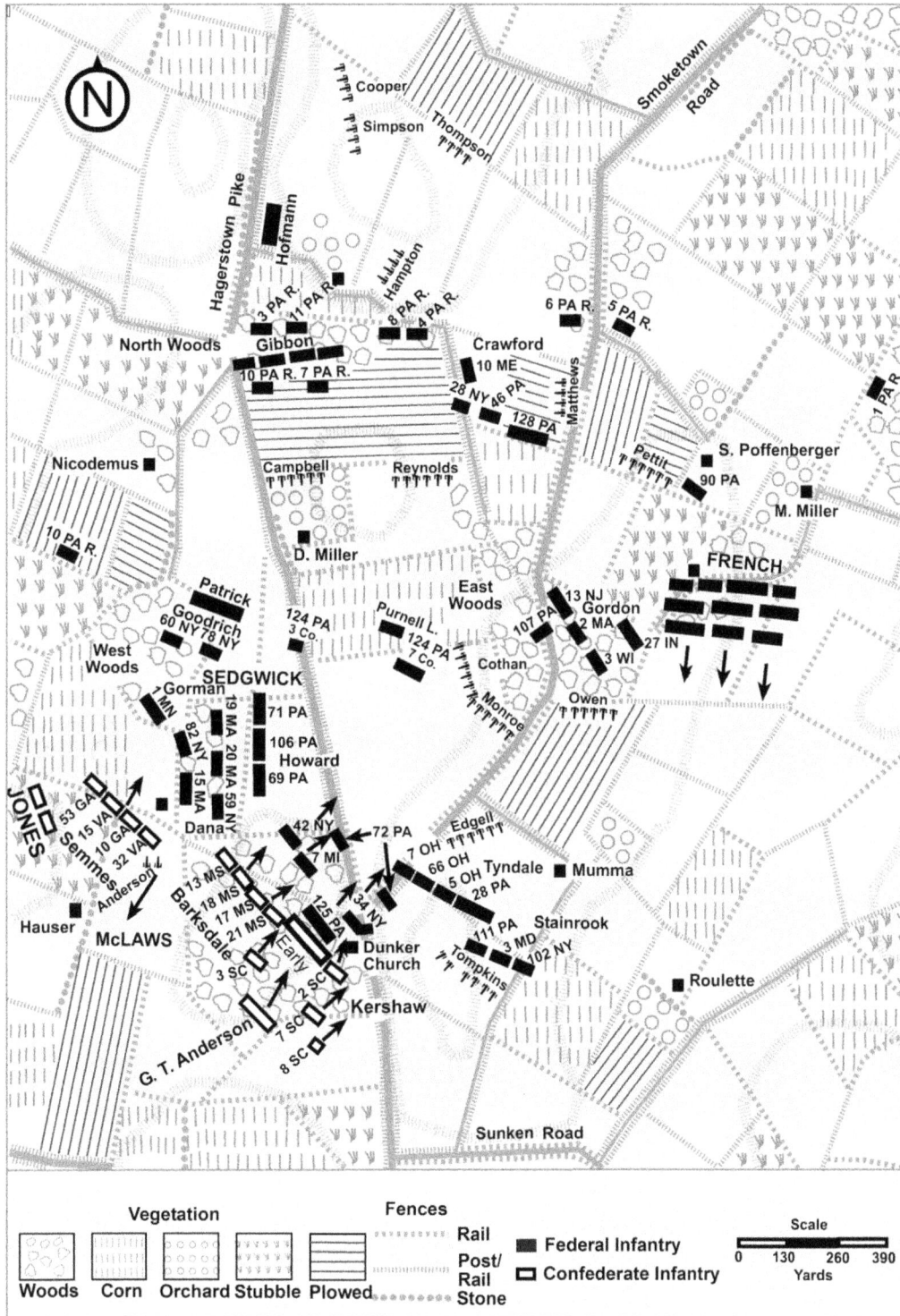

Cooper

Simpson

Thompson

Smoketown Road

Hagerstown Pike

Hofmann

3 PA R. 11 PA R.

8 PA R. 4 PA R.

Hampton

6 PA R. 5 PA R.

North Woods

Gibbon

Crawford

10 ME

1 PA R.

10 PA R. 7 PA R.

28 NY 46 PA

Matthews

128 PA

Nicodemus

S. Poffenberger

Campbell

Reynolds

Pettit

90 PA

M. Miller

10 PA R.

D. Miller

East Woods

FRENCH

Patrick

124 PA

Purnell L.

107 PA

13 NJ Gordon

Goodrich

3 Co.

124 PA

2 MA

60 NY 78 NY

7 Co.

Cothan

3 WI

27 IN

West Woods

SEDGWICK

Gorman

1 MN

19 MA

71 PA

Monroe

Owen

JONES

82 NY 20 MA 59 NY

106 PA

15 MA

Howard

69 PA

53 GA

5 VA 10 GA

Dana

42 NY

72 PA

Edgell

32 VA

7 MI

7 OH

Semmes

Anderson

66 OH

Tyndale

Mumma

13 MS

5 OH

125 PA

34 NY

28 PA

Hauser

Barksdale

18 MS

17 MS

Dunker Church

Stainrook

McLAWS

21 MS

Early

111 PA

3 MD

3 SC

2 SC

Tompkins

102 NY

Kershaw

Roulette

G. T. Anderson

7 SC

8 SC

Sunken Road

## Vegetation

Woods  Corn  Orchard  Stubble  Plowed

## Fences

Rail

Post/ Rail

Stone

■ Federal Infantry

□ Confederate Infantry

## Scale

0   130   260   390

Yards

20

# MAP 16: ANTIETAM (SEPTEMBER 17, 1862): 10:00 – 10:30 a.m.

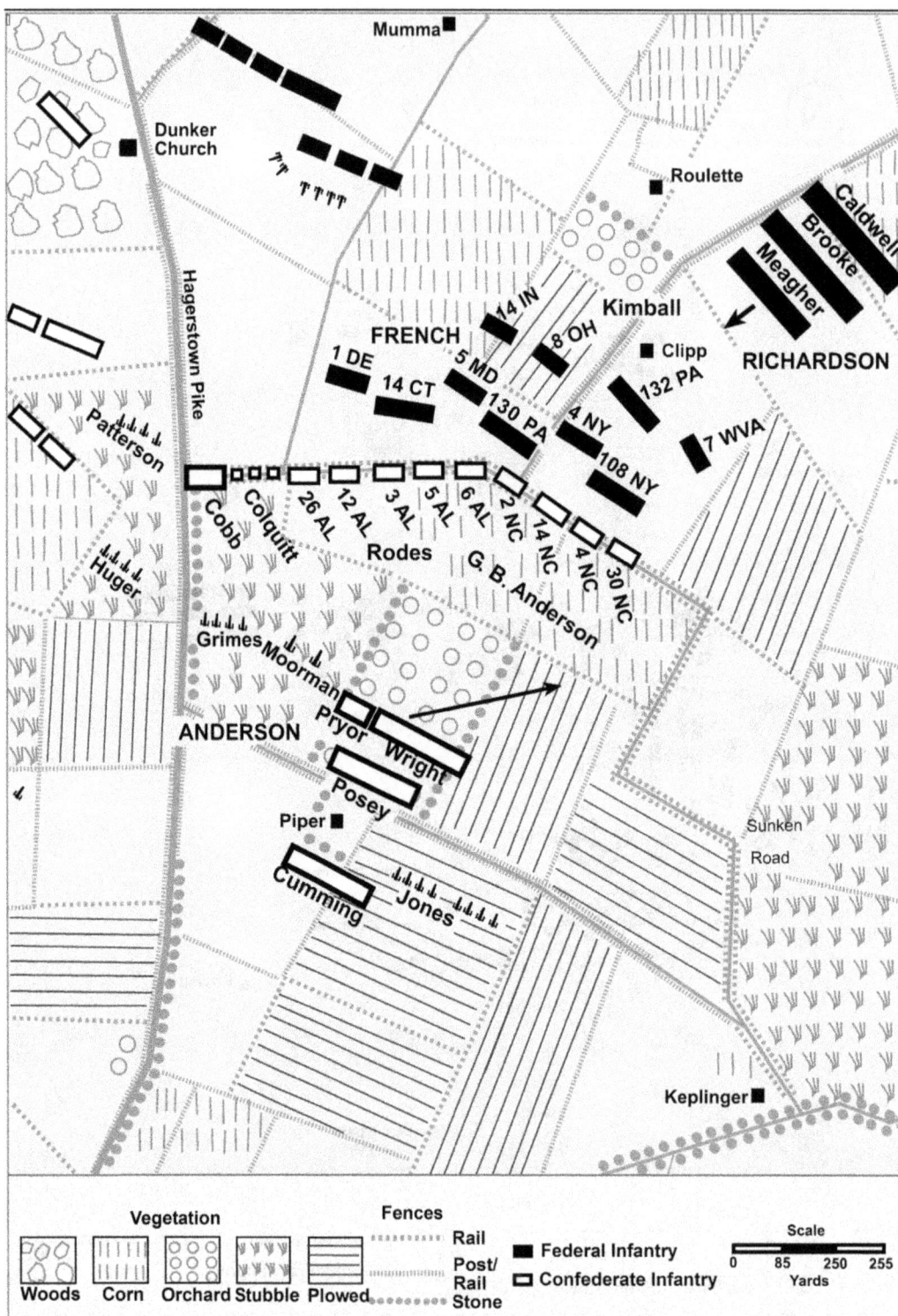

Mumma

Dunker
Church

Roulette

Caldwell
Brooke
Meagher
RICHARDSON

14 IN
Kimball

FRENCH
8 OH
Clipp

1 DE
5 MD
132 PA

14 CT
130 PA
4 NY
108 NY
7 WVA

Hagerstown Pike

Patterson

Cobb
Colquitt
26 AL
12 AL
3 AL
5 AL
6 AL
2 NC
14 NC
4 NC
30 NC
Rodes
G. B. Anderson

Huger

Grimes
Moorman

ANDERSON
Pryor
Wright
Posey

Piper

Sunken

Road

Cumming
Jones

Keplinger

## Vegetation

## Fences

Woods  Corn  Orchard  Stubble  Plowed

Rail
Post/
Rail
Stone

■ Federal Infantry
□ Confederate Infantry

Scale

0    85    250   255
Yards

21

# MAP 17: ANTIETAM (SEPTEMBER 17, 1862): 9:00 – 9:30 a.m.

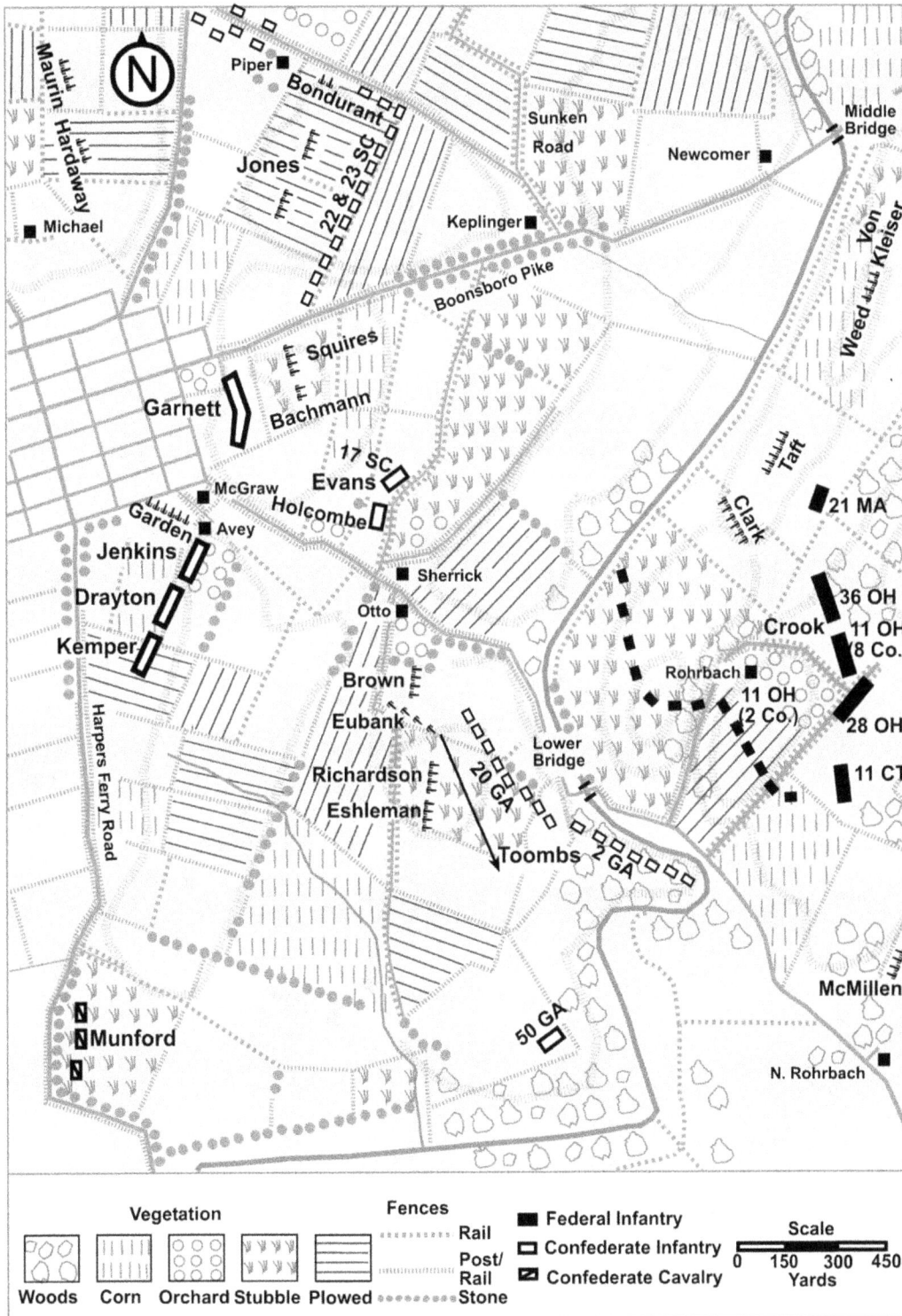

Maurin
Hardaway

Piper

Bondurant

Jones

22 & 23 SC

Michael

Sunken
Road

Newcomer

Middle
Bridge

Keplinger

Boonsboro Pike

Von Kleiser

Weed

Squires

Garnett

Bachmann

Taft

17 SC

Evans

Holcombe

Clark

21 MA

McGraw

Garden

Avey

Jenkins

Sherrick

36 OH

Crook

11 OH
(8 Co.)

Drayton

Otto

Rohrbach

11 OH
(2 Co.)

Kemper

Brown

28 OH

Eubank

Lower
Bridge

Richardson

20 GA

11 CT

Eshleman

Harpers Ferry Road

Toombs

2 GA

McMillen

Munford

50 GA

N. Rohrbach

## Legend

**Vegetation**

Woods  Corn  Orchard  Stubble  Plowed

**Fences**

Rail
Post/
Rail
Stone

■ Federal Infantry
□ Confederate Infantry
▨ Confederate Cavalry

**Scale**

0  150  300  450
Yards

22

# MAP 18: ANTIETAM (SEPTEMBER 17, 1862): 3:30 – 4:00 p.m.

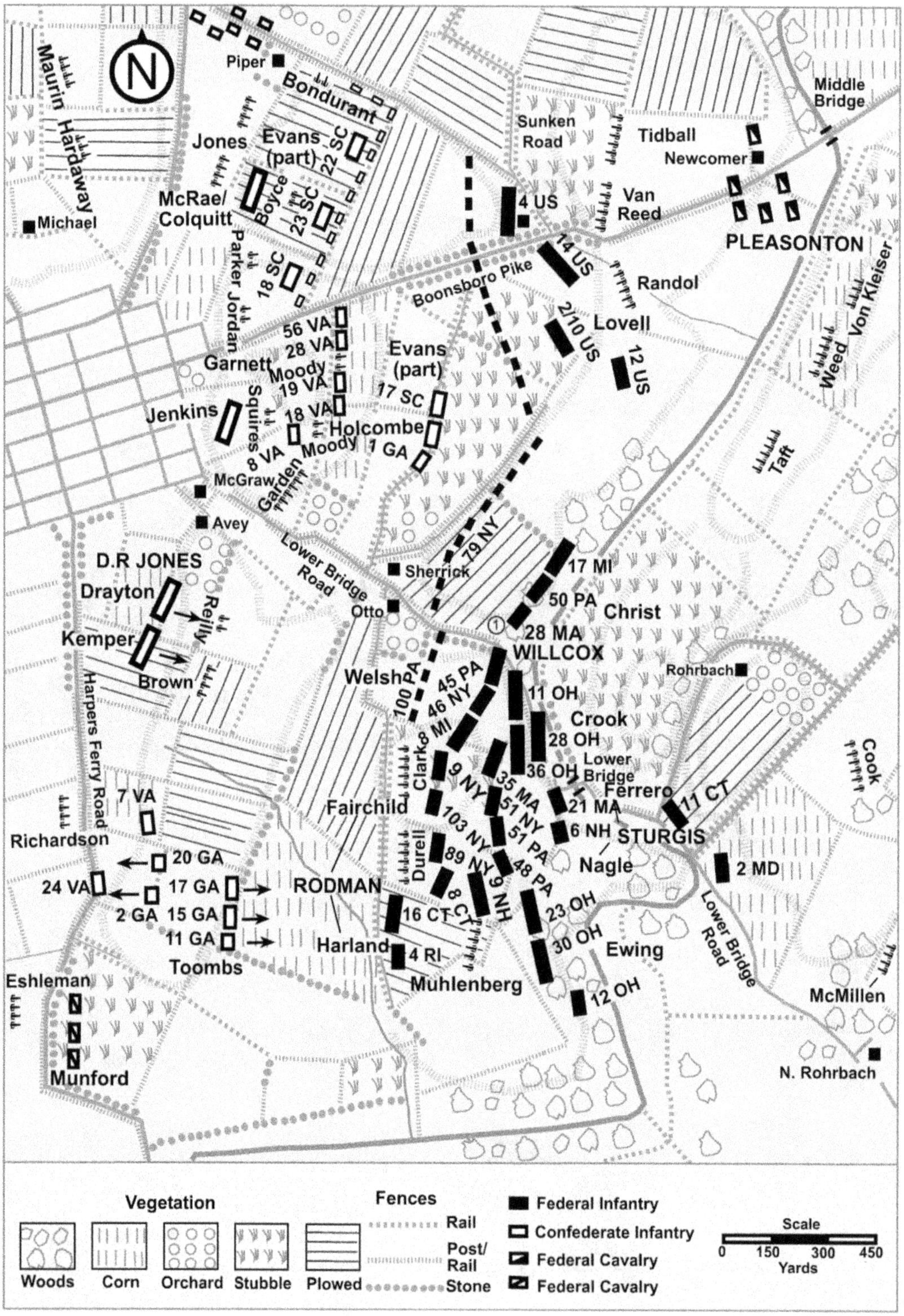

Piper

Bondurant

Maurin

Hardaway

Jones

Evans (part)

22 SC

Sunken Road

Tidball

Newcomer

Middle Bridge

McRae/ Colquitt

Michael

Boyce

23 SC

Van Reed

PLEASONTON

Parker Jordan

18 SC

Boonsboro Pike

4 US

14 US

Randol

Weed

Von Kleiser

56 VA

28 VA

2/10 US

Lovell

12 US

Garnett

Moody

19 VA

Evans (part)

Jenkins

Squires

18 VA

17 SC

Taft

8 VA

Moody

Holcombe

1 GA

McGraw

Garden

Avey

79 NY

D.R JONES

Sherrick

17 MI

Drayton

Reilly

Lower Bridge Road

Otto

50 PA

Christ

Kemper

① 28 MA

WILLCOX

Rohrbach

Brown

Welsh

45 PA

100 PA

46 NY

11 OH

Crook

Cook

28 OH

Harpers Ferry Road

Clark

8 MI

36 OH

Lower Bridge

Ferrero

11 CT

7 VA

Fairchild

9 NY

35 MA

51 NY

21 MA

STURGIS

Richardson

Durell

103 NY

51 PA

6 NH

Nagle

2 MD

20 GA

89 NY

48 PA

24 VA

17 GA

8

9 NH

23 OH

2 GA

15 GA

RODMAN

16 CT

30 OH

Ewing

11 GA

Harland

4 RI

McMillen

Toombs

Muhlenberg

12 OH

N. Rohrbach

Eshleman

Munford

| Vegetation | | | | | Fences | | | |
|---|---|---|---|---|---|---|---|---|
| | | | | | | Rail | ■ | Federal Infantry |
| | | | | | | Post/ Rail | ☐ | Confederate Infantry |
| Woods | Corn | Orchard | Stubble | Plowed | | Stone | ◣ | Federal Cavalry |
| | | | | | | | ◳ | Federal Cavalry |

Scale

0    150    300    450

Yards

23

# MAP 19: ANTIETAM (SEPTEMBER 17, 1862): 4:00 – 5:00 p.m.

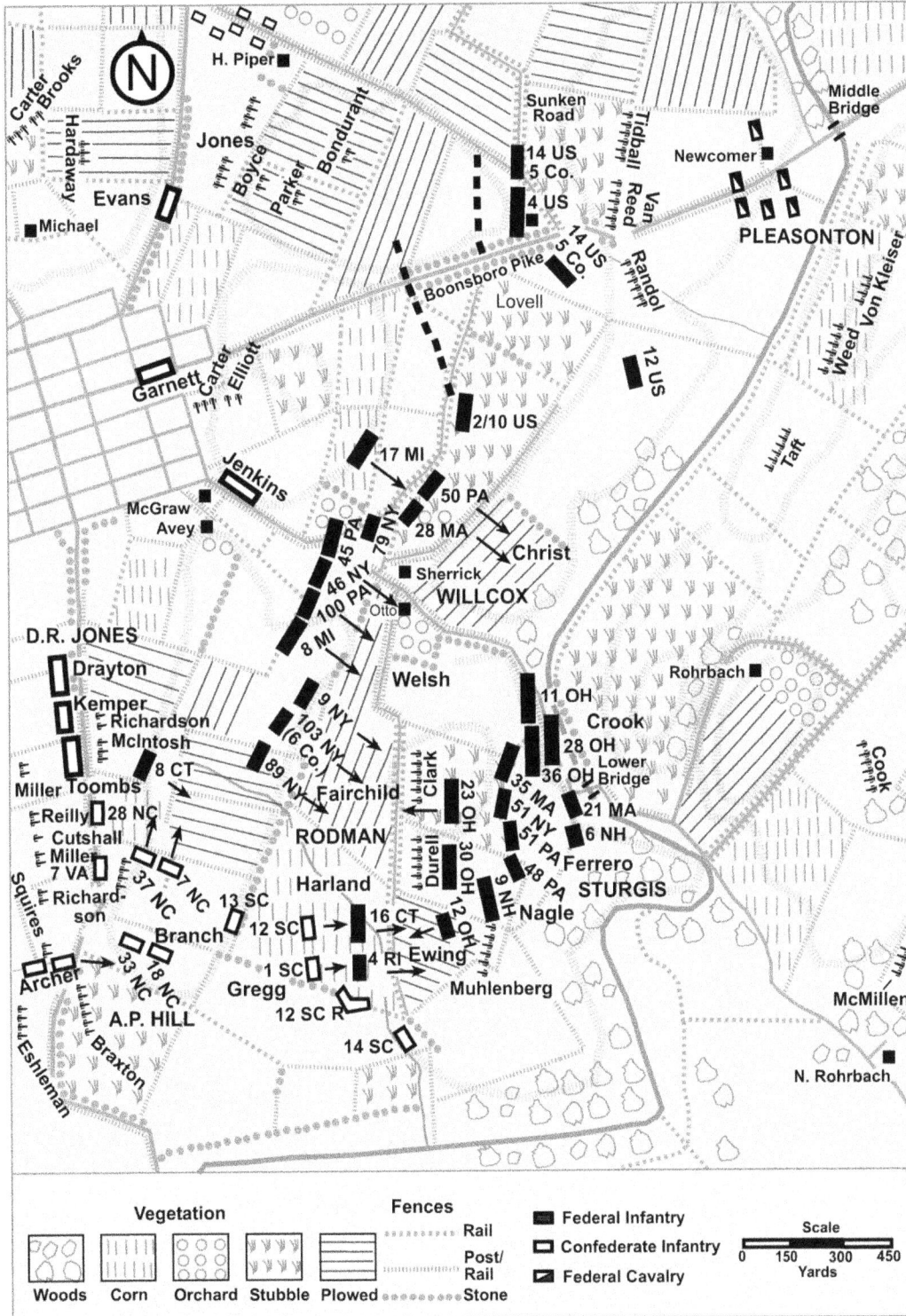

# MAP 20: SHEPHERDSTOWN (SEPTEMBER 20, 1862): 9:00 – 9:30 a.m.

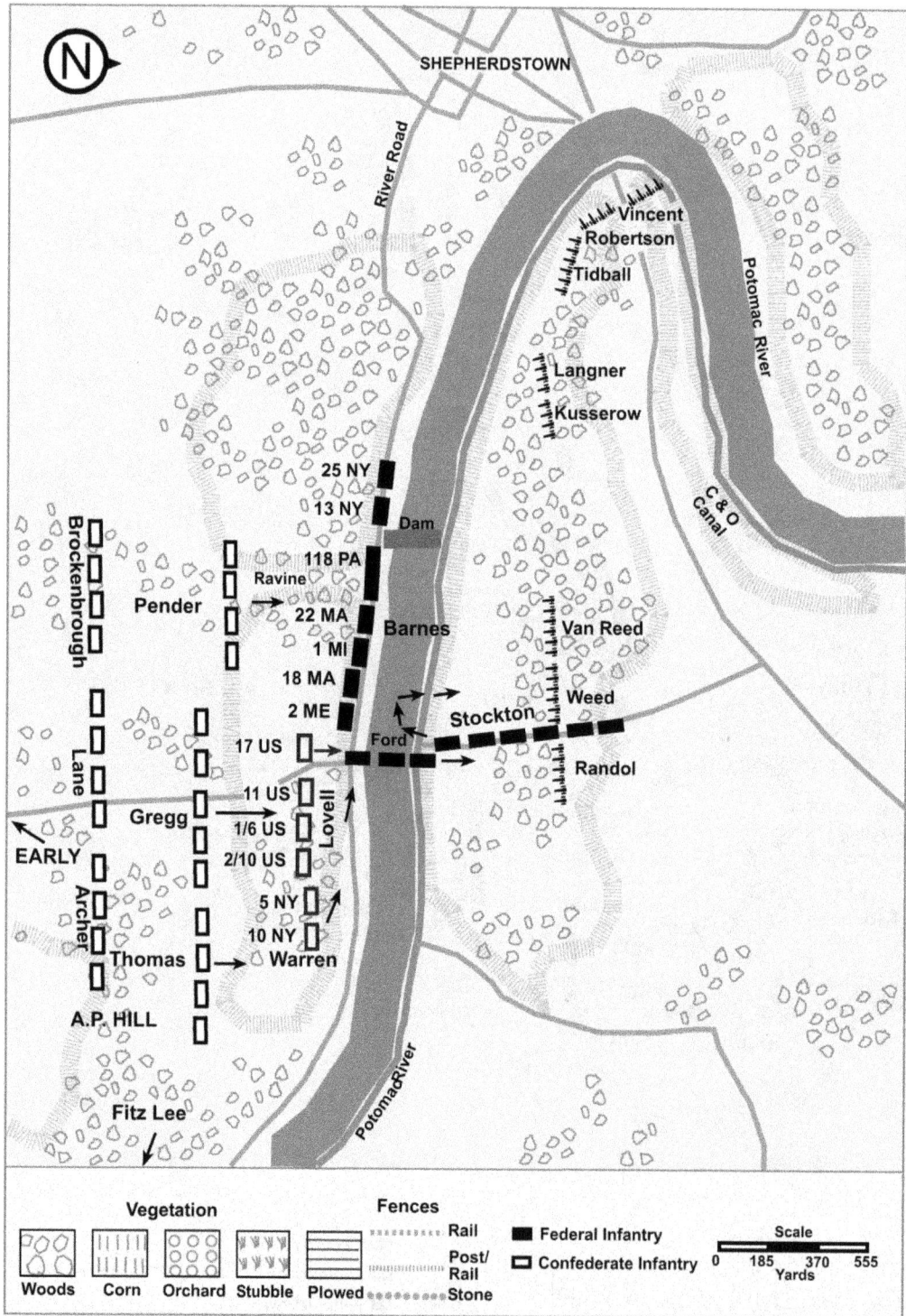

SHEPHERDSTOWN

River Road

Vincent
Robertson
Tidball

Potomac River

Langner

Kusserow

C & O Canal

25 NY
13 NY
Dam
118 PA
Ravine
22 MA
Barnes
Van Reed
1 MI
18 MA
2 ME
Weed
Stockton
17 US
Ford
Randol
11 US
Gregg
1/6 US
Lovell
2/10 US
5 NY
10 NY
Warren

Brockenbrough

Pender

Lane

EARLY

Archer

Thomas

A.P. HILL

Fitz Lee

Potomac River

## Vegetation

| Woods | Corn | Orchard | Stubble | Plowed |

## Fences

Rail
Post/Rail
Stone

■ Federal Infantry
□ Confederate Infantry

### Scale

0   185   370   555
Yards

# I CORPS—

## Major General Joseph Hooker

### * * *

Major General Joseph "Fighting Joe" Hooker, an 1837 West Point graduate from Massachusetts with war-fighting experience in the Seminole and Mexico Wars, had no lack of confidence. As the story goes, during a trip to Washington to offer his military services after the war broke out, but finding little encouragement, he requested a meeting with President Lincoln where he said, "I was at the Battle of Bull Run the other day, and it is neither vanity nor boasting in me to disclose that I am a better general than you, sir, had on that field." His bold words hit their mark. Hooker was commissioned brigadier general of volunteers in August, 1861 backdated to May 17, and given division command in the III Corps of the Army of the Potomac shortly thereafter.[1]

Hooker and his division saw hard fighting during the summer of 1862 in the Seven Days Battles and Second Bull Run. Of special note, the Battle of Williamsburg "established the fame of Hooker as a fighting commander," according to historian Ezra A. Carman, leading to his promotion to the rank of major general on July 26, backdated to May 5. On September 6, Hooker was given command of the I Corps, Army of the Potomac, as the last of Gen. Robert E. Lee's Confederates climbed over the north banks of the Potomac River into Maryland.[2]

Hooker's division commanders at the start of the Maryland Campaign were Brig. Gen. John Reynolds, commanding the Pennsylvania Reserves division, Brig. Gen. John Hatch, and Brig. Gen. James Ricketts. Before the I Corps' first engagement with the enemy in the Maryland Campaign at South Mountain on September 14, Reynolds was called away by Governor Andrew Curtin of Pennsylvania and replaced by Brig. Gen. George Meade. Hatch was severely wounded on South Mountain and replaced by Brig. Gen. Abner Doubleday. Meade, Doubleday and Ricketts would be the line up for the Battle of Antietam on September 17.[3]

On September 10, as part of Maj. Gen. George McClellan's Right Wing under Gen. Ambrose Burnside, the I Corps pushed northeast through Maryland, arriving at the Monocacy River, east of Frederick, around noon on September 13. The corps marched west along the National Road at daylight on September 14, reaching Middletown around 1:00 p.m., several miles east of where the IX Corps was fiercely engaging the right flank of the enemy at Fox's Gap.[4]

Hooker's corps entered the fight on South Mountain around 5:00 p.m., pushing the left flank of Maj. Gen. D.H. Hill's stubborn Confederates up and over the uneven mountain ridges to the north of the National Road, with Meade's division on the right, Hatch's on the left, and Ricketts' in reserve. As Meade's and Hatch's divisions neared the summit, Brig. Gen. John Gibbon's brigade, which had been temporarily detached from Hatch's division by Burnside, advanced up the National Road toward Turner's Gap on the I Corps' left flank, where, as Hooker reported, "the resistance of the enemy was continued until after dark, and only subsided on his being driven from his position." The I Corps' victory on South Mountain cost 878 casualties.[5]

The next morning, September 15, Maj. Gen. Edwin Sumner's II Corps and Brig. Gen. Alfred Pleasonton's cavalry division passed through Hooker's lines atop South Mountain. The I Corps fell in line behind them for the march southwest toward Sharpsburg and Lee's troops making a stand there. At Keedysville, east of Antietam Creek, the corps marched to the right of Boonsboro Pike, crossed Little Antietam Creek over a stone bridge, and bivouacked in the forks of the Little Antietam and Antietam Creek.[6]

Hooker's 9,000-10,000 men crossed Antietam Creek during mid-afternoon of September 16 to "attack the enemy on his left flank," which lay somewhere beyond the west banks of the creek. Meade's and Ricketts' divisions crossed over the Upper Bridge; Doubleday's waded across the creek at Pry's Ford, south of the bridge. Hooker took advantage of a visit from McClellan to request reinforcements, telling his commander that "if another attack was not made on the enemy's right, the rebels would eat me up." In response, McClellan sent Maj. Gen. Joseph Mansfield's XII Corps across the creek around midnight in support of Hooker.[7]

As the corps marched southwest toward the farms of Samuel and Joseph Poffenberger, probing for Lee's left flank, Brig. Gen. Truman Seymour's brigade (Meade's division) encountered Confederate infantry and cavalry attempting to slow Hooker's advance. The two sides skirmished until dark in the East Woods, while the rest of the corps remained farther north, moving into the fields north of the North and East Woods. Hooker established his headquarters in Joseph Poffenberger's barn and planned for the next day's battle. As he retired for the night, Hooker told his staff, "Gentlemen, we are through for tonight, but tomorrow we fight the battle that will decide the fate of the Republic." The victory on South Mountain had bolstered the morale of the men, and now they had Lee with his back to the Potomac River.[8]

Before dawn on September 17, musket fire from the East Woods ushered in the day as the skirmish from the previous evening resumed. Fifteen minutes later, the rumble of Confederate cannon from Nicodemus Heights on Hooker's right (west) shook the earth. Hooker brought up artillery to answer the rebel cannon to his right and clear enemy pickets from D.R. Miller's cornfield to his front. A half mile beyond the cornfield was his initial objective, a plateau adjacent to the little white Dunker Church populated with Confederate artillery. The plateau was key terrain which, as Hooker described, "commanded the position of the enemy on his retreat from South Mountain." Once the cornfield was cleared of rebels, Hooker launched his two-pronged attack toward the plateau, with Ricketts on the left, Doubleday on the right, and Meade in reserve.[9]

Though confident in himself, Hooker did not underestimate his opponent. He had great respect for the discipline and spirit of Lee's army on the field, stating prior to Antietam that although the Confederate soldiers were "vastly inferior to our own, intellectually and physically … they had acquired a character for steadiness and efficiency unsurpassed … in modern times."[10]

As if to illustrate Hooker's assessment, Maj. Gen. Thomas "Stonewall" Jackson, commanding Lee's left flank, had "swung his left flank 180 degrees to the north" at sunrise to support the artillery on Nicodemus Heights, complicating what Hooker had likely intended as an attack on Lee's left flank. Instead, the I Corps smashed head-on into Jackson's divisions of Brig. Gen. J.R. Jones and Brig. Gen. Alexander Lawton, with Confederate artillery pounding Hooker's front and right flank. With both sides essentially on the offense, "the battle took on a life of its own, changing into bestial savagery that characterized the entire morning and yielded the bloodiest day of the war," as described by historian Joseph Harsh.[11]

Shortly before 7:00 a.m., with thousands of casualties already littering the field, elements of Doubleday's and Rickett's divisions finally pushed through D.R. Miller's cornfield, which would forever be known as the Cornfield, the epicenter of casualties on America's bloodiest day. Their objective was within reach, about a quarter mile ahead, when a strong counterattack by Brig. Gen. John Hood's division sent them reeling back through the Cornfield. Quick action by Meade's division, some of Doubleday's troops across Hagerstown Pike, and Union artillery nearly obliterated Hood's division, but another Confederate counterattack, this time by several brigades of Maj. Gen. D.H. Hill's division, soon followed.

The XII Corps had moved forward that morning with the first sounds of the cannon. As Meade's reserves and other I Corps elements beat back Hood's division, Hooker ordered Brig. Gen. Alpheus Williams to deploy his XII Corps to meet the enemy. Williams had assumed command only moments earlier, after Mansfield was mortally wounded near the East Woods. The XII Corps' arrival was not a moment too soon;

the I Corps had little strength left to thwart Hill's brigades and many of Hooker's units were streaming north.[12]

Meanwhile, a wound to Hooker's foot caused him to nearly lose consciousness. With a vague recollection of seeing the II Corps arrive on the field, Hooker was whisked off to the Pry House on the east side of Antietam Creek for treatment.[13]

McClellan was pleased with Hooker's performance at Antietam, as his official report suggests: "Had you not been wounded when you were, I believe the result of the battle would have been the entire destruction of the rebel army, for I *know* that, with you at its head, your corps would have kept on until it gained the main road." Historian Scott Hartwig considers Hooker's performance to be the best of any corps commander at Antietam. "He had his fingers on the pulse of the battle like no other commander, seemed to be everywhere along the front of his corps, and 'saw' the battlefield with a clarity few generals possess."[14]

As Hooker recovered from his wound, Reynolds returned from Pennsylvania and assumed permanent command of the I Corps. Hooker recovered in time to lead a Grand Division, composed of the III and V Corps, at Fredericksburg in December, 1862.[15]

**Laura Marfut**

* * *

# 1ST DIVISION—

## Brigadier General John Hatch, Brigadier General Abner Doubleday

The 1st Division was formed at the same time as the I Corps on March 3, 1862 and spent its initial period near Washington, while George McClellan drove his Army of the Potomac south toward Richmond. The division transferred to the Department of the Rappahannock a month later, and then it joined the newly created Army of Virginia on June 26 as part of the III Corps. The division did not see action until the Second Bull Run Campaign, where it lost more men (2,728) than any other Union division. The III Corps was reclassified as the I Corps when McClellan reorganized the army in early September 1862.

Brigadier General Rufus King was the division's first commander. Born in 1814, King graduated from Columbia College and then completed his studies at West Point in 1833. He resigned from the army in 1836 and pursued careers in railroads, newspapers, and public education. Lincoln appointed him Minister to the Papal States in 1861 and he was on his way to Italy when the war erupted. King quickly returned to the United States to become brigadier general of the Wisconsin militia. He received the same rank in the U. S. Army and raised a brigade of Wisconsin and Indiana regiments that would become known as the Iron Brigade, and he became its first commander. King was plagued by epilepsy, causing him to miss the Second Bull Run Campaign. As the episodes became more frequent and extreme, King missed additional time with his troops. He was removed on September 14 and replaced by Brig. Gen. John Hatch, just hours prior to the Battle of South Mountain.[16]

Born in 1822, Hatch was a New Yorker like King. An 1845 West Point graduate, he saw extensive service in the Mexican War and then was assigned to posts in the west. After initially serving in the cavalry at the outbreak of the Civil War, he was promoted to the rank of brigadier general in September 1861 and given command of a cavalry brigade. He commanded Maj. Gen. Nathaniel Banks' cavalry during the 1862 Valley Campaign, and after a couple of failed cavalry raids, was transferred to the infantry, commanding a brigade during the Second Bull Run Campaign. Hatch assumed temporary command of the division during the Battle of Second Bull Run when King experienced a series of seizures, and continued serving in that capacity until he officially replaced King on September 14, during the Maryland Campaign.[17]

The division performed well under Hatch at Second Bull Run and began the Maryland with four brigades under Brig. Gen. Marsena Patrick, Brig. Gen. John Gibbon, Brig. Gen. Abner Doubleday, and Col. Walter Phelps. The division left its camps along the Monocacy River at 6:00 a.m. on September 14 and reached the Catoctin Mountains at 12:30 p.m., where it halted for two hours. King was replaced by Hatch during this period. The column resumed its march westward toward South Mountain. Enemy artillery atop the mountain poured shells onto the division, causing it to turn right onto Mount Tabor Church Road. Before the division made its turn, Wing Commander Maj. Gen. Ambrose Burnside detached Gibbon's brigade, which later drove up the National Road toward the summit of Turner's Gap. The rest of the division marched past Joseph Hooker and his staff at the Mount Tabor Church.

Hatch deployed his three remaining brigades, which he estimated to number less than 3,500 men, at the base of the mountain. Two of Patrick's regiments were thrown forward on a skirmish line and sent up the mountainside, followed by the brigade's remaining two regiments. Phelps' brigade followed Patrick's during its ascent. Because of the rugged terrain, Patrick's brigade became separated and, unbeknownst to Phelps, his advance drove between the two wings of Patrick's brigade. The two brigades climbed South Mountain toward Frosttown Plateau with Doubleday's brigade in reserve and encountered Brig. Gen. Richard Garnett's brigade of Virginians behind a fence at the edge of a woodlot. Hatch noted the "firing was very heavy, the enemy making a desperate resistance, and our troops advancing with determined courage." Brig. Gen. James Kemper's Virginia brigade also arrived, but its orientation precluded it from becoming actively engaged.[18]

Hatch ordered a charge but "the resistance of the enemy being so much more determined than anticipated," he called up Doubleday's brigade to add its weight to the fight, and it drove the Virginians from behind a fence. Hatch went down with a leg wound and he relinquish division command to Doubleday. Col. William Wainwright of the 76th New York assumed command of Doubleday's brigade. The brigade relieved Phelps' brigade beyond the fence once held by Garnett's men. The latter made a desperate countercharge and, according to Doubleday, his men "allowed the enemy to charge to within about 15 paces, apparently under the impression that we had given way. Then, at the word, my men sprang to their feet and poured in a deadly volley, from which the enemy fled in disorder, leaving their dead within 30 feet of our line." James Ricketts' 2nd Division came up after dark and relieved the 1st Division, ending its activities along Frosttown Plateau.

While Hatch's three brigades were engaged on Frosttown Plateau, the 4th Brigade (Gibbon's) was ordered up the National Road to clear Turner's Gap. It encountered Col. Alfred Colquitt's brigade on the side of the mountain. Nightfall put an end to the stalemate. The division lost a total of 496 men (63 killed; 390 wounded; 43 missing) on September 14. Col. Wainwright was among the wounded, so command of the 2nd Brigade devolved to Lt. Col. William Hofmann of the 56th Pennsylvania.[19]

The division headed to Antietam Creek the following day, crossing it at Pry's Ford on the afternoon of September 16. Doubleday slid his division westward toward Hagerstown Pike, where his men spent the night between it and Joseph Poffenberger's home. Doubleday's division was tasked with attacking south on the right of Ricketts' division on the morning of September 17. Difficult sight-lines and tremendous artillery fire delayed the full attack until after 6:30 a.m. Enemy skirmish fire from the right of the road caused Doubleday to split Gibbon's brigade in half and the westerners advanced on either side of Hagerstown Pike. Patrick's brigade followed the half of Gibbon's brigade on the right (west side) of the road; Phelps' brigade followed Gibbon's regiments on the left (east side). Driving forward, the division dislodged portions of Alexander Lawton's division and J.R. Jones' division from their positions south of the Cornfield and the advance continued toward Dunker Church and the high ground beyond. John Hood's Confederate division materialized from the West Woods and counterattacked, driving Doubleday's troops on the east side of Hagerstown Pike back through the Cornfield. However, Doubleday's troops on the right (west) side turned and hit Hood's left flank, forcing it to retreat. Elements of Gibbon's and Patrick's brigades advanced across Hagerstown Pike, but were driven back by Brig. Gen. Roswell Ripley's brigade (Maj. Gen. D.H. Hill's division) which was rushed from the area near the Mumma farm lane. Only three of the 1st Division's brigades were fully engaged at Antietam—Hofmann's brigade was detached to support the Union artillery.[20]

The division fell back and reformed near the Joseph Poffenberger house where it supported the massive array of artillery deployed there. This ended the Maryland Campaign for the 1st Division. The division lost a total of 812 men at Antietam (140 killed; 638 wounded; 34 missing). Hatch never returned to the Army of the Potomac, so Doubleday continued commanding the division until replaced by Brig. Gen. James Wadsworth. Doubleday then was assigned command of the 3rd Division, I Corps.[21]

**Bradley M. Gottfried**

✳ ✳ ✳

## 1st Brigade: Colonel Walter Phelps, Jr.

**Units:** 22nd New York, 24th New York, 30th New York, 84th (14th Brooklyn) New York, 2nd U.S. Sharpshooters
**Strength:** 400 – 425[22]
**Losses:** 249 (50k–187w–12m)[23]

Colonel Walter Phelps Jr. was born in Vermont in 1832, lived in Connecticut, attended Trinity College and was a lumber merchant in Glens Falls, New York before the war. After leaving Trinity in 1847-48, Phelps traveled as a civilian aboard the USS Saratoga to California, but was soon back in Glens Falls where he joined the militia before the Civil War. He mustered in as Colonel of the 22nd New York in May, 1861. One of his first military duties was serving as a pall bearer for Col. Elmer Ellsworth, the first Union officer killed in the war. Phelps had the advantage of learning from Regular Army officers who previously commanded his brigade, including E.D. Keyes, C.C. Augur, and J.D. Hatch, easing his transition to brigade commander. Phelps' letters describe the rigorous training and difficult marches as part of Maj. Gen. Irvin McDowell's corps in and around Fredericksburg, Virginia in the spring and summer of 1862.[24]

The three New York regiments, raised in Oswego, Saratoga and several northern counties mustered into Federal service during the spring of 1861 to serve for two years. The fourth regiment, the 84th New York, which was almost always referred to as the 14th Brooklyn, was enlisted for three years, and merged into another brigade in 1863. It was a veteran regiment, having served at the Battle of First Bull Run. The 2nd U.S. Sharpshooters was attached in the spring of 1862, but was often detached, serving as skirmishers for the division.

The brigade acquired the sobriquet "Iron Brigade" during the spring of 1862. However, it is John Gibbon's brigade of the same division that is usually associated with that name. Several sources claim Phelps' brigade acquired the nickname first, and was known as such throughout its service. No less authority than William A. Fox, a veteran of the war, including Antietam, noted historian and author of several authoritative books, wrote, "in justice to Hatch's brigade, it should be stated that it was the original Iron Brigade and that Gibbon's brigade was not known by that until after Antietam, at which time it was so designated by a war correspondent who was apparently unaware of his lack of originality."[25]

There are several stories concerning the origin of the nickname. At least two cite a long and difficult march by the brigade, from Catlett's Station to Falmouth Virginia, ending in a minor fight. A witness remarked, "Your men must be made of iron

30

to make such marches, to which Col. [Edward] Frisbee of the 30th N.Y. replied, 'Yes, this is the Iron Brigade.'"[26]

The brigade did not participate in the Peninsula Campaign and suffered very little until thrown into the maelstrom of Second Bull Run. Brigade commander John Hatch was elevated to division command, replacing the ailing Rufus King, but Phelps was home on leave and Col. Timothy Sullivan of the 24th New York assumed command of the brigade. In one of the many blunders committed on August 29, Sullivan's and Abner Doubleday's brigades were sent in a confused attack late in the afternoon that proved deadly to the New Yorkers. Their attack on the unfinished railroad cut the next day only created more losses. Col. Edward Fowler of the 14th Brooklyn was wounded, Col. Edward Frisbee of the 30th New York and Lt. Col. Gorton Thomas, commanding the 22nd New York, were killed, and the 772 losses were nearly a third of the brigade. Many demoralized survivors apparently straggled or deserted because by September 14 nearly 1,000 more men simply disappeared from the brigade.[27]

Phelps took his 22nd New York's devastation at Manassas hard as he believed he should have been there to share its fate. He had arrived in Washington on August 28, but Brig. Gen. James Wadsworth refused to let him leave the city to find his regiment due to the uncertain circumstances. When he finally reached the 22nd New York he found himself in command of the brigade. It was little more than a shattered group of survivors, badly demoralized by their confused fight on August 29. Phelps headed into the Maryland Campaign under a cloud as someone in Glens Falls publicly accused him of shirking his duty, leaving him to fight a battle in his rear while advancing towards his first real battle as an untried brigade commander.[28]

The Iron Brigade departed its camp on Upton's Hill, Virginia on September 6 as part of the III Corps, Army of Virginia, soon to be designated the I Corps, Army of the Potomac, under new commander, Joseph Hooker. Having survived their first big battle, many of the exhausted sick and dispirited remained in Washington or straggled on the march. The same cannot be said of Phelps, who wrote to his wife Emmaline, "If I was unfortunate to be absent when my regiment was engaged in the last battles, it is possible I may have an opportunity to distinguish myself as a brigade commander."[29]

Camped eight miles outside of Frederick on September 13, Phelps boasted about his brigade's discipline. "We marched 18 miles yesterday in heavy marching order, no straggling, no falling out of ranks. Our excellent marching was remarked." Considering the entire brigade numbered only 400 men, this may be a lesser accomplishment than might otherwise be the case.[30]

## South Mountain

As part of Wing Commander Maj. Gen. Ambrose Burnside's September 14 plan of attack on the Confederate troops holding Fox's and Turner's Gap on South Mountain, Hooker's I Corps was ordered to flank Turner's Gap from the north via Frosttown Gap, and the New York Iron Brigade found themselves marching a circuitous and difficult route after diverging northward from the National Pike. Hatch, now commanding the 1st Division, was ordered to follow George Meade's Pennsylvania Reserves Division. When Marsena Patrick's brigade reached the base of the ravine leading to the gap, Hatch ordered it forward in line of battle with Phelps to follow in support by "column of divisions," essentially a dense marching formation. They were confronted by the newly arrived Virginia brigades of James Kemper and Richard Garnett. Patrick drove the Confederates uphill to the edge an open field, bordered at the opposite edge by a stone fence. Patrick's regiments split and diverged and Phelps suddenly found his brigade advancing in column with no skirmishers or other Union troops in their front as they drove between Patrick's two wings into the front line. Hatch arrived and ordered Phelps to deploy and advance upon the Confederate line across the open field.[31]

Historian Ezra Carman explained what happened next: "Phelps now ordered his men to attack ... But they needed no urging, they leaped forward with a

31

hearty cheer, poured in a hot fire, were given a hot volley in return, followed by a heavy and continuous fire, which was as heavily responded to." Virginians began drifting back from their stone wall after about 15 minutes. "Phelps now ordered a charge," according to Carman, "the stone fence was carried, and the entire line of Garnett driven back some 200 yards." Phelps' men now held the fence and a number of prisoners. They were soon relieved by Doubleday's brigade.[32]

Prior to their attack, Lt. Col. William Searing of the 30th New York evidently recognized the Confederate regimental flags and called out to his regiment, "Boys, the men who killed your Colonel [Edward Frisbee] are now in front of you. Let us avenge his death!" Phelps ordered the 14th Brooklyn to flank the rebel line on the left and the Iron Brigade drove off the Confederates, whose numbers were similar to Phelps. The body of Col. William Strange of the 19th Virginia was found behind the stone wall wearing boots with Col. Frisbee's name stenciled on them. The boots were returned to Frisbee's widow.[33]

Phelps not only survived his first battle, he had successfully exercised command of the brigade and exulted to his wife, "The brigade has covered itself with glory. My brigade remained on the battlefield during the night, the 22d behaved splendidly. They killed two rebel officers, one a Col. Strang[e] of the 19th Va. The rebel dead lay in heaps in front of my brigade line, the 22d lost 12 men killed and 26 wounded. I took occasion yesterday to compliment the brigade upon their splendid fighting, the 14th did finely, in fact all the regiments behaved as well as I could have wished. I got one ball through my coat, with that exception escaped." The victory gained exacted a heavy price as the brigade suffered 95 casualties, almost 25% of their strength engaged. Little did they know the worst was yet to come.[34]

## Antietam

The brigade marched along the National Road to Boonsboro the following morning, and turned towards the Potomac River on Boonsboro–Shepherdstown Turnpike. According to S.E.

Chandler of the 24th New York, more men left the brigade: "After 'South Mountain' the boys were out of rations & permission was granted the men to 'fall out' & get food 'long the way and you know how easy it easy to _not_ catch up in a line like that." With the rest of Hooker's corps they bivouacked that night near the junction of the Little Antietam and Antietam Creeks.[35]

Hooker's I Corps was ordered to cross Antietam Creek on the afternoon of September 16 to approach the left flank of Lee's line near the Dunker Church. Following the other divisions, Doubleday, who now commanded the division because of Hatch's wounding, ordered his men to bivouac that night on a bluff behind Joseph Poffenberger's house, parallel to Hagerstown Pike. Phelps described the situation on the morning of September 17: "At 5.30 a.m. Wednesday the enemy's batteries opened upon our lines, and I was ordered by General Doubleday to move to the support of Gibbon's brigade, which had already advanced to attack the enemy's lines." The brigade moved by the flank through an open field, passed into a cornfield, and formed line of battle. The 2nd U. S. Sharpshooters fastened its right on Hagerstown Pike in support of Gibbon's brigade, which Phelps described as 25 paces to the front. Gibbon's brigade had already driven the Confederates out of the Miller Cornfield and were heading toward the Dunker Church with Phelps' men behind them.[36]

A line of Confederates, Brig. Gen. William Starke's Louisiana brigade, moved from the West Woods to flank Gibbon's line, and Phelps ordered Col. Henry Post of the 2nd U. S. Sharpshooters to move west and confront the rebel brigade. In doing so, Col. Post was wounded, and Lt. Lewis Parmalee was killed. A Sharpshooter described his death; "Adj't. Parmalee was shot while trying to carry off a rebel flag he had seized fastened to a fence post, but unfortunately for him and others, the rebels were behind that fence, and the gallant adjutant had five bullets put in him." The Sharpshooters also supported Battery B, 4th U.S., where one of them remembered, "Gibbon fired the first round of canister, I saw the air was filled with hats, caps, everything soldiers have. I saw an arm go 30 feet into the air and fall back again. It looked as though it had been torn off up close up to the shoulder, it was just awful."[37]

The rest of the brigade conformed their movements to the 2nd and 6th Wisconsin of Gibbon's brigade in their front, and eventually mingled with them. Maj. Rufus R. Dawes of the 6th Wisconsin described the crisis when John Hood's Confederate division marched out of the West Woods and counterattacked the two brigades; "The Fourteenth Brooklyn Regiment, red-legged Zouaves, came into our line, closing the awful gaps. Men and officers of New York and Wisconsin are fused into a common mass." Hood's men drove Gibbon's and Phelps' brigades from the clover field, through the Cornfield and toward the North Woods.[38]

Phelps was again conscious of his behavior in light of the accusations made against him at home. In a letter to his wife he noted, "Fortunately I am very cool under fire & the fact of my quietly lighting my pipe when the shot & shell were flying about cutting down my men seemed to enspirit the men and gave them confidence. A shell struck between the Qr. Master[']s horse & my own yesterday on the field, but did no damage. I had two orderlies shot at my side."[39]

Morale problems persisted in the brigade. According to John Bryson, "Lt. Col. Searing (30th New York), was taken sick after the Battle of South Mountain. Capt. John H. Campbell of Co. A commanded the Reg't. at Antietam, I think. The regiment however, took little part in the battle." Another member of the regiment recalled, "Col. Wm. M. Searing & J.M. Andrews [Lt. Co. D] was not in the fight, that I know, as there were only about 80 men present for duty." Perhaps it was something more serious because after the battle Phelps had charges and specifications drawn up to court martial Searing for refusing to lead his regiment in the battle. Among the specifications was testimony stating that Searing said "… he had already lost his horse and refused to risk his life again to lead 50 men in battle." Research does not show the court martial ever took place, but Phelps may have used the charges to subsequently force Searing to do his duty.[40]

Phelps' brigade lost an additional 154 men at Antietam. Therefore, the brigade lost a total of 249 men during the campaign. Phelps probably summed up the feelings of many men in the brigade when he wrote, "I do not know how I escaped. I assure you that at night I offered the most fervent prayer of thanksgiving for my wonderful preservation through the dangers of the battle fields." Despite letters from Gens. King, Hatch, Reynolds, Hooker and a number of others encouraging Lincoln to promote Phelps to the rank of brigadier general, Phelps remained a colonel and left the army when his regiment was mustered out of service in 1863. He became involved in iron making for the next 16 years until he suddenly died on February 25, 1878. While most of the regiments mustered out in 1863, the 14th Brooklyn and 2nd U.S. Sharpshooters earned lasting fame on several battlefields.[41]

**Thomas G. Clemens**

\* \* \*

## 2nd Brigade: Brigadier General Abner Doubleday, Colonel William Wainwright, Lieutenant Colonel J. William Hofmann

**Units:** 7th Indiana, 76th New York, 95th New York, 56th Pennsylvania
**Strength:** 1,298[42]
**Losses:** 10 (0k-10w–0m)[43]

Brigadier General Abner Doubleday's brigade, minus the 7th Indiana, first saw action at Second Bull Run. The Hoosiers were added just prior to the Maryland Campaign. All were veteran units, having seen action in at least one battle prior to the

Maryland Campaign. Doubleday was a seasoned West Pointer who had the distinction of being second in command at Fort Sumter at the outset of the war.[44]

While still in Virginia, the men were provided with four days of welcome rest, reviving them in "body and spirit." According to the historian of the 76th New York, the rations they received here were the first issued in twenty days. At 6:00 p.m. on September 6, the division was ordered to leave Upton Hill in Virginia and cross the Potomac River into Washington. The march was a difficult one as other troops clogged the road. The men were given a short rest at 2:00 a.m. while in front of the White House. The column then proceeded up Seventh Street, past Fort Massachusetts and into Maryland. A soldier complained to his father, "[we] marched all night and all the next day without any rations, not even a hard cracker to eat."[45]

The brigade did not spend much time in Frederick when it arrived on September 14, for it was immediately marched through town. The men's spirits were buoyed by the civilians: "Flags were waving throughout the day, from almost every house; handkerchiefs were fluttering, while ever and anon a beautiful bouquet would be tossed by the fairest hands of Maryland's loyal daughters. These were answered by cheer upon cheer from the happy patriots, until they cheered themselves hoarse in the attempt to show their appreciation of the reception." The column continued on at a double-quick pace toward and through Middletown, which it reached about noon.[46]

## South Mountain

The column continued on to South Mountain. A soldier in the 76th New York wrote home, "We found that the enemy had posted themselves on the top of what is called South Mountain . . . From this place our tired and exhausted division was ordered to drive them off." Hooker's I Corps was tasked with forcing its way through South Mountain and Meade's division on the right was already engaged when John Hatch's division moved into action at

about 5:30 p.m. Doubleday's brigade was last in line, so the men were unable to observe the initial fight of Patrick's and Phelps' brigades against Garnett's and Kemper's undersized Confederate brigades. These enemy troops were dog tired as they left Hagerstown earlier that morning and were now thrown into combat. Despite fighting up hill, Patrick's and Phelps' men pushed the enemy from their positions, but the enemy rallied and was still full of fight. The Confederates were reinforced by newly arriving troops from Col. Joseph Walker's brigade. Hatch wrote the "resistance of the enemy being so much more determined than had been anticipated, Doubleday was ordered up."[47]

At about the same time, the adjutant of Phelps' brigade saw Doubleday's brigade waiting to go in and screamed, "Our Brigade cannot sustain itself much longer, as we are nearly out of ammunition! For God's sake, to the front!" Hatch was wounded just as he ordered up the 2nd Brigade so Doubleday assumed command of the division and Col. William Wainwright of the 76th New York took over the brigade. The men were tired from their 90-minute trek up the mountainside, but they were ordered to toss aside their knapsacks and prepare for action. The conditions were less than ideal, as they were fighting on an incline as the sun began to set. The enemy was fighting from behind a stone wall, so Doubleday's men did not realize they outnumbered the Confederates by three to one.[48]

The brigade was deployed, from left to right: 76th New York- 7th Indiana- 95th New York- 56th Pennsylvania. The officers encouraged the men as they advanced, yelling "Steady, boys, steady!" They moved up and replaced Phelps' brigade, coming within 30 to 40 paces of the enemy line. The Confederates saw the movement and launched several unsuccessful attacks against the new arrivals. Doubleday explained how he "ordered the troops to cease firing, lie down behind the fence, and allowed the enemy to charge to within about 15 paces, apparently under the impression that we had given way. Then, at the word, my men sprang to their feet and poured in a deadly volley, from which the enemy fled in disorder, leaving their dead within 30 feet of our line."[49]

Wainwright ordered a charge, and when the 76th New York on the left hesitated, flagbearer Sgt. Charles Stamp rushed forward alone. When only sixteen yards from the enemy line he yelled back to his men, "There, come up to that!" A bullet drilled into Stamp's forehead almost immediately and he fell dead. It only became worse for the New Yorkers when they detected the enemy attempting to get around their left flank. The regiment pivoted, along with a portion of the 7th Indiana next to it, and their musketfire halted the enemy's attempt to flank them. Col. Wainwright was wounded during this portion of the fight and was replaced by J. William Hofmann of the 56th Pennsylvania.[50]

It was now so dark the men could only fire at the approximate location of the enemy as indicated by their musket flashes. The brigade's ammunition was rapidly becoming depleted, so Ricketts' division advanced to replace Hofmann's men. The fight continued for about another half an hour, but the battle was over for the brigade. It lost a total of 59 men in the fight.[51]

### Antietam

After an uneventful march to the battlefield, the brigade crossed Antietam Creek with the rest of Doubleday's division on September 16. It went into bivouac "behind a fence in a depression of the earth, on Hagerstown Pike," according to the 76th New York's historian. The brigade remained in its sheltered position along the pike until 10:00 a.m. as a brisk artillery duel sent projectiles streaking over the men's heads. Some of the shells fell prematurely, "scattering the dust and stones promiscuously over the" men, but none exploded. At 10:00 a.m. the brigade was ordered across the pike to support a battery. One of the men admitted that his regiment "was not under infantry fire at this battle" and therefore sustained few casualties—about ten in all.

The men buried the dead for two days after the battle by digging long trenches and rolling the corpses into the depression. The brigade spent the next several weeks resting and being restocked with supplies. The ten men lost at Antietam were the lowest for any brigade on the battlefield.[52]

**Bradley M. Gottfried**

\* \* \*

## 3rd Brigade: Brigadier General Marsena R. Patrick

**Units:** 21st New York, 23rd New York, 35th New York, 80th New York (20th Militia)
**Strength:** 1,523[53]
**Losses:** 234(30k-187w-17m)[54]

The brigade was organized under George McClellan on October 15, 1861 as Col. James Wadsworth's brigade in Irvin McDowell's division. Three of the regiments, the 21st, 23rd, and 35th New York, were organized as two-year regiments during the spring and summer of 1861. The 80th New York was a three-year regiment organized in September, 1861. All four regiments were brigaded together from the start of their enlistment. Marsena Patrick seems to have assumed command of the brigade shortly after his promotion to brigadier general on March 17, 1862. Wadsworth assumed command of the defenses of Washington a day earlier. Although a stable unit, it did not see action until the Second Bull Run Campaign.[55]

Patrick was described by the historian of the 35th New York State Volunteers as "large of stature, with a somewhat fierce appearance and manner, and voice heavy and powerful. General Patrick was harsh and exacting in his discipline."[56]

The brigade, with the rest of the division, left Virginia for Washington at 2:00 a.m. on September 6. The 16-mile march ended at Leesboro (now Wheaton), Maryland at 5:00 p.m. Col. William Rogers of the 21st New York called the march "one of the most fatiguing and harassing of the campaign." By its conclusion, only 50 men of the 80th New York were in the ranks. From September 6 through the morning of September 14, the brigade made five short marches, totaling 46 miles and bivouacked on the shores of the Monocacy River for 36 hours. The brigade marched through Frederick on September 14 on its way to the fight with Maj. Gen. D.H. Hill's division on South Mountain.[57]

## South Mountain

Patrick's brigade led Hatch's division's march from the Monocacy River on September 14. It arrived at Catoctin Mountain at 12:30 p.m. and after a two-hour rest, the men made their way to South Mountain. The column turned right onto Mt. Tabor Church Road, reaching the church at about 3:30 p.m. Patrick was ordered to throw out two regiments as skirmishers, to be followed by the remaining two regiments, and Phelps' brigade marched 200 paces behind them as they headed up the south spur of the mountain.

The 21st New York, supported by the 80th New York, marched on the right of the 35th New York, which was supported by the 23rd New York. With officers on horseback, flags waving proudly in the breeze and the men in perfect lockstep, it was an imposing sight. D.H. Hill later noted, "there was not a single Confederate soldier to oppose the advance of General Hatch." He did have artillery on the mountain and Capt. John Lane's guns opened fire on the approaching New Yorkers. Hill noted the guns were "as harmless as blank cartridge salutes in honor of a militia general … the enemy did not honor by so much as a dodge." Hill brought up additional guns from Lt. Col. A. S. Cutts'

battalion but they were ineffective because their barrels could not be depressed enough to fire into Patrick's men. He called the artillery fire "the worst he ever witnessed."[58]

A ravine stood between the two sides of the brigade, forcing it to break apart. Patrick saw this occurring and ordered the 80th New York in the second line to veer left to help cover the gap and at the same time, the 35th and 23rd New York were to angle right. Before these actions could be completed, Phelps' brigade drove forward into the gap and continued north. Around this time, Gen. Longstreet brought up Garnett's and Kemper's brigades from Maj. Gen. D.R. Jones' division and sent the 850 men down the mountain to a stone wall to face Hatch's division.[59]

On the left side of Patrick's brigade, the 35th and 23rd New York's movement toward the right brought the regiments in contact with the left of Phelps' brigade and they fastened themselves to it while Patrick's 80th and 21st New York fought on Phelps' right. The two Union brigades came under a "galling fire from the Confederates above, posted behind trees, among rocks and under the shelter of stone walls." The problems were compounded by the "steepness of the ascent and the heat of the day, added to the long march of the marching," which slowed the advance, according to historian Ezra Carman.[60]

It was getting dark as Patrick's left two regiments came up to the fence held by Phelps' men and they fired into a cornfield held by Garnett's brigade. When the enemy's return fire slackened, the officers told the men to cease fire. Patrick's two regiments on the right roughly handled Kemper's skirmish line but did not engage the brigade's main line. Total darkness put an end to the fighting but not before the enemy was pushed back to a new position. Although dramatically outnumbered, the Confederates held out until nightfall, when they abandoned their positions and headed for Boonsboro.

Patrick's losses were modest: three killed, nineteen wounded, and one missing for a total of twenty-three. He would write in his report, "The officers and men, although fatigued, pushed rapidly up the mountain, went into the engagement with spirit, and their conduct was such as to meet my entire approbation."[61]

The brigade reunited on the morning of September 15 and moved down to the National Road where it "ate a frugal breakfast," according to the historian of the 80th New York. Victory was a rare commodity to these soldiers so they were exuberant. The historian of the 21st New York noted the men "took up the march in excellent spirits; the joy and satisfaction everywhere evident, the jokes at the expense of the enemy … this was not a retreat, but an actual pursuit of a flying enemy." The men then headed through Boonsboro and camped three miles beyond, "supperless." Patrick's men awoke on September 16 and headed for Antietam Creek, where they were placed behind a ridge to avoid enemy artillery shells. The brigade, with the rest of the I Corps crossed Antietam Creek at about 3:00 p.m. and marched west and then south, resting near the Joseph Poffenberger farm. Patrick's brigade led Doubleday's division, removing fences along the way. Col. William Rogers of the 21st New York recalled the night of the battle: "I moved my regiment inside the edge of the woods where we bivouacked for the night, the men lying on their arms. It was a very unquiet night frequent collisions taking place between the pickets of the opposing armies. The rumbling of the artillery wheels seemed to indicate that positions were being taken for the morrow[']s conflict. The alarms were frequent and were distinctly heard in our position, indicating that we were but short distance from the enemy's lines."[62]

## Antietam

The Confederates welcomed Patrick's men to September 17 with a barrage of artillery fire that included round-shot, shell, and canister that wounded some of the men. An unidentified soldier in the 23rd New York wrote home, "At 6 ½ A.M. our brigade was ordered to advance and occupy a piece of woods in front. Rifle balls were whistling through them, and the shells of the enemy were bursting in them. Finding no enemy in our immediate front, we lay down and awaited orders." The brigade was now ordered to march south. Because the brigade led the division the day before, it now followed in the rear, behind Gibbon's and Phelps' brigades. The men halted in a shallow depression between a peach orchard and the D.R. Miller cornfield that later became known as "Bloody Corn Field". Patrick recalled his men could not have been here for more than five to seven minutes when he was ordered to "march my brigade rapidly across the road, and hold the woods at a little distance on the right of the road." This movement included half of Gibbon's brigade (19th Indiana and 7th Wisconsin) and Patrick's men formed behind the westerners. Doubleday wanted a regiment to help support Capt. Joseph Campbell's battery, so he sent the 20th New York. Patrick's remaining three regiments were up against the Stonewall Division's (now under Brig. Gen. J.R. Jones) first line, which faced north. The five Union regiments quickly scattered Jones' two brigades on the first line, which numbered, at most, 500 men. Patrick saw some enemy soldiers to his right in a cornfield and informed Hooker, who ordered a regiment in that direction. Patrick selected the 23rd New York.[63]

Patrick was down to two regiments, the 21st and 35th New York, which continued following Gibbon's two regiments on the west side of Hagerstown Pike. They encountered the two remaining brigades of the Stonewall Division, and with the help of the rest of Gibbon's brigade across the road, drove them to the rear. Looking to his left, Patrick saw a fresh line of enemy troops on the opposite side of Hagerstown Pike. These were troops from John Hood's division who were now chasing Phelps' brigade and the 2nd and 6th Wisconsin of Gibbon's brigade to the rear. To protect his men, Patrick, "threw my whole command, including the Seventh Wisconsin and Nineteenth Indiana, across the open space and under the rocky ledge, perpendicular to my former position and parallel to the road, when I was joined at double-quick by the Twenty-third, now relieved on the right by General Meade."[64]

The five regiments now faced three regiments of Col. William Wofford's brigade (John Hood's division) driving north through the Cornfield. The sudden appearance of Union troops on their left caused them to wheel to face them. The two Iron Brigade regiments climbed over the ledge along the road and fired into Wofford's men. The two sides exchanged fire for several minutes, when the 19th Indiana and 7th Wisconsin fell back. Patrick's men came up behind them, passed through their ranks and assumed the position along the side of the road and drove the enemy back toward the Dunker Church. The historian of the 21st New York wrote, "Forward we went through the woods, out into the open field, and we were face to face with the enemy on a fair field. With bayonets fixed, rapidly we charged forward. Two fences lined the turnpike road in our front, on the other side of which the enemy was posted. We reached the first fence, forced them back and scaling that and the one on the other side, continued to pour deadly fire into their ranks. General Patrick at this time rode up and ordered us to fall back to the road, as our line was in advance of that on our left, and we were running into the line of fire of our own artillery." A soldier in the 23rd New York recalled, "Halting at the fence we saw that the rebels had halted on the crest of a hill, and had reformed. There must have been a brigade or two large regiments of them. Lying down behind the fence, we opened fire upon them and again drove them . . ."[65]

Patrick thought the enemy was simply reforming, but he was now facing a fresh Confederate brigade under Roswell Ripley. He ordered his men back across the stone ledges. With pressure growing along his flank and rear, Confederate artillery fire tearing at his ranks, and with ammunition running low, Patrick pulled his three regiments back fifteen rods to a low meadow near the D.R. Miller barn, where the men were protected by rock ledges at right angles to Hagerstown Pike. The men brewed coffee while awaiting ammunition and reinforcements, because, as Patrick reported, "they

having moved so early as to fail of breakfast." Hooker's I Corps now was out of the fight, except for the two brigades of Maj. Gen. George Meade's division in reserve and Patrick's brigade.[66]

The XII Corps was now entering the fight. Hooker requested support for Capt. Joseph Campbell's battery and Col. William Goodrich's brigade (Brig. Gen. George Greene's division) was sent west, forming in front of Patrick's men, who would provide them with support. Patrick knew the terrain well and the location of the enemy. He tried to explain this to Goodrich and suggested he "advance cautiously, forming his skirmishers, until I could get reinforcements to go in on his left and front in sufficient force . . ." Patrick then rode across Hagerstown Pike in search of reinforcements. Goodrich was in no mood to wait, so he waved his command forward through the West Woods with Patrick's three regiments behind them. When Patrick returned he found Goodrich dead and the men of the two brigades barely holding on. A soldier in the 23rd New York wrote home about this portion of the battle. "We waited a half hour, but no cartridges came. – An awful crash of musketry followed—the brigade [Goodrich's] gave way and came fleeing toward us. We were ordered forward to the cliff again, and taking position, we fully returned fire. The stampede was stopped for a moment, but our right was being flanked by a large force." The enemy, Brig. Gen. Jubal Early's brigade, with remnants of the Stonewall Division, was fortunately content to simply fire at the Union troops and not mount a charge.[67]

Patrick's and Goodrich's troops remained on the west side of Hagerstown Pike when portions of Sedgwick's division, defeated in the West Woods, barreled into them. Patrick reported: "All were retiring rapidly before the enemy along the same line as in the preceding engagement, and I once more threw my brigade under the ledge, partly to rally the retiring troops and partly to hold with our remaining cartridges until order could be restored. But few of the troops rallied, however, and after holding my command here until the enemy were

38

close upon our right flank, the brigade was withdrawn in an unbroken line to the wood on the other side of the road, and took position to arrest the flight of stragglers." Col. Rogers of the 21st New York later wrote that all efforts to stop Sumner's troops' flight were ineffective. "It was a complete rout," he wrote, "and they passed on out of sight." Patrick's troops were prevented from firing into the Confederates as they were following Sumner's men so closely.[68]

Historian Ezra Carman praised Patrick and his men, writing, "Patrick was a tenacious and resourceful fighter and undoubtedly would have checked the farther advance [of the enemy] … had the right not been turned by the 53rd Georgia." With increasing pressure on his front and his flank turned by Brig. Gen. Paul Semmes' brigade (Maj.

Gen. Lafayette McLaws' division), Patrick ordered his men to retire by the right flank. Most of the men had expended their ammunition by this point. Semmes' men were not about to let Patrick get away so easily and fired into the New Yorkers, causing a number of casualties among the retreating troops.[69]

Patrick pulled his men back to the North Woods where they rejoined Doubleday's division. The brigade remained in the area for several weeks before moving toward the Potomac on October 20. Meanwhile, the historian of the 21st New York noted, on "Wednesday October 8, the boys were turned out to say good-bye to their old General, who, having been assigned to duty at headquarters as Provost Marshal General of the army, on that day relinquished his command to Colonel Rogers."[70]

**Joseph Stahl**

\* \* \*

## 4th Brigade: Brigadier General John Gibbon

**Units:** 19th Indiana, 2nd Wisconsin, 6th Wisconsin, 7th Wisconsin
**Strength:** 1,729[71]
**Losses:** 348 (68k-275w-5m)[72]

Arguably one of the most celebrated and finest fighting units in the Union Army, the "Iron Brigade" or the "Iron Brigade of the West," as some called them, deserved its well-earned moniker after fighting at the Battles of Brawner's Farm, South Mountain and Antietam between August 28 and September 17, 1862. The four regiments comprising the Iron Brigade, the 2nd, 6th and 7th Wisconsin, and the 19th Indiana were brigaded together October 1, 1861 under the command of Rufus King, a New York native, who stood fourth in the West Point Class of 1833. The 2nd Wisconsin was the only regiment of the four that had seen combat prior to Brawner's Farm. It was engaged at First Bull Run July 21, 1861 as part of Col. William Sherman's brigade.

The Iron Brigade, the only brigade in the Army of the Potomac composed entirely of western regiments, was forged into a formidable fighting

force by John Gibbon, who replaced King on May 7, 1862, when King ascended to division command. Gibbon completed King's process of outfitting the men in frock coats and tall black Hardee hats, pinned back on one side and sporting a black ostrich feather. The unit was feared and respected by the enemy who referred to them as "Those Damned Black Hats." Light Company B, 4th United States Artillery under Capt. and aide-de-camp Joseph Campbell joined the brigade after Gibbon took command. It would remain associated with the Iron Brigade for much of the rest of the Civil War. Together they were a redoubtable pair.[73]

The brigade also had another distinction: John Gibbon. Gibbon was born in Holmesburg, Pennsylvania in 1827 and moved with his family to Charlotte, North Carolina when he was a youth. Gibbon was appointed to West Point and graduated in 1847, ranking 20 out of 38 cadets. Gibbon, a professional to the core, brought the soldiers of the brigade under regular army regulations, teaching them the rudiments of what it meant to be a well-trained, disciplined soldier. He respected the volunteers, writing in his memoirs, "The first marked feature I noted was their quick intelligence. It was only necessary to explain a thing but once or twice to enable them to catch the idea." While the men did not especially like him at first, the volunteers came to understand after a while, what Gibbon taught them saved lives and won battles. They stayed connected with Gibbon long after he moved up to higher command, and each would remember the other fondly during their waning years.[74]

At the August 28, 1862 Battle of Brawner's Farm, the Iron Brigade (III Corps of the Army of Virginia) stood toe to toe against Maj. Gen. Stonewall Jackson's Wing of the Army of Northern Virginia, including his vaunted Stonewall Brigade. Gibbon noted in his memoirs, "This fight was the 'baptism of fire' for my brigade and we paid a heavy price for it. Out of the 1,800 men I took into action about one third (725 men) were killed or wounded in the space of one hour and a half." Jackson also lost about one third of the 3,500 men engaged. Following the Second Bull Run Campaign, the Iron Brigade withdrew to the defenses surrounding Washington, arriving there on September 2. While in Washington, the III Corps became the I Corps of the Army of the Potomac and Gibbon's brigade was designated as the 4th Brigade of the 1st Division.[75]

The Iron Brigade and other I Corps units left the defenses of Washington on September 6, 1862. Gibbon noted, "Our Division marched out the 7th Street road and all night long the men plodded wearily. We reached Leesburg [Leesborough] the next day at 2 o'clock. Our corps moved along by short marches and reached New Market on the road to Frederick (Maryland) on the 12th." The "exhausted brigade" arrived on the outskirts of Fredrick on Saturday, September 13. "They camped in a plowed field near the banks of the Monocacy River within sight of the church spires of Frederick." Rufus Dawes of the 6th Wisconsin wrote home, "There are few fairer landscapes in the country than this." He also heard the sounds of battle coming from the west where the rear guard of Lee's army engaged the advancing elements of McClellan's forces. As the men lay down to a fitful sleep they knew another battle would soon be in the offing.[76]

The men were up early on September 14 and by 8:00 a.m., they were marching through Frederick with the six Model 1857 Light 12 Pounders of Light Company B, 4th U. S. Artillery in tow, headed westward on the National Road toward Turner's Gap in South Mountain. As they marched through town, past houses gaily decorated with American flags, they were greeted by citizens smiling and waving handkerchiefs. By afternoon, the brigade had traveled eight miles and passed through Middletown, Maryland, where the men could plainly hear the roar of battle emanating from Fox's Gap. After leaving Middletown, the Iron Brigade marched about a mile and a half toward South Mountain and then was allowed to stop and "orders were given to build fires for coffee." The fires were barely lit before the orders were countermanded. The troops reformed and continued the advance.

## South Mountain

As the I Corps neared the mountain passes around three in the afternoon, units were separated from the columns and formed in line of battle. Most of the I Corps took a right on a road that branched off the National Road that ran parallel to South Mountain in the direction of Frosttown Gap. Gibbon's command was detached from the 1st Division and ordered to report to Wing Commander, Ambrose Burnside, whose forces were heavily engaged since morning to the southwest in an attempt to take Fox's Gap. Gibbon halted adjacent to the road and awaited Burnside's orders.

The terrain over which the Iron Brigade marched as they advanced toward the base of South Mountain was rolling, open farm fields. At the base of the hill, the fields to the north of the National Road were replaced with densely timbered lands. South of the road was open ground and some timbered areas which provided shelter and concealed troop movement and placement. Rock

40

outcroppings and large boulders were evident in the open fields.[77]

Gibbon described in his after-battle report what happened upon receipt of Burnside's orders: "Late in the afternoon (about 5:00 p.m. when the general advance was made by Hooker) I was ordered to move up the Hagerstown Turnpike [National Road] with my brigade and one section of Gibbon's battery (Light Company B, 4th U.S.) to attack the position of the enemy in the gorge [Turners Gap]." He placed the 7th Wisconsin on the right of the National Road and the 19th Indiana on the opposite side of it, preceded by two companies of skirmishers from the 6th and 7th Wisconsin. The Hoosiers were supported by the 2nd Wisconsin and the Badgers by the 6th Wisconsin, each advancing about 200 yards in the rear. Gibbon worried about his left flank, so Capt. W.W. Dudley's company of the 19th Indiana was thrown in that direction as flankers. A section of Campbell's battery under Lt. James Stewart followed in the rear of the first line. The skirmishers soon encountered Alfred Colquitt's brigade's (D.H. Hill's division) skirmish line and Gibbon ordered his artillery into action. Colquitt's five regiments were deployed on the mountainside behind a stone wall, about 850 yards from the summit. Dusk was settling on the battlefield as Gibbon's men prepared for action.[78]

The 7th Wisconsin skirmish line advancing on the right of the National Road was stopped in its tracks by volleys from the 23rd and 28th Georgia skirmishers in its front and by portions of the 27th Georgia across the road to the left. They returned the fire but could go no further while the rest of the 7th Wisconsin deployed behind them. Across the road, the 19th Indiana drifted to the left, so the 2nd Wisconsin advanced and closed the gap with the National Road. The two regiments moved cautiously forward and drove Colquitt's skirmish line away, allowing the 7th Wisconsin across the road to continue its advance against the left side of Colquitt's line. The 7th Wisconsin halted again when it was hit by a devastating frontal fire from the 23rd Georgia and an enfilade fire from the 28th Georgia. The 2nd Wisconsin, which had cleared the

enemy from its front, changed front to the right, and now parallel to the National Road, opened fire on the 23rd Georgia across the road to relieve pressure on the 7th. Because these Wisconsin boys were on lower ground and the Georgians were well protected by their stone wall, the impact was minimal. The 2nd Wisconsin expended their ammunition and fell back and the 19th Indiana moved up to take their place, but they too had no success in driving the 23rd Georgia from its position.

Gibbon brought up the 6th Wisconsin and shoved it onto the right flank of the 7th Wisconsin to enfilade the 28th Georgia. Col. Edward Bragg divided his regiment into two wings, with one behind the other and each leap-frogged the other toward the enemy. Sgt. James Sullivan of the 6th Wisconsin wrote of this maneuver: "Part of the men would fire and then rush forward while the others covered them and had at the rebels and then the rear line would pass through to the front and lay down while the other line kept up the fire, and in that way it was a steady advance." Ammunition was giving out, as was daylight, so Gibbon ordered his men to halt and maintain their position, thus ending their action at Turner's Gap.

Gibbon wrote in his report, "Thus the fighting continued until long after dark, Stewart using his guns with good effect over the heads of our own men. We had made our way up to the gorge of the pass, then the fire on both sides gradually died down." The Iron Brigade lost more men at South Mountain than any other I Corps brigade—318 (37 killed, 251 wounded and 30 missing), or about 25 percent of its strength, without forcing Colquitt to withdraw. The brigade did win lasting fame and a new name on the bloody slopes of South Mountain. Formerly referred to as the "Black Hat Brigade" it now earned the name of "Iron Brigade." The story behind the name is unclear, but it may have originated with McClellan himself as he watched the brigade moving up the mountainside. It was first officially used in a newspaper article a little more than a week after the battle.[79]

## Antietam

When the sun rose on September 15, 1862 it was evident the Confederate forces opposing the Iron Brigade the previous evening had abandoned their positions on South Mountain. The brigade, with the rest of the division, marched down the mountain's western slope, through Boonsboro and then made a left onto Sharpsburg Pike. When they reached Antietam Creek, the men observed Confederate artillery atop the ridges on the west side of the stream. Gibbon and his men spent the night of September 15, until about mid-afternoon on September 16, bivouacked near Sharpsburg Pike, as "shells from the enemy's guns now and then passed over our heads." The brigade numbered about 970 at this time.[80]

About 4:00 p.m., the Iron Brigade received orders to cross the stream with other brigades of the I Corps. Gibbon's command waded across Antietam Creek at a ford downstream of the Upper Bridge. Gibbon noted, "Moving by the flank toward the Sharpsburg-Hagerstown pike by way of Smoketown they [the men] found cover in a range of hills. Marching through an orchard the men filled their pockets and near-empty haversacks with apples." The men bivouacked for the night in a drizzling rain in an open field near Hagerstown Pike on the Joseph Poffenberger farm with their 1st Division comrades.[81]

Gibbon wrote, "The next morning we needed no reveille, for at the earliest dawn firing commenced, the shells commencing to scream over our heads" from Confederate batteries on Nicodemus Heights. Maj. Dawes recalled, "Doubleday came galloping along the line and ordered our brigade be moved from its exposed position. We had marched ten rods when whiz-z-z! bang! Burst a shell over our heads; then another; then a percussion shell struck and exploded in the very center of the moving mass of men. It killed two men and wounded eleven" from the 6th Wisconsin. "The column moved on to the shelter of" the Poffenberger barn. "For a few moments it was checked but "the shock was but momentary" and as Bragg wrote to his wife, the

men advanced, "leaving the mangled bodies of their comrades on the ground." "About 6:00 a.m., at the voice of its Lt. Colonel, the 6th moved on again, followed by the rest of the brigade" southward into and through the North Woods, to an open field beyond. The six guns of Light Company B, 4th U. S. Artillery advanced southward following the brigade. The farm of D.R. Miller looming in front of them and, beyond it, a large cornfield that blocked them from seeing Col. Marcellus Douglass' brigade (Alexander Lawton's division) deployed beyond it.[82]

When Gibbon's brigade reached the plowed field immediately south of the North Woods, on the east side of the Hagerstown Pike, the 6th Wisconsin was deployed in line of battle with two companies thrown out as skirmishers. The brigade's adjutant, Lt. Frank Haskell, pulled up to Lt. Col. Bragg and ordered him to "advance as far as it was safe." Bragg replied through gritted teeth, "Give General Gibbon my compliments, and tell him it has been damned unsafe for the last thirty minutes!" Bragg tugged on the brim of his hat and ordered his regiment forward, followed by the brigade's other three regiments, obliquing to the right until its right flank reached Hagerstown Pike, and then the advance shifted southward. The 6th's skirmishers reached D.R. Miller's farm buildings and drove off Confederate skirmishers. The regiment pushed on over the open field, which was swept by artillery fire from Stuart's guns on Nicodemus Heights and Capt. William Poague's guns in their right front. The right wing of the 6th Wisconsin passed to the right of D.R. Miller's garden without difficulty but the left wing was delayed by a picket fence that surrounded the garden. As the two wings united in the orchard south of the garden the men could see Confederate skirmishers disappear into the western part of a thick, head-high cornfield to their front. "The other three regiments of the brigade followed the 6th Wisconsin and halted, closed in mass, in the open space between Miller's orchard and the cornfield, while the 6th Wisconsin skirmishers were searching the corn," reported historian Ezra Carman.[83]

The 6th Wisconsin followed their skirmishers into the corn, supported on their left by the 2nd Wisconsin. The 6th Wisconsin was immediately hit by enemy fire in their front and an enfilading fire on their right from Confederates lying along the fence paralleling Hagerstown Pike and others behind a rock ledge that paralleled the road to the west. To counter this threat, Gibbon sent the 7th Wisconsin and the 19th Indiana, who were following in the second line, across Hagerstown Pike to its west side. With the 19th Indiana on the right and the 7th Wisconsin on the left, the two regiments pushed forward against the forward Confederate brigades (Col. Andrew Grigsby and Capt. John Penn's brigades of Brig. Gen. J.R. Jones' Stonewall Division). Outnumbered and flanked, the Virginians scrambled from the protection of their rock ledges, and headed southward into the northern edge of the West Woods.[84]

Across the road, the 6th and 2nd Wisconsin approached the southern edge of the Cornfield. Dawes recalled what occurred next: "a long line of men in butternut and gray rose up from the ground." These were the Georgians from Douglass' brigade. "Simultaneously, the hostile battle lines opened a tremendous fire upon each other," Dawes continued. "Men, I can not say fell; they were knocked out of the ranks by dozens. But we jumped over the fence, and pushed on, loading, firing, and shouting as we advanced." Douglass' men had been battling for almost an hour and had lost about half of their effectives, including Douglass. The sight of this new line of enemy troops caused them to take flight. Dawes noted in his men a "great hysterical excitement, eagerness to go forward, and a reckless disregard of life." After a short halt, the Wisconsin men continued their advance with Walter Phelps' brigade behind them to lend support. The 2nd and 6th Wisconsin with the 2nd U. S. Sharpshooters on their right, now headed toward Dunker Church and the high ground beyond. They were almost immediately hit on their right flank by an intense fire from William Starke's and Col. J. Jackson's Confederate brigades across the road that had rotated to the right to face Hagerstown Pike.

Savage fighting, which lasted for about fifteen minutes, erupted on both sides of Hagerstown Pike. The 19th Indiana and 7th Wisconsin, with support from Marsena Patrick's brigade and Campbell's battery, drove into the enemy's left flank and rear, creating scores of casualties and forcing them from their positions.

With the threat to their flank neutralized, the 2nd and 6th Wisconsin, with Phelps' brigade continued toward the Dunker Church. The men and officers were becoming increasing concerned about their rifles becoming fouled and, according to Dawes, it took "a hard pounding to get the bullets down." The Wisconsin men of the Iron Brigade and Phelps' New Yorkers approached Smoketown Road when a "long and steady line of rebel gray, unbroken by the fugitives who fly before us, comes sweeping down through the woods around the church," according to Dawes. These men were from Brig. Gen. John Hood's division who "delivered such a business like fire that the pursuing forces halted, then fell back in some disorder, those on the left through the corn" those on the right retreating to D. R. Miller's farm. Dawes was more graphic in describing the initial interaction with Hood's men. "They [Hood's men] raise the yell and fire. It is like a scythe running through our line … It is a race for life that each man runs for the cornfield." Hood's men followed.[85]

As the left of Hood's division (Col. William Wofford's brigade) followed the 2nd and 6th Wisconsin northward, it passed the left flank of the skirmish line of the 19th Indiana on the higher ground in the West Woods. The Hoosier skirmishers observed the movement and reported it to their commander, Col. Alois Bachman, gathered the 7th Wisconsin and Patrick's three regiments together, changed front to the left and opened fire on Wofford's left flank. The Union troops then charged toward the fence lining Hagerstown Pike. Seeing this movement, Col. Wofford ordered his Hampton Legion, 18th Georgia, and 4th Texas to move obliquely to the open ground bordering the road where the two sides fired into each other. Campbell's battery fired double canister into

Wofford's flank, and with intense small arms fire in its front, Wofford was forced to withdraw his brigade. The 19th Indiana and some of Gen. Patrick's troops pursued across the pike to the brow of the ridge on the east side of Smoketown Road where they encountered fresh Confederate re-enforcements from Roswell Ripley's brigade. Ripley's men opened fire, mortally wounding Bachman and forcing the 19th Indiana to fall back across Hagerstown Pike where it rejoined what was left the 7th Wisconsin and Patrick's brigade.

Meanwhile, the 2nd and 6th Wisconsin retired through the Cornfield to a shallow swale where they rallied prior to moving across Hagerstown Pike to support Campbell's Light Company B, which was engaged in a desperate struggle with Wofford's infantry. Gibbon was able to extricate Light Company B from its perilous situation, limber up the guns and move them to the rear by 7:30 a.m., allowing the Iron Brigade's four regiments to disengage and move to the rear near the North Woods where they remained until about 1:00 p.m. before moving with the rest of Doubleday's division to the high ground north of the Joseph Poffenberger Barn.

The brigade lost an additional 348 men at Antietam (68 killed, 275 wounded, 5 missing). With the 318 casualties at South Mountain, the brigade lost a total of 666. It had performed well, earning its new moniker.[86]

**Sharon A. Murray**

* * *

# 2ND DIVISION—

## Brigadier General James Ricketts

Brigadier General James Ricketts should have been home, recuperating from battlefield wounds, not in command of the 2nd Division during the Maryland Campaign. Born in New York City on June 21, 1817, Ricketts graduated from West Point in 1839 and served in Florida, seeing action during the Mexican War. He commanded a battery at the Battle of First Bull Run, positioned on Henry Hill, that was overrun by Brig. Gen. Thomas Jackson's brigade. Ricketts sustained four wounds, including a serious leg injury. He was captured and recuperated in Richmond under his wife's care. Exchanged in January 1862, he was promoted to the rank of brigadier general for "gallant and meritorious conduct" at First Bull Run. He mounted a horse for the first time in April 1862 and joined his new command, a division in Irvin McDowell's III Corps in the Army of Virginia, the following month. He commanded his division at Cedar Mountain and Second Bull Run, but continued suffering from his wounds as he marched north at the head of his division during the Maryland Campaign.[87]

The division, with the rest of the I Corps, was in reserve at Brookville, Maryland until September 11, when it marched ten miles to Cooksville. The following day's march took the men to Ridgewood, about 15 miles southeast of Frederick, and then to the Monocacy River on September 13. The division was on the road early on September 14, passing over the Catoctin Mountains and through Middletown.[88]

The division arrived at the base of South Mountain at about 5:00 p.m. after the 17-mile march and formed into line of battle. It played a minor role in the fight for Turner's Gap and the

Frosttown Plateau as most of the fighting involved John Hatch's and George Meade's divisions. While in reserve, Ricketts placed Brig. Gen. Abram Duryee's brigade on the right, Brig. Gen. George Hartsuff's in the center, and Col. William Christian's on the left. Meade believed he was being flanked on his left and requested support from Hooker. The I Corps commander quickly responded by sending Duryee's brigade to bolster his line. According to historian Ezra Carman, "Owing to the distance to be marched, Duryee did not arrive until just at the close of the engagement, and was then thrown in" to the battle line. It engaged portions of Brig. Gen. Robert Rodes' brigade and helped drive it back up the mountain. Christian's brigade was called into action in the fading light to relieve Abner Doubleday's brigade on the left, which was running out of ammunition. Christians' men threw a few volleys at the Confederates, but night ended the fighting. Ricketts' last brigade, Hartsuff's, was brought up after dark and formed as a bridge between Hatch's division on the left and Meade's division on the right. Ricketts' division lost only 35 men on South Mountain because of its reserve capacity.[89]

Ricketts' division marched with the remainder of the I Corps through Turner's Gap to the shores of Antietam Creek on September 15. It followed Meade's division across the creek on the Upper Bridge at about 4:00 p.m. on September 16 and swept west where it spent the night just beyond the North Woods. Christian's brigade was on the left, Hartsuff's on the right and Duryee's in reserve. According to historian Ezra Carman, "Hartsuff's and Duryee's brigades were directed to flank to the right out of the [Samuel] Poffenberger woods, and then advanced south, Hartsuff, in deployed line, leading with Duryee, in column of divisions, in close support on the right. Christian's Brigade was to go directly forward on the left of the Smoketown Road."

The plan quickly went awry when Hartsuff was wounded and Christian exhibited erratic behavior, halting their advance, so only Duryee drove forward. It battled elements of Col. James Walker's and Col. Marcellus Douglass' brigades (Alexander Lawton's division), but was ultimately forced to withdraw. Hartsuff's brigade could not advance until Col. Richard Coulter of the 11th Pennsylvania assumed command. It then swept toward the Miller Cornfield, where it battled Douglass' and Brig. Gen. Harry Hays' brigades. Col. Peter Lyle of the 90th Pennsylvania took command of Christian's brigade and it drove forward into the East Woods. The two brigades held their positions as ammunition dwindled, but were forced to retreat in the face of John Hood's division's counterattack after 7:00 a.m. Ricketts' men made their way to the rear, where they remained during the rest of the battle.[90]

One of Edwin Sumner's (II Corps) aides sought out Hooker as John Sedgwick's division arrived near the East Woods. Unable to find the wounded Hooker, he came upon Ricketts who exclaimed only 300 men of the I Corps could be mustered. Historian Ezra Carman believed this statement was true, if confined to Ricketts' division and unjustly claimed, "The division commander seems to have lacked the disposition or energy to gather his regiments, which were in the woods and fields in the rear." Carman may not have been aware of Ricketts proximity to the action, resulting in two horses being shot out from under him. The second horse fell on him, reinjuring his prior wounds. He probably retained command of his division because he did not believe any of his subordinates were up to the task.[91]

The division carried 3,158 men into battle and lost a total of 1,051 (153 killed and 898 wounded). The 2nd Division carried on without Ricketts after the Maryland Campaign. He never fully recuperated from his wounds and requested a leave of absence on October 19, 1862. He did not return to the army until the Shenandoah Valley Campaign of 1864.[92]

**Bradley M. Gottfried**

\*\*\*

## 1st Brigade: Brigadier General Abram Duryee

**Units:** 97th New York, 104th New York, 105th New York, 107th Pennsylvania
**Strength:** 1,574
**Losses:** 327 (59k-223w-35m)[93]

Volunteers for the 1st Brigade came forward in late 1861 from New York and early 1862 from Pennsylvania. These men were largely "farmers, mechanics and woodsmen of a rugged hardy physique, many familiar with the use of a rifle, accustomed to daily toil and skilled in the use of mechanical tools." The New York volunteers hailed from small towns and rural communities in the central and western parts of the state. The Pennsylvanians enlisted from the south-central counties along the Maryland border, north through the coalfields and all the way to Bradford County at New York's border. The men spent late 1861 through early 1862 in their home states. The regiments were fully mustered into service by the second week of March and were transported via rail to the nation's capital. Forts in the defensive boundary of Washington served as quarters until April 16 when orders arrived forming the four regiments into the brigade.[94]

The brigade's initial commander was Brig. Gen. Abram Duryee, an ambitious and successful businessman. Born in New York City in 1815 of French Huguenot stock, he was well educated and became a profitable businessman in the mahogany trade. Duryee was fascinated by military matters and served in several militia regiments, including the famous 7th New York prior to the war. He quickly rose in rank from non-commissioned and junior officer to colonel in 1849. The 7th New York was known for its drilling proficiency and its status as a destination for some of the city's well-to-do sons. The regiment was called upon numerous times to quell disturbances in the city, including the unfortunate and deadly Astor Place riot in 1849. Duryee remained in command until 1859. At the outbreak of the Civil War he became colonel of the 5th New York, known as "Duryee's Zouaves." His soldiers received as much notice for their mastery of drill as for their gaudy attire. The regiment was one of the first to see action in the war at Big Bethel in June. Duryee's expertise in drill led to his promotion to the rank of brigadier general on August 31, 1861. He was given a brigade the following spring.[95]

Duryee spent three weeks drilling the brigade at Camp Reliance, near Alexandria, Virginia. The brigade became part James Ricketts' division of Irvin McDowell's III Corps in the newly formed Army of Virginia commanded by Maj. Gen. John Pope in late June. The brigade played a minor role at Cedar Mountain in early August, where Duryee was slightly wounded, and again at Thoroughfare Gap. Second Bull Run was the first major encounter for the brigade, where a massive Confederate onslaught overwhelmed Duryee's brigade, which left the field precipitously after sustaining a loss of 391. Most of the losses, over 200, were men missing or captured.[96]

Orders to "Pack up and fall in" were barked unexpectedly at twilight on September 6 and the brigade was on the road toward Washington City. It crossed the Aqueduct Bridge to 7th Street in Washington and then turned north, toward Maryland, marching at a frenetic pace. Dozens dropped from the ranks exhausted while others, who could not resist the luxuries of food and drink, left the ranks along Washington's streets to indulge. The column finally halted at daybreak and the fatigued men and opportunists caught up with their respective commands.[97]

After marching four miles on September 7, the soldiers heard news they were under the command of George McClellan. The men greeted this change of command with "lively satisfaction." The soldiers were feted as "deliverers" in Maryland. At Mechanicsville (now Olney), the Star-Spangled Banner floated from roofs or was "waved by gentle hands" as they passed. Each hamlet or town "greeted them with cheers of welcome and tokens of hospitality." The soldiers were struck by the "home-like dwellings and well-stocked barns," in contrast to the depleted and ravaged Virginia countryside. In just a few days the men saw the "patriotism with these good people is not an abstract theory, but is a living fact," according to the brigade's historian. The column reached the vicinity of Frederick on September 13.[98]

## South Mountain

Reveille sounded at 3:00 a.m. on Sunday, September 14 and the army was moving by sunrise. The column marched through Frederick and the citizenry was jubilant at the sight of the soldiers. The brigade reached Middletown on the National Road, about eight miles away, after frequent stopping and starting. The men could hear gunfire in the distance as South Mountain came into view. Duryee's brigade was summoned at approximately 4:00 p.m. The men took a narrow road paralleling the base of South Mountain where a member of the Pennsylvania "Bucktails" led the brigade deftly up the slopes as the sound of gunfire grew closer. George Meade's Pennsylvania Reserve Division was slugging it out on the steep mountainside with Brig. Gen. Robert Rodes' tenacious Alabama brigade. Duryee's men were called into action at about 5:30 p.m. The 105th New York and 107th Pennsylvania fixed bayonets and advanced side by side up the

steep terrain, led by Duryee on horseback. The remaining regiments followed.[99]

"Cheering like mad men," the regiments charged up the mountainside through a gap between Brig. Gen. Truman Seymour's and Col. Thomas Gallagher's brigades of Meade's division. Duryee led from the front, "yelling the loudest of any of us" remembered Lt. James Thomas of the 107th Pennsylvania, perhaps realizing this influx of fresh troops might break the obstinate Confederate line. "The enemy were scattered and in much confusion ... flying before us," wrote Capt. James MacThomson commanding the 107th. The 12th Alabama rallied behind a stone fence directly in front to make one more stand. In unison with Meade's resolute fighters attacking from the flanks, Duryee's men made a dash toward the stone fence and then climbed over it. Confederate resistance collapsed. It was now nearly dark and despite some lingering resistance by some of Rodes' men, the fighting ceased. After the 17-mile march since daybreak and the exhilaration of battle, the soldiers collapsed on ground "strewn with rebel dead." Duryee's brigade lost 5 killed and 16 wounded in the fighting. They had finally tasted victory.[100]

The army was on the move again by 9:00 a.m. the following day. The Confederates had abandoned the mountain during the night and were in full retreat toward Sharpsburg. Droves of Confederate stragglers were taken prisoner along the crowded road winding down the west side of the mountain. The line of blue soldiers following the National Road down to Boonsboro, turned left and headed for Keedysville and Sharpsburg. The column halted at about 1:00 p.m. before reaching Keedysville to wait as other troops streamed past. The march resumed that night, as the men trudged through Keedysville, turned right off the main road and crossed a stone bridge over Little Antietam Creek to bivouac in an open field.[101]

## Antietam

After sporadic bugle calls and an "irregular cannonade" throughout the day on September 16, orders finally arrived sometime after 3:00 p.m. to pack up and move. The I Corps crossed Antietam Creek using the Hitt (Upper) Bridge and a nearby fording site, heading generally west. Duryee's brigade, with the rest of Ricketts' division, crossed Antietam Creek at the bridge and marched west until it reached Smoketown Road, where it turned left and approached the Joseph Poffenberger homestead, where it bivouacked. Few men slept that night. A light rain began after nightfall and pickets exchanged fire a few hundred yards south of where Duryee's and Ricketts' other brigades lay.[102]

At dawn, Duryee's brigade formed into a marching column of two companies abreast and advanced across a plowed field, towards a small woods just south of the Joseph Poffenberger farm. George Hartsuff's brigade was on its left, preparing to advance toward the East Woods. William Christian's brigade was to follow. Abner Doubleday's division was further to the right and with Ricketts,' would smash into Lee's left flank. Trouble began almost immediately, for enemy artillery fire rained down on the brigade as it entered an open plowed field south of the North Woods. "We halted for about five minutes, the enemy's shot and shell flying about us like hail, killing and wounding some of our poor fellows," recalled MacThomson, a 28-year-old schoolteacher. In the absence of any field grade officers, MacThomson led the 190 men of the 107th Pennsylvania into the fight. "One shot exploded beneath the muzzle of a gun in [Capt. James] Thompson's battery taking down three artillerymen," remembered John Delaney, also of the 107th. The 105th New York provided volunteers to replace the fallen artillerymen.[103]

Duryee's brigade advanced through the batteries and down a slope to the north fence of a cornfield and formed lines of battle. The 107th Pennsylvania was on the right of the brigade, followed by the 97th New York, 104th New York and 105th New York on the left of the line close to the East Woods. The men laid down when they reached the north fence of the Cornfield as two Pennsylvania batteries on the rise of ground behind them fired

over their heads to drive away the Confederate skirmishers in the Cornfield. Duryee's men were up and on their feet at 6:00 a.m. and quickly entered the Cornfield, driving south toward the enemy. "The corn was taller than our heads and very dense," recalled Henry Shaefer of the 107th Pennsylvania. The line moved quickly through the corn, but limited visibility and artillery fire made alignment difficult. Upon reaching the south fence, Marcellus Douglass' brigade (Alexander Lawton's division) lying in the clover field in front of them, rose and fired a deadly volley into the brigade's ranks that staggered it. The two New York regiments on the left recovered quickly and climbed the fence and headed for the Georgians. The 104th New York advanced about 120 yards and the 105th New York about 160 yards in the face of a murderous fire. Now on open ground, the two regiments drew more attention from Confederate artillery and the right of Douglass' line poured an incessant fire. Two regiments of James Walker's brigade on Douglass' right opened fire onto the 105th New York's exposed left flank. Col. Howard Carroll of the 105th New York went down with a severe wound. With seemingly no support on their left, the two New York regiments withdrew to the Cornfield fence line and lay down to return fire, bringing Carroll with them.[104]

Withering blasts from the three left regiments of Douglass' brigade stopped the 107th Pennsylvania and 97th New York at the Cornfield's south fence. Men fell and were knocked from the ranks as officers and non-commissioned officers scurried to restore order. The men returned the Georgians' fire from the scant protection of the fence, some taking a knee to shoot into the smoke-filled pasture at their adversaries. The 97th New York fired their Enfield rifles "with coolness free from all perturbation." They did not, however, venture from the fence line and "each side just stood and fired upon the other" The 38th Georgia regiment suddenly charged, and was cut to pieces by the New Yorkers' and Pennsylvanians' fire. Part of the 107th Pennsylvania was separated from the rest of the regiment by a limestone ledge over four feet in height. This bit of elevation gave those men an initial advantage by permitting them to shoot into the left of Douglass' battle line. The 26th Georgia regiment soon scampered up the slope on their part of the field and delivered a destructive fire into the Pennsylvanians and the right of the 97th New York. There was more trouble for the 107th New York as men from Andrew Grigsby's brigade (J.R. Jones' division) west of Hagerstown Pike dashed to the post and rail fence along that road and fired into their unprotected right flank.[105]

Duryee did not unnecessarily endanger himself in the fighting, keeping a respectable distance in rear of his brigade. After about half an hour of intense fighting, word reached him that his left regiments were in danger of being flanked and erroneously informed him they were giving way. Without investigating, he sent a staff officer to order their withdrawal. Duryee might well have perceived that Hartsuff's brigade was delayed in moving into the East Woods on his left and Doubleday's attack was stalled on the right. His brigade was completely unsupported when two regiments of Truman Seymour's brigade in the East Woods repositioned and allowed Walker's men to enter the woods and endanger the 105th and 104th New York. Those two regiments knew their situation was precarious but not insurmountable, if and when supporting troops arrived. Their accurate and deadly fire forced Douglass to pull back the right of his line and the two regiments Walker sent forward were withdrawn. Still, when Duryee's adjutant arrived with word to pull back, the two regiments complied. "How I or any of the boys came out of that carnage alive is more than I can tell you," wrote H. W. Burlingame of the 104th.

Things did not go smoothly when the adjutant reached the lines of the 97th New York and 107th Pennsylvania with orders to retire. Those two regiments were fully engaged and not all of the men received the orders. The density of the corn made seeing anything to the left difficult. Only parts of the regiments pulled back at first. A slackening of the enemy's fire made them realize that something occurred to their left. Capt. R.S. Eggleston of the 97th New York investigated and found "only the dead remained" on his regiment's left, so he ran up the "roll of ground" on the right to see that none of the Pennsylvanians were there. At that point, the 97th New York closed ranks and left the field, as did a remnant of the 107th Pennsylvania.[106]

As Duryee's men retired, they encountered a portion of Hartsuff's brigade moving south into battle. Hooker, riding about the field, mistook Duryee's survivors for reinforcements and ordered them back into battle before realizing his mistake. Some of the men did rejoin the battle, but most took positions in support of batteries north of D.R. Miller's house and were not called upon again. Of the estimated brigade strength of 1,100 men, nearly 30 percent were killed, wounded or missing. There is little doubt that withdrawing to the fence line and lying down to return fire spared the 104th and 105th from many more losses. The men spent September 18 gathering the wounded and "nothing was omitted which science or humanity could suggest to alleviate their suffering," noted the brigade's historian.

The brigade marched to Mercerville, Pennsylvania on the Potomac River a week later and camped there until the army marched into Virginia again in November. Duryee requested a 30-day leave of absence beginning on October 3, and never returned to command the brigade. Angered and insulted when passed over for command of a division and replaced as brigade commander, Duryee resigned his commission in January 1863.[107]

**William Sagle**

***

## 2nd Brigade: Colonel William Henry Christian, Colonel Peter Lyle

**Units:** 26th New York, 94th New York, 88th Pennsylvania, 90th Pennsylvania
**Strength:** 1,417[108]
**Losses:** 254 (38k-197w- 29m)[109]

The 2nd brigade was formed in May 1862 with Brig. Gen. Zealour B. Tower in command of the original three regiments. The 94th New York was not added until early September 1862. All were three-year regiments with the exception of the 26th New York, whose men were mustered in for two years. Col. William Christian assumed command after Tower was wounded in action on August 30, 1862 at the Battle of Second Bull Run. Thirty-six year old Christian joined the 26th New York Infantry as its colonel on May 21, 1861. Prior to the war he was a civil engineer living in Utica.[110]

The brigade, with the rest of James Ricketts' division, crossed the Potomac River on September 5 and left Washington the following day for the long march north to Frederick, Maryland. According to the historian of the 26th New York, "The weather was beautiful, the cornfields were full of roasting ears, and the fruit trees hung heavy with their bounty." The men were given soft bread on September 8—the first the men had enjoyed since July 4. The 12-mile march through Mechanicsville (now Olney) and Brookville brought the brigade to beyond Cooksville. The historian of the 88th Pennsylvania noted the "people all along the road expressed the greatest surprise at the number of men passing, saying they never thought there were that many men in the whole country." The column finally reached the "thrifty little city of Frederick" on September 14 on its way to South Mountain.

### South Mountain

The division marched 12 miles to Turner's Gap, where the I Corps was battling units from Maj. Gen. James Longstreet's wing. Christian's brigade arrived at the base of South Mountain at about 6:00 p.m., but was held in reserve during the combat so the men pulled off their knapsacks and rested. The brigade was brought up to relieve Doubleday's brigade in the fading light. It fired a few volleys into the enemy until nightfall ended the fighting.[111]

### Antietam

Christian's brigade encamped on the mountain until daylight next morning when it marched to Boonsboro and camped about a half mile outside of Keedysville. During the march through Turner's Gap, the men observed the "Great numbers of Rebel dead [that] lay on the field … ghastly pale in death." McClellan rode past the brigade at Keedysville and, according to John Vautier of the 88th Pennsylvania, "all cheered him." The entire I Corps crossed Antietam Creek on the afternoon of September 16 and moved forward to a position north of the Samuel Poffensberger farm where they laid on their arms all night in the woods.[112]

On the morning of the battle, Christian's brigade was in the rear of George Hartsuff's brigade on the east side of Smoketown Road; Abram Duryee's brigade was on the opposite side of the road. Ricketts' ordered his division south toward the enemy positions just beyond the East Woods and Cornfield at 6:00 a.m. The brigade was shy a regiment as the 90th Pennsylvania was sent southwest to support Capt. Ezra Matthews' battery. Upon entering the Samuel Poffenberger woods, the men were exposed to falling limbs, torn off trees by enemy shells. John Vautier of the 88th Pennsylvania recorded in his diary how the shells were "howling and shrieking as they went on their mad course. Soon the zip, zip, zip, zip of the musket balls sound around our ears." The men could see a line of enemy skirmishers in the distance.[113]

Christian brought the three regiments forward into the open field and formed them in column of division. The Confederate artillery on Nicodemus Heights to the west and the high ground beyond Dunker Church saw these movements and opened a deadly cross-fire that created confusion within the ranks. Vautier recorded the confusing series of commands issued to the brigade: "First it was 'forward guide center,' then 'by the right flank,' and then 'Forward guide center' again, then we would oblique to the left and so on." To the men's amazement, Christian rushed to the rear. Vautier explained long after the war, "He [Christian] had seen too much combat and was not able to maintain his composure when the shell began to fall among the brigade … He took the brigade in, in good shape, but when the fire got very hot he "walked Spanish", cut and ran, an example that fortunately was not followed by his brigade." An officer in the 26th New York wrote after the war, Christian "showed the 'white feather' and when we received the first fire he turned and fled to the rear and almost created a stampede among some troops in the rear; by shouting that our flank was turned and the lines completely broken." Others recalled "[a]fter abandoning his men on the field, Christian was later found cowering behind a tree." It appears that Peter Lyle of the 90th Pennsylvania assumed command of the brigade.[114]

As the brigade entered the East Woods, it deployed into line of battle, from right to left: 88th Pennsylvania- 94th New York- 26th New York. The brigade straddled Smoketown Road as it marched through the East Woods, and passed through Seymour's Pennsylvania Reserve brigade (Meade's division), which was heading for the rear. Lyle's men reached the fence at the southern edge of the woods and encountered Col. James Walker's brigade (Alexander Lawton's division), which had been fighting in this sector since first light. To Walker's right rear, Roswell Ripley's brigade (D.H. Hill's division) stood, awaiting orders to advance. Christian's brigade opened fire on the two enemy brigades, felling many of their men. Hartsuff's brigade stood to Christian's right.[115]

Hartsuff's brigade had gone in prior to Christian's and was "melting away" under enemy attacks. Richard Coulter, now in command of that brigade after its commander's wounding, needed help and when he saw the 90th Pennsylvania returning to its (Christian's) brigade through the East Woods, he begged for assistance. Lyle quickly complied and moved his regiment west to come in line with Coulter's men. It did not stop at the fence line at the edge of the corn, but continued its advance about 60 yards beyond it into the clover field. According to historian Ezra Carman, the regiment "planted the colors on a rock ledge and, facing southwest, opened fire upon [Harry] Hays and [Alexander] Lawton."[116]

Coulter's decimated brigade fell back, leaving the 90th Pennsylvania exposed in the clover field. The rest of Christian's brigade was to its left, taking a breather after driving Walker's brigade from its front. A cloud of enemy troops from Col. Evander Law's brigade (John Hood's division) soon approached. They had been summoned from the West Woods to drive the Yanks out of the East Woods and Cornfield. Without support and with their ammunition almost expended, Christian's men retraced their steps through the East Woods and headed for the rear. Lt. William P. Gifford of the 26th New York explained, "Our regiment did not retire in a body, it gradually wasted away. There was [sic] no field officers in sight, and the companies were not fully officered so that it became a sort of a go as you please . . ." Gifford recalled the brigade halting in the "vicinity of the ammunition train and spent the greater part of the day reorganizing and replenishing our ammunition, and rations." The brigade then moved back to a position north of the Joseph Pofferberger house where it supported the I Corps artillery and remained there the rest of the day.[117]

The historian of the 88th Pennsylvania related a post-battle incident. The men were issued green coffee on September 18 but had no way of preparing it, so they went about "crushing the berries as best they could. One group of grinders had improvised a cracker-box and a huge elongated shell for duty as a coffee-mill, and were doing a brisk business in ground coffee when a red-edged artilleryman passing by examined the shell, and informed the astonished grinders that it was primed with a perfect percussion-cap, which needed but a slight blow to explode it. Business in that shop was suspended without further ceremony."[118]

**Joseph Stahl**

\* \* \*

## 3rd Brigade: Brigadier General George Hartsuff, Colonel Richard Coulter

**Units:** 16th Maine, 12th Massachusetts, 13th Massachusetts, 83rd New York, 11th Pennsylvania
**Strength:** 1,913[119]
**Losses:** 599 (82k-497w-20m)[120]

The Massachusetts, New York, and Pennsylvania units under Brig. Gen. George Hartsuff's command entered the Maryland Campaign a shell of their former selves. These four regiments faced their first test fighting James Longstreet's command of the Army of Northern Virginia at Thoroughfare Gap on August 28, 1862. Two days later, the brigade participated in the action atop Chinn Ridge at Second Bull Run, losing 657 men.[121]

Hartsuff did not lead the brigade into action during the prior campaign. Instead, he suffered "from some disease of the stomach" and rode in an ambulance during most of the Second Bull Run Campaign. His illness prevented him from joining the brigade until September 7. Though Hartsuff was not perfectly healthy during the Maryland Campaign, he still brought years of army experience to the brigade. Born in New York State in 1830, Hartsuff graduated from West Point in 1852. He served with the 4th United States Artillery in Texas and Florida prior to the Civil War, receiving a serious wound during the latter campaign. Though it did not kill him, it plagued him for the rest of his life and led to his death in 1874.[122]

To offset the losses of the previous campaign and increase the brigade's numbers, the green 16th Maine joined the brigade on September 9. However, the Mainers were detached from the rest of the brigade almost immediately and remained at Ridgeville to protect "against raids of rebel cavalry and guerrillas," wrote a member of the regiment.

The rookies did not rejoin the brigade until September 19.[123]

Like Hartsuff, the brigade's veterans needed rest after their trial at Second Bull Run. However, Robert E. Lee did not grant them that wish as he began his invasion of Maryland. The early marches into Maryland taxed the men. As part of Ambrose Burnside's Right Wing, they reached the outskirts of Frederick on September 13 and camped along the Monocacy River.[124]

### South Mountain

An early reveille stirred Hartsuff's men from their slumber along the banks of the Monocacy River outside Frederick on September 14. The men consumed their rations and prepared coffee while they awaited the orders to "Fall in." Around daybreak, Hooker put his corps in motion towards South Mountain. The I Corps stood in battle formation by 5:00 p.m. that day, preparing to assault the Confederate forces posted on the slope of the mountain. Ricketts' division assumed a reserve role to George Meade's and John Hatch's frontline divisions. Hartsuff's brigade participated only in the tail end of the action when it advanced to connect Hatch's and Meade's divisions as darkness descended on the field. The brigade suffered minimal casualties—two killed and four wounded.[125]

The next morning's dawn found Hartsuff's men shaken out in a skirmish line. Orders reached the brigade from corps headquarters to advance and ascertain if the enemy remained in its front. Hartsuff's line advanced unmolested over the wreck of the previous day's battle into Turner's Gap itself. Maj. Gen. Israel Richardson's II Corps division took up the pursuit from there, allowing Hartsuff's

52

men to break ranks and eat their morning rations. Hooker's corps joined the rest of the army's pursuit of the enemy toward Antietam Creek. The men reached Keedysville on the stream's eastern bank about 3:00 p.m. on September 15.[126]

The Army of the Potomac's victory on the slopes of South Mountain buttressed its shaky morale. "The *espirit de corps* of this fine body of troops was now particularly high," recalled Pvt. George Kimball of the 12th Massachusetts. "The men felt that if any shadow of discredit had attached to them on account of the disaster at Manassas, it had been swept away by the brilliant flank movement at South Mountain." Hartsuff's men now prepared themselves for their next test.[127]

## Antietam

Hooker put his corps in motion for the west side of the creek at 2:00 p.m. on September 16. Hartsuff's brigade crossed the stream at the Upper Bridge and, following in the footsteps of Meade's division, bivouacked on either side of the Smoketown Road in the rear of Truman Seymour's brigade. "The march had been a short one," conceded Pvt. Kimball, "but much time was consumed in waits and measures and the day was far spent" by the time the brigade bivouacked for the night. The soldiers slept without removing their accoutrements in preparation for battle. The night of September 16-17 was an uncomfortable one for the men. "Picket-firing, and movements of artillery and troops, gave little chance for sleep that night," recalled one 12th Massachusetts soldier.[128]

Hooker ordered Ricketts' division forward at dawn. Ricketts intended Hartsuff's and Duryee's formations would advance side-by-side. However, shortly after beginning the movement, Hartsuff halted his brigade while he personally reconnoitered the ground in front of him. Nearing the northern edge of the East Woods, Hartsuff was wounded in the left hip. He stayed mounted on his horse but the loss of blood soon forced him to the ground. Two soldiers came forward to help him rearward. Hartsuff placed his arms around their shoulders as

support, but blood spurting from the wound stopped him again. A few nearby men secured a blanket and carried him to an ambulance. While he passed to the rear, the general "begged of those who carried him not to tell his brave men of his mishap, feeling that their love for him and their confidence in his leadership might perhaps create a temporary feeling of discouragement."[129]

Hartsuff's fall was a great loss to the men of the brigade. Furthermore, it delayed the brigade's advance for 30 minutes, thus shattering the idea of it moving in concert with Duryee's brigade. After halting for a half-hour, Richard Coulter of the 11th Pennsylvania assumed command and Ricketts ordered the brigade forward to support Duryee's beleaguered men.[130]

Each regiment threw two companies of skirmishers out to the front and advanced. The brigade encountered a stout post and rail fence along the Poffenberger farm lane. While under fire, the soldiers found the fence too sturdy to be torn down and suffered many casualties in attempting to climb over it. Once over this obstacle, Coulter's line, moving "as one man, and as if on parade" passed through both the East Woods and the open ground north of the Cornfield.[131]

Marcellus Douglass' brigade's (Lawton's division) skirmishers peppered the brigade's advance but gave way under the renewed forward movement. The 12th Massachusetts held the brigade's right and its left connected with the 11th Pennsylvania. These regiments advanced through the Cornfield. The 13th Massachusetts moved partially through the corn and partially through the East Woods while the 83rd New York, holding the brigade's left, marched under the mature trees of the East Woods.[132]

The 12th Massachusetts, on the right of the brigade, held the advantage of advancing through slightly easier ground and thus deployed into action first. It held "a swell of ground" fifty yards south of the Cornfield's southern boundary, its right slightly more advanced than its left. The 11th Pennsylvania quickly joined on the left of the 12th Massachusetts in the open ground. Coulter's two left regiments, upon reaching the Pennsylvanians' right flank, wheeled to the right and formed, facing west, along the edge of the East Woods, causing the brigade's formation to be concave in shape. According to battle historian Ezra Carman, this deployment "was executed in good order" and in less than three minutes. The entire line immediately opened fire.[133]

As Coulter's line completed its deployment at 6:40 a.m., Harry Hays' Louisiana brigade (Lawton's division) advanced past Douglass' right and against the right center of Coulter's brigade. The two brigades slugged it out with successive volleys at close quarters.

Col. Stephen Lee's battalion's guns posted on the Dunker Church Plateau played great havoc in the ranks of the 12th Massachusetts. Its commander, Maj. Sidney Burbank, fell mortally wounded early in the fight. The regimental colors, prominently displayed in the center of the line out in the open and floating above the darkening battle smoke, became the only visible target to hit for the Confederates. "As fast as the men would fall they would close towards the centre on the colors," wrote Capt. Benjamin Cook. This centered more men into the terrific fire of Hays' Louisianans and shortened the regiment's line, enough so that when it withdrew from the field it was no longer in touch with the rest of the brigade.[134]

However, Coulter's concave line held the advantage of position, and the men poured a deadly fire not only into Hays' front but, thanks to the left of the 13th Massachusetts' and the 83rd New York's west-facing disposition, they also hit Hays' right flank. Hays' command suffered staggering losses in approximately 20 minutes of action, much of it from the fire of Coulter's line.[135]

Little maneuvering occurred following Hays' initial advance and repulse. Both sides maintained a tremendous fire, as the casualty lists attest, particularly among Coulter's two right regiments fighting entirely in the open, and the lines shrunk under the intense, close-quarters combat. Fighting with the 13th Massachusetts deployed in the open ground west of the East Woods, Pvt. Prince Dunton recalled of the action, "I fired 28 rounds

and came out of it without a scratch. One ball just grazed my shoe. The men that stood each side of me both got shot. I do not see how any of us got out alive. The shot and shell fell about us thick and fast, I can tell you, but I did not think much about getting shot after the first volley."[136]

The 83rd New York on the left of the line carrying .69 caliber Harpers Ferry muskets loaded with buck and ball, were in an excellent position to completely enfilade the Louisianans in front of them. Pvt. William Prince of that regiment wrote that of the approximately 20 rounds he fired before being wounded, "I took deliberate aim at some one every time."[137]

Despite the pounding Hays' men took at the expense of Coulter's line, the Confederate fire also took its toll in the ranks of these four regiments. Richard Coulter recognized the plight of his brigade. The incessant pleas of the regimental commanders for more ammunition added urgency to Coulter's search for support. Spurring away from the front lines, Coulter rode into the East Woods where he found Peter Lyle, commander of the 90th Pennsylvania (William Christian's brigade). "For God's sake Colonel, come and help us out, our ammunition is exhausted," Coulter yelled. Lyle quickly ordered his regiment forward to relieve Coulter's command. As soon as the 90th Pennsylvania assumed its position south of the Cornfield, the survivors of Coulter's brigade withdrew and took stock of the firefight through which they had just passed.[138]

Fighting on the brigade's right, the most exposed position, the 12th Massachusetts suffered dearly, losing 222 men of the 262 engaged for a loss of 84.7% (Company H served at brigade headquarters and missed the action). The 11th Pennsylvania suffered approximately 53% casualties while the brigade's two other regiments' losses were proportionally lower because of the protection afforded by being adjacent to the East Woods.[139]

The brigade's losses were not restricted to the line soldiers, however. Of the 51 officers the brigade carried into action, excluding Hartsuff and his staff, 22 (43%) were casualties of the battle. Of course, the loss of Hartsuff early in the action further decapitated the brigade's officer corps. [140]

The men replenished their ammunition, then the brigade supported the Federal artillery clustered on the northern end of the battlefield in the afternoon. When the officers called roll at 3:00 p.m. to assess the brigade's strength, only 298 men were present.[141]

Hartsuff's brigade is not usually one of the first brigades to come to mind for visitors to the Antietam battlefield. But in its 20 minutes of action, the brigade suffered higher proportionate losses than any other Union brigade on the field that day. The action on the brigade's front was particularly intense. Little to no maneuvering occurred between Hays' and Hartsuff's commands. Instead, as the 12th Massachusetts' George Kimball described it, "This was no accidental or forlorn hope affair, but a square stand-up fight." The casualty figures of Hartsuff's brigade bear this out. Thus, the brigade deserves more attention than it has previously received.[142]

**Kevin R. Pawlak**

* * *

## Pennsylvania Reserves Division—

### Brigadier General George Meade

Born in Caditz, Spain on December 31, 1815, George Meade was raised in Pennsylvania and was appointed to the U.S. Military Academy in 1831. After graduating in 1835, Meade saw action in Florida with the 3rd Artillery, but decided that military life was not for him. He resigned from the army in 1836 to pursue a career in the private sector, but returned to the military in 1842 as a topographical engineer. Meade served in the War with Mexico in 1846-47 then returned to his engineering duties. He was promoted to captain in 1856 and placed in charge of the U.S. Lakes Survey until the outbreak of the Civil War. Meade was promoted the rank of brigadier general in August 1861 and placed in command of a brigade in the Pennsylvania Reserves Division. His brigade saw heavy action in Maj. Gen. Fitz John Porter's V Corps during the Seven Days Battles and he was severely wounded at Glendale. Meade recovered to lead his brigade at Second Bull Run and assumed command of the division during the march in Maryland when John Reynolds was summoned to command the Pennsylvania militia.[143]

The division rested in the vicinity of Arlington Heights and Munson's Hill, Virginia on September 2 after its arduous ordeal during the Second Bull Run Campaign. The long roll drumbeat got the men to their feet late on September 5 to begin the pursuit of the Confederate army in Maryland. The division, now part of Joseph Hooker's I Corps, passed through Washington in the early morning hours of September 6 and took up the line of march through Maryland in subsequent days. Reynolds bade the division farewell on September 12 and reluctantly headed north to Pennsylvania under orders to organize the state's militia. Hooker protested Reynolds' loss in a message to the War Department, "He commands a division not of the best character. I have no one to replace him." This swipe at the Reserves' demeanor was also a slap in the face to Meade, who was next in order of rank to command the division. Hooker had harbored misgivings toward the Reserves since June and disparaged its fighting abilities in a battle report. Despite apprehension and wounded feelings in the higher ranks, the division plodded on, reaching the west bank of the Monocacy River near Frederick on September 13.[144]

The Reserves formed marching columns early on September 14 and headed toward Frederick City, and then followed the National Road over Catoctin Mountain. The division reached a stream beyond Middletown before 1:00 p.m., after marching more than 15 miles. After a pause of about two hours, the Reserves, with the rest of Hooker's corps, headed toward the enemy in position along South Mountain's ridgelines and gaps. Any reservations that Hooker had regarding the division's fighting ability were cast aside as the division prepared to assault Brig. Gen. Robert Rodes' tough Alabama brigade. Two narrow roads snaked up the mountainside with a large ravine between them. Forming in open fields, the men faced terrain of parallel ridges, boulders, rocks, stone fences and swales, which was better suited to the defenders' advantage. "When to these features are added heavily wooded portions and frequent depressions in the ground, some idea might be gathered of the task laid upon the division," recorded the regimental historian of the 13th Pennsylvania Reserves. The terrain was intimidating even without an armed enemy to defend it. Truman Seymour's brigade, on the right of the division's line, attacked the left of Rodes' line anchored on a spur near northernmost Frosttown Road. Col. Thomas Gallagher's brigade in the center and Col. Albert Magilton's on the left drove straight ahead toward the largely concealed Confederates. Col. Peter Stevens' 550-man South Carolina brigade arrived and formed on Rodes' right, in the path of Magilton's men.

Seymour sent skirmishers from the 13th Pennsylvania Reserves – the "Bucktails" – forward first and met intense resistance from the Alabama skirmishers. The "Bucktails" soon brought their breech-loading rifles to bear and advanced. Seymour recognized the importance of the road running up the spur to Rodes' left and moved his brigade to flank the Confederate line. Rodes shifted the weight of his brigade to meet Seymour's attack, but the Pennsylvanians won the fight for the road and compromised the Confederate position. Still the Alabamians and Carolinians fought tenaciously using every terrain feature to advantage. "A murderous fire of musketry was opened on us," recalled Sgt. A.F. Hill of the 8th Reserves, as Confederates mowed down his regiment from behind a stone fence. Hill added, "With a wild shout we dashed forward while volley after volley poured upon us…we rushed madly on."

Lt. Col. Robert Anderson took over Gallagher's brigade when that officer went down with a severe wound. Cohesion within the brigades was difficult and visibility limited, as the division ground its way up the mountain. Capt. A.J. Bolar remembered how the Confederates only gave ground when met with "balls or bayonets from our men." By nightfall, the division reached the summit as the remaining Confederates withdrew. The Reserves' success drew praise from Hooker who wrote that though the enemy disputed their advance, "he did not check it."[145]

The division was in action again during the late afternoon of September 16. The Reserves crossed the Upper Bridge spanning Antietam Creek in pursuit of their foe with the "Bucktails" and the 3rd Pennsylvania Reserves leading the way. The remainder of the division marched in columns of divisions, pushing south across fields toward the East Woods and Joseph Poffenberger farm. A sharp firefight developed as the "Bucktails" encountered elements of John Bell Hood's division near the East Woods. Anticipating an attack, Meade deployed the rest of the division that stretched to Hagerstown Pike. Artillery roared from both sides as Seymour's brigade pushed Confederates from the East Woods under a terrific din of gunfire. Darkness put an end to the nasty late day encounter and saved the Reserves and all of Hooker's vulnerable corps from an attack.

At first light, Seymour's brigade caught a glimpse of James Walker's and Marcellus Douglass' brigades (Alexander Lawton's division) deployed in front of them in low pasture and plowed fields in front of the East Woods. Seymour's men opened fire and an intense clash ensued-- the deadliest single day in American history now began. Just before 6:00 a.m., in the growing daylight, Hooker unleashed his main attack. Abner Doubleday and James Ricketts' divisions advanced through the prone men of Anderson's and Magilton's brigades in and near the North Woods. The attack got off to a ragged start, but gained momentum by 6:30 a.m. George Hartsuff's brigade (Ricketts' division) relieved Seymour's stalwart fighters in the East Woods and the Confederate line yielded as Doubleday's troops advanced out of the Cornfield on their right.

At approximately 7:00 a.m., Hood's division sprang to the attack and quickly regained much of the ground garnered by Hooker's onslaught. As the Union assault collapsed, Meade ordered Magilton's and Anderson's brigades forward. The Pennsylvanians formed battle lines along the north fence of the Cornfield and waited until retreating Union troops cleared their front. "The enemy advanced to within a few paces of our lines," recalled Lt. Col. Samuel Jackson of the 11th Reserves. Anderson's men then let loose destructive salvos stopping the 1st Texas regiment about 30 yards from the fence. With matter-of-fact understatement, Jackson said the enemy "retired in confusion" after his men fired. Magilton's brigade was struck by two hard-hitting Mississippi regiments from Evander Law's brigade, breaking their formation. The veterans regained their composure and stopped a Confederate incursion in the East Woods. Anderson's brigade charged through the Cornfield with the 9th Reserves advancing beyond its south fence. Hood's attack, which Meade called, "one of the most critical moments of the morning" was stopped.[146]

The arrival of the XII Corps allowed the withdrawal of the Pennsylvania Reserves to the Joseph Poffenberger farm, within sight of mountains of their home state. They were not engaged again in the campaign. Meade's division was the last to engage the enemy on September 16 and the first to fire on them the next morning. Although Hooker had indirectly disparaged Meade before the Battle of Antietam, he wrote in his report, "I desire to make special mention of Brigadier General Meade for the great intelligence and gallantry displayed by him."[147]

**William Sagle**

**\* \* \***

## 1st Brigade: Brigadier General Truman Seymour

**Units:** 1st Pennsylvania Reserves; 2nd Pennsylvania Reserves; 5th Pennsylvania Reserves; 6th Pennsylvania Reserves; 13th Pennsylvania Reserves (a.k.a., 1st Pennsylvania Rifles and "Bucktails")
**Strength:** 1,902[148]
**Losses:** 155 (24k-131w)[149]

The men of Brig. Gen. Truman Seymour's brigade awoke near the Monacacy River, finished their coffee, scoured out their tin cups with a bit of Maryland sand, and took their place in the long blue column marching west in search of Robert E. Lee's main body on the morning of September 14. Their steps were lively; for the first time, they were heading toward battle in friendly territory, enjoying warm receptions from the civilians in Frederick, Middletown, and other towns along their route. "Union flags [were] displayed out of nearly every window, the people seemed to be very much rejoiced at us driving the rebels before us and getting the clear of them." The day would bring a victory for George McClellan's army on South Mountain and high praise for the brigade, setting the stage for Seymour's troops to open the Battle of Antietam two days later.[150]

Seymour, an accomplished painter from Vermont, was a graduate of the illustrious West Point class of 1846. He remained on active duty in the years following his West Point graduation and was an artillery captain at Fort Sumter when it was attacked. In April of 1862, he was promoted to brigadier general of volunteers and given command of a brigade that included the 1st, 2nd, 5th and 6th Pennsylvania Reserves. By the time the Maryland Campaign began five months later, these soldiers were hardened veterans. As part of the Pennsylvania Reserves Division, the brigade fought under the I Corps in the Peninsula Campaign Battles of Mechanicsville, Gaines' Mill, Glendale, and Malvern Hill (where Seymour was temporary division commander), and under the III Corps at Second Bull Run/Manassas. A fifth veteran regiment, the 13th Pennsylvania Reserves "Bucktails," joined the brigade on September 7. Legendary for their marksmanship skills, buck tail hats, and breech-loading Sharps rifles, the companies were now reunited as a regiment after several months of split special assignments with the I, III and V Corps in the Peninsula Campaign, Shenandoah Valley, and Manassas.[151]

## South Mountain

Seymour's brigade approached the small village of Bolivar, east of South Mountain along the Old National Road, around 2:00 p.m. on September 14. The road climbed to the crest of the mountain two miles ahead and then through Turner's Gap. Union cavalry reported the gap heavily defended. All day, Confederate observers watched Union IX Corps troops snake south at the crossroads in Bolivar, on their way to Fox's Gap to attack the Confederate right flank. Now they watched as Union troops from Hooker's I Corps turned north at the crossroads to attack their left flank north of Turner's Gap. Seymour's position on the far right of the Union line meant success or failure was on his shoulders.[152]

Seymour's brigade led the rest of George Meade's division and the I Corps northwest about a mile and a half, stopping near the Mt. Tabor Church where Meade, Hooker, and Wing Commander, Ambrose Burnside, conferred. They could hear the guns and see puffs of white smoke from the IX Corps' action on Fox's Gap. The road ahead curved up the mountain to Frosttown Gap, about three quarters of a mile north of Turner's Gap. Seymour could see Confederate artillery and infantry posted behind strong positions on the hill, and they could see him. Hooker described the scene: "In front of us was South Mountain, the crest of the spinal ridge of which was held by the enemy in considerable force. Its slopes are precipitous, rugged, and wooded, and difficult of ascent to an infantry force, even in absence of a foe in front."[153]

Behind rocks and stone walls on the mountainside, Confederate Robert Rodes' brigade of Alabama regiments, about 1,200 men strong, stretched in a thin line between Turner's and

Frosttown Gaps. Wide gaps yawned between Rodes' regiments and he knew he couldn't hold on for long. Rodes was counting on the rough terrain and obstacles to buy time until reinforcements came or darkness fell.[154]

Around 5:00 p.m., Meade ordered his division to attack Frosttown Plateau in a three-brigade front, with Seymour on the right, Magilton on the left, and Gallagher in the middle. Seymour deployed to the north side of the road leading to Frosttown Gap, with the Bucktails (Col. Hugh McNeil) in front as the division's skirmishers, supported by the 2nd Pennsylvania Reserves (Capt. James Byrnes), and part of the 1st Pennsylvania Reserves (Col. R. Biddle Roberts). Behind them, left to right, were the rest of the 1st Pennsylvania Reserves, the 5th Pennsylvania Reserves (Col. Joseph Fisher), and the 6th Pennsylvania Reserves (Col. William Sinclair).

The Bucktails' advance brought artillery shells raining down on them from the crest, as muskets flashed from skirmishers behind a stone wall at the mountain's base. The Bucktails dove for cover behind the rocks and trees, but their breech-loading rifles gave them an edge as they picked off Confederate skirmishers who had to stand to reload. The Pennsylvanians charged, dislodging the Confederates from their first line of defense and driving them up the mountain. The rest of Seymour's brigade advanced behind them.[155]

Rodes watched the Union advance from the mountaintop and saw Seymour's line extending beyond his left flank, which rested on Frosttown Gap. He ordered the 6th Alabama (Col. John Gordon) across the gap and onto the knoll to the north, supported by artillery. As Gordon's men moved into position, they charged their surprised attackers. The skirmish that followed had a devastating effect on the Bucktails, especially from the enemy's supporting artillery. Seymour wrote, "The exposure was great, and a number fell under the accurate fire of the shell from these guns."[156]

Seymour ordered the 6th Pennsylvania Reserves to charge around the north side of the 6th Alabama and take the knoll. Sinclair's regiment "dashed like a steed released from his curb against the very muzzles of their guns," sending the 6th Alabama reeling. The Bucktails and 6th Pennsylvania Reserves took the hill commanding Rodes' left flank and rear, capturing many prisoners along the way. [157]

About the same time, Seymour ordered the 1st, 5th and 2nd Pennsylvania Reserves to change the direction of their ascent to the left and charge into a cornfield where he saw a concentration of Confederate soldiers, telling Col. Roberts (1st Pennsylvania Reserves), "Col., put your regiment into that cornfield and hurt somebody!" Volleys were fired, bayonets were leveled, and the whole line drove the enemy up and over the crest. "All order and regularity of the lines were soon destroyed. From wall and rock the enemy was driven, until the summit was reached and the loud cheer of victory rising from the crest, rolled down the mountainside."[158]

The sun was setting as all five of Seymour's regiments crested the mountain and began pushing Rodes' men southward toward Turner's Gap. They had achieved Meade's objective, with Hooker as their witness: "From its great elevation and the dense smoke which rose over the stop of the forest, the progress of the battle on this part of the field was watched with anxious interest for miles around, and while it elicited the applause of the spectators, they could not fail to admire the steadiness, resolution, and courage of the brave officers and men engaged." As darkness fell, Seymour's exhausted troops ended the pursuit.[159]

The soldiers spent a cold night on the mountain, sleeping on their arms and expecting the contest to resume in the morning. When dawn broke the following day, Seymour's men discovered the enemy was already gone, beating a hasty retreat toward Sharpsburg with the Union II Corps in hot pursuit.

Success on South Mountain cost Seymour 171 casualties, with the heaviest toll in the 6th Pennsylvania Reserves (54 casualties) and the 13th Pennsylvania Reserves "Bucktails" (50 casualties). Seymour's troops buried their dead as they awaited orders to join the column.[160]

Around noon, Seymour's brigade descended the western slope of the mountain and marched to Keedysville, where, as a 2nd Pennsylvania Reserves soldier recalled, "the boys were most liberally supplied with hot cakes and bread by Mr. John Cost, a good Union citizen of that place, and from whom Capt. Byrnes got liquer enough to give the men a ration." The troops set up bivouac along the east side of Antietam Creek. On the west side, less than two miles away, John Hood's infantry division and Brig. Gen. W.H. Fitzhugh Lee's cavalry brigade held down Lee's left flank. In less than 24 hours, a clash between them and Seymour's brigade would open the prelude to America's bloodiest day.[161]

## Antietam

Frequent artillery barrages began at daybreak on September 16 as Seymour's men ate their rations of coffee, sugar and crackers, and waited. McClellan ordered the I Corps to cross Antietam Creek around 2:00 p.m. and attack Lee's left flank. Meade's division crossed the Upper Bridge on the Keedysville-Williamsport Road by 3:00 p.m. Seymour's brigade led the column, with the Bucktails thrown forward as skirmishers and the 3rd Pennsylvania Reserves, from Magilton's brigade, in support to their right. Elements of the 3rd Pennsylvania Cavalry scouted the roads ahead.[162]

Seymour's troops followed the winding road about a mile to the Susan Hoffman farm where McClellan himself directed them off the road and southwest, over the rolling hills of the picturesque, 284-acre farm, toward Smoketown Road. By morning, this peaceful, tidy farm would be a place of horror and chaos as a field hospital for hundreds of wounded soldiers, described by New York Times journalist Charles Coffin as "an appalling site" where "the wounded were lying in rows awaiting their turns at the surgeons' tables."

The 3rd Pennsylvania Cavalry suddenly came under fire while riding ahead of the brigade. Confederate cavalry scouts had watched Hooker's crossing earlier in the afternoon and sent word to Lee, who issued a rush of orders for reinforcements to contest the advance. By the time Seymour's troops reached Smoketown Road, the 9th Virginia Cavalry (Fitz Lee) was waiting less than a mile ahead, with Hood's skirmishers (from his own brigades of William Wofford and Evander Law, and Alfred Colquitt's skirmish battalion) massing in the East Woods behind them. An officer from the 9th Virginia Cavalry wrote, "These gallant men, who were destined to meet the first furious onslaught of McClellan's troops, occupied rising ground, partly in the woods, and partly in the open fields, with an open valley winding in front of them … in the distance could be seen the heavy column of the advancing troops."[163]

Hooker ordered the Bucktails and 3rd Pennsylvania Reserves to deploy their skirmish lines, the latter moving off to the right with the rest of Meade's division. McNeil deployed four companies in the fields on both sides of Smoketown Road, leaving six in reserve, and moved steadily south under increasing fire. As the Bucktails passed Samuel Poffenberger's farmhouse, cavalrymen from the 9th Virginia charged forward and nearly overran them before being driven back. McNeil brought up his six reserve companies and prepared to charge, just as two Confederate artillery batteries unlimbered near the East Woods. Capt. Dennis McGee, McNeil's second in command, wrote, "… the enemy's pickets were discovered extending in a line across a plowed field. No sooner had we formed a line of battle than we were opened upon by two batteries, one upon our right, with grape and canister, the other on our left, throwing shell."[164]

The Confederate guns opened fire around 4:30 p.m., causing the Bucktails to hug the ground for 15 minutes while the rest of the brigade caught up. McNeil ordered his men to rise and charge to drive the enemy from the East Woods. The Bucktails rushed forward, their battle lines falling apart under the heavy artillery and musket fire. Seventy-five yards from their goal, the fire became so intense that the men dropped to the ground, rising to run a few feet, only to drop again, pouring shot after shot from their breech loaders. McNeil remained in front of his regiment and called out, "Forward, Bucktails, forward!" just as a bullet struck his heart, killing him instantly. The popular 32-year-old Yale graduate from New York was the first Union officer to die at Antietam, and his death was a heavy blow to the brigade. In a letter home, McGee wrote, "A braver man than him the army did not hold."[165]

McNeil's men continued their charge without their commander and cleared the fence line along the north edge of the woods of enemy soldiers. Seymour deployed the rest of his brigade, from right to left: the 6th Pennsylvania Reserves - 1st Pennsylvania Reserves (behind and to the right of the Bucktails) - 5th Pennsylvania Reserves. The 2nd Pennsylvania Reserves supported Capt. James Cooper's battery near the northwest corner of the East Woods.[166]

Seymour's toughest fight was on his right, where the Bucktails and the 6th Pennsylvania Reserves faced stubborn resistance from the 4th and 5th Texas Infantry (Wofford's brigade) in the D.R. Miller Cornfield, while the left of Law's brigade pressed their front. Confederate artillery pounded Seymour's troops in the East Woods as Meade shifted his batteries to silence them.

McClellan watched the sharp contest unfold from the Pry House on the east side of Antietam Creek until about 6:15 p.m., when darkness obscured his view. The fighting decreased after dark, but didn't stop. Historian Joseph Harsh wrote, "the flare of bursting shells and burning fuses streaking the night sky set a grand but ominous prologue for the morrow's morning."[167]

As darkness fell, the threat in the Cornfield to his right forced Seymour to withdraw the 6th Pennsylvania Reserves about 100 yards to the northwest part of the woods, leaving a strong picket line along the fence between the woods and the cornfield. The 5th Pennsylvania Reserves, who had been under heavy fire on open ground throughout most of the fight, moved up to the woods and formed along the north fence.

Hooker visited Seymour's brigade, isolated in its advanced position, at about 9:00 p.m., and found the picket lines of the two armies so close they could hear each other move about. "I found Seymour's officers and men keenly alive to their proximity to our enemy, and seemed to realize the responsible character of their services for the night." Hooker was probably hearing Alexander Lawton's brigades of Marcellus Douglas and James Walker replacing Hood's men, who had barely eaten or slept in the last few days.[168]

The soldiers on both sides spent a fitful, drizzly night in the East Woods just yards apart, occasional bursts of rifle fire causing casualties and making sleep impossible. A soldier in the 1st Pennsylvania Reserves wrote, "So near were the pickets of the contending forces, that a squad of six men of the enemy were captured, having approached unawares to our line."[169]

The nervous bursts of musket fire intensified and were joined by artillery toward dawn; then the bloody battle of September 17 seemed to begin automatically as the Bucktails fired into the pickets of Walker's brigade in the southern edge of the woods. The 6th Pennsylvania Reserves advanced south and fired into the left flank of the pickets of the 31st Georgia (Marcellus Douglass' brigade, Lawton's division), who had replaced the 4th and 5th Texas. The Confederate pickets to Seymour's right and front were driven out of the East Woods and into the open fields to the south, as the 1st Pennsylvania Reserves moved up between the Bucktails and the 6th and fired into the main lines of Douglass' right and Walker's left. The 5th Pennsylvania Reserves advanced to the southern edge of the woods, to the Bucktails' left, where they fired on Walker's exposed men across a plowed field to their front.

The Bucktails were running low on ammunition and Seymour sent in the 2nd Pennsylvania Reserves to replace them. A soldier in the 2nd Pennsylvania Reserves wrote, "… we crept on our bellies to our position, and opened a heavy fire upon the enemy, both parties keeping the ground and maintaining their positions." Col. Fisher of the 5th Pennsylvania Reserves saw the Bucktails pull back but could not see the 2nd's advance. Misinterpreting the move as a retreat, Fisher pulled back to the Samuel Poffenberger farm and out of the action. This caused the commander of the 2nd Pennsylvania Reserves to withdraw a short distance to protect his left flank. Sensing an opportunity, Walker wheeled his regiments to the left, "taking shelter under a low stone fence … directing their fire at the wavering Yankee regiment, with the view of breaking the enemy's line at this point." The 2nd, along with skirmishers from the 1st and 6th Pennsylvania Reserves, fell back further.[170]

Reinforcements finally arrived about 6:00 a.m. Hooker ordered Ricketts's division to support Seymour with a three-brigade attack, but various factors caused a delayed and piecemeal arrival. As Seymour's regiments fell back, Duryee's brigade marched through the Cornfield to Seymour's right and engaged Lawton's troops. Nearly 40 minutes later, Christian's brigade marched haltingly into the East Woods and was pressed into action by Seymour, who then withdrew his regiments to the Samuel Poffenberger farm. Although three of his regiments later rallied to support Brig. Gen. Samuel Crawford's XII Corps brigade in the East Woods, Seymour's men were not heavily engaged in the chaos for the rest of the day.[171]

Seymour and his brigade deserved every bit of the praise they received from senior commanders following the battles. In three major engagements over four days, they had crushed the Confederate left flank on South Mountain, found the enemy at Antietam and shaped the fight on September 16, and then remained engaged on the following day through the bitter fighting of the I and XII Corps.

The cost was high. The brigade suffered 155 casualties in and around the East Woods at Antietam, for a total of 326 casualties between South Mountain and Antietam. Once again, Col. Sinclair's 6th Pennsylvania Reserves bore the brunt with 69 casualties.[162]

**Laura Marfut**

**\*\*\***

## 2nd Brigade: Colonel Albert Magilton

**Units:** 3rd Pennsylvania Reserves, 4th Pennsylvania Reserves, 7th Pennsylvania Reserves, 8th Pennsylvania Reserves
**Strength:** 1,770[173]
**Losses:** 222 (41k-181w)[174]

The men of the 3rd, 4th, and 7th Pennsylvania Reserves in Col. Albert Magilton's brigade hailed from Philadelphia, and eastern and north-central Pennsylvania. The 11th Pennsylvania Reserves, which would be replaced by the 8th Pennsylvania Reserves in the summer of 1862, came from Pittsburgh. The state initially uniformed and equipped these regiments until they were accepted into national service in July 1861. The men were transported to a camp of instruction at Tenallytown, Maryland and assigned to George Meade's brigade. The Regular Army taskmaster and disciplinarian instructed the officers and drilled the men to exacting demands. Picket duty, drill, inspections, marches, and skirmishes occupied the fall and winter. The brigade relocated to Manassas Junction in March 1861 and Falmouth in May. On June 10, the brigade, with the entire division, joined George McClellan's forces on the Virginia peninsula. Just over two weeks later, the brigade, as part of Porter's V Corps, fought at Mechanicsville, Gaines' Mill, and Charles City Crossroads, incurring heavy losses. After the Seven Days Battles, the 8th Reserves, with scarcely one hundred men in the ranks, was transferred to the brigade in place of the 11th Reserves. The Reserves reinforced John Pope's army and fought well at Second Bull Run, in McDowell's corps. Their losses, with respect to their declining numbers, moved Pope to state how they "were so broken down and diminished in numbers that they are of little use in effective service whatsoever." Meade, in a letter to his wife, stated the men were "pretty well used up, and ought to be withdrawn, reorganized, filled up with recruits, and put into efficient condition." Circumstances would not permit such accommodation as these

battered and defeated soldiers plodded toward Washington.[175]

In West Point's stellar class of 1846, with such luminaries and notables as George McClellan, "Stonewall" Jackson, Jesse Reno, and George Pickett, the name Albert Magilton is somewhat overlooked. Born in New Castle, Delaware in 1826, the son of an Irish-born carpenter, Magilton grew up in Philadelphia and earned an appointment to the U.S. Military Academy. He did well at the Academy, ranking 18th at graduation in a class of 59. Posted as a 2nd Lt. to the 4th Artillery, Magilton earned brevets for his service at Contreras and Cherubusco in the War with Mexico. He served in Florida during the Seminole Wars and on the plains during the troubles in Kansas. Promoted to captain in June 1857, Magilton resigned his commission in December of that year. Magilton was appointed lieutenant colonel of the 2nd Pennsylvania Reserves in April, 1861 and became colonel of the 4th Reserves in October. A history of the 4th Reserves states, "Under his skillful discipline, the regiment acquired a marked professionalism." He led the 4th in the desperate fighting of the Seven Days Battles, where he was wounded at Charles City Crossroads, and again at Second Bull Run. Considered a "chum" and confidant of Meade and Reynolds, Magilton, as ranking colonel, assumed brigade command for the Maryland Campaign when Meade moved up to division command.[176]

Magilton and his brigade rested only a few days after the arduous Bull Run Campaign. Late in the day on September 6, the Reserves joined McClellan's army in pursuit of Robert E. Lee's army, now in Maryland. As part of Joseph Hooker's I Corps, the men followed the National Road toward Frederick, reaching Lisbon on September 12 and bivouacking near Frederick the next day. The citizens welcomed the men marching through the town early on September 14 and Griffin Baldwin of the 7th Reserves noted, "a great display of flags some of which have been used for many months showing that the owners' patriotism was not gotten up for the occasion." The column of troops proceeded on the National Road over Catoctin Mountain, finally coming to a rest at 1:00 p.m. near a creek one mile west of Middletown. The brigade was on its feet again two hours later, marching, with the division and corps, another two miles to the hamlet of Bolivar where a narrow road to the right led to the base of South Mountain. Battle lines formed to attack the Confederate position on the heights and the Pennsylvania Reserves led the way. Meade deployed his division with Magilton's brigade on the left of his divisional line.[177]

## South Mountain

"We entered the woods at the foot of the mountain and were opened upon by the enemy," wrote Lewis Baldwin as the brigade advanced. "The mountain is covered by woods, underbrush and trees," and, he added, "is very rough, with heavy stones serving as breastworks for both parties." Baldwin and the 7th Reserves were in the center of the brigade line, with the 4th Reserves on the right and 8th on the left guiding on Dahlgren Road. The 3rd Reserves were detached from the brigade and sent to the right of the line to watch for enemy activity. The 13th Reserves of Truman Seymour's brigade, with their breach-loading rifles, dispatched Confederate skirmishers.

It was nearly 5:00 p.m. when the attack began and mountain shadows could soon become a factor in the fighting. "A few hundred feet from the base of the mountain was a stone fence," remembered Sgt. Archibald Hill of the 8th Reserves, "below this the ground was clear. When within fifty yards of the fence, a murderous fire was opened on us by rebels who lay concealed behind it." The 8th Reserves were caught in the open ground by this fusillade from the 17th South Carolina regiment of Brig. Gen. Nathan Evans' brigade. "Bullets whistled past our ears," wrote Hill. Then, the 8th bolted forward and, in Hill's words, "with a wild shout, while volley after volley was poured upon us, we rushed madly

on." The 8th reached the wall as the Confederates scampered up the mountainside, using rocks and trees as cover to reform their line. The 8th Reserves pursued them. The left of the South Carolinians' line gave way and the right companies of the 8th dashed forward to outflank them. "We were within twenty to thirty steps of them, directly on their left," Hill recalled, "they did not see us. Then we mowed them down."

The carnage was gruesome and evoked some sympathy from the Pennsylvanians as their prey fell with some becoming wedged between rocks. George Darby of the 8th was awed by the sight of so many of their foes struck in the head by bullets. Lt. Col. Robert Means of the 17th South Carolina was among the wounded. Although the 8th bore much of the fight, the 7th in the center and the 4th Reserves on the right also had their hands full. "As we entered the wooded portion of the hill, they opened on us with a brisk fire," remembered Bates Alexander of the 7th Reserves. "They had a fine opportunity to select their targets in our line," he recalled. Lt. Col. Henry Bollinger of the 7th Reserves was wounded in the chest and passed command of the regiment to Maj. Chauncey Lyman. Despite the barrage, Magilton's men pushed relentlessly up the rugged mountainside, driving their resolute foe to the top. Baldwin claimed the Battle at South Mountain "required all my physical effort that I could muster." Confederate resistance dissipated near the spine of the mountain until darkness ended the day's hostilities. Magilton counted 89 casualties in his brigade. Baldwin summarized the feeling of many in the brigade by stating the fighting at South Mountain, "served to encourage our boys after the defeat at Bull Run and before Richmond."[178]

Lee's army withdrew from the mountain during the night; the Reserves did not pursue until 10:00 a.m. on September 15. Joining the National Road at Turner's Gap, "we marched up the pike towards Pennsylvania as far as Boonsboro where we filed left towards the Potomac," recalled Lewis Baldwin. The men eventually passed through Keedysville and made a right turn onto the road taking them over a stone bridge across Little Antietam Creek. They bivouacked on the ground between the Little Antietam and Antietam Creek until the afternoon of September 16.

At 2:00 p.m., the Pennsylvanians crossed over a bridge at Antietam Creek and proceeded west on Williamsport Road until contact was made with enemy skirmishers in the vicinity of the George Line farm near the Smoketown Road. Four companies of the 3rd Reserves deployed as skirmishers on the right of the road as the column turned left and advanced, in columns of battalions, toward Lee's main body of troops. Magilton's brigade formed into battle line at the Joseph Poffenberger farm as artillery fire whistled in on them at the south edge of the North Woods. "I never found myself in a place that I felt so uneasy" wrote Baldwin, as shot and shell struck the ground in front and trees overhead. The men were urged to lie down until Union artillery dispatched the enemy's guns. With the exception of skirmish firing, the confrontation ended after sunset. Three of Magilton's regiments spent the night in the North Woods while the 8th spent the night on open ground at the Poffenberger farm.[179]

## Antietam

Artillery fire punched the air just after dawn, and Hooker's attack lines, composed of Doubleday's and Ricketts' divisions moved south. Magilton's and Anderson's brigades were kept in reserve. The Pennsylvanians opened spaces for Ricketts' troops as they advanced. Meade's two reserve brigades were ordered to advance by 6:30 a.m. Frank Holsinger in the 8th Reserves wrote, "It was quite early when we left, closed in mass, passing through a depression in the (North) woods and coming to the open ground in rear of D.R. Miller's." Ricketts' and Doubleday's divisions were driving the enemy, gaining ground against their tenacious foe. Everything changed at 7:00 a.m. John Hood's division attacked Hooker's extended and depleted battle lines and, within minutes, sent them flying northward in retreat. Magilton's brigade joined

Anderson's brigade at the fence lining the north edge of the Cornfield to provide a buttress and rallying point for their reeling comrades. "Soon, men began to pour out of the field," recalled Holsinger, "They had big hats and feathers." These were black-hatted Wisconsin soldiers who, with other troops of Doubleday's and Ricketts' divisions, retreated through the Reserves' positions. Union artillery ceased firing, lest they hit their own men in the Cornfield. This pause gave Hood's men time to gain ground on the retreating boys in blue. Magilton's brigade waited for Hood's approach. "We had not been in position along this line of the Cornfield fence ten minutes when the order was given to move to the left on the double quick and rally in the (East) woods," wrote Holsinger.[180]

Hood's ferocious attack now compromised Union resistance in the East Woods. Meade saw the threat and sent word to Magilton to move there. At the order, the men rose, shouldered their weapons, left-faced into column and double-quicked toward the woods with the 8th Reserves in the lead. Suddenly, two Confederate regiments sprang from the Cornfield and, "poured upon us the most withering volley we had ever felt," recalled Sgt. Hill. "Another and another followed and a continuous rattle rent the air," said Hill, "we could not stop to reply — we could but hurry on." With Magilton's men in a marching column four abreast, they were nearly defenseless against two Mississippi regiments from Evander Law's brigade who lay in wait to fire point blank into them. The 3rd and 4th Reserves gave way under the fusillade and bolted up the rise of ground north of the Cornfield with the 2nd Mississippi on their heels. The 7th Reserves, last in the column, were able to form a battle line on the left of Anderson's brigade to slow the 2nd Mississippi and fire into the 11th Mississippi at the fence. The 8th Reserves made it almost to the woods, but had a nasty surprise waiting for them. The 6th North Carolina, straddling the western edge of the East Woods and Cornfield, allowed the 8th to get within thirty feet before blasting them. Well-placed volleys from the Carolinians "decimated our ranks," recalled Hill. The 8th began to run and Hill said, "I did not expect to stop this side of the Pennsylvania line." Maj. Silas Baily, commanding the 8th, managed to steady enough men to fight back. Hill remembered, "a tall, thin, young soldier, cool as a cucumber, his hat off which he was swinging lustily who yelled, 'Rally boys, rally! Die like men; don't run like dogs!'" The 8th Reserves reformed their battle line and returned fire. The 3rd and 4th Reserves joined them and, with the help of Capt. Dunbar Ransom's stalwart Battery C, 5th U.S. Artillery, brought Hood's attack to a standstill. Just past 7:30 a.m., elements of Brig. Gen. Joseph Mansfield's XII Corps arrived and, with remnants of Meade's Reserves and Ricketts' division, drove Hood's beleaguered survivors from the Cornfield and allowed the battered Pennsylvanians to retire from the field.[181]

Magilton's men withdrew to the Joseph Poffenberger farm. They were not called to fight anymore that day, but were under fire as battery support. Two hundred and twenty-two names on the brigade's roster did not answer roll call the next morning. The Reserves were not used in the effort to pursue Lee's army on September 19 and eventually moved into camps near Sharpsburg to recuperate.

Meade still felt that the Reserves should be withdrawn from field service to properly recover from their strenuous campaigning and to refill their depleted ranks. Pennsylvania's governor, Andrew Curtin, felt likewise and petitioned both the president and McClellan to no avail. Visitors and aid societies from Pennsylvania brought food and goods to the men encamped near Sharpsburg and these luxuries alleviated some of their needs. President Lincoln visited the army in early October and reviewed the men. Two regiments – the 121st and 142nd Pennsylvania– were added to the brigade to increase its numerical strength. When the army departed Maryland in late October, the Reserves were still part of it and fought well at Fredericksburg. Albert Magilton resigned his commission on December 23, 1862. On February 8, 1863, the Pennsylvania Reserves were withdrawn from field service and sent to the defenses of Washington to refit and recruit.[182]

**William Sagle**

* * *

## 3rd Brigade: Colonel Thomas Gallagher, Lieutenant Colonel Robert Anderson

**Units:** 9th Pennsylvania Reserves, 10th Pennsylvania Reserves, 11th Pennsylvania Reserves, 12th Pennsylvania Reserves
**Strength:** 1,635[183]
**Losses:** 175 (37k-136w-2m)[184]

The regiments comprising Brig. Gen. George McCall's Pennsylvania Reserve Division assembled at Tenallytown, Maryland in August 1861. Col. John McCalmont, a 39 year-old West Point graduate from Franklin, Pennsylvania, laid the groundwork for turning citizens into soldiers. Instruction and drill began in earnest and classes were instituted to familiarize newly minted officers with the intricacies and demands of military manuals. McCalmont commanded the third brigade of the division, then composed of the 6th, 9th, 10th and 12th Pennsylvania Reserve regiments. Western Pennsylvanians filled two regiments. Eight of the ten companies of the 9th Reserves were recruited in Pittsburgh. The 10th came from the northwestern part of the state, including counties bordering Ohio and southwestern New York. The 6th Reserves hailed from northeastern and central Pennsylvania. The 12th regiment was a polyglot with companies recruited from northeastern, western and central regions of the state. The brigade relocated to Camp Pierpont in northern Virginia on October 9, 1861 where, according to the division's historian, "the organization was perfected and the troops instructed by drills, and by frequent foraging expeditions and reconnaissances [sic]."[185]

Brig. Gen. Edward Ord assumed command of the brigade in November, 1861. An 1839 West Point graduate, Ord served in Florida and saw extensive service on the west coast with the 3rd Artillery and in surveying expeditions. Ord's brigade first tasted blood on December 20, 1861 when it engaged and defeated Confederate Brig. Gen. Jeb Stuart's forces at Dranesville, Virginia. In the two-hour, largely overlooked action, the brigade performed well and received accolades from military and civilian circles craving any military success after the Bull Run and Ball's Bluff debacles. Secretary of War Cameron concluded a congratulatory letter stating, "other portions of the army will be stimulated by their brave deeds and men will be proud to say that at Dranesville they served under McCall and Ord." The men were instructed to paint "Dranesville" in gold on their regimental flags.

Spring brought changes to the brigade as it relocated to Falmouth and then to Fredericksburg, Virginia in May 1862. Truman Seymour, a West Point graduate in the illustrious class of 1846, replaced Ord who was promoted and reassigned. The Reserves sailed to the Virginia Peninsula to reinforce George McClellan's army the following month. Within two weeks of joining McClellan's growing army, the brigade helped stop determined Confederate attacks at Mechanicsville and was involved in the gruesome fighting at Gaines' Mill and actions at White Oak Swamp and Glendale. Lt. Col. Adoniram Warner of the 10th Reserves expressed pride in the brigade and the Pennsylvania Reserves, noting, "there was never better fighting done…our men rallied and fought when everything was against them." The 6th Reserves did not participate in the fighting with the brigade during the Seven Days Battles, making the 559 losses suffered by the remaining three regiments even more telling.[186]

The 3rd Brigade, with the rest of McClellan's army, reassembled at Harrison's Landing during the first week of July. The men were re-equipped during their stay here and soldiers' aid societies provided fruit and other luxuries. The men remained here until they boarded transport ships on August 16 and returned to Falmouth to become part of John Pope's Army of Virginia. Recently promoted, Brig. Gen. Conrad Jackson, formerly colonel of the 9th Reserves, led the brigade as Seymour moved to the 1st Brigade. The 11th Reserves, another war-weary western Pennsylvania regiment, replaced the 6th Reserves who went with Seymour. After landing at Falmouth, the men endured a tough five-day forced march toward Manassas Junction and took part in the Second Bull Run Campaign, suffering 287 casualties. Jackson became incapacitated by a burst blood vessel, so the brigade fought successively under colonels Martin Hardin and James Kirk. Both were wounded, leaving 45 year-old postmaster and Mexican War veteran, Lt. Col. Robert Anderson, of the 9th Reserves in charge. The exhausted brigade formed for battle again at Chantilly on September 1 before withdrawing to bivouac on familiar ground at Arlington Heights.[187]

Any recuperation the Pennsylvania Reserves anticipated was cut short late on September 6 when marching orders arrived to follow the Confederate army into Maryland. Grumbling soldiers packed their belongings and fell into line. The column passed through Georgetown and Washington on its way to Maryland. The Reserves were back in the Army of the Potomac as the 3rd Division of Joseph Hooker's I Corps. The brigade spent two days at Brookeville, Maryland where the ailing Thomas Gallagher of the 9th Reserves returned and, as ranking officer, assumed command of the brigade. Gallagher suffered from a kidney stone, making riding a horse an excruciating endeavor. Division commander John Reynolds left for Pennsylvania on September 12 to organize its militia, leaving George Meade in command of the division.[188]

## South Mountain

The brigade arrived at the Monocacy River near Frederick on September 13 and, with the division and corps, bivouacked on the east bank. The men were on the road by 8:00 a.m. the next morning, marching through Frederick toward a pass in the Catoctin Mountains on the National Road. A grueling march of about 15 miles brought them to a stream west of Middletown in the early afternoon. They rested until about 3:00 p.m., and then the men were on their feet and on the march toward the sounds of cannon fire at South Mountain. The column filed off the main highway onto a narrow road to the right that paralleled, and then eventually crossed South Mountain. The division formed the right of Hooker's battle line. "We were shelled while moving into position," recalled Lt. Col. Warner, of the 10th Reserves.

Gallagher formed the middle brigade with Seymour's on the right and Albert Magilton's on the left of the division. The plan was for Seymour's brigade to outflank the Confederate line on a mountain spur while Gallagher's and Magilton's men attacked straight ahead up the mountainside. With the 9th Reserves on the right of the line, 11th in the center and 12th on the left, the line went forward. The 10th Reserves was initially sent toward the right, but was ordered by Meade to join in the main attack. "The lines advanced in good order and soon became hotly engaged," wrote Warner. "I moved my regiment forward and soon received a shower of bullets from across a ravine in our front." Tenacious Alabama soldiers from Robert Rodes' veteran brigade (probably portions of the 3rd, 12th, and 26th Alabama) disputed their advance. The enemy was well concealed by rocks and the late-day shadows on the mountainside made them difficult to see. Some enemy soldiers were posted behind a stone fence.

Officers offered a particular target to the Alabamians. A bullet struck Gallagher, disabling him, and Anderson resumed command of the brigade. Seven officers in the 11th Reserves went down, two of them killed. "The firing was incessant," recalled Capt. A.J. Bolar of the 12th Reserves, "the rebels yielding their positions only when routed by balls or bayonets from our men." The brigade faltered at first then surged forward toward the enemy driven into their path by Seymour's men. The 9th Reserves gained possession of the stone fence and peppered a log house in the distance with gunfire, chasing Confederates from it

and capturing fifteen others. Warner described the climax of the fighting: "In a few minutes, confidence took the place of hesitation and all pressed wildly forward driving the enemy and fast gaining the mountainside." Darkness put an end to the arduous battle fought on very difficult terrain. That night, the Confederates withdrew from the mountain. The 3rd Brigade lost 132 men during its fight for the summit of South Mountain.[189]

## Antietam

The next morning, details from the brigade buried their own dead on a battlefield for first time before taking up the line of march. Lee's forces withdrew toward Sharpsburg near the Potomac River and McClellan's army followed them. At Boonsboro, the brigade took the road that led to Sharpsburg. "There was much straggling," Warner recalled, "more than seemed fitting for a victorious army." The column halted near Keedysville and Warner snatched a refreshing forty-minute nap before the march resumed. It was nearly dark when the Reserves bivouacked in a field within sight of the Upper Bridge. On September 16, Warner noticed, "Rebels on distant hills scanning our movements." The men sensed another battle looming with "resignation such as the true soldier brings himself." The men received rations and by 4:00 p.m. the brigade was under arms and ready to go.

The men crossed the Upper Bridge and followed the road leading to Williamsport. Hooker and his staff passed hurriedly through the column. The men continued on, veering left as they approached Hagerstown Pike. They swept across open fields until artillery fire greeted them near the Joseph Poffenberger farm. Skirmishers were dispatched beyond the North Woods and all anticipated a fight. The brigade bivouacked on the uneven ground of the Poffenberger farm. Rain fell at about 9:00 p.m. making rest difficult.[190]

The skirmishers were recalled at daybreak as artillery fire resumed. Hooker planned to retain Magilton's and Anderson's brigades in reserve as

Seymour's brigade marched through the East Woods and Ricketts' and Doubleday's divisions advanced from the North Woods to smash into the Confederate line and gain a rise of ground east of Dunker Church. Anderson formed his brigade at about 6:30 a.m. and with Magilton's on his left and Battery C, 5th U.S. Artillery, marched through the North Woods toward the fighting. The 10th Reserves were detached and sent about 700 yards to the right to protect the I Corps' flank. Hooker's attack got off to a ragged start, but gained momentum as both sides took heavy losses. The Confederates slowly yielded ground. Hooker's attack unraveled at 7:00 a.m. when a powerful counter-thrust by John Bell Hood's division sent Rickett's and Doubleday's exhausted and depleted troops reeling back through the Cornfield. Anderson's men were called into action and they advanced across an open field and down a slope to a basin of ground just south of the D.R. Miller farmhouse. Division commander Meade saw Hooker's dilemma as masses of disorganized Union soldiers were in full retreat. He ordered Anderson to form his brigade along the north fence of the Cornfield to cover the withdrawal of the fleeing Union troops. Black-hatted Wisconsin soldiers retreated over a portion of fence held by Capt. Samuel Dick's 9th Reserves, whose right was near Hagerstown Pike. Red-legged New Yorkers, among others, retreated through Lt. Col. Samuel Jackson's 11th Reserves in the center of the line. Capt. Richard Gustin's 12th Reserves held the left of the line, waiting next to Magilton's brigade.[191]

It was difficult to determine the location of the enemy because of the smoke, confusion, and corn. The 1st Texas regiment had broken loose from Hood's main attack and pursued retreating bluecoats. "The enemy advanced to within a few paces of our lines before we discovered them to be foes," recalled Lt. Col. Jackson. His 11th Reserves rested their .69 caliber smoothbore muskets on the fence rail and waited. At the signal, the entire brigade let loose a crushing volley that stopped the Texans in their tracks. They stood and returned the Pennsylvanian's fire until their numbers were severely reduced. The fire from the 11th Reserves smoothbores directly in front of the Texans was particularly devastating. The 9th Reserves on the right of the brigade fired obliquely into the Texans. The understated Jackson wrote, "After a few well directed volleys from our lines" the enemy "retired in confusion." The loss sustained by the 1st Texas was staggering with over 80% casualties.

The 12th Reserves on the left of the line helped seal a break in Magilton's line by two Mississippi regiments of Evander Law's brigade turning its fire to the left. The last of Hood's men in the Cornfield were forced to withdraw and Anderson's three regiments went after them. The 9th Reserves charged through the Cornfield at its western edge and advanced 75 yards beyond its south fence. They halted on the high ground near the pike and fired on advancing troops of D.H. Hill's division. Anderson told Capt. Dick that he would try to get help, but seeing the 11th and 12th Reserves on his left had withdrawn and no troops on the right, the captain ordered his men to retire.[192]

Troops of the XII Corps took up the fight as Anderson's brigade withdrew. The 10th and 11th Pennsylvania Reserves regrouped near the North Woods, while the 9th and 12th halted at the north edge of the Poffenberger farm. The brigade was not called upon the rest of the day and bivouacked not far from where they spent the previous night. The brigade lost another 175 men during the morning fight at Antietam. The veteran brigade fought as would be expected at both South Mountain and Antietam and received praise for its actions.[193]

**William Sagle**

∗ ∗ ∗

# II CORPS—

## Major General Edwin Sumner

The II Corps was one of the initial five corps formed by Abraham Lincoln on March 13, 1862. It subsequently saw extensive service during the Peninsula/Seven Days Campaign, fighting at Seven Pines, Savage's Station and Glendale. It did not arrive in time to participate in the Second Bull Run Campaign. The corps was led by Maj. Gen. Edwin Sumner, the only commander the unit ever knew. At the age of 65, Sumner was the oldest general on either side at Antietam. Sumner's roots were in Massachusetts and New York, and he entered the army as a second lieutenant in 1819, seeing action in the Black Hawk War. He also served as a cavalry instructor at Carlisle Barracks (Pennsylvania) and then was garrisoned in the west until the Mexican-American War broke out, where he was as major in the 2nd Dragoons. A bullet bounced off his head during the Battle of Cerro Gordo, gaining him the sobriquet, "Bull." Sumner was a colonel commanding the 1st U. S. Cavalry at the outbreak of the Civil War.[1]

Historian Ezra Carman, a contemporary of Sumner's, noted that despite his age he was "still vigorous and active." He wrote glowingly of his personality: describing him as "of fine presence, consciousness of his high rank showed in all his movements, he was courageous as a lion; and self assertive, whether for himself or his men, yet never arrogant, or unkind, and always accessible to his soldiers, who believed in and loved to follow him." Historian Scott Hartwig had a different opinion of Sumner, noting, "His management of the corps through the Peninsula Campaign and the Seven Days Battles left much to be desired. Although always courageous and a model subordinate, he displayed poor judgment on more than one occasion. McClellan appreciated his bravery but thought little of him as a general."[2]

By the beginning of the Maryland Campaign, the II Corps had developed a reputation as a dependable and effective unit. Two of its division commanders, Maj. Gen. John Sedgwick and Maj. Gen. Israel Richardson were considered to be among the finest in the army. Brig. Gen. William French and his 3rd Division were newcomers to the corps and had yet to develop a reputation. The division was formed on September 10 and contained a mix of combat veterans, garrison troops, and rookies.[3]

The corps was ordered across the Potomac River to Tennallytown, District of Columbia, on September 3, and then headed to Rockville, Maryland on September 5. It passed through Middleburg on September 9, Clarksburg on September 10, Urbana on September 12 and entered Frederick on September 13. Francis Walker recalled "no soldier who entered Frederick on the morning of the 13th will ever forget the cordial welcome with which the rescuing army was received by the loyal inhabitants." Sumner was assigned command of a wing composed of his own corps and the XII Corps, and it left Frederick on September 14. The congestion was so great on the National Road that Sumner was ordered to detour to Shookstown Road. Many of the units were forced to backtrack as they had already passed the intersection. The road proved to be a poor thoroughfare for troops. A soldier recalled, "such a road you never saw—rocks & steep pitches going up & down" over Catoctin Mountain. The corps did not see action during the fight for South Mountain.[4]

Richardson's division spearheaded the Union army's advance toward Sharpsburg as Sumner and his other two divisions marched to Keedysville, where the men were permitted to rest. As McClellan developed his battle plan, he envisioned the I and XII Corps carrying the initial fight, supported by Sumner's II Corps and possibly Franklin's VI Corps. Sumner's strength at Antietam was just over 16,000 men.[5]

McClellan sent the XII Corps to support Hooker's I Corps on the evening of September 16, and Sumner requested permission to cross Antietam Creek with it, but was told to wait. He spent an uneasy night, awaiting orders. Sumner finally mounted his horse at 6:00 a.m. and headed to McClellan's headquarters at the Pry house. According to historian Ezra Carman, "Sumner waited, walking to and fro on the veranda of the Pry house, or sitting on the steps" waiting for orders. Finally, at 7:20 a.m., Sumner received the orders he anxiously awaited—"You will cross in as solid a mass as possible and communicate with Genl. Hooker immediately." Sedgwick crossed Antietam Creek at a ford south of the Upper Bridge, followed by French's division; Richardson's division remained behind until relieved. Sumner was in such a hurry to enter the fray that he immediately put Sedgwick's division into column and marched directly west to the ford, rather than rely on country roads. Sumner drove the men forward, not permitting them to remove their shoes and socks before crossing. French's inexperienced division took longer to form into column and fell behind. Sumner's six batteries were not with him as he had sent them across Antietam Creek with Mansfield's XII Corps the night before.[6]

As Sumner approached the East Woods at the head of Sedgwick's division, he began realizing all was not as supposed, for the sounds of battle were coming from the north, not from the south. Sumner received a message, marked 8:30 a.m., from McClellan's headquarters to push south on Hooker's left flank toward the burning house [Mumma] and push on towards Sharpsburg. As Sumner approached the East Woods he was not so sure this was the best idea.[7]

Sedgwick's division was aligned in three lines with a brigade forming each, and Sumner and Sedgwick rode on the right side between the first and second lines. While halting his lines near the East Woods, Sumner sent out aides to secure information from I and XII Corps officers about the status of affairs, and he rode forward to reconnoiter. The fighting in the Cornfield/East Woods had abated and two Union brigades from Brig. Gen. George Greene's division were driving south. After conferring with George Meade, now commanding the I Corps, and a staff officer from the XII Corps, he decided to continue driving west, enter the West Woods in its middle section, clear out any lingering enemy troops, pivot left and drive south on the right of the brigades he had seen when he first arrived at the East Woods.[8]

Brig. Gen. Willis Gorman's lead brigade stepped off on its march to the West Woods. Brig. Gen. Napoleon Dana's brigade was supposed to march 50 yards behind it. When Sumner looked back, Dana's brigade was nowhere to be seen. Sumner yelled out, "Where is my second line," and sent an aide back to bring it and Brig. Gen. Oliver Howard's brigade forward. The historian of the 19th Massachusetts recalled seeing Sumner, "hat in hand, with his long gray locks streaming in the wind, his smiling face looking as if the noise of howling shell and screeching shrapnel was sweet music to him. He was the picture of soldierly courage."[9]

As Sumner rode behind the 1st Minnesota he noted its sheathed flags and roared, "In God's name, what are you fighting for? Unfurl those colors!" Gorman's brigade entered the West Woods and encountered the remnant of the Stonewall Division. Dana's and Howard's brigades were now up and deployed behind Gorman. Sumner began considering his next moves. French's division had reached the East Woods and it headed south where a new line of Confederates could be seen forming. Sumner sent aides to Greene to prepare to continue his division's advance.[10]

Maj. Gen. Lafayette McLaws' division, which had only arrived from Harpers Ferry that morning, was sent through the West Woods to reinforce the sector when it smashed into Sedgwick's front and left. The sudden attack shocked all in Sedgwick's division. Sumner was near Gorman's line and quickly realized the extent of the danger, yelling "My God, we must got out of this!" He then rode to Howard's third line to try to reposition it to withstand the attack. He was too late and all he could yell to the Pennsylvanians was, "Back boys! For God's sake move back; you are in a bad fix!" Sumner spent the next half hour frantically attempting to move his men to safety. The division lost over 2,200 men in a matter of minutes. Sumner has been criticized for sending Sedgwick's division to its destruction, but after a careful analysis, historian Marion

Armstrong believed he made the "right decision at the right time," given the information available to him.[11]

French's division, meanwhile, passed the Mumma and Roulette farms, deployed in three lines with a brigade in each. Brig. Gen. Max Weber's brigade advanced against the Sunken Road first, but was bloodily repulsed, as was French's second brigade, under Col. Dwight Morris. Sumner sent a message to French to press the attack to take some of the pressure off of Sedgwick, so he sent in his most experienced brigade under Brig. Gen. Nathan Kimball, which was only able to achieve a stalemate.[11]

Meanwhile, Richardson's division was relieved by a V Corps division, crossed Antietam Creek, and added its weight to the Sunken Road fight. After the repulse of the Irish Brigade, Brig. Gen. John Caldwell's brigade was able to break the enemy's Sunken Road defensive line. Intensive fighting primarily involving Caldwell's brigade occurred around the Piper farm fields until Richardson was wounded and the men were running low on ammunition. Col. John Brooke's brigade, in Richardson's third line, was sent toward the Dunker Church to help blunt an attack against French's flank.

This ended the II Corps' fight at Antietam. It earned a special place in the annals of history for its defeat in the West Woods and ultimate victory at the Sunken Road. It paid the price though, losing 5,138 men—more than any other corps in McClellan's army.[12]

**Bradley M. Gottfried**

\*\*\*

# 1ST DIVISION—

## Major General Israel B. Richardson, Brigadier General Winfield Hancock

The 1st Division was a stable and highly effective fighting unit. Organized under Israel Richardson as part of the II Corps on March 13, 1862, it saw extensive action during the Seven Days Battles but arrived too late to participate in the Second Bull Run Campaign. Richardson was the only commander it ever knew. Born the day after Christmas in Fairfax, Vermont in 1815, Richardson was a career army officer. He graduated from West Point in 1841, saw service in the Seminole War, and received two brevets for his heroic actions during the Mexican War. He received the moniker, "Fighting Dick," during this period. He later served on the western frontier until he retired in 1855 and took up farming near Pontiac, Michigan. Some speculated the death of his young wife and infant caused him to quit the army and settle near family in Michigan.

Upon the outbreak of the Civil War, Richardson helped recruit and organize the 2nd Michigan Infantry. He commanded a brigade during the First Bull Run Campaign, which saw action at Blackburn's Ford, and helped cover the army's retreat. Richardson was subsequently promoted to the rank of brigadier general on August 9, 1861 and assigned command of the 1st Division during the late winter of 1861. He whipped the division into an effective fighting force and during the Seven Days Battles. For example, Richardson "displayed the iron courage which endeared him to the rowdy Irish of Meagher's brigade." He was promoted to the rank of major general on July 5, 1862. Richardson enjoyed mingling with his men, wearing "a jacket, an old straw hat, and trousers, the side pockets of which his hands are generally thrust," according to a soldier. He disliked pomp and circumstance and believed in leading by example.[13]

The division's enlisted men were among the finest the Army of the Potomac had to offer, but their brigade officers were a mixed bag. None of the three had formal military training prior to the war. Brig. Gen. John Caldwell later rose to division command the following year and Brig. Gen. Thomas Meagher captured his men's loyalty, but was considered rash. The best of the bunch may have been Col. John Brooke who quickly learned his trade and became an effective brigade commander.

The 4,039-man division marched from Frederick, Maryland on September 14 toward Middletown via the National Road. The congested road caused the division to detour over Catoctin Mountain on Shookstown Road. The narrow, rocky, and steep road slowed the division's pace, but it soon returned to the National Road near Middletown. At Bolivar, Richardson's division pushed right to Mt. Tabor Church to support the I Corps slugging it out with the enemy around Turner's Gap on South Mountain. Night put an end to the fighting and the enemy's hold on South Mountain before the division could become engaged. Richardson's division was summoned to spearhead the advance toward Boonsboro the following day, climbing the steep and rocky small road from the church to the Mountain House on the National Road. The division encountered some troopers of Brig. Gen. Fitz Lee's cavalry brigade as it descended the western side of the mountain toward Boonsboro and pushed them back. Fitz Lee brought up artillery, forcing Richardson to halt and deploy the 5th New Hampshire (Caldwell's brigade) for action and he sent it forward, only to find the enemy had abandoned its positions.[14]

Confederates could be seen across Antietam Creek when Richardson's men reached Keedysville later that day (September 15). They were joined by Brig. Gen. Alfred Pleasonton's cavalry division. Two Union batteries deployed for action while Richardson's men rested. Two additional batteries from the Artillery Reserve and Brig. Gen. George Sykes' division (Maj. Gen. Fitz John Porter's V Corps) also arrived. Richardson's division rested on the right of Boonsboro Pike and Sykes' men were on the left of the road. When Sumner finally received orders to cross Antietam Creek with his II Corps at 7:20 a.m. on September 17, Richardson's division was left behind to support the artillery until it was relieved by Brig. Gen. George Morell's division (V Corps) at 9:00 a.m. Richardson led the division to a ford south of the Upper Bridge and crossed within half an hour. The division headed southwest with Meagher's brigade on the right; Caldwell's on its left and Brooke's brigade behind Caldwell's. The column halted when it reached a cornfield on high ground overlooking the Roulette farm and formed into battle lines. Brig. Gen. William French's division (II Corps) was still engaging Confederates in the Sunken Road to the right, as Meagher's brigade made the division's first attack. Appearing at the top of the hill, the brigade was hit by heavy small arms and artillery fire, sustaining heavy losses—some regiments lost as many as 62% and the entire brigade could muster fewer than 500 men after the battle.[15]

Caldwell's brigade was initially on the Irish Brigade's left and rear, protected by the brow of a hill. When called into action, Caldwell began a slow wheel to the right. Some officers believed a more energetic movement could have hit the right flank of the enemy troops in the Sunken Road. Before completed, Richardson ordered Caldwell to relieve Meagher, so he filed his men to the right and behind the beleaguered Irishmen. Caldwell then ordered his men to turn and attack the Sunken Road. The remnants of Meagher's brigade formed behind them. Pressure from the 61st/64th New York near the enemy's flank and the 29th Massachusetts in their front caused the enemy line in the Sunken Road to collapse.[16]

Richardson's division surged forward to engage the enemy in the fields around the Piper farm, southwest of the Sunken Road. Thomas Livermore of the 5th New Hampshire, looked over his right shoulder and "saw that gallant old fellow [Richardson] advancing on the right of our line, almost alone, afoot with his bare sword in his hand, and his face was as black as a thunder cloud; and well it might be . . . I shall never cease to admire that magnificent fighting general who advanced with his front line, with his sword bare and ready for use, and his swarthy face, burning eye, and square jaw . . ."[17]

While most of Caldwell's brigade engaged the enemy at the Piper farm, Brooke's and some of Caldwell's men helped thwart an attack by the enemy emerging from the West Woods. The division was recalled about 1:00 p.m. and reformed near the Roulette farmhouse.[18]

The division lost 1,165 at Antietam (210 killed; 939 wounded; 16 missing). Richardson was among the casualties. Several days earlier, Richardson had been accidently kicked by a soldier in the Irish Brigade and the two subsequently shared a pull from a whisky bottle. He sustained a more serious wound near the Sunken Road, when he was hit in the chest by a ball from a spherical case shot while conversing with Capt. William Graham, whose battery was near the left of his original line. Richardson purportedly sent an aide to tell McClellan, "I have been doing a Colonel's work all day, and I'm now too badly hurt to do a General's." Richardson was taken to the Pry House, where Lincoln made a point of visiting him in early October. Richardson died on November 3, 1862 after developing pneumonia and other complications. Richardson was replaced by Brig. Gen. Winfield Hancock of the VI Corps during the afternoon of September 17.[19]

**Bradley M. Gottfried**

* * *

## 1st Brigade: Brigadier General John Caldwell

**Units:** 5th New Hampshire, 61st/64th New York 7th New York, 81st Pennsylvania
**Strength:** 1,551[20]
**Losses:** 323 (43k-280w)[21]

Still on the east side of Antietam Creek at 7:40 a.m. on September 17, Brig. Gen. John Caldwell's men could hear the crash of artillery from the battle raging on the other side when orders arrived for Richardson's division to march, once relieved from its key position near the Middle Bridge. Richardson's division had helped set the stage for this battle by pursuing Lee's retreating forces from South Mountain to the Antietam Creek two days earlier. As a veteran of the 61st New York recalled, "We were close on the rear of the enemy and saw the last of him go over the hill ahead of us. At the time we did not know that we were on the banks of the – to be celebrated - Antietam." The brigade would soon play an even more important role by nearly breaking the center of Lee's line.[22]

By 9:30 a.m., Caldwell's brigade was wading across the creek at a ford south of the Upper Bridge. After a brief stop to wring water from their socks, the troops marched south along the creek, past Henry Neikirk's farm, and into a ravine where they took position behind high ground overlooking the Roulette farmhouse. They were about 700 yards northeast from the Sunken Road, where William French's division had been trying for nearly an hour to dislodge Maj. Gen. D.H. Hill's stubborn resistance. Caldwell's brigade would break the impasse in less than two hours' time.[23]

Caldwell was only 29 years old, the youngest of McClellan's generals at Antietam. With no military experience, this Maine schoolteacher entered service in the fall of 1861 as Colonel of the 11th Maine Infantry. Caldwell was well suited to military leadership and in less than a year, was promoted to general officer and given command of a brigade. By Gettysburg, he would command a division.[24]

Caldwell had an enviable line-up of regimental commanders. Col. Francis Barlow, commander of the 61st New York and 64th New York, would become a division commander after Antietam and one of the few to rise from enlisted private to general officer. Lt. Col. Nelson Miles, who would take command of Barlow's regiments after he was wounded at Antietam, would receive the Medal of Honor for bravery at Chancellorsville and rise to the position of Commander in Chief of the U.S. Army by the end of the century. Col. Edward Cross, 5th New Hampshire, whose regiment formed the skirmish line during the pursuit of Lee from South Mountain, catching Fitzhugh Lee's Confederate cavalry off-guard at Boonsboro, would take over the brigade after Caldwell, but receive a mortal wound at Gettysburg. Maj. Henry McKeen of the 81st Pennsylvania would be promoted to the rank of colonel and take over the brigade after Cross' death, but suffer a mortal wound at Cold Harbor. Lastly, Capt. Charles Brestel, in temporary command of the 7th New York, would hold his own among the more senior officers at Antietam with his regiment's capture of three battle flags.[25]

This solid leadership team had fought together since Caldwell took command of the brigade in June of 1862, earning praise for their performance during the Peninsula Campaign over the summer. Their experience and cohesion would serve them well in the hours ahead.

Caldwell marched his brigade toward the sounds of battle from its position east of the Roulette farm, using the rolling hills as cover. As Caldwell's men ascended the long hill where, up ahead and to the right, the Irish brigade was already engaged, shots rang out from an isolated tree to their left front, killing an officer and wounding several men. The officer was Capt. Manton Angell of the 61st New York, who had "told his friends he knew he would be killed in this fight." Barlow ordered a dozen marksmen to fire into the tree and two Confederate snipers fell to the ground. There was "no more trouble from that source."[26]

Following orders by Richardson to form to the left of Thomas Meagher's Irish Brigade, Caldwell pushed forward with the 61st New York and 64th New York (Barlow) on the right, the 5th New Hampshire (Cross) on the left, the 7th New York (Brestel) at right center, and the 81st Pennsylvania (McKeen) at left center.

Caldwell advanced to the left and rear of the Irish Brigade, along the northeast side of a rise that blocked his view of the enemy in the Sunken Road. Finding no enemy to his front, he began to slowly wheel his brigade to the right, feeling his way, when Richardson ordered him to relieve Meagher's thinning line.[27]

It was about 10:30 a.m. when the order came. By this time, Irish Brigade casualties had mounted to the point where one regiment had nearly melted away. A soldier from the 61st New York recalled hearing Meagher, who would soon be knocked from his horse and borne from the field, call out to Barlow, "Col! For God's sake come and help me!"[28]

Caldwell wasted no time. Under severe fire, he moved his brigade by the right flank to the rear of the Irish Brigade, passed through its line and, with swords in the air, drove up and over the crest of the hill overlooking the enemy troops massed in the Sunken Road. A soldier from the Irish Brigade described Caldwell's advance: "Now the rush of troops we heard in the rear … the air was rent with wild yells. It was altogether too much of a shock for the enemy; they broke, and fled for the cornfield. The next moment, Caldwell's Brigade, led by Gen. Richardson in person, with Cross, Barlow, and all its other heroes, came sweeping up behind the sheltered lines of the Irish Brigade."[29]

Most of the fleeing Confederates were from Richard Anderson's division, sent in to reinforce George B. Anderson's brigade on the Confederate right (eastern) half of the Sunken Road. The division's deployment and initial movements got off to a bad start. Many of the officers fell early, including Richard Anderson himself, and the confused troops bunched into the road already crowded with George B. Anderson's men. The sight of Caldwell's brigade cresting the hill was the last straw; they broke and ran, taking two regiments of Anderson's brigade with them.[30]

The Confederate line broke along Caldwell's entire front, except on the extreme right, where some of George B. Anderson's troops and Robert Rodes' brigade, on the western half of the road, remained. Barlow's 61st and 64th New York regiments conducted a change of front that flanked the Confederates still in the road. Barlow wrote in his report, "Our position giving us peculiar advantages for attacking in flank this part of the enemy's line, my regiments advanced and obtained an enfilading fire upon the enemy." With support from French's troops and the Irish Brigade shooting into the road, the result was like "shooting sheep in a pen." Barlow's troops captured close to 300 prisoners and two stands of colors. Second Lt. Theodore Greig of the 61st New York would receive the Medal of Honor for capturing the flag of the 44th Alabama, despite being wounded in the neck.[31]

Some Confederate remnants still held on in the western half of the road, but with Federal troops to their front and rear, and few officers left to command them, it wasn't long before they fled toward Hagerstown Pike.

The Sunken Road fell into Union hands sometime between 11:00 - 11:30 a.m. Caldwell's men were among the first to witness the carnage of two hours of bitter fighting in that confined space. Thomas Livermore, 5th New Hampshire, wrote, "In this road there lay so many dead rebels that there formed a line which one might have walked on as far as I could see."[32]

As Barlow's command swept the road, the rest of the brigade pushed southward into the Piper cornfield. The Confederates fired desperately on the advancing line with muskets and artillery. Charles Hale, 5th New Hampshire, recalled the destructive fire: "Just then a strand of canister went over our heads, and that was my dread; I could endure rifle bullets, but when the big iron bullets went swishing through the air with a sound as though there were bushels of them, it made me wish I was at home." The artillery was having its desired effect on the advancing units. Caldwell wrote, "The 7th New York wavered for a few minutes, but I rallied them and led them forward in person." The New Yorkers did indeed rally, capturing three battle flags as they pushed through the corn.[33]

According to historian Ezra Carman, confusion "reigned supreme" among the Confederates as Hill and James Longstreet tried to rally their infantry to slow Richardson's advance. Cross's 5th New Hampshire had scarcely reached its position in the cornfield, on the left of the brigade, when the enemy attempted to outflank the division with a strong force. Cross wrote, "They had, in fact, advanced within 200 yards of the left of our lines, and were preparing to charge." Hill's official report indicates that Hill himself led this attack. Desperate to "stop the Yankees from reaching the hill that commanded Sharpsburg and the Confederate rear (Cemetery Hill)," Hill pulled together about 200 men who were willing to attack if he would lead them. However, his band met with a "warm reception," as Cross ordered a change of front to the rear, advanced toward them and drove them back.[34]

Caldwell's brigade now stretched nearly 600 yards across the cornfield, with large gaps between the regiments. Richardson called up his reserve brigade, under John Brooke, to reinforce Caldwell. Brooke sent in the 2nd Delaware and 52nd New York to fill the gaps.

On the right, Barlow marched his command southwest into the cornfield to join the rest of the brigade. Brooke's two regiments were already there. Barlow noted in his report that the regiments of both brigades were "joined together without much order … none having favorable opportunities to fire." While finding a position, he spotted a significant enemy force moving to his right. What Barlow saw were the commands of Col. John Cooke and Brig. Gen. Howell Cobb, hastily launching an attack organized by Longstreet to strike the right flank of French's division and Richardson's rear.[35]

Barlow quickly moved to the right oblique to the crest of a hill about 300 yards distant, to the right of the 52nd New York of Brooke's brigade, where he could "use his fire to advantage," resting his right on the Sunken Road where Rodes' brigade had been before their retreat. The 61st and 64th New York opened fire on the attackers as other Federal troops did the same. Hit from three sides, Cooke's and Cobb's commands were forced to retreat.[36]

On the other side of the field, remnants of D.H. Hill's and R.H. Anderson's divisions launched another attack on Caldwell's left. Col. Cross, whom Thomas Livermore described as "the glorious man standing erect with a red handkerchief, a conspicuous mark, tied around his bare head," and his 5th New Hampshire, this time with the assistance of the 81st Pennsylvania, drove the enemy back with heavy loss, capturing the flag of the 4th North Carolina in the process.[37]

Hearing the fighting on the left, Barlow changed front once more and returned to the cornfield to assist the brigade, taking his place to the right of the 7th New York. About the same time, Brooke sent in two additional regiments, the 57th New York and 66th New York, which blocked out the 7th New York and became the center of the line. Brooke's

57th New York connected with Barlow's left and the mixed regiments pushed forward, driving the enemy out of the cornfield and through Piper's orchard under "very hot artillery fire and a scattering of fire from musketry," according to Ezra Carman.[38]

Case and canister from Confederate artillery slowed the advance of Richardson's division, particularly the four guns of Capt. M.B. Miller's battery of Washington Artillery. Longstreet, who was holding the reins of the horses while his staff filled in for Miller's casualties and worked the guns, witnessed Barlow's advance. Longstreet wrote, "Capt. Miller charged and double-charged with spherical case and canister until his guns at the discharge leaped into the air from 10 to 12 inches." Barlow went down during this advance, with a serious wound in the groin by grapeshot that would take several months to heal.[39]

Richardson had no artillery to silence Lee's guns at this point, and ordered the advancing regiments to halt. It was about 1:00 p.m., and the infantry fight was over. Caldwell drew his brigade back to a line near the cornfield, where they remained exposed to heavy artillery fire for the remainder of the day.[40]

Richardson received a mortal wound from Confederate artillery shortly after ordering the withdrawal. With Richardson down and Meagher wounded, command of the division fell briefly to Caldwell until Brig. Gen. Winfield Hancock made his way from the northern end of the field to relieve him.

Since wading across Antietam Creek that morning, Caldwell's brigade had lost nearly a quarter of its strength. Cross's 5th New Hampshire, which led the repulse of Hill's flank attacks on Richardson's left, suffered the most, with 37% casualties. In this day's fighting, the brigade had taken the Sunken Road, captured over 300 prisoners and six battle flags, advanced to the high ground above the Piper farmhouse, and seriously threatened Lee's center.[41]

**Laura Marfut**

* * *

## 2nd (Irish) Brigade: Brigadier General Thomas Francis Meagher

**Units:** 63rd New York, 69th New York, 88th New York, 29th Massachusetts
**Strength:** 1,516[42]
**Losses:** 540 (113k-422w-5m)[43]

Thomas Francis Meagher originated the idea of the Irish Brigade and became its first commander. Born in 1823 to a wealthy family in southern Ireland, he was convinced that Ireland's freedom from Great Britain could only be achieved through violent revolution and became a revolutionary. He was captured, tried and sentenced to death in 1849 but his sentence was commuted and he was exiled to Tasmania. Meagher escaped and fled to New York in 1852, where he started a new life as a free man. His revolutionary leanings branded him a hero in his new land and had a significant influence on his ability to raise troops for the Union cause.[44]

Meagher commanded an "Irish Zouave" company of the famed 69th New York State Militia at the First Battle of Bull Run. This spirited group of mostly Irish Catholics with capable military experience was very effective in acting as the Union Army's rear guard following the debacle of what most believed would be a Union rout, and the unit became known as the "Fighting Irish." Capt. Meagher returned to New York following the battle, where he conceived the idea of forming an all-Irish brigade commanded by an Irish officer. Hundreds of Irish signed up for three-year enlistments. Many were second-generation United States citizens or migrated south from Canada; still others were directly from Ireland. Capt. David P. Conyngham observed: "so great was the rush of Irishmen to the ranks of the Brigade, that recruits came from Albany, Utica, Buffalo, Pittsburgh, and other remote towns and places." The New York regiments were issued Meagher's favorite infantry weapon, the .69 caliber smoothbore musket which could fire "buck 'n ball" with lethal effect at close range. The brigade included many veterans of the United States Army; some having fought in the Mexican War and the Seminole Wars. Some recruits in Company D, 69th New York, were parolees who had served in the 23rd Illinois, which had been captured in the western theater earlier in the war.[45]

Crucial to this all-Catholic brigade were its chaplains. Father William Corby, an American born priest of the Congregation of Holy Cross left his teaching position at Notre Dame College to become chaplain to the 88th New York. Corby was most notable and often rode at the front of the column with Meagher. The chaplains brought cohesion between Catholicism and patriotism that infused the fighting nature of the troops and inspired them in battle. Corby and others were known for exposing themselves to extreme danger while shot and shell whizzed about as they went from one casualty to another giving absolution to the dying or other aid, earning enormous respect from Irish soldiers.[46]

The brigade was comprised initially of the 63rd, 69th, and 88th New York regiments. Meagher was commissioned brigadier general in February, 1862 and the brigade soon headed for the Virginia Peninsula to join George B. McClellan's Army of the Potomac as the 2nd Brigade, 1st Division, II Corps. The bond between the brigadier and his men was unquestionably the strongest in the II Corps, if not the AoP, and they were about to "see the elephant" (baptism of fire) for the first time in the Battle of Seven Pines (Fair Oaks) on May 31 – June 1, 1862. Two regiments charged several hundred yards across open ground with fixed bayonets, pausing to form their lines and then cut loose a horrific fire into the enemy, sending them in retreat. Another Irish charge resulted in flying musket butts and bayonets that overcame the enemy. Meagher was elated: "The fire of the two regiments was so

telling that the enemy were compelled to retire, leaving their dead and wounded piled in the wood." The brigade's performance left an indelible impression on the Union high command.[47]

The 29th Massachusetts Volunteers joined the Irish Brigade after the Battle of Seven Pines but they were anything but Irish. They were the blue bloods of Boston and mostly Protestant as was their chaplain. The men of the 29th were issued .577-caliber British Enfield rifled muskets.[48]

The Irish brigade played an active role during the Seven Days Battles around Richmond. When the V Corps was under a vicious attack at Gaines' Mill, the Irish Brigade was one of the units sent to reinforce the besieged Federals and was instrumental in aiding the withdrawal of the AoP. The brigade continued distinguishing itself time and again on the Virginia Peninsula with its distinctive Gaelic yell that could be heard above the din of battle at places like White Oak Swamp and Malvern Hill, invoking such comments as from one Confederate officer: "Steady, boys, here comes that damned green flag again." The Irish favored the bayonet and it was so feared by the Confederates when escorted with the green banner. Such performance came with a heavy price. An officer of the 88th New York observed: "Our heroic brigade left 700 of its bravest officers and men on the bloody fields behind."[49]

McClellan once expressed to Meagher, "I wish I had twenty thousand more men like yours." Lincoln's high regard for Meagher's brigade was evident in his July 1862 visit to the AoP when he kissed the "bullet-riddled green battle flag" of the 69th and declared "God Bless the Irish Flag!" According to Captain Conyngham, "The regimental flags were of deep rich green, heavily fringed, having in the centre a richly embroidered Irish harp, with a sunburst above it and a wreath of shamrock beneath[.] Underneath, on a crimson scroll, in Irish characters, was the motto: 'They shall never retreat from the charge of lances.'" The Confederates never captured the Irish Brigade's flag.[50]

Meagher returned to New York City seeking new recruits in the summer of 1862 to replenish his regiments. Meanwhile, the brigade was among a number of the Army of the Potomac units that were hastily summoned from Virginia to secure Washington.[51]

## Antietam

The Irish Brigade marched out of Rockville, Maryland on September 9 with the rest of Richardson's division in pursuit of Lee. The men arrived to a warm welcome in Frederick on the morning of September 13 and bivouacked northwest of town. On Sunday morning of September 14, the II Corps was ordered to detour northward over the Catoctin Mountains by way of Shookstown, forcing the entire corps to march as a single column, slowing the pace until it resumed its march west on the National Road near Middletown.[52]

Early on the morning of September 15, the Irish Brigade "had the honor of leading the pursuit of the rebels from South Mountain through Boonsboro and Keedysville" to Antietam Creek. Meagher deployed the 88th and 63rd New York regiments on the left side of Boonsboro Pike while posting the 69th New York and 29th Massachusetts regiments on the right, just east of the creek. The brigade bivouacked at these locations until the morning of September 17 and was continuously harassed by enemy artillery, "losing several good men."[53]

The Battle of Antietam began at first light on September 17. By 9:30 a.m., John Sedgwick's veteran division (also II Corps) had experienced heavy losses in the West Woods. II Corps commander, Edwin Sumner, directed William French's newly formed 6,300-man division to press its attack on the sunken road in the Confederate center, soon to be known as "Bloody Lane." Two brigades totaling about 2,024 battle-hardened men of D.H. Hill's division occupied a roughly 800-yard front with Robert Rodes' five small Alabama regiments on the left and George B. Anderson's four North Carolina regiments on the right. The defenders had dismantled the snake rail fences on either side of the narrow road and employed them as part of a formidable breastwork. Despite the two-to-one advantage, French could not dislodge Hill's men after an hour of fighting, suffering about 30% casualties by the end of the day. Richard Anderson's division came to Hill's aid by 10:15 a.m.[54]

Sumner had ordered reveille for the entire II Corps at 2:00 a.m. Meagher emerged from his tent in a resplendent uniform. A soldier recalled he had "gotten up most gorgeously … with a gold shoulder belt." He had an orderly brush off his uniform, saying "we'd all have a brush soon." Richardson's division was held in reserve until it received marching orders at 9:10 a.m. The Irish Brigade led the advance, crossing Antietam Creek at a ford "a mile or so to the right of the bivouac." The men knew it would be a hot day so they filled their canteens with the creek's cool water. They then headed toward a ravine behind the high ground overlooking Roulette's house, hidden by rising ground between them and the enemy, "where Richardson ordered that everything but cartridge boxes should be thrown off." The 69th New York led the column, followed by the 29th Massachusetts, 63rd New York and 88th New York. Richardson deployed his division just before 10:00 a.m., with Caldwell's brigade deployed on the left, Meagher's on the right and Brooke's held in reserve.[55]

Meagher deployed his regiments in line of battle on the edge of a cornfield, from left to right: the 88th New York, 63rd New York, 29th Massachusetts, and 69th New York, and moved about 200 yards into the corn as bullets clipped the stalks around them. About 300 yards before reaching the Confederates, the brigade encountered a split rail fence impeding its advance and volunteers rushed forward to dismantle it in the face of deadly enemy sharpshooters inflicting casualties among them. Pvt. Samuel Wright, 29th Massachusetts, exhibited particular boldness and later received the Medal of Honor for his bravery. He later remembered, "as one would grasp a rail it would be sent flying out of his hands by rifle shots." The brigade pressed onward over an open clover field as casualties mounted.[56]

The brigade then ascended a hill within 75 to 100 yards of the Sunken Road, fully exposed with men constantly falling as they were hit by enemy fire. Meagher stood tall in his saddle and yelled out to his men, "Boys! Raise the colors and follow me!" He was clearly "relying on the impetuosity and recklessness of Irish soldiers in a [bayonet] charge" and "felt confident that before such a charge the rebel column would give way and be dispersed." He couldn't have been more wrong. Still, he instructed his officers to order two volleys fired into the enemy followed by a fixed bayonet charge. Instead, he permitted the 69th New York to deliver five or six volleys then ordered the men to charge while bringing up the 88th and 63rd New York. Since the 69th New York was at a slight oblique angle to the enemy line, the left of the brigade was closer to the enemy and sustained higher casualties.

In the face of a galling fire, which, according to Meagher, "literally cut lanes through our approaching line," the brigade reached within 30 yards of the enemy with officers and men falling at every step. Meagher had triggered a bloodbath and while demonstrating conspicuous bravery, soon found himself carried from the field after his was horse shot out from under him, falling heavily to the ground, and command devolved to Col. John Burke of the 63rd. In addition to running head-on into George B. Anderson's North Carolina troops, Richard Anderson's division of about 3,600 troops had moved up on the Confederate right in the Sunken Road. Col. Carnot Posey's Mississippians (Richard Anderson's division) abruptly attacked the left flank of the 63rd New York but were checked by well-placed shots from the 69th New York and the attack of the 88th. The brigade's close proximity to the lane brought murderous sheets of flame and lead that tore through the ranks. Still, above the din of battle came the Irish cry "Faugh-a-Ballagh" (Gaelic for "clear the way"). The brigade's steadfast determination to conquer inspired many in French's division and they fell-in alongside the Irish, refusing to withdraw.[57]

The Irishmen occupying the high ground in the area of the 63rd began firing southwesterly, raking the Alabama troops with a flanking fire. French's men on the right began firing into the left flank of the North Carolina troops as a deadly crossfire began to take its toll on the enemy line. After advancing another 30 yards under withering fire, the 69th New York was ordered back to its original position. The left of the regiment was thrown forward again to within 100 yards of the Sunken Road while the right stood fast.

The 63rd and 88th New York on the left of Meagher's line were also ordered to charge the Sunken Road. Before they could obey, they were decimated by enemy fire, which severely thinned their ranks. The 88th New York advanced into the deadly fire, but its commander, Lt Col. Patrick Kelly, realized the 63rd New York had not stepped off. He rushed back to determine why and was told the regiment's commander and second in command were both struck down, leaving a leadership void. Kelly found Capt. Joseph O'Neill on the regiment's left flank and he agreed to charge if someone stepped forward to command the regiment. Kelly realized it was a forlorn effort by this point, and ordered both regiments back.[58]

The 69th New York "nearly melted away and but a few heroic Irishmen were left huddling about the two colors," according to historian Ezra Carman. The enemy in the Sunken Road yelled out, "bring them colors here" and the two flagbearers advanced a few yards, shook their banners in the Confederates' faces and replied, "Come and take them you damned rebels!" The exchange worried Lt. Col. Joseph Barnes of the 29th Massachusetts who thought it might provoke an enemy charge that would sweep away the remnants of the Irish Brigade.

For some reason, Meagher never ordered the 29th Massachusetts into battle. It occupied a depression in the hill in front of the Sunken Road and could not see the road or be seen, so it sustained few casualties. Barnes watched the destruction of the brigade and according to the regiment's history, he, "feeling a deep responsibility, saw at once that something must be done to prevent disaster, he knew, though he had received no orders since entering the fight … he called upon the regiment for three cheers … Barnes then gave the order, 'forward!' The regiment's historian remembered. "The shout of our men, and their sudden dash toward the sunken road, so startled the enemy that their fire visibly slackened, their line wavered, and squads of two and three began leaving the road and running into the corn."[59]

As the Irish casualties continued to escalate, Caldwell brought his brigade into position to attack the Sunken Road. As the 29th Massachusetts, together with the remaining Irish troops still on the firing line, charged the road, Caldwell's 61st/64th New York began a flanking movement on the enemy's right flank, dislodging many of them from the Sunken Road. The combined efforts of the effective troops remaining in both Richardson's and French's divisions eventually drove all the Confederates from the road and held the position for the remainder of the battle.[60]

The brigade suffered enormous losses. Meagher's entire staff had become casualties and the 69th New York lost 12 color-bearers. Fewer than 50 men remained in the 63rd. Lt. Col. Henry Fowler reported "our colors, although in ribbons, and staff shot through, were still there, sustained at a bloody sacrifice, 16 men having fallen while carrying them." The 63rd New York sustained the greatest losses in the brigade with 202 casualties, nearly 60 percent of its number. The 69th New York was second with 196 casualties while the 88th New York lost 104, about one-third of its strength. The 29th Massachusetts suffered the fewest casualties at 40, owing to the terrain it occupied during the battle. The brigade lost a total of 542 casualties; 113 killed, 422 wounded, and 5 missing—the most of the three brigades of Richardson's division.[61]

**Gary W. Rohrer**

\* \* \*

## 3rd Brigade: Colonel John R. Brooke

**Units:** 2nd Delaware, 52nd New York, 57th New York, 66th New York, 53rd Pennsylvania
**Strength:** 1,650[62]
**Losses:** 305 (52k-244w-9m)[63]

Richardson's 3rd Brigade consisted of five veteran regiments that had seen extensive combat prior to the Maryland Campaign. Recruitment of the 2nd Delaware began in May of 1861 and it headed to Washington in September. The remaining four regiments mustered into service in November, 1861. The New York regiments were assigned to French's brigade in February 1862. The 2nd Delaware and 53rd Pennsylvania were added to the brigade under the President's order that defined the organization of the army dated March 8, 1862. It became the 3rd Brigade of Richardson's division. French remained in command of the brigade until September 6, 1862 when he was elevated to command of the 3rd Division. Col. John R. Brooke

of the 53rd Pennsylvania assumed command of the brigade as it prepared for the Maryland Campaign.[64]

Brooke's brigade marched north with the division from Rockville, Maryland and reached Frederick via Shookstown Road. Josiah Favill of the 57th New York recorded in his diary on September 5: McClellan "has an immense army, well equipped and disciplined and eager for the fray; brains and genius only are only wanting to accomplish the greatest results." The brigade, with the rest of the II Corps, arrived in Frederick on the afternoon of September 13. "As we entered the main street the drums sounded attention, and the troops marched in regular order, with bands playing and colors flying," noted Favill. The citizens were "beside themselves with joy."[65]

The column moved north on the National Road, and then west to Bolivar. Richardson's division pushed ahead to Mt. Tabor Church in support of the I Corps, which was fighting for control of

Turner's Gap. The next day, September 15, the brigade, with the rest of the division, moved over South Mountain to Boonsboro and then Keedysville, taking position on the high ground east of Antietam Creek near the Middle Bridge. Brooke threw out a picket line. Capt. David Stricker of the 2nd Delaware recalled, "On the morning of the 16th Gen. Richardson personally ordered me to withdraw my picket and return with my regiment to our former position in rear of the battery. We lay there all day and night, under a heavy artillery fire, losing 1 man killed and 1 wounded."[66]

The brigade came under enemy artillery fire as the men lay on the east bank of Antietam Creek. Favill noted the Confederates "are liberal in the expenditure of ammunition." Brooke's brigade finally crossed Antietam Creek on the morning of September 17 with the remainder of Richardson's division. Col. Paul Frank of the 52nd New York reported his regiment "crossed the creek and was drawn up in line of battle in a corn field, half an hour after which it advanced." This advance was made under a "heavy fire" of artillery. The brigade came on the field with the 53rd Pennsylvania on the left of the line, the 66th New York to their right, followed by the 57th New York, 2nd Delaware, and the 52nd New York forming the right of the line. The brigade remained in reserve while Thomas Meagher's Irish Brigade and then John Caldwell's brigade battled the Confederates defending the Sunken Road.[67]

According to Brooke, "General Richardson then ordered me to move forward, which was done with great precision under a terrific fire of shot and shell," probably around the time the Sunken Road defensive line was beginning to break. Favill recalled his reaction when the order was given to advance, with "teeth firmly set and without a word spoken, we marched steadily forward. As we approached the Irish brigade, it opened files and we passed through, immediately coming under terrific fire of musketry and artillery." Brooke ordered his men to again lie down.

Just then, the 27th North Carolina and 3rd Arkansas under the command of John Cooke (Van Manning's brigade) appeared on the division's vulnerable right flank. Col. Frank apparently saw the threat first. He reported, "Advancing in close line for about half a mile under a heavy fire, it [52nd New York] entered a corn field on the crest of a hill, when I received intelligence that two rebel regiments were on our right, on a lower ground. Col. Brooke, commanding brigade, was in the center of the line, but too far off for me to report for orders. I therefore took the Fifty-second on the high ground to our right and opened fire on the flank of the rebel regiments ... After about half an hour's fighting the rebel lines broke, and seeing our forces deploying out of a corn field in front of the rebels, I ceased firing, and shortly afterward was ordered back for a fresh supply of ammunition." Frank claimed his men used "an average of from 50 to 60 rounds [of ammunition] per man."[68]

Winfield Hancock told a slightly different version. "Colonel Brooke, observing it [the enemy piercing French's troops on the right of Roulette's house], applied for orders to General Richardson to repair the accident, and immediately led three regiments in that direction, and formed line of battle on the crest in front of Roulette's house and inclosures [sic], sending one regiment (the Fifty-third Pennsylvania, commanded by Lieutenant-Colonel Richards McMichael) to dislodge the enemy, who had then gained a foothold in the corn-field in rear of those buildings. The enemy was promptly driven out by this regiment, which held the ground until ordered subsequently to march to another part of the field."[69]

Brooke modestly reported his action: "the enemy charged and drove back the troops on our right, when the Fifty second New York and the Second Delaware, under Colonel Frank, changed front to meet this attack." The 53rd Pennsylvania also joined in this attack. Historian Ezra Carman singled out its importance, noting it was ordered to "hold at all hazards the Roulette barn and orchard, the barn being used as a hospital." The regiment "advanced under a shower of musketry gained the barn, reached high ground in the orchard and opened fire upon the left of the 27th North Carolina ..." Other units converged on Cooke's men as well, hitting its front, flank, and rear, and driving it back toward the West Woods.[70]

A new threat materialized in the cornfield south of the Sunken Road when several Confederate regiments mounted a counterattack to retake their old positions. Brooke reported he "advanced the Fifty-seventh and Sixty-sixth New York to relieve Caldwell's lines, which were now fiercely assailed by fresh troops of the enemy." These two regiments swept across the Sunken Road and into the cornfield beyond it. The 57th New York with the 66th New York on its left attached itself to the left of the 61st/64th New York. Brooke sent Favill to see Francis Barlow, commanding the latter regiments with orders to "move by the left and close up the gap. To my surprise, he refused to budge, saying he did not recognize Colonel Brooke's authority. The balls were whistling around me as I stood arguing with him, almost beside myself for chagrin, when Brooke suddenly made his appearance. I told him the colonel refused to recognize his authority, and he, very angry, ordered him instantly to move forward." The regiments advanced and crashed into the enemy, driving them in disorder back toward the Piper barn. Favill recalled the regiments moved rapidly down the "slope, over a sunken road strewn with dead and dying, and into a cornfield pell mell we went, driving the flying rebels before us in splendid shape, bayoneting all who did not promptly surrender." Maj. Alford Chapman of the 57th New York proudly proclaimed, "Animated by the presence of both their brigade and division commanders, the regiment moved forward with a determined enthusiasm I have never seen excelled." Brooke's New Yorkers captured the flags of the 12th Alabama and 5th Florida during the bitter fighting and collected scores of prisoners.[71]

Brooke sought permission from Richardson to withdraw the 57th New York and 66th New York because the threat was gone, but they were now "exposed to a cross-fire of the enemy's batteries." Richardson concurred and Brooke pulled them back beyond the Sunken Road. They were sent back to support Capt. William Graham's battery to the left. Maj. Chapman reported, "I filed round the foot of the hill under a terrible fire of grape and canister, which fortunately caused us comparatively slight loss, being aimed too high. Arriving on the left of the battery, I found General Richardson, who was in the act of assigning me my position, when he was badly wounded and carried from the field."[72]

The battle was now over for Brooke's brigade. He noted in his report, "Nothing now occurred except an occasional interchange of shots on the line of pickets. It gives me pleasure to say that every man did his duty unflinchingly. About 2,000 stands of arms were captured, as also a great number of prisoners, who were sent through the ranks to the rear."[73]

The brigade had fought well at Antietam. Although it did not participate in directly driving the enemy from the Sunken Road, it was involved in staunching two Confederate counterattacks made against the II Corps' right flank and front. It lost 305 men in the fight.

After the battle, the brigade was engaged for two days interring the dead. The brigade then marched to Harpers Ferry and remained at Bolivar Heights until Oct. 30. Brooke did not remain in command as he was returned to command of the 53rd Pennsylvania within a month.[74]

**Joseph Stahl**

***

# 2ND DIVISION—

## Major General John Sedgwick, Brigadier General Oliver Howard

Major General John Sedgwick had just celebrated his 49th birthday as his 2nd Division of Sumner's II Corps crested South Mountain and drew close to Antietam Creek. Well-trained for the tasks ahead of him in the coming days, Sedgwick brought experience to the officers and men of his command. After graduating in the West Point Class of 1837, Sedgwick started his career in the artillery before moving to the cavalry where he earned two brevets for gallantry and merit in Mexico. The opening of the Civil War found him serving as colonel of the 1st U.S. Cavalry. He soon added infantry to his command experience when commissioned brigadier general and then major general of volunteers. He was wounded in the arm and leg at the Battle of Glendale (Frayser's Farm) during the Seven Days Campaign.[75]

Sedgwick managed his division with a small staff that included his cousin, William Dwight Sedgwick. The division was composed of three brigades. All were mostly veterans of the Army of the Potomac's campaigns and one went all the way back to First Bull Run. Willis Gorman's brigade brought 1,691 men to Antietam; Oliver O. Howard's Philadelphia Brigade numbered 1,800; and Napoleon Dana's came in with 1,946 under arms. The brigades contributed four regiments from Pennsylvania, four from New York, three from Massachusetts, and single regiments from Michigan and Minnesota. The 15th Massachusetts and 1st Minnesota also had contingents of sharpshooters. Additionally, John Tompkins' 1st Rhode Island Light, Battery A and George Woodruff's 1st U.S. Battery I provided artillery support. In all, the division totaled 6,634 officers and infantry and 244 artillery officers and men.[76]

The division began the Maryland Campaign in the fields surrounding the little hamlet of Tennallytown in the District of Columbia. Located on Rockville Road, the surrounding fields, woodlands, and good water sources provided the perfect assembly point for George McClellan's Army of the Potomac.[77]

On September 5, with news of Confederates crossing the Potomac in force, General-in-Chief Henry Halleck ordered McClellan to move General Sumner's II Corps in pursuit. The men marched along Rockville Road in the direction of Frederick, Maryland. Sedgwick's division entered Hyattstown on September 11 where it made the initial contact with Lee's army by driving off some pickets from Brig. Gen. Wade Hampton's cavalry brigade. From that point on, the road to Frederick was wide open. The division, along with the rest of the II Corps, rested west of town on the night of September 13. At 8:45 p.m. that night the corps received orders to march west to Middletown as part of McClellan's pursuit of Lee's army. Sumner and the rest of the corps stepped off on the National Pike at 7:00 a.m. the following day.[78]

They soon ran into heavy traffic on the two-lane road, about two miles west of Frederick. McClellan directed Sumner to detour to Shookstown Road that ran parallel to the pike leading to Middletown. The corps counter-marched against traffic to find the new route. Once on it, however, they found little improvement for its rocky surface and steep pitches slowed them to a crawl and the column made little more than two miles that day.[79]

By the evening of September 14, Sedgwick and the rest of the II Corps were concentrated in Bolivar along the National Pike, a couple miles east of Turner's Gap. McClellan ordered Sumner to move to Boonsboro at 8:45 a.m. on September 15. He was told that if he found any retreating Confederates, he was to "push on after the enemy as rapidly and far as possible, keeping your corps well in hand and doing them all the injury possible." Before Sedgwick and the rest of Sumner's command could get to Boonsboro, however, he had to get his command through the congestion of infantry, artillery, and supply wagons crowding the top of the mountain pass.[80]

Reaching the summit at the Mountain House, Sedgwick found Hooker's I Corps blocking the way, brewing morning coffee and cooking breakfast. After some delay, the division crossed the pass and followed the road down the mountain to Boonsboro where it turned south on the Boonsboro-Sharpsburg Turnpike. By late afternoon, the division overlooked Antietam Creek just outside of Keedysville. Beyond the creek, the men observed a Confederate line facing them "in large force" stretching for about a mile and a half. Sedgwick's men spent the night in the farm fields owned by Philip Pry, lying on their arms and ready to go at first light.[81]

A little after 6:00 a.m. of September 17, Sumner along with his son, Capt. Samuel Sumner and some members of his staff, went to the Pry house for orders. As Sumner paced impatiently on the veranda of the house, he could clearly hear the artillery on their right. All of Sumner's divisions, including Sedgwick's, had been ready to go hours earlier. The officers and men spent time in the dank darkness of intermittent drizzle making coffee, writing letters, and catching a little shut eye.[82]

Orders came down directing Sumner to move his command to support Hooker's I Corps at 7:20 a.m. Hooker's men had been engaged for over an hour in the fight for Miller's Cornfield and East Woods. Sumner had two of his three divisions on the move in a short time. As they made their way down the steep bluffs to a ford crossing Antietam Creek, Sedgwick's division took the lead while William French's newly-formed division followed. Crossing the creek, at least one brigade halted "for the purpose of giving the men time to shake the water from their shoes and clothing."[83]

"The advance moved forward with very little wavering," reported one of the commanders, "under a fire from the enemy's batteries, which at first were concealed from us by a skirting of woods." Nearing the battlefield, they entered the East Woods where they were "considerably crowded" into a space not more than "40 paces" wide.[84]

Despite the crowding, Sedgwick aligned his division for the attack. Gorman's brigade led the way, followed by Dana's brigade, and Howard's Philadelphia Brigade brought up the rear. With Sumner and Sedgwick at the fore, the entire division stepped off at the double quick; it was a little after 9:00 a.m. Their destination was a body of woods that lay past Hagerstown Pike, about 500 yards and directly to their west.[85]

Years later, Captain James Hope, a professional artist on the field that day, sketched the advance of the three brigades crossing the open fields to the West Woods. What he could not show, however, was the speed at which they were moving. But Lt. H.W. Sanford of Co. E, 34th New York, described the mad dash as his comrades "rushed forward at the top of their speed in broken order, one company in rear of the other, out of breath and almost fainting."[86]

After crossing the high post and rail fences along Hagerstown Pike, the brigades proceeded westward and halted when Gorman's brigade emerged from the western border of the woods and encountered Confederates at the Alfred Poffenberger farmstead. These were the approximate 200 survivors of the Stonewall Division, commanded by Andrew Grigsby. The Virginians had survived the bloody fight with portions of the Iron Brigade and Marsena Patrick's brigade west of the Cornfield and were still full of fight. Grigsby's men used the farmstead buildings, orchard, and limestone ridges for cover. Further to the west, a line of Confederate artillery crowned Hauser's Ridge. As Gorman's brigade stepped out of the protection of the woods, the combined fire of artillery and infantry slowed the Union advance to a halt.[87]

While Gorman's line dealt with Grigsby's Virginians, Dana and Howard in the rear became aware of an increasing commotion on the left of the division, down by the Dunker Church. Two Union regiments from different brigades were down that way and bore the brunt of a Confederate attack by G. T. Anderson's, Joseph Kershaw's, and William Barksdale's brigades. In very little time, the flanked regiments broke and the collapse spread northward as the Confederates moved on the left flanks of all of the regiments.[88]

Sumner attempted to get Howard's Philadelphia Brigade turned to meet the attackers but it was too late.

Compounding matters, Sedgwick was struck down by enemy fire at the division's left. Dana was also hit as he tried to steer his brigade to a defensive position. Wounds for both were serious, and they would survive but their loss further diminished any hope of righting things.[89]

As companies, then regiments, then brigades splintered and fell back, individual leaders emerged. Col. Thomas Sully of the 1st Minnesota rallied remnants of New York and Pennsylvania regiments north of the woods to make a stand on the colors. A bit further to the east, Col. Turner Morehead of the 106th Pennsylvania patched together another firing line that halted the Mississippi and Virginia pursuers. But these were fall-back actions and in short time, the remnants of the division retired to the protection of the North Woods or supported artillery batteries coming into action east of the Pike. By 11:00 a.m. the division was all but wrecked.[90]

Sedgwick's advance to the West Woods cost 2,183 officers and men or 40% of the number that crossed Antietam Creek that day. By noon, the division's brigades were reassembled near the Joseph Poffenberger farmstead. Gorman's brigade rested along the farm lane bordering the North Woods while Dana and Howard's brigades deployed facing west a little over 200 yards to the east, or left, of Gorman's flank. After the West Woods withdrawal, the division did not participate in subsequent actions.[91]

John Sedgwick was lucky to have survived the battle. One bullet struck him in his leg and another broke his wrist. Still on his horse, a surgeon examined his wounds and told him that he should leave the field to get proper medical attention. Refusing this advice, Sedgwick changed horses but could not handle the reins with his shattered wrist. A third wound soon followed, this one to his shoulder, convincing him it was time to leave the field. He eventually made it back to his Connecticut home where his sister attended to his convalescence for the next three months. Returning to duty in mid-December, he remarked, "If I am ever hit again, I hope it will settle me at once. I want no more wounds." On May 9, 1864 he was "settled" at Spotsylvania; his last words were "they couldn't hit an elephant at this distance." He is buried in Cornwall Hollow, Connecticut.[92]

**James M. Buchanan**

*  *  *

## 1st Brigade: Brigadier General Willis Gorman

**Units:** 34th New York, 15th Massachusetts, 82nd New York, 1st Minnesota, Minnesota Sharpshooters (Second Company), Massachusetts Sharpshooters (Andrew's)
**Strength:** 2,027[93]
**Losses:** 740 (134k-539w-67m)[94]

Willis A. Gorman brought military experience to the command, having served as a major of the Third Indiana Volunteers in Mexico. After the war, he organized another state regiment, served two terms in Congress, and became governor of the territory of Minnesota. The outbreak of the Civil War brought Gorman back into military service as the commander of the First Regiment of Minnesota Volunteers. Breveted a brigadier general after the Battle of First Bull Run, he took charge of the brigade that bore his name.[95]

Gorman's brigade, composed of James A. Suiter's 34th New York, John W. Kimball's 15th Massachusetts, Henry W. Hudson's 82nd New York, and Alfred Sully's 1st Minnesota, was a well-trained and veteran outfit totaling 2,027 officers and men. A small group of aides de camp that included his sons, James and Richard, helped Gorman manage the brigade.[96]

Gorman's brigade followed the rest of Sedgwick's division as it made its way from Washington to Antietam Creek. The men were usually uncertain about their destinations, as described by Ed Walker of the 1st Minnesota. "... [W]e began to think that we were going to Edwards Ferry again and perhaps picket duty this winter, but waiting awhile the movements of the Secesh, we were marched to Frederick City." The men had a good experience in the town, according to Walker, as the inhabitants "welcomed us with enthusiasm, flags hung from most every house, sidewalks covered with women and children the fact is Maryland will *blow* about sympathizing with Secesh, but when they come to have war on Maryland, they had rather be excused."[97]

## Antietam

September 17 found Gorman's brigade leading Sedgwick's division down the steep bluffs from its encampment to the east side of Antietam Creek a little after 7:30 a.m. The division then crossed a ford and moved west through fields and over fences. Nearing the battlefield, they moved into the East Woods. There the brigades were "considerably crowded" into a space not more than "40 paces wide." [98]

Sedgwick now aligned his division for the attack. Gorman's brigade led the way, followed by Dana and Howard's Philadelphia Brigade. With Sumner and Sedgwick riding point, the division stepped off at the double quick at approximately 9:00 a.m. Gorman's men "rushed forward at the top of their speed in broken order, one company in rear of the other, out of breath, and almost fainting," recalled the historian of the 34th New York. Their destination was a body of woods that lay beyond Hagerstown Pike, 500 yards directly to their west.[99]

As Gorman's brigade raced across the field, the regiments were arrayed from left to right: the 34th New York, 15th Massachusetts, the 82nd New York, and the 1st Minnesota. Sumner rode on the right flank with Sully's 1st Minnesota, when he saw its colors still encased and in a voice heard for quite a distance, shouted: "In God's name, what are you fighting for? Unfurl those colors!"[100]

Whether or not the boys of the 34th New York heard Sumner's admonition is unknown as they were on the far left of the brigade. Suiter rode his horse, Old Billy, at the front of the line and aligned

his command on the Smoketown Road on his left as his command sped west across stubble fields.[101]

Dunker Church, adjacent to a large wood lot of ancient oaks and maples, loomed ahead. The ground here was rolling and uneven with swales, limestone outcroppings, and ravines of intermittent streams. Suiter and his command suspected the clouds of white smoke rising above the trees and the crash of volleys spelled trouble ahead. Reaching the church, Suiter noticed something was not right: "From some cause to me unknown, I had become detached from my brigade" and instead found himself to the left rear of the 125th Pennsylvania, a XII Corps rookie outfit who had entered the woods less than 30 minutes before and were now tangling with Confederates in its front.[102]

Suiter perceived he was unsupported by artillery or infantry, and worse, he suspected the Confederates were moving to flank him on his left. Lt. Church Howe from Sedgwick's staff thought "they were our friends." Amid the rising din and smoke, Lt. William Wallace, Co. C, volunteered to reconnoiter "to make what discovery he could." With Wallace scouting his left, Suiter placed Sgt. Charles Barton at the regiment's center to display the colors and steady the line. Barton was a veteran of all of Suiter's battles and his presence was sure to steel the men.[103]

Wallace returned with alarming news: "the enemy were moving upon [the] left flank with a strong force." This was Kershaw's 2nd South Carolina (McLaws' division) and Suiter immediately ordered his command to refuse its left to meet him. Brig. Gen. William Barksdale's Mississippi brigade then arrived. "Old soldiers" all, the Confederates delivered well-timed and well-aimed volleys into the ranks of Suiter's men, and the rookie Pennsylvanians, who broke for the rear.[104]

The 34th New York, separated from the rest of the brigade, stood its ground; 50 yards behind it and to its right stood the left flank of the 72nd Pennsylvania. One South Carolinian remarked "the first Union line was very quickly driven [the 125th Pennsylvania], but an oblique line [the 34th New

York] apparently older soldiers, was not so easily moved and checked us."[105]

In the middle of this rapidly deteriorating situation, Lt. Richard Gorman, Willis Gorman's Aide-de-Camp and son, rode up. Suiter told him to take a message up the line that he was being flanked. The alarm must have been received since Sedgwick appeared next on the scene. Moving down Suiter's line, Sedgwick quickly saw it could not hold much longer and ordered it to retire. With the South Carolinians breathing fire 50 feet away, the order came none too soon for Philip Crewel of Co. K: "We had to fall back … and if we hadn't, they would have killed all of us." Among those left on the field was Sgt. Charles Barton. The stalwart color bearer had been struck five times but would survive his wounds.[106]

From the perspective of the left wing of the 72nd Pennsylvania behind them, the 34th did not retire, but rather they "came back in great disorder." Breaking through the Pennsylvanians' line and carrying most of it away with them, the New Yorkers crossed the road and headed back up Smoketown Road in the direction they had come. Officers desperately grouped companies of the 34th and 72nd Pennsylvania to support Monroe's and Woodruff's batteries across the Pike.[107]

The 34th New York may have been the first of the brigade to go, but it was not the last. As the attackers grew in numbers, the same fate befell other regiments in other brigades north along the line near Hagerstown Pike. The Confederate tide continued sweeping north through the woods and along the Pike washing over regiment after regiment.

The rest of Gorman's brigade formed along the western border of the woods, about five hundred yards northwest of the right flank of the 34th New York. The 15th Massachusetts was on the left; the 82nd New York in the middle, and the 1st Minnesota on the right. About the time the 34th New York pulled up to the Dunker Church, the rest of the brigade emerged from the western edge of the woods along a fence line. Before them a gentle slope led down to a wood road.[108]

Opposite the 15th Massachusetts, just beyond the road stood the Alfred Poffenberger farmstead of a cabin, outbuildings, hay stacks, and a small orchard. Fifty yards to the south stood a large bank barn serving as a Confederate aid station. About 200 survivors of the Stonewall Division, commanded by A. J. Grigsby, were scattered in and around the farmstead. Grigsby surveyed the blue lines emerging from the dark woods, figuring he could hold his position, but not for long.[109]

Grigsby, however, did have some backup. Behind him, less than 600 yards to the west, stood Hauser's Ridge presenting no less than 13 artillery pieces to Gorman's front. These guns opened up with shell and case shot as Gorman emerged from the protection of the woods. They had the range on them and were very accurate.[110]

Despite the artillery fire, Kimball advanced his 15th Massachusetts, led by skirmishers and a company of Andrew's Sharpshooters. Grigsby's thrown-together line started giving way but not without inflicting casualties on the Massachusetts "men [who] were falling thick and fast."[111]

Not all casualties, however, came from Confederate muskets. After volleying with Grigsby's defenders for about 25 minutes, Dana's brigade, which had been halted 30 to 40 yards in the rear, started advancing again and pulled up close on Kimball's left rear. Dana's 59th New York halted immediately behind and to the left of the 15th Massachusetts and it opened fire on both the Confederates and the 15th in their front. Kimball described what happened next: "Many of my men were by this maneuver killed … and my most strenuous exertions were of no avail either stopping this murderous fire or in causing the second line to advance to the front." Sumner riding nearby heard Kimball's frantic shouts and got control of the errant regiment by ordering it to retire that "was executed in considerable confusion."[112]

As Brig. Gen. Paul Semmes' brigade advanced from Hauser's Ridge to the Alfred Poffenberger farmstead, it sent a deadly fire into Kimball's front. Semmes' Virginians and Georgians had had little sleep and sustenace "for the two or three nights and days previous," but their adrenaline was up, and they attacked with a fury. Simultaneously, Brig. Gen. Jubal Early's Virginians hit Gorman's left flank.[113]

Sgt. Jonathan Stowe of the 15th Massachusetts saw "shells fly past me every few seconds carrying away limbs from trees and scattering limbs around," and concluded, "we had a bad place." Turning around, Gorman saw Dana's brigade being flanked as well and Howard's Philadelphians, further to his rear, were also getting hit along their flank and rear. As regiments from these commands broke to the north or east across the Pike, the left of Gorman's line became fully exposed.[114]

"Without orders of any kind from any one" Gorman knew he had to act quickly to escape the "enemy's fire … pouring hotly on our left flank and rear." He commanded his brigade to move out by the right flank, but in the confusion of noise and smoke it "reached no one but Colonel Sully" of the First Minnesota at the far right of the line.[115]

Kimball's regiment, receiving "no orders to retire, held its position until the other two Regiments on its [the] right had withdrawn, and then … fell back in order to protect themselves, being entirely unsupported." While most of the 15th moved off in an orderly fashion, at least some broke and broke fast. Roland Bowen recorded in his diary that "no God Damned Southerner is going to catch me unless he can run 29 miles an hour."[116]

As the depleted 15th Massachusetts moved north through the woods to escape the Confederate attackers, Kimball formed a defensive line facing south along an east-west fence that ran from Hagerstown Pike to the middle of the West Woods. This stand slowed the Confederate pursuers, but the line soon gave way to the Confederate artillery fire raining down on it from the high ground to their west. By 11:00 a.m., the 15th Massachusetts had found its way to the relative safety of the North Woods and the Joseph Poffenberger house and barn. For them, this day was over.[117]

The brigade's two remaining regiments fought on. Col. Henry Hudson, commander of the 82nd New York, looked to his left to find that his companies closest to the 15th Massachusetts had fallen back through the 19th Massachusetts just a few yards to their rear. The greater part of his regiment still stood firm but not for long; the wave of the rebel attack was too much for his command and his men began peeling northward to the outer edge of the wood, not in a rout but with a measured retreat.[118]

Hudson looked around for Gorman but could not find him and, receiving no direction, turned to Sully of the 1st Minnesota. As the senior officer present, Sully, who *had* heard Gorman's orders, directed Hudson to form his colors on his left.[119]

Since arriving in the West Woods, the Minnesotans had exchanged fire with the 13th Virginia, one of Jubal Early's regiments, located in a strip of dense timber on Hauser's Ridge and a cornfield in their front. Sully and his commanders heard the commotion on their left but could not see very far up the brigade line as the rise of the ground and the tall trees in that direction blocked any view. As the noise increased to an ominous pitch, the scope of the disaster soon revealed itself to the Minnesotans. "As I saw it," one commander recalled, "the whole Division except our [Minnesota] Regiment was broken into a mob, madly pressing to the rear followed closely by the enemies lines."[120]

With the 82nd New York joining them, Sully ordered an about face and marched the two regiments to the rear at the double quick. As they moved out, canister showered them from Confederate batteries that stalked them northward along the high ground to the west. Clearing the woods and moving north about 100 yards through an open field, they found a rock ledge. The 82nd formed on Sully's left, and both turned around twice to deliver volleys at their pursuers. The 13th Virginia shadowed them in the ravines to the west and fast-moving horse artillery batteries leap-frogged on the high ground, opening on them as they moved, and in their rear, Semmes' regiments followed in hot pursuit.[121]

A rough road leading to the Nicodemus farmstead loomed ahead of the Minnesotans and New Yorkers. To Sully, this looked like a good place to make a stand, as its farmhouse, outbuildings, and grain stacks could give some defensive cover. But they had to get there first. As one witness recounted, they rushed "through the farm yard under a shower of cannister, tumbled over the stone fence in front and in less than 20 seconds formed on our colors in the road, every man in his place."[122]

They then almost immediately moved by the right flank to the corner of the North Woods extending to the west of the turnpike, where they were joined by the 19th Massachusetts on their left. Together the three regiments faced about to check the pursuing Confederates. Capt. James Cooper's battery joined the fray and came up on the right of the improvised line. The Confederate battery following them was soon put out of action by Cooper's battery but a fight with Confederate sharpshooters ensued for the next 20 minutes as each side exchanged a deadly fire. Using the woods to the right of the Union line to their advantage, the sharpshooters exacted "a considerable loss" on the Union line before they too were depleted. As the fighting subsided, the regiments moved farther north to rejoin the division.[123]

All totaled, the brigade losses amounted to 740 men—134 dead, 539 wounded, and 67 captured or missing.[124]

As for Willis Gorman, Antietam was his last command in the Army of the Potomac. In November 1862 he left to command the district of Arkansas at Helena. Poor health forced him to resign his commission in May 1864 and he again took up the practice of law in St. Paul, Minnesota. Yet, Gorman never really left his first command, the First Minnesota, and he joined their post-war reunions. Fourteen years later he was laid to rest in the town's Oakland Cemetery where many of his old comrades came to express their respect and devotion to their leader.[125]

**James M. Buchanan**

* * *

## 2nd (Philadelphia) Brigade: Brigadier General Oliver O. Howard, Colonel Joshua Owen

**Units:** 69th Pennsylvania, 71st Pennsylvania, 72nd Pennsylvania, 106th Pennsylvania
**Strength:** 2,650[126]
**Losses:** 545 (93k-379w-73m)[127]

The Philadelphia Brigade was originally organized as the California Brigade by Oregon Senator Edward Baker in July 1861. Baker, a former resident of California, wanted the Golden State to be represented in the Union Army. Despite its name, the California Brigade recruited men from Philadelphia and by October consisted of four regiments, the 1st, 2nd, 3rd and 5th California. The brigade first saw action at Ball's Bluff where Baker was killed. With Baker's death, Philadelphia claimed the four California regiments as part of its quota, renamed it the Philadelphia Brigade, and renaming its regiments. The 1st became the 71st Pennsylvania, the 2nd the 69th Pennsylvania, the 3d the 72nd Pennsylvania, and the 5th the 106th Pennsylvania. Brig. Gen. William Burns was assigned command of the brigade, which saw action at the Peninsula, Seven Days, and covered Pope's retreat after Second Bull Run. They then embarked with the rest of the Army of the Potomac on the Maryland Campaign.[128]

Burns was wounded at Savage Station during the Seven Days and 31-year-old Oliver Otis Howard assumed command of the brigade. Howard was born in Maine and graduated from Bowdoin College before entering West Point with the Class of 1854. His experiences in the Seminole War were put to use as colonel of the 3rd Maine and he commanded a brigade at First Bull Run. Howard lost an arm at Seven Pines, but returned to command the Philadelphia Brigade at the end of the Second Bull Run Campaign.[129]

Howard's brigade moved out of its encampment at Tennallytown along with Sedgwick's other brigades on September 5 and headed north. The men camped near the Fox's Gap battlefield on the night of September 14-15 and they never forgot the sights and smells when they awoke. One of the men recalled a blacksmith shop converted into a field hospital and outside a window, amputated limbs "still lay in a blue festering heap that would have filled two or three army wagons." The brigade reached the banks of Antietam Creek on the late afternoon of September 16 where the men set up camp on the Pry farm.[130]

## Antietam

The brigade was in motion by 7:30 a.m. the following day. It formed the division's third line after it crossed Antietam Creek from its encampment at the Pry House. The brigade formed for the attack after crossing fields and fences for about a mile and entered the East Woods. The objective was a large woodlot 800 yards to the west called the West Woods.

As the brigade advanced from the East Woods, the 71st Pennsylvania under Col. Isaac Wistar, was posted on the right; Col. DeWitt Baxter's Fire Zouaves, 72nd Pennsylvania, took up the extreme left. The right center was occupied by Col. Turner Morehead's 106th Pennsylvania. The 69th Pennsylvania, under Col. Joshua T. Owen, on the left center, completed the brigade formation.[131]

The brigade "eagerly pressed forward" in good order as it crossed the field. Howard urged the lines to keep steady and cautioned everyone to "be careful not to step on those poor men" of both sides that lay wounded on the field.[132]

Halfway across the field, an aide from General Sumner ordered Howard to "detach a regiment to support" Joseph Mansfield's XII Corps. Howard halted the 71st Pennsylvania "in the place indicated on the right of [the brigade's] line." But shortly afterwards, Sedgwick ordered Howard to move up his entire line including the 71st Pennsylvania. Howard delayed the brigade long enough to allow the 71st to come up and then moved on toward the West Woods.[133]

Ahead, two stout post and rail fences bordered both sides of Hagerstown Pike. The brigade struck the fence obliquely with the 71st Pennsylvania reaching it first and began climbing the high rail fences. As the men crossed, a Confederate battery delivered an enfilading fire. One veteran wrote "[we] continu[ed] across the open field beyond and into the woods, fulfilling General Sedgwick's orders to 'Push into the woods,' which sheltered us from their artillery fire, they also using canister with terrible effect."[134]

The rest of the brigade followed suit, regiment by regiment. All along the fence extending south along the Pike toward the Dunker church, a long line of men in blue climbed up and over the six rails. Howard, riding with the 106th Pennsylvania, second regiment in line, spoke quietly to the men saying: "Steady men, don't hurry;" "Get over the fence carefully;" "Be careful of your guns;" "Keep the muzzles well up;" "Don't hurt any one with your bayonets."[135]

Ahead, the men could hear heavy infantry volleys coming from Gorman's lead brigade "showing that the first line was already hotly engaged." As Howard turned to his left, he saw "quite a large body of men falling back. I judged them to be troops that our division was relieving." What Howard saw was the 125th Pennsylvania, a rookie outfit, breaking back from the West Woods just north of the Dunker Church. To Howard, their movement did not appear to be anything but a field maneuver having been "relieved" by his division.[136]

Not fully realizing the nature of the affairs to his left, Howard "pushed the [brigade] on a little farther, and into the woods beyond the turnpike." From this position, "their [the enemy's] infantry [in our front] could not be seen, only the flash of their guns as they poured volley after volley into our division. This checked our advance and our brigade was instructed to lie down."[137]

Other commanders saw the commotion on the left too. Capt. James C. Lynch of Company A of the 106th Pennsylvania, called over to Col. Owen of the 69th Pennsylvania, alerting him to a Confederate column, "now plainly visible on [the] left flank; Colonel Owen said he saw them and had called General Howard's attention to them," and "immediately suggested the propriety of moving the brigade obliquely to the left." Howard, however, "replied that he knew it, but his orders were to move right oblique." And so the brigade continued in "good order," dressing by the right of Dana's brigade to their front.[138]

The havoc on the left became more and more apparent over the next few minutes. While the green 125th Pennsylvania streamed back out of the woods, the veteran 34th New York from Gorman's brigade and Howard's own 72nd Pennsylvania held steady.

As the brigade marched toward the West Woods, the 72nd Pennsylvania on the far left drifted south from the rest of the brigade and aligned itself behind and to the right of the 34th New York of Gorman's brigade. This alignment brought the regiment just north of the Dunker Church. Not only were they separated from the rest of their brigade, but for some unknown reason, the regiment had split in two: the left close to the church and the right in line on its right flank but separated by 50 yards.[139]

Lt. John Lockhart of the 72nd Pennsylvania recalled, "on arriving on the line of battle, we could not fire for a short time, as some of our troops were in our front." But once cleared, they opened fire on the Confederates. But, recalled Pvt. Sylvester Byrne, 72nd Pennsylvania, "after about five or ten minutes the enemy came around us on the left flank." For Thomas Eaton, Co. H, 72nd Pennsylvania, the collapse crested from the front as the 34th New York "broke through our lines throwing us into great disorder." The line now breached, the left wing of "the regiment fell back carrying the right wing with them." According to

Byrne, "There was no order maintained," and the Philadelphians were quickly swept away by the rising butternut and gray tide.[140]

Meanwhile, the rest of the brigade was lying down for about half-an-hour and reserving its fire as Gorman's front line brigade dueled with Confederates at the Alfred Poffenberger farmstead on the western edge of the woods. As more Confederates assaulted their position from the west and the south, Gorman's lead brigade was forced to retire. As it did, their men "fell back through Dana's brigade, carrying it with them in confusion, and together they came back through the line of [Howard's] Brigade."[141]

With the field cleared of their comrades in the first two lines, the Philadelphia Brigade stood and unleashed a volley into the advancing Confederates. Just then Sumner accompanied by an aide rode up and "his hat in hand [and] gave an order which our men thought was to charge, and answered him with a cheer, rose up, began to fix bayonets."[142]

With Sedgwick trying to fix the situation on the left of the division, Sumner, tried to manage the growing crisis in the center, directing Howard to change position to meet the Confederate regiments pushing from the south and "indicated … the point where the stand was to be made." Howard, at the center of the line near the 106th Pennsylvania, tried to obey Sumner's orders, but "the noise of the musketry and artillery was so great that I judged more by the gestures of the general as to the disposition he wished me to make than by the orders that reached my ears."[143]

It was too late, as the regiments from his and Dana's brigades on their left were breaking up quickly and Confederates under G.T. Anderson, William Barksdale, Kershaw's 3rd South Carolina and Jubal Early pushed north while Paul Semmes' brigade drove in from the west.

The confusion of noise and smoke amplified the unfolding disaster, as the left-most regiments of Howard's brigade's became exposed and began to break too. Commanders of the 69th and 106th Pennsylvania described "a terrific fire of canister from batteries they had rushed into position on our left flank [that had a] terrible effect." At the 69th Pennsylvania's position, "the fire was coming from our rear, left, and front, and we were obliged to retire to the right."[144]

With smoke obscuring the landscape and tall trees dappling the woods with light and shadows, men on both sides moved in a confused mass of individuals, companies, and regiments.

A witness saw "Sergeant Charles E. Hickman of Company A, 106th Pennsylvania who with his gun in both hands across his body, marching backwards all the way, called upon his men to keep steady, and by his example kept the company closed up, and then in good order retired, firing as they fell back. Here Sergeant Hickman gave his life for his country, being instantly killed."[145]

Morehead was injured when his horse was shot out from under him, and was helped off the field by a sergeant and two corporals. Nearly to safety, he realized his sword, presented to him by the regiment, was missing. Declaring he had vowed to "protect it with my life and never see it dishonored," he turned back to where his horse lay and retrieved it. Yards away, Confederates demanded his surrender. He refused and walked back to his line under fire from his would-be captors.[146]

As parts of the brigade retreated northward, and other small groups headed to the safety of the East Woods, Howard took command of the division after Sedgwick was seriously wounded. Assuming his new duties, Howard delegated the brigade command to Joshua Owen who "speedily as possible … restored the brigade to order."[147]

Amid this confusion of men and commanders, the brigade found ways to rally and resist. Pvt. John Reilly of the 69th Pennsylvania recalled "the confusion for the time being was so that they reformed without regard to formation of regiments or brigade, about a half mile up the Hagerstown Pike." Color Sgts. Benjamin Sloanaker, William

Rose, and James J. Foy planted the 106th's colors along a worm fence running perpendicular to the pike, about 600 yards from their initial position. Detachments from other regiments soon joined them. A small band from the 15th Massachusetts (Gorman's brigade) was led to the line by a captain, "who was almost instantly killed upon reaching there by a round shot." Morehead, back from his sword adventure, and assisted by Lt. Lyndford Tyler, stood with the 106th as it began to pour "volley after volley in quick succession into the advancing enemy, who, thinking they had struck our second line, checked their advance, and finally fell back under cover of the wood."[148]

The stands by these Philadelphia regiments came at a high cost. For the 106th, "one-third of the entire regiment was stricken down, and at the conclusion of the engagement the dead lay in line as they had stood in the fight." The 71st, with "all of its field officers … wounded and left on the ground, were lead off by its sole surviving captain." The 72nd suffered the most: 237 or nearly half became casualties that day.[149]

Years later, Howard wrote: "I came in command of [Sedgwick's] division [at Antietam] and evidently was too new at that command to do the thing that would have been best, namely, move slowly and steadily forward again. Had anybody ordered Sumner's corps straight forward, after their slight discomfiture, the maps would have been different and the results more complete." Probably many in II Corps would have found a better description for their bloody experience than as a "slight discomfiture."[150]

**James M. Buchanan**

## 3rd Brigade: Brigadier General Napoleon J.T. Dana, Colonel Norman Hall

**Units:** 7th Michigan, 42nd New York, 59th New York, 20th Massachusetts, 19th Massachusetts
**Strength:** 1,713[151]
**Losses:** 898 (142k-652w-104m)[152]

The 3rd Brigade consisted of Norman Hall's 7th Michigan, George Bomford's 42nd New York (Tammany Regiment), William Tidball's 59th New York (The Union Guards), Edward Hinck's 19th Massachusetts, and William Lee's 20th Massachusetts (The Harvard Regiment). Dana's brigade was formed from various units who were operating in and around the District of Columbia and guarding the Potomac River crossings to the north during the early months of the Civil War. Four of the five regiments that formed the brigade at Antietam were in place by March, 1862; the 59th New York joined in July, 1862.[153]

Napoleon Jackson Tecumseh Dana (1822-1905) seemed destined from birth for a military life as he came from a military family and was named after three well known warriors of his day. The West Point graduate (Class of 1842) was so severely wounded while storming the entrenchments at Telegraph Hill during the Mexican War that he was left for dead. Following the war, he served for a time at Ft. Snelling, Minnesota before resigning his commission. He then entered banking but remained active in military affairs by leading a state militia outfit. When Willis Gorman left the 1st Minnesota to assume brigade command at the start of the war, Dana took over. He did not stay long, however, and soon moved up to command the 3rd Brigade in Sedgwick's division.[154]

The 1,713 officers and men of Dana's brigade stepped off from the Tennallytown heights in the District of Columbia on September 5. In a series of marches north along Rockville Road, they made Frederick with the rest of the II Corps on the 13th. The next morning they took Shookstown Road across Catoctin Ridge to Middletown and then continued over South Mountain and into Boonsboro. Turning south at Boonsboro, they arrived at the fields just north of farmer Philip Pry's house where they set up camp on the evening of the 16th.[155]

### Antietam

The brigade made its way down the steep bluffs of Antietam Creek west of their encampment at 7:30 a.m. on September 17. After crossing the stream, the brigade halted "for the purpose of giving the men time to shake the water from their shoes and clothing." Next, the brigade closed ranks "to preserve accurately the line of battle before advancing." The brigade assumed the second line of battle, approximately 75 yards behind Gorman's brigade in front of it. Howard's Philadelphia Brigade brought up the division's rear. The regimental order was from right to left, the 19th Massachusetts, 20th Massachusetts, 59th New York, 42nd New York, and the 7th Michigan.[156]

Gradually climbing westward out of the Antietam Valley, the men traversed rolling and open fields to higher ground. They could easily see Confederate batteries to the south playing on Gorman's brigade. Dana soon came under the same fire. Capt. John Adams of the 19th Massachusetts explained, "we advanced in three lines of battle, over walls and fences, through fields, under a terrible fire of artillery" until they reached the safety of the East Woods. The artillery raining down unnerved some of the men and Adams recalled that "[t]he regiment was growing nervous but did not break. Colonel Hincks halted us, put us through the manual of arms, ending with parade rest." This steadied the men as they advanced.[157]

As Dana's command moved at the double quick across the field, they encountered "a line of troops lying on the ground." Dana thought they were from Gorman's brigade and "I accordingly halted and ordered my men to lie down." Sumner looked back from his position riding with Gorman's brigade and, seeing this, ordered Dana in no uncertain terms to get his men up and moving at the double-quick. For Sumner, this kind of confusion in his brigades was just the start of a long day ahead for him.[158]

Nearing Hagerstown Pike, Dana saw the West Woods up ahead, and noted the "outline of the woods was irregular, presenting a salient point where the left of my line first entered." Ahead he could see Gorman's brigade already "hotly engaged." Just as Dana was taking all this in, a "tremendous musketry fire opened on [his] left and front."[159]

The fire came from Mississippi regiments under William Barksdale. Dana had crossed the Pike just as the Mississippians engaged the 125th Pennsylvania. Barksdale realized the danger to his left posed by Dana's brigade, especially the 7th Michigan, so he ordered his left two regiments, the 18th and 13th Mississippi, to turn and meet this new threat. George T. Anderson's Georgia brigade came up on Barksdale's right and together they threw 1,000 muskets into the fight on the Union flank.[160]

The 7th Michigan under Norman Hall pulled up to the left flank of the Pennsylvanians. After facing their line to the south, they delivered an oblique fire to the left. Anderson's and Barksdale's men responded with well aimed volleys that carried away the right flank of the Pennsylvanians and "struck down nearly half of the 7th Michigan.[161]

For Dana, "there was no time to wait for orders; the flanking force whatever it was, was advancing its fire too rapidly on my left." Dana sent his right three regiments (19th, 20th Massachusetts, 59th New York) to move on to support Gorman's brigade, then in a firefight to the west. He stayed with the 42nd New York and 7th Michigan, trying to steady them as they met the "fury on my left flank."[162]

Falling back a few feet, the 7th rallied and got off several return volleys. The right wing of the 72nd Pennsylvania from Howard's brigade came up on the Michigander's left and poured in additional fire

of their own. But the contest was too much for both regiments and both broke; the remnants of the 7th Michigan retreated east across the Pike "leaving one half the regiment dead or wounded in the woods or on the road."[163]

Moving through an open field to the west of the 7th Michigan, Dana ordered the George Bomford's 42nd New York, known as the Tammany Regiment, "to change front to support the Michiganders in resisting the flank attack." But before the regiment could fully align, the full brunt of Barksdale's Mississippians and Kershaw's 3rd South Carolina fell upon them. The first volley took every fifth New Yorker and the second volley further thinned the ranks, causing the line to waver. With the 7th Michigan giving way, the left flank of the New Yorkers was fully exposed. Bomford attempted to rally the depleted ranks but a series of volleys broke them completely. Although wounded, Bomford carried the Tammany's colors to the rear over the Pike, leaving behind 181 officers and men or 52% of the number carried into action just a few minutes earlier.[164]

The Confederate flank attack severely wounded Dana, when a round entered his leg midway between the knee and ankle and lodged in the tibia bone. Riding slowly off the field, Dana told the 7th Michigan commander, Norman Hall, the brigade was now his. Or at least that is what Hall thought he heard. He learned later, however, that the general had said "this *wing* of the brigade" not "the brigade." In any event, receiving "no orders whatever on the field" Hall assigned command of the Michiganders to Capt. Charles Hunt. "One half of [the] regiment lay dead or wounded in the woods or on the road" and Hunt moved the remnants across the Pike and rallied on the colors south of Miller's Cornfield. They were soon joined by members of the brigade's other shattered regiments where they supported Woodruff's artillery until relieved.[165]

Meanwhile, Hall bounded around the field, locating and placing brigade regiments in an attempt to form defensive lines. Along the way, two aides from Dana's staff briefly joined his efforts. Hall soon encountered William Lee of the 20th Massachusetts, and as Lee was his senior, Hall offered him the command but "he positively declined to relieve me." Finally, he found Oliver Howard now commanding the division after Sedgwick's wounding, who told him "to continue in command."[166]

While the 7th Michigan and 42nd New York were fighting for their lives, the 59th New York pulled in behind Gorman's 15th Massachusetts and engaged the two hundred Confederate survivors from Jackson's division under Col. A.J. Grigsby.

Col. William Tidball's 59th New York committed a unit's worst mistake—friendly fire. For some reason, confusion, incompetent officers, or a mix of both, the men of the 59th advanced in such a way that they came up and overlapped the rear of their comrades then engaging Confederates in the farmstead to the west. The 59th's right wing then "began firing through the left wing of the 15th Massachusetts, upon the [Confederates] in front." Despite "the most strenuous exertions" of front line commanders to halt the fire, they fired off seven or eight volleys and nothing seemed to stop "the murderous fire." Only when Sumner saw the disaster unfolding and galloped into the fray to order a cease fire, did the killing stop. The men of the 59th retired from their position in "considerable confusion" as Sumner "cussed them out by the right flank." Years later, a veteran of the 59th told historian Ezra Carman that Tidball "felt much chagrined even to the end about the way he had been treated at Antietam. He being the Senior officer of the Brigade after Dana was disabled, and not given the command."[167]

With the 59th New York ordered off the field, the 20th and 19th Massachusetts were now 200 to 400 yards respectively from the now vacated 59th's position and even further from the brigade's deteriorating left flank formed by the 7th Michigan and 42nd New York.

For the 20th Massachusetts, especially, it was not a good position to be in, as it was jammed up with the 15th Massachusetts in its front and Howard's brigade's 71st and 106th Pennsylvania in its rear. To make things even worse, the 3rd Delaware (William Goodrich's brigade, George Greene's division, XII Corps), pulled in close to the right and rear of the 71st, adding to the claustrophobic formation. One historian described this situation as "telescoping" as the four regiments stacked up on one another, similar to a jam up caused by an unexpected and sudden stop of traffic on a modern highway. Capt. Samuel Sumner, his father's Aide de Camp, offered another perspective: "It was the duty of brigade commanders to preserve proper intervals, but there is always confusion in such movements when under fire, and the natural instinct of the men is to close together."[168]

The 106th Pennsylvania crumbled under the weight of Barksdale's, the 3rd South Carolina, and Early's assaults on their left flank. The 20th Massachusetts, seeing the danger, faced around to direct its fire at the Confederate attackers. One eyewitness recalled, "in less time than it takes to tell it, the ground was strewn with the bodies of the dead and wounded."[169]

At this point, the field had become a mass of confusion suffused with smoke, noise, and men wild in panic and others steady of purpose. The noise of battle was so great that Lt. Henry Patten of the 20th Massachusetts noted the "noise prevented their hearing the order to retire." The swirl of smoke and the mixture of volleys and shouting in the dark woods created so much confusion that Capt. Norwood Hallowell of the 20th Massachusetts recalled after getting "knocked out," he merely walked "to the rear through the Rebs who, in much confusion of formation, were advancing and firing." After ten minutes of "slow walking" he took refuge in the Nicodemus farm house, 600 yards north of their firing line. There he found his friend, Captain Oliver Wendell Holmes, shot through the neck. Holmes, uncertain if he could maintain consciousness, scribbled a note to whoever might find him: "I am Capt. OW Holmes 20th Mass. son of Oliver Wendell Holmes Boston."[170]

Back on the field, the regiment's commander Col. Lee was doing all he could to bring order out of the growing chaos. But the flanking attack was too much and the regiment broke, some going through the 19th Massachusetts directly to their north.[171]

Hinck's 19th Massachusetts formed the right flank of the brigade and was behind Gorman's brigade's 1st Minnesota. It was nearly 400 yards from the 59th New York, which was positioned at the far left end of the brigade line, so the Bay Staters were out of sight of the rest of the brigade. The smoke and noise coming from the woods on its left informed the regimental commanders that a serious fight was afoot but nothing more. The answer soon came as the 1st Minnesota, in its front, abandoned its position and headed north out of the woods.[172]

Hincks immediately ordered the 19th to change front and fall back with Sully's Minnesotans and Hudson's 82nd New York. The three regiments left the woods and entered an open field at the double quick. They formed on their colors on a slight elevation in an open field just north of the wood line and turned and fired two volleys to try and slow down their pursuers from Semmes' brigade. The 53rd Georgia, Semmes' largest regiment did the most damage, slamming into the line's right, and firing well-placed volleys that further decimated Sully's defensive line. To this was added the shower of canister from enemy artillery on their right, and Early's 13th Virginia threatened their rear. "An order was given for the entire line to fall back." At this point, Hincks was severely wounded and the command devolved to Arthur Devereux who reported the situation to Sully, as the most senior officer on the field. A short while later, Devereux was hit and Capt. H.G.O. Weymouth took over.[173]

The final stand of Sully's band was made along the intermittent creek that ran westward across the field from the D.R. Miller farmstead to the Nicodemus property. It was short lived, and the men soon filed off to the protection of the North Woods. A pursuing Confederate battery was silenced by Cooper's battery along the present-day Mondale Road. The battery's infantry supports established a line in some dense woods to their front but were silenced after about 20 minutes by Hoffman's brigade, joined by survivors of Sedgwick's division.[174]

By noon it was all over for the brigade. The 19th Massachusetts, the last of Dana's brigade in action, finally could find some rest. The brigade's shattered regiments slowly regrouped in the open field just east of the Smoketown Road where they faced to the west with Howard's brigade on their right flank.[175]

During the course of a little over two hours, Dana's brigade lost 128 killed, 650 wounded, and 124 missing. Of the three brigades in Sedgwick's division, Dana suffered the highest number of casualties, accounting for 40% of the division's casualties.[176]

Napoleon Dana rode off the field seriously wounded in the left leg. The wound took two months to heal, but Dana was finished with the Army of the Potomac. He died in Portsmouth, New Hampshire on July 15, 1905 and is buried there.[177]

**James M. Buchanan**

* * *

# 3RD DIVISION—

## Brigadier General William French

"Old Blinky" was born in Baltimore, Maryland in 1815 and graduated in the middle of his 1837 West Point class. He was posted in the artillery and saw service in the Florida Seminole Wars and the War with Mexico, earning brevets of captain and major for "gallantry and meritorious conduct." At the outbreak of the Civil War, French took it upon himself to move his troops from Eagle Pass, Texas, to the mouth of the Rio Grande River over 16 days and then put them on ships to Key West, Florida. He was promoted to the rank of brigadier general in September 1861 and given a brigade in the II Corps that fought during the Peninsula Campaign. He performed well during the Battle of Seven Pines (Fair Oaks) where his brigade repelled several determined Confederate attacks. That was essentially the extent of French's Civil War battlefield experience. However, on September 10, McClellan placed him in command of a new cobbled together II Corps division. A historian called French a "choleric-looking old regular with a facial tic . . . Alcohol was a problem for French and in time it would sully his reputation."[178]

French's new division was composed of an odd combination of units. Brig. Gen. Max Weber's brigade had army experience, but it was primarily garrison duty and his men had not fired a gun in battle. Col. Dwight Morris' brigade was totally green, having been recruited only a few weeks before the Maryland Campaign. Only Brig. Gen. Nathan Kimball's brigade was a battle-hardened unit, but its effectiveness was somewhat dissipated by the addition of a new nine-month regiment. What the division lacked in experience, it made up in numbers. At 5,700 men, it was the largest division in the army.[179]

After completing its formation at Clarksburg, Maryland on September 10, the new division marched with the rest of the II Corps to Urbana on September 12 and entered Frederick the following day. The division took the road to Snookstown with the rest of the II Corps, and arrived at the base of South Mountain after dark on September 14, too late to participate in the battle near Bolivar. The division headed for Turner's Gap from Bolivar at 8:45 a.m. on September 15, and halted near Keedysville by 3:00 p.m. that day.

George McClellan carefully arranged his troops on the east side of Antietam Creek on the afternoon of September 16. The II Corps straddled Boonsboro Pike-- French's men occupied the left (south) side of the road. French had his men up and ready to move at daybreak on September 17. He finally received orders from Edwin Sumner, the II Corps commander, at close to 7:30 a.m. to ford Antietam Creek below the Upper Bridge. French's division marched behind John Sedgwick's division, attempting to keep up with its veteran comrades. To expedite the crossing and subsequent march west, French put his division into three columns of brigades. Weber's brigade marched on the left; Kimball's on the right and the inexperienced Morris' in the middle. The division struggled along the mostly uphill route toward the battlefield. French halted his division after it had traveled about a mile from the ford and turned it to the left, putting Weber's brigade on the front line, Morris's in the second and Kimball's in the third. In so doing, French followed influential West Point instructor, Dennis Hart Mahan's doctrine: the reserve "should, in all cases, be composed of the best troops of the army, since upon its efforts depend our own safety and the defeat of the enemy."[180]

French apparently reached the East Woods at about 9:15 a.m. and was moving south about 15 minutes later. Although the division crossed Antietam Creek behind Sedgwick's division, it fell behind and lost sight of it. A variety of reasons have been hypothesized to explain why French did not follow Sedgwick to the West Woods, instead turning south and heading toward the Sunken Road. These explanations, however, are beyond the scope of this work. Enemy artillery opened fire on the division as it marched south. French guided the men slightly southeast to skirt the burning Mumma farm buildings and then turned them south again, as the William Roulette farm loomed ahead. Enemy skirmishers opened fire around the farm and French's men pushed them away. The orientation of the division caused most of the regiments to march on the west side of Roulette's farm lane, but four of the division's 10 regiments advanced on the opposite side. Maj. Gen. D.H. Hill, whose Confederate division protected this sector, watched French's advance and recalled it "advanced in three parallel lines, with all the precision of a parade day."[181]

Weber's three regiments continued their advance to the top of the hill overlooking the Sunken Road as Confederate Robert Rodes' and George B. Anderson's men rose up and fired a devastating volley into them.

The historian of the 1st Delaware explained the volleys were "so destructive that even veteran troops would have been repulsed." The brigade shrunk back to the opposite side of the hill where the officers attempted to reform the shattered ranks and then brought the men forward again. The Confederates counterattacked, and Weber's men helped beat back these scattered and uncoordinated drives. Weber's officers ordered the men to the ground where they attempted to maintain a constant fire against the Alabamians and North Carolinians.

Morris' brigade, following at a distance of about 200 yards, now approached the firing line. Several men were hit by Confederate overshots before they reached their positions. The sudden fire unsettled the rookies, some of whom were carried away by a number of Weber's men stampeding for the rear. The 14th Connecticut, on the right of Morris' line, opened fire and most of the shots plowed into the backs of men in Weber's 1st Delaware, causing them to fall back through the new arrivals' line. All was chaos by this time and it is unclear what French was doing, other than ordering the two brigades forward.[182]

A historian described the confusion as the "fight for the sunken road now became a contest of firepower, with the force on the Federal side a confusing, swirling combination of what little remained of Weber's regiments and the newly arrived line of Morris' brigade, both intermingled on the crest of the ridge overlooking the enemy . . ." Another noted, the two brigades had "lost heavily and, being new troops, had become confused and much broken; many of the men had gone to the rear, but enough of them remained on the firing line to resist the enemy, though without sufficient aggressive force." Sumner's son, Samuel, pounded up to French with orders. According to French's report, Capt. Sumner "communicated to me, from the general commanding the corps, that his right divisions [Sedgwick's] were being severely handled, and directed me to press the enemy with all my force." French now brought up Kimball's veteran brigade and sent it forward. The men and their officers realized to stand atop the hill and exchange volleys was folly, so in the words of a Pennsylvanian, they decided to "lie down just under the top of the hill and crawl forward and fire over, each man crawling back, reloading his piece in this prone position and again crawling forward and firing." This maneuver took its toll on the Sunken Road's defenders, but it became a stalemate, as neither side was able to drive the other from their positions.[183]

The stalemate was finally broken when Israel Richardson's division arrived on French's left and eventually drove the enemy from the road. This was not the end of French's fight, for during the early afternoon, several regiments of Van Manning's brigade (John Walker's division) charged out of the West Woods toward French's right flank. John Caldwell's brigade, William Irwin's brigade from the newly arrived VI Corps, and several of French's regiments, turned and sent the attackers back the way they came. French reformed his shattered division near the Roulette farm.[184]

The division lost 1,750 men in its first battle. French threw his three brigades against a strong defensive position but had little to show for the losses, as each attempt to take the Sunken Road was repulsed.[185]

**Bradley M. Gottfried**

* * *

# 1st Brigade: Brigadier General Nathan Kimball

**Units:** 14th Indiana, 8th Ohio, 7th (West) Virginia, 132nd Pennsylvania,
**Strength:** 1,751[186]
**Losses:** 639 (121k- 510w- 8m)[187]

The 8th Ohio, 14th Indiana, and 7th West Virginia Volunteer Infantry were organized and mustered into service during the summer and late fall of 1861. They hailed from the southern parts of Ohio, Indiana and from the western portions of Virginia. The 4th Ohio had been part of the brigade, but an inordinate amount of sickness forced it to return to Washington. It was replaced by the 132nd Pennsylvania, a brand new regiment that entered the service in August of 1862.[188]

Brig. Gen. Nathan Kimball commanded this multi-state brigade. An 1841 graduate of Indiana Asbury College (now DePauw University), Kimball went on to study medicine and established a successful medical practice near his hometown of Fredericksburg, Indiana. Kimball served honorably as a company commander during the Mexican War and then returned to civilian life shortly after its conclusion. At the outbreak of the Civil War, Kimball again answered the call of duty and raised a company of soldiers near his hometown. He was named colonel of the 14th Indiana on June 7, 1861.[189]

After handing Thomas "Stonewall" Jackson a rare defeat at the Battle of Kernstown (Virginia) in the spring of 1862, Kimball was promoted to brigadier general and given a brigade. That June, Kimball's brigade was transferred from the Shenandoah Valley to the Army of the Potomac. Arriving late in the Peninsula Campaign, the brigade saw little action. It was recalled to Washington at the end of August and became the first brigade of William French's 3rd Division of the Army of the Potomac's II Corps. The 132nd Pennsylvania joined the brigade on September 7 in Rockville, Maryland, nearly doubling the brigade's numbers.[190]

"The men arrived at Rockville apprehensive but not fully aware of Lee's serious threat to the North. The rebels were at Frederick City with a reported 100,000 men. Lee had to be stopped at once," explained the historian of the 14th Indiana. By September 10, most of the Army of the Potomac was in Maryland and on its way to Frederick to confront the invading Confederates.[191]

The II Corps reached the outskirts of Frederick by September 12. According to Col. Franklin Sawyer, commander of the 8th Ohio, "Our brigade soon advanced, keeping up a good battle front, and felt its way along the Monocacy [River]."[192]

## South Mountain

The entire II Corps marched through Frederick on September 14, then toward Hagerstown along the National Road and the fields on either side of it. The men then struggled up and over Catoctin Mountain and into the Middletown Valley. According to Frederick Hitchcock, Adjutant of the 132nd Pennsylvania, "We heard heavy cannonading all day, and part of the time could see our batteries, toward which we were marching." The men did not know it, but they were seeing and hearing portions of the Battle of South Mountain.[193]

The II Corps was ordered to support Joseph Hooker's I Corps at Turner's Gap, but it arrived too late in the day to do so. In uniform less than a month, Hitchcock would later write, "Here I saw the first dead soldier. Two of our artillery men had been killed while serving their gun. Both were terribly mangled ... this first vision of the awful work of war stills remains."[194]

That night, Kimball's men lay on their arms near Bolivar, a few miles east of Turner's Gap along the National Road, but few would find restful sleep. The sunrise on September 15 revealed the Confederates had retreated west off the mountain. Edwin Sumner's II Corps now led the pursuit through Turner's Gap and on towards Boonsboro, with Israel Richardson's division out in front. Sedgwick's and French's divisions followed a distance behind. Together with some cavalry, Richardson's division pushed the Confederate rearguard toward Boonsboro, and some skirmishes occurred when the vanguard came too close. Leaving Boonsboro, Kimball's brigade marched west on Boonsboro Pike, passing Keedysville and arriving near the banks of Antietam Creek around 3:00 p.m.[195]

## Antietam

In the early morning hours of September 16, McClellan wired General-in-Chief Halleck: "This morning a heavy fog has thus far prevented us doing more than to ascertain that the enemy are still there." As the fog lifted, Confederate troops across Antietam Creek could be seen maneuvering. An artillery exchange occurred during the afternoon. Col. Sawyer of the 8th Ohio wrote, "The men were kept down out of sight, the artillery directing their fire mainly at each other."[196]

The men of Kimball's brigade spent another night along Boonsboro Pike, about a half mile east of Antietam Creek. The night of September 16-17 was a somber, reflective time for the soldiers. Hitchcock recalled, "Letters were written home, many of them 'last words' and quiet talks were had, and promises made between comrades." Thomas Galwey of the 8th Ohio recorded in his diary how quiet the men were. "Everybody knows that there must be fought a bloody battle tomorrow and all are therefore anxious to save their strength for the contest."[197]

Exploding shells and musket fire greeted the sunrise of September 17, but the men of Kimball's brigade had been awake for several hours. McClellan had given Sumner orders to be ready to move his II Corps at dawn to the right in support of the I and XII Corps, and possibly join them in driving the enemy south toward the town of Sharpsburg. As the fighting intensified in the open fields to the north, Sumner's men stood idle. Finally, at 7:20 a.m., orders arrived and the impatient Sumner wasted no time in leading two of his three divisions west across the creek. Sedgwick's division crossed first, followed by French. Richardson was held back about an hour until Morell's division (V Corps) arrived to take the division's place in support of the Union center.[198]

French's men followed Sedgwick's division west, up the slopes from Antietam Creek, and arrived at the East Woods at about 9:15 a.m. French organized his brigades into line of battle, sending Max Weber's three untested regiments into the first line, Dwight Morris' three newly mustered in nine-month regiments, in the second, and Kimball's more seasoned regiments remained in reserve. Placing new troops in front of seasoned comrades was in accordance with established military doctrine.[199]

French's three brigades marched south from the East Woods, past the burning Mumma farm buildings, and then the Roulette farm, where they encountered Confederate skirmishers, pushing them back. Ahead of them in the distance was the Piper farm. They could also not see a dip in the terrain in front of them.[200]

Weber's regiments in the first line marched through a cornfield on the right, and an open field on the left, reaching the crest of a hill with their bayonets fixed. Suddenly, a long line of Confederates in a sunken road rose and delivered a murderous fire into the startled Union troops. These were two brigades from D.H. Hill's division. Robert Rodes' Alabamians occupied the left (west) in the Sunken Road and G.B. Anderson's men were to their right (east). Weber's men took heavy losses and were stopped cold in their tracks, forcing the entire brigade to seek shelter behind a ridge line 50 to 80 yards from the Confederates. Despite this initial set-back, French's division outnumbered the Confederate defenders by nearly two to one.[201]

French now ordered Morris' brigade forward, following Weber's brigade's path toward the Sunken Road, but it fared no better. Historian Marion Armstrong wrote, "The two brigades of Weber and Morris had made spirited efforts to drive the enemy but were brought to a stand, had lost heavily and, being new troops, had become confused and much broken; many of the men had gone to the rear, but enough of them remained on the firing line to resist the enemy, though without sufficient aggressive force to advance."[202]

Sumner recognized Sedgwick's division needed help in the West Woods, so he ordered French to step up his attacks on the Sunken Road. French complied by sending in his veterans. The Roulette farm lane split the brigade in two, with the 8th Ohio and 14th Indiana on the right (west) of the lane and the 132nd Pennsylvania and the 7th West Virginia on the left (east) of it. The brigade numbered nearly 1,800 men strong. Kimball rode out in front of his brigade, exhorting his men, "Now boys, we are going in now, and we'll stay with them all day if they want us to!" Bayonets were fixed and a determined advance was ordered.[203]

The commander of the 132nd Pennsylvania, Col. Richard Oakford, was almost immediately mortally wounded, yet his rookies continued their advance in line with the veteran regiments of the brigade through "grape and canister, shot and shell, screaming and whistling and turning the air dark." Cresting the final knoll, the units were met by a devastating volley of muskets from Confederates in the Sunken Road and from reinforcements in the cornfield beyond. In writing his mother, Sgt. William Houghton, 14th Indiana recalled, "I saw my brave boys fall like sheep led to the slaughter." Forced backward, "we were ordered to lie down just under the top of the hill and crawl forward and fire over, each man crawling back, reloading his piece in the prone position and again crawling forward and firing," remembered Frederick Hitchcock of the 132nd Pennsylvania.[204]

Kimball's entire brigade extended nearly 300 yards across the ridgeline fronting and nearly parallel to the Sunken Road. Kimball's men had taken heavy losses but from this elevated and relatively protected position they were able to fire down into the Confederate defenders in front of them and enfilade others on either end of the road. Richard Anderson's Confederate division crossed the cornfield south of the Sunken Road to give succor to the two brigades ensconced there. Kimball noted in his official report, "The enemy, having been reinforced, made an attempt to turn my left flank … which I met and repulsed." Kimball was referring to a desperate charge made by a portion of Ambrose Wright's brigade (Anderson's division), which had taken up a position on the right (east) side of the Sunken Road. The veteran 7th (West) Virginia saw Wright's men approaching their vulnerable left flank, pivoted, and threw several destructive volleys into the Georgians, halting the attack in its tracks. Hitchcock of the 132nd Pennsylvania recalled, "Soon our men began to call for more ammunition, and we officers were kept busy taking from the dead and wounded and distributing to the living."[205]

Reinforcements finally arrived after French's division had confronted the Rebels in the Sunken Road, alone for more than an hour. Richardson's division was finally permitted to cross Antietam Creek and was now moving forward in line of battle on the left side of the Roulette farm lane. Thomas Meagher's Irish Brigade (Richardson's division) raced ahead and relieved the 132nd Pennsylvania and 7th West Virginia, but took heavy casualties and could not drive the enemy from the Sunken Road. The 8th Ohio and 14th Indiana on the opposite side of the Roulette lane held their positions and continued exchanging volleys with the enemy. Richardson now brought up John Caldwell's brigade and attacked the center and flank of the Confederates in the Sunken Road. A number of Kimball's men were swept up in the ensuing charge that finally dislodged the Confederate forces in the Sunken Road. Houghton of the 14th Indiana recalled the "men yelled like demons and fought like infuriated mad men, the Rebels at last broke and ran like sheep from the squad that was left of our brigade."[206]

As men pursued the enemy retreating south toward the Piper farm, Kimball went about reorganizing and resupplying his tired brigade near the Sunken Road. At about noon, while moving his brigade back toward the Roulette farm, a contingent of Confederate infantry charged from the high ground to the north. Joined by several regiments from different brigades, Kimball quickly ordered the 8th Ohio and the 14th Indiana to change front and face the oncoming charge. Together with support from newly arriving artillery and the first units of the VI Corps, this minor flare-up was quickly doused.[207]

Hitchcock of the 132nd Pennsylvania later recorded, "Our work, so far as this battle was concerned, was done." Kimball gathered his brigade near the Roulette farm and told his men how proud he was of their actions. Sumner complimented the brigade by bestowing on it the moniker of the "Gibraltar Brigade" in recognition of their steadfast and determined performance on the field at "Bloody Lane."[208]

The survivors rested that night and prepared for continued bloodshed the following day. September 18 was quiet and the men learned on the morning of September 19 that Lee had taken his army back to Virginia. The brigade lost the most men in French's division--- 639.

The historian of the 14th Indiana penned the following solemn description that could have applied to all of Kimball's regiments: "Antietam profoundly affected the regimental spirit [by] instilling in the men a deep new sense of comradeship. In a few minutes scores of regimental or lifetime friends were gone – shot to pieces or left to die untended on the darkened field. The sense of anguish and helplessness on the part of their comrades was great. But for the living comrades a new feeling was born, a sense of debt and respect. These men from southern Indiana had held the line for the Union and for each other on the greatest day of slaughter in the Civil War."[209]

**Mac Bryan**

*** *** ***

## 2nd Brigade: Colonel Dwight Morris

**Units**: 14th Connecticut, 108th New York, 130th Pennsylvania
**Strength**: 2,765[210]
**Losses**: 531 (80k-356w-95m)[211]

The 2nd brigade consisted of three regiments composed of new recruits. The 14th Connecticut mustered into service on August 23, the 108th New York on August 16 to 18, and the 130th Pennsylvania on August 15, 1862. The men of the first two regiments enlisted for three-year terms; the Pennsylvania unit would serve only nine months. Of the nine field officers, only four had previous military service in other units. Col. Dwight Morris was made brigade commander on September 7, 1862 when the brigade was formed in Rockville, Maryland.[212]

Dwight Morris was born in Connecticut on November 22, 1817 and graduated from Union College in 1838 at the age of 21. He was a lawyer when the war broke out and was appointed colonel of the 14th Connecticut Infantry on May 23, 1862.[213]

After its formation, the brigade marched with the Army of the Potomac north to meet the Confederate army. Several days of marching brought the brigade to Frederick on September 13, where they were welcomed with open arms by the residents: "Miniature stars and stripes flags fluttered as plentifully from buildings as leaves on trees, and 'May God bless you,' welled up on all sides," recalled the 108th New York's historian. The brigade, with the rest of the division, left Frederick on September 13. Climbing South Mountain on September 15, the rookies saw dead soldiers at Turner's Gap where fighting occurred the day before. Sgt. Benjamin Hirst of the 14th Connecticut explained, "I cannot describe my feelings, but I hope to God never to see the like again." He would not get his wish. The men's interactions with their own comrades were not always positive on the march. For example, men of the Irish Brigade (Richardson's division) taunted them with the name "blue-legged devils" and claimed they would not stand long once they encountered "Bobbie Lee." McClellan issued orders about respecting the civilians' property, but Col. Oliver Palmer could not allow his men of the 108th New York to bivouac in a muddy field, so he allowed them to collect straw from a stack in the same field. He was later arrested for this transgression but he good-naturedly remarked, "I did not think there was any harm for the boys to get a little straw to lay upon, instead of in the mud." [214]

### Antietam

The brigade proceeded about a mile beyond Keedysville on September 15, where it halted in a field on the right of Boonsboro Pike, not far from McClellan's headquarters. The brigade remained there until the early morning of the battle. It was there that the brigade first came under enemy artillery fire: "treatment very unwelcome" recalled one of the veterans after the war.

The men were awake at 2:00 a.m. on the morning of the battle; each received 96 rounds of cartridges and 45 caps. They were also provided with additional rations-- "enough in weight to double a man up," recalled a veteran. The regiment forded Antietam Creek at about 8:00 a.m. The water was deep and the banks steep and slippery. Some men filled their canteens. A two-mile march brought the men to the East Woods. Along the way, they were halted and ordered to "unsling knapsacks" into a pile. Not to worry, they were told, as they would return to retrieve them, which did not happen. The brigade formed into line of battle with the 108th New York on the left, the 14th Connecticut on the right and the 130th Pennsylvania in the middle. The line scrambled over a series of post and rail fences and passed down a small hill that brought the men to low marshy ground between the Mumma and Roulette houses. Some of the men passing through Mr. Mumma's orchard grabbed an apple or two and quickly munched on them as they march onward.[215]

Private John Hemmingen of the 130th Pennsylvania wrote in his diary that they "laid hold of the fence and with a mighty pull the entire fence came down and fell on Thomas Boyles." Later in the entry for September 17, he wrote: "In the line of advance a number of beehives were over turned, and the little fellows resented the intrusion, and did most unceremoniously charge upon us, accelerating our speed through the orchard toward the entrenched position of the enemy."[216]

The brigade passed the Roulette house and guided along its farm lane with the 14th Connecticut and 130th Pennsylvania on the right of the house and the 108th New York on the left. The Nutmeggers passed through a cornfield that limited their sight lines. As the division deployed with Weber's brigade in front, then Morris's and Kimball's, they were not able to see the Confederates of Rodes' Alabama brigade and Anderson's North Carolina brigade crouching in what is now known as the "bloody lane." In front of Morris' men, Max Weber's brigade came to the top of a hill, where the men stumbled upon the Sunken Road and were immediately hit by devastating volleys from the Confederates stationed there. The historian of the 14th Connecticut recalled, the "line of troops in front had passed well into the open field. It seemed to melt under the enemy's fire and breaking many of the men ran through the ranks of the Fourteenth toward the rear." This must have been a difficult time for the rookie Nutmeggers, as they could have broken and bolted to the rear with Weber's fleeing men. The fleeing 5th Maryland was especially troublesome, as it carried three companies on the right of the 14th Connecticut to the rear, where they were rallied and returned to the line.[217]

Most of the rookies did not flee and instead moved forward. "No enemy could be seen," wrote the 14th Connecticut's historian, "only a thin cloud of smoke rose from what was afterwards found to be their rifle-pits." A veteran recalled, when "the Fourteenth reached the fence it received a smashing fire full in the face." The line halted in the open field beyond the cornfield and opened fire, which probably had little impact as the enemy troops were fairly protected by the Sunken Road. Bullets continued to whistle by and into the line, creating casualties that mounted by the minute because the "withering storm of bullets was smiting them." Realizing the futility of remaining out in the open, the officers ordered the men back to the fence lining the cornfield and ordered them to "load and fire at will."[218]

Historian Ezra Carman summed up Morris' (and Weber's) efforts at the Battle of Antietam when he wrote they "made spirited efforts to drive the enemy but were brought to a stand; had lost heavily and, being new troops, had become confused and much broken; many of the men had gone to the rear, but enough of them remained on the firing line to resist the enemy, though without sufficient aggressive force to advance."[219]

The brigade ceased to operate as a unit from this point to the end of the battle. Nathan Kimball's brigade, French's last brigade, now moved forward to take on the enemy in the Sunken Road. As that brigade began running out of ammunition, Morris ordered the 14th Connecticut to advance to a stone wall "and hold it." Richardson's division arrived on the left of Roulette's farm lane and relieved the 108th New York, which fell back about 550 yards to rest, but was soon ordered to march to the front and fill a gap that appeared on the left of Richardson's line. The regiment remained there until dark, under a severe shelling. It was then thrown out on the skirmish line until 9:00 a.m. on September 18. The 130th Pennsylvania became separated from the rest of the brigade when it fell back to the Roulette house. Kimball saw the large Pennsylvania unit idling around the house, so he ordered it to fall in with the rest of his brigade, where it remained until the following morning when Morris' brigade was reconstituted.[220]

The brigade lost 529 men at the Battle of Antietam. One of the wounded was 2nd Lt. Samuel Porter of Company F of the 108th. In a letter he wrote on September 20 he described his wound this way: "My own feelings were so complex that it would be impossible to describe them but the thought of fear never entered my head. I had several two or three, pretty close calls but with the exception of a bullet hole through the fleshy part of my foot, received no particular damage. I was struck by a spent ball that hurt a good deal at the time but only just drew blood. Since the fight I have had a pretty dull time and expect that it will be so for some time to come."[221]

After the battle, the brigade remained in the area for several days and then began the movement back to Virginia. But these men were now veterans! They had seen the elephant and done it within about a month of entering the service of their country. Experience came hard and fast to these men. Morris would not remain with his brigade after the battle, as he is not listed as being in command at Fredericksburg. He commanded the brigade again on January 31, 1863 but was not at Gettysburg. Morris was discharged as disabled on August 14, 1863. One source describes him as suffering from chronic diarrhea.[222]

**Joseph Stahl**

* * *

### 3rd Brigade: Brigadier General Max Weber, Colonel John Andrews

**Units:** 1st Delaware, 4th New York, 5th Maryland
**Strength:** 1,800[223]
**Losses:** 582 (100k-449w-33m)[224]

Max Weber was born in 1824 in the village of Achern in what is now southern Germany. Educated at a military school, he joined the revolutionaries of 1848 and fled to New York after the Prussian army put down the revolt. Weber organized the 20th New York in May 1861 and led the regiment to Fort Monroe as part of the Department of Virginia. He was promoted to the rank of brigadier general of volunteers in April 1862, and became commandant of Fort Monroe. He later assumed command of a brigade that included the 1st Delaware and the 4th New York. On September 7, General-in-Chief Halleck ordered Maj. Gen. John Dix, commander of the Department of Virginia, to send the 1st Delaware, 3rd New York and 4th New York to Washington. Dix protested that these regiments were the "flower of command" and his "main reliance if Suffolk is to be defended." He proposed sending the 5th Maryland in place of the 3rd New York, to which Halleck assented. On September 9, Weber and the three regiments that would comprise his brigade at Antietam traveled by transport to Washington.[225]

The 1st Delaware organized in spring 1861, its initial term of service expiring after three months. In August 1861, the regiment reorganized for a three-year term under the command of Lt. Col. John Andrews. The regiment arrived at Fort Monroe in October and later witnessed the naval clash between the *Virginia* and several U.S. Navy warships, capped off by its fight with the ironclad *Monitor* at Hampton Roads. During the 1st Delaware's summer 1862 occupation of Suffolk, situated on the edge of the Great Dismal Swamp, "fully three-fourths of the regiment suffered with fevers in some form or another." The regimental historian noted that when ordered northward to Washington, "never did soldiers pack their knapsacks for a march to meet the enemy with lighter hearts or more genuine enthusiasm than did the First Delaware on this occasion."[226]

The 4th New York was mustered into service in May 1861 for a two-year term, its men recruited mostly from New York City. Embarking first for Newport News, Virginia, the regiment also spent parts of 1861 in Havre de Grace and Baltimore, Maryland. The regiment served at Fort McHenry in Baltimore during the spring of 1862 and later moved to Suffolk. The 5th Maryland was organized in Baltimore in September 1861 for three years' service and remained there until March 1862, when it moved to Fort Monroe. Weber's brigade thus consisted of mostly veteran troops by the time of the Maryland Campaign but, like four of the other regiments in French's division, had yet to see combat.[227]

## Antietam

From Washington, Weber's regiments "took up the line of march in the wake of the Army of the Potomac" and caught up with the army as the Battle of South Mountain raged on September 14. The brigade bivouacked near Middletown for two days before crossing South Mountain and reaching Keedysville around mid-day on September 16, where it was assigned to French's division. While near Boonsboro Pike, the brigade was "subjected to a severe artillery fire from over the hills in the direction of Sharpsburg." The eagerness to taste combat cost Lt. James Lewis of the 1st Delaware, who went "to the brow of a hill to witness the firing, [and] was struck by a cannon ball which tore away part of his foot." To his great regret, for "there was not an officer in the Regiment more anxious to meet the foe than he," Lewis would miss the impending battle.[228]

II Corps commander Edwin Sumner put Weber's brigade, along with the rest of French's division, "in motion by orders" at about 7:30 a.m. on September 17. As Company I of the 5th Maryland was forming, Sgt. William Purnell told his men, "Steady now boys, we will soon see what you are made of." After fording waist-deep Antietam Creek, the brigade, on the left of the division, advanced approximately a mile to the area of the East Woods. French's division formed "left in front" in "three lines of battle." This maneuver put Weber's brigade "in the advance line," so it would be the first to confront any Confederates ahead. Fifth Maryland veteran George Graham remembered a delay resulting from the need to bring up ammunition for his regiment, which was armed with Austrian .54 caliber rifles and thus could not be supplied from the normal stores of corps ordnance. Though for a time it appeared the regiment might have to drop out of line, a courier arrived with the needed cartridges "slung across his horse's back" and each man received 80 rounds.[229]

The brigade cleared the East Woods sometime after 9:00 a.m. and advanced southward under artillery fire from Confederate batteries south of the

Piper farm and west of Hagerstown Pike. A captain in the 1st Delaware wrote that when they were ordered to fix bayonets, "We began to think something was to do." The 1st Delaware was on the right, the 5th Maryland in the center, and the 4th New York on the left. Weber ordered the 5th Maryland's color bearer, "a heavy built [G]erman man of over six feet and weighing nearly 300 pounds," to use "the [William] Roulette dwelling house as his point of direction." As the color bearer "was very deliberate in his movements," the brigade bowed outward to the left and right, a shape that would conform to the Confederate line ahead. Driving Confederate skirmishers from around the Roulette buildings, Weber's three regiments paused to fix bayonets, then "charged double quick." The 1st Delaware, taking fire from their right as they went forward, moved through a cornfield before scaling a fence "on the edge of the field." The 5th Maryland had to clear the Roulette orchard before advancing across a plowed field and then "rushed with a yell up the hill" to their front. The 4th New York on the left moved across an open field, separated from the rest of the brigade by the Roulette farm lane, and "with a cheer and a rush … reached the brow of the hill destined to be [their] position that day."[230]

When the brigade reached the crest, Graham remembered they were "met by a murderous fire, which made the bravest shrink for a moment." Weber's men had stumbled upon two Confederate brigades: Robert Rodes' Alabamians and George B. Anderson's North Carolinians occupying a sunken portion of a farm lane that connected Boonsboro Pike and Hagerstown Pike. Col. Andrews of the 1st Delaware described the Confederates as "posted in a road or ravine four feet below the surface of the adjoining field, with a third line in a cornfield in the rear, the ground gradually rising, so that they were able to fire over the heads of those in the ravine." To Rodes' left, retreating survivors of the morning's melee in the Cornfield from Col. Alfred Colquitt's and Col. Duncan McRae's (Garland's) brigades, as well as the arriving but depleted brigade of Brig. Gen. Howell Cobb, occupied the lane in the

direction of Hagerstown Pike. Rodes' and Anderson's troops had improved their position in what was afterward known as the "Bloody Lane" by piling fence rails in their front.[231]

The 1st Delaware faced the right and center of Rodes' men, the 5th Maryland was up against the right of Rodes' brigade and left of Anderson's and the 4th New York took fire from the center and right of Anderson's line. Edwin Osborne of the 14th North Carolina recalled that when Weber's men appeared "within good musket shot," he and his comrades "rose and delivered our fire with terrible effect." Col. John Gordon of the 6th Alabama wrote how his men's "rifles flamed and roared in the Federals' faces like a blinding blaze of lightning accompanied by the quick and deadly thunderbolt. The effect was appalling." Weber's men went no further. The ridgeline they had just crested provided cover to the 4th New York and 5th Maryland. The 1st Delaware had less cover to their front and withdrew further back to the edge of the Mumma cornfield. Those of Weber's men who could use the slope to protect themselves against the "heavy shower of bullets" lay down to open fire from their position overlooking the lane, a range of 50 to 80 yards.[232]

The opposing lines of infantry tore into each other, neither side able to drive their counterpart from the field. Their regimental flags "about 30 feet to the front," the men of the 5th Maryland "crawled forward and dressed on the colors." At one point, Rodes' Alabamians charged out of the sunken lane to seize the prize, but the color bearer pulled out of harm's way "while the boys in line met the venturesome rebels and sent them back quicker than they came." Some of Anderson's North Carolinians also rushed forward out of the lane against the 4th New York but fell back like the Alabamians to their left. All of the 1st Delaware color bearers were dead or wounded, the colors lying within "yards of the frowning lines of muskets, surrounded by the lifeless bodies of nine heroes, who died while trying to plant them in that road of death." The Confederates made several attempts to seize the 1st Delaware's colors from in front of their line, each time repulsed by fire from the 1st Delaware and the 5th Maryland. Under the covering fire of twenty or so comrades, the 1st Delaware's Lt. Charles Tanner ran forward to rescue the colors, and later recalled making "the best eighty-yard time on record," receiving three wounds in the process. Lt. Tanner received the Medal of Honor for his actions. As the 1st Delaware hammered away at the Confederates in the lane, Capt. James Rickards took pity on a seemingly wounded Confederate limping toward Weber's line, striking the weapon of a sergeant before he could "drop that fellow." As the captain did so, the Confederate "leveled his gun and shot Captain Rickards, who died a few minutes afterwards. The dastard rebel fell in his tracks, riddled with bullets."[233]

Weber's troops were the first Federal wave to break upon the Confederate line in the lane. French had two more brigades to send forward, the next under Dwight Morris. Instead of reinforcement, however, Morris' brigade added to the confusing maelstrom, at least initially. The commander of the 1st Delaware reported the "new levies" coming up behind his men, and "instead of supporting our advance, fired into our rear." The swirling firefight and undulating terrain undoubtedly confused the advancing green troops. Ahead were the dead and wounded of Weber's brigade along with the brigade's survivors, some of whom were struggling to establish a firing line from the crest while others were withdrawing. Morris reported the 5th Maryland "fell back early in the action, passing through the right wing of the Fourteenth Connecticut." A contemporary newspaper account reported the 5th Maryland, with the exception of two companies, "took a panic and ran at the first fire." In his account, George Graham denied this claim, stating the 5th Maryland "remained in action under its company officers." Another 5th Maryland veteran, J.K. Polk Racine, remembered the "green troops" coming up behind Weber "began firing while we were still between, and there was great danger of us being massacred by our own men." Racine admitted that, "in our haste to get from between we dodged through [Morris's brigade] just

wherever we could and passed off of the bloody field in a go-as-you-please style."

Regardless of the claims of friendly fire and wavering soldiers, Weber and other officers were able to rally enough men to hold their position on the crest overlooking the sunken lane as successive waves of French's men, who told them to "get to the rear you fellows," arrived to assault the Confederate line. Weber's men who stayed, eventually became part of a firing line formed by troops from French's entire division. By the time the brigades of Richardson's division assaulted the lane around 10:30 a.m., the 5th Maryland and 4th New York were withdrawing from the crest and re-forming near the Roulette buildings. The 1st Delaware fell back to the Mumma cornfield through which it had passed during its advance.[234]

The brigade command structure suffered along with the enlisted men. A bullet shattered the right arm of Weber, who was carried from the field. Weber later served in limited capacity in Washington and took command of Harpers Ferry in April 1864, but had to take leave because of complications from his wound. He left the army in May 1865 and never regained full use of his right arm. The commander of the 5th Maryland, Maj. Leopold Blumenberg, suffered a leg wound that fractured his thigh. After some convincing, Blumenberg persuaded the surgeon not to amputate, though he would be crippled for life. The senior captain of the 5th Maryland, William Bamberger, was also wounded. In the 1st Delaware, Lt. Col. Oliver Hopkinson was wounded, three captains were killed and four wounded, and four lieutenants were wounded. The 4th New York lost a captain and lieutenant killed and six other officers wounded. At the cost of approximately 600 casualties, Weber's brigade had battered the Confederates in the sunken lane, but the glory of breaking that line went to other II Corps troops following in their wake.[235]

Weber's regiments spent the night of September 17 not far from where they had fought, still on the west side of Antietam Creek. A soldier of the 5th Maryland wrote home that, "we slept last night amidst hundreds of dead rebels, who are partially decomposed and cause an awful stench." The 1st Delaware marched to Harpers Ferry on September 19. The 4th New York and 5th Maryland did the same on September 22, crossing the Potomac River opposite the village and encamping on Bolivar Heights. For the rest of September and much of October, the brigade recovered from the battle, "replenishing stores, recruiting for the army, and improving its efficiency." During that period of rest and refitting, President Lincoln visited the troops and a 4th New York soldier observed that the "many riddled and torn colors of the various regiments must have given Mr. Lincoln a pretty good idea of the way the bullets flew at Antietam."[236]

**J.O. Smith**

\*\*\*

# V Corps—

## Major General Fitz John Porter

George McClellan called Maj. Gen. Fitz John Porter, "probably the best general officer I had under me." Despite this strong support, Porter was under a cloud as the Maryland Campaign began. Charges were brought against him by John Pope, the commander of the now defunct Army of Virginia, and he was relieved of command of the V Corps on September 5, 1862, pending a hearing. McClellan had to act quickly when he integrated the two armies as the Confederate army headed deeper into Maryland, so he restored Porter to command. The charges would stand, but Porter would at least be able to command his corps during this all-important campaign.[1]

Porter was born on June 13, 1822 in New Hampshire, the son of a naval captain. He graduated from West Point in 1845 and saw extensive service in the artillery during the Mexican War and was brevetted twice for gallantry. He spent considerable time at West Point after the war as an instructor and then served in Kansas and Utah. During his inspection of the defenses of Charleston, South Carolina in November 1860, he recommended against occupying Fort Sumter and Castle Pinckney. At the outbreak of the war, he served as chief of staff for Gen. Robert Patterson and then was appointed colonel of the 15th U. S. Infantry on May 14, 1861. Three days later, Porter was appointed brigadier general and assigned to duty in Washington. He assumed command of a III Corps division in the Spring of 1862 and accompanied it to the Virginia Peninsula, where on May 18, Porter was placed in charge of the newly constituted V Corps. Porter effectively led his corps during the Seven Days Battles and won his second star on June 27. Historian Ezra Carman noted, "he displayed a rare ability and unflinching courage." A favorite of McClellan, Porter became a convenient scapegoat for John Pope's defeat at Second Bull Run.[2]

The V Corps' divisions were split up and operated independently during the Maryland Campaign. While Porter and most of his V Corps remained near Washington, Brig. Gen. George Sykes' division headed north with the army on September 11. The Reserve Artillery was attached to it during the journey. Later that day, in response to McClellan's request for additional troops, Maj. Gen. Henry Halleck promised to send the rest of the V Corps. Only Brig. Gen. George Morell's division was ready to march, so Porter accompanied it north at 6:00 a.m. on September 12. As Porter and Morell's division headed north, Sykes' division reached Frederick on September 13, and followed the IX Corps to Fox's Gap the following day, halting at Middletown. Porter and Morell reached Frederick on September 14, and while the men rested, Porter continued on to reach Sykes' men.[3]

Sykes' division was not engaged at the battle for Fox's Gap, but was ordered to follow the IX Corps through the gap to Boonsboro on the morning of September 15. The division was on the road at 9:00 a.m. and reached Fox's Gap by noon. Porter and Sykes found, to their surprise, Burnside's men still camped in the gap. McClellan pulled up about this time and Porter requested permission to march past the IX Corps. A thoroughly annoyed McClellan assented about 30-minutes later. Porter reached Porterstown at 5:30 p.m. and found Israel Richardson's division (II Corps) in position on the right side of Boonsboro Pike, so Porter ordered Sykes to form across the road.[4]

Porter and McClellan studied the enemy's lines through field glasses atop a hill McClellan established as his headquarters. The two men apparently conferred and decided against offensive actions on September 15 as only two divisions were up.[5]

George Morell's division arrived on the battlefield at noon on September 16. It had crossed the Potomac River on September 4 and reached Rockville the following day. It remained there, blocking a possible enemy thrust toward Washington until September 13, when it continued its march north to reunite with the rest of the army. Upon arrival at the battlefield, it was assigned a position near the Middle Bridge. It relieved Israel Richardson's division on the morning of September 17, but was not engaged.[6]

Porter's artillery was active through September 17. He noted in his report, "From early in the morning of the 17th till dark the artillery was engaged with great effect upon that of the enemy, or upon his infantry, whenever it showed itself." Sykes' men remained inactive until the afternoon, when Brig. Gen. Alfred Pleasonton advanced several horse artillery batteries over the Middle Bridge to shell the town of Sharpsburg and Porter sent an infantry battalion from Maj. Charles Lovell's brigade (Sykes' division) and later, one from Lt. Col. Robert Buchanan's brigade. Rather than merely support the artillery, Sykes' regulars pushed toward Sharpsburg, driving Confederate infantry from their positions. Sykes was concerned about the vulnerability of these troops and pulled them back across Antietam Creek.[7]

With the IX Corps crossing at the Lower Bridge and its attack on Lee's right flank, Pleasonton believed the time was right for a push against Lee's center. He hoped to smash through Lee's line, capture Cemetery Hill, and place his artillery on the heights to enfilade Lee's right flank, thus helping facilitate the IX Corps' success. He requested infantry support, but Porter could not comply. Porter explained in his report, "the tide of battle had changed. Our troops on the left under Burnside had been driven from the heights which they had so gallantly crowned, while those on the immediate right, under Sumner, were held in check. The army was at a stand. I had not the force asked for, and could not, under my orders, risk the safety of the artillery and center of the line, and perhaps imperil the success of the day by further diminishing my small command, not then 4,000 strong—then in the front line and supported, and protecting all our trains."[8]

Porter has been criticized for his inaction at the Middle Bridge, but historian Ezra Carman defended him, noting, "General Porter has been severely and unjustly blamed for his inaction at Antietam. All the operations at the middle bridge were ordered by McClellan."[9]

Staff officer, D.H. Strother, recalled seeing the V Corps commander during the battle, within a "small redan built of fence rails, behind which sat General Fitz John Porter, who, with a telescope resting on the top rail, studied the field with unremitting attention, scarcely leaving his post during the whole day. His observations he communicated to the commander [McClellan] by nods, signs, or in words so low toned and brief that the nearest by-standers had but little benefit from them."[10]

During the evening of September 17, McClellan again sought the counsel of only Porter in determining what actions to take the following day. The army commander ultimately decided not to renew the fight. Andrew Humphreys' division arrived on September 18, and Porter sent it to relieve Morell's division. The latter moved south to relieve the IX Corps near the Lower Bridge.[11]

When McClellan received reports of Lee's retreat across the Potomac River, he sent Porter's corps through Sharpsburg at about noon on September 19. The men were to take up defensive positions beyond the town in support of Pleasonton's cavalry. During the afternoon, Porter relieved Pleasonton, so he sent his infantry toward the river. Some of Lee's men defended Shepherdstown Ford with "artillery well posted," and Porter "determined to clear the fords, and, if possible, secure some of the enemy's artillery. With this view I caused the banks of the river and canal to be well lined with skirmishers and sharpshooters, supported by portions of their respective divisions (Morell's and Sykes'), while their artillery and that of the reserve was posted to control the opposite bank." These batteries on the bluffs overlooking the river were commanded by Brig. Gen. William Pendleton. Porter sent detachments from Lovell's, Warren's, and Barnes' brigades across the river, where they drove the enemy's infantry and artillery into retreat and captured some of the guns on

September 19 and 20. Several units, particularly Barnes' brigade, were attacked by Maj. Gen. A.P. Hill's division and forced to retreat back across the river. This was the last action of the Maryland Campaign.[12]

It would also be the last action for Fitz John Porter. He was relieved from command in November 1862 and placed under arrest for his perceived short-comings during the Second Bull Run Campaign that purportedly led to the army's defeat. The Radical Republicans ensured he would be found guilty, and he was dismissed from the army on January 21, 1863. Porter spent the rest of his life seeking vindication and he finally received his wish after a military board overturned his conviction 16 years later. Abraham Lincoln's personal aide, John Hay, wrote of Porter, "the most magnificent soldier in the Army of the Potomac, ruined by his devotion to George McClellan."[13]

**Bradley M. Gottfried**

* * *

# 1ST DIVISION

## Major General George W. Morell

George Webb Morell had a distinguished military lineage. His maternal grandfather was a general officer during the Revolutionary War and his father, a major general in the New York Militia. Young George was born in Cooperstown, New York on January 8, 1815 and graduated from West Point in 1835 at the top of his class. After serving a mere two years in the military, Morell resigned to pursue a railroad career and later studied law. He held the rank of colonel and was a staff officer early in the Civil War and then assisted in the Washington defenses. Morell was promoted to the rank of brigadier general on August 9, 1861 and was later given a brigade in the V Corps. He saw action during the summer and fall of 1862, and was promoted to the rank of major general on July 25, 1862. During the trial of Fitz John Porter, Morell would not toe the prosecutors' line and he was denied a field command. He later commanded the defenses of the upper Potomac and was finally mustered out of service on December 15, 1864. Morell was a farmer after the war and died on February 11, 1883.[14]

Morell's footsore men were left behind when McClellan pushed his army north in early September. The division remained in and around the Washington defenses on the Virginia side through September 12. On that morning, the men received orders to pack up, cross the Potomac River and they marched rapidly through Washington, Silver Spring, Seneca Run, reaching Frederick on September 14. The division was on the road at 3:00 a.m., heading for Middletown. It crossed South Mountain at Fox's Gap and then headed to Boonsboro, and reached Antietam Creek on the afternoon of September 16.

The division was not engaged during the Battle of Antietam. It remained near Keedysville until it was ordered to relieve Richardson's division along Antietam Creek. It arrived shortly after 9:00 a.m. and remained in this position for the remainder of the battle. Two brigades, Col. Thomas Stockton's and Brig. Gen. Charles Griffin's, were detached and sent to the right to support Sumner's II Corps, but they did not see action. During the morning of September 18, the division marched to the left to reinforce the IX Corps. Morell's men crossed the Lower Bridge and advanced toward Harpers Ferry Road, only to learn the enemy was gone. The division finally rejoined the rest of the V Corps on the morning of September 19 and advanced through Sharpsburg to the Potomac River. Some members of Col. James Barnes' brigade crossed the river on September 19 and assisted in capturing some of Lee's artillery pieces. The entire brigade crossed the Potomac River the following day in pursuit of the Confederate rearguard, when it was set upon by Maj. Gen. A.P. Hill's division and almost destroyed.[15] **Bradley M. Gottfried**

***

## 1st Brigade: Colonel James Barnes

**Units:** 2nd Maine, 18th Massachusetts, 22nd Massachusetts, 1st Michigan, 13th New York, 25th New York, 118th Pennsylvania, Massachusetts Sharpshooters (Second Company)
**Strength:** 2,020[16]
**Losses:** 320 (66k-124w-130m)[17]

During the course of the Seven Days' and Second Manassas Campaigns, the 1st Brigade (minus the 118th Pennsylvania) fought dearly and suffered heavily. It lost 886 men in action at the gates of Richmond in late June and early July and an additional 576 men at Manassas in August. The brigade served under two different commanders in those campaigns and would have a third at the beginning of the Maryland Campaign.[18]

That man was Col. James Barnes, a 60-year-old Massachusetts native and a member of the United States Military Academy's Class of 1829. He remained at West Point as an instructor before he resigned from the United States Army in 1836. In the prewar years, Barnes worked as a civil engineer for railroads across the country. He became colonel of the 18th Massachusetts in July 1861 and, by way of seniority, came to command this veteran brigade in the Maryland Campaign. It was his first campaign in charge of a unit this size.[19]

The 118th Pennsylvania was assigned to help offset the brigade's losses on September 6, 1862, just three days after it reached the defenses of Washington and six days after mustering into Federal service.[20]

The brigade and its parent division left the vicinity of Washington City on September 12. The first march taxed the brigade's newcomers. "Three men to a company, as the 'strength present for duty,' was a most creditable showing when the final halt was made," recalled the 118th's regimental historian of one unit's earliest marches in the campaign. One straggler recognized Gen. George Morell and asked if he knew where the 118th Pennsylvania was. "Certainly, my man," replied the general, "everywhere between here and Washington."[21]

### Antietam

Despite the early lack of chemistry between the veterans and rookies, the brigade reached the Army of the Potomac, posted on the east bank of Antietam Creek on the afternoon of September 16. Morell's division assumed the position of Israel Richardson's II Corps division overlooking the Middle Bridge at 9:00 a.m. on September 17. The division's other two brigades reached the army's right near 4:00 p.m., while Barnes' men presumably remained near the Middle Bridge. The division was not engaged during the Battle of Antietam. Once the day's fighting quieted down, elements of the 18th Massachusetts performed picket duty on the west bank of Antietam Creek near the Middle Bridge.[22]

### Shepherdstown

Barnes' men marched to the army's left with the rest of the division on September 18 before rejoining the V Corps in its pursuit of the enemy towards Boteler's Ford on the Potomac River, a mile downstream from Shepherdstown on September 19. Near dusk, some members of the brigade participated in the Union charge across the ford that scattered the Confederate rearguard and netted some Confederate artillery pieces and limbers, an enemy flag, and 400 arms.[23]

The next morning, corps commander Fitz John Porter dispatched elements of Morell's and Sykes' divisions across the river to march in the directions of both Shepherdstown and Charlestown to "report what is to be found there." Barnes' brigade was the second Federal brigade to cross the ford that morning after Col. Charles Lovell's brigade of Regulars. Led by the 18th Massachusetts, the brigade's soldiers did not anticipate any action south of the Potomac River. "There was no haste or excitement," a member of the 22nd Massachusetts said. "The weather was pleasant, and we anticipated an agreeable incursion into a beautiful section that was new to us."[24]

Immediately upon reaching the Potomac's south shore, Maj. Joseph Hayes, commanding the 18th Massachusetts, learned from operation commander, Brig. Gen. George Sykes that the enemy was advancing in force towards the river. Hayes sent Sykes' aide to Barnes who received the information and informed Sykes that if he desired it, Barnes would change course away from Shepherdstown to support the rest of the Union forces. Sykes agreed to this change and ordered Barnes' 18th Massachusetts to the top of the bluffs to face the threat.[25]

Once atop the bluff, the 18th Massachusetts stood alone while the rest of the brigade navigated the broken ravines and terrain to deploy. Hayes engaged the enemy with his skirmishers before ordering his regiment to fix bayonets and fully engage Ambrose Hill's advancing division. Soon, the rest of the brigade extended the line with the 13th and 25th New York and the 118th Pennsylvania occupying the brigade's right while the other regiments filed onto their left.[26]

The battle soon raged across Barnes' entire front. Sykes quickly realized the plight of the men with steep cliffs and a river at their backs, and issued orders for the entire reconnoitering force to withdraw. Upon receiving the orders, Barnes personally ordered the left half of the brigade to disengage and begin recrossing the Potomac River. He dispatched Lt. Walter Davis of his staff to order the two New York regiments on the extreme right to fall back. En route, Davis noticed the 118th Pennsylvania fully engaged. He passed Barnes' orders along to Lt. Henry Kelly of that regiment before proceeding to the New Yorkers.[27]

Lt. Kelly found his commanding officer, Col. Charles Prevost, and relayed Barnes' order. Prevost, however, believed the orders came through an improper chain of command. "[I]f Colonel Barnes has any order to give me," he said, "let his aide come to me." While the rest of Sykes' force headed for the river, the green 118th Pennsylvania stood alone against Hill's veteran division.[28]

Hill's Confederates reached as close as fifty yards to Prevost's line and began enveloping the regiment's right, temporarily throwing it into a confused panic. Prevost grabbed the regimental colors to rally his men but was seriously wounded in the process. The wounded Prevost met Col. Barnes as he headed to the river. When Barnes realized the 118th Pennsylvania was not withdrawing, he personally rode to the regiment to extricate it from the worsening situation. As if the untenable situation was not bad enough, some of the men's guns also malfunctioned during the fight.[29]

Lt. Col. James Gwyn, Prevost's successor, had just ordered a charge to steady his men and was directing the regiment's fire towards a growing threat on its left when he received Barnes' second order. The regiment, now pressed on both its flanks, immediately broke for the river. Many ran for the ravine the regiment used to reach the top of the bluffs, where "the slaughter became dreadful," wrote Capt. Francis Donaldson. "Others again were driven headlong over the bluff." Gwyn reported that while crossing the river at a milldam, the enemy fired on the regiment from the bluffs above "with great effect."[30]

Except for the 118th Pennsylvania, Barnes' men "recrossed the river in good order." The veteran regiments escaped mostly unscathed, as the Pennsylvanians' losses totaled 269 of the brigade's 320 losses.[31]

The experience of Barnes' brigade at Shepherdstown demonstrates the dangers a lack of chemistry between commands and commanders can have on a battlefield, as evidenced by the unfamiliarity between Barnes and Prevost that led to the 118th Pennsylvania remaining atop the bluffs while the rest of the brigade retired. It also illustrates that despite the bloody results of Antietam, the Army of Northern Virginia was still a formidable and dangerous foe.

**Kevin Pawlak**

113

* * *

## 2nd Brigade: Brigadier General Charles Griffin

**Units:** 2nd District of Columbia, 9th Massachusetts, 32nd Massachusetts, 4th Michigan, 14th New York, 62nd Pennsylvania
**Strength:** 2,060[32]
**Losses:** 0[33]

The 2nd Brigade was initially commanded by Brig. Gen. John Abercrombie until he was wounded at Malvern Hill on June 26, 1862. He was wounded earlier at Seven Pines, but was able to remain with his command. With his second wound, Charles Griffin assumed command of the brigade. Griffin was born in December 1825 in Ohio, and after a short stint at Kenyon College, entered West Point and graduated in 1847. He entered the artillery and served under Winfield Scott in Mexico and then in posts in the southwest. Griffin returned to West Point in 1860 as an instructor, but with the possibility of a war, Griffin left to organize a field battery of U.S. Regulars that served at First Bull Run. He switched to the infantry and received the rank of brigadier general to rank from June 9, 1862 and assumed command of the 2nd Brigade upon Abercrombie's wounding in late June.[34]

The 2nd Brigade was composed of regiments from five states. The 14th New York was mustered into service in May 1861, followed by the 4th Michigan and 9th Massachusetts in June, the 62nd Pennsylvania in August, and the 32nd Massachusetts in November. These regiments entered the war in a variety of brigades, but were banded together under Abercrombie by May 1862. The brigade fought in the Peninsula, Seven Days and Second Bull Run Campaign. The 2nd District of Columbia was the oddball of the group. It was mustered into service in February 1862 and spent its entire term in the defenses of Washington, except during the Maryland Campaign, when it was attached to the 2nd Brigade.[35]

The brigade played a minor role in the campaign—see the divisional description for additional information.

**Bradley M. Gottfried**

* * *

## Third Brigade: Colonel T.B. Stockton

**Units:** 20th Maine, 16th Michigan, 12th New York, 17th New York, 44th New York, 83rd Pennsylvania, Michigan Sharpshooters
**Strength:** 1,675[36]
**Losses:** 0[37]

Unlike many of the brigades during this period of the war, the 3rd Brigade had gone through a number of commanders (four) during its short existence. Col. T. B. Stockton assumed command of the brigade on eve of the Maryland Campaign. He was born in New York State in 1805 and graduated from West Point in 1827. Stockton served as a quartermaster until resigning from the army in 1836. He reentered the service during the War with Mexico and commanded the 1st Michigan Volunteers. Stockton again left the army in 1848 and upon the outbreak of the war, helped organize the 16th Michigan Volunteers and became its colonel.[38]

Most of the regiments were brigaded together in May 1862. The 12th New York had the most experience, as it was mustered into service before the others (May 1861) and was involved in the First Bull Run Campaign. The 17th New York also entered the service in May, but spent about six months as part of the Washington garrison. The other regiments mustered into service in September 1861 (16th Michigan and 83rd Pennsylvania), October 1861 (44th New York). These units saw action during the Peninsula, Seven Days, and

Second Bull Run Campaign. The 20th Maine arrived in August 1862, so the Maryland Campaign was its first experience in the army.[39]

The brigade played a minor role in the campaign—see the divisional description for additional information.

**Bradley M. Gottfried**

\* \* \*

# 2ND DIVISION—

## Brigadier General George Sykes

Born in Dover Delaware, George Sykes graduated with the famous West Point Class of 1842, which included James Longstreet, D.H. Hill and John Pope. Sykes served credibly with the 3rd U.S. Infantry in the Seminole and Mexican Wars, earning a brevet for gallantry in the latter conflict. One of his officers described him as "so thoroughly and simply a soldier unsympathetic and methodical, a man of details, diligent and untiring, but never hurried, never flurried; one of the coolest men in danger or confusion that we had in the whole army. He enforced discipline like a machine and had apparently no more sentiment than a gunstock." Sykes commanded a battalion of regular infantry at First Bull Run/Manassas and formed the rear guard, successfully holding off the victorious Confederates. With the arrival of additional regular infantry in March 1862, Sykes successively commanded the Regular Brigade and then in May 1862, the newly created division of regular troops.[40]

Sykes' division fought during the Seven Days Battles "with all the obstinacy of the regulars" and was afterward sent with the V Corps to John Pope's Army of Virginia. Once again, his "badly crippled" troops formed the rear guard at Second Bull Run/Manassas. The regulars were not assigned to the Army of the Potomac until September 6 when Sykes was ordered "to report in person to the general commanding ... and [the division] will constitute a reserve under the personal orders of the general." Sykes remained under McClellan's direct command until V Corps commander, Fitz John Porter reached the army on September 14.[41]

The division left the Manassas battlefield on September 2 and marched to Hall's Hill, Virginia, where Lt. Col. Robert Buchanan's and Col. Gouverneur Warren's brigades received badly needed reinforcements. It crossed the Chain Bridge on September 5, and made a night march through Washington D.C., arriving at Tenallytown the next day. The division continued its march on September 7, marching to Rockville, where it remained until September 11. For the next two days, Sykes' men marched under sunny skies and warm temperatures through the villages of Middlebrook and Urbana. The Federals received a warm welcome from the citizens in Frederick upon arriving there on September 13. Sensing a fight, the regulars marched on to Middletown on September 14 as artillery and musket fire thundered ahead of them in the South Mountain gaps. McClellan originally ordered Sykes' division to follow the IX Corps through Fox's Gap in pursuit of the defeated rebels on September 15. However, when Sykes' division reached the summit around noon, Ambrose Burnside's troops were still burying their dead and issuing rations. McClellan was impatient to resume his pursuit of the enemy, so he ordered Sykes' three brigades to push through the IX Corps and proceed toward Sharpsburg.[42]

Sykes' division reached Boonsboro Pike around 5:00 p.m. on September 15 and established itself on the high ground south of the road overlooking Antietam Creek. One battalion of Buchanan's brigade was advanced to the Middle Bridge that evening and established a skirmish line on the west bank of the creek.[43]

The division supported the Union Artillery Reserve on September 16 with one battalion at the Middle Bridge throughout the day, and sent Col. Gouverneur Warren's small brigade of zouaves to the left to link up with Burnside's IX Corps to cover the approaches to Harpers Ferry.[44]

As the Battle of Antietam opened on the morning of September 17, one battalion of Lt. Col. Robert Buchanan's brigade was across the Middle Bridge and maintained a skirmish line on the west bank of Antietam Creek. The remainder of Sykes' division held the high ground on the east bank and supported the batteries of the Artillery Reserve.[45]

When Brig. Gen. Alfred Pleasonton's cavalry division and horse artillery crossed Antietam Creek after noon, Sykes sent a battalion of Maj. Charles Lovell's brigade across to drive back Confederate sharpshooters who were annoying the gunners. Later in the afternoon, Porter ordered Sykes to send two of his divisional artillery batteries across the creek when the horse artillery batteries ran low on ammunition. Sykes complied with the order "against his judgment." Lt. Alanson Randol's guns were in action a short period of time, but Lt. William Van Reed's battery remained at the front for the rest of the day supporting the regular infantry.[46]

Around the same time, about 2:00 p.m., Sykes ordered Capt. Hiram Dryer and his 4th U.S. Infantry across the creek with the remainder of Buchanan's brigade to drive off Confederate sharpshooters who were still within range of his artillery batteries. Pushing through the Union guns, Dryer continued advancing his elated regulars toward the crest of Cemetery Hill. From Sykes' vantage point, Dryer was exceeding his orders and did not have sufficient troops to support this further advance. He ordered Dryer to "draw in his pickets" which Dryer immediately proceeded to do, pulling back "about 75 yards and putting his whole line under cover." Dryer's infantry and Van Reed's battery remained in their positions until dark when all were withdrawn to the east bank.[47]

Warren's brigade meanwhile remained detached throughout the day. In the afternoon, it advanced to the high ground overlooking the Rohrbach (Lower) Bridge as the IX Corps resumed its advance west of Antietam Creek. Lovell's brigade, less one battalion, continued supporting the guns of position on the east bank of Antietam Creek for the remainder of the day.[48]

Sykes pushed his division to the Potomac River on September 19 in pursuit of the retreating Confederates. Lovell's brigade, supported by Warren's zouaves, took the lead with Weed's three artillery batteries in close support. The artillery took position on the high ground overlooking Boteler's Ford and engaged Confederate artillery and infantry on the opposite bank.[49]

The following day, Porter ordered Sykes across the Potomac River to reconnoiter along the opposite side. He threw Lovell's brigade across at 7:00 a.m. and it advanced in line of battle to a wood line about a mile from the river. Here they encountered Ambrose Hill's division preparing to advance. Sykes ordered Lovell to fall back slowly to the crest of the riverbank and sent Warren's brigade across to support Lovell's left flank while Weed's artillery supported the two brigades from the Maryland side of the river. Porter watched Hill's division advance against Lovell and Warren and ordered Sykes to pull his troops back across the river. The two Union brigades executed the retrograde in good order despite heavy fire from the advancing Confederates. By early afternoon, the regulars were back in their original positions on the Maryland side of the Potomac.[50]

Sykes' division was rightly regarded as the best-drilled and most professional command in the Army of the Potomac. While they did not play the decisive role that perhaps many of the officers and men felt they should have on September 17, they did not disappoint their leaders. Their key position in the center of McClellan's line was critical in maintaining an unbroken connection between the II and IX Corps. The regulars' aggressive skirmish line tied down a significant amount of Lee's already diminished artillery, preventing it from supporting other endangered points. Sykes' men competently executed their reconnaissance mission at

Shepherdstown on September 20 and, unlike other formations of Porter's corps, escaped across the Potomac with relatively few losses.

**James A. Rosebrock**

* * *

## 1st Brigade: Lieutenant Colonel Robert Buchanan

**Units:** 3rd U.S., 4th U.S., 12th U.S., 14th U.S.
**Strength:** 1,391[51]
**Losses:** 39 (4k-35w)[52]

The core of Lt. Col. Robert Buchanan's brigade can be traced back to a battalion of regular army infantry troops who fought at First Bull Run under Maj. George Sykes. By March of 1862, enough regulars from other regiments reached Washington from the frontier to organize them into the Regular Infantry Reserve Brigade of the Army of the Potomac. In addition to the 3rd and 4th U.S. from the old army, the War Department assigned two "New Army" infantry regiments, the 12th and 14th U.S. to the brigade. Instead of the traditional ten-company regimental establishment, the new regiments were organized into two battalions of eight companies each. The men were new recruits led, in many cases, by equally green officers.

On May 20, 1862, the Regular Infantry Reserve Brigade became the 1st Brigade of George Sykes' division, under the command of Lt. Col. Robert Buchanan of the 4th U.S. Buchanan graduated from West Point in 1830 and served in the 4th U.S. his entire career. A veteran of the Mexican War with two brevets for gallantry, the Marylander was a tough, no nonsense disciplinarian. Buchanan was Ulysses Grant's commanding officer when the young captain from Ohio resigned from the army in 1854. Upon observing the arrival of the bedraggled 2-14th U.S., Buchanan thundered to its commanding officer, Capt. John O'Connell, "I will make them Regulars," and that is what he did.[53]

Buchanan changed his opinion of his two new regiments after their first Battle at Gaines' Mill. Two months later, the brigade formed the rear guard of Pope's army on Henry Hill at the Second Battle of Bull Run. Buchanan described his brigade as being "cut to pieces" in heavy fighting that further heightened the reputation of his regulars.[54]

The 2-12th U.S. joined the brigade prior to the march north, bringing 320 badly needed soldiers to its thin ranks. The brigade began its march after Lee's army at 9:00 p.m. on September 6, reaching Rockville, Maryland the following evening. Sgt. Thomas Evans of the 12th U.S. described the severity of the trek as the "the worst dry march of the campaign…the heat intense, and the perspirations started in gushes at every pore." The brigade remained in Rockville until September 11, which gave Buchanan three days to drill the new recruits and ready the brigade for its next fight. Morale soared when the soldiers learned their Rockville camp was near McClellan's headquarters and they were designated as a reserve under his personal command.[55]

The brigade left Rockville on September 11 and marched seven miles to Seneca Creek. The pace quickened the next day as the regulars reached Hyattstown, 12 miles up the road. The following morning they marched 14 miles to Frederick, bringing the Artillery Reserve with them. According to Sgt. Charles Bowen, his 12th U.S., "marched through Frederick with banners flying, music playing, & all the pomp of war … The inhabitants filled our canteens with cool water, the young ladies threw flowers and waved handkerchiefs, & I tell you it made us feel as though we could whip all creation & the rebs throwed in."[56]

The brigade awoke to the rumble of artillery and musket fire on September 14. Sykes ordered Buchanan to march his brigade west to Middletown, seven miles west of Frederick. Reaching the summit of Catoctin Mountain at Braddock Heights,

Buchanan's sweating troops observed the vast panorama of the Middletown Valley in front of them and the distant South Mountain engulfed in haze. Artillery and musket fire flashed along its slopes as Ambrose Burnside's wing battled for control of the mountain passes. The regulars quickened their pace and reached Middletown late in the afternoon.

Early the next day, Sykes ordered Buchanan's brigade to follow the IX Corps through Fox's Gap in pursuit of Robert E. Lee's defeated troops. The brigade scaled the mountain and reached the gap at noon only to find the road blocked by Burnside's troops. Despite being ordered to pursue with the "utmost vigor" Burnside instead spent the morning burying his dead and issuing rations. Frustrated at the delay, McClellan gave orders at 12:30 p.m. for Sykes "to push by them and put his division in front."[57]

## Antietam

Buchanan led his brigade down South Mountain, across Pleasant Valley and over Red Hill. The tired men reached Porterstown at 5:30 p.m., at the intersection with Boonsboro Pike, where Buchanan found Richardson's division across the pike facing Antietam Creek. He ordered Capt. John D. Wilkins' 3rd U.S. Infantry to relieve the 5th New Hampshire on picket duty at the Middle Bridge. Wilkins' regiment remained at the bridge all night until relieved the following morning.[58]

At 7:00 a.m. on September 16, Buchanan ordered Capt. Hiram Dryer's 4th U.S. to relieve Wilkins' men. Five companies passed through the 3rd U.S. picket line and two companies led by Lt.'s John Buell and Robert McKibbin advanced across the bridge, 300 yards further up the ascending road toward Sharpsburg. They suddenly encountered enemy pickets from George B. Anderson's brigade (D.H. Hill's division). A few shots were fired before the enemy troops fell back. Confederate artillery on Cemetery Hill under Col. James Walton spotted the Union advance and opened fire on Dryer's skirmishers. Union batteries of the Artillery Reserve

immediately returned fire, prompting James Longstreet to order Walton to cease firing to conserve his ammunition. At 5:00 p.m., the 1-12th U.S., commanded by Capt. Matthew Blunt, relieved Dryer's regiment.[59]

On the fateful morning of September 17, Buchanan's brigade (all but the 1-12th U.S.) formed the right of Sykes' division. It was deployed behind the crest of the ridge overlooking Antietam Creek south of Boonsboro Pike. The buildings of the Ecker farm stood immediately in front of the brigade line. Capt. William Graham's, Lt. Marcus Miller's and Lt. William Van Reed's Napoleons were in battery across Porterstown Road behind the brigade. The 1-12th U.S. continued to picket the west bank of Antietam Creek around the Newcomer farm buildings.

Around 10:00 a.m., Buchanan's men watched Pleasonton's cavalry division and the four horse artillery batteries below them, clatter down the pike and cross Antietam Creek at the Middle Bridge. The cavalry passed through the 1-12th U.S. picket line, taking up positions around the Newcomer farm buildings. The horse batteries went into action on the high ground further up the road. On their left, Confederate skirmishers from the 1st Georgia opened a severe fire from a stone wall opposite the guns, killing a number of artillery horses.[60]

Pleasonton asked Blunt to advance a line of skirmishers to drive the rebels back. Capt. Frederick Winthrop deployed his company and advanced through the fields to the left (south) of the pike taking the enemy skirmishers under fire. Shortly afterward, Sykes ordered Blunt to advance the rest of his battalion to support the batteries. Sgt. Bowen described how his men "advanced skirmisher order, & the devils fought until we were right up to the fence; one fellow poked his musket right in my face & pulled trigger, the ball just grazed my head & the powder burnt my face he was so close. One of the boys put a ball into him almost the same moment."[61]

Blunt's skirmishers were unable to dislodge the well-protected enemy sharpshooters from the stone wall, so Sykes ordered some units from Lovell's brigade to bolster Blunt's position. They successfully pushed the Georgians from the stone wall toward the Sherrick farm lane.[62]

On the right (north) of the pike, two horse artillery batteries took fire from three regiments of Shank's Evans' South Carolina brigade. Only one squadron of cavalry stood between the Union guns and the South Carolinians. Buchanan ordered the 2-14th U.S., commanded by Capt. David McKibbin, to relieve the cavalry at 1:00 p.m. After crossing Antietam Creek, McKibbin's battalion filed to the right at the Newcomer house and halted behind the artillery. He then sent Capt. Horace Thatcher's Company B through the gun line to relieve the cavalry squadron in front of it and they soon engaged the 1st Georgia skirmish line on their left and the 18th, 22nd, and 23rd South Carolina on the high ground in front.[63]

Around 2:00 p.m., Sykes and Buchanan determined that a heavier force of infantry was needed to support the divisional artillery, which had replaced Pleasonton's horse artillery. Buchanan tapped Capt. Hiram Dryer, the senior captain in the 4th U.S., to cross the bridge with his regiment and Capt. Harvey Brown's 1-14th U.S. and assume command of all regular infantry on the west side of the creek. Dryer was regarded as one of the "coolest and bravest officers in our service." Buchanan ordered him to support the artillery and dislodge the enemy still hiding among the haystacks in front of the Sherrick farm lane. Dryer's command totaled 1,640 men when he got all his men across the creek at about 3:00 p.m. Buchanan held the remainder of his brigade, the 3rd U.S. and 2-12th U.S., on the east bank of Antietam Creek to support the Federal guns of position.[64]

The two regiments steadily advanced under heavy fire in column over the Newcomer Ridge into a ravine that cut across Boonsboro Pike at the intersection with the Sunken Road. As Dryer's infantry moved forward, several horse batteries completed their resupply and dropped trail on the west bank of Antietam Creek and resumed firing.

As elements of Lovell's brigade advanced on the left, Dryer ordered Lt. Caleb Carlton to move the three leading companies of the 4th U.S. (K, I, G from left to right) up the right side of Boonsboro Pike to the crest of the ridge in their front. The young Ohioan led his companies through a three-acre triangular shaped cornfield adjacent to the end of the Sunken Road, driving Evans' skirmishers before him. His little command then steadily advanced thru the open fields to the high ground about 150 yards past the little cornfield. Carlton halted to await further orders as he came on line with Lovell's men in the Sherrick farm lane across Boonsboro Pike.[65]

Dryer meanwhile advanced the five remaining companies of the 4th U. S. to the west of the triangular cornfield and concealed them in the tall corn. To their left, Brown's battalion of the 14th U.S. moved into a deep ravine, just behind the Sherrick lane. To the right, Capt. David McKibbin's 2-14th U.S. advanced through Van Reed's battery and took position in the same ravine. He pushed a skirmish line to the crest of the ridge in his front that came under a steady fire from the 22nd and 23rd South Carolina of Evans' brigade and a section of Capt. Robert Boyce's South Carolina battery.

Dryer meanwhile ordered Carlton's skirmish line to advance to the crest overlooking Sharpsburg. As they moved forward, Evans' infantry and most of the Confederate artillery pulled back to the reverse slope of the high ground under the fierce artillery fire of the guns of position and horse artillery. Under lessening Confederate fire, Carlton's three companies gained the crest. The regulars could see the Lutheran church a mere 450 yards ahead. Dryer characteristically was with the skirmish line and noted the apparent weakness of the Confederate position, with "but one battery and two regiments in front of Sharpsburg."[66]

Blunt's battalion remained well behind on the bank of Antietam Creek. Dryer now proposed to Blunt that his battalion join the 4th and 14th U.S. and immediately charge the rebel position on Cemetery Hill. Unknown to Dryer, Blunt "preferred asking for orders" and sent a note back to Buchanan requesting instructions. He felt his mission was limited to protecting the Union batteries and not moving forward.[67]

Across the creek, Sykes and Buchanan could see Dryer "pushing his men forward on each side of the pike towards the crest occupied by the enemy, with a view, as it was afterwards understood, to charge and take a battery there." While Dryer and Carlton saw an open road into Sharpsburg, Buchanan and Sykes had a bigger picture. From their vantage point, the two officers could see not just one battery, but eighteen guns in front of Carlton. Dryer's thin line was just too far forward to be adequately supported.[68]

Just then, Buchanan received Blunt's note. He passed it to Sykes who at the time was talking with McClellan and Porter some distance away. Sykes, "very annoyed," ordered Lt. William Powell, Buchanan's assistant adjutant general, to ride over to Dryer with orders to suspend the attack and withdraw his troops to the ridge where the artillery was located.[69]

Dryer, standing in the middle of the pike under heavy fire, had just ordered elements of Lovell's brigade to resume its advance. He was about to lead the remainder of the 4th U.S. forward to Carlton's position when he saw a mounted officer galloping furiously toward him. Lt. Powell wheeled up to Dryer and delivered Sykes' order. The captain asked if he had any discretion to continue the attack. When informed that the order was imperative, Dryer immediately ordered Carlton to fall back.[70]

At 5:30 p.m., the 4th U.S. held the center of the brigade line in the triangular cornfield. McKibbin's battalion to its right was posted in the Sunken Road. To the left, Brown's battalion held a position in the ravine behind the Sherrick lane with Blunt's battalion anchoring the brigade left. The brigade held these positions until the artillery withdrew. At 7:30 p.m., Dryer and his men crossed over the Middle Bridge carrying their dead and wounded with them.

The actions of Buchanan's brigade around the Middle Bridge are often overlooked in the overall scheme of the Battle of Antietam. While the number of troops committed and casualties incurred was relatively low, the brigade forged a critical link between the offensive operations of the II and IX Corps on its flanks. The aggressive skirmishing of Buchanan's regulars was a constant threat that Lee could not ignore. Perhaps Sykes said it best when he reported Dryer's troops "behaved in the handsomest manner, and had there been an available force for their support, there is no doubt he could have crowned the Sharpsburg crest."[71]

**James A. Rosebrock**

* * *

## 2nd Brigade: Major Charles S. Lovell

**Units:** 1st & 6th U.S. (combined), 2nd & 10th U.S. (combined), 1-11th U.S., 1-17th U.S.
**Strength:** 1,288[72]
**Losses:** 56 (8k-47w-1m)[73]

Maj. Charles Lovell's brigade was the second brigade of regular infantry organized and assigned to the Army of the Potomac. The brigade was constituted on May 20, 1862 with Lt. Col. William

Chapman of the 3rd U.S. as its commander. The 2nd Brigade included bits and pieces of the old 1st, 2nd, 6th, and 10th U.S. and a battalion from each of the new 11th and 17th U.S. regiments. The four old regiments were so under-strength that they had to be consolidated into two battalions. One company of the 1st U.S. was attached to the 6th U.S. to form the 1st and 6th U.S. Nine companies of the 2nd

U.S. and three companies of the 10th U.S. formed the 2nd and 10th U.S.[74]

The brigade suffered heavy casualties in the Peninsula and Second Manassas Campaigns and large numbers of men were absent due to illness as it started the Maryland Campaign. Chapman turned over command to Charles Lovell, then commanding the 2nd and 10th U.S., when the brigade reached Rockville, Maryland on September 7. Chapman had been plagued by illness since the Peninsula Campaign and was too sick to remain in command.[75]

Lovell was the only brigade commander in Sykes' division who did not attend West Point. The native of Hull, Massachusetts enlisted in the 2nd U.S. Artillery in 1830 at the age of 19 and rose to the rank of regimental sergeant major in just seven years. Lovell was commissioned in the 6th U.S. in 1837 and commanded an infantry company with General Winfield Scott in the Mexico City campaign of 1847. Known for his "remarkable coolness in action," and as "a modest and retiring man ... loved among his men," the 51-year-old was a worthy leader for the regulars of the 2nd Brigade.[76]

The brigade left Rockville on the morning of September 11 and marched under sunny skies and warm temperatures over the rolling terrain of central Maryland, passing through little hamlets like Middlebrook, Clarksburg and Hyattstown. Lovell's men crossed the Monocacy River and entered Frederick on September 13 where they received a warm welcome typical of all Union troops who passed through that Unionist city.[77]

Lovell's brigade advanced to Middletown on September 14 as Ambrose Burnside's wing of the Army of the Potomac battled Rebel troops arrayed along the South Mountain passes. The brigade headed to Fox's Gap on the morning of September 15 but had to wait for Burnside's troops to clear the road before the men could advance. They subsequently followed Robert Buchanan's brigade into Pleasant Valley and over Red Hill along the Porterstown Road. Reaching Boonsboro Pike, the brigade turned left (south) and climbed to the top of a ridge overlooking Antietam Creek.

Lovell's brigade formed a line on the left of George Sykes' division and occupied a 500-yard front between two fence lines on the Ecker farm. The "Maine Regulars" of the 1-17th U.S anchored the left. Named because the regiment was first recruited at Fort Preble, Maine in late 1861, these eight companies were commanded by Maj. George Andrews. Andrews, a Missouri businessman at the beginning of the war, commanded a volunteer regiment at the Battle of Wilson's Creek before accepting a regular commission. Next in line was the 1-11th U.S., commanded by Maj. De Lancey Floyd-Jones. Floyd-Jones was a West Point classmate of McClellan. He served in the 4th U.S. for many years with U.S. Grant as a fellow company commander. To the right of Floyd-Jones was the 1st and 6th U.S. commanded by Capt. Levi C. Bootes. Bootes, a former sergeant in the Mounted Rifles, had served with Lovell in the 6th U.S. for many years. Capt. John Poland, commanding the 1st and 10th U.S., held down the right of the line. Until ten days before, Poland had been Chapman's aide-de-camp and was elevated to command when Lovell took over the brigade. Poland's officers were described as a collection of boys appointed from civilian life and old soldiers commissioned from the ranks.[78]

## Antietam

On September 16, the brigade remained in position supporting three batteries of the Artillery Reserve engaging rebel batteries on Cemetery Hill. Three of Lovell's four battalions, the 1st and 6th U.S., 11th U.S. and the 17th U.S., remained on the east bank of Antietam Creek the following day supporting the artillery. Lt. Duncan Vance of the 11th U.S. recalled the action: "We were supporting the batteries on a high range of hills, where we had a view of the whole battlefield and only suffered from the enemy's shells which they sent over us thick and fast ... We saw the whole battlefield – our infantry advancing – rebel infantry broken and retreating – our infantry charging on rebel batteries, repulsed, rallied, and finally carried them. I would not have missed the sight for anything."[79]

Around 1:00 p.m. on September 17, Lovell ordered Poland's 2nd and 10th U.S. to reinforce a battalion of Buchanan's brigade supporting four horse artillery batteries on the west bank of Antietam Creek. Upon crossing the Middle Bridge, the regulars shook out a skirmish line of seven companies as Poland kept his other five companies back in reserve. The 26-year-old lieutenant pushed his regiment into an open field to the left of Boonsboro Pike. They immediately came under a harassing fire from a battalion of Georgia skirmishers positioned behind a stone wall, and several enemy batteries on Cemetery Hill. With the support of Federal horse artillery, Poland pushed the stubborn Georgians back from the wall toward the Sherrick farm lane. Later, when the horse batteries withdrew, Poland continued supporting one of Sykes' divisional batteries sent to replace them.[80]

Capt. Hiram Dryer of the 4th U. S. (Buchanan's brigade) assumed command of all regular infantry on the west bank of Antietam Creek at 3:00 p.m. He ordered Poland to take possession of some haystacks in a field about 150 yards in front of the Sherrick lane. Poland committed his five reserve companies with the other seven forming an extended skirmish line. The Federals advanced under a steady fire from the Georgia infantry at the stone wall and two South Carolina regiments from Nathan Evans' brigade positioned in the lane. Reaching the haystacks, more enemy infantry, hidden in a cornfield further up the slope, took them under fire. Two Confederate batteries of rifled guns on Cemetery Hill opened with "a heavy fire of case shot and canister." Poland reported Musician George Miller of Company G seized a musket on the field and used it with good effect during the hottest part of the engagement. Sgt. Patrick Breen of Company C, 2nd U.S. recalled, "we got down to work and silenced their battery, but at what a sacrifice! The rebel infantry, in the mean time holding the cornfield, kept picking away at us and we at them." Poland's men moved through the haystacks, capturing some of the Georgia sharpshooters and driving the South Carolinians out of Sherrick lane.[81]

Several companies on Poland's right, led by Irish-born Lt. George McLoughlin and First Sgt. Francis Lacey, didn't hear the captain's orders to halt in the lane and continued moving forward. They executed a crisp left wheel into the pasture in front of the cornfield and their men's enfilading fire, coupled with the musketry of Poland's main line, caused the enemy artillery near the crest to limber up. A Virginia regiment remained in their front, but Poland could see the enemy pulling their artillery off Cemetery Hill. McLoughlin's little skirmish line was soon compelled to fall back as shells from the Union batteries fell short and landed in their ranks.[82]

Around 4:30 p.m., the 17th Michigan (Col. Benjamin Christ's brigade, Brig. Gen. Orlando Willcox's division, IX Corps) joined Poland's left in the Sherrick Lane. Poland reported his men running short of ammunition, so Dryer ordered him to suspend further forward movement and withdraw a short distance behind the ridge to await ammunition resupply. Around dusk, Poland received a further order to fall back to the bridge, and during the movement, was ordered to return to camp on the east bank.[83]

First Sgt. Breen was disappointed. "Some of us of that field knew of our own observation from the position at the sunken road at the edge of the cornfield that the rebels were weak at that point and that if prompt orders had been given the Regular regiments then and there and engaging the enemy, that his center could be broken."[84]

## Shepherdstown

On September 19, Lovell's brigade moved through Sharpsburg and bivouacked near the Potomac River opposite Boteler's Ford. Very early on the morning of the 20th, the brigade was ordered across the Potomac River at the ford. Sykes ordered Lovell to advance up Charlestown Road to "the second belt of woods" on the plateau

122

overlooking the river, about a mile and a half inland. The brigade advanced in column from the ford up a narrow rocky path with the 11th U.S. in the lead. They approached the belt of woods by about 7:30 a.m.[85]

Lovell spotted movement in the wood line and immediately deployed the 11th U.S. as skirmishers. Lt. George Head's Company D, at the very front of the skirmish line, was just 40 paces from the woods. Head and his men had a feeling the enemy held the woods in front in great strength. John Ames recalled, "indeed I could see the grey devils trotting up to us." Looming up ahead in the woods was Maj. Gen. A. P. Hill's entire Light Division.[86]

Lovell coolly snapped out a line of battle. The 2nd and 10th U.S. formed the left and the 1st and 6th U.S. was next to them. The 11th U.S. occupied the center of the line, and to the right of the road, in a cornfield, was the 17th U.S. There was no movement or response by the Confederates in the trees ahead as the brigade moved into line.

Lovell turned to aide Lt. Edward Sellers and ordered the young officer to ride back to Sykes at the river and ask for instructions. The old regular knew he faced a large Confederate force and was clearly outnumbered. After what seemed like an eternity, Sellers galloped back up the road with orders from Sykes to slowly fall back to the crest of the riverbank.[87]

With parade ground precision, Lovell's brigade about-faced and slowly fell back in good order. Major Bootes recalled, "the enemy's pickets were advancing very fast, supported by a battery, cavalry and a large force of infantry." At two different positions, the line turned around and faced the pursuing Confederates. When the Federals reached the open ground on the heights near the river, Hill's men opened a heavy fire. Lovell found that Porter had ordered Col. James Barnes' brigade (George Morell's division) across the river to cover his right flank. Col. Gouverneur Warren's brigade from

Lovell's own division also crossed to support his left.[88]

As the Confederates emerged into the open from the wood line, Union artillery on the east bank of the Potomac spotted them and opened fire. Lovell's men continued pulling back as artillery shells flew overhead with some rounds falling into their ranks. The brigade finally reached a position on the bluff overlooking the river around 11:00 a.m. Lovell now received word from Sykes to withdraw across the river. The regulars scampered down the steep bluff under a shower of enemy musketry from Brig. Gen. Maxcy Gregg's brigade (Hill's division), and splashed into the Potomac River.[89]

Covered by a heavy volume of artillery fire, the brigade threaded its way across the swiftly flowing river. Poland's battalion formed the rear guard. As his men prepared to enter the river, First Sgt. Daniel Burke of Company B volunteered to return and spike an abandoned Confederate gun. Under a hail of gunfire, Burke and a lone New York officer dashed back up the slope and managed to jam a ramrod into the gun vent. Sprinting back to the Potomac shore, Burke found he was about the last man standing on the Virginia side. To the astonishment and cheers of his comrades and under a flurry of enemy bullets, the Connecticut Yankee sprinted across Boteler's Mill Dam to the safety of the Maryland shore. For Burke's feat of bravery he was awarded the Medal of Honor.[90]

Lovell's small brigade of regulars, ably led by professional officers and sergeants, demonstrated their unparalleled expertise as skirmishers at both Antietam and Shepherdstown. Many of the rank and file felt they could have done much more had they been allowed, particularly in the fields in front of Cemetery Hill. Their skill as the rear guard holding off Hill's division's advance at Shepherdstown was the one bright spot in an otherwise dismal Union reverse on that field of battle. **James A. Rosebrock**

**\*\*\***

## 3rd Brigade: Colonel Gouverneur K. Warren

**Units:** 5th New York, 10th New York
**Strength:** 523[91]
**Losses:** 0[92]

There were not enough regular troops to organize a third brigade when George Sykes' division was organized on May 20, 1862. To round out the division, two well drilled and disciplined zouave regiments, the 5th and 10th New York, were formed into a small demi-brigade which became the 3rd Brigade of Sykes' division. Sykes appointed Col. Gouverneur Warren, the commander of the 5th New York, as the brigade commander.

Warren, a brilliant and temperamental New Yorker, graduated second in the West Point class of 1850 and was commissioned in the elite topographical engineers. He surveyed the Mississippi Delta and compiled maps and reports of the Pacific Railroad explorations and Dakota and Nebraska territories. The 31-year-old lieutenant was teaching mathematics at West Point at the outbreak of the Civil War and was appointed lieutenant colonel of Abram Duryee's 5th New York. Duryee was frequently absent during the regiment's formative period, leaving Warren in command. Warren was a strict disciplinarian and drillmaster and relentlessly whipped the fledgling zouaves into shape. He helped established the regiment's reputation as one of the foremost volunteer outfits in the Army of the Potomac. Warren was promoted to colonel and given command of the regiment when Duryee was appointed a brigadier general. A protégé of George McClellan, Warren moved up to command the newly organized third brigade of Sykes' division in May, 1862.

The 5th New York's reputation was unequaled by any other volunteer regiment. The regiment emulated the uniform and drill of Elmer Ellsworth's Chicago Zouaves, a precision drilling company that gained a huge popular following in the United States before the Civil War. Artillery officer Charles Wainwright observed, "the Fifth New York is equal in all respects to the regulars and better drilled ... very showy in their red trousers and white turbans." The 10th New York ("National Zouaves") was not as well known but had an equally solid reputation. Their colorful zouave uniforms were accidentally burned with a large amount of supplies when the army abandoned the Peninsula in August of 1862, leaving the men to wear the standard blue uniform of the Union infantry.[93]

Sgt. Charles Cowtan of the 10th New York recalled, "the boys hardly liked the nick-name of 'regulars,' which was immediately applied to them by the volunteers of the neighboring camps, and some of the more pugnacious proceeded to vent their discontent upon their comrades of the regular regiments ... and although rivalry existed to a certain extent always, a good feeling grew between the Tenth and their regular comrades."[94]

Warren's zouaves quickly gained renown as fierce and determined fighters in battle. "The regular officers can't speak to[o] highly of us," wrote Pvt. Richard Ackermam of the 5th New York after Gaines' Mill. Warren's brigade attained immortality at Second Manassas. The New Yorkers were virtually destroyed in a brief and forlorn stand against John Hood's Texas brigade on Chinn Ridge. With over 300 casualties, the 5th New York emerged from the battle little more than an oversize company. The 10th New York was not much better off. Warren wrote to his brother on September 5, "I feel so bad about our losses and the desperate state of things."[95]

Arriving at Hall's Hill, Virginia on September 3, the brigade found a contingent of some 200 poorly armed and equipped recruits sent down from New York City to reinforce the 5th New York, doubling the size of the regiment. Warren and a few regimental officers had until September 6 to show the new men the rudiments of drill before they were off to pursue Lee's army as it moved into Maryland.

124

The brigade rejoined Sykes' division at its Rockville, Maryland encampment on September 9.[96]

The brigade took up the march two days later, passing through Middlebrook and Urbana. Twenty more recruits for the 5th New York caught up with brigade at Frederick on September 13. One of them, Arthur Hendricks, was shocked at the condition of the regiment, "sunburned and weather-beaten, their uniforms spoiled and ragged beyond description."[97]

Warren's brigade brought up the rear of Sykes' division as it continued its advance. The men reached Middletown on September 14 and advanced over Fox's Gap the next day, following the Union victory at South Mountain. Passing a line of dead rebels sprawled along the mountain road, young Hendricks recalled, "my impression as a man (or boy) new to the business, was not favorable to war as a regular occupation."[98]

## Antietam

The brigade reached Boonsboro Pike late in the afternoon of September 15 and established a battle line in the rear of the two regular brigades. The next morning, stray rounds of Confederate artillery fire fell among Warren's men. Sykes ordered the brigade moved further back to an oak grove covering the approaches from Harpers Ferry. Lt. Alanson Randol's divisional battery reported to Warren and unlimbered to the right of his brigade.

During their move, the soldiers of the 10th New York recognized Joseph Mansfield, their old commander from Fort Monroe, as he cantered by with his staff. "His soldierly form and patriarchal beard were at once recognized by the regiment, and officers and men cheered him lustily, and crowded around him to tender a true soldierly greeting. The old general seemed much affected by the tribute from his old friends and returned their salutation with many hearty words and sturdy grips of the hand."[99]

As the battle raged across Antietam Creek on September 17, Warren's men stacked arms and awaited further orders. Gen. Porter finally detached the brigade from Sykes' division at 2:00 p.m. and ordered it to the left to support the IX Corps as Ambrose Burnside's men prepared to resume the advance west of the Lower Bridge. Warren's brigade moved 1,600 yards southwest to a position on the high ground overlooking the bridge. The men expected to be ordered into the attack and get "wiped out." Instead, when Ambrose Hill's division attacked the IX Corps and stragglers began streaming over the bridge, Warren pulled the brigade off the high ground to an open field near the Henry Rohrbach farm and established a straggler's line. Capt. Cleveland Winslow reported, "stopping all stragglers from going to the rear, [and] forming them as they came off the battlefield irrespective of regiment or division." The brigade held that position for the rest of the day.[100]

## Shepherdstown

The brigade moved through Sharpsburg on September 19 and formed line of battle on the left of Sykes' division. The men bivouacked near the Potomac River on a hill overlooking Blackford's Ford. Reaching the bluff, enemy artillery opened fire and struck down Warren's orderly. The brigade opened fire on the enemy across the river and the new recruits fired their muskets in anger for the first time. Their fire reduced the enemy's small arms fire and prevented enemy cannoneers from manning their guns.[101]

Sykes ordered Warren's brigade across the Potomac River around 10:00 a.m. on September 20 to support Lovell's brigade, which was falling back to the river under heavy Confederate pressure. Sensing some unsteadiness in the ranks of his nervous recruits, Warren drew his revolver and shouted, "Men we are about to cross the river, if any man does not want to cross, let him step out." Properly motivated, the zouaves crossed the waist-deep river, scaled a sheer bluff using both hands and feet, and took position on the left of Lovell's brigade. Throwing out a skirmish line, the brigade was met by a sharp fire of musketry from Brig. Gen. Edward Thomas' Georgians on the right side of Hill's advancing division. Lt. Col. John Marshall, commanding the 10th New York, calmly stood with folded arms in the regiment's rear, "a well-defined mark for the enemy's fire." Cowtan recalled, "all hands retained an unpleasant recollection of the Union disaster at Ball's Bluff, in 1861, and did not wish for a repetition in this instance."[102]

Porter arrived and immediately ordered his troops back across the Potomac River to the Maryland side. Tumbling down the bluff, Warren's two regiments effected the movement without loss. Warren stood in the middle of the river and personally guided his men across the narrow line of the ford. Company E of the 5th New York was sent across the river again at 4:00 p.m. to protect a party of stragglers from the regiment who were sent over to retrieve an abandoned 6-pound brass howitzer. The rest of the brigade was posted behind the embankment on the canal, connected to Buchanan's brigade on the left.[103]

Because Warren's brigade was a shadow of its former self after Second Manassas, Sykes was wise to limit its role at Antietam. Though it performed capably holding back stragglers at the Lower Bridge, the undermanned brigade could serve as little more than an effective skirmish line at Shepherdstown. Sgt. George Mitchell spoke for the entire 5th New York when he wrote, "the regiment will never again be the regiment it has been."[104]

**James A. Rosebrock**

\* \* \*

# VI Corps—

## Major General William B. Franklin

Major General George McClellan created two new provisional corps on May 18, 1862 after receiving permission from the Lincoln Administration. One was the VI Corps, assigned to Brig. Gen. William Franklin. Born in York, Pennsylvania on February 27, 1823, Franklin graduated first in his West Point Class of 1843 and was assigned to the Army Corps of Topographical Engineers. Zachary Taylor recognized him for gallantry in his official report during the Mexican War. Franklin was an excellent engineer, who served with distinction in a number of roles, such as the Architect for the Capital building, but despite his many years in the army, Capt. Franklin had never commanded infantry by the time the winds of war began blowing in 1860. Shortly after the surrender of Fort Sumter, Franklin was one of three officers appointed by Lincoln to draft a plan to expand the regular army. He was promoted to colonel on May 14, 1861 and given command of the 12th U. S. Infantry. Gov. Curtin of Pennsylvania simultaneously telegraphed an offer appointing him major general of Pennsylvania forces, which he declined. Before taking command of the VI Corps, Franklin gained limited experience as a brigade commander under Brig. Gen. Samuel Heintzelman. But for the 1st Minnesota, his brigade's performance was anything but effective.[1]

The VI Corps' first engagement, albeit limited, was at the Battle of Gaines' Mill, where Brig. Gen. Henry Slocum's division was sent across the Chickahominy River to support the V Corps, and lost heavily, while Brig. Gen. William "Baldy" Smith's division engaged the enemy with long range artillery. The VI Corps saw no further action in the Seven Days Battles. Franklin was promoted to major general on July 4, 1862. In late June, due to the administration's dissatisfaction with McClellan's performance, Maj. Gen. John Pope was summoned from the west to command the newly formed Union Army of Virginia. McClellan became embroiled in disputes with the high command over sending troops to Pope and withheld the VI Corps until August 30. As a result, Franklin arrived just in time to cover the Federal retreat. In the aftermath of the Second Manassas fiasco, Franklin was one of three officers accused by Pope of misconduct and Lincoln relieved him of command on September 5, 1862. Much to the objection of his cabinet, Lincoln saw no choice but to restore McClellan to command of the Federal troops around the Capital in the face of the first Confederate invasion of Maryland. Franklin had been a loyal subordinate to McClellan and the latter wrote of Franklin, "… he was one of the best officers I had; very powerful. He was a man not only of excellent judgement, but of remarkably high order of intellectual ability." By contrast, Maj. Gen. Phil Kearny saw a different Franklin: "believe me that [he] is no soldier. With all his mind he feels it, and in the hour of need, he dreads to show up." Still, McClellan's pleadings convinced Lincoln to suspend the proceedings against Franklin.[2]

As part of his plan to seek out the Army of Northern Virginia, McClellan established three "wings" and set them in motion out of Washington and through Maryland. Franklin commanded the southernmost or left wing, comprised of the VI Corps and Maj. Gen. Darius Couch's division (IV Corps), moving along the Potomac River. The VI Corps camped near Alexandria, Virginia between September 2-6, then crossed the Potomac River to begin the 1862 Maryland Campaign. The VI Corps marched from Georgetown through Tennallytown, Rockville, Darnestown, Licksville, Barnesville, and finally Buckeystown, where it went into camp. Upon receiving a copy of Lee's Special Order 191, McClellan put his army in motion with the general intent to "… cut the enemy in two and beat him in detail." Little Mac ordered Franklin to move at daybreak

127

on September 14 by way of Jefferson and Burkittsville, through Crampton's Gap to enter Pleasant Valley. McClellan's dispatch included a complicated set of scenarios that, in the end, caused the already overly cautious Franklin to *overthink* his assignment. McClellan wanted Franklin to synchronize his attack with those taking place at the northern gaps, overtake Maj. Gen. Lafayette McLaws' Confederate forces and relieve Col. Dixon Miles' Harpers Ferry garrison. Miles' troops were then to join Franklin, destroy bridges on the Potomac River, leave troops to guard fords the rebels might use, and head for Boonsboro by way of Rohrersville. He was then to march "… to either Sharpsburg or Williamsport to cut off D.H. Hill and Longstreet or prevent Jackson from reinforcing them." Historian Scott Hartwig wrote: "It is doubtful McClellan expected all this to be accomplished in one day, but Franklin's mission and the force he was given to complete it might have daunted even Stonewall Jackson."[3]

The VI Corps marched at first light (about 5:30 a.m.) on September 14 over Catoctin Mountain at Mountville Pass and halted about three miles west of Jefferson. Contrary to McClellan's orders, he waited for two and a half hours for Couch's division to arrive, but it never did. Franklin squandered precious daylight with perfect weather before continuing his march on to Burkittsville. Slocum's division led the column, arriving two miles east of the village around noon. Skirmishers drove enemy pickets back through the town and up the base of South Mountain while a Confederate battery greeted the Federals. Franklin was convinced the enemy was in force, when in fact he outnumbered Col. Thomas Munford's small force by about 12:1 and McLaws' entire force by 3:1. Franklin established headquarters in Martin Shafer's yard and ordered Slocum's division forward through Burkittsville. Given the steepness of the ascent, Franklin knew the Federal guns would not be effective, necessitating an infantry attack. Col. Joseph Bartlett, commanding Slocum's old brigade, was summoned to headquarters. He recalled finding Franklin, Smith, Slocum, Brig. Gens. William T.H. Brooks, Winfield Scott Hancock, and John Newton "resting on the ground … smoking cigars." They wanted to know "on which side of the road and leading over the pass I would attack." Bartlett immediately replied, "on the right," whereupon Franklin declared that to be the point of attack and designated Bartlett to lead it.

McClellan had by now ordered Franklin to mass his troops and "carry Burkittsville at all costs" along with vague alternatives. Bartlett launched his attack in late afternoon while Franklin ordered two of Baldy Smith's brigades to protect Slocum's flank. Bartlett and Col. Alfred Torbert launched a bayonet charge over open ground as Newton's brigade followed Bartlett's and supported Torbert's right flank. Newton's brigade charged forward as Bartlett's men expended their ammunition and fell back. Franklin could not see his troops as they entered the woods and began their climb after the fleeing enemy troops. McLaws certainly understood the importance of protecting Crampton's Gap. Upon hearing word of the Union attack, he sent orders at noon to Brig. Gen. Howell Cobb at Sandy Hook to hold the gap if it cost the lives of every man in his command. Cobb's 1,300 Georgians arrived as darkness enveloped the battlefield and the fighting intensified. By 5:20 p.m., Franklin doubted his ability to take Crampton's Gap and sent word to Little Mac, "the force of the enemy is too great for us to take the pass tonight I am afraid." Despite Franklin's impressions, his troops prevailed. Cobb's troops were almost annihilated and Munford's were scattered, resulting in 179 Confederate dead, 317 wounded, nearly 400 prisoners, 700 stands of arms, 3 stand of colors, and one artillery piece at a cost of 533 Union casualties. Franklin boasted in a letter to his wife: "one of the prettiest fights of the war and I arranged the details of it myself." Franklin appears not to have considered how he failed to achieve his primary assignment: "to cut off, destroy or capture McLaws' command and relieve Col. Miles." Miles surrendered his garrison early the following morning. Franklin's poor generalship enabled the Confederate capture of Harpers Ferry.[4]

Franklin claimed he did not reach the top of the gap until 7:00 a.m. on September 15. He and Baldy Smith determined an attack on the Confederates in Pleasant Valley would be suicidal, as they continued believing the enemy outnumbered them by a factor of at least two to one. McLaws stretched troops clear across the Pleasant Valley during the night to protect his rear, with only a quarter of the VI Corps' strength. As the Army of the Potomac's main body moved toward Sharpsburg, the VI Corps stood fast guarding its left flank. McLaws withdrew his forces and crossed the Potomac River early on Tuesday, September 16. Historian Steven Stotelmyer believes Franklin's pending court-martial and potentially even more serious allegations may have influenced his overly cautious moves at Crampton's Gap.[5]

McClellan directed Franklin to send Couch's division to Maryland Heights while the VI Corps marched to Keedysville at first light on September 17. Smith's division led the column and arrived at 11:00 a.m. on the battlefield to support John Sedgwick's division (II Corps). A short time later, McClellan pulled Brig. Gen. Winfield S. Hancock from his brigade to replace mortally wounded Israel Richardson. Slocum's division arrived on the field soon afterward and was sent to the Union right. Around midday, Longstreet ordered the 27th North Carolina and the 3rd Arkansas to make an attack on the Union right flank at the Sunken Road. As Nathan Kimball's brigade (William French's division, II Corps) responded, the 7th Maine of Col. William Irwin's brigade moved to the Dunker Church plateau, faced west and delivered a punishing fire on the Confederate left flank, that helped end the Confederate attack.[6]

Franklin was firmly convinced his corps could smash Lee's left and contemplated an attack upon it. He positioned Newton's and Torbert's brigades of Slocum's division to carry the West Woods and take Nicodemus Heights. Sumner arrived and ordered a postponement of the attack, launching a disagreement among the two corps commanders. Franklin was so determined he requested McClellan's intervention. McClellan soon arrived on the scene and after considering both arguments, consented to making the attack the following morning. Newton's, Hancock's, and Torbert's brigades remained in support of the Union batteries positioned along the edge of the East Woods. Around 5:00 p.m., Irwin ordered the 7th Maine to attack Confederate skirmishers in Piper's orchard and around the buildings that menaced Lt. Edward Williston's battery on the Mumma farm. The charge carried them over open ground for 600 yards to the orchard and a half mile between their starting position and the barn. The Mainers were exposed to 30 minutes of severe fire and suffered 88 casualties, without having an effect on the enemy.[7]

McClellan rescinded his approval of the VI Corps' attack on the Confederate left on the night of September 17. After a standoff overnight and through September 18, Lee quietly slipped back across the Potomac River by way of Shepherdstown Ford back into the Old Dominion. The VI Corps lost a total of 533 men at Crampton Gap on September 14 and another 439 at Antietam.[8]

Upon the removal of McClellan on November 7, new army commander, Maj. Gen. Ambrose Burnside reorganized the army and gave Franklin command of the "Left Grand Division." Formal charges were never filed against him.[9]

**Gary W Rohrer**

* * *

# 1st DIVISION—

## Major General Henry Slocum

The 1st Division was initially commanded by William Franklin, but upon his ascension to command the VI Corps during the Army of the Potomac's reorganization, brigade commander Brig. Gen. Henry Slocum assumed command of the division. The unit lost heavily (2,000 men out of 8,000) at the Battle of Gaines' Mill, but did not see action in the other Seven Days Battles. One of its brigades, the First New Jersey Brigade, was engaged on August 27 at Second Bull Run, but the rest of the division was in Washington at the time. Slocum's division was a veteran unit by the start of the Maryland Campaign, but most had not seen action for over two months.[10]

Henry Slocum was born in New York, a direct descendent of one of the first Englishmen who arrived in America in 1637. He attended a seminary and then taught for several years before securing an appointment to West Point, where he graduated in 1852. He resigned in 1856 to begin a law practice. Slocum also joined the New York State Militia and rose to the rank of colonel. He assumed command of the 27th New York with the rank of colonel in May 1861. The two-year outfit saw action at First Bull Run, where Slocum was wounded in the thigh. Upon returning to duty, Slocum was given a brigade in Franklin's division, and later assumed command of the division during the spring of 1862, and was promoted to the rank of major general in July. Slocum was described as "small and rather spare" having sparkling brown eyes that gave him "magnetic power over his troops." To those close to him, Slocum was self-contained, unemotional, and highly cautious.[11]

Slocum's division broke camp at Centreville, Virginia at sundown on September 1 and marched to Fairfax Court House. It reached Alexandria, Virginia the following day, and then crossed the Long Bridge into Washington on September 6, camping beyond Tennallytown the following evening. The division continued its march and traveled through Muddy Run, Seneca Run, and Barnsville on successive days, reaching the Monocacy River in Maryland on September 12. Slocum's division broke camp the following day and marched to the foot of Catoctin Mountain, near Jefferson.

September 14 would prove to be a pivotal day in the division's history. It was tasked with fighting its way through South Mountain at Crampton's Gap to allow the entire VI Corps, plus Couch's division, to enter Pleasant Valley and lift the siege of Harpers Ferry, and possibly destroy isolated enemy units. The men were up early, marching through Jefferson and reaching Burkittsville that afternoon.[12]

Col. Joseph Bartlett's brigade led the column toward Burkittsville and it threw out the 96th Pennsylvania to drive the enemy pickets out of town. The remainder of the division remained a half-mile east of the village, concealed from the enemy's artillery deployed at Crampton's Gap. Slocum deployed his division for the attack at 3:00 p.m. Bartlett's brigade was on the front line, followed by Brig. Gen. John Newton's brigade and then Col. Alfred Torbert's First New Jersey Brigade. Each brigade was deployed in two lines, 200 yards apart. Slocum's division advanced to within 300 yards of the enemy's position at the base of the mountain. He did not know it at the time, but he faced a weak combined force of Col. Thomas Munford's cavalry brigade (Maj. Gen. James "Jeb" Stuart's cavalry division), Brig. Gen. William Mahone's infantry brigade (under Col. William Parham; Maj. Gen. R.H. Anderson's division), and a portion of a regiment from Brig. Gen. Paul Semmes' brigade (Maj. Gen. Lafayette McLaws' division). Munford commanded the weak sector, but reinforcements from Brig. Gen. Howell Cobb's brigade (McLaws' division) were on the way.

The Confederate artillery half way up the mountainside opened fire on the 1st Division, but Slocum had no remedy, as he had left his artillery in the rear. Slocum sized up the enemy position and feared "the stone wall behind which the enemy had taken cover would prove an insurmountable obstacle to the advance of my lines," so he "at once used every effort to bring forward a battery, with the view of driving the enemy from his position." He didn't need the battery, as Bartlett launched the charge before it could drop trail. Slocum beamed in his official report how the enemy was "overcome by a most gallant charge of the infantry, and the enemy were fleeing in confusion up the mountain, closely pursued by every regiment of the division except the one in reserve, each vying with the other in the pursuit."[13]

It was a bit more complicated than explained by Slocum in his report. Bartlett's brigade outpaced Newton's by 600 yards—far more than the ordered 200 yards. This forced a halt to allow Newton's brigade to catch up. Bartlett's ammunition was running low, so Newton's regiments moved forward to replace them. Prior to the charge, Torbert's Jerseymen swung to the left and attacked on Bartlett's left, thus extending the line in that direction. Slocum called for support and received Brig. Gen. William Brook's Vermont brigade from Maj. Gen. William Smith's division and it trotted into position on Torbert's left.

Few engagements are as decisive as the one on September 14 at Crampton's Gap. Not only did Slocum's men drive Munford's men from their defensive line at the base of the hill, they drove them up the mountainside, destroying at least one enemy unit arriving to reinforce Munford, and driving away the others. The Confederates lost 873 men compared with Slocum's 514 (112 killed; 400 wounded; 2 missing).[14]

The division camped at Crampton's Gap that evening and remained there until ordered to join McClellan's army near Antietam Creek on the morning of September 17. The men arrived on the battlefield about noon and took position near the Dunker Church. "Our infantry, though not actively engaged, were exposed to a heavy artillery fire from the enemy until sundown, and are entitled to great credit for their gallantry under a severe fire, which they were unable to return," Slocum stated in his report. Although the infantrymen fired not a shot, the enemy's artillery took its toll, causing 65 casualties (5 killed; 58 wounded; 2 missing).[15]

Slocum's division may not have played a role at the Battle of Antietam, but the potential strategic value of its victory at Crampton's Gap cannot be overstated. By taking the gap, the VI Corps had access to Harpers Ferry and the rear of two isolated Confederate divisions. Harpers Ferry, however, capitulated on September 15, denying the VI Corps further glory in the Pleasant Valley.

**Bradley M. Gottfried**

* * *

## 1st Brigade: Colonel Alfred Torbert

**Units:** 1st New Jersey, 2nd New Jersey, 3rd New Jersey, 4th New Jersey
**Strength:** 1,513[16]
**Losses:** 19 (2k-17w-0m)[17]

The "First New Jersey Brigade" was one of the few brigades with units from the same state, and this gave the unit its unique moniker. All four regiments were recruited from around New Jersey from May through August 1861. The first three regiments were not on the First Bull Run battlefield, but formed the army's rearguard. The brigade first saw action at Gaines' Mill during the Seven Days Battles, where the entire 4th New Jersey was captured and its men forced to march through Richmond amid the taunts of its citizens. The unit was exchanged during the second week in August 1862, in time to participate in the Second Bull Run Campaign. Early in the campaign, the brigade was sent to the bridge over Bull Run where it ran into Maj. Gen. "Stonewall" Jackson's entire wing. It was forced to beat a hasty retreat, but not before it lost a number of men, including its commander, Brig.

Gen. George Taylor, who was mortally wounded. The brigade was a solid unit that had the bad luck of being sent into difficult situations. That would change during the Maryland Campaign.[18]

Col. Alfred Thomas Archimedes Torbert was an enigma. A Delaware native, Torbert graduated from West Point in 1855 and served in Texas, Florida, Missouri, Utah, and New Mexico until the outbreak of the war. He took a leave of absence from the army from February 25, 1861 through April 17, 1861, and during this time, he apparently gained an appointment as a lieutenant of artillery in the Confederate army. When he returned to the Union army in April, he was sent to New Jersey to muster in new recruits and on September 16, became the colonel of the 1st New Jersey. He led his regiment through the Second Bull Run Campaign, and assumed command of the brigade upon the death of Taylor. He would cut his teeth in higher command during the Maryland Campaign. Torbert was respected by his men and superiors and rose in rank, eventually commanding a cavalry division in 1864.[19]

Torbert's brigade, with the rest of Henry Slocum's division, began its trek north on September 6 when it crossed the Potomac River via Long Bridge and entered Washington. In subsequent days, the brigade passed through Tenallytown, Darnestown, Barnesville, and Urbana, reaching Catoctin Mountain on September 13.

## South Mountain

The men broke camp at 6:00 a.m. on September 14 at Buckeystown and reached the village of Burkittsville, at the foot of South Mountain. VI Corps commander, William Franklin, tasked Slocum's division with capturing Crampton's Gap to gain entry into the Pleasant Valley. Once in the valley, the division could turn south and swoop down toward Harpers Ferry. Slocum began deploying his men at 4:00 p.m. just outside the village of Burkittsville. Joseph Bartlett's brigade would lead the attack, followed by John Newton's and then Torbert's, with 200-yards between each brigade. Just prior to the attack, Torbert's brigade, in the rear, swung to the left and formed on Newton's left flank. The column then marched a half-mile closer to the gap and halted when it was within 300 yards of the thin line of Confederate defenders. Torbert's brigade was deployed in two lines of regiments. The 1st and 2nd New Jersey formed the first line and the 3rd and 4th New Jersey formed the second, separated by about 150 paces.[20]

Thomas Munford, in temporary command of Brig. Gen. Beverly Robertson's cavalry brigade, was in command of the Confederate defenses. He also had infantry at his disposal. Munford chose to position his men at the bottom of the mountain rather than the top, with three Virginia units lined up behind a high fence on Mountain Church Road: the 16th Virginia Infantry, the 12th Virginia Infantry (both from William Parham's/William Mahone's brigade; R.H. Anderson's division), and the 2nd Virginia Cavalry of Robertson's brigade. Eight companies of the 10th Georgia (Paul

Semmes' brigade; Lafayette McLaws' division) were deployed further to the left. Confederate reinforcements were rushing to Crampton's Gap, but would they arrive soon enough to make the difference?[21]

The 1st and 2nd New Jersey were ordered to lie behind a low stone wall until ordered to advance, but the men could not restrain themselves. Hopping on the wall, they shook their fists at the Virginians and taunted them to come out and fight. Several shots rang out and a couple of Jerseymen toppled from the wall while the rest quickly hunkered down behind their protective barrier. This began a small arms fire fight that lasted about 25 minutes. Confederate artillery on the heights made matters worse when they rained shells down on the Union position. Slocum quickly realized he had erred in not bringing up his own artillery, thinking the terrain was too difficult. He finally ordered up his guns, but they would arrive too late to have an impact.[22]

Bartlett rode over from the right of the division to confer with Torbert and they concluded the only way to end the bombardment would be to capture the enemy's defensive line at the base of the mountain and then drive up to its summit. Torbert agreed and ordered his second line forward, leapfrogging over his first. The 3rd and 4th New Jersey jogged toward the enemy line yelling "Avenge Kearny," referring to their fallen initial brigade leader, Maj. Gen. Phil Kearny, who had fallen at the Battle of Chantilly, and "Remember Manassas and Gaines' Mill;" two particularly upsetting defeats. The brigade had never tasted victory since mustering into service and the men sensed this was their opportunity. The newly released men of the 4th New Jersey also yelled, "Remember Belle Island and Richmond." The 1st and 2nd New Jersey picked up the yells as they advanced about 150 yards behind the first line.[23]

The men were pounded by enemy artillery and small arms fire, but were not to be denied. The commander of the 3rd New Jersey reported the enemy sharpshooters "delivered their fire with great rapidity. But nothing could withstand the onset of our men." The veteran Virginian defenders knew a hopeless situation when they saw one and began leaving their positions to scramble up the side of the mountain. A Jerseyman wrote home to his local newspaper: the enemy "broke and run like sheep, and we after them." The commander of the 4th New Jersey reported, "We leaped the walls and continued in pursuit over the mountain into the gorge and up the next ascent to its summit, the enemy retreating in disorder into the valley below." While accurate, it does not fully describe the desperate defense of the enemy along the east side and top of the mountain.[24]

Confederate reinforcements arrived and moved down the steep mountainside to support Munford's men, but they arrived too late. Cobb's Legion (Howell Cobb's brigade; Lafayette McLaws' division) was about halfway down the mountain, when it encountered Torbert's men rushing after Munford's. The regiment's commander, Lt. Col. Jefferson Lamar, made a fateful decision—he would halt his men and give battle to allow the Virginians time to get to safety atop the mountain. The Jerseymen were almost immediately on the Georgians, attacking on three sides. While the 4th New Jersey took on the Georgians' front, the 1st and 2nd New Jersey hit their flank and the 3rd hit their rear. The Legion bent itself back to form a "V" to take on the enemy soldiers. The steep mountainside made footing difficult and fighting hazardous. Realizing the futility of further resistance, Lamar ordered his men to retreat, but not before he was mortally wounded. The Legion lost 33 killed or wounded and 156 fell into the Jerseymen's hands. Cobb's Legion was almost destroyed, sustaining a loss of 76%.[25]

Another of Cobb's regiments, the 16th Georgia, loomed in front of Slocum's division, half-way up the mountainside. While the Jerseymen attacked its right flank and rear, the rest of Slocum's men attacked its front. These Georgians quickly retreated up the hill with heavy losses. Cobb rallied a number of his men at the top of the mountain in a clearing called Padgett's Field. Torbert's brigade shifted a bit to the left and headed up the mountain on Gapland Road. A small enemy cannon deployed on Gapland Road, given the name "Sallie Craig" by its cannoneers, fired into the Jerseymen, but it failed to halt their advance. It quickly limbered and headed to the rear after firing about seven shots. Torbert's men surged up to the top of the mountain, and with the rest of Slocum's men, fell on Cobb's men, forcing them to flee down the west side of the mountain.[26]

The victory was complete. After so many defeats, the Jerseymen had shown the valor and stamina needed to drive the enemy from their front. The brigade lost 172 (38 killed, 134 wounded) but inflicted hundreds of casualties and captured hundreds more.[27]

Franklin chose not to follow the enemy into Pleasant Valley as his men were exhausted and it was already dark. The victorious Jerseymen grabbed supper and then fell into a deep sleep. The following day, the men scrounged the battlefield, collecting about 700 valuable Springfield rifles. Many were given to members of the 4th New Jersey who were armed with smoothbore muskets. Torbert wrote of the regiment, "which lost its colors before Richmond, captured two colors during this engagement." In a congratulatory note to his men, Torbert wrote: "you dashingly met and drove the enemy at every point. Your advance in line of battle, under a galling artillery fire, and final bayonet charge, was a feat seldom if ever surpass[ed] … You have sustained the reputation of your State and done great credit to your officers and yourselves."[28]

## Antietam

Harpers Ferry fell on the morning of September 15, so Torbert's men were permitted to remain on the battlefield—something they had never experienced in the past. Franklin received orders to rejoin the army, cross Antietam Creek, and deploy on the Antietam battlefield on September 17. Slocum's division arrived at 11:00 a.m., halting near D.R. Miller's infamous Cornfield. Torbert's brigade was deployed east of Hagerstown Pike, relieving a portion of the II Corps. The men expected a

Confederate attack, but it never materialized. The Jerseymen spent the next six hours supporting Union artillery in this sector, being pounded by enemy counter-artillery fire all the while. An enlisted man from the 3rd New Jersey noted the "shells flew thick and fast around us as we lay drawn up on three or four lines of battle." Another soldier in the same regiment called it a "very unpleasant situation."[29]

So ended the Maryland Campaign for the First New Jersey Brigade. After being heavily engaged at Crampton's Gap, it played only a minor role at Antietam, losing only 19 (2 killed, 17 wounded). The men would always savor their victory at Crampton's Gap, but it would be the first of many.[30]

**Bradley M. Gottfried**

$* * *$

# 2nd Brigade: Colonel Joseph Bartlett

**Units:** 5th Maine, 16th New York, 27th New York, 121st New York, 96th Pennsylvania,
**Strength:** 2,744[31]
**Losses:** 10 (1k-9w-0m)[32]

The 16th New York, 27th New York, and 5th Maine each saw action at First Bull Run in different brigades. The 16th New York had been part of Col. Thomas Davies' brigade (Dixon Miles' division), and suffered relatively few losses. Col. Henry Slocum's 27th New York (Col. Andrew Porter's brigade) lost 130 men. The 5th Maine (Col. Oliver Howard's brigade) suffered over 400 casualties. The regiments were combined the following month to form Col. Samuel P. Heintzelman's brigade, occupying a camp near Fort Lyon, southwest of Alexandria, Virginia. Brig. Gen. Henry Slocum took command of the brigade in October 1861.[33]

The 96th Pennsylvania joined the brigade in November 1861 and the 121st New York arrived in time to witness the fighting at Crampton's Gap. Slocum's brigade took part in McClellan's advance to Manassas before joining the rest of the army at Yorktown. The VI Corps was organized on May 7, 1862 and Slocum was given command of Maj. Gen. William Franklin's former division. Col. Joseph Bartlett of the 27th New York replaced Slocum as the brigade commander.[34]

Bartlett was a twenty-seven year old lawyer from Binghamton, New York. He was appointed captain of what would become Company C, 27th New York in June 1861, and upon the organization of

the regiment, became its major. When Slocum was wounded at First Bull Run, Bartlett assumed command of the regiment. He was promoted to the rank of colonel of the regiment when Slocum was promoted to brigade command in September 1861.[35]

The four-regiment brigade saw its first action as a unit at Eltham's Landing where it was lightly engaged and sustained only 16 casualties. During the Seven Days, however, Bartlett's brigade lost 546 men at Gaines' Mill, White Oak Swamp, Glendale, and Malvern Hill. The brigade returned to Alexandria in late August 1862 and joined John Pope's Army of Virginia near Bull Run. It arrived too late to participate in the battle and retreated with the rest of the army.[36]

Bartlett's brigade began the Maryland Campaign late on September 6, crossing the Long Bridge over the Potomac River and bivouacking near Tenallytown after a 15-mile march. Their route over the next seven days took the men through Rockville, Darnestown, Hyattstown, and Urbana, on the Army of the Potomac's left flank. On September 13, the brigade marched through Buckeystown, and camped that night on the eastern side of Catoctin Mountain. [37]

## South Mountain

Before dawn on September 14, Bartlett's brigade led the VI Corps over the Catoctin Mountain on the march to Burkittsville, at the foot of South Mountain. Although nearing the enemy, the men had time to admire the scenery. Color bearer William Morse of the 5th Maine noted, "It is the richest and most beautiful country I ever saw, fine farms with an abundance of fruit." Bartlett's brigade, with the rest of the VI Corps, was tasked with punching through South Mountain at Crampton's Gap to enter Pleasant Valley. Once there, the corps could relieve the Union garrison under siege at Harpers Ferry. The march resumed after a brief rest about noon, southwest of Jefferson. The 12th Virginia Cavalry (Munford's brigade) opened a sporadic fire on the column as it neared Burkittsville, at the base of South Mountain. The brigade was brought into line on the left side of the road. The 96th Pennsylvania, already thrown forward as a skirmish line, soon received additional fire from two Confederate batteries on the side of the mountain.[38]

While the 96th Pennsylvania advanced into Burkittsville, the remainder of the brigade withdrew to the safety of Samuel's Run Ravine. Bartlett was summoned to VI Corps headquarters and informed he would lead the assault on Crampton's Gap. He chose to attack on the right (north) side of Burkittsville Road, over the mountain, and "suggested the formation of the three brigades in column of regiments deployed, two regiments front, at 100 paces interval between lines…" Bartlett's brigade began forming up in a large field about 2:00 p.m. The 27th New York formed a skirmish line in front. The 5th Maine on the left, and the 16th New York on the right, following in line 200 yards behind. The 96th Pennsylvania joined the column as it passed Burkittsville. Newton's brigade was 200 yards behind Bartlett's, followed by Torbert's.[39]

The attack began at about 3:30 p.m., as the brigade passed north of Burkittsville through the ridge cut by Burkitt's Run. George Bicknell of the 5th Maine recalled that "(d)uring the forward movement, which was a distance of over three-quarters of a mile from the point where we formed our line of battle, we climbed over five rail fences, marched through a large cornfield, which, under peaceable circumstances, would have caused a great deal of difficulty in keeping any sort of a decent line, and yet all in good order … we advanced with quick strides, until we reached a fair position within about three hundred and fifty yards, perhaps, of the enemy's lines, where, scarcely waiting for the word of command, we opened a fearful fire of musketry." Bartlett ordered the returning 96th Pennsylvania to form on his right.[40]

The enemy regiments were positioned in front of Bartlett's brigade, behind a stone wall along Mountain Church Road. These included the thin 12th and 6th Virginia regiments of William Parham's (Mahone's) brigade (R.H. Anderson's division), the 10th Georgia Regiment (Paul Semmes' brigade; Lafayette McLaws' division), and some troopers of the 2nd Virginia Cavalry (Munford's brigade). A couple of batteries, Capt. Cary Grimes and Capt. Roger Chew's Virginia artillery units, were farther up the mountain, adding to the brisk fire. For some reason, Newton's brigade had not stepped off on time, and failed to come up for nearly half an hour. With no more cover than the rail fence, Bartlett's brigade suffered heavy casualties. Ammunition began running low, and soon, as Bicknell noted, every "round had been expended; and as the soldier sought in vain for another charge in his own box, he eagerly sought the cartridge boxes of the killed and the wounded, discharging their contents as rapidly as possible."[41]

When Newton's brigade finally arrived, its 18th and 32nd New York regiments took position between Bartlett's 16th New York and the 96th Pennsylvania, and his 31st New York and 95th Pennsylvania formed to the left of Bartlett's 5th Maine and 27th New York. Torbert's brigade moved up on the left. Slocum had not thought to bring up artillery, but he quickly called for it and while waiting, Bartlett and Torbert consulted with Newton and decided in short order that only an immediate infantry assault could alleviate the difficult situation. However, when the advance was ordered, only three or four companies of the 27th New York had formed up.[42]

Bicknell recalled, "'Forward,' rang out upon the air, and in a moment the entire division was in motion... our troops moved down a slightly-inclined plane toward the enemy, like an avalanche."

The ground in front of the 96th Pennsylvania on Bartlett's far right presented many obstacles and Col. Henry Cake twice stopped and reformed his regiment so it would not hit the rebel line disorganized. Upon emerging from a cornfield directly in front of the Confederate position, the 96th Pennsylvania received a volley that momentarily staggered the regiment. But, with the rest of the line to their left, it pushed forward and drove the rebels from the road and back up the mountain. The historian of the 27th New York recalled, "As our men went over the wall, some of the rebels tried to retreat, and others threw down their arms and surrendered. Those on the retreat were exposed to our fire from behind, and very few of them made their escape." [43]

"The men fought nobly and pressed on up the steep ascent under a perfect shower of bullets, and their example encouraged others, who faltered before the terrors of the enemy and the steepness of the hill, to follow," wrote the 16th New York's Lt. Col. Joel Seaver. The historian of the 27th New York recalled the side of the mountain was so steep that "the men had to pull themselves up by taking hold of the bushes." As they pushed up the slope, the 15th North Carolina, 16th Georgia and 24th Georgia regiments (Howell Cobb's brigade; McLaws' division) rushed into line before them. "'Down' went the men at my order, and down came a volley from a full regiment or more, and we returned the fire. We had them started, and — they could not help it — they ran," Seaver wrote. They followed the panicked rebels up and through the gap, before darkness halted further pursuit. "The victory was decisive and complete," reported Bartlett, "the routed enemy leaving arms, ammunition, knapsacks, haversacks, and blankets in heaps by the roadside." The 16th New York also captured a battle flag. [44]

Bartlett's brigade had suffered 217 (51 killed; 166 wounded) casualties. It camped on the western slope of South Mountain, where it would stay until the morning of September 17. [45]

## Antietam

Bartlett's brigade followed Torbert's and Newton's on the march from Crampton's Gap to the Antietam battlefield on the morning of September 17. The men saw most of the homes in Keedysville filled with wounded men and the streets clogged with ambulances. Arriving on the field about midday, the brigade was initially diverted by Edwin Sumner to stabilize the right of his badly mauled II Corps. Franklin, however, was awaiting Bartlett's arrival to use it as a reserve for his own assault on the West Woods. The two corps commanders debated the issue until it was decided by McClellan, who ultimately sided with Sumner, saying the attack wasn't necessary, as the battle was already progressing in the Army of the Potomac's favor. The 5th Maine's George Bicknell remembered differently, though, as "[r]umor ran along our lines that the Sixth Corps had all the ammunition there was in the army; that all the other corps had expended theirs, and that the fortunes of the day hung upon the ardor and faithfulness of our corps." [46]

Bartlett's brigade was eventually moved to a position behind Newton's brigade along the East Woods, north of the Smoketown Road. About 3:00 p.m. the 5th Maine and 16th New York were moved to support William Irwin's brigade (Smith's division; VI Corps), with Torbert's brigade on their right and their left resting on the Mumma Lane. They held this position until late afternoon of September 18. Confederate batteries maintained a heavy fire, but the men stayed prone throughout, and there were only ten casualties in the brigade at Antietam. "[W]e passed the night [September 17-18] with no blankets to cover us, nothing to shelter, our supper consisting of hard bread and raw salt pork, surrounded by dead men and horses, in line, in as disagreeable a condition as it is possible to conceive," remembered Bicknell. [47]

Lee's army was discovered gone on the morning of September 19, so Bartlett's brigade marched to the Potomac River, opposite Shepherdstown, Virginia. The brigade, with the rest of the division, made a forced march to Williamsport, Maryland beginning at midnight on September 20. It remained there until September 23, when it moved to Bakersville, northwest of Antietam, and camped there until late October.[48]

**Robert Gottschalk**

*** *** ***

# 3rd Brigade: Brigadier General John Newton

**Units:** 18th New York, 31st New York, 32nd New York, 95th Pennsylvania
**Strength:** 1,759[49]
**Losses:** 21 (1k-20w-0m)[50]

The 18th, 31st, and 32nd New York Infantry Regiments were among the first Union volunteers to enlist following Fort Sumter. All were accepted by the State of New York as two-year regiments. Upon arriving in Washington prior to the end of June 1861, they were brigaded with the 16th New York in Thomas Davies' brigade (Dixon Miles' division). Although present at Fairfax Court House, Blackburn's Ford, and First Bull Run, no soldiers died and only a handful were wounded during their first campaign.[51]

William Franklin briefly took command of the brigade in August 1861, after Davies and the 16th New York were reassigned. Upon Franklin's promotion to division command in October, John Newton replaced him as brigade commander. The New Yorkers were joined by the 95th Pennsylvania at the end of that month. The 95th was a three-year regiment, largely recruited in the Philadelphia area.[52]

Forty-year-old Virginia native John Newton graduated second in the West Point Class of 1842, and remained there as an engineering instructor for the following three years. He later served in the Army Corps of Engineers, married, and worked on military installations along the Atlantic Coast and the Great Lakes. In 1858 he served as chief engineer on the Utah Expedition. The outbreak of war in 1861 found Newton at Fort Delaware, as Chief Engineer of the Department of Pennsylvania. In spite of his limited field experience, Newton was promoted to brigadier general in September 1861 and took command of the brigade the following month.[53]

Newton's brigade was camped below Alexandria, Virginia during the winter of 1861-62, and assisted in the construction of Ft. Ward. After taking part in McClellan's advance on Manassas in March 1862, it joined the rest of the army at Yorktown in late April. Newton's brigade saw its first real battle on May 7 at Eltham's Landing, on the Pamunkey River, where it sustained 166 casualties. It lost heavily (409) at Gaines' Mill and lost a couple hundred more at White Oak Swamp and Malvern Hill. The brigade arrived back in the Washington area on August 30, too late to take part in Second Bull Run.[54]

The Maryland Campaign began for Newton's brigade late on September 6, when the VI Corps crossed the Long Bridge over the Potomac River and headed north. The VI Corps served as the army's left flank, and by nightfall of September 13, was camped near Licksville, Maryland, on the eastern side of Catoctin Mountain. After reviewing a copy of Lee's Special Orders Number 191 which split his army, McClellan tasked the VI Corps with driving through South Mountain at Crampton's Gap and entering Pleasant Valley to relieve the Harpers Ferry garrison.[55]

## South Mountain

The VI Corps, with Slocum's division in the van, began its march to Burkittsville, at the foot of South Mountain, before dawn on September 14. The vanguard reached Jefferson at 8:00 a.m. and halted to allow the rest of the corps to catch up. The march resumed about 10:30 a.m. [56]

The division arrived behind the ridge along Broad Run Village Road, near Burkittsville, about noon. The men were permitted to rest and prepare food and coffee while the corps' senior officers planned the assault on Crampton's Gap. Col. Bartlett of the 2nd brigade would oversee the assault, probably because Newton was ill and traveling with the column in an ambulance. Bartlett chose to attack in columns of brigades, with his brigade in front and Newton's 200 yards behind it. Newton's would be close enough to provide support, when and if needed.[57]

Newton's brigade began forming up behind Bartlett's at about 2:00 p.m. in a large field, two regiments across and two deep. The first line was composed of the 18th New York on the left and the 32nd New York to its right. The second line had the 95th Pennsylvania on the left and the 31st New York to its right. It would be a nearly two-mile advance, passing north of Burkittsville through the ridge cut by Burkitt's Run. Newton decided to lead his brigade's advance, mustering enough energy to leave the ambulance and mount his horse.[58]

Bartlett's men stepped off at 4:00 p.m., but for reasons unknown, Newton's brigade failed to advance in a timely manner and a gap of nearly 1,000 yards opened between the two brigades. Bartlett's men approached a flimsy rail fence, where they slugged it out alone with the thin Confederate line at the foot of the mountain along Mountain Church Road. Newton finally arrived within a half hour, just as Bartlett's two front regiments (5th Maine and 16th New York) were running low on ammunition. Newton's 32nd New York and 18th New York on the front line advanced to spell them. Col. Alfred Torbert's brigade also came up on their left about this time. Newton's 31st New York and 95th Pennsylvania also arrived and formed on the left of the brigade. The Confederate artillery on the mountainside pounded the men, but Slocum had no way of stopping it, because he had left his own artillery behind.[59]

A consultation among the three brigade commanders ended with an agreement that an immediate attack was needed to avoid a battle of attrition. Slocum's men were up against a thin line of Confederates behind a stone wall lining Mountain Church Road, including the small 12th and 6th Virginia infantry regiments of Parham's (Mahone's) brigade (Anderson's division), and the 10th Georgia infantry regiment of Semmes' brigade (McLaws' division). Bartlett carefully aligned his attack column. Bartlett's 96th Pennsylvania was on the far right, with Newton's 32nd New York and 18th New York on its left. To the left of Newton's 18th New York were another three regiments of Bartlett's brigade, followed by the 95th Pennsylvania and 31st New York. Torbert's New Jerseymen were on the left of the line.[60]

With all in readiness, Bartlett gave the order to charge. Lt. Col. Francis Pinto of the 32nd New York reported, "I instantly gave the order to charge, which was promptly obeyed by jumping a fence and passing through a corn-field with an unearthly yell." Newton added, "The charge was short and decisive, and the enemy was driven from his stronghold in a very few moments, although our loss was severe in accomplishing this object." Capt. Edward Tilley of the brigade staff claimed, "The boys went up the hill with a will and did not stop until everything in sight in the shape of a rebel, was cleaned out." Sgt. Frank Seymour of the 18th New York boasted at how "our bodies seemed endowed with supernatural strength, and forward up the mountains we pushed, the Rebels flying like frightened hares before us." Newton's regiments became intermingled, but the brigade drove on. A second Confederate line along the Arnoldstown Road, composed of the 15th North Carolina and 24th Georgia (Cobb's brigade; McLaws' division), was also overrun, but not before it inflicted losses on the right of the brigade, where Col. Roderick Matheson of the 18th New York and Maj. George Lemon of the 32nd New York fell mortally wounded, the former yelling "You've got 'em boys, push on!"[61]

The 31st New York and 95th Pennsylvania pushed to the summit of the mountain where they received canister blasts from a section of the Troup Artillery of Georgia. Most of the deadly missiles overshot the regiments, and Col. Gustavus Town of the 95th Pennsylvania proclaimed his "line recoiled but for a moment, and then, with shouts, charged upon it, firing as it advanced, the shots being directed by the flash of the artillery, as it was now too dark to distinguish the gunners at that distance." As the 95th Pennsylvania closed in, one of the guns, a lone 12-lb. howitzer marked, "Jennie," was abandoned. With darkness enveloping the battlefield, Bartlett halted the advance.[62]

The victory was complete, and the enemy was routed. Francis Pinto of the 32nd New York reported his regiment alone rounded up 130 prisoners. The entire brigade lost 124 men (24 killed, 98 wounded, 2 missing) in achieving its smashing victory. The 18th New York on the right of the line sustained 58 casualties—the most in the brigade. Newton reassembled his brigade after the battle and the men camped below the gap on the western side of South Mountain, where they remained for the next two days.[63]

### Antietam

Newton's brigade began its march to join the army along Antietam Creek at about 5:30 a.m. on September 17. It passed through Keedysville and crossed Antietam Creek at the Upper Bridge, arriving on the Antietam battlefield between 11:00 a.m. and noon. According to Slocum, the brigade was immediately "formed in column of attack" along the western edge of the East Woods, in preparation for an assault on the West Woods near the Dunker Church. Torbert's brigade formed on its left, astride the Smoketown Road. Left to right in front of Newton's men were Consolidated Batteries A & C, 4th U.S. Artillery, Battery A, Maryland Light Artillery, and Battery B, Maryland Light Artillery.[64]

II Corps commander Edwin Sumner, the ranking officer on the Union right, diverted Bartlett's brigade to help stiffen his own badly mauled right flank, and postponed any VI Corps attack. Slocum wrote, "Our infantry, though not actively engaged, were exposed to a heavy artillery fire from the enemy until sundown, and are entitled to great credit for their gallantry under a severe fire, which they were unable to return." Bronson Mills of the 18th New York wrote how the shelling was "the severest that our boys ever received, shell and solid shot were everywhere visible." The brigade lost 21 men at Antietam.

Newton's brigade remained in this position until the morning of September 19, when it was discovered the Army of Northern Virginia was gone. The 31st New York pushed into the West Woods, where it skirmished with the Confederate rearguard and took some prisoners.[65]

The overall casualties in Newton's brigade in the Maryland Campaign were light—145. After the battle, the brigade briefly moved to the Potomac River near Boteler's Ford, and after several days, marched to Bakersville, a few miles northwest of the battlefield. The brigade had finally tasted victory after sustaining a series of losses at the hands of the enemy.[66]

**Robert Gottschalk**

\* \* \*

# 2ND DIVISION—

## Major General William Smith

The VI Corps' 2nd Division was formed during the Army of the Potomac's reorganization in March 1862. It was a stable veteran organization; its three brigades were essentially the same from the start and two of its three brigade commanders, Brig. Gen. Winfield Hancock and Brig. Gen. W. T. Brooks, had served from its inception. Only Col. William Irwin of the Third Brigade was new to his command—he was appointed just after the Peninsula Campaign. Smith was one of the most experienced leaders in the army. Born in Vermont in 1824, Smith graduated from West Point in 1845, standing fourth in his class. He served in a variety of engineering posts and as a West Point instructor prior to the war. Nicknamed "Baldy" for his thinning hair during his days at West Point, Smith began the war as colonel of the 3rd Vermont and served on Maj. Gen. Irvin McDowell's staff. He quickly rose to brigade and then division command. He cultivated a friendship with George McClellan, who noted he "possessed great personal courage & a wonderfully quick eye for ground & for handling troops." Smith could also rub others the wrong way, which would lead to his removal from command later in 1862. Hancock and Brooks were also seasoned and effective leaders who would both rise to corps command later in the war. After an effective performance at Antietam, Irwin was wounded in the foot at Fredericksburg and resigned his commission in October, 1863.[67]

Smith's division marched north with the rest of the VI Corps, passing through Alexandria, Virginia, over the Chain Bridge to Washington and then to Rockville, Maryland. The division subsequently tramped through Barnesville, Buckeystown, and Jefferson. The marches exhausted the men, who were "forced beyond their powers to endure," causing many to fall by the roadsides. Those who remained in the ranks were buoyed by their receptions at Maryland towns along the way. James Anderson of the 5th Wisconsin wrote home that while passing through Jefferson, the men "were greeted with the greatest enthusiasm [as] flags floated from nearly every window and the ladies waved their handkerchiefs from every balcony." He admitted, "this aroused our patriotism which was becoming dormant." Anderson noted a change in the men as "The sallowness of face has given place to flush, the grumbling of dissatisfaction to joyous hilarity, [and] camp at night, even after our long marches resounds with mirth and music." [68]

The VI Corps marched through Jefferson on September 14, heading for battle at the South Mountain pass of Crampton's Gap. After Slocum's division took the gap, the division, with the remainder of the corps was tasked with entering the Pleasant Valley (on the west side of South Mountain) and drive south to relieve the siege of Harpers Ferry. Smith's division reached Burkittsville, at the foot of Crampton's Gap at about 1:00 p.m. The division remained in reserve until a brigade was needed to support the 1st Division's left flank. Brooks' brigade was detailed for this duty and it moved forward on the left side of Burkittsville Road with the 4th Vermont in the van. Brooks sent out skirmishers and the brigade followed, advancing "under a sharp fire of skirmishers." The Vermonters, with Col. Irwin's support, marched to the top of the mountain, where they encountered enemy troops behind a stone wall at Padgett's Field in the dying light, and with Slocum's men from the 1st Division, were able to clear the enemy from the top of the mountain. Brook's brigade lost a total of 19 men at Crampton's Gap (1 killed; 18 wounded). The division rested on the mountain and the next day was sent down to spread across the Pleasant Valley, facing portions of Lafayette McLaws' and Richard Anderson's divisions extended across the valley. Franklin chose not to engage these Confederate troops and the Harpers Ferry garrison fell soon after.[69]

Smith's division, with the rest of the VI Corps, camped near Rohrersville in the Pleasant Valley on September 15 and 16, then headed toward Sharpsburg at 6:00 a.m. on the morning of September 17 at the head of the corps. It arrived at the Middle Bridge over Antietam Creek at 10:00 a.m., after the ten-mile march and was ordered to rest on the left (south) of Boonsboro Pike. From this position, the division could send troops wherever the threat was greatest. While waiting here, Hancock gave his men a rousing speech: "Boys, do as you have done before; be brave and true, and I think this will be your last battle." The men did not have time to rest for they were ordered to the aid of John Sedgwick's division (Edwin Sumner's II Corps). The division, with Hancock's brigade in the van, crossed Antietam Creek at a ford between the Upper and Middle Bridges. During the division's advance from the East Woods, Smith rode behind the 20th New York.

Hancock's brigade was peeled off and sent north to support Capt. Andrew Cowan's and Capt. John Frank's New York batteries north of the Miller Cornfield. The 49th Pennsylvania, 43rd New York, and 137th Pennsylvania formed around the guns, and the 5th Wisconsin and 6th Maine formed behind their comrades in the East Woods.

Smith believed the quick action by Hancock's brigade saved the two Union batteries. When William French division (II Corps), attacking the Sunken Road, ran out of ammunition, Brooks' brigade was sent forward to assist, forming on its right flank. Alpheus Williams, commanding the XII Corps at this time, recalled when Smith's division arrived, the men "fairly rushed toward the left and front. I hastily called his attention to the woods full of Rebels on his right as he was advancing." Irwin's brigade, initially between Hancock's and Brooks' brigades, was now ordered to charge the enemy formations in the West Woods. After completing these deployments by 11:00 a.m., Smith decided to bring up Brooks to support Irwin, but learned, to his dismay, it was ordered away without his knowledge. He wrote disparagingly in his report, "It is not the first or second time during a battle that my command has been dispersed by orders from an officer superior in rank to the general commanding this corps, and I must assert that I have never known any good to arise from such a method of fighting a battle, and think the contrary rule should be adopted of keeping commands intact."[70]

Irwin's brigade did most of the subsequent fighting. It attacked the West Woods, but was quickly beaten back. The 7th Maine was later sent to the Piper farm and almost destroyed when it was set upon by enemy troops on three sides and beat a hasty retreat.

This ended the activities of Smith's division during the Maryland Campaign. Except for minor actions by two of Smith's brigades and an important advance by Irwin's brigade at Antietam, the division played a minor role. It lost 373 men at Antietam (65 killed, 277 wounded, 31 missing/captured), but most (342) of the casualties were in Irwin's brigade.[71]

**Bradley M. Gottfried**

* * *

## 1st Brigade: Brigadier General Winfield Hancock, Colonel Amasa Cobb

**Units:** 6th Maine, 43rd New York, 49th Pennsylvania, 137th Pennsylvania, 5th Wisconsin
**Strength:** 2,570
**Losses:** 6 (0k-6w-0m)[72]

The 1st Brigade formed at the same time as the division, in March 1862, under Winfield Hancock. A twin, Hancock was born outside of Philadelphia in February 1824. He attended West Point and graduated in 1844 and had the distinction of being the youngest cadet in his class (20 years old). He spent a couple of years in the west and then fought in the War with Mexico, earning several brevets. Hancock fought in the Seminoles conflicts and then became a quartermaster. His association with George McClellan led to his promotion to the rank of brigadier general and a mixed brigade in

September 1861. Hancock had already served with distinction in several campaigns and was seen as a rising star.[73]

Hancock's brigade consisted of a odd concoction of units whose origins stretched from the far eastern part of the U.S. (Maine), to the far western state (Wisconsin), with New York and Pennsylvania troops added for good measure. The 6th Maine and 5th Wisconsin mustered into service in July 1861 and the 43rd New York and 49th Pennsylvania entered the following September. These four regiments were brigaded together under Hancock and fought during the Seven Days (Gaines Mill, Savage Station, White Oak Swamp, and Malvern Hill). They also assisted in John Pope's retreat during the Second Bull Run Campaign. The 137th

Pennsylvania did not muster into service until August 1862, so the Maryland Campaign was its first war experience.[74]

When infantry supported was requested by cavalry commander, Alfred Pleasonton, on September 11, Hancock's brigade was selected for the mission. The show of force caused the Confederate cavalry to abandon the strategically important Sugar Loaf Mountain. Historian Ezra Carman summarized the role of the brigade on September 14, when portions of the VI Corps captured Crampton' Gap: "Hancock's brigade was in reserve, [and] did not participate in the engagement and remained east of the mountain."

The brigade led the VI Corps' march to Antietam Creek on September 17, arriving near Keedysville at about 9:00 a.m. When Lt. Col. Benjamin Taylor of

Edwin Sumner's staff requested support for a line of batteries in and north of the Cornfield, Hancock's men were dispatched to the area. The brigade's left flank was in the East Woods; its line curving in a northwest direction, and the right flank rested in the field north of the Cornfield. Hancock's skirmishers moved cautiously forward and came under fire from the Confederates along Hagerstown Pike. The losses sustained by the brigade were primarily from the intense enemy artillery fire. When Hancock was called upon to command Richardson's division, Col. Asa Cobb of the 5th Wisconsin assumed command of the brigade.[75]

**Bradley M. Gottfried**

* * *

## Second Brigade: Brigadier General W. T. Brooks

**Units:** 2nd Vermont, 3rd Vermont, 4th Vermont, 5th Vermont, 6th Vermont
**Strength:** 2,188
**Losses:** 25 (1k- 24m-0w)[76]

The 2nd Brigade formed in March 1862, at the same time as the 2nd Division. Unlike most of the brigades in the Army of the Potomac, it was composed of units from only one state. The 2nd Vermont formed first, mustering into service in June 1861, seeing action at First Bull Run as part of Oliver Howard's brigade. The 3rd Vermont was mustered into service in July and it joined the 2nd Vermont in William Smith's brigade and both fought during the skirmish at Lewinsville, Virginia. The 4th and 5th Vermont were mustered into service in September and the 6th Vermont in October. All five regiments were brigaded together in Brooks' brigade in March 1862. The brigade saw action at Williamsburg and during the Seven Days Campaign (Garnett's Farm, Savage Station, White Oak Swamp, and Malvern Hill). By the Maryland Campaign it was a veteran unit whose reputation would grow as the war progressed.[77]

Brig. Gen. William Brooks was born in Ohio in January 1821 and graduated from West Point in 1841. Upon graduation he was sent to Florida, where he participated in a number of military actions. He won several brevets for gallantry during the War with Mexico and then returned to the frontier. Brooks won promotion to the rank of brigadier general on September 28, 1861 and became the brigade's original commander.[78]

The brigade played a minor role in the Battle of Crampton's Gap. While Henry Slocum's division attacked the Confederates defending the base of the gap, Brooks' brigade was thrown forward on Slocum's left, on the left of Burkittsville Road. Upon encountering enemy skirmishers, Brooks deployed his brigade for action and sent the 4th Vermont forward on the skirmish line, supported by the 2nd Vermont. The brigade drove the sparse enemy from its front and remained at the base of the mountain as Crampton's Gap fell to Slocum's men. The brigade moved up South Mountain in the darkness, and the 4th Vermont continued moving left along the top of the mountain, rounding up prisoners and capturing the 16th Virginia's flag. The entire brigade then moved down the western slope into the Pleasant Valley. The brigade lost 19 men (1 killed; 18 wounded).[79]

During the Battle of Antietam, Brooks' brigade was detached from the division and sent to support William French's division (II Corps). It took up a position on the south edge of the Mumma cornfield on the right of French's men. The men were about 170 yards from the Sunken Road. According to Brooks, the men were "subjected to quite a galling fire of both artillery and sharpshooters, causing numerous casualties. . ."[80]

**Bradley M. Gottfried**

* * *

## 3rd Brigade: Colonel William Irwin

**Units:** 7th Maine, 20th New York, 33rd New York, 49th New York, 77th New York
**Strength:** 2,164[81]
**Losses:** 342 (64k-247w-31m)[82]

Colonel William Irwin's brigade was an experienced unit, whose regiments were mustered into service between May 9, 1861 and November 23, 1861. They participated to varying degrees of all combat during the Peninsula Campaign and Seven Days Battles.

Pennsylvanian William Howard Irwin was born in 1818 and attended Dickinson College for two years before returning home to study for the bar. He entered the army in February 1847 and received a commission in the 11th U.S. Infantry. Irwin was seriously wounded during the Battle of El Molino del Rey on September 8, 1847, during the War with Mexico, while leading his company. He received a brevet to major for his bravery and returned to Pennsylvania to practice law until the outbreak of the Civil War when he again donned a uniform. He enlisted as a private after the fall of Fort Sumter but quickly rose to the rank of colonel of the 7th Pennsylvania Volunteers, a ninety-day unit that participated in the early advance on the Shenandoah Valley in June and July 1861.

After the regiment mustered out, Irwin assisted in raising and organizing several Pennsylvania units. He was appointed colonel of the 49th Pennsylvania in late 1861. Several of his subordinates brought charges against him for drunkenness and "conduct prejudicial to good order and military discipline." He was acquitted on the first charge but convicted on the second, drawing an inconsequential suspended punishment. He went on to lead the 49th with distinction in the Peninsula Campaign. He was given a brigade in the 2nd Division in the VI Corps prior to the advance into Maryland.[83]

Irwin's brigade left Camp California, near Alexandria, Virginia and eventually crossed the Potomac River at Long Bridge, camping near Georgetown on September 7. The column subsequently marched through the Maryland towns of Rockville, Barnesville, Darnestown, and Jefferson, toward Catoctin Mountain. On September 14, the brigade trudged through Burkittsville to support William T. H. Brooks' brigade (also of Smith's division) at Crampton's Gap. The brigade was subjected to enemy artillery fire as it hurried through the town but sustained no casualties. The men spent the afternoon and evening supporting Capt. Romeyn Ayres' divisional artillery and camped at the gap until Wednesday, September 17, when they began their march toward Antietam Creek. Irwin's brigade reached its destination at 10:00 a.m. and crossed Antietam Creek at Pry's Ford, where it was called into action by Smith to relieve troops from George Greene's division (XII Corps).[84]

### Antietam

Brig. Gen. William French's division (II Corps) launched charge after charge against the Sunken Road during this time. To relieve pressure on D.H. Hill's two brigades defending the road, wing

143

commander James Longstreet directed a counter attack meant to land on French's vulnerable right flank. John Cooke of the 27th North Carolina led his regiment and the 3rd Arkansas (Van Manning's brigade; John Walker's division) out of the West Woods and against French's flank. The ambitious band assisted in routing the left of Greene's division holding the Dunker Church and then crossed Hagerstown Pike, setting their sights on the Union soldiers clearing out the Sunken Road.

Irwin threw the 33rd and 77th New York out as skirmishers on the right of the brigade along Smoketown Road. The rest of the brigade was oriented south-southwest with its right on the road. The large 20th New York led the advance, the 49th New York followed on its right and the 7th Maine advanced on its left *en echelon*. The 20th New York cleared the East Woods with Smith riding behind the regiment. As the three regiments dashed past the southern edge of the East Woods they encountered retreating elements of Greene's division. They then moved through Lt. Evan Thomas' 4th U. S. Artillery, Battery A, firing at the enemy in the West Woods. Further south, Cooke's Confederate assault force climbed over the fences lining Mumma Lane and entered a cornfield. Before Cooke's men could attack French, they were hit by John Brooke's brigade (Israel Richardson's division; II Corps) that was rushed toward the Roulette farm buildings from the east to halt the two enemy regiments. The 7th Maine also rushed forward to add its support from the north. While Brooke's men fired into the enemy's front, the 7th Maine fired into the left flank of the 27th North Carolina. The intense fire in their front and flank was more than Cooke's men could handle and they broke in confusion, followed closely by Irwin's men.

While the 7th Maine was engaged with Cooke, the 20th New York came to a rise in the ground just to the east of Hagerstown Pike that had sheltered Greene's men earlier in the day. It was ordered to halt there, but the New Yorkers kept going until they were driven back by small arms fire from Manning's brigade and an enemy battery stationed near the West Woods. The New Yorkers quickly retraced their steps to the high ground and lay down behind the hill. They were soon joined by the 49th New York who also took cover. After repulsing Cooke and clearing the Mumma farm buildings, the 7th Maine also returned to the brigade, lying down behind the hill on the left of the 20th New York.[85]

The 33rd and 77th New York, on the skirmish line to the right of the rest of the brigade, had their own share of excitement. As they headed toward the West Woods, with the 33rd New York on the right of Smoketown Road and the 77th New York on its left, they were closely watched by the 49th and 35th North Carolina (Robert Ransom's brigade; John Walker's division). The tar heels hopped behind a rail barricade they had previously built just north of the Dunker Church. Irwin explained what happened next: "A severe and unexpected volley from the woods on our right struck full on the Seventy-seventh and Thirty-third New York, which staggered them for a moment, but they closed up and faced by the rear rank, and poured in a close and scorching fire." Lt. Col. Joseph Corning of the 33rd New York reported his regiment was "in columns at the time, marching by the right flank. This sudden and unexpected attack caused a momentary unsteadiness in the ranks, which was quickly rectified. The battalion faced by the rear rank and returned the fire." Capt. Nathan Babcock of the 77th New York claimed the two lines were so close that "you could see the white of their eyes." The historian of the 49th New York claimed its two fellow New York regiments were "losing frightfully, and would doubtless have been annihilated had not General Smith seen their predicament and sent an aide to their rescue, who faced them by the rear rank and placed them behind the ridge, at right angles with the other regiments of the brigade." The brigade reformed in the safety of the Mumma swale.[86]

The swale sheltered Irwin's men from the enemy's small arms fire but not from their artillery and sharpshooters. The brigade also found itself in the uncomfortable position between dueling Union and Confederate artillery, causing considerable uneasiness amongst the men in the ranks. A

Confederate battery fired along the flank and through the line of the 20th New York, which, from the nature of the ground, was compelled to refuse its left, and thus received the fire along its entire front. Sharpshooters from the woods to the right and to the extreme left also opened upon the brigade. Shell, grape, and canister swept from left to right. The enemy fired quickly and accurately, causing Irwin's losses to accelerate. The historian of the 49th New York recalled, "the whirring shells and screaming shrapnel going both ways over their prostrate forms, reduced the most corpulent of the men to very thin proportions."[87]

Maj. Thomas Hyde and his 7th Maine found themselves better protected by large boulders along their line and were able to see the Irish Brigade's (Richardson's division; II Corps) notable colors and the Union line finally breaching the Sunken Road, as well as artillery playing along the right of the line from Confederate batteries near the Dunker Church. The Germans of the 20th New York on the right, having only flat ground to lie on for protection, suffered mightily, and a stream of wounded headed for the rear. The regiments occupying protected terrain, such as the 7th Maine, lost but few men. At one-point, Hyde suggested to Col. Ernest Vegesack of the 20th New York that the Confederates could possibly be sighting in on the 20th's regimental colors being held high.[88]

Most of the brigade remained in this position, subjected to heavy artillery and sharpshooter fire for twenty-four hours, until relieved by a brigade from Darius Couch's IV Corps division (attached to the VI Corps) on September 18. The 7th Maine did not stay inactive, however. The rugged men were dead shots and were deployed as sharpshooters against the Confederate artillery positions. One Maine sharpshooter known by the name of "Knox" drove every man from the guns of one section and knocked an unknown general officer from his horse in the distance.

At around 4:30 p.m., Col. Irwin became concerned about Confederate troops he could see moving across Reel Ridge to the west, on the other side of Hagerstown Pike, who appeared to threaten the division's left flank. Heavy fighting could be heard in the direction of Sharpsburg. The hills blocked most views of troop movements to the left, where the V and IX Corps were in action. Irwin watched the Confederate columns and worried they could be supporting Lee's right flank, now under attack. Irwin sent word to Smith requesting artillery support, and the division's Chief of Artillery, Capt. Emery Upton, complied. Capt. John Wolcott's Maryland Light battery arrived as ordered and dropped trail with its three rifled guns. These guns threw a destructive cannonade against the enemy positions for half an hour before being replaced by Lt. Edward Williston's 2nd U.S. Artillery's six Napoleons.[89]

Enemy sharpshooters from D.H. Hill's Confederate division began firing at the cannoneers from the Piper orchard, causing Irwin to look to his best unit available to put an end to the sniping. He again turned to the 7th Maine. Hyde selected one of his companies to clear out enemy sharpshooters from the orchard, when Irwin suddenly changed the order. Irwin stated, "That is not enough, sir; go yourself; take your regiment and drive them from those trees and buildings." The order astonished Hyde, as he did not believe he had enough men to clear the entire area of the enemy that two divisions had failed to do earlier. He asked Irwin to repeat his order and point out the ground again. Irwin did so, adding with an oath, "Those are your orders, sir." This, he purportedly repeated several times.[90]

Hyde led his men toward the new target, the Piper farm building complex, about half a mile away, firing while crossing the Sunken Road filled with enemy dead and dying. Hyde regretted his horse stepping on some of the bodies as it crossed the bloody road. He halted his men in the trampled cornfield beyond the road to reform his ranks and then gave the order to charge. Using the right corner of the Piper barn as the guide the brave task force descended into the deep "cup shaped bowl," a topographical feature much like the swale protecting their regimental brothers. The beginning of the 7th Maine's memorable charge began as badly as it ended, with supporting Union guns accidently firing into Hyde's men, dropping four.

Enemy soldiers in front of, and to the left of, Hyde's men realized they were in danger of being cut off and ran for safety, clearing out the orchard. The Confederates lining Hagerstown Pike to the right did not run and, instead, poured a volley into Hyde's men. It did little damage and Hyde quickly obliqued his men to the left to take cover behind a ridge, on the south rim of the cup, running from behind the Piper barn to Hagerstown Pike. As Hyde rode up the high ground, he quickly took in the danger around him. Lying down in front of his men was a line of enemy troops from G.T. Anderson's brigade and another body led by D.H. Hill himself, rushing along Piper Lane to his left in an effort to cut off his retreat.

With the enemy in front, and closing on his right, Hyde quickly realized it was time to retreat. He ordered the regiment to move by the left flank before Hill's men saw them, and double-quickened his men past the Piper barn, through a forced opening in the picket fence, and into the orchard. Additional troops, remnants of Cadmus Wilcox's and Ambrose Wright's brigades (both of Richard Anderson's division), still full of fight, headed for Piper Lane and opened fire just as Hyde's men passed through the fence. Hyde's men returned the fire and then Hyde instantly sent his men up the hill in the middle of the orchard, where they again halted to fire into G.T. Anderson's men and others who were hurrying toward them. Hyde's men were now receiving fire from three sides. His horse was shot from under him, causing Hyde to fall behind his men who were making their way to the north fence line, using their unique sabre bayonets to pry

and hack their way through the barrier. In the manic pursuit through the expanse of the orchard, Confederate troops were now between Hyde and his men and were about to close in on him. He would have been captured, were it not for Sgt. Henry Hill, who quickly ordered his men to push the barrels of their Windsor rifles through the picket openings and fire while he cut an opening in the fence and collected Hyde. Union artillery once again opened fire, helping to stall the enemy's final assault, and allowing Hyde and the remnants of his regiment to quickly retrace their steps back across the Sunken Road to the safety of the rest of the brigade hunkered down in the Mumma farm swale.[91]

Of the 181 men Hyde brought forward with him on the advance, 88 were killed, wounded or missing. The 7th Maine won accolades for its actions at the Piper farm and Hyde received the Medal of Honor, albeit at great cost.[92]

Irwin's brigade occupied the battlefield for twenty-six hours until relieved at noon on September 18 by Couch's division. Irwin summed up his brigade's actions during the battle: "It was under fire constantly during this time in a most exposed position, lost 311 in killed and wounded, yet neither officers nor men fell back or gave the slightest evidence of any desire to do so. My line was immovable, only anxious to be launched against the enemy. I forbear comment on such conduct. It will commend itself to the heart and mind of every true soldier." [93]

**Martin Pritchett**

# IX CORPS—

## Major General Ambrose Burnside, Major General Jesse Reno, Brigadier General Jacob Cox

Major General Ambrose Burnside was born on May 23, 1824 in Indiana to a father who owned slaves in South Carolina, but sold them and moved north to the Hoosier state. After a short stint as a tailor, Burnside gained entry to West Point and graduated in 1847. He pulled garrison duty during the Mexican War and this continued in the Southwest after the war. He resigned his commission in 1853 to concentrate on developing and manufacturing a breech-loading rifle that carried his name. His friend, George McClellan, hired him to work for the Illinois Central Railroad, and he organized the 1st Rhode Island at the start of the Civil War. It became part of a brigade he commanded at First Bull Run. Burnside received his first star on August 6, 1861, and because of his positive interactions with Lincoln, was tapped to lead an expedition to the North Carolina coast in early 1862. The successful campaign resulted in Union control of the North Carolina sounds, which was a severe blow to Confederate blockade runners. Burnside assumed command of the IX Corps in July 1862 which combined troops from his own Department of North Carolina with the Department of the South. Burnside was promoted to major general and Lincoln offered him command of the Army of the Potomac at least twice that summer. Burnside, apparently not as enamored of his own abilities as perhaps others were, declined both offers.

The IX Corps supported John Pope's campaign in central Virginia during the late summer of 1862. The corps arrived at Aquia Creek on August 3 and nine days later, Burnside sent twelve regiments and four batteries under Maj. Gen. Jesse Reno to reinforce Pope, while Burnside remained with seven regiments of infantry and six companies of cavalry to man a line stretching from Fredericksburg and Falmouth to the depot at Aquia Creek. The corps suffered more than 1,500 casualties in Pope's campaign, including the death of division commander, Brig. Gen. Isaac Stevens at Chantilly, on September 1, and it subsequently joined the retreat to Washington. These units reunited with Burnside, whose regiments had departed Aquia Creek, leaving the depot in flames. Over the next several days, the corps reorganized with new leadership and additional troops. Brig. Gen. Orlando Willcox, recently exchanged after more than a year as a Confederate prisoner, replaced the fallen Stevens as commander of the 1st Division. Brig. Gen. Samuel Sturgis, in command of Pope's Reserve Corps during the Second Bull Run Campaign, took over the 2nd Division after Reno ascended to corps command. Brig. Gen. Isaac Rodman, recently recovered from illness, assumed command of the 3rd Division in place of Maj. Gen. John Parke, who became Burnside's chief of staff. Brig. Gen. Jacob Cox's Kanawha Division joined the corps on September 5. Each of the corps' four divisions consisted of two brigades.[1]

As the Federal army began its pursuit of the Army of the Northern Virginia, the IX Corps and I Corps comprised the Right Wing and led the way into Frederick, with Burnside in command of the wing and Maj. Gen. Jesse Reno in command of the IX Corps. The corps left Washington on September 7 and passed through Leesborough, Brookville and Damascus before reaching Frederick in the early afternoon of September 12. There, the Kanawha Division skirmished with a rearguard of Confederate cavalry, resulting in the capture of Col. Augustus Moor, one of the division's brigade commanders. When the Confederates retreated, the jubilant townsfolk of Frederick greeted Burnside's men by "waving their handkerchiefs and the national flag" and bringing "fruits and refreshments for the marching soldiers." A private in Rodman's Third

Division wrote the "reception of our troops was extremely enthusiastic and the soldiers who could get out into the city were dragged into the houses and given everything that would fill empty stomachs."[2]

On September 13, Rodman's division, followed by the rest of the corps, moved west from Frederick on the National Road to support Union cavalry reconnoitering toward South Mountain. Cox sent Col. Eliakim Scammon's brigade to report to Brig. Gen. Alfred Pleasonton, commander of the Union cavalry, at 6:00 a.m. on September 14, as the army continued its westward advance from Middletown. Receiving a veiled warning from the newly paroled Moor of a sizable number of Confederates holding the mountain, Cox brought up his other brigade, commanded by Col. George Crook. Meanwhile, Pleasonton posted artillery on "a high knoll," including Lt. Samuel Benjamin's IX Corps battery of four 20-lb. Parrott rifles, and directed Scammon's brigade, soon followed by Crook's brigade, to detour off the National Road and head toward Fox's Gap, a pass over South Mountain. The Kanawha Division battled Samuel Garland's North Carolina brigade all morning for possession of the gap. By noon, Cox's troops had wrecked Garland's brigade, inflicting 379 casualties, including the mortal wounded Garland. Hindsight suggests Cox could have seized control of the gap at this time, but instead a "lull" fell over the field for several hours as both sides brought up reinforcements. Further assaults by Willcox's and Sturgis' men secured Fox's Gap by nightfall. The IX Corps sustained a total of 889 casualties according to the official returns, while shattering Thomas Drayton's Confederate brigade, which suffered 643 casualties. Only one Union regiment lost more men during the fighting on September 14 than the 1st Division's 45th Pennsylvania, and four of the five Union regiments that suffered the highest number of casualties that day were from the IX Corps. A singular casualty late in the evening darkened the Union victory. Reno was struck in the chest by a bullet near the road passing over the mountain at Fox's Gap and died a short time later, bidding a resolute farewell to Sturgis as his life ebbed away, "Hallo Sam, I'm dead . . . good bye!"[3]

McClellan sent Burnside three communications with expectations the IX Corps would follow the enemy toward Sharpsburg on the morning of September 15. The men were instead permitted to tarry at Fox's Gap. Cox later claimed his men were tired, without provisions, and needed to bury their dead. This frustrated McClellan so much that he authorized George Sykes to "push by" the IX Corps with his V Corps division in the early afternoon. The IX Corps' march began at 2:00 p.m., taking the "road from Rohrersville," and by evening, the men were "encamped in the rear of the extreme left of the whole line of the Army of the Potomac, close to the hills on the southeast side of the valley of the Antietam," according to Cox. McClellan's displeasure with Burnside continued on September 16, when a headquarters missive admonished him for not having his men in their "designated position" by noon and noted "there was a delay of some four hours in the movement of your command yesterday." The communication demanded "explanations of these failures on your part to comply with the orders given you." That day, "the whole corps, except Willcox's division, was moved forward to the left and front . . . and took up a new position upon the rear slope of the ridges on the [east] bank of the Antietam, the center of the corps being nearly opposite the [Lower Bridge]," reported Cox. With the death of Reno, Cox assumed temporary command of the corps, which perhaps contributed to the clumsy handling of the troops as McClellan's orders came to Burnside, who read them, and then passed them along to Cox. In arraying his army for battle along Antietam Creek, McClellan sent the IX Corps south to form his left flank.[4]

As the battle opened around the Miller Cornfield and East Woods to their right on the morning of September 17, the IX Corps confronted a predicament their compatriots did not. Cox's men were "alone at the only place on the field where the Confederates had their line immediately upon the stream which must be crossed under fire," explained Cox. They would have to fight their way across Antietam Creek. Further complicating matters, the Lower (Rohrbach) Bridge narrowed the bluecoats' avenue of advance to a 12-foot wide span in the face of a steep slope, an imposing defensive position. Confederate artillery on high ground further back also had the range of this ground. An additional crossing was needed to flank the Confederate position. Union engineers identified a supposed ford downstream from the bridge on September 16. Cox decided to push Rodman's division, supplemented by Col. Hugh Ewing's brigade across the ford and flank the enemy defenders, while Crook's brigade (Kanawha Division) and Sturgis' division stormed the bridge.

Rodman positioned his command at the designated ford, but he quickly learned the banks were too steep to cross a large body of infantry and thus led his division further downstream. Meanwhile, Burnside reported, "[a]t 10 o'clock [a.m.] I received an order from the general commanding to make the attack" on the bridge. The timing of that order became a matter of dispute. McClellan's initial report of October 15, 1862 concurred with Burnside as to the 10:00 a.m. timing of the order. McClellan's subsequent report, dated August 4, 1863, revised the time of the order to 8:00 a.m. The truth is probably in between (Cox timed the order at 9:00 a.m.), but the discrepancy illustrates the second-guessing aimed at McClellan and Burnside for supposedly missing an opportunity to destroy Lee's army before Maj. Gen. A.P. Hill's division arrived from Harpers Ferry.[5]

Whatever the timing of the order, it took the IX Corps at least three assaults before the two Georgia regiments defending the bridge withdrew, "affirm[ing] that the Confederate position was virtually impregnable to a direct attack over the bridge." In short, the first assault by Crook's brigade was misdirected (part of the attacking force coming into position too far upstream), the second assault used the road running alongside the creek (exposing the attackers' flank to heavy rifle fire before reaching the bridge), and the third assault carried the bridge in the early afternoon when the Georgians were low on ammunition and flanked by Rodman's division, now across the creek.

Cox's men next faced a 200-foot undulating climb to reach the main part of the Confederate right. Two corps batteries lined a ridge and banged away at Confederate artillery that had the advantage of higher elevation. Organizing the infantry advance took two hours, and it was not until after 3:00 p.m. when the IX Corps went forward in a battle line that stretched nearly a mile. Willcox's division was on the right, supported by Crook's brigade, slightly ahead of Rodman's division on the left, supported by Scammon's Kanawha Division. Willcox and the right half of Rodman reached the heights of Sharpsburg, the 8th Connecticut capturing one of Hill's newly-arrived batteries along Harpers Ferry Road. The regiments on the left of the IX Corps were another matter. Caught in low ground amidst tall corn in a 40-acre field, the month-old 16th Connecticut and the veteran 4th Rhode Island to its left received Hill's lead brigade of South Carolinians. Rodman rode back to rally his regiments lagging in the low ground when he was hit in the chest, a wound that proved fatal several days later. Two more brigades from Hill's division arrived, and along with rallied elements of Brig. Gen. D.R. Jones' division and strong artillery support, stabilized the Confederate line as the sunlight receded. Although the Kanawha Division fought off counterattacking Confederates, and Sturgis's division moved forward from the bridge to add its weight to the Federal line, Burnside reported "the command was ordered to fall back to the crests above the bridge" despite protests from Willcox and others whose men had fought their way up to the heights and streets of town.[6]

The IX Corps suffered 438 killed, 1,796 wounded and 115 missing at Antietam while inflicting more than a thousand Confederate casualties. The Kanawha Division also indirectly contributed to the fighting on the Union right by so wrecking Garland's brigade at Fox's Gap that it was largely ineffective. Willcox's destruction of Drayton's brigade on September 14 thinned the Confederate right on September 17 before Hill's arrival. No Union brigade on September 17, save perhaps one, suffered a higher percentage of casualties than Col. Harrison Fairchild's of Rodman's division. The IX Corps was the van of the Army of the Potomac in its pursuit of the Army of Northern Virginia into Maryland. Its attacks unraveled the Confederate line at Fox's Gap and nearly broke the Confederate right on the heights of Sharpsburg, while costing the lives of two of its general officers. Ahead for Burnside was one more opportunity to take command of the Army of the Potomac.[7] **J.O. Smith**

✳ ✳ ✳

# 1ST DIVISION—

## Brigadier General Orlando Willcox

The 1st Division of the IX Corps was officially formed on July 22, 1862 under the command of Brig. Gen. Isaac Stevens, who lost his life in a hail of Confederate bullets at Chantilly on September 1, 1862 while grasping the flag of the 79th New York. He was temporarily replaced by Col. Benjamin Christ until Brig. Gen. Orlando Willcox took command of the division on a permanent basis during the early phase of the Maryland Campaign. The division initially comprised three brigades of two regiments each, but was reorganized during the Second Bull Run Campaign to bring it in line with the other IX Corps divisions. The three brigades were consolidated into two and Col. Thomas Welsh's 45th Pennsylvania was added to bolster the division's strength. Because of the wounding of two brigade commanders at Second Bull Run, Welsh rose to command the 2nd Brigade while Christ retained command of the 1st Brigade during the Maryland Campaign.[8]

Willcox was born in Detroit, Michigan, "a frontier military town not yet greatly altered from the ancient French place" at the time of his birth in 1823. Willcox graduated from West Point in 1847 alongside a number of future Civil War notables, including A. P. Hill, Henry Heth, John Gibbon, and future IX Corps commander, Ambrose Burnside. Remaining in the army for the next 10 years, Willcox served in Mexico, Boston, the Plains and Florida. He resigned his commission, but civilian life enervated him; he titled his journal entries for 1857-1858, "Citizen Willcox: Life among the Lunatics." Returning to military service at the outbreak of war, Willcox helped organize and became colonel of the 1st Michigan Infantry Regiment in April 1861. Willcox was wounded while leading a brigade at First Bull Run and fell into Confederate hands. After he was exchanged in August 1862, he was assigned command of the 1st Division of the IX Corps. He caught up with his new command on September 8.[9]

The division left the Chantilly battlefield on September 2, marched to Alexandria, and then crossed the Long Bridge into Washington on the night of September 4. The men left their camp on Meridian Hill in northwest Washington on September 7 and marched 10 miles to Leesborough (present-day Wheaton), Maryland and then continued northward to Brookville on September 9.[10]

The next day, Christ's brigade was reinforced by the 17th Michigan, a green regiment that had left Detroit only a few weeks earlier. Willcox's troops reached the outskirts of Frederick on September 12 and moved to Middletown, west of Frederick, where they bivouacked on the evening of September 13. IX Corps commander, Jesse Reno, ordered Willcox forward on Sunday, September 14 "to the base of South Mountain to support [Jacob] Cox's [Kanahwa] division." Cox advised Willcox to keep his command "near the main pike or Cumberland road, and consult with General Pleasonton as to taking a position." Willcox conferred with the cavalry commander near the latter's batteries, and dropped off Lt. Samuel Benjamin's four 20-lb. Parrott rifles before sending his two infantry brigades forward along the National Road toward Turner's Gap. Ambrose Burnside soon recalled Willcox and sent his division up Old Sharpsburg Road toward Fox's Gap. Arriving after the Kanawha Division's morning assault, Willcox's men renewed the attack up the mountain in the late afternoon. One of Willcox's veterans remembered how "[d]uring the thickest of the fight," Willcox "sat on his horse like a statue while the shots of the enemy cut the rails of the fence behind him into slivers." Confederate reinforcements hurrying from Hagerstown prevented a rout, but vacated Fox's Gap after nightfall. The Union victory came at the cost of "the gallant and beloved Reno," felled near sunset just a few yards from the summit. Cox replaced him as commander of the IX Corps.[11]

The division lost a total of 355 men at Fox's Gap. After spending the night on the mountain where they had fought, Willcox's division marched a short distance on September 15 toward Porterstown. By evening of the next day, the division and the rest of the IX Corps caught up with the army, "halting at sunset close to the hills on the southeast side of Antietam Valley, and on the left of the old Sharpsburg road, in rear of the left of Sykes' [V Corps] Division." Benjamin's long-range guns took part in the artillery engagement on September 16.[12]

The IX Corps on the army's left flank had to fight its way across Antietam Creek on September 17. Willcox's division remained in reserve during the corps' early actions. The Lower Bridge fell around 1:00 p.m., and the division finally crossed Antietam Creek about an hour later. Once across, Willcox's two brigades formed the IX Corps' right flank, deployed on either side of Lower Bridge Road leading from the bridge into Sharpsburg, and began their advance about 3:00 p.m. The men were subjected to considerable Confederate artillery fire from batteries on the high ground in their front (west). Although a series of ravines protected the division as it advanced, the uneven terrain complicated Cox's ability to coordinate a battle line that stretched nearly a mile in length. Some of Willcox's division penetrated the main Confederate defensive line, reaching the streets of town. But the IX Corps' attack soon unraveled from left to right, as the arrival of A. P. Hill's division sparked a series of blows the Union high command was unable to answer.[13]

Reflecting on the Maryland Campaign eight days after Antietam, Willcox wrote his wife, "my division has been the most successful in its work of any in the corps." From the late afternoon of September 17 forward, however, a hint of lost opportunity emanated from Willcox and his men. Willcox believed he could have countered the effect of Hill's attack, and recalled telling Isaac Rodman's brigade commanders and Kanawha Division commander, Eliakim Scammon, that he could "assist the left by a charge bayonet (our ammunition being exhausted) . . . when we were *ordered* to fall back near the bridge." Willcox questioned the order to stand down twice before obeying. Marie Willcox visited her husband in early October when his division's camps were not far from where they had fought. Willcox toured the battlefield with his wife and "showed [her] the exact position of his command." Mrs. Willcox expressed more plainly the regret of her husband and others in his division, calling it a "great shame that he was not permitted to drive the enemy as he wanted to."[14]

The division lost a total of 338 at Antietam. The lighter casualty figures of Christ's and Welsh's brigades, relative to the losses suffered by Rodman's two brigades to their left (1,077), suggest Willcox's division could have accomplished more.[15]

**J.O. Smith**

* * *

## 1st: Brigade: Colonel Benjamin Christ

**Units:** 28th Massachusetts, 17th Michigan, 79th New York, 50th Pennsylvania
**Strength:** 2,482[16]
**Losses:** 244 (43k-198w-3m)[17]

Schuylkill County, Pennsylvania native Benjamin Christ was born in 1822. He helped organize the 50th Pennsylvania Infantry in September 1861, and was its first colonel. Christ's personal history seems largely unknown; he may have been a coal merchant and hotelier before the war. Christ moved up to

brigade command in the summer of 1862, not long after the 50th Pennsylvania departed Beaufort, South Carolina and became part of Ambrose Burnside's IX Corps. During the ensuing Second Bull Run Campaign, Christ's brigade contained only two regiments: the 50th Pennsylvania and the 8th Michigan. Following George McClellan's reorganization of the Army of the Potomac in early September 1862, two additional regiments, the 28th Massachusetts, recruited in 1861 as part of Thomas

Francis Meagher's effort to enlist Irish immigrants, and the 79th New York, known as the "Highlanders" for their large number of Scottish-descended recruits who wore kilts on parade, were added to the brigade. These regiments had been in Col. Addison Farnsworth's brigade, who was wounded at Second Bull Run.[18]

After leaving the Chantilly battlefield on September 2, Christ's brigade, along with the brigade that Col. Thomas Welsh would eventually command during the Maryland Campaign, spent two days in Alexandria, Virginia, before encamping on Meridian Hill in Washington from September 5 until the morning of September 7. The 17th Michigan joined the brigade on September 10. The 17th was a new regiment that had assembled in Detroit the month before. A recruit noted the men were without uniforms as of August 12. With the addition of the 17th Michigan, which left Detroit in late August with 982 officers and men, Christ's total strength grew to approximately 2,400 men; the toll of the campaign would diminish that strength considerably by the time the brigade reached Antietam. Continuing its move northward into Maryland, the brigade advanced to the Monocacy River, within two miles of Frederick, on September 12.[19]

## South Mountain

After bivouacking a mile and a half east of Middletown on the night of September 13, the brigade began its westward march around 8:00 a.m. the next morning toward South Mountain. Willcox's two brigades initially advanced along the National Road toward Turner's Gap before Burnside diverted them southward to support Jacob Cox's Kanawha Division, which was attempting to take Fox's Gap that morning. Had Willcox continued toward the thin Confederate line defending Turner's Gap in the early afternoon, the battle, and the course of the campaign, might have played out very differently. Instead, the weight of the IX Corps hammered Fox's Gap while the other corps in Burnside's wing, Joseph Hooker's I Corps, attacked Turner's Gap and points north.[20]

Willcox arrived behind Cox's division at Fox's Gap on Old Sharpsburg Road at about 2:00 p.m. Under fire from Confederate artillery on Ridge Road, which runs from Fox's Gap northward for approximately one mile to Turner's Gap, and from an elevated position near Turner's Gap, Christ's brigade deployed in support of two guns from Capt. Asa Cook's battery trying to answer the Confederate salvos. A member of the 17th Michigan remembered the Confederate artillery fire cutting "the leaves of corn until [they] were quite thoroughly covered." A shell disabled one of Cook's guns, and for a time it appeared they would be lost. To meet the approaching Confederate infantry, Christ put the 17th Michigan north of Old Sharpsburg Road while the 79th New York linked with Welsh's brigade on the south side of the road. Ordered to silence "at all hazards" the nearby Confederate battery of Capt. J.W. Bondurant, Willcox was understandably skeptical of the 17th Michigan's fighting abilities at this nascent stage of its service. Greeting the 17th's Col. William Withington, his "old friend and fellow prisoner of war," Willcox asked:

"Glad to see you, Colonel. But what can you do?"

"We can march by a flank and load and fire, General."

"All right, sir. You see that battery up in the gap? Now if you can steal up through the woods and pick off some of the cannoneers, that will help a good deal."

"All right."

Willcox sent the 17th Michigan forward with support from the 45th Pennsylvania (Welsh's brigade). Withington "led his Wolverines . . . through the woods, where the crack of their rifles was soon heard, causing an evident abatement of the [Confederate] artillery fire, and some mysterious movement of [Confederate] infantry."[21]

Thomas Drayton's brigade (David Jones' division) of approximately 1,300 Georgians and South Carolinians faced Willcox. Initially deployed in an L-shaped line facing south and east, Drayton's men received orders to attack from D. H. Hill, who "felt anxious to beat the force on [his] right [at Fox's Gap] before the Yankees made their grand attack, which [he] feared would be on [his] left." Hill directed Drayton, along with the brigades of G.T. Anderson (D.R. Jones' division) and Roswell Ripley, "to follow a path until they came in contact with [Thomas] Rosser, when they should change their flank, march into line of battle, and sweep the woods before them." As part of Drayton's brigade advanced southward to attack Burnside's Corps, the 50th and 51st Georgia shifted their position from a stone fence facing east, to Old Sharpsburg Road, the embankments on either side of which appeared to make for a naturally strong defensive position. The Georgians did not see the 17th Michigan advancing out of the woods and into a field on their left flank and rear. The road devolved into a slaughter pen, with Drayton's brigade suffering more than 50% casualties, many of them inflicted by the 17th Michigan. Christ reported the 17th Michigan "opened a fire on the enemy with terrible effect, piling the road and field with his dead and wounded, and finally completely routing him, driving him in the utmost confusion across the field into the woods, and capturing a number of prisoners." A newspaper account just days after the battle reported, "Drayton's South Carolina brigade is entirely gone, either killed, wounded or prisoners. The 17th Michigan—a new regiment—done up this brigade, first with bullets and finally with bayonets." Willcox praised the 17th Michigan, a regiment that "had not been organized a single month, and was composed of raw levies," for having "performed a feat that may vie with any recorded in the annals of war, and set an example to the oldest troops." Confederate reinforcements from John Hood's division stabilized the situation after the rout of Drayton's men, enabling the Confederates to retreat off the mountain after dark. Christ's brigade suffered 26 killed and 136 wounded at Fox's Gap. Most of the casualties were sustained by the 17th Michigan.[22]

Christ's brigade, along with the rest of the IX Corps, spent the night on the Fox's Gap battlefield and left the area after noon on September 15, marching toward Porterstown and then the Boonsboro Pike. Christ's brigade spent September 16 on picket duty as the two sides exchanged artillery fire and moved into position.[23]

## Antietam

As the battle unfolded on the morning of September 17, the IX Corps on the Union left was charged with attacking the Confederate right flank. After the IX Corps captured the Lower Bridge in the early afternoon, Burnside personally ordered Willcox to move his division across Antietam Creek. Christ's men crossed at about 2:00 p.m. and filed up Lower Bridge Road toward Sharpsburg. The brigade fanned out to the right of the road as it continued toward Sharpsburg. The 79th New York led the brigade in a double skirmish line, followed by the 17th Michigan on the right, the 50th Pennsylvania in the center, and the 28th Massachusetts on the left next to the road. Welsh's brigade was across the road to their left.[24]

Despite Burnside's intent that the divisions of Isaac Rodman and Willcox move forward in an unbroken line, the IX Corps advance was uneven. Christ later reported on the lack of support on his left, where Welsh's brigade should have been, while Welsh reported a lack of support on his right, where Christ's brigade should have advanced. The undulating terrain made it difficult to keep the lines together. Moving up from the banks of the Creek, Christ's men came into view of, and under fire from, Confederate batteries posted on high ground to their front. The 79th New York skirmishers advanced on the left of troops from Charles Lovell's brigade (Sykes' division, V Corps) and together they drove detachments from the brigades of Nathan Evans (independent brigade, Longstreet's Wing) and G.T. Anderson (D.R. Jones' division) out of the Sherrick farm lane. The Confederates retreated to a house and stone mill straddling Lower Bridge Road leading into Sharpsburg. Lacking authority to continue the advance, Lovell's men went no further. Richard Garnett's Confederate brigade (D.R. Jones' division) waited above in support of two 3-inch rifles of Capt. G.V. Moody's battery (Col. Stephen Lee's artillery battalion) that had begun the day arrayed on the plateau opposite the Dunker Church. Nearby, Joseph Walker's South Carolinians, along with Capt. C.W. Squires' and Capt. H.R. Garden's batteries, occupied high ground on Cemetery Hill.[25]

Christ's brigade advanced to within a few hundred yards of the enemy batteries, but halted due to a lack of support south of the road into Sharpsburg. In this exposed position, Confederate artillery fire "commanded [Christ's] whole line from left to right" and put Christ's men "under a most severe fire of round shot, shell, grape, and canister." An artillery shell took off both legs of Capt. James Ingham of the 50th Pennsylvania, leaving the dying officer to exhort his men, "Forward, Company K, aim, fire." The day after the battle, Elon Mills, a private in the 17th Michigan, wrote, "[w]e were marched up under a most galling cross-fire, which raked our ranks severely" and "I was struck on the shoulder with a piece of a shell (the meanest thing in the world). It spoiled my fun for that day, for I did not fire a gun, but had to leave." When Welsh advanced south of the Sharpsburg road, the 17th Michigan, supported by the 50th Pennsylvania and the 28th Massachusetts, closed on the Confederate guns to their front and compelled them to limber up and retire. A rise provided cover that prevented Christ's men from shooting the horses and the cannoneers. Christ's brigade went no further. Its commander curiously cited the reason as "the woods were lined with [enemy] sharpshooters, and I would only have exposed my command to their fire without gaining anything."[26]

Christ's brigade suffered 244 casualties for the day. No doubt the rolling terrain on that part of the field limited the exposure of Christ's men at various points during the fighting. Perhaps that is why the men of the 17th Michigan and Lt. Col. David Morrison of the 79th New York hinted that the attack should have been pressed further. Despite the initial success of Christ's and Welsh's attacks, as well as that of Col. Harrison Fairchild's brigade just to their south, the IX Corps attack would falter in the fading afternoon light as reinforcements bolstered Confederate resistance beginning at the left end of the Union line. Christ's brigade spent the evening of September 17 and most of the next day near its fighting ground before re-crossing Antietam Creek around 5:00 p.m. on the 18th. On September 19, they moved back to the west side of the creek, camping within a mile of the Shepherdstown Ford across the Potomac River, not far from the closing act of the Maryland Campaign.[27]

**J.O. Smith**

* * *

## 2nd Brigade: Colonel Thomas Welsh

**Units:** 8th Michigan, 46th New York, 45th Pennsylvania, 100th Pennsylvania
**Strength:** 2,057[28]
**Losses:** 93 (3k-86w-4m)[29]

Born in 1824, Thomas Welsh hailed from the Susquehanna River town of Columbia, Pennsylvania. After three months' service in the 2nd Pennsylvania, Welsh became the first colonel of the 45th Pennsylvania Infantry in October 1861. It departed for South Carolina in December 1861 and served there until returning to Fort Monroe, Virginia in July 1862. The regiment became part of the newly formed IX Corps in early August 1862. The 100th Pennsylvania, or the Round Heads, was recruited in the southwestern part of the state in August 1861, also served in South Carolina, including in the campaign to take Port Royal in late 1861, and took part in operations against

Charleston, along with regiments that later became part of Willcox's division—the 8th Michigan (organized in September 1861), the 50th Pennsylvania and the 79th New York. The 8th Michigan and the 100th Pennsylvania, along with the 46th New York, a German American regiment known as the Fremont Rifles, also saw action at Second Bull Run and Chantilly.[30]

Leaving the battlefields of Northern Virginia, the 1st Division, consisting of Welsh's brigade (minus the 45th Pennsylvania, which would not depart from Aquia Creek, Virginia until September 6) and Col. Benjamin Christ's brigade, spent two days in Alexandria, Virginia before encamping on Meridian Hill in Washington from September 5 until the morning of September 7. From there, the brigade moved northward into Maryland and reached the Monocacy River, within two miles of Frederick, on September 12.[31]

## South Mountain

The men of Welsh's brigade stirred from their bivouac east of Middletown on the morning of September 14. After a breakfast of "roasted corn, crackers and coffee," the men marched westward at around 8:00 a.m. Welsh reported that upon "[a]rriving in front of and within range of the enemy's guns, in position on the South Mountain, commanding the [National] [R]oad leading to Hagerstown, I received orders to lead and attack the enemy's batteries on the right of the turnpike." The Round Heads led the way as skirmishers along the road. Welsh soon received an order "recalling my command and directing me to follow Christ's brigade to the support of General Cox's division" in the assault on Fox's Gap to the south. Jacob Cox's Kanawha Division had battled for possession of Fox's Gap since morning, and Willcox's troops would now join in the effort, while Joseph Hooker's I Corps attacked Turner's Gap and points north of the National Road.[32]

Advancing up Old Sharpsburg Road toward Fox's Gap, Welsh placed his troops to the left of Christ's brigade. The right of the 45th Pennsylvania

was on Old Sharpsburg Road, the left of the 46th New York "extending toward the command of General Cox," and the 100th Pennsylvania in reserve. Willcox sent the 8th Michigan, which was transferred from Christ's brigade to Welsh's brigade on September 16, as well as the 50th Pennsylvania (Christ's brigade) further to the left to reinforce Cox. Lt. Col. Joseph Gerhardt of the 46th New York reported his line was "under a very heavy fire of shot and shell" and so "covered themselves behind fences and hills till the order was given to advance." A veteran of the 45th Pennsylvania remembered, "orders were given to unsling knapsacks which were piled and a man from each company detailed to guard them." Confederate artillery fire from along Ridge Road, intersecting Old Sharpsburg Road at Fox's Gap, and from an elevated position near Turner's Gap a mile to the north, fell among Willcox's men. Two guns from Capt. Asa Cook's division battery went forward to answer the Confederate artillery. Welsh was in the front line with his old regiment and "[h]ardly had [Cook's] guns unlimbered, however, when a volley of musketry and a dose of grape and canister sent guns, gunners, caissons and horses pell mell back down the road." Fortunately for the bluecoats, Welsh "by a few cool assuring words allayed whatever excitement might have prevailed among the men." Around 4:00 p.m., when "all had become ominously silent all along the line," Welsh and Christ received orders to advance. Two companies of the 45th Pennsylvania advanced as skirmishers. With the 17th Michigan (Christ's brigade) north of Old Sharpsburg Road, Welsh's men went forward while Confederate artillery fire from their right "made sad havoc among the tree-tops scattering limbs in all directions or plowing ugly furrows in the ground in dangerous proximity to [Welsh's] line."[33]

After defending Fox's Gap with a single North Carolina brigade in the morning fight, D.H. Hill decided to deploy newly arriving reinforcements from Longstreet's command, including the approximately 1,300 Georgians and South Carolinians of Thomas Drayton's brigade. Hill envisioned a sweeping multi-brigade attack to knock the Yankees back down the mountain. Unfortunately for Hill, confusing terrain, winding roads, sightline-obscuring trees and slopes, and wanting leadership among his brigade commanders produced nothing more than a bloody melee that ultimately yielded the Gap to the bluecoats. Part of Drayton's brigade advanced southward from Old Sharpsburg Road before reorienting to take cover behind a stone fence facing east from a lane that ran south of the road. Caught in the open for a time and exposed to the fire of Willcox's men from three sides, Drayton's brigade suffered more than 50% casualties. Still, Drayton's men inflicted a heavy toll on Welsh. In particular, the 45th Pennsylvania suffered 134 casualties. Only the 7th Wisconsin lost more men at South Mountain on the Union side. Though the 8th Michigan, which had been sent to the left in support of the Kanawha Division along with the 50th Pennsylvania, did not directly participate in this action, Cox wrote of the "meritorious conduct" of the 8th's Lt. Horatio Belcher, who "rallied about 100 men and led them up to the front." Separated from his brigade, Belcher reported to Cox "and asked a position where he might be of use until his proper place could be ascertained," eventually supporting one of Cox's batteries. Samuel Sturgis's division's advance allowed Welsh's men to withdraw, though not without some hazard. Gerhardt reported the 9th New Hampshire "commenced firing before they had taken our position," and the men of the 46th New York "only saved themselves by throwing themselves down on the ground." Willcox was proud of his division's performance at South Mountain, writing to his wife that his men had gathered more than 1100 rifles and muskets and "took some hundreds of prisoners that were turned over without count."[34]

## Antietam

After spending the night of September 14 on the Fox's Gap battlefield, the brigade made its way to Sharpsburg via Porterstown and arrived with most of the IX Corps on September 16. When the IX Corps attempted to force its way across Antietam Creek the following day, Welsh's brigade, with the rest of Willcox's division, remained in reserve until Burnside ordered it forward. Crossing the Lower Bridge at about 2:00 p.m., Welsh's troops climbed "a steep hill on the left side of the [Lower Bridge] road" leading into Sharpsburg. The 100th Pennsylvania led the way as skirmishers, followed by the 45th Pennsylvania on the right, the 46th New York in the center and the 8th Michigan on the left. Christ's brigade was across the road to their right.[35]

After assembling on the west side of the creek, the IX Corps advanced at about 3:15 p.m. Welsh's men confronted difficult terrain and "an incessant fire of [Confederate] artillery [that had] the exact range of the valley and the ravines." Gerhardt of the 46th New York reported "a galling fire of shot and shell" as soon as his regiment came into view of a Confederate battery posted on Cemetery Hill. The brigade drove the 15th South Carolina skirmishers from near the Otto farm buildings before facing a number of enemy units, including Micah Jenkins' South Carolina brigade (under the command of Joseph Walker) and Col. F.W. McMaster's detachment (17th South Carolina and Holcombe Legion of Nathan Evans' brigade, and a detail from the 1st Georgia of G.T. Anderson's brigade), which Christ's troops had forced out of the Sherrick farm lane. The combined Confederate force took position in and around an orchard, stone house, and mill next to the Lower Bridge Road leading into town. Two guns of Cook's division battery under Lt. John Coffin went forward with the infantry and unlimbered near the Otto house. Willcox watched Coffin's guns fire on Confederate artillery on Cemetery Hill and the Confederate infantry confronting Welsh. The 45th Pennsylvania, with support from the 100th, carried the stone house and mill, taking several prisoners. Welsh wrote of his men "charging the enemy and driving them rapidly in the direction of Sharpsburg, my troops advancing to the edge of the town and capturing the rebel Captain [Hansford] Twiggs and several soldiers." Twiggs, who was part of McMaster's detachment that Christ's men had driven from the Sherrick farm lane, was wounded and lying inside the stone house when he was captured by "stragglers from a Pennsylvania regiment which marched passed (sic) the house in column." Welsh's skirmishers then advanced to the first street in town, just a few hundred yards away.[36]

The advance of Christ's brigade to Welsh's right compelled the withdrawal of Confederate infantry and artillery from Cemetery Hill. Richard Garnett (D.R. Jones' division), whose brigade was on Cemetery Hill near Boonsboro Pike, wrote of the danger Welsh and Christ presented: "the Federals had turned our extreme right, which began to give way, and a number of the Yankee flags appeared on the hill in rear of the town and not far from our only avenue of escape. I ordered the brigade to fall back, deeming it in imminent danger of being surrounded and captured, as it would have been impossible for it to have held its position without the support of the troops on the right." Walker withdrew his brigade to take up a position parallel to the road connecting the bridge with the town. Cox noted this ascendant moment for the IX Corps: "On the right, General Willcox and Colonel Crook quickly repulsed the enemy and drove back their artillery, pushing victoriously forward nearly to the village. On the left, General Rodman and Colonel Scammon likewise advanced rapidly, driving the rebels before them."[37]

With no more than two hours before sunset, the window of opportunity for the IX Corps was closing. Still, Willcox liked their chances: "With two batteries on the roadway, my two brigades on either side, and a similar formation under Scammon, the command was ready to start." Welsh's casualties were relatively light to this point, and with the 45th Pennsylvania's men reaching the town, the Confederates might have been unable to rally. But

then, according to Willcox, Burnside halted the advance. Willcox "sent back an aide-de-camp to explain the situation—a clear front and signs of confusion at Sharpsburg, and to insist upon our going ahead." The aide returned to deliver "another order to halt, with a message that McClellan concurred—for the reason that he expected an attack on our left from A. P. Hill, coming over from Harper's Ferry." In Willcox's estimation, "this was the time when we felt the loss of Reno." Hill's attack on the left of the IX Corps thus inflicted not only heavy casualties on Isaac Rodman's division, but also apparently unnerved the Union high command. Had Willcox been unleashed into the streets of Sharpsburg, his division might have wreaked havoc in the ranks of the Army of Northern Virginia.[38]

Casualty returns for Welsh's brigade were just under 100. The rolling terrain that slowed Welsh's advance also provided more cover than was available to attacking Union forces on other parts of the field. Positioned on Welsh's immediate left, Fairchild's brigade suffered one of the highest casualty rates of all the Union brigades at Antietam. Welsh, as well as Christ, suffered far less. Welsh reported "great difficulty in restraining the ardor of my troops, who seemed anxious to charge through the town and capture the batteries beyond." But Willcox and Welsh had to obey Burnside's orders. Welsh withdrew his men back to the creek that evening and re-crossed toward the end of the next day. Back on the west side of the creek on September 19, Welsh's brigade encamped within a mile of the Shepherdstown Ford across the Potomac River, as the Maryland Campaign drew to a close.[39]

**J.O. Smith**

157

***

# 2ND DIVISION—

## Brigadier General Samuel Sturgis

Samuel Sturgis was born in Shippensburg, Pennsylvania on June 11, 1822 and graduated from West Point in 1846. He served as a Lieutenant of Dragoons during the Mexican War and was captured and held for eight days as a prisoner of war. After the war he served in the West and took part in several campaigns against the American Indians. When the Civil War broke out, Sturgis was in command of Fort Smith (Arkansas). Sturgis watched numerous colleagues defect to the Confederacy, but he was duty bound, and led his men and government supplies out of the fort and traveled to Fort Leavenworth in Kansas. Sturgis was rewarded with a promotion to the rank of major. He was promoted to the rank of brigadier general of volunteers in March 1862 and assigned to the defenses of Washington. Sturgis was ordered to support John Pope at Second Manassas in August. He was temporarily placed in command of the Reserve Corps attached to the V Corps. While waiting for a train to carry his men to Pope, Sturgis was told his men were not a priority, as other troops were being sent forward. Sturgis boldly stated, "I don't care for John Pope one pinch of owl dung."[40]

A number of changes occurred after Pope's defeat and elevation of McClellan to reorganize the Army of the Potomac with units of the Army of Virginia early in the campaign. One was Maj. Gen. Jesse Reno's elevation to IX Corps command, leaving his division without a commander, so Sturgis was selected to lead the 2nd Division, consisting of Brig. Gen. James Nagel's 1st Brigade and Col. Edward Ferrero's 2nd Brigade. Both brigades consisted of battle-hardened veterans who had served with Burnside during his North Carolina Expedition. The brigades saw limited action at Second Manassas, but were heavily engaged at the battle of Chantilly. Due to attrition from heavy campaigning, each brigade received a rookie regiment to augment its fighting strength.[41]

The two rookie regiments, 35th Massachusetts and 9th New Hampshire, added to the division spent several days rapidly marching to catch up to their battle-tested comrades. They completed their trek on September 13, a day before the battle of South Mountain. The next morning started leisurely, as the division was encamped west of Middletown, Maryland. Reno sent the Kanawha Division forward to cross South Mountain, where it encountered enemy troops at Fox's Gap. Sturgis received word at about 1:00 p.m., to move his command forward, ". . . to the support of General Willcox, then hotly engaged on the slope of the mountain . . ." The division arrived at the foot of the mountain around 3:30 p.m. Reno detached the 2nd Maryland and 6th New Hampshire to support Union artillery along the National Road, as Sturgis directed the rest of his men onto Old Sharpsburg Road, leading to Fox's Gap, to shore up other hotly engaged IX Corps units. Sturgis ordered Ferrero's brigade into battle while holding Nagle's brigade in reserve. As the battle progressed Sturgis noted, "The infantry fire had now become so warm and the ground so stubbornly disputed that General Nagle's brigade was brought forward, and the whole line engaged." The gunfire ceased around 9:00 p.m., and Sturgis wrote in his report, ". . . our valiant troops slept on the ground and on their arms." The next morning greeted the men with sights of dead Confederates in "ghastly numbers scattered on the field," whose comrades had withdrawn from the mountain. Sturgis reported a divisional loss of 151 at the battle for Fox's Gap.[42]

The division headed for Boonsboro in pursuit of the Confederates after noon on September 15. The IX Corps eventually reached the banks of Antietam Creek, where the men went into bivouac. September 16 found the division shifting further to the left of the IX Corps' line to an open field concealed from Confederate observations by a large cornfield. Sturgis reported on September 17, "… the enemy opened a heavy artillery fire, from which their projectiles fell thick in our camp." Though the Confederates could not directly observe the IX Corps units, they had a general sense of their location. Sturgis received orders from Burnside to push to the left and advance with the goal of capturing the Lower Bridge. Crook's brigade (Kanawha Division) had already tried and failed to take the bridge. Sturgis repositioned his division's artillery, Capt. George Durell's Pennsylvania Light, Battery D and Capt. Joseph Clark 4th United States, Battery E, to pound the Confederates.

Sturgis' division's 3,354 men played a major role in securing the Lower Bridge. He selected Nagle's brigade to lead his attack at about 11:00 a.m., but it failed. Sturgis reported, "They [Nagle's men] made a handsome effort to execute this order, but the fire was so heavy on them before they could reach the bridge that they were forced to give way and fall back." Undeterred by the past failures of capturing the bridge, Burnside ordered Sturgis, ". . . to carry the bridge at all hazards." Sturgis turned to Edward Ferrero's twins (the 51st New York and the 51st Pennsylvania) and ordered them to "charge with the bayonet." Observing their charge, Sturgis wrote, "They started on their mission of death full of enthusiasm, and taking a route less exposed than the regiments which had made the effort before them." Sturgis anxiously watched his men descend the ridge and made their dangerous charge. Cheering erupted along the IX Corps line as the Stars and Stripes could be seen racing across the bridge. The 1st Brigade crossed the bridge and moved to the left, ascending the high ground, while the 2nd Brigade moved to the right along the road after it crossed.[43]

Battle-weary men and empty cartridge boxes made Sturgis' division incapable of further action until properly resupplied and rested. The IX Corps' final attack was led by Orlando Willcox's and Isaac Rodman's divisions, while Sturgis' men waited in the rear, subjected to an intense Confederate artillery barrage of, ". . . canister and grape, shell and railroad iron, and the vehicles of destruction fell like hail among them, killing and wounding large numbers and fairly covering us with dust, yet not a man left his place except to carry off his wounded comrade." Disaster struck as victory was within the IX Corps' grasp. A.P. Hill's division, newly arrived from Harper's Ferry, hit the IX Corps' exposed left flank. Thunderstruck, the IX Corps' line collapsed left to right like a row of dominoes. Sturgis' division was called back into action to stabilize the line and prevent the loss of hard-fought ground. Nagle's brigade was sent to the left to support Rodman, and Ferrero's brigade to the right to support Willcox. With the line stabilized and with darkness descending across the fields, America's bloodiest day came to an end.

The division lost 673 men at Antietam. Sturgis' report of the battle began, "It is impossible to refer to the many individual acts of heroism displayed by the officers and men throughout these few eventful days . . ." He praised his men for going days at a time without food, continuously marching and fighting "in the brilliant victories of Roanoke, Camden, New Berne, and Chantilly." The Maryland Campaign brought these battle-hardened veterans additional laurels while the rookies saw the elephant.[44]

**Jason Campbell**

* * *

### 1st Brigade: Brigadier General James Nagle

**Units:** 2nd Maryland, 6th New Hampshire, 9th New Hampshire, 48th Pennsylvania
**Strength:** 2,289[45]
**Losses:** 204 (39k-160w-5m)[46]

Three of the four regiments in Brig. Gen. Nagle's brigade were battle-hardened. The 2nd Maryland mustered into service in September 1861 in Baltimore, Maryland, for a three-year term. Once the regiment completed its training, it joined Gen. Ambrose Burnside's IX Corps command in North Carolina and took part in his expedition. The 6th New Hampshire also joined Burnside in North

Carolina after mustering into service in November 1861. The 48th Pennsylvania responded to President Lincoln's call for 600,000 men in July 1861 and mustered into service in October 1861. Once equipped, the regiment joined Burnside in North Carolina. The remaining regiment, the 9th New Hampshire was green. It mustered into service in August 1862, and many of those boys had never fired their muskets prior to going into their first combat, but quickly became battle-hardened veterans. The four regiments were brigaded together when McClellan reorganized the army in early September 1862, and all four remained in the IX Corps until the end of the war, fighting in both the eastern and western theaters.[47]

James Nagle was born on April 5, 1822, in Reading, Pennsylvania and became a painter and paper hanger. He had a distinguished career as a soldier, serving his country during the Mexican War and the Civil War. He organized the Washington Artillery Company in 1842 and served with distinction as a captain in Company B, 1st Regimental of Pennsylvania Infantry. Responding to President Lincoln's initial call for 75,000 troops after the attack on Fort Sumter, Nagle once again offered his services by becoming colonel of the 6th Pennsylvania Infantry. After the initial troops' three-month terms of enlistment expired, Lincoln was forced to call upon the states for additional enlistments. Pennsylvania Governor Andrew Curtin, eager to meet this call for more men, turned to Nagle to raise a new regiment. Nagle went to work recruiting men from within his home area of Schuylkill County. The 48th Pennsylvania was mustered into service with Col. Nagle in command in October 1861. He rose to brigade command prior to the Second Bull Run Campaign and was rewarded for his actions with promotion to brigadier general on September 10.[48]

## South Mountain

Nagle's brigade consisted of only three regiments when the Maryland Campaign began—the 9th New Hampshire did not receive orders to join it until September 6, arriving on September 13, the day before its baptism by fire. Nagle's three regiments were battle-tested, but attrition had dwindled their numbers. The addition of the 9th New Hampshire gave the brigade "the advantage of numbers if not experience, for it doubled the length of the line," reported the regiment's historian.[49]

Nagle's brigade left Middletown on the National Road at 1:00 p.m. on September 14, and advanced toward the sounds of Battle at South Mountain, reaching its foot by 3:00 p.m. The 2nd Maryland and 6th New Hampshire were detached and continued along the National Road towards Turner's Gap. The green troops of the 9th New Hampshire were paired with the veterans of the 48th Pennsylvania and held in reserve. While in this position, the 9th New Hampshire was ordered to load its muskets. Many of the young farm boys had never loaded or fired a gun before and were shown how to do so very quickly. Once the guns were loaded, the men watched Burnside sighting a gun of Lt. Samuel Benjamin's battery. For the men, "nothing so stirs the blood of the true soldier as the cannon's voice." This was especially true for the boys of the 9th New Hampshire, who were mesmerized by the cannons' roar and the sounds of battle.[50]

They soon had a much different experience as they began to encounter casualties-- lines of wounded passed to the rear with bloodstained uniforms and mangled forms. A young boy on a stretcher passed by, and though wounded, he had strong words of encouragement for the Granite State boys: "Lying upon a stretcher, he is borne on the shoulders of comrades. Mere boy as he seems, his voice has all the electric thrill of command as he shouts: 'Go in, boys! They can't stand the bayonet!'"

Nagle's two regiments were soon ordered to head for Fox's Gap to support Ferrero's brigade, assuming a position on the left of Old Sharpsburg Road. The 46th New York (Thomas Welsh's brigade; Orlando Willcox's division) was deployed in front of the 9th New Hampshire. When its ammunition ran low, the Granite State boys moved up to replace it. In their haste to engage the enemy, the rookies opened fire too soon. Lt. Col. Joseph Gerhardt of the 46th New York reported the rookie 9th "commenced firing before they had taken our positions…" and recalled, "our soldiers…only saved themselves by throwing themselves down on the ground." The 9th New Hampshire then rushed forward as the "Zip, Zip" of passing musket balls sought out victims. "Here and there a man drops his rifle, clasps a hand to his leg, arm, or side, and falls to the rear, or sinks to the ground." The 48th Pennsylvania moved up on the left of the 9th New Hampshire against Thomas Drayton's brigade of David Jones' division.[51]

The various IX Corps units began fighting alongside other units outside their command as the struggle continued. For example, the 9th New Hampshire and 48th Pennsylvania found themselves fighting alongside the 100th Pennsylvania of Welsh's brigade. The 46th New York returned to the firing line after replenishing its ammunition. The combined firepower of the mixed units of Nagle's and Welsh's brigades delivered the final punishing blow to Drayton's brigade. Division commander, Sturgis noted, "The enemy made several charges with the hope of driving our brave troops from their position, but were driven back with great slaughter behind a stone fence, where he reformed, but was driven again even from that shelter, and we occupied the highest point of the mountain." Darkness descended upon the mountain, bringing an end to the Battle of South Mountain. The 9th New Hampshire and 48th Pennsylvania lost a combined 41 men. The 2nd Maryland and 6th New Hampshire were held in reserve along the National Road, and though they saw no action, were subjected to galling fire from Turner's Gap.[52]

**Antietam**

Nagle's brigade bivouacked on the eve of the battle near the Lower Bridge. During the morning of September 17, the 2nd Maryland led the slow advance down a lane from the Rohrbach's farm, followed by the 6th New Hampshire, 48th Pennsylvania and the 9th New Hampshire. The 2nd Maryland came to a halt along the lane; its right resting on the southwest corner of a cornfield. The 6th New Hampshire halted behind it. A plowed field with a slight hill to the west of the lane offered protection from stray fire. The 48th Pennsylvania stepped off the lane and advanced through the cornfield and came to a halt near a small log cabin in close proximity to the 2nd Maryland. The last regiment in the column, the 9th New Hampshire, continued down the lane and halted at a chestnut post-rail fence bordering Rohrersville Road. This road led to the Lower Bridge about 375 yards to the north of the 9th New Hampshire's position. Once the men of the 9th New Hampshire took position behind the fence, they begin engaging the Georgians of Robert Toombs brigade (David Jones' division) across the creek. Nagle's brigade held its positions as the first unsuccessful attacks on the bridge were made by the 11th Connecticut and Crook's brigade.[53]

Nagle's brigade was called to action around 11:30 a.m. Burnside believed a charge from the south would face less of a concentrated fire then the previous direct assaults. The 2nd Maryland received orders to countermarch 200 yards back up the lane they had earlier descended to reduce the time spent under the Georgians' flanking fire. The Marylanders then halted beside the 6th New Hampshire, who remained under the protection of the plowed hill on the west side of the lane. The 2nd Maryland and 6th New Hampshire each had 150 men for the impending charge towards the bridge.

Sturgis ordered them to "move over at a double-quick and with bayonets fixed." Complying, the 2nd Maryland and 6th New Hampshire advanced over the plowed hill. Descending the opposite side, they came to a halt in its southwest corner. The same strong fence that the 9th New Hampshire used for protection further south, now stood in front of them, bordering the road to the bridge The historian of the 6th New Hampshire reported the terrain, "turning at right angles, it [the road] ran along the bank with only the narrow stream between it and the enemy's position." Officers raced ahead to tear down a section of the fence to allow the men following behind them to get through the gap. Once through, the men turned right onto the road and charged towards the bridge about 300 yards to the north. The men quickly saw the challenge before them. "The opposite bank was a steep, high bluff, covered on its top and sides with forest trees. Behind these trees, and behind barricades of stone and logs, the rebels were strongly posted, their fire covering every inch of ground over which our troops must march to reach the bridge," reported the 6th New Hampshire's historian.[54]

The 2nd Maryland surged toward the gap in the fence, funneling them into its limited opening, making them vulnerable to the Georgians' withering fire. Dozens of men fell victim to this heavy onslaught of lead, causing those in the rear to become unsteady. The men began pushing and elbowing their way out of the ranks to avoid the hail of musket balls directed at them. Their cool, calm and steady officers quickly regained control and issued bursts of orders. The men began double-quicking along the road, receiving fire from the west bank of the creek to their left that paralleled the road. The Georgians in the rock quarry and the cliff above the bridge unleashed a torrent of lead. The Marylanders lost a third of their strength after traversing a mere 100 yards, but they continued to push forward, determined to reach the bridge. Their momentum began to slow when within 250 feet of the bridge as their column became decimated. The 6th New Hampshire behind them met the same fate, receiving a devastating fire while proceeding through the fence gap. Its historian wrote, "They fixed bayonets, and, moving at the double quick, passed through a narrow opening in a strong chestnut fence-which there was no time to remove-and charged in the most gallant manner directly up the road to the bridge." The historian continued, "Of the first hundred men who passed through the opening in the fence, at least nine tenths were either killed or wounded. Such sweeping destruction checked the advancing column." The fire from the Georgians was described as having a "murderous

effect" upon the men. Survivors of the regiments began frantically searching for any protection available; fence posts, fallen logs, and anything that could stop a musket ball. Once they found a protected position, those able to fight proved their resilience by maintaining a steady fire at the well-concealed Georgians. Observing their actions from the rear, Nagle explained, "The Second Maryland and Sixth New Hampshire Volunteers were placed in a perilous position near the bridge, and are entitled to commendation for their soldier-like bearing and bravery displayed." Sturgis further noted, "They made a handsome effort to execute this order, but the fire was so heavy on them before they could reach the bridge that they were forced to give way and fall back."[55]

The 9th New Hampshire remained in reserve, positioned along the far end of the lane once occupied by the 2nd Maryland and 6th New Hampshire. Their left flank rested 100 yards away from the road; their right flank extended up the lane to the former position of the 2nd Maryland. A hill to the west protected the entire line from stray fire, but the men slowly crawled up its side to provide support and covering fire for their comrades. Nagle noted in his report how the 9th New Hampshire, ". . . opened a destructive fire directly upon the enemy, and expended nearly all of their ammunition during a gallant resistance of an hour." The 48th Pennsylvania also provided supporting fire. These men advanced further north to support Capt. Seth Simmonds' battery, also supported by five companies of the 28th Ohio (Crook's brigade). The 48th Pennsylvania became engaged with the 20th Georgia directly opposite of them. During this brisk exchange of fire, Capt. James Wren became a conspicuous target and had several close calls. "I came near losing my life with 3 difrent [sic] musket Balls," said Wren, who continued: "Coming right over whear [sic] I was firing with the musket & the men said, 'Captain they have range on you.'" Officers handling muskets was frowned upon as they were expected to provide leadership, not additional firepower. Wren however, could not resist the urge to assist his men in this deadly dual.

Aware that his position has been spotted, Wren "watched Closly [sic] & saw a Soldier on the other side of the Crick [sic], alongside of the Bridge, step to the one side from behind a tree & fire & the Bullet whistled over my head." Now aware of who was shooting at him, Wren was determined to eliminate the threat to his well-being. Wren reloaded the musket and "secured a safe place & had my gun at a rest & lined for the tree & when he Came out to fire again, I fired but was too slow." Wren then said, "I loaded again & Keept [sic] my gun lined on the tree & Just as he moved I drew tricker [sic] & I saw him Double up at the root of the tree." Wren then proudly concluded "that Ball Ceased Coming over my head."[56]

With the repulse of Nagle's attack, the 2nd Maryland, 6th New Hampshire and the 9th New Hampshire returned to their original locations in the lane, where they provided supporting fire for other IX Corps units. The 48th Pennsylvania remained in its position on the crest of the ridge as support for Simmonds' battery. It also provided additional firepower to support Ferrero's brigade's attack on the bridge. With the success of this attack, the entire IX Corps crossed Antietam Creek. The 2nd Maryland, having suffered severely in its earlier charge and having very little ammunition remaining, was held in place on the east side of the creek. The 48th Pennsylvania was the first of Nagle's regiments to cross the bridge, followed by the 6th New Hampshire and the 9th New Hampshire. The historian of the 6th New Hampshire recorded, "As the regiments crossed the bridge they filed to the right and left," Nagle's brigade turned left once across the bridge, while previous units had turned right and followed the road leading to Sharpsburg. Nagle's men ascended the high ground and formed a line of battle, coming under very strong and persistent artillery fire. The brigade sought the protection of a ridge to shelter it from the artillery fire. Skirmishers pushed forward to engage the Confederates roughly 350 yards to their west, behind a stone fence. The 48th Pennsylvania's skirmishers engaged those from George T. Anderson's brigade (David Jones' division). Due to

its earlier engagement, Sturgis' division was considered unfit for another attack, so its exhausted men with spent ammunition were held in reserve. Fresh troops would make the assault. After being resupplied with ammunition, Sturgis' men were brought up to support Willcox's division.[57]

Willcox's division surged forward toward Sharpsburg around 3:30 p.m. under heavy fire from both small arms and artillery. Isaac Rodman's division advanced on the left, gaps begin forming in his lines and Sturgis' division was sent forward to plug them. Nagle's brigade took position on the left and Ferrero's on the right of the division's line. After replenishing its ammunition, the 2nd Maryland crossed the bridge and joined the 6th New Hampshire as the brigade's reserve. The 48th Pennsylvania formed in the rear of the 51st Pennsylvania (Ferrero's brigade), creating a second line of support. The 9th New Hampshire was supporting Lt. Charles Muhlenberg's battery, but now moved up to protect the 51st Pennsylvania's left flank and the right of the 12th Ohio (Hugh Ewing's brigade; Kanawha Division). The 9th New Hampshire was forced to lie down to avoid the heavy artillery fire directed at them. Once the 51st Pennsylvania exhausted its ammunition, the 48th Pennsylvania crawled forward to relieve their fellow Pennsylvanians. The 51st Pennsylvania crawled to the rear and held the ground previously occupied by the 48th Pennsylvania.

As the sun began setting, the 12th Ohio withdrew from the battle line, followed soon after by the 9th New Hampshire. Both regiments withstood a severe bombardment from Confederate batteries in their front and from three guns of Capt. W.J. Pegram and Capt. Carter Braxton (A.P. Hill's division) near Snavely's Ford, to the southeast. The 9th New Hampshire's withdrawal was disorganized. Confusion caused some of the men to re-cross the creek at a ford below the bridge, while the rest of the men reformed between a ridge and a 40-acre cornfield. Darkness slowly settled across the field of battle as the 2nd Maryland and 6th New Hampshire were thrown forward as skirmishers on the ridge overlooking the cornfield. As their surroundings faded in the darkness and the guns grew silent, the men began hearing the cries of the wounded. This ended Nagle's brigade's activities at the Battle of Antietam and the Maryland Campaign.[58]

Nagle's brigade performed well during the Maryland Campaign, beginning at the Battle of South Mountain, where only half of it saw action. The green troops of the 9th New Hampshire met the elephant on the mountain and did not shirk from their duty, though their inexperience almost resulted in a friendly fire incident. The entire brigade saw action at the Battle of Antietam, participating in the assaults on the Lower Bridge and the Final Attack. The brigade lost 245 (39 killed, 194 wounded, 12 captured or missing) men during the Maryland Campaign, 41 at South Mountain and another 204 at Antietam.

Nagle effectively led his brigade at Fredericksburg in December, but a heart condition forced him to resign from the army in May 1863. Nagle once again served his country during the Gettysburg Campaign when he organized a 90-day militia regiment. He did the same when Jubal Early invaded Maryland in 1864. Nagle lost his fight with heart disease in 1866, when he was only 44 years old. The monument to the 48th Pennsylvania regiment at Antietam National Battlefield bears his likeness.[59]

**Jason Campbell**

* * *

## 2nd Brigade: Colonel Edward Ferrero

**Units:** 21st Massachusetts, 35th Massachusetts, 51st New York, 51st Pennsylvania
**Strength:** 2,285[60]
**Losses:** 469(95k-368w-6m)[61]

Edward Ferrero's brigade was a veteran unit as it marched into Maryland in early September. The 21st Massachusetts, 51st New York, and 51st Pennsylvania regiments mustered into service between July and October 1861, and were sent to Annapolis, Maryland for training. They were assigned to Burnside's North Carolina expedition in early 1862 and then traveled north to Virginia, but saw limited action at Second Bull Run, but were heavily engaged at the Battle of Chantilly.[62]

The 35th Massachusetts was a new addition to the brigade. It was mustered into service in August 1862, as part of President Lincoln's July call for 300,000 men. The regiment arrived in Washington in late August and assisted in garrisoning the capital. During McClellan's reorganization of the army, the regiment was assigned to Col. Edward Ferrero's brigade on September 8.[63]

Edward Ferrero was born in Spain to Italian parents. His father was a world-renowned dance master. The family immigrated to New York while Ferrero was still an infant. The senior Ferrero established a dance studio and young Edward followed in his father's footsteps, becoming a gifted dancer in his own right. Edward also taught dance classes, but part-time at West Point. The attack on Fort Sumter inspired Ferrero to raise the 31st New York militia, also known as the "Shepherd Rifles." Ferrero was selected colonel of the regiment when it was re-designated the 51st New York Infantry.[64]

### South Mountain

The green troops of the 35th Massachusetts caught up to Ferrero's brigade on September 13. The battle-tested veterans of the brigade informed the green troops of the brigade's nickname: "The Bloody Second Brigade" and scared the recruits by telling them it is "death to belong to it [the brigade]." A Bay Stater said, "with mouths open with amazement we swallowed the startling information."[65]

Ferrero's brigade bivouacked in the fields around Middletown on the night of September 13. The Sabbath morning of September 14 started out leisurely. Cattle were driven into a nearby field for slaughter and the men began boiling their beef, but the distant rumblings were ominous signs of pending action. The Kanawha Division had left town earlier in the morning and proceeded westward toward South Mountain. By 9:00 a.m., the men could also hear the unmistakable sounds of an intensifying battle. Ferrero's brigade, about 1,650 strong, received orders at 3:30 p.m. to advance toward the mountain along the National Road and as they approached South Mountain, they were ordered to prepare for battle. According to one of the men, "leaving the turnpike. . . we began to ascend the thousand feet of elevation that we had to climb." Ferrero's men passed Union artillery "fuming like furnaces," launching shells toward Turner's Gap off to the right, and into the woods that surround Fox's Gap further above them.[66]

Ferrero's brigade turned onto Old Sharpsburg Road and ascended the mountain toward Fox's Gap amid the sounds of a furious battle up ahead. "Our brigade was now moved out of the line of rebel artillery fire, and massed, just off the road in an open space below the summit," recalled a Bay Stater. About halfway up the mountainside, the column passed a wounded man on a stretcher being carried to the rear, yelling: "Forward, boys, forward! We're driving them! Don't let this scare you, give' em hell! They can't stand cold steel!"

The 35th Massachusetts received orders to "feel the woods" for Confederate activity up ahead; the rest of the brigade remained in reserve. Their officers yelled to the men to, "Throw off your packs!" and this was quickly followed with, "Fix bayonets!" The 35th Massachusetts, with its right resting on a sunken portion of Old Sharpsburg Road, passed dead and wounded Confederates from earlier fighting. A random gunshot rang out and a soldier fell. The men, believing the shot came from wounded Confederates, lunged toward them with leveled bayonets. "Hold, men, don't strike a wounded man!" someone yelled, in time to prevent needless bloodshed. "The dead and wounded, their cadaverous faces and pale gray clothing, arms thrown up for mercy, and the little cloud of smoke dissipating above, left a vivid impression," remembered a rookie Bay Stater.

The men searched for Confederates in the surrounding woods to the right of Old Sharpsburg Road at the crest of Fox's Gap. "We had penetrated far within the original Confederate line, and the foe in this front had fled down the road to the left. If any remained in position we were well within their left flank," remembered the historian for the 35th Massachusetts. Having accomplished their reconnaissance and finding no Confederates, the men returned to the brigade. However, the descent and thick underbrush of the woods caused the lines to become disorganized and men became separated from their companies. Men called out, "Company A!" . . . Company B!" The 35th Massachusetts finally emerged from the woods and returned to their brigade, drawn up in line of battle.[67]

The 51st Pennsylvania supported George Durell's battery on the right of Old Sharpsburg Road while the 35th Massachusetts was on reconnaissance within the woods at the crest of the mountain. The men lay down in front of the guns to avoid being hit by their own artillery fire as they engaged in a duel with Confederate guns at Turner's Gap. The 51st Pennsylvania then received orders to continue ascending the mountain toward Fox's Gap, where it was held in reserve. IX Corps commander, Jesse Reno, was not satisfied with his men's progress, so he ordered the 51st Pennsylvania to cross to the right side of Old Sharpsburg Road. The 51st Pennsylvania and 51st New York were positioned on the frontline holding the IX Corps' right flank, separated by Old Sharpsburg Road. The 21st Massachusetts was behind them on the second line.[68]

After crossing Old Sharpsburg Road, the 51st Pennsylvania entered the field in front of the woods recently vacated by the returning 35th Massachusetts. The regiment's historian recalled "a most murderous fire of musketry was poured into them from the enemy, who was concealed in a thicket that skirted the field." The unexpected burst of flashing muskets erupting from the darkened woods froze the men momentarily.. A Bay Stater recalled "their bullets cut the earth about our feet," and a Pennsylvanian added, the "blinding flashes of their guns," was the only way to pinpoint the location of the hidden enemy. They were up against John Hood's division, who had arrived to reinforce the Confederates holding Fox's Gap. The 21st Massachusetts on the second line dropped for cover, as the "Twin" 51st regiments on the frontline quickly responded, pouring "a deadly volley into them [Hood's men] that soon cleared the skirt of woods of all rebels." The 51st Pennsylvania had other worries. As the green troops of the 35th Massachusetts, "believing they were attacked, opened a deadly fire in the direction from which the balls were coming," and they "returned fire, aiming over the heads of the line in front," recalled a Bay Stater. The Pennsylvanians found they were sandwiched in a deadly crossfire between friend and foe "getting shot like dogs." remembered the Keystone State historian.[69]

Many of the Pennsylvanians dove to the ground to save themselves. The 51st New York arrived and quickly interceded, threatening to shoot members of the 35th Massachusetts if they did not cease fire. Panic and confusion reigned as conflicting commands to, "Fire!" and "Cease fire!" were heard. A Pennsylvanian explained, "God only knows when the slaughter would have ceased." Reno was mortally wounded when he was struck in the chest by a musket ball around this time. The musket fire gradually ceased as the mountain became darker and colder, but the men remained alert for sounds of enemy movement. Ferrero's brigade lost 116 men (10 killed, 83 wounded, and 23 missing/captured) at the Battle of Fox's Gap. Two companies from the 21st Massachusetts were detached to escort Confederate prisoners to Frederick, further decreasing the brigade's effective force at Antietam.[70]

**Antietam**

The brigade received orders to pursue the Confederates at 1:00 p.m. on September 15. The historian of the 21st Massachusetts recalled, "we moved down the mountain, and marching some five miles towards Sharpsburg, went into bivouac in a beautiful spot, about a mile from Antietam Creek." The brigade awoke on September 17 to a cloudy day with fighting taking place to their north. The IX Corps' sector remained quiet until 8:00 a.m. when the corps' artillery went into action. The 21st Massachusetts supported Durell's battery, while some had an opportunity to read recently delivered mail from home. A shell exploded within the regiment's color guard, but fortunately, one by one, its members sat up with no injuries. The regiment rejoined the brigade around noon, about the time that Ferrero was ordered to prepare for an assault on the Lower Bridge. The 35th Massachusetts was held in reserve and its men watched as the brigade's veteran regiments: 51st New York, 21st Massachusetts, and 51st Pennsylvania advanced towards the bridge. The three units halted behind a low hill in a cornfield, but some stray shells caused the brigade's first casualties of the battle.[71]

Across Antietam Creek, the Georgians of Robert Toombs' brigade (David Jones' division) held a strong defensive position on a bluff. Ferrero's men were not aware of the several prior attempts to capture the bridge, but numbers of fallen comrades on the field told them the challenge would be formidable. Ferrero thundered up to his brigade and shouted, "the 51st to forward," and galloped off. Colonels Robert Potter (51st New York) and John Hartranft (51st Pennsylvania) looked at each other, amused, as "the state was not designated," recalled Hartranft. Potter said he "smiled and turned around to his regiment" content to remain in place. Ferrero returned, demanding in a roar "Why in hell don't you 'forward?'" Hartranft responded, "Who do you want to forward?" Ferrero replied, "the 51st Pennsylvania." Hartranft retorted, "Why don't you say what you mean when you want me to move?" The 51st Pennsylvania moved only a short distance toward a nearby barn where they were joined by the remainder of the brigade. A courier approached Ferrero and delivered orders and he rode up to both 51st regiments, yelling, "It is General Burnside's special request that the two 51sts take that bridge.

Will you do it?" Cpl. Lewis Patterson (Co. I, 51st Pennsylvania) called out, "Will you give us our whiskey, Colonel if we take it?" Ferrero spun his horse around to look at Patterson, "Yes, by G-d, you shall all have as much as you want, if you take the bridge." Ferrero was adamant they would get the whiskey from the commissary wagons, or if "I have to send to New York to get it, and pay for it out of my own private purse." The men immediately yelled, "Yes!" Units from Nagle's brigade (2d Maryland, 6th New Hampshire and the 9th New Hampshire), involved in earlier attacks on the bridge, provided additional firepower from their protected positions. The two Bay State regiments also added their firepower.[72]

The "twin 51st" regiments marched to a position overlooking the bridge while under enemy fire. Col. Potter reported, "We formed on the hill directly opposite the bridge, at a spot where a dip in the ground concealed us from sight." The men tossed their knapsacks onto a quickly growing pile and formed near the 48th Pennsylvania (Nagle's brigade), who supported Simmonds' battery. The Kentucky battery and others pounded the opposite side of the creek. The "Twins" took the measure of the terrain. They would traverse 300 yards of open field to reach the bridge, all the while under a storm of lead. The men soon heard their officers scream "Charge!" and a blue wave of men rolled down the hill. A Union soldier recalled the men were "cheering and dropping at every step as [we] descended the plowed hill in full view of the enemy." He and the line raced into the storm of lead and "seemed to melt away like a thread of solder before a blowtorch." Potter reported, "As soon as we come pouring over the hill, rushing upon the bridge, the enemy greeted us with so hot a fire," that the attack's momentum began to slow. The narrow opening of the bridge entrance forced the two regiments to break like a wave upon rocks. The 51st Pennsylvania gathered behind a stone fence to the right of the bridge entrance; the New Yorkers raced for a post-and-rail fence to the left of the bridge entrance. As the men dove for cover, Potter ordered his New Yorkers to engage the

Georgians. The men responded by opening "a rapid fire into the opposite quarry" across the bridge.[73]

The 21st Massachusetts, just south of the bridge, poured a continuous fire into the Rebels across the creek. The historian for the 21st Massachusetts remembered, "The bank opposite the 21st was covered from the water's edge with a thicket of brush and trees, presenting a mass of foliage impenetrable to the eye," forcing the men to fire "from twenty to thirty rounds into the wall of shining leaves." Union artillery hammered the west bank with canister, and a few stray rounds hit the Bay Staters. The 21st Massachusetts was then ordered to support the 51st New York, which they did "on the double-quick through a withering fire . . . which dotted the field around us with little puffs of dust as the hissing bullets entered the ground; and pierced the bodies of more than twenty of our little band marked the path . . ." The men successfully connected with the left of the 51st New York. Ferrero's men now engaged the Confederates in a "desultory sharp-shooting fire . . . for ten or fifteen minutes."[74]

Sensing the Confederate fire slackening, and seeing many of them withdrawing "from their position by twos and threes," Potter believed the time to rush the bridge had arrived. "I saw Col. [John] Hartranft, I asked him what was the matter. He replied that 'he had experienced so hard a fire that it had checked his advance and forced his men to seek shelter, which he could not get them to leave.'" Potter walked to the center of the bridge opening, where a hot fire still poured down from the heights, but the intensity had definitely diminished. Potter returned to Hartranft, the senior officer, and requested permission to storm the bridge with his men. Hartranft gave his consent, and according to Potter, "I turned towards my men, rushed to the center of the bridge, and waved my sword to them to come." A captain of the right-most company ran up to Potter and asked, "what do you want?" Potter replied, "I want you to come over the bridge with me." The captain returned to his company and ordered his men to double-quick to the bridge entrance. As they neared it, the 51st

167

Pennsylvania saw their twin surge towards the opening and the men sprang-up and also ran toward the bridge entrance. The regimental colors of both regiments, side-by-side, surged across the bridge. A defiant Lt. Col. William Holmes of the 2nd Georgia raced down the hill to the water's edge, brazenly waving his sword at the crossing Union troops. A shower of bullets dropped Holmes whose body was then stripped of all valuables. The "Twins" climbed the bluff, capturing Confederates concealed in the trees and in the quarry. Many signaled surrender, raising their ramrods into the air with scraps of white paper on the ends. Ferrero's men gazed back across the bridge to the east side and saw a trail of scattered blue bodies lying along the length of the bridge. The 21st Massachusetts did not cross with the "twins," but remained on the east side of the creek. Its ammunition was depleted, so the men searched fallen comrades' cartridge boxes. The 35th Massachusetts crossed over the bridge and joined the "Twins" on the west side of the creek.[75]

The remainder of the IX Corps also crossed Antietam Creek. The exhausted men and their depleted ammunition precluded the brigade, and the rest of the division, from participating in the Final Attack. Orlando Willcox's and Isaac Rodman's fresh divisions were tasked with carrying the attack into Sharpsburg. Ferrero's brigade remained in reserve. All was going according to plan when A. P. Hill's division arrived from Harpers Ferry and slammed into the attacking units of the IX Corps. Sturgis' division was brought up to stabilize the line and blunt Hill's attack. Ferrero's brigade advanced and took a position along a Virginia worm fence. The 51st Pennsylvania's historian explained how the men, "Advanced to the brow of the hill that overlooked the large 40-acre cornfield that ran along the John Otto farm lane, where the enemy were as thick as bees in a hive." The men were forced to lie down due to the "most violent discharges of case-shot and shells from the enemy that it [the 51st Pennsylvania] ever was under up to that time." The Pennsylvanians held the brigade's left, with the 51st New York on its right and then the 21st Massachusetts (now up after being resupplied with ammunition), and the 35th Massachusetts. Potter reported, "we drove the Confederates who were pursuing Rodman's division to their entrenchments." Ferrero's men stubbornly held their ground while under heavy fire from both infantry and artillery, "A rebel battery of six guns on our right, played upon us with a miscellaneous collection of missiles, varying between canister, shell, pieces of railroad iron, and scraps of all kinds," explained the historian of the 21st Massachusetts. Potter added, "The firing was very sharp and at short range, and our losses very severe." When the sun began setting, the men were troubled by their diminishing supply of ammunition. Potter's men "were obliged to husband those we had, to reply to any attack made on us." The 35th Massachusetts on the right of the line, with their full cartridge boxes, blazed away at the Confederate artillery on Cemetery Hill, and the main Confederate line consisting of the 37th North Carolina (Lawrence Branch's brigade; A.P. Hill's division), Toombs' brigade and James Archer's brigade (A.P. Hill's division). Darkness put an end to the fighting. Sturgis' division was replaced by the Kanawha Division, which allowed Ferrero's brigade to fall back to the heights above the bridge.[76]

The veteran regiments in Ferrero's brigade performed well at the Battle of South Mountain, but the rookie 35th Massachusetts caused additional and unnecessary casualties when its men opened fire on their comrades. During the Battle of Antietam, Ferraro's brigade met a daunting challenge at the Lower Bridge and during the Final Attack; however, their resilience and determination, resulted in the IX Corps' success in taking and holding the hard-fought bridgehead. The brigade lost 585 men (105 killed; 451 wounded; 29 missing), about a third of their strength during the Maryland Campaign (116 at Fox's Gap and another 469 at Antietam). The 35th Massachusetts, after the Maryland Campaign, understood the brigade's nickname, as they truly were, "The Bloody Second Brigade."[77]

**Jason Campbell**

* * *

# 3RD DIVISION—

## Brigadier General Isaac P. Rodman, Colonel Edward Harland

The 3rd Division was formed on April 2, 1862 after the start of Burnside's North Carolina Campaign. It was initially commanded by Brig. Gen. John Parke, but when he became Burnside's Chief of Staff prior to the Maryland Campaign, Brig. Gen. Isaac Rodman assumed command of the division.[8]

Rodman was born in South Kingston, Rhode Island on August 18, 1822 and followed his father into the world of business as a young man. He also became involved in politics, rising to state senator. Rodman was a deeply religious Quaker who taught Bible study classes and was a superintendent of a Sunday school. He was forced to search his soul before joining the military. He ultimately determined he could not enjoy the comforts of home if he did not protect his country. Rodman helped raise a company in the 2nd Rhode Island and was commissioned its captain on June 6, 1861. His unit first saw action at First Bull Run. Rodman was promoted to the rank of colonel in October 1861 and given command of the 4th Rhode Island, which he molded into an effective fighting unit. Rodman and his regiment accompanied Burnside in his North Carolina Campaign, and he claimed fame during the final charge at the Battle of New Bern on April 28, 1862. After his promotion to brigadier general, Rodman contracted typhoid fever during his service in the Carolinas, so he returned home to recuperate. Burnside wrote to Rodman about the need for seasoned officers prior to the Maryland Campaign, so although still not well and against the advice of his doctors, Rodman returned to the army. Upon his return in August 1862, he was given a division in the IX Corps.[79]

Rodman's 3rd division joined the IX Corps' march from Washington and was among the first Union troops to reach Frederick, Maryland on September 12. The following day, Rodman spun off Col. Harrison Fairchild's brigade to Jefferson, to assist in driving the enemy's cavalry toward Crampton's Gap. The division left Frederick at 3:00 a.m., and after a short rest, reached Middletown at 10:00 a.m. After resting there for four hours, the march continued to Fox's Gap. Rodman and his men finally arrived between 4:00 and 5:00 p.m., the last of Burnside's divisions to arrive. Col. Edward Harland's brigade was sent to the right to support Orlando Willcox's division, but saw no action. Fairchild's brigade was sent to the opposite end of the line to support Capt. Joseph Clark's battery, just as it was coming under attack by G.B. Anderson's brigade of North Carolinians, which it helped repulse. The division sustained 20 casualties at Fox's Gap (two killed and eighteen wounded).[80]

The division's seven regiments and two batteries numbering 2,791 men, arrived east of the Lower Bridge with the rest of the IX Corps on the evening of September 15. Rodman's men formed the extreme left of the Union line on a low ridge behind the Rohrbach farm. On September 16, McClellan and Burnside devised a battle plan that would send a division west along Antietam Creek to a ford, three-quarters of a mile south of the bridge, selected by the army's engineers. Once across, the men would flank the enemy in front of the Lower Bridge, ensuring a swift passage by the IX Corps across Antietam Creek. Why Burnside selected Rodman, a non-West Pointer, to lead the flanking effort across Antietam Creek is unknown. It could have simply been expedient because the division was already closest to the ford. Their personal friendship may have also played a role. Both Burnside and Rodman were native Rhode Islanders and had fought together since First Bull Run. It was no secret that Burnside lobbied for Rodman's promotion to brigadier general and encouraged him to return to the army from his medical leave of absence.[81]

On the morning of September 17, Rodman marched his men toward the ford designated by McClellan's engineers. Col. Hugh Ewing's brigade from the Kanawha division was added to the flanking column. The IX

Corps' leadership listened intently for indications of Rodman crossing the ford. They heard none and would only learn later that the designated ford was unsuitable for crossing. Rodman heard about a suitable ford further downstream, so he continued moving his column in that direction. In the meantime, a second attack on the bridge was repulsed. Rodman finally approached Snavely's Ford and prepared to cross. The men pushed aside the Confederate sharpshooters defending the fording site and the crossing went fairly smoothly. With Rodman across Antietam Creek, and growing losses among the Confederates defending the bridge, the IX Corps was able to successfully take the Lower Bridge and climb the ridges to get into position for the final assault on Lee's right flank.[82]

Rodman's division occupied the IX Corps' left flank during the Final Attack; Willcox's division would attack on the corps' right flank. Rodman deployed his division with Harland's brigade on the left, Fairchild's on its right, and Ewing's in reserve. According to historian Ezra Carman, "Willcox . . . should move directly upon Sharpsburg, and that Rodman, supported by Ewing, should follow the movement of Willcox, first dislodging the enemy in their immediate front, and then inkling to the right, so as to bring the left wing in echelon on the left of Willcox." Fairchild stepped off smoothly, but confusion reigned in Harland's brigade and only one of its regiments moved forward toward the enemy line. The regiments advancing toward the enemy positions achieved limited success before being thrown back by the newly arriving troops of A.P. Hill's division.[83]

Rodman's division lost an additional 1,077 men at Antietam (220 killed; 787 wounded, 70 missing/captured). Rodman was among the wounded. He rode up to the 8th Connecticut, far in advance of the rest Harland's brigade, and was struck in the chest by a ball that passed through a lung. No one saw him fall, but two enlisted men, Seth Bingham and T. H. Hawley, heard his cries and took him to a sheltered position under the ridgeline where he was protected. Fairchild believed Rodman had crossed to the west side of a heavily contested stone wall, placing himself in harms way. Rodman died on September 30, 1862.[84]

**Bradley M. Gottfried**

✳ ✳ ✳

## 1st Brigade: Colonel Harrison Fairchild

**Units:** 9th New York, 89th New York, 103rd New York
**Strength:** 1,099[85]
**Losses:** 455 (87k-321w-47m)[86]

Harrison Fairchild, born in Cazenovia, New York in 1820, assumed command of the 1st Brigade when Col. Rush Hawkins took leave on September 7, 1862. Fairchild helped organize the 89th New York (Dickinson Guard) in November 1861, and it served in North Carolina during much of 1862. The origins of the 9th New York date to July 1860 when Hawkins organized a company of "Zouaves," the name taken from an Algerian tribe noted for its fighting qualities. Following President Lincoln's call for volunteers after Fort Sumter, the 9th New York was sworn into service in late April 1861 under the command of Hawkins. The regiment was involved in some of the earliest actions of the war, covering the Union retreat from Big Bethel in June 1861, and later served in Burnside's 1862 campaign in eastern North Carolina. The 103rd New York (Seward Infantry) was organized in early 1862 and served in North Carolina that summer. During the Maryland Campaign, the 103rd was below full strength, as at least three of its companies remained in North Carolina. The 9th New York, 89th New York and 103rd New York all became part of the 1st Brigade in July 1862. The Maryland Campaign would mark the brigade's first combat together.[87]

The brigade arrived in Washington on September 5 and bivouacked on Meridian Hill, before heading north, into Maryland, two days later. A 9th New

York veteran noted they were a "portion of a great river of men rolling down toward Frederick." Once more in a "friendly country," the troops "sauntered along leisurely enjoying the rural scenes and the pleasing sight of men pursuing their daily vocations, while women and children stood in doorways or leaned from windows to watch them pass." The brigade reached the outskirts of Frederick on September 12, and a historian of the 9th New York recalled the "streets bloomed out as profusely as a garden with flowers, and everywhere the army was received with a joyous outburst that will be remembered for many a day." A saloonkeeper even hung a colorful engraving of the 9th New York in action on Roanoke Island, North Carolina to celebrate the newly arrived bluecoats.[88]

## South Mountain

On September 13, Fairchild detailed the 9th New York to support a cavalry detachment under Col. R.H. Rush, scouting a few miles outside of Frederick toward Jefferson that had run into a small Confederate cavalry force under Thomas Munford. Three companies of the 9th deployed as skirmishers, and John Parke, Burnside's chief of staff, ordered the rest of the brigade forward in support. The Confederates withdrew northward toward Middletown before Fairchild's men could do much damage. Though the brigade netted only a prisoner or two, the excursion afforded a grand view of the Middletown Valley from Catoctin Ridge. A Zouave recorded that "[b]eneath us was ten miles of country checkered with fields of grain of various hues, some having already yielded their harvests, thus imparting a stranger brilliancy with the contrast to the rest. Through them all were scattered beautiful groves and the farmers' home-like looking barns and cottages; and the Blue Ridge [South Mountain], in its massive, dark-blue shade, seemingly dividing this spot from the ever-changing landscape of the Heavens."[89]

Fairchild's brigade backtracked to Frederick that evening, as "the men sung [sic] their customary marching songs and the woods rang with the choruses." Eager for sleep after a full day of marching, the men threw "themselves on the hard earth" and "enjoyed that sweet rest which worn and footsore soldiers can so well appreciate." A fire at the Frederick city jail during the night interrupted their rest and required the aid of three companies of the 9th New York to guard prisoners and douse the flames. The brigade was on the march again by 3:00 a.m. on September 14 and arrived at Middletown about 10:00 a.m. The men enjoyed a view of the Middletown Valley similar to the day before, but they also "could see the white puffs of smoke and catch the dull sound of which we all knew the meaning."[90]

The sights and sounds of the Battle of South Mountain lay before Fairchild's brigade, which spent a few hours at Middletown before proceeding toward Fox's Gap during the mid-afternoon. About 4:00 p.m., Jacob Cox ordered the brigade to the far left of the Union line to support Capt. Joseph Clark's four-gun battery. The 9th New York deployed on the right, facing west, the 103rd was in the center and the 89th New York on the left, facing south. Fairchild reported that "while forming line of battle we were attacked on the left by Second, Third, Thirteenth, and Thirtieth North Carolina Regiments, their object being to capture the battery, it having been in position some time without support." G.B. Anderson had directed these North Carolinians (three regiments from his own brigade, one from Samuel Garland's) from their positions on Old Sharpsburg Road, up the hillside through "woods [that] were very dense" and ground that was "very rugged and mountainous." To the Confederates, Clark's battery, with its attention drawn northward toward the fighting around the gap, appeared vulnerable.[91]

The 89th New York, under the temporary command of Maj. Edward Jardine of the 9th New York, received the brunt of the Confederate attack and was still getting into position when the North Carolinians struck. When some of the 89th halted at "the sudden and unexpected dash of the enemy," Jardine jumped on top of a stone wall and yelled, "Eighty-ninth New York, what in hell are you about? Continue the movement!" A private in the 89th New York wrote that when the Confederates opened fire, "we dropped to the ground" and then "rose up and let into them." Clark's battery let loose with double canister, until the butternut attackers "recoiled and fell back suffering great loss." David Thompson of the 9th New York remembered hearing for the first time the "high shrill yelp" of the Rebel yell. The Confederates lost approximately 70 men in this sharp attack. Only the 89th New York suffered any losses in the brigade: 2 killed and 18 wounded. As Thompson astutely observed, "the whole day's battle had been merely an effort of the enemy to check our advance till he could concentrate for a general engagement."[92]

The 9th New York was on picket duty that night, guarding the left end of the IX Corps' line. Firing between the two sides continued until several hours after dark. On September 15, the brigade rested for much of the day and then moved out around 5:00 p.m., halting six hours later. By the next evening, the brigade was again at the far left of the Union line and bivouacked in a cornfield, not far from the bluffs overlooking Antietam Creek. A regimental historian of the 9th New York recorded how the movements during the evening of September 16 were made "in almost absolute darkness," when "it was too dark to see either one's comrades, the bushes through which we forced our way, or the stumps and inequalities of the ground over which we stumbled." Fairchild ordered Lt. Col. E.A. Kimball of the 9th New York to throw out a company of skirmishers, who ended up "frequently engaging the enemy's sharp-shooters during the night, and keeping them at bay."[93]

## Antietam

Beginning at daylight on September 17, the brigade endured Confederate artillery fire for the first of several times throughout the day. Fairchild reported the brigade not only received a "brisk shelling" but was also "saluted by the bullets of [enemy] sharpshooters" from across Antietam Creek. Pvt. Charles Johnson of the 9th New York

wrote of the Confederate shells, "[e]very one of them exploded just as nicely as they could wish, squarely over our heads." The brigade suffered 36 casualties before moving to a less exposed position. Cox sent Fairchild's brigade, along with Harland's, across Antietam Creek downstream from the Rohrbach (Lower) Bridge which would be under attack by other IX Corps troops later that morning. Locating a suitable crossing, however, was not so simple. The assigned ford immediately below the bridge featured banks too steep for a large body of troops and their equipment to traverse. Instead, Fairchild and Harland tramped two miles farther south to find Snavely's Ford. The ground was difficult, so the movement consumed valuable time and enabled the 2nd Georgia and 20th Georgia (Toombs' brigade, D.R. Jones' division) to give their full attention to defending the bridge.[94]

During the search for a practical crossing site, Capt. James Whiting's battery (five 12-lb. boat howitzers, two rifled and three smoothbore cannons), attached to Fairchild's brigade, shelled the west side of the creek to suppress the Confederate artillery fire and skirmishers. Some of Whiting's rounds reached the Confederate defenders upstream at the bridge. Once skirmishers from the 8th Connecticut had located Snavely's Ford, Whiting's battery moved to an elevated position below the ford to cover the brigade's crossing. The 9th New York crossed first. Though the ford was only waist-deep, a veteran remembered "it was quite an effort to stem the current." A thin line of Confederate skirmishers—men from the 50th Georgia and some sharpshooters from Jenkins' brigade of South Carolinians—harassed the crossing with a "rather scattering" fire, which Fairchild's men did not stop to answer.[95]

Once across the creek at around 1:00 p.m., the brigade filed to the right while under cover of the bluff. The ascent came next. Pvt. Johnson recorded the men "with considerable difficulty scrambled up" a steep and rocky hillside, 185 feet above the creek. The brigade came under Confederate artillery fire as it had at the beginning of the day. Many of the shells falling among the brigade were overshoots directed at Joseph Clark's and George Durell's batteries. The 9th New York formed in line on the right of Clark's guns, the 103rd in the center behind Clark and Durell, and the 89th New York on the left of Durell's guns. In addition to taking a toll on Clark and Durell, the Confederate fire from Capt. J.S. Brown's and Capt. James Reilly's batteries inflicted a number of casualties on Fairchild's brigade, including Kimball's horse. The brigade's field officers impatiently paced behind their lines, eager to go forward. Rodman sent out a company of the 9th as skirmishers and then gave the command, "First brigade! Forward!" Matthew Graham of the 9th New York remembered how he had been "lying on my back, supported on my elbows, watching the shells explode overhead and speculating as to how long how I could hold up my finger before it would be shot off."[96]

From the plateau where Clark and Durell were in battery, the brigade crossed Otto's farm lane, descended into another ravine and then drove 7th Virginia skirmishers of James Kemper's brigade from the stone and rail fences that ran from the western edge of the 40-acre cornfield to Lower Bridge Road. Fairchild ordered a charge. Drayton's and Kemper's under-strength Confederate brigades, totaling about 600 men, waited for Fairchild in a ravine that was behind yet another slope the bluecoats had to ascend. As Fairchild's men approached, Drayton's and Kemper's troops took position behind stone and rail fences just east of Harpers Ferry Road, where they delivered "a crashing volley of musketry." Charles Johnson of the 9th New York wrote the "air was filled with a deluge of bullets, grape, canister and shell." Fairchild reported his brigade "charged over the fence, dislodging [Kemper and Drayton] and driving them from their position down the hill toward the village, a stand of regimental colors belonging to a South Carolina regiment being taken by Private Thomas Hare, Company D, Eighty-ninth New York Volunteers, who was afterward killed." Fairchild's brigade, though much depleted, had gained a foothold on the heights of Sharpsburg; only a few elements of the IX Corps—the 8th Connecticut, some of the 45th Pennsylvania—had managed to make it that far.[97]

Fairchild's men recorded sights as horrific as any on the field that day. David Thompson of the 9th New York, whose likening of the battle scenes to a "whole landscape for an instant turned slightly red" echoed down the years, recalled the "dreadful spectacle" of grape-shot that "plowed a groove in the skull of a young fellow" who "never stirred from his position, but lay there face downward." Charles Johnson saw a man hit in the groin by an artillery round, "severing his limbs completely from his body." Capt. Henry Sand of the 103rd New York grabbed a flag from a fallen color bearer and ran along the line, holding the flag aloft to inspire his men. He fell wounded and wrote to his mother from the field:

> "Dear Ma,
> Here I lay on the field, shot through the thigh. My wound is painful but not mortal I believe—however. I send you these lines to bid you all goodbye in case I never see you again.
> I hear our men cheering and hope the day is ours—if we only have a great victory, I am contented. Goodbye. My love and kiss to all . . ."

Capt. Sand died of his wound six weeks later. The 9th New York's Capt. Adolph Libaire raised the regimental flag and shouted to his company, "Up, damn you, and forward." He was awarded the Medal of Honor in 1898.

As some of Fairchild's men, along with some of those from Welsh's brigade, pushed toward town, the Confederates rallied to their left along Harpers Ferry Road. The lines of Fairchild's brigade, broken by casualties and terrain, became jumbled and in need of readjustment. While the 89th and 103rd dealt with the growing pressure on the left, Kimball gathered up the 9th's survivors "on the ground which had been occupied by the enemy's line of battle, and while still exchanging shots with the scattered groups of the enemy, waited anxiously for the reinforcements which were momentarily expected to appear." Kimball recalled how the 89th, under the command of Jardine, faced the attacking Confederates on the left and "gave them the bayonet." Kimball's hoped-for reinforcements did not arrive. With the Confederates gathering strength as A.P. Hill's division arrived, Fairchild "ordered the brigade to retire about 250 yards to the rear." Kimball said his men had "tears in their eyes at the necessity which compelled them to leave the field they had so dearly won."[98]

Fairchild's brigade took up a position that evening next to Antietam Creek in the rear of Sturgis' division. Like others in the IX Corps, Fairchild's men withdrew "with curses on their lips" at yielding the ground they had won. The sacrifice they made was among the greatest of any Union brigade at Antietam-- nearly 50%. The 9th New York lost more than 60% of its men who went into action, the 89th lost 28%, and the 103rd lost 58%. Fairchild's men crossed and re-crossed Antietam Creek over the next two days before pitching camp along the creek further downstream, where they could "lay back on their laurels for a few days." Though they had not gained the complete victory for which they had hoped, the brigade delivered some of the final blows that ultimately drove the Confederates back across the Potomac and ended the Maryland Campaign.[99] **J.O. Smith**

**✳ ✳ ✳**

## 2nd Brigade: Colonel Edward Harland

**Units:** 8th Connecticut, 11th Connecticut, 16th Connecticut, 4th Rhode Island
**Strength:** 2,240[100]
**Losses:** 618 (194k-139w-285m)[101]

The majority of the 2nd Brigade came from regiments that participated in Burnside's successful North Carolina Expedition. The 8th Connecticut, 11th Connecticut, and 4th Rhode Island were veteran regiments; the 8th Connecticut and 4th Rhode Island had served for almost a year. These three regiments participated in the Battles of Roanoke Island and New Berne in the early months of 1862. Likewise, the 8th Connecticut and 4th Rhode Island further proved themselves in the capture of Ft. Macon in April 1862. These men stood in stark contrast to the final regiment of their brigade. The 16th Connecticut was one of the regiments formed to answer President Lincoln's July 1, 1862 call for more volunteers. The men of the regiment spent the month of August encamped in Hartford and officially mustered in on August 24. They left home four days later, totally unaware of the fate that awaited them.[102]

The commander of the brigade, Col. Edward Harland, began his military career as captain of Company D, 3rd Connecticut Volunteer Infantry. Though he had no military experience, the Norwich native raised the 3rd Connecticut in the spring of 1861. The regiment completed its term of service and was disbanded, so Harland mustered in as colonel of the 8th Connecticut in October 1861. He led the regiment to success in Burnside's North Carolina Expedition and received command of the brigade in the months before Antietam.[103]

Harland's brigade arrived in Washington, D.C. during the first week of September, part of Rodman's division of the IX Corps. It left its encampment at Meridian Hill and began the march to Leesborough, Maryland on September 7. The corps moved again on September 8 and 9, traveling from Leesborough to Rockville and from Rockville to Goshen. Having left home only two weeks prior, the men of the 16th Connecticut were unaccustomed to the hard life of a soldier and dozens suffered from exhaustion and fell out the ranks. The IX Corps left New Market and arrived in Frederick on September 12. As the first Union troops to arrive, the 8th Connecticut, 11th Connecticut, and 4th Rhode Island entered Frederick in time "to see the last of the rebel cavalry dash out of the streets pursued by our own," while the 16th Connecticut had yet to join the brigade.[104]

## South Mountain

September 14 began early for the men of Harland's brigade. Called on to support fellow IX Corps divisions, the men began marching west from Frederick at 3:00 a.m. and arrived in Middletown by 10:00 a.m. After a four-hour pause, the brigade resumed its march and arrived at Fox's Gap between 4:00 p.m. and 5:00 p.m., where a battle had been raging for several hours. Rodman led Harland's men into the fray to support Orlando Willcox's and Samuel Sturgis's divisions engaged with D.H. Hill's men. The brigade deployed to the right of Old Sharpsburg Road and went into line of battle with "bullets cutting the branches of the trees overhead," according to Walter Yates. Darkness quickly brought an end to the fighting at Fox's Gap as Harland's brigade waited in reserve.[105]

Harland's brigade began its descent down the mountain the following day and passed through the detritus of battle. Wolcott Marsh of the 8th Connecticut wrote home about passing by "hundreds of dead secesh lying beside stone walls in narrow lanes and scattered through the woods," as they passed the Fox's Gap battlefield. For the 16th Connecticut, this was their first exposure to the horrors of war. Lt. Bernard Blakeslee recounted: "We could here begin to form some idea of that great army, the 'Army of the Potomac,' and the fearful destruction that an army can make." The other regiments of the brigade reached Antietam Creek by the morning of September 16 and were later joined by the 16th Connecticut, whose men reportedly loaded their muskets for the first time. The brigade was ordered into line of battle on the extreme left of the Union line, a quarter of a mile from Antietam Creek, on a low ridge behind the Rohrbach farm. The men spent the night resting on their arms, no doubt unable to sleep knowing what the morrow would bring.[106]

## Antietam

Harland's brigade were welcomed into the battle of Antietam by a Confederate 12-lb solid ball that crashed through the men of the 8th Connecticut, killing three and wounding four. Their position at sunrise on September 17 left the troops in range of Confederate artillery, and the brigade was obliged to move back and to the left into a more covered position. Pvt. Marx Neisener of the 16th Connecticut recounted the enemy fire "came like rain—round shot, shells, shrapnel, grape and all. The regiment fell flat and the shot went over them." The men were ordered to lie down to avoid the ongoing enemy artillery fire, and spent two hours in this position with a clear view of the enemy.[107]

Around 10:00 a.m., Burnside ordered Col. Henry Kingsbury to detach his 11th Connecticut from the brigade and head toward the Lower Bridge. It would act as a skirmish line to drive the Confederates from the bridge before George Crook's brigade (Kanahwa Division) attacked. A force of around five hundred men opposed them from Robert Toombs' brigade. The regiment advanced in left and right wings down the hill opposite the bridge. The right side of the regiment reached a low stone wall running along the creek. Though the wall provided some protection, the position was too exposed, and Capt. John Griswold jumped on the stone wall and called for his men to follow him into the creek. Few of the men followed Griswold and most of the men attempting to wade the creek were shot down or forced to turn back. Griswold was mortally wounded, and he alone made it across the creek before collapsing among the rebels. The left wing of the regiment arrived at the creek with Kingsbury leading it. He was shot four times as he approached the bridge and was carried from the field. Losing their beloved commander further shattered the already collapsing line of the 11th Connecticut, and the men retreated from the bridge. Though the 11th Connecticut's assault on the bridge lasted less than thirty minutes, the regiment lost more than one third of its men.[108]

Around the time the 11th Connecticut was detached, Rodman ordered Harland to cross the creek at a ford McClellan's engineers found the previous day. The ford proved to be impassible and Harland was instructed to locate another place to cross. Two companies of the 8th Connecticut completed this task by locating Snavely's Ford, further south from the original ford. The process of finding a suitable ford slowed Rodman's division, which did not cross the creek until around 1:00 p.m. with the help of the 8th Connecticut acting as skirmishers. Although a more suitable ford, some of the men, such as George Merriman of the 16th Connecticut, still complained about wading the "river nearly to our waist." Once across the creek, the brigade moved right and halted in the woods behind Fairchild's brigade. Harland received orders around 3:00 p.m. to form his brigade on the left of Fairchild's and prepare for an advance *en echelon* in conjunction with the rest of the IX Corps. Harland maneuvered his brigade into position and linked the 8th Connecticut with the left of Fairchild's 89th New York. The 16th Connecticut and 4th Rhode Island settled into position in a 40-acre cornfield to the left of the 8th Connecticut. This formation placed Harland's men at the extreme left of the Union line.[109]

Harland's brigade, along with the rest of the IX Corps, was tasked with advancing several hundred feet up steep, rocky slopes toward the town of Sharpsburg. David Jones's small division awaited the attack, supported by nearly 40 cannons. Rodman waved Fairchild's and Harland's brigades forward at 4:00 p.m. The 8th Connecticut on the right of Harland's line, veered slightly to the northeast to avoid moving into a large cornfield. Harland reported, "The Sixteenth Regiment Connecticut Volunteers, and the Fourth Regiment Rhode Island Volunteers, both of which regiments were in a cornfield, apparently did not hear my order . . . This delay on the left placed the Eighth Regiment Connecticut Volunteers considerably in the advance of the rest of the brigade." Harland asked Rodman if he should halt the 8th Connecticut and wait for the rest of his men to catch up, but was

told to stay with the 8th Connecticut and he would personally hurry the 16th Connecticut and 4th Rhode Island forward. Rodman found the 16th Connecticut lying down at the edge of the cornfield attempting to avoid heavy artillery fire. While urging the 16th Connecticut forward, Rodman spotted Confederates moving toward the left of the federal line. These men were from Maxcy Gregg's brigade, the lead element of A.P. Hill's Light Division, arriving from Harpers Ferry. Rodman ordered Col. Francis Beach of the 16th Connecticut to shift his men to the left to meet this new threat. Rodman then hurried forward to return to the 8th Connecticut but was struck down with a mortal wound, and command of the division now fell to Harland. The 16th Connecticut, in the army less than a month, panicked under fire and was unable to follow orders. A rookie recalled orders "were given which few of the men understood, for we were almost wholly ignorant of regimental movements, having been less than three weeks in the service, and the greatest confusion prevailed." According to 16th Connecticut historian Lesley Gordon, "One officer cried out in desperation, "Tell us what you want us to do and we'll try to obey you." "I want my men to face the enemy," Beach replied."[110]

While advancing with the 8th Connecticut, Harland spotted the lead elements of Gregg's brigade entering the 40-acre cornfield behind him, occupied by the 16th Connecticut and 4th Rhode Island. He quickly turned his horse around and hurried back to warn the rest of his command, but his horse was shot from under him. Though delayed, Harland arrived in time to order the 16th Connecticut to change front to face left and meet the 12th and 1st South Carolina (Maxcy Gregg's brigade; A. P. Hill's division), now entering the corn. The Nutmeggers inflicted serious damage to the enemy's front and flanks and compelled them to fall back. However, the South Carolinians rallied and advanced again but were quickly checked for a second time. The arrival of the 4th Rhode Island on the left of the 16th compelled the 12th South Carolina to fall back out of the corn. As the Rhode

Islanders came up to join with the 16th Connecticut and prepared to engage the enemy, someone mistook the 1st South Carolina for friendly troops, as its men were purportedly wearing Union blue (captured at Harpers Ferry) and their flag appeared to be the Stars and Stripes, so the men ceased firing. They soon discovered their error and poured a deadly fire into the 1st South Carolina's right flank, forcing it to retreat from the cornfield. While preoccupied with these Carolinians, the Rhode Islanders were unaware that Gregg had sent the 1st South Carolina Rifles forward to provide support. The Rifles swung around and slammed into the vulnerable left flank of the 4th Rhode Island, driving its men from the field. The 16th Connecticut, now alone in the cornfield, soon followed the 4th Rhode Island in a disorganized retreat. Sgt. Jacob Bauer told his wife the men accomplished their retreat "in a Bull run fashion."[111]

The 8th Connecticut fared little better in its advance toward Sharpsburg. The regiment was the only one of Harland's three regiments to hear his call to advance, and the regiment, following the 89th New York of Fairchild's brigade, moved forward without the 16th Connecticut and 4th Rhode Island. The men headed toward Capt. David McIntosh's Pee Dee battery posted along Harpers Ferry Road. McIntosh shifted to fire into the 8th Connecticut, but they approached so rapidly that he was forced to abandon the guns. The Nutmeggers would have seized the guns, had they not been in such a vulnerable position. Without the 16th Connecticut and 4th Rhode Island moving up on their left and Fairchild's brigade now falling back on their right, the 8th Connecticut was now isolated on the high ground along Harpers Ferry Road. Portions of Kemper's, Drayton's, and Toombs' brigades, along with artillery, battered the 8th Connecticut's front and then the newly arrived 7th and 37th North Carolina (Lawrence Branch's brigade; A.P. Hill's division) arrived and poured volley after volley into their left flank. Despite this tremendous fire, the 8th Connecticut made a valiant stand as described by Capt. Henry Jones: "The color guard falls! Another seized the standard, he too falls! A third! A fourth! and with him the standard goes down. But Private Charles H. Walker, of Company D, seizes the staff and waves the riddled banner in the very face of the foe." Henry Hall recalled the regiment's desperate situation as the enemy approached "steadily upon us from three sides and in a few moments the open space between us and our friends would have been filled with foes when our Major gave the command to retreat but not until the order had been three times repeated did our gallant fellows obey." Walcott also recalled a number of men refusing to fall back, shouting "Boys Lets Never Retreat. No Never," but as the regiment was about to be overwhelmed, Maj. John Ward eventually persuaded the men to "follow their colors" in an orderly retreat from the field after loss of almost fifty percent.[112]

Harland attempted to rally the elements of his command on the western side of Antietam Creek, including the 11th Connecticut, which he had not seen since it was detached for its fatal assault on the bridge. The brigade's casualties included the loss of the colonels of the 11th Connecticut and 4th Rhode Island and the lieutenant colonel of the 8th Connecticut. September 17 ended for Harland's brigade back on the east side of the Antietam Creek as "arms were stacked, and the tired soldiers laid down to rest." According to Lt. Blakeslee of the 16th Connecticut, the night after the battle of Antietam was: "Of all gloomy nights … the saddest we ever experienced." The brigade lost fully a third of its men at Antietam with little to show for it. The 8th Connecticut lost the most (194), but the rookies of the 16th Connecticut lost almost as many (185).[113]

**Claire Affinito**

✱ ✱ ✱

# KANAWHA (4TH) DIVISION—

## Brigadier General Jacob Cox, Colonel Eliakim Scammon

Jacob Cox was born in Montreal, Canada in 1828, where his father supervised roof construction and carpentry work on the Church of Notre Dame. Upon graduating from Oberlin College in 1851, Cox moved to Warren, Ohio to become the superintendent of public schools. Also active in politics, Cox helped organize the Republican Party, won a seat in the Ohio Senate in 1859 and became good friends with Gov. William Dennison. Dennison appointed Cox a brigadier general in the Ohio State Militia in the spring of 1860. The appointment amused Cox's friends, who dubbed him the "future Napoleon," and they descended upon a local bookstore to purchase military books for him. Although purchased in jest, Cox thoroughly examined and devoured the books. Though Cox thought the jokes about his appointment humorous, he expressed concerns over the rising tension with the South. Cox pursued his appointment with a determined mindset, and devoted himself to mastering the art of war, studying alongside future president James Garfield.

The attack on Fort Sumter and the subsequent call-to-arms reverberated through the country. On April 23, 1861, Cox was appointed to the rank of brigadier general of Ohio State Volunteers. Family and friends tried to convince him not to serve, citing his frailness, but he was adamant that men were needed to serve and he would be one of them.[114]

Many of the Buckeyes mustering into service in 1861 were sent to the Great Kanawha River Valley (present day West Virginia), where they were formed into the Kanawha Division under Cox. These green troops became battle-hardened veterans when they participated in the first victories for the Union war effort, protecting the vital railroad infrastructure in the Kanawha Valley. The success of the Kanawha Division gained national attention and helped army commander, George McClellan, become a recognized and respected figure. He was summoned to Washington in the latter half of 1861 to assume the command of the Union armies.

The Kanawha Division was summoned to Washington in August 1862 after Lee's success at Second Bull Run. As McClellan reorganized the Army of the Potomac, the Kanawha division was incorporated into Burnside's IX Corps. The corps had recently arrived from North Carolina, and Cox's unit became its 4th Division. The army left Washington marching in a northwesterly direction toward western Maryland, where on September 12, advance units of the IX Corps made first significant contact with the Confederate rear guard in Frederick.[115]

The 2,700-man Kanawha division was composed of two brigades: Col. Eliakim Scammon's 1st brigade and Col. George Crook's 2nd Brigade. Scammon was ordered on the morning of September 14 to report to Pleasanton's cavalry with his brigade. The brigade had spent the night camped west of Middletown and now headed west along the National Road toward South Mountain. As it crossed over Catoctin Creek, a surprise awaited. Cox noted, "Just as Scammon and I crossed Catoctin Creek I was surprised to see Colonel [Augustus] Moor standing at the roadside." When Moor led his 11th Ohio into Frederick on September 12, he was captured by Confederates during a skirmish. Cox thundered up to Moor and peppered him with questions. Moor explained he had been taken to the mountain after his capture, but was paroled the previous evening and was heading back to the army. Moor then asked Cox, "But where are you going?" Cox responded by telling him of Scammon's mission to support the cavalry reconnaissance toward Turner's Gap.

Moor was shocked by what he heard and exclaimed, "My God! Be careful!" However, by the terms of his parole, Moor was honor-bound not to disclose any pertinent information to his comrades. After he caught himself, Moor relayed no further information and continued on his way. Alerted to the potential danger ahead, Cox said, "I galloped to Scammon and told him that I should follow him in close support with Crook's brigade." Cox then rode off to bring up Crook's brigade. As Cox rode along the advancing columns, he warned every regimental commander to be prepared for anything, "it might be a skirmish, it might be a battle."[116]

After delivering orders to Crook, Cox sent a message to Jesse Reno, commander of the IX Corps, warning him that he "…suspected we should find the enemy in force on the mountain top, and should go forward with both brigades instead of sending one." Cox found Scammon and Pleasanton and joined them in a discussion along the road. By mutual agreement, they determined it was unwise for the infantry to continue on its current course. Pleasanton decided to use his cavalry to demonstrate on the road toward Turner's Gap, while the Kanawha Division stepped off the main road and used Old Sharpsburg Road to reach Fox's Gap. If successful, this movement would outflank the Confederate position at Turner's Gap. Cox decided to advance with his entire division, not knowing if, or how many Confederates might be present. Having made this decision, Cox said he would take full responsibility for whatever may happen.[117]

Cox's and his Kanawha Division's role in the Maryland Campaign began with their fight at Fox's Gap against elements of D.H. Hill's division. The Kanawha Division carried on the battle alone for most of the morning and performed well, helping the IX Corps secure the mountaintop. However, Reno's mortal wounding at the end of the battle created a leadership change. Cox assumed command of the IX Corps, Scammon became the Kanawha Division's commander, and Colonel Hugh Ewing of the 30th Ohio took over the 1st Brigade.

Scammon graduated from West Point in 1837 and served in the Seminole and Mexican Wars. On June 4, 1856, he was dismissed from military service for disobedience of orders. He became a professor at St. Mary's College in Ohio, and later, president of Cincinnati College, a position he held until the outbreak of the Civil War. Dennison appointed Scammon to the position of colonel of the 23rd Ohio, where two of his subordinates were future Presidents of the United States. Having served well in the Kanawha Valley, Scammon was promoted to brigade command in the fall of 1861. Promotion to brigadier general came after the Maryland Campaign.[118]

Scammon led the division at Antietam, where it was fully engaged. Crook's brigade participated in the early assaults on the Lower Bridge, although it was unsuccessful in its attempt. After the IX Corps secured the bridge, the division was placed in reserve. However, it was thrown back into the Final Attack when its manpower was needed to save the army from potential disaster.

Unbeknownst to the Union army, A.P. Hill's division made an unfortunate appearance on the exposed Union left flank. Hitting with the force of a sledgehammer, Hill shattered the Union line from left to right. Cox, watching pending victory slip away, quickly sent the Kanawha Division forward to reinforce the line. Ewing's brigade anchored the Union left, while Crook anchored the Union right. The resilience of the Kanawha division blunted Hill's attack, while also saving the IX Corps from a ruinous retreat across the Antietam.[119]

**Jason Campbell**

* * *

## 1st Brigade: Colonel Eliakim Scammon, Colonel Hugh Ewing

**Units**: 12th Ohio, 23rd Ohio, 30th Ohio
**Strength**: 1,308[118]
**Losses**: 182 (28k-134w-20m)[120]

The 12th Ohio and the 30th Ohio were organized between June-July 1861 and were formally mustered into three years of service at Camp Dennison and Camp Chase, respectively, in Ohio. The 23rd Ohio, organized in Columbus, began forming in June 1861, but was not complete until March 1862, when it was mustered into service. All three regiments were sent to the Great Kanawha River Valley in what is now West Virginia. These Ohioans first tasted combat there, slowly transforming into battle-hardened veterans. In August 1862, the brigade was transferred to Washington and attached to John Pope's Army of Virginia where it saw limited action. Under McClellan's reorganization, Col. Eliakim Scammon, a brigade commander since the fall of 1861, and his brigade were attached to the IX Corps as part of the Kanawha Division led by Jacob Cox, on September 9.[121]

The death of IX Corps commander, Jesse Reno, at the Battle of South Mountain created a leadership void that led to a chain of successive command changes. Cox left the Kanawha Division to command the IX Corps and Scammon took his place. Col. Hugh Ewing of the 30th Ohio now headed up the 1st Brigade.[122]

Ewing came from a prominent family that had adopted future general William Tecumseh Sherman. Sherman later married Ewing's sister, making the two men brothers-in-law. Ewing entered West Point in 1844, but dropped out of school in his final year after failing an exam. He caught gold fever, and traveled to California in 1849 to participate in the Gold Rush. He later returned to the East and studied law, joined the bar, and practiced law in St. Louis. In the first year of the Civil War, Ewing became a Brigade Inspector with the rank of major.

He traveled into what is now West Virginia, where he joined McClellan. On August 15, 1861 Ewing was promoted to colonel, assuming command of the 30th Ohio. Having achieved several successful victories in the Kanawha River Valley, McClellan was summoned to Washington. The Kanawha Division was later called to Washington and reunited with McClellan.[123]

### South Mountain

The brigade bivouacked on the evening of September 13 near Middletown. Orders arrived the following morning to advance westward towards South Mountain to support Union cavalry operations. Lt. Samuel Benjamin's battery unlimbered between the National Road and the Old Sharpsburg Road and went into action against Confederate artillery at Turner's Gap. Capt. Seth Simmonds' Kentucky battery, composed of two 20-pound Parrots and two 10-pound Parrots, travelled with Scammon's brigade. The two 10-pound Parrotts were unlimbered next to Benjamin's battery and their combined firepower was directed at Fox's Gap. The two 20-pound Parrots removed to the rear and directed their fire towards Turner's Gap. At about 7:00 a.m., Scammon's brigade headed toward Fox's Gap, on Old Sharpsburg Road when it came under artillery fire from the mountaintop. Crook's brigade, on the march, about a half-hour behind, also turned onto Old Sharpsburg Road and followed Ewing. Of the ascent to the top, Cox wrote, "We had fully two miles to go before we should reach the place where our attack was actually made, and it was a pretty sharp ascent." The climb was very tough and the men were forced to take several breaks on the way up. During one of the breaks a courier from Reno pounded up with the corps commander's support of Cox's decision to proceed towards Fox's Gap. Reno subsequently

180

brought the entire IX Corps forward to support the Kanawha Division.[124]

Scammon was within a half-mile of Fox's Gap when his brigade, numbering about 1,500 men, came under case-shot fire from Confederate artillery. He detached the 30th Ohio and sent it forward on Old Sharpsburg Road towards the gap. The rest of the brigade turned onto another country road paralleling the ridgeline, which allowed it to move further left to outflank the Confederate position at Fox's Gap. The use of the forest on the side of the mountain allowed Scammon to conceal his brigade's movements from the Confederates who held the high ground. The trees eventually gave way to an open field. Brig. Gen. Samuel Garland had his North Carolina brigade (D. H. Hill's division) deployed on the opposite side of the field, further up the mountainside, behind the protection of a stone fence. The 23rd Ohio, under the command of future president, Lt. Col. Rutherford B. Hayes, deployed on the left of the line. Hayes had been instructed to keep to the woods and to seek out the Confederate flank. Once found, Hayes was to launch an attack and turn it. Col. Carr White and his 12th Ohio formed on Hayes' right and became the center of the line. These Ohioans launched their attack towards the stone fence as the 30th Ohio slid into position on the 12th Ohio's right flank. Ewing and his 30th Ohio received orders to advance against Capt. John Bondurant's Confederate battery at the crest of Fox's Gap.[125]

Hayes pushed his skirmishers through the woods and made contact with the 5th North Carolina skirmish line at about 9:00 a.m. Alerted to the heavy exchange of gunfire on his right, Garland ordered the rest of the 5th North Carolina to move forward into the woods. The heavy growth of trees disrupted the North Carolinians' line of battle, as the 23rd Ohio advanced towards them from the opposite side of the field. Cox noted: "Hayes, being in the woods, was not seen till he had passed over the crest and turned upon the enemy's flank and rear." Like two aggressive rams on top of a mountain, a brutal collision occurred between the Buckeyes and Tar Heels. The Ohioans' well-maintained line unleashed a volley into the disjointed North Carolinians, who responded with a less effective volley. Men fell on both sides as the fight gained in intensity. Many of the conscripts in the 5th North Carolina panicked when hit by their first hostile fire and fled from the field. This caused the rest of the regiment to break and fall back onto a secondary line. Hayes quickly gathered his men and reformed his line to continue the fight. The intensity of the fight drastically heightened and Hayes ordered a charge. "Here was a sharp combat, but our men established themselves upon the summit and drove the enemy before them," said Cox. The charge was made in gallant style that broke the 5th North Carolina's line and caused some of its men to break for the rear. The charge came at a steep price. Hayes was severely wounded in the left arm when a musket ball shattered it above the elbow. Though badly injured, Hayes remained on the field and continued leading his men.[126]

With no time to cool, the guns of the 23rd Ohio went back into action and battled two other regiments of Garland's brigade to the right of the 5th North Carolina, the 12th North Carolina on the latter's right and the 23rd North Carolina, which continued the line to the east. The small 70-man 12th North Carolina, was led by an inexperienced Capt. Shugan Snow, fired a volley at the 23rd Ohio and then broke for the rear, creating a gap between the 5th North Carolina and the 23rd North Carolina. Hayes feared a charge by the 23rd North Carolina, only 100 yards away, behind a stone fence on a hill, so he ordered his men back into the woods. Suffering from a loss of blood, Hayes laid down unwittingly between the opposing lines. Hayes said: "I soon felt weak, faint, and sick to the stomach." He requested help to bring him back to his line, but all attempts brought forth a heavy fire from the North Carolinians. Musket balls thudded into the ground around him, spraying him with dirt. Hayes' men were eventually successful in returning him to the safety of his own line. Weak from loss of blood, Hayes turned command of the regiment over to Maj. James Comly."[127]

Meanwhile, the 12th and 30th Ohio, on the right of the 23rd Ohio, "charged over the open under a destructive fire of musketry and shrapnel," Cox later reported. In the center of the line, the 12th Ohio drew the assignment of attacking the stone fence in its front, under a galling storm of lead from the 23rd North Carolina, which also contended with the 23rd Ohio on the left of the 12th Ohio. The two Ohio regiments now advanced against the Tar Heels. The 12th Ohio was briefly halted under an intense fire until the 30th Ohio moved up onto their right. Cox noted, "Our front was hollow, for the two wings were nearly at right angles to each other." With his flanks secured, Cox felt confident in continuing the fight, although the 30th Ohio on the right was exposed. However, its commanding position allowed its men to sweep the field in front of them. The entire brigade now surged toward the stone fence with Crook's newly arrived brigade. The 12th Ohio, with fixed bayonets, stormed the stone fence and engaged in vicious hand-to-hand fighting. The determined attack caused Garland's line to finally collapse. The 30th Ohio, on the right of the line, raced up the mountainside to capture Bondurant's battery. Anticipating the danger, Capt. Bondurant fired a parting shot, limbered his guns and escaped up the mountain road, heading towards Turner's Gap. The Buckeyes were denied the prized battlefield trophies they actively sought.[128]

After three hours of marching, ascending a mountainside and heavy fighting, the men of the Kanawha Division were exhausted. Cox, speaking on the conduct of his division said: "The two Kanawha brigades had certainly won a glorious victory, and had made so assured a success of the day's work that it would be folly to imperil it." The division was replaced by Orlando Willcox's division. The hard fought victory gained the mountaintop but resulted in 265 casualties for the 1st Brigade.[129]

## Antietam

With Reno's death and Scammon's rise to division command, Ewing took over the 1st Brigade on September 15. The men observed the aftermath of the previous day's fight as they crossed the gap and headed down the mountain on their way toward Antietam Creek. Ewing's brigade did not participate in storming the Lower Bridge on September 17 as it was sent downstream with Isaac Rodman's division to find a ford across Antietam Creek to outflank Robert Toombs' Georgians guarding the bridge. Rodman's division finally crossed the creek at Snavely's Ford, followed by Ewing's men. "We crossed the ford of the Antietam under a shower of grape, and after being held under a trying fire from the enemy's batteries [Capt. Benjamin Eschleman's battery]…" Ewing commented later about the overwhelming mass of Union troops crossing the creek forcing the enemy guns to retire.[130]

The troops involved in attacking the Lower Bridge were exhausted and out of ammunition, so Cox brought up fresh soldiers to continue the fight. He aligned his troops on the ridges west of the bridge and prepared them for action. The majority of the IX Corps had gone without food for at least a day, so Sgt. William McKinley, the commissary officer of Ewing's brigade, and a future President, decided to bring up much needed food and hot coffee for the famished men. He raced two miles to the supply trains and with the aid of stragglers, loaded his own wagons with cooked meat, beans, crackers and fresh coffee. Once his wagons were loaded, McKinley called out for a volunteer to help him transport the wagons to the men. John Harvey of the 23rd Ohio offered his services. As the two raced back toward their starving men on the front line, they were stopped several times and told their mission was just too dangerous. Harvey later wrote: "The regiment was almost in sight of us." As McKinley looked ahead and saw the men, he became all the more determined to reach them. Harvey recalled McKinley "was so anxious to carry out his point and give the half-starved boys something to eat." McKinley appealed to Harvey to finish their journey and "he himself risking his life in taking the lead, I following and the horses going at full speed." Harvey continued, "We had the back end of the wagon shot away by a small cannon shot." The two men successfully reached their comrades and quickly dispersed the food to the hungry men.[131]

The IX Corps' final attack was launched about 3:00 p.m., with Rodman's division on the left of the line. Ewing's brigade was held in reserve on a ridge a half-mile behind Rodman to provide support. From this position the brigade watched its comrades push towards the town; success appeared imminent, but the tide was about to change. Cox recalled, "The view of the field to the south was now obstructed by fields of tall Indian corn, and under this cover, Confederate troops [from Maj. Gen. A.P. Hill's division arriving from Harper's Ferry] approached the flank in line of battle." Cox continued, "Scammon's [Ewing's] officers in the reserve saw them as soon as Rodman's brigades echeloned." Rodman's echelon deployment was meant to help support the right of the Union line, but this movement exposed Rodman's left flank to the unexpected arrival of Hill's men.[132]

Cox recalled, "Those [Confederates] first seen by Scammon's [Ewing's] men were dressed in the National blue uniforms which they had captured at Harper's Ferry; and it was assumed that they were part of our own forces till they began to fire." Ewing's men, lying behind a ridge that overlooked the impending doom to Rodman's left, quickly responded to Rodman's dilemma. As Rodman's line broke, the Ohioans' fire temporarily forced Hill's men to withdraw. Maxcy Gregg's brigade led the advance of Hill's division and was the first to be thrown into battle. With Gregg's men temporarily checked, the Buckeyes seized the opportunity to advance. The enemy's retrograde movement permitted the Ohioans to advance down the ridge, through a gully of corn, and up a slope to a stone fence that provided some protection. The 23rd Ohio raced across 375 yards of challenging terrain while under both musket and artillery fire. Once they arrived at the stone fence, the left side of their line rested on the west edge of the 40-acre cornfield through which they just passed. The right side of the line extended up along a nearby hill. The 30th Ohio advanced along the left side of the 23rd Ohio and they too encountered the same challenging terrain. They were also forced to navigate through the broken remnants of the 16th Connecticut (Rodman's division). Meanwhile the 12th Ohio advanced to the John Otto farm lane where they were held in reserve. Because they occupied high ground overlooking the cornfield, they could add support fire if needed.[133]

Maj. George Hildt of the 30th Ohio stated, "…we were ordered to charge the enemy, who were distant one-half mile, on the slope of a cleared hill facing us, a part of which was planted in corn, and served to screen both the enemy and ourselves." The 30th Ohio emerged from the protection of the ridge and advanced against the combined firepower of the rallied troops of Toombs, and James Archer's brigade (A.P. Hill's division). They soon received "a severe fire from the enemy the moment we moved over the brow of the hill," noted Hildt. The 30th Ohio raced down the ridge under fire and into the gully of corn, where they encountered the remnants of the 16th Connecticut, whose dead and wounded dotted the field. The Buckeyes continued their charge to the stone fence. Here "we delivered our fire with great precision, and for a time checked the advancing enemy," said Hildt. The 30th Ohio's slugfest against Toombs and Archer's commands took its toll on the Confederates; Archer lost about one-third of his strength trying to charge the well-positioned Ohioans. A Confederate soldier caught in this storm of lead recalled the Ohioans "posted in a heavy, dark line behind a rock fence." Hildt explained, "Our men were at this time utterly exhausted from the effect of the double-quick step across the plowed field." After the first volley was fired, Hildt continued: "…our colors erected at the wall, a withering fire was directed upon us from our left flank, and from which we suffered most severely."[134]

Archer reformed his shattered ranks, and with the support of Gregg's brigade to his right, launched another attack upon the Ohioans. Gregg's South Carolinians delivered a volley into the exposed left flank of the 30th Ohio holding the left of the brigade line and tore into the 23rd Ohio on the right of the same line. The outflanked Buckeyes were forced to retire from the stone fence. Comly of the 23rd Ohio watched soldiers approaching the 30th Ohio from his elevated position on the hill on the brigade's right flank. He later reported assuming the unknown men were additional Union forces and told his men to hold their fire. The subsequent Confederate volley ripped through both Ohio regiments. Ewing ordered Comly to change front to face this new threat, aligning his men perpendicular to the rear. As the men completed this movement, Lt. Col. Theodore Jones brought the 30th Ohio's line backwards and connected his right to the left of the 23rd Ohio. The four right-most companies heard this order and obeyed it, but the rest did not hear the order over the sounds of battle and held their position. Ewing realized the danger posed to the 30th Ohio's line and sent Lt. Reese Furbay to extract the now isolated six companies of the 30th Ohio. Furbay was killed on his way to deliver the order and the Ohioans withstood the storm of lead as long as possible. With two color bearers shot down and Archer bearing down upon them, the Ohioans fell back to the gully and once again encountered the remnants of the 16th Connecticut. Though Gregg's men delivered a flanking fire upon the exposed left flank of the 30th Ohio, they inadvertently exposed their own right flank to the 12th Ohio. The 12th Ohio's Carr White said, "My regiment was then ordered to form a line at right angles with the main line, to advance and engage a flanking column of the enemy [Gregg], which was promptly done under a shower of shell and canister that threatened the destruction of the regiment." Having checked Gregg's advance, White said, "With a view to a better position, the regiment was withdrawn to a fence [Otto's farm lane runs parallel to this fence] 50 yards in the rear, and put in position." This position proved to be just as hazardous as its previous one, so the 12th Ohio fell back further to the brigade's original position on the ridge.

Jones estimated his 30th Ohio delivered 12 to 15 shots per man before retreating. He became separated from his command when the line collapsed and was captured. Ewing's brigade, having lost the protection of the stone fence, fell back to its original position on the ridge. Darkness put an end to the fighting.[135]

Ewing's brigade faced numerous challenges during the Maryland Campaign: fighting a battle while ascending South Mountain, fighting on challenging terrain at Antietam, and leadership transitions at the corps, division and brigade levels. The men of the brigade were tough and resilient. The brigade lost a total of 447 men (90 killed, 329 wounded, 28 and missing) during the Maryland Campaign (265 men at Fox's Gap and another 182 at Antietam).

Ewing was later transferred to the Western Theater, where he remained until the end of the war. He later became the American Minister to Holland, serving from 1866 to 1870. Afterward, Ewing settled down on a farm in Lancaster, Ohio and pursued a writing career. He wrote several books including; *The Gold Plague*.[136]

**Jason Campbell**

* * *

## 2nd Brigade: Colonel George Crook

**Units:** 11th Ohio, 28th Ohio, 36th Ohio, Kentucky Light Artillery; Simmonds' Battery
**Strength:** 2,004[137]
**Losses:** 73 (8k-58w-7m)[138]

The 11th and 36th Ohio regiments were mustered into service in 1861, and the 28th Ohio entered into service in March 1862. The three regiments spent their early years of the war fighting in the Kanawha River Valley, in what is now West

Virginia. In August 1862, the regiments received orders to board trains for Washington, garnering tremendous excitement among the men looking forward to joining the Army of the Potomac. The men arrived on August 24, 1862 and the three regiments were brigaded together within weeks of their arrival, under the command of Col. Augustus Moor, and attached to the IX Corps.[139]

On September 7, the Army of the Potomac left Washington and began its chase of Lee's army, which had crossed the Potomac River into Maryland. The IX Corps marched in a northwest direction that carried it into Western Maryland, covering an easy five to six miles a day. The corps arrived on the outskirts of Frederick on September 12, which was occupied by Lee's rear-guard, consisting of Wade Hampton's cavalry brigade. Moor, whose brigade led the IX Corps, ordered the 11th Ohio to follow him in an aggressive charge into the city. A brisk skirmish erupted between the Union infantry and Confederate cavalry resulting in the first bloodshed for Union infantry in the campaign. Both sides sustained several casualties, but none greater than the capture of Moor. Leaderless, and within days of major combat, the brigade needed a new commander. Col. George Crook of the 36th Ohio was tapped to lead the brigade into its first major battle.[140]

Crook graduated from West Point in 1852 and had the dubious distinction of being the lowest ranked graduate to become a Major General, and the only person of this rank to be captured by Confederates. The majority of Crook's military career, both before and after the Civil War, involved American Indian affairs, bringing him fame. Crazy Horse once said of Crook, he was more "feared by the Sioux than all other white men." His reputation amongst the American Indians earned Crook the name "three stars." During one of many battles with the American Indians, Crook was struck by a poison-tipped arrow, but his legend only grew when he fought off the effects of the poison and recovered fully, though the arrowhead remained inside of him to his dying day.[141]

## South Mountain

On September 14, Crook's brigade marched to Fox's Gap in support of Scammon's brigade, which led the IX Corps' column. Scammon's men encountered Garland's North Carolina brigade at the gap and the two began slugging it out. Crook's brigade was called up to tip the balance in the IX Corps' favor. As his brigade arrived on the battlefield, it lost its fighting cohesion when each regiment was detached and sent to a separate, but critical spot on the frontline. The 11th Ohio was sent to support the 23rd Ohio on the far left of the division's line, while the 36th Ohio was sent to plug a gap that had formed between the 12th Ohio and the 30th Ohio in the center. Crook's last regiment, the 28th Ohio, was sent to support the 30th Ohio on the far right of the division's line, and assumed a position in the rear of that regiment. The musketry fire from both sides was extremely heavy and the casualties for both sides mounted. Under the full onslaught of the Kanawha Division's firepower, Cox's entire division surged forward against Garland's position. The 11th Ohio, on the far left of the line, executed a flanking movement that broke Garland's Carolinians and forced them back towards the cabin of farmer Daniel Wise, where they took refuge behind a stone fence. The subsequent savage hand-to-hand combat fighting dislodged the Tar Heels from their mountaintop position, then fresh troops arrived to relieve Crook's brigade. Crook's first action in brigade command was a success, but it came at a price. The brigade lost 84 men during the intense fighting at Fox's Gap.[142]

## Antietam

The brigade made its way toward Antietam Creek after the Battle of Fox's Gap. By the morning of September 17, it was camped in the vicinity of the Henry Rohrbach farm. Crook's men heard an ominous sound to the north, not a storm of nature, but one of human creation, as the Battle of Antietam had begun. Crook's success on South

Mountain had earned his brigade the honor of leading the first attack on the Lower Bridge. The question of when the attack would begin was soon answered when a staff officer of Cox's arrived with orders for Crook.[143]

Due to miscommunication, Crook believed he was to support Samuel Sturgis' division's attack on the Lower Bridge, not actually lead the attack. The initial plan called for the 11th Connecticut (Harland's brigade; Rodman's division) to charge the bridge, drawing the Confederate fire towards them. Crook would then lead his men on a direct frontal charge upon the bridge and storm across it. Crook recalled receiving his orders at "About ten A.M.," as one of Gen. Cox' staff "came to see me, and said. 'The General wishes you to take the bridge.' I asked him what bridge. He said he didn't know. I asked him where the stream was, but he didn't know. I made some remarks not complimentary to such a way of doing business, but he went off, not caring a cent." An annoyed Crook further added: "The consequence was that I had to get a good many men killed in acquiring the information which should have been supplied me from division headquarters." Crook launched his advance in the direction the staff officer had ordered. Crook noted, "We had not proceeded far before we came across the dead and wounded of Gen. Sturgis' Division [the 11th Connecticut of Rodman's division]. I went sufficiently far in advance to see the situation and to convince myself that the bridge could not be taken from that point." This was the first time Crook actually saw the terrain, as his view from his original position, to the east on the Rohrbach farm, was obscured by the wooded ridge.[144]

Crook decided to place the 36th Ohio in reserve near an orchard by the Rohrbach farm and send his other two regiments against the bridge. Maj. Lyman Jackson of the 11th Ohio reported his unit advanced "in line across a plowed field and hill, the right and left divided." Crook split up his two regiments when they reached the west side of the ridge overlooking the bridge. According to Crook, "I left the 11th Ohio where it was and took the 28th

Ohio and a section of Simmonds Battery to the right of the 11th and up the creek into some small hills…" This caused the men to advance further to the north of the bridge and to the right of 11th Connecticut, whose dead and wounded Crook had seen earlier. The Buckeyes were subjected to an intense Confederate fire that further decimated it. Having missed their objective of charging the bridge straight on, Lt. Col. A.H. Coleman led his 11th Ohio northeast of the bridge. Two companies of the 11th Ohio had previously been sent to the wooded crest overlooking the bridge to monitor the Confederates, and they forced several enemy skirmishers who had crossed the bridge, to scramble back to the other side. This action took place prior to the unsuccessful attack of the 11th Connecticut. Jackson reported "under conflicting orders, the right moving to our skirmishers forward on the right, the left moving to the base of the hill by the creek." Jackson led the right wing up to the skirmish line which had not only found the bridge, but also the Confederates, resulting in a lively exchange between the Buckeyes and the Georgians defending the bridge.[145]

Meanwhile, Coleman led the left wing of the 11th Ohio charging toward the bridge, not from due east as originally intended, but slightly from the northeast. The Ohioans descended the slope of the ridge, into an open field, and then dashed towards the bridge. The men come under a galling fire from the Confederate defenders located directly across the creek and from the bridge defenders to the southwest. Coleman was shot in his right arm while leading the left wing across the field and would be dead within an hour. On the loss of Coleman, Jackson later wrote, "I must say of him that no better, braver, truer officer ever served our country, and no regiment can feel a loss more sorely." Those who survived this charge fell back to find protective covering and continued firing until they exhausted their ammunition. Jackson reported, at "the base of the hill I found myself in a useless position with a part of the regiment, and recrossed the field to a point of the hill opposite the bridge." With his ammunition spent, Jackson received orders to withdraw back onto the 36th Ohio, which had moved up into a position of support behind the ridge. Both regiments held their positions until the Confederates were dislodged from the bridgehead. Henry Benning, the Confederate commander responsible for the defense of the bridge, later wrote of the failed attempt: "This attack [referring to the previous attempt by the 11th Connecticut] was succeeded by two bodies of troops and with like results, the last of the two extending above the bridge to the upper part of the line."[146]

Benning was describing the 11th and 28th Ohio's movements. The latter had trailed behind the 11th Ohio during its advance. Five companies of the 28th Ohio had been sent forward as skirmishers to the right of the 11th Ohio. The Confederate fire from the opposite side of the creek was extremely intense, forcing the 28th Ohio's skirmishers back to the other side of the ridge. Capt. John Amrine said of this movement: "Immediately however as the skirmishers reached the open ground a little to the northeast of the bridge they became exposed to a fierce enfilading fire not only from well posted sharpshooters but also from the main force of the enemy posted on the heights and commanding the eastern approach to the bridge." Amrine was seriously wounded from this fire and carried off the field.[147]

The other five companies of the 28th Ohio received orders to help Capt. Seth Simmonds' Kentucky battery establish a position on the wooded crest of the ridge. They struggled to get two Parrott Rifles into a commanding position to pour a destructive enfilade fire into the Georgians above the bridge. The men responsible for this hard work then took up a position on the reverse slope in support of these guns. As the 11th Ohio's right wing advanced, so too did the five companies from the 28th Ohio who had earlier skirmished by the creek. During its attack, the 28th Ohio headed, not towards the bridge, but 300 yards above it. Under a severe fire, the Ohioans scrambled to identify protection, which they found in a sandy ridge and a fence along the side of the creek. Cox reported, "Later in the contest, his men [Crook's brigade]

lining the stream, made experiments in trying to get over, and found a fordable place a little way above, by which he got over five companies of the Twenty-eighth Ohio at about the same time as the final and successful charge." Cox was referring to the charge of the 51st Pennsylvania and the 51st New York.[148]

With the capture of the Lower Bridge, the IX Corps swarmed across Antietam Creek. Crook's men crossed the creek at the recently found ford, 300 yards above the bridge. A lull, lasting about two hours, settled across the fields as the men prepared for the assault against Lee's right flank, in what many hoped would be an end to the war.

With Rodman's division on his left and Willcox's on his right, Crook's brigade held the center and pushed forward to the town of Sharpsburg. Jackson described the attack: "our army had then driven the enemy from the creek. We charged across the open fields west of the creek, where we were halted close to a stone fence." The momentum was on their side and victory was at hand, when a sledgehammer in the form of A.P. Hill's division struck the advancing Union left flank with such force that it sent shockwaves rippling down the Union line.[149]

As the troops on Crook's left flank collapsed, Jackson quickly assessed the vulnerability of the line, "Under some indications that the enemy were about to follow up the charge on our flank, I wheeled the regiment left and backward, the right standing fast on the line of battle, so as to oppose a front to any such flank movement." Soon, the 35th Massachusetts (Ferrero's brigade; Sturgis' division) arrived and assumed a position on the left of the 11th Ohio, which helped secure the left of Crook's line. However, this lone regiment was soon under heavy Confederate fire from both infantry and artillery. With its losses mounting the regiment broke and fell back, exposing Crook's left. With this new danger to the left, Jackson once again took immediate action. "I then resumed a position fronting the left, at right angles to and resting on our line." After A.P. Hill's advance was checked, Crook's brigade received orders to fall back to the eastern slope of the hill on the west side of the creek. The brigade remained in this position until the following afternoon when it was relieved by other units.[150]

Crook's brigade performed quite well during the Maryland Campaign. They lost a total of 157 men (25 killed; 122 wounded; and 10 missing) during the Maryland Campaign (84 at Fox's Gap and another 73 at Antietam).[151]

**Jason Campbell**

* * *

# XII Corps—

## Brigadier General Joseph Mansfield, Brigadier General Alpheus Williams

The XII Corps had its genesis on March 13, 1862 when a corps structure was approved for the Army of the Potomac. One of the five included the divisions of Brig. Gen. Alpheus Williams and Brig. Gen. James Shields and was designated the Fifth Corps under the command of Maj. Gen. Nathaniel Banks. The corps was shipped to the Shenandoah Valley, where it fought Stonewall Jackson in the spring of that year, besting him in the Battle of Kernstown. President Lincoln subsequently designated it the Second Corps of the Army of Virginia on June 26, 1862. It fought Jackson again at the Battle of Cedar Mountain on August 9, 1862, coming close to again defeating him. The corps' losses were heavy, though, almost 2,400. The veteran unit was designated the XII Corps of the Army of the Potomac when it was integrated into the Army of the Potomac.[1]

At 7,600 effectives, the XII Corps was the smallest corps in McClellan's army during the Maryland Campaign. Its two divisions were commanded by veterans. Williams had commanded the 1st Division since its formation and George Greene had seen action through the war, but had never commanded a division in battle. A total of five brigades with 25 regiments populated the two divisions. The corps received five new regiments, more than any other corps. It also counted seven batteries in the artillery arm. The corps marched to Fairfax on September 1 where it spent the night. Then on successive days, it marched through Washington until it reached Frederick. The two divisions took slightly different routes that will be covered in their narratives.[2]

Williams commanded the XII Corps in the absence of Banks, who was assigned command of the Washington defenses. That changed on September 15, when Joseph Mansfield arrived in Middletown to take command of the corps. Williams wrote to his daughters, "I went back to my division, rather pleased that I had got rid of an onerous responsibility." Williams called Mansfield a "veteran-looking officer, with head as white as snow." He soon learned that "our new commander was very fussy . . ."[3]

Fifty-nine year old Joseph Mansfield was a "blue blood" from Connecticut who graduated from West Point in 1822 and served as an engineering officer for most of his career. He saw action at Fort Brown, Monterey, and Buena Vista during the Mexican War, winning brevets to major, lieutenant colonel, and colonel. He was wounded in the leg during the action on September 21, 1846. After the war, he became an inspector general and gained the strong support of Gen. Winfield Scott, commander of the U. S. Army. This relationship gained Mansfield the rank of brigadier general in May 1861. He was assigned command of the Washington garrison and effectively crafted a ring of forts around Washington. While successful in these endeavors, Mansfield craved a military command. According to a modern historian, Mansfield "may well have been viewed, rightly or wrongly, as too much a creature of the peacetime army, dependable and fit for routine duty but lacking the physical dynamism, youth, and charisma needed for field command." His chance came in March 1862, when he was given a brigade in the Department of Virginia, but it did not see action. Mansfield was elevated to corps commander when McClellan headed north after Lee's army. His experience in the Mexican War caused him to take a dim view of volunteers until they sustained rigorous training or gained battlefield experience.[4]

McClellan decided to send Mansfield's XII Corps across the Upper Bridge after dark on September 16 to support Joseph Hooker's I Corps. The column slowly made its way west until it reached the Hoffman and

Line farms, about a mile in Hooker's rear at 2:00 a.m., where the men were permitted to rest in "column of companies, closed in mass." It does not appear that Hooker ever directly interacted with Mansfield. According to a modern historian, Mansfield had "only the vaguest directions as to what would be expected of him and little sense about the overall plan of battle." The men were up and on the move at first light of September 17, moving to the front "by battalions in mass . . . over ground of intermingled woods, plowed fields, and corn-fields," according to Williams. The latter's own 1st Division led the column down Smoketown Road. Williams was a savvy commander, so he knew the dangers posed by Mansfield's orders, which made "a regiment look like a solid mass" and therefore highly susceptible to enemy artillery fire. The enemy artillery immediately opened fire, but fortunately missed their target, for Williams believed if a single shot struck "our massed regiments, dozens of men would have been killed."[5]

Mansfield, according to Williams "had a very nervous temperament and a very impatient manner," but he could not stand by and watch his men being massacred. "I begged him to let me deploy them in line of battle, in which the men present but *two* ranks or rows instead of *twenty*, as we were marching, but I could not move him." The men went into action without food or coffee after a sleepless night. The corps crossed Smoketown Road and continued west a short distance and then swung south, still in massed formations. The movement was slow, as the cautious Mansfield frequently halted his command. Mansfield rode ahead to reconnoiter and confer with Hooker when the corps reached an open field west of the Samuel Poffenberger woods. The I Corps' plight was obvious as his "general officers were hurrying toward us begging for support in every direction. First, one would come from the right; then over from the center, and then one urging support for a battery on the left," according to Williams.[6]

Mansfield returned and headed over to Crawford's experienced regiments and led them into position. It was an odd activity for a corps commander, but he had a very small staff and had never commanded troops in battle, at least not since the Mexican War, and never so many as now. Upon placing the 10th Maine in position, he hurried over to lead the 128th Pennsylvania into position. Mansfield was mortally wounded at some point during the morning's fighting. Where he fell is very much in contention for as many as seven places have been claimed as the spot of Mansfield's wounding. Maj. John Gould of the 10th Maine probably makes the most compelling case. Having returned from guiding the 128th Pennsylvania into position, Mansfield ordered the Maine regiment to cease firing because he thought they were firing into George Meade's troops in the East Woods. When his men pointed out his error, Mansfield allowed them to continue, but he was almost immediately wounded in the chest. Surgeons believed his punctured lung meant certain death. When informed of his dire condition, Mansfield purportedly said, "It is God's will, it is all right." He died at the Line farm at about 8:00 a.m. on September 18.[7]

Williams was now back in charge of the XII Corps and Col. Samuel Crawford assumed command of the 1st Division. Williams rode back and conferred with Hooker. He deployed the 1st Division in the East Woods/Cornfield on the left, with Brig. Gen. George Gordon's brigade on his right behind the Cornfield and Crawford's brigade to its left extending into the East Woods. Greene's 2nd Division now arrived and Williams sent it to the East Woods. A messenger arrived from John Gibbon seeking "re-enforcements to the right,"-- across Hagerstown Pike. Williams sent Greene's 3rd Brigade under Col. William Goodrich in that direction and the 124th Pennsylvania toward the D.R. Miller farm to add additional support and "hold the ridge as long as practicable."[8]

Pitched fighting occurred between the 1st Division and elements of D.H. Hill's division in and around the Cornfield. The arrival of Greene's division tipped the balance in the Union's favor and the Confederates were forced from their positions. Greene's two remaining brigades (Lt. Col. Hector Tyndale's and Col. Henry Stainrook's) drove south, capturing the high ground around Dunker Church, where the men were permitted to rest. Williams was pleased by the performance of his men but noted the "new regiments were badly broken up, but I collected about one-half of them and placed them in support of the batteries."[9]

In response to calls for reinforcements from Greene, Williams sent several regiments from Gordon's brigade. Greene and these troops were eventually forced from their forward positions in the West Woods. With the arrival of William Smith's division (VI Corps) in the afternoon, Williams pulled the XII back to regroup, replenish the men's ammunition and eat, all but ending the XII Corps' fight during the Battle of Antietam. The small XII Corps lost 1,746 during the battle (275 killed, 1,386 wounded and 85 missing) or about 23% of its effectives. Williams was passed over for command of the corps and although he would command a corps from time to time until the end of the war, he was never officially assigned a large command.[10]

**Bradley M. Gottfried**

* * *

# 1st Division—

## Brigadier General Alpheus Williams, Brigadier General Samuel Crawford, Brigadier General George Gordon

Born in 1810 in Connecticut, Alpheus Williams graduated from Yale University, studied law and opened a successful practice in Detroit, Michigan. His pre-war career was filled with adventure, travelling extensively in Europe and serving as a probate judge, newspaper owner, postmaster of Detroit, and lieutenant colonel of the 1st Michigan Volunteers that arrived too late to see action in the Mexican War. At the outbreak of the Civil War, Williams was asked to head up Michigan's military board, preparing the state for its part in the conflict. He received a commission as brigadier general in the U. S. Army on August 9, 1861, to date from May 17, and was placed in command of a division that fought in the Shenandoah Campaign of 1862 and at Cedar Mountain. His men called him "Old Pap" because he obviously cared about their well-being. Some believed, including McClellan, perhaps too much so. In battle he was an effective leader who garnered praise from all levels.[11]

Williams retained his division when the Army of Virginia was integrated into the Army of the Potomac. He assumed temporary command of the XII Corps at the beginning of the Maryland Campaign when Nathaniel Banks was assigned command of the Washington defenses. The two-week period after Cedar Mountain was especially difficult for Williams and his men. He wrote to his daughter about being "without pen, ink, or paper—almost without food—sleeping every night in our clothes—often without taking off my spurs!" Times did not get much better after the army took off after Gen. Lee's army. Williams wrote home on September 12: "for over three weeks we have been scarcely a day without marching—for at least seven days without rations, except what a poor country afforded to a very large and hungry crowd."[12]

After leaving Fairfax, Virginia, Williams' division marched through Alexandria, Georgetown, and Tennallytown, reaching Rockville, Maryland on September 5. It remained there until September 9, when it was on the move again, this time to Middlebrook and then Damascus, where it remained on September 10 and 11. It was again on the road the following day to Ijamsville, and the division finally reached Frederick on September 13 where it camped for the night. The corps was ordered to South Mountain to support the fighting there on September 14, but it was not called into action. September 15 found the XII Corps at

Keedysville, near Antietam Creek. During its passage through Boonsboro on September 15, Williams recalled, "we were greatly cheered . . . the whole population seemed rejoiced. . ."

Joseph Mansfield arrived during this period and assumed command of the XII Corps, returning Williams to division command. The 1st Division settled in around Keedysville, and on September 16, it moved "hurriedly to the front, Gen. Mansfield, in an excited and fussy way, announcing that we should be in a general engagement in half an hour," according to Williams. The men could easily see the enemy positions across Antietam Creek. A tired Williams turned in for the night when "along came a message to get under arms at once. Oh, how sleepy I was, but there is no help at such times." The column formed, crossed the Upper Bridge over Antietam Creek and eventually camped more than a mile behind the I Corps.[13]

It was a difficult march in the dark night and all were relieved to halt in a ploughed field, where Williams was told to put his men "in column in mass." Williams recalled it "took a long time as I had five regiments who knew absolutely nothing of maneuvering." The men were up early on September 17 and on the move to the front with Samuel Crawford's brigade in the lead. The men moved by "column of companies, closed in mass." Upon reaching Hooker's position, Williams ordered his men deployed into line of battle while Mansfield departed to confer with the I Corps commander, but when Mansfield returned, he angrily told him to reform into the block-type formation. Williams resorted to gathering the commanders of his veteran units under a tree to explain how he wanted them deployed when the time came.

The veteran units deployed for action effortlessly, but Williams realized the rookies needed help. He took hold of one and ordered Gordon and Crawford to assist the others. Williams told his daughters, "I got mine in line pretty well by having a fence to align in on and having got it in this way I ordered the colonel to go forward and open fire the moment he saw the Rebels." This was apparently the 128th Pennsylvania. Williams recalled the regiment "was split in two by coming in contact with a barn . . . [and] they fell into inextricable confusion and fell to the rear, where they were easily rallied." There was hope, for Williams wrote home, "The men were of an excellent stamp, ready and willing, but neither officers nor men knew anything, and there was an absence of the mutual confidence which drill begets."[14]

Williams, like Mansfield, spent considerable time moving troops into position. For example, he grabbed hold of the 124th Pennsylvania and personally led it west toward the D.R. Miller farm and Hagerstown Pike. He apparently neglected to inform brigade commander Crawford of the movement, for the latter reported the regiment "was detached from my brigade by some superior order unknown to me." Once the Pennsylvanians were in position, Williams sought out the 125th Pennsylvania, which had wandered to the right. He learned of Mansfield's mortal wounding about this time. Williams did not realize his veterans were already heavily engaged with Alfred Colquitt's brigade (D.H. Hill's division). He departed again, this time to check on the well-being of William Goodrich's brigade (Greene's division), which had been sent west to help support Abner Doubleday's division (I Corps).[15]

Williams' division performed well during the morning hours of September 17. It went into action at 7:30 a.m. and held Confederate reinforcements in check in the East Woods and Cornfield until Greene's division came up and delivered the knock-out punch. Williams pulled his men back at 9:10 a.m. to rest and resupply their ammunition. Edwin Sumner (II Corps commander) requested assistance from Williams during John Sedgwick's division's drive into the West Woods and he complied by sending the 13th New Jersey, 2nd Massachusetts, and Purnell's Legion of Gordon's brigade, but they were ultimately forced to withdraw. Some of these regiments entered West Woods at 11:00 a.m. to support Greene's division, but were driven back by John Walker's division's counterattack .

This ended the fighting for Williams' division. It later occupied the East Woods and supported the VI Corps. The division lost a total of 1,077 during the fight (159 killed, 864 wounded, 54 missing).[16]

**Bradley M. Gottfried**

* * *

## 1st Brigade: Brigadier General Samuel W. Crawford, Colonel Joseph Knipe

**Units:** 10th Maine, 28th New York, 46th Pennsylvania, 124th Pennsylvania, 125th Pennsylvania, 128th Pennsylvania
**Strength:** 4,246[17]
**Losses:** 430 (88k-315w-27m)[18]

The 1st Brigade was comprised of six regiments during the Maryland Campaign. Three (10th Maine, 28th New York and 46th Pennsylvania) were veteran units, mustered into service during the summer and early fall of 1861; the remaining three regiments, the 124th, 125th and 128th Pennsylvania were composed of new troops organized in Harrisburg, Pennsylvania during early August 1862, as part of President Lincoln's call for 300,000 volunteers in July.[19]

Samuel W. Crawford was born on November 8, 1827 in Fayetteville, Pennsylvania (just east of Chambersburg), the son of a Presbyterian minister. He entered the University of Pennsylvania at the tender age of 14 and eventually studied medicine. After graduating with his medical degree in 1850, Crawford joined the army, serving in Texas and New Mexico as an assistant surgeon. Crawford was assigned to command the batteries at Fort Sumter in Charleston, South Carolina and was present during the bombardment. He later became the Assistant Inspector General of the Department of Ohio where he first served under George McClellan, and then a major in the 13th U. S. Infantry. In April 1862 Crawford was promoted to brigadier general of Volunteers and given a brigade in the Department of the Shenandoah under Nathaniel Banks. The brigade was later assigned to John Pope's Army of Virginia during the summer of 1862 and it fought bravely in a losing cause at Cedar Mountain where the brigade's casualties exceeded 50%.[20]

The brigade's three veteran regiments (10th Maine, 28th New York and 46th Pennsylvania) crossed the Potomac River into Maryland, where their depleted ranks were augmented by the three new regiments from Pennsylvania on September 6 and 7. Straggling was a major issue for the Union army during the early days of the Maryland Campaign. While still encamped in Rockville, Maryland on September 9, Crawford wrote to his superiors in a manner that underscored his training as a doctor: "There are many men belonging to the command who cannot, from absolute want of muscular tone, follow in its marches. Men never known to fall behind, upon previous marches, do so now…There is nothing which keeps them together but the common interest and association, and I have no hesitation in saying that unless some opportunity is afforded these regiments to rest and to reorganize, their regimental character will cease to exist."[21]

These were hot days of marching on dry, dusty roads and frequent breaks were necessary. The friendly and sympathetic local residents offered the soldiers fruit and cheese to supplement their frequent diet of foraging for green corn and apples when the commissary wagons lagged behind.[22]

Crawford's brigade marched through Frederick early on September 14 to the sounds of church bells and cheering crowds. The men were obliged to march in the fields adjacent to the National Road, leaving the roadway open for ammunition trains and other supplies intended for the soldiers fighting on South Mountain. "As the men pressed forward, over fences and brooks, and through fields and woods, they could see and hear the engagement up the mountain side," according to Pvt. Charles Boyce of the 28th New York.[23]

The XII Corps moved quickly through the Middletown Valley, but the battle for the South Mountain gaps ended as the sun set. The historian of the 125th Pennsylvania remembered, "About three o'clock in the morning [September 15th] a halt was ordered in a field near the village of Bolivar, where the old Hagerstown Road diverges to the

193

right and the old Sharpsburg Road to the left. Here we lay until day light."[24]

## Antietam

The march on September 15 brought the brigade past the scenes of the Battle at Turner's Gap the day before. Crawford's brigade eventually reached Boonsboro, at the base of the western slope, around 4:00 p.m. and turned left onto Boonsboro Pike toward Keedysville. The delaying action of the Confederate rear guard slowed the Union advance and clogged the pike. The brigade bivouacked in the fields adjacent to the pike, about two miles east of Keedysville.[25]

Earlier that day, the men first saw their new corps commander, Joseph Mansfield, who quickly gained their respect and confidence. "We well remember how favorably impressed we were with his fine fatherly appearance and with the deep interest he took in us," wrote the historian of the 125th Pennsylvania.[26]

The men awoke early on the morning September 16 to a dense fog that obscured the enemy lines. The brigade advanced and joined the rest of the II Corps near Antietam Creek. Brisk artillery fire heightened the men's anxiety, but they were not called into action until 10:00 p.m. The men crossed Antietam Creek at the "Upper" or "Pry" Bridge and marched northwest to the George Line farm, about a mile northeast of Hooker's command. Crawford's brigade again led the corps. Pvt. Frederick Crouse of the 128th Pennsylvania remembered, "After the regiment was formed we was marched off in the darkness, and it was terriable [sic] dark, we went groping through the bushes, over fences, around ditches, fields, creeks and through woods. We were finely [sic] halted about two o'clock in the morning in a freshly plowed field, and ordered to lay down on our arms."[27]

It was impossible to sleep, as a private in the 125th Pennsylvania later recalled, "We were massed . . . in a cornfield; the night was close, air heavy, some fog and the smoke from the skirmish firing of the late evening and picket firing of the night . . .

We made our beds between the rows of corn and did not unbuckle or remove accoutrements."[28]

As the first rays of light filtered through a cloudy sky on September 17, the heavy crash of musket and artillery fire interrupted the pre-dawn stillness. Division commander Alpheus Williams later reported, "At the first sound of cannon at daylight . . . the command was put in movement, each regiment, by order of General Mansfield, marching in column of companies, closed in mass." The men went into action without coffee or breakfast after an almost sleepless night. Crawford's brigade again led the corps as it marched south in close-order along the Smoketown Road. Mansfield rode ahead to report to Joseph Hooker and learned the I Corps was already "hard pressed and that he would be called upon to relieve it."[29]

The fight for Miller's Cornfield and the surrounding woods can be best described as a series of attacks and counter attacks, each seemingly more desperate and bloodier than the one before it. By the time the XII Corps approached the front along Smoketown Road at about 7:15 a.m., the I Corps was wrecked and "much of it streaming to the rear." As the 125th Pennsylvania arrived, its historian remembered, "Men were falling rapidly, and sad and ghastly were the sights that met our view, only to be multiplied afterward."[30]

Crawford initially led the 125th Pennsylvania forward with its left on Smoketown Road and its right almost to the Joseph Poffenberger farm. It then advanced toward the East Woods while exposed "to a most terrific fire of musketry, shot, and shell," according to its commander, Col. Jacob Higgins. Entering the East Woods, the Pennsylvanians encountered the 4th Alabama (Evander Law's brigade; John Hood's division), 21st Georgia (James Walker's brigade; Alexander Lawton's division), and 5th Texas (William Wofford's brigade; Hood's division) on the opposite side and were wisely ordered to retreat to their former position.[31]

Col J.F. Knipe of the 46th Pennsylvania reported the three rookie regiments "should move to the front when wanted, and the old ones should follow at a proper distance in the rear, contributing, as it were, a reserve for the brigade." This did not materialize, as Hooker was worried about the East Woods and wanted Crawford's veterans there. The three rookie Pennsylvania regiments were shoved to the right to the Cornfield, where they relieved George Meade's Pennsylvania Reserves. George Gordon's brigade was brought up to support Crawford's brigade. Mansfield and Williams disagreed about how to deploy Crawford's brigade. The latter wanted to deploy them in line of battle in the open fields north of the fighting, but Mansfield felt it was too dangerous, especially for green troops.[32]

Williams received a request from John Gibbon (Abner Doubleday's division; I Corps) and personally led the 124th Pennsylvania to the right where it straddled Hagerstown Pike. It soon came under fire from enemy troops in the West Woods from Jubal Early's brigade (Alexander Lawton's division) and portions of J.R. Jones' division, which had been wrecked in earlier fighting. Meanwhile, Mansfield personally led the three veteran regiments and the 128th Pennsylvania into their front-line positions. The four regiments initially marched south, through a ten-acre cornfield, just east of the northern part of the North Woods. Mansfield rode with the 10th Maine, which remained on the east side of Smoketown Road. The remaining units crossed Smoketown Road at about 7:30 a.m., still in closed mass to a plowed field, where they deployed in line of battle. The 28th New York formed on the opposite side of Smoketown Road with the 10th Maine on its left, and the 46th Pennsylvania extending the line to the right. Mansfield left the 10th Maine and rode to the 128th Pennsylvania, which was still a bit to the rear, and ordered it to fill the hole between the 10th Maine and 28th New York. The New Yorkers and the 46th Pennsylvania were slugging it out with the 1st and 3rd North Carolina (Roswell Ripley's brigade; D.H. Hill's division) at the north end of Miller's Cornfield at the time.[33]

Historian Ezra Carman explained the importance of Crawford's entrance into this portion of the battle: "It had not fired a shot, but its movement in front and on the Confederate flank, steadied Meade's left, what little there was of it, enabled Magilton to partially reform his shattered brigade; held at bay by Law's Confederate brigade, and finally, with the appearance of the 10th Maine, compelled Law to withdraw."[34]

The 128th Pennsylvania's commander and then his second in command were struck down, leaving Maj. Joel Wanner in command. These rookies had never been in battle before and, without leadership and with lead pouring in on them, they crowded to the right behind the 28th New York and 46th Pennsylvania. Mansfield had already left the regiment, so Col. Knipe of the 46th Pennsylvania took control. He reported, "seeing the uselessness of a regiment in that position I took the responsibility of getting it into line of battle the best way circumstances would admit," and he led the regiment to a position on the right of his own, behind the fence lining the northern boundary of the Cornfield. Knipe suggested a charge to Wanner and he agreed. The men fired several volleys into Ripley's men, climbed the fence and rushed into the Cornfield, where they were met by a tremendous fire. Although they came close to reaching the southern edge of the Cornfield, they were ultimately pushed back. A veteran explained, "Fresh from civil life, hardly a month in service, with two of their commanding officers stricken down before their eyes, and comrades falling on every hand, the men fell into some confusion." Instead of returning to their original position, they shifted left to cover the space between the 10th Maine and 28th New York.[35]

The 10th Maine remained in the southern portion of the East Woods, slugging it out with three small enemy regiments (5th Texas, 21st Georgia, 4th Alabama), the only foes left in the East Woods. Mansfield was mortally wounded around this time and Williams assumed command of the XII Corps while Crawford took over Williams' division. Knipe took over Crawford's brigade. Williams told Knipe "to retire to the rear of the woods and then reform." Terrain and distance hampered Knipe's control over his new command, but he realigned the regiments as best he could in a cornfield just north and west of Smoketown Road near the Samuel Poffenberger farm. The brigade was still without the services of the 124th Pennsylvania, which was along Hagerstown Pike, and the 125th Pennsylvania (see below).[36]

Except for its initial aborted advance, the 125th Pennsylvania had remained in the rear, moving about to several positions. According to the regiment's historian, it was "moved quickly to the rear and right, and then obliquely to the left, and then further to the left front." The regiment was not in this location long when, according to Jacob Higgins, the unit's commander, "some colonel, whose name I do not know, told me that his troops were falling back for want of ammunition, and asked me to advance to his support. I immediately reported this to General Crawford, who ordered me to advance at once." Lt. Thomas McCamant of the 125th Pennsylvania later recorded, "As we approached Smoketown road, a brass gun battery came out [on] the road and took position on a rising ground in front of us, and this battery we were ordered to support." He was referring to J. Albert Monroe's 1st Rhode Island battery consisting of six twelve-pound Napoleons. Hooker arrived and asked Higgins if any troops were in the West Woods and he replied, "None but Rebels." As the two were conversing, Hooker's horse was wounded.[37]

Higgins received orders to move into the West Woods a short time later. He threw out a skirmish line and cautiously followed with the rest of the regiment. After driving back the Georgia and South Carolina skirmishers, the 125th Pennsylvania entered the West Woods. Higgins halted his men and rode forward to seek out the enemy. He found them "in force in my front and on my right. On looking around I discovered myself without support either in my rear or right." He quickly gave his horse to an aide with instructions to get back to the general [and] "inform him of my situation, and ask him to send me support immediately, or I would be unable to hold my position, and that the enemy would certainly flank me and cut me off . . ."

Higgins did not realize he was directly in the path of Jubal Early's brigade, the lead elements of G.T. Anderson's brigade (D.R. Jones' division), and Lafayette McLaws' division. The 34th New York (Willis Gorman's brigade; John Sedgwick's division, II Corps), which had drifted away from its brigade, took up a position to the rear and left of the 125th Pennsylvania and joined in the fight. The Confederates rushed forward several times, were stopped, fell back and then rushed forward again when additional reinforcements arrived, tipping the scales in favor of the Rebels.[38]

The 125th Pennsylvania now faced Early's brigade to its front and at least the 2nd South Carolina of Joseph Kershaw's brigade (McLaws' division) on its left and G.T. Anderson's brigade on his right. The 125th Pennsylvania maintained a constant fire while being forced back into the 34th New York on their left and the newly arriving 7th Michigan of Napoleon Dana's brigade (Sedgwick's division) on their right, leaving no room to maneuver. Higgins reported, "I held him here for some time, until I discovered two regiments of them moving around my right, while a brigade charged on my front. On looking around and finding no support in sight, I was compelled to retire. Had I remained in my position two minutes longer I would have lost my whole command." South Carolinians of Kershaw's brigade followed Higgins' men from the West Woods, but they quickly ended their pursuit when Union batteries belched canister loads into their ranks. Monroe asked the Pennsylvanians to halt behind his guns to provide support, which, according to the regiment's historian, "This we did, though more or less confusion reigned . . ." The stunned Pennsylvanians had occupied the West Woods for about half an hour.[39]

As darkness descended, the two detached regiments, the 124th and 125th Pennsylvania, rejoined their brigade near Samuel Poffenberger's farm and rested on their arms. Crawford, wounded in his thigh during the battle, reported, "It was now night; the action had ceased . . . I reported to the general commanding the corps, and left the field."

Awakening the next day, every soldier expected a renewal of hostilities, yet as the hours past, no more than scattered skirmishing disturbed the sullen and dreadful tasks of recovering the wounded and burial of the dead. "Stunned and dazed by the shock of the furious battle ... neither side wished to provoke the other."[40]

The brigade lost 430 men during the battle of Antietam. As expected, the 125th Pennsylvania, overwhelmed in the West Woods, lost the most—145, followed by the 128th Pennsylvania (118) which made the dash into the Cornfield against Ripley's brigade. The 28th New York and 46th Pennsylvania, which primarily held a defensive line along the north edge of the Cornfield, lost only 12 and 19 men, respectively. The 10th Maine and 124th Pennsylvania lost a moderate number of men (72 and 64, respectively).[41]

**Mac Bryan**

* * *

### 2nd Brigade: Brigadier General George Henry Gordon, Colonel Thomas Ruger

**Units:** 27th Indiana, 2nd Massachusetts, 13th New Jersey, 107th New York, 3rd Wisconsin
**Strength:** 3,479[42]
**Losses:** 646 (71k-548w-27m) [43]

Brigadier General George Gordon's brigade was an odd mixture of veterans and new recruits. The 2nd Massachusetts, 27th Indiana, and 3rd Wisconsin were all mustered into service in 1861 and saw action in the Shenandoah Valley Campaign and the Second Bull Run Campaign. The 13th New Jersey and 107th New York were mustered in during the summer of 1862 and had little or no training by the time they marched north to meet Lee's army. The historian of the veteran 27th Indiana recalled the appearance of the new recruits: "The new uniforms, their enormous knapsacks, and their seeming excess of equipments of all kinds, attracting more attention by their inexperienced way of bundling them up and caring for them . . . No less in contrast were their bleached faces and soft, white hands. Would such dainty, effeminate fellows ever make soldiers?"[44]

Massachusetts resident George Gordon graduated from West Point in 1846 and served with distinction in the War with Mexico. He resigned from the army in 1854 and became an attorney. At the outbreak of hostilities, Gordon organized and became colonel of the 2nd Massachusetts. After guarding the Upper Potomac River, the regiment was transferred to Nathaniel Banks' army and saw action during the Shenandoah Valley Campaign. Gordon was promoted to brigadier general in July, 1862, and given command of the brigade. He temporarily led the division after Joseph Mansfield was mortally wounded.[45]

The brigade, with the rest of the division, marched out of Washington and headed to Rockville on September 5. It was a difficult 14-mile march; made more so by the warm weather that took its toll on most every soldier. Many fell out of ranks to seek shelter or relief from the scorching temperatures. The rookies of the 13th New Jersey managed the hardship by taking care of each other through the natural camaraderie that hard times always seem to foster, but nevertheless, only 200 were present when the march ended a couple of miles north of Rockville. The remainder of the regiment caught up later that night. The brigade reached Frederick on September 13 and while setting up camp, Sgt. John Bloss and Pvt. B.W. Mitchell of the 27th Indiana had the distinction of finding a copy of Lee's Special Orders Number 191 -- the "Lost Orders"-- in a clover field.[46]

The brigade, with the rest of the division, broke camp on September 14 and marched through Frederick on its way to South Mountain to attack Lee's army. Van Willard of the 3rd Wisconsin recalled civilians "came out to shake hands with us and bid us good bye and 'God speed' on our dangerous mission," as flags fluttered from almost every home. Gordon's brigade did not participate in the Union victory at South Mountain later that day, but they were keen observers from their perch atop Catoctin Mountain. It was an unsettling 16-hour march over the mountain through Turner's Gap as the landscape was littered with broken muskets, disabled caissons and other indications of battle; the slopes were littered with the corpses of dead soldiers. Willard noted the "dead of both sides lay in heaps, or scattered thickly over the ground, lying side by side." The column marched through Boonsboro to Keedysville on September 15 where it went into bivouac. George McClellan appeared during this phase of the march and, according to Capt. Henry Comey of the 2nd Massachusetts, "the men cheered loudly and threw their caps in the air. We all seemed to believe that at last we had a general who could lead us to the victories we deserve."[47]

## Antietam

On the evening of September 16, the men were awoken at 10:00 p.m. by their officers stooping down to their tents and calling them in subdued tones. Gordon's brigade crossed Antietam Creek about two hours later. Willard recalled, "No one was allowed to speak above his breath; every gun was loaded; and we were prepared for any emergency." The men reached the Hoffman farm, approximately a mile behind Joseph Hooker's I Corps, by 2:30 a.m. on September 17 and were permitted to lie down in the rain for a few hours of rest. Few men slept well that night. Edward Cromwell of the 13th New Jersey recalled, "I didn't sleep much that night. I could think of nothing but fighting and being shot." In just a few hours the rookies of the 107th New York and 13th New Jersey, 34 and 22 days from home, respectively, representing two fifths of the brigade, would fire their muskets for the first time and receive their "baptism by fire."[48]

The men grumbled because they were called into action on that misty September morning without their beloved coffee, and only nearly raw meat to eat. The cautious advance was made in column with occasional stops and starts as some regiments were detached to the woods bordering the flanks, then brought back into the fold. The head of the column stopped in an open field just west of Samuel Poffenberger's wood lot as Joseph Mansfield, XII Corps commander, rode forward to reconnoiter. The brigade was then thrown into columns of division and the "hurry up and wait" cycle began in earnest. The brigade's slow and cautious movements with frequent halts did not permit the men to make coffee.

The men halted at 6:30 a.m. and were finally permitted to make small fires to brew coffee, eat crackers and cook the raw pork from their haversacks. The soldiers knew it could be their last meal. The nervous ones could not finish but a single mouthful while others consumed as if it was their last meal. Seeing streams of wounded men passing by on their way to the rear and the constant stream of enemy cannon shells exploding in front of them did not help the men's appetites.[49]

The brigade, with the rest of the division, prepared for action at 7:15 a.m. Crawford's brigade advanced first, followed by Gordon's. One of Hooker's aides galloped up to Gordon, imploring him to move rapidly to support the beleaguered I Corps. The sound of musketry suggested the steady approach of the enemy. Confederate shouts of exultation, the famous blood curdling rebel yell, could be distinctly heard. Gordon deployed his brigade from column to line of battle in the open fields just south of the North Woods. He posted the 2nd Massachusetts on the right, the 3rd Wisconsin in the middle and the 27th Indiana on the left. The two rookie regiments remained in reserve: The 107th New York supported Cothran's battery near the edge of a piece of woods on the left, north of the East Woods, while the 13th New Jersey was held in reserve near the line until 8:00 a.m., when it moved forward to join the rest of the brigade.[50]

Three Confederate brigades from D.H. Hill's division rapidly approached the D.R. Miller Cornfield to blunt George Meade's Pennsylvania

Reserves' advance at this time. The Pennsylvanians had routed John Hood's division and were now following them toward Dunker Church. Roswell Ripley's brigade appeared first, followed by Alfred Colquitt's and Duncan McRae's (commanding Samuel Garland's small brigade), supported by George Moody's battery. Gordon's three veteran regiments engaged Ripley's brigade, supported by three Union batteries: Dunbar Ransom's, Joseph Campbell's and George Cothran's. Colquitt's brigade relieved Ripley's and they continued pouring a heavy fire into Gordon's men. According to historian Ezra Carman, Gordon's men "stood on higher ground than the Confederates, the sky behind them, in good musket range, a good target, not yielding an inch, giving and taking punishment." While Gordon's three regiments now battled Colquitt's brigade, George Greene's division (XII Corps) arrived, and by maneuvering south-southwest on the Smoketown Road slammed into Colquitt's exposed right flank held by the 6th Georgia. The Georgians were torn apart by short range musket fire and hand-to-hand combat. Colquitt's left was also suffering greatly from Gordon's 2nd Massachusetts and 3rd Wisconsin. The 2nd Massachusetts was especially effective in shooting up the 13th Alabama and 28th Georgia. The historian of the 3rd Wisconsin noted the "enemy were handicapped by the fact that they were moving diagonally across our front instead of directly towards us and our fire was terribly severe."[51]

Colquitt's men could not sustain such heavy fire against their flanks and fell back. Gordon reported, "Before the impetuous charge and the withering fire of our line, the enemy halted, wavered, fled in confusion, and sought shelter in the woods opposite from whence he had emerged." Seeing his veterans in need of support, Gordon called up his two rookie regiments, and he reported, "We now held possession of the field, had driven the enemy into the concealment of the woods, and, by a partial change of front forward on our left, were advancing toward the center of the general line of battle."[52]

It was now about 8:45 a.m. and the Cornfield was in Gordon's possession. With no enemy in front, and John Sedgwick's division (II Corps) sweeping past, Gordon allowed his men to withdraw to the relative safety of the East Woods. The men observed the carnage all around them. According to Robert Shaw of the 2nd Massachusetts, the Cornfield "was full of their dead and wounded . . . beyond the cornfield was a large open field, and such a mass of dead and wounded men, mostly rebels, as were lying there, I never saw before; it was a terrible sight, and our men had to be careful to avoid treading on them. Many were mangled and torn to bits by artillery but most by infantry fire."[53]

The reprieve for Gordon's brigade in the East Woods was short-lived, as Sedgwick's division was soon in need of assistance. At approximately 9:45 a.m., Alpheus Williams, now in command of the XII Corps after Mansfield's mortal wounding, ordered the 13th New Jersey and the 2nd Massachusetts to support Sedgwick. The regiments advanced through the Cornfield to Hagerstown Pike; the 13th New Jersey on the right and the 2nd Massachusetts on the left. They were unaware they faced the 49th North Carolina, 35th North Carolina and 25th North Carolina of Robert Ransom's brigade (John Walker's division) across the Pike, hidden from view by a ledge of rock. As the two Union regiments unsuspectingly crossed the fence bordering the pike and came into view, the North Carolinians let loose a withering fire. "Suddenly something occurred that seemed almost supernatural. A vast number of the enemy appeared to rise straight up out of the solid earth, and they poured into us a deadly volley of leaden hail. It is not believed that there is another geological formation like that particular spot on the face of the earth." The unexpected volleys left nine Jerseymen dead and another 60 wounded. Among the dead was the beloved Capt. Hugh Irish, who had led the charge with raised sword. Some of his men braved torrents of bullets to retrieve his belongings and his body.[54]

Sedgwick's men were nowhere in sight and with enemy reinforcements streaming into view behind the Tar Heels, the two regiments briefly returned the fire. The commander of the 13th New Jersey recalled his men behind the fence "were being shot by a foe they could not see, so perfectly did the ledge protect them; they scarcely knew how to load their muskets and were doing little or no execution." He concluded "to hold them longer under fire would be murder," so he ordered his men to fall back 300 to 400 yards to the East Woods. The commander of the 2nd Massachusetts did the same. Moments after reaching the woods, Gordon received a plea for help from Greene, whose men were in the West Woods. Gordon reformed the 13th New Jersey and sent them back across the fields to support Greene. The Jerseymen crossed Hagerstown Pike at approximately 10:30 a.m. and entered the woods adjacent to Dunker Church, positioning themselves on Greene's right. The regiment's left flank was not in physical contact with Greene's right flank. The Jerseymen began seeing what appeared to be enemy troops approaching their right flank and communicated this sighting to Greene, who came over to observe

the situation. He told the Jerseymen they were not to fire into their right under any circumstances because, he thought, Sedgwick's division occupied the woods in that direction.[55]

He was wrong, and the enemy struck hard at the 13th New Jersey's right flank at noon. These men were from the same brigade (Ransom's) that had attacked and devastated them along Hagerstown Pike. The 13th New Jersey was forced to retreat, and Greene's division was not far behind it. Gordon's brigade was relieved by elements of the VI Corps at 1:30 p.m. and retired to the rear to rest and be resupplied.[56]

Gordon's brigade had played a major role in blunting D. H. Hill's counterattack and attempt to recapture the Cornfield. Subsequently, two regiments were unexpectedly attacked in ill-advised advances, losing heavily in the process. The brigade lost 646 men during the battle.[57]

**Martin Pritchett**

* * *

# 2nd DIVISION—

## Brigadier General George S. Greene

At 61 years old, Brig. Gen. George Sears Greene was one of the oldest officers on the field at the Battle of Antietam. Born in Apponaug, Rhode Island on May 6, 1801, George Greene's family was financially ruined by the War of 1812, forcing him to find work in New York rather than attend Brown University. He received an appointment to West Point in 1819 and graduated second in his class in 1823. Though assigned to the 3rd Artillery, Greene spent most of the next 13 years as an engineering instructor at West Point and on garrison duty at various east coast facilities. Greene resigned his commission in 1836 to become a civil engineer, and was involved in numerous projects throughout the South and along the east coast.[58]

Greene worked as the chief engineer in the Croton Aqueduct Department of New York City that constructed the Central Park reservoir. He offered his services to New York Governor Edwin Morgan in 1861, but did not receive a command until January 18, 1862, when he became colonel of the 60th New York Infantry. Greene immediately instituted rigorous drills and inspections for his regiment. His no-nonsense approach to drill and his efforts to properly supply and equip his soldiers, quickly endeared him to his men. [59]

Greene was promoted to the rank of brigadier general on April 28, 1862—a rank he held for the majority of his Civil War service. He was ordered to report to Nathaniel Banks, commanding the V Corps in the

Department of Shenandoah, but initially there was no command for him. Greene assumed command of the 3rd Brigade, 1st Division, V Corps following the Union defeat at First Winchester in late May. This appointment was only temporary, however, but a day later he received orders to command the 3rd Brigade of the 2nd Division in John Pope's new Army of Virginia's II Corps. His new brigade included his old regiment, the 60th New York Infantry, and other units from New York, Delaware, Maryland, and the District of Columbia.[60]

Greene's new brigade's first taste of battle occurred at Cedar Mountain on August 9, 1862, but it mainly served in a reserve capacity. Greene's division commander, Brig. Gen. Christopher Augur spoke highly of Greene in his after action report, stating, "Greene, who, with his little command, so persistently held the enemy in check on our left." Augur was wounded during the battle, so Greene assumed command of 2nd Division.[61]

With McClellan's integration of the Army of Virginia into the Army of the Potomac, Banks' II Corps became the XII Corps. Banks remained in Washington to oversee its defenses and Alpheus Williams assumed command of the corps until Joseph Mansfield arrived to take command of the corps on September 15.[62]

Prior to Mansfield's arrival, the XII Corps had passed through Frederick, Maryland on September 13, where the corps received an enthusiastic welcome by the citizenry. They then marched over the Catoctins and on to Middletown, where the XII Corps encamped behind the I Corps following the Battle of South Mountain on September 14. Up at dawn the following day, they found "the dead lay thick in our front" prior to moving down South Mountain into Boonsboro. There the citizens of Maryland, "received us with great rejoicing."[63]

Now under Mansfield, the XII Corps was ordered over Antietam Creek to support the advance of Joseph Hooker's I Corps on the night of September 16. Ordered up around 11:00 pm, in a drizzling rain the men advanced, "Silently and half asleep the column moved off in the darkness, and crossing the Antietam on one of the upper bridges arrived at their designated position after a three-hour march . . . the men threw themselves down in the wet grass for a few hours sleep." At daybreak on September 17, 1862, Greene's three brigades, which had been at the rear of the XII Corps column, awoke on the George Line farm to the sound of artillery fire coming from the south.[64]

Greene reported his division consisted of 2,504 men in three brigades at Antietam. The 1st Brigade was commanded by Lt. Col. Hector Tyndale, the 2nd Brigade by Col. Henry J. Stainrook, and the 3rd Brigade was under Col. William B. Goodrich. Marching south down Smoketown Road in column of companies, the XII Corps vanguard reached the field around 6:30 a.m., and by 7:30 a.m., both XII Corps divisions, approximately 7,600 men, were on the field and pushing south, helping to shore up the I Corps lines and driving back the remaining Confederates.[65]

Goodrich's brigade brought up the XII Corps' rear. As Greene's division began deploying north of the East Woods, John Gibbon requested assistance, and Goodrich's brigade was broken off and marched through the North Woods to Hagerstown Pike. The Federal right had been partially driven back and needed support. Goodrich remained separated from Greene's division for the rest of the battle, and according to Greene, reduced his effective strength to 1,727 men. Mansfield's mortal wounding and Williams' assumption of XII Corps command delayed Greene's deployment. Tyndale's brigade finally deployed with its right attached to Gordon's brigade, just north of the Cornfield, and its left stretching east to Smoketown Road. Stainrook's brigade deployed into line on Tyndale's left, moving south over the rocky fields north of the East Woods.[66]

The XII Corps' arrival had not gone unnoticed by the Confederates. As Alfred Colquitt's Confederate brigade slugged it out with Gordon's troops, Tyndale's brigade succeeded in taking Colquitt's line in the flank, crushing the 6th Georgia in the northeast corner of the Cornfield. Greene's brigades' advance also spooked

Duncan McRae's North Carolina brigade. The much reduced brigade was attempting to support Colquitt's advance, but was jittery after its devastating defeat at Fox's Gap and loss of its commander, Samuel Garland. Seeing Tyndale's men advancing towards them with Stainrook's brigade stretched beyond their right, McRae's men panicked and fell back, forcing the withdrawal of Roswell Ripley's brigade and Colquitt's hard pressed troops. Greene's advance also swept away the last of John Hood's division grimly holding on in the East Woods.[67]

With Confederate forces falling back, Greene's brigades surged south, passing through the East Woods and into the fields north of the burning Mumma Farm. Swinging to the southwest, following the curve of Smoketown Road, the brigades began climbing the long slope of Sharpsburg Ridge that had previously been held by Stephen Lee's artillery battalion. The Confederate guns had been withdrawn by this time, and the high ground near the Dunker Church was being utilized by Albert Monroe's Battery D, 1st Rhode Island Artillery's six Napoleons. These guns hammered Confederate infantry trying to reorganize in the West Woods around the Dunker Church, as Greene's men came up in support. As Greene's brigades caught their breath between 8:45 and 9:00 a.m., Sedgwick's division (II Corps) swept across the field moving from the East Woods, toward the West Woods in battle lines that stretch nearly half a mile.[68]

Beyond Sedgwick's advance, on the north side of the West Woods, Goodrich's brigade deployed west of Hagerstown Pike, near the D.R. Miller farm. Pushing south with Patrick's brigade (Doubleday's division, I Corps) in support, they ran into the only organized Confederate resistance still in that portion of the field, Jubal Early's Virginia brigade, supported by the remains of the Stonewall Division, then under the command of Andrew Grigsby. Early's men briefly stopped the Union advance, killing Goodrich in the process. With the growing threat to the West Woods, Early redeployed his brigade back towards the Dunker Church, leaving Grigsby to once more give ground to the Federal advance. Goodrich's men advanced to the north end of the West Woods where they and Patrick's brigade attempted to assist Sedgwick's division as they plunged into the same woods south of them.[69]

As Sedgwick's division drove into the West Woods, a Confederate counter attack led by Lafayette McLaws' troops, slammed into its flank and rear between 9:00 and 9:30 a.m. Joseph Kershaw's brigade (McLaws' division) poured out of the West Woods around the Dunker Church and became separated from the rest of the division. The South Carolinians attacked John Tompkins' six, 10 pound Parrotts, which vented their fury on the advancing Confederates. They were joined by Tyndale's and Stainrook's brigades who rose up from behind the crest of Sharpsburg Ridge and stopped the Confederate advance at a distance of 70 yards, causing Kershaw's brigade to suffer, "immense loss."[70]

With the repulse, Greene's brigades dropped back below the lip of Sharpsburg Ridge. Kershaw's South Carolina troops were not the only Confederates in the West Woods, however. Vannoy Manning's brigade (John Walker's division) had raced north from its position near Snavely's Ford that morning to help stem the tide of the Union advance. Manning's soldiers swept through the West Woods and reached the fences lining Hagerstown Pike. Once more Greene's brigades rose up from behind the crest of Sharpsburg Ridge, taking advantage of the fence and rock outcroppings that topped it, and poured volley after volley into the advancing Confederates, throwing them back. Manning was wounded in this advance and his brigade suffered more than 900 casualties.[71]

With the Confederates withdrawing, Greene ordered an advance. Cresting Sharpsburg Ridge, the two brigades drove into the West Woods past the Dunker Church around 10:30 a.m. Greene believed his right flank was secure because the woods were held by Sedgwick's division, who had advanced about an hour before. Greene was not aware of Sedgwick's defeat and his troops now were isolated. Greene pushed his brigades approximately 200 yards beyond Dunker Church and refused his left flank to defend from an attack from the south. Greene held his brigades here, the Union prize, though several regiments were forced to withdraw from the woods for want of ammunition and took position along the Sharpsburg Ridge once more. Greene repeatedly requested reinforcements to help exploit his toe hold, but acting corps commander Williams had few troops to send. He was able to mobilize the Purnell Legion, separated from Goodrich's brigade, and the 2nd Massachusetts and 13th New Jersey from Gordon's brigade. The 13th New Jersey brought news of Sedgwick's defeat and repeatedly warned of Confederate movements in the West Woods to Greene's front and right flank.[72]

Greene did not initially believe Sedgwick was forced to retreat, but prior to 12:30 p.m. it became clear this was the case. Having used the lull in the fighting to their advantage, Confederate troops, spearheaded by Robert Ransom's brigade, slammed into Greene's right flank, using the rolling terrain and rock ledges in the West Woods to draw as close as possible before engaging. The Purnell Legion on Greene's right was crushed by Ransom's attack which was aided by several regiments of Manning's brigade and the 46th North Carolina which struck Greene's front. After Greene's men held their positions for almost two hours, and with ammunition nearly depleted, the line buckled under the multi-pronged attack. The brigades fell back across the open fields to the East Woods as the Confederate pursuit gobbled up a cannon from Lt. James McGill's battery. The XII Corps' massed cannon and newly arriving units of the VI Corps forced the Confederates to break off their pursuit. The longest breach of the Confederate lines at Antietam was over.[73]

The men of the division were praised for their conduct in both Greene's and Williams' after-action reports. This gallantry under fire came with a high cost. Of the 2,504 men Greene's division carried into the battle, 651 became casualties (26%). The XII Corps withdrew from the battlefield on September 19, 1862 and reoccupied Harpers Ferry on September 22, where it remained for several months. Greene took ill in October and when he returned to the XII Corps, he was no longer in command of the 2nd Division and resumed command of his 3rd Brigade.[74]

**Matthew Borders**

* * *

## 1st Brigade: Lieutenant Colonel Hector Tyndale

**Units:** 5th Ohio, 7th Ohio, 66th Ohio, 28th Pennsylvania
**Strength:** 2,256[75]
**Losses:** 376 (61k-308w-7m)[76]

Hector Tyndale was born on March 24, 1821 in Philadelphia. He had every intention of attending the United States Military Academy. In 1837, at the age of 16, he was offered an appointment to West Point, but his mother persuaded him to turn it down. She had aspirations of him joining the family business, which was buying and selling china, pottery, and glass.

Even though Tyndale was not a professional soldier, he gravitated toward being a citizen soldier in his free time. While assisting his father with the import business, he became a member of an artillery corps in Philadelphia and quickly rose through the ranks. During the anti-Catholic riots in 1844, Tyndale commanded a ward of the citizens police force whose job it was to keep the peace between the anti-immigrant mobs and Irish-Americans.[77]

During the spring of 1845, Maj. Edwin Sumner, commander of the 1st Dragoons, invited Tyndale to accompany him on an expedition to the Northwest. Upon his return home, he again set aside military endeavors and became the head of the family business after the death of his father. In 1851, Tyndale toured Europe for several months with the goal to "improve his knowledge and cultivate his taste." He visited numerous art galleries and manufacturing houses of fine china and it was this trip that provided him the newfound knowledge and wisdom to become one of Philadelphia's largest and most respected importers of fine materials.[78]

203

While he did not consider himself an abolitionist, Tyndale was very supportive of the anti-slavery movement. Following the capture and conviction of John Brown in 1859, Brown's wife traveled through Philadelphia on her way to Virginia to see her husband before his execution and to bring his remains home. Tyndale, encouraged by Brown's wife, believed it was his responsibility to escort Mrs. Brown on her trip. He provided safe passage for the party back to Philadelphia and saw them off to New York.[79]

The Civil War broke out while Tyndale and his wife were traveling in France. A strong sense of duty and recognizing the importance of the situation back home forced an early end to their trip. Shortly following his return, Tyndale was instrumental in raising and providing the initial funding for the 28th Pennsylvania Regiment. He was commissioned major of the regiment in June 1861. Tyndale was then promoted to lieutenant colonel in April 1862, which was his rank at Antietam, even though he commanded a brigade. Col. Charles Candy actually commanded the brigade, but in his absence, Tyndale oversaw it at Second Bull Run and Antietam.

On September 1, 1862, the brigade left the area around Bull Run and over the next fourteen days, marched from Alexandria, Virginia to the base of South Mountain. It was later remembered, "during the tedious march of about 125 miles, in the hottest season of the year, they passed through . . . Alexandria, Long Bridge . . . Ijamsville, Frederick, and Boonsboro. They also crossed Cotoctin [sp] and South mountains, and waded the Monocacy and other streams."[80]

On September 14, the brigade moved out of Frederick, Maryland with church bells ringing behind them and cannon fire booming out from the action at Harpers Ferry and South Mountain. The march, though not long, was made difficult by the amount of traffic. Veterans recalled, "The roads were occupied by cavalry, artillery and ammunition trains. The infantry moved across fields and through tall standing corn, where the still, close air intensified the suffocating heat."[81]

The men crossed over South Mountain on September 15, continued through Boonsboro, and marched to a point east of the Antietam Creek. J. Hume, a soldier in the 7th Ohio, wrote a letter home describing the field where the fighting unfolded around Turner's Gap. "We beat them bad . . . they lost two to our one. I came through there on Tuesday after and there was thirty or forty dead Rebels laying in the Woods and behind a Stone wall not buried . . . the citizens was trying to have them buried."[82]

## Antietam

Very late on the evening of September 16th, Tyndale and his brigade crossed Antietam Creek by way of the Upper Bridge and took up position in and around the Hoffman and Line farms.

On the following morning, Tyndale's brigade consisted of the 5th, 7th, and 66th Ohio numbering about 425 men total. The 28th Pennsylvania took on to the field 766 troops for a brigade total of 1,191, far fewer than at the start of the campaign.[83]

Lt. Col. Eugene Powell of the 66th Ohio recalled the men could hear the battle unfolding to their front as they stood around small campfires making their coffee. It was at that point, around 6:30 a.m., that the brigade was ordered to move. Their drinks were quickly snatched up and consumed on the way to battle. While confusion in the XII Corps' deployment unfolded due Joseph Mansfield's wounding, the last Confederate brigade to hold the Cornfield was moving onto the field.[84]

Col. Alfred Colquitt's brigade (D.H. Hill's division) of a little more than 1,300 men from Georgia and Alabama started their morning in the Sunken Road near the Roulette Lane. Around 7:30 a.m. they advanced across the Mumma Farm, through the southwest corner of the East Woods and into the fight. The 6th Georgia was on the far right of the line and it held the northeastern corner of the Cornfield. To their left and stretching southwest back toward the southern edge of the Cornfield was the 27th, 23rd, 28th Georgia and on the far left was the 13th Alabama.[85]

The deployment of Tyndale's Federal soldiers had the 7th Ohio on the far right. The 66th Ohio was next, then the 5th Ohio, and on the far left the 28th Pennsylvania. As the men moved across the Poffenberger Lane and into the East Woods, they had no idea what was on the other side of the woodlot. As they broke out of the woods Powell recalled, "mist and fog of the early morning rendered everything obscure and uncertain; but, peering through that cloud of vapor, I saw a line of the enemy . . . just beyond and behind a rail fence."[86]

The three Ohio regiments fired a volley into the men of the 6th Georgia and very quickly, the large 28th Pennsylvania appeared on their left flank. A hand-to-hand melee broke out with men using the bayonet and those without, resorted to clubbing the enemy with their muskets. Quickly, the Confederate line broke and Colquitt's brigade retreated toward the Dunker Church.

Tyndale's men followed the retreating Confederates through the corn and into the open pasture north of Smoketown Road. A part of the 28th Pennsylvania and the 111th Pennsylvania (Henry Stainrook's brigade) captured two Confederate artillery pieces that had been detached from the large group of Stephen Lee's command posted on the high ground east of the Dunker Church. The sight of Greene's division advancing south and the effects of the long-range Federal artillery finally drove Lee's guns from this position, which they had held all morning.

By this point in the fight, Tyndale's men had run out of ammunition so they and Stainrook's men moved into the low ground south and west of the Mumma Farm. Here they were resupplied, and from this position some of the men saw John Sedgwick's (II Corps) over 5,000 troops move out of the East Woods and head toward the West Woods.

Shortly after 9:30 a.m., Tyndale, along with Stainrook's brigade advanced toward the high ground to the west, the same ground held by Stephen Lee's artillery earlier in the day. Just as they crested the ridge the Federals could see that in the West Woods, just on the other side of Hagerstown

Pike and south of the Dunker Church, Confederate forces were reorganized and readied for an advance. These men were part of Kershaw's brigade of South Carolinians, including the 2nd, 7th, and 8th regiments.

Greene's division was halted and ordered to the east side of the ridge to lie in wait for the Confederates. Eventually, the enemy pushed across Hagerstown Pike and up the slope, Maj. Orrin Crane of the 7th Ohio reported, "when within a short range our troops were quickly thrown forward to the top of the hill, where we poured into their advance columns volley after volley. So terrific was the fire of our men that the enemy fell like grass before the mower." After a short, deadly engagement, the Confederates fell back."[87]

Tyndale's men had just enough time to catch their breath before a second advance was made by regiments from Van Manning's brigade (John Walker's division). Their attack originated from around the church with the 48th North Carolina on the right, 30th Virginia around the Smoketown Road intersection of the pike and the 46th North Carolina on the far left. Up the slope they charged only to be met again by Tyndale's Buckeye soldiers and once again the Confederate advance was driven back into the woods.[88]

At approximately 10:45 a.m., Greene moved his division down the slope, across Hagerstown Pike and into the West Woods. Stainrook's men were on the left along the south edge of the woods facing south. The 28th Pennsylvania was to Stainrook's right and faced southwest. By this time, the Ohio regiments had so reduced, that reinforcements were called up to replace them to help secure the right. The 13th New Jersey and Purnell Legion, other regiments from the XII Corps, were placed to the right of the 28th Pennsylvania, facing west in the woods, a little less than 200 yards from the Dunker Church.

The two brigades of Greene's division, held onto this position until about 12:30 p.m. While Tyndale and Greene attempted to get some artillery support posted on the far left of the described line, a Confederate attack struck both Federal flanks simultaneously. On the right, the remainder of Tyndale's troops were hit by Brig. Gen. Robert Ransom's North Carolina brigade. The pressure was too much, and Greene's troops fell out of the West Woods and back toward the East Woods. Sgt. W.H.H. Fithian in the 28th Pennsylvania wrote of the Confederate attack, "We were congratulating ourselves upon our success and cheer after cheer went fourth with a will at the sight of our old battery [Knapp's]. The enemy however took notice of it, and before the boys got their piece into position their sharpshooters began to pick off the men and shoot the horses . . . superior forces being sent against us, we were compelled to fall back."[89]

As Tyndale's men fell back, he was wounded for a second time that day. The first hit him in the hip, not causing much damage. The second hit him in the back of the head and was thought to be mortal. He survived the wounds and after a long recovery was back in the field by June 1863. Eventually, the wound he received at Antietam forced him to resign from service in August 1864.

Two soldiers in Tyndale's brigade were awarded the Medal of Honor for their actions at Antietam. Pvt. John Murphy of the 5th Ohio captured the flag of the 13th Alabama during the fighting around the Cornfield and Cpl. Jacob Orth of the 28th Pennsylvania captured the flag of the 7th South Carolina during the fight on the ridge east of the Hagerstown Pike.[90]

**Brian S. Baracz**

* * *

## 2nd Brigade: Colonel Henry Stainrook

**Units:** 3rd Maryland, 102nd New York, 111th Pennsylvania
**Strength:** 1,325[91]
**Losses:** 176 (30k-121w-16m)[92]

The size of brigades varied greatly at Antietam. Henry Stainrook had one of the smaller commands on the field with only 536 men on the morning of the battle. Stainrook was born in Pennsylvania in 1826 and served as a private in the First Pennsylvania Infantry during the Mexican War. This experience served him well during the Civil War. Following the Mexican War, Stainrook was a painter and grainer, painting wood grain on non-wooden materials.[93]

Shortly after the first shots of the war were fired, Stainrook joined a three-month regiment, the 22nd Pennsylvania, and served as captain of Company C. In the first part of December 1861, Stainrook, who was living in Philadelphia, became the recruiter for the 109th Pennsylvania. Every company but two were raised from that city. He was commissioned colonel of the regiment, which was dated back to November 8, 1861.

Throughout the spring of 1862, the brigade as detailed to hold and secure the area around Harpers Ferry. In August 1862, the brigade was commanded by Brig. Gen. Henry Prince, part of Brig. Gen. Christopher Augur's division, XII Corps. Prince and his men were engaged at the Battle of Cedar Mountain and the brigade suffered close to 500 casualties, including two members of Prince's staff killed, one wounded, and Prince was taken prisoner.[94]

In late August during the Second Bull Run Campaign, the brigade was in reserve and assisted with guarding trains and saw little action in the lead up to the Maryland Campaign. Stainrook, who had quickly recovered from a wound at Cedar Mountain, was placed in command of the brigade shortly before September 1, 1862. His brigade at this point consisted of the 3rd Maryland, 102nd New York, and the 109th and 111th Pennsylvania.[95]

After the reorganization of the Federal Army after Second Bull Run, and with word of the

Confederates crossing the Potomac River into Maryland, Union forces pressed out of Washington in pursuit. Adj. John Boyle of the 111th Pennsylvania commented on the march out of the capital city toward Frederick: "The marches had been short, the weather though warm, was pleasant, and the men felt rested and were in good spirits." On September 13, the men crossed the Monocacy River, near Frederick, and camped there for the night. It was also on this day that Stainrook's home regiment, 109th Pennsylvania, was detached and did not return to the brigade before Antietam.[96]

On September 14, the XII Corps made its way out of Frederick and was not engaged during the combat at South Mountain. The Federals pressed Lee's forces back toward Sharpsburg and eventually the corps was posted on the east side of Antietam Creek on September 16. Stainrook's men settled in for a quiet evening, remembered a member of the 3rd Maryland, "Pickets were stationed: beef were killed and distributed among the troops, who enjoyed a square meal – the last that many a poor fellow ever ate."[97]

## Antietam

An unwelcome call to get up and move came to Stainrook's men just past midnight, and in the early hours of September 17 they crossed Antietam Creek by way of the Upper Bridge and moved in on the left of Hooker's I Corps. "The regiments spread their damp blankets onto the soaked ground and extracted such comfort as they could from their hard tack and water, before sinking into the forgetfulness of exhaustion," remembered John Boyle of the 111th Pennsylvania. They spent the rest of the dark, rainy morning near the Hoffman and Line Farms, northeast of the East Woods.[98]

The sounds of battle stirred the men in the early light of the morning. Hooker's troops moved first and engaged the Confederates for the initial two hours of the battle in the Cornfield and East Woods. The XII Corps, over 7,000 men, advanced to assist Hooker shortly before 8:00 a.m. Alpheus Williams led the way with his division followed by George Greene's division, which included Goodrich's, Tyndale's, and Stainrook's brigades.

Following the wounding of Mansfield very early in the deployment of the XII Corps, Williams took over command. After consulting with Hooker and others, Greene was ordered to send one of his brigades west, toward Hagerstown Pike to assist men from the I Corps to shore up that section of the line. Tyndale and Stainrook continued forward through the East Woods, following sections of Smoketown Road, searching for the foe.

Tyndale's brigade of three Ohio regiments, 5th, 7th, and 66th, and the 28th Pennsylvania were on the right moving south; Stainrook was on the left. The 111th Pennsylvania was on the right of the brigade, in close contact with the left of Tyndale, the 3rd Maryland was in the middle, and the 102nd New York covered the left flank.

The push south was slightly easier for Tyndale's troops than it was for Stanrook's, as they moved through the eastern section of the East Woods. The 111th Pennsylvania and a small part of the 28th Pennsylvania encountered resistance from two Confederate regiments: the 4th Alabama (Evander Law's brigade), and the 5th Texas, (William Woffords's brigade), both of John Hood's division, who fought stubbornly to stop the Federal advance.

The Pennsylvanians eventually pushed back their foe and at about the same time, the other regiments from Stainrook's brigade moved in on the left of the 111th Pennsylvania in a concerted effort to drive toward the Dunker Church. As the brigade pushed southwest in the direction of the artillery on the high ground east of the church, the 111th Pennsylvania, along with the 28th Pennsylvania, captured two pieces of Confederate artillery. The section had been sent forward to a position near the intersection of Smoketown Road and Mumma Lane by Lee to provide close support for the Confederate infantry. It managed to fire only a few rounds before losing the guns.[99]

As evident by the official report of the 3rd Maryland, this regiment and the 102nd New York were further east around the Mumma buildings. Lt. Col. Joseph Sudsburg recalled, "Our left rested on a burning farmhouse, said to have been the commissary store-house of the enemy, who had, before leaving, set fire to the same and thrown his salt in the well."[100]

This action brought a lull onto the field. Tyndale's and Stainrook's brigades hunkered down in a swale between the Hagerstown Pike and the Mumma Farm Lane. The division was resupplied over the course of the next hour or so, and at around 9:30 a.m., just as Federal soldiers from French's division made the initial assault on the Sunken Road, Greene started his men west up to the top of the high ground previously held by S.D. Lee's Confederate artillery.

Six guns from a Rhodes Island battery commanded by Capt. John Tompkins, were posted to the left of Stainrook's men to suppress Confederate artillery on the Piper Farm, just south of the Sunken Road. Shortly after moving to the high ground, the infantry came under a Confederate attack that originated from the West Woods. Portions of the 2nd, 7th, and 8th South Carolina, part of Joseph Kershaw's brigade, pressed toward Stainrook and the artillery.

The struggle that ensued was so close that a hand to hand fight commenced on the right and center of Stainrook's line. Maj. Thomas Walker of the 111th Pennsylvania remembered, "They were allowed to approach within 30 feet (my men in the mean time having fixed bayonets), but at the proper time we rushed forward to the mouths of the cannon, handsomely repulsing their charge…when the enemy began to waver we advanced."[101]

After Stainrook's men drove back this attack, another assault hit Tyndale's men who also held. Greene's men marched across Hagerstown Pike and into the West Woods around the Dunker Church at approximately 10:45 a.m. The division formed the shape of the letter 'L' when it finally settled in the woods. Two companies from the 102nd New York anchored themselves to Hagerstown Pike, along the south edge of the West Woods and faced south.

The 3rd Maryland was next in line and finally the 111th Pennsylvania. Tyndale's men formed the angle of the line in the woods, and then extended it north to a point even with the church, and west of it.[102]

Greene's division held this advanced position for about the next ninety minutes. A section of Capt. Joseph Knap's Pennsylvania battery was sent toward the woods to help bolster Stainrook's line and quiet two regiments of Confederates, the 3rd Arkansas and 27th North Carolina (Van Manning's brigade), who were pestering the right of the line. Lt. James McGill, who commanded these two guns on the left, protested the placement of the guns. Tyndale wanted the guns posted in the woods, but McGill argued that in between trees was no place for artillery. Tyndale won this brief argument and one gun was placed in the middle of the pike about 100 yards south of the church and the other gun moved into the West Woods. Just as McGill decided where to place his piece, Manning's Confederates fired into the artillery and then pushed toward the Federal line.[103]

While this action unfolded on the left, another Confederate attack struck the far right of Greene's division. These two attacks forced Stainrook and Tyndale to fall out of the woods. McGill's gun in the woodlot was captured after getting pinned down by limbs that had fallen on it and because several artillerymen and horses were killed in the initial Confederate volley. In his after-action report, Sudsburg recalled, "In this woods, I lost most of my men."[104]

Greene's men made their way back across the ground they had fought earlier to gain and eventually reformed around the Joseph Poffenberger farm. As the day drew to a close, the 3rd Maryland lost 28 men, 102nd New York counted 37 casualties, and the 111th Pennsylvania, who fired over 160 rounds per man and had their battle flag pierced by 25 bullets, lost the most, 110 men.[105]

**Brian S. Baracz**

***

## 3rd Brigade: Colonel William B. Goodrich, Lieutenant Colonel Jonathan Austin

**Units:** 3rd Delaware, Purnell Legion (Maryland), 60th New York, 78th New York
**Strength:** 1,469[106]
**Losses:** 99 (18k-6w-65m) [107]

Brigade commander, Col. William Goodrich, had an interesting pre-war career. Trained as a seminarian, he became a teacher, mercantile businessman, lawyer, and newspaper publisher. He put it all aside with the outbreak of the war with Mexico and served as the adjutant of the Missouri Infantry Battalion. He entered the Civil War as lieutenant colonel of the 60th New York and he and his unit saw action during the Shenandoah Valley Campaign of 1862 and the Second Bull Run Campaign, as did the brigade's other regiments. Goodrich was promoted to the rank of colonel in May 1862 and elevated to brigade command on the eve of the Maryland Campaign. The brigade had been commanded by George Greene until he was given a division. Col. James Tate of the 1st District of Columbia Infantry had assumed command of the brigade for only a little more than a month before being replaced by Goodrich on September 12. The Maryland Campaign would therefore be Goodrich's first experience leading a large unit into battle, but he had a premonition it would be his last. His brigade was a mix of men hailing from three states. The brigade had also contained the 1st District of Columbia Volunteers, but division commander George Greene explained it had "entirely disappeared from the command by sickness and desertion." The other regiments were also reduced in size. For example, the 3rd Delaware was consolidated into four companies with 30 men each. The Purnell Legion had 209 men in the ranks, the 78th New York counted 218, and the 60th New York, 231.[108]

## Antietam

The brigade's march to the Antietam battlefield was unremarkable and followed the rest of Greene's division and XII Corps. After Joseph Mansfield was mortally wounded on the morning of September 17, Alpheus Williams took over the corps and was "strongly solicited" by John Gibbon, commander of a brigade in the I Corps to send reinforcements to Abner Doubleday's division, but probably more specifically to protect Campbell's battery, which Gibbon once commanded. Williams selected Goodrich's brigade, which was just arriving on the battlefield and sent it to the right (west) to bolster Hooker's right flank. Goodrich was ordered to report to any "general officer found on the field indicated." As the brigade approached Hagerstown Pike with the 60th New York in the lead, the Purnell Legion was detached and sent to support the 124th Pennsylvania of George Gordon's brigade (Williams' division), preparing for action at the rear of Miller's Cornfield. Most of Doubleday's division, including Gibbon's brigade, were gone when Goodrich's men arrived near Hagerstown Pike. Goodrich initially deployed his brigade for action in a plowed field just in front of the North Woods, then shifted it further right to form along Hagerstown Pike, where it supported Campbell's and Cotham's batteries. Whether through orders or Goodrich's initiative, the brigade attempted to cross the pike, but the strong post and rail fence disordered the lines and created some initial chaos until the officers sorted things out.[109]

Once across the road, Goodrich deployed the brigade with the 60th New York on the right, the 3rd Delaware on the left and the 78th New York in the center. Goodrich encountered Marsena Patrick whose brigade (Doubleday's division, I Corps) had fought in this sector, so he was familiar with the terrain and how the enemy was using it to their best advantage. Patrick stated, "Knowing the ground well I directed Col. Goodrich to advance cautiously forming his skirmishers, until I could get reinforcements to go in on his left and front in sufficient force to drive through the corner, where the enemy appeared to hold in masses." Patrick could not find Doubleday so upon his return he crossed Hagerstown Pike to the sound of rapid gunfire. He quickly realized Goodrich had not followed his suggestion and had launched his small brigade forward.[110]

A company or two from each regiment were thrown on the skirmish line and they moved forward with the rest of the brigade behind them, followed by Patrick's 21st, 23rd, and 35th New York. Angling a bit to the right through the northern portion of the West Woods, Goodrich's men engaged the remnants of J.R. Jones' division, reinforced by Jubal Early's fresh brigade (Alexander Lawton's division). Goodrich was mortally wounded around this time and was first taken to the D.R. Miller barn and then further to the rear. Lt. Col. Jonathan Austin of the 78th New York assumed command of the brigade. Patrick returned about this time and ordered both brigades to hold their positions, despite heavy firing from the woods in front of them. The enemy showed no interest in advancing or retreating. Early had bigger fish to fry as the large 125th Pennsylvania entered the West Woods to the south and he turned his command to meet it.[111]

After Early's brigade and Lafayette McLaws' division devastated Sedgwick's division a short time later, many of the survivors barreled through Goodrich's lines. Patrick wrote how they "put to rout the 78' & 60'—Everything now was in the wildest disorder." Lt. Col. Charles Brundage of the 60th New York believed the brigade was on the field for about 90 minutes after Goodrich's death. The men of the terribly disordered brigade first headed to the Miller house and then beyond to Joseph Poffenberger's.[112]

One of Goodrich's regiments, the Purnell Legion, saw considerably more action after it was detached, and sent to support the 124th Pennsylvania along Hagerstown Pike. The large Keystone unit straddled the pike, extending into the Miller Cornfield, while the much smaller Maryland unit formed on its right, on the right (west) side of the pike. The veteran Marylanders may have been selected to help harden the resolve of the rookie Pennsylvanians. While along the pike, the men were under a constant fire from Early's and J.R. Jones' men-- the same gunfire that was also directed toward the rest of Goodrich's brigade, deployed off on the right of the Marylanders.[113]

The Legion crossed the road and reformed near Woodruff's battery during the attack on Sedgwick's division. It helped blunt a determined attack on the battery by the 3rd South Carolina of Joseph Kershaw's brigade (McLaws' division). The Marylanders were then sent into the West Woods near the Dunker Church in response to Sedgwick's urgent plea for reinforcements to help extend his flank. Williams, now in command of the XII Corps, could only provide the 13th New Jersey and the Purnell Legion, which marched into the woods at about 11:00 a.m. The Legion formed the right flank of the line in the quiet woods, but was not lined up with the Jerseymen. The colonel of the 13th New Jersey was certain that troops hovering around his right flank were hostile, but Greene believed they belonged to Sedgwick's division, which in reality, had already been driven from the woods.[114]

Lt. Col. Benjamin Simpson, who commanded the Legion, sent skirmishers through the woods to his right and they quickly returned with a report of a regiment—the 49th North Carolina—"lying down in the woods, well concealed, very near the right and front, beyond a ravine, where it had lain the entire time that Greene was in the woods." They also observed other troops moving into position on the enemy's left flank. These were part of Walker's division, which had been rushed up from Snavely's Ford to counter the Union thrust toward the Dunker Church. The men of the Purnell Legion could not know that other units from Walker's division were also approaching Greene's left flank, putting the units in the West Woods in a vise.[115]

Because of the undulations in the ground, the 13th New Jersey and Purnell Legion could not see the 49th North Carolina rise and head for their right flank, but they could hear them approaching. The adjutant of the 13th New Jersey and an officer of the Purnell Legion quickly advanced to determine the identity of the approaching troops. They saw the glistening gun barrels and the gray and butternut uniforms and quickly retreated to their units yelling, "they are rebs!" The Tar Heels were equally surprised as they were expecting to drive through the woods and then capture two guns of Lt. James McGill's battery in action near the church. The Marylanders were able to get off three or four volleys before being forced from the woods because of the flank attack. Simpson's short report simply stated, "the enemy appeared in overwhelming numbers and compelled it [the regiment] to retire."

This encounter ended Goodrich's brigade's actions at Antietam. The brigade eventually was ordered back to the division from its resting position behind the Joseph Poffenberger farm. It sustained the least casualties of any XII Corps unit-- 99 killed, wounded, and missing.[116]

**Bradley M. Gottfried**

* * *

# CAVALRY DIVISION—

## Brigadier General Alfred Pleasonton

**Units:** 8th Illinois Cavalry, 3rd Indiana Cavalry, 1st Massachusetts Cavalry, 1st Maine Cavalry, 1st New York Cavalry, 4th Pennsylvania Cavalry, 6th Pennsylvania Cavalry, 8th Pennsylvania Cavalry, 12th Pennsylvania Cavalry, 5th United States Cavalry, 6th United States Cavalry
**Strength:** 3,828
**Losses:** 108 (17-78-13)[1]

When McClellan brought his army north on September 7, the cavalry division was in name only as several regiments were still making their way north from the Virginia Peninsula. According to historian Scott Hartwig, the brigades "were administrative, not tactical. Only Col. John F. Farnsworth's 2nd Brigade operated as a tactical unit throughout the campaign, but even it rarely had all four of its regiments together." McClellan's cavalry division is therefore considered as a whole.[2]

The cavalry was still evolving during the Maryland Campaign. McClellan insisted on breaking his cavalry into small units, which were usually whipped or outmaneuvered by Jeb Stuart's horsemen. Prior to the movement north after Lee's army at the start of the Maryland Campaign, McClellan formed his cavalry into a division with four brigades. He appointed Brig. Gen. Alfred Pleasonton to lead the new unit. Pleasonton seemed a good choice. The 38-year-old West Point graduate had served in the cavalry almost his entire 18-years of service. Pleasonton and his 2nd U. S. Cavalry came to McClellan's attention when they were attached to his headquarters. McClellan began giving him increasingly complex assignments, such as reconnoitering prior to the Battle of Malvern Hill and helping with rearguard duty during the army's retreat toward Harrison's Landing at the end of the Seven Days Battles. McClellan wrote to his wife on August 18, 1862, that Pleasonton "is a most excellent soldier & has performed a very important duty most admirably." The new cavalry leader's men were not as generous, calling him a bully, toady, mean, and incompetent as he "can't see the truth & tell the truth."[3]

Determining Lee's position, strength, and movements fell on Pleasonton's shoulders. Although he had significant strength on paper, the equivalent of four regiments were detached, usually company by company for headquarters guard, escort, provost, and courier duty. This left Pleasonton with 3,600 men to perform his responsibilities, although it was probably much lower as many of the horses were in poor condition and not fit for service. Historian Tom Clemens noted, "Pleasonton was relying on a few understrength regiments to not only discover the intentions of the Confederates, but also to guard the ford of the Potomac and screen the advance of the Union army."[4]

The cavalry's mission of watching the Potomac River fords fell to the 1st Massachusetts Cavalry, fresh from service in South Carolina. Its commander, Maj. H. Higginson, received orders on September 2 to collect two days' rations and picket all of the fords from Great Falls to Harpers Ferry. He was told, the mission "intrusted to you is of the highest importance, and not a moment must be lost in proceeding to the scene of your duties." This was a tall order to picket such a wide stretch of territory with two small battalions, but he collected a number of sightings of enemy troops moving northward toward Leesburg.[5]

McClellan decided to move Pleasonton across the Potomac River to operate on the Maryland side. He was ordered to leave Fort Albany in Virginia and ride to Falls Church on September 4. The Bay State troopers were returning from their mission around this time. After crossing the Potomac River, Pleasonton was to head north to determine the intentions of the enemy. He had the 6th United States Cavalry with him and collected the 8th Illinois Cavalry and 8th Pennsylvania Cavalry at Falls Church. They had skirmished with Fitz Lee's cavalry brigade under Thomas Munford north of town. Pleasonton correctly predicted the enemy was flexing his muscle to hide the real movement further north. Pleasonton crossed the Potomac River as ordered and rode north.[6]

Pleasonton initially picketed the area from Seneca Mill on the Potomac River to Cooksville on the National Road, a distance of 25 miles, between September 4 and 6. On September 5, a detachment of 100 men from the 1st Massachusetts Cavalry was sent through Poolesville on its way to guard the fords across the Potomac River. They ran into Munford's cavalry brigade outside of town and stampeded back through it, losing about a third of their men during the fray. The minor skirmish had a tremendous impact on Pleasonton's men: "Some of my cavalry are so nervous I cannot make much of their reports," he wrote.[7]

Pleasonton welcomed the 1st New York Cavalry from the Peninsula on September 6 and pushed it up to Middleburg and Clarksburg. The 1st U. S. Cavalry headed to Brookville and the 8th Illinois Cavalry and 3rd Indiana Cavalry headed for Darnstown on their way to Poolesville and the fords along the Potomac River. The movements in search of Lee's army continued on September 7. A couple of squadrons from the 8th Illinois Cavalry and 3rd Indiana Cavalry stirred up some excitement when they charged into Poolesville, Maryland, capturing two enemy cavalry vedettes. It was not much of a prize as Pleasonton admitted they were "all of the enemy in the town at that time." John Farnsworth followed up on September 8 by bringing both regiments into Poolesville. As they approached the town they saw enemy cavalry leaving in the opposite direction and dashed after them. The two sides deployed artillery and the Union guns silenced the enemy's. The Confederates beat a hasty retreat, followed closely by Farnsworth's troopers. The pursuit abruptly ended when the "westerners" ran into the 7th and 12th Virginia Cavalry and two cannon, deployed for action and itching for a fight. Another artillery duel transpired and again the Confederate guns fell silent. The 3rd Indiana Cavalry now charged and almost captured the Confederate artillery when the two Virginia regiments turned and counterattacked, driving the Hoosiers from the field. Farnsworth brought up the 8th Illinois Cavalry and it quickly routed the 12th Virginia Cavalry and almost captured the two cannon, but they were driven back by a desperate charge by the 7th Virginia Cavalry. The Virginians had more than enough and retreated, followed by Farnsworth's men. The pursuit continued until darkness put an end to the action.[8]

Farnsworth was not yet done with the enemy troopers, for at first light on September 9, he had his men in the saddle and riding after Munford's troopers. They encountered the 12th Virginia Cavalry and again routed it, capturing its battle-flag in the process. The 9th Virginia Cavalry arrived to put an end the action. Further east, a battalion of the 1st New York Cavalry dashed into Hyattstown and routed troops from Brig. Gen.

Wade Hampton's cavalry brigade. Hampton returned the following day, and the New Yorkers, supported by a squadron from the 1st United States Cavalry, again drove them back.[9]

Pleasonton's men collected important information about Lee's movements during this period. He reported on the morning of September 6, how he had "just learned that Lee's corps, said to number 30,000, crossed above yesterday, and moved down in the direction of Pooleville; and that Jackson is on the move by the Frederick road, the design being an attack on Washington." McClellan reassured President Lincoln on the evening of September 8 that Pleasonton "guards every approach [to Washington] carefully, and will keep me full advised." With the knowledge that Lee's army was across the Potomac River and in Maryland, McClellan pushed his infantry north on September 9. Pleasonton's troopers were already there, screening and collecting information, much of it incorrect.[10]

Pleasonton's estimate of Lee's strength in Maryland swelled to 100,000 the evening of September 8, but he was reticent about revealing how he arrived at this figure. McClellan understood the best way to confirm his cavalry chief's estimate would be to take Sugar Loaf Mountain and look down on the enemy. It could also be used as a signal station. Pleasonton was ordered to take the eminence and complied by sending the 6th U. S. Cavalry, a squadron of the 8th Illinois Cavalry, and two cannon on September 10. Thomas Munford's small 2nd and 12th Virginia Cavalry and a battery of horse artillery defended the mountain and they easily drove off the regulars. The VI Corps' arrival changed the math and McClellan made it clear to William Franklin about the importance of taking the mountain: "accomplish the important object if it can be done without incurring the risk of losing your command." He was also told to use Darius Couch's division (IV Corps), if needed. Franklin chose not to push the issue, depriving McClellan the eyes that could have seen Lee's army leaving Frederick and moving north toward Boonsboro and Harpers Ferry. John Farnsworth's brigade arrived and with support from Winfield Hancock's brigade (VI Corps), finally drove Munford from the mountain on September 11.[11]

Pleasonton entered Frederick on the evening of September 12. Farnsworth's brigade was already present and the cavalry chief brought the 1st New York Cavalry and a portion of the 12th Pennsylvania Cavalry, part of Col. Andrew McReynolds' brigade, with him. Pleasonton now had eight cavalry regiments—the largest assemblage of Union horsemen up to this point in the war. However, Pleasonton was forced to scatter them for various missions. The 6th U. S. Cavalry remained with the VI Corps, screening its movements north. He sent McReynolds' brigade (1st New York Cavalry, 8th Pennsylvania Cavalry, a portion of the 12th Pennsylvania Cavalry, and a horse artillery battery) northeast toward Gettysburg to follow what was thought to be a portion of Munford's brigade riding in that direction. The newly arrived 6th Pennsylvania Cavalry was sent to assist the 6th U. S. Cavalry in supporting the VI Corps. The 1st Maine Cavalry was retained in Frederick on provost duty, and the remainder of the 12th Pennsylvania Cavalry supported the II Corps. Only the 8th Illinois Cavalry, the 3rd Indiana Cavalry, and the 1st Massachusetts Cavalry, with two horse batteries, remained with Farnsworth.

McClellan now had possession of Lee's Special Orders Number 191 and he ordered Pleasonton to determine "whether this order of march has thus far been followed by the enemy." He counseled Pleasonton to approach South Mountain "with great care." Pleasonton rode northwest along the National Road toward Catoctin Mountain with Farnsworth's brigade. They had ridden only three or four miles when the column was shelled by a couple of cannon supported by the Jeff Davis Legion (Hampton's brigade; Stuart's division) holding the Catoctin Mountain gap at Fairview. Pleasonton dismounted a few squadrons from the 3rd Indiana Cavalry and 8th Illinois Cavalry and sent them up the ridge, and at the same time, ordered a couple of batteries to drop trail and open fire on the enemy artillery. By 2:00 p.m., the dismounted troopers reached a point above the enemy's guns and fired down on them, forcing them to pack up and immediately retreat. Hampton arrived with additional cavalry and they made another stand just east of Middletown. Jeb Stuart arrived as Pleasonton deployed his men to drive Hampton from the field and ordered a retreat. Stuart and Hampton were merely conducting a holding action to buy time for D.H. Hill to deploy his infantry in and around Turner's Gap.[12]

The 6th U. S. Cavalry and 6th Pennsylvania Cavalry were also engaged with some of Stuart's troopers. After being driven from Sugar Loaf Mountain, Munford brought his 2nd and 12th Virginia Cavalry to the Catoctin Mountain gap near Jefferson, about 15 miles to the northwest, on September 12. Pleasonton's two regiments were supported by Harrison Fairchild's infantry brigade (Isaac Rodman's division; IX Corps), sent down from Frederick. They made quick work of Munford's men and opened the mountain gap. Munford pulled back to Burkittsville, about seven miles away, at the base of South Mountain to defend Crampton's Gap. The "6's" followed Munford's men during their retreat.[13]

By the end of September 13, Pleasonton had driven the enemy from Catoctin Mountain to the foot of South Mountain, allowing a clear avenue for the infantry to advance the following day. Pleasonton informed McClellan of his belief that the enemy would make a stand at Turner's Gap. He requested support from the IX Corps and while waiting, sent some skirmishers up the mountainside, where the two sides exchanged small arms fire. Pleasonton was unsure of the enemy's strength on South Mountain, so he decided to wait for the IX Corps before risking destruction on the mountain side, and instead camped at the foot of the mountain.[14]

Pleasonton was aware of a second gap in South Mountain to the left of Turner's Gap and recommended the IX Corps use it to enter Pleasant Valley. Eliakim Scammon's brigade (Kanahwa Division, IX Corps) was sent toward Fox's Gap while Pleasonton demonstrated in front of Turner's Gap in an attempt to distract the enemy. Pleasonton with Farnsworth's brigade, camped at Bolivar on the National Road on the evening of September 14 and the following morning marched through Turner's Gap to Boonsboro where they tangled with several regiments of Fitz Lee's cavalry brigade forming the rearguard. The Union troopers drove them through Boonsboro in a spirited action, causing more casualties than any other action up to this point. Pleasonton followed orders and moved cross country and joined Israel Richardson's division at Keedysville. Richardson's artillery was in the rear, so Pleasonton ordered up Tidball's horse artillery battery to engage several enemy batteries of Col. Stephen Lee's artillery battalion. Pleasonton spent the night just west of Keedysville and described his actions the following day in one sentence in his report: "On the 16th instant my cavalry was engaged in reconnaissances, escorts, and supports to batteries." One of the reconnaissances may have been across the Middle Bridge at dawn that day.[15]

## Antietam

As the battle raged in the fields north of Sharpsburg, Pleasonton was ordered to march toward the Middle Bridge. The bridge was covered by Confederate snipers and an artillery crossfire. Around noon, McClellan ordered Pleasonton across the bridge to support Sumner's attack on the Sunken Road. Pleasonton complied by sending a squadron of the 4th Pennsylvania Cavalry galloping across the bridge, followed by Tidball's horse artillery to drive away enemy skirmishers. The troopers took up defensive positions behind stone walls at the base of the bridge. The regiment's commander, Col. James Childs, brought the remainder of his men across the bridge a short time later and halted them on the right of Boonsboro Pike. He realized it was not an optimal place for cavalry and as he turned to report this observation to Pleasonton, a shell exploded, mortally wounding him.[16]

Three other batteries crossed Middle Bridge to pound the Confederates in and around Sharpsburg, and were engaged for at least two hours. The rest of Pleasonton's men followed the artillery across the bridge and deployed on the left of Boonsboro Pike. This included the 5th and 6th U. S. Cavalry, 3rd Indiana Cavalry, 8th

Illinois Cavalry, 1st Massachusetts Cavalry and a portion of the 8th Pennsylvania Cavalry. They quickly came under a destructive enemy artillery fire due to their proximity to the batteries they were supporting. Artilleryman John Tidball noted, "The cavalry that had crossed the bridge, finding itself greatly exposed and without the power of acting, took shelter in hollows and under the banks of the creek. At this period of the war the cavalry had not yet fallen into the hands of those who knew the proper use to make of it." A cavalryman complained, "instead of being posted, according to the practice of the centuries, on the flanks of the infantry, we was used throughout the day in support of its own horse batteries, in the rear of the Federal center, and in a position from which it would have been impossible for it to have been used as cavalry, or even to have emerged mounted."[17]

Shortly after 3:00 p.m., Pleasonton surveyed the situation and felt a push against the enemy's center was in order. The enemy in front was weak, he felt, and the IX Corps' attack on Lee's right was about to begin. He therefore petitioned McClellan for infantry support to attack Lee's center. McClellan forwarded his answer at 3:30 p.m.—the army commander "has no infantry to spare." McClellan suggested Pleasonton approach V Corps commander, Fitz John Porter for troops. He did so at about 4:00 p.m., but received no assistance. While some U. S. Regulars from Sykes' division were engaged in front, they were only a handful of units. No full scale attack was therefore made against Lee's center. Pleasonton pulled back across Antietam Creek at 7:00 p.m. and returned to Keedysville for the night.[18]

Pleasonton's cavalry were engaged in collecting stragglers and testing the Confederate line on September 18. Realizing the enemy was gone the following day, Pleasonton headed for the Potomac River, too late to cut off Lee's retreat, but he did round up almost 200 prisoners, a cannon, and one battle-flag.[19]

**Bradley M. Gottfried**

***

# LONGSTREET'S WING—

## Major General James Longstreet

James Longstreet and Thomas Jackson commanded the Army of Northern Virginia's two "wings," since the Confederate Congress had not yet designated corps formations. Longstreet's wing was composed of five divisions: Maj. Gen. Lafayette McLaws', Maj. Gen. Richard Anderson's, Brig. Gen. David Jones', Brig. Gen. John Walker's, and Brig. Gen. John Hood's. The wing structure was actually quite flexible, and each division fought under the wing commander who happened to oversee a particular sector. For example, Hood's division fought under Longstreet at Fox's Gap, but with Jackson at Antietam.[1]

By the Maryland Campaign, James Longstreet had developed a reputation as a steady and reliable subordinate, able to handle large bodies of troops. To his nickname of "Old Pete" was added "Lee's War Horse." He was born on January 8, 1821 in South Carolina and spent his boyhood years in Georgia living with his parents, but when his father died, he was sent to live with his uncle. He attended West Point, graduating a low 54 out of 62 in his Class of 1842. Longstreet served in a variety of posts in Missouri, Louisiana, and Florida after graduating from West Point. His star rose during the Mexican War, where his exploits earned him a wound and brevets to captain and major. Longstreet was promoted to the rank of captain in 1852 and assigned to service fighting Native Americans in Texas. He then accepted the post of paymaster with the rank of major. Longstreet resigned from the Union army on June 1, 1861 and joined the Confederacy. He was commissioned a brigadier general on June 17, 1861 and given a brigade. His unit was the first to see action during the First Bull Run Campaign when it repelled an enemy attempt to cross Bull Run at Blackburn's Ford on July 18, 1861. Longstreet's steady hand led to promotion to major general on October 7, 1861 and command of a division. Tragedy struck in January 1862, when three of his children died of scarlet fever, causing him to become much more reserved. Longstreet distinguished himself the following spring at the Battle of Williamsburg, but confusion arose in his command at the Battle of Seven Pines, and his attacks were poorly coordinated. He redeemed himself during the Seven Days Battles around Richmond. Longstreet was given the "right" wing of the Army of Northern Virginia prior to Second Bull Run, where his men delivered a crushing counterattack on August 30. By the start of the Maryland Campaign, he was a well-respected member of Lee's inner circle.[2]

Longstreet was plagued by an ugly looking sore on his foot made by the chafing of his boot. He finally resorted to wearing a carpet slipper and occasionally rode side-saddle. His aide declared, "a wobbly carpet slipper was not a good-looking thing for a commander on the field."[3]

Longstreet followed Jackson's men from Chantilly to Leesburg. McLaws marched by way of Gum Springs, while Anderson's and Jones' division marched closer to the Potomac River to the east, via Dranesville. Hood's division and Brig. Gen. Nathan Evans' brigade, both unattached, accompanied Longstreet during the Maryland Campaign. The usually defensive-minded Longstreet warmly supported the foray into Maryland, and with Jackson's support, Lee decided the time was right for the invasion. Longstreet's men waded across the Potomac River at White's Ford, beginning on the morning of September 6 and then marched to Frederick by way of Buckeystown, arriving there on September 7.[4]

During the ride north to Frederick, Lee consulted with Longstreet about the possibility of organizing an expedition to capture the Federal garrison at Harpers Ferry. Longstreet thought it too risky an endeavor, and when Lee did not respond, thought the issue was settled. He happened by Lee's headquarters on September 9 and was summoned to attend a meeting to discuss the idea with Jackson, who was already present. "They had gone so far that it seemed useless for me to offer any further opposition," he wrote after the war. McLaws' and Walker's divisions were to accompany Jackson, and rather than contest the movement, Longstreet suggested attaching Anderson's division to McLaws' to strengthen the effort. Hood's and D.R. Jones' divisions joined D.H. Hill at Boonsboro, forming the army's rearguard. Longstreet's command was covered in bullet point IV of Special Orders Number 191: "General Longstreet's command will pursue the main road as far as Boonsborough, where it will halt, with reserve, supply, and baggage trains of the army."[5]

Longstreet, with Hood's and Jones' divisions, left Frederick on National Road behind Jackson's column on September 10. The two divisions bivouacked between Middletown and Turner's Gap that evening, and were again on the march the following day. Their destination was not Boonsboro, but Hagerstown. Lee learned of massive quantities of flour there and heard a rumor of a large Union force marching from Pennsylvania. Longstreet was none too pleased about Lee's army being further separated and apparently told Lee, "General I wish we could stand still and let the damned Yankees come to us!" Longstreet was in Hagerstown on the evening of September 13, when Lee learned of McClellan's movements toward South Mountain. Lee ordered Longstreet to head for Boonsboro the next morning to reinforce D.H. Hill at Boonsboro.[6]

D.R. Jones' division led the grueling march from Hagerstown to Boonsboro, followed by Hood's division. D.H. Hill, tasked with holding the South Mountain gaps, was already engaged at Fox's Gap and a second front was about to open at Turner's and Frosttown Gaps. Longstreet alerted Hill of his imminent arrival, as the van approached Boonsboro at about 3:00 p.m. Longstreet rode up Turner's Gap to confer with Hill and quickly saw "everything was in such disjointed condition that it would be impossible for my troops and Hill's to hold the mountain against such forces as McClellan had there. . ." After some confusion, Jones' men were sent into the fray. Lee ordered Longstreet to break up Jones' division, sending Drayton's and G.T. Anderson's brigades south to Fox's Gap, where they encountered the Union IX Corps. The former brigade was roughly handled in subsequent action. Garnett's, Kemper's, and Jenkins' brigades were retained around Turner's Gap and fought on the heights, just north of it. Nathan Evans' independent brigade attached to Longstreet's wing, also fought around Turner's Gap. When Hood's division arrived, it was quickly sent south to help arrest the successful thrust of the IX Corps at Fox's Gap. The division, aided by the growing darkness, managed to halt the Union drive through the gap, and its troops may have fired the shots that killed Maj. Gen. Jesse Reno. Longstreet claimed in his report, "Had the command reached the mountain pass in time to have gotten into position before the attack was made, I believe that the direct assaults of the enemy could have been repulsed with comparative ease. Hurried into action, however, we arrived at our positions more exhausted than the enemy."[7]

Longstreet and Hill met with Lee soon after the hostilities ended. Hill explained his troops' untenable positions on the heights and Longstreet suggested an immediate retreat. Lee agreed and an all-night march began. Longstreet rode ahead of his troops and found Lee on Cemetery Hill at 9:30 a.m. on September 15. When Lee explained his desire to stand and fight at Sharpsburg, Longstreet immediately went to work posting his batteries. His troops began crossing Antietam Creek at the Middle Bridge: Jones' division crossed first, at 10:00 a.m., and formed on Cemetery Hill, southeast of Sharpsburg; Hood's division crossed about an hour later and deployed on Jones' right. With word of the Union I Corps' crossing of Antietam Creek during the afternoon of September 16, Hood's division was thrust northward, spread between Hagerstown Pike and Smoketown Road. Its position was directly in front of Truman Seymour's brigade, which advanced through the East Woods on the evening of September 16. Darkness put an end to the lively skirmishing.[8]

Stonewall Jackson oversaw the northern fields. Longstreet theoretically had 17,646 in his wing during the battle. However, because he exercised operational control south of the Dunker Church, he commanded far fewer troops—only D.R. Jones' and D.H. Hill's divisions, despite the vast area under his control. Hood's divisions had already been sent north and operated under Jackson, and when McLaws' and Walker's divisions appeared, they too were eventually sent to Jackson, after arriving from Harpers Ferry. Longstreet did retain control over Richard Anderson's division when it finally appeared from Harpers Ferry on the morning of the battle.[9]

Three of D.H. Hill's brigades were sent north to help blunt the I Corps attacks through the Cornfield and East Woods, leaving only two brigades, Brig. Gen. George B. Anderson's, and Robert Rodes' under Longstreet's control. These two brigades settled into the Sunken Road, and with the remnants of Howell Cobb's (McLaws' division) and Alfred Colquitt's (D.H. Hill's division) brigades initially fought Brig. Gen. William French's division (II Corps). Historian Joseph Harsh summed up the leadership at the Sunken Road as "Neither Longstreet, nor D.H. Hill, who were both present and directing throughout, seem to have coordinated their units effectively." Harsh was especially critical of Longstreet's handling of Anderson's division. Anderson's division arrived at Sharpsburg on the morning of the battle, and after a short rest, was sent to reinforce the Sunken Road sector. Anderson was wounded almost as soon as the division made its way toward the sector, giving way to Roger Pryor who apparently knew nothing about the division's orders or how to get his new division to the Sunken Road. Longstreet apparently did little to help coordinate the division's change in command and movement to the Sunken Road, which Harsh called "confused and inefficient."[10]

Although Longstreet never mentioned it, he ordered Rodes to make what proved to be a fool-hardy charge against French's division. The charge was disjointed; at least one of Rodes' regiments did not hear the order and remained glued to the Sunken Road and the others attacked in an uncoordinated fashion. The repulse was bloody and achieved nothing. When Longstreet noted Union pressure on the left of the Sunken Road line, he ordered another charge against French's right flank to relieve the pressure, this time by Cobb's brigade and portions of Manning's brigade (Walker's division), which was also bloodily repulsed.[11]

During the desperate fight at the Sunken Road, Longstreet ordered Capt. M. Miller's battery on Cemetery Hill into action in the Piper orchard. Many of the cannoneers were soon stricken by counterbattery fire and two guns fell silent. Longstreet ordered his five aides off their horses to man one of the pieces while Longstreet held their horses' reins. When replaced by actual cannoneers, the aides quickly remounted.[12]

At the collapse of the Sunken Road, Longstreet's two divisions fell back to the Piper farm where desperate fighting continued. Historian Ezra Carman acknowledged "regiments and brigades were intermingled one with another and considerably disorganized and demoralized by the loss of an unusually large number of officers and many men."[13]

While Longstreet was preoccupied with his sector, Hood's, McLaws', and Walker's divisions were engaged in the area north of Dunker Church. Their activities are highlighted in each divisional entry. All three achieved initial success before pulling back. Longstreet was also directly responsible for the area east and south of Sharpsburg. Portions of D.R. Jones' division and Evans' (under Stevens) brigade helped defend Boonsboro Pike against incursions by U.S. Regular Infantry. The rest of Jones' division spread out south of Sharpsburg, where it engaged the IX Corps, which had crossed the Lower Bridge and was heading for the town. Longstreet confided in his report, "The enemy was then met by Brig. Gen. D.R. Jones with six brigades. He drove back our right several times, and was himself made to retire several times badly crippled, but his strong re-enforcements finally enabled him to drive in my right and occupy this part of my ground." The arrival of A. P. Hill's division from Harpers Ferry saved the day.[14]

Longstreet's wing was the first to recross the Potomac River on the night of September 18-19, completing the process by 2:00 a.m. The wing performed fairly well during the Maryland Campaign. It helped stabilize D.H. Hill's line at Turner's and Fox's Gaps and performed as well as could be expected at Antietam. The wing lost 5,384 men for a casualty rate of 31%.[15] **Bradley M. Gottfried**

# McLAWS' DIVISION—

## Major General Lafayette McLaws

Lafayette McLaws was named after the famed French general of the American Revolution, the Marquis de Lafayette, who once held the young McLaws on his knee during a visit to his hometown of Augusta, Georgia in 1825. Family records indicate McLaws learned to write at the age of four and "wrote on the walls or his books, 'Gen. Lafayette McLaws'," not realizing that he would one day become a general.[1]

McLaws graduated from West Point in 1842, along with his friend James Longstreet, under whose command he would serve throughout most of the Civil War. He chose the military as a career, serving in the Mexican War and Mormon uprising before resigning his commission as a captain to join the Confederate States Army upon the outbreak of the war. On June 17, 1861, McLaws was promoted to colonel and given command of the newly formed 10th Georgia Infantry Regiment. He rose quickly in rank and responsibility, receiving a promotion to brigadier general and brigade command on September 25, 1861 and another promotion to major general and division command on May 23, 1862.[2]

McLaws' division, consisting of the brigades commanded by Brig. Gen. Joseph Kershaw and Brig. Gen. Paul Semmes, fought in the Seven Days Battles, June 25 – July 1, 1862 as part of Longstreet's command in the Army of Northern Virginia. The brigades of Col. William Barksdale and Brig. Gen. Howell Cobb were transferred to his division following the Seven Days. Though none of McLaws' brigade commanders were professional soldiers, the division built a solid reputation as a capable fighting unit on the field.[3]

The division spent the first half of August 1862 opposite George McClellan's Army of the Potomac along the James River near Richmond. McLaws' division marched north to reunite with Lee's army in late August, a nine-day trek of 145 miles that took it through the bloody aftermath of Second Bull Run. The division reached Leesburg on September 3, the day before the first Confederate troops splashed across the Potomac River and into Maryland. McLaws' men crossed the river on September 6 at White's Ferry and Cheek's Ford, still badly worn from their long march from Richmond. In a letter to his wife, McLaws wrote: "Many of our men are without shoes, and all of them are very ragged."[4]

The men reached Frederick, Maryland on September 7, and then marched southwest toward Harpers Ferry on September 10 to fulfill what was arguably the most difficult assignment in Lee's Special Orders Number 191. Leading an independent command composed of his own division and Maj. Gen. Richard Anderson's, McLaws was directed to "possess himself of the Maryland Heights, and endeavor to capture the enemy at Harpers Ferry and vicinity." McLaws' command was one of three Confederate prongs ordered to converge on Harpers Ferry from different directions, but his was the only one operating on the Maryland side, which meant any Union relief effort would come from his rear. Additionally, Maryland Heights would likely be heavily defended. Recognizing the difficulties McLaws faced, Longstreet added three brigades to Anderson's division, increasing McLaws' strength to ten brigades. Longstreet recalled McLaws' robust command marching off in high spirits, "singing, as they marched through the streets of Frederick, 'The Girl I Left Behind Me.'"[5]

The long column snaked through Middletown, Burkittsville, and then through South Mountain at Brownsville Pass before reaching the town of Brownsville, at the mountain's western base in Pleasant Valley, by nightfall on September 11. About two miles to the west and running parallel to South Mountain sits Elk Ridge, with Maryland Heights on its southern tip, looming over the Potomac River and Harpers Ferry beyond. McLaws observed, "so long as Maryland Heights was occupied by the enemy, Harpers Ferry could never be occupied by us. If we gained possession of the heights, the town was no longer tenable to [the enemy]."[6]

All ten brigades were in motion at sunrise on September 12. From his own division, McLaws selected Kershaw's and Barksdale's brigades to ascend Elk Ridge through Solomon's Gap and take possession of Maryland Heights, four miles to the south, while Cobb's brigade kept pace with their advance from the valley below. To protect his rear, McLaws ordered Semmes' brigade, along with Col. William Parham's brigade of Anderson's division, to guard the South Mountain passageways at Brownsville Pass and Crampton's Gap to the northeast. A regiment was also sent to guard Solomon's Gap on Elk Ridge. The rest of Anderson's brigades moved south toward the Potomac River.[7]

After bitter fighting along the narrow summit of Elk Ridge, Kershaw and Barksdale took possession of Maryland Heights around 3:30 p.m. on September 13, as the Union defenders streamed down the mountain's southwestern slope and crossed the Potomac River to the Union garrison. A reporter who witnessed the scene wrote, "I could not but think they were marching to the funeral of Harpers Ferry."[8]

The three Confederate prongs were now in possession of the high ground surrounding Harpers Ferry – McLaws to the north, Brig. Gen. John Walker to the south, and "Stonewall" Jackson to the west – and spent the morning of September 14 positioning their artillery on the heights. The barrage began around 2:00 p.m. from all three directions. Over the din, McLaws could hear cannon fire to the northeast, but was not overly concerned "as there were three brigades of infantry in the vicinity, besides cavalry of Col. Munford and Gen. Stuart, who was with me on the heights and [having] just come from above, told me he did not believe there was more than a brigade of enemy."[9]

The enemy force estimated as a brigade by Jeb Stuart was actually William Franklin's VI Corps. By the time McLaws and Stuart started toward Brownsville to assess the situation, Franklin's overwhelming numbers had forced the defenders from Crampton's Gap. McLaws sent in Cobb's brigade, which had been pulled from its position near the base of Maryland Heights hours earlier, but as historian Ezra Carman described, Cobb's men reached the field "when it was practically lost, were thrown into some disorder by the unexpected…and yielded only when one fourth of the number were killed or wounded." It was too late to stop the Federal tide descending into Pleasant Valley as darkness fell.[10]

With Harpers Ferry in front and Franklin's corps in his rear, McLaws was trapped in enemy territory. Lee received word of McLaws' predicament in Pleasant Valley and halted the retreat of his forces in Keedysville (several miles east of Sharpsburg) rather than leave McLaws isolated in Maryland. Carman wrote, "McLaws could not now join him by the road up Pleasant Valley, and it would not do to leave him to his fate; his extrication was of grave necessity."[11]

To counter the threat to his rear, McLaws withdrew Kershaw and Barksdale from Maryland Heights (leaving one regiment and two artillery pieces behind) after dark on September 14, and ordered up Anderson's reserve brigade. Joining these brigades with the remnants of Cobb, Semmes, and Parham, he formed a battle line across Pleasant Valley as a show of strength, about one and a half miles south of Crampton's Gap, and waited.[12]

To McLaws' front (south), Anderson's remaining brigades continued to guard the Potomac River, but the withdrawal of Cobb from the base of Maryland Heights left uncovered an avenue of escape to the west. Union cavalry from Harpers Ferry took full advantage of the gap, and approximately 1,500 horsemen quietly slipped across the pontoon bridge at the base of Maryland Heights after dark on September 14, and turned left (west) on the Sharpsburg Road, making their way to safety and capturing one of Longstreet's reserve trains near Williamsport, Maryland along the way.[13]

The next morning, September 15, McLaws received a telegraph message around 10:00 a.m. that Harpers Ferry "had hoisted the white flag." McLaws mounted his horse and crossed the river to receive orders from

Jackson, who directed him to "proceed to Sharpsburg with all possible dispatch." Still facing Franklin's corps, McLaws began withdrawing his troops around 2:00 p.m. and cleared Pleasant Valley by the early hours of September 16, relieved but astounded that Franklin did not attack. Years later, McLaws blamed Franklin's reticence for the battle that occurred two days later, ". . . if Franklin had pushed his advantages gained, when he found Crampton's Gap in Maryland in my rear – Gen. Lee would have had to retreat across the Potomac…the Battle of Sharpsburg would not have been fought."[14]

The division bivouacked four miles west of Harpers Ferry at Halltown, Virginia around 8:00 a.m. on September 16, while McLaws tried unsuccessfully to find provisions for his tired and hungry men. The march resumed toward Sharpsburg about 3:00 p.m., and halted a couple of miles from Shepherdstown once it got too dark to see the road. Around midnight, McLaws received orders from Lee to hasten forward, so after a short rest but still no provisions, the men trudged on. Sgt. John Parham of Semmes' brigade recalled the disappointment when they turned toward Maryland, as he and his comrades "thought they would be marching toward Richmond" instead.[15]

The men crossed the Potomac River by torchlight early on September 17, as McLaws rode ahead to receive orders. He found Lee at his headquarters west of Sharpsburg, and was told to rest his men. Lee added, "I will send for you when I want you." McLaws' men were badly in need of rest. Kershaw and Barksdale had been in battle or in battle line from September 12 through the 15th, and Cobb and Semmes had been badly mauled at Crampton's Gap. Hundreds of exhausted, hungry and sick men were left along the route from Harpers Ferry. Col. James Nance of the 3rd South Carolina wrote, "Our division was never in a poorer plight to go into battle." However, a rest was not in the cards.[16]

McLaws settled into the tall grass and fell asleep, only to be awoken less than an hour later by Maj. Walter Taylor of Lee's staff, who informed him that his division was already marching north toward the fight on Lee's left flank. McLaws quickly mounted his horse and rode to the front of the column along Taylor's Landing Road (present day Mondell Road). It was about 8:30 a.m. when the troops obliqued northeast and witnessed a desperate scene: wounded streaming by on stretchers, soldiers dragging guns to the rear, spilling from the West Woods in the face of an advancing enemy.[17]

A staff officer from D.H. Hill's staff pointed out McLaws' position, but not knowing the terrain or troop dispositions, McLaws needed more information. He found John Hood, riding alone after his division's crushing defeat in the Cornfield, who identified the line of advance. McLaws formed his division from right to left -- Cobb, Kershaw, Barksdale, Semmes, and advanced northeast toward the West Woods. Cobb's brigade, however, veered too far to the right and into the Sunken Road, a detachment that would last until that night. About this time, McLaws received orders from Jackson to send a brigade to support Stuart's cavalry and artillery on his (and the Confederate army's) far left, a mission McLaws assigned to Semmes.[18]

McLaws wrote, "As the enemy were filling the woods so rapidly, I wished my troops to cross the open space between us and the woods before they were entirely occupied." He ordered a regiment forward from Kershaw's brigade to check the Union advance while his brigades deployed. The 2nd South Carolina advanced and fired into the left flank of the 125th Pennsylvania (Samuel Crawford's brigade; Alpheus Williams' division; XII Corps) and the 34th New York (Brig. Gen. Willis Gorman's brigade; Maj. Gen. John Sedgwick's division, II Corps). Jubal Early's brigade fired into the front and right of these Union regiments. Seeing the attack underway, McLaws waived his handkerchief in the air to signal the advance of his division.[19]

Barksdale advanced into the West Woods to the left of the 2nd South Carolina, "merry as hunters on a fox chase," according to Albert Henley of the 13th Mississippi. Barksdale's right wing obliqued to the right to assist Early. Three more regiments from Sedgwick's left were drawn into the engagement as George T. Anderson's brigade (Longstreet's command) joined the fray. The Union troops fell back in confusion and the

2nd South Carolina pushed briefly across Hagerstown Pike near the Dunker Church, before retreating west of the church. They would charge again with the rest of Kershaw's brigade a half hour later.[20]

The conflagration between the intermingled Confederate brigades of Barksdale, Kershaw, Anderson and Early, and five Union regiments from three brigades and two separate corps, took place between 9:00-9:30 a.m. in the southern, widest portion of the West Woods between the Dunker Church and a large clearing about 450 yards to the north, west of Hagerstown Pike (present day Philadelphia Park).[21]

During the engagement, Barksdale looked to his left and saw the rest of Sedgwick's division marching west through the large clearing, unaware of the Confederate menace in the woods. Barksdale swung his left wing north and slammed into Sedgwick's flank. Early moved up on Barksdale's left and the 3rd South Carolina of Kershaw's brigade took position on Barksdale's right rear. The Confederate line pressed forward through the clearing as Sedgwick's men, taking fire from their flank and rear, fled north in confusion toward the D.R. Miller barn. After advancing about 225 yards through open fields, heavy enfilade fire from Union artillery and infantry to the east checked and repulsed the rebels' advance.[22]

Around 9:30 a.m., as Barksdale and the 3rd South Carolina sought cover in the clearing, Kershaw ordered the rest of his brigade to attack east from the vicinity of the Dunker Church, across Hagerstown Pike, and over the plateau. The bold charge collided with George Greene's troops and II Corps artillery, forcing Kershaw's men to fall back through the woods with heavy losses.[23]

McLaws still had one more brigade in position to change the outcome in the West Woods. Moments earlier, Semmes' men had been in a severe fight with the 15th Massachusetts of Sedgwick's lead brigade (Gorman's) near the Alfred Poffenberger farm when Barksdale, Early and the 3rd South Carolina smashed into Sedgwick's flank and rear in the clearing, forcing the Union division's retreat. Semmes' 1862 took advantage of the confusion and pursued the fugitives northeast, nearly 400 hundred yards beyond Barksdale's furthest point of advance and toward the D.R. Miller farm, protected by a rocky ledge running north to south to their right and Stuart's artillery to their left. Semmes' men drove past the D.R. Miller barn and farmhouse, capturing "thirty-six prisoners, including a lieutenant colonel and first lieutenant," before the lack of support to their right and sheer exhaustion forced them to pull back.[24]

By 10:30 a.m., McLaws' men had retired to the rocky ledges and stone walls to the west and south of the woods. His division lost 38% of its strength.[25]

Historian William C. Davis described the Confederate actions in the West Woods, mostly involving McLaws' division, as "the greatest southern tactical triumph on the field." Ezra Carman acknowledged the significance, especially of Semmes advance, in forcing Union remnants out of the West Woods and nearly turning the Union right.[26]

**Laura Marfut**

* * *

### Kershaw's Brigade: Brigadier General Joseph Kershaw

**Units:** 2nd South Carolina, 3rd South Carolina, 7th South Carolina, 8th South Carolina
**Strength:** 1,712[27]
**Losses:** 355 (57k-292w-6w)[28]

The men of Brig. Gen. Joseph Kershaw's South Carolina brigade stripped naked and bid adieu to Virginia as they waded across the Potomac River at White's Ferry and into Maryland on September 6, 1862.[29]

After hard fighting in the Seven Days Battles in June and July, the brigade had enjoyed a relaxing month near Richmond, watching McClellan's troops as Lee's main body contended with Pope in northern Virginia. They finally marched north to rejoin the army in Leesburg in late August, a journey that took them through the bloody aftermath of Second Bull Run. They arrived in time for the river crossing. Kershaw's men were in high spirits to be back with the army and taking the fight to the North. D. Augustus Dickert wrote, "Never before had an occurrence so excited and enlivened the spirits of the troops as the crossing of the Potomac into the land of our sister, Maryland.[30]

The South Carolina regiments – the 2nd, 3rd, 7th and 8th - had been brigaded together in Lafayette McLaws' division since early summer of 1861, along with three non-South Carolina regiments. Col. Joseph Kershaw, a self-taught lawyer and politician with militia experience, commanded the 2nd and 8th South Carolinians, which helped break the Union line at Henry House Hill, leading to a Confederate victory at First Bull Run. His actions attracted the attention of his superiors, and he was promoted to the rank of brigadier general and given command of the South Carolina brigade in January 1862, which by then consisted of only the four South Carolina regiments.

Once in Maryland, Kershaw's men marched north about 25 miles to Frederick, arriving on September 7 to a much more subdued welcome than the "greatest enthusiasm imaginable" they had received in Leesburg. Robert Shand recalled the mixed reception, "Our friends were out on balconies and at open windows; our enemies looked at us through closed blinds."[31]

After a short stay in Frederick, the brigade marched southwest toward Harpers Ferry by late morning on September 10. Lee's Special Orders Number 191 directed McLaws, Stonewall Jackson, and John Walker to force the surrender of the Union garrison there by seizing the high ground around it. McLaws was ordered to take Maryland Heights, looming hundreds of feet over Harpers Ferry from the north. In two days, McLaws would show his faith in Kershaw by selecting him for the honor of taking the Heights.[32]

The column marched about 13 miles in the heat and dust, reaching Middletown around midnight.

Waking early on September 11, the men experienced "ridicule from the local women" in Burkittsville, Mac Wyckoff noted, and continued west over South Mountain and into Pleasant Valley. Kershaw's troops made camp in Brownsville, a small town on the western base of South Mountain where, to their relief, sympathizers provided them with much appreciated fruit and corn.[33]

## Harpers Ferry

Elk Ridge, a small mountain range running parallel to South Mountain, lies less than two miles west of Brownsville across Pleasant Valley. Maryland Heights looms over Harpers Ferry at the southern tip of Elk Ridge. On the morning of September 12, McLaws ordered Kershaw's brigade, supported by William Barksdale's Mississippians, to ascend Elk Ridge through Solomon's Gap and force its way to the Maryland Heights overlook four miles to the south.[34]

The brigades crossed Pleasant Valley without resistance and climbed toward Solomon's Gap, cutting their way along an old coal road. Tally Simpson, on the picket line, wrote, "It was the hardest work I have ever done. The mountain was high and steep and the laurel and ivy bushes were so thick and closely matted together that it was almost impossible to pass through them." Kershaw's skirmishers encountered Union pickets as they neared the top and pursued them over the mountain. Barksdale's skirmishers moved up and Kershaw advanced south toward Maryland Heights, along the very narrow ridge that, at some points, was only 25 yards wide.[35]

After about a mile, the Mississippi skirmishers hit an abatis (an obstacle of tangled brush and felled trees) with Union defenders behind it from Col. Thomas Ford's brigade of the Harpers Ferry garrison. Kershaw's column moved right, off the ridge, to bypass the obstacle while the skirmishers confronted the Union pickets. With no trail, the terrain became even more challenging. "Almost impassable woods, rock – no road – blind path and no path," wrote Henry L.P. King. The commander of the 3th South Carolina, Col. James Nance, wrote, "The men had to pull themselves up precipitous inclines by the twigs and undergrowth that lines the mountainside."[36]

Around 6:00 p.m., Kershaw's troops reached a narrow summit where the ground flattened. The Mississippi skirmishers, back in the lead, encountered a second abatis, this time with stiffer Union resistance. Satisfied that the enemy was there in force, Kershaw deployed his battle lines and prepared for the morning, as daylight was growing scarce. The ridge was only about 50 yards wide and Kershaw's line reached from side to side: the 8th (Col. John Henagan) on the right and the 7th (Col. D. Wyatt Aiken) on the left in front, and the 3rd (Nance) on the right and the 2nd (Col. John Kennedy) on the left in back. Barksdale's brigade followed in reserve.[37]

Darkness fell quickly on the mountain. The troops were exhausted; they had clawed their way approximately three miles along the ridge, with still a mile to go and an enemy to dislodge before reaching the Maryland Heights overlook. To add to their misery, there was no water other than what could be retrieved from the foot of the mountain.[38]

The two sides slept on their arms on the rocky ridge, not more than 100 yards apart. Captured Union prisoners reported about 1,200 defenders from Ford's brigade lay in wait beyond the abatis, the 126th New York and 32nd Ohio regiments forming their front line. The morning would bring the first major battle of the Maryland Campaign and seal the fate of Harpers Ferry.[39]

The fighting on September 13 commenced about 6:30 a.m. when Kershaw ordered his line to advance, while Barksdale's assumed its position along the eastern slope. Kershaw wrote in his report that because of the narrow ridge, the 8th South Carolina, on the brigade's right front, "encountered a ledge of rock which cut them off," causing the regiment to move down the western slope to bypass it. The 7th, now alone on the crest, "moved briskly forward under heavy musket fire, surmounted a difficult abatis and drove the enemy from position in about 20 minutes."[40]

The Union troops fell back about 400 yards, behind yet a third barrier -- a much stronger position "built of great stones and logs," as described by D. Augustus Dickert. Nearly out of ammunition, Col. Aiken of the 7th South Carolina requested relief and Kershaw sent in the 3rd South Carolina, which struggled to pass through the 7th in the narrow space while under deadly fire. "Men had to cling to bushes while they loaded and fired. But with their usual gallantry they came down to their work. Through the tangled undergrowth, through the abattis (sic), and over the breastworks they leaped with a yell," wrote Dickert. But despite the enthusiasm of the men of the 3rd South Carolina, the stubborn Union resistance wore them down. [41]

The tide turned in favor of Kershaw around 10:00 a.m. Barksdale's advance along the eastern slope positioned his men to the Union right flank and rear while, at the same time, the 8th and 2nd South Carolinians appeared at the crest on the enemy's left flank. Kershaw saw an opportunity to capture the entire Union force and ordered a cease-fire so Barksdale's regiments could move up without encountering friendly fire. However, Barksdale's troops fired prematurely. A sharp skirmish erupted and the commander of the 126th New York, Col. Eliakim Sherrill, was seriously wounded. With their leader out of the fight, the outflanked Union defenders fled down the mountain. Kershaw's men knew the worst of the fighting was over; "The 7th gave three cheers to the 3rd South Carolina, and Kershaw hurried over to congratulate Nance," wrote Wyckoff.[42]

Kershaw began his final push toward the Maryland Heights overlook around 10:30 a.m. The effort took several hours as the soldiers encountered scattered Union resistance, captured stragglers, and grabbed up rifles, blankets, and other equipment from the abandoned enemy positions. Ford and Miles attempted to rally their men at the Union naval battery about two-thirds of the way down the southwest slope of the mountain and send them back up, but met with little success.[43]

McLaws reported that Kershaw's command, by 4:30 p.m., "had possession of the entire heights, the enemy going down a road which they had constructed on the side opposite the ferry . . . fired on by our skirmishers as they crossed the pontoon bridge to Harpers Ferry town." The South Carolinians paused to appreciate the view from the overlook, described by Col. Nance as "the finest in America, if not the world." Later that day, the soldiers discovered three abandoned heavy guns in the Union naval battery, which had been turned uphill during Kershaw's advance with little effect, had been destroyed.[44]

Thus ended the first fight for possession of Harpers Ferry. The toll was heavy for Kershaw's brigade-- 213 casualties. The 7th South Carolina took the brunt with 113 casualties, earning the sobriquet, "The Bloody 7th." The wounded suffered more than usual that night because of water shortages and no road to bring up ambulances and medical supplies.[45]

As the sun rose on September 14, the Union flag continued waving over Harpers Ferry, despite being surrounded by McLaws, Walker and Jackson. Two days behind Lee's timetable in Special Orders Number 191, the Confederates scrambled to drag artillery onto the heights to speed the Union surrender. By 2:00 p.m., after herculean efforts to cut a road and haul the guns up by hand, four Parrot guns were on Maryland Heights and a coordinated barrage from three directions soon commenced.[46]

A situation was developing to the north that threatened to derail the siege: ". . . all during the day . . . we heard continually the deep, dull sound of cannonading in our rear," recalled Dickert. The Battle of South Mountain had opened at dawn at Fox's Gap about 12 miles to the northeast, and by evening, as Confederate artillery bombarded Harpers Ferry, the Union VI Corps had forced its way through Crampton's Gap, only five miles to the north, potentially trapping McLaws between them and Harpers Ferry.[47]

McLaws bought time by withdrawing Kershaw's and Barksdale's brigades from the heights after dark, leaving one of Barksdale's regiments and two guns behind, and forming a line across Pleasant Valley, about a mile south of the VI Corps' position. Remnants of the four brigades that had tried to slow the VI Corps' advance formed a second line behind them. This was a ruse to give the impression of a strong defensive line, and it worked. The VI Corps did not attack at daylight on September 15; however, Kershaw's men felt the strain of their bluff. Robert Shand wrote, "We felt that we were in a trap and that by night those who were not killed would be prisoners. We all realized our great peril and hence were as quiet as a moral village at midnight."[48]

Harpers Ferry finally surrendered around 8:00 a.m. on September 15, but Kershaw's men remained in their precarious position in Pleasant Valley for the rest of the day, waiting their turn to withdraw to the south and march toward Sharpsburg, where Lee was gathering his forces. Shand wrote, "About nightfall we marched across the Potomac on a pontoon bridge into harper's (sic) Ferry, passing on our way the 11000 paroled federal soldiers who had been surrendered that day. They were overcome but not whipped; they gibed us as they passed and promised to come back and whip us to (sic) soon as exchanged."[49]

According to historian Ezra Carman, Kershaw, who carried the bulk of the fighting on Maryland Heights, lost 35 killed and 178 wounded.[50]

**Antietam**

The march from Harpers Ferry to Sharpsburg was arduous and mostly without sustenance. Mac Wyckoff explained, "The commissary wagons caught up with the men late (on the night of the 16th) during a brief rest stop, but before they could draw rations the order came to 'fall in,' and their march resumed." Many of Kershaw's troops fell out along the way.[51]

Kershaw's men waded back into Maryland at Boteler's Ford at dawn on September 17, as the fighting opened between Jackson and the Union I Corps about six miles to the northeast. Upon reaching Lee's headquarters near Sharpsburg, McLaws' division was directed toward the battle.[52]

As McLaws' men neared the West Woods at about 9:00 a.m., they saw the chaos up ahead. McLaws wrote, "Just in front of the line was a large body of woods, from which parties of our troops . . . were seen retiring, and the enemy, I could see, were advancing rapidly, occupying the place." John Sedgwick's Union division had entered the West Woods from the east, intent on turning Lee's left flank, and the 125th Pennsylvania (Samuel Crawford's brigade; Alpheus Williams' division; XII Corps) occupied the southern edge of the woods around the Dunker Church to McLaws' right front.[53]

Kershaw, on the right of McLaws' division, was ordered to charge. Kershaw "detached the 2nd South Carolina and hurried them forward at the double quick into the woods." It drove into the left flank of the 125th Pennsylvania minutes after the 125th's right flank had been attacked by Jackson's troops. The Pennsylvanians fled northeast, carrying three of Sedgwick's regiments with them. The 2nd South Carolina then faced northeast and pursued the 125th Pennsylvania out of the West Woods and briefly across Hagerstown Pike, close to the Smoketown Road, before George Greene's Union infantry division (XII Corps), to their right (east) sent them reeling back into the woods.[54]

As the 2nd headed northeast, the 3rd South Carolina drove north, smashing into Sedgwick's left and rear. Nance reported his regiment "pushed clear of the woods and out into the open field beyond, where the enemy gave way with considerable disorder." But the 3rd's rapid advance exposed its right flank to heavy Union artillery fire and remnants of Sedgwick's division east of Hagerstown Pike. Amid the firestorm, the 3rd South Carolina faced east and took cover in a hollow. Within minutes, Nance saw the rest of the South Carolina Brigade appear to his right, south of the Dunker Church, advancing "most beautifully through the woods up the slope beyond."[55]

It was about 9:30 a.m., when Kershaw ordered the 2nd South Carolina (Maj. Franklin Gaillard in command after Kennedy's wounding) once more across Hagerstown Pike to the northeast, this time supported by the 7th and 8th on its right. "The troops made constant progress along the whole line, driving in column after column of the enemy," wrote Kershaw. The 3rd South Carolina rose from the hollow when they saw Greene's division break to the southeast and attacked across Hagerstown Pike, north of the Smoketown Road, while the rest of the brigade advanced south of the Smoketown Road.[56]

The 2nd and 7th South Carolinians advanced northeast and up a ridge, unseen by John Tompkins' Union battery, which was just over the crest and firing south toward the Sunken Road. Kershaw wrote, "Col. Aiken's regiment approached within 30 yards of one of the batteries, driving the men from the guns." The surprised Tompkins pivoted his cannons and "with a sharp fire of canister opened upon them, causing them to retire in confusion." At the same time the 2nd South Carolina, to the left of the 7th, re-engaged with Greene's infantry, which had repelled them earlier, and the 2nd South Carolinians were pushed back again with heavy loss.[57]

In the confusion, the 8th South Carolina veered to the right, crossed Mumma farm lane and, all alone, fired several volleys into the flank of Max Weber's Union brigade (William French's division; II Corps) as it approached the Sunken Road. The approximately 60-man 8th South Carolina made a significant impression on Weber's flank before pulling back with the rest of the brigade. French reported his right was "exposed to the sudden and terrible fire . . . by troops which had succeeded in breaking the center division of the line of battle."[58]

By 10:00 a.m., the 2nd, 7th and 8th South Carolinians had fallen back through the West Woods. Finding protection from Union artillery behind a stone wall to the southwest, their fight was over. The 3rd South Carolina also withdrew, under fire from two Union batteries that, even 33 years later, Y.J. Pope could vividly remember as "the heaviest (he) had seen during the entire war . . . cannonballs dancing over the ground."[59]

In little over an hour, Kershaw's South Carolina brigade suffered 355 casualties (57 killed; 292

wounded; 6 missing). Once again, the "The Bloody 7th" suffered the most with 140 casualties, including its commander, Col. Aiken, who was wounded and captured. That night, Kershaw's men had their first meal since they left Pleasant Valley, described by

Robert Shand as a "good supply of bread and meat which we ravenously devoured," and slept on the battlefield with the dead all around them.[60]

**Laura Marfut**

$$* * *$$

## Cobb's Brigade: Brigadier General Howell Cobb

**Units:** 16th Georgia, 24th Georgia, Cobb's Georgia Legion, 15th North Carolina[61]
**Strength:** 1,631[62]
**Losses:** 147 (16k-121w-10m)[63]

Brigadier General Howell Cobb's brigade consisted of four veteran regiments organized in the spring and summer of 1861, and the men became veterans fighting on the Virginia peninsula and in the Seven Days' Battles around Richmond. The brigade moved north from Richmond with the rest of McLaws' division around August 19 to join Lee's army. Under the overall wing command of Maj. Gen. Daniel Harvey Hill, the large reinforcing column set out on a forced march that lasted nine days and covered 145 grueling miles. Cobb's brigade left Richmond with nearly 2,000 men, but lost almost a third of its strength enroute before reaching Lee on September 2. This would have a profound impact on the brigade's performance during the Maryland Campaign.[64]

Howell Cobb was already a man of prominence and achievement by the time he volunteered for Confederate service. Born in Jefferson County, Georgia in 1815 he graduated from the University of Georgia in 1834 and practiced law. He was elected to the U. S. Congress in 1843 and became Speaker of the House in 1849 for one term before being elected governor of Georgia. Cobb returned to Congress in 1855 and was appointed Secretary of the Treasury by President James Buchanan in 1857. He was a moderate and opponent of secession during his entire political career, but the election of Lincoln in 1860 effectively reversed his view to one of immediate secession. He was a strong candidate

for the presidency of the new Confederacy, but was determined to take up arms to protect his new country. He organized the 16th Georgia Infantry and became its colonel in July 1861 and a brigadier general in early 1862.[65]

As part of McLaws' division, the brigade reached Big Spring, north of Leesburg, Virginia, on September 3, crossed the Potomac River at White's Ford on September 6, and ultimately reached Frederick. The brigade left Frederick with the rest of the division on September 10, and marched to Pleasant Valley. Cobb's brigade was not part of the force that attacked Maryland Heights on September 12, but was directed to maintain communication with Joseph Kershaw's brigade and "give support if possible," and "serve as a rallying force should any disaster render such necessary." After the capture of Maryland Heights on September 13, Cobb's brigade was sent to Sandy Hook along the Potomac River to guard the eastern roads out of Harpers Ferry.[66]

### South Mountain

Cavalry commander, Jeb Stuart, believed Crampton's Gap was the most likely entry point for the Federals to enter Pleasant Valley to attack McLaws and lift the Harpers Ferry siege. He sent a note to McLaws mid-morning on September 14 requesting infantry reinforcements. Paul Semmes, occupying Brownsville Pass (one mile south of Crampton's Gap), also reported the appearance of William Franklin's Union VI Corps moving west toward his position. At noon, McLaws ordered Cobb to march from Sandy Hook back "to the camp near the point where the road came into the

[Pleasant] valley." Cobb left with his brigade about 1:00 p.m. and made it to Brownsville at the western foot of South Mountain by 4:00 p.m. The big Georgian was directed to take command upon his arrival at Crampton's Gap. Despite the sounds of fighting on the east side of the mountain, Cobb did not attempt to personally reconnoiter the ground at the gap. This lack of understanding would have grave results.[67]

At 5:00 p.m., Cobb received a request for reinforcements from Thomas Munford who commanded a cavalry brigade heavily engaged on the east side of the gap. Cobb promptly ordered his two largest regiments, the 16th Georgia, numbering 368 men and the 15th North Carolina with 402 men, to move north to Crampton's Gap. Cobb had no sooner given the order when he received an urgent request from William Parham, temporary commander of William Mahone's brigade, whose three small Virginia regiments were defending the base of the gap. Parham stated he was up against overwhelming numbers and needed all the help he could get. This last message removed all doubt about the Federal objective and prompted Cobb to order his two remaining regiments, the 24th Georgia and Cobb's Legion, to proceed quickly to Crampton's Gap. Just as the troops began moving, a final message arrived from McLaws ordering Cobb to "hold the gap if it cost the life of every man" in his command.[68]

It took Cobb's men a half hour to reach the summit of South Mountain where utter confusion reigned. Through the woods below him, Cobb could see long lines of Union soldiers charging the hopelessly outnumbered Confederate defenders, overlapping their flanks. These troops were Henry Slocum's VI Corps division's troops, hailing from New York, Pennsylvania and New Jersey. Munford gave a quick explanation of the troop dispositions and turned his command over to the newly arrived brigadier general. Not knowing the ground, Cobb asked Munford to place his men, which he did by sending the first two regiments down Arnoldstown Road to the left and the two others down the road to the right (Gapland Road). Both roads descended to the valley below at oblique angles. Unfortunately for the new arrivals, the entire Confederate line at the base of the mountain just then collapsed. The right two regiments of Cobb's line had barely arrived before being overrun with retreating men and oncoming enemy troops, flush with success and pressing their quarry up the slope.[69]

Cobb's Legion was the smallest unit in Cobb's brigade with 248 effectives. Its commander, Lt. Col. Jefferson Mirabeau Lamar, attempted to place his men in a battle line, unaware in the growing darkness that he was now the right of the entire Confederate line. Firing down the mountain, the small band did not realize 1,200 New Jerseymen from Alfred Torbert's brigade were almost upon them. Almost immediately, the Georgians received fire from the flank and the rear. Not willing to jeopardize the rest of the brigade by retreating out of the vise, Lamar chose to stand and fight. Men fell in heaps from bullets flying from all directions. Sgt. Benjamin Mell of Company D was shot through the chest and arm, but told his comrades, "Boys, I know I must die, but don't leave the field." Lamar was hit in the leg and went down. With annihilation a real possibility, Lamar gathered his strength and shouted for a retreat before another bullet plowed into his chest. The survivors of the Legion attempted to retreat back over the gap, but many were captured in the melee. The casualties were appalling—72%.[70]

As the Gapland Road portion of Cobb's line crumbled, his left was being equally pressed. Four Union regiments (16th, 18th, and 32nd New York and 96th Pennsylvania) piled into the woods and thrust themselves up the slope toward the Confederates posted on Arnoldstown Road. After exchanging several volleys, the Southerners began to waver. A sudden burst of rifle fire on their right revealed the absence of any flank protection. Lt. H.C. Kearney (Company E, 15th North Carolina) stated they were so focused on the troops in their front that the first volley caught them completely unaware. "The first knowledge we had of the situation on the right was a terrible volley of musketry from the rear and right flank, which was at first thought to be from our own troops . . . but such thoughts were dispelled by seeing the Federal flag in the rear," wrote Kearney. What was already a nervous disposition from the Confederate line now became a complete collapse, and men either surrendered outright or frantically made their way over the crest. [71]

As wounded and frantic men streamed through the gap, Cobb and other officers attempted a vain rally for a final stand. Some men posted behind a stone wall at the far end of Padgett's Field, but most ignored their commander's pleas and continued their flight into the darkness, down the western slope. Eli Landers, a private in Co. H of the 16th Georgia, described the desperation of the men in retreat. "It made me feel awful to think that they [his comrades] was all in the hands of the enemy but I could not redeem them with sympathy for I come very near being with them. I stopped once to give up for I nearly give out but the nearer the Yanks came the worse I was scared so I tried it again." With no hope of further support, the Confederate command realized retreating into Pleasant Valley and reestablishing a new defensive line was its best and only alternative. Fortunately for the Southerners, they were given a few minutes of precious time with the arrival of two guns of the Troup Artillery. These two small howitzers were posted to cover both approaches to Crampton's Gap. In the consuming darkness, each gun fired four or five rounds of canister into the oncoming Federals, inflicting considerable casualties and momentarily checking their advance. As quickly as the guns arrived, they limbered back up and bolted back down the mountain. Although some Union men attempted to pursue, the scattering of units, lack of ammunition, descending darkness and complete exhaustion compelled the victors to reform and hold their position on the mountain. [72]

Despite his earlier dismissal of cannon fire to the northeast, McLaws' concern steadily increased as the din of battle at Crampton's Gap continued to swell. He decided to leave Maryland Heights and investigate in person. Accompanied by Jeb Stuart, the burly Georgian rode into Pleasant Valley. Upon

nearing Brownsville, the entourage began encountering the remnants of the Crampton's Gap defenders. Not knowing if the Federals were still in pursuit, McLaws commenced to cobble the forces together into a defensive line that would eventually cross the width of the valley. McLaws bolstered his line with Cadmus Wilcox's brigade from Richard Anderson's division, the two brigades that had taken Maryland Heights, Kershaw's and William Barksdale's, Semmes' and the remnants of Cobb's brigades. As dawn approached on September 15, Franklin saw the impressive battle lines, and thinking himself outnumbered, determined not to attack. Harpers Ferry surrendered mid-morning, and McLaws was ordered to evacuate his troops to that place. By early morning of September 16, the division had bivouacked near Halltown, about four miles distant. The fight at Crampton's Gap had been devastating for Cobb's brigade. Losses totaled 686 men (52%) and there was still more fighting ahead.[73]

## Antietam

The brigade, with the rest of McLaws' division, marched to Sharpsburg, arriving at the vicinity of Lee's headquarters at sunrise on September 17. The division rested west of town and was designated by Lee as a reserve division for the army. The men could easily hear the sound of fierce combat to the northeast. Sometime around 8:45 a.m., McLaws received orders to march toward the vicinity of the West Woods. Cobb's brigade was in the van, but the Georgian was not in command, nor even present. He stated in his official report that he was "necessarily absent" and did not rejoin his men until the morning of September 18. Command devolved to Lt. Col. Christopher C. Sanders of the 24th Georgia. The brigade, now numbering only 357 men, formed the right flank of the division for the impending assault on the woods to the north with the left of its line guiding on Hagerstown Pike. Unfortunately, Sanders never heard the order to face front. Instead of moving north, the brigade continued east and joined the left of Robert Rodes' brigade in the Sunken Road. "We were thus separated from the division, and did not join it until the next morning," lamented Lt. Col. William MacRae of the 15th North Carolina.[74]

The brigade was posted behind a stone wall with its left anchored on Hagerstown Pike. For about an hour the men endured shelling from the long-range Union guns across Antietam Creek. They were not exposed to small arms fire, mostly due to a large hill immediately to their front. Nearer to 10:00 a.m., Rodes' Alabama brigade moved out of the Sunken Road and attempted to flank the oncoming Federal brigades of Max Weber and Dwight Morris both of William French's II Corps division. Cobb's brigade (and the remnants of Alfred Colquitt's brigade, now sandwiched between Cobb and Rodes) participated in the advance. Cobb's men made it to the top of the hill and engaged the enemy "amid a galling and destructive shower of balls." It remained there until Rodes' Alabamians retreated back to the Sunken Road with severe loss. Being unsupported, Sanders ordered the brigade back to the protection of the road and fence from which it had come.[75]

The 250 survivors of the brigade watched as the entire Confederate line along the Sunken Road give way. To protect their right, the entire brigade changed front to the east and took protection behind a stone wall along the Hagerstown Pike. No sooner had this maneuver been executed, when Maj. Gen. D.H. Hill "rode up and ordered us forward to check the advance of the enemy. Sanders, though very unwell, had gallantly remained on the field . . . until this moment, when he was much too exhausted to remain any longer." Command now devolved upon MacRae, who advanced the small brigade northeast over the same hill and toward the Mumma Farm Lane at about noon. The 27th North Carolina and 3rd Arkansas (Van Manning's brigade; John Walker's division) formed on MacRae's left and joined the attack. The two regiments were led by John Cooke, of the 27th North Carolina.

MacRae attacked the 1st Delaware (Weber's brigade), still on the field after suffering heavily in the first assault on the Sunken Road. The Delaware men held at first, but Cooke's threat to their right and rear compelled them to retire. MacRae's advance got no farther than the Mumma Farm Lane as portions of John Caldwell's and John Brooke's brigades (Israel Richardson's division; II Corps) approached. Running low on ammunition and pressured from front and flanks, MacRae and Cooke were compelled to retire. MacRae claimed, "We left the field with not more than 50 of the 250 men. We fell back about 300 yards and joined Colonel Cooke . . . remaining with his shattered regiment." Cobb's brigade remained in position west of Hagerstown Pike until moved to the northwest corner of the West Woods to help anchor and extend the Confederate line sometime between 4:30 and 5:00 p.m.[76]

What was left of Cobb's brigade crossed the Potomac into Virginia late on September 18. Through the course of two pitched battles in four days, the unit lost 833 men of the 1,310 listed as engaged – a brigade casualty rate of 63.6%. Most of the losses were sustained during its sacrificial stand at Crampton's Gap. The brigade would survive and fight again, proving its toughness and courage through a total of twenty engagements before surrendering at Appomattox Court House two-and-a-half years later. Cobb left the brigade soon after the conclusion of the Maryland Campaign. Shouldering the blame for the defeat at Crampton's Gap, and with a desire to return to his native state, Cobb transferred south and was eventually made commander of the District of Georgia until the end of the war.[77]

**Lucas I. Cade**

*** 

## Semmes's Brigade: Brigadier General Paul Semmes

**Units:** 10th Georgia, 53rd Georgia, 15th Virginia, 32nd Virginia
**Strength:** 1,717[78]
**Losses:** 314 (53k-255w-6m)[79]

Forty-eight year old Paul Jones Semmes brought his brigade into combat at South Mountain and Antietam. A banker and plantation owner, Semmes was also active in the Georgia militia before the war. He was colonel of the 2nd Georgia Volunteer Infantry Regiment when war broke out, and by the spring of 1862, he commanded Lafayette McLaws' old brigade at Williamsburg and at Savage's Station. Semmes so exhausted himself at the Battle of Malvern Hill that he had to be helped back to camp by his men. McLaws recognized his abilities as a field commander, commending "his cool courage and knowledge of his duties."[80]

During the Maryland Campaign, Semmes' brigade consisted of the 10th Georgia under command of Maj. W.C. Holt at South Mountain and Lt. Col. Henry Thomas at Antietam, the 53rd Georgia under Lt. Col. Thomas Sloan, the 15th Virginia led by Capt. E.M. Morrison, and the 32nd Virginia under Col. E.B. Montague.

The brigade crossed the Potomac River on the night of September 6. William Stilwell of the 53rd Georgia wrote to his wife that the river was "not more than waist deep . . . it was as clear as crystal . . . best of all, to see about fifty thousand men pull off their socks, britches and hold up their shirt tails. . ." Upon reaching the Maryland shore the men let out "such a yell [that] was never heard which rent the air and echoed down the long extending banks of the river." The men were buoyed by the "ladies who had gathered on horseback along the road with Confederate flags flying and cheers for the Southern army."[81]

### South Mountain

As McLaws moved his division in the direction of Maryland Heights on September 11, he ordered Semmes "to take care of his rear by occupying both Crampton's and Brownsville gaps" with his own and William Mahone's (under William Parham) brigades. At that time, Semmes did not have enough men in his brigade to adequately cover both gaps, so he ordered almost his entire brigade to Brownsville Gap except for the 10th Georgia. That regiment was assigned to cover Rohrersville Road "and other avenues leading down [the mountain] into Pleasant Valley." On September 13, Parham reported to Semmes and his 41st Virginia was dispatched to picket Solomon's Gap to the south.

The morning of September 14 "was rife with rumors of the Union advance" And soon scouts reported a large force advancing in their direction from Jefferson five miles off. This was William Franklin's VI Corps.

Thomas Munford, whose cavalry brigade occupied the base of South Mountain at Crampton's Gap, posted Mahone's Virginia regiments behind the stone walls and rail fences along the road at the eastern base of the mountain. Semmes' 10th Georgia was ordered to support Parham. Intercepting its commander, W. C. Holt, Parham directed him to send two companies to the "Colored Church on the road to Rohersville" and place the rest of his command on the left of Parham's brigade. While these preparations were underway, Montague's 32nd Virginia established a picket of about 200 men along the eastern base of the mountain near the crossroads hamlet of Burkittsville. Munford's cavalry vedettes were to their left.[82] After some initial probing by skirmishers on Munford's right, the Federals began their assault between 3:00 and 4:00 p.m., shifting their attack to Munford's left and away from Montague's line. As the main attack on the Confederate defensive line grew, Munford's left crumbled and soon fled up the mountainside. The 10th Georgia, holding the far left flank, came under attack by the 96th Pennsylvania and the rest of Joseph Bartlett's brigade (Henry Slocum's division; VI Corps). The Confederate defenders offered shot and shell to the advancing Union lines but after delivering a final punishing volley, Munford's Virginians and Semmes' Georgian's were overrun by the rushing Union lines. Routed, the Confederates pulled back up the mountain with Bartlett's brigade in close pursuit.[83]

That evening, Semmes' regiments joined other commands from Lafayette McLaws' and Richard Anderson's divisions, to "form a line of battle across Pleasant Valley, about 1 1/2 miles below Crampton's Gap" in order to block Franklin's VI Corps from advancing down the Valley and relieving the Harpers Ferry garrison. The formation appeared "so formidable . . . that it deterred Franklin from attacking it," according to historian Ezra Carman. Of Semmes' regiments, only the 10th Georgia suffered casualties during the battle for Crampton's Gap: 3 killed, 19 wounded, and 37 missing.[84]

Since the Union VI Corps did not advance on the Confederate battle line stretched across Pleasant Valley on September 15, McLaws gradually withdrew his troops to a new line across the foot of the Valley between Maryland Heights and Weverton. The units remained there until near 2:00 p.m. when they marched across the Potomac River, through Harpers Ferry, and finally to Halltown, four miles northwest of Harpers Ferry, where they made camp at 8:00 p.m.[85]

McLaws later reported that by the time his division (including Semmes' brigade) had gotten to Halltown it was much fatigued. "A large number had no provisions, and a great portion had not had the time or opportunity to cook what they had. All the troops had been without sleep during the night previous." A full night's sleep was not in the offing at Halltown, for the column was in motion on a forced march in the direction of Sharpsburg at midnight. The brigade crossed the Potomac River at Boteler's Ford, marched along the C&O Canal to opposite the town, where they paused a short time to fill canteens and get a bite to eat before continuing on to Sharpsburg about four miles away.[86]

## Antietam

Semmes, along with the rest of the division, arrived in Sharpsburg about 5:30 a.m. on the morning of September 17, and halted just west of town. After a brief rest, they were called into battle to help support Jubal Early's brigade on the left flank near the West Woods. McLaws, however, had fallen asleep in the high grass and could not be located. Ensign John Parham of the 32nd Virginia described what happened next. "When we got a half mile of the field of battle, Gen. Stonewall Jackson . . . had the command halted and by his order we got in a light fighting trim, unloading our baggage (haversacks and canteens excepted). We then moved forward at a double-quick, marching by the right flank across fields, creeks, woods, stone walls and other fences. Gen. Jackson riding along with us and seeming by his manner impatient for our division to reach Gen. Early as soon as possible. I well remember his appearance as he rode with us, some times ahead of us, mounted on his little sorrel, leaping fences, fording streams and jumping ditches." At some point, McLaws caught up with his command. Seeing the pace of his command, he "was fearful that our rapid marching would break the men down before we reached the field of action [and] ordered us to march at quick time instead of at a full gait, and we slacked our gait a little . . . but Gen. Jackson soon had us on the trot again."[87]

McLaws moved northeast to the West Woods, where he deployed his division. Semmes was placed on the far left of the line and directed to support Jeb Stuart's cavalry and artillery, then on the extreme left of the Confederate line.[88]

The march brought Semmes' men to the Hauser farmstead, situated on a ridge by the same name, overlooking the western border of the West Woods, 350 yards to their right. They waited for McLaws to give the signal, by waving his handkerchief, to begin the attack.[89]

From his vantage point from the Hauser farmstead, Semmes could see the border of the woods ahead full of Union troops from John Sedgwick's II Corps division. The 59th New York from Napoleon Dana's brigade was closest to Semmes, and to it right stood the 15th Massachusetts and 82nd New York (Willis Gorman's brigade). Semmes observed the sharp infantry engagement underway at the Alfred Poffenberger farmstead, involving about 200 Confederate infantry under the command of A.J. Grigsby attempting to stem the advance of Sedgwick's lead regiments advancing out of the West Woods towards them. The Confederates used the buildings in the farmstead and nearby rock ledges as cover. Semmes realized if he moved quickly, he could join the fight from these protected positions, but first he had to cross 350 yards of open fields. The movement would place his men at the mercy of Sedgwick's infantry in the wood line. Semmes deployed his brigade of 709 officers and men on the high ground of the Hauser farmstead and waited for McLaws' signal to advance. From left to right the 53rd Georgia, 15th Virginia, 10th Georgia, and 32nd Virginia made up the line.[90]

When McLaws waved his handkerchief, Semmes immediately gave the order "'by company into line' followed by 'forward into line' which movements were made by the regiment under a most galling fire from the enemy's sharpshooters" that caused a "severe loss in killed and wounded." As the brigade passed through the Hauser apple orchard, it came "under a severe fire from the 15th Massachusetts and 82nd New York." Semmes then ordered his command to commence firing even though it was nearly at the extreme range of the men's muskets. Nevertheless, recalled Semmes, it was "for the purpose of encouraging the men and disconcerting the enemy, and the effect was visible in the diminished number of killed and wounded."[91]

Dashing down the heights to the open fields below, the brigade crossed a fence that ran in a nearly north-south direction, just to the east of the Hauser property. As the men did so, they came under "a murderous fire" from Gorman's brigade. Once free of the fence, they continued their charge across "a stubble field, men falling at every step" until they came to the protection of some "haystacks and piles of rocks" near the Poffenberger barn, where they opened fire on the Union regiments across the road. The "conflict here was at close quarters and very severe" as the brigade absorbed volleys from the 15th Massachusetts and 82nd New York on their front and left and the 59th New York on their right. Semmes came up to Ensign John Parham of the 32nd Virginia standing with the colors. "He asked me where the federals were," recalled Parham, "I told him behind the fence [and] he remarked 'yes' and they will kill the last one of us and that we must charge them."[92]

Semmes ordered a charge, and the men obeyed, halting by a lane just east of the Poffenberger cabin, where they maintained their fire for ten to fifteen minutes. Just as Semmes moved into the road, Early's Virginians attacked from the south, hitting Gorman's brigade's front and left flank. The infantry attacks, combined with artillery pounding, were too much for the Federal defenders and they slowly retreated northward. By now, nearly half of Semmes' brigade were killed or wounded. The 10th Georgia and the 15th Virginia were especially hard hit, "each losing more than one half their number."[93]

As Gorman's and Dana's men scattered northward, Semmes' men pushed close behind. Once exposed in the open fields north and east of the woods, however, most Confederate outfits were checked by Union artillery and infantry east of Hagerstown Pike. Ezra Carman noted, "farther pursuit was left to Semmes and the artillery under Stuart."

The terrain protected Semmes. A ridge running parallel and 100 yards from Hagerstown Pike masked his advance, at least to the vicinity of the D.R. Miller farmstead. In addition, Stuart's artillery moved along Hauser's Ridge on his left flank and provided effective support as Semmes' infantry headed north. The pursuit toward the northeast, however, "was not in [a] connected line, there being wide intervals between some of the regiments, and these became much scattered in the pursuit, some parts of them forging ahead of the others," according to Carman.[94]

At points along the way, Sedgwick's commanders formed fall back lines. One such line was formed by the 1st Minnesota, the 82nd New York, and the 19th Massachusetts that faced the 53rd Georgia on Semmes left flank. The regiment was Semmes' largest, containing twice the number of any of the other regiments. The Georgians fought independently from the rest of the brigade, but was supported on the high ground to the west by Stuart's artillery and Early's 13th Virginia. The combined Confederate infantry and artillery quickly pushed the Union regiments further north and the 53rd Georgia in pursuit. [95]

As the 53rd Georgia and its artillery support pounded the cobbled together Union line, the rest of Semmes' regiments, the 32nd Virginia on the far right and then the 10th Georgia and 15th Virginia, halted near a fence on open ground south of the Miller barn to survey Marsena Patrick's brigade deployed for action in front of them. Semmes' three regiments were reduced to 250 men with few cartridges remaining in their boxes. After exchanging volleys, Patrick observed the fall back line of the 82nd New York, 1st Minnesota, and 19th Massachusetts to his west heading north, exposing his right flank, so he withdrew his command. Carman describes what happened next: "As soon as Semmes' men saw that Patrick was retiring from his position . . . they rushed forward, cheering and firing."[96]

As Semmes' men rushed north, the covering terrain on his right began to give out and his movements became more exposed to Union artillery east of the pike, exposing them to a "terrible front and enfilading fire" that inflicted on the brigade a "great loss." By now the 32nd Virginia was reduced to 50-80 men. The 10th Georgia and 15th Virginia swung around to the left of the 32nd and the Miller barn, outbuildings, and hay stacks and halted behind the prominent rock ledges running north/south—the same ledges that Patrick had recently occupied. Pvt. Callom Jones of the 15th Virginia described finding a "right many wounded federal Soldiers, and some dead" at the straw stacks south of the barn. The 32nd Virginia captured 36 men including a lieutenant colonel.[97]

Stuart, who had been directing the artillery outfits that accompanied Semmes northward, came riding out of the woods "at full speed," halting at the 32nd Virginia and "inquired for Semmes." Just as Stuart arrived, Battery B of the 4th U.S. Artillery under command of James A. Campbell maneuvered into position on the high ground across from Semmes. Campbell "loaded his guns with canister, [and] waited until he saw four stands of colors in their front and began firing." Under fire, Stuart directed Semmes to take the battery, but Semmes replied that his men had been "very severely engaged" and were nearly out of ammunition. He pointed out that Barksdale was in the woods 350 yards south from him and not engaged. Hearing this, Stuart took off after Barksdale.[98]

Reinforcements, however, were not coming. Carman reported that Semmes found the continued showers of "cannister to be very annoying" and so, without support, Semmes pulled his regiments back to the protection of the West Woods. As they withdrew, Stewart followed "them with cannister until they were out of sight." The D.R. Miller farm would be Semmes' high tide. The brigade moved back through the West Woods to the Alfred Poffenberger farmstead, where it was held in reserve through September 18. Remarkably, Semmes with Lt. Benjamin F. Davis and six men of the 10th Georgia remained at the front for an hour longer before withdrawing to the rest of the command. Semmes and his small band may have been hoping for reinforcements from the south but they never came.[99]

Despite Semmes' failure to turn the Union right and advance any further beyond the Miller farmstead, his efforts had important tactical value. As Carman pointed out, Semmes advance "forced the front or turned the right flank of all the detachments that had united in checking the advance of Barksdale and the 3rd South Carolina, and that finally expelled [Col. William] Goodrich and Patrick from the north body of the West Woods."[100]

Semmes' brigade advanced farther to the northern front than any other Confederate command and stayed in the fight continuously for two and half hours. The lack of support from other commands ended its efforts. Semmes, perhaps somewhat bitterly, remarked that "if he'd been supported with another 2,500 or 3,000 troops, he could have crushed the Federal right flank." Semmes' boys paid a steep price at Antietam: 314 killed, wounded, and missing or 44% of those engaged. Three of the four regimental commanders were wounded and one, Thomas Sloan, of the 53rd Georgia, was mortally wounded.[101]

**James M. Buchanan**

* * *

## Barksdale's Brigade: Brigadier General William Barksdale

**Units:** 13th, 17th, 18th, and 21st Mississippi Infantry
**Strength:** 2,280[102]
**Losses:** 294 (33k-257w-4m)[103]

The men in Brig. Gen. William Barksdale's Mississippi brigade were footsore before they crossed the Potomac River into Maryland. Left behind near Richmond a month earlier to guard the Confederate capitol against rumored Union attacks, they had marched 145 miles in nine days to catch up with Lee in northern Virginia as he consolidated his forces for his first invasion of the north.[104]

McLaws' division reunited with Lee's army in Leesburg, Virginia on September 3. As the division marched down Main Street, the crowd erupted when they spotted Barksdale and his Mississippians. According to James Dinkins of the 18th Mississippi, they swarmed among the men, temporarily disrupting the march to welcome the Heroes of Ball's Bluff, who had soundly defeated the Union troops and saved Leesburg the previous October.[105]

William Barksdale was well known in the south for more than his military victories. McLaws called him "the fiery, impetuous Mississippian," which described both his military and civilian careers. As editor of a pro-slavery newspaper and a U.S. Congressman from 1853-1861, Barksdale was considered one of the most ferocious States' Rights Democrats in the House of Representatives, even participating in a brawl on the House floor that ended when two Republicans pulled off his hairpiece.[106]

Barksdale resigned from Congress when the war broke out. He immediately joined the rebellion, first as an officer in the Mississippi Militia, and then as Colonel of the 13th Mississippi Infantry. Barksdale assumed command of the Mississippi Brigade, which included the 13th Mississippi (Lt. Col. Kennon McElroy), 17th Mississippi (Lt Col. John Fiser), 18th Mississippi (Lt. Col. William Luse) and 21st Mississippi (Col. Benjamin Humphreys), after its commander, Brig. Gen. Richard Griffith, was mortally wounded at the Battle of Savage's Station in June of 1862. Following a courageous charge at Malvern Hill on August 12, Barksdale was promoted to brigadier general and his command became known as "Barksdale's Mississippi Brigade."[107]

Barksdale's Mississippians crossed the Potomac River into Maryland on September 6. "Our haversacks full of rations, we were again set into motion," recalled Albert Henley of the 13th Mississippi. McLaws' division crossed at Cheeks Ford, rather than White's Ferry, five miles to the south, which was clogged with the tail end of Lee's long column that had begun crossing on September 4.[108]

The men camped near the river, and then marched 18 miles the next day to the outskirts of Frederick, arriving to a disappointing welcome from the town's civilian population. Mike Hubbert of the

13th Misssssippi wrote, it was without "the enthusiasm which we expected," including the lack of recruits they were expecting from their oppressed Maryland brothers. At least part of the brigade was excited when Maj. Gen. "Jeb" Stuart hosted a ball in nearby Urbana on September 8, and selected the 18th Mississippi band to provide the music. The hall was decorated with the Mississippians' battle flags.[109]

Barksdale's men rested near Frederick until late morning on September 10, when they fell in line to the bugle calls and marched west to fulfill the duties assigned to them in Lee's Special Orders Number 191. McLaws' division, with Richard Anderson's division in support, was to seize Maryland Heights north of Harpers Ferry as part of a three-pronged attack to force the surrender of the Union garrison there, and sweep up Union soldiers escaping to the north and east.[110]

The march behind Jackson's and Longstreet's commands on Hagerstown Pike was slow, but the pace picked up as the Mississippians turned southwest toward their bivouac in Middletown. Henley wrote, "We were treated very cool there. They refused to sell us anything or take our money. Marched 14 miles today. Wrote to Ma."[111]

Rising early on September 11, the Mississippians marched south through Burkittsville, turned west over South Mountain, and encamped for the night in the small town of Brownsville in Pleasant Valley. As Barksdale's men wrote letters or tried to sleep, Union pickets in Pleasant Valley were alerting the Maryland Heights defenders of their presence. [112]

**Harpers Ferry**

At daylight on September 12, Barksdale's Mississippi brigade marched west behind Joseph Kershaw's South Carolinians toward Solomon's Gap, their access point to Elk Ridge. The fate of McLaws' assignment in Special Orders Number 191 was in the hands of his two most trusted brigades.[113]

At 1,400 feet, Maryland Heights looms over Harpers Ferry and commands the surrounding elevations. McLaws knew taking the Heights would

doom the Harpers Ferry garrison. Kershaw and Barksdale made the four-mile trek from Solomon's Gap to Maryland Heights, while Howell Cobb's brigade kept pace in the valley below, east of the mountain. The two brigades were on their own on the narrow, rocky ridge, with no room for additional support or artillery. Even the horses were sent back down to the valley, "as no one can ride here," wrote Capt. Henry King.[114]

The men hacked their way up the mountain to Solomon's Gap, meeting no resistance until near the crest, where Kershaw's skirmishers took fire from the 1st Maryland Cavalry pickets. Kershaw's skirmishers pursued the Union pickets over the ridge as Barksdale's skirmishers from the 13th Mississippi, led by Maj. John M. Bradley, moved to the front of the column. They turned left at the crest and began clawing their way south toward Maryland Heights, pushing back scattered Union resistance along the ridge.[115]

Near nightfall, still about a mile from Maryland Heights, the Mississippi skirmishers encountered a strong defensive position, behind which lay about 1,200 Union troops from Col. Thomas Ford's brigade. Kershaw and Barksdale halted for the night and prepared for morning. Although the fight with the enemy was light during the day, the men were exhausted from the rugged terrain and lack of food and water. Settling in on the rocky ridge, Barksdale's troops looked down on the campfires dotting Pleasant Valley below and up South Mountain to the east, where the rest of McLaws' command guarded the escape routes from Harpers Ferry.[116]

Kershaw's and Barksdale's men advanced around 6:30 a.m. on September 13, opening the battle for Maryland Heights in earnest. To compensate for the narrow ridge, Barksdale's men descended part way down the east side of the mountain and advanced south toward the enemy's right flank, climbing over boulders and crawling along the mountain's steep slope.[117]

By around 10:00 a.m., Ford's troops had fallen back behind sturdy fortifications, thwarting Kershaw's advance on the ridge. About that time, Barksdale sent word that he, with great labor, had overcome the difficulties of the route and reached the desired position, but that he could not bring his men up without coming under friendly fire from the 3rd South Carolina. Kershaw saw that Barksdale was in position to capture the entire Union line and ordered a ceasefire, but shots erupted from the 17th Mississippi into Union snipers from the 126th New York on a rocky outpost, igniting a fire fight up and down the line. During the exchange, the commander of the 126th New York, Eliakim Sherrill, was badly wounded, leaving the Union defenders without a senior commander on the mountaintop.[118]

In the confusion, the Union troops were ordered to withdraw. Morris Brown, 126th New York, wrote, ". . . the order was given to leave the works, and retreat down the hill. At once, every one in the regiment, from the highest officer to the lowest private in the ranks, saw that to give up Maryland Heights was to lose all; but we must obey, and down the hill we started." One last attempt was made to stop the Confederate advance, but according to Morris, "the rebels appeared and after firing 2-3 rounds, we were ordered to retreat across the Potomac to our camp."[119]

Barksdale's brigade was directed to occupy the point of the Heights overlooking Harpers Ferry, a task the men accomplished with little resistance. By 3:30 p.m., the battle was over. James Dinkins, 18th Mississippi, recalled the soldiers helping themselves to what was left behind in the Union retreat, "We scrambled over bread crusts, onion peels and meat skins the enemy had thrown away."[120]

The battle for Maryland Heights on September 13 was the first major fight between Union and Confederate soldiers in the siege of Harpers Ferry. Because of Barksdale's supporting role and the Union retreat, his casualties were light: two killed and 15 wounded.[121]

Efforts to drag artillery up to Maryland Heights, deemed an impossible task by McLaws' engineers the day before, commenced early on the 14th. Dinkins described the labor involved in hauling the heavy guns up the rocky mountainside: "The mountain was very steep. We carried up the wheels

and axels one at a time, and 100 or more men would pull guns up with ropes." Shortly after 2:00 p.m., the Confederate artillery on Maryland Heights joined the barrage coming from John Walker's guns on Loudoun Heights and Jackson's guns on Schoolhouse Ridge.[122]

Around 5:00 p.m., a serious threat developed to McLaws' rear when the Union VI Corps forced its way through Crampton's Gap and spread out through Pleasant Valley, about five miles to the north. Feeling trapped, McLaws once again relied on his trusted brigades. Leaving the 13th Mississippi and two guns from Capt. John Read's battery on Maryland Heights to continue the barrage in the morning, he ordered Barksdale and Kershaw off the mountain around midnight to form a defensive line across the valley, about a mile south of the VI Corps position. The remnants of six of McLaws' other brigades formed a second line. Barksdale's men were so close to the overwhelming Union force that, when the sun came up, they "could see the enemy's camp and his guns stacked," according to Dinkins.[123]

Harpers Ferry surrendered at about 8:00 a.m. the next morning, September 15. McLaws' division withdrew cautiously away from the Union VI Corps and toward Harpers Ferry throughout the day, delayed from crossing the pontoon bridge over the Potomac River while thousands of paroled Union soldiers crossed from the other side. In the meantime, the 13th Mississippi withdrew from the mountain and re-joined the brigade. Barksdale's men finally entered Harpers Ferry in the early hours of September 16 and marched to join Lee at Sharpsburg.[124]

At least one of Barksdale's regiments, the 18th Mississippi, marched in high spirits as rumors spread that they were headed west to the Shenandoah Valley and the ash cakes and apple butter they'd heard so much about. "As night came on, we sang all kinds of plantation songs, "Rock the Cradle, Julie," and "Sallie, Get Your Hoe Cake Done," wrote Dinkins, until they reached a fork in the road and headed northwest toward

Shepherdstown and the men grew quiet, knowing "the war wasn't over."[125]

Despite the temporary high spirits of the 18th Mississippi, the labor and lack of food during the previous few days had taken their toll. Hubbert wrote that they stopped in Shepherdstown around 4:00 a.m. on September 17 and ate some rations, "which was the first in three days . . . Many of our best men had given out and fallen by the way side during the dark and tiresome march."[126]

Barksdale's men re-crossed the Potomac River into Maryland at daylight, toward the little town of Sharpsburg. Pvt. Albert Henley wrote, "The roar of artillery was meanwhile sounding ahead of us."[127]

### Antietam

After reaching Sharpsburg, the Mississippians stopped briefly near a small cemetery on the north end of town to fill their canteens, then marched north with the division for several hundred yards, toward Lee's beleaguered left flank. Dinkins recalled seeing "General Lee occupied with the Richmond howitzers as we passed him." They encountered the 11th Mississippi (John Hood's division) retreating toward them, "who had shot away all their ammunition and were in the act of leaving . . . the Yankees had followed them up a short distance to their rear," wrote Henley.[128]

McLaws' division was directed toward the West Woods, where the 125th Pennsylvania (Samuel Crawford's brigade; Alpheus Williams' division; XII Corps) was in line in the southern tip of the West Woods. John Sedgwick's division (II Corps) approached from the east.[129]

It was about 9:00 a.m. as McLaws approached over open fields to within several hundred yards of the West Woods. Taking raking fire from Union artillery and seeing the enemy "advancing rapidly, occupying the place," he was in a hurry to attack. McLaws ordered the 2nd South Carolina into the West Woods to drive the enemy out while he formed his battle line. Barksdale was in the center of the line, between the Hauser farmhouse and the southern tip of the West Woods, with Semmes'

brigade to his left and Kershaw's to his right. By the time McLaws waved his handkerchief to signal the advance, the 125th Pennsylvania was already taking fire from the 2nd South Carolina on its left and Jubal Early's brigade (Alexander Lawton's division; Jackson's Wing) on its right.[130]

Barksdale advanced into the woods with the 18th, 13th, 17th and 21st Mississippi from left to right, pausing briefly behind a rail fence south of the Alfred Poffenberger barn to ensure Semmes' was advancing on his left. Once convinced his left flank was secure, Barksdale's men drove forward at the double-quick.[131]

About 150 yards into the woods, Barksdale saw Early's men attacking, falling back, and attacking again. Barksdale ordered his right wing, the 17th and 21st Mississippi, to oblique to the right and assist in driving out the 125th Pennsylvania and the 34th New York (Willis Gorman's brigade), one of Sedgwick's regiments that had veered off course. On these two regiments' left flank, the 2nd South Carolina continued its attack, joined by Col. George T. Anderson's brigade (D.R. Jones' division; Longstreet's Wing), which was rushed from Lee's center. Edward Burrows of the 21st Mississippi expressed no mercy for the enveloped Union troops, "The cowardly dogs hardly gave us fight enough to make it interesting but a battery opening just then upon our left & front made it a little more than interesting – Still we kept on through the woods, driving the Yankees before us like sheep."[132]

As the 125th Pennsylvania and 34th New York fell back, Barksdale's Mississippians shifted northeast and smashed into three more of Sedgwick's regiments, the 7th Michigan, 42nd New York (both from Dana's brigade) and the 72nd Pennsylvania (Oliver Howard's brigade), about 100 yards west of Hagerstown Pike. Dana attempted to re-form the 42nd New York, but to no avail, ". . . whilst it was in disorder, the enemy was close up on it, and the fire which was poured upon it and the 7th Michigan was the most terrific I ever witnessed." The 17th and 21st Mississippi pursued the enemy across an open field (present day Philadelphia Park).[133]

At about the same time, wrote Barksdale, "I discovered that a very large force of the enemy were attempting to flank me on the left." As the 17th and 21st Mississippi attacked the remnants of the 7th Michigan, 42nd New York and 72nd Pennsylvania, Barksdale wheeled the 13th and 18th Mississippi to the left (north) and into the left flanks of the 59th New York (Dana's brigade) and 69th Pennsylvania (Howard's brigade). The commander of the 69th Pennsylvania, Col. Joshua Owen, wrote, "The panic which I had observed on the left ultimately spread along the line, and the impetuous advance of the enemy's column threatened to turn our left flank."[134]

Early's brigade moved up on Barksdale's left, the 3rd South Carolina moved up on Barksdale's right rear, and the 13th and 18th Mississippi advanced north along the edge of the woods, in the open between the woods and Hagerstown Pike to the east. At this point, the 17th and 21st Mississippians were still battling the 7th Michigan, 42nd New York and 72nd Pennsylvania to the right (east), near Hagerstown Pike.

The chaos and noise in the West Woods were unimaginable. The brigades of Barksdale, Early, Kershaw and G.T. Anderson were intermingled in a space not much larger than half a square mile, but they had the advantage and momentum as the attackers. Sedgwick's division was in bad shape. Caught by surprise by Confederate regiments materializing from deep ravines to their front, flank and rear, with no clear line of fire without hitting their own men, the survivors fled north. The Union II Corps commander, Edwin Sumner, who had ridden forward to check the progress of Sedgwick's men, saw the disaster unfolding and yelled, "Back boys, for God's sake move back; you are in a bad fix!"[135]

Barksdale led the 13th and 18th Mississippi north in hot pursuit for several hundred yards, toward the D.R. Miller barn, before realizing he had outpaced his support. During the pursuit, the 17th and 21st Mississippi had been forced to pull back to avoid a flank attack from Union forces massing east of Hagerstown Pike. Early's brigade had stopped at a rock ledge about half way through the woods, and the 3rd South Carolina had turned east in an attempt to rejoin the rest of Kershaw's brigade south of the Dunker Church.[136]

Without support and checked by Union artillery and infantry fire from the north and east, Barksdale withdrew his regiments. Semmes' brigade appeared on Barksdale's left (west) and continued its pursuit while all four of Barksdale's regiments fell back to a stone wall southwest of the southern tip of the West Woods, near where they had launched their attack about 90 minutes earlier.[137]

Barksdale's Mississippi Brigade suffered 294 casualties, or one out of every three men, between 9:00 a.m. and 10:30. Barksdale's reputation for leading from the front was intact, along with his brigade's reputation for hard fighting. William Cage wrote in a letter, "General Hill says that if the other troops had fought as Barksdale's (brigade) it would have been the most complete rout that the Yankees ever had."[138]

**Laura Marfut**

* * *

# ANDERSON'S DIVISION—

## Major General Richard Anderson

A South Carolinian by birth, Maj. Gen. Richard H. Anderson graduated from West Point, and then fought in the Mexican, Mormon, and Comanche Wars. Upon Southern secession, Anderson resigned his U.S. Army commission and joined the Confederacy, prior to the bombardment of Ft. Sumter, and was present at its fall. He remained in South Carolina and commanded its forces at the beginning of the war. Ordered to join the army in Virginia, Anderson was assigned a brigade of South Carolina regiments and led them at the Battles of Williamsburg, Seven Pines, Gaines' Mill, and Frayser's Farm. After distinguishing himself on those fields, it was just a matter of time before he received a division. Anderson briefly commanded Longstreet's division during the Peninsula Campaign, was promoted to the rank of major general on July 14, 1862, and given command of Huger's division, consisting of three brigades.[1]

Prior to the Maryland Campaign, Anderson's division made a long march from Richmond to Leesburg, where the Army of Northern Virginia was assembling. The division reached Chantilly, Virginia on September 1, and continued to Dranesville the following day. The trek continued on September 3, when the men crossed Goose Creek and bivouacked about a mile beyond it. The division reached Leesburg on September 4, making camp not far from the Potomac River. There would be no rest, though, for Anderson's men crossed the Potomac River at White's Ford on September 5, and then marched an additional eight miles toward Frederick, Maryland, before resting for the night. The division was in poor shape when it crossed the Potomac River, and many men were left behind at Leesburg because they lacked shoes. Those somewhat shod men suffered from exhaustion from the long summer campaign, and combined with poor food, many fell out of the ranks or straggled behind the column. The men were smelly and in rags, as they had not changed clothes or bathed in over a month. The soldiers savored their rest on September 6 and 7, camped three miles west of Frederick on the Monocacy River, where they could finally bathe, swim, and wash their tattered uniforms.[2]

Anderson's division was selected to accompany Maj. Gen. Lafayette McLaws and his division on the mission to invest Harpers Ferry from Maryland Heights. Wing commander, Maj. Gen. James Longstreet, worried that McLaws' and Anderson's divisions were not strong enough for their mission, so he convinced Lee to combine Wilcox's three-brigade division (composed of Cadmus Wilcox's, Roger Pryor's and Winfield Featherston's brigades) with the rest of Richard Anderson's division, giving it six brigades. This was probably a fairly easy decision, as Wilcox was ill at the time, although he was still with his troops.[3]

Beginning the march southwest on September 10, the division crossed South Mountain at Brownsville Pass on September 12, and entered Pleasant Valley, where the men spent the night, a mere six miles from their destination. The march continued on September 13 down Pleasant Valley, ending when the division reached the Potomac River. Anderson deployed his division between Sandy Hook and Weverton, but it was not directly involved in the investiture of Harpers Ferry. Its mission was to support McLaws' division and guard Weverton Gap, through which George McClellan could send reinforcements to break the Harpers Ferry siege. On September 14, William Franklin's Union VI Corps, broke through Crampton's Gap and entered Pleasant Valley the following day, threatening McLaws' rear. The portly Georgian hustled six brigades from his two divisions to the rear, to form across Pleasant Valley and block the VI Corps from driving south. Two of Anderson's brigades, Wilcox's and Mahone's, were part of this contingent, although they did not see action, as Franklin did not offer battle.[4]

With the siege over, and Harpers Ferry in Confederate hands, the division crossed the pontoon bridge over the Potomac River and entered Harpers Ferry on the morning of September 16. The men were permitted to rest about a mile and a half west of the town until sunset. Ezra Carman estimated the division numbered 3,672 infantry and 328 artillerymen at Antietam. With Lee preparing for battle in Sharpsburg, Anderson's men were put on the road and marched most of the night to reach the battlefield. The division crossed the Potomac River at about 7:00 a.m. on September 17, after the "tedious and wearisome march," and halted briefly near Lee's headquarters at the western edge of Sharpsburg. The men grumbled when they were called into action at 10:00 a.m., without being permitted much time to rest or a chance to grab a bite to eat. The division was needed at the Sunken Road, so it crossed open fields to reach Hagerstown Pike and then headed for the Piper farm. Anderson was severely wounded with a thigh injury during this movement and Brig. Gen. Roger Pryor was thrust into command of the division.[5]

Historian Robert K. Krick believed Anderson's division was heading toward William French's vulnerable right flank and could have rolled up his division, effectively ending the fighting at the Sunken Road. Anderson's wound ended that possibility, because from that time, the division "ceased to act as a unit. It sustained heavy casualties and it kept up scattered, sporadic fire . . . but it lacked leadership, drive or striking-power," according to historian Douglas Freeman. Whether Pryor knew he was in command is uncertain. Longstreet recalled that Pryor was "not advised of his new authority," although his memory may have faded somewhat (see below), and Maj. Gen. D.H. Hill merely wrote "command devolved upon General Pryor." Pryor never filed an after-action report, nor did Anderson or any of his regimental or brigade commanders, save two.

Either way, Anderson of "modest competence that might have met the needs of the hour . . . was replaced by the incomparably incompetent Roger A. Pryor," according to Krick. The division did not hit the Union line's right flank, but instead the brigades moved into action without firm direction, in an uncoordinated fashion. In fairness to Pryor, he probably was not briefed about Anderson's intended tactics, even if he was aware of his new responsibilities. Later in the fight, a member of Anderson's staff recalled a short conversation between Pryor and Longstreet. Pryor sent word that "he would hold his position until the last man was taken." Longstreet knew Pryor's mettle and responded, "We do not come here to be taken or surrender, we came here to fight."[6]

The division's effectiveness was frittered away and was never really a factor in the fight. The division almost immediately broke apart as the brigades approached the Sunken Road using different routes. Pryor's brigade was the first in line, reaching Hagerstown Pike about 350 yards south of the Piper farm lane and passed by the barn and into the orchard; Wilcox's/Cumming's brigade followed, but did not turn north on Hagerstown Pike, instead crossing it and heading for the Piper farm buildings. It was followed by Featherston's/Posey's brigade. Wright's brigade brought up the rear, reaching Hagerstown Pike further north and crossing over it, north of the Piper farm lane. Union artillery fire raked the men as they headed to the Piper buildings and orchard, and casualties mounted, especially among the officers.[7]

Wright's brigade was the first to begin heading toward the Sunken Road, but it took multiple efforts to reach the depression because of the artillery pounding and small arms fire. It slid into position on the right of George B. Anderson's brigade. Pryor's brigade, with Parham's small brigade attached to it, halted in the orchard until Rodes rode back to hasten its entry into the fight. Wilcox's/Cumming's brigade appears to have split in half with the 8th Alabama and 9th Alabama forming on the right of Wright's brigade and the remaining two regiments forming behind Posey's brigade. The new additions crammed themselves into the Sunken Road and just behind it. Thomas Galwey of the 8th Ohio (Nathan Kimball's brigade; William French's division; II Corps) recalled how "Line after line of enemy's troops are advancing along the ridge through the corn. They come up opposite us and sink out of sight in the sunken lane. It is a mystery that so many men could crowd into so small a space."

Casualties mounted among the Sunken Road defenders until the 29th Massachusetts (Thomas Meagher's brigade; Israel Richard's division; II Corps) and the 61st/64th New York (John Caldwell's brigade; Richardson's division; II Corps) drove Anderson's division and George Anderson's brigade from the Sunken Road. Most of the division sought refuge between the Piper farm buildings and Hagerstown Pike. Two of Anderson's regiments, 9th Alabama and 5th Florida, and two of George Anderson's, attacked part of Caldwell's brigade, but were driven back. The division spent the night of September 17, and the following

day, near the Piper farm along Hagerstown Pike, and began retreating toward the Potomac River that night. Of all of Lee's divisions that fought at Sharpsburg, Anderson's probably turned in the worst performance.[8]
**Bradley M. Gottfried**

\* \* \*

## Wilcox's Brigade: Brigadier General Cadmus Wilcox, Colonel Alfred Cumming, Major Hilary Herbert

**Units:** 8th Alabama, 9th Alabama, 10th Alabama, 11th Alabama
**Strength:** 1,392[9]
**Losses:** 244 (34k-191w-29m)[10]

Brigadier General Cadmus Wilcox's brigade was perhaps the most stable in the Confederate army. All four regiments were mustered into service in June 1861, and all but the 8th Alabama were banded together into Wilcox's brigade in April 1862. The 8th joined in June, and all served together through the Peninsula Campaign, Seven Days Battles, and Second Bull Run. Most of the regiments knew only Wilcox as their brigade commander. A North Carolinian by birth, he graduated from West Point in 1842 and was recognized for his bravery during the War with Mexico. Wilcox served at First Bull Run and was promoted to brigadier general in October 1861. The brigade was a cohesive and effective combat unit under a veteran leader. Wilcox was elevated to divisional command prior to the Second Bull Run Campaign, but apparently also remained in charge of his brigade.[11]

The brigade marched with the rest of Wilcox's division to Leesburg on September 4, and crossed the Potomac River at White's Ford the following day. Marching north on September 7, the men bivouacked on the Monocacy River, about three miles west of Frederick, where they were given a well-deserved rest. However, food was problematic as only green corn and green apples were available, which often wreaked havoc on digestive systems. Wilcox rode into Maryland at the head of his division, but was very ill. He probably hoped to recover during the invasion, but his condition worsened during the march to Harpers Ferry. His

failing health, coupled with the loss of his division (see Anderson's divisional entry) caused him to leave the army on September 11, and head for Hagerstown where he checked into a hotel to recuperate. Wilcox was replaced by Col. Alfred Cumming of the 10th Georgia (Paul Semmes' brigade; Lafayette McLaws' division). Cumming was a good temporary replacement for Wilcox. A West Point graduate in the class of 1849, he had seen extensive service during the Peninsula Campaign.[12]

### Harpers Ferry

The brigade's reprieve at the Monocacy River ended on September 10, when the men joined the rest of Anderson's division on its march to the Potomac River, just east of Harpers Ferry. After a long uneventful march, the division arrived in the Pleasant Valley and was spread between Weverton Pass and Sandy Hook, just east of Maryland Heights. Maj. Hilary Herbert of the 8th Alabama recalled the men's anxiety during the Harpers Ferry siege: "The river in front of the 8th Alabama as we laid across the Pleasant Valley Road could not be crossed except by the single bridge leading into the town and held by the enemy. Such was our situation for two days, we (Major General Lafayette) McLaws and Anderson's Divisions, about three thousand of the besiegers cooped up, hemmed in and apparently at the mercy of the enemy. Our salvation depended upon the fall of the post; every officer and private knew it, and the suspense was awful."

Wilcox's men were assigned the middle of Anderson's line, but did not see any action. Cumming, now in command, was apparently told

242

the brigade could be called upon to help defend Crampton's Gap against the Union VI Corps' hammer blows pounding the outnumbered Confederate defenders. McLaws did order Cumming north to help defend the gap, but it arrived too late to stop the Union onslaught. Late on September 14, McLaws spread six brigades, including Cumming's, across Pleasant Valley to block the VI Corps' movement south. On the morning of September 15, the VI Corps' commander, William Franklin, realized Harpers Ferry had fallen, so did not press against McLaws' formidable line. Cumming's brigade was on the right of the first line, but was not engaged, although a few men may have been captured.[13]

## Antietam

With the siege over, the brigade joined the rest of Anderson's division and crossed the pontoon bridge over the Potomac River into Harpers Ferry on the morning of September 16. Cumming rested his brigade for the remainder of the day, about a mile and a half west of town. At sunset, the tired and hungry men were back on their feet to began the difficult all-night march to Sharpsburg. "It was tramp, tramp, the whole night long; mounted officers dozed on their horses, and the men fell asleep as they stood at every one of the momentary halts caused by the temporary and vexatious stoppings of the jaded teams that intervened along the line," recalled Herbert.

Reaching Shepherdstown the morning of September 17, the brigade approached the swiftly flowing Potomac River. A dam crossed the river, but the portion on the Virginia side was destroyed, so according to Bailey McClelen of the 10th Alabama, the men jumped "from rock to rock which were projecting above the water . . . and it was a very careful job to make it to the near end of the dam," which they climbed and easily headed the rest of the way to the Maryland shore. The march continued east to Sharpsburg, which the men reached at about 10:00 a.m. Their pace was made livelier by the continuous rumble of artillery in front

of them. The men dropped their knapsacks and blankets by the side of the road under guard, and continued on.[14]

The size of the brigade at this point is unknown, but Z. Abney of the 11th Alabama recalled how the members of the regiment who trudged into Sharpsburg were "fagged out" from their march from Harpers Ferry, at the "quick step" and noted "many had straggled and when we formed in line of battle, more than half our regiment was missing." Herbert stated that only 120 men in the 8th Alabama answered roll call that morning.

Cumming and his men followed Pryor's brigade through Sharpsburg, marching by the right flank to Hagerstown Pike where the men passed Robert E. Lee who was "standing on a rock. We cheered him as we passed," recalled Maj. Hilary Herbert of the 8th Alabama. "He stood with his hat off, the light of battle in his eyes, his gray hair glittering in the sunling [sic]; and I have always remembered him as he stood then, as the noblest figure that is imprinted on my memory. The brigade then followed a different path to the Piper farm as the 8th and 9th Alabama led the column, followed by the 11th Alabama and the 10th Alabama. The brigade immediately crossed Hagerstown Pike and marched east for about 400 yards and finally took up a position under the protection of a ridge running southeast of the Piper house. After a short rest, the brigade passed through the Piper apple orchard and into a cornfield. Abney recalled how the men now advanced through a "perfect hail storm of bullets— it appeared to me that every ear of corn was perforated by a bullet—many of our men were killed before we got through it." Union artillery and small arms fire also killed and wounded a number of men traversing the cornfield to get to the Sunken Road. McClelen of the 10th Alabama recalled a "storm of bullets and shells and exploding shells . . . and canister shot . . . high and low" permeating the ranks. The brigade's actions after this point are unclear. One historian believed the brigade broke in half; the 8th and 9th Alabama moving to the right of Wright's brigade, beyond where the Sunken Road bent south. The 10th and 11th Alabama continued forward and formed within the Sunken Road behind many of Anderson's brigade and other troops of Anderson's division. Alexander Chisholm of the 9th Alabama recalled, "We advanced obliquely across the Hagerstown Pike and took an advanced position along an old rail fence the field open in our front and sloping gradually down to some woods some 2 or 300 yards distance between which and our position we could plainly see 2 or 3 blue lines of battle . . ." The men were there long enough to expend their ammunition, forcing them to scrounge for replacements from the dead and wounded's ammunition boxes. The Alabamians were initially successful in holding out against the Irish Brigade (Israel Richardson's division; II Corps), but soon fresh troops from John Caldwell's brigade (Richardson's division) appeared. Chisholm recalled, "that old familiar sound hip hip huzzah told us that some thing had to be done, and that quickly for the Federals were on their feet their colors up and they were coming fast." The Confederate line was hit in both flanks and the center, and gave way. "All of us that could got away from there, every man looking out for himself," recalled Chisholm.[15]

Cumming was already wounded as the men deployed around the Piper orchard. Maj. Jeremiah Williams of the 9th Alabama then assumed command of the brigade, and when he was wounded, Herbert took over. The men scrambled back through the cornfield and orchard, toward the Piper barn. Herbert rallied about a hundred of them and brought them forward into the orchard again. "Pouring a volley into them and charging them with a shout, we routed them completely." According to Herbert, he "ordered the regiment back when our left was observed to be giving away. I tried very hard to keep the regiment in line as we went back, but I was behind the line towards the enemy and we were much exposed in falling back, and consequently did so in much confusion." Herbert halted his men behind a rock fence on the opposite ridge about 100 yards distant. Their stay there was not long, as the small arms fire and constant stream of artillery projectiles flying in their direction,

caused the brigade to "gradually melt away." Herbert now ordered the remaining 50 men to their feet, and again they advanced to the Piper orchard, and again they were driven back. He noted, "When we got down under the brow of the hill over which we retreated we had only eight men around my colors."[16]

Some of the men's blood was still up, and they followed Herbert north with members of the 4th Georgia to counter another Union thrust, this one from the 7th Maine (William Irwin's brigade; William Smith's division, VI Corps). According to Herbert, "The enemy now came confidently forward. We were in line just in front of them but concealed by the crest of a hill. When they arrived within thirty yards of us we rose, poured a volley into, and charged them. They fled in confusion, leaving us in possession of the oft-disputed apple orchard and seventeen prisoners besides their wounded." This effectively ended Wilcox's brigade's action at Sharpsburg. The brigade returned to Hagerstown Pike, near the Piper farm, where the men bivouacked with the remainder of Anderson's division, and fell back across the Potomac River during the night of September 18.[17]

The brigade lost almost 40% of its men at the Battle of Antietam, but the losses were probably not evenly spread among the regiments. For example, Herbert stated his 8th Alabama lost 78 men of the 120 it carried into battle (65% loss), but the 11th Alabama lost only 34 (its initial strength is unknown). The brigade did well during the campaign, despite being poorly led at the divisional level. It is unclear who, if anyone, commanded the brigade at Antietam. Cumming went down with a wound and so did a series of officers. Herbert claimed to assume command of the brigade by the end of the battle.[18]

Wilcox returned to his brigade after the battle, and commanded it until given a division prior to the Overland Campaign of 1864. Cumming showed so much promise that he was given a star in October 1862, and placed in command of a brigade in Mississippi. He surrendered with his command at Vicksburg, but was paroled, and then fought again at Missionary Ridge and the Atlanta Campaign. Cumming was wounded a third time in the latter campaign, ending his war days.[19]

**Bradley M. Gottfried**

✳ ✳ ✳

## Mahone's Brigade: Colonel William Parham

**Units:** 6th Virginia, 12th Virginia, 16th Virginia, 41st Virginia
**Strength:** 1,500[20]
**Losses:** 24 (3k-18w-3m)[21]

Brigadier General William Mahone's men knew no other brigade commander until he was wounded at Second Bull Run. The brigade was initially assigned to the Department of Norfolk, where it helped repel a Federal naval squadron attempting to approach Richmond. Later, the brigade was transferred to the Army of Northern Virginia in time to participate in the Battle of Seven Pines. Mahone's brigade performed poorly at Glendale, but redeemed itself at Malvern Hill, when it drove to within 75 yards of the enemy.[22]

The brigade often functioned under a cloud, as "Little Billy" Mahone was thought to be a commander who put concerns for his men above orders. After Mahone was wounded at Second Bull Run, senior regimental commander, Col. William Parham, a planter before the war, assumed command. Parham had only recently returned to the army after being wounded at Malvern Hill and was not fully healed, but felt honor bound to return to his men. Parham was described as a "glorious, brave man, a good fellow and the best curser when he chose." The historian of the 12th Virginia noted the interesting relationship between Mahone and Parham: "Parham obeyed or disobeyed Mahone's orders as Parham pleased and Mahone kept his mouth shut about it." Parham was promoted to colonel of the 41st Virginia as recently as July 25, 1862, and this would contribute to the general uneasiness about the brigade's effectiveness as it marched into Maryland.[23]

Parham's brigade marched with the rest of Anderson's division to Leesburg and waded across the Potomac River at White's Ford on September 6, reduced by scores of shoeless men who were ordered to remain behind in Virginia. Some of the less ardent pulled off their shoes and tossed them away, while some shoeless men crossed anyway. With their wagons in the rear and Lee's strict orders against foraging, the men subsisted on apples and green corn. The brigade reached Frederick and, according to Philip Brown of the 12th Virginia, the men "made a handsome spectacle, as we marched through the streets, open order, arms resting on knapsacks. By this maneuvre [sic] four men abreast extended across the street, and caused our force to look much larger than it really was."

### South Mountain

The brigade, with the rest of the division, left Frederick on September 10, marched west through Brownsville Pass through South Mountain, and into Pleasant Valley to support the siege of Harpers Ferry. The men suffered greatly during these marches. The sharp pebbles and stones of Maryland's turnpikes cut those who marched barefoot. Many who were lucky enough to have found shoes, suffered because they were stiff and raised blisters. Like most of Lee's men, they had not changed their clothes in weeks, and washing was a luxury they did not have.[24]

As part of the siege plan, Lafayette McLaws, with ten brigades in his own and Anderson's divisions, was tasked with taking Maryland Heights at the southern end of Elk Ridge. Once accomplished, he would post artillery there to bombard Harpers Ferry. McLaws deployed his and Anderson's divisions across Pleasant Valley, from Elk Ridge to South Mountain to prevent the enemy from attacking his rear and relieving the siege. Paul

245

Semmes was tasked with overseeing the defense of Brownsville Pass and Crampton's Gap to prevent the Yanks from entering Pleasant Valley. He left the 41st Virginia at Brownsville Pass and sent the 16th Virginia to guard Crampton's Gap, to the north. Parham's remaining two regiments, the 6th and 12th Virginia, later joined the 16th Virginia behind a stone wall at the base of the mountain. The Virginians were spread about eight feet apart, as there were not enough men to defend the broad front on the east side of the mountain. Parham arrived later with the 10th Georgia (Semmes' brigade; McLaws' division) and the 2nd and 12th Virginia cavalry regiments under Col. Thomas Munford. The men saw dust clouds beyond Burkittsville, in front of them, but thought it signified only enemy cavalry.

As senior officer, Munford assumed command of the small Confederate fighting force. He carefully laid out his defensive line along Mountain Church Road, starting at the intersection with Burkittsville Road and extending to the north. The 2nd Virginia Cavalry was divided, with one half on the right of the line, south of Burkittsville Road. The 16th Virginia formed on its left, straddling the road, and then came the rest of the 2nd Virginia Cavalry. The 12th Virginia on its left, stretched to its extreme, and the 6th Virginia came next. Eight companies of the 10th Georgia anchored the far left of the line. Sensing danger at Crampton's Gap, McLaws sent Howell Cobb and his brigade to reinforce the skeletal force there. Cobb adopted a slow approach as the Union threat drew closer.[25]

As Munford quickly organized his line of defense at the base of South Mountain, Henry Slocum's division (VI Corps) approached Burkittsville from the east. Union VI Corps commander, William Franklin, was ordered by George McClellan to drive through Crampton's Gap into Pleasant Valley, then turn south and head for McLaws' and Anderson's divisions at its southern end, destroy them if he could, and relieve the siege of Harpers Ferry. Slocum deployed his three brigades, Col. Alfred Torbert's, Col. John Newton's, Col. Joseph Bartlett's, from left to right respectively. When

Company C, of the 16th Virginia rashly attacked Slocum's left flank, Franklin brought up William Brook's brigade (William Smith's division) and deployed it to the left of Torbert on the front line. It was quite a mismatch, as Franklin had 9,500 men to take the gap defended by 550 men of Mahone's brigade (three regiments), a few hundred more from the two small Virginia cavalry units, and a portion of the 10th Georgia—probably under 1,200 men. Franklin's men outnumbered Munford's by a factor of over 8:1. Reinforcements were arriving for Munford, but they would not reach the foot of the mountain in time to assist.[26]

The two sides fired into each other at the base of the mountain for almost two hours while Franklin assessed the situation. The cautious VI Corps commander worried his men were facing a large number of enemy troops. Torbert's Jerseymen jumped up on a stone wall in front of them, and shaking their fists at the Virginians, yelled to "come out and fight." The Confederate response came in the form of well-aimed volleys, knocking several men from atop the wall. A portion of the fence in front of the 12th Virginia caught fire, and several men were shot while attempting to extinguish the flames.

The Union brigade commanders realized "nothing but a united charge would dislodge the enemy and win the battle." Franklin unleashed Slocum's attack at about 5:30 p.m., and all three of Slocum's brigades headed toward Munford's line. A soldier in the 12th Virginia looked up and yelled, "Look yonder, boys! They are coming across the field." Many of the Jerseymen yelled, "Avenge Kearny!" as they loped toward the Virginians, in reference to their first commander, Phil Kearny, who was killed at Chantilly a couple of weeks before. Others yelled, "Remember Manassas and Gaines' Mill," as these attackers had yet to taste victory on any battlefield.[27]

The 6th and 12th Virginia were up against Newton's and Bartlett's brigades; further south, the 16th Virginia battled the left flank of Newton's brigade and Torbert's entire brigade. The men were ordered to "fix bayonets" and prepare to engage the enemy. Robert Brown of the 12th Virginia recalled, "Finally a great cheering, as if greeting some welcome reinforcements, swelled along the [enemy] line, and over the fence they clambered, and started for us at double quick time. When they had advanced about fifty yards, a deadly rifle fire hurled them back, leaving a line of killed and wounded." There were just too many Union troops, and Torbert explained what happened next: "the enemy, although holding a very strong position, and having the advantage of artillery, could not stand these charges, so broke and fled up the mountain side in great disorder." Realizing the futility of attempting to hold out against such overwhelming odds, the officers yelled to the men to retreat up the mountainside. Torbert described in his report how the Virginians were "closely pursued by our men, who drove them through the pass, and some distance of the valley on the other side." It was chaos and every man for himself during those tense moments. Most of the casualties probably occurred as the men scrambled up the side of the mountain, in full view of the enemy's muskets. Many were chased down and forced to surrender or killed or wounded in combat.[28]

Only darkness put an end to the pursuit. Parham's brigade lost heavily at Crampton's Gap-- 203 men (5 killed, 74 wounded, and 124 captured or missing). The 12th Virginia lost 87 men or 57% of its men. The brigade reformed on the morning of September 15, and even though its losses were heavy and the emotional toll great, the brigade was called upon to stop a southward thrust by Franklin's VI Corps. Parham's brigade was thrown onto the second line of the six-brigade front across Pleasant Valley near Brownsville Pass, and awaited the enemy's onslaught. When Franklin realized the Harpers Ferry garrison had capitulated, he ended his pursuit.[29]

## Antietam

Parham's brigade headed south to recombine with the rest of Anderson's division after its action in Pleasant Valley. It was but a skeleton of its former self, so Anderson consolidated it with Roger Pryor's brigade. The division crossed the pontoon bridge from Harpers Ferry as darkness was falling on September 16, and headed toward Sharpsburg, arriving the following morning after an all-night march. Some veterans believed the brigade numbered under 85 men when it went into battle with Pryor's brigade on September 17. The consolidated unit did not perform well at Antietam (see Pryor's brigade's entry). After being driven from the Sunken Road, a number of men congregated along Hagerstown Pike, near the mouth of Piper Lane. This number grew as additional men from Anderson's division arrived. Lt. William Chamberlaine of the 6th Virginia, recalled thinking "how near our lines were to the Potomac River." Fortunately, the enemy soldiers of the II Corps who had driven the Confederates from the Sunken Road were recalled before testing the Confederate line along Hagerstown Pike. The small unit lost an additional 24 men at Sharpsburg (3 killed, 18 wounded, 3 missing), with Parham among the wounded.[30]

The brigade performed as well as could be expected during the Maryland Campaign. It was placed in an untenable situation at Crampton's Gap and suffered mightily. The small unit that marched to Sharpsburg with Pryor's brigade was again placed in a difficult position that was exacerbated by poor leadership at the brigade and division levels.

**Bradley M. Gottfried**

✳ ✳ ✳

## Featherston's Brigade: Brigadier General Winfield Featherston, Colonel Carnot Posey

**Units:** 12th Mississippi, 16th Mississippi, 19th Mississippi, 2nd Mississippi Battalion
**Strength:** 1,565[31]
**Losses:** 319 (45k- 238w- 36m)[32]

All four Mississippi regiments were recruited in mid-1861, but were initially deployed in four different brigades. While the 2nd Mississippi Battalion (which later became the 48th Mississippi), 12th and 19th Mississippi were sent directly to Joseph Johnston's army and participated in the Peninsula Campaign and the Battle of Seven Pines, the 16th Mississippi became part of Trimble's brigade and fought in the Shenandoah Valley. All but the 16th Mississippi were placed in Brig. Gen. Winfield Featherston's brigade just prior to the Seven Days Battles, and saw action at Gaines' Mill and Glendale. The 16th Mississippi was added to the brigade prior to the Second Bull Run Campaign. The brigade marched into Maryland with Featherston in command, but he became sick during the journey to Harpers Ferry and Col. Carnot Posey of the 16th Mississippi assumed command of the brigade during the remainder of the campaign.[33]

Featherston was an attorney by trade, who organized the 17th Mississippi Infantry in 1862 and was given a general's commission and a brigade the following year. Posey was also an attorney, but had prior military experience as a lieutenant in the Mexican War, and it did not hurt that he had served under Jefferson Davis. Posey entered Confederate service as a captain in the 16th Mississippi and rose to command the regiment in June 1861. He saw continuous combat until elevated to brigade command when Featherston was transferred elsewhere after the Maryland Campaign because Lee was never pleased by his performance.[34]

Featherston's brigade marched with the rest of Anderson's division to White's Ford on September 5 and crossed the Potomac River. Some men stopped to remove their trousers, wrapped them around their ammunition, and held the bundle above the 2-4 foot deep water. Barefoot men, about a third of the brigade, were left behind at Leesburg, and with the excessive straggling, the brigade's strength was sapped. After crossing the river, the men marched north toward Frederick, Maryland. Many roads were hard-surfaced, wreaking havoc on the men's feet. "Men without shoes don't make very good soldiers," recorded Austin Riley of the 16th Mississippi in his diary.[35]

The brigade arrived at the Monocacy River on September 7, where it bivouacked, and the men were able to bathe. The column reached Frederick on September 8, as the regimental bands played "Maryland, My Maryland" and "Dixie," and the men gave a throaty Rebel Yell, frightening the townspeople. "We are dirty, unshaven, tired; our clothes are smelly; toes gap from our shoes," is how Riley described the soldiers as they marched through Frederick. "Gen. Jackson . . . looks just as bad," he noted, and as a result, we "have not made a very favorable impression on the Marylanders." Despite the bounty all about, the men subsisted on roasted ears of corn and green apples until they reached Frederick, when they were rewarded with beef, bacon, flour, and coffee.[36]

### Harpers Ferry

The soldiers were roused by drums beating at 4:00 a.m. on September 10, but road congestion delayed the march until noon. Their destination was Pleasant Valley, a narrow strip of land between South Mountain and Elk Ridge to its west, leading south to Harpers Ferry on the Potomac River. The men noticed a change in locals' attitudes as they passed through Middletown. While some Frederick residents were openly pro-South; the Middletown civilians were decidedly pro-Union, and according to James Kirkpatrick of the 16th Mississippi, "some

248

of the ladies expressed their opinions quite freely." The men crossed South Mountain through Brownsville Pass on September 12 and began their march down Pleasant Valley, which had earned its name, in the men's estimation. The men did not know their mission, but the division was deployed midway between Weverton and Sandy Hook at the southern end of the valley. Some of McLaws' division captured Maryland Heights, and although the Harpers Ferry garrison was under siege, there was not much to do for the soldiers in the valley. The men heard heavy cannonading to the west, and on the morning of September 15, all was quiet as the Union garrison at Harpers Ferry surrendered.[37]

## Antietam

The brigade, with the rest of the division, broke camp in Pleasant Valley at daybreak on September 16, marched west to the Potomac River, and crossed on the pontoon bridge to Harpers Ferry. Most of the men had never crossed a river on a pontoon bridge, so it was a new experience for them. The column then marched west toward Charlestown. After a few rest breaks, the trek continued all night, until the brigade forded the Potomac River at Shepherdstown at daybreak on September 17, and reached Sharpsburg between 7:00 and 8:00 a.m. "We were foot-sore and weary," wrote one of the men, "but the booming of cannon and rattle of musketry suppled our joints." Wounded soldiers they passed yelled, "Hurry up boys, you are badly needed at the front." Casualties began mounting even before the brigade entered the fray. Kilpatrick recalled how the "shot & shell in abundance causing many muscular contractions in the spinal column of our line. But all the dodging did not save us. Occasionally a shell, better aimed than the rest would crash through our line making corpses & mutilated trunks."[38]

At 10:00 a.m., the brigade, with the rest of the division, was called in to support Robert Rodes' and G.B. Anderson's brigades in the Sunken Road, who were up against both William French's and Israel Richardson's II Corps divisions. Posey's brigade followed Wilcox's/Cumming's brigade through the town to Hagerstown Pike, crossing it south of the Piper farm buildings and then headed for the Piper Orchard, halting near the Alabamians. Posey deployed his brigade for action from right to left: 2nd Mississippi Battalion- 19th Mississippi- 12th Mississippi- 16th Mississippi. The line then moved rapidly through a cornfield, approached the Sunken Road on the right of the Roulette farm lane, and joined Anderson's brigade in the Sunken Road.

The men did not halt when they reached the Sunken Road however. They surged up its bank and moved directly against the Irish Brigade, stalled on a rise in front of the road. Some estimated the brigade traveled 30 – 40 yards beyond the Sunken Road and fought there for about five minutes before retreating back to the road. Col. Risden Bennett of the 14th North Carolina (Anderson's brigade) recalled how Posey's men "flowed over and out of the road and many of them were killed in this overflow. The 16th Mississippi disappeared as if it had gone into the earth." Bennett's observations were hardly exaggerated; the 16th Mississippi brought 228 into battle, and 144 of them were killed or wounded in a matter of minutes. The commander of the regiment, Capt. Abram Feltus, reported, how the brigade "confronted the enemy in line of battle [Irish Brigade], who were drawn up some 300 yards from the road, pouring a destructive fire in our ranks . . . A murderous fire of grape, canister, shell, and small-arms played on us." A soldier in the 16th Mississippi claimed all the men could see of the Irish Brigade was their "heads and shoulders" as they used the rise of ground in front of the Sunken Road for protection.[39]

The brigade then fell back into the Sunken Road where they used the fence rails for protection. "Sometimes even a ¾" rail will stop a Minnie ball," noted Austin Riley of the 16th Mississippi. The Sunken Road was becoming increasingly cramped with dead and wounded bodies interfering with the deadly work of the healthy. Lt. James Shinn of the 4th North Carolina (G.B. Anderson's brigade) recalled how the addition of Posey's men into the Sunken Road, "created some confusion." John

Caldwell's brigade now appeared at the top of the rise and bore down on the Confederates in the road. According to historian Ezra Carman, "Colonel Posey, observing the crowded conditions of the troops in the road, subjected to so much loss, ordered his own brigade to retire." This would not be easy because the men were again forced to traverse the cornfield under heavy musketry and artillery fire. Posey halted his shattered brigade near the orchard and reformed his ranks.[40]

Posey's brigade, with the rest of the division, spent the night and the following day along Hagerstown Pike behind the Piper property and crossed over the Potomac River that evening. So ended the Maryland Campaign for Posey's brigade. J.J. Wilson of the 16th Mississippi wrote home to his family, "It was the hottest place I ever was in or ever want to be again soon." He added a couple of caveats. The food was plentiful-- "we could get anything we wanted to eat or drink and very cheap at that." Many of the survivors replaced their smoothbore muskets with Springfield and Enfield rifles during the battle. Posey's brigade lost 45 killed, 238 wounded, and 36 missing for a total of 319, which exceeded any other brigade in Anderson's division. The 16th Mississippi lost 63% of its men.[41]

**Bradley M. Gottfried**

* * *

## Armistead's Brigade: Brigadier General Lewis Armistead, Colonel James Hodge

**Units:** 9th Virginia, 14th Virginia, 38th Virginia, 53rd Virginia, 57th Virginia
**Strength:** 2,146[42]
**Losses:** 35 (5k- 29w- 1m)[43]

Brigadier General Lewis Armistead's brigade was a veteran unit. All five of its regiments were mustered into service between the spring and winter of 1861, and all were brigaded together under Armistead by June 1862. They fought together at Seven Pines, the Seven Days, and Second Bull Run.[44]

Lewis Armistead was a 45 year-old who was almost a West Point graduate. He was dismissed for breaking a plate over the head of classmate Jubal Early, but had this incident not occurred, Armistead probably would have been tossed out anyway because of failing grades. Military service was in his blood. He received a commission in 1839 and distinguished himself in the Mexican War. Armistead then spent many years in frontier posts until Virginia seceded in 1861. During this period, Armistead made strong friendships with many associates, including Winfield Hancock and Albert Sidney Johnston. After making the arduous journey from Los Angeles to throw his lot with the Confederacy, Armistead received the rank of colonel and was placed in charge of the 57th Virginia Infantry. He led the regiment for a few months in North Carolina and Western Virginia until he was promoted to brigadier general and given a brigade. Armistead gained notice at the Battle of Seven Pines, when the rest of his brigade stampeded to the rear, leaving him and 30 men behind to face an entire enemy brigade. He was later tapped to lead the charge at Malvern Hill with his brigade. Twenty-two years in the old army made Armistead crusty, blunt, and prematurely gray. At least one senior colonel resigned from the army after several run-ins with Armistead.[45]

Lee must have respected Armistead's abilities as a no nonsense officer, for he named him provost marshal as the army marched north. General Orders Number 103, prepared on September 6, 1862, gave Armistead "authority to call for guards, take all proper measures to correct irregularities against good order and military discipline, and prevent depredations upon the community."[46]

### Harpers Ferry

Armistead's brigade, now temporarily under Col. James Hodges of the 14th Virginia, traveled with the rest of Anderson's division from the Second Bull Run battlefield to Leesburg, and then across the Potomac River. It spent some time resting near Frederick, Maryland, and then joined Anderson's column on its march over South Mountain into Pleasant Valley, and then south to the Potomac River. The brigade formed the right of Anderson's line that stretched from Weverton to Sandy Hook, but saw no action.[47]

## Antietam

After the fall of Harpers Ferry on September 15, the brigade joined the rest of Anderson's division, crossing the Potomac River on the pontoon bridge into Harpers Ferry. After resting until sunset, the brigade marched all night to Sharpsburg at the rear of Anderson's column. Armistead was probably back leading his brigade by this time. Because his was the last brigade to arrive, it was not sent with the rest of the division toward the Sunken Road, but was ordered north to the West Woods. Lafayette McLaws' and John Walker's divisions had already driven John Sedgwick's division (II Corps) from the woods, but George Greene's division (XII Corps) had reentered it and remained in the southern portion. As Walker's division prepared to attack Greene's men, Armistead deployed his brigade behind it, just east of the Hauser home, ready to provide support, if needed. The brigade was guided into position by the adjutant of the 35th North Carolina (Robert Ransom's brigade; Walker's division). The men came under enemy artillery fire and sustained some losses, including Armistead, who was wounded. According to one of the soldiers, Armistead "saw the ball as it came rolling down the hill, and could not have moved out of its course with all care, but, probably thinking it a shell and likely to explode, stood as one transfixed and did not move his foot or a muscle." Hit in the foot, Armistead was carried to the rear, and Hodges again assumed command of the brigade. The severe shelling caused disorder and confusion in the brigade's ranks, and some of the men may have scampered to the rear. Hodges moved the brigade

to the left to relieve Jubal Early's brigade. It is doubtful the brigade fired a shot in anger during the battle.[48]

The brigade crossed the Potomac River during the early morning of September 19 and was ordered to report to Brig. Gen. William Pendleton, whose artillery crowned the high ground overlooking the river. Col. Marcellus Douglass' brigade and Armistead's, with barely 600 men between them, were ordered to "picket the ford, and, screening themselves as well as possible, to act as sharpshooters on the bank." Pendleton also told the brigade commanders "not to fire merely in reply to shots from the other side, but only to repel any attempt at crossing, and to guard the ford."[49]

While most of the men of the two brigades remained behind a hill, the two commanders sent about 200 men forward to the river, where they skirmished with troops in Gouverneur Warren's brigade (George Sykes division; V Corps). Thomas Munford of the 2nd Virginia Cavalry watched the activities along the river and became alarmed. He was particularly concerned about Boteler's Ford, so he requested some manpower from Hodges' brigade to reinforce his skirmish line. Hodges complied by sending the 9th Virginia Infantry, numbering fewer than 60 men. When the V Corps pushed across the river in large numbers, Hodges' men fired their weapons and then headed for the rear. A handful of men were no match for the thousands now crossing the river. The brigade retreated and caught up with the division, and continued its march toward Winchester. The brigade's losses at Shepherdstown are unknown, but were probably light. Douglass' brigade lost about seven wounded.[50]

Armistead's small brigade played a small role in the campaign. While in position at Sandy Hook and the West Woods, it was not engaged, but sustained some casualties in the latter fight. The undermanned brigade saw some action at Shepherdstown.

**Bradley M. Gottfried**

* * *

## Pryor's Brigade: Brigadier General Roger Pryor, Colonel John Hately

**Units:** 14th Alabama, 2nd Florida, 5th Florida, 8th Florida, 3rd Virginia
**Strength:** 2,625[51]
**Losses:** 382(48k-285w-49m)[52]

Brigadier General Roger Pryor's brigade was an odd concoction of regiments, led by an even odder commander. Most Confederate brigades were composed of regiments from the same state, sometimes from two states, but Pryor's hailed from three. The 14th Alabama, 2nd Florida, and 3rd Virginia regiments were mustered into service during the summer of 1861. Two other Florida regiments, the 5th and 8th, entered in May-June 1862. While the initial three regiments were all at the Battle of Seven Pines, only the 14th Alabama served in Pryor's brigade; the 2nd Florida and 3rd Virginia fought in two other brigades. The three regiments were combined prior to the Seven Days Battles, and the 5th Florida and 8th Florida were added just prior to Second Bull Run. The Maryland Campaign would be the first time all five regiments would fight together.[53]

Pryor had absolutely no military experience when he joined the army in 1861. An attorney and also the editor of the powerful *Richmond Enquirer*, Pryor was appointed to the United States House of Representatives to fill an unexpired term. He joined Gen. P.G.T. Beauregard's staff during the attack on Fort Sumter and had the opportunity to fire the first shot on the fort. Pryor was elected to the Provisional Confederate Congress, but resigned to assume command of the 3rd Virginia, and in the spring of 1862 was given command of the mixed brigade. His performance at the Battle of Williamsburg earned him the rank of brigadier general. Although commended for his initial actions at the Battle of Seven Pines and the Seven Days Battles, at Second Bull Run, he and Winfield Featherston were criticized for "drifting away from their designated line of advance and for failure, later in the day, to strike the rear of Federals who were

attacking Jackson." Although Pryor rode into the Maryland Campaign with extensive combat experience, Lee and others were not convinced of his effectiveness.[54]

### Harpers Ferry

Not much is known about Pryor's brigade's crossing of the Potomac River with the rest of Anderson's division, its activities around Frederick, or its march toward Harpers Ferry. The brigade waded the Potomac River at White's Ford on September 6, reaching Frederick the following day. It joined the march to invest Harpers Ferry on September 10. Anderson's division was charged with holding the area of Maryland east of Harpers Ferry, from Sandy Hook to Weverton. The men marched down Pleasant Valley on September 12, and by the evening of the following day, Pryor's brigade was in position on the division's left flank at Weverton with Ambrose Wright's brigade. The town was near a gap formed between the southern edge of South Mountain and the Potomac River that could be used by Union reinforcements to attempt to rescue the Harpers Ferry garrison. Wright's brigade occupied the heights of South Mountain overlooking Weverton; Pryor's brigade took position in the town. Sgt. Isaac Auld of the 5th Florida wrote home, "We were there [at Harpers Ferry], but were not engaged. We were placed to guard a gap in the mountains expecting the enemy every minute, but well for them they did not come." After the fall of Harpers Ferry on September 15, the brigade crossed the pontoon bridge into Harpers Ferry, rested briefly, and began the march to Sharpsburg on the evening of September 16.[55]

Straggling among the brigade was excessive, particularly among the inexperienced 5th and 8th Florida. Auld wrote home, "they traveled very fast and . . . about half of the regiment broke down that night." A Mississippi soldier recorded in his diary that Pryor was so frustrated by the number of men falling out of his ranks that he "ordered his brigade to fire into them."[56]

## Antietam

Pryor's brigade, with the rest of the division, reached Sharpsburg on the morning of September 17 and was sent to support D.H. Hill's troops in the Sunken Road at 10:00 a.m. Pryor's brigade was in the van, followed closely by Cumming's (Wilcox's) and Posey's (Featherston's) brigades. They cut across open fields to reach Hagerstown Pike under a blistering artillery fire from Tompkins' battery, to the north. The brigade marched 100 yards north on the pike and turned right onto the Piper farm lane. Upon reaching the barn, the brigade again turned north and finally halted to the left of the Piper orchard. Wright's brigade took the lead in advancing to the right side of the Confederate line in the Sunken Road and was almost immediately hit by enfilade fire on its left. The men were told to hold on, as Pryor's brigade would soon join their left and halt the damage. Pryor's men did not budge from the orchard, however.

The brigade was deployed from left to right: 2nd Florida- 8th Florida- 5th Florida- 3rd Virginia- 14th Alabama. William Mahone's brigade under Col. William Parham, badly mauled at Crampton's Gap, was fastened to Pryor's right flank. Before it could enter the action, the brigade adjusted its front to orient to the contours of the Sunken Road and this may have contributed to its tardy entrance into the fight. The orchard and cornfield helped mask the alignment activities and reduced casualties.

It is unclear whether Pryor knew his division commander was wounded and he now commanded the division. Historian Ezra Carman believed Col. John Hately of the 5th Florida commanded the brigade. Hately was not in command long, as he was shot through both thighs. The regimental leadership was also battered. Lt. Col. Georges Coppens of the 8th Florida was killed near the Piper barn, and he was replaced by Capt. Richard Walker, who died "with the colors of the regiment draped over his shoulders." Capt. David Lang next assumed

command, but he was wounded. All of these command changes occurred before the regiment reached the Sunken Road. So great were the leadership losses, that Sgt. Henry Geiger directed the 2nd Florida at the end of the battle. Carman noted, "every regiment suffered great loss."

With the brigade now formed for action, it moved forward into the cornfield where it was hit by Tompkins' battery and small arms fire from Nathan Kimball's brigade (French's division) and Thomas Meagher's Irish Brigade (Richardson's division), leading the Union advance.[57]

The brigade's left flank, composed of the 2nd and 8th Florida, did not advance with the remainder of the brigade. Robert Rodes realized his Alabama brigade on the left side of the Sunken Road needed reinforcements and he spied these two units in his rear. "I noticed troops going in to the support of [G.B.] Anderson or to his right, and that one regiment and a portion of another, instead of passing on to the front, stopped in the hollow immediately in my rear and near the orchard. As the fire on both sides was, at my position at least, now desultory and slack, I went to the troops referred to, and found that they belonged to General Pryor's brigade. Their officers stated that they had been ordered to halt there by somebody, not General Pryor. Finding General Pryor in a few moments, and informing him as to their conduct, he immediately ordered them forward."[58]

The left of Pryor's brigade apparently settled in behind the right wing of the 14th North Carolina of G.B. Anderson's brigade. Some of Pryor's men reaching the Sunken Road apparently climbed its bank and attacked the Irish Brigade, but were driven back into the road. Dead and wounded piled up in the Sunken Road, creating difficulties for the men attempting to defend their positions. A short time after the brigade arrived at the Sunken Road, a final push by John Caldwell's brigade (Richardson's division) and the 29th Massachusetts of the Irish Brigade, sealed the fate of the road's defenders. Risden Bennett, now commanding Anderson's brigade, noted in his report, the "Sixteenth Mississippi and Second Florida, of that command

[Anderson's division], coming to our succor, broke beyond the power of rallying after five minutes' stay. In this stampede, if we may so term it, the Fourth North Carolina State Troops and Thirtieth North Carolina Troops participated. The hour of 1 p. m. had arrived."[59]

Although driven from the Sunken Road, many of Pryor's men continued the fight. The counterattack by the 5th Florida on the 5th New Hampshire and 81st Pennsylvania (Caldwell's brigade) is perhaps most notable. The Floridians were joined by elements of three other brigades, the 12th Alabama of Rodes' brigade, 9th Alabama of Wilcox's brigade, and 4th North Carolina of G.B. Anderson's brigade. These exhausted troops were no match for the fresh Yanks, who were quickly reinforced by four other Union regiments, and were driven from the field. Scattered units desperately attempted to halt the Union advance toward the Piper barn. D.H. Hill reported on a "farcical" experience involving Pryor. The latter "had collected quite a respectable force behind a stone wall on the Hagerstown Pike" with a regiment from G.T. Anderson's brigade. "A Maine regiment came down to this hill wholly unconscious that there were any Confederate troops near it. A shout and a volley informed them of their dangerous neighborhood. The Yankee apprehension is acute; the idea was soon taken in, and was followed by the most rapid running I ever saw."[60]

Pryor's brigade fell back, and spent the night of September 17 and the next day on the east side of Sharpsburg, until the men marched to the Potomac River and crossed at Boteler's Ford. The small brigade lost 382 men at Antietam: 48 killed, 285 wounded, and 49 missing. The rookie 5th Florida may have lost as many as two-thirds of its men, tallying only 26 able-bodied men at Shepherdstown on September 19.[61]

Pryor's brigade was broken up during the army's subsequent reorganization. Col. Edward Perry of the 2nd Florida was given command of a new brigade comprising the three Florida regiments; the remaining two regiments were sent to other brigades, leaving Pryor without a unit to command. Lee apparently made no effort to find a place for Pryor, suggesting that he might be used in a new small army Gen. Gustavus Smith was forming in southern Virginia. Pryor would eventually resign his commission.[62]

**Bradley M. Gottfried**

* * *

## Wright's Brigade: Brigadier General Ambrose Wright, Colonel Robert Jones, Colonel William Gibson

**Units:** 44th Alabama, 3rd Georgia, 22nd Georgia, 48th Georgia
**Strength:** 1,468[63]
**Losses:** 258 (32- 192- 34)[64]

The 3rd and 22nd Georgia regiments were organized between May and August 1861; the others during the following spring. Their initial assignments included Norfolk, North Carolina, Georgia, and Florida. By June, 1862, all but the 48th Georgia were in Wright's brigade. The latter regiment was transferred to the brigade prior to the Second Bull Run Campaign.[65]

Born and raised in Georgia, Ambrose Wright was an attorney and politician who enthusiastically supported secession. He enlisted as a private in the 3rd Georgia, and was elected the regiment's colonel within a few weeks. Wright performed well in his early engagements and was promoted to brigadier general on June 3, 1862 and given a brigade in time for the Seven Days Campaign. The brigade was known as a tough fighting unit under effective leadership.[66]

## Harpers Ferry

Little has been written about the brigade's experiences leaving Virginia, entering Frederick, Maryland, and moving against Harpers Ferry. A member of the 48th Georgia wrote to his local newspaper on September 8: We are now in Maryland . . . We have now marched over one hundred and fifty miles, waded the Rapidan, Rappahannock, and Potomac, besides [a] number [of] streams of smaller size." He further wrote of Frederick, "Supplies seem plentiful and at living prices, and Confederate money will purchase anything, so far, in Maryland."[67]

Wright's brigade followed the rest of Anderson's division, and its movements can be found in the Anderson's division's entry. Upon crossing South Mountain at Brownsville Pass and entering into Pleasant Valley, Wright's brigade moved south to the Potomac River. Once there, Wright and his men were ordered to ascend South Mountain again, and march with two small mountain howitzers, each pulled by one horse, to Weverton Gap overlooking the Potomac River. While Wright's men looked down on the town of Weverton, Pryor's brigade secured it. According to historian Ezra Carman, this was "the route by which McClellan's left column might be expected to attempt the relief of the garrison at Harpers Ferry."[68]

## Antietam

With the surrender of Harpers Ferry on September 15, Wright's brigade, with the rest of the division, crossed the pontoon bridge over the Potomac River and entered Harpers Ferry on September 16. After resting until near sunset, the column set off toward Sharpsburg, marching all night in what one of the officers called a "tedious and wearisome march," reaching Boteler's Ford, near Shepherdstown, at daylight. After a short rest around 10:00 a.m., the brigade, with the rest of the division, was ordered forward to assist with defending the Sunken Road. Instead of traveling along Hagerstown Pike to Piper Lane, the brigade bore to the right and avoided the lane. The artillery fire from Tompkins' guns to their north, and the guns of position across Antietam Creek, nevertheless, played havoc on Wright's men. The brigade encountered the Piper apple orchard and tore down a fence to enter it, sustaining losses all the while from the never-ending artillery fire. The brigade was deployed from left to right: 22nd Georgia- 44th Alabama- 48th Georgia- 3rd Georgia. As a result of its movements, the brigade approached the Sunken Road before Anderson's other units.[69]

Once in the orchard, the brigade moved in a northeast direction and then entered the cornfield. While climbing a rise in the cornfield, enemy artillery fire rained havoc on the brigade and many "comrades were falling on the right and left killed and wounded," according to Col. William Gibson of the 48th Georgia. When less than a hundred yards from the Sunken Road, a shell tore Wright's horse to pieces, throwing the general to the ground. After disengaging himself, Wright rose and led his men on foot the rest of the way. The left of Wright's line approached the right of G.B. Anderson's brigade in the Sunken Road, manned by the 30th North Carolina. The small arms fire, probably from the Irish Brigade, and the artillery fire were so devastating, that it knocked this part of Wright's brigade back into the cornfield. The men rallied and moved forward again. Wright was wounded as he approached the road, and then his second in command, Col. Robert Jones, was hit as well. The remnants of the brigade, as few as 250 men, now settled down in the Sunken Road, forming the right of the line.[70]

The twice-wounded Wright, insistent on remaining with his troops in the Sunken Road, lay on a litter while giving orders. Up ahead, the 7th West Virginia, on the left of Nathan Kimball's line (French's division, II Corps), sent a blistering frontal fire into the Georgians, while the Union guns of position enfiladed the line with bursting shells. The men were told to hold on as Pryor's brigade would soon be up to assist them, but they were slow in arriving. Growing more desperate as the losses mounted, Wright ordered an audacious charge to drive the West Virginians from his front. For some reason, only the 3rd Georgia and perhaps part of the 48th Georgia on the right of the line rose, and after adjusting its line to fall on the 7th's unprotected left flank, charged. The West Virginians saw this small enemy band approaching, and quickly wheeled to face it, and then counter-charged, sending the Southerners back to the road with losses that included the 3rd's commander, Col. R. B. Nisbet. Kimball reported, "The enemy having been re-inforced, made an attempt to turn my left flank by throwing three regiments forward entirely on to the left of my line, which I met and repulsed, with loss, by extending my left wing, 7th West Virginia and 132nd Pennsylvania, in that direction."[71]

The brigade was in rough shape. Its commander was wounded, all of its regimental commanders killed or wounded, and many companies were commanded by sergeants or corporals. Yet, according to historian Ezra Carman, the brigade "remained in the road and kept up a warm fire." Gibson reported "with our cartridges exhausted, upon seeing a new formation of the enemy in our front, of a very large force, and a movement by our right flank . . . I withdrew the brigade, in order, to a stone fence in the rear, which position was held during the day." The force in front and flank was John Caldwell's brigade (Richardson's division, II Corps). Its 61st and 64th New York under Col. Francis Barlow approached the front and right flank of the 3rd Georgia, making the brigade's position untenable. A soldier from the 22nd Georgia wrote home, "our ranks being so reduced by marching the night before, the men falling out by the wayside, and having no reinforcements, we were compelled to fall back, after sustaining a very severe loss."[72]

The enemy made several charges against the stone wall now occupied by Wright's men. The Georgians were able to repulse all of them, aided by an abandoned cannon that Lt. William Chamberlaine of the 6th Virginia (Mahone's brigade), fired several times into the Federal ranks. The action, "seemed to surprise the enemy very much," according to one of Wright's men. Unfortunately the gun and the dogged defense "drew upon our lines a severe shower of shot and shell for thirty minutes or more, which was kept up all the evening at intervals, occasionally wounding and killing a man," according to Gibson.[73]

The brigade spent the night of September 17 and the following day in position near Hagerstown Pike with the rest of Anderson's division. The men crossed the Potomac River into Virginia at Boteler's Ford on September 18. Alva Spencer of the 3rd Georgia wrote to his future wife on September 29, 1862, that he had crossed the Potomac River "three or four times" and concluded "I do hope we will not be compelled to cross it again. I'm perfectly willing to remain on this side, for a while at least." Most of Lee's men probably harbored these sentiments.[74]

**Bradley M. Gottfried**

* * *

# D.R. JONES' DIVISION—

## Major General David R. Jones

Thirty-seven year old David Jones received the odd middle name, "Rumph," to honor his maternal grandfather who fought in the Revolutionary War. Although David was born in South Carolina, his family moved to Georgia when he was a boy. He graduated from West Point in 1846 with the likes of "Stonewall" Jackson, George Pickett, and George McClellan, and fought in the War with Mexico, taught at West Point and served in the Adjutant General's office. He married well, wedding the niece of President Zachary Taylor (and cousin of Jefferson Davis' first wife). He resigned from the United States Army on March 16, 1861 to join the Confederacy, and was present at the initial bombardment of Fort Sumter. Jones presented the terms of surrender to Union Maj. Robert Anderson, and is said to have lowered the Stars and Stripes after the capitulation. Promoted to the rank of brigadier general and given a brigade, Jones saw action during the First Bull Run Campaign. In late March 1862, Jones was promoted to the rank of major general and given a two-brigade division composed of Brig. Gen. Edward Thomas's brigade and Col. G.T. Anderson's brigade, which saw action during the Seven Days Battles and Second Bull Run. His division expanded to three brigades during this period with the addition of Brig. Gen. Robert Toombs' brigade. Even with these new additions, the division remained small, fielding only 3,392 men. William Palmer of the 1st Virginia (Kemper's brigade) exaggerated somewhat when he recalled its numbers, "did not make one good brigade."[1]

Jones' division left the Chantilly, Virginia battlefield on September 3 and headed for Leesburg, reaching it by the evening of the following day. The men were given a well-deserved rest, then headed for the Potomac River on the morning of September 6 and crossed at White's Ford. Jones welcomed three additional brigades that day: Brig. Gen. James Kemper's, Brig. Gen. George Pickett's (commanded by Brig. Gen. Richard Garnett) and Brig. Gen. Micah Jenkins' (commanded by Lt. Col. James Walker). The expanded division marched through Buckeystown and encamped that night on the banks of the Monocacy River. September 7 found the division at Monocacy Junction, just east of Frederick. The men were again permitted to rest, and then on the morning of September 10, marched through Boonsboro and finally reached Hagerstown on September 12.

As part of James Longstreet's command, the division left Hagerstown on the morning of September 14 to retrace its steps back to South Mountain to reinforce D.H. Hill's division, holding Turner's and Fox's Gaps. Jones left Toombs' brigade at Hagerstown and then headed south. Reaching Boonsboro, Drayton's and G.T. Anderson's brigades were detached and sent to Fox's Gap. Jones' remaining three brigades (Garnett's, Kemper's and Walker's brigades) were sent to a South Mountain gap about a mile south, where enemy troops were rumored to be attempting to enter Pleasant Valley. The report proved incorrect and Jones hustled them back north just in time to put them on Frosttown Plateau, to the north of the National Road, to repel a determined attack by the Union I Corps on the weakly held Confederate line.

Jones explained what happened next: "While taking position my troops were exposed to severe shelling, and shortly afterward to a heavy infantry attack in overwhelming numbers. Despite the odds, they held their ground till dark, when, the brigades on my left giving way, they were withdrawn in comparatively good order to the foot of the mountain." This was somewhat true. The Union I Corps drove up the mountain, pushing back Robert Rodes' and Nathan Evans' Confederate brigades before them. Kemper's brigade arrived and slid into position first and it was soon followed by Garnett's, forming a "V." They were almost immediately attacked by John Hatch's division (I Corps). Walker's brigade also arrived to provide support. As night fell, the Union attack broke Jones' position and many assumed a new position behind a stone wall and prepared to stop another Union attack as darkness enveloped the area.[2]

While three of Jones' brigades were tangling with the I Corps on the Frosttown Plateau, the two others, Drayton's and G. T. Anderson's, sent south to reinforce Hill's division at Fox's Gap. Hill's men had been tangling with elements of the Union IX Corps all morning. Hill put Brig. Gen. Roswell Ripley in command of a column of four Confederate brigades (two from Hill's division and two from Jones' division) with orders to sweep around the Union flank and drive it away. G.T. Anderson's was third in line and Drayton's brigade brought up the rear. Drayton's brigade was to be the lynchpin on which the three other brigades would pivot. However, a large gap formed between Anderson's and Drayton's brigades, and as the latter approached Fox's Gap, it was attacked by overwhelming numbers of IX Corps units. Drayton chose to stand and fight and his brigade was almost destroyed in the subsequent fighting. G.T. Anderson's brigade later attached itself to John Hood's division's left flank and fought with it until night put an end to the fighting.[3]

Jones was relieved when he realized the enemy had no intention of following up its victory, so he pulled his men off the mountain and marched them first through Boonsboro and then to Antietam Creek, reaching Sharpsburg on the morning of September 15. G.T. Anderson's brigade remained with Hood's division during the retreat, acting as the rearguard. Toombs arrived with only two of his regiments, the 2nd and 20th Georgia; the others were sent with Longstreet's wagons to Williamsport. Jones' division began crossing Antietam Creek at 10:00 a.m. and formed on Cemetery Hill, southeast of Sharpsburg. Jones placed Kemper's, Jenkins' and Drayton's brigades in the first line and Garnett's in the second. Jones counted only 2,430 men in his six brigades on the morning of the battle. The line became weaker when Toombs' two regiments, the 50th Georgia (Drayton's brigade) and half a company of sharpshooters from Walker's South Carolina brigade were sent south to guard the army's exposed right flank near the Lower Bridge.[4]

While resting near Sharpsburg, the division was harassed by Union artillery on September 16. Maj. Palmer recalled, "we were annoyed by the fire of 20 pound Parrott pieces on a hill above and to our left of the bridge, Burnsides bridge. We had no guns on our part of the line of sufficient range to reach them, and they amuse themselves by firing at single horsemen, or a few men, and sometimes at a single man."[5]

While the contingent south of town battled the enemy during the late morning of September 17, Jones waited for an attack against his front line. Garnett's brigade was detached and sent to the front of town, leaving only Kemper's, Drayton's and Walker's brigades to stop an enemy attack from the Lower and Middle Bridges. Two more regiments of Toombs' brigade arrived, the 15th and 17th Georgia, as did five companies of the 11th Georgia of Anderson's brigade.  They were sent to aid in the defense of the Lower Bridge, but Burnside's IX Corps had already bullied its way across Antietam Creek before these units could come into action.

Later in the afternoon, just as A.P. Hill's division arrived from Harpers Ferry and began to form on Jones' right, the IX Corps made a surge toward Jones' line. Jones admitted that Kemper's and Drayton's brigades were "driven back through the town." The 15th South Carolina rallied and helped the rest of Drayton's brigade reform. Jones noted, "Jenkins' brigade held its own, and from their position in the orchard poured a destructive fire on the enemy." Toombs, with his 15th and 17th Georgia, charged the enemy who had driven the cannoneers from Capt. David McIntosh's battery, forcing them to abandon the newly captured guns. Darkness put an end to the fighting. Jones' division had bent but not broken, despite being so dramatically outnumbered.[6]

The division held its position south of town through September 18 and at 9:00 p.m., took up the march to the Potomac River. It encamped near Shepherdstown by daylight the following day. The small division lost 1,435 during the campaign. Most of the casualties (531) were sustained by Drayton's brigade, which had been manhandled at Fox's Gap on September 14.[7]

Ironically, Col. Henry Kingsbury of the 11th Connecticut, who was Jones' brother-in-law (they married sisters), was among the first Union attackers to be mortally wounded at the Lower Bridge. The two men were very close and Jones mourned his passing. Jones suffered a major heart attack in October 1862 and died on January 15, 1863, leaving the two sisters widows.[8]

**Bradley M. Gottfried**

\*\*\*

## Toombs' Brigade: Brigadier General Robert Toombs, Colonel Henry Benning

**Units:** 2nd Georgia, 15th Georgia, 17th Georgia, 20th Georgia
**Strength:** 1,221[9]
**Losses:** 160 (16k-122w-22m)[10]

Brigadier General Robert Toombs' brigade of four Georgia regiments received its baptism of fire during the Seven Days Campaign and was likewise heavily engaged in the Second Bull Run Campaign. It was a cohesive unit formed between May – August 1861. The first three regiments (2nd, 15th and 17th Georgia) were immediately brigaded together under former Confederate presidential candidate, Robert Toombs. The 20th Georgia was transferred from Jubal Early's brigade in June 1862. Col. Henry Benning held nominal command of the brigade during the Maryland Campaign as Toombs believed he commanded a small division of three brigades, including his own, during the campaign.[11]

Benning exercised tactical command of the four Georgia regiments during the Battle of Antietam. The 48-year old was a prewar lawyer in Georgia. Most notably, he served as a justice on the state's Supreme Court. Benning played an active role in Democratic politics during the 1860 election and also participated in Georgia's secession convention. He "exhibited considerable reluctance to encourage secession until the die was absolutely cast," according to historian Ezra Warner. When war began, Benning accepted the colonelcy of the 17th Georgia Infantry.[12]

The brigade crossed the Potomac River on September 6 and encamped on the outskirts of Frederick. On September 10, the brigade marched with the rest of Jones' division to Hagerstown, reaching it two days later.[13]

When James Longstreet's column departed Hagerstown on the morning of September 14, destined for Boonsboro, Benning's Georgians did not accompany it. They served on picket duty around the city the previous evening and thus received orders, along with the 11th Georgia Infantry and 1st Virginia Cavalry, to remain there. The Georgians listened all day to the thunder of artillery to the southeast but sat on the sidelines. At 10:00 p.m., orders arrived from Jones to march to Sharpsburg and rejoin the Army of Northern Virginia reassembling there.[14]

### Antietam

Leaving behind the 11th Georgia of George T. ("Tige") Anderson's brigade, informally attached to Benning's command, the four Georgia regiments marched south on Hagerstown Turnpike and arrived at Antietam Creek before sunrise on September 15. Benning posted his brigade on the ridge southeast of Sharpsburg and awaited orders. The men only had a few hours to rest before Jones ordered Benning to send two of his regiments to Williamsport to protect the wagon train. Benning selected the 15th and 17th Georgia for the task; Col. William T. Millican, 15th Georgia, led the detached regiments. Millican's command marched 13 miles to Williamsport, but the wagon train was already in Virginia when they arrived, so the two regiments remained in the Old Dominion with it until September 17.[15]

Jones sent Benning's two remaining regiments, the 2nd and 20th Georgia, forward to the banks of Antietam Creek, where they assumed an advantageous position on the bluffs overlooking the western entrance of the Lower Bridge. If these 357 men guarding the main crossing of the creek southeast of Sharpsburg should be compelled to fall back, they would reform on a higher hill about 500 yards south of the bridge overlooking Antietam Creek. If forced from this position, Benning had orders to fall in on the right of Jones' division. Benning's force at the bridge was therefore the first level of a multi-layered defense south/southeast of Sharpsburg.[16]

The bluff upon which the Georgians assumed their positions stood approximately fifty feet above Antietam Creek and the Lower Bridge. A line of "thinly scattered trees" topped the slope and the quarry pits, which supplied the stone used to build the bridge. The depression afforded some cover to no more than thirty men. Immediately upon reaching their new position, a thin skirmish line marched across the bridge to the creek's eastern bank. The rest of the command improved their position. The Georgians disassembled a nearby fence and "built [it] up against such trees as were in suitable situations, and where there were no such trees the rails were laid in simple piles," Benning reported. "These rude barricades, few and far between, afforded to men lying behind them tolerable shelter against small-arms."[17]

While the skirmish line across the creek shielded the Federals' eyes to the bridge's approaches, Benning placed his thin line of troops on the hillside. Col. John Cumming's 20th Georgia held the line directly facing the bridge's entryway, and occupied the quarry pits, while his left extended forty to fifty yards above the bridge. Lt. Col. William Holmes' 2nd Georgia extended the line to the south for about 300 yards. Benning's force was overextended and did not have enough men to cover the ground assigned to it. Thus, it did not fight in lines of battle but in "a more open order than was desirable," said Toombs.[18]

Jones attempted to bolster Benning's forward position as best he could. The 100-man 50th Georgia (Thomas Drayton's brigade), which suffered extensive losses at Fox's Gap on September 14, extended beyond the 2nd Georgia's right along the creek. Additionally, a company from Micah Jenkins' brigade was split: half took position between the 2nd and 50th Georgia; the other half watched Snavely's Ford, approximately one and a quarter mile downstream from the bridge. Three Confederate artillery batteries backed up Benning's line as the sun rose on September 17.[19]

Benning's men busily prepared their position as they braced for an attack. Occasional Federal artillery shells crashed into their position on

September 15 and 16 and Confederate skirmishers east of the creek traded shots with probing Union scouting parties.[20]

The contest for the bridge began in earnest between 9:00 and 10:00 a.m. on September 17. Advancing Union skirmishers—Companies F and I of the 11th Ohio—drove the Georgia pickets from their positions east of the bridge before the Federals launched their first assault. Benning's meager command first repulsed a disjointed attack by the 11th Connecticut and George Crook's brigade. Confederate fire poured onto the open plain east of the bridge, devastating the 11th Connecticut. Of the 430 men it carried into the battle, it suffered 139 casualties, including its commander, Col. Henry Kingsbury, who was mortally wounded.[21]

It was now Samuel Sturgis' division's turn to attack the bridge. He first sent in James Nagle's brigade. The 2nd Maryland and 6th New Hampshire charged up Sharpsburg-Rohrersville Road under cover of friendly infantry and artillery fire. The Georgians still held firm and leveled their muskets and rifles into the flank of the assaulting column, which disintegrated before the van of the attack reached the bridge's eastern end. The two regiments' combined total of 300 soldiers attacked, and Benning's men cut down nearly a third of them.[22]

Near noon, another Federal attack commenced, this one led by the 51st New York and 51st Pennsylvania (Edward Ferrero's brigade), supported by various other regiments and 26 artillery pieces that pounded the Georgians' hillside position at an average range of 600 yards. This concentrated artillery fire greatly harassed the men of the two Georgia regiments. "[W]e suffered badly," noted Lt. Theodore Fogle of the 2nd Georgia. The Union guns "were pouring grape shot, shell and cannister [sic] into us & our artillery could not silence them." This fire, coupled with that of the Union infantry posted on the creek's eastern bank, began to take effect in Benning's ranks.[23]

After fighting for nearly three consecutive hours, Benning's line began to crack. In the 2nd Georgia, Lt. Fogle reported, "So many of the men were shot that the officers filled their places & loaded & fired their guns." Additionally, at this time, the Georgians' ammunition supply neared its end. Near 1:00 p.m., Federals began streaming across Antietam Creek at the bridge, at a newly discovered ford 350 yards north of it, and downstream at Snavely's Ford. Accordingly, Benning ordered a retreat.[24]

The orders reached the 2nd Georgia first, now under command of Maj. William Harris after Lt. Col. Holmes was mortally wounded leading a forlorn charge down to the bridge itself. Benning ordered the 2nd to withdraw and "pass the order on down the line" to the 20th Georgia on their left. The men on the left of the 2nd failed to convey this order, but pockets of Cumming's regiment saw what was happening and withdrew. A small force of sixteen men led by Lt. Robert McCrimmon did not receive the message and surrendered to the ensnaring Federals.[25]

The advance of Isaac Rodman's Union division from Snavely's Ford deprived Benning's men of the chance to withdraw to their previously appointed hill south of the bridge. Instead, they fell back to the western edge of a 40-acre cornfield, 900 yards west of their recently vacated position. Benning's two regiments lost 120 men while inflicting 500 casualties on their Federal attackers during the fight for the bridge. After three hours of action, Benning's fight was not yet over.[26]

As the bridge defenders reached their fallback position, the 15th and 17th Georgia, which had been guarding the wagon train in Virginia, arrived to greet them. Half of the 11th Georgia also arrived and fought alongside the brigade for the remainder of the battle. The 2nd and 20th Georgia temporarily marched rearward to replenish their ammunition.[27]

Benning's advanced command skirmished with the IX Corps as it deployed for its assault on the heights southeast of Sharpsburg. This attack began north of Benning's position and, before A.P. Hill's division arrived to relieve his command, Jones ordered the Georgians to fall back to Harpers Ferry Road and support his division's crumbling right flank.

As they reached the road, the survivors of the 20th Georgia rejoined the brigade, their refilled cartridge boxes ready for another fight. Toombs now received news of the defeat of Jones' right flank. The brigadier ordered his men to shoulder their rifles as they ran—"not double-quicked," a member of the 11th Georgia specified—north on the Harpers Ferry Road. Less than halfway to Sharpsburg, Toombs and Benning saw three abandoned rebel guns of Capt. David McIntosh's Pee Dee Artillery and the 8th Connecticut ready to pounce on them. Benning recognized the meagerness of his force, but he sprang into action, deploying the brigade into line and yelling for his Georgians to commence firing. "The fire soon became general," Benning reported. "It was hot and rapid."[28]

Benning's men held the advantage of position during this firefight. "We were sheltered by a fence and embankment," recalled a soldier of the 11th Georgia regarding their position in Harpers Ferry Road. This cover aided the Georgians "so much so that we mowed them down, and they scarcely harmed us." Besides holding an advantageous position over the 8th Connecticut, remnants of Drayton's and James Kemper's brigades fell in on the Georgians' left and added their firepower while the 7th and 37th North Carolina of Lawrence Branch's brigade (A.P. Hill's division), which had just arrived from Harpers Ferry, hit the Connecticut regiment's left flank and rear. "They stood our fire about ten minutes," noted one Georgian, "when they began to retire in a pretty good order, then to run."[29]

The fight along the Harpers Ferry Road freed McIntosh's guns from the 8th Connecticut. Benning's men leapt forward at the opportunity to reclaim the pieces. Millican of the 15th Georgia drew his sword and "advanced ten paces before the colors." He turned to his men and "told them to follow their officers, and if they fell to march forward over their bodies." Toombs, now on foot after being admonished by future Georgia governor Capt. Henry McDaniel of the 11th Georgia for "unnecessarily exposing yourself," likewise strode out in front of his men. The sight of the backs of the 8th Connecticut spurred the Georgians and the remnants of Kemper's and Drayton's brigades to advance to the former position of the Connecticut regiment.[30]

Benning's new position placed his men below the crest of the hill, which shielded their view from what lay on the other side. Toombs' blood was up and he ordered the charge to continue. Benning, who exercised closer tactical command over the brigade, urged caution. He "knew a very large force of the enemy must be somewhere below" the crest. Additionally, he reported, the brigade was "so small and it had no supports behind it." Benning suggested sending "only the men armed with long-range guns" to the crest to pepper the Federals below. Toombs assented.[31]

Despite the recent gains, Toombs still chomped at the bit to achieve more. He peered over the crest of the hill and saw a Union line reforming east of the 40-acre cornfield and he ordered most of his command forward, leaving Benning in the rear with a small reserve force. Down the hill they charged to a stone fence bordering the west side of the cornfield and opened fire on the 35th Massachusetts (Ferrero's brigade) 300 yards distant. "The men were going half bent in order to be protected by the stone fence," remembered John Lokey of the 20th Georgia. The fight at the wall raged for some time even though the combatants engaged at a great distance. Lokey fired twenty rounds alone from behind the wall. After fighting all day, "I had fired sixty rounds with my old Enfield rifle," he remembered, "and my right shoulder was kicked blue."[32]

This action claimed the life of a second regimental commander that day. As Col. Millican of the 15th Georgia urged on his men, "He was shot through the breast, and died in a short time after," wrote a member of the brigade. Darkness finally brought an end to the killing. During the night, Benning's men were ordered to leave the stone wall and withdraw to Cemetery Hill.[33]

Skirmish fire kept the command under cover for much of the next day. Towards nightfall, as the Army of Northern Virginia prepared to depart Maryland, Toombs and his staff rode to the front and became lost. Toombs rode his mount, Gray Alice, along the outskirts of Sharpsburg. Suddenly, a small force of mounted men dashed upon Toombs' entourage. Silence greeted the Confederates' entreaties for the party to identify themselves. Capt. James Troup, one of Toombs' aides, drew his revolver. "Don't shoot," yelled a voice in the thickening darkness. "We are Massachusetts men." Toombs reached for his own weapon as Troup opened fire. The Federals quickly responded before withdrawing for the rear. Their scattered shots proved accurate, wounding Toombs in his rein-hand, and another of Toombs' staffers, Lt. Robert Grant, was also wounded.[34]

The stand of Toombs' and Benning's men at the Burnside Bridge is immortalized in the story of Antietam, yet they performed a greater service to the Confederate army after their position at the bridge collapsed. As the right flank of Lee's army caved in, the remnants of these four Georgia regiments, bolstered by half of the 11th Georgia, stood strong and slowed the Federal attack south of Sharpsburg, creating a favorable situation for A. P. Hill's arriving command.

**Kevin Pawlak**

* * *

## Drayton's Brigade: Brigadier General Thomas F. Drayton

**Units:** 3rd South Carolina Battalion, 15th South Carolina, Phillips' (Georgia) Legion, 50th Georgia, 51st Georgia
**Strength:** 1,464[35]
**Losses:** 198[36]

South Carolinian Thomas Drayton owed much of his success to his friendship with President Jefferson Davis. Both were West Point graduates in the class of 1828. Unlike Davis, Drayton barely scraped through, graduating 28 out of 33. He served but eight years in the military and then resigned his commission to return home to the family plantation. Drayton did not immediately offer his services to the Confederacy, but when he did, Jefferson Davis appointed him to the rank of brigadier general on September 25, 1861. Until July 15, 1862, Drayton commanded the Military District of Port Royal. The defenses of Port Royal Sound were the scene of the first U.S. thrust against the Confederate States' coastline. During a massive bombardment, Drayton was fired on by his brother, who was in command of the S.S. Powhatan, in Federal service off the coast of South Carolina.

The 3rd South Carolina Battalion, 15th South Carolina, and Phillips' Legion were mustered into service during the late summer/fall of 1861. The 3rd South Carolina Battalion was known generally in the army as James' Battalion in honor of its commander, Lt. Col. George James. The 50th and 51st Georgia regiments joined the brigade in March 1862. The South Carolina elements of the brigade eventually traveled north to join the Army of Northern Virginia in July 1862; the Georgia units did not arrive until August. It was a troubled brigade because the combination of Georgia and South Carolina troops did not mix well.

The entire brigade's first battle together was at Second Bull Run where it sustained the fewest casualties of any brigade in Lee's army. Called upon by division commander D.R. Jones "again and

again," Drayton arrived "too late to accomplish the results contemplated." Jones subsequently lost faith in Drayton, thinking him "slow and perhaps even lacking in intelligence," according to his biographer. The brigade would march north into Maryland as an inexperienced unit under the command of an officer judged lacking in the "capacity to command" by his superiors. This would prove disastrous on September 14 at Fox's Gap.[37]

Drayton's brigade joined the rest of D.R. Jones' division's trek to Leesburg on September 3 and crossed the Potomac River at 8:00 a.m. on September 6 via White's Ford. Lee ordered barefooted soldiers to remain behind and the numbers were sizable. A soldier in the 50th Georgia recalled the group looked as large as a brigade. Maj. Gen. James Longstreet issued orders "that all barefoot, weak and inefficient of each regiment be left with the baggage in charge of an officer." Lt. Alex Erwin of Phillips' Legion was that officer and he oversaw about 150 of Drayton's troops, observing, "They then ordered all that were left, about five thousand in all to Winchester."[38]

The rest of the brigade trudged slowly toward Frederick, Maryland. The Reverend George G. Smith, chaplain of Phillips' Legion sadly recalled, "many of our men were sick, many were ragged and barefooted, and our army was not half the size of the Army with which we had left the field of Second Manassas." Despite the bounty around them, many of the men subsisted on raw or uncooked crops and intestinal problems soon took their toll. Capt. Henry Young with the Phillips' Legion wrote his wife that "one day's rations has often supplied three days and this has forced the men to live on green apples and corn which together with this miserable limestone water has resulted in diarrhea among the men."

Reaching Monocacy Junction, the men were given a well-deserved rest where they could swim, bathe, and wash their tattered clothes. Pvt. Solomon

263

Marsh of the 51st Georgia informed his wife on September 8, "I pulled off one of my shirts, under drawers & washed them in the river." The men passed through Frederick on their way to Boonsboro on September 10 and then headed for Hagerstown. The sympathy of the citizens of Maryland towards the Southern cause, like beauty, seemed to be in the eye of the beholder. Col. William DeSaussure, commanding the 15th South Carolina, observed, "We saw but little enthusiasm among the people, the majority looking sour and sullen as we passed through the towns." However, Chaplin Smith noted the "long, straggling village of Boonsboro," where he "found quite a number of southern sympathizers."

Drayton's brigade arrived on the outskirts of Hagerstown on September 12. Because many of the pro-Union citizens had fled across the Pennsylvania border, many of those who remained harbored sympathy for the Confederates. A southern correspondent commented that many citizens of Hagerstown, "have thrown open their houses to us...There is strong Southern feeling in this town and vicinity."[39]

**South Mountain**

Shortly after entering Maryland, Pvt. Marsh of the 51st Georgia shared some camp gossip in a letter to his wife: "we are getting a long ways from home but if we have luck . . . we will not stay in this country more than a month or two longer." He then declared, "Our General says that he is going to try and get his brigade back on the sea coast & if he does we will be close [to] home again." One can only imagine Marsh's surprise when on the morning of September 14, only six days after writing those lines to his wife, the brigade received orders for the retrograde march back to Boonsboro. All were disappointed when told to collect their belongings and form into line. The brigade, with the rest of the division, marched rapidly south toward the South Mountain passes where George McClellan's army was attempting to force the gaps, defeat Lee's

scattered army in detail, and rescue the Harpers Ferry garrison.[40]

Drayton's brigade likely led the march from Hagerstown, followed by G.T. Anderson's brigade. They were the first of James Longstreet's troops to reach Boonsboro, arriving about 3:00 p.m. after a hot, dusty march of 10 miles. The men were immediately sent up the mountain to Turner's Gap. Due to excessive straggling because of the forced march, and the climb up the western slope of the mountain, the combined effective force of the two brigades was probably somewhere around 1,900 men. D.H. Hill personally brought them south to Fox's Gap. Hill planned to have two of his brigades, Roswell Ripley's and G.B. Anderson's, combine with Longstreet's two newly arrived brigades to participate in an attack on the IX Corps at Fox's Gap. Hill believed the main attack against him would fall on his left and he was anxious to dispose of the Federal force on his right before this could happen. He placed Ripley in charge of the four brigades at Fox's Gap, giving him precise orders on how to attack and then he rode north, back to his headquarters at Turner's Gap.[41]

The four brigades deployed along Old Sharpsburg Road westward below Fox's Gap and faced south. G.B. Anderson took the farthest position down the western slope, followed by Ripley and George T. Anderson. Drayton's brigade remained in the gap. Hill's plan apparently called for both Andersons and Ripley to counterattack by moving south and then wheel east over the crest with Drayton's men holding the gap, forming the lynchpin of a great sweeping movement that would drive the Federals off the mountain.[42]

Things immediately went wrong and Ripley's movement stranded Drayton at Fox's Gap. The full responsibility for the success or failure of the counterattack fell on Drayton. As the lynchpin, or anchor of the movement, he was instructed to deploy his men at the gap for an assault. Drayton soon confronted the greater part of three divisions of Jesse Reno's IX Corps.

Drayton initially deployed in an inverted L-shaped formation that took advantage of stone walls on the southern and eastern edges of the northern field opposite the Daniel Wise farmstead and adjacent to Old Sharpsburg Road. It was a strong defensive position. Old Sharpsburg Road was deeply sunken, and the eastern wall faced a steep, formidable ravine. Part of Jacob Cox's Kanawha Division occupied the forested area across Wise's field south of Old Sharpsburg Road, the same area Hill intended Ripley to assault with the sweeping movement. As Drayton recognized the increasing interval between Ripley's forces and his own, he took steps to fill the Old Sharpsburg Road with three regiments. At this point the 50th and 51st Georgia still occupied the crucial position at the stone wall facing his eastern flank.

The rest of Reno's corps arrived by 4:00 p.m. and prepared to attack at the same time Drayton launched an assault of his own. Why he did this, and more particularly the way he did this, remains one of the battle's unexplained mysteries. One thing however is certain, he had been accused previously of being late and lacking capacity to command and it is safe to assume he was determined not to suffer those accusations again. Led by the regiments in the Old Sharpsburg Road (3rd and 15th South Carolina plus Phillips' Legion) Drayton's attack opened with a furious charge straight south through Wise's field and the timber behind the Wise cabin. Drayton then shifted the pair of Georgia regiments from their defensive position at the eastern stone wall into Old Sharpsburg Road. This is the mysterious and controversial part of Drayton's action. He had to be aware of the massive Federal forces on his left, but still positioned his troops so as to leave that flank with no defenders.[43]

When the end came for Drayton's brigade, it was swift and overwhelming. At one point Drayton's men in Old Sharpsburg Road took fire from their front, flank, and rear. The 17th Michigan passed through a ravine, over the eastern wall, into the field, and wheeled to the left to arrive behind the Georgians in Old Sharpsburg Road. In a maelstrom of flying lead, Drayton's men broke in disorder and streamed to the rear, including the three regiments that led the assault. The most shocking description

of conditions in Old Sharpsburg Road is provided by Lt. Peter McGlashen of the 50th Georgia. "The Fiftieth were posted in a narrow path washed out into a regular gully," wrote McGlashen, "and were fired into by the enemy from the front, rear and left flank." His soldiers stood their ground the best they could, but the outcome was inevitable. "Out of 210 carried into the fight over 125 were killed and wounded in less than twenty minutes," declared the young lieutenant, "A man could have walked from the head of our line to the foot on their bodies." A desperate last stand was attempted in an intersecting road near the gap. Ridge Road, as it came to be known, ran south along the mountain crest and was bordered on either side by substantial stone walls. The commander of the 3rd South Carolina Battalion, Lt. Col. George James, tried to rally his men and the retreating forces between the stone walls. The weight of the Federal numbers was too much, and James was shot in the chest and perished on the field later that night.

Drayton's brigade was brutally injured and its effectiveness as a unit was crippled. Out of the 1,464 men the brigade carried into the battle, Drayton could muster only 710 at Antietam three days later. This translates to a loss of 52%.[44]

## Antietam

The brigade crossed Antietam Creek on September 15 and took position with the rest of Jones' division on the high ground approximately 500 yards south of Sharpsburg and roughly parallel to the Harpers Ferry Road. Jones detached the 98 soldiers of the 50th Georgia to Robert Toombs the following day. They were posted with the 2nd and 20th Georgia along the high ground above Antietam Creek near the Lower Bridge. The brigade's remaining 612 soldiers remained in their positions.[45]

The morning of September 17 found Drayton's brigade posted between James Kemper's brigade on its right, and Jenkins brigade on its left. Throughout the morning and into the afternoon the men heard "a terribly magnificent battle," as Col. DeSaussure described it. The role of the 50th Georgia, commanded by Lt. Col. Francis Kearse, to the south of the Lower Bridge, has been overlooked. The regiment was deployed on the right flank of the 2nd Georgia, about 650 yards due south of Burnside Bridge on the ridge above the creek. A half company of South Carolina sharpshooters from Jenkins' brigade formed on either side of Kearse's men, who were in an open order on an incredibly thin picket line running west approximately 500 yards (more than a quarter mile). A rough farm ford ran about 350 yards due south of Kearse's left flank and another ford, Snavely's, was about 650 yards downstream. Kearse occupied the high ground overlooking this stretch of the Antietam, approximately 150 vertical feet below, on the morning of the battle. Robert Toombs was in overall command of the whole line.[46]

Lt. William O. Fleming of the 50th Georgia was under the impression the creek was fordable on "the whole line of our picket," and that the only course of action should the enemy attempt a crossing, "would be to fall back to a point where the picket could be concentrated to keep the enemy at bay without danger of being surrounded." No doubt, after the regiment's experience at Fox's Gap, being surrounded was uppermost on their minds. Between "10 and 11 o'clock" Fleming observed Isaac Rodman's Union division moving "in large force" towards Snavely's Ford. The sounds of battle had been ongoing from the direction of the bridge. About two hours later, with the regiment under "an incessant fire of shot and canister" the enemy "commenced his advance, the cannonade rather increasing in rapidity," wrote Fleming. A false report reached Kearse that the left of the line was falling back; consequently, he ordered the whole line to fall back. Fleming estimated the line had withdrawn about 150 or 200 yards when "one of Gen. Toombs' aids rode up and said to Col. Kearse that it was Gen. Toombs' order for him to resume his position on the creek."

Kearse immediately marched his men back to their former position "under a fearful storm of grape," and as Fleming noted, "not a man refusing to return." Upon reaching the creek, the men noted the enemy had reached the Antietam and were crossing. Harrison Fairchild's brigade (Rodman's division) formed on their right, and Hugh Ewing's brigade of the Kanawha Division formed on their left. While Rodman's division crossed at Snavely's ford, the Ohio troops had performed the near impossible feat of crossing at the farm ford and scaling the steep slope in their front (the equivalent of a ten-story building). Looking upon at least 20 times his number forming for an assault against him, Kearse must have decided that discretion was the better part of valor and, as Fleming remembered, he "had the moral courage to give the order to fall back again." The regiment was just being formed under the brow of a small hill when Toombs' aide returned with the same order as before. According to Fleming, "Col. Kearse told the aide to say to Gen. Toombs that he would be cut off if he returned, and did not feel disposed to sacrifice his command."[47]

Toombs appeared in person within a few minutes and had "scarcely commenced conversation" with Kearse when his aide arrived with news of the Federals forcing the passage at the bridge and crossing the creek. Henry Benning, commanding the 2nd and 20th Georgia, had already decided to withdraw in the face of superior numbers. Toombs "at once ordered Col. Kearse to support his regiments as he drew them off from the creek." The 2nd and the 20th Georgia were ordered to the rear to replenish their ammunition and, presumably, the 50th Georgia accompanied them and managed to rejoin Drayton's brigade in time for the Final Attack.[48]

Conditions had become dire for D.R. Jones by 3:00 p.m. when the IX Corps crossed Antietam Creek and, with elements of George Sykes' division (V Corps), the Federals formed for the Final Attack. The 2,430 Confederate defenders south of Sharpsburg faced four times their number advancing in a line of battle roughly a mile wide. Consequently, Jones moved Garnett's brigade north to counter some of Sykes' Regulars thrown across Antietam Creek at the Middle Bridge, leaving only

Drayton's, Kemper's, and Jenkins' brigades in position. By 3:30 p.m., while Toombs' men were still to the south, Drayton's men could see troops from the IX Corps moving into position to attack. It was a desperate time for Lee as the combined V and IX Corps were forming against Jones' thin, understrength brigades. Incredibly, some of these Federals were the same troops Drayton had tangled with three days before at Fox's Gap.[49]

Drayton's brigade was sheltered in the safety of a ravine most of the day. To meet the advance of the Federals, they were moved to a stone wall on the crest, about 400 yards due east of Harper's Ferry Road where they received the full brunt of the Federal assault. First contact was made when the 8th Michigan (Thomas Welsh's brigade; Orlando Willcox's division) and the 9th New York (Harrison Fairchild's brigade; Rodman's division) drove part of the 15th South Carolina on the skirmish line, about 130 yards from the Otto barn, back toward the main line. About this time, the 50th Georgia rejoined Drayton, and a portion of Toombs' brigade arrived and formed on Kemper's right. The left of Drayton's line was anchored on an orchard. Intense shelling from Union artillery on both sides of Antietam Creek caused the men to lie down to seek cover. The defensive position was a good one, rising 70 feet above Fairchild's brigade and the men had the additional protection of a stone wall. As Fairchild's men approached, Drayton's men rested their rifle barrels atop the stone wall and opened fire when the enemy was about 50 yards away. The devastating blasts caused Fairchild's brigade to recoil. The Union officers reformed their shattered ranks and came on again, driving Drayton's and Kemper's men from their positions. "For about 5 to 10 minutes," recalled Capt. Henry E. Young of Drayton's staff, "we were swept back for about 1/2 mile by overwhelming numbers." Jones noted in his report, "Kemper and Drayton were driven back through the town."

Things looked dire for the brigade, but then another legendary Antietam event occurred. "But very soon had two brigades of A P Hill (Archer's, Branch's) came up and Gregg's brigade," wrote Young, "and these three brigades together with odd troops there drove the enemy back with terrible carnage, regaining every foot of ground and slaughtering them with grape and canister." Many of Drayton's men returned to their former positions and stabilized the Confederate line. According to Lt. Fleming of the 50th Georgia, "Colonel Kearse . . . when the color bearer had been shot down, took the flag himself, and waving it, cheered on the men to the end of the charge." By the end of the battle the regimental colors "were pierced by seven balls, and one through the staff."[50]

Drayton's brigade suffered 28% casualties at Antietam. Understandably, the 50th Georgia suffered the most-- 43% of their number. The entire brigade endured 65% casualties in the Maryland Campaign.

Drayton's brigade, with the rest of the division, remained in position along Harpers Ferry Road on September 18 and then began its retreat toward the Potomac River after dark. This would be the last battle for Drayton's brigade. It was broken up and the regiments distributed to other brigades. Drayton was transferred to court-martial duty and then given some districts in the South, probably because Lee hoped that "some duty may be found for him . . . which he may be able to perform." Lee knew he was unfit for field command, noting the brigade had been a "source of delay and embarrassment from the time the army left Richmond."[51]

**Steven R. Stotelmyer**

\* \* \*

## Pickett's Brigade: Brigadier General Richard Garnett

**Units:** 8th Virginia, 18th Virginia, 19th Virginia, 28th Virginia, 56th Virginia
**Strength:** 1,739[52]
**Losses:** 78 (9k-69w)[53]

The first four regiments of Brig. Gen. George Pickett's brigade had an identical history: formed in May 1861, transferred to Confederate service in July 1861, and brigaded with each other under Brig. Gen. Philip St. George Cocke. These regiments were at First Bull Run, Seven Pines, Seven Days, and Second Bull Run. Pickett was placed in command after St. George Cocke resigned his commission. The brigade had proven itself to be a dependable and effective unit on many battlefields. The 56th Virginia formed in September 1861 and was immediately sent west to Kentucky, where it garrisoned Ft. Donelson for a few days in February 1862, before being transferred back to Virginia to serve in Pickett's brigade in June 1862. Pickett was wounded at Gaines' Mill and Col. Eppa Hunton commanded the brigade until Brig. Gen. Richard Garnett was named its temporary commander.[54]

Richard Garnett is often confused with his cousin, Robert Garnett. Both grew up together in Virginia and both attended West Point at the same time. Richard was born in 1817 and graduated from West Point in 1841. He pulled garrison duty in Florida and the West prior to the Civil War. Unlike his cousin, he did not see action in the Mexican War. Garnett resigned his commission in the U.S. Army in May 1861 and became a major in the Confederate army. He was promoted to the rank of brigadier general on November 14, 1861 and was sent to the Shenandoah Valley to command the "Stonewall Brigade." His first action ended badly. Outnumbered and outgunned, Garnett pulled his men from the Battle of Kernstown, one of Stonewall Jackson's rare defeats. An irate Jackson removed him from command and placed him under arrest. The almost constant maneuvering and

fighting over the next several months precluded a court martial and Garnett stewed without a command. A court martial was finally convened, but quickly ended when the Second Bull Run Campaign erupted. Lee finally released Garnett from arrest over Jackson's strenuous objections, who claimed Garnett, "so incompetent an officer" that he would turn any good brigade into a bad one. Some have claimed Jackson sought a scapegoat for his Kernstown defeat and Garnett conveniently filled that role. With Pickett out with a shoulder wound sustained during the Seven Days Battles, Lee found an able replacement. He would serve under a cloud of uncertainty until his life ended at the Battle of Gettysburg.[55]

The brigade was in poor shape when the Maryland Campaign began. "Officers were scarce. Many of them were at home or in hospitals . . . The companies had been much reduced by the casualties of war, and in some instances two companies were thrown into one temporarily, in order to have a commissioned officer to command," recalled Lt. William Wood of the 19th Virginia. The men's uniforms were often in tatters, leading Randolph Shotwell to admit, "we were a hard-looking set!" The men enjoyed their short reprieve around Leesburg on September 4, and then headed for White's Ford the following day, where most stripped off their clothing before fording the Potomac River. Many of the men were excited to be crossing the Potomac. According to Shotwell, "At last we were assuming the forward and offensive, which of itself was inspiriting after eighteen months of patient warding off of blows, or repulsing of invaders!"[56]

The brigade camped for several days along the Monocacy River in Maryland where the men could swim, bathe, and wash their tattered rags of uniforms. The town of Frederick was nearby and Lt. Wood recalled, "We made visits to Frederick in small squads." Most of the men did not have money so, according to the historian of the 56th Virginia, would stand "for hours in front of well-stocked shop windows and gawked at things they had not seen for months." The men were ordered to break camp on September 11 and marched first to Boonsboro and then to Hagerstown, arriving there on September 12. Curious townspeople came out along the route, from Frederick to Hagerstown to watch the ragged column pass by. The men's diet during this time consisted mainly of corn and green apples, which wreaked havoc on their digestive tracts.[57]

## South Mountain

The men heard the ominous rumble of artillery on the morning of September 14 and orderlies soon pounded up with orders to pack up and form into column for the forced march back south. Garnett called it a "hot, dusty, and fatiguing march of some 18 miles." The column reached Boonsboro about 4:00 p.m. and a short distance beyond it, several of D.R. Jones' brigades (James Kemper's, then Garnett's and finally Micah Jenkins'), were ordered on a road "running perpendicular to the pike," according to Garnett. After several additional miles on various roads, a staff officer approached Garnett with orders to "about-face, and to return the way I came until I reached a path, which I must take. He was unable to give me any information respecting the path in question, but said he would go forward and try to obtain some. I did not, however, see him again." It appears the three brigades were first sent south to assist in Fox's Gap defense, but after marching and countermarching, Longstreet decided the three brigades were needed to the north, at the Turner's Gap sector.

Garnett finally found the road he thought he should take but by then "my troops were almost exhausted. I consequently lost the services of a number of men by straggling." After a short rest, Garnett led his men up the side of the mountain toward Turner's Gap on the National Road and then turned onto another road that brought his command to an even higher summit. He finally filed his brigade by the right flank to his assigned position. Enemy artillery took his position under fire and he lost several men. Longstreet pointed out their positions on the right of Robert Rodes' brigade on Frosttown Plateau. Garnett quickly positioned his men with their right flank resting in a thick woods and his left in a cornfield. The exact position of the brigade's deployment is unclear. The 8th Virginia formed Garnett's right flank, adjacent to the woods and the 56th Virginia formed the opposite flank, closest to Kemper's brigade with the 28th Virginia on its right. The relative positions of the 18th and 19th Virginia are uncertain but were between the 8th and 28th Virginia.[58]

It was almost sunset when Garnett threw out a skirmish line to find the enemy and then received orders from Jones to slide the 56th Virginia to the left to connect with Kemper's right flank and then withdraw the rest of the brigade to a wooded ridge to his left and rear. Just as Garnett was about to comply with the second part of the order, the enemy skirmish line appeared with a strong line of battle behind it. There was no time for Garnett to redeploy, so he decided to fight it out on less than optimal ground, although the men did have the protection of a stone fence. Garnett was up against two brigades: Marsena Patrick's and Walter Phelps' (John Hatch's division; I Corps). The 3,500-man division (Abner Doubleday's brigade was in reserve) was up against Garnett's and Kemper's combined force of perhaps 975 men.[59]

Phelps' men needed no encouragement and immediately mounted a charge. The Virginians responded with heavy volleys that halted Phelps' advance. The two sides poured volleys into each other for about 15 minutes. Capt. Henry Owen of the 28th Virginia recalled Garnett's brigade held its own until a second line came up behind Phelps' first and "the Confederates, being greatly outnumbered, gave way . . . and rushed back in the open field." During the desperate fighting along the stone fence, Col. J.B. Strange of the 19th Virginia was killed and Gen. Hatch seriously wounded. Owen noted the "great confusion" of the men and how "the broken ranks were hard to rally and reform." Had Hatch's men continued their charge, Owen believed, they would have driven all of the Confederates from the ridge. However, Phelps' men were spent and in no shape to continue the attack and time was wasted as Doubleday's brigade came up to take over the front line. This delay gave Garnett's and Kemper's men time to reform behind another fence. Owen estimated Garnett's brigade could only muster 200 men at this point—the rest had continued their retreat to the rear. The Confederates, according to Owen, fought "in squads of a dozen or more, with great gaps between them, and were scattered along behind the fence and bushes for half a mile, while the enemy had a strong line in front and outflanked our position on both the right and left."[60]

Jenkins' brigade arrived and slid into position and Garnett was ordered to retire. It was now nightfall and the fighting had all but ended. Garnett explained his new brigade's gallantry in his official report: "It had marched (a portion of the time rapidly) between 22 and 25 miles before it went into action, much oppressed by heat and dust; readied its position a short time before sunset under a disheartening fire of artillery, and was attacked by a much superior force as soon as it was formed in line of battle. That it bravely discharged its duty is fully attested by the number of casualties which occurred during the engagement." Garnett's men lost 196 men during their short stay on Frosttown Plateau (35 killed; 164 wounded; 176 missing). Col. Eppa Hunton of the 8th Virginia explained, "we had a most unsatisfactory fight at that point, by reason of the forced march." D.H. Hill bemoaned the defeat of Longstreet's men: "I had now become familiar with the ground, and knew all the vital points, and, had those troops reported to me, the result might have been different. As it was, they took wrong positions, and, in their exhausted condition, after a long march, they were broken and scattered."[61]

## Antietam

Garnett's brigade had bent but not broken, and marched down the western slope of South Mountain in the darkness. It began its march through Boonsboro on the National Road after midnight and then turned left onto Boonsboro Pike to Keedysville. The exhausted men crossed Antietam Creek at the Middle Bridge after dawn on September 15 and took up positions on Cemetery Hill, on a second line behind Kemper's, Jenkins', and Drayton's brigades where they supported batteries of the Washington Artillery.[62]

On September 17, Union artillery opened fire on Lee's artillery line on Cemetery Hill, but Garnett said the brigade was "sheltered in a hollow in the rear of the artillery" with its right flank on Lower Bridge Road. The brigade remained in this position for four to five hours, probably until noon, and although somewhat protected, took several casualties from exploding Union ordnance. Lt. William Wood, 19th Virginia, called the artillery fire, "save one single occasion, the heaviest I ever witnessed." Garnett moved his command further to the rear. A heavy skirmish line of U. S. Regulars from George Sykes' division materialized in front of Cemetery Hill and a request was made to Garnett for skirmishers to protect some of Col. Stephen Lee's pieces. The 56th Virginia moved forward on this mission. Another, larger threat materialized to Garnett's right, when the IX Corps, having crossed Antietam Creek, prepared to attack Jones' division, south of Sharpsburg. Garnett put the 56th and 28th Virginia, perhaps totaling 100 men, in the cornfield in front of two guns from Capt. George Moody's battery; the 19th and 18th Virginia, perhaps numbering 120 men, were placed to the right of the guns at about 3:30 p.m. The 8th Virginia Infantry, numbering only 20 men at this time, was placed behind the 18th Virginia on the second line. The 56th, 28th and part of the 19th Virginia faced east, against the Regulars' right and center; the remaining men faced southeast and took on the Regulars' left and portions of the IX Corps. The fighting was intense here and several units lost between a third and a half of their men.[63]

Fearing his entire command would be engulfed by the IX Corps' advance, Garnett pulled his brigade back into the town. Union artillery commanded the town, forcing Garnett to move his men along cross streets to the north side. He reported finding "troops scattered in squads from various parts of the army, so that it was impossible to distinguish men of the different commands." When he learned Jones' division was forming south of town to combat Ambrose Burnside's men, Garnett gathered as many able bodied men as he could muster and moved in that direction, arriving after the last of the IX Corps had been thrown back. The brigade was subsequently ordered to reoccupy Cemetery Hill.[64]

Garnett lost another 78 men at the Battle of Sharpsburg (9 killed; 69 wound). The undersized brigade fought as well as expected at South Mountain and again at Sharpsburg. In both cases, it was placed in difficult situations where it was outnumbered and outflanked.[65]

**Bradley M. Gottfried**

* * *

## Kemper's Brigade: Brigadier General James Kemper

**Units:** 1st Virginia, 7th Virginia, 11th Virginia, 17th Virginia, 24th Virginia
**Strength:** 1,362[66]
**Losses:** 69 (10k-43w-16m)[67]

Brigadier General James Kemper's brigade had a long and distinguished history in Confederate service. All of the regiments were mustered into action between April and July 1861, with all but the 7th Virginia initially part of James Longstreet's brigade. The 7th Virginia began the war as part of Jubal Early's brigade but was transferred to Longstreet's brigade after First Bull Run. The brigade did not see action at that battle, but was actively engaged at Blackburn's Ford three days before. Four of the brigades's original regimental commanders would go on to command at least brigades (Montgomery Corse, Samuel Garland, Jubal Early, and James Kemper). Ambrose Powell Hill commanded the brigade after Longstreet received a division, and he led it during Battles at Williamsburg and Seven Pines. The brigade was especially effective at the former battle when it "swept away a Union attack." When Hill received a division, James Kemper received the brigade, which he led during the Seven Days Battles.[68]

Virginian James Kemper was born in 1823 and graduated from what is now Washington and Lee University. Kemper eventually went into law, but he put his practice aside to volunteer for the War with Mexico, serving as quartermaster of the 1st Virginia Infantry with the rank of captain. Kemper did not see action, but learned important lessons that would serve him well in the future. He went into politics, serving five successive terms in the Virginia House of Delegates and rose to become the Speaker of the House. He initially opposed secession but his position changed after Fort Sumter and Lincoln's call for 75,000 volunteers. Kemper entered Confederate service as commander of the 7th Virginia, and saw action on Chinn Ridge at First Bull Run. Upon his promotion to brigadier general on June 2, 1862, Kemper took over Hill's brigade. His seniority put him in command of a three-brigade division during the Second Bull Run Campaign, but it was combined with D.R. Jones' division on September 5, so Kemper returned to his brigade.[69]

The men embarked on the invasion of Maryland in a sorry state. Alexander Hunter of the 17th Virginia called it a "direful and shameful blunder." Supplies were scarce, so the men were forced to forage on their own. Without new clothes, especially shoes, "thousands were barefooted and obliged to fall behind because of their stonebruises," and "instead of having a thoroughly equipped army to invade the North, there were long lines of limping, starving soldiery, streaming wearily on, as disheartened and miserable in feeling as they looked; there was no elasticity or vim in the crowd." The brigade was only a shadow of its former self, mustering fewer than 500 men. The venerable 1st

Virginia numbered only 60 men and the other regiments, not much more.

After a short rest at Leesburg, Virginia, the brigade continued its march to White's Ford. Excessive straggling robbed the brigade of many of its men. John Dooley of the 1st Virginia never forgot that march. "I do not remember any march that so prostrated me as that of this first day of the invasion of the north." Hunter recounted every "hundred yards or so some soldier would drop unquestioned from the ranks . . . To a casual observer the army seemed to be going to pieces; to such an extent was straggling carried on that it looked more like the retreat of a demoralized legion than a body of troops flushed with success and advancing to conquest." [70]

Kemper's brigade reached the Monocacy River on September 7 and remained there for two days. During the march, "country people lined the roads, gazing in open-eyed wonder upon the long lines of infantry that filled the road for miles; as far as the eye could reach rose the glitter of the swaying points of the bayonets," according to Hunter. The somewhat refreshed men broke camp on September 10 and marched through Frederick, where they received a cool reception, camping at the base of South Mountain that evening. The column broke camp the next morning at 5:00 a.m. and marched through Boonsboro, ending the day just south of Hagerstown. Back on the road on September 12 at 7:00 a.m., the brigade passed through Hagerstown, halting just north of it. The reprieve close to the Pennsylvania border was a short one, for the men received orders to break camp and form column on the morning of September 14. The subsequent march back to Boonsboro was a difficult one for the men. "The day was hot, the road hard and dusty, the march rapid—so much so that many of the men broke down, falling by the wayside," according to David Johnston of the 7th Virginia. Although Lee issued strict orders against foraging, George Wise of the 17th Virginia noted, "it would have been an impossibility to have prevented starving men from helping themselves whenever an opportunity presented itself." [71]

## South Mountain

The brigade reached Boonsboro at 2:00 p.m. on September 14 and undertook a series of confused movements toward Fox's Gap (South Mountain) that exhausted the men, but did not bring them into battle. According to Johnston, "with other troops we were hurried up the mountain to the right of the main gap (Turner's), and after getting near the firing line, and finding Confederate troops there holding the enemy in steady fight, our steps were retraced to the Gap." As the brigade ascended South Mountain, the men passed a stream of wounded soldiers which "discouraged" the men, according to Dooley. Reaching the summit of South Mountain, the men were led down to their position in a cornfield to the left (north) of Turner's Gap. Enemy artillery fire plagued the men as they moved into position. The men slid into their defensive position behind a post and rail fence astride Old Hagerstown Road as John Hatch's Union division (I Corps) made its way up the mountainside from the east. When the men realized they had not been ordered to load their guns, they quickly rectified the situation. The brigade appears to have been deployed, from right to left: 17th Virginia- 11th Virginia- 1st Virginia- 7th Virginia- 24th Virginia. [72]

Garnett's brigade slid into position on their right and Robert Rodes' brigade was off to their left. Few enemy formations were deployed in Kemper's front. Hunter of the 17th Virginia recalled a "feeble attack was undertaken" but it was "easily checked." The same was not true to the right, where Garnett's small brigade was forced backward, causing Kemper to also pull his men back to join Garnett's Virginians. The men held this position until after dark. According to Col. Montgomery Corse of the 17th Virginia, the brigade was exposed to a "severe fire of musketry obliquely on our right flank and in front." Corse received orders to pull back up the mountain at 7:30 p.m. The brigade lost 75 men (11 killed, 57 wounded, 7 missing) on September 14. [73]

## Antietam

Kemper's brigade, in company with Garnett's, traveled down National Road to Boonsboro and then made a left onto Boonsboro Pike. The brigade crossed Antietam Creek at about 10:00 a.m. on September 15 and formed the right of the Confederate army on Cemetery Hill. The men were behind a post and rail fence in a deep ravine, about 175 yards from Harpers Ferry Road. Jenkins' and Drayton's brigades were to their right. The men rested the remainder of September 15 and 16 and were inactive through the morning of September 17. Suddenly, at about 10:00 a.m., Hunter recalled the "musketry at the bridge broke out fiercely, rising and swelling into full compass" as Burnside's IX Corps stormed the Lower Bridge. When Robert Toombs' brigade finally retreated from the bridge at about 1:00 p.m., Kemper's men expected to go into action immediately, but it took several hours for the men of the IX Corps to cross the creek and climb the ridges to assume their pre-attack positions. The 7th and 24th Virginia, 263-strong, were detached from the regiment and sent south along Harpers Ferry Road to shore up Lee's right flank and support some artillery. This left the 11th Virginia-1st Virginia- 17th Virginia, from left to right, in position to face the Union onslaught. These three regiments numbered only 210 officers and men.

Many of the men moved about to stretch their legs when they heard their officers yell, "Quick, men, back to your posts." Orlando Willcox's division advanced off to their left while Harrison Fairchild's brigade headed directly for their position. Kemper watched their advance and ordered his three regiments back toward Harpers Ferry Road. The 11th Virginia on the left took up a position where a stone wall and rail fence met; the rest of Kemper's men formed on its right. Drayton's brigade also sprinted up the hill and again formed on Kemper's left flank. Kemper's Virginians rested their rifles on the lowest rung of the fence and awaited orders to open fire.[74]

Fairchild halted his brigade to dress his line before continuing to ascend the slope toward Drayton and Kemper. Their orders were to halt, fire a volley, and then charge with fixed bayonets. Confederate artillery fire had already subtracted almost a third of Fairchild's men, but now they advanced at a quick step as if on parade. Hunter recalled his emotions as he watched the "onset of solid ranks of blue," and "felt his heart sink within him and grow faint." The men heard their officers yelling, "Men, we are to hold this position at all hazards. Not a man [should] leave his place. If need be, we will die together in this road," recalled Johnston. The historian of the 17th Virginia described the scene: "The first thing we saw appear was the gilt eagle that surmounted the pole, then the top of the flag, next the flutter of the Stars and Stripes itself slowly mounting—up it rose; then their hats came in sight; still rising, the faces emerged; next a range of curious eyes appeared, then such a hurrah as only the Yankee troops could give broke the stillness, and they surged towards us." Corse yelled, "Keep cool, men—don't fire yet," and then gave the order when the New Yorkers were within 50 yards.[75]

The murderous volley staggered Fairchild's men. Many fell; others ran for the rear, but according to Hunter, "the majority [of the New Yorkers] sent a stunning volley at us, and but for that fence there would have been hardly a man left alive." He estimated the volley hit at least half of the men of the 17th Virginia. The two sides were now but 30 yards apart when the 89th New York, directly in front of Kemper's men, charged. Because the New Yorkers' left flank overlapped the right of Kemper's, they were able to pour in an enfilade fire that made the position untenable, and the Virginians began making their way into Sharpsburg, which was becoming awash with confusion from many converging, defeated units. Dooley recalled, "Oh, how I ran!" He expected the Yanks to be on his heels but they halted at the fence—"they began to give regular methodical cheers, as if they had gained a game of base ball."[76]

Kemper rallied some of his men and returned them along Harpers Ferry Road where they confronted the 8th Connecticut (Edward Harland's brigade; Rodman's division) and assisted in repelling its attack. Additional Virginians joined Kemper and he returned them to their original position behind the fence along Harpers Ferry Road. The detached 7th and 24th Virginia also returned. They had not been engaged, and according to a member of the former regiment, "suffered a few casualties in killed and wounded, mostly from the artillery fire, a few by musket balls."

Kemper's brigade lost an additional 69 men (10 killed, 43 wounded, 16 missing) at Antietam—the lowest number of any of D.R. Jones' brigades. The brigade spent September 18 skirmishing with the enemy, and at 11:00 p.m., left its position and headed for the Potomac River. The small brigade was only slightly engaged at South Mountain on September 14, but, at Antietam on September 17, was driven from its position south of town by a determined Union charge during the "Final Attack."[77]

**Bradley M. Gottfried**

* * *

## Jenkins' Brigade: Colonel Joseph Walker

**Units:** 1st South Carolina Volunteers, 2nd South Carolina Rifles, 5th South Carolina, 6th South Carolina, 4th South Carolina Battalion, Palmetto Sharpshooters
**Strength:** 1,786[78]
**Losses:** 216 (26k-184w-6m)[79]

Brigadier General Micah Jenkins' brigade was a fairly homogenous South Carolina unit formed during the spring and summer of 1861. Most were initially placed in David R. Jones' brigade, which became Jenkins' when the former was elevated to division command. The 1st South Carolina was the exception. It was present at the Fort Sumter bombardment in April 1861 and remained in South Carolina until sent north to Lee's army in August 1862. The Maryland Campaign would be the last for the 4th South Carolina Battalion as it disbanded a short time later. The brigade saw action in several Seven Days Battles and at Second Bull Run, so it was an experienced fighting unit.[80]

Jenkins was severely wounded at Second Bull Run, so Col. Joseph Walker of the Palmetto Sharpshooters commanded the brigade during the Maryland Campaign. Walker was a successful businessman before the war, but gave it up to join the 5th South Carolina as a company commander in April 1861.[81]

The brigade, with the rest of Maj. Gen. D.R. Jones' division reached Leesburg on September 4. Col. James Hagood of the 1st South Carolina Volunteers recalled the brigade's reception: "Beautiful ladies entered the ranks as the troops marched down the main street, distributing refreshments and cheering the wearied soldiers with kind words." The men reciprocated by yelling and cheering until they were hoarse. The brigade spent the night along the Potomac River and forded the wide expanse on September 6 at White's Ford, and headed toward Frederick, about 20 miles away. Richard Lewis of the Palmetto Rifles wrote home to his mother: the men "plunged into it [the Potomac River] with the spirit that characterizes a good soldier, coming out on this side with nothing but the sun of high heavens to comfort them and to dry their dripping and wet clothes." The men were not happy to leave their baggage behind in Virginia. Frank Mixson of the 1st South Carolina Volunteers complained, "we had nothing but a haversack, canteen and a blanket or oil cloth, besides the accoutrements -- gun, cartridge box and scabbard. You will see from this that we were prepared for *quick marching.*" The men reached Frederick City on September 8. Mixson recalled the brigade's reception: "As we passed through the town everybody was out to see us; streets crammed, doors and windows full; some cheering and waving

Confederate flags; others jeering us and waving United States flags."[82]

## South Mountain

The men remained near Frederick until ordered to join the rest of the division for the march to Boonsboro on September 10. It was then onto Hagerstown, reaching it at midday on September 12, where it went into camp two miles beyond the town. The column reformed on the morning of September 14 and made a forced march back to Boonsboro. Walker's brigade brought up the division's rear. One by one, Jones' brigades were thrown into battle at the South Mountain gaps. Kemper's and Garnett's Virginia brigades were pushed into position to the left (north) of Turner's Gap where they almost immediately battled elements of Ricketts' division (I Corps). When Walker's brigade arrived at about 5:00 p.m., Jones immediately sent it to the west side of Turner's Gap, near the Mountain House, after the long march in the intense Maryland heat. The men were completely worn out and James Longstreet recalled how the men had "dropped along the road, as rapidly as if under severe skirmish." After only a few minutes of rest, the men were ordered to their feet and sent across the National Road, to the north, to support Kemper's and Garnett's brigades who were barely holding their own against overwhelming numbers.[83]

The 1st, 5th, and 6th South Carolina descended the mountain marching by the left flank along a side road. The Virginians gave way just as the South Carolinians were forming into line of battle. The line was pounded by Union artillery as it advanced. The three regiments advanced about 200 yards and took position behind the stone wall that had sheltered Garnett's men. A number of Virginians returned and formed alongside the South Carolinians. Ricketts' men approached to within 20 steps of Walker's men, who opened a brisk fire. This halted the Union advance and before the enemy could recover, the 1st and 6th South Carolina charged. Hagood claimed the "enemy was

driven some distance but rallied after crossing a ravine which became impassable to the Confederates under the fire which now greeted them." Walker ordered his men to lie down and the two sides exchanged gunfire for the next two hours. Hagood thought the distance between the combatants was less than 15 to 30 paces at this time. When the fighting ended, Walker tallied 32 casualties (3 killed and 29 wounded).[84]

## Antietam

Longstreet ordered a general retreat of all units on the mountain at about midnight. Hagood recalled the men "silently crept away under the protection of the rocks and gullies." The men halted by the Mountain House and the 2nd South Carolina Rifles moved a short distance down the east side of the mountain until its men encountered a heavy cloud of Union skirmishers. The rest of Walker's men remained near the top of Turner's Gap as the rearguard until relieved by elements of Fitzhugh Lee's cavalry at about 4:00 a.m. on September 15, and then made their way to Boonsboro. They turned left onto Boonsboro Pike and headed for Sharpsburg—the last of Jones' division to make this trek. The brigade reached Sharpsburg about 11:00 a.m. on September 15 and was positioned on Cemetery Hill, to the right (south) of Boonsboro Pike with Garnett's brigade. Later that afternoon, Walker moved the brigade further right, across a ravine to the right of the road leading to the Lower Bridge. The brigade remained here until 3:00 p.m., "under a heavy fire of shot and shell."[85]

Walker received orders to return his brigade to its original position, closer to town, where it supported Capt. George Moody's battery and a section of the Washington Artillery. The brigade was moved again at about 3:30 p.m., advancing about 400 yards to an apple orchard while exposed to small arms fire and pounded by enemy artillery. The IX Corps had crossed the Lower Bridge, scaled the ridge between it and the town, and now prepared to advance. Walker's men faced Orlando Willcox's division— Benjamin Christ's brigade was deployed in their front and Thomas Welsh's brigade to their right. Walker reported, "Perceiving the enemy in force in several positions, from any of which we were assailable," he decided to deploy the brigade at a 90-degree angle, with the 1st South Carolina, 5th South Carolina, and 6th South Carolina on the left, facing east and Christ's brigade. The right, composed of the 2nd South Carolina Rifles and Palmetto Rifles faced southwest to "meet him [Welsh] in the center and on the right."

An officer in the 6th South Carolina explained how his unit on the left wing "went boldly forward, down the hill, through an orchard, to a good stone fence, where [we] were halted and began firing." Hagood claimed the "attacking column [Christ's] at last began to move and with unbroken front and steady tread to ascend the hill. The enemy's artillery ceased its fire and a horrible stillness pervaded the scene." Mixson noted the enemy was "moving on it at a double quick and a regular dress parade line." According to Walker, the regiments "continued pouring a destructive fire into the ranks of the enemy, at short range." Christ's men returned the fire, but Walker's men were protected by a stone fence.[86]

While Walker's men were able to keep Christ's men at bay, Welsh's brigade continued approaching and according to Walker, was "steadily driving back the brigades of Generals Kemper and Drayton" on Walker's right, forcing him to pull his troops back to form perpendicular to Harpers Ferry Road. They opened a destructive enfilade fire and helped drive back the enemy columns. The brigade than changed front again to face Antietam Creek at a right angle to the Lower Bridge Road, and threw out a line of skirmishers. A.P. Hill's division appeared by this time and Burnside's men were forced back toward the creek, thus ending the battle.[87]

The brigade held this position on September 18, burying the dead, caring for the wounded and maintaining a brisk fire with Burnside's troops. Walker received word from Jones to cover the division as it pulled back after dark and Walker held his position until the morning of September 19. The brigade was relieved by Fitz Lee's cavalry brigade and marched to the Potomac River, crossing a little after sunrise.[88]

The brigade lost an additional 216 (26 killed, 184 wounded, 6 missing) at Sharpsburg for a total of 248 for the campaign. Despite its small size, it fought well at South Mountain and again at Sharpsburg.[89]

**Bradley M. Gottfried**

* * *

## G.T. Anderson's Brigade: Colonel George T. Anderson

**Units:** 1st Georgia, 7th Georgia, 8th Georgia, 9th Georgia, 11th Georgia
**Strength:** 1,381[90]
**Losses:** 87 (8k-77w-2m)[91]

George T. ("G.T." or "Tige") Anderson's brigade was a veteran unit whose roots extended back to the First Battle of Bull Run, where the 7th and 8th Georgia served in Col. Francis Bartow's brigade. Brig. Gen. Samuel Jones assumed command of the brigade after the battle and the 9th and 11th Georgia were added. After a short stint under D.R. Jones, the brigade was assigned to Anderson. The brigade fought at Yorktown and Williamsburg and charged up Malvern Hill, but had better luck when it helped take on John Pope's army at the Battle of Second Bull Run.[92]

"Tige" (short for "tiger") Anderson was born in Georgia in 1824. He served in the War with Mexico and later commanded a company in the regular army. At the outbreak of the war Anderson was a wealthy landowner. Anderson began the war as colonel of the 11th Georgia, but took over the brigade just prior to the Seven Days Battles. A tough fighter, he was well liked by his men.[93]

The brigade, with the rest of the division, reached Leesburg on September 3 and was across the Potomac River three days later. Sgt. William Andrews recalled how the men stripped down prior to entering the four-foot deep water. "Don't think the picture would be suitable for the parlor," he later wrote. The men marched to the Monocacy River in Maryland where they rested. Many took baths in the river and Andrews recalled their ranks stretched for more than a mile in the water. Food remained an issue. One of Anderson's soldiers wrote home, "We had a hard time for provisions on the march; but the soldiers made the apples fly when passing orchards. Many times we were turned loose upon cornfields, where the cobs were left in heaps." The men reached Frederick and then marched to Hagerstown, arriving in the vicinity on September 12. The 11th Georgia was detailed as guard for D.H. Hill's commissary wagons being sent to safety in Martinsburg. It would miss the Battle of Fox's Gap and operate independently of the rest of the brigade at Sharpsburg.[94]

## South Mountain

D.R. Jones' men did not remain at Hagerstown for long, as James Longstreet was ordered back to Boonsboro on September 14 to help defend the South Mountain passes. "What a march we had, a great deal of time on the double-quick, the distance being about 25 miles," according to Andrews. The brigade, along with Thomas Drayton's, was at the van of the column when it arrived at Hill's headquarters at the Mountain House at about 3:30 p.m. Hill called the commanders of G.B. Anderson's, G.T. Anderson's, Drayton's, and Roswell Ripley's brigades together to explain his expectations. Because Hill commanded a wide front, he placed Ripley in charge of the four brigades and sent them south toward Fox's Gap. Upon arriving on the battlefield, G.T. Anderson dutifully led his brigade south on Old Sharpsburg

Road, following Ripley's. But Ripley marched the column too far down Old Sharpsburg Road, and a 300-yard gap opened between G.T. Anderson's and Drayton's brigades. When Ripley realized Drayton was under attack, he ordered Anderson into the woods in front of him, followed by a move by the left flank toward Drayton's beleaguered brigade, which was being attacked by overwhelming numbers of infantry from the Union IX Corps. Anderson threw out half of the 1st Georgia Regulars as skirmishers, but almost immediately learned that Drayton's right was turned and his front, left, and rear were in danger. Ripley's brigade was more than 400 yards away and could provide no assistance, so Anderson pulled his men back to Old Sharpsburg Road and changed front to the left. As he was about to order his men forward to assist Drayton, Anderson encountered John Hood's division, marching to the contested gap. Anderson noted in his report, "Not knowing where to find General Ripley or General Drayton, I reported to General Hood for instructions, and was requested by him to hold my position to protect his left flank," which he did as the sun was setting. The brigade's losses were slight—three wounded and four missing.[95]

## Antietam

G.T. Anderson's brigade remained attached to Hood's division and therefore formed part of the rearguard, leaving Fox's Gap at about 1:00 a.m. on September 15. It headed toward Boonsboro Pike using roads and cutting across farmers' fields. The brigade crossed Antietam Creek at the Middle Bridge and assumed a defensive position on Cemetery Hill on the east side of Sharpsburg, with its left anchored on Boonsboro Pike, supporting the Washington Artillery. Nathan Evans' brigade was on its left and Richard Garnett's was on its right. On September 17, Anderson reported receiving orders at 7:30 a.m. to support Hood. Anderson was given neither guide nor directions, but followed the sounds of fighting in the West Woods. He succeeded in finding Hood, who "pointed out the position he wished me to occupy."[96]

The men approached their designated position along the southwest corner of the West Woods, where they were fired upon by the 125th Pennsylvania's (Samuel Crawford's brigade; Alpheus Williams' division; XII Corps) skirmish line coming through the woods. Anderson ordered his brigade's sharpshooters forward by yelling, "Sharpshooters to the front." The rest of the brigade made its way to the fence at the southwest corner of the woods. The men tore down the fence to create a barricade as their sharpshooters continued advancing. Jubal Early's brigade appeared from the north and also fired into the rookie Pennsylvanians. Joseph Kershaw's brigade (Lafayette McLaws' division) came up behind the Georgians and pitched into the West Woods, driving the enemy before it. Anderson's men followed the Carolinians beyond the Dunker Church, moving by the left flank at the double-quick along a fence and helped seal the hole between the 2nd and 3rd South Carolina (Kershaw's brigade). According to historian Ezra Carman, Anderson's men pitched into John Sedgwick's division (II Corps), helping defeat the 34th New York (Willis Gorman's brigade) and the 72nd Pennsylvania (Oliver Howard's brigade). These regiments formed Sedgwick's first and third lines of his left flank. Andrews noted the ground was "covered in blue" as each man "killed a yankee [with] the first shot." Anderson merely reported, his men "engaged the enemy and drove them for about a half mile, my men and officers behaving in a most gallant manner." The men then rested in a cornfield south of the Dunker Church and west of Hagerstown Pike.[97]

An officer rode up to Anderson with news of Kershaw's repulse of his thrust out of the West Woods and informed him of the very real possibility of an enemy attack on his vulnerable right flank. Anderson pulled his brigade back toward its original position on the edge of the West Woods, but this time facing east. An aide to Longstreet ordered the men to move to a new position along the west side of Hagerstown Pike, just south of the Sunken Road.

Anderson explained how "the enemy opened an enfilade fire on my position with long-range artillery, and I was forced to change [position], moving down the road toward Sharpsburg under the crest of the hill."

The men spied an abandoned 6-pounder cannon, and with the help of Lt. William Chamberlaine of the 6th Virginia (Mahone's brigade), they repositioned the gun on a hill, about a hundred yards up Hagerstown Pike, and opened fire on Richardson's division. After a couple of shots, the men realized the position was too exposed, so they ran it down to the intersection with the Sunken Road and opened fire on the skirmishers from the 57th and 66th New York (Brooke's brigade; Richardson's division; II Corps) who were in the process of crossing the road and heading toward the Piper house. The fire had the desired effect, and the skirmishers fell back. The men again repositioned the gun further north on Hagerstown Pike to again fire on the rest of Brooke's brigade. According to Anderson, the men "served it most beautifully until the ammunition was exhausted."[98]

Some time between 2:00 and 3:00 p.m., D.H. Hill gathered remnants of Richard Anderson's division (probably Alfred Cumming's, Carnot Posey's, and Roger Pryor's), who had fought in the Sunken Road and placed them under G.T. Anderson's command. The brigade remained aligned parallel to Hagerstown Road until Hill ordered it to occupy a hill "to my right and rear." This was probably Reel Ridge. Anderson noted in his report "I moved to the position and sent forward skirmishers, but failed to find the enemy; and the enemy opening a cross-fire of artillery from the left on us . . ." Hill permitted Anderson to abandon the hill and was directed across the road to a new position along the Sunken Road where it intersects with Hagertsown Pike. The brigade was not here long before "General [D.H.] Hill, who, riding forward to the crest of the hill in our front, called my attention to a line of the enemy advancing apparently to attack us." This was the unsupported 7th Maine (William Irwin's brigade; William Smith's division; VI Corps) approaching the Piper farm. Anderson quickly

278

shifted his brigade's position so it faced northeast and noted in his report, "Suffering them to come near us, I ordered my command to charge them, which they did in splendid style and good order, killing and wounding many of the enemy, taking several prisoners, and routing the remainder." The beleaguered Union regiment was attacked on three sides and forced to beat a hasty retreat. Anderson ordered his men forward after the retreating Maine soldiers, but they "could not pursue them as far as I wished, because of the severe fire of artillery directed against us from long-range guns that we could not reach."[99]

While most of Tige Anderson's brigade fought north of Sharpsburg, two detachments were engaged elsewhere: a portion of the 11th Georgia fought further south with Robert Toombs' brigade and 85-100 men of the 1st Georgia Regulars under Capt. H.D. Twiggs, was sent out on picket duty between the town of Sharpsburg and Antietam Creek, just south of Boonsboro Pike. George B. Anderson's brigade straddled the pike east of Sharpsburg until about 9:00 a.m., when it was sent to the Sunken Road, leaving Twiggs' skirmish line as the first line of defense in this sector. A squadron of the 4th Pennsylvania Cavalry approached on Boonsboro Pike around noon. Twiggs selected 20 of his best marksmen and sent them forward to the pike, where they deployed behind stone walls on either side of it. They drove the troopers back, but a section of Capt. John Tidball's Union battery arrived. Twiggs responded by bringing up his entire command, deploying it behind the stone walls. The Georgians promptly shot a number of cannoneers, forcing the remainder to take cover. Its artillerymen inched forward to try to retrieve their abandoned cannon, but were driven back by Confederate artillery on Cemetery Hill dropping shells on them. The remainder of the 4th Pennsylvania Cavalry approached on the right of the pike, accompanied by the remaining two sections of Tidball's battery, but they too were hit by Twiggs' small arms fire and the massed Confederate artillery on Cemetery Hill.[100]

Twiggs' men kept the Union troops pinned down until Capt. Stephen Weed's battery across Antietam Creek enfiladed the Georgians' position and forced them from their protective stone walls. The men fell back to a small road trailing off from Boonsboro Pike and again opened fire. The 17th South Carolina and Holcombe Legion from Nathan Evans' brigade joined them on their left as additional Union artillery crossed Antietam Creek dropped trail west of it. V Corps division commander, George Sykes, ordered his 2nd and 10th United States Regular Infantry across Antietam Creek to drive Twiggs' men away and perhaps neutralize the Confederate artillery on Cemetery Hill. They were soon joined by the 4th United States Regulars and the 1st Battalion of the 14th United States Regulars. The Regulars totaled about 1,640 men—far more than the 200 men Twiggs and the Carolinians could muster. The small force assumed a defensive position behind stone walls and haystacks and continued battling the Regulars. The Regulars were finally pulled back across the Antietam Creek, but a skirmish line from the 79th New York (Benjamin Christ's brigade; Orlando Willcox's division; IX Corps) materialized in their front and right, tasked with attacking Lee's right flank. Twiggs' men retreated to a stone structure where they battled units of Thomas Welsh's brigade, also of Willcox's division. Twiggs was wounded and taken prisoner during this action.[101]

The 11th Georgia had been detached at Hagerstown on September 14 to guard D.H. Hill's commissary trains heading for Martinsburg, Virginia. Maj. F.H. Little split his regiment, sending half to Martinsburg to accompany the train; retaining the other half at Shepherdstown. The regiment was recalled on the night of September 16. Little waited for the half of his regiment to arrive from Martinsburg, but when it did not appear, he made his way to the battlefield at 8:00 a.m. on September 17. Upon arriving on the battlefield, one of D.R. Jones' aides guided the five companies to the right, where they assumed a strong position behind a stone wall on the right of Toombs' 15th Georgia and 17th Georgia. The latter regiments had also only recently arrived on the battlefield. It was about 1:00 p.m. and the IX Corps was now crossing Antietam Creek.[102]

The 48th Pennsylvania (James Nagle's brigade; Daniel Sturgis' division; IX Corps) crossed Antietam Creek and appeared in Little's front. Little noted in his report, "Our skirmishers were run in; the enemy's skirmishers advanced to within about 125 yards of us; a full line of battle was drawn up in their rear. We quietly awaited their advance, but the efforts of their officers to move them forward were unavailing. We did not fire upon them until they began to fall back, and then a portion of the men fired with great coolness and precision, evidently doing execution." A.P. Hill's men arrived about 4:00 p.m., and the 11th Georgia moved north and assisted in defeating the 8th Connecticut, which was driving toward David McIntosh's battery. Little explained what happened next: "We moved up in double-quick, fronted the enemy, who were moving forward in handsome style without opposition, our opposing troops having retired. Our arrival was just in time to save one of our batteries, name not known. We immediately opened upon them a well-directed fire, which the enemy stoutly resisted for awhile, but soon broke and fled. General Toombs immediately gave the order to charge, which the men, with loud and long-continued cheers, as promptly obeyed, continuing the chase until ordered by General Toombs to halt." A soldier wrote home how the Connecticut soldiers "stood and fought us very bravely for awhile. We were sheltered by a fence and embankment, so much so that we mowed them down, and they scarcely harmed us."[103]

The battle was now over for Tige Anderson's brigade. It fought well in all of its actions at Fox's Gap and again in several Antietam sectors. It lost only seven men at Fox's Gap, and another 87 (8 killed, 77 wounded, 2 missing) at Antietam.[104]

**Bradley M. Gottfried**

* * *

# WALKER'S DIVISION—

## Brigadier General John G. Walker

John G. Walker was born in Missouri on July 22, 1822 and was educated at the Jesuit College in St. Louis. He entered the army in 1846, fought in the Mexican War, and remained in the army until his resignation to go south on July 31, 1861. He initially served as a captain in the 8th Texas Cavalry (better known as Terry's Texas Rangers) and was subsequently elected its lieutenant colonel.[1]

Walker received his star in January 1862, and a brigade in the Department of North Carolina. The brigade was sent to Drewry's Bluff, Virginia during the first days of June where it kept watch on the Union navy operating on the James River. The unit was part of Brig. Gen. Theophilus Holmes' division, which was lightly engaged at the Battle of Malvern Hill, but suffered under the combined bombardment of the Union field artillery as well as the big guns of the Union navy. Walker himself met with an unspecified, "painful accident," on July 1 that forced him to relinquish command, as the brigade returned to Drewry's Bluff on July 3, 1862.[2]

Walker apparently recovered from his injury by August and received command of Holmes' division when the latter was given command of the Trans-Mississippi Department. The division remained near Richmond after the Seven Days battles, so it missed the Second Bull Run Campaign. It was ordered north to join Lee's army at Leesburg, but with only two brigades (Walker's own, now under Col. Vannoy Manning of the 3rd Arkansas, and Brig. Gen. Robert Ransom Jr.'s); Brig. Gen. Junius Daniel's brigade was detached and left behind to guard Richmond. Walker and his diminished command reached Leesburg, Virginia on September 6 at the start of the Maryland Campaign.[3]

Walker's men crossed the Potomac River into Maryland on September 7 at Cheek's Ford, approximately three miles above White's Ford and went into camp near Buckeystown, Maryland that night. Walker pressed on to Monocacy Junction the next day and reported to General Lee. The division was ordered back to the Potomac River on September 9 to destroy the Monocacy Aqueduct of the Chesapeake & Ohio Canal at the mouth of the Monocacy River.[4]

Walker reached the aqueduct by 11:00 p.m. that night, where some of his men skirmished with an enemy cavalry detachment guarding it. In his official report, Walker stated that following the skirmish, "Working parties were at once detailed, and set to work to drill holes for blowing up the arches, but, after several hours labor, it was apparent that, owing to the insufficiency of our tools and the extraordinary solidity and massiveness of the masonry, the work we had undertaken was one of days instead of hours." Walker did not have days however, so he prepared to withdraw from the aqueduct at 4:00 a.m. on September 10, unable to accomplish his mission to break the Chesapeake & Ohio Canal.[5]

With orders to rejoin General Lee by way of Jefferson and Middletown, Maryland, Walker marched his command towards Adamstown, Maryland, where he received his copy of Special Orders 191 early on September 10. The orders referenced Walker's command in Part Six of the document: "General Walker, with his division, after accomplishing the object in which he is now engaged, will cross the Potomac at Cheek's Ford, ascend its right bank to Lovettsville, take possession of Loudoun Heights, if practicable, by Friday morning, Key's Ford on his left, and the road between the end of the mountain and the Potomac on his right. He will, as far as practicable, cooperate with General McLaws and Jackson, and intercept retreat of the enemy."[6]

Walker knew the Cheek's Ford crossing would be risky because of the apparent approach of Federal forces from Poolesville, Maryland. Walker chose to instead ford at Point of Rocks, Maryland. According to Walker, his crossing was "effected during the night of the 10th and by daylight on the 11th, but with much difficulty, owing to the destruction of the bridge over the canal and the steepness of the banks of the Potomac." The division rested after the crossing on September 11, and then moved to Hillsborough, Virginia the next morning. Walker guided his division on a less direct route, using a better road, arching north from Hillsborough on Harpers Ferry Road. The lead elements of Walker's division occupied Loudoun Heights on the morning of September 13, 1862.[7]

On the morning of September 14, Walker ordered, "three Parrott guns and two rifled pieces" placed on Loudoun Heights. As the battery was being established, the Confederate signal corps got to work around 8:00 a.m., trying to open communication with Thomas Jackson's command on Schoolhouse Ridge. The wigwagging of the signal flags drew the attention of Battery A, 5th New York Artillery, whose shells sent the signalmen scampering back into woods.[8]

Walker's signal station reported his guns were in position at 10:30 a.m., and requested permission to open fire. Jackson wished to coordinate a simultaneous artillery bombardment from Loudoun, Maryland Heights, and Schoolhouse Ridge, so he ordered Walker to wait as communications from Maj. Gen. Lafayette McLaws' forces on Maryland Heights had yet to be established. When McLaws reported firing in his rear, likely the struggle for the South Mountain gaps, around noon, Walker again requested permission to open fire, but was again denied. By 12:30 p.m., Walker heard distant artillery fire and reported his concerns of a potential Federal advance in his own rear from Purcellville, Virginia. Though Jackson's original instructions stated, "I do not desire any of the batteries to open until all are ready on both sides of the river," they also contained the caveat, "except you should find it necessary, of which you must judge for yourself."[9]

Watching the Confederate artillery on Loudoun Heights, including the frequent communications of the signal corps, the Federal artillery on Camp Hill within Harpers Ferry opened fire. This fire, along with perceived threats to the Confederate rear, spurred Walker to act on his own discretion. He wrote, "About 1 p.m. I therefore gave orders to open fire upon the enemy's batteries and the troops upon Bolivar Heights." Shortly thereafter, Jackson's own batteries opened fire and about an hour later, the four guns McLaws had manhandled to the top of Maryland Heights, joined in. Walker described how the Confederate guns were, "served admirably and with great rapidity." This duel however was not without cost, as several of his officers and men were killed or wounded.[10]

Walker's cannonade did more than demoralize the Federal garrison, it also helped cover Maj. Gen. Ambrose Hill's division's flanking movements against the strong Union position on Bolivar Heights during the afternoon of September 14. Additional Confederate artillery, ten pieces in all, were sent across the Shenandoah River to the base of Loudoun Heights that night, causing Hill to quip, "the fate of Harpers Ferry was sealed."[11]

The Federal garrison opened fire around 6:00 a.m. on September 15, 1862. Walker's artillery did not respond until 8:00 a.m. due to a heavy mist, and then continued firing for about an hour. The firing became more intermittent until, "about 9:30 o'clock we observed a white flag displayed from a large brick building in the upper town, when our batteries immediately ceased their fire . . . after a short time we had the extreme satisfaction to see the head of Maj. Gen. A.P. Hill's column approaching the town along the Charlestown turnpike."[12]

Walker's division remained on Loudoun Heights for part of September 15, 1862, and then marched north that evening, crossing the Shenandoah River later that night. The command continued its march at 1:00 a.m. the following night, reaching Shepherdstown, Virginia by 1:00 a.m. on September 17. After crossing the river, the division pushed on through town to reunite with the rest of the army around Sharpsburg, Maryland.[13]

Walker's division, led by Ransom's brigade, was ordered to the extreme right of the Confederate line, about a mile and a half south of Sharpsburg, at around 3:00 a.m. on September 17. Walker reported his line extended "from a wood on the right to a group of barns, stables, and outhouses on the left, in such way as to cover the ford over the Antietam Creek and to be within supporting distance of the command of Brigadier-General Toombs . . ." The division covered Snavely's Ford that morning, south of the Lower Bridge, its batteries placed on the heights northwest of the creek to cover the roads from the east, and a battalion of sharpshooters was posted along the wooded banks of Antietam Creek. Walker wrote proudly, "While we were in this position, the enemy made no attempt to cross the stream."[14]

As dawn broke over western Maryland, the roar of battle had been building for almost half an hour. Walker's division waited for three hours. He later wrote, "the only evidence of his [the enemy] being in our front was his artillery fire at long range . . . about half a mile to my left." This reprieve was not to last, for at about 9:00 a.m., the division was ordered to the left of the line, where Jackson's wing was heavily engaged.[15]

As the division pushed north, passing through Sharpsburg, the sounds of battle became increasingly distinct. A half mile north of Sharpsburg, Walker divided his division. While Manning deployed his brigade in a line of battle and advanced northeast into the West Woods to support the brigades of George T. Anderson and Joseph Kershaw, Ransom's brigade headed directly north towards the break in the line caused by the advance of John Sedgwick's division (II Corps). Ransom's brigade was ordered to change front to the right by regiments and advance into the West Woods. They re-established the Confederate line sometime after 10:00 a.m. as McLaws' division drove the outflanked Federals north. Ransom's men subsequently succeeded in repulsing the 2nd Massachusetts and 13th New Jersey (George Gordon's brigade; Alpheus Williams' division, XII Corps) as they advanced across the open fields east of the West Woods. Ransom's men then settled down along the edge of the woods behind a limestone outcropping.[16]

Manning's brigade was involved in two bloody repulses during the day. As it initially approached the West Woods, two of its regiments, the 3rd Arkansas and 27th North Carolina, were detached to plug a gap in the line between the Sunken Road and the West Woods. The remainder of the brigade continued into the West

Woods, forming on the right of Ransom's brigade. Seeing enemy troops on a hill in front of him (on the ground now occupied by the Maryland monument), Manning ordered a charge of the 46th North Carolina, 48th North Carolina, and 30th Virginia. The commander of the former regiment, realizing the folly of the endeavor, ordered his men to remain behind an improvised barricade, while the other two regiments charged the hill, only to be devastated by artillery and small arms fire from Greene's division and several nearby batteries. The two regiments lost over half their men in this charge.[17]

Greene's men advanced into the West Woods in pursuit of Manning's men and several of its regiments held the woods by 11:00 a.m. The Federal presence around the Dunker Church drew the attention of Ransom's brigade. Around noon, Ransom's men attacked and succeeded in driving back Greene's men, recapturing the area of the Dunker Church for the last time. Riding this success, the 27th North Carolina and 3rd Arkansas were ordered to attack the exposed Federal flank near the Sunken Road. This attack was bloodily repulsed around 1:00 p.m. By the end of the day, Walker's division had suffered over 1,100 casualties. However, throughout the campaign its hard marching and fighting helped to force the capitulation of Harpers Ferry and stabilized the Confederate line at a desperate moment of the Maryland Campaign.[18]
**Matthew Borders**

✳ ✳ ✳

## Walker's Brigade: Colonel Vannoy Hartrog Manning

**Units:** 3rd Arkansas, 27th North Carolina, 46th North Carolina, 48th North Carolina, 30th Virginia
**Strength:** 2,959[19]
**Losses:** 917 (140k – 684w – 93m)[20]

At the start of the 1862 Maryland Campaign, Robert E. Lee had been in command of the army for a little over three months. According to Antietam scholar, Joseph Harsh, he had not yet determined how he was going to organize his army. In the fall of 1862, he had two commands, Longstreet's, and Jackson's, as well as four independent divisions that, for the most part, answered directly to Lee. Brig. Gen. John George Walker led one of these commands. It was a small division of two brigades, one of which was Walker's brigade, commanded by Col. Vannoy Hartrog Manning.[21]

Colonel Van Manning was born on July 26, 1831, in Wake County, North Carolina. His family moved when Manning was quite young to Mississippi. Following his schooling at the University of Nashville where he studied law, he settled down in Arkansas. After the war started, Manning and a good friend, Dr. W.H. Tebbs, recruited and raised the 3rd Arkansas Infantry with all of the men hailing from Arkansas, except one company comprised of troops from both Tennessee and Kentucky.[22]

Manning started his military career as a captain in the 3rd Arkansas. After it organization was completed, the regiment marched to Vicksburg, Mississippi with the thought of joining other Confederate forces in the area. However, upon their arrival, the men were turned away. The war would be short, was the prevailing thought, and there were already enough men to finish the fight. This answer was not acceptable to Manning and Tebbs and so they enlisted the help of a politician friend, Albert Rust.

Rust was promoted to the rank of colonel and the regiment was welcomed into the army and promptly sent to Lynchburg, Virginia for training. Manning was promoted to major in July 1861 and to colonel on March 11, 1862 after Rust was made a brigadier general. The 3rd Arkansas was the only regiment from the state to fight in Army of Northern Virginia. It saw action in every major battle of the war. Manning was wounded at Antietam, Gettysburg, and Wilderness. He was captured during the latter battle and remained a prisoner until July 24, 1865.[23]

Manning rose to command one of Walker's brigades during the Maryland Campaign, which included the 3rd Arkansas, 27th North Carolina, 46th North Carolina, 48th North Carolina, and the 30th Virginia. Manning's brigade, and the other brigade in Walker's division, Brig. Gen. Robert Ransom's Jr., were fortunate enough to be among the few Confederates put on trains from Richmond to join Lee's Army around Manassas following the Battle of Second Bull Run.

Walker's division was the last to cross the Potomac River into Maryland on September 7. One of the soldiers from North Carolina remarked on the memorable event, "Passed the Potomac River . . . very shallow to about knees, or half thigh deep, the infantry stripped off pants, drawers, shoes and stockings and the sight was comical to see the boys wading like cranes over the rocky ford and cringing as their tender fee struck the rocky bottom . . . our bands played 'Dixie and Maryland' as we arrived on the shores of the U.S."[24]

When Lee issued Special Orders Number 191, which divided his army across the Maryland countryside, Walker's division was tasked with assisting in the siege of the Federal garrison at Harper's Ferry. His task was to move his men to Loudoun Heights to assist in encircling the garrison from the Virginia high ground looking down into the town.[25]

## Harpers Ferry

The division set out from the area around Frederick, Maryland on September 10 and reached its designated Potomac River crossing point at around 10:00 a.m. Upon reaching this point, however, the men encountered Federal artillery and cavalry guarding the crossing. This forced Walker to march to another crossing at Point of Rocks, Maryland, but it was a difficult journey. It was well after dark, there was no bridge, and the banks of the river were quite steep. To make matters worse, it was raining.[26]

A welcome rest day greeted the men on September 11, and they were again on the move toward their objective by the next day. Finally, on September 13, at approximately 10:00 a.m., Walker's division, including Manning's brigade, reached the base of Loudoun Heights. Col. John R. Cooke was placed in charge of a two-regiment detachment comprised of the 27th North Carolina and the 30th Virginia tasked with occupying and holding the top of Loudoun Heights. They held this position throughout the night, while the rest of the division guarded the banks of the river to block any escape attempt by the Federal garrison.

A member of the 27th North Carolina recalled of the siege, "As soon as we gained our position, which was accomplished by a circuitous route up the steep and ragged mountain, the enemy in and around Harper's Ferry, opened fire upon us from their batteries. Owing to the extreme elevation, most of their shells fell short; a few burst over us, but did no damage." According to Walker's report, there were four total casualties for the brigade and French's battery which was posted on the heights, during this operation. Following the surrender of the garrison, Walker's division made its way toward Sharpsburg.[27]

## Antietam

Throughout the night of September 15 and early morning hours of the 16th, Manning's brigade marched from Loudoun Heights to rejoin the Army of Northern Virginia at Sharpsburg. The division was forced to recross the Potomac River again and this time it was a little more problematic. "We crossed the Potomac at Shepherdstown, where the water was swift and deep. One man drowned, and several others were swept off their feet," a soldier from the 30th Virginia recalled. The brigade eventually posted up just west of Sharpsburg by approximately 3:00 p.m. on September 16.[28]

The brigade stayed in this area with Ransom's brigade until summoned to the far-right end of Lee's line to guard Snavely's Ford. Walker received this order at roughly 3:00 a.m. on the morning of

September 17. When the battle started, this end of the line was relatively quiet, and due to the heavy engagement on the opposite end of the line, Lee made the decision to move Walker's division north in an attempt to bolster his left flank. There was a lull in the battle at the time Walker received his order. The fighting for control of the Cornfield and East Woods had simmered down and the Federal II Corps was about to arrive on the field. Walker's division shift north began at 9:00 a.m. and within the hour, elements of Manning's brigade were engaged.

In moving from the fields south of Sharpsburg toward the faltering left flank, Walker was ordered by Thomas Jackson to leave a small force between the area of the Sunken Road and West Woods thus connecting the two parts of Lee's forces. Walker selected the 3rd Arkansas and 27th North Carolina for this duty and Col. Cooke was placed in command of this detachment. The remaining three regiments of Manning's brigade continued northward and entered the southwest corner of the West Woods, shortly after Federal troops from Sedgwick's division had been routed from the woodlot.[29]

Upon entering the woods and swinging north and east, Manning and his three regiments moved in on the left of Kershaw's brigade, which was reforming in the woods, south of the Dunker Church. At approximately 9:30 a.m., Kershaw moved out of the woods, heading east across Hagerstown Pike to attack John Tompkins' six-gun battery. After quickly falling back toward the shelter of the woods following a brief engagement with Federal infantry and the right half of the battery, Manning's three regiments attacked in the same fashion as Kershaw's troops.

Capt. Benjamin Rawlings of the 30th Virginia remembered the advance, "We charged on the double-quick over fences, keeping our line as well as we could. As we got within sixty or seventy yards of the top of the hill, the enemy line that had been lying down raised up and fired point blank at us . . . Our Colonel gave orders to retreat to prevent all of us from being killed." The men Rawlings referenced

where part of George Greene's division (XII Corps).[30]

Manning's brigade moved out of the woods, with the right regiment, 48th North Carolina, splitting into two parts to move past the Dunker Church. The 30th Virginia in the middle of the line crossed the pike where Smoketown Road branches off toward the East Woods. The 46th North Carolina advanced out of the woods and crossed Hagerstown Pike, moving in a southeastern direction, but they were unable to lend support to the other two regiments and didn't make it across the Smoketown Road due to the heavy fire from Hector Tyndale's brigade (Greene's division; XII Corps).

Rawlings wrote of his narrow escape, "I could see a part of a rail fence about thirty yards ahead and was making good time toward it, humped up to expose no more of my body than necessary. I picked out a place on the top rail to spring over, but in this place about twenty bullets had struck the rail . . . I thought that if I went over there, the enemy would get me on the wing, so I moved a little to the right, where there was a break in the fence." Manning's three regiments were engaged for a short period, not more than 30 minutes, against Greene's division, and they suffered severely, losing 387 out of 1503. Many of the casualties were in the 48th North Carolina and the 30th Virginia. The battle flag of the 30th Virginia had a corner shot off and was riddled with 15 bullet holes.[31]

While all the action around Hagerstown Pike and Dunker Church unfolded, the 3rd Arkansas and 27th North Carolina held their ground, continuing to provide a connection to Jackson's men on the north end of the field and Longstreet's troops covering the south end. It wasn't long before these two regiments became engaged and gained some revenge for their comrades.

Greene's troops, who followed the retreating three regiments from Manning's brigade into the West Woods, took up a new position around the church. The left of the Federal line sat on Hagerstown Pike about 200 yards south of the Dunker Church. It ran along the south edge of the woods for about 200 yards and then bent at a right angle and continued north with the end of the line roughly even with the church, about 175 yards in the woods. Adding strength to the left of the line, the Federals pushed one cannon into the woods, in an attempt to silence Cooke's regiments who were skirmishing with troops from Stainrook's brigade (Greene's division).

Shortly after the Confederate line in the Sunken Road broke, James Longstreet ordered Cooke's two regiments, the 3rd Arkansas and 27th North Carolina to charge. His thinking was twofold. First, drive Greene's men from the woods and second, relieve some of the pressure on Lee's center due to the Federal breakthrough at the Sunken Road. A member of the 27th North Carolina remembered, ". . . the enemy attempted to sneak up a section of artillery to the little woods upon our left. Colonel Cooke, watching the movement, ordered the four left companies of the regiment up to the fence and directed them to fire upon this artillery. At the first fire, before they had gotten into position, nearly every horse and more than half the men fell . . . the infantry line …showed evident signs of wavering."[32]

As Cooke's regiments hit Greene's left flank, another attack hit the right flank. A scattering of troops from the 46th North Carolina and 30th Virginia and Ransom's brigade rushed forward, and these simultaneous attacks drove Greene from the West Woods. The attack that hit the right didn't pursue much beyond Hagerstown Pike, but Cooke's detachment followed the Federals across the pike. The Confederates continued east over the ridge where Manning's three regiments attacked a few hours before. They continued down the hill over the Mumma Farm Lane and into Mumma's cornfield.

A soldier in this advance recalled, "After pushing on this way for a while we found ourselves opposed by a large body of troops behind a stone wall in a corn-field. Stopping to contend with these, we found that we were almost out of ammunition. Owing to this fact, and not being supported in our charge, we were ordered to fall back to our original position." The troops the Confederates ran into were men from Nathan Kimball's brigade (French's division; II Corps) who after breaking through the Confederate line in the Sunken Road, were pulled back to a position along the Roulette Farm Lane to meet Cooke's advance. The 3rd Arkansas lost 217 men and the 27th North Carolina left 150 casualties on the field.[33]

Following the brigade's action around the Dunker Church and West Woods, the regiments were reunited and held the southwest corner of the woods for the remainder of the day. Later in the day when Lee attempted to test the Federal right flank, the 48th North Carolina was sent to assist the artillery. This mission turned out poorly for the Confederates and the 48th was back with its brigade by nightfall.

Following his release from prison after the war, Van Manning was elected to U.S. Congress three times and in 1883 returned to practicing law in Washington D.C. He died in Branchville, Maryland on November 3, 1892 and was buried in Glenwood Cemetery, Washington D.C.[34]

**Brian S. Baracz**

### Ransom's Brigade: Brigadier General Robert Ransom, Jr.

**Units:** 24th North Carolina, 25th North Carolina, 35th North Carolina, 49th North Carolina, Branch's Petersburg (VA) Artillery, 46th North Carolina (attached during Battle of Antietam)
**Strength:** 2,018[35]
**Losses:** 186 (41-141-4)[36]

Brigadier General Robert Ransom's North Carolina brigade was a new addition to the Army of Northern Virginia. It was organized on April 9, 1862, following the Confederate disaster on the Outer Banks that winter. Though the 24th and 25th North Carolina served the Confederacy since the summer of 1861, and the 35th North Carolina since November 1861, the 49th North Carolina was not formed until the winter of 1862. The new brigade's 26th and 35th North Carolina had already received their baptism of fire at the Battle of New Bern, North Carolina on March 14, 1862. The entire brigade first saw action during the opening skirmishes of the Seven Days and at the Battle of Malvern Hill on July 1, 1862. The brigade suffered heavy losses during the latter battle when it charged Federal artillery positioned on the heights. Prior to the assault General Ransom inspired his men, by telling them to wait to open fire until they could, "see the whites of their eyes, and d—n it, give it to them."[37]

Robert Ransom, Jr. was born in Warren County, North Carolina on February 12, 1828. After his graduation from West Point in 1850, he was assigned to the cavalry and eventually rose to the rank of captain in the 2nd Dragoons. He resigned his commission at the outbreak of war and joined the Confederate army as captain in the Regular Army. He was then commissioned colonel of the 1st North Carolina Cavalry, later known as the 9th North Carolina Volunteers. Ransom received his brigadier general wreath in March 1862, and was sent to Kinston, North Carolina, following the fall of New Bern. Ransom received command of the brigade while there. It would bear both his and his brother's surname, until the end of the war.[38]

Following the bloodletting on the Peninsula, Ransom's North Carolina brigade was ordered into the defenses of the capital and did not participate in the Second Bull Run Campaign. It instead built fortifications around Richmond and Petersburg. The regiments suffered significantly from sickness in the ranks and the 26th North Carolina was transferred from the brigade on August 26, 1862.[39]

Ransom's brigade was ordered north to join the Army of Northern Virginia on August 27, 1862, and reached it at Leesburg, Virginia, on the evening of September 6. The brigade was assigned to John Walker's division, whose old brigade, now commanded by Vannoy Manning, made up the other half of the division.[40]

Crossing the Potomac River on September 7 at Cheek's Ford, approximately three miles above White's Ford, Capt. William Burgwyn of the 35th North Carolina later noted how the river was "a quarter of a mile wide and waist deep." As the men reached the Maryland shore, "they gave the 'rebel yell'." The brigade, with the rest of the division, headed to Monocacy Aqueduct where elements of the 24th North Carolina engaged in a slight skirmish with what was likely a detachment of the 1st Massachusetts Cavalry guarding the aqueduct. The regiment lost an officer and several of its men—the brigade's first casualties of the Maryland Campaign.[41]

### Harpers Ferry

The division then marched toward Loudoun Heights to assist in reducing Harpers Ferry, but did little. Branch's battery was ordered to the heights on the morning of September 14 and shelled the town the following day. The Union artillery opened fire, wounding several cannoneers. The Union garrison surrendered at 9:30 a.m. on September 15.[42]

## Antietam

Walker's division remained on Loudoun Heights and apparently did not participate in the revelry or resupply that occurred in a portion of Stonewall Jackson's command following the fall of Harpers Ferry. The division began its march north on the evening of September 15 and crossed over the Blue Ridge Mountains and Shenandoah River, and continued its trek all night. The command reached Shepherdstown, Virginia by the morning of September 16, pushing on through the town and over the Potomac River once more. Captain William Burgwyn of the 35th North Carolina recalled the regiment was, "wading the Potomac for the third time within nine days." Shortly thereafter, Walker's brigades reunited with Robert E. Lee's forces taking position around Sharpsburg, Maryland on September 16.[43]

Ransom's brigade led Walker's division to the extreme right of the Confederate line, about a mile and a half south of Sharpsburg, around 3:00 a.m. on September 17. It remained here for about six hours, when the division was called north to reinforce Stonewall Jackson's men near the Dunker Church. Ransom again led the column's movement, with the 49th North Carolina at the head of the brigade. The men marched through Sharpsburg as the sounds of battle swelled ahead of them. According to Judge Walter Clark, then a 16 year old adjutant in the 35th North Carolina, "All this time there was the steady booming of the cannon, the whistling of shells, the pattering of fire-arms, and the occasional yell or cheer rising above the roar of battle as some advantage was gained by either side." When Ransom's men marched about half a mile north of Sharpsburg, they were told to drop their packs and form in line of battle. The line was deployed under a severe artillery fire and continued north along Hauser's Ridge until it was west of the West Woods. John Sedgwick's division had succeeded in penetrating the Confederate line in the West Woods, so Ransom's brigade was ordered to change front to the right by regiments. This maneuver was accomplished by the majority of the brigade; the

49th North Carolina leading off and the 35th and 25th North Carolina following suit.[44]

In its enthusiasm, the 24th North Carolina did not swing to the right, but continued north, came in contact with the enemy, and opened fire. Although many North Carolinians claimed Ransom's brigade drove out the remains of Willis Gorman's Federal brigade from the West Woods, this seems unlikely. Ransom's brigade did not arrive until almost 9:30 a.m. and Gorman, along with the rest of Sedgewick's division, was already being driven back by Lafayette McLaws' division and Jubal Early's brigade. The 24th North Carolina may have engaged some of Sedgwick's fleeing soldiers heading north. Ransom noted in his after-action report how the 24th North Carolina proceeded north and attached itself to the left flank of William Barksdale's Mississippi brigade. In actuality, the regiment was attached to the right of Paul Semmes' brigade, which pursued the retreating federal troops northward to a stone fence in the vicinity of the D.R. Miller home. There, the 24th North Carolina helped repulse Marsena Patrick's brigade trying to cover Sedgewick's retreating troops. Ransom headed north to collect his wayward regiment and may have witnessed its charge against the Federal troops near the fence. Cpl. William Rose claimed Jeb Stuart and Ransom observed the charge and, "General Stuart remarked to General Ransom that every soldier in that command was worthy to be made a commander. Ransom replied, 'God bless the gallant boys, I will never curse them any more'." The 24th North Carolina remained detached from Ransom's brigade for the rest of the day, helping to protect the Confederate positions on Nicodemus Heights, where the batteries of Branch and French were sent. The regiment suffered a severe shelling late in the day and was withdrawn 500 yards to the rear at nightfall to rejoin the rest of Ransom's brigade.[45]

While the 24th North Carolina charged north, the rest of Ransom's brigade became engaged with Federal troops sent double-quicking west across the open fields south of the infamous Bloody Cornfield. The 2nd Massachusetts and 13th New Jersey

(George Gordon's brigade; Alpheus Williams' division; XII Corps) were sent to aid Sedgewick's division in the West Woods, or at least help cover its retreat. With Federal troops fleeing north, these reinforcements were now dangerously exposed. As the two regiments approached the fences paralleling Hagerstown Pike, Ransom's regiments lined the eastern edge of the West Woods, about 100 yards from the road, well positioned behind a rock ledge. The Tar Heels opened what their commander called, a "crushing fire," upon the approaching Union troops that drove them back. Ransom left to find the wayward 24th North Carolina after this action, leaving his brother, Col. Matt Ransom, in charge of the brigade.[46]

During the brigadier's absence, Ransom's brigade was subjected to a tremendous artillery barrage for about thirty minutes, prior to another enemy advance around 10:30 a.m. This advance was likely made by the Purnell Legion (Marylanders), who were on the right flank of George Greene's division's advance into the West Woods, just south of Ransom's position near the Dunker Church. Ransom's men had the advantage of the West Woods, the rock ledge and the undulating ground, with its numerous dips and ravines. The Confederates were unnoticed as Greene's men entered the West Woods. Greene's advance was backed by Federal cannon on rising ground east of Dunker Church and two guns of Capt. Joseph Knap's Pennsylvania artillery. One of these pieces advanced into the West Woods around noon, and Col. Ransom wanted that cannon.[47]

The 49th North Carolina, the right most regiment in the brigade line, was ordered to file down a ravine, change front to face south, and charge towards the Dunker Church. The 35th and 25th North Carolina regiments were to follow. This movement allowed Ransom's brigade to advance upon the Purnell Legion's right flank, almost unseen. However the presence of the Federals seems to have surprised Ransom's men as well. Both sides did not initially fire in the gloom and smoke of the West Woods, but sent officers forward to ascertain who was moving in their front.

This confusion ended when the 49th North Carolina, still trying to change its front, opened upon the Federals, pouring two volleys into their ranks and charging directly into the Purnell Legion's flank, which quickly gave way. Ransom's brigade was aided in this attack by the 46th North Carolina, which had become separated from Manning's brigade. The attack on Greene's right was supported by a Confederate effort led by Colonel John Cooke with the 27th North Carolina and the 3rd Arkansas infantries on Greene's left as well. This drove the Federal troops out of the West Woods and back to the rising ground east of Dunker Church. Ransom's brigade pursued the Federals to the post and rail fences along Hagerstown Pike. The attack also helped overwhelm McGill's guns near the Dunker Church, forcing one to be abandoned as the other cannon and caissons retreated down the Smoketown Road, back toward the Federal lines in the East Woods. McGill's lost piece was the only Federal cannon captured by Confederate forces during the battle. The presence of reforming Federals on the ridge to the east, as well as the massed Union batteries on the edge of the East Woods convinced those few North Carolinians that tried to pursue the Federals further, to break off.[48]

The fighting around Dunker Church was the last attempt by McClellan's troops to clear the West Woods. Throughout the rest of the day, Ransom's brigade held its position in the West Woods, being intermittently shelled by Federal guns near the East Woods, or across Antietam Creek. Gen. Ransom was called upon, at least twice, to take the battery in his front by storm. These were either the guns of Battery G, 1st Rhode Island Artillery, or the massed Federal guns along the East Woods, but the orders were rescinded. Late in the day, word spread to be prepared to advance when Jackson's guns were heard striking the Union right, but again this did not occur, and the North Carolinians remained where they were. The brigade withdrew further back from front late in the day.

The brigade suffered one last tragedy before the terrible day was over. According to Thomas Roulhac of the 49th North Carolina, "here the gallant Lieutenant Greenlea Flemming . . . was killed, and a dozen men of his company were killed or wounded by a shell which fell in its ranks as the brigade was moving by the flank to change its position just before sunset." Roulhac believed the shell, fired from across Antietam Creek, was directed by the Union Signal Corps, attracted by the "moving line of bayonets, glistening in the setting sunlight."[49]

Ransom's brigade returned to its position in the West Woods on September 18th and remained there throughout the day. Capt. Burgwyn recalled that night "we were again on the march, with orders to follow our file leader and ask no questions; daylight the next morning finding us once again across the Potomac near Shepherdstown." Ransom's brigade marched to Martinsburg, Virginia and then pressed on to Winchester, where it went into camp for ten days, when the men could finally rest and recuperate.[50]

Ransom's brigade sustained almost 200 casualties during the Maryland Campaign. The vast majority occurred at the Battle of Antietam. Ransom's, and later his brother's, use of the terrain in the West Woods provided excellent protection from both infantry and artillery fire over the course of the battle. The brigade was praised for its stubborn defense of the West Woods in division commander, John Walker's after-action report: "To Brigadier-General Ransom's coolness, judgment and skill we are in a great degree indebted for the successful maintenance of our position on the left, which, to have been permanently gained by the enemy, would, in all probability, have been to us the loss of the battle."[51]

**Matthew Borders**

\* \* \*

# HOOD'S DIVISION—

## Major General John B. Hood

John Bell Hood has become synonymous with aggressiveness and, at times, recklessness. The Kentuckian was born in 1831 and graduated from West Point in 1853. He narrowly escaped expulsion with 196 of 200 permissible demerits. Commandant Robert E. Lee likely inspired Hood's turnabout and successful completion of his studies. These two officers later served together in the United States Army in Texas and in the Confederate army through the middle of the Civil War.[1]

Hood resigned his commission in the United States Army after the outbreak of the Civil War and was commissioned a captain in the Confederacy, commanding cavalry under Brig. Gen. J.B. Magruder on the Virginia Peninsula, where he established an early reputation as an aggressive commander who was not shy about personally leading his troops into battle. Within a short period, he climbed through the ranks and eventually became colonel and commander of the 4th Texas Volunteers in September 1861. Hood became commander of the Texas Brigade on March 12, 1862, and was promoted to brigadier general in May 1862.[2]

Hood led the Texas Brigade through a number of crucial battles in the Peninsula Campaign where the unit soon gained its fabled reputation. Two months after his promotion to brigadier general, he was given command of a division. In addition to the Texas Brigade, now under the command of Col. William Wofford of the 18th Georgia, the division also included Col. Evander Law's brigade and Maj. Bushrod W. Frobel's artillery command. The division was part of Maj. Gen. James Longstreet's wing and fought in the Battles of West Point (Eltham's Landing), Seven Pines, Gaines' Mill, Malvern Hill, and Second Bull Run.[3]

During the Second Bull Run Campaign, Hood's division delivered a devastating blow to the left flank of Union Army of Virginia, leaving it in shambles and leading to its rapid retreat back across the Potomac River.[4]

On September 1, the division joined the rest of the army on the march through Dranesville, Virginia to Leesburg, Virginia, where the men bivouacked and rested. Hood's men acted as Lee's rearguard, being the last to wade across the Potomac River at White's Ford on September 6. The division bivouacked southeast of Frederick near the B&O Railroad bridge at Monocacy Junction on the evening of September 7.[5]

Hood was not riding at the head of the column when the division entered Maryland. Hood's men had captured Union ambulances following the battle of Second Bull Run and Brig. Gen. Nathan "Shanks" Evans, to whom Hood was reporting, demanded that he turn over the ambulances to his brigade. When Hood refused, Evans complained to Longstreet. The latter arrested Hood and ordered him to be court-martialed. The matter put Lee in a difficult situation, wanting to avoid losing one of his best division commanders in mid-campaign but not wanting to interfere with Longstreet's authority, so he ordered Hood to ride at the rear of his unit.[6]

As a result of Special Orders 191, James Longstreet's two divisions (Hood's and D. R. Jones') and D.H. Hill's division headed for Boonsboro. The prospect of supplies and threats of Pennsylvania militia along the Mason-Dixon Line caused Longstreet to leave Hill's division as the rearguard at Boonsboro with the supply train. Lee and the reserve artillery headed for Hagerstown, Maryland with Longstreet's command. The unexpected advance of George McClellan's army on September 13 forced Lee to order Longstreet back to Boonsboro. Hood's and Jones' divisions left Hagerstown the following morning and raced southeast to aid D.H. Hill's men holding off several Federal corps attempting to break through Turner's and Fox's Gaps on South Mountain. Longstreet raced 12 miles in seven grueling hours, arriving late afternoon, just in time to

291

reinforce Hill's beleaguered troops. Longstreet lost hundreds to heat stroke and fatigue along the way and later wrote, "We marched as hurriedly as we could over a hot and dusty road . . . the troops [were] much scattered and worn."

Hood's men were about to give battle for the first time in two weeks, but knew their beloved commander was still riding at the rear of the column. Marching past Lee at the foot of the mountain, the men of the Texas Brigade shouted, "Give us Hood!" to which Lee responded, "You shall have him, gentlemen." Lee summoned Hood and offered his release if he would but express regret for the incident with Evans, but Hood refused. Lee acquiesced and suspended the arrest.[7]

The sun was beginning to set when Hood's division arrived at Turner's Gap where it turned south along Wood Road to Fox's Gap, about a mile distant. Hood's men passed stragglers from Thomas Drayton's brigade (D.R. Jones' division), who warned them of conditions in the gap. In the waning daylight, Hood resolved to press on and took position in a tree line north of Old Sharpsburg Road, regaining a portion of ground lost by Drayton, with minimal casualties. Many have credited Hood's division with mortally wounding Federal IX Corps commander, Jesse Reno, as he rode forward to find out what had stalled his troops. Hood's division held its position until nearly midnight when it was ordered to quietly withdraw under the cover of darkness. After taking councel with Longstreet and D.H. Hill, Lee ordered a withdrawal and headed for the Old Dominion by way of Sharpsburg to the Potomac River. Hood's division and other units served as Lee's rearguard.[8]

Hood's division crossed Antietam Creek shortly after 11:00 a.m. at the Middle Bridge on September 15 and took up a position on Lee's far right, above the Lower Bridge, behind Robert Toombs' brigade. The division was eventually ordered to Lee's left flank in the vicinity of the Dunker Church. On Tuesday, September 16, the division was spread across the fields in line of battle between the Hagerstown Pike and Smoketown Road, and slightly beyond. The Texas brigade was stretched across D.R. Miller's Cornfield, facing north; Law's brigade was on its right. The division clashed with Truman Seymour's brigade (George Meade's division; I Corps) in the East Woods in the evening, and after a brief firefight, drove the enemy to the far side of the woods.[9]

As darkness fell, Hood grew concerned about the physical stamina of his men, who sorely needed rest and sustenance. They had experienced exhausting marches and some fighting over the previous few days, so Hood appealed directly to Lee for permission to withdraw his troops to rest and draw rations. Lee referred him to Jackson who granted conditional permission. All knew the morrow would mean battle.[10]

Early in the morning of Wednesday, September 17, a most sanguine day for both sides, Hood's division was in the midst of preparing a meager breakfast behind the Dunker Church in the West Woods. The provisions had barely arrived when Hood's men were summoned to the front. The request originated from Alexander Lawton, whose division had replaced Hood the evening before. The Confederate left flank was evaporating in front of Joseph Hooker's I Corps. The starving troops were violently angered at the interruption of their long-awaited meal, threw down their provisions when ordered to "fall-in" and march across Hagerstown Pike. The men formed along the Smoketown Road and faced north toward the enemy. A soldier from the 4th Texas remembered it was "the hottest place I ever saw on earth or want to see ... there were shot, shells, and minie balls sweeping the face of the earth; legs, arms, and other parts of human bodies were flying in the air like straw in a whirlwind."

Hood's division charged unrestrained through David Miller's pasture, screaming a blood-curdling rebel yell, with the Texas Brigade on the left and Law's brigade on the right. The counter-attack was swift and without hesitation as the men trailed arms along the way. Hood later wrote, "It was here that I witnessed the most terrible clash of arms, by far, that occurred during the war." They pursued elements of Abner Doubleday's and James Ricketts' divisions, who had exhausted their ammunition, into the Cornfield, a scene which

Stonewall Jackson described as "a terrific storm of shell, canister, and musketry." After the division had inflicted heavy casualties on the enemy, portions of the Federal I Corps nearly decimated the Texas Brigade and much of Law's brigade before driving them from the field after about 45 minutes. Two of Law's regiments held on with one of Isaac Trimble's (James Walker's) brigade's regiments for another hour on the south edge of the East Woods, east of the Smoketown Road.[11]

The division rapidly withdrew to the woods behind the Dunker Church, where it remained inactive until the arrival of fresh Confederate troops. It then withdrew to a position just north of Sharpsburg on the west side of Hagerstown Pike. There it remained until the army withdrew back into Virginia late on the night of September 18. The night before, Lee met with his commanders to assess the condition of his army. When he heard of Hood's casualties, he cried out, "Great God General Hood, where is your splendid division?" To which Hood replied: "They are lying on the field where you sent them."[12]

Longstreet's aide, Maj. Thomas Goree, wrote of Hood's command to his mother on October 10, 1862: "it was always in front and in the thickest of the fight," in every battle. "It is very probable that Genl. Hood will be promoted to Major Genl. for his gallantry in these various contests. No man deserves it more. He is one of the finest young officers I ever saw . . ."[13]

**Gary W. Rohrer**

✳ ✳ ✳

## Hood's Texas Brigade: Colonel William T. Wofford

**Units:** 1st Texas, 4th Texas, 5th Texas, 18th Georgia, Hampton (South Carolina) Legion
**Strength:** 2,177[14]
**Losses:** 548 (68k-417w-62m)[15]

Hood's original brigade was also known as the Texas Brigade, as it contained the only Lone Star regiments in the Army of Northern Virginia. The Texans were a unique and independent breed within the Confederate army who rejected the practice of the Confederate high command choosing senior officers without giving the men a voice in the matter. For whatever reason, the Texans were endeared to Brig. Gen. John Bell Hood. As brigade historian Joe Polley (Co. F, 4th Texas) put it, Hood was "well versed in human nature and thoroughly [understood] the peculiarities of Texans' character. He knew not to draw the reins of true military discipline very tight at first – issuing few orders and those quite lenient for some time but gradually increasing." While there were other Texas regiments in the Civil War, they either remained in Texas to guard its southern border from Indian raids or served in the western theater. The men of the three

Texas regiments considered Virginia to be "the seat of the war," the more "decisive" arena, and thus wanted to be where they felt they could contribute most to the war effort.[16]

The men of the brigade came from all walks of life, laborers to professionals, slaveholders to non-slaveholders. The comradery of the brigade was forged in the fall/winter of 1861-1862 while serving in mundane duty along the Potomac River. The weather was harsh and unforgiving, diseases such as typhoid and measles were common. The men endured loneliness, homesickness, and the crude winter quarters. The Texans were more than a thousand miles from home and had already experienced countless hardships in the weeks of travel to reach Virginia. Passionate about their cause, they were full of fight when they arrived.[17]

During the Maryland Campaign, the Texas Brigade comprised more than Lone Star regiments, initially including the 1st, 4th, and 5th Texas and the 18th Georgia. The latter was formed in April 1861 in Cobb County and was led by Col. William T. Wofford. The Texans initially harbored some reservations when the Georgians were added to their brigade, but it dissipated when they realized the new arrivals were ardent believers in the southern cause. The Texans and Georgians forged such a strong bond that the 18th Georgia was referred to as the "3rd Texas."[18]

The Hampton Legion (South Carolina) joined the brigade in late June 1862. Wade Hampton was a wealthy South Carolina plantation owner who formed the Hampton Legion in the spring of 1861 with his own funds. It initially consisted of infantry, cavalry, and artillery units, but the Confederate high command eventually separated the units and assigned them to like units. The infantry unit became part of the Texas Brigade under the command of Lt. Col. Martin W. Gary but it retained its identity as the Hampton Legion.[19]

The brigade "saw the elephant" for the first time in May 1862, during the minor action at the Battle of West Point, or Eltham's Landing. The brigade was truly baptized by fire at Gaines' Mill, where it inflicted significant damage to the Federals while suffering heavy losses. The heavy losses in the 4th Texas earned it the nickname, "Lee's Grenadier Guard." The Hampton Legion found itself in the thick of the fighting at the Battle of Second Bull Run, but the 5th Texas inflicted and received the most casualties, earning the nickname, the "Bloody Fifth." When Hood was promoted to brigadier general and given command of the division, Col. William Wofford of the 18th Georgia took his place. Wofford had been a practicing attorney in Cassville, Georgia and served as a captain in the Mexican War. He had voted against secession as a legislator but took up the banner when the war began, becoming colonel of the 18th Georgia.[20]

As Lee moved northwesterly toward Leesburg, Virginia after Second Bull Run, the brigade had rapidly developed the reputation as the feared "shock troops" of the Army of Northern Virginia. The brigade, with the rest of the division, bivouacked in Leesburg, and then crossed the Potomac on September 6 and marched to Frederick City where the men spent the next several days. The entire army received strict orders to be on its best behavior to win favor of the local citizens. After an uneventful three days southwest of Frederick, the brigade received orders to march northwestward on National Road.

The men obtained a few ripe melons as they passed through Frederick on their way to South Mountain. Many of the local citizens tended to be unfriendly to Lee's army but exhibited a strong curiosity. It became obvious that the Texans' ferocious reputation had preceded them when a youngster blurted out, "Oh, Mama, they look just like our folks." The brigade continued west over the mountains of Western Maryland along the National Road as far as Middletown where the men bivouacked on September 10. An early start on September 11 allowed the brigade to reach Boonsboro early that morning. The march continued to Funkstown where the men bivouacked. The brigade, with the rest of Hood's division, reached its final destination just south of Hagerstown on September 12.[21]

## South Mountain

The Union army's attempted thrust through the South Mountain gaps forced the Texas Brigade to march back to Boonsboro on the morning of September 14. It was a brutal, seven-hour forced march back to Turner's Gap in dust and scorching heat. The men reached the gap at about 4:00 p.m. and initially took up a position on the left (north side) of the road. Hooker's Federal I Corps was pressuring the Confederate left at Turner's Gap and the Frosttown Plateau while Jesse Reno's IX Corps mangled D.H. Hill's thin line on the Confederate right flank at Fox's Gap. David R. Jones' division arrived first at Turner's Gap so Hill sent several of its brigades to shore up the Confederate right, only to have them get lost in the maneuver. They eventually found the Wood Road that led to Fox's Gap. Hood's men followed after they arrived. He described it as a "pig path," but it was the perfect avenue of approach to move his troops quickly south. The Texans clearly heard the jubilant shouts of the Federals as they drove through the Confederate line, sending the men in grey down the western slope. Upon reaching the edge of the tree line north of the Old Sharpsburg Road, Hood deployed his men across the Wood Road, sending Wofford's brigade to the right. Although Hood's men effectively stymied the Federal advance at Fox's Gap, Lt. Col. Philip Work, commanding the 1st Texas, later wrote, "the part taken by the 1st Texas in the [battle] … was so uneventful as scarcely to merit mention." The division held its position until withdrawing under the cover of darkness as Lee's rearguard. It is impossible to know the number of casualties sustained by the brigade as none of the regimental commanders mention them in their reports, but casualties were likely light.[22]

The brigade marched all night toward Sharpsburg by way of National Road back to Boonsboro then turning south on Boonsboro Pike. It held the honored post as the rear of the rearguard all the way to Sharpsburg, crossing Antietam Creek on the Middle Bridge around noon on September 15. With the Federal skirmishers of Israel Richardson's division in pursuit, the brigade was periodically forced to form a line of battle.

## Antietam

After crossing Antietam Creek, the men ascended a ridge where they took up a position on the south side of the Pike, facing east. Richardson's skirmishers arrived about two hours later and halted on the east side of the creek. The Texas Brigade rested at this location before moving north to the vicinity of the Dunker Church on the left of the Confederate line, again facing east. The men received very little supplemental clothing or supplies from home and were among the most threadbare units in Lee's army. There were no rations that evening and they had to tolerate shelling from the long-range Federal guns.[23]

Late in the day on September 16, the brigade marched with the rest of the division, less than a half-mile up Hagerstown Pike to the left of its previous position behind the church, formed line of battle parallel to the pike, and advanced into David

Miller's Cornfield. They deployed from left to right: the Hampton Legion, 18th Georgia, 1st Texas (on high ground), the 4th Texas, and the 5th Texas on the right flank. Around 7:00 p.m., the brigade moved forward under heavy fire to engage the 13th Pennsylvania "Bucktails" of Truman Seymour's brigade (George Meade's division, I Corps). Law's men supported the Texas Brigade as it drove the "Bucktails" about 200 yards through the East Woods and emerged into a wide-open clover field beyond. Col. Hugh McNeil of the "Bucktails" was shot through the heart during this engagement, becoming the first Union regimental commander to fall at Antietam. The "Bucktails" were packing single-shot breach-loader Sharps rifles and pushed back into the East Woods. About 100 skirmishers of the 4th Texas, Company K, under Capt. "Howdy" Martin moved forward into the woods in front and to the left of the 5th Texas and were "hotly engaged" but held their ground. The 1st Texas surged forward ahead of both flanks.

A light rain began falling about 9:00 p.m. and lasted until the wee hours of the morning. Hood arranged for his men's withdrawal by this time so they could rest and draw rations. Marcellus Douglass' and Isaac Trimble's (now under James Walker) brigades, part of Alexander Lawton's division, replaced Hood's men.[24]

Hood's famished troops withdrew back to the woods behind the church only to realize the rations had not yet arrived. The angry men finally received their rations about 4:00 a.m. and immediately began baking hoecakes on the end of sticks and ramrods, only to have Federal guns begin shelling the woods. A desperate call for reinforcements from Lawton put an end to their breakfast.[25]

Hood's men were ordered to fall in at about 7:00 a.m., angering those still cooking and consuming their rations. Jackson permitted Hood to move his men back to the church the night before with the condition they would return to the field when needed. Abner Doubleday's and James Ricketts' Federal divisions slammed into Lawton's division east of Hagerstown Pike and the Stonewall Division (now under J.R. Jones) on the west side. Hood was quickly summoned.

Doubleday's division and George Hartsuff's brigade (Ricketts' division) overpowered Lawton's men and had driven through the Confederate left flank after marching south through Miller's Cornfield. Doubleday's troops posed the greatest threat, entering the pasture south of the Cornfield and heading for the high ground near the church. Hood marched his men through a gap in the fence to form in line of battle on the north side of Smoketown Road. A tremendous artillery duel shrieked overhead involving Hooker's nine batteries, joined by about two dozen long-range Federal guns on the heights east of Antietam Creek, slugging it out with Stephen Lee's 19-gun battalion on a plateau east of Hagerstown Pike, opposite the Dunker Church, and John Pelham's 15 guns on Nicodemus Heights, about three-quarters of a mile northwest of Miller's Cornfield. The noise was deafening and Pvt. William Hamby of the 4th Texas later wrote, "the earth and sky seemed to be on fire."[26]

The Texas Brigade dressed its left on Hagerstown Pike facing north, with the Hampton Legion next to the Pike, and continuing to its right: 18th Georgia, 1st Texas, 4th Texas, and 5th Texas. The brigade faced five Federal brigades commanded by John Gibbon, Walter Phelps, Marsena Patrick (Doubleday's division), George Hartsuff, and William Christian (Ricketts' division). Meade's division was also heading south, but was not yet in view of the Texas Brigade. Hood was convinced he was facing not less than two corps. Wofford called out as his men formed up, "It is the Yankees who have taken your breakfast; make them pay for it!" The remnants of Douglass' brigade fled back through Hood's line, blocking their line of fire and impeding the counterattack. The brigade was not to be denied; their long awaited, meager breakfast had been interrupted and they were madder than hornets. Rufus Dawes of the 6th Wisconsin (Gibbon's brigade; Doubleday's division, I Corps), later described the scene: "A long and steady line of rebel grey, unbroken by the fugitives who [flew]

before us [came] sweeping down through the woods around the church; raising the rebel yell and firing. It [was] like a scythe running through our line." Before Wofford could give the command to move out, the regiments broke for the enemy. W.D. Pritchard of the 1st Texas described the advance: "The command to forward dispels all fear, and from the first volley all traces of that fear and dread are gone, all is lost in the excitement." Lt. Col. Solon Ruff of the 18th Georgia called out "Looky there boys, at them black hats! Let's go knock 'em off!" The brigade charged with wild laughter and the piercing "Rebel-Yell," as they fired from the hip.[27]

The "Black Hats" of Gibbon's Iron Brigade had been on the field for more than an hour and, besides building up a crust in the weapons that slowed reloading, they had expended their ammunition. Their only alternative was to withdraw from the attack, and rapidly, or face annihilation. It was every man for himself heading back through Miller's Cornfield and beyond. The Texas Brigade was right on their heels. The Hampton Legion and the 18th Georgia began drawing horrific fire from Patrick's brigade and half of Gibbon's on the left flank, on the opposite side of Hagerstown Pike as they reached the top of the hill. Pvt. Scott of the Hampton Legion remembered, "it seemed the whole world was in arms against us." In the thick smoke and hail of bullets, three of the Legion's color-bearers were shot down. Maj. J. H. Dingle, Jr. grabbed the flag, charging ahead shouting: "Legion, follow your colors!" Dingle was killed within 50 yards of the enemy line. Hood ordered the 4th Texas to move to the far left to protect that flank. Battery B, 4th U.S. Artillery poured case shot and canister into the brigade from across Hagerstown Pike. J. M. Polk of the 4th Texas said, "the air was full of shot and shell . . . it seemed almost impossible for a rat to live in such a place." Despite taking heavy casualties from the artillery just 20 yards on the other side of the fence, the Hampton Legion and the 18th Georgia were dishing it out as the battery endured forty casualties.[28]

As the three regiments on the left turned to face the Federals on the opposite side of Hagerstown

Pike, the 1st Texas was in hot pursuit of the 2nd and 6th Wisconsin troops who were running for the fence on the far side of Miller's Cornfield. In their quest, the Texans failed to maintain a uniform pace and managed to advance about 150 yards in advance of the regiments on either side of them. They found themselves in a precarious situation with two fresh brigades of Meade's Pennsylvania Reserves awaiting them behind a fence on the far side of the field; their guns arrayed high and low behind the rails. Capt. Dunbar Ransom's Federal battery poured death into the Texans' ranks from the hill behind Meade.

The 1st Texas not only exposed its own flanks but also the right flank of the 18th Georgia. When the Texans arrived within about thirty yards of the fence, the Federals released a devastating volley that decimated them and caused the loss of their colors. Thirteen Texans lay dead within reach of the colors, one of which lay stretched across it. Col. Philip Work sent repeated cries for reinforcements but there would be none, and his men stood erect and shot it out with Meade's men. In his report, Work said, "They fought bravely, and unflinchingly faced a terrible hail of bullets and artillery until ordered by me to retire." Seeing the dilemma of the four regiments on his right, Wofford ordered them to retire by the left flank and they did so all the way to the woods behind the church. The regiment's stand in Miller's Cornfield proved to be the costliest of any regiment on either side during the Civil War.[29]

Capt. "Ike" Turner's 5th Texas charged into the fight up the right (east) side of Smoketown Road and linked with the 4th Alabama (Law's brigade) and the 21st Georgia (Walker's brigade). Together they drove William Christian's brigade through the East Woods. As the Federal XII Corps appeared, the three regiments put up a stubborn resistance that lasted for at least another hour after the rest of the Texas Brigade's departure. Pressured by the growing presence of George Greene's division (XII Corps), Turner called for reinforcements multiple times, but to no avail. D.H. Hill had ordered Brig. Gen. Samuel Garland's brigade (commanded by Col. Duncan McRae) to provide support, but the unit exhibited "battle fatigue" after its devastating losses at South Mountain on September 14, and turned and ran. The 5th Texans were furious and had to be restrained from firing upon their stampeding comrades. Out of ammunition, the enemy within 100 yards, and no reinforcements in sight, Turner withdrew his men back to the woods behind the church to join the rest of their brigade.[30]

No one was prepared for the grim report of casualties when the brigade mustered. The 5th Texas lost 82 of 175 men (47%); the Hampton Legion, 55 of 77 (71%); 4th Texas, 107 of 200 (54%); and the 18th Georgia, 101 of 176 (57%). The 1st Texas lost 186 of 211 (88%); one survived from Company A, two from Company C, three from Company E, and none for Company F. Of the 854 men who reported for duty on that September morn, 530 (62%) were casualties.[31]

**Gary W. Rohrer**

***

## Law's Brigade: Colonel Evander Law

**Units:** 4th Alabama, 2nd Mississippi, 11th Mississippi, 6th North Carolina
**Strength:** 1,394[32]
**Losses:** 473 (53k-390w-30m)[33]

Evander Law's brigade was one of the most experienced in the army, as all of its regiments had served since First Bull Run. The brigade was originally commanded by Brig. Gen. William Whiting. When Whiting was given a division, Law stepped up to command the brigade in June 1862. Law was a South Carolina native and graduate of the Citadel. He assisted in founding a military high school and when the war broke out, recruited a company of its students. He was elected lieutenant colonel of the 4th Alabama regiment and was severely wounded at First Bull Run. He returned to command the brigade at Seven Pines, Gaines' Mill, Malvern Hill, and Second Bull Run, and was recognized as an effective commander.[34]

Law's brigade left the Second Bull Run battlefield on September 1 along with the rest of Hood's division and headed for Leesburg, Virginia, where it bivouacked for a couple of days. It crossed the Potomac River on September 6 as part of the rearguard. The men rested for several uneventful days southeast of Frederick, Maryland and found the citizens of Maryland a bit dubious and not so hospitable. One Confederate officer observed: "We were not received with cheers or songs or other evidences of approbation, but instead they looked on us in self-evident pity." With the issuance of Special Orders No. 191, the army left Frederick on September 10. The brigade joined the rest of Hood's division and D.R. Jones' division on the march to Middletown that evening. It was on the road early the next morning, reaching Funkstown by evening and Hagerstown early the next day.[35]

## South Mountain

Law's men were part of the column that marched southeast from Hagerstown to Boonsboro on the morning of September 14. It was a horrific seven-hour forced march under intense heat and clouds of dust, causing half of Longstreet's command to become stragglers. As the column arrived at the South Mountain summit at Turner's Gap shortly before 4:00 p.m., the brigade, with the rest of the division, was sent to the north side of the pike for a brief stand. The Union IX Corps was overpowering Fox's Gap to the south, so Hood was sent down Wood Road, a "pig path" to bolster the Confederate right at Fox's Gap.

Hood's division encountered demoralized troops from Thomas Drayton's brigade warning of a dire situation at the gap, and they heard the jubilant Federals in the distance, but Hood's men were not deterred. The sun was beginning to set when they reached the edge of the tree line just north of Old Sharpsburg Road where Hood deployed his men across Wood Road. Law's brigade was thrown to the left (east) side of the line with Wofford's brigade on their right, all with fixed bayonets. In the brief exchange of gunfire, Lt. Col. O.K. McLemore of the 4th Alabama fell mortally wounded, and it is plausible a shot from one of Law's men mortally wounded IX Corps commander, Jesse Reno. The brigade lost a total of 19 men at Fox's Gap (3 killed; 11 wounded; 5 missing). R.T. Cole of the 4th Alabama believed the casualties were light because the men used a sunken road for cover.

Both sides kept up a desultory fire into the night because ammunition was running low on both sides. Hood wanted to ensure the enemy knew his men were still in position and full of fight. The exhausted men had trouble staying awake, after their strenuous march to the battlefield and the subsequent stress of battle. The officers, who tried hard to keep the men awake, probably appreciated

298

the midnight orders to vacate their positions and head down the mountain. Hood made sure a skirmish line remained in place to deceive the enemy. Pvt. Andrew Baker of the 11th Mississippi was one of the unfortunates left behind. He estimated a space of less than 50 yards between the combatants. For those leaving their positions, silence was of utmost importance because the enemy was so close. Cole recalled, as the "men were awakened, they were ordered to go quietly one at a time down to the main road, which led to Sharpsburg and there reform." They were among the last Confederate troops to withdraw under the cover of darkness.[36]

## Antietam

The brigade crossed Antietam Creek on the Middle Bridge around noon on September 15, ascended the ridge east of Sharpsburg and, along with the rest of the division, was sent to the far-right flank. Later in the afternoon, Lee positioned Hood's division about a mile north of Sharpsburg along Hagerstown Pike with the right of the brigade resting at the Dunker Church and the line extending north along the pike.[37]

When elements of Truman Seymour's Federal brigade moved into the East Woods late in the afternoon of September 16, Hood sent a company of the 2nd Mississippi and one from the 6th North Carolina up Hagerstown Pike, through D.R. Miller's Cornfield and the grass field beyond. About 100 skirmishers of the 4th Texas and others joined them to check the Federals. When the 13th Pennsylvania "Bucktails" and the 3rd Pennsylvania Reserves charged forward with support from their brigade, Hood ordered the remainder of Law's brigade forward with Wofford's men to occupy the edge of the same woods, and a fire fight ensued. George Smalley of the *New York Tribune* wrote: "The fight flashed, and glimmered, and faded, and finally went out in the dark." Law's casualties were light, but they included Col. P.E. Liddell of the 11th Mississippi, who according to historian Ezra Carman, "was struck by a chance shot."[38]

The fighting subsided as darkness fell and Law's brigade was withdrawn to the woods behind Dunker Church. The men were exhausted and hungry from days of marching and fighting. Hood had managed to gain a respite for his troops but rations did not arrive until 4:00 a.m. Law's men were still struggling to enjoy their meager breakfast on the morning of September 17, when they were ordered forward into an open field across Hagerstown Pike. Two divisions of Joseph Hooker's I Corps had overrun the Confederate line and Alexander Lawton (commanding Richard Ewell's division) pleaded for reinforcements. Law's brigade followed the Texas Brigade across the pike and, as Hood stretched 2,000 men across the pasture to the East Woods, Law's brigade formed the right flank. The order of battle from left to right was: 2nd Mississippi, 11th Mississippi, 6th North Carolina, and 4th Alabama. According to Law, "On reaching the road, I found but few of our troops on the field, and these seemed to be in much confusion, but still opposing the advance of the enemy's dense masses with determination." The brigade headed northeast toward the East Woods when Hood halted it and ordered it to face left toward the southeast corner of the D.R. Miller Cornfield. The 90th Pennsylvania's (William Christian's brigade; James Ricketts' division, I Corps) volleys cut down Law's men, so Hood ordered the change in direction. All of the regiments turned except the 4th Alabama, which continued up Smoketown Road, apparently "crowded out of line," and moved northeast into the East Woods.

The rest of the line headed for the 90th Pennsylvania in the Cornfield. Billy Ellis of the 11th Mississippi recalled his regiment "charged through the bloody wreckage of the dead and wounded from earlier fighting. They lay so thick that we had to watch our every step so as not to step on them." Pvt. D. C. Love recalled his 11th Mississippi formed line of battle without halting. Law's combined firepower decimated the Pennsylvanians' front and flanks, and when they began lapping around their flanks, the Pennsylvanians retired slowly back through the East Woods after losing nearly half their men. Law's men also descended upon the 6th Pennsylvania Reserves (Seymour's brigade) in similar fashion and forced it from the East Woods.[39]

Law's left three regiments paused at the fence lining the Cornfield for about five minutes, firing all the while. Law then ordered the three regiments into the Cornfield where they pushed the remaining 100 men from the 104th and 105th New York (Abram Duryee's brigade; Ricketts' division, I Corps) from the field. Hood's division had now driven Ricketts' entire division from the field, and it continued moving north toward the northern edge of the Cornfield. Joseph Hooker, commander of the I Corps, now brought up his reserve—two brigades of George Meade's Pennsylvania Reserves. Albert Magilton's brigade left its position at the North Woods and headed south, and then moved by the left flank across Law's front behind the fence on the north side of the Cornfield. "An infantry line appeared on the crest and engaged our line," remembered the 11th Mississippi's Pvt. Love. "The flag of the regiment opposing [us] was shot down or lowered at least a half a dozen times before it disappeared behind a hill." Capt. Ezra Matthews' six-gun battery was deployed on the ridge just behind Magilton's brigade and unleashed double canister into the Confederate ranks, thinning them badly, but they continued onward.[40]

Law's men delivered a horrific fire causing two of Magilton's regiments, the 3rd and 4th Pennsylvania Reserves, to retreat in disorder. "As we neared the grove . . . a regiment of rebels, who had lain concealed among the tall corn, arose and poured upon us the most withering volley we ever felt," reported Ashbel Hill of the 8th Pennsylvania Reserves. "Another and another followed . . . we could not stop to reply – we could but hurry on," he recalled. About 50 men of the 8th Pennsylvania Reserves managed to reach the cover of the East Woods and returned fire on Law's troops as they approached the Cornfield's north fence. The 6th North Carolina occupied the "hot spot," where the northeast corner of the Cornfield meets the East

Woods and the exhausted Tar Heels took on the 8th Pennsylvania.

To their left, some of the 2nd and 11th Mississippi men crossed the fence and were hit by a blast of canister from Matthews' battery before the cannoneers were forced to abandon their guns. Capt. Dunbar Ransom's battery on Matthews' right flank trained its guns on Law's Mississippians. The undaunted Mississippians spotted the 150 men of the 7th Pennsylvania Reserves on their left who had been following the 3rd and 4th Pennsylvania Reserves before they were routed. The two sides fired upon one another, and about half of the Pennsylvanians were killed or wounded, and the rest forced to flee.[41]

With the Pennsylvania Reserves gone from their front, the Mississippi regiments lay down behind the fence lining the north of the Cornfield. The 1st Texas continued slugging it out to their left and the 6th North Carolina continued battling the 8th Pennsylvania Reserves, who were joined by members of the defeated 3rd and 4th Pennsylvania Reserves. Law was pleased with the results: "So far, we had been entirely successful and everything promised a decisive victory. It is true that strong support was needed to follow up our success, but this I expected every moment." Reinforcements did arrive, but not for Law. Joseph Mansfield's XII Corps now arrived with Alpheus Williams' division in the van. Law reported how at "this stage of the battle, a powerful Federal force (ten times our number) of fresh troops was thrown in our front." A decision had to be made and Law reluctantly made it. "Our losses up to this time had been very heavy; the troops now confronting the enemy were insufficient to cover properly one-fourth of the line of battle; our ammunition was expended; the men had been fighting long and desperately, and were exhausted from want of food and rest." The men scrounged about obtaining ammunition from the cartridge boxes of the dead and wounded around them, but Law realized, "this state of affairs could not long continue." He weighed his options: "To remain stationary or advance without it would have caused a useless butchery, and I adopted the only alternative—that of falling back to the wood from which I had first advanced." This was a bitter moment for Law, whose brigade had never been forced from a field of battle.[42]

While Law's three regiments returned to the West Woods, the 4th Alabama in front of the East Woods hunkered down on the east side of Smoketown Road with the 21st Georgia and Turner's 5th Texas on its right. After driving Christian's brigade through the East Woods, all was quiet. Cole recalled the "nervous condition of the regiment from want of food and rest caused them to fight desperately, even savagely." The reprieve ended with the appearance of the left side of Samuel Crawford's brigade (Williams' division; XII Corps). The three regiments again joined forces to put up a stubborn resistance that lasted for at least another hour after the rest of Hood's division departed. They were cheered to see Garland's brigade, now commanded by Col. Duncan McRae, approaching. However, the men exhibited "battle fatigue" after their devastating losses at South Mountain on September 14, and turned and ran. The defenders were irate about fighting it out alone. The 10th Maine was among the enemy regiments the 4th Alabama faced in the East Woods. The regiment's adjutant, Maj. John Gould recalled, it "was an awful morning; our comrades went down one after another with a most disheartening frequency, pierced with bullets from men who were half concealed, or who dodged quickly back to a safe cover the moment they fired . . . they were all good marksmen and the constant call of their officers to aim low appeared to us entirely unnecessary."

The three regiments held their own until Mansfield's second division under George Greene drove down through the East Woods. The 4th Alabama was out of ammunition, and with Greene's men within 100 yards and no reinforcements in sight, was forced to withdraw.[43]

Law's brigade lost 454 at Antietam, and with the 19 casualties at Fox's Gap on September 14, the brigade lost a total of 473 during the Maryland Campaign. The 2nd Mississippi had the dubious honor of being on the list of regiments losing the greatest percentage of men, 73%[44]

Law penned an appropriate conclusion to his brigade's actions at Sharpsburg: "The good conduct of my brigade in this battle has not been surpassed by it in any previous engagement. Weak and exhausted as they were, and fighting against fearful odds, the troops accomplished and endured all that was within the limits of human capacity."[45]

**Gary W. Rohrer**

* * *

## Evans' Brigade (Independent Command): Brigadier General Nathan Evans, Colonel Peter Stevens

**Units:** 17th South Carolina, 18th South Carolina, 22nd South Carolina, 23rd South Carolina, Holcombe Legion (South Carolina)
**Strength:** 1,058[1]
**Losses:** 65 (11k-43w-11m)[2]

Brigadier General Nathan "Shanks" Evans' regiments were brigaded together almost from the time they entered the Confederate service during the winter of 1861-62. The brigade was initially stationed in South Carolina, but was transferred to Lee's army in July 1862. According to historian Douglas Freeman, the four regiments "for some reason, were left as an 'Independent Brigade'," which first saw action during the Second Bull Run Campaign where it lost nearly 300 men.

Evans was an enigma. While at West Point he was given the nickname "Shanks" because of his skinny legs. On the frontier he gained a reputation as an effective combat officer and rose in rank to captain in the 2nd U. S. Cavalry. At the outbreak of the Civil War he raised the 4th South Carolina and with the 1st Louisiana Battalion, became immortal because of his bold actions at First Bull Run. He followed that battle with another solid performance at the Battle of Ball's Bluff in command of three Mississippi regiments. The governor of South Carolina wanted his distinguished war hero home, where he assumed command of a brigade of South Carolina troops he was to bring to Virginia later that year. Although a proven leader, promotion came slowly. He "possessed crudeness and conceit. He spoke his mind and made opponents." Equally disturbing, he enjoyed the bottle, and was followed by an aide carrying a one-gallon jug of liquor Evans dubbed his "barellita."[3]

Evans' brigade was part of James Longstreet's wing that crossed the Potomac River at White's Ford and reached Frederick on September 7. A reporter for a Charleston newspaper accompanying the troops noted a Maryland civilian watching the crossing and saying, "I've been to shows and circuses and theaters and all them things, but I never seen such a sigh'n all my life. Why you've got soldiers enough to whip all creation; but look yere, won't these fellers hurt us Marylanders?" Before taking off, the gentlemen said, "To tell the truth, I don't care to leave my farmhouse."[4]

## South Mountain

After leaving Frederick and crossing South Mountain, the brigade moved north with the rest of Longstreet's column and reached Hagerstown on September 12. The men had a reprieve from the intensive marching while camped there. Lt. William DuBose recalled, "the opportunity of a bath in a nice mountain stream and at last a little change of apparel." Longstreet's men were ordered south on September 14 to Boonsboro, arriving there at 3:00 p.m. amid heavy fighting going on to the east. Evans was not in charge of his brigade during this phase of the invasion. He commanded Hood's two brigades and his own to form a "provisional" division. Col. P.F. Stevens of the Holcombe Legion commanded the brigade, but as the division approached Turner's Gap, Longstreet informed Evans that Hood's two brigades were being detached and sent to Fox's Gap. His own South

Carolinians were ordered to continue marching up the mountain to Turner's Gap. Evans apparently remained behind at Boonsboro, so Stevens continued leading the brigade. The commander of the 17th South Carolina called the march from Boonsboro to Turner's Gap "most fatiguing" and when the brigade reached the gap at 4:00 p.m., it was without some of the men who "broke down" during the trek up the side of the mountain. Stevens reported to D.H. Hill and was sent to the left to support Robert Rodes' brigade, which was slugging it out, single-handedly, on Frosttown Plateau, against the three brigades of George Meade's division of Pennsylvania Reserves.[5]

DuBose recalled the climb to its position: "It was quite a steep climb to the top of the mountain as we ascended it, and on the top there was a tolerably large plateau bounded on the eastern edge by a line of rocky cliffs." The brigade halted behind this cliff. Stevens received an order from Evans to halt the brigade when about half the distance to its position in support of Rodes, but at the same time another message arrived from Rodes, urging him forward. This was a new commander's nightmare. Stevens halted his small, 550-man command and requested additional orders from Evans and then sent word to Rodes about his reasons for halting. Meade's troops, specifically Albert Magilton's brigade, forced the issue. Stevens reported, "I found that the enemy were in the valley below on my right and were already threatening my position." He quickly threw his old regiment, the Holcombe Legion out on the skirmish line and aligned his brigade from left to right: 23rd South Carolina- 22nd South Carolina- 18th South Carolina- 17th South Carolina. The position was along the brow of the mountain side, with his left "very nearly" joining Rodes' right. Stevens thought this could buy time until Evans responded to his query, but the Pennsylvanians attacked almost immediately. Stevens was on the right of his line, near the 17th South Carolina, which seemed to be holding its own against the 8th Pennsylvania Reserves. Moving to the left of his line, Stevens found a very different situation as the 22nd and 23rd South Carolina were being driven back by the 4th and 7th Pennsylvania Reserves after holding their positions for about 30 minutes. The two regiments rallied about 30 yards in the rear, but when Lt. Col. T.C. Watkins of the 23rd South Carolina was mortally wounded, the line again fell in disarray. The left of the line rallied two or three times before being forced to give up and continue scrambling up the side of the mountain.

The fight was essentially over when Magilton's men broke the 18th South Carolina in the middle of the line. Stevens noted, "from that time the fight was a retreating one until the enemy occupied the mountain and we were driven from it." He added that "General Rodes was at the same time forced back on my left." Some of the 23rd South Carolina that had been on the brigade's left, fell in with some of Rodes' retreating Alabamians. Stevens was horrified by the behavior of some of his men: "after once falling back I cannot commend the behavior of the men. Some two or three bravely faced the foe, but a general lack of discipline and disregard for officers prevailed all around me." The 17th South Carolina on the left of the line was the exception. Its commander, Col. F.W. McMaster, reported: "after fighting for about an hour, and after the other regiments of the brigade had broken and retired, and we were about being flanked by the enemy, I ordered my regiment to retire, firing." A Union soldier in the 8th Pennsylvania Reserves provided additional texture to the horror on the mountain that night. "We were within twenty or thirty steps of them [the 17th South Carolina], directly on their left, and they did not see us; then we mowed them down. Poor fellows! I almost pitied them, to see them sink down by the dozens at every discharge." McMaster attempted to rally his men for another stand, about 300 yards in the rear, but he was soon flanked by the approaching enemy and forced to continue his retreat.[6]

The brigade rallied near the Mountain House on the National Road. Of the 550 men Stevens brought into battle, it lost 216 of them or 40% (23 killed, 148 wounded, 45 missing). The effectiveness of Evans'/Stevens' brigade high atop South Mountain has been debated. D.H. Hill reported,

"they took wrong positions, and, in their exhausted condition after a long march, they were broken and scattered." Rodes reported how the right of his line "mingled in utter confusion with some South Carolina stragglers on the summit of the hill, who stated that their brigade had been compelled to give way, and had retired." In actuality, it would have been difficult for any troops to have halted the Pennsylvanians' determined drive. The men were exhausted from their long march from Hagerstown, were thrown into position in the growing dusk without the ability to reconnoiter, and were almost immediately set upon by overwhelming enemy numbers. They probably did all that could have been expected of them.

Sometime after 11:00 p.m., Lee decided to determine whether the enemy still occupied the mountain or had retreated. This would determine his next actions. Stevens was ordered to send a reconnaissance party down the mountain, and he selected a company of the Holcombe Legion under DuBose. The young officer led his men forward, and then halted them as he descended the mountain on his own. He got his answer when shots rang out and he quickly scrambled back up the mountain with the information. Evans' brigade with Hood's division, formed the rearguard as Longstreet's command made its way toward Keedysville during the all-night march.[7]

## Antietam

Evans' brigade supported batteries around Cemetery Hill on September 16. It was not much of a brigade, numbering at best 280 men. Stevens explained, "sickness, fatigue, and the casualties of battle had reduced the brigade to a mere skeleton." Evans returned to command his brigade and Stevens assumed direct oversight of the Holcombe Legion. Evans had quite a bit of real estate to defend with his small brigade on the morning of the battle, so he split it into two wings. The left wing on the left (north) of Boonsboro Pike included the 18th, 22nd, and 23rd South Carolina. The 17th South Carolina, which had done so well at South

Mountain, and the Holcombe Legion were on the right of the road. Evans described how he was ordered at 2:00 p.m. to "rally the troops then flocking to the town from our right [left] and bring them into action. After considerable exertion, with the assistance of my entire staff, I succeeded in collecting about 250 men and officers." He formed these men into two companies under the command of Alfred Colquitt and Alfred Iverson and placed them behind his three regiments on the left of the road.[8]

Maj. M. Hilton of the 18th South Carolina asserted, "during most of the time [the brigade] was between the fires of our own and the enemy's batteries, and exposed to the heavy and continuous shelling of the enemy." Toward 3:00 p.m., a handful of U. S. Regular regiments from Sykes' division (V Corps) totaling about 1,640 men, slowly moved up Boonsboro Pike, where they encountered Evans' three small regiments, Richard Garnett's small brigade, and the men Evans had rounded up for a total of fewer than 800 men. A decisive Union thrust could have shoved aside these relatively few Confederate defenders, taken Sharpsburg and split Lee's army. The Regulars' steady advance concerned Evans so much that he launched at least one counterattack that temporarily halted the enemy's advance. It continued, pushing the makeshift unit commanded by Colquitt and Iverson into Sharpsburg's streets. Evans pulled his three regiments back and redeployed them along Hagerstown Pike. The Regulars' advance came to a halt before pushing their way into town.[9]

The situation on the right of Boonsboro Pike was becoming dire for the 17th South Carolina and the Holcombe Legion. Sometime about 3:15 p.m., the IX Corps launched its final attack on D.R. Jones' small division south of town. The two small South Carolina units were up against the 17th Michigan (Benjamin Christ's brigade, Orlando Willcox's division) on the extreme right of the IX Corps'

advance. Col. McMaster of the 17th South Carolina reported, "the enemy flanked my command on the right, and, after firing a few moments, the Holcombe Legion and a few of the Seventeenth Regiment, in spite of my efforts, broke and ran." Seeing the futility of maintaining his position, McMaster ordered the remnants of the two regiments back to an apple orchard about 200 yards in the rear. He estimated having only 40 to 50 men here. After holding this position for about half an hour, he was flanked on both sides, so McMaster ordered his men to a "stone house" which "I converted into a fort, and fought for some time, until Drayton's brigade, on the right, and Jenkins' brigade, on the left, had completely abandoned the ground, and the enemy had almost entirely surrounded my little band. When resistance on our part was entirely futile, I gave the order to retreat." Fortunately, the Union attack was spent, so Willcox's men did not drive into Sharpsburg.[10]

The battle was now over for Evans' brigade. It lost a total of 65 men at Sharpsburg (11 killed, 43 wounded, and 11 missing). Evans rounded up his shattered brigade on the morning of September 18 and marched it back to its original position east of town. They were pulled out of line at 10 p.m. and ordered to the Potomac River, which it immediately crossed.

Evans' brigade was transferred to Weldon, North Carolina in November 1862 and would not return to the Army of Northern Virginia until the fighting unfolded around Petersburg in 1864. Stevens would not be with the brigade, as he resigned his commission on October 8, 1862 and returned to the ministry. He had volunteered to defend his native South Carolina, not to fight in Virginia and Maryland.[11]

**Bradley M. Gottfried**

*** 

# Jackson's Wing—

## Major General Thomas Jackson

Born on January 21, 1824, Thomas Jackson's early life was difficult. His father died when he was a boy and his destitute mother could not raise him so he was sent to live with an uncle. He entered West Point in 1842 and after graduation fought in the Mexican War as an artillery officer. He was recognized for bravery on several battlefields. An argument with his superior officer caused Jackson's resignation from the army and he became a professor at the Virginia Military Institute. He quickly developed a reputation as a rigid and colorless instructor who broached no transgressions or laziness. With the outbreak of the Civil War he became a colonel of Virginia militia and then almost immediately was appointed to the rank of brigadier general and command of what came to be known as the Stonewall Brigade. He performed well in his early engagements and assumed command of a division and then a Wing. Lee used Jackson's aggressive nature to help balance James Longstreet's more conservative approach.[1]

Stonewall Jackson's wing consisted of three divisions that varied in size and command effectiveness. Strengths varied from 3,904 infantry in Alexander Lawton's division, 2,231 infantry in A.P. Hill's to only 1,784 infantry in J.R. Jones' Stonewall Division. Jackson knew his senior leadership was suspect. Only A.P. Hill had considerable experience at the divisional level; the other two divisions were commanded by men who were simply filling in and had no prior experience commanding large numbers of troops in battle conditions. Five of his eight brigades were commanded by colonels.[2]

Jackson led his column north toward Leesburg on September 3 and spent the night just north of Dranesville, Virginia. He summoned his three division commanders to his headquarters that evening and laid out the details for the next day's march. All synchronized watches with his to ensure compliance with his orders. With the Union army in Washington, Jackson expected rapid marches to distance his troops from the enemy. The men were to begin their march at a specific hour, continue for 50 minutes and rest for ten through the day. He sternly told his divisional commanders he would tolerate no breeches of these orders. Things went awry right from the start when the lead division, A.P. Hill's, did not begin the march at the appointed time (see A.P. Hill's entry). The column finally reached Leesburg on the afternoon of September 4 and continued to Big Spring, a source of fresh water for both men and horses. Jackson had his men on the march toward White's Ford on the Potomac River the following day and continued to Three Springs, about eleven miles south of Frederick. September 6 brought misery to Jackson. A local admirer gave him a horse to replace his lost Little Sorrel. The new horse would not budge, so Jackson touched its flank lightly with his spur and it reared, throwing the animal and Jackson backward. Jackson sustained no broken bones, but was so sore, he and spent the rest of the day riding in an ambulance.[3]

The column reached Frederick that day. The Stonewall Division camped outside of the town; the other two divisions bivouacked near the Monocacy River railroad bridge, watching for enemy troops approaching from Washington. The men remained here until the morning of September 10, when Jackson's three divisions made their way toward Harpers Ferry to capture its garrison. Jackson decided to take a round-about route to Harpers Ferry, swinging around to the north and then south to attempt to capture the garrison at Martinsburg. He led the column from Frederick, through Middletown, Boonsboro, and Williamsport, where the three divisions again crossed the Potomac River. Jackson split his command on September 11. Hill's division marched directly on Martinsburg as the other two headed for the North Mountain Depot (B&O

Railroad), about seven miles northwest of Martinsburg. He hoped to bag the garrison the following day, September 12, but Gen. Julius White and his men slipped away before he could accomplish his mission. Although unsuccessful in capturing almost a couple of thousand men, John Worsham of the 21st Virginia (Penn's brigade; Jones' division) noted, "we captured from the enemy a good lot of stores, they retreating to Harper's Ferry." Jackson's report noted how "abandoned quartermaster's, commissary, and ordnance stores fell into our hands."[4]

The march to Harpers Ferry continued on September 13 and by 11:00 a.m., the van of his column could see the enemy in position on Bolivar Heights. The three divisions camped near Halltown, about two miles from the enemy. Jackson was now able to coordinate the movements of the other two prongs under Lafayette McLaws and John Walker. Jackson deployed his three divisions in front of Bolivar Heights. Hill's division was on the right, with its right on the Shenandoah River, the Stonewall Division on the left, with its left on the Potomac River, and Lawton's division in the center. During the night of September 14-15, Col. Stapleton Crutchfield, Jackson's chief of artillery brought up his guns. Ten guns crossed the Shenandoah River across from Bolivar Heights and the remainder dropped trail on Schoolhouse Ridge in front of the enemy. Jackson's infantry did not have the opportunity to storm the enemy's position, as the garrison surrendered early on September 15, after Crutchfield's guns and those on Loudoun Heights and Maryland Heights, opened fire.[5]

Lee desperately needed Jackson's troops at Sharpsburg, so after resting his troops during the afternoon, two divisions embarked on a forced march to Sharpsburg that evening. Hill's division was left behind to collect supplies and parole the garrison. Lawton's and Jones' divisions reached Sharpsburg the morning of September 16 after an exhausting all-night march. Even the demanding Jackson called the march "severe." Lee directed Jackson's two divisions north, to the area north of the Dunker Church. The small Stonewall Division was placed on the left of Hagerstown Pike in two lines of two brigades each. That night, Jackson later brought up half of Lawton's division (James Walker's and Marcellus Douglass' brigades), to relieve Hood's division, which had been deployed between Hagerstown Pike and Smoketown Road, in front of the Miller Cornfield and East Woods. Truman Seymour's brigade of Pennsylvania Reserves occupied the East Woods in front of Walker's men so the men spent a restless night in their vulnerable positions. The remainder of Lawton's men, Hays' and Early's brigades, spent the night in the West Woods.[6]

The fight began early on September 17 between Jackson's two advanced divisions, consisting of six brigades, versus most of the Union I Corps. Coordination of the two divisions was almost impossible given the rolling terrain and the 120-yard gap between them. The Stonewall Division was beaten and driven back. Stonewall Jackson's biographer described how the "Federals tore apart the Stonewall Division almost effortlessly. . ." After a bold stand, the three brigades of Lawton's division (Hays' brigade was brought up to the front line) were also forced to withdraw after sustaining heavy losses in front of the Cornfield and East Woods. Only Early's brigade remained intact, off to the northwest, protecting Stuart's artillery on Nicodemus Heights. It teamed up with the remnants of the Stonewall Division to battle some I and XII Corps units north of the West Woods and then played an active role in driving the enemy out of the West Woods. Both of Jackson's division commanders were wounded during this fighting. Col. Andrew Grigsby assumed command of the Stonewall Division and Early took charge of Lawton's division. Six of the eight brigade commanders were wounded, and in most of them, multiple officers stepped up only to be stricken.[7]

While the two divisions rested during the afternoon, A.P. Hill's division marched north to Boteler's Ford near Shepherdstown. It reached the battlefield about 2:30 p.m., just as the IX Corps was pushing D.R. Jones' division back toward Sharpsburg. The situation looked bleak until Hill arrived and pushed each of his brigades into action as they came onto the field. They smashed into the victorious Union troops, ending their surge toward Lee's vulnerable right flank. Jackson's Wing was the last to cross the Potomac River at Boteler's

Ford on September 19. As the column made its way toward Martinsburg, a portion of the Union V Corps crossed the Potomac River. Jackson sent A.P. Hill's division back four miles toward the river, followed by Lawton's (Early's) division. Hill drove the enemy units back across the river with heavy losses, thus ending the Maryland Campaign.[8]

Jackson's Wing started the fighting on September 17 and ended it on September 19. His Wing lost a total of 2,403 at Antietam.[9]

**Bradley M. Gottfried**

***

# EWELL'S DIVISION—

## Brigadier General Alexander Lawton, Brigadier General Jubal Early

Major General Richard Ewell's division was a dependable, hard-hitting unit whose four veteran brigades had served together since Jackson's Shenandoah Valley Campaign. Ewell provided steady leadership until he was severely wounded during the Battle of Second Bull Run, on August 28, 1862. Brig. Gen. Alexander Lawton commanded the division during the Maryland Campaign.[1]

Lawton was born near Beaufort, South Carolina on November 4, 1818 to a well-to-do family. They secured his appointment to West Point, where he graduated in 1839 and was subsequently commissioned in the U.S. Army. He served only two years, and then headed to Harvard University's Law School. After graduation, he settled in Savannah Georgia, and within seven years, became the President of the new Augusta & Savannah Railroad. Lawton became a Georgia state legislator until the war erupted and became colonel of the 1st Georgia Volunteers. He gained a reputation by capturing Fort Pulaski, although it was only defended by a sergeant and a caretaker. Lawton caught the attention of President Jefferson Davis, who appointed him brigadier general on February 17, 1861. He was assigned command of a brigade of Georgia troops that fought with Stonewall Jackson in the Shenandoah Valley. Lawton performed exceptionally well at Gaines' Mill during the Seven Days Battles and was elevated to divisional command because of his seniority when Ewell went down with a severe leg wound. His ascent to division command would last less than last three weeks, as he was wounded during the opening hours of the Battle of Antietam.[2]

Because Lawton's division had seen service on many a battlefield, its numbers were decimated, particularly among the officer corps. Brig. Gen. Jubal Early and Brig. Gen. Harry Hays were able brigade commanders who led their units during the Maryland Campaign, but the other two brigades were led by experienced regimental officers who had never led a large number of troops in battle. These included Col. Marcellus Douglass, who commanded Lawton's own brigade, and Col. James Walker, who commanded Brig. Gen. Isaac Trimble's brigade, while the latter recuperated from a wound sustained at Second Bull Run.

The division marched north with the rest of Stonewall Jackson's wing. It crossed the Potomac River on September 5 at White's Ford and encamped about three miles from the Baltimore & Ohio Railroad. The division then headed to the Monocacy River to seize the railroad bridge. As part of Special Orders Number 191, Lawton joined Jackson's two other divisions marching through Frederick on September 10. After passing through Middletown, the division reached the Potomac River at Williamsport on September 11. The command eventually passed through Martinsburg, Virginia and camped a mile from Halltown, Virginia on the evening of September 13. The following afternoon, Lawton arranged his division in three columns, with Hays' brigade on the left of the turnpike leading into Harpers Ferry, Douglass' on the right of the road, and Walker's marching on the road. Early's brigade followed in a second line. The division continued in this fashion until it reached the woods on Schoolhouse Ridge, opposite the main Union defensive position on Bolivar Heights, where Lawton deployed his division into line of battle. Early's brigade remained in the second line behind Douglass' brigade. The men lay on their arms in the woods during the night of September 14. Jackson brought up his artillery that night and Lawton advanced his line out of the woods on the morning of September 15. Douglass' brigade moved by the right flank to support Maj. Gen. A.P. Hill's division advancing adjacent to the Shenandoah River. The men did not get very far before they saw white flags fluttering along the enemy's position.[3]

Lawton received orders on the afternoon of September 15 to march to Sharpsburg where his troops were urgently needed. The hungry men needed rations before the march could begin. Douglass' and Walker's men drew rations from Harpers Ferry and began their march around sunset, but Hays' and Early's were told to wait until the commissary wagons arrived. Douglass' and Walker's men marched into the night and finally went into camp about four miles from Shepherdstown. Early's and Hays' men did not receive their rations until later that evening, and then needed to cook them, so they did not begin their march until 1:00 a.m. on September 16. They finally reached Douglass' and Walker's camp, and then the entire division completed its march to the Potomac River. The men crossed at sunrise on September 16 and halted in woods, about a mile from town, where they joined J.R. Jones' division.

The men were permitted to rest until the late afternoon of September 16, when they were ordered back into line and marched through fields north of Sharpsburg to Hagerstown Pike, and then to the West Woods around the Dunker Church, probably in response to the Union I Corps' crossing of Antietam Creek. The division rested until sometime between 10:00 and 11:00 p.m., when Douglass' and Walker's brigades were ordered out of the West Woods to replace John Hood's men in front of the Miller Cornfield and East Woods. Occasional skirmishing occurred during the night. Hays' and Early's men remained in reserve in the West Woods.[4]

Soon after daybreak on September 17, Lawton watched Union troops making their way south toward Walker's and Douglass' brigades. Early's brigade was sent northwest toward Nicodemus Heights to support Jeb Stuart's artillery platform there. Hays' brigade remained in reserve in the West Woods, just northwest of the Dunker Church until ordered to support Douglass' brigade at about 6:15 a.m. Lawton was in an exposed position with his three brigades when he was severely wounded by an artillery shell, so Jubal Early assumed command of the division. Douglass' and Walker's men were barely holding their own when Hays' men appeared. Douglass suggested a charge and Hays agreed. Hays soon found his men in a crossfire from George Hartsuff's brigade in the Cornfield and Truman Seymour's brigade in the East Woods. The charge did not last long, but it cost the brigade over 50% of its men. Both Douglass' and Hays' brigades were decimated by the artillery pounding and overwhelming small arms fire, forcing them to vacate their positions and fall back toward Smoketown Road, leaving Walker's men in place in front (south) of the East Woods. The brigade remained here as Hood's division appeared on their left and drove the enemy from the Cornfield. The brigade pulled back as Roswell Ripley's brigade (Brig. Gen. D.H. Hill's division) approached.[5]

Lawton's remaining brigade, Early's, left its supporting position near Nicodemus Heights and headed back toward Hagerstown Pike where it battled William Goodrich's brigade (George Greene's division; XII Corps), supported by Marsena Patrick's brigade (Abner Doubleday's division; I Corps). Early's Virginians were supported by the remnants of J.R. Jones' Stonewall Division in halting Goodrich's thrust south. Early's brigade, now under Col. William Smith of the 49th Virginia, was ordered south to stop the 125th Pennsylvania's (Samuel Crawford's brigade; George Greene's division; XII Corps) advance through the West Woods. It effectively did so, but a new threat materialized in the form of John Sedgwick's Union division (II Corps) advancing toward the West Woods. The brigade joined with Lafayette McLaws' division to repel this advance.

Early next rode to the rear to hunt up the remnants of his division. It would take until the following morning for the division's survivors to assemble. Under orders from Jackson, Early marched his division back toward the Potomac River, crossing at Boteler's Ford just after sunrise, ending the activities of Lawton's division during the Maryland Campaign. The division went into action at Sharpsburg with fewer than 4,000 men and lost 1,338, or about a third of its numbers.[6]

**Bradley M. Gottfried**

\*\*\*

## Lawton's Brigade: Colonel Marcellus Douglass, Major John Lowe, Colonel John Lamar

**Units:** 13th Georgia, 26th Georgia, 31st Georgia, 38th Georgia, 60th Georgia, 61st Georgia
**Strength:** 1,781
**Losses:** 567 (106k-440w-21m)[7]

The brigade was recruited and organized in a span of eleven months, June 1861 to May 1862, representing every quadrant of the "Peach State." The 13th regiment was most experienced, serving in western Virginia early in the war, but then returned to Georgia due to the men's illness and need of equipment. With Alexander Lawton in command, the six regiments entrained for the seat of war in time for the Seven Days Battles. The brigade saw significant action at Gaines' Mill and the Second Bull Run Campaign in late August, making seasoned soldiers of the men.[8]

Col. Marcellus Douglass, a forty-one year-old lawyer turned soldier, led the brigade. Described as a small, fair-skinned man with light blue eyes and blonde curly hair, Douglass did not fit the mould of a fighting man by appearance. A resident of Cuthbert in Randolph County and graduate of the University of Georgia, he began a law practice in 1847, was appointed notary, and became a member of the local Ways & Means Committee. Elected to the town council, he was a delegate to Georgia's secession convention, voting against leaving the Union. Putting his personal feelings aside, he entered the Confederate army as captain, Company E, 13th Georgia Infantry. He became colonel of the regiment in February 1862.[9]

The trek to Maryland for Douglass and his Georgia brigade began on September 5 with reveille before dawn. A speedy crossing of the Potomac River was expected and, although there was scant opposition to the Confederate entry into Maryland, the shallow water brought the troops to rather steep riverbanks that slowed the column's progress. Once ashore, the men were put to work destroying a railroad bridge and then treating themselves to some captured stores. The men headed toward Frederick City across the pleasant Maryland countryside to a rather mixed reception. "There is not much feeling for the South in Maryland," Sgt. Harrison Wells of the 13th Georgia wrote, adding, "there are some few patriots in Maryland, but they are far and few between." Wells also noticed that some of the residents, "had Union flags hanging from their windows and would sing Union songs," and added, "The boys treated them gentlemanly and did not appear to notice." Three uneventful days near Frederick ended on September 10 when the entire Confederate force in Maryland was put in motion.[10]

### Harpers Ferry

An ambitious plan unfolded to subdue a large Union army garrison at Harpers Ferry. Stonewall Jackson led three divisions, including Lawton's, north on the National Road through Frederick, toward the Potomac River, crossing at Williamsport, Maryland. The brigade advanced to a railroad depot at North Mountain, Virginia on September 11, and in the process, helped in "running some yanks off to Harper's Ferry," according to Sgt. Wells. This action was intentional as Jackson hoped to corral as many Union troops as he could at Harpers Ferry. A march of over sixty-two miles brought the soldiers to the outskirts of Harpers Ferry on September 13. Douglass' brigade was in line of battle west of the garrison town the next day. Confederate artillery overwhelmed the Union defenders and forced their surrender without the need of a large-scale infantry assault. Wells commented, "We had the garrison hemmed in and compelled them to surrender on the 15th." Speaking for many in the Confederate ranks he continued, "I was much relieved when I saw their white flag. This affair was most glorious."[11]

## Antietam

"Before we had time to rest, we were ordered forward again to help our friend Longstreet in Maryland," stated Wells. "We hurried forward and crossed the Potomac a third time on the 16th near Shepherdstown." In Maryland again, Douglass led the troops into fields west of Sharpsburg with the rest of Lawton's division, followed by other troops of Jackson's command. The men were ordered to form ranks during the late afternoon. Although originally ordered to the right of the Confederate battle line, south and east of Sharpsburg, the column of Georgians marched through the town until directed north to reinforce James Longstreet's beleaguered command, then in command of the sector.[12]

Proceeding into thick woods north of the whitewashed Dunker Church at about sunset, the Georgians stacked arms and settled in to get some rest. New orders at 10:00 p.m. changed everything. The men formed ranks, shouldered their weapons, followed a narrow trail out of the dark woods, and crossed Hagerstown Pike. They passed through an opening in the turnpike fence into a low pasture to relieve the famished soldiers of John Hood's division. Lt. Col. John Crowder's 31st Georgia advanced to suppress picket firing on the brigade's front. Eight companies formed a reserve in advance of the main brigade line, while two companies, under Lt. William Harrison, deployed as skirmishers. Harrison's line extended from the East

Woods to near Hagerstown Pike, penetrating some 50 feet into the corn. Some of the skirmishers crept a bit too close to the Union lines. Suddenly, voices from Union pickets commanded them to halt. "They told us to throw down our guns and be quick about it," recalled Sgt. Willis Martin. "There seemed to be a whole battle line a few paces from us," he recalled and, along with Harrison and some others, Martin complied with the request of their blue-coated adversaries. The troops that Martin observed were Pennsylvanians of Truman Seymour's tough, battle-tested 1st Brigade of Pennsylvania Reserves, commanded by George Meade, waiting for daybreak to attack the Georgians' line.[13]

Union artillery fired canister into the Cornfield at dawn on September 17, causing Douglass' remaining skirmishers to withdraw to the main body of the 31st Georgia, south of the Cornfield and 100 hundred yards in advance of the brigade line. Seymour's Pennsylvanians advanced through the East Woods and laid an accurate fire onto the 31st Georgia. Crowder deployed his regiment along the edge of the East Woods and repelled the first attack. The blue line was reinforced and the Georgians, without concealment, were no match for the savvy Pennsylvanians. The 31st rejoined the brigade line amid shouts of "what's the matter?" and "what are you running for?" from jeering comrades. "You'll soon find out!" was their reply.[14]

The vulnerable position of Douglass' brigade became apparent at daybreak. The brigade was positioned approximately 225 yards south of the Cornfield fence in what amounted to a basin. The ground was slightly lower than the Cornfield, bordered by the East Woods on the right and high ground to the left where the Hagerstown Pike ran. Stone "protuberances" and ledges gave the men some protection and they pulled down a rail fence to use as a breastwork. "Our brigade was stretched out in a very thin line with wide intervals between the regiments to occupy as much space as possible," remarked Gordon Bradwell. The left of the brigade line, held by the 26th Georgia, was initially located at the foot of high ground 120 yards east of Hagerstown Pike. The nearest Confederate brigade was part of J.R. Jones' division and it was on the west of the pike, out of visual contact with Douglass' line. The 38th Georgia under Capt. William Battey was on the immediate right of the 26th, and the 61st Georgia commanded by Col. John Lamar was next. These three regiments faced the Cornfield. Then the line angled slightly toward the East Woods with the 60th Georgia under Capt. Watters Jones, the 13th led by Capt. D.A. Kidd, and on the right of the line was the aforementioned 31st Georgia. A gap of more than 60 yards existed between the right of Douglass' line and the left of James Walker's brigade of Lawton's division.[15]

Union artillery "opened with great fury" in advance of Joseph Hooker's attack. The thump of Confederate artillery from high ground behind the brigade line announced an imminent threat to the I Corps' infantry. Gunners of S.D. Lee's Confederate artillery battalion spotted a large formation moving south through the Cornfield toward Douglass' brigade and opened fire. The target was Abram Duryee's brigade of New York and Pennsylvania infantry (James Ricketts' division). Confederate artillerymen tried to blunt the impact of the attack, blasting the blue battle line traversing the Cornfield. "Colonel Douglass ran from regiment to regiment exhorting the men not to fire until the enemy reached the fence and began to get over it – to shoot low and make every bullet count." The men were urged to pick out rows of corn and fire at them. Two New York regiments reached the fence near the eastern portion of the Cornfield and advanced closer to the waiting Georgians. When they reached effective range, Douglass gave the order to fire. The Georgians unleashed a crushing volley, which made the bluecoats "stagger and hesitate." The firing became general. "That's right, my brave boys," yelled Douglass, "pour it into them!" Soon, this Union thrust "broke into a disorderly mass helped on by our cheering and yelling." The Union troops rallied and advanced, firing at close range. Rifle smoke hung in the moist early morning air obscuring the battle lines. The soldiers, at times, fired at muzzle flashes seen in the haze of battle smoke. Duryee's two right regiments

did not venture far from the Cornfield fence and the 26th Georgia moved obliquely to the high ground near the Hagerstown Pike to take advantage of that position. The 26th fired a destructive enfilading fire into the right flank of Duryee's line, which was also receiving frontal fire from the 38th and 61st regiments. At one point, the 38th Georgia attempted to advance to the cover of a rock ledge, but was driven back by the intense fire from Duryee's right regiments. The right side of Douglass' brigade suffered under Duryee's frontal fire and Truman Seymour's flank fire from the East Woods. Under the Georgians' concentrated fire, with assistance from Walker's brigade on the right, Duryee's men withdrew. This action lasted approximately thirty minutes; it was now about 6:30 a.m. Casualties mounted from the "distressing artillery fire from the Union batteries in front and from the long range guns beyond the Antietam," according to historian Ezra Carman. Jubal Early reported how the Douglass' brigade was subjected to a "terrible carnage."[16]

Skirmishers from Douglass' brigade followed Duryee's retreating soldiers into the corn. The remainder of the brigade followed. The Georgians, with the help of Walker's brigade, had dealt Duryee's men a punishing blow and sought to inflict even more losses on the decimated bluecoats. Douglass requested that Hays' brigade, which had been in reserve, join in the counter-attack. Soon, the Georgia skirmishers encountered another Union brigade pushing south through the Cornfield. The skirmish line withdrew slowly from the corn as George Hartsuff's brigade (Ricketts' division; I Corps), now commanded by Col. Richard Coulter, bore down on them. With approximately 1,000 men in the ranks, this contingent of Massachusetts, New York and Pennsylvania troops replaced Duryee's shattered brigade. Douglass' men returned to the pasture field south of the Cornfield as Confederate artillery pounded Hartsuff's line.[17]

The Georgians blasted the right of Hartsuff's line as Hays' Louisiana brigade surged forward. Some of Douglass' men joined this attack while others resumed their original positions. While the right of

Hartsuff's brigade received severe punishment in this stand-up firefight, two of his regiments took positions in the East Woods and enfiladed the Confederate battle line. To make matters worse, constant Union artillery fire from positions north of the Cornfield and from long-range artillery beyond the creek pounded every foot of ground. Scores of Georgians and Louisiana soldiers were killed or wounded by this devastating fire. One of the casualties was Douglass. A ball struck him in the abdomen, yet he stayed on his feet and encouraged the men, urging them to make every cartridge count. He was struck in the chest with another shot that knocked him to the ground. The twice-wounded colonel, "refused to leave the field, when suddenly a shell burst nearby, mutilating one of his legs." Struck eight times by enemy fire, Douglass died on the field with his men around him.[18]

With the right of the Georgians' line subjected to a withering fire, the left of the brigade wheeled obliquely toward the turnpike to face a new threat. John Gibbon's brigade (Abner Doubleday's division), soon to be dubbed the "Iron Brigade," moved south in line of battle, extending from the turnpike into the Cornfield. The 2nd and 6th Wisconsin led the attack. The left of Douglass' line occupied the high ground east of the pike and lay in wait as the "Badger State" men wearing regulation U.S. Army headgear – high-crowned, wide brimmed black hats – neared the southern edge of the Cornfield. Rufus Dawes of the 6th Wisconsin described the encounter with Douglass' line, "As we appeared at the edge of the corn, a long line of men in butternut and gray rose up from the ground." Upon sight of each other to two battle lines let loose ferocious volleys. "Men, I cannot say fell; they were knocked out of the ranks by the dozens," recalled Dawes. The Wisconsin men surged forward over the Cornfield fence a short distance, then "by common impulse" fell back to the Cornfield and lay down behind the low rail fence. The Wisconsin men, joined by Walter Phelps' small brigade of New Yorkers and U.S. Sharpshooters (Doubleday's division), went forward again. "There is a rattling fusillade and loud cheers. 'Forward' is the word,"

recalled Dawes. The Union line fired with "demonical fury" and the men were "shouting and laughing hysterically" as they mowed down the Georgians in front of them. Douglass' line was a shambles. William Christian's brigade (Ricketts' division) arrived in the East Woods and poured an unrelenting fire on Douglass' front and flank. Lt. Col. Crowder of the 31st Georgia, "a man destitute of fear," was wounded and removed from the field.

All told, five of the six regimental commanders in Douglass' brigade were killed or wounded. The brigade, desperate for ammunition, offered only pockets of resistance as it was bent into a defensive arc with "only a man every ten feet or more" resisting this onslaught. Finally, with half of the brigade killed or wounded, the Georgians gave way. The field was "covered with rebels fleeing for life, into the (West) woods," wrote Dawes. Many were shot trying to climb the sturdy turnpike fence. At last, Hood's division dashed out of the West Woods and formed lines to advance, replacing Douglass' brigade. These were the same troops the Georgians relieved the night before. The time was shortly after 7:00 a.m. and Douglass' brigade had been engaged since daybreak.[19]

Unwounded survivors of the brigade found their way to a position southwest of the Dunker Church and Maj. John Lowe of the 31st Georgia, the ranking officer, assumed command. With a loss of more than 49% of its effective strength, the brigade was not called upon to fight the rest of the day. On September 18, under truce flags, Douglass' body was removed from the field with scores of wounded Georgians. Dr. William Scaife of the 31st Georgia described the medical facilities as two tents: one used for surgeries and the other used to hide amputated limbs from the eyes of the men.[20]

### Shepherdstown

For the fourth time in two weeks, the Georgians crossed the Potomac River on the morning of September 19, reaching Virginia's shore south of Shepherdstown with approximately 250 men fit for duty. The Georgians were used as a rearguard at the river's bluffs with Col. John Lamar of the 61st Georgia in command. A Union effort was made to pursue Gen. Lee's army. On the afternoon of September 19, Union batteries were positioned on the Maryland side and a large number of troops appeared at the river. No sustained action occurred as the Georgians were instructed not to expend ammunition needlessly or at long range. They were soon withdrawn from the river's bluff and began the march toward Winchester, Virginia, ending the Maryland Campaign.[21]

Douglass' brigade had the distinction of firing the first shots during the battle of Sharpsburg on September 17. They performed exceptionally well, considering their exposed position and the overwhelming numbers of Union troops they battled.

**William Sagle**

* * *

## Early's Brigade: Brigadier General Jubal Early, Colonel William Smith

**Units:** 13th Virginia, 25th Virginia, 31st Virginia, 44th Virginia, 49th Virginia, 52nd Virginia, 58th Virginia
**Strength:** 1,794[22]
**Losses:** 194 (18k-167w-9m)[23]

The brigade was comprised of seven small Virginia regiments. All but the 58th Virginia were mustered into service in the summer of 1861 and all but the 49th Virginia had begun their service in the mountains of West Virginia. The 13th Virginia had the distinction of initially serving under Col. A.P. Hill and several companies of the 49th Virginia fought at First Bull Run. All had seen extensive action in multiple campaigns. The seven regiments were brigaded together under Brig. Gen. Arnold Elzey during the spring of 1862 and fought together through the Seven Days Campaign, where Elzey was desperately wounded, and Jubal Early was elevated to brigade command.[24]

Jubal Anderson Early was a West Point graduate class of 1837 and combat veteran, having served during the Second Seminole and the Mexican-American Wars before volunteering his services to the Confederate army in May 1861. A lawyer and politician by trade, Early "showed himself tenacious, cool and hard hitting" as a military leader. He did however, possess an abrasive personality and quick temper which caused him difficulty with his superiors and, at times, with his peers, but he was well liked and respected as a commander, particularly by his men who affectionately called him "Old Jube."[25]

Early's Brigade crossed the Potomac River into Maryland on September 5, 1862 and proceeded north to Frederick, arriving the following day. The brigade made camp a few miles away, near Monocacy Junction, where it remained for several days resting and resupplying. The brigade then joined Jackson's column heading for Harpers Ferry on September 10.

### Harpers Ferry

The brigade arrived at Halltown, Virginia, about three miles west of Harpers Ferry on September 13 with the remainder of Lawton's division and went into bivouac. The division deployed for action on Schoolhouse Ridge on September 14 with Marcellus Douglass' and James Walker's brigades on the right of the turnpike leading to Harpers Ferry and Harry Hays' brigade on the left of it. Early's brigade was in reserve behind Douglass'. The entire line now advanced toward Bolivar Heights. Early's brigade was then shifted across the road to form behind Hays' Louisianans. Lawton brought up artillery during the night for the final attack, which was to come on the morning of September 15, but before the advance could commence, white flags appeared along the enemy's line. Early recalled in later years that the area to be traversed would have been difficult at best as the valley between Schoolhouse Ridge and Bolivar Heights "was cleared . . . the enemy's works was steep and over thick brush that had been felled so as to make a formidable assault." He found the prospect of taking the heights, "by no means comforting."[26]

"After the white flag went up, we started almost immediately to rejoin Gen. Lee in Maryland and a most trying march it was," recalled Capt. Samuel Buck of the 13th Virginia. Lt. Wray Lacy of the 44th Virginia recalled, "[T]he marches of this period were undoubtedly the severest, in every particular . . . The command frequently marched all day and all night. The privations were also of the most painful and distressing nature. They were often without provision for several days in succession and subsisted upon green corn." Straggling was severe, sapping the brigade's strength.[27]

Early's brigade, with the remainder of Lawton's division, crossed the Potomac River just south of Shepherdstown at Boteler's Ford and arrived in Sharpsburg on the morning of September 16, tired but prepared for combat.

## Antietam

Jackson positioned two of Lawton's four brigades south of D. R. Miller's Cornfield and east of Hagerstown Pike in the open fields between the East and West Woods. He retained the other two brigades in reserve west of Hagerstown Pike, including Early's Virginians, who were camped near the Alfred Poffenberger cabin. According to Jackson, his men slept "upon their arms disturbed by the occasional fire of the pickets of the two armies who were in close proximity to each other."[28]

Before dawn on September 17, Jackson personally ordered Early's brigade to Nicodemus Heights, about a mile to the northwest, to support over 12 cannon deployed during the night by Jeb Stuart. When Early arrived, he spied the batteries dueling with Northern artillery just beyond the Joseph

Poffenberger barn. At Stuart's suggestion, Early formed a line behind the eminence and remained there for an hour. During this time the 23rd New York (Patrick's brigade; Doubleday's division) ventured forward to protect Joseph Hooker's I Corps' right flank. Stuart responded by repositioning a battery to face it and Early threw out the 100-man 13th Virginia on the skirmish line, neutralizing the threat.[29]

A bigger concern materialized when Marsena Patrick's and John Gibbon's brigades (Abner Doubleday's division; I Corps) began driving south. Stuart decided it would be more productive to reposition his artillery closer to Sharpsburg along Hauser Ridge, so he moved Early's brigade with him, deploying it in woods about 425 yards northwest of the Alfred Poffenberger's cabin. Lawton was wounded around this time while leading his men in a desperate fight in the Cornfield and Jackson tapped Early to take command of the division. Early assigned Col. William "Billy" Smith of the 49th Virginia Infantry to command his brigade, instructing him "to resist the enemy at all hazards."[30]

J.R. Jones' Stonewall division was now under heavy attack, so Early moved his brigade (now commanded by Smith) to the south, leaving the 13th Virginia Regiment with Stuart. The six regiments formed in the West Woods north of the Dunker Church, perpendicular to Hagerstown Pike, facing north. J. R. Jones' men were defeated by the time Early's men arrived, so he ordered the 200-300 remaining men from the division to form on his left. Soon, "A considerable body of the enemy's troops was seen in the field in my front, as thus presented, which was evidently endeavoring to make a movement on our flank and rear." This was Patrick's brigade, but it showed little interest in advancing. What did concern Early was the advance of the XII Corps, which threatened his right flank. He directed Smith to refuse the 49th Virginia so it faced Hagerstown Pike, at a right angle with the remainder of the brigade.[31]

Early rode about looking for his new division, but found few survivors scattered in the rear with no organized presence. He wrote in his report, "I ascertained that these brigades had fallen back some distance to the rear for the purpose of reorganizing, and that they were probably not in a condition to go into the fight again." Early then rode back to Jackson and reported the conditions on the field. "I found the General on a hill in rear of the Dunkard Church . . . he directed me to return to my brigade and resist the enemy until he could send me some reinforcements, which he promised to do as soon as he could obtain them."[32]

William Goodrich's brigade (Greene's division, XII Corps) and three companies of the 124th Pennsylvania supported by Patrick's brigade appeared in front of Early's brigade and the remnants of J.R. Jones' division. The remainder of the large Pennsylvania regiment marched south on Hagerstown Pike, supported by the Purnell Legion of Goodrich's brigade. This was a desperate time as there were no organized Confederate troops between Early and the Sunken Road. Fortunately, the Union threat never materialized, as the Yanks were content to simply engage in long range skirmishing with Early's men.[33]

Early wrote in his report, "I kept an anxious eye on the column on my right, as well as on the one moving up in my front, and very soon I saw the column on my right move into the woods in the direction of the church. I looked to the rear for the re-enforcements, and could not see them coming." The new column Early observed was the rookie 125th Pennsylvania (Samuel Crawford's brigade; Alpheus Williams' division; XII Corps), which entered the empty southern portion of the West Woods near the Dunker Church alone, threatening to isolate Early from the rest of Lee's army. It was about 8:30 a.m. and the field in front of Early's men was littered with dead and wounded soldiers from both sides. Early hoped for reinforcements to address the 125th Pennsylvania's threat, but when they did not materialize, he left the few hundred men of J. R. Jones's Stonewall Division, now under Andrew Grigsby, and his own 31st Virginia Infantry

to confront the threat to the north and marched the remainder of his brigade south, taking advantage of the rocky outcroppings and shelter of the rolling terrain in the West Woods. The 49th Virginia regiment led the column south.[34]

As his men approached the Pennsylvanians, Early realized they were "concealed from his [the enemy's] view, and it was evident that my presence . . . was not suspected." His skirmish line pushed the Pennsylvanians' counterparts back. Just then Early saw G.T. Anderson's brigade (D.R. Jones' division; Longstreet's Wing) approach from the southwest—the first of Jackson's promised reinforcements. As Anderson's men deployed, Early "ordered the brigade to face to the front and open fire, which was done in handsome style and responded to by the enemy." This was all Early intended to do. However, he changed his mind when he observed some of Anderson's troops "which had come up to re-enforce me preparing to advance into the woods from the direction of my right flank." The movement concerned Early as it could expose "my brigade to their fire, and that the two movements would throw us into confusion, as they would have been at right angles." The subsequent attack by both Early and Anderson was too much for the rookie Pennsylvanians and they began breaking for the rear. To Early's dismay, the brigade, "which I have always found difficult to restrain, commenced pursuing, driving the enemy in front entirely out of the woods. Notwithstanding my efforts to stop the[m]."[35]

According to historian Ezra Carman, Early's success was not as clear-cut as Early made it appear. "Early was making a vigorous attack on the 125th Pennsylvania, advancing and falling back, and again advancing, then lying down. The left regiments were in some confusion, when Captain Lilley, 25th Virginia, observing a line coming up, called his own men to hold on a littler longer, as help was coming, and in a moment Barksdale [brigade] came up on the left and joined the attack." Grave danger now approached, from beyond the West Woods, John Sedgwick's Union division (II Corps) headed in Early's direction. It was about 9:15 a.m. when Early shifted his brigade's front once again and, joined by several brigades of reinforcements from Lafayette McLaws' division, aimed their fury north, striking Sedgwick's unsuspecting brigades on their left flank. The results were fairly predictable as the Federal division was hit in its front, flank, and rear by strong Confederate reinforcements. Several of Early's regiments participated in the attack that drove Sedgwick from the West Woods, most notably the flank attack on the 15th Massachusetts and likely the 59th New York.[36]

With the repulse of Sedgwick's division, Early's brigade returned to its former position, parallel to Hagerstown Pike, about 130 yards south of the middle body of the West Woods. The men lay on their arms behind the rocky outcroppings and awaited the aerial storm of Federal shot and shell from in front of the East Woods to subside. Captain Henry Wingfield, commander of the 58th Virginia regiment asserted, "We formed line again holding the old battleground. We remained in line of battle all night, the cries of the wounded and dying rendered the position a most unpleasant one." When Lee ordered a consolidation of his lines, "Early's Brigade …was moved to a reserve position south of the Dunker Church and west of the Hagerstown Turnpike, where it would be available to support either Jackson or Longstreet."[37]

### Shepherdstown

Lee began his retreat on September 18 and Early's brigade was one of the last to wade the Potomac at Boteler's Ford—the same crossing they used to enter Maryland three days before. The campaign was not yet over for Early's brigade, for it was called upon to support A. P. Hill's division in repelling a portion of the Union V Corps intent on attacking Lee's rear on September 20. The men were not engaged but endured some shelling from the Union batteries across the river."

Early's brigade did all that could be asked of it during the Maryland Campaign. In his after action report Robert E. Lee singled out Early, stating he "… attacked with great resolution the large force opposed to him." Fellow Virginian, Jeb Stuart wrote, ". . . Early behaved with great coolness and good judgment, particularly after he came in command of his division." Jackson added, ". . . General Early attacked with great vigor and gallantry the column on his right and front." Early claimed in his report, "I hope I may be excused for referring to the record shown by my own brigade, which has never been broken or compelled to fall back or left one of its dead to be buried by the enemy, but have invariably driven the enemy when opposed to him, and slept upon the ground on which it has fought."[38]

**Mac Bryan**

***

## Trimble's Brigade: Colonel James Walker, Captain Isaac Feagin

**Units:** 15th Alabama, 12th Georgia, 21st Georgia, 21st North Carolina, 1st North Carolina Battalion Sharpshooters
**Strength:** 707[39]
**Losses:** 237 (27k-202w-8m)[40]

Brigadier General Isaac Trimble's brigade was a veteran unit that had seen action in several campaigns, including the Shenandoah Valley, Seven Days, and Second Bull Run. Most of the units were mustered into service between June and September 1861. The 1st North Carolina Battalion Sharpshooters were the exception as they were not formed until April 1862. The brigade played a major role during the Battle of Cross Keys when it blunted a Union attack and then successfully counterattacked. It was also heavily engaged at Cedar Mountain and played a major role in Stonewall Jackson's capture of Manassas Junction during the Second Bull Run Campaign.

Sixty-year-old Isaac Trimble was severely wounded in the leg on August 29, 1862 and recuperating during the Maryland Campaign. He was replaced by Col. James Walker. Born in 1832, Walker attended the Virginia Military Institute but was expelled by Jackson, just weeks before his graduation. Walker was so incensed that he tried to kill Jackson by throwing a brick at him from his dormitory window and spoke of shooting him. He pursued a variety of professions until he became a lawyer. He entered the war as a captain in the 4th Virginia Infantry but soon rose to command the 13th Virginia Infantry. He performed exceptionally well and when Trimble went down, Walker was plucked from another brigade to take over.[41]

The brigade rested a few days near Leesburg, Virginia and then crossed the Potomac River at White's Ford on September 5. The march continued the next day to Frederick. The reception was anything but warm as children waved the U. S. flag at the gray-clad invaders. Capt. Ujanirtus Allen of the 21st Georgia wrote home, "Frederick is guarded and the doors of all business houses closed." Still he believed "Everything of service will be pressed for the army." Allen was especially impressed by the stately homes and the barns, which were "frequently more costly than the dwellings." Walker joined his new brigade while it rested around Frederick.[42]

### Harpers Ferry

The brigade, with the rest of Lawton's division, left Frederick on September 10 and headed toward Middletown and eventually reached Halltown, Virginia about three miles west of Harpers Ferry, where the men camped on September 13. They were in position on Schoolhouse Ridge the following afternoon. Lawton's division straddled Charlestown Turnpike, with the left of Walker's brigade touching it. Marcellus Douglass' brigade was on its right and Harry Hays' brigade was on its left. The men lay on their arms that night, awaiting the morning signal to advance. September 15 dawned bright and the Confederate batteries opened fire. The Harpers Ferry garrison capitulated before Walker's men were waved forward to take Bolivar Heights.[43]

### Antietam

The men marched all night during September 15-16 and upon arriving at Boteler's Ford, were permitted to rest for a few hours. They crossed the Potomac River before daylight on September 16. The men never had an opportunity to visit Sharpsburg, as the column turned left and headed for the Dunker Church in the West Woods. Jackson agreed to relieve John Hood's division in front of the East Woods and Miller's Cornfield on the evening of September 16 and Douglass' and Walker's brigades were selected for the mission. Walker's men marched northwest, where they replaced Evander Law's brigade in front of the East Woods. They settled down for the night with Douglass' brigade on their left and Roswell Ripley's brigade (D.H. Hill's division) behind them near the Mumma farmhouse. It was an uneasy night as twice the pickets of Truman Seymour's Union brigade (George Meade's division; I Corps) attacked Walker's pickets and firing occurred throughout the night. Few men were probably able to sleep.

Walker's brigade was deployed from left to right: 12th Georgia- 21st Georgia- 21st North Carolina- 15th Alabama. The three right regiments were deployed in a plowed field on the right of Smoketown Road facing northeast; the 12th Georgia was on the left of the road in a clover field. The right flank of the 15th Alabama rested on the Mumma graveyard. The left flank of the 12th Georgia did not link with the right flank of Douglass' brigade, creating a 50-yard gap between the two. The officers saw the problem in the morning and moved quickly to fill it by sliding troops in that direction. There was also a gap between the 12th Georgia and the rest of the brigade.[44]

Skirmishing between Seymour's and Walker's brigades began in earnest at first light on September 17 and continued until sunrise, when the Pennsylvanians advanced a line of battle, driving Walker's pickets back to their main line. The Union guns of position on the opposite side of Antietam Creek opened fire and enfiladed Walker's line. He noted in his report, "my command was exposed to full view of their gunners and had no shelter." He found this fire to be "very annoying, but less destructive than I at first apprehended it would be." Walker was more irritated by the fire of Capt. Ezra Matthews' Union battery deployed on high ground just beyond the Miller Cornfield. A new threat materialized when the 5th and 13th Pennsylvania Reserves (Seymour's brigade), advanced to the edge of the East Woods and opened a brisk fire. Walker noted Seymour's men "opened fire upon us, to which my men replied with spirit and effect, holding them in check."[45]

At about 6:00 a.m., Abram Duryee's brigade advanced through the Miller Cornfield to the left of the brigade. The 105th New York on the brigade's left flank actually advanced beyond the edge of the Cornfield. The 2nd Pennsylvania Reserves was on its left in the East Woods and both fired into Walker's brigade. Walker watched how effectively the 12th Georgia on the left of his line was playing on the enemy, so he ordered the 21st Georgia and 21st North Carolina to advance into the plowed field and swing to the left to take a position behind the same stone wall perpendicular to their original position, where they opened fire on Duryee's New Yorkers and the 2nd Pennsylvania Reserves. The retreat of Seymour's 5th and 13th Pennsylvania Reserves from the edge of the East Woods allowed Walker's men to concentrate on the New Yorkers and Pennsylvanians. At this point, three of Walker's regiments were facing northwest and only the 15th Alabama faced north from its original position near the Mumma cemetery.[46]

Harry Hays' Louisiana brigade arrived between Walker's left and Douglass' right and launched an attack. Walker ordered his men to prepare to charge but "the fresh troops [Hays'], which were advancing in such good order at first, gave way under the enemy's fire and ran off the field before they had been halted by their officers and almost before they had fired a gun." Without support on his left, Walker aborted his charge. William Christian's Federal brigade's (James Ricketts' division; I Corps) now arrived and moved through the East Woods, threatening Walker's right flank, and forcing him to pull his units back to the position they occupied earlier that morning, after about an hour behind the stone wall. Walker received reports of his men running out of ammunition, so he ordered his men to scrounge the cartridge boxes of the dead and wounded and continue the fight. Walker was wounded around this time and headed for the rear, leaving Capt. Isaac Feagin of the 15th Alabama in command of the brigade. Desperate times call for unusual measures, and Walker's officers, for the first time in the war, picked up muskets and used them against Christian's men. Walker's men were relieved to see Ripley's brigade advance at about 7:30 a.m., permitting them to fall back to beyond the burning Mumma farm buildings to replenish their ammunition.[47]

Gen. D.H. Hill, accompanying Ripley and two of his other brigades, rode toward the 15th Alabama and when he saw the men lying on the ground, he exclaimed. "My God, is this an Alabama regiment lying here?" They explained they were awaiting the arrival of ammunition, but Hill just waved them off, and told them to use bayonets and then rocks, if necessary. The men loudly disparaged Hill's remarks as he rode away.[48]

Walker's brigade, except for the 21st Georgia, eventually retired to the fence along Smoketown Road in their rear, and then continued their movement south with Hays' and Douglass' brigades to beyond Reel Ridge, just north of Sharpsburg. The 21st Georgia was still full of fight and did not retreat with the remainder of the brigade. Its commander was wounded so Capt. James Nisbet commanded what was left of the regiment. Nisbet apparently approached Capt. William Robbins, now in command of the 4th Alabama (Evander Law's brigade; John Hood's division) for orders and he was told to form his men on the right. The 5th

Texas slid into position on the Georgians' right and the three regiments marched into the East Woods. Nisbet ordered his men to "take cover behind a tree or any kind of shelter they could find and open on them [the enemy] as soon as they got in range." They were up against the 10th Maine (Samuel Crawford's brigade; Alpheus Williams' division; XII Corps). The two sides blazed away at each other until Henry Stainrook's brigade (George Greene's division; XII Corps) arrived and flanked the three regiments. Taking fire from front and both flanks, the three regiments were forced to fall back at about 8:30 a.m.[49]

This ended the fighting by Walker's brigade. By the time the battle ended, its commander was wounded and three of the four regimental commanders were also out of action. The regiment lost 237 men of the 700 or so they brought into battle. Walker transferred out of the brigade and assumed command of the venerable Stonewall Brigade. Trimble's brigade was later broken up and its units distributed to three other brigades.[50]

**Bradley M. Gottfried**

* * *

### Hays' (1st Louisiana) Brigade: Brigadier General Harry Hays

**Units:** 5th Louisiana Infantry, 6th Louisiana Infantry, 7th Louisiana Infantry, 8th Louisiana Infantry, 14th Louisiana Infantry
**Strength:** 1,677[51]
**Losses:** 336 (45k-289w-2m)[52]

The 6th, 7th, 8th, and 9th Louisiana Infantry were first grouped under the command of Col. Isaac Seymour, following the Battle of First Bull Run. They were soon joined by Maj. Roberdeau Wheat's "Louisiana Tiger" Battalion. In November 1861, Seymour was replaced by Brig. Gen. Richard Taylor, son of Zachary Taylor. The Louisianans spent the winter in the Centreville area and then saw

considerable combat during the 1862 Shenandoah Valley Campaign and Seven Days Battles. Large-scale changes occurred during July 1862 when the 9th Louisiana was transferred to the newly formed 2nd Louisiana Brigade, and Wheat's decimated battalion was disbanded and replaced by the 5th and 14th Louisiana Infantry Regiments. The 5th, formerly of Paul Semmes' brigade, had seen action at Lee's Mill, New Bridge, and White Oak Swamp. The 14th, organized as the 1st Regiment, Polish Brigade in June 1861, had served under Roger Pryor at Williamsburg, Seven Pines, Mechanicsville, Gaines' Mill, and Frazier's Farm. At about the same time the brigade was reorganized, Richard Taylor

319

was transferred to the Trans-Mississippi Department, and command passed to Brig. Gen. Harry Thompson Hays.[53]

Harry Hays was born in Wilson County, Tennessee in 1820, and was raised by an uncle in Mississippi after his parents died. He attended St. Mary's School in Baltimore, Maryland and afterwards studied law. He then established a law practice in New Orleans, served in the Mexican War, and became active in the Whig Party. Hays became colonel of the 7th Louisiana Infantry, or "Pelican Regiment" in June 1861. He led it at First Bull Run and through Stonewall Jackson's Valley Campaign, where he was wounded at Port Republic. Hays was promoted to the rank of brigadier general and given command of the 1st Louisiana Brigade in July 1862 while recuperating from his wound. He did not return to the army to assume command of his brigade until two days before the Battle of Antietam.[54]

Col. Henry Forno of the 5th Louisiana commanded the brigade during the Second Bull Run Campaign. The Louisianans suffered a total of 14 casualties at Cedar Mountain on August 9, but during the following three weeks in actions at Bristoe Station, Second Bull Run, and Chantilly they lost 361 more, including Col. Forno, who was wounded. Col. Henry Strong of the 6th Louisiana assumed command of the brigade.[55]

On September 3, Richard Ewell's division, under the command of Alexander Lawton, began its march north, camping for the night near Dranesville, Virginia. The brigade marched through Leesburg and crossed the Potomac River at White's Ford on September 5. Lt. George Ring of Company K, 6th Louisiana proudly wrote, "we . . . at last put foot on Yankee soil." The brigade marched to the Baltimore and Ohio Railroad junction on the Monocacy River, two miles southeast of Frederick on September 6, and remained there for the next three days.[56]

Father James Sheeran, Chaplain of the 14th Louisiana, noted observed Maryland's "numerous cornfields growing abundant crops, the well-stocked pasture ground, the numerous and beautiful orchards whose trees were growing under the weight of delicious fruit, the granaries and barnyards thronged with poultry and swine presented a pleasing contrast with the desolate fields and plundered habitations of North Eastern Virginia." Observing the faces of the Marylanders, Father Sheeran wrote, "we saw some friendly countenances, but the greater number looked upon us with seeming indifference."[57]

## Harpers Ferry

Hays' brigade, with the rest of Lawton's division, decamped early on September 10 and began its march west, spending that night just east of Boonsboro. The next day the Louisianans covered 23 miles, re-crossing the Potomac at Light's Ford near Williamsport. The subsequent march to North Mountain Depot, Virginia put it in the position to help block any northward escape attempt by the Federal garrison at Martinsburg. The garrison fled to Harpers Ferry and the Louisianans passed through Martinsburg the following day, and camped overnight on the banks of Opequon Creek. The advance continued to Halltown, only about three miles west of Harpers Ferry, on September 13. Camp was made along the Shepherdstown Turnpike, north of the town.[58]

Jackson's siege lines began tightening around Harpers Ferry during the late afternoon of September 14. The 1st Louisiana Brigade advanced to Schoolhouse Ridge in column, north of Charlestown Turnpike. Jubal Early's brigade was just behind the Louisianans on the ridge, and Lawton temporarily placed the Louisianans under his command. Early reported his brigades "lay on their arms" in the woods along Schoolhouse Ridge during the night of September 14. With the dawn, the Louisianans formed on the eastern edge of the woods, ready for the assault, which never came. After a short bombardment, the Union garrison surrendered. "We were not in this fight except as spectators," Ring wrote.[59]

Later that afternoon, Early was ordered by Lawton to prepare his and Hays' brigades for the march to Sharpsburg. Hays finally joined his command on September 15 after riding up from Winchester. It was night by the time the men received their rations and then they set off for Boteler's Ford. The Louisianans halted for several hours of rest, four or five miles short of the ford, and crossed soon after dawn on September 16.[60]

## Antietam

After crossing the Potomac River, Hays' brigade proceeded up the road to Sharpsburg, halting and stacking arms in woods on the west side of the road, about a mile south of the town. They spent the better part of September 16 here, until later that afternoon, when the division marched north, following Early's brigade around the western side of Sharpsburg to the West Woods, halting there about dusk. The men bivouacked in the woods behind the rest of the division.[61]

The battle opened at dawn on September 17 with Hays' brigade in reserve. Jackson summoned the brigade to support Marcellus Douglass' Georgia brigade, formed in line of battle east of Hagerstown Pike. Hays' men crossed the pike about 100 yards north of the Dunker Church and headed north. The Louisianans were to initially fill a gap between the 26th Georgia on Douglass's left and the pike, but after some confusion and counter orders, Lawton ordered them further to the right, where they initially formed behind the Georgians. Hays' right rested on Smoketown Road, near the Mumma Lane, where the brigade received fire from Capt. James Thompson's Pennsylvania Light Artillery, Batteries C and F. Ring later wrote to his wife, "(W)e were ordered out into a ploughed field and told to lie down in a line of battle. We were about three hundred yards behind a Georgia brigade. We lay in that position with a fire from three Yankee batteries and one from a battery of our own answering, firing over our head, besides a fire of infantry on the brigade in front of us. I thought, darling, I'd heard at Malvern Hill heavy cannonading, but I was mistaken. That half hour that we were lying in that field taught me to the contrary." The men could not

see much in front of them as dense smoke enveloped the area.[62]

Douglass' brigade was pushing back Abram Duryee's brigade (James Ricketts' division, I Corps) at about 6:15 a.m., when Douglass urged Hays to advance with him on his right. Hays agreed. Ring recounted Hays' men "advanced some three hundred and fifty yards and then commenced firing upon the enemy, who were in front of a wood about two hundred yards off, protected by a battery." They met newly arriving George Hartsuff's Union brigade (Ricketts' division) advancing through the East Woods and Cornfield. The Louisianans hit the 12th Massachusetts, 11th Pennsylvania, and the right of the 13th Massachusetts regiments. The former was hit particularly hard. Its commander, Maj. Elisha Burbank, was killed and the regiment's entire color guard decimated.[63]

Hays' men were also taking losses. Capt. George Wren, who commanded a company of the 8th Louisiana recalled, "I had never seen so many falling in as little a time in any instance before [but] . . . there was a continual shout of forward from different commanders until we were near the enemy and had commenced firing."

Hays men did not see Hartsuff's left flank advancing through the western edge of the East Woods. Part of the 13th Massachusetts and the 83rd New York folded around Hays' right flank and unleashed terrible volleys into it. Wren noted, "Our brigade had become very small being thinned out so fast that we were in an angle the enemy had formed, they were shooting us from two directions." Scores of Louisianans were hit. Ring wrote, "We stood there about half an hour and found ourselves cut all to pieces." Strong, leading the 6th, was slain, along with his horse. While attempting to recover the colonel's personal items, Ring was hit by no fewer than four minie balls.[64]

Both Douglass' and Hays' brigades were forced to stubbornly fall back. William Christian's brigade (also of Ricketts' division) extended Hartsuff's left along the western edge of the East Woods, and added to the firepower. Douglass was killed and

Lawton severely wounded by this time and command and control was breaking down as other leaders fell, including all of Hays' regimental commanders and his entire staff. Although most of Hays' brigade was forced to retreat, Hays, with about 40 of his men, held their original position in front of the Cornfield. Hood's division appeared at this time and swept Hays' and Douglass' tormenters from the field.[65]

The role of Hays' brigade in the fighting at Sharpsburg was over. The brigade's losses exceeded 60%. Wren reported, "Out of eighteen men [in my company] only three were left unhurt that came off the field. The whole brigade fared a similar fate." The survivors retreated to the area behind the West Woods, where they rested with Douglass' and Walker's brigades and replenished their ammunition. In the afternoon, the brigade took up a position behind Hood's now battered division in the West Woods, about 400 yards west of the Dunker Church. "We remained in the front exposed to frequent shelling from the enemy until 5 o'clock p.m. when we fell back to a less exposed position," recalled Ring. Hays' men then shifted south along the western edge of the Hagerstown Pike, across from the Sunken Road.[66]

On the morning of September 18, Early, now commanding Ewell's/Lawton's division, ordered Hays' brigade to form on the left of his old brigade in the West Woods. It remained there until late that night, when it received orders to retire. The Louisianans yet again crossed the Potomac at Boteler's Ford about sunrise on September 19.[67]

### Shepherdstown

After first moving toward Martinsburg, Virginia, Jackson ordered the brigade back to Boteler's Ford early on September 20 to assist A.P. Hill's division during its fight with the Union V Corps. The brigade deployed on the right side of Charlestown Road leading to the ford, but they played no part in the Battle of Shepherdstown. The brigade continued its march toward Martinsburg that afternoon, making camp after midnight near Opequon Creek. The Louisianans remained there until September 24, when they moved to a new position on the Williamsport Pike, six or seven miles north of Martinsburg.[68]

By September 27, Hays' brigade was camped at Bunker Hill, between Martinsburg and Winchester. The brigade slowly regained its strength. On September 30, 1,317 officers and men were present for duty in the brigade. In October, the 9th Louisiana Infantry Regiment returned to the brigade and the 14th was sent to join the 2nd Louisiana Brigade.[69]

**Robert Gottschalk**

*** ***  ***

# A.P. HILL'S DIVISION—

## Major General Ambrose Powell Hill

Few divisions in the Army of Northern Virginia received a special designation; one was A.P. Hill's command, called the "Light Division." The division was created on May 27, 1862 when Brig. Gen. J.R. Anderson's (later commanded by Edward Thomas), Lawrence Branch's, Charles Field's and Maxcy Gregg's brigades were placed in the new unit. Hill named the division and used it on his first dispatch on June 1, 1862. The reason for the name is unclear, but the division's biographer believed Ambrose Hill may have wanted to avoid confusion with D.H. Hill's division. A member of the division later wrote, "We are lightly armed, lightly fed, but march rapidly, and fight frequently!" Two additional brigades—Dorsey Pender's and James Archer's were added on June 11, 1862. The division under Hill's able leadership developed a reputation for being one of the finest fighting forces in Lee's army.[1]

Maj. Gen. A.P. Hill quickly became one of Lee's most effective division leaders. After graduating from West Point in 1847, Hill served in Mexico and fought the Seminoles. He resigned his commission and threw his lot with his native Virginia when it entered the Confederacy. Hill rapidly rose in rank from commander of the 13th Virginia Infantry to brigade command on February 26, 1862. After distinguished service during the Peninsula Campaign, he was given the newly created Light Division. Lee regarded Hill as his best division commander, telling Jefferson Davis, "He fights his troops well and takes good care of them." Physically, Hill was narrow-chested and frail. He wore his hair long and brushed straight back, causing James Longstreet to joke there was "a good deal of 'curled darling'" about Hill. When in battle, Hill donned a red wool hunting shirt, calling it his "battle shirt" and the men knew they were in for a fight when he wore it. He suffered from a case of untreated gonorrhea, which flared up when he was under stress—often when in battle. Hill was beloved by his men because of his "warm manner and his thoughtfulness." But he had another side, jealously guarding his "rights." He could be excessively proud and jealous and this got him in trouble with many of his superiors, including both James Longstreet and Stonewall Jackson. The latter's relationship with Hill was particularly tempestuous. With the death of Stonewall Jackson, Hill ascended to corps command.[2]

Hill's bickering with Stonewall Jackson reached a high point during the march toward Leesburg on the night of September 3. Although the men appreciated Jackson's success, they felt he was overly harsh in his expectations of them. Dorsey Pender wrote home to his wife that he did not care for Jackson "for he forgets that one ever gets tired, hungry or sleepy." Jackson summoned his three division commanders to his headquarters on September 2 and told them to be on the road by 4:00 a.m. the following morning with Hill's division in the lead. When Jackson rode to Hill's camp at the appointed hour, he found the men just standing around and one brigade had not yet broken camp. He was inquiring why they were not on the march, when Hill rode up. Jackson "mildly" reprimanded Hill for not promptly following his orders. An observer noted Hill "took this reprimand rather sullenly, his face flushing up, but he said nothing." Jackson was not yet done, speaking up in a loud voice he said, "There are but few commanders who properly appreciate the value of celerity!"

Beginning the march, Hill rode at the front of his division, setting a fast pace so he would not again be criticized, but all it did was raise Jackson's ire even further because the column became strung out. The men were supposed to halt for a rest at noon, but Hill kept on marching, so Jackson halted the column without informing Hill. This was Hill's last straw. Dismounting, he stomped up to Jackson and offered him his sword saying, "If you take command of my troops in my presence, take my sword also." Jackson calmly replied, "Put up your sword and consider yourself in arrest" and galloped off. A courier soon arrived with orders for Branch to assume command of the division while Hill marched on foot behind it with "an old white hat slouched down over his eyes, his coat off and wearing an old flannel shirt, looking as mad as a bull." This was the second time in two months that Jackson arrested Hill. He was released from arrest and re-assumed command as the division left Frederick on its march to Harpers Ferry on September 10.[3]

The division marched with Jackson's wing to Halltown Virginia, about two miles from Bolivar Heights on September 13, and Hill deployed his division on the afternoon of the following day. While four of his brigades headed directly for the Union position at Bolivar Heights, Gregg's and Branch's climbed the bluffs, to its east, adjacent to the Shenandoah River, in an attempt to flank the enemy position. Hill pushed his men forward during the late afternoon of September 14, but nightfall put an end to the effort. With artillery in place, Hill kicked off his advance on the morning of September 15, but it ended abruptly when white surrender flags fluttered all along the enemy's works. The Light Division lost 3 killed and 66 wounded at Harpers Ferry.

Hill's division was left at Harpers Ferry September 15 to collect supplies and parole the prisoners while Jackson's other two divisions headed for Sharpsburg and a reunion with Lee's army. Why Jackson would leave his finest division behind has never been satisfactorily explained. Lee ordered Hill to make a forced march to Sharpsburg at 6:30 a.m. on September 17. He and his men were on the march an hour later, leaving Thomas' brigade behind to finish the work. The column began crossing the Potomac River into Maryland at 2:00 p.m. after marching the 17 miles to Blackford's Ford south of Shepherdstown. Historian Joseph Harsh criticized Hill for taking so long to arrive on the battlefield: His men were clearly not ready to march when Lee's order arrived, the road he took was difficult to traverse and it probably took more time than the direct route Jackson's other troops had followed. As a result of the long hard march, Hill lost as many as 40% of his men along the way.[4]

The division was only a skeleton of its former self for other reasons. Like the rest of the army, its almost exclusive reliance on a diet of green apples and corn produced severe attacks of diarrhea and dysentery. Compounded by the relapses common in soldiers who had not completely recovered from their sicknesses, many became stragglers. The men did not have the physical stamina needed to endure the forced march and they fell out of ranks by the score.[5]

Three of Hill"'s five brigades were thrown into the fray as they arrived south of Sharpsburg on Miller's Sawmill Road. Gregg's brigade was in the van, followed by Branch's, and finally Archer's, totaling 2,000 men. According to Hill, these were the only troops to see combat on afternoon of September 17. With the division so spread out, Pender's and Fields' brigades arrived after the fighting was over.

Gregg's brigade attacked through a 40-acre cornfield against the left flank of the IX Corps, driving back the 16th Connecticut and 4th Rhode Island (Edward Harland's brigade; Isaac Rodman's division). Some of these South Carolinians then turned and attacked north while Archer's and Toombs' brigade attacked from the west to drive reinforcements from the area. Branch's brigade was split up and the regiments sent where needed. One regiment supported McIntosh's battery and a couple more drove the 8th Connecticut (Harland's brigade) back to its lines. The division lost 63 killed and 283 wounded for a total loss of 346. It had lost many more men on other battlefields, but never was its entry more pivotal to the outcome of a battle.[6]

Hill's division was the last of Lee's army to recross the Potomac River on the morning of September 19. After marching several miles, it was tasked with turning and dealing with several V Corps brigades harassing Lee's rear. Deployed in two lines, with Pender's, Gregg's, and Thomas' in the first and Field's, Lane, and Archer in the second, the division drove forward under a heavy artillery barrage and drove the enemy back across the Potomac River, inflicting heavy losses. Hill lost an additional 261 men (30 killed and 231 wounded) during this action at Shepherdstown, for a total of 676 men during the campaign.[7]

**Bradley M. Gottfried**

* * *

### Branch's Brigade: Brigadier General Lawrence Branch, Colonel James Lane

**Units:** 7th North Carolina, 18th North Carolina, 28th North Carolina, 33rd North Carolina, 37th North Carolina
**Strength:** 1,754[8]
**Losses:** 104 (21k- 79w-4m)[9]

Brigadier General Lawrence Branch's brigade was a veteran unit that had fought as a cohesive unit since March 1862, but without much early success.

It first saw action during the New Bern Campaign when Ambrose Burnside's small army shoved the brigade aside and captured the town. The brigade was transferred to Piedmont, Virginia, but was never called upon to join Stonewall Jackson's forces. The brigade was next sent to Hanover Court House, where it was thoroughly thrashed by a large Federal force at the Battle of Mechanicsville. Later, Branch's brigade was transferred to A.P. Hill's Light

Division and fought well, earning victories at Gaines' Mill and Frayser's Farm during the Seven Days Campaign. It also played an important role in the Confederate victory at Cedar Mountain and saw action at Second Bull Run.[10]

Some of the regiments received new recruits as a result of the Confederate Conscription Act of April 1862. For example, the 18th North Carolina received 90, and the 7th North Carolina, 130. These troops probably played but a small role in the campaign, as they were untrained in marching and fighting and few had weapons or accoutrements when they arrived just prior to the Maryland Campaign. Many would form the large body of stragglers unable to keep pace with the veterans of their new units.[11]

After graduating from Princeton University, Branch became an attorney and newspaper editor. He went on to represent North Carolina in the U.S. Congress until 1861, when his state seceded from the Union. While a Congressman, he rejected invitations by President Buchanan to be Secretary of the Treasury and Postmaster General. He joined the Confederate Army, and although not a West Pointer, was highly intelligent and quickly grasped military concepts. Branch was a respected officer who was destined for higher command. He began the war as commander of the 33rd North Carolina and was promoted to brigadier general in November 1861. Branch has been described as a "hard-hitting brigadier as well as a good follower."[12]

After its march to Leesburg, Branch's brigade, with the remainder of the division, crossed the Potomac River on September 5. James Harris (7th North Carolina) recalled the brigade entered the waist-deep water at 4:00 p.m., and Nicholas Gibbon (28th North Carolina) observed men "with their shoes and pants hanging on their guns, others with theirs rolled up above their knees and others wading through the clear stream without seeming to care whether they got wet or not." The brigade marched north and stopped outside of Frederick, guarding the intersection of the Baltimore & Ohio Railroad Bridge and Georgetown Pike. Having marched 272 miles in the past 30 days, the men were given a well-deserved rest from September 7-9. Charles Mills (7th North Carolina) complained that Stonewall Jackson "marches them so hard that they are nerly [sic] broke down before they get to the battle field."[13]

## Harpers Ferry

The reprieve ended on September 10, when Branch's brigade, and the rest of Stonewall Jackson's wing, followed a circuitous route west, crossed the Potomac River at Williamsport. The men continued marching south through Martinsburg, and finally southeast to invest Harpers Ferry. Some of these marches were grueling, particularly the 23-mile trek on September 11. A.P. Hill divided his division in two as it advanced toward Bolivar Heights on September 14. While Pender's, Archer's, and Field's (under John Brockenbrough) brigades advanced, Branch's and Gregg's marched along the Shenandoah River, and following the railroad, attempted to get in the enemy's rear. The men reached their jumping off point at about midnight and were permitted to rest. Branch's men were back in position and ready for action by 3:00 a.m. on September 15, a mere 400 yards from the enemy's position on Bolivar Heights. White flags fluttered from the enemy positions before Jackson could unleash his men against the beleaguered garrison. The brigade lost four men wounded during this phase of the campaign. The men were impressed by the largess of Harpers Ferry during their two days of paroling prisoners and inventorying captured Union goods. Branch wrote home to his wife about the captured Yanks who were the "best-dressed and best-provided soldiers I ever expect to see." Austin Jones (7th North Carolina) boasted, "We boys were turned loose on these good things and you may be sure we availed ourselves of them."[14]

## Antietam

The brigade was second in line behind Gregg's Gamecocks during the march north to Sharpsburg at 7:00 a.m. on September 17. Col. James Lane (28th North Carolina) called it a "very rapid and fatiguing march," as Hill pushed his men toward their destination. The column began crossing the Potomac River at 2:00 p.m., and this time, there was no slowing down to remove clothing as they splashed across the wide river. A veteran recalled the men's "clothing was saturated with water from the hips down . . . [the] up-hill foot-race from the river to the battle-field, caused none but those of unquestioned endurance to be there to go into action." Because of the combination of sickness and stragglers, the 28th North Carolina fielded only 50 men by the time it reached the contested fields. Branch halted his brigade as it crossed the Potomac River and sought out Hill. He did not find him, but Hill found the 28th North Carolina at the rear of the brigade, preparing to cross. He immediately ordered it north along Harpers Ferry Road to help support McIntosh's battery. It would encounter no Yanks and play no further part of the battle.[15]

The 7th and 37th North Carolina were sent across Harpers Ferry Road and then turned left as the 8th Connecticut (Harland's brigade; Rodman's division) in front of them surged toward McIntosh's battery. As the Tar Heels deployed for action, the left flank of the 7th was hit by Union artillery fire and thrown into temporary disarray. The rest of the two regiments hit the Nutmeggers' flank and rear, sending the unit flying into retreat with heavy losses. The two regiments were soon on the receiving end of volleys fired from a regiment to their right behind a stone wall, possibly the 23rd Ohio (Ewing's brigade; Scammon's division). The two North Carolina regiments fell back about a hundred yards and reformed. As they did so, several of Gregg's and Archer's regiments attacked the Buckeye regiment, forcing it from its protective wall. Branch led the two regiments forward to the stone wall in the face of heavy enemy artillery fire. A member of the 7th North Carolina recalled a "shell was exploded in its ranks with destructive effect and some confusion ensued . . . First Sergeant Thos. P. Mallory . . . who had borne the colors with conspicuous courage throughout the campaign,

placed himself in front and appealed to the men to align themselves on the colors which they did under fire, then moving forward, the regiment occupied the stone wall." After reaching the wall, the 37th North Carolina went over and advanced into a cornfield where it was met by a "warm fire" and was forced back.[16]

The 18th and 33rd North Carolina appeared and joined their comrades behind the wall, where the men remained hunkered down with the remnants of Archer's and Toombs' brigades and the 7th and 37th North Carolina. The 18th and 33rd North Carolina also arrived. They initially formed a reserve along Harpers Ferry Road, but then drove forward and planted their flags on the stone wall.[17]

Darkness ended the fighting. The brigade lost 104 men during its fight against the IX Corps' left flank (21 killed, 79 wounded and 4 missing). Branch was among the dead, but the circumstances are unclear. According to one account, he was viewing the enemy positions through his field glasses in company with Gregg and Archer, when a bullet passed through his right cheek and entered behind his left ear, killing him instantly. Another explanation had him conferring with officers of Gregg's brigade when he was struck, and a third account claimed a stray bullet killed him. Historian Michael Hardy believed "a Federal soldier, spotting a clump of enemy officers in the dusk, took a timely shot at the group and hit Branch." James Lane of the 28th North Carolina assumed command of the brigade and would lead it through the remainder of the war.[18]

The brigade spent the following day ensconced behind the stone wall, trying to keep under cover from the occasional sniper bullet. During Lee's retreat back into Virginia, Branch's brigade, along with Archer's and Gregg's, formed the army's rearguard, and did not cross the Potomac River until 10:00 a.m. on September 19. It halted about five miles beyond the town of Shepherdstown that evening.[19]

**Shepherdstown**

The men received word they would be heading back to the Potomac River at 6:30 a.m. on September 20. Two hours later, the Light Division was deploying in two lines of brigades, advancing on part of the V Corps that had crossed the river and had gained the bluffs on the Virginia side. Branch's brigade was in the second line between Field's and Archer's brigades. Pender on the left flank of the first line believed his brigade was being flanked, so he called upon the second line to provide support. An officer in the 33rd North Carolina wrote, "We never forgot the feeling that ran through us about the time we got the order to go forward. We had hardly started before the bullets began to whiz about our heads, which did not help to soften the first feeling." The advance was made under a tremendous enemy artillery fire. Lane reported "Finding that he [Pender] was outflanked on the left, we then moved by the left flank until we unmasked his brigade. The men, on reaching the top of the hill, raised a yell and poured a deadly fire into the enemy, who fled precipitately and in great confusion to the river."[20]

As the line approached the 118th Pennsylvania, a member of the 18th North Carolina recalled seeing "the Yankees lay on the field in heaps and piles. He noted, "The bombs burst around our heads with terrific fury and showers of grape canister fell mingled with limbs of trees thick about us." Despite the danger, the men "shot as long as we could see a blue coat." Branch's brigade was able to make its way to the bluff overlooking the river and spent the remainder of the day there. The brigade lost three killed and 71 wounded in this engagement.[21]

This ended the Maryland Campaign for Branch's brigade. It played a minor role during the attack on Harpers Ferry and was split into pieces when going into action at Sharpsburg. The brigade ended the campaign fighting cohesively at Shepherdstown.

**Bradley M. Gottfried**

✳ ✳ ✳

## Gregg's Brigade: Brigadier General Maxcy Gregg

**Units:** 1st South Carolina (Provisional Army), 1st South Carolina (Rifles), 12th South Carolina, 13th South Carolina, 14th South Carolina
**Strength:** 984[22]
**Losses:** 165 (28k-135w-2m)[23]

The distinguished brigade of South Carolinians had its roots at Ft. Sumter, where the 1st South Carolina (Provisional) was present. The regiment's commander, Col. Maxcy Gregg, was chagrined when only half of his regiment consented to accompany him to Virginia. Promoted to brigadier general, Gregg received a brigade composed of the 12th, 13th, and 14th South Carolina. After spending the winter in South Carolina, Gregg returned to Virginia, where the 1st South Carolina Provisional and 1st South Carolina Rifles were added. The brigade performed brilliantly at the Battle of Gaines' Mill and received additional accolades when it anchored the Confederate left at the Battle of Second Bull Run and beat off attack after attack.

"Fire-eater" Maxcy Gregg was born into South Carolina's aristocracy. After graduating from what is now the University of South Carolina, Gregg became an attorney. He served as a major in the 12th U.S. Infantry during the Mexican-American War, but did not see combat. Historian James Robertson described him as "jocular, thickset, and blue-eyed, with graying hair that made him look older than his mid-forties. He appeared quiet and slovenly until battle began; then an all-but-total transformation took place." Gregg was also more than slightly hard of hearing and it would contribute to his death at the Battle of Fredericksburg when his brigade was unexpectantly attacked.[24]

The brigade, with the rest of Hill's Light Division, crossed the Potomac River on September

5. The brigade's historian recalled the army's spirit "always high in spirit, was now jubilant. . . They plunged into the water waist-deep, and waded over, cheering lustily and singing 'My Maryland.' They felt themselves doubly conquerors now; for they had not only driven the Federal army from Southern soil, but they were carrying the war across Northern thresholds." After resting around Frederick, the brigade joined the march toward Harpers Ferry on September 10.[25]

## Harpers Ferry

The Light Division was tasked with taking pivotal Bolivar Heights. Hill sent most of the division straight ahead toward the ridgeline while Gregg's and Branch's brigades moved with their right on the west bank of the Shenandoah River, scaling the tall bluffs the Yanks thought would prevent an enemy advance from the southeast. The demi-brigade's orders were to get around the enemy's weakly defended left flank and attack its flank and rear. The brigade angled into position until 2:00 a.m. on September 15. At daylight, the men were treated to a special sight while occupying the bluff. "The view [of the Pleasant Valley and Harpers Ferry] was magnificent, presenting such a spectacle as is rarely seen," recalled Col. Samuel McGowan of the 14th South Carolina. The Confederate batteries surrounding Harpers Ferry opened a converging fire on the beleaguered garrison, and just as the orders to advance were about to be given, white flags could be seen fluttering on the Union works. Staff officer, Maj. Andrew Wardlaw, heard "One loud, long continuous shout from the hills around." Gregg's brigade lost not a man during the operation.[26]

Moving down into Harper's Ferry, the brigade "fared sumptuously" on the abundance of food, clothing, and accouterments, captured from the Union garrison. Hill's division was left behind to collect supplies and parole the prisoners on September 16 and the following day was on the road early to rejoin Lee's army. Gregg's brigade led the grueling march. Wading across the Potomac was not the same jubilant event experienced earlier, as

noted by the brigade's historian: "We waded the river at once and rapidly, although the current was quite swift, and the ledges of rock, cropping out at a sharp angle, rendered the passage both difficult and painful. Climbing up the slippery bank on the Maryland side." Then it was a double-quick to the battlefield. Gregg estimated the van of the brigade reached the actual battlefield at 3:40 p.m.[27]

## Antietam

Gregg's brigade, probably numbering about 800 men, arrived on the scene "not a moment too soon for the fortunes of the day," as D.R. Jones' 2,000-man division was all that was available to halt the progress of the 13,000-man IX Corps. The brigade was hit by Federal artillery fire upon reaching Harpers Ferry Road, so the men rushed across it and took cover about 250 yards beyond it. Alexander Haskell, Gregg's Chief of Staff recalled seeing a Union soldier perched on one of David McIntosh's cannons and "flap his arms and crow, this of course hurried up the line as it was adding insult to injury." He recalled the men "firing as it got into line and pressing forward."

The first regiment in line, the 14th South Carolina, was thrown to the right of the line to protect the flank. It found refuge behind a stone wall and would remain there for the remainder of the battle, even though it was on the enemy's left flank. Gregg now formed three of his remaining four regiments in a line: the 13th South Carolina on the left, the 1st South Carolina on the right, the 12th South Carolina in the middle and the fourth regiment, the 1st South Carolina Rifles, remained in reserve. Historian Ezra Carman estimated these four regiments contained about 750 men. Pegram's battery galloped into position along Harpers Ferry Road to provide support.[28]

Up ahead loomed a 40-acre cornfield that precluded seeing what enemy troops lurked within it. Gregg's men could not know the corn held the veteran 4th Rhode Island and rookie 16th Connecticut forming the IX Corps' left flank. As the three Confederate regiments were about to enter the cornfield, the 13th South Carolina on the left halted at a stone wall, while the 1st South Carolina and the 12th South Carolina continued forward, moving northeast. The dense corn may have caused the two units to fight independently even though they were in close proximity to each other. The Gamecocks pushed the 16th Connecticut skirmish line back. Although the rookie Nutmeggers were somewhat disordered by shifting their line to face the suddenly appearing enemy, they opened a ragged fire on the 12th South Carolina. Maj. W.H. McCorkle of the 12th South Carolina reported, "The enemy now appearing in force on the opposite hill, and at the fence in the intervening ravine, the Twelfth, at once and alone, advanced down the hill and to the fence in front. In this charge we were subjected to a terrible cross-fire in front and from both flanks. After reaching the fence we were compelled to fall back to prevent being flanked on the right, the enemy on the left having been driven back." The two Union regiments now advanced to the fence. The 12th South Carolina again charged and, according to McCorkle, "drove them back a short distance, but were not able to reach the fence, as in the first charge." Perceiving the threat of being flanked on his right, McCorkle ordered another retreat, this time to the top of the hill in their rear. The regiment attacked yet again and this time, with the help of the 1st South Carolina and 1st South Carolina Rifles (see below), forced the inexperienced men of the 16th Connecticut to stampede to the rear, taking the 4th Rhode Island with them.[29]

The 1st South Carolina on the right of the 12th South Carolina fought independently of each other. The men came upon the enemy behind a fence in the cornfield and the two sides exchanged volleys. Col. D.H. Hamilton was made aware of a large Union force on his right, so he ordered his right three companies refused and continued the fight. The men were firing so rapidly, the charges began clogging in their rifle barrels, forcing them to pound them down with rocks. According to Hamilton, "Just at this time, it was reported to me by one of my officers that another regiment had gained the

hill in my rear. This sounded like danger. I looked, but instead of the enemy there floated our own bonny blue flag. The Rifles had come to our assistance, and not one moment too soon, for in a few moments my fire must have ceased for want of ammunition."[30]

Lt. Col. James Perrin's 1st South Carolina Rifles, which had been in reserve, picks up the narrative: "The regiment advanced across the field in good order, moving rapidly, as Colonel Hamilton, on our left, had already engaged the enemy. So soon as we ascended to the crest of the hill in our front, we discovered a regiment of the enemy who had succeeded in turning Colonel Hamilton's right, and were delivering a destructive fire on his flank. Our advance was such as to completely turn the left flank of this regiment. We delivered a destructive volley into it before our presence seemed to be realized." The three South Carolina regiments had cleared their front. Perrin noted "this large, well equipped regiment failed to rally, broke and fled from the field in the utmost confusion, leaving their guns, knapsacks, and dead and wounded in large numbers on the field.[31]

The fight was not yet over for the three South Carolina regiments, as Hugh Ewing's Ohio brigade moved forward to support the IX Corps' left flank. Although not clear from the several official reports filed by the regimental leaders, historian Ezra Carman believed the three South Carolina regiments turned north and drove against the Buckeyes' flank while parts of Archer's, Branch's, and Toombs' brigades hit their front, pushing the Union forces back as darkness fell. After resting on their arms on September 18, the brigade had the distinction of being the last of Lee's brigades to cross the Potomac River at 9:00 a.m. on the 19th. Gregg's brigade lost more men at Sharpsburg, 165 (28 killed, 135 wounded, 2 missing) than any of A.P. Hill's other brigades.[32]

## Shepherdstown

The brigade marched another five miles after crossing the Potomac River on September 19 and

329

camped for the night. During the subsequent battle at Shepherdstown the following day, Gregg's brigade was again in one of the hottest spots—the center of the first line, with Thomas' brigade on its right and Pender's on its left. The brigade's historian believed the brigade was deployed from left to right: 14th South Carolina- 13th South Carolina- 1st South Carolina- 12th South Carolina, and the 1st South Carolina Rifles was on the skirmish line. As the first line of brigades advanced to drive portions of the V Corps back north across the Potomac River, the "batteries of the enemy on the Maryland side poured upon them a terrible fire of grape, round shot, and shell," reported Samuel McGowan.

"Their practice was remarkably fine, bursting shells in the ranks at every discharge. Because the 14th South Carolina occupied the most open terrain on the left of the brigade, it suffered the greatest casualties-- 55 of the 63 total casualties sustained by the brigade. Gregg proudly wrote, "When the artillery made gaps in their ranks, they closed up like veterans, and marched on without confusion or in the least losing distance." It is ironic that the only regiment that sustained no losses, at Antietam, was badly hammered at Shepherdstown. Overall, the brigade lost 228 (38 killed; 188 wounded; 2 missing) during the Maryland Campaign.[33]

**Bradley M. Gottfried**

\* \* \*

## Field's Brigade: Colonel John Brockenbrough

**Units:** 40th Virginia, 47th Virginia, 55th Virginia, 22nd Virginia Battalion
**Strength:** 1,336[34]
**Losses:** Minimal[35]

Charles Field's brigade was one of the most cohesive and well-led units in the Army of Northern Virginia. The 40th Virginia, 47th Virginia, and 55th Virginia had fought together since May 1862 and had distinguished themselves on several battlefields. Two changes occurred in August 1862 when the 22nd Virginia Battalion was added, and Field went down with a serious wound at the battle of Second Bull Run. The brigade marched north under the temporary leadership of Col. John Brockenbrough of the 40th Virginia. While not the optimal choice, he had seniority over the other colonels. Because of Brockenbrough's questionable leadership, his brigade saw little action throughout the campaign.[36]

The march to Frederick and Harpers Ferry mirrored the remainder of A.P. Hill's brigades. Capt. Wayland Dunaway (40th Virginia) recalled that during the three day march, "no rations were issued, and our only food was ears of green corn roasted or boiled without salt. These served for

supper, and breakfast, but we had nothing for dinner, for if when we started in the morning we put the cooking corn in the haversacks it soured under the hot rays of the sun." The brigade, along with James Archer's and Dorsey Pender's, were placed under the latter's command on September 14, as they advanced toward the Union position on Bolivar Heights. The brigade was positioned behind Pender's and beside Archer's. The advance scattered the Union skirmish line, but Union reinforcements rushed to the heights and countered the advance. The men slept on their arms that night and the advance continued the following day. The Confederate line approached to within 150 yards of the Union defenses when white flags appeared on Bolivar Heights, signaling the surrender of the garrison.

### Antietam

Brockenbrough's brigade brought up the rear during the division's forced march to Sharpsburg— an appropriate spot for a brigade with an uncertain commander. Because of its trailing position, the brigade did not arrive until after the fighting ended on September 17. The men slept on their arms during the night and remained in reserve the following day. The 40th Virginia was sent to a hill near Snavely's Ford to support some batteries, but was not engaged and was pulled back after dark, spending the night at a stone mill south of town. The 47th Virginia was ordered to Snavely's Ford on September 18, sustaining some losses there: five wounded and nine were captured.[37]

## Shepherdstown

The campaign was not yet over for Hill's division. When several V Corps brigades crossed the Potomac River after Lee's army, the Light Division turned back and deployed for action. Brockenbrough's brigade was placed on the second line, behind Pender's brigade during the subsequent attack. It ultimately participated in the fray, helping to push the Union troops back across the River.[38]

The brigade saw some action at Harpers Ferry and Shepherdstown, but its losses were minimal. A.P. Hill's reluctance to use the brigade is understandable, given his concerns about Brockenbrough's effectiveness.

**Bradley M. Gottfried**

\* \* \*

## Archer's Brigade: Brigadier General James Archer, Colonel Peter Turney

**Units:** 5th Alabama Battalion, 19th Georgia, 1st Tennessee (Provisional Army), 7th Tennessee, 14th Tennessee
**Strength:** 1,149[39]
**Losses:** 105 (15k-90w-0m)[40]

The brigade could trace its roots to Brig. Gen. Samuel Anderson's brigade in the summer of 1861. Composed initially of the 1st, 7th, and 14th Tennessee, the brigade first tasted combat under Robert E. Lee in the mountains of western Virginia. It fought well at the Battle of Cheat's Mountain and later participated in the Romney Campaign in January 1862. The brigade transferred to Gen. Joseph Johnston's army in late February and fought with John Hood's brigade at Eltham's Landing during the Peninsula Campaign. Anderson resigned his commission because of ill health and was replaced by Brig. Gen. Robert Hatton, commander of the 7th Virginia. Entering into thick, tangled woods during the Battle of Seven Pines, the brigade blundered into a fresh Union division and forced to beat a hasty retreat, but not before Hatton was killed instantly. Additional units were added to the brigade, including the 5th Alabama and the 19th Georgia, along with a new commander. Princeton graduate and attorney by trade, Marylander James Archer had served as a captain in the Mexican War. He remained in the army in that capacity and rose to the rank of colonel of the 5th Texas. He served in this capacity at the outbreak of the war. Historian James Robertson described him as "a slightly built man with thin face and elongated beard, the humorless Archer was a . . . dependable but unexciting brigadier." Although he had seen limited service in the war, Archer was promoted to the rank of brigadier general on June 3, 1862 and given Hatton's brigade.

Archer's brigade saw action in A.P. Hill's division at Mechanicsville and Gaines' Mill, where it launched bloody charges against strong Federal positions. Additional casualties were sustained at Frayser's Farm, where its counterattack helped stabilize the Confederate line. The brigade lost over 500 men in the week of fighting. Another counterattack helped win the day at the Battle of Cedar Mountain and later, the brigade beat back several Federal attacks during the Battle of Second Bull Run.[41]

## Harpers Ferry

Archer's brigade, with the rest of Hill's division crossed the Potomac River into Maryland on September 5, 1862 and headed north to Frederick. The men subsisted on green corn, cooked over fence rails. After spending several days in and around Frederick, the brigade marched northwest, crossed the Potomac River at Williamsport, and continued via Martinsburg to Harpers Ferry. After camping at Halltown, Virginia the night of September 13, the brigade, along with Field's (under John Brockenbrough) and Pender's brigades were placed under Dorsey Pender, and ordered to advance toward the main Union defensive position on Bolivar Heights. Hill observed the position on the left of the Union line was weakly held, devoid of breastworks and artillery, and only an "abatis of fallen timber" obstructed their passage. Archer formed his brigade into line of battle and sent it forward, driving the enemy picket line before it. Union reinforcements arrived to bolster the Union left flank. As Archer's men ascended Schoolhouse Ridge, they could easily see the Union line, and attempted to flank the enemy's artillery by advancing through the woods. Archer reported his line "continued to advance, as rapidly as the rough ground and abatis would permit." Darkness put an end to the action. Despite his division commander's denigration of the enemy works, Archer noted his men "had become entangled in the almost impenetrable abatis" before they halted for the night, within 400 yards of the enemy position.

At daybreak, the repositioned Confederate batteries opened fire on the Union positions "while I was struggling through the abatis, endeavoring to execute an order from General Hill to get in rear of the guns," Archer reported. White flags soon fluttered in the breeze as the Union garrison realized the futility of further resistance and surrendered. The brigade lost one killed and 22 wounded at Harpers Ferry. Maj. James Neal, commander of the 19th Georgia, reported how his regiment "was under a tolerably heavy fire from the artillery of the enemy," but sustained relatively few casualties, "owing to the protection afforded by the crest of the hill." Archer's men, with the rest of the division, were left behind to help secure the prisoners and supplies. This gave the men a false sense of security. Felix Motlow of the 1st Tennessee believed, "there would be no more fighting for at least several months."[42]

## Antietam

Motlow would not get his wish, for on the morning of September 17, the brigade began an 18-mile forced march with the rest of the division to the Sharpsburg battlefield, leaving behind the 5th Alabama Battalion to guard the captured cannon and help prepare them for shipment to Richmond. Blue uniforms abounded, as the men has shucked their tattered rags for fresh blue garments scavenged from Union supplies. Archer handed command of the brigade to Col. Peter Turney of the 1st Tennessee on September 16, as he became "too unwell for duty." Archer told his mother months after the battle, "I had been sick in bed all the day before [September 16], & was too weak & sick to mount my horse, but rode in an ambulance & had to stop on the way and lie down for an hour." The day was hot and the pace fast, causing scores of men to fall by the wayside. Archer counted only 350 men present for duty when the brigade reached the battlefield. G.W. Gleaton claimed his 19th Georgia led Archer's brigade.[43]

The brigade was third in line during the march, and when as it arrived, Hill immediately shoved it into action on the left of the division. When Archer "heard the sound of the battle . . . & the thought of my troops going in without me I got well again—mounted my horse & overtook my brigade just before it came up with the enemy." Trotting north along Harpers Ferry Road, the men halted when they reached Robert Toombs' brigade, about to launch its men against the 8th Connecticut (Edward Harland's brigade; Isaac Rodman's division; IX Corps) which had advanced further than most of the rest of the IX Corps. According to Archer, the brigade, "Marching by flank, right in front, along the Sharpsburg road, the brigade was halted and faced to the right, forming line of battle faced by the rear rank" and with a narrow cornfield to its front, threw out a skirmish line. The four regiments scaled a board fence and passed through the cornfield. Upon emerging, the 14th and 7th Tennessee on the left were alone, as the right, composed of the 1st Tennessee and 19th Georgia, had mistakenly fallen back to the road after hearing commands meant for the 37th North Carolina of Branch's brigade. Archer saw the two confused regiments approach the road and immediately sent them back through the corn, where they eventually linked up with the right of the two other regiments. Archer now ordered the four regiments forward toward a stone wall, 300 yard away, on the opposite side of a wide plowed field. Toombs' brigade joined the advance on the brigade's left. The 23rd and 30th Ohio were behind this wall, throwing a storm of lead against the Tennesseans and Georgians, felling about a third of them. Just as the Confederate attack began wavering, the 12th South Carolina and the 1st South Carolina attacked the Buckeye's left flank and rear, forcing the right of the 30th Ohio from the stone wall.[44]

Archer's men briefly halted at the wall. Seeing members of the 23rd Ohio still holding a portion of it to their left, and the left wing of the 30th Ohio on their right, they opened a blistering fire, forcing both from the wall. Motlow recalled how the men fired at the retreating Ohioans: we "picked them off with unerring aim by the score before they got out of range of these guns." Archer ordered his skeletal brigade forward across the cornfield where they were mowed down by the reformed 30th Ohio. Archer wisely ordered his men back to their hard won stone wall. As night descended on the battlefield, Edward Ferrero's Union brigade advanced toward Archer's position. The latter jumped atop the fence and attempted a counterattack, but was driven back, ending the action of September 17. Archer's brigade lost 15 dead and 90 wounded at Sharpsburg. Among the "casualties" was Archer himself, who wrote home. "I never felt better or stronger than during the whole time the battle lasted [but] when it was over I found myself completely prostrated, and lay almost in a stupor all the next day." Archer again turned the brigade over to Turney, which remained in position on September 18 and formed the army's rearguard with Gregg's and Branch's brigades when the army recrossed the Potomac River.[45]

## Shepherdstown

Archer was back in command of his brigade when Hill's Light Division deployed for battle against several V Corps brigades on September 20. Hill placed Archer in command of his division's second line, composed of his own brigade on the right, Field's (Brockenbrough) on the far left, and Lane's brigade in the center. When Pender worried about the well-being of his left flank, Archer promptly advanced his brigade, followed by the two others under his command. According to Hill, the final charge against the 118th Pennsylvania, the sole unit still on the west side of the Potomac River, was made by Pender's and Archer's brigades. The brigade lost another six killed and 49 wounded in this battle, many by intense artillery fire from cannon on the opposite side of the Potomac River.[46]

The brigade served well during the Maryland Campaign and was one of the few that saw actions on three separate battlefields.

**Bradley M. Gottfried**

333

## Pender's Brigade: Brigadier General Dorsey Pender

**Units:** 16th North Carolina, 22nd North Carolina, 34th North Carolina, 38th North Carolina
**Strength:** 1,596[47]
**Losses:** 30 (2k-28w-0m)[48]

With the exception of the 38th North Carolina, every regiment in Dorsey Pender's brigade was mustered into service in 1861. The 16th and 22nd North Carolina served in Virginia; the 34th North Carolina and 38th North Carolina served in North Carolina until brigaded together in June 1863. The four regiments saw considerable service during the Seven Days Battles, Cedar Mountain, and Second Bull Run. It was a veteran unit under a commander whose star was on the rise.

William Dorsey Pender was born in North Carolina on February 6, 1834. After clerking in his brother's general store in Tarboro, Pender received an appointment to West Point. He graduated in 1854 with the likes of Jeb Stuart and Oliver Howard. He entered the army with the rank of 2nd lieutenant of the 1st U. S. Artillery. After a series of posts and units, Pender was sent to fight Native Americans in Washington State. In one of his three fights, he subdued an Indian leader with his bare hands. Pender entered the Confederate army as a captain of artillery in March 1861. He was soon after elected colonel of the 3rd North Carolina (later designated the 13th North Carolina). He caught President Jefferson Davis' eye during the Battle of Seven Pines, where he exhibited effective leadership. Davis greeted him after the battle by saying, "General Pender, I salute you." His promotion became official on July 22, but was backdated to June 3. He was given command of a new brigade, which he effectively led through the many battles in June through August, 1862. Pender has been described as being "twenty-eight, erect, with a thin frame, an olive complexion, a pointed beard, and a kindly expression that belied his strict sense of discipline."[49]

The brigade bivouacked near Big Spring, near Leesburg, Virginia on the evening of September 4. Pender received orders to cross the Potomac River into Maryland with the rest of the Light Division, but before he did, he called his officers to his headquarters. He told them about the move into Maryland, and how "they must act as officers and gentlemen, keeping a firm hand on the men of their commands, and that he would hold them responsible for their conduct." The brigade formed into line at about 10:00 a.m. on September 5, and reached Edward's Ferry by 2:00 p.m. Once across the Potomac River, the column continued north until midnight, when the men were permitted to go into bivouac. The men helped themselves to a field of green corn, which they roasted and consumed for a late supper. What was left was stashed for breakfast. The column continued to Frederick, on September 6, which it reached at noon. The men were not given much time to enjoy the sights or the stores, as they spent several days along the Baltimore and Ohio Railroad, doing as much damage, destroying the rail lines, as they could. Capt. George Mills ruefully recalled, "The men were not allowed to leave the camps or enter the city or to forage in the country."[50]

### Harpers Ferry

Pender's brigade was ordered to break camp on September 10, and the men began the long march from Frederick to the Potomac River. The brigade, with the rest of the division, reached Harpers Ferry on September 13. During the afternoon of the following day, Hill observed the Union left on high ground on Bolivar Heights devoid of artillery and earthworks. Only an abatis of "slashed timber" provided the defenders with cover. Hill immediately ordered Pender to collect Archer's and Field's (Brockenbrough's) brigades along with his own, and advance toward the Union position, keeping their right flank on the Shenandoah River. Pender's brigade led the attack, followed by the other brigades. Union brigade commander, Brig. Gen. Julius White saw Pender's men scatter his skirmish line, so he rushed the 9th and 32nd Ohio, with a section of Rigby's battery to the left to protect the ridgeline. The fighting continued until dark, but Pender able to capture high ground. Pender noted in his report, "My brigade advanced within about 60 yards of the breastwork on the west point of Bolivar Heights, having exchanged shots with the enemy several times on their way there."[51]

Hill brought up artillery during the night of September 14 and reorganized his division for action. The men slept on their arms and the historian of the 16th North Carolina recalled, "Though chilled and shivering, we were eager for the fray." At first light on September 15, Pender again advanced his three brigades to within 150 yards of the Union defensive works on Bolivar Heights. The undulations in the ground helped reduce the number of Confederate casualties, as did the fire by two Confederate batteries that charged forward and deployed for action within 400 yards of the Federal works. As Pender began his final push, white flags of surrender appeared above the Federal works-- Col. Dixon Miles, the garrison's commander, finally realized the futility of further resistance, given the Confederate artillery surrounding it from west of Bolivar Heights, on Maryland Heights, and on Loudoun Heights. A Tar Heel noted: "We found them [Miles' men] drawn up in line, with arms stacked and discoursing music of a patriotic sort—from their point of view. It was in fact quite a splendid reception, but what a contrast! The enemy was spotlessly dressed in brand-new uniforms, shoes and buttons, and gold and silver trappings glistening in the morning sun, while we were almost naked; a great many of us without shoes, without even a faded emblem on our ragged coats to tell even rank or official command."[52]

## Antietam

As Jackson and two of his divisions marched to Sharpsburg, Hill's division was left behind at Harpers Ferry to parole the Union prisoners and secure the captured supplies. The force march to Sharpsburg began on the morning of September 17. The rapid pace left many stragglers in its wake, and the historian of the 34th North Carolina recalled that his regiment, "owing to hard marching and exhausting fighting, was a mere skeleton." Pender's brigade was the fourth of Hill's brigades to reach Sharpsburg, and by the time it arrived, the battle was all but over. When some Union troops surged forward, endangering the artillery, Pender's brigade was ordered from the right to the center to protect them, but the attack was already receding by the time they arrived. Pender's men lay on their arms during the night of September 17-18, between Brockenbrough's brigade on their left and Lane's brigade on their right. The men spent September 18 dodging sharpshooter bullets.[53]

## Shepherdstown

In retreat, Lee began crossing the Potomac River after dark on September 18. When portions of the Union V Corps followed across the Potomac River on September 20, Hill's division was ordered to turn and face the threat. Pender's brigade was again on the first line, but this time the three brigades forming this battle line were commanded by Maxcy Gregg. The men advanced 300 yards toward the Potomac River under a tremendous Union artillery barrage. Pender's brigade, on the left, attacked James Barnes' brigade (George Morell's division; V Corps), but its line was too short. When the right of the Union line began flanking Pender's, he refused his left two regiments to face this threat. Hill called up his second line and they extended Pender's left flank. As they moved forward they enveloped the beleaguered Union brigade, pinning it against the river. The Union troops suffered heavy losses and the 118th Pennsylvania was almost destroyed. Hill reported, a "daring charge was made and the enemy driven pell-mell into the river. Then commenced the most terrible slaughter that this war has yet witnessed. The broad surface of the Potomac was blue with the floating bodies of our foe." The historian of the 16th North Carolina remembered, "Rushing over the river bank, we intended giving the enemy the bayonet, but before reaching him he fled in the wildest confusion, some plunging headlong into the river and others attempting to cross on a foot-bridge purposely erected for their retreat if events should require."[54]

This ended the Maryland Campaign for Pender's brigade. Although the brigade was not involved in the Antietam fight, it was heavily engaged at Harpers Ferry and Shepherdstown, performing well in both battles.

**Bradley M. Gottfried**

* * *

### Thomas' Brigade: Brigadier General Edward Thomas

**Units:** 14th Georgia, 35th Georgia, 45th Georgia, 49th Georgia
**Strength:** 1,205[55]
**Losses:** 0[56]

Most of the regiments of Brig. Gen. Edward Thomas' brigade entered the war as part of Brig. Gen. Joseph Anderson's brigade. The brigade initially served in North Carolina, but was transferred to Virginia in early May 1862, and was positioned near the Rappahannock River to watch Irwin McDowell's Federal Third Corps. The brigade was called upon to reinforce the Army of Northern Virginia and was placed in A.P. Hill's division, seeing action at the Battles of Mechanicsville, Gaines' Mill, and Frayser's Farm. The brigade was less engaged in these battles than other units in Hill's division, and it lost relatively few men.

Anderson resigned his commission on July 19, 1862 and Col. Edward Thomas of the 35th Georgia was given command of the brigade. Thomas quickly showed he was a hard-hitting fighter, and he and his brigade performed well at the Battles of Cedar Mountain and Second Bull Run. The brigade was stationed behind the unfinished railroad in the latter battle and helped beat back several determined attacks.[57]

Thomas' brigade moved north with the rest of the army, reaching Leesburg on September 4. Draughton Stith Haynes noted the "citizens of the town appeared very glad to see us, and many had biscuits & coffee for the soldiers as we passed through." The brigade crossed the Potomac River as the sun was setting on September 5. The men first removed their pants, shoes and socks, causing Haynes to claim, "Never did I behold so many naked legs in my life." The men finally halted for the night at 11:00 p.m. They subsisted on green corn, which Haynes said were "not quite substantial enough for a soldier." While in Frederick the men rested, and on Sunday, September 8, many attended a prayer meeting.[58]

Thomas' brigade joined the rest of Hill's division for the long march to Harpers Ferry, beginning on September 10. The men were on the road at 3:00 a.m. and marched all day. "We are upon a mountain, which looks down upon one of the prettiest vallies [sic] I have ever seen," wrote Haines in his diary. The brigade crossed the Potomac River at Williamsport on September 11. "Our troops are very tired and some of the boys have failed to come up," noted Haynes. At Martinsburg, the men were given rations of hard bread and then it was on to Harpers Ferry. Despite the long march the men were "in good health & fine spirits," except that "our feet are very sore from marching." Thomas' brigade, with the rest of the division, advanced on Bolivar Heights on September 15, occupying a reserve position in the rear. The Union batteries quit firing by 8:30 a.m. and the garrison surrendered a short time later. Haynes saw Hill ride past "(in his shirt sleeves as he always goes) with three Yankee officers dressed as fine as could be, quite a contrast." James Kimbrough noted, "We had a great time there, plenty to eat but little to do." The men were permitted to fraternize with the enemy and "exchanged many little tokens of remembrance."[59]

The role of Thomas' brigade during the seminal Battle of Sharpsburg is summarized by one sentence written by Marion Fitzpatrick of the 45th Georgia to his wife: "Our brigade was left at Harper's Ferry to guard the place for four days." When Hill was summoned to Sharpsburg on the morning of September 17, he left Thomas' brigade behind to finish collecting the ample supplies.

The brigade rejoined the division during its retreat from Sharpsburg. When two Union V Corps brigades crossed the Potomac River to follow Lee's army on September 20, Hill's division turned and attacked in what became known as the Battle of Shepherdstown. Thomas' brigade was on the right of the first line and advanced with the rest of the division under a tremendous artillery fire. With no enemy troops in front of them, Thomas wheeled the men in his right regiments and attacked Charles Lovell's brigade's left flank, while Maxcy Gregg's South Carolinians and the rest of Thomas' men hit their front. Fitzpatrick wrote home, "On we went still routing them till we drove them across the river."[60]

The brigade played a small role during the Maryland Campaign losing just a handful of men.
**Bradley M. Gottfried**

* * *

## Stonewall Division—

### Brig. General J.R. Jones, Brigadier General William Starke, Colonel Andrew Grigsby

The venerable Stonewall Division was first commanded by Stonewall Jackson and then by Brig. Gen. Thomas Winder during the Seven Days Battles and Cedar Mountain, where he was killed. Brig. Gen. William Taliaferro finished the battle and brought the division into Second Bull Run, where he was wounded. This elevated Brig. Gen. J.R. Jones to command of the division during the Maryland Campaign.[1]

Historian Robert K. Krick wrote, "Stonewall Jackson's numerous military virtues did not include an aptitude for identifying and nurturing promising subordinates . . . None was more disappointing than John Robert Jones." Jones was born in Harrisonburg, Virginia on March 12, 1827 and graduated from the Virginia Military Institute with "distinction." He became a teacher in several schools before the Civil War. With the outbreak of the war, Jones organized an infantry company at Harrisonburg that became incorporated into the 33rd Virginia of the Stonewall Brigade. As captain of the company, he fought at First Bull Run and was promoted to the rank of lieutenant colonel on August 21, 1861. He curried Jackson's favor, which came in handy after the regimental elections of spring 1862. He was passed over as colonel, lieutenant colonel and major of the regiment so he petitioned Jackson for help. Because of Jackson's urgings, President Jefferson Davis promoted Jones to the rank of brigadier general and gave him command of a brigade in the Stonewall Division over several deserving colonels who had shown competence on recent battlefields. This action on June 23, 1862 dismayed and angered many of the brigade's officers. They would get the last laugh, however, as Jones' promotion was never officially confirmed by the Confederate Congress. Jones led his brigade at Gaines' Mill and Malvern Hill. A slight wound kept him out of action during Cedar Mountain and Second Bull Run and he entered the Maryland Campaign in charge of the Stonewall Division because of seniority.[2]

As the division moved north to Leesburg on September 3, it did so under the dubious leadership of Jones. The situation was not much better at the brigade level, as only one brigade was led by a permanent commander who held the appropriate rank of brigadier general. Two other brigades in the division were led by their senior colonels and one by a captain. The men were not in much better shape as their numbers were decimated by months of hard campaigning and fighting and their uniforms were in tatters. Many did not have shoes. This poorly led, poorly equipped, and decimated division would be one of two Confederate divisions that opened the fight at Sharpsburg.

Jones' division crossed the Potomac River at White's Ford on September 5 and bivouacked near Three Springs, Maryland. The division reached Frederick on September 7 and camped at the Best farm, about a mile outside of town. Jones' brigade, under Col. Bradley Johnson, entered the town and acted as provost guard. The division remained there until September 10 when it broke camp and headed for Harpers Ferry. The division, with the rest of Jackson's command, marched to Williamsport, Maryland where it crossed the Potomac River and aimed for Martinsburg, Virginia, which the Federal garrison had abandoned earlier in the morning. Jones paused in his official report of the campaign to cite a story in the *New York World* published on December 15, 1862: "The ragged, half-starved rebels passed through Maryland without disorder or marauding, without injury to the country, showing their excellent discipline. The well-fed, well-clothed Union soldiers laid waste everything before them, plundering houses, hen-roosts, and hog-pens, showing an utter want of discipline."

The division reached Schoolhouse Ridge, about a mile west of the Union defensive line on Bolivar Heights on September 14 and was placed on the left of Jackson's line. Although the Union artillery opened fire on the division, Jones reported not a single casualty. The division shifted to the left, closer to the Potomac River after dark. William Starke's brigade was ordered to straddle River Road to prevent enemy troops from attempting to escape. The garrison surrendered around 9:00 a.m. on September 15 to the relief of the men. The division headed back to its camp at Halltown, about three miles west of Harpers Ferry and prepared two days rations. The men were on road to Sharpsburg at 1:00 a.m. The all-night march brought them to the Potomac River at sunrise on September 16 and the division hurriedly crossed. Jones would write in his report, "Never has the army been so dirty, ragged, and ill-provided for as on this march, and yet there was no marauding, no plundering. The rights of person and property were strictly respected…"

The men were permitted a well-deserved two-hour rest in woods about a mile from Sharpsburg and then headed to the left with their right flank resting on Hagerstown Pike. Jones divided his division in two, two-brigade lines. Col. Andrew Grigsby's Stonewall Brigade formed the right of the first line with its right touching Hagerstown Pike. Capt. John Penn's brigade formed on its left, with its left touching the northernmost portion of the West Woods. Jones placed Grigsby in charge of this line. The second line was about 200 yards behind the first and was composed of Col. Alexander Taliaferro's brigade, under Col. Edward Warren, on the right, with its right touching Hagerstown Road, and Brig. Gen. William Starke's brigade on its left. Starke commanded these two brigades.[3]

The division's skirmishers were engaged all night, causing few of Jones' men to get much sleep. September 17 opened with an intense enfilade fire thrown against the division by enemy artillery in front, right, and from the Union guns of position across Antietam Creek. Jones' batteries responded quickly. Jones wrote in his report, "It was during this almost unprecedented iron storm that a shell exploded a little above my head, and so stunned and injured me that I was rendered unfit for duty, and retired from the field, turning over the command to Brigadier-General Starke . . ." This continued Jones' trend of finding ways to avoid being with his troops when it entered combat.

Jones' skirmishers awoke a giant when they fired into the right flank of Abner Doubleday's division marching south on the opposite side of Hagerstown Pike. The two rear regiments of John Gibbon's brigade (19th Indiana and 7th Wisconsin) were detached and sent across the road, followed by Marsena Patrick's brigade (both of Doubleday's division). The Stonewall Division was in rough shape that morning. Lt. Thomas Dunn, acting adjutant of the division, estimated the unit numbered about 1,500 men. "The troops were in the worst possible condition for a fight, having been under arms two nights in succession, one of which, at Harper's Ferry, it rained all night, while the march from Harper's Ferry to Sharpsburg was forced."[4]

Penn's and Grigsby's brigades, about 500 men in all, gamely held their positions against a growing host, but when the 19th Indiana wheeled and attacked the line's left flank, the fewer than 250 survivors were forced to retreat into the West Woods behind them. This first line fell back after about 30 minutes of fighting. The situation only became worse for the division when Starke saw the rest of Gibbon's brigade (2nd and 6th Wisconsin), followed by Walter Phelps' brigade (Doubleday's division), making its way south on the opposite side of Hagerstown Pike. Starke quickly wheeled his two reserve brigades to the right, to face Hagerstown Pike and the enemy's right flank across the road. All was chaos as Starke's two brigades became intermingled. They finally reformed along the fence lining the west side of Hagerstown Pike and fired into the flank of the Wisconsin regiments. These troops quickly turned to face Starke's men. Joseph Campbell's battery, less than a hundred yards from Starke's left flank, fired canister into the Virginians and the rest of the Iron Brigade and part of Patrick's brigade advanced against his left flank and rear. Starke frantically attempted to shore up his line, grabbing a battle flag and galloping forward with it, only to fall mortally wounded. According to Jones' report, the "gallant and generous Starke fell, pierced by three balls, and survived but a few moments. His fall cast a gloom over the troops."

The survivors of the Stonewall Division retreated into the West Woods. Stonewall Jackson wrote of the division's fight: "With heroic spirit our lines advanced to the conflict, and maintained their position, in the face of superior numbers, with stubborn resolution, sometimes driving the enemy before them and sometimes compelled to fall back before their well-sustained and destructive fire. Fresh troops from time to time relieved the enemy's ranks, and the carnage on both sides was terrific."

As ranking officer, Col. Grigsby assumed command of the division after Starke fell. He reformed his shattered division and led it forward again. Jubal Early's brigade (Alexander Lawton's division), which had been off to the left supporting the artillery on Nicodemus Heights, marched east to assist in repelling the Union charges. Grigsby quickly advanced with what was left of the Stonewall Division on the left of Early's line. Jackson wrote, "Colonel Grigsby, with his small command, kept in check the advance of the enemy on the left flank . . ." This was William Goodrich's brigade (George Greene's division, XII Corps), sent across Hagerstown Pike to support Doubleday's division. The Stonewall Division veterans opened fire, killing Col. Goodrich and ending any consideration of an advance south.[5]

John Sedgwick's division (II Corps) advanced toward the West Woods and was met by Lafayette McLaws' division, with support from Early's brigade and John Walker's division. Grigsby marched his division south sometime between 9:00 and 9:30 a.m. and reformed the men behind a fence just to the west of the southern projection of the West Woods. Although not engaged, the division was prepared to assist if needed. The men remained there until about 1:00 p.m. when Jackson ordered the division to march west to the Cox house to recover, "as it had been much thrown into disorder, to replenish . . . ammunition, [and] to get something to eat." The men moved again, sometime after 4:00 p.m. to the southeast to support several batteries "just above Hauser's farmhouse" on Hauser Ridge.[6]

The Stonewall Division remained in position through September 18 and crossed the Potomac River back into Virginia the following morning. Jones concluded, "In this bloody conflict the 'Old Stonewall Division' lost nothing of its fair name and fame," but it came at a price, as the battle closed "with a colonel commanding the division, captains commanding brigades, and lieutenants commanding regiments. In this fight every officer and man was a hero . . ." At least 12 officers commanded the four brigades at one time or another during the battle, and every brigade was commanded by as many as three officers. The division lost a total of 614 men or almost 40% of the number of men in position at the start of the battle.[7]

**Bradley M. Gottfried**

* * *

## Stonewall Brigade/Winder's Brigade: Colonel Andrew Grigsby, Lieutenant Colonel R. D. Gardner, Major Hazael J. Williams

**Units:** 2nd Virginia, 4th Virginia, 5th Virginia, 27th Virginia, 33rd Virginia
**Strength:** 1,160[8]
**Losses:** 88(11k-77w-0m)[9]

The "Stonewall Brigade" was perhaps the most famous unit in the Army of Northern Virginia. It was molded by Thomas Jackson into an effective fighting force that had fought in many battles, from First Bull Run, Shenandoah Valley Campaign, the Seven Days, Cedar Mountain and Second Bull Run. The hard campaigning had taken its toll on the unit, as it was just a shadow of its former self at the onset of the Maryland Campaign. Charles Winder led the brigade from the time Jackson departed to command a division until Cedar Mountain, where he was "frightfully mangled" by a shell on August 9, 1862 and died within a few hours. Winder's loss was mourned by both Lee and Jackson, as he was considered to be an efficient and effective commander. Col. Andrew Grigsby was thrust into command of the brigade. He had seen service during the Mexican War and was a farmer before the war. Grigsby enlisted as a private in the 7th Virginia in April 1861 and was quickly appointed major in the 27th Virginia. He fought with his regiment at First Bull Run and through the brigade's campaigns until he was wounded at Malvern Hill on July 1, 1862. Grigsby returned to action in time to command the brigade during the Maryland Campaign.[10]

The small brigade struck north from Ox Hill, Virginia on September 4 and marched through Leesburg the following day. September 6 found the men crossing the Potomac River "in excellent order and high spirits," according to Maj. H.J. Williams of the 5th Virginia. After passing through Frederick on September 7, the men rested about two miles north of the town on the road to Emmitsburg, Maryland. Williams noted the change in the men during their short hiatus here: "Our short sojourn in the land of promise wrought a salutary change in the general appearance and condition of the troops. The ragged were clad, the shoeless shod, and the inner man rejoiced by a number and variety of delicacies to which it had been a stranger for long, long weary months before."

### Harpers Ferry

The men were on the march again on September 10, heading for Harpers Ferry. The division passed through Martinsburg, Virginia on September 13, and the 2nd Virginia remained there as provost guard while the rest of Grigsby's brigade and the division headed for Harpers Ferry. The following day, according to Jackson's report, the brigade was to "secure a commanding hill to the left of the heights near the Potomac. Promptly dispersing some cavalry, this eminence, from which the batteries of William Poague and John Carpenter subsequently did such admirable execution, was secured without difficulty." The brigade took shelter from the enemy artillery shells by remaining behind the hill. That night, the men avanced to within half a mile of Bolivar Heights, the main Union defensive line at Harpers Ferry. They awaited the daylight, when Grigsby's men knew they would be ordered to make a dash toward the enemy's positions. As the men prepared to storm the heights on September 15, white flags fluttered on the high ground. Grigsby apparently did not see the white flags and ordered Poague's battery to continue firing at Harpers Ferry. Jackson sent word of the truce and Poague sent an aide to Grigsby to ask what to do with his loaded cannon. Grigsby purportedly said, "Tell him to fire them off the way they are pointed. He won't kill more of the damn Yankees than he ought to!"[11]

340

The Stonewall Brigade, with the rest of the division, returned to Halltown, about three miles west of Harpers Ferry, where the men prepared rations. The march to join Lee at Sharpsburg began at 2:00 a.m. on September 16 and continued all night until the men crossed the Potomac River at Shepherdstown around sunrise.[12]

## Antietam

Grigsby's brigade rested in a wooded grove just north of Sharpsburg until 3:00 p.m. on September 16, when it moved more about two miles northwest of town to take position on Jackson's front line. J.R. Jones' division occupied two lines of brigades north of the Dunker Church, perpendicular to Hagerstown Pike. The men rested in an unprotected clover field, with the Stonewall Brigade on the right of the first line with its right flank attached to Hagerstown Pike. John Penn's brigade extended the line to the left. William Starke's and Edward Warren's (William Taliaferro's brigade) brigades were about 250 yards in the rear. Poague's battery dropped trail between the brigade's main line and its skirmishers and opened an effective fire against an enemy battery (probably Dunbar Ransom's) and silenced it, but awoke a sleeping giant as several Union batteries, only a quarter of a mile away, opened fire on Poague's battery and Grigsby's men until after dark on September 16. Maj. Williams of the 5th Virginia called the enemy artillery fire, "grand and comparatively harmless, except to the stragglers in [the] far rear." The quiet of the night was occasionally broken by skirmish fire. In several cases, the men jumped from their blankets to prepare to get into line of battle.[13]

As daylight of September 17 approached, the officers woke the men and told them to prepare their rifles for action. It had briefly rained and the men made sure their loads were dry. Poague's battery moved forward again and threw a few rounds at the enemy and then fell back and redeployed between Jones' two lines of brigades. Grigsby noted a large gap between his right on Hagerstown Pike and Marcellus Douglass'

(Alexander Lawton's division) left and called attention to it, without success. He asked again when he saw the enemy advancing against his position and this time Harry Hays' brigade (Lawton's division) was ordered from its reserve position in the West Woods to fill the void. Its orders were countermanded and Hays instead headed toward the right of Douglass' line; the gap remained intact.

Lt. E.E. Stickley of the brigade's staff never forgot the first appearance of the 19th Indiana and 7th Wisconsin (John Gibbon's Iron Brigade), followed by Marsena Patrick's brigade (Abner Doubleday's division; I Corps). "The spectacle now presented was one of splendor and magnificence, for as the enemy advanced we beheld one of the most brilliant displays of troops we had ever seen. The Federals in apparent double battle line were moving toward us at charge bayonets, common time, and the sunbeams falling on their well-polished guns and bayonets gave a glamour and a show at once fearful and entrancing."[14]

The men in Jones' front line were lying down for concealment and protection, but as the enemy approached, they were ordered to their feet and according to Williams, "poured in a staggering volley, which stopped his advance." The 19th Indiana advanced against the first line's left flank, so Grigsby's men were hit in their front and flank. Artillery shells plowed through the line and exploded above it. Grigsby sent Lt. J.M. Garnett of his staff to Starke, now in charge of the Stonewall Division, with a message that he could not hold on much longer. As Garnett delivered his message, he looked up and saw the front line retreating across the open field. Williams saw the futility of further defense and suggested to Grigsby that he order a general retreat. The brigade commander would not take responsibility for falling back, probably knowing the attitude of Stonewall Jackson toward leaders who allowed their men to retreat. Williams ordered his own regiment to fall back to the West Woods behind them and the entire brigade followed suit.[15]

Later that morning, the remnants of the brigade with other members of the Stonewall Division ventured forward and formed on the left of Jubal Early's brigade (Lawton's division) and battled William Goodrich's brigade (George Greene's division, XII Corps), supported by Patrick's brigade. Their actions discouraged a full-scale attack by these two brigades. The men later pulled back and turned their orientation from north to east, taking position behind a fence in reserve while Lafayette McLaws' division hammered John Sedgwick's division (II Corps) in the West Woods. Although not engaged, Grigsby's men were were close enough to do so.[16]

This ended the fighting for Grigsby's brigade. The brigade, with the rest of the division, fell back to the Cox house, just west of the West Woods, where the men rested and were resupplied with ammunition. The men also welcomed the arrival of provisions. One of the famished soldiers wrote, "Some salt bacon was issued to us. In default of cooking utensils we cooked it . . . on forked sticks and I never knew bacon to taste sweeter." The brigade moved again shortly after 4:00 p.m., this time to Hauser Ridge to support a number of batteries.

The Stonewall Brigade lost 71 men during the intense fighting west of Hagerstown Pike. While forced to relinquish its position, it only did so when faced with overwhelming numbers of enemy infantry and artillery.[17]

Although Grigsby performed capably during his short stint as brigade commander during the Maryland Campaign, he was passed over for the permanent position. Jackson strongly recommended Maj. Elisha Paxton of his staff. Grigsby was "mad as thunder," and all of the other colonels of the brigade immediately resigned. Grigsby swore, "as soon as the war ends, I will challenge Jackson to a duel." He took his grievance directly to Jefferson Davis and the resulting meeting did not go well. Grigsby resigned his commission in November, 1862.[18]

**Bradley M. Gottfried**

* * *

### Jones' Brigade: Colonel Bradley Johnson, Captain John Penn, Captain John Page, Captain Robert Withers, Lieutenant John Booker

**Units:** 21st Virginia, 42nd Virginia, 48th Virginia, 1st Virginia Battalion
**Strength:** 812[19]
**Losses:** 71 (9k-62w-0m)[20]

Brigadier General J.R. Jones' original brigade was a veteran unit, whose regiments were mustered into service in April and May, 1861. The brigade saw extensive action prior to the Maryland Campaign, including during Stonewall Jackson's Shenandoah Valley Campaign, Seven Days Battles, Cedar Mountain, and Second Bull Run. It was a cohesive brigade that had the distinction of fighting in each of these campaigns under a different leader. Col. Bradley Johnson was the current commander, but he served as Provost Marshal at Frederick, and did not command the brigade at Antietam.[21]

By virtue of his seniority, Capt. John Penn initially commanded the brigade at Antietam. Born in 1837 in Virginia, Penn attended Randolph-Macon College and the University of Virginia before becoming a lawyer. He enlisted in May 1861 and became a captain in the 42nd Virginia Infantry. Penn would lose a leg at Antietam and be captured. After he was exchanged in January 1863, he was promoted to the rank of major and attempted to return to his unit, but he was forced to resign his commission because of his debilitating wound. Penn later served in the Virginia State Senate and died in 1895.[22]

The brigade was one of the smallest in Lee's army. An historian of the 21st Virginia called it "a company size regiment that formed part of a regimental size brigade." The brigade had not yet recuperated from its horrendous losses at the Battle of Cedar Mountain as it marched north to Leesburg on September 3. Another reason for its small size was the number of soldiers who refused take part in the invasion. They had enlisted for the defense of Virginia, not to invade Maryland. The brigade, with the rest of the division, crossed the Potomac River on September 5 at White's Ford and made its way to Frederick, Maryland where it camped north of town. Guards were placed around the town to prevent troops from "visiting," but many were able to get through and enjoyed seeing the sites.[23]

## Harpers Ferry

The brigade left the pleasant surroundings of Frederick on September 10 and headed northwest on a circular course as part of Stonewall Jackson's advance on Harpers Ferry. Reaching Schoolhouse Ridge, a mile west of the main Harpers Ferry defensive line on Bolivar Heights, J.R. Jones' division was on the left of Jackson's line, adjacent to the Potomac River. Penn's brigade occupied the second line and was not called upon to advance against the enemy position. The men exchanged fire with enemy troops until late into the evening of September 14 and then slept on their arms, aware that the morrow would bring a full-scale attack on the Union garrison. Before the men received orders to advance, they saw white flags fluttering in the distance. Many of Penn's soldiers greeted the news of the garrison's surrender on September 15 with a hearty rebel yell. They rested the remainder of the day and then were ordered to prepare three days rations, and completed this task by midnight. The division moved out between 1:00 and 2:00 a.m. on September 16, marched all night, and crossed the Potomac River at Shepherdstown at sunrise.[24]

## Antietam

After resting, the Stonewall Division marched north and deployed "about two hours before night," according to Jones. Jones deployed his division in a double line north of the Dunker Church. The first line was composed of Penn's brigade and the Stonewall Brigade. The latter brigade was on the right, with its right flank touching Hagerstown Pike. The brigade extended about 150 yards to the left (west), where it connected with Penn's brigade, which continued the line west until it reached the West Woods. The two brigades' line ran about 400 yards and occupied a clover field with little cover. Jones' remaining two brigades formed the second line, about 210 yards in the rear, where they were better protected. Penn threw out a skirmish line, which engaged the enemy until dark.[25]

Lt. John Roberts of the 48th Virginia recalled, "The Yankees gave us a good bombing while we were lying in the line . . . [continuing] the fire long after dark, the bombs bursting all around us. After night we could see them coming for a mile. They described a beautiful curve with the fire of the burning fuse streaming out behind. The scene was very grand, but not altogether pleasant to us, as pieces of bombs, dusk and brush were flying all around us." The cannonade did little damage to the brigade, except to fray the men's nerves.[26]

September 17 dawned bright with a ground haze that obscured the terrain in front of Penn's men. The Union artillery opened fire at 5:30 a.m. John Worsham of the 21st Virginia, recalled, "It seemed that the air was alive with shells!" One of the shells knocked division commander J.R. Jones out of action when it exploded over his head. Abner Doubleday's Union division (I Corps) initially advanced south on the opposite (east) side of Hagerstown Road, but Penn's and Grigsby's skirmishers fired into its flank, causing the division to break into two pieces. Half of John Gibbon's Iron brigade (19th Indiana and 7th Wisconsin) crossed over to the west side of Hagerstown Pike, followed by Marsena Patrick's brigade. These 1,315 men vastly outnumbered the 600 men in Penn's and Grigsby's two brigades on the front line. Roberts recalled, "The Yankees threw forward a heavy column of infantry and a battery that made grape-shot rain around us."[27]

The men of the two brigades lay in the grass awaiting orders from their officers to rise and send volleys into the advancing Union troops. As the distance closed, the officers finally gave the order and the men "poured a staggering volley, which stopped [the] advance." John Worsham recalled the Union artillery opened again while the enemy regrouped. If the numerical disadvantage was not bad enough, the Union troops advanced at an oblique angle through the upper portion of the West Woods against Penn's left flank. With frontal and flank fire, Penn's men were forced to slowly withdraw toward the division's second line. Penn went down with a leg wound and Capt. Archer Page of the 21st Virginia assumed command of the brigade, but he too was wounded in the leg and carried to the rear, leaving Capt. R. Withers of the 42nd Virginia in charge.[28]

When the Stonewall Brigade fell back to the West Woods, just north of the Dunker Church, at about 6:45 a.m., Penn's men followed. Here, Roberts recalled the brigade was "exposed to a terrific storm of grape, canister, and shell" for about half an hour.

Some of Penn's men joined a portion of the Stonewall Division's advance with Jubal Early's brigade (Alexander Lawton's division) that helped keep William Goodrich's brigade (George Greene's division; XII Corps) at bay. Roberts described it as "a long and severe fight with a heavy force. We were reinforced just in time to save us from falling back again." The brigade, with the rest of the division, headed to the Cox house, west of the West Woods to reform, and refit. Penn's brigade later supported the Rockbridge Artillery on Hauser Ridge.[29]

The battle was now over for Penn's brigade. It was now commanded by Lt. John Booker, the brigade's fourth commander since daybreak, since Withers was severely wounded. Roberts called it a "very hard battle." The brigade's 71 casualties reduced its numbers after the battle to under 130 men. The 48th Virginia mustered fewer than 25 men and the other regiments fared little better. The brigade, with the rest of the division, crossed the Potomac River at Boteler's Ford just after dawn on September 19 and made its way to Martinsburg and then to Bunker Hill in the Shenandoah Valley. Lt. D. Garrett of the 42nd Virginia predicted, "I don't think we are to rest long for it seems that there is not rest for us."[30]

**Bradley M. Gottfried**

* * *

### Taliaferro's Brigade: Colonel Edward Warren, Colonel James Jackson, Colonel James Sheffield

**Units:** 47th Alabama, 48th Alabama, 10th Virginia, 23rd Virginia, 37th Virginia
**Strength:** 1,543[31]
**Losses:** 168 (41k-127w-0m)[32]

William Taliaferro's mixed brigade of Alabama and Virginia troops had seen action in several campaigns. The three Virginia regiments were all mustered into Confederate service on July 1, 1861, but served in different brigades. The 10th Virginia was in Brig. Gen. Kirby Smith's brigade and saw service at First Bull Run. The two other Virginia regiments served in Taliaferro's brigade, which was part of the Army of the Northwest. The two Alabama regiments were mustered into service on May 20 and May 22, 1862 and were immediately placed into Taliaferro's brigade. The Virginia regiments saw extensive action during Stonewall Jackson's Shenandoah Valley Campaign and the Seven Days Battles, and the entire brigade saw action at Cedar Mountain and Second Bull Run.[33]

William Taliaferro officially commanded the brigade but he was wounded at Second Bull Run. His men thought him too strict and he became unpopular with them. He also ran afoul of Stonewall Jackson, who unsuccessfully attempted to block his promotion to brigadier general. Col. Edward Warren of the 10th Virginia assumed command of the brigade during the Maryland Campaign. Warren was born in 1829 in Rockingham County, Virginia and practiced law before the war. He was appointed lieutenant colonel of the 10th Virginia at its formation and assumed command of the regiment during the Shenandoah Valley Campaign when its commander was killed at the Battle of McDowell.[34]

Little is known of Warren's brigade's march to the battlefield as none of its leaders filed an official report of the battle and few left recollections.[35]

**Antietam**

J.R. Jones' division was deployed for action on the west (left) side of Hagerstown Pike in two lines, facing north, on the morning of September 17. Warren's brigade occupied the right of the second line, about 210 yards behind the first line, with its right touching Hagerstown Pike. William Starke's brigade was deployed on its left. Stonewall Jackson and his staff rode by and told the men, "Be ready, we will move up soon."

Warren's men watched the first line battle portions of John Gibbon's "Iron Brigade" and Marsena Patrick's brigade (both of Abner Doubleday's division; I Corps). Danger also loomed across Hagerstown Pike, for the rest of the Iron Brigade and Walter Phelps' brigade (also Doubleday's division) had driven Marcellus Douglass' brigade (Alexander Lawton's division) to the rear and was now heading toward the high ground near the Dunker Church. Warren ordered his men to their feet and with Starke's brigade, made a right wheel to face the pike. During the confused movement, the right of Starke's brigade became intermingled with the left of Warren's, causing confusion until the officers straightened

things out. Starke was again on Warren's left flank and the two brigades advanced toward Hagerstown Pike. According to historian Ezra Carman, "the two brigades, under a murderous fire, thinning its ranks at every step, reached the high and strong post and rail fence of the road and came face to face with the Wisconsin men [2nd and 6th] across the road, only 30 – 75 yards away." The 14th Brooklyn (Phelps' brigade) rushed out of the corn and joined the Wisconsinites by the fence. Carman called the fighting "fast, furious, and deadly." The two sides stood toe to toe for about 15 minutes, neither side willing to give an inch. Some Confederates mounted the fence to charge the enemy, but were quickly cut down. R.P. Jennings of the 23rd Virginia wrote to a Union soldier after the war, "You fellows just mowed us down."[36]

Starke's brigade on the left was now in desperate straits as it not only faced Union troops across Hagerstown Pike in its front, but Joseph Campbell's battery dropped trail on its left. The Union regiments who had routed J.R. Jones' two brigades on the first line had regrouped and now descended upon Starke's left flank and rear, forcing its men to stampede for the rear.[37]

The storm now descended upon Warren's brigade and it too was overwhelmed and forced to retreat. Parts of the brigade subsequently reformed in the West Woods; other men were scattered around the battlefield and some fought with other units. Those men still with the brigade advanced again with the remainder of the division and engaged Goodrich's brigade. The brigade then pulled back to Hauser's Ridge. The fighting was now over for Warren's brigade. It had lost 168 men in about half an hour of intense fighting.[38]

The brigade, with the rest of the Stonewall Division, crossed the Potomac River during the night of September 18-19 and rested along Opequon Creek between Shepherdstown and Williamsport, where they were reinforced.[39]

**Bradley M. Gottfried**

## Starke's (2nd Louisiana) Brigade: Brigadier General William Starke, Colonel Jesse Williams, Colonel Leroy Stafford, Colonel Edmund Pendleton

**Units:** 1st Louisiana Infantry, 2nd Louisiana Infantry, 9th Louisiana Infantry, 10th Louisiana Infantry, 15th Louisiana Infantry, Coppens' Battalion
**Strength:** 1,623
**Losses:** 304 (83-204-17)[40]

The 2nd Louisiana Brigade was formed in July 1862 by pulling regiments scattered throughout several brigades. The 1st Louisiana, previously part of Ambrose Wright's brigade, spent most of the war's first year near Yorktown, and had seen action only during the Seven Days Battles. The 2nd Louisiana had also spent nearly 11 months in the Yorktown area as part of Howell Cobb's brigade. Paul Semmes' brigade contributed the 10th Louisiana, which had also spent many months at Yorktown before seeing combat during the Seven Days. The 9th Louisiana, transferred from Richard Taylor's brigade (now the 1st Louisiana Brigade), was the new brigade's most veteran unit, having seen hard service in Stonewall Jackson's Valley Campaign and the Seven Days. The 15th Louisiana had only recently been mustered into service in July, by the amalgamation of the 3rd Louisiana Infantry Battalion and two companies of the 7th Louisiana Infantry Battalion. Its members had previously fought at Mechanicsville, Gaines' Mill, and Frazier's Farm. Coppens' Zouave Battalion had most recently served in Roger Pryor's brigade, and had seen combat at Williamsburg, Seven Pines, and during the Seven Days. Most of these units had also been at Malvern Hill.[41]

The new brigade's commander, William Edwin Starke, was born in Brunswick County, Virginia in 1814. He emigrated south in the 1840's, settling in Mobile and New Orleans. He became a successful stagecoach operator, cotton broker, and businessman. Starke returned to Virginia after its secession, and became an aide to Robert Garnett

and Robert E. Lee in western Virginia. He was appointed colonel of the 60th Virginia Infantry in October 1861. Starke led the regiment through the Seven Days, and was wounded at Frazier's Farm. Perhaps because he had a long association with Louisiana, Starke was appointed brigadier general of the 2nd Louisiana Brigade in August 1862.[42]

A part of Stonewall Jackson's Wing, Starke's brigade marched north from Gordonsville, Virginia, in early August, suffering only 20 casualties at Cedar Mountain on August 9. The brigade resorted to throwing rocks at Second Bull Run when its men ran out of ammunition. Starke assumed temporary command of the division when William Taliaferro was wounded. On September 1, the brigade fought another brief action at Chantilly, Virginia. The Louisianans lost a total of 400 men in the Second Bull Run Campaign.[43]

From Chantilly, Starke's brigade marched to Leesburg, Virginia and crossed the Potomac River at White's Ford on September 5. The brigade reached Frederick on September 7. After marching through the city, the Louisianans made camp about a mile beyond it. Controversy arose almost immediately when Jackson placed Starke under arrest for refusing an order to return his command to the city, so irate citizens might identify Confederate soldiers who had supposedly looted and insulted them. Starke retained his command through the campaign, but remained under arrest.[44]

The brigade's stay in the area was brief. At 3:00 a.m. on the morning of the September 10, the Louisianans began the march west from Frederick, on their way to Harpers Ferry. They passed through Middletown and camped near Boonsboro that night, before crossing the Potomac River at Light's Ford, near Williamsport, the next day. To prevent the escape of the Union garrison at Martinsburg, Virginia, J.R. Jones and Alexander Lawton's divisions marched to North Depot, seven miles northwest of the town. After bivouacking there for the night, the brigade marched into Martinsburg on September 12. J.R. Jones paid tribute to his division, writing in his report, "Never has the army been so dirty, ragged, and ill-provided for as on this march, and yet there was no marauding, no plundering. The rights of person and property were strictly respected…"[45]

## Harpers Ferry

The brigade left Martinsburg at first light on September 13 and arrived near Harpers Ferry in the afternoon. It camped behind Schoolhouse Ridge, about a mile west of the main Union defensive line on Bolivar Heights, along Charlestown Road. About 2:00 p.m. on September 14, J.R. Jones' division was ordered to move up in support of the Baltimore Light Artillery, on the far right of the ridge, overlooking the Federal position on Bolivar Heights. After darkness fell, the brigade was shifted to the Potomac River to seal the River Road from any Federal escape attempt.[46]

The Harpers Ferry garrison surrendered early on the morning of September 15. In the mid-afternoon, Starke's Louisianans were told to prepare two days rations and be ready to march. At 1:00 a.m. on September 16, the brigade set off on the march to Sharpsburg, reaching Boteler's Ford at first light and again crossing into Maryland.[47]

## Antietam

Starke's brigade, with the rest of Jones' division, rested about a mile southwest of Sharpsburg for several hours on September 16, then marched to the West Woods area during the mid-afternoon and formed on the left of John Hood's division near the Dunker Church. The dispositions were made between 4:00 and 5:00 p.m., with the Louisianans and Edward Warren's Brigade (on their right) composing the second line of the division, facing north. About 100 yards in front of them stood the Stonewall Brigade (under Andrew Grigsby) and Jones' brigade (under John Penn) in the open fields

along Hagerstown Pike. While in this position, the brigade suffered from the effects of an artillery duel between the Rockbridge Artillery and Federal batteries near the North Woods. Union over-shots caused several casualties, including brigade Assistant Adjutant General, Lt. Archibald Gordon, who lost both legs and subsequently bled to death.[48]

As darkness settled over the field, Jubal Early's brigade (Alexander Lawton's division) took position on Starke's left. That night the men rested on their arms as best as they could. Union artillery occasionally clipped the treetops over their heads, and the pop-pop-pop of skirmishing lasted until dawn.[49]

Artillery fire began shortly after first light on September 17. J.R. Jones was stunned by a shell burst very early on, so he turned the division over to Starke. Jesse Williams, 2nd Louisiana, assumed command of the brigade. Abner Doubleday's division (I Corps) advanced south on Hagerstown Pike, slowly forcing back Penn's and Grigsby's small brigades. Sometime between 6:00 and 6:30 a.m., Starke received a desperate message from Grigsby stating the Stonewall Brigade could not hold much longer. Being pressed by the 19th Indiana and the 7th Wisconsin of John Gibbon's "Iron Brigade," Grigsby's and Penn's brigades fell back into the West Woods.[50]

The 2nd and 6th Wisconsin regiments, with the 2nd United States Sharpshooters, advanced south on the opposite side of the Pike at the same time, pushing the remnants of Marcellus Douglass' brigade (Lawton's division) back toward the Dunker Church. Starke decided to attack their vulnerable right flank adjacent to Hagerstown Pike. With Warren's brigade on the right, the Louisianans swept northeast out of the West Woods, aiming directly for the southwestern edge of the Cornfield. Edmund Pendleton of the 15th Louisiana, who later commanded the brigade, wrote, "We had scarcely emerged from the woods in which we had rested during the night, when we found ourselves face to face with the enemy, heavily massed and within close musket range." The attack pushed obliquely to the right, and the two brigades became intermingled. Pendleton reported how the men "charged forward in the face of a murderous fire, which thinned our ranks at every step, until our progress was arrested by a lane on either side of which was a high, staked fence stretching along our whole front, to pass which, under the circumstances, was an impossibility."[51]

Starke grabbed a flag and carried it forward, only to be hit by three bullets. He was carried to the rear, where he died within the hour. Pendleton called him a "brave and chivalric leader . . . loved and honored by every man under his command." A bitter, short-range firefight took place across Hagerstown Pike. The 14th Brooklyn of Walter Phelps' brigade (Doubleday's division) joined the Wisconsin men across Hagerstown Pike, shifting the balance even more toward the Union troops. The 1st Louisiana, on the left of Starke's line, came face to face with the 2nd U.S. Sharpshooters, who also helped stabilize the Union line. Other elements of Phelps' brigade fell in on their left. Some of the Louisianans scaled the fence, although few, if any, lived to cross back.[52]

A threat was materializing on Starke's left flank, as a section of Battery B, 4th U.S. Artillery under Lt. James Stewart, supported by men of the 80th New York, dropped trail and fired spherical case shot into the 1st Louisiana as skirmishers from the 19th Indiana advanced into the Louisianans' rear. Pendleton noted, "Not a man was seen to flinch from the conflict. By some mistake or misapprehension, the troops which were intended, as I have since been informed, to support us on the left, failed to get in position as early as was expected, and, our left being unprotected, we were about to be outflanked, when the order to retire was given and obeyed, the men withdrawing in tolerable order, and fighting as they fell back." The retreat was by the right flank southwest into the portion of the West Woods they had previously occupied. As the badly mixed Federal units advanced after them, they came upon Hood's division, fresh on the field.[53]

In the aftermath of Hood's charge, the Louisianans reformed their shattered ranks and prepared for another onslaught. According to Pendleton, other troops came to his support and "we gathered our strength for a fresh charge upon the rapidly advancing and exulting foe, and, with a determination to win or die, hurled ourselves against his lines with an impetus which first staggered, then drove him, fleeing, from the field, and leaving behind him hundreds of his dead and wounded." This fight just north of the West Woods was against the right wing of the Iron Brigade as it stood gathered in Hagerstown Pike. Starke's brigade, with the rest of the division, was pulled back through the West Woods to the Alfred Poffenberger farm, where the men reformed and received ammunition. Col. Leroy Stafford of the 9th Louisiana reported the brigade "remained in line of battle all night of the 17th."[54]

In addition to nearly 300 casualties, Col. Jesse Williams of the 2nd Louisiana, who commanded the brigade after Starke replaced J. R. Jones, was wounded by a bullet in the chest. His replacement, Col. Stafford, was wounded in the foot. Command finally devolved upon Edmund Pendleton of the 15th Louisiana. Not an officer of the brigade was unwounded during the intense fighting. Sgt. Edward Stephens of Company C, 9th Louisiana thought his regiment "is almost destroyed." The 1st Louisiana's flag was captured by the 2nd U.S. Sharpshooters on Hagerstown Pike.[55]

## Shepherdstown

Starke's brigade again crossed the Potomac River at Boteler's Ford early on the morning of September 19. The brigade was held in reserve during the Battle of Shepherdstown, then continued to Martinsburg on September 21, followed by a march to Bunker Hill in early October. The 9th Louisiana Infantry returned to Harry Hays' 1st Louisiana Brigade later that month and it was replaced by the 14th Louisiana.[56]

**Robert Gottschalk**

***

# D.H. HILL'S DIVISION—

## Major General Daniel Harvey Hill

Daniel Harvey Hill was born into a wealthy South Carolina plantation family on July 12, 1821. His father died four years later, leaving the family in dire financial straits, causing Hill to recall, "I had no youth." He graduated from West Point in 1842 and joined the artillery. Hill saw extensive action during the Mexican War and remained with the army until he resigned in 1849 to join the math faculty of Washington College in Lexington, Virginia before moving to Davidson College in North Carolina. Along the way he published three books, including an algebra textbook. His last job before the Civil War was superintendent of the newly formed North Carolina Military Institute. Upon the outbreak of the war, Hill received the rank of colonel and command of the North Carolina camp of instruction in April 1861. He was subsequently elected colonel of the 1st North Carolina on May 11, 1861 and led his unit in its successful skirmish with Union troops at Big Bethel on June 10, 1861. The action propelled him into the public eye and a promotion to brigadier general. He subsequently commanded several posts along the coast of North Carolina and near Leesburg, Virginia. He received his second star on March 26, 1862 and with it, a division stationed near Yorktown, Virginia.

Hill was described as five feet, ten inches tall with a slight stoop from a chronic spinal issue. He was Stonewall Jackson's brother-in-law, and like him, was devoutly religious. He fought well on the Peninsula and during the Seven Days Campaign. His division was sent to the Department of North Carolina, but Lee requested Hill's services. Hill and his division were reunited in time for the Second Bull Run Campaign. A hard fighter who always seemed to "go from choice into the most dangerous place he could find on the field," Hill was described by a contemporary as "harsh, abrupt, often insulting in the effort to be sarcastic" and another admitted he would "offend many and conciliate none."[1]

Hill's division was considered among the finest in the army after its gallant service at Seven Pines, Williamsburg, Gaines' Mill and Malvern Hill. At five brigades, Hill's division was among the largest in the army. With the exception of Brig. Gen. Roswell Ripley, each brigade was headed by a highly competent leader. Hill's division was among the first to cross the Potomac River on September 4, and it was then ordered to the mouth of the Monocacy River to destroy the canals and locks of the C & O Canal. The lack of tools and explosive powder caused the mission to fail. The division marched to just outside of Frederick on September 5. Because Jackson had fallen from his horse and was temporarily disabled on September 6, Hill assumed command of the wing until Jackson recuperated. The division was designated in Special Orders Number 191 as the army's rearguard and protector of the "immense" wagon train. Hill's command left Frederick on September 10 and camped that night east of South Mountain. The division marched through Turner's Gap on September 12 and reached the town of Boonsboro. Hill's orders were to "distribute my five brigades so as not only to protect the wagons and guns, but also to watch all roads leading from Harper's Ferry, in order to intercept the Federal forces that might make their escape before Jackson had completed the investment of that place." The orders forced Hill to disperse his five brigades south and west to cover the major roads.

On September 13, Lee ordered Hill to position his division to "prevent the escape of the Yankees from Harpers' Ferry, then besieged, and also to guard the pass in the Blue Ridge near Boonsborough." Cavalry leader, Jeb Stuart, informed Hill that day of two Union brigades approaching Turner's Gap and requested a brigade to halt their advance at South Mountain. Hill responded by sending Col. Alfred Colquitt's and Brig.

Gen. Samuel Garland's brigades up to the summit of South Mountain. He estimated his division numbered about 5,000 men on the morning of the Battle of South Mountain on September 14.[2]

Lee sent a note to Hill around midnight of September 13 indicating he was unhappy with the "condition of things on the turnpike or National road," and ordered him to ride up the mountainside the next morning to "assist Stuart in its defense." Hill left "very early on the morning of the 14th" and quickly realized "it could only be held by a large force, and was wholly indefensible by a small one," so he called up Brig. Gen. George B. Anderson's brigade. He left Brig. Gen. Robert Rodes' and Ripley's brigades at the base of the mountain until he had more definitive information on the "strength and design of the Yankees." Hill was surprised to hear firing from his right at Fox's Gap at about 7:00 a.m., so he quickly dispatched Garland's brigade down Wood Road to block the gap. Garland was killed and his command scattered during the heavy morning fighting. Hill called Garland a "pure, gallant, and accomplished Christian soldier" who "had no superiors and few equals in the service." Hill sent Anderson's brigade to reinforce Garland's brigade and halt the Union thrust through Fox's Gap. Jacob Cox, whose Kanawha Division, battled for the gap all morning, chose to await reinforcements, rather than continue his push through the gap.[3]

With the Union I and IX Corps assailing the mountain, Hill called up Ripley's and Rodes' brigades. He sent the former down to reinforce the Fox's Gap sector and the latter up to Frosttown Plateau to stop an enemy flanking attempt. Longstreet with his two divisions began arriving from Hagerstown between 3:00 to 3:30 p.m. David R. Jones' division was broken up: two brigades moved south to Fox's Gap and three others headed north to form on the right of Rodes' brigade, battling the Pennsylvania Reserves. Because Hill could not oversee both fronts, he assigned Ripley oversight of the afternoon defense of Fox's Gap. Ripley did a poor job of it, leading to two brigades not directly engaged and one almost destroyed. Hill remained angry with Ripley 25 years after the battle, writing how he was "sent for in hot haste . . . but he was a coward and did nothing."

Hill's single division, with help from Longstreet's command, faced two Union corps, and although his troops at Frosttown Plateau were bested, the stout defense along Old Sharpsburg Road (Fox's Gap) and National Road (Turner's Gap) continued until after dark. Hill and Longstreet met with Lee that night and informed him the mountain could no longer be held. Lee agreed and ordered Hill to march his shattered division toward Sharpsburg. "Should the truth ever be known, the battle of South Mountain, as far as my division was concerned, will be regarded as one of the most remarkable and creditable of the war." Hill's losses on September 14 were approximately 124 killed, 456 wounded, and 404 missing for a total of 984. Although forced to vacate the South Mountain gaps, Hill's men put up a furious fight until dark, buying time for Jackson's troops to reduce the Harpers Ferry garrison.[4]

Hill's division was the first unit to vacate the mountain, beginning at about 10:00 p.m. Rodes marched his brigade and Colquitt's down the National Road to Boonsboro and then picked up Boonsboro Pike to Sharpsburg. After crossing the Middle Bridge shortly before sunrise, Colquitt's brigade continued its march through Sharpsburg and halted near Blackford's Ford, west of town. Rodes' brigade assumed high ground southeast of town. The division's remaining three brigades moved on country roads from Old Sharpsburg Road to Boonsboro and then followed Rodes' contingent toward Sharpsburg. After crossing the Middle Bridge, the brigades marched right when about a mile short of town and occupied high ground there. Rodes' and Colquitt's brigades later rejoined the division, whose right was anchored on Boonsboro Pike. When Lee realized the danger to his left flank, he ordered Hill to extend his line to the left to support Stonewall Jackson's men. Ripley's brigade moved during the night of September 16-17 to a position about 150 yards west of the Mumma house.[5]

Because of his losses at South Mountain and excessive straggling, Hill estimated his division numbered only 3,000 muskets on the morning of the Battle of Antietam. What he lacked in infantry, he made up in artillery, as he had 26 cannon under his command and he carefully deployed them. The see-saw battle for the Miller Cornfield and East Woods had chewed up three Confederate divisions by about 7:30 a.m., when Hill was ordered to provide troops to battle Meade's division (I Corps) and the newly arriving XII Corps. Hill led Ripley's brigade by the left flank in column of fours to the scene of the combat and they drove Meade's Pennsylvania Reserves through the Cornfield and battled the XII Corps at a distance. Colquitt's brigade arrived and it dashed past Ripley's men into the Cornfield where its men slugged it out with Alpheus Williams' division (XII Corps). Garland's North Carolinians, now under Col. Duncan McRae, followed Colquitt toward the East Woods, but the men headed to the rear when an officer yelled they were being flanked. All alone, Colquitt's men battled overwhelming numbers of enemy troops until finally ordered to retire. Colquitt's men would be the last Confederate troops to enter the Cornfield, and when they were forced to withdraw, the XII Corps overran the field and held it for the remainder of the battle.[6]

As Hill's three brigades were being overrun by the XII Corps, Rodes received orders to advance and support them. He noted in his report, "I had hardly begun the movement before it was evident that the two latter had met with a reverse, and that the best service I could render them and the field generally would be to form a line in rear of them and endeavor to rally them before attacking or being attacked." He took up a position in the Sunken Road and G.B. Anderson's brigade formed on his right. The remnants of Colquitt's and McRae's brigades formed further to their left, adjacent to Hagerstown Pike. The Sunken Road line was first attacked by William French's division's (II Corps) onslaught and then by Israel Richardson's division (II Corps). A combination of heavy casualties, especially among the officers, mistaken commands, and a flanking action caused the defensive line to fall back, abandoning the Sunken Road.[7]

Rodes, Hill, and several other officers rounded up a number of survivors and led them against Richardson's troops advancing through the Piper farm fields. The situation was so desperate that Hill picked up a musket and led 200 men in a counterattack. Hill recalled the little band was met "with a warm reception, and the little command was broken and dispersed." The Union troops soon were ordered to withdraw, ending the fighting.[8]

During a counsel of war at the conclusion of the bloody day, Hill purportedly told Lee, "his division was cut to pieces; that his losses had been terrible and he had no troops to hold his line against the great odds against him." He strongly recommended crossing the Potomac River and end the invasion. Hill's division was indeed just a shadow of its former self, losing 2,310 men (352 killed; 1,439 wounded; 519 missing) at Sharpsburg. The division had played a major role in the campaign, fighting at Turner's Gap, Frosttown Plateau, Fox's Gap, the Miller Cornfield, the East Woods, the Sunken Road, and the fields of the Piper farm.[9]

**Bradley M. Gottfried**

✳ ✳ ✳

## Ripley's Brigade: Brigadier General Roswell Ripley

**Units:** 4th Georgia, 44th Georgia, 1st North Carolina, 3rd North Carolina
**Strength:** 2,334[10]
**Losses:** 776 (121k-531w-124m)[11]

The 4th Georgia, 1st North Carolina, and 3rd North Carolina were all mustered into service between May and June 1861. The 4th Georgia spent the early months of the war in the Department of Norfolk; the North Carolina regiments were in the Department of Fredericksburg. The 44th Georgia was not formed until March 1862, and was added to the brigade in July 1862. The brigade saw action on several battlefields during the Seven Days Battles. It did not participate at the Battle of Second Bull Run.[12]

Roswell Ripley was a prickly officer who always seemed to be at odds with his immediate superiors and subordinates. Born in Ohio in 1823, he graduated from West Point and was twice brevetted for gallantry in the Mexican War. He published a two-volume history of the conflict soon after the end of the conflict. After service in various posts in the South, Ripley married into a Charleston family and resigned his commission to become a businessman. He joined the South Carolina militia and was present during the bombardment of Ft. Sumter. Promotion did not come quick enough for Ripley, so he threatened to resign, but President Jefferson Davis interceded and promoted him to the rank of brigadier general. Ripley commanded the South Carolina Department, but it was consolidated with others and he came under the command of Gen. John Pemberton. Conflict began almost immediately and Ripley requested a transfer. He was given a brigade in D.H. Hill's division, which he led through the Seven Days. Although Ripley was considered a "skillful and competent field officer" he did not perform well at Gaines' Mill. He marched with his brigade north during the Maryland Campaign with a bit of a cloud hanging over his head.[13]

## South Mountain

The brigade's activities after leaving Leesburg through September 13 mirrored the rest of D.H. Hill's division and can be found in its entry. Ripley's brigade, with Robert Rodes' and G.T. Anderson's were ready to be sent into action near Boonsboro on September 13. Ripley was ordered to send a regiment to Hamburg Pass (sometimes called Orr's Gap), more than three miles north of Turner's Gap on the morning of September 13. Ripley selected his veteran 4th Georgia for this mission. The rest of Ripley's command remained near Boonsboro until Hill knew more about the "strength and design of the Yankees." As the fighting at Fox's Gap intensified on September 14, Hill brought Ripley's and Rodes' brigades up the side of South Mountain. Rodes' men were sent to the left to Frosttown

Gap/Plateau and Ripley was ordered to the right, toward Fox's Gap, marching behind G.B. Anderson's brigade, which subsequently supported Samuel Garland's brigade in its fight with Jacob Cox's division (IX Corps) in the morning.

The van of D.R. Jones' division arrived about 3:30 p.m. and Hill sent Thomas Drayton's brigade and G.T. Anderson brigades south by the right flank to reinforce Fox's Gap. Hill accompanied these 1,900 men toward Ripley's brigade, which was near Old Sharpsburg Road. Hill held a meeting with the brigade commanders and then returned to his headquarters at the Mountain House. Because of his seniority, Ripley was put in charge of the four brigades. G.B. Anderson's brigade was on the right, and Ripley's on its left, were to slide to their right along Old Sharpsburg Road to create room for G.T. Anderson's brigade and then Drayton's. The plan had the column marching west along Old Sharpsburg Road, halting, and then swinging to their left to hit the enemy line at Fox's Gap.[14]

G.B. Anderson's and Ripley's brigades headed down Old Sharpsburg Road with G.T. Anderson's men double quicking to catch up with them. A 300 yard gap opened with Drayton's brigade bringing up the rear of the column. The IX Corps exploited this error by driving into Drayton's front, flank, and rear. G.B. Anderson realized he was too far from the action and without orders, ordered his men to the left, into the thickets and up the mountainside and G.T. Anderson attempted to retrace its steps to provide support. Ripley's men became disoriented and never came close enough to engage the enemy. Ripley wrote in his report, "General Anderson's and my own brigade pushing forward through dense thickets and up very steep acclivities to outflank the enemy and come into General Drayton's support. The natural difficulties of the ground and the condition of the troops prevented these movements being made with the rapidity which was desirable..."[15]

Calvin Leach of the 1st North Carolina recorded the brigade's confusion in his diary, "We were now ordered by the right flank and marched on to the top of the mountain . . . going over rocks and cliffs and some of the worst places I ever saw. We were marched forward and backward across the mountain and were marched to the top of it by the left flank in a line of battle, waited there till near sundown then back again." It was dark by the time Ripley's men reached the scene of the fighting, so it did not participate in the defense of Fox's Gap. The brigade subsequently filled the gap between John Hood's division and G.B. Anderson's brigade. Hill bitterly wrote in his report, "Anderson soon became partially and Drayton hotly engaged, but Ripley did not draw trigger; why, I do not know." Col. William DeRosset of the 3rd North Carolina claimed after the war, ". . . we had no opportunity to [draw a trigger in the fight because] I verily believe, purposely as I have no doubt we were at Second Manassas." He pinned the blame squarely on Ripley's shoulders.[16]

Members of the 4th Georgia were also upset with Ripley. The regiment was sent to Hamburg Pass, and according to its historian, "The entire regiment came very near being captured that night, however, for, when our army was ordered to evacuate the position, General Ripley forgot all about us and started with the rest of the brigade for Sharpsburg." The writer went on to praise DeRosset, who "discovered our absence and a courier was dispatched to notify us."[17]

## Antietam

Hill's division was the first to make the trek to Boonsboro during the evening hours of September 17. Ripley's brigade was between Garland's brigade and G.B. Anderson's during the trek to the small town, arriving via small country roads. Upon arriving at Sharpsburg, Hill deployed the three brigades near Boonsboro Pike. G.B. Anderson's was on the pike and Ripley's was behind it. Hood's division's skirmishing in front of the East Woods on the evening of September 16 caused Hill to move Ripley, Colquitt, and Garland's brigades closer to the fighting. Ripley led his men toward the rear of Hood's division, about 150 yards west of the Mumma house, with his right resting on Mumma's

farm lane and his left extending northwest, almost to the Smoketown Road. That night, James Walker's brigade (Alexander Lawton's division) replaced Hood's men in front of Ripley's brigade.[18]

The Union guns of position across Antietam Creek wreaked havoc on Ripley's men during the morning of September 17. Ripley reported, they "opened a severe enfilading fire on the troops of my command, the position which we had been ordered to occupy being in full view of nearly all of his batteries. This fire inflicted serious loss before the troops were called into positive action, the men lying under it, without flinching, for over an hour, while the enemy plied his guns unceasing." Ripley ordered the 3rd North Carolina to set the Mumma farm buildings "on fire to prevent them [from] being made use of by the enemy."[19]

Walker's brigade retreated at about 7:00 a.m. and Ripley's men advanced to replace it. Ripley claimed his men "sprung to their arms with alacrity and moved forward through the burning buildings in our front, reformed on the other side, and opened a rapid fire upon the enemy." The 4th Georgia was on the left, followed to the right by the 44th Georgia, 1st North Carolina, and 3rd North Carolina. The latter faced an orchard; the rest of the brigade was on the edge of a plowed field, oriented in a northeast direction. William Christian's brigade (James Ricketts' division, I Corps) had occupied the East Woods until driven away by Hood's division, but Meade's division of Pennsylvania Reserves appeared at the northern edge of the Cornfield, extending into the East Woods.

Ripley received a wound in his neck during the movement toward the contested area and relinquished command of the brigade to Col. George Doles of the 4th Georgia. Doles aimed the men toward the East Woods and the brigade was about half-way there when Gen. Hill rode up and ordered the men to march by the left flank, in column of fours, across Smoketown Pike, toward the Cornfield, marching in a northwest direction. The 4th Georgia was exposed to a tremendous small arms fire that killed and wounded a number of its men. The brigade was also hit by canister fire from Dunbar Ransom's battery of Napoleons deployed on a hill beyond the Cornfield.[20]

Ripley's advance caught Col. Robert Anderson's brigade of Pennsylvania Reserves near the southern end of the Cornfield. The left side of the line (4th Georgia, 44th Georgia, part of 1st North Carolina) hit the 9th Pennsylvania Reserves on higher ground near Hagerstown Pike, south of the Cornfield and drove it back into the corn. A Georgia soldier recalled the Pennsylvanians "gave way like chaff before a cyclone." A soldier in the 44th Georgia wrote home, "our boys fell as regularly and as fast as counting one, two, three." The right side of the brigade, with its right almost to the East Woods attacked the 11th and 12th Pennsylvania Reserves in the Cornfield and drove them back to its northern fence without entering the corn. The left side of the brigade also forced the 19th Indiana of the Iron Brigade back across Hagerstown Pike. To avoid a repeat of the flank attacks on Starke's brigade earlier in the morning and Wofford's brigade a bit later, the 1st North Carolina was moved from the center of the line to the left, to face Hagerstown Pike so it was at right angles with the rest of the brigade.[21]

Doles now sent his skirmishers forward into the Cornfield, where they encountered Samuel Crawford's brigade (Alpheus Williams' division) of the newly arriving XII Corps, approaching the northern boundary of the Cornfield. Ripley's men opened a blistering fire against the new arrivals but were ordered to cease fire so they could shift their orientation from facing northwest to north and the new threat. Crawford's men, particularly the 46th Pennsylvania and 128th Pennsylvania took advantage of this momentary confusion and fired into the right of Ripley's line, composed of the 3rd North Carolina. The rookies of the 128th Pennsylvania now launched an ill-advised attack into the Cornfield, reaching the southern part of the field before being forced back by Ripley's massive small arms fire.[22]

Still another fresh XII Corps brigade, George Gordon's (Williams' division) appeared at the northern fence and opened fire on Ripley's men who were running out of ammunition and growing tired from their efforts in halting the Union advances. Hill saw the worsening condition of Ripley's men and brought up Alfred Colquitt's brigade. With the new arrivals dashing into the Cornfield, Doles ordered his men to the rear. Leach recorded in his diary, "our Reg got cut up very severely and the Brig was ordered to retreat back when we met reinforcements coming in and I was glad to see them for I was nearly tired to death." The left of Ripley's brigade aimed for the Dunker Church, but the 3rd North Carolina and perhaps part of the 1st North Carolina on the right remained in position and fought with Colquitt's men for several minutes. Ripley returned after 90 minutes to find his brigade resting just west of Sharpsburg. He relinquished command again to Doles in the afternoon after he became faint.[23]

The historian of the 44th Georgia wrote "About three o'clock p.m. the brigade was moved to the front and formed line of battle, and so remained until late in the afternoon. Late in the night of the 18th, the Fourth Georgia and First and Third North Carolina (except two companies of the last named regiment) were detached and moved to some other point, leaving the Forty-fourth Georgia and the two companies of the Third North Carolina to hold the ground occupied by the brigade, until about daylight on the morning of the 19th, when they marched to the Potomac . . ."[24]

Ripley's men fought three enemy brigades in toe-to-toe combat at Antietam, losing 740 men in the process, or over 50% of its initial strength. As expected, the 3rd North Carolina on the right flank suffered the highest casualties, losing over 250 of its men. Ripley never returned to the army after the Maryland Campaign. Lee had lost faith in his abilities and so had his men. One of his officers called him a "bully, coward, a whoremaster; a coward or a traitor . . . and a Yankee by birth" after the war, and several suggested he tried to avoid combat whenever possible.[25]

**Bradley M. Gottfried**

## Rodes' Brigade: Brigadier General Robert Rodes

**Units:** 3rd Alabama, 5th Alabama, 6th Alabama, 12th Alabama, 26th Alabama
**Strength:** 1,803
**Losses:** 203 (50k-132w- 21m)[26]

Robert Rodes' brigade became an all-Alabama unit in mid-June 1862 when the 3rd and 26th Alabama regiments were added to the 5th, 6th, and 12th Alabama. The three original regiments had started their service as part of Richard Ewell's brigade during the summer and fall of 1861 and saw service together at Yorktown, Williamsburg, and Seven Pines. The eight companies of the 26th Alabama formerly in Brig. Gen. Gabriel Rains' brigade also participated in these battles. The 3rd Alabama began its service near Norfolk in May 1861, and had seen action at Drewry's Bluff and Seven Pines as part of William Mahone's brigade. The brigade was part of D.H. Hill's division by mid-June 1862.[27]

Robert Emmet Rodes was a 33-year old native of Lynchburg, Virginia, who had graduated from the Virginia Military Institute in 1848. He served as an Assistant Professor there for the next three years before becoming a civil engineer for the Southside Railroad. In 1856, Rodes became chief engineer for the Alabama & Chattanooga Railroad and married the following year. Upon Alabama's secession, Rodes became a captain in a militia company, and was appointed colonel of the 5th Alabama when that regiment was formed in May 1861.[28]

During the Seven Days Battles Rodes' brigade suffered few casualties until Malvern Hill, where, even without the detached 12th Alabama, it suffered more than 1,000 casualties. Remaining in the environs of Richmond following the Seven Days, the brigade helped guard the capital and Petersburg against any further incursions by the Army of the Potomac, while Robert E. Lee launched the Army of Northern Virginia in an offensive against John Pope's Army of Virginia at Second Bull Run. Hill's division left Hanover Junction to rejoin Lee's army on August 26 and reached it near Chantilly, Virginia on September 2. It continued to Leesburg the next day.[29]

Hill's division was ordered to cross the Potomac at Cheek's Ford on September 4, and the 3rd Alabama became the first Confederate regiment to step foot on Maryland soil. The rest of that day and part of the next were spent breaking down the banks of the Chesapeake and Ohio Canal, and making a futile attempt to damage its stone aqueduct over the Monocacy River. Late on September 5, the brigade marched on, encamping within a few miles of Frederick and entered the city the following morning.[30]

When the Army of Northern Virginia left Frederick on September 10, Hill's division acted as the rear guard and escort for the army's wagon train. By September 13, Rodes' brigade was camped about half a mile west of Boonsboro, to prevent an escape by the Union garrison at Harper's Ferry, and, if necessary, to reinforce Alfred Colquitt's brigade, which guarded the South Mountain pass at Turner's Gap.[31]

### South Mountain

Hill faced an imminent assault on the area around Turner's Gap by the Union I Corps, and he ordered Rodes' brigade to march there at midday on September 14. Lt. Thomas Taylor of Co. G, 6th Alabama recalled "We were all seemingly resting very quietly when we got orders to fall in. We double quicked towards Boonsborough. We passed through this little place & and went up a mountain …" Upon reaching the gap, probably after 1:00 p.m., Hill positioned the brigade on the left of National Pike on Hill 1280, supporting part of Lt. Col. A.S. Cutts' Artillery Battalion. The 6th Alabama held the left of the line, with the 5th, 3rd, 26th and 12th to its right. Lt. Robert Park of the

12th Alabama was ordered to form an extended skirmish line (comprised of 4 men from each of the regiment's 10 companies) further to the left, in order to cover Frosttown Road. Although Cutts' guns attracted some counter-battery fire, few casualties were incurred.[32]

After the better part of an hour, Rodes' brigade was ordered to move nearly three-quarters of a mile north, because, as Hill later reported, "a solitary peak on the left, which, if gained by the Yankees, would give them control of the ridge commanding the turnpike. The possession of this peak was, therefore, everything to the Yankees, but they seemed slow to perceive it." This move left a yawning gap between the brigade's right flank and Cutts' guns at Turner's Gap that Nathaniel Evans' South Carolina brigade was to cover. Before the Alabamians had advanced far, Evans issued contradictory orders that halted his brigade. Rodes was forced to recall that part of the 12th Alabama not with Park's skirmishers to help cover this space.[33]

George Meade's 4,000-man Pennsylvania Reserve Division (I Corps) faced the Alabamians. If Meade's men swept around the Confederate left and pressed down Zittlestown Road to the National Pike, they would be behind the Confederate defensive position at Turner's Gap and could sever any easy route of retreat.[34]

Meade's division outflanked Rodes by nearly half a mile on both sides. Heavy skirmishing opened on the brigade's front at about 3:00 p.m. Six companies of the 13th Pennsylvania Reserves, better known as the "Bucktails" acted as Meade's skirmishers. They were all marksmen, well-armed with Sharps rifles. Rodes worried the enemy could gain possession of Hill 1360, still further to his left, so he ordered Col. John Gordon to extend his 6th Alabama to cover it. This caused a division in the 5th Alabama, which stretched further to fill the left. That part on the right was isolated for a time.[35]

After an hour or more of skirmishing, Meade's division began its advance. Rodes' men drove the Pennsylvanians back more than once, only to see them rally and come on again. Although the boulder strewn hillsides gave the heavily outnumbered Alabamians ideal defensive positions, the sheer weight of Meade's numbers slowly drove them back. Otis Smith of the 6th Alabama wrote "the pat, pat of the bullets against the rocks sounded like hail."[36]

Despite Gordon's best efforts, his 6th Alabama was slowly forced to relinquish its hold on Hill 1360. Taylor wrote ". . . we stop & are almost surrounded . . . skedaddle & halt fight & skedaddle again." The 5th Pennsylvania Reserves and the Bucktails fired into the Alabamians' flank, as Truman Seymour's brigade's other regiments advanced on their front. The center also suffered. Park was captured while helping a wounded fellow skirmisher. Capt. Edward Ready and 15 members of the 3rd Alabama were captured at the Haupt House on Frosttown Road when the 9th Pennsylvania Reserves (Thomas' Gallagher's brigade) surged over them. Col. Cullen Battle of the 3rd, only recently returned to the regiment after being wounded at Seven Pines, received a painful wound when his belt plate was struck by a minie ball. Finally relieved on the right by Nathaniel Evans' South Carolina brigade, the 12th Alabama took a position between the 3rd and 5th Alabama where Col. Bristor Gayle was slain. He was replaced by Lt. Col. Samuel Pickens, who was badly wounded shortly afterwards. Col. Edward O'Neal of the 26th Alabama was also wounded, and Battle took over direction of that regiment in addition to his own.[37]

The sun set at 6:11 p.m. Rodes wrote that by this time the Federals "were nearly on top of the highest peak [Hill 1500] and were pushing on, when Gordon's regiment, unexpectedly to them, opened fire on their front and checked them. This last stand was so disastrous to the enemy that it attracted the attention of the stragglers, even many of whom Col. Battle and I had been endeavoring to organize, and who were just then on the flank of that portion of the enemy engaged with Gordon, and for a few minutes they kept up a brisk enfilading fire upon the enemy . . . it was now so dark that it was difficult to distinguish objects at short musket range, and both parties ceased firing."[38]

When total darkness fell, the brigade held a line only 200 yards from National Pike. The stand had cost the brigade 422 of its 1,200 men, or about a third of its original numbers. Hill wrote in his report, "Rodes handled his little brigade in a most admirable and gallant manner, fighting, for hours, vastly superior odds, and maintaining the key-points of the position until darkness rendered a further advance of the Yankees impossible. Had he fought with less obstinacy, a practicable artillery road to the rear would have been gained on our left and the line of retreat cut off."[39]

The brigade began its descent back down the mountain to Boonsboro at about 11:00 p.m. and was ordered to Sharpsburg, where the Union cavalry escaping from Harpers Ferry had caused some concern. The exhausted men halted for about an hour's rest near Keedysville, then proceeded to Sharpsburg with Colquitt's brigade, bivouacking southwest of the town about dawn of the September 15.[40]

## Antietam

After a brief rest, the brigade moved to fortify the heights north of Boonboro Pike, overlooking Antietam Creek. The men remained here until the morning of the battle, "subsisting on green corn mainly and under an occasional artillery fire," reported Rodes."[41]

The battle opened at dawn on September 17, more than a mile to the north. Rodes' brigade was ordered to its left before 9:00 a.m. to support Ripley's, Colquitt's, and Garland's brigades, who were rushed north to assist in stemming the Union thrust against the East Woods and Cornfield. The Alabamians moved through a ravine east of the Piper Farm, to a sunken side road that connected Hagerstown and Boonsboro Pikes. Taylor remembered it simply as "an old road that runs through a cornfield." Moving by the left flank, the 26th Alabama led the column, followed by the 12th, 3rd, 5th, and 6th Alabama; George B. Anderson's North Carolina brigade filed into position on their right. Taylor noted as they moved into the new

position "the enemy could be seen marching slowly but steadily on to us."[42]

It soon became apparent that Hill's three brigades sent north "had met with a reverse," wrote Rodes, "and that the best service I could render them and the field generally would be to form a line in rear of them and endeavor to rally them before attacking or being attacked." Some of the remnants of these shattered units returned, and were placed on the Alabamians' left.[43]

Rodes' brigade held the length of the Sunken Road from the Mumma Farm Lane to nearly the Roulette Farm Lane. "Sunken" might be something of an exaggeration, as horses' hooves, wagon wheels, and erosion had probably not worn this section of the road to more than a foot or two deep. The Alabamians strengthened their defenses facing north by stacking rails from the snake fences that lined both sides of the lane. As the men prepared for the inevitable, Hill walked through the lane, telling them they had "fought well on Sunday, but today you must fight harder."[44]

After its losses at South Mountain, the brigade line could muster but a thin line. One company of the 3rd Alabama was down to three men, and another had only eight. In all, there were probably no more than 800 men in Rodes' line.[45]

Cullen Battle noted that in front of most of the brigade, "(N)ot a shrub obscured the vision or offered shelter." The 6th Alabama on the right descended to a sharp bend in the road and connected with the left of the 2nd North Carolina (Anderson's brigade). The ground to its front rose sharply, limiting the regiment's vision to little more than 50-60 yards. The bend in the road would at the same time expose their flank to the ridgeline farther to their right. It would ultimately prove to be an adverse position.[46]

Capt. R. Boyce's South Carolina battery was probably in the brigade's center-left front, engaged in counter-battery fire when the brigade arrived. Max Weber's brigade (French's division; II Corps) "deployed in our front in three beautiful lines, all vastly outstretching ours, and commenced to advance steadily," noted Rodes. Boyce turned his guns toward the enemy infantry, but he withdrew when they came under fire from Federal skirmishers.[47]

Gen. Hill reported that Weber's brigade, never before engaged in combat, "advanced in three parallel lines, with all the precision of a parade day." Gordon of the 6th Alabama wrote. "The men in blue . . . formed in my front, an assaulting column four lines deep. The front line came to a 'charge bayonets,' the other lines to a 'right shoulder shift.'" Weber, he continued, "...superbly mounted, placed himself in front..." Taylor claimed, "...I could see column after column advancing toward us . . . I thought they had me this time, but determined that my life should cost them dearly."[48]

The Federals advanced to the edge of the hill, within 80 yards of the Alabamians, when they received the first volley. Gordon wrote "the effect was appalling. The entire front line, with few exceptions, went down in the consuming blast." The Federals "fell back a short distance, rallied, were driven back again and again, and finally lay down just back of the crest, keeping up a steady fire." The 1st Delaware's right flank ended directly in front of Rodes' center, causing it to suffer from both frontal and enfilade fire. Eight of its company commanders were killed or wounded as was its entire color-guard. The 5th Maryland to its left suffered nearly 25% casualties in the first volleys.[49]

James Longstreet, commanding the Confederate center and right, witnessed the confusion and disorganization that swept the Federal lines and ordered a bayonet charge by the road's defenders. The bulk of Rodes' brigade rushed forward, but the men soon found themselves exposed to overwhelming Federal small arms fire as Dwight Morris' brigade (French's division, II Corps) advanced behind Weber. The 14th Connecticut came into line behind the 1st Delaware, and the 130th Pennsylvania came up to the line held by what was left of the 5th Maryland. James Tompkins' Battery A, 1st Rhode Island Light Artillery added to the firepower. The 6th Alabama did not hear the command and never advanced. Similarly, despite Rodes' personal exhortations to rouse them, he

reported, "Colquitt's men did not advance far enough." Those Alabamians who did attack were forced to fall back to the safety of the road after their bloody repulse, leaving Capt. Exton Tucker, commanding the 12th Alabama, dead on the field. Longstreet's failed bayonet attack probably accounted for a large percentage of the brigade's casualties at Sharpsburg.[50]

The battle now became one of steady attrition. Battle noted the opposing lines "stood up and looked into each others' eyes, and delivered their fire with coolness and precision." Three of the 3rd's color bearers became casualties. "We made the Yankees 'smell brimstone,' though we smelled it also," Battle recalled.[51]

From their positions on the ridgeline to the right of the brigade, enemy soldiers were able to enfilade the portion of the lane held by the 6th Alabama. Casualties mounted. Gordon received five bullet wounds, the last passing through left check and out his jaw, leaving him with a disfiguring scar. He crawled out of the lane and through the cornfield to the rear.[52]

Shortly before noon, Lt. Col. James Lightfoot, now in command of the 6th Alabama, sought and received Rodes' permission to "refuse" the right half of the regiment to face this enemy fire. Lightfoot hastened back and gave the order: "Sixth Alabama, about face; forward march." Maj. Edwin Hobson of the 5th Alabama saw the troops on his immediate right withdrawing from the road. He rushed over to Lightfoot, and after ascertaining what was happening, "asked him if the order was intended for the whole brigade; (Lightfoot) replied, 'Yes,' and thereupon the Fifth, and immediately the other troops on their left, retreated."[53]

What started as a realignment became a rout. The three remaining regiments watched the soldiers to their right streaming to the rear, and fearing the line had been broken or a retreat ordered, soon joined the others. Rodes returned to the line after helping severely wounded aide Lt. John Birney to the rear and was shocked to see the brigade "without visible cause to me, retreating in confusion…" Lightfoot was badly wounded during this retreat.[54]

Rodes quickly made his way to Hagerstown Pike, where he, Hill, Hobson, and others attempted to rally whatever troops they could for a defense of Lee's center. Rodes found that "with the exception of a few men from the Twenty-sixth, Twelfth, and Third, and a few under Major Hobson, not more than 40 in all, the brigade had completely disappeared from this portion of the field."[55]

After rallying a force of about 200 men, 150 of whom were probably members of Rodes' brigade, Hill, musket in hand, led a last ditch counterattack through the Piper Orchard that did little to stem the Federal advance, and as he later reported "was broken up and dispersed."[56]

When the battle ended, Rodes' brigade reformed in a defensive line some distance behind its Sunken Road position. There were now probably fewer than 600 men of all ranks.[57]

The men rested on their arms without incident until nightfall of September 18, when they retreated across the Potomac River near Shepherdstown. The march continued to near the Opequon Creek, and several days later, the brigade moved on to Bunker Hill and Winchester. The brigade had done well during the campaign, twice being placed in untenable situations, but in both cases, the men performed well.[58]

**Robert Gottschalk**

\* \* \*

### Garland's Brigade: Brigadier General Samuel Garland, Jr., Colonel Duncan McRae

**Units:** 5th North Carolina, 12th North Carolina, 13th North Carolina, 20th North Carolina, 23rd North Carolina
**Strength:** 2,507[59]
**Losses:** 84 (9k-42w-32m)[60]

Samuel Garland was born in 1830 and entered the Virginia Military Institute at age 15, graduating third in the class of 1849. After earning a law degree from the University of Virginia he started a practice in Lynchburg. Garland organized the Lynchburg Home Guard after John Brown's raid on Harpers Ferry. The unit became Company G in the 11th Virginia Volunteer Infantry, and Gov. John Letcher commissioned Garland the colonel of the regiment on May 8, 1861. His wife died on June 12 and his infant son died two months later, both of influenza. Garland soon after earned a reputation for being calm under fire with a reckless disregard for his own safety. His recklessness gave rise to speculation that he may have harbored a death wish, an overwhelming desire to join his wife and son. Although wounded in the elbow at the Battle of Williamsburg, May 5, 1862, Garland refused to leave

the field. His actions earned him promotion to brigadier general and command of a North Carolina brigade in D.H. Hill's division.[61]

The 12th and 13th North Carolina (formerly the 2nd and 3rd Volunteers) mustered into service during May 1861. The 5th, 20th and 23rd North Carolina in July 1861. After individual service and participation in two different brigades prior to, and at, the Battle of Williamsburg, the five regiments found themselves together under Garland. The brigade first fought during the Seven Days' Battles, but did not participate in the Battle of Second Bull Run because Hill's division was left behind as part of the force guarding Richmond.[62]

Initially assigned to Stonewall Jackson's command, Hill's troops were the first to cross the Potomac River on September 4. Garland's brigade splashed across the river at Noland's Ferry near the mouth of the Monocacy River and spent the next day destroying the locks and breaching the banks of the Chesapeake & Ohio Canal. Hill took advantage of the unharvested bounty of the Maryland countryside. As a soldier in the 23rd North Carolina recalled some years later, "One of General Hill's first acts after crossing the Potomac into Maryland, was to buy a large field of corn and turn in his division." Diplomatically, Hill paid the farmer in U.S. currency.[63]

Garland's brigade was among the first Confederates to enter Frederick on September 6. During the army's occupation of the town, Lee issued Special Orders Number 191, dividing his army, and embarking upon the Harpers Ferry operation. These orders detached Hill's division to "form the rear guard of the army, pursuing the road taken by the main body," that is James Longstreet's command. Garland's Tar Heels departed Frederick on September 11 as part of the rear guard. Dr. Lewis H. Steiner, a civilian observer, noted in his diary that Hill's men when compared to Lee's entire army, "showed more of military discipline . . . the men marched in better order had better music and were fairly clothed and equipped." Garland's brigade camped two miles east of Turner's Gap on the evening of September 11. The next day the brigade resumed its march on the National Turnpike.[64]

Garland's brigade, with the rest of the division, marched westward through Turner's Gap on September 12 and passed through the town of Boonsboro. Hill established his headquarters tent about four miles west of the town. He was ordered "to distribute my five brigades so as not only to protect the wagons and guns, but also to watch all roads leading from Harper's Ferry, in order to intercept the Federal forces that might make their escape before Jackson had completed the investment of that place." These objectives required Hill to place his brigades with a "considerable separation." Consequently, the division's camps were spread out south and west to cover the roads to Pleasant Valley, Sharpsburg, and Williamsport.[65]

Sometime around noon on September 13, Hill received a surprising dispatch from J.E.B. Stuart. The Confederate cavalry commander had withdrawn from Frederick the previous day and was now approaching Turner's Gap. Stuart claimed, "he was followed by two Brigades of Federal infantry." The dispatch requested a brigade from Hill to assist in "defending" Turner's Gap. Hill responded by sending Colquitt's brigade. Later that evening Hill received a dispatch from Colquitt advising him "that Genl. Stuart must have been mistaken as to the strength of the enemy." Hill responded by sending Garland's brigade. Although the brigade bivouacked in the vicinity of Boonsboro, Garland rode to Turner's Gap to confer with Colquitt later that evening. Colquitt no doubt informed Garland of the "heavy clouds of dust rising from the turnpike for a long distance" he observed in the direction of Frederick. It was much more dust than one would associate with two brigades of infantry. Regardless, both men were able to see "the whole Middletown Valley lighted with camp-fires far in excess of what would have been necessary for the two brigades." According to George D. Gratton (Colquitt's AAG) those campfires only increased as the night advanced.[66]

**South Mountain**

Garland's brigade joined him at Turner's Gap early on the morning of September 14, at "about sunrise," meaning a three-mile march in the dark, or at the very least early morning twilight. The brigade numbered 1,119 at this time. Garland had his men in position at the Mountain House atop Turner's Gap and Hill immediately set out on a reconnaissance of the area, which took him south towards Fox's Gap. Soon after his departure the soldiers of Garland's brigade heard the boom of artillery fire. Upon Hill's return, he sought out Garland and explained the situation. Hill discovered the Old Sharpsburg Road about a mile south. The road could permit the enemy to pass through Fox's Gap and turn the position at Turner's Gap. Hill was convinced the enemy was moving to take possession of Fox's Gap and ordered Garland "to sweep through the woods, reach the road, and hold it at all hazards." Hill later recalled that Garland departed "in high spirits and I never saw him again. I never knew a truer, better, braver man."[67]

The brigade marched south on Wood Road, a nineteenth century road, for about a mile to Fox's

Gap where it intersected the Old Sharpsburg Road at the cabin and farm of Daniel Wise. Garland was now presented with two unexpected surprises. Unknown to anyone, Stuart had sent Col. Tom Rosser and his 5th Virginia Cavalry and a few guns of the Horse Artillery to "occupy" Fox's Gap. Strong circumstantial evidence suggests it was Rosser's artillery, commanded by Maj. John Pelham that was heard at Turner's Gap earlier that morning. While the addition of Rosser's men and Pelham's artillery was welcome news, what Garland learned next was not. There was another road known locally as the Loop Road about a mile due south. The Loop Road passed over the mountain crest and down the western slope. By using this road an enemy force could turn any position at Fox's Gap. Tom Rosser and Sam Garland took a few minutes to discuss the situation under the shade of a chestnut tree.[68]

Garland's tactical situation required dividing his forces to cover the two roads. Garland decided to send his largest regiment, the 5th North Carolina commanded by Col. Duncan McRae, to cover the Loop Road south of Fox's Gap. McRae followed Ridge Road, which ran along the mountain crest from the Wise farm to the Loop Road. McRae noted the Loop Road "seemed good for Artillery and general transportation." His attention was next drawn to "considerable bodies of troops" about a mile distant, and he responded by sending Rosser to the extreme right to occupy the high ground just south of the Loop Road. Rosser deployed his 250 dismounted cavalry and artillery to cover the approach to the east. McRae's 5th North Carolina was placed on the left side of Rosser, just north of the Loop Road. The 12th and the 23rd North Carolina were on the left of the 5th. The 20th and 13th North Carolina remained at Fox's Gap. Due to the nature of the ground and the duty to be performed, Garland did not have a continuous line. For example, there was an interval of almost 500 yards between the left flank of the 23th North Carolina and Fox's Gap. The intervals between the regiments at the Loop Road were partially filled by the arrival of Bondurant's Alabama battery.

Bondurant's two 3-inch Ordnance Guns and two 12-lb. smoothbore Howitzers were placed in an open field on the left of the 5th North Carolina. All-in-all, with a reserve of a little over 360 infantry at Fox's Gap, and with the addition of Rosser's forces, Garland was able to muster a force at the Loop Road of approximately 900 rifles and six guns.[69]

The troops Garland observed were the 1,500 infantry belonging to Eliakim Scammon's brigade (Kanawha Division; IX Corps). The 23rd and 12th Ohio assaulted Garland's forces at the Loop Road around 9:00 a.m. while the 30th Ohio made its way up the southern side of the Old Sharpsburg Road towards the Wise farm at Fox's Gap. Although most of the 5th North Carolina were green conscripts, terrain and artillery worked to the advantage of the Confederates. The first assault resulted in a stalemate. During this combat the colonel of the 23rd Ohio, future president Rutherford B. Hayes, received a wound that removed him from the battle. Both sides took advantage of a temporary lull in fighting to re-enforce their lines. Garland positioned the 20th North Carolina on the left flank of the 23rd while Cox deployed his other brigade under George Crook. The 11th and 36th Ohio joined the Loop Road assaulting force; the 28th was kept in reserve. Meanwhile, the 30th Ohio continued its advance along the Old Sharpsburg Road.[70]

Garland returned to Fox's Gap to bring up the 20th North Carolina to support the 23rd. He next brought the 13th into an open field in the vicinity of the Wise cabin. Skirmishers of the 30th Ohio were immediately in front of them (to the east). As the Tarheels and Buckeyes exchanged fire, Col. Thomas Ruffin, Jr., commanding the 13th, warned Garland, "Why do you stay here, you are in great danger." It was to no avail, as D.H. Hill later observed "with Garland the post of danger was the post of honor." Understandably, Garland's reply was succinct: "I may as well be here as yourself." Ruffin was wounded and momentarily distracted. He heard a groan and looked to see Garland on the ground "wounded and writhing in pain." With his dying

361

breath Garland uttered, "I am killed, send for the senior colonel and tell him to take command," which was Duncan McRae of the 5th.[71]

The first attack forced Bondurant's battery to withdraw, so it could no longer support the Loop Road force. McRae was outnumbered at least two to one and later reported, "I felt all the embarrassment which the situation was calculated to inspire." Due to Garland's aides transporting his body back to Turner's Gap, part of that embarrassment included a lack of adequate staff for brigade command and the inability to immediately communicate with subordinate commanders or Hill. From his vantage point, McRae was keenly aware the enemy "was preparing a heavy movement against us."

Two-thirds of the Kanawha Division, as reported by McRae, "with a long extended yell, burst upon our line." The combat at Fox's Gap was among the most tenacious, violent, and savage of the entire war and actual hand-to-hand combat occurred with a ferocity rarely seen. "Men from both sides fell from bayonet wounds," wrote McRae, "the enemy's strength was overpowering and could not be resisted." A soldier with the 23rd North Carolina remembered, "It was here . . . that bayonets and clubbed muskets were so freely used in the vain struggle to repel outnumbering foes." Col. Alfred Iverson, commanding the 20th North Carolina, recalled, "There was nothing to do but to get away or surrender." Some men broke and ran. Others attempted a more orderly withdrawal. "As I turned to go I was called upon frequently to halt and fired at within 50 paces," wrote Iverson. He admitted "I made terrific leaps down that mountain. I saw Col. McRae some distance in advance of me. I must have been the fastest runner for I caught up with him and together we went to the foot of the mountain."[72]

Garland's brigade resisted as best they could, but the outcome was inevitable. Outnumbered and demoralized by the loss of their commander, the men withdrew down the western slope of the mountain. Shortly after winning the crest of Ridge Road the Ohioans regrouped and turned their attention to Fox's Gap. The 11th, 12th, and 36th moved north to join the 30th Ohio and press an attack on the last Confederate defenders at the vicinity of the Wise cabin. Moments before, the 2nd and 4th North Carolina of George B. Anderson's brigade arrived from Turner's Gap to re-enforce Ruffin. The Federals pressed their attack between 11:30 a.m. and noon, resulting in another furious fight with more hand-to-hand combat. The 2nd and 4th North Carolina withdrew "through a heavy fire, men falling at every few steps" to the safety of several stone walls north of the gap. Ruffin and the 13th North Carolina were left to face a dire situation, "We numbered, only, two hundred and twelve men, and were assailed by a regiment in our front, one on our right, and one on our left at the same moment," recalled Ruffin, "I thought the game was a hopeless one and determined to surrender with my whole command, and was on the point of doing so, as I could not bear to see my men falling all around me!" At that moment one of his subordinates asked Ruffin to order a charge instead. An incredulous Ruffin was reassured the men would indeed charge if ordered to do so. As Ruffin explained to his father a month later, "I gave the order; and they did make it beautifully and drove the enemy in our front back, wheeled to the right charged the enemy then and there, and then about-faced charged those on our left and got out."[73]

Ruffin reported to G. B. Anderson north of the Old Sharpsburg Road and "asked to be taken under his command, to which he assented, and we remained with him the rest of the day." The rest of Garland's brigade, under the command of McRae, headed to the rear and rendered no further service. Hill later commented, "The brigade was too roughly handled to be of any further use that day." Indeed, *roughly handled* is an often-employed euphemism used to describe the brigade's experience at South Mountain. Cpl. Edward Dugand of the 5th North Carolina graphically explained the meaning of the phrase: "The assaulting party being Ohio troops and right there was the first and only instance I witnessed during my four years experience of war;

two men of the 23rd N.C. run through with bayonets while retreating."[74]

The brigade lost 43 killed, 168 wounded, and another 168 missing which translates to a 34% casualty rate. The 12th North Carolina suffered 68% casualties-- 58 of its 92 men present for duty. Samuel Garland, Jr., became the first of four Confederate brigadier generals to perish during the Maryland Campaign. If Garland possessed a death wish, it was granted him at Fox's Gap on the morning of September 14, 1862.[75]

## Antietam

McRae commanded the brigade through the remainder of the campaign. He was a native North Carolinian who was a civilian attorney and former U.S. Consul General in Paris, France at the start of the war. The brigade crossed Antietam Creek on September 15 and took position with Hill's division along a sunken country road that afterwards became known as Bloody Lane. McRae occupied the portion of the road running directly east from the intersection of Roulette Farm lane to a bend that turned south (the location of the modern observation tower). The men remained here through September 16. Historian Ezra Carman gives the brigade strength at Antietam as 756 officers and men.

By 7:00 a.m. on September 17, three of Hill's brigades, Ripley's, Colquitt's, and McRae's, were moving to support John Hood's division in the Cornfield. Although they arrived too late to be of any assistance to Hood, they moved into the maelstrom that was swirling in and around the Cornfield. By 8:00 a.m. Ripley's brigade formed a line just south of the Cornfield on high ground east of, and roughly askance in a northeast direction from Hagerstown Pike. Colquitt's brigade occupied the center and northeast corner of the Cornfield, his extreme right abutting the East Woods. McRae's brigade followed, formed line of battle near the Mumma Cemetery, the 5th North Carolina on the right, moved across a plowed field, over the fences of the Smoketown Road, and into the East Woods.

As Carman succinctly noted, "Here great confusion ensued."[76]

McRae blamed the confusion on "conflicting orders" and "a general panic." As the brigade caught sight of the enemy it opened fire, "but, unaccountably to me, an order was given to cease firing," wrote McRae. Lt. Vines Turner of the 23rd North Carolina claimed that when the Federals came within view some retreating Confederates emerged from the corn and begged the Tar Heels not to fire, "saying that their men were in our front." According to Turner, "Someone in a regiment to the right of us also shouted: 'Cease firing. You are shooting your own men.'" The constant enemy artillery fire grew in intensity at this time. Concurrently, the right of the brigade began falling back in disorder. Capt. Thomas Garrett in command of the 5th North Carolina remembered the confusion and conflicting orders. He also noted the movements of the brigade seemed "vacillating and unsteady." Clearly, the men had not recovered from their experience on South Mountain and it may account for what transpired next. This was about the time the Union XII Corps was coming on the field and were observed by McRae's men on their front and flank. "At this moment," reported Garrett, Capt. Thompson, "came up to me, and in a very excited manner and tone cried out to me, 'They are flanking us! See, yonder's a whole brigade!'" As Garrett explained, "The men before this were far from being cool, but, when this act of indiscretion occurred, a panic ensued, and, despite the efforts of the file-closers and officers, they began to break and run." Even the sometimes acerbic Hill understood what happened. "The alarm over being flanked spread like an electric shock along the ranks," bringing up vivid recollections of the flank fire at South Mountain. In a moment they broke and fell to the rear." McRae later referred to it as, "the most unutterable stampede." In some parts of the brigade the ensuing panicked rout became known as the unaccountable "run back."[77]

McRae's brigade ceased functioning as a cohesive unit. Some of the men retreated to the West Woods while others continued all the way to Sharpsburg.

Portions rallied in the section of Bloody Lane between the Hagerstown Pike and the Mumma Farm Lane. Portions of the 5th and 20th North Carolina were rallied in the streets of Sharpsburg and later re-enforced Nathan Evans' brigade east of town on the heights of Cemetery Hill. Worse yet was the effect the "run back" had on future events. It set up a series of cascading events resulting in the withdrawal of Hill's other two brigades in the Cornfield area, allowing George Greene's division to advance along the Smoketown Road and wrest control of the Dunkard Church plateau from the Confederates.[78]

McRae was wounded "by a piece of shell [that] struck me in the forehead," while rallying some of his brigade in the streets of Sharpsburg, but remained on the field. The brigade lost significantly fewer men, compared to South Mountain: 84 killed, wounded, or missing (12.5%) of those engaged. Overall, the brigade lost 40% of those engaged during the campaign.[79]

Many of the officers laid the poor performance of the brigade on McRae. Some believed that while McRae "was a man of commanding gifts," he harbored "strong prejudices, and the whole brigade knew of his prejudices against the Twelfth Regiment." Iverson blamed the South Mountain defeat on McRae. "I ascribe the disaster to Gen. Garland's death," wrote Iverson, "for had he been alive *he would have known where to put, and how to handle his troops.*" Ruffin of the 13th North Carolina did not mince any of his words: "He is a bad, bad, man and as sheer a coward as ever hid or ran." However, Hill included a special commendation for McRae, pointing out his "good conduct" at South Mountain and made special mention of the colonel gathering up stragglers and personally rendering "much efficient service" at Sharpsburg. Hill declared that McRae, "was struck in the forehead, but gallantly remained on the field." Garrett who succeeded McRae to command of the 5th North Carolina provided the most heartfelt tribute, reporting, at South Mountain, "I observed, as throughout the day, your admirable self possession and command of your facilities in the midst of danger, and I am greatly indebted to you for valuable aid rendered me."[80]

Garland was placed in an impossible situation at South Mountain and it cost him his life. As a result, McRae was presented with a hopeless task at the height of a particularly savage enemy assault with inadequate resources and staff. His traumatized brigade never fully recovered in time for Antietam and that manifested itself in the "run back." Rightly, or wrongly McRae was passed over for promotion, and citing failing health, resigned on November 13, 1862.[81]

**Steven R. Stotelmyer**

* * *

## G.B. Anderson's Brigade: Brigadier General George Burgwyn Anderson

**Units:** 2nd North Carolina, 4th North Carolina, 14th North Carolina, 30th North Carolina
**Strength:** 1,427[82]
**Losses:** 475 (9k-245w-173m)[83]

George Burgwyn Anderson was born just outside of Hillsdale, North Carolina on April 12, 1831. He began his formal education at the University of North Carolina in 1847, but within the year, received an appointment to the United States Military Academy at West Point. Anderson graduated tenth in his class of 1852 and because of his high standing, was able to select his preferred arm of the service, and he choose the Dragoons.[84]

After attending a few months of cavalry school, Anderson was detailed by Secretary of War, Jefferson Davis, to assist with finding a practical route for a railroad in California. He participated in the project for close to two years before rejoining his cavalry regiment and subsequently spent considerable time in the West.[85]

Anderson married Mildred Ewing in November 1860 and resigned his commission the following April, after the fall of Ft. Sumter. The couple traveled to North Carolina, and on May 18, Anderson was commissioned as colonel of the 4th North Carolina Regiment. The men missed First Bull Run but arrived in the area a few days later. The Confederates remaining after the battle were charged with building fortifications in the area and Anderson was appointed commandant of that post where he and the 4th remained until March 1862.[86]

The Battle of Seven Pines, May 31, 1862, was the first time that Anderson and the men from the 4th North Carolina were heavily engaged. Without a brigade commander, Anderson was placed in charge at this battle, and the unit saw heavy combat. The brigade entered the fight with 520 men and lost 462. Anderson's gallantry and valor during this battle earned him a promotion to brigadier general on June 9, 1862. The regiments assigned to him consisted of the brigade he commanded at Antietam: 2nd, 4th, 14th, and 30th North Carolina Regiments. All of these regiments saw action throughout the Peninsula Campaign, but were not present for Second Bull Run.[87]

Even though Anderson's troops were some of the first of Lee's Army to head north during the Maryland Campaign, they were the last Confederate soldiers to actually cross the Potomac River. They were sent just about twenty miles further up the river, on the Virginia side, to act as a decoy.

While the main body of the Army of Northern Virginia splashed across the Potomac between September 4-6, Anderson's North Carolinians skirmished with Federal soldiers, tried to disrupt communications, and attempted to pester the B&O Railroad that ran close along the Potomac River. The brigade eventually crossed the Potomac on September 7 and made its way toward Frederick, Maryland, setting up camp near Buckeystown, Maryland.

## South Mountain

Anderson's brigade was part of D.H. Hill's division and in accordance with Special Orders Number 191, moved up and over South Mountain, and was just miles from Hagerstown by September 13. An officer from the 2nd North Carolina, who within a few weeks of being wounded at Antietam, wrote of the march outside of Frederick: "We marched all day over a beautiful mountain turnpike that, at times, gave us beautiful views of the scenery . . . having passed through, during the day, several little villages that lay nestled down among the valley, the largest being Middletown, a village of about 1000 inhabitants that showed by their signs, that they were, for the greater part, hostile to our cause."[88]

During the early morning hours of September 14, Anderson and his men, along with Rodes' brigade were miles from South Mountain. They were left behind to watch roads out of Harpers Ferry and guard fords along the Antietam Creek, while D.H. Hill's remaining brigades were sent before daybreak to Turner's Gap.

Following a quick survey of the area on top of the mountain, Hill quickly called for Anderson and Rodes to move their men back to Turner's Gap. Upon reaching the top of South Mountain, Anderson was instructed to split his brigade. The 2nd and 4th, roughly 450 men, were sent further south to Fox's Gap. An unnerving sight presented itself to Capt. John Gorman of the 2nd North Carolina as the men made their way into position: "We pass lots of wounded limping down the mountain, trickling blood at every step, then again a stretcher containing some more desperately wounded, and as I bend over one, I catch the pale face of the gallant Garland who is being carried down desperately wounded in the breast."[89]

The arrival of the two regiments, around 11:00 a.m., helped Samuel Garland's troubled brigade, now under Duncan McRae, for a short while, but still more assistance was needed to help stop the advance of Jacob Cox's Kanawha Division (IX Corps). In attempting to shore up their defensive line in Fox's Gap, Col. Charles Tew, commanding Anderson's two regiments, and McRae were unable to decipher a note from Anderson who was back at Turner's Gap. During this time of confusion, regiments were shifted and gaps created in battle lines, allowing the Federals to cause serious damage to the Confederate line.

After repositioning further back toward Turner's Gap, Tew's men were able to fire into the flank of an Ohio regiment as it pushed forward. Col. Bryan Grimes of the 4th North Carolina wrote, "After remaining in our new position for perhaps half an hour, the enemy in front, from 100-200 yards distant, and my best marksmen shooting them whenever they appeared, I have reasons to believe they killed several."[90]

The arrival of the other two regiments from Anderson's brigade added the much-needed support to this part of the line and the volleys between the two sides ended, for the time being, at approximately noon.

At this point, Anderson's full brigade was posted on the far right of the line (about three-quarters of a mile south of the gap) with three other brigades, under the command of Roswell Ripley. Fighting erupted again in the middle of the afternoon and it was the sound of battle at the gap that sent Anderson into action. Without direct orders, he started moving his men north, back toward Fox's Gap.

The mountain terrain, boulders, mountain laurel, and thick vines, caused great difficulty in returning to the fight. Eventually, Anderson's men reached a point where they drove off a few Federal regiments right around dark, but then New Yorkers from Harrison Fairchild's brigade (Isaac Rodman's division; IX Corps) put a stop to Anderson's push and the fighting ceased for the day. The brigade lost 90 men at Fox's Gap (7 killed, 54 wounded and 29 missing).[91]

After retreating off of South Mountain that night, Lee's men gathered on the high ground east of Sharpsburg through the next two days. G.B. Anderson's four regiments crossed Antietam Creek at daybreak on September 15 and took their initial position along the Sunken Road. The right flank rested on Boonsboro Pike and extended north up the road. The troops faced east. Maj. W.W. Sillers, 30th North Carolina recalled, "In these movements, made very rapidly and in the heat of the day, some of the men became exhausted and fell out of the ranks."[92]

## Antietam

Throughout the day and night of September 16, Anderson's men remained in position along the far southern end of the Sunken Road/Boonsboro Pike intersection. The skirmishers on a forward ridge had fields of fire eastward toward the Middle Bridge.

Early on the morning of September 17, an artillery exchange between Federal guns east of the Antietam and Confederate pieces posted on the high ground to the west of Anderson's men, put the North Carolinians into motion. Anderson moved his troops north through the Piper farm pastures and eventually through a cornfield just south of the Sunken Road.

Upon reaching this section of the Sunken Road, the brigade took position to the right of Rodes' men; the 2nd North Carolina was positioned opposite the Roulette Lane. The line ran east with the 14th, 4th, and 30th to the right of Tew's regiment. The men undoubtedly knew the battle was eventually going to move their way. "I then felt sure we would do honor to our noble old State that day, though we would not live to see it again," recalled an officer in the 2nd, who was wounded in the fight that day.[93]

Anderson's men moved into the lane at approximately 9:00 a.m. and had little time to prepare for William French's division's (II Corps) onslaught. With over 15,000 men, the II Corps was the largest corps fielded by the Union army, and as they moved into the fight, they became separated with one division heading toward the West Woods; the remaining two attacked the Confederate position in the Sunken Road.

French's three brigades attacked first, with Weber's brigade in the lead. "They did not see our single line of hungry, jaded, and dusty men, who were lying down, until within good musket shot, when we rose and delivered our fire with terrible effect. Instantly the air was filled with the cries of wounded and dying," remembered Capt. E.A. Osborne of the 4th North Carolina. Anderson's men sent the Federals back for cover behind a slight ridge not more than 100 yards north of the road.[94]

The same fate greeted the next Federal attack and it wasn't until the third Union assault that Anderson's men had to make an earnest attempt to hold their position in the lane. These troops were veteran soldiers of Nathan Kimball's brigade, and rather than fire a volley and charge the lane, they fired upon Anderson's men from behind the cover of the ridge north of the lane. Over the course of the next thirty minutes, both sides fired volley after volley toward their foe attempting to gain an upper hand. A soldier in the 2nd North Carolina recalled, "Our men are protected by . . . the ware of the road, but that is great protection; they fire cautiously, and are apparently as cool as if shooting at squirrels, taking sure to aim every fire."[95]

Richard Anderson's division arrived in the Sunken Road around this time and Ambrose Wright's brigade extended G.B. Anderson's line further to the right. Confederate leadership commanding the action in the Sunken Road started to crumble at this time. G.B. Anderson was wounded at approximately 10:30 a.m. while returning to the Sunken Road after meeting with D.H. Hill. Anderson was hit in the ankle as he made his way through the northeast corner of the Piper Orchard. Before being removed from the field, Anderson sent a message forward to the lane, instructing Col. Tew of the 2nd North Carolina, to take command of the brigade. The messenger, Fred Phillips, eventually found Tew at a point where the Roulette Lane runs into the Sunken Road and informed him of Anderson's wounding and he was now in charge of the brigade. Almost immediately after taking command, Tew was mortally wounded. Eventually, Col. R.T. Bennett of the 14th North Carolina, took command.[96]

More trouble arrived at about 11:00 a.m., when a third II Corps division, Israel Richardson's, approached the Sunken Road. Bennett and his line held until about noon when a series of events forced them to retreat from their position in the Sunken Road. First, reinforcements from R.H. Anderson's division did not add much to strengthen the Confederate line in the lane and in some cases added to an already mounting confusing situation due to the loss of numerous commanders. Second, two Federal regiments, the 61st and 64th New York, part of Caldwell's brigade, the fifth brigade to attack the Confederate position, broke through the North Carolinians' line.[97]

Richardson's men's determined attack on the right of the Sunken Road line forced Wright's brigade to retreat. The confusion spread to Anderson's two regiments to their left. Bennett reported, "In this stampede, if we may so term it, the Fourth North Carolina State Troops and Thirtieth North Carolina Troops participated." Bennett attempted to hold his left two regiments in the lane, but Rodes' brigade on their left was finally forced to break to the rear at approximately 12:00 p.m. G.B. Anderson's brigade, along with those that could be gathered up from D.H. Hill's division, spent the rest of the battle around the Piper barnyard and along the Hagerstown Pike." The brigade lost an additional 475 men at Antietam—more than double of Rodes' casualties (203).[98]

Anderson's brother, Lt. Col. Robert Anderson, was also wounded at Antietam. He assisted George to Shepherdstown, Virginia, then to Staunton and finally back to Raleigh, North Carolina. During the trip home, Anderson's wounded foot became much worse. In an attempt to save his life, doctors amputated Anderson's leg, but he was unable to survive and died on October 16, 1862. His funeral was "[o]ne of the largest public meetings in Raleigh testified the sorrow of the citizens at the great public loss." He was buried in the City Cemetery. Tragically, Anderson's son was born a couple of days after his death.[99]

**Brian S. Baracz**

***

## Colquitt's Brigade: Colonel Alfred Colquitt

**Units:** 13th Alabama, 6th Georgia, 23rd Georgia, 27th Georgia, and 28th Georgia
**Strength:** 1,474[100]
**Losses:** 722 (111k-444w-167m)[101]

Colonel Alfred Holt Colquitt's brigade was already a veteran unit when it waded across the Potomac at White's Ford late on the evening of September 5, 1862. Each regiment mustered into service in 1861 and had received its baptism of fire during the Peninsula Campaign and Seven Days' battles. The 13th Alabama, 6th Georgia and 23rd Georgia were initially assigned to Gabriel Rains' brigade in the spring of 1862; the 27th and 28th Georgia were in Winfield Featherston's brigade. Rains was relieved of command after the Battle of Seven Pines and replaced with Colquitt of the 6th Georgia. The five regiments were combined in mid-June under Colquitt and fought together during the Seven Days as part of D. H. Hill's division. This brigade structure remained unchanged throughout the Maryland Campaign.[102]

Born to a prominent family in 1824 near Monroe, Georgia, Alfred Colquitt followed his father's path to the legal profession and then politics. He graduated from Princeton University in 1844, just in time to volunteer for service in the Mexican-American War. He served as a staff major during that conflict and returned to Georgia to commence his law practice. Elected to both the U. S. Congress and the Georgia legislature in the 1850s, his pre-war political service ended as a member of the state secession convention. Colquitt volunteered and was elected captain of Company H of the 6th Georgia and then rose to colonel of the regiment in May 1861.[103]

After the battles around Richmond, Hill's division remained as part of the defense of that city while most of Robert E. Lee's army moved north to engage the forces of John Pope and the Army of Virginia. Ordered to join Lee's command, Hill's division did not travel together. Colquitt's brigade and Roswell Ripley's brigade left their camps on August 19 and traveled by train to Orange Court House. The two brigades remained there until August 26 when they resumed their march, arriving at Manassas two days after Pope's defeat. Colquitt's and Ripley's brigades did not reunite with Hill until September 6 near Buckeystown, Maryland. Hill's men enjoyed three days of much needed rest while camped just southeast of Frederick.[104]

### South Mountain

On September 9, Gen. Lee issued his infamous Special Orders Number 191, part of which specified Hill's division as the army's rear guard. It would also protect the reserve artillery, ordnance and supply trains as they moved west on National Road. The division crossed South Mountain at Turner's Gap on September 11 and Hill arranged his units at strategic points between Boonsboro and Hagerstown to intercept any Federals attempting to escape the Harpers Ferry trap set by Stonewall Jackson's command. Hill's objective changed on September 12 to include defending Turner's gap when Jeb Stuart reported his cavalry was pressed aggressively enough to suggest a general advance by the Army of the Potomac. Hill remained largely unconcerned stating, "Major General Stuart reported to me that two brigades only of the Yankees were pursuing us, and that one brigade was sufficient to hold the pass." Late in the morning of September 13, Hill ordered Colquitt and a battery of artillery to the summit of South Mountain to assist Stuart in defense of the gap.[105]

The brigade reached the mountain crest at approximately 4:00 p.m. and Colquitt met Stuart arriving from the east. After a brief conference, Stuart assisted in deploying Colquitt's men on either side of National Road, about 700 yards up from the base of the east slope of the mountain. George

Grattan, a 2nd lieutenant in the 6th Georgia and an aide-de-camp on Colquitt's staff, recalled Stuart "reported there were no troops following him but cavalry and that Col. Colquitt would have no difficulty holding the pass with his brigade." At the appearance of Confederate infantry, Alfred Pleasonton's Federal troopers made no further attempt to engage before nightfall. After assessing the situation, Colquitt determined that holding Turner's Pass was more easily stated than done. Good roads leading over the mountain crest, north and south of National Road, could be used to turn his flanks. He threw out strong pickets toward both roads, left a line of skirmishers in his front, and retired his main body back up near the mountain crest.[106]

With his evening dispositions complete, Colquitt observed the large number of campfires appearing in the Middletown Valley to the east. Despite Stuart's assurances, Colquitt correctly surmised the force in his front far exceeded two brigades. Spread out over the valley floor were actually three of Jesse Reno's four IX Corps divisions totaling close to 10,000 men. Colquitt rushed a courier to Hill describing the situation and requesting reinforcements. This request prompted Hill to further consolidate his forces toward Boonsboro and send Samuel Garland's North Carolina brigade to the mountain where its men bivouacked halfway up the western slope.[107]

At first light, Colquitt sent his brigade back down the mountain to the position it occupied the day before. The Georgian had an eye for terrain for he chose his defensive positions well. He placed two of his regiments on the north side of the road near a sharp bend that enabled a terrific field of fire on any enemy approaching up the National Road. He anchored the left with the 28th Georgia against a steep slope of the mountain and the 23th Georgia extended the line to the pike. A stone wall running perpendicular to the road provided cover for the entire length of the 23rd and almost half of the 28th. Three companies of skirmishers were sent forward – one north of the road and two south of it. On the south side of the pike the ground

dropped into a deep ravine cut by a mountain stream, requiring the remaining three regiments (6th Georgia, 27th Georgia and 13th Alabama respectively) to post about 200-300 yards to the rear and southwest of the 23rd and the 28th. Finally, the brigade's permanent skirmish battalion under Capt. W.M. Arnold of the 6th Georgia was deployed forward to cover the ravine and prevent two regiments north of the road from being flanked. Colquitt was ordered to connect his right with the left of Garland's brigade now posting up at Fox's Gap to the south. Unfortunately, there were too few men to carry out this order, resulting in a gap of 400 yards.[108]

All through September 14, Colquitt's men heard fighting to their right, where the IX Corps assaulted Fox's Gap. Later in the afternoon, two divisions of the I Corps attacked up the hills to Colquitt's left. Early in the fight for Fox's Gap, Colquitt's skirmishers south of the pike made contact with some of the advancing enemy troops to their right under Jacob Cox. About 4:00 p.m. Colquitt saw a large body of men moving up and astride the National Road with a line of skirmishers in their front. This force was John Gibbon's brigade (Doubleday's division; I Corps), composed of western regiments: 2nd, 6th and 7th Wisconsin, and the 19th Indiana. Though not yet known by their future sobriquet, the Iron Brigade, these tough men in their black Hardee hats were about to show the mettle that earned them their reputation. The 19th Indiana on the left of National Road and the 7th Wisconsin on the right of it steadily advanced, supported by the 2nd and 6th Wisconsin, similarly aligned, about 200 yards behind. The sun was already setting behind South Mountain when both sides' skirmishers clashed with the rest of Gibbon's men pushing steadily up the mountain behind them. The incessant fire from Arnold's skirmish battalion south of the pike caused the 19th Indiana to veer left, so the 2nd Wisconsin obliqued to the right to fill the gap adjacent to the National Road. Stubborn skirmish resistance on both sides of the road slowed the forward pace and caused the 7th Wisconsin to temporarily change front to the road, thus exposing its right flank to 23rd Georgia concealed behind their stone wall. The Georgians leveled their muskets and delivered a punishing volley into the flank of the Badgers. Simultaneously, the 28th Georgia shifted in the woods to the north and fired directly into the backs of the unfortunate Wisconsin men, causing another change of front back to their original position. The 6th Wisconsin came up on the 7th's right and, as Colquitt simply wrote, "the fight opened in earnest."[109]

Both sides blazed away at each other in the consuming darkness. Having driven the skirmishers south of the road, both the 19th Indiana and the 2nd Wisconsin changed front to the north and attempted to fire into the flank of the Georgians behind the stone wall. Owing to the differences in elevation, most of this fire was ineffectual, and both units soon exhausted their ammunition. Despite the massed firepower, Gibbon's men could not move the Georgians from their position. In a letter to his wife, Maj. Tully Graybill of the 28th stated, "the old 28th and 23rd met them like men and held them at bay for three long hours." Even as the ammunition ran low, neither side was willing to give, as both Colquitt's and Gibbon's men remained in place with fixed bayonets. Gibbon's men performed courageously, but the Confederate advantage of position and the tenacity with which the gray clad opponents fought, could not be overcome. While both Confederate flanks on South Mountain had been turned, Colquitt's stand meant the army could retreat intact toward Sharpsburg in the darkness. Colquitt lost 109 men during its fierce defense of Turner's Gap.[110]

**Antietam**

Colquitt's brigade was ordered to withdraw from its position on South Mountain to commence the march to Sharpsburg at about 10:00 p.m. Colquitt and Robert Rodes led the van from Boonsboro to Keedysville, passing through the latter at about 1:00 a.m. on September 15. The bone-weary men of both brigades got little relief from their battle exertions of the day as they were ordered on to

Sharpsburg arriving around daybreak. Posted south of town near the Shepherdstown Ford, Colquitt's men were finally able to rest; however, the respite was short lived. About 8:30 a.m. on September 16, the brigade was ordered back through Sharpsburg and placed in a sunken farm road that connected Hagerstown and Boonsboro Pikes. The brigade faced north from its position just south of the William Roulette farm to help protect Lee's vulnerable left flank. Joseph Hooker's I Corps began crossing the Upper Bridge during the afternoon, causing John Hood's men to deploy in various positions from Hagerstown Pike, east along the north edge of D.R. Miller's Cornfield, and then southeast into and through the East Woods. As part of this effort, Colquitt's skirmish battalion under Arnold moved into the East Woods and attached themselves to the right of 4th Texas skirmishers. They were soon engaged in a brisk engagement with the 13th Pennsylvania Reserves (Truman Seymour's brigade; George Meade's division; I Corps). As darkness fell, the battalion withdrew and bivouacked at the Roulette farm.[111]

The expected battle opened just after 5:00 a.m. on September 17 with a resumption of musket firing in the East Woods and artillery fire along the Confederate and Union positions around the open ground between the Confederate left and the Union right. Colquitt's men were out of sight in their sunken lane, but could clearly hear the intense struggle going on just over the ridge to their north. R. V. Cobb of the 27th Georgia heard a man remark with considerable understatement that it was "getting pretty warm down there." Colquitt received his orders at 7:00 a.m. to support Hood's division in the cornfield and East Woods. Marching by the left flank, the brigade filed between the Roulette farm and the burning Mumma farm buildings and then turned north. Cresting the ridge along Smoketown Road, the men saw Roswell Ripley's brigade already heavily engaged in the clover field and at the southern end of farmer David Miller's Cornfield. Hastening to Ripley's aid, the 13th Alabama leading Colquitt's column passed the 3rd North Carolina and obliqued to the left across Ripley's front to give room for the entire brigade to come on line. Unfortunately, the 6th Georgia bringing up the rear was forced to enter the East Woods, where some adroit maneuvering managed to bring it back in line to the right.[112]

Colquitt's men now faced front and commenced firing. Opposing them on the plowed field north of the cornfield were more westerners, the 3rd Wisconsin and the 27th Indiana, both from George Gordon's brigade (Alpheus Williams' division; XII Corps). These troops had already fought it out with Ripley and now fully engaged Colquitt's men. Colquitt gave the order to advance into the Cornfield but the movement was checked by the blistering fire in the brigade's front, which now included canister from Dunbar Ransom's Battery C, Fifth U.S. Artillery. After a few minutes, Colquitt saw Samuel Garland's North Carolina brigade approaching the East Woods to support his right, and the Georgian renewed his efforts to push Gordon from the field. Casualties mounted on both sides due to the intense concentration of firepower. Colquitt pushed farther into the Cornfield, but the support on either flank never materialized. Most of Ripley's men remained in the clover field south of the Cornfield and did not advance, and Garland's men, believing they were being flanked, fled the field. Despite the pressure in front, the 6th Georgia and a portion of the 27th Georgia made it to the fence on the north end of the Cornfield. The rest of the brigade line faced diagonally southwest to northeast. Ben Miliken of the 27th Georgia lamented later, "Oh I tell you truly it was a perfect hail of bullets shot and shell from the time I got in until I was hit." For the next few minutes, both sides poured volleys into the other, neither side willing to give way. Finally, Hector Tyndale's brigade (George Greene's division; XII Corps) arrived and broke the stalemate. Entering the north end of the East Woods, Tyndale's right units, the 66th and 7th Ohio regiments, could see the exposed right flank of the 6th Georgia. The two small regiments fired almost point blank into it and then charged into the Georgians. According to Ezra Carman, "the fighting in the northeast corner of the

corn was now fast and furious and hand to hand." In the ensuing melee, Colquitt stated the lines became "scarcely distinguishable," and the 6th Georgia was almost wiped out. Colquitt spied the remainder of Tyndale's brigade approaching through the East Woods to threaten his rear. With no support and in danger of being surrounded, Colquitt reluctantly ordered a withdrawal from the field, and his men "made their best way out." The fragmented Georgians and Alabamians attempted to rally but the enemy's pressure was unrelenting. Some remnants of the brigade made it to where the Sunken Road connected to Hagerstown Pike and formed on Robert Rodes' brigade's left.[113]

Rodes assumed command of the remnants of Colquitt's and Garland's brigades as they filed into the western end of the Sunken Road. The survivors fought in the defense of that road and retreated with the rest of Rodes' brigade when the position collapsed later that morning. Of Colquitt's original force, only about 200 rallied at the Sunken Road, and 50 of those became additional casualties. Colquitt's only other engagement with the enemy occurred about 3:30 p.m. when fragments of his brigade assembled in Sharpsburg and were sent east of town onto Cemetery Hill to assist Nathan Evans' brigade's defense of Boonsboro Pike. Colquitt and Alfred Iverson of the 20th North Carolina brought about 250 men to assist Evan's South Carolinians, who were being pressed by Lt. C.H. Carlton's skirmish line of the 4th U. S. Infantry (George Sykes' division; V Corps). After a brief engagement, Colquitt and Iverson retreated from the field.[114]

The Antietam losses to Col. Colquitt's brigade were appalling, especially for the short duration of time actually engaged with the enemy. In a span of about thirty minutes in the Miller Cornfield, every field officer but one was killed or wounded. Colquitt lamented in his official report that "their loss is irreparable." Of the 1,320 officers and men Colquitt brought into battle, he lost 111 killed, 444 wounded and 167 missing for a total of 722 or about 55%. The 6th Georgia went into battle with about 250 men and lost 78% killed and wounded. Without embellishment, a survivor wrote, "the regiment fought as bravely as ever men fought, and held their ground until none were left to hold it."[115]

The brigade's survivors crossed the Potomac River back into Virginia on September 19, ending their part of the Maryland Campaign. The veteran brigade had exhibited mettle and bravery, particularly in their critical stand at Turner's Gap and in Miller's Cornfield. In October, Colquitt achieved promotion to brigadier general to rank from September 1 and led his brigade to the close of the war.[116]

**Lucas I. Cade**

* * *

# STUART'S DIVISION—

## Major General James E. B. Stuart

James Ewell Brown (Jeb) Stuart was the only cavalry commander the Army of Northern Virginia ever knew. Born on February 6, 1833 in Virginia, Stuart was only 29 years old during the Maryland Campaign. He graduated from West Point in 1854 and spent most of the pre-war years as an officer with the 1st U.S. Cavalry in Texas and Kansas. Stuart was somewhat of an inventor, perfecting the design of a saber hook, which allowed cavalrymen to rapidly and easily remove the scabbard from its belt. He ultimately sold the patent rights to the government for $5,000. Stuart volunteered to be an aide to Robert E. Lee during the capture of John Brown in 1859. He resigned his commission when Virginia seceded and received the rank of colonel of the 1st Virginia Cavalry. He served under Gen. Joseph Johnston in the Shenandoah Valley and performed meritoriously at First Bull Run. He later collected vital information about enemy formations and their locations. Stuart was promoted to the rank of brigadier general and assigned command of Lee's new cavalry brigade. Promotion to major general came on July 25, 1862 and command of the newly formed cavalry division. Stuart quickly gained legendary status that rivaled Stonewall Jackson's by the start of the Maryland Campaign.[1]

Stuart's 5,000-man cavalry division was divided into three brigades with a horse artillery battery assigned to each. Fitzhugh Lee, Wade Hampton, and Beverly Robertson each commanded a brigade. The first two officers were experienced and talented leaders. Robertson was not up to Stuart's standards and he lobbied hard to get him reassigned. Lee finally consented on September 5 and Thomas Munford commanded the brigade during the Maryland Campaign. Stuart's cavalrymen were confident and experienced, and their efficient organization created an effective information gathering apparatus, along with undertaking screening and in some cases, fighting activities.[2]

While Lee's infantry made their way to Leesburg, Stuart's men were in the saddle, screening the army's rear and making a thrust south toward Washington to confuse and upset Lincoln and Halleck. Munford's brigade traveled almost to Falls Church. Because of the myriad tasks assigned to Stuart, his three brigades never operated as a whole during the campaign. After a well-deserved rest on September 4, Fitz Lee's and Hampton's men were back in the saddle the following day, heading for Leesburg. They crossed the Potomac River at Edward's Ferry, about seven miles below White's Ford the following afternoon. Fitz Lee's brigade headed to Poolesville, Maryland, while Hampton's men continued crossing the river. Fitz Lee's troopers encountered three companies of the 1st Massachusetts Cavalry and drove them through the town, capturing over 30 and sustaining just under 10 casualties—the first casualties of the campaign.[3]

Stuart's three brigades fanned out on September 7 with orders to guard Lee's rear. Fitz Lee rode northeast, occupying New Market, with pickets spreading out from there, Hampton was centered at Urbana with strong outposts at Hyattstown and pickets in surrounding areas, and Munford's brigade occupied the area east of the Monocacy River. By the morning of September 7, Stuart's screen extended about 30 miles. The increasingly aggressive Union cavalry skirmished with Stuart's men at Hyattstown and Poolesville on September 8-10. Pleasonton set out to capture strategically important Sugar Loaf Mountain on September 10 and after several persistent cavalry thrusts, supported by infantry, Munford abandoned the high ground. Stuart apparently neglected to inform Lee of these increasingly aggressive thrusts by the Union army.[4]

Stuart loved parties and the ladies, so he threw a large ball in Urbana, Maryland on the evening of September 8 that was briefly interrupted when half of the 1st U. S. Cavalry dashed into Hyattsville and drove north. Stuart and his officers quickly left the festivities to direct the action, but he eventually returned to the party. Fighting occurred later on September 9 in Hyattsville, as the Union cavalry continued their aggressive push north. Several modern historians conclude Stuart was negligent in providing a flow of incorrect information to Lee prior to the formulation of Special Orders Number 191. As a result Lee did not worry about dividing his army when in fact McClellan was moving north to contest his movements in Maryland.[5]

Stuart's command was a major component of Lee's Special Orders Number 191: "General Stuart will detach a squadron of cavalry to accompany the commands of Generals Longstreet, Jackson, and McLaws, and, with the main body of the cavalry, will cover the route of the army, bringing up all stragglers that may have been left behind." Stuart put his division into action on September 10. Hampton's brigade remained behind as the army left Frederick to operate as the rear guard and retard the enemy's movements toward Frederick. Hampton then fell back to screen the rear of Lee's army on the National Road, including defending Hagan's Gap in the Cactoctin Mountains from an incursion by Union cavalry. Munford's brigade was sent west to protect the army's right flank at Jefferson, and Fitz Lee remained near the army's left flank at New Market. Stuart again faltered, allowing Lee to form the impression that McClellan was moving the bulk of his army toward Harpers Ferry, and as a result, created the possibility of each of Lee's columns being defeated in isolation of each other.

After a series of fights with Union cavalry pursuing along the National Road to beyond Middletown, Stuart sent Hampton toward Burkittsville. He followed on the morning of September 14 and after reaching Burkittsville, contined to Weverton, where Hampton was sent to guard McLaws' command's rear. Hampton continued hovering around McLaws' rear during its march to Sharpsburg after Harpers Ferry's capture.[6]

Because Stuart was a bit confused about McClellan's movements, he sent Fitz Lee's brigade on September 11 on a reconnaissance around McClellan's right flank. The men then undertook an arduous ride to Shookstown at the foot of Catoctin Mountain, through Hamburg Pass, and then to Boonsboro, arriving there on September 14. The exhausted men served as the rearguard to protect Longstreet's and D.H. Hill's troops retreating from South Mountain toward Sharpsburg on September 15. The brigade fought a pitched battle with Union cavalry in the streets of Boonsboro, but it was routed and forced to flee to the Middle Bridge over Antietam Creek.

Of the three brigades, historian Joseph Harsh declared "Munford faced a truly formidable task." With only two of his regiments remaining, numbering perhaps 300 men, and three cannon of Chew's battery, Munford was ordered to anchor Lee's right flank. It had already fought hard at Sugar Loaf Mountain and was pushed back by overwhelming enemy troops, including infantry. Munford now headed for Burkittsville with Union cavalry relentlessly following and nipping at his heels. Hampton's brigade arrived and assisted before moving on to the Pleasant Valley. Munford continued to Crampton's Gap and deployed his men at the base of the mountain. He was joined by portions of William Mahone's (under William Parham) and Howell Cobb's infantry brigades, but both commanders yielded to Munford. The young cavalry commander had perhaps 1,200 men against the VI Corps, boasting 12,000 men. The result was predictable, as the Union infantry drove Munford's command up the side of the mountain. Stuart heard the fighting while still at Weverton with

Hampton and he immediately "rode at full speed" to reach Crampton's Gap, arriving there after dark. The fight was over and the Confederates were defeated. Stuart decided to turn and head over to Harpers Ferry, where he met with Stonewall Jackson on September 15. Jackson sent him to Sharpsburg to deliver information about the situation at Harpers Ferry.[7]

Meanwhile, Fitz Lee's brigade, so roughed up at Boonsboro, arrived at Sharpsburg before the rest of Stuart's command. After a brief rest, the brigade was broken apart to guard both of Lee's flanks. Munford's men arrived next and were sent south to guard the area below the Lower Bridge, freeing Fitz Lee to recombine his command. The brigade headed to Nicodemus Heights to support Stuart's horse artillery, and remained there until relieved by Jubal Early's infantry brigade. After another short rest, the brigade was sent north and joined Hampton's newly arrived brigade on the aborted attempt to turn the Union right flank later in the day.[8]

Stuart's cavalry crossed the Potomac River during the night of September 18-19; Fitz Lee's brigade had the honor of forming the rearguard and was the last unit of Lee's army to cross the Potomac River on September 19.[9]

Stuart's troopers performed effectively during the Maryland Campaign. It did a good job of screening Lee's army's move north, collected important intelligence, and fought. When it did the latter, it generally held the Union cavalry at bay. Stuart's effectiveness has been called into question, particularly with regard to understanding the enemy's movements and more importantly, communicating what he knew to Lee. Stuart, somewhat disingenuously stated, "Every means was taken to ascertain what the nature of the enemy's movement was; whether a reconnaissance feeling for our whereabouts, or an aggressive movement of the army. The enemy studiously avoided displaying any force, except a part of Burnside's corps, and built no camp-fires . . ." Stuart would continue collecting accolades, but his shortcomings in communicating the enemy's location and intentions would also plague Lee during his second invasion of the North in 1863.[10]

**Bradley M. Gottfried**

* * *

## Hampton's Brigade: Brigadier General Wade Hampton

**Units:** 1st North Carolina Cavalry, 2nd South Carolina Cavalry, 10th Virginia Cavalry, Cobb's Legion Cavalry, Jeff Davis Legion Cavalry
**Strength:** 1,445[11]
**Losses:** 30 (7-20-3)[12]

Hampton's brigade was formed in late July 1862 during the reorganization of the Army of Northern Virginia's cavalry arm. The cavalry, previously organized as an oversized brigade of seven regiments, one battalion, and cavalry from three different legions, became a division of two brigades.[13]

Forty-four year old South Carolinian Wade Hampton III was a third generation aristocrat, and possibly the wealthiest man in the South. A graduate of South Carolina College and an avid sportsman, Hampton doubted the future of slavery and entered South Carolina politics to counter the fire-eaters so prevalent in South Carolina. When war came, however, he immediately raised the Hampton Legion: six companies of infantry, four of cavalry, and a battery of artillery, all he equipped with the finest arms and materials at his own expense. Although he had no prior military experience, Hampton proved an able leader and was promoted to the rank of brigadier general in May 1862. He commanded an infantry brigade through Seven Pines, where he was wounded in the foot.[14]

Hampton's new command was composed of an unusual set of units. The 1st North Carolina Cavalry had seen active service in Virginia since October

1861. The 2nd South Carolina was only organized on August 22, 1862 with the consolidation of the 4th South Carolina Cavalry Battalion, the Hampton Legion Cavalry Battalion, and two independent companies. Cobb's Legion Cavalry of Georgia had grown since its recruitment from four companies to eleven and had been active since Yorktown. The Jeff Davis Legion was first organized with three Mississippi companies and one Alabama company as the 2nd Mississippi Cavalry Battalion in October 1861. More companies from Alabama and Georgia were added after its arrival in Virginia, and it was designated the Jeff Davis Legion in late 1861. The 10th Virginia Cavalry rounded out the brigade. It was organized in May 1862 from the Wise Legion and the 8th Virginia Cavalry Battalion.[15]

Hampton's brigade remained in the Richmond environs following the Seven Days Campaign to keep an eye on the Army of the Potomac camped on the James River. When D.H. Hill's and Lafayette McLaws' divisions started north on August 18 to reinforce the Army of Northern Virginia, the brigade covered the march.[16]

Hampton's men joined Stuart, who was with Fitzhugh Lee's brigade at Fairfax Court House on September 2. They came across retreating elements of the Union II Corps at Flint Hill, and with a section of Maj. John Pelham's battery, pursued them into the evening hours. As darkness fell, Col. Lawrence Baker's 1st North Carolina rode into an ambush prepared by the 71st Pennsylvania, ending the day's engagement. It was the brigade's first battle as a unit.[17]

Moving north by way of Hunter's Mill and Dranesville, Hampton's brigade arrived in Leesburg on September 5. Before crossing the Potomac River at Conrad's Ford, the 10th Virginia Cavalry was detached from the command. The brigade camped on the evening of September 5 about two miles east of Poolesville, Maryland, and marched toward Frederick the following day. The bulk of the brigade camped at Urbana, with outposts established at Damascus, Hyattstown, and Clarksburg, guarding the most direct approaches from Washington.[18]

Jeb Stuart threw a ball at the Landon School in Urbana on the evening of September 8, inviting many local females and a large cadre of his own cavalry officers. Not long into the festivities, five companies of the 1st U.S. Cavalry dashed into Hyattstown, driving Hampton's pickets back to within three miles of Urbana. Although the 1st North Carolina drove the Federals back, Stuart paused the ball and rode out to review the situation with his staff. The ball resumed by 1:00 a.m. on the morning of September 9. A few of the wounded were attended to by the belles of the ball.[19]

Later that day, a battalion of the 1st New York Cavalry charged into Hyattstown and drove out Hampton's pickets. Hampton's troopers returned with artillery the next day, and a sharp action occurred. The New Yorkers were reinforced by a squadron of the 1st U.S. Cavalry, and the southerners again fell back. The Federals later returned to Clarksburg.[20]

**Preliminary Actions**

The last of the Army of Northern Virginia's infantry, D. H. Hill's division, with the army's trains, marched westward out of Frederick on September 10 and Hampton's brigade pulled back to that city on September 12, to cover the infantry's withdrawal and delay the Army of the Potomac's advance. Hampton's troopers observed the Union IX Corps marching along National Pike at about 4:00 p.m. Hampton had positioned two squadrons of cavalry, about 50 men, with Hart's battery near the Monocacy River on Urbana Pike, and Hampton worried they might be cut off. He sent an additional rifled gun and a squadron of the 2nd South Carolina to their aid as the rest of Hampton's troopers fell back along both roads. This led Col. Augustus Moor, commanding the 2nd Brigade of the Kanawha Division, to launch a hasty charge at the head of the Chicago Dragoons (1st West Virginia Cavalry), supported by a single gun. Scattered by a countercharge of the Jeff Davis Legion and part of the 2nd South Carolina Cavalry, led by Capt. David Waldhauer, Moor was unhorsed and captured, the gun was abandoned, and the Union troopers sustained about 25 casualties. A Legion member remembered the Federals "ran over each other, upsetting cannon and horses, and firing off their cannon in their own midst, with not a Confederate within fifty yards of them." The Confederates lost two killed and three wounded.[21]

With the Union advance blunted, Hampton's brigade withdrew westward along National Pike. Hampton left the Jeff Davis Legion under Lt. Col. William Martin and a section of Hart's battery at Hagan's Gap to hold the Catoctin Mountain pass while he led the rest of his brigade to Middletown. On the morning of September 13, Stuart urged Hampton to return to Hagan's Gap with most of his brigade to delay the Federals as long as possible, and he rode there with him. Martin was already making a successful stand against the Union cavalry, holding back skirmishers of the 3rd Indiana Cavalry, 8th Illinois Cavalry, and 1st Massachusetts Cavalry of John Farnsworth's brigade, supported by two batteries of the 2nd U.S. Artillery.[22]

The Federals slowly gained the upper hand in the afternoon, forcing Hampton to retire to the approaches of Middletown. He placed Hart's battery along National Pike with Baker's 1st North Carolina Cavalry as support. The rest of the brigade fell back to Catoctin Creek, west of Middletown. Pleasonton pursued closely and he deployed Batteries C & G, 3rd U.S. Artillery to silence Hart's guns. Skirmishers advanced, and after a brief action, Hampton ordered a retreat. Baker's 1st North Carolina Cavalry was designated as rear guard and they steadily fell back through Middletown, briefly taking a position along Catoctin Creek with Hart's battery. Farnsworth's brigade followed. Union batteries came up, forcing Baker to burn the bridge over the pike. Some skirmishing followed briefly and then the 1st North Carolina Cavalry followed Hampton. This action cost the brigade 13 casualties.[23]

After the Middletown fight, Jeb Stuart ordered Hampton to take his brigade, with the cavalry trains in tow, southwestward toward Burkittsville, where it would rendezvous with Thomas Munford's brigade.

The Jeff Davis Legion, with one section of Hart's battery, were detached earlier by Stuart and ordered to Turner's Gap.[24]

Hampton became aware that four companies of the 8th Illinois Cavalry and 3rd Indiana Cavalry were following him on a parallel road to the east. Near Quebec Schoolhouse, about two miles southwest of Middletown, Maj. William Medill, leading the Union troopers, decided he was outnumbered, and reversed his column. At the same time, Hampton sent the Cobb Legion into the Federals' rear. It was a close-quarters fight; a thrust and parry fight that cost the Legion 13 casualties, including Lt. Col. Peirce Young, whose horse was killed under him and he lost several teeth to a saber blow. The Federals lost between 20 and 30 men.[25]

Hampton reformed his column and rode on to Burkittsville later that day, where the brigade was nearly fired on by its own Chew's battery. The men camped that night below Crampton's Gap; the Jeff Davis Legion camped near Boonsboro.[26]

## South Mountain

Jeb Stuart feared the Federals would march directly on besieged Harpers Ferry via Weverton Gap and ordered Hampton's brigade south to guard McLaws' rear on September 14. The men remained here until the morning of September 16, when they followed McLaws across the across a pontoon bridge into Harper's Ferry.[27]

The Jeff Davis Legion and Hart's battery were sent to Solomon's Gap to picket the roads leading north from Harpers Ferry. At about 10:00 p.m. on September 14, some of the Legion's pickets west of the gap exchanged shots with Union cavalry escaping from Harpers Ferry, under Col. Benjamin Davis. Martin was perplexed that a large Union force was to his west, so he decided to withdraw toward Hagerstown. The Legion followed a route that led past Keedysville, over the Upper Antietam Bridge, and through Smoketown and Bakersville. Near Williamsport, the Legion stumbled upon the part of Longstreet's ordnance train that Davis' Union cavalry hadn't captured. After a brief pursuit of Davis's cavalry, Martin turned the Legion and crossed the Potomac. Riding to Shepherdstown, they again forded the river and joined Lee's army at Sharpsburg on September 16.[28]

## Antietam

Acting as the rear guard and escort for McLaws' division, Hampton's brigade crossed the Potomac River at Knott's and Boteler's Fords late in the morning of September 17 and joined Stuart on the army's left flank north of Sharpsburg at about 1:00 p.m. The brigade was ordered to advance around the Union right flank, but the movement was aborted because of the heavy presence of Union artillery, so it remained unengaged throughout the day. It was reunited with the Jeff Davis Legion after dark and the 10th Virginia rejoined the brigade late on September 17, or early the following day, after its circuitous ride from Leesburg via Winchester.[29]

## Williamsport

Following the Battle of Sharpsburg, Robert E. Lee hoped to reenter Maryland and gain a better foothold than his position at Sharpsburg offered. Hampton's brigade crossed the Potomac River late on September 18 and proceeded up the south side of the river to Mason's Ford near Williamsport. The brigade crossed back into Maryland and joined Jeb Stuart, in command of a mixed force of cavalry, infantry, and artillery. Making a demonstration on the 20th, the Confederates were confronted by nearly 2,000 Union cavalry and Darius Couch's IV Corps division. The brigade sustained no casualties and returned to Virginia late in the day.[30]

The Maryland Campaign was over. Mississippian E.A. Turner of the Jeff Davis Legion summed it up best, writing home "Since I wrote last I have seen and gone through a great deal. Our trip to Maryland was not a very pleasant one. There was not much rest for men nor horse day nor night. Our horses wore the saddle nearly all the time. We had picket and cavalry fighting almost every day." Hampton's brigade established camp along the Opequon Creek between Shepherdstown and Martinsburg, Virginia. In October, Phillips' Georgia Legion joined the brigade, and in November the 10th Virginia Cavalry left to become part of Brig. Gen. W.H.F. Lee's new brigade. Each unit in the brigade also contributed a detachment for Stuart's Chambersburg Raid, October 10 – 12.[31]

**Robert Gottschalk**

\* \* \*

## Fitzhugh Lee's Brigade: Brigadier General Fitzhugh Lee

**Units:** 1st Virginia Cavalry, 3rd Virginia Cavalry, 4th Virginia Cavalry, 5th Virginia Cavalry, 9th Virginia Cavalry
**Strength:** 1,959[32]
**Losses:** 80[33]

Fitzhugh Lee's brigade contained the venerable 1st Virginia Cavalry, first led by Jeb Stuart that participated in First Bull Run. It was formed in July 1861, with the 3rd Virginia Cavalry. The 4th Virginia Cavalry was added in September of that year, but the remaining units did not join until the following year. Stuart initially commanded the brigade, which first saw action at the Battle of Seven Pines (Fair Oaks) in late May/early June 1862. Only the 1st, 2nd, and 4th Virginia Cavalry comprised the brigade at the time and they were joined by the Jeff Davis Legion, the Hampton Legion, and Wise's Legion. The entire brigade saw action during the Seven Days' Battles. When the large cavalry brigade was split into two brigades prior to Second Bull Run, Fitzhugh Lee was given command of one of them.[34]

Fitzhugh was the nephew of Robert E. Lee. Born on November 19, 1835 in Alexandria, Virginia, Lee attended West Point, barely graduating because he enjoyed the "carefree life." Lee's subsequent life in the U.S. Army was anything but ordinary. After a stint at the Carlisle Barracks in Pennsylvania, he was shipped south to Texas to fight Comanches. He received an arrow wound that pierced both lungs leaving him thinking, "I was going to die." After recuperating from his wound, he headed back to West Point as a cavalry instructor and was there when the war broke out. Fitz Lee immediately offered his services to the Confederacy and became an aide to Brig. Gen. Richard Ewell. He later became the lieutenant colonel of the celebrated 1st Virginia Cavalry led by Jeb Stuart. When Stuart left to command the cavalry brigade, Lee was promoted to colonel and assumed command of his regiment on April 23, 1862. He and his horsemen joined in the ride around McClellan's army, continuing to impress Jeb Stuart in the process. Fitz Lee was promoted to brigadier general on July 24, 1862 and given his own cavalry brigade. Not everyone approved of his elevation. Col. Thomas Cobb noted, "I confess that I was a little annoyed this morning by the announcement . . . I suppose in a few days we will see the balance of the Lee's promoted also." His performance at Second Bull Run was anything but stellar, causing Stuart to barely escape capture. His superior scolded his "dilatory behavior." The Maryland Campaign would be Fitz Lee's opportunity for redemption.[35]

## Preliminary Actions

Fitz Lee's men were in the saddle and heading toward Alexandria on the morning of September 3 to demonstrate in that sector. The brigade was recalled and headed back to Leesburg, and on September 5, it was the first of Stuart's brigades to cross the Potomac River at Edward's Ferry. The 5th Virginia Cavalry was in the van and the 9th Virginia Cavalry brought up the rear. After crossing, the brigade rode to Poolesville where it encountered a detachment of the 1st Massachusetts making its way

through town. The outnumbered Bay Staters immediately turned and retreated but obstructions in the town caused the horses to lose their footing and the Virginians caught up with them, capturing over 30 men and wounding eight or nine more. Lee lost seven men during this encounter. Fitz Lee's men then reunited with Hampton's brigade and both headed north to Urbana, screening the rear of Lee's army. Lee's brigade formed Stuart's right flank (facing north), and remained at New Market, southeast of Frederick on the Baltimore and Ohio Railroad until September 12. The 1st Virginia Cavalry was apparently detached while the brigade was still at New Market on September 10 and sent north with James Longstreet's column to Hagerstown to protect his flank and rear from a possible enemy movement from Pennsylvania.

## South Mountain

Fitz Lee received orders on September 11 to hover around the enemy's right flank to ascertain its strength and the meaning of its movements by gaining "the enemy's rear from his position on the left." This information was vital to D.H. Hill holding Turner's Gap at South Mountain. Lee's men were in the saddle at 11:00 a.m. that day, riding north, skirting Frederick and halting for the night at Liberty. He then led his men west toward Frederick on September 12, and after remaining in its outskirts for most of the day, led his command to Shookstown, at the foot of Catoctin Mountain, as the sun rose on September 13. Lee permitted his men to rest until 2:00 p.m., when the column rode north along the base of the mountain to Hamburg Pass. The brigade reached it by sunset, and then headed up the pass, camping on the eastern slope of the mountain. The march resumed at dawn on September 14, when the men reached the top of the pass and rode down the western side of the mountain to an apple orchard where they rested until 4:00 p.m. The march continued over South Mountain to Boonsboro, which the column reached about sunset. Fitz Lee was called to meet with Robert E. Lee that evening who told him the army was pulling back from the South Mountain gaps and he was to move his command up the mountainside and replace the infantry pickets facing the Union army.[36]

The brigade was missing yet another regiment, for while it was still at New Market on September 11, Col. Tom Rosser's 5th Virginia Cavalry was sent toward Westminster with two cannon. Stuart ordered Rosser's men to turn around and head to Fox's Gap that evening and they were in position on the morning of September 14 as the IX Corps headed in their direction. The two cannon opened fire on the approaching troops and Rosser held his position until Samuel Garland's North Carolina brigade arrived.[37]

Fitz Lee marched his three regiments from Boonsboro toward Turner's Gap on the National Road just after midnight on September 15. The Virginians were ordered to halt about a mile and a half east of Boonsboro and prepare for action at daylight on September 15. The brigade was tasked with buying time for Longstreet's men to make their way to safety. The 3rd Virginia Cavalry held the front and flanks of the brigade, the 9th Virginia Cavalry was behind it in the road in column formation, and the 4th Virginia Cavalry was further in the rear, nearest Boonsboro. Two cannon were strategically placed on high ground near the National Road. Micah Jenkins' brigade (under James Walker) passed the brigade as daylight approached, so there were no Confederate infantry troops between Fitz Lee and the Union army. Israel Richardson's division (II Corps) was the first unit to march through Turner's Gap that morning. The enemy pushed hard against the 3rd Virginia Cavalry's skirmish line and came under fire from Lee's two cannon. The stubborn Confederate defense forced Richardson to halt. He brought up the crack 5th New Hampshire and deployed it as skirmishers on either side of the road. Their determined advance caused Lee to limber his two cannons, followed by the supporting 4th Virginia Cavalry, and all headed for Boonsboro. The 9th Virginia Cavalry then turned and followed, and the 3rd Virginia Cavalry brought up the rear.

Richardson's men moved off the road to allow the 8th Illinois Cavalry to gallop down the National Road and into Boonsboro where they encountered the 3rd Virginia Cavalry. The Illinois boys were eventually forced to break off the attack and fall back. They were not yet finished, for they reformed and charged again, and this time they drove the 3rd Virginia Cavalry from town.

Fitz Lee's other two regiments, the 4th and 9th Virginia Cavalry, exhausted from their exertions over the past four days, had dismounted in the town when they were ordered to "Mount! Mount!" Before they could do so, the 3rd Virginia Cavalry barreled into them creating havoc. Young Lt. George Beale of the 9th Virginia Cavalry recalled, "in an incredibly short time the street became packed with a mass of horses and horsemen, so jammed together as to make motion impossible for most of them." Gunfire erupted from some of the buildings and the 8th Illinois Cavalry arrived and emptied their carbines into the mass of helpless Virginians. The 4th Virginia Cavalry was finally able to untangle itself and open a way for the rest of the men to gallop to safety. It was complete chaos. According to historian Ezra Carman, "Here and there in the pell-mell race, blinded by the dust, horses and horsemen dashed against telegraph poles and fell to the ground to be trampled by those behind." A charge by most of the 9th Virginia Cavalry and a squadron of the 4th Virginia Cavalry helped cool the Illinois troops' ardor. The historian of the 9th Virginia Cavalry recalled the "column became a confused mass, hurrying without order down the pike, and many escaping through the fields." The Illinois horsemen followed for about a mile before turning back. Fitz Lee was able to rally his men near Keedysville on Boonsboro Pike and then head for Sharpsburg. The historian of the 8th Illinois Cavalry claimed Fitz Lee lost 30 dead and 50 wounded.[38]

While most of Fitz Lee's men covered the National Road, Tom Rosser's 5th Virginia Cavalry, which had opened the fight at Fox's Gap, was still in the area, and ordered to assume the rearguard for the infantry and artillery which carried the subsequent bitter fight. The regiment did not encounter the same enemy pursuit as Fitz Lee's other regiments.

**Antietam**

The battered brigade finally reached the Middle Bridge over Antietam Creek about noon on September 15 and bivouacked in the fields near the Dunker Church. Because Fitz Lee arrived on the battlefield before Munford's and Hampton's brigades, his men were thrown out on both flanks of the army—south beyond the Lower Bridge and north toward the Upper Bridge. Upon Munford's arrival, Fitz Lee concentrated his units on Lee's left flank, covering Hagerstown Pike and Smoketown Road. . Stuart positioned over a dozen cannon on Nicodemus Heights during the night of September 16-17 and ordered Fitz Lee to defend them by deploying his men on the west side of the hill. With his men in position, Fitz Lee rode up the hill and went to sleep under a small tree. He was later joined by Stonewall Jackson. The brigade remained near Nicodemus Heights until Jubal Early's brigade arrived on the morning of September 17. The brigade then moved further west, near the Cox house where the men rested. The 9th Virginia Cavalry was sent to Jackson who ordered it to round up stragglers, who were moving through Sharpsburg. These men were resupplied with ammunition and sent back to the front. [39]

Stuart assembled seven of his regiments to attack the Union right flank at about 1:00 p.m. Fitz Lee contributed three of his regiments (3rd, 4th, and 5th Virginia Cavalry) who were near River Road. The column reached New Industry, when it turned to the right to take on the enemy. The massed Union artillery opened fire, ending the attempt.

The 1st Virginia Cavalry missed most of the latter part of the campaign. After accompanying Longstreet's wagon trains across the Potomac River on September 15, it continued its march the following day through Martinsburg to Shepherdstown, where it recrossed the Potomac River and rejoined Fitz Lee's brigade on the left of the army.

According to Stuart, Fitz Lee handled the "the delicate and difficult duty of covering the movement" of the army across the Potomac River on the evening of September 18. It finally crossed the river on the morning of September 19. The brigade had performed effectively in its mission of screening the army and seeking the location of McClellan's army. Its performance at Boonsboro became, however, a black mark on Fitz Lee's record. [40] **Bradley M. Gottfried**

* * *

## Robertson's Brigade: Colonel Thomas Munford

**Units:** 2nd Virginia, 7th Virginia, 12th Virginia, 17th Virginia Battalion
**Strength:** 1,647[41]
**Losses:** Under 50[42]

Brig. Gen. Beverly Robertson's brigade was an effective fighting unit under the command of a questionable leader. The 2nd Virginia Cavalry began its Confederate service on July 1, 1861 as the 30th Virginia Mounted Infantry, but changed its designation on October 31, 1861. The 7th Virginia Cavalry also began its service on July 1 and initially contained 29 one-year companies. Ten of these companies were cleaved off to form the 12th Virginia Cavalry and another seven to form the 17th Virginia Battalion. These units fought together under Thomas Jackson's command in the Shenandoah Valley.[43]

Robertson received orders on September 5 to report to the Department of North Carolina where "his services are indispensably necessary for the organization and instruction of cavalry troops . . ." This was a convenient way for Lee to rid his army of a leader "not deemed a very efficient officer."

One of Stuart's staff officers noted Robertson "was an excellent man in camp to train troops, but in the field, in the presence of the enemy, he lost all self-possession, and was perfectly unreliable." Col. Thomas Munford of the 2nd Virginia Cavalry took over the brigade as it rode deeper into Maryland. Munford was born in Virginia on March 28, 1831 and graduated from the Virginia Military Academy. Formerly a planter, Munford entered the war as lieutenant colonel of the 30th Virginia Mounted Infantry which became the 2nd Virginia Cavalry. He fought in nearly every engagement from First Bull Run to Appomattox.[44]

**Preliminary Actions**

The brigade got off to a bad start when on the night of September 2, "by a misapprehension of the order [it] returned to the vicinity of Chantilly" rather than bivouacking with the rest of the division at Fairfax Court House. Munford and his regiment were sent north to Leesburg ahead of the army to rout "a party of marauders" under Captain S.C. Means who had "long infested that country and harassed the inhabitants." Munford successfully drove these troops from the town with few losses. Robertson's brigade camped near Dranesville, Virginia on the night of September 3 and headed south toward Falls Church to deceive the enemy into thinking an attack on Washington was imminent and, in the words of Gen. Robertson, "hold him in check while our army was crossing the Potomac above." The brigade then headed north to Leesburg, crossed the Potomac River on the afternoon of September 6, and continued toward Poolesville. The now Robertson-less brigade arrived at Urbana that day, where it camped with the rest of Stuart's command. Munford's new command occupied the right of Stuart's line (as it faced south). It held the important Sugar Loaf Mountain, valued by both armies as an observation post, with pickets extending as far south as Poolesville. When Stuart realized the enemy's cavalry were pushing north to occupy Poolesville, he pushed Munford's brigade toward that town on September 8. The brigade was reduced to only the 2nd, 7th and 12th Virginia Cavalry, as the 17th Virginia Cavalry Battalion was on detached service.[45]

Munford's advanced units reached Poolesville and encountered the 3rd Indiana Cavalry and 8th Illinois Cavalry (John Farnsworth's brigade). Munford quickly brought up his 7th and 12th Virginia Cavalry and deployed them for action. He had a howitzer and a Blakely Rifle from Roger Chew's battery with him and they opened fire on the enemy troopers. Farnsworth responded by bringing up a section of Battery M, 2nd U. S. Artillery under Lt. Robert Chapin, who opened fire on Chew's guns. The Union troopers almost immediately charged Chew's howitzer. It fired two rounds of canister, dampening their ardor and causing them to quickly withdraw. Munford quickly brought up the 7th Virginia Cavalry and later reported the regiment "charged them handsomely." Another body of enemy troopers charged the Blakely, but was driven off by the 75 men of the 12th Virginia Cavalry. Munford praised the regiment's commander but reported that a portion of the regiment "behaved very badly." Munford retreated toward Barnesville, followed by Farnsworth, who attacked on the morning of September 9, who drove back the 12th Virginia and captured its flag.[46]

Munford's brigade lost another chunk of its manpower when the 7th Virginia was detached and sent north to accompany Stonewall Jackson's column to Harpers Ferry on September 10. Munford deployed his remaining two regiments at the crossroads leading to Sugar Loaf Mountain, which he was ordered to defend. The 2nd Virginia Cavalry occupied the crossroads, southeast of the Mountain, its men protected by fence rails they assembled into a barricade. The 12th Virginia Cavalry was deployed to their right-rear. On September 10, a portion of the 6th U. S. Cavalry attempted to take the crossroads, but they were driven away by the Virginia sharpshooters. The brigade faced an insurmountable challenge on September 11 when Union infantry appeared. Pleasonton informed McClellan the day before of his inability to take the high ground after three attempts, so the army commander ordered William Franklin (VI Corps) to assist. Franklin sent a brigade of Darius Couch's division (IV Corps) with the promise that the entire command could be used, if Pleasonton needed it. Couch, Franklin, and Pleasonton apparently did not share McClellan's urgency, and waited until September 11 to begin the effort. The delay prevented the Union signal corps from seeing Lee's army leave Frederick, bound for destinations to the west and north. The push was finally made during the afternoon, when Farnsworth's cavalry brigade, supported by Winfield Hancock's brigade (William Smith's division; VI Corps) advanced and quickly ended the Confederates' hold on Sugar Loaf Mountain. Stuart ordered Munford to fall back to Jefferson to guard the gap in the Catoctin Mountain there and screen the rear of the army.[47]

## South Mountain

Munford's men did not remain long in Jefferson as he realized his 400 or so men were no match for Farnsworth's cavalry brigade, including the 6th U. S. Cavalry, 6th Pennsylvania Cavalry and Harrison Fairchild's infantry brigade (Isaac Rodman's division, IX Corps) sent from Frederick to support the cavalry. Munford wrote in his report how the enemy appeared on September 12 with the "enemy's infantry pressing us on three roads." Munford quickly left the hamlet and headed to Burkittsville at the foot of Crampton's Gap in South Mountain the following day with Farnsworth's men nipping at his heals the whole way. Munford also worried about his brigade's wagons, which accompanied the two regiments. The Virginians stubbornly resisted the enemy's pursuit. Upon reaching Burkittsville, Munford sent his vulnerable wagons through Crampton's Gap, deployed his artillery pieces half way up the mountain, and scattered his two regiments at its base behind a stout stone wall. Stuart apparently gave Munford the opportunity to stay or ride to assist McLaws. He chose to stay and ordered the

horses to the rear because his men would fight as infantry. On the morning of September 14, Munford received a message from Stuart that he was to "hold the gap at all hazards."[48]

Farnsworth's cavalry was relieved and Fairchild's brigade returned to Frederick. Munford did not know it, but another body of cavalry, composed of the 8th Illinois Cavalry and a portion of the 3rd Indiana Cavalry on their way to Harpers Ferry from Turner's Gap, were now approaching his position. Fortunately, Wade Hampton's brigade was in the area and it pitched into the Union cavalry, driving them from the field.[49]

This was a difficult time for Munford. He wrote in his report, "As soon as his [the enemy's] skirmishers were deployed, he advanced one regiment of infantry in line of battle, which was immediately followed by four others. In half an hour five other regiments appeared on their left and advanced in the same way, and in a very short time another brigade appeared in rear of those who had preceded them." Munford did not know it but he would soon be facing four VI Corps infantry brigades. Some help was on the way. William Mahone's small Virginia brigade, under the command of Col. William Parham, arrived as did eight companies of the 10th Georgia. Munford deployed his two regiments on either side of Burkittstown Road leading from the town that crossed over Crampton's Gap to Pleasant Valley. Munford positioned his two cavalry regiments on opposite flanks to act as sharpshooters: the 2nd Virginia Cavalry was on the right and the 12th Virginia Cavalry on the left. Parham's infantry extended the line to the left. Howell Cobb would send additional regiments to assist, but until they arrived, Munford's 1,200 infantry and cavalry would be up against the Union VI Corps with 12,000 Union troops, supported by 13 artillery pieces.[50]

Three of the Union brigades made their attack at about 3:00 p.m. Driving forward against the small force of defenders, the Yanks quickly drove them from their positions at the base of the mountain. The Confederates scrambled up the hillside, but those moving too slowly were captured or bayoneted. Reinforcements from Cobb's brigade arrived and were either overwhelmed as they got into position, or beat a hasty retreat. Munford blamed Cobb for the defeat, noting in his report, "Had General Cobb's brigade given the support to the first troops engaged which they deserved, the gap would have been held." He added, "Had General Cobb come up in time, the result might have been otherwise."

How ardently Munford's cavalry held the gap is debatable. Munford noted, "The fight we had at Crampton's Gap was the heaviest I ever engaged in, and the cavalry fought here with pistols against rifles." However, he lists only three casualties in the 2nd Virginia Cavalry and none for the 12th Virginia Cavalry, suggesting they may have skedaddled as the Union infantry approached. Given the mismatch in numbers, they cannot be blamed for their actions.[51]

## Antietam

Munford and his brigade passed through Crampton's Gap to Pleasant Valley. He received a message from Robert E. Lee at 10:15 p.m. that night: "Hold your position at Rohrersville, if possible, and if you can discover or hear of a practicable road below Crampton's Gap by which McLaws, at Weverton at present, can pass over the mountains to Sharpsburg, send him a messenger to guide him over immediately." Munford knew of no such road and immediately informed Lee and McLaws. Lee subsequently ordered Munford to remain in Rohrersville until morning and then rejoin the army at Sharpsburg. Daylight of September 15 found Franklin's VI Corps moving into the Pleasant Valley, hastening Munford's ride to Sharpsburg via what is now called "Burnside Bridge Road." The route took the brigade through Porterstown to the Lower Bridge, where it formed on the right of Robert Toombs' brigade and guarded the approaches to Sharpsburg from the east and south. The brigade occupied a large cornfield, facing due east, just above Myers' Ford, 500 yards southwest of

Snavely Ford, with its right at the Antietam Furnace near the Creek. Munford sent his skirmish line through the corn to its eastern edge. These men opened fire on Edward Harland's brigade (Isaac Rodman's division; IX Corps) who crossed Antietam Creek at Snavely Ford and were moving inland. It appears that Munford's command was strengthened by the temporary addition of Col. Matthew Butler's 1st South Carolina Cavalry.[52]

The 7th Virginia Cavalry returned to the Sharpsburg area on the afternoon of September 16 when it crossed the Potomac River at Shepherstown Ford and headed north to Ground Squirrel Church along Hagerstown Pike. The men dismounted and assumed a defensive position on both sides of the pike. The troopers did not realize they were only 600 yards south of a portion of the 3rd Pennsylvania Cavalry and a half mile north of Abner Doubleday's division (I Corps). The men understood their plight at first light on September 17 and quickly headed north to New Industry on the Potomac River and remained there until the afternoon, when the unit moved south to rejoin the brigade near the Blackford house, about a mile south of Sharpsburg on Miller's Sawmill Road. Munford claimed he conferred with A.P. Hill when he approached the battlefield in the afternoon.[53]

Munford's brigade played an important role in the Maryland Campaign. It screened Lee's right flank and rear as the army left Frederick. The brigade also defended Sugar Loaf Mountain longer than could have been expected, given his small command. Its fight at Crampton's Gap was not auspicious, but was probably as good as could be expected, given the overwhelming disparity in numbers. During the Battle of Antietam, the brigade protected Lee's extreme right flank along Antietam Creek. Munford performed credibly and while he would effectively command a brigade at several points during the war and ended it commanding a division, he was never promoted to the rank of brigadier general.[54]

**Bradley M. Gottfried**

# ENDNOTES

## I Corps

1. Ezra Carman, *The Maryland Campaign of 1862*, Thomas Clemens, ed. 3 volumes (El Dorado Hills: Savas Beatie, 2010, 2012), vol. I, 151. President Lincoln was impressed with Hooker's self-confidence. In Lincoln's January 26, 1863 letter to Hooker, appointing him to command the Army of the Potomac, Lincoln wrote, "You have confidence in yourself, which is a valuable, if not an indispensable quality."

2. Carman, *The Maryland Campaign*, vol. I, 148, 151. The III Corps, which had been temporarily assigned to the Army of Virginia from June-September, 1862, was redesignated the I Corps, Army of the Potomac. It's commander, Maj. Gen. Irvin McDowell, was relieved following the defeat at Second Bull Run.

3. Carman, *The Maryland Campaign*, vol. I, 204.

4. United States War Department: *The War of the Rebellion: A Compilation of the Official Records of the Union and Confederate Armies*, 128 volumes (Washington: U.S. Government Printing Office, 1880-1901), vol. 19, pt. 1, 214, hereafter *OR*.

5. *OR* 19, pt. 1, 215.

6. Carman, *The Maryland Campaign*, vol. I, 411.

7. *OR* 19, pt. 1, 217, 475; Carman, *The Maryland Campaign*, vol. II, 27, 573. Hooker gives his strength upon crossing Antietam Creek as between 12,000-13,000 in his official report, but the aggregate of the division reports is 9,438.

8. James M. McPherson, *Crossroads of Freedom: Antietam, The Battle That Changed the Course of the Civil War*, (New York, NY: Oxford University Press, 2002), 117. Hooker quoted in *New York Times* article, September 20, 1862.

9. Joseph L. Harsh, *Taken at the Flood: Robert E. Lee & Confederate Strategy in the Maryland Campaign of 1862*, (Kent, OH: The Kent State University Press, 1999), 370; *OR* 19, pt. 1, 218.

10. D. Scott Hartwig, *To Antietam Creek: The Maryland Campaign* (Baltimore, MD: The Johns Hopkins University Press, 2012), 80.

11. Harsh, *Taken at the Flood*, 372.

12. *OR* 19, pt. 1, 475.

13. *OR* 19, pt. 1, 219; Walter H. Hebert, *Fighting Joe Hooker* (Indianapolis, IN: The Bobbs-Merrill Company, 1944), 142-43.

14. Scott Hartwig personal communication, 9 December 2020.

15. *OR* 19, pt. 1, 219; Janet B. Hewett, Noah Andre Trudeau, and Bryce A. Suderow, eds., *Supplement to the Official Records of the Union and Confederate Armies*, 100 volumes (Wilmington, NC: Broadfoot Publishing Company, 1994), vol. 3, 456. Hereafter, *OR Suppl.*

16. John H. Eicher and David J. Eicher, *Civil War High Commands* (Stanford, CA: Stanford University Press, 2001), 333; *OR* 12, pt. 2, 254; Ezra J. Warner, *Generals in Blue: Lives of the Union Commanders* (Baton Rouge, LA: Louisiana State University Press, 1991), 269-70. King resigned his commission on October 20, 1863 and resumed his post as Minister to the Papal States. He died in 1876.

17. Warner, *Generals in Blue*, 216-17. Hatch recovered from his leg wound in February, 1863 but was assigned light duty until July of 1864 when he led the Union forces at the Battle of Honey Hill and later fought under General William Sherman.

18. *OR* 19, pt. 1, 220-21.

19. *OR* 19, pt. 1, 184, 220, 221-22. Hatch was one of the few generals who earned the Medal of Honor, which he received in 1893. His citation read: "Was severely wounded while leading one of his brigades in the attack under a heavy fire from the enemy." https://www.cmohs.org/recipients/john-p-hatch.

20. *OR* 19, pt. 1, 223-26.

21. *OR* 19, pt. 1, 190; Frederick H. Dyer, *A Compendium of the War of the Rebellion*, 3 volumes (New York: Tomas Yoseloff, 1959), vol. 1, 184, 284.

22. Col. Phelps reported his strength at South Mountain as less than 400, but he also reported his strength at Antietam as 425. This may be caused by the 2nd USS being detached at South Mountain, but included in his Antietam strength. *OR* 19, pt. 1, 232, 234.

23. Phelps' initial report stated the brigade at Antietam lost 10 officers killed and wounded, 147 men killed and wounded, and 29 men missing, but the figures were revised to 95 total casualties in a later total. Phelps listed far more missing in his initial report for a total of 186, the true number is more likely the former. *OR* 19, pt. 1, 189, 234.

24. Roger D. Hunt and Jack R. Brown, *Brevet Brigadiers in Blue* (Gaithersburg, MD: Olde Soldier Books, 1990), 479. Through the generosity of Phelps' great granddaughter, his diary, papers, letters and scrapbook are in the U.S. Army Military History Institute in Carlisle PA. See Walter

Phelps Jr. Papers, Manuscript Division, U.S. Army Military History Institute (hereafter USAMHI).

25. William F. Fox, *Regimental Losses in the Civil War* (Dayton, OH: Morningside Press, 1985), 117.

26. S.E. Chandler, *Brooklyn Eagle*, April 25, 1898. Several other sources refer to the same march and use the term Iron Brigade. C. V. Tevis and D. R. Marquis, *History of the Fighting Fourteenth* (Brooklyn: Brooklyn Eagle, 1911), 34-5; Samuel R. Beardsley letter dated August 13, 1862, near Culpeper C.H. Samuel R. Beardsley Papers, USAMHI. A host of post war memorabilia, including badges, ribbons, and medals are labeled First Iron Brigade, or New York Iron Brigade, author's collection. For a more thorough discussion see Tom Clemens, "'Black Hats' Off to the Original 'Iron Brigade,'" *Columbiad*, vol. 1, Number 1, (Spring, 1997), 46-58.

27. The strength of the brigade on Aug. 28 was 2,475, and with 772 casualties deducted, and they went into the fight at South Mountain with a mere 400 men, leaving roughly 1,300 men absent men as unaccounted. Again the counts may not include the 2nd U.S. Sharpshooters. *OR* 12, pt. 2, 254; *OR* 19, pt. 1, 232.

28. Walter Phelps Jr. to Emmaline, Aug. 29, 1862, USAMHI.

29. Walter Phelps Jr. to Emmaline, Sept. 6, 1862, USAMHI.

30. Walter Phelps Jr. to Emmaline, Sept. 13, 1862, USAMHI.

31. Carman, *The Maryland Campaign,* vol. I, 360; *OR* 19, pt. 1, 231-2.

32. Carman, *The Maryland Campaign,* vol. I, 360-62.

33. *OR* 19, pt. 1, 231-32; John Bryson, "Manuscript History of the 30th New York Infantry Regiment," New York State Library, Albany, NY.

34. Walter Phelps Jr. to Emmaline, Sept. 16, 1862, USAMHI; *OR* 19, pt. 1, 232. The brigade losses at South Mountain were 20 killed, 67 wounded, and 8 missing, or 25-percent.

35. S. E. Chandler to J.M. Gould, April 15,1893, John Gould Papers, Dartmouth College Library, Andover, NH.

36. *OR* 19, pt. 1, 232.

37. David P. Craig to John M. Gould, Jan. 15, 1892; Wm. H. Humphrey to John. M. Gould, March 23, 1893.

38. Dawes, Rufus R. *Service with the Sixth Wisconsin Volunteers* (Marietta, Ohio: E. P. Alderman & Sons, 1890), 90. Although Dawes called them Zouaves because of the red trousers, in fact the 14th Brooklyn's trousers were a style called "chasseur" which were not the true Zouave style. It was a common mistake, then and now.

39. Walter Phelps Jr. to Emmaline, September 18, 1862, USAMHI. The Quartermaster, as Phelps called him, was James W. Schenck Jr., who was the quartermaster for the 22nd New York, and also Phelps' brother in law.

40. John Bryson to John M. Gould, October 18, 1893; John Dargan to John M. Gould, October 4, 1893; Phelps Papers, USAMHI.

41. The breakdown of Antietam losses was: 30 killed, 120 wounded and 4 missing. *OR* 19, pt. 1, 189; Walter Phelps Jr. to Emmaline, September 18, 1862, USAMHI; Thomas Reed, *The Original Iron Brigade* (Madison, NJ: Fairleigh Dickinson University Press, 2011), 156. Phelps' lack of success obtaining a general's star may be attributed to most of his brigade mustering out, but also he was a Democrat and his letters often expressed his commitment to McClellan commanding the army. By the spring of 1863 these views were not compatible with promotion in the Army of the Potomac.

42. Hartwig, *To Antietam Creek*, Appendix B, Strength of Union and Confederate Forces. Hartwig estimated the brigade numbered 829 at Antietam, but see Carman, *The Maryland Campaign*, vol. II, 572.

43. *OR* 19, pt. 1, 189. The brigade lost an additional 59 men on September 14 (3k; 52w; 4m). *OR* 19, pt. 1, 184.

44. Dyer, *A Compendium of the War of the Rebellion*, vol. 1, 284; vol. 3, 1120, 1434, 1442, 1593.

45. A. P. Smith, *History of the Seventy-Sixth Regiment New York Volunteers: What it Endured and Accomplished* (Cortland, NY: Jacob Miller, Binder, 1866), 147-48; *Cherry Valley Gazette* (NY), October 1, 1862.

46. Smith, *History of the Seventy-Sixth Regiment New York Volunteers*, 148- 49.

47. *Cherry Valley Gazette*, October 1, 1862; *OR* 19, pt. 1, 220.

48. Smith, *History of the Seventy-Sixth Regiment New York Volunteers*, 152; Matthew Hurlenger Diary, September 14, 1862 entry, copy in the 56th Pennsylvania file, Antietam National Battlefield Library, (hereafter ANB Library).

49. *OR* 19, pt. 1, 222, 234-35; Edward L. Barnes, "The 95th New York," *National Tribune*, January 7, 1886.

50. *OR* 19, pt. 1, 235; Smith, *History of the Seventy-Sixth Regiment New York Volunteers*, 153; *Cherry Valley Gazette*, October 1, 1862.

51. Orville Thomson, *From Philippi to Appomattox: Narrative of the Service of the Seventh Indiana Infantry in the War for the Union* (Baltimore, MD: Butternut & Blue, 1993), 126-27; *OR* 19, pt. 1, 239.

52. Smith, *History of the Seventy-Sixth Regiment New York Volunteers*, 164-169; *Cherry Valley Gazette*, October 1, 1862. Matthew Hurlenger Diary, September 17, 1862 entry; *OR* 19, pt. 1, 189.

53. Hartwig, *To Antietam Creek*, Appendix B, Strength of Union and Confederate Forces. Hartwig estimated that Patrick's brigade numbered 750 at Antietam.

54. *OR* 19, pt. 1, 189. The brigade lost an additional 23 men on September 14 (2k; 19w; 1m).

55. Dyer, *A Compendium of the War of the Rebellion,* vol. III, 1413, 1417, 1436; *OR* 5, 15-16, 57. *OR* 19, pt. 1, 184.

56. Albert D. Shaw, *A Full Report of the First Re-union and Banquet of the Thirty-Fifth N. Y. Vols.* (Watertown N.Y.: Times Printing and Publishing House, 1888; Reprint Higginson Book Company Salem Massachusetts 1998), 25.

57. Theodore B. Gates, *The "Ulster Guard" [20th N. Y. State Militia] and the War of the Rebellion* (New York: Benj. H. Tyrrel, 1879), 286-87, 293; J. Harrison Mills, *Chronicles of the Twenty-First Regiment New York State Volunteers Embracing the Full History of the Regiment* (Buffalo, NY: The 21st Reg't Veteran Association of Buffalo, 1887), 277-78.

58. *OR*, 19, pt. 1, 241-242; Carman, *The Maryland Campaign*, vol. I, 358-59; Daniel Harvey Hill, "The Battle of South Mountain, or 'Boonsboro,'" *Battles & Leaders of the Civil War*, vol. 2, 573-74.

59. Carman, *The Maryland Campaign*, vol. II, 360. As the men of the 21st New York headed up the hill they encountered an old woman who was obviously frightened. She inquired about the nature of their mission and an officer told her they were "only going up the hill." "Don't you go up there," she warned. "Some of you will get hurt" as she had seen the Rebels descending from the top of the mountain. Mills, *Chronicles of the Twenty-First Regiment*, 280.

60. *OR* 19, pt. 1, 231-32, 241-42; Carman, *The Maryland Campaign*, vol. II, 360-61.

61. Carman, *The Maryland Campaign*, vol. I, 362-63, 379; *OR* 19, pt. 1, 241, 242.

62. Gates, *The "Ulster Guard"*, 308, 310; Mills, *Chronicles of the Twenty-First Regiment*, 289; W. L. Rogers to Ezra Carman, January 19, 1893, NA-AS.

63. *OR*, 19, pt. 1, 243-44; R. L. Murray, *New Yorkers in the Civil War A Historic Journal* (Wolcott, NY: Benedum Books, 2004), vol. 4, 77-78; Edmund J. Raus, Jr., *Banners South A Northern Community at War*. (Kent OH: The Kent State University Press 2005), 202-203.

64. *OR*, 19, pt. 1, 244.

65. Carman, *The Maryland Campaign*, vol. II, 105-07; Mills, *Chronicles of the Twenty-First Regiment New York State Volunteers*, 290; Murray, *New Yorkers in the Civil War*, 77-78.

66. *OR*, 19, pt. 1, 244; Carman, *The Maryland Campaign*, vol. II, 107, 109, 158.

67. Murray, *New Yorkers in the Civil War*, 77-78; Carman, *The Maryland Campaign*, vol. II, 159-61.

68. *OR*, 19, pt. 1, 244; Carman, *The Maryland Campaign*, vol. II, 216; Rogers to Ezra Carman, January 19, 1893, NA-AS..

69. Carman, *The Maryland Campaign*, vol. II, 217, 219, 221.

70. Mills, *Chronicles of the Twenty-First Regiment New York State Volunteers*, 308.

71. Hartwig, *To Antietam Creek*, Appendix B.

72. *OR* 19, pt. 1, 189.

73. Alan T. Nolan and Marc Storch, "The Iron Brigade Earns its Name," *Blue and Gray Magazine*, vol. XXI, Issue 6 (2004), 6-7.

74. John Gibbon, *Personal Recollections of the Civil War* (Dayton, OH: Morningside Bookshop, 1988), 14.

75. Gibbon, *Personal Recollections*, 55.

76. Alan T. Nolan and Marc Storch, "The Iron Brigade Earns Its Name", *Blue & Gray Magazine*, 7; Alan T.

Nolan, *The Iron Brigade: A Military History* (Bloomington, IN: Indiana University Press, 1961), 115-17.

77. Nolan and Storch, "The Iron Brigade Earns Its Name," 11.

78. *OR* 19, pt. 1, 247-248; Carman, *The Maryland Campaign*, vol. I, 363; Nolan, *The Iron Brigade*, 121-22; Dawes, *Service with the Sixth Wisconsin Volunteers*, 81; Craig L. Dunn, *Iron Men, Iron Will: The Nineteenth Indiana Regiment of the Iron Brigade* (Indianapolis, IN: Guild Press, 1995), 94-97.

79. Carman, *The Maryland Campaign*, 365-67, 379; Gibbon, *Personal Recollections*, 77-79; William J. K. Beaudot and Lance J. Herdegen, eds., *An Irishman in the Iron Brigade: The Civil War Memoirs of James P. Sullivan, Sergt., Company K, 6th Wisconsin Volunteers* (New York: Fordham University Press, 1993), 60; *OR* 19, pt. 1, 247-248, 252-53, 253-54, 256; Dawes, *Service with the Sixth Wisconsin Volunteers*, 83-84; Lance J. Herdegen, *The Iron Brigade in the Civil War and Memory: The Black Hats from Bull Run to Appomattox and Thereafter* (El Dorado Hills, CA: Savas Beatie, 2012), 235-36; *Cincinnati Daily Commercial*, September 22, 1862; . Colquitt reportedly suffered 110 casualties.

80. *OR* 19, pt. 1, 247-248; Gibbon, *Personal Recollections*, 79-80. Nolan and Storch, "The Iron Brigade Earns Its Name," 19; Hartwig, *To Antietam Creek*, Appendix B.

81. *OR* 19, pt. 1, 247-248; Gibbon, *Personal Recollections*, 80. Nolan and Storch, "The Iron Brigade Earns Its Name," 19-20; Hartwig, *To Antietam Creek*, Appendix B.

82. *OR* 19, pt. 1, 247-248; Gibbon, *Personal Recollections*, 81-82. Nolan and Storch, "The Iron Brigade Earns Its Name," 20. Carman, *The Maryland Campaign*, vol. II, 69; Dawes, *Service with the Sixth Wisconsin Volunteers*, 87; Edward Bragg to wife, September 21, 1862, copy at ANB Library. The shells thrown at the Iron Brigade on the morning of September 17 came from Balthis and Wooding's batteries on James Stuart's artillery line on Nicodemus Heights.

83. Carman, *The Maryland Campaign*, vol. II, 71-75; Herdegen, *The Iron Brigade in Civil War*, 251-52.

84. Carman, *The Maryland Campaign*, vol. II, 76-77; Herdegen, *The Iron Brigade in Civil War*, 254.

85. Carman, *The Maryland Campaign*, vol. II, 80, 89-99; Dawes, *Service with the Sixth Wisconsin Volunteers*, 90-91.

86. Carman, *The Maryland Campaign*, vol. II, 104-106; Alan D. Gaff, *On Many A Bloody Field: Four Years in the Iron Brigade* (Bloomington, IN: Indiana University Press, 1996), 186-88; *OR* 19, pt. 1, 189.

87. Jack D. Welsh, *Medical Histories of Union Generals* (Kent, OH: Kent State University Press, 1996), 279; Warner, *Generals in Blue*, 403-04.

88. Carman, *The Maryland Campaign*, vol. I, 179, 188, 197, 347.

89. *OR*, 19, pt. 1, 258; Carman, *The Maryland Campaign*, vol. I, 353, 363, 375.

90. Carman, *The Maryland Campaign*, vol. II, 27, 57; *OR* 19, pt. 1, 258-59.

91. Carman, *The Maryland Campaign*, vol. II, 164.

92. *OR* 19, pt. 1, 259.

93. Hartwig, *To Antietam Creek*, Appendix B, Strength of Union and Confederate Forces; Carman, *The Maryland Campaign*, vol. II, 58; *OR* 19, pt. 2, 190. The brigade lost an additional 21 men on September 14 (56k; 15w). *OR* 19, pt. 1, 185.

94. Isaac Hall, *History of the Ninety-Seventh Regiment New York Volunteers*, (Utica, NY: L.C. Childs & Son, 1896), 11-13, 20-24; Franklin Hough, *History of Duryee's Brigade During the Campaign in Virginia Under General Pope and in Maryland Under General McClellan in the Summer and Autumn of 1862*, (Albany, NY: J. Munsell, 1864) 29; Historical Data Systems, Inc., http://civilwardata.com/active/product.html Conkling was a congressman from New York and Wadsworth was a philanthropist, politician, and general from Livingston County where some of the 104th New York were recruited, LeRoy was a training depot for the 105th New York. New York State Military Museum and Veterans Research Center, https://dmna.ny.gov/historic/mil-hist.htm;

95. Hough, *Duryee's Brigade*, 9-20, 28-29. Duryee is spelled *Duryea* in some accounts. Jacob Duryee commanded the 2nd Maryland in the IX Corps, which made an attack on Burnside's Bridge later in the morning. He is buried at in the Antietam National Cemetery.

96. Hough, *Duryee's Brigade*, 29, 39, 49, 52-55, 94-103; Hall, *History of the Ninety-Seventh*, 30-33; *OR* 12, 255.

97. Hough, *Duryee's Brigade*, 107-8; Hall, *Ninety-Seventh*, 81-2.

98. Hough, *Duryee's Brigade*, 108-9; Hall, *Ninety-Seventh*, 82-3.

99. Hartwig, *To Antietam Creek*, 392; Hall, *Ninety-Seventh* 87; Mary Warner Thomas & Richard A. Sauers (eds.), *The Civil War Letters of First Lieutenant James B. Thomas, Adjutant 107th Pennsylvania Volunteers*, (Baltimore, MD: Butternut & Blue, 1995), 93-94; Hough, *Duryee's Brigade*, 109-113.

100. Hartwig, *To Antietam Creek*, 392-3; Hall, *Ninety-Seventh*, 87-88; Thomas & Sauers, *Civil War Letters*, 94; Hough, *Duryee's Brigade*, 113; *OR* 19, pt. 1, 258, 261-62.

101. Hough, *Duryee's Brigade*, 114-16; Hall, *Ninety-Seventh*, 88-9.

102. Hough, *Duryee's Brigade*, 116-18; Hall, *Ninety-Seventh*, 89-91; Harsh, *Taken At The Flood*, 350-51; Joseph L. Harsh, *Sounding the Shallows: A Confederate Compendium for The Maryland Campaign* (Kent, OH: The Kent State University Press, 2000), 16-17.

103. Carman, *Maryland Campaign*, vol. II, 51-57; *OR* 19, pt. 1, 261-62; John Delaney to Battlefield Board, March 27, 1891, Gould Papers.

104. Hall, *Ninety-Seventh*, 91; Carman, Maryland Campaign, vol. II, 58-60; Henry Shaefer to Ezra Carman, Dec. 20, 1894, NA-AS. Carroll, a civil engineer from Dublin, Ireland, died of his wounds on September 29, 1862. Capt. James MacThomson commanded the 107th Pennsylvania; Maj. Charles Northrup commanded the 97th New York; Maj. Lewis Skinner commanded the 104th New York and Col. Howard Carroll commanded the 105th New York.

105. Hall, *Ninety-Seventh*, 22, 92-93; Carman, *The Maryland Campaign*, vol. II, 60-62.

106. *The Maryland Campaign*, vol. II, 60, 62; Hall, *Ninety-Seventh*, 93; H.W. Burlingame, "Personal Reminiscences of the Civil War," 41, copy at the ANB Library.

107. Hall, *Ninety-Seventh*, 94, 108-9; Hough, *Duryee's Brigade*, 122-23, 126-28; *OR* 19, pt. 1, 190. The 97th New York took 203 men into battle and lost 107 in the fighting. The 107th Pennsylvania had 113 men answer roll call after taking 190 into battle. The 104th suffered 74 casualties and the 105th lost 64 men. Brig. Gen. John Gibbon was promoted to command of the 2nd Division after Ricketts was transferred. Brig. Gen. Nelson Taylor replaced Duryee as brigade commander. Duryee complained to Gen. Ambrose Burnside who assumed command of the Army of the Potomac, but the army was on the move in November and nothing was resolved. There appears to have been some obvious but undocumented dissatisfaction with Duryee in the higher echelon of command and, seemingly, an effort to replace citizen generals, like Duryee, with professional soldiers. Could his absence on the field at Antietam have played a role?

108. Hartwig, *To Antietam Creek*, Appendix B, Strength of Union and Confederate Forces. The brigade had about 680 men at Antietam. Unit files at Antietam National Battlefield Park.

109. *OR* 19, pt. 1, 190. The brigade lost an additional eight men (2k; 6w) on September 14. *OR* 19, pt. 1, 185.

110. Dyer, *Compendium of the War of the Rebellion*, vol. III, 1414, 1442, 1603, 1603-04; Civil War Data Base accessed on April 19, 2020. Brig-General 3/13/1865 by Brevet http://www.civilwardata.com/active/hdsquery.dll?Soldier History?U&1443356

111. *OR* 19, pt. 1, 263; Carman, *The Maryland Campaign*, vol. I, 363; Paul Taylor, *Glory Was Not Their Companion The Twenty-Sixth New York Volunteer Infantry in the Civil War* (Jefferson, NC: McFarland & Company, Inc., 2005), 74-75; Michael N. Ayoub, *The Campfire Chronicles: The Words and Deeds of the 88th Pennsylvania 1861-1865* (n.p.: Xlibris Corporation, 2010), 118; John D. Vautier, *History of the 88th Pennsylvania Volunteers in the War for the Union 1861-1865* (Philadelphia: J.B. Lippincott Company, 1894), 70. According to Lt. Col. Richard Richardson of the 26th New York, his left wing fired 20 rounds and his right wing only four. *OR* 19, pt. 1, 263.

112. Ayoub, *The Campfire Chronicles*, 119-20.

113. Carman, *The Maryland Campaign of 1862*, vol. II, 57, 81; Ayoub, *The Campfire Chronicles*, 126; Capt. Jacob Davis to John Gould, October 31, 1892, Gould Papers; Cope Map #1 (Daybreak).

114. Ayoub, *The Campfire Chronicles*, 126; John Vautier to John Gould, December 5, 1892, Gould Papers; Lt. William Gifford to John Gould, March 7, 1893. Gould

Papers; Taylor, *Glory Was Not Their Companion*, 84; *OR* 19, pt. 1, 259, 265-66. Gifford also wrote, "Before night of that day he had been requested by the line officers to resign and had handed in his resignation. Which was promptly accepted (and he went home in disgrace)."

115. Capt. E. R. Shurly to John Gould, undated letter, Gould Papers; Carman, *The Maryland Campaign*, vol. II, 81.

116. Carman, *The Maryland Campaign*, vol. II, 82-83.

117. Lt. William Gifford letter to John Gould, March 7, 1893, Gould Papers; Carman, *The Maryland Campaign*, vol. II, 83. An officer in the 90th Pennsylvania noted his regiment retired after the rest of Christian's brigade. Carman, *The Maryland Campaign of 1862*, vol. II, 84, note 56.

118. Vautier, *History of the 88th Pennsylvania Volunteers*, 78.

119. Hartwig, *To Antietam Creek*, Appendix B, Strength of Union and Confederate Forces. The brigade probably numbered about 1,000 at Antietam, Carman, *The Maryland Campaign*, vol. II, 64.

120. *OR* 19, pt. 1, 190. The brigade also lost two men killed and four men wounded in the Battle of South Mountain. These numbers are not factored into the 599 losses counted above. *OR* 19, pt. 1, 185.

121. John Hennessy, *Second Manassas Battlefield Map Study* (Lynchburg, VA: H. E. Howard, Inc., 1985), 456. The brigade was commanded by Col. John W. Stiles as Gen. Hartsuff was ill.

122. George E. Craig, *In Memoriam: Maj. Gen. George L. Hartsuff* (Norwood, MA: Charles G. Wheelock, 1875), 5-6; George Kimball, *A Corporal's Story: Civil War Recollections of the Twelfth Massachusetts*, Alan D. Gaff and Donald H. Gaff, eds., (Norman, OK: University of Oklahoma Press, 2014), 165; Warner, *Generals in Blue*, 212-13.

123. A. R. Small, *The Sixteenth Maine Regiment in the War of the Rebellion* (Portland, ME: B. Thurston & Company, 1886), 33, 35. "From the Maine 16th—Antietam," *Lewiston (ME) Daily Evening Journal*, October 16, 1862.

124. George Cramer to wife, September 4, 1862, in 11th Pennsylvania Infantry File, ANB Library; Benjamin F. Cook, *History of the Twelfth Massachusetts Volunteers (Webster Regiment)* (Boston, MA: Twelfth (Webster) Regiment Association, 1882), 67.

125. Carman, *The Maryland Campaign*, vol. I, 346, 363, 379.

126. Carman, *The Maryland Campaign*, vol. I, 397-98, 403.

127. Kimball, *A Corporal's Story*, 167.

128. Carman, *The Maryland Campaign*, vol. II, 27; Cope Map #1 (Daybreak); Kimball, *A Corporal's Story*, 171; Francis W. Pee Account, 11th Pennsylvania Infantry File, ANB Library; Cook, *History of the Twelfth Massachusetts Volunteers*, 72.

129. Carman, *The Maryland Campaign*, vol. II. 57, 63; Welsh, *Medical Histories of Union Generals*, 156; Kimball, *A Corporal's Story*, 179-80.

130. *OR* 51, pt. 1, 142; Carman, *The Maryland Campaign*, vol. II, 63-64.

131. Kimball, *A Corporal's Story*, 176; John Hendrickson to Ezra Carman, December 6, 1894, NA-AS.

132. Carman, *The Maryland Campaign*, vol. II, 64-65. Carman specifically mentions the 12th Massachusetts' deployment of skirmishers. Reference to the 11th Pennsylvania doing the same is found in the September 17, 1862 entry, 11th Pennsylvania Infantry Morning Reports, copy in 11th Pennsylvania Infantry File, ANB Library. It is thus inferred that the brigade's two other regiments followed suit.

133. Carman, *The Maryland Campaign*, vol. II, 64-65.

134. Carman, *The Maryland Campaign*, vol. II, 65, 110; Benjamin F. Cook to J. S. E. Rogers, September 18, 1862, in "Co. K, 12th Reg.," *Cape Ann Light and Gloucester (MA) Telegraph*, September 27, 1862; James B. Dorr to Ezra Carman, December 6, 1899, NA-AS.

135. Carman, *The Maryland Campaign*, vol. II, 65; *OR* 19, pt. 1, 979.

136. Carman, *The Maryland Campaign*, vol. II, 82; Prince A. Dunton to Byron Milliken, September 24, 1862, 13th Massachusetts Infantry File, ANB Library.

137. George A. Hussey to John M. Gould, May 21, 1892, Gould Papers; William Prince to Mother, September 22, 1862, William R. Prince Papers, New York State Library.

138. Carman, *The Maryland Campaign*, vol. II, 82-83; Alfred Sellers to Ezra Carman, September 30, 1897, NA-AS.

139. Carman, *The Maryland Campaign*, vol. II, 83; Kimball, *A Corporal's Story*, 170.

140. *OR* 51, pt. 1, 141-42.

141. 11th Pennsylvania Infantry Morning Reports, copy in 11th Pennsylvania Infantry File, ANB Library.

142. Kimball, *A Corporal's Story*, 184.

143. George Cullum, *Biographical Register of the Officers and Graduates of the U.S. Military Academy at West Point, NY* (Boston: Houghton Mifflin, 1891), vol. 1, 601; Hartwig, *To Antietam Creek*, 375; John David Hoptak, *The Battle of South Mountain* (Charleston, SC: The History Press, 2011), 89.

144. Samuel P. Bates *History of Pennsylvania Volunteers 1861-65*, 5 volumes (Harrisburg, PA: B. Singerly, Printer, 1869), vol. 1, 698, 748, 790; Joseph Gibbs, *Three Years In The Bloody Eleventh* (University Park, PA: The Pennsylvania State University Press, 2002), 167-71.

145. Hartwig, *To Antietam Creek*, 375-92; Hoptak *South Mountain*, 87-109. The 13th Pennsylvania Reserves, composed mostly of accomplished marksmen from western Pennsylvania and equipped with Sharps rifles, were conspicuous by a deer tail affixed to their caps.

146. Carman, *The Maryland Campaign*, vol. II, 32-44, 87-110; Gibbs, *Bloody Eleventh*, 183-85; *OR* 19, pt. 1, 269-70. The mountains of southern Pennsylvania are clearly visible from the northern section of Antietam Battlefield.

147. Carman, *Maryland Campaign*. vol. II, 11; *OR* 19, pt. 1, 216.

148. Hartwig, *To Antietam Creek*, Appendix B, Strength of Union and Confederate Forces. The brigade numbered

about 1,107 at Antietam, taking into account the losses of 171 on South Mountain. Carman, *The Maryland Campaign*, vol. II, 573. The estimate is further derived by comparing the strength numbers given for each of Seymour's regiments in the unpublished Ezra Carman manuscript with Meade's overall division strength in *The Maryland Campaign*, vol. II.

149. *OR* 19, pt. 1, 191. Figure does not include South Mountain, where Seymour's brigade had 171 casualties (38k-133w-0m). *OR* 19, pt. 1, 185.

150. Edwin A. Glover, *Bucktailed Wildcats: A Regiment of Civil War Volunteers* (New York, NY: T. Yoseloff, 1960), 14; Samuel Waters Memoir, Civil War Miscellaneous Collection, USAMHI, 6.

151. Bates, *History of Pennsylvania Volunteers*, vol. I, 918.

152. *OR* 19, pt. 1, 1020.

153. Glover, *Bucktailed Wildcats*, 145; *OR* 19, pt. 1, 214.

154. *OR* 19, pt. 1, 1034.

155. Howard Thomson and William H. Rauch, *History of the "Bucktails:" Kane Rifle Regiment of the PA Reserve Corps (13th Pennsylvania Reserves, 42nd of the Line)* (Philadelphia, PA: Electric Printing Co., 1906), 204.

156. *OR* 19, pt. 1, 272, 1034-1036.

157. *OR* 19, pt. 1, 272, 1034; Bates, *"History of Pennsylvania Volunteers, vol. I, 698.*

158. *OR* 19, pt. 1, 272; Bates, *History of Pennsylvania Volunteers*, vol. I, 584, 669.

159. *OR* 19, pt. 1, 269, 215; Samuel Waters Memoir, 5-6.

160. *OR* 19, pt. 1, 185, 267, 215.

161. E.M. Woodward, *Our Campaigns: The Marches, Bivouacs, Battles, Incidents of Camp Life, and History of our Regiment during its Three Years Term of Service* (Philadelphia, PA: John E. Potter, Publisher, 1865), 201.

162. *OR* 19, pt. 1, 217.

163. R.L.T. Beale, *History of the Ninth Virginia Cavalry in the War Between the States*, (Richmond, VA: B.F. Johnson Publishing Co., 1899), 46-47; Carman, *The Maryland Campaign*, vol. II, 127.

164. *OR* 19, pt. 1, 155; Carman, *The Maryland Campaign*, vol. II, 33.

165. Thomson, *History of the "Bucktails,"* 210; William J. Tenney, *The Military and Naval History of the Rebellion in the United States*, (New York, NY: D. Appleton & Co., 1865), 736; Carman, *The Maryland Campaign*, vol. II, 35; *OR* 19, pt. 1, 269, 156.

166. *OR* 19, pt. 1, 270.

167. Harsh, *Taken at the Flood*, 352; *Columbia Democrat* (Bloomington, Pennsylvania), September 27, 1862.

168. *OR* 19, p. 1, 218.

169. Bates, *History of Pennsylvania Volunteers*, vol. I, 550. J.T. Baynes of the 5th Pennsylvania Reserves wrote home, "every little while during the night [the rebels would] come down towards us and fire a few shots at us but we would return their fires so quick they did not do us much harm with the exception of killing 1 Lt. and wounded two or three of the men that was on picket."

J.T. Baynes to Lizzie, September 25, 1862. Copy at ANB Library.

170. Woodward, *Our Campaigns*, 206; James Miles Smith to "Dear Friends," September 20, 1862, copy at ANB Library.

171. Carman, *The Maryland Campaign*, vol. II, 81, 82, 110; Doug Kauffman, *Tobias's Story: The Life and Civil War Career of Tobias B. Kaufman* (Bloomington, IN: Xlibris, 2012), 34-35. Christian's brigade halted twice on their approach to the East Woods, in columns of division on open ground and under heavy artillery fire. After being ordered once more to advance, they entered the woods and halted again. At that point, Seymour rode up and ordered the regiments to deploy in line and go forward.

172. *OR* 19, pt. 1, 191.

173. Hartwig, *To Antietam Creek*, Appendix B, Strength of Union and Confederate Forces. The brigade probably numbered 952 at Antietam. The literature does not contain accurate information for each brigade, so the figure stated divides Meade's strength on the morning of the battle by three (number of brigades). Carman, *The Maryland Campaign*, vol. II, 573.

174. *OR* 19, pt. 1, 191. The brigade lost an additional 89 men on September 14 (25k-63w-1m). *OR* 19, pt. 1, 185.

175. Pennsylvania raised more volunteers in the first call for soldiers than required for the federal government quota, so the governor retained enough men to fill thirteen regiments thus becoming the Pennsylvania Reserves. When the Reserves were mustered into U.S. service they received numerical designations that differed from that of the State (32nd, 33rd, 36th, 37th and 40th Pennsylvania Infantry). The men preferred their state designation: 3rd, 4th, 7th, 8th & 11th Pennsylvania Reserves respectively. The original division commander and all three brigade commanders of the Reserves were West Point graduates. The brigade lost 1,400 during the Seven Days Battles including 672 captured. The loss at 2nd Bull Run was 185; *OR* 12, pt. 2, 32, 256; Bates, *History of Pennsylvania Volunteers*, vol. I, 609-10, 636, 720-27, 756-60; Hartwig, *To Antietam Creek*, 376; J.R. Sypher, *History of the Pennsylvania Reserve Corps* (Lancaster, PA: Elias Barr & Co, 1865), 355.

176. McClellan finished second in the West Point Class of 1846, Jackson finished seventeenth, one place higher than Magilton. Truman Seymour was one place behind Magilton, and Pickett was last in the class. Cullum, *Biographical Register of the Graduates of the U.S. Military Academy*, vol. 2, 269; Francis Heitman, *Historical Register and Dictionary of the United States Army 1789-1903* (Washington, D.C.: U.S. Government Printing Office, 1903), vol. 1, 684.

http://antietam.aotw.org/officers.php?officer_id=899, Col. Robert G. March of the 4th Reserves resigned due to illness and Magilton was made colonel. The 4th Reserves were involved in a particularly nasty bayonet fight on June 30 at Charles City Crossroads, Virginia. Reynolds was in command of the Pennsylvania Reserves

Division after the Seven Days until called back to Pennsylvania to take over the militia early in the Maryland Campaign. Hartwig, *To Antietam Creek*, 376.

177. *Civil War Diary of Griffin Lewis Baldwin*, copy in the ANB Library; Carman, *The Maryland Campaign*, vol. I 345-56;

178. Robert Eberly, Jr. *Bouquets From The Cannon's Mouth* (Shippensburg, PA: White Mane Publishing, 2005) 126-29; OR 19, pt. 1 185, 266-68, 273-74; OR 51, pt. 1 148; Carman, *Maryland Campaign*, vol. I, 349-56; Hartwig *To Antietam Creek* 381-91; *Civil War Diary of Griffin Lewis Baldwin*; Lt. Col. Means, the son of the South Carolina governor, died of his wounds. The 8th Reserves reported 50 of the 89 losses reported in the brigade.

179. OR 19, pt. 1., 30, 267-69, 273-74; Carman *Antietam Campaign*, vol. I, 411; Carman *Antietam Campaign*, vol. II, 29-37.
Hartwig *To Antietam Creek*, 607-8; *Civil War Diary of Griffin Lewis Baldwin*; Tablet, Antietam National Battlefield.

180. Frank Holsinger to John M. Gould, February 29, 1892, Gould Papers; Carman, *The Maryland Campaign*, vol. II, 93.

181. OR 19, pt. 1, 269-70, 274; Carman *Maryland Campaign*, vol. II, 93-99; Eberly, *Bouquets From the Cannon's Mouth*, 131-32; Bradley M. Gottfried, *The Maps of Antietam: An Atlas of the Antietam Campaign Including the Battle of South Mountain, September 2 – 220, 1862* (El Dorado Hills, CA: Savas Beatie, 2012), 154-57; Silas Baily ran a jewelry shop in Waynesburg, Pennsylvania before the war and was praised in the after-action reports for his efforts at South Mountain and Antietam. He was promoted to the rank of colonel of the 8th to date from September 14. Sypher, *Pennsylvania Reserves*, 401-02.

182. Sypher *Pennsylvania Reserves*, 397-99, 405-07, 428. Albert Magilton in 1864 became a tactics instructor at Philadelphia Pennsylvania Free Military School that helped train officers for African-American regiments, Cullum, *Biographical Register*, vol. 2, 151.

183. Hartwig, *To Antietam Creek*, Appendix B, Strength of Union and Confederate Forces. The brigade's strength at Antietam was probably 952. The literature does not contain accurate information for each brigade, so the figure stated divides the Meade's strength on the morning of the battle by three (number of brigades). Carman, *The Maryland Campaign*, vol. II, 573.

184. OR 19, pt. 1, 191. The brigade lost an additional 132 men on September 14 (32k-100w). OR 19, pt. 1, 186.

185. Sypher, *Pennsylvania Reserves*, 86, 89-90, 123, 127; Bates *History of Pennsylvania Volunteers*, vol. I, 21, 693, 784, 814; Uzal Ent *The Pennsylvania Reserves in the Civil War A Comprehensive History* (Jefferson, NC: McFarland & Company, 2012), 358; Cullum, *Biographical Register of the Officers and Graduates of the U.S. Military Academy at West Point*, vol. 2, 137.

186. Cullum, *Biographical Register*, vol. 2, 6-7, 270; Biography, Arlington National Cemetery, http://www.arlingtoncemetery.net/ecoord.htm; Sypher, *Pennsylvania Reserves*, 129-41, 187-193, 210-214; OR 12, pt. 2, 32; James Casey, ed., "The Ordeal of Adoniram Judson Warner, His Minutes of South Mountain and Antietam," *Civil War History*, vol. XXVII, no. 3 (1982), 214.

187. Sypher, *Pennsylvania Reserves*, 318-23, 329; Bates, *Pennsylvania Volunteers*, vol. I, 789-90, 881-83; Gibbs, *Three Years In The Bloody Eleventh*, 168-69. George McClellan and Thomas "Stonewall" Jackson were among Seymour's classmates at West Point. The 11th Reserves was almost entirely captured at Gaines' Mill and exchanged on August 5. McCall was captured and exchanged, but due to failing health, did not resume command of the division. Hardin was from a distinguished military family and an 1859 West Point graduate who replaced Col. John Taggart as commander of the 12th Reserves, who lost an arm at 2nd Bull Run. Kirk was colonel of the 10th, but his wounds prevented him from resuming command. OR 12, pt. 2, 256.

188. Hartwig, *To Antietam Creek*, 36, 168-69; Gibbs, *Bloody 11th*, 167-71; Sypher, *Penna. Reserves*, 361; The report stated, "after an ineffectual attack, the whole of McCall's division was routed and many of the fugitives rushed down the road where my right was resting." Hooker further implied that the Reserves' poor performance endangered his troops. McCall published a small book on the Pennsylvania Reserves in an effort to clear their name. Lt. Col. Anderson resumed command of the 9th Reserves. Some accounts give September 7 as the date that Reserves received marching orders.

189. Casey, "The Ordeal of Adoniram Judson Warner," 217-18; OR 19, pt. 1, 185-86, 274-75; OR 51, pt. 1, 149-154; Carman, *The Maryland Campaign*, vol. I, 349-51; Gibbs, *Bloody 11th*, 174-78. The brigade reported 132 casualties at South Mountain.

190. Carman, *The Maryland Campaign*, vol. II, 27-41; Casey, "The Ordeal of Adoniram Judson Warner," 219-224; Gibbs, *Bloody 11th*, 179-81.

191. Carman, *The Maryland Campaign*, vol. II, 93-103; "The Ordeal of Adoniram Judson Warner," 224-227; Gibbs *Bloody 11th*, 182-84; Samuel Jackson was the maternal grandfather of the famous movie actor James Stewart.

192; OR 19, pt. 1, 269-70; OR 51, pt. 2, 150-54; Carman, *The Maryland Campaign*, vol. II, 107-109; Bates *Pennsylvania Volunteers*, vol. I, 850; Gibbs *Bloody 11th*, 183-85; Cope Map #4 (7:20 a.m.).

193. OR 19, pt. 1, 191, 213-19, 270-71; Martin Hardin *History of the Twelfth Regiment, Pennsylvania Volunteer Reserve Volunteer Corps* (New York: By Author, 1890), 128-29.

**II Corps**

1. Dyer, *A Compendium of the War of the Rebellion*, vol. I, 287; Carman, *The Maryland Campaign*, vol. I, 152.

2. Carman, *The Maryland Campaign of 1862*, vol. I, 153; Hartwig, *To Antietam Creek*, 142.

3. Francis A. Walker, *History of the Second Army Corps in the Army of the Potomac* (New York: Charles Scribner's Sons, 1886), 97-98; Dyer, *A Compendium of the War of the Rebellion*, vol. I, 291.

4. Carman, *The Maryland Campaign*, vol. I, 132; Walker, *History of the Second Army Corps*, 92-93; Hartwig, *To Antietam Creek*, 334.

5. George B. McClellan, *McClellan's Own Story: The War for the Union* (New York: Charles L. Webster, Company, 1887), 586; Carman, *The Maryland Campaign*, vol. II, 576.

6. OR 19, pt. 1, 283, 308; OR 51, pt. 1, 839; Samuel S. Sumner, "The Antietam Campaign," *Papers of the Historical Society of Massachusetts* (Wilmington, NC: Broadfoot Publishing Company, 1990), 10; Carman, *The Maryland Campaign*, vol. II, 171; Marion V. Armstrong, *Unfurl Those Colors! McClellan, Sumner, & the Second Corps in the Antietam Campaign* (Tuscaloosa, AL: University of Alabama Press, 2008), 167; Thomas K. Tate, *General Edwin Vose Sumner, USA* (New York: McFarland & Company, 2013), 165.

7. *Joint Committee on the Conduct of the War*, pt. 1, 581-82; Armstrong, Jr., *Unfurl Those Colors*, 172.

8. Armstrong, Jr.., *Unfurl Those Colors*, 175-79; Sumner, "The Antietam Campaign," 10. Marion Armstrong posited that Sumner rode on the right of Sedgwick's line because most of the firing and smoke was from that direction and he wanted to reposition the division quickly, if needed. Armstrong, Jr., *Unfurl Those Colors*, 179-80.

9. Gibbon, *Personal Recollections*, 87-88; Ernest L. Waitt, *History of the Nineteenth Regiment Massachusetts Volunteer Infantry 1861 -1865* (Salem, MA: The Salem Press, 1906), 134.

10. Carman, *The Maryland Campaign*, vol. II, 193; Armstrong, Jr. *Unfurl Those Colors*, 184-85; Sumner, "The Antietam Campaign," 11.

11. OR 19, pt. 1, 306; Oliver Howard, "Personal Reminiscences of the War of the Rebellion," *National Tribune*, April 3, 1884; Carman, *The Maryland Campaign*, vol. II, 207-08; Armstrong, *Unfurl Those Colors*, 191-92; Tate, *General Edwin Vose Sumner*, 171-72.

12. Carman, *The Maryland Campaign*, vol. II, 601.

13. Fox, *Regimental Losses in the American Civil War*, 67; Warner, *Generals in Blue*, 402-03; Jack C. Mason, *Until Antietam: The Life and Letters of Major General Israel B. Richardson, U. S. Army* (Carbondale, IL: Southern Illinois University Press, 2009), 121, 132; https://www.civilwarmed.org/richardson/ accessed February 11, 2021.

14. Carman, *The Maryland Campaign*, vol. I, 370, 397-99; vol. II, 351. Gen. Caldwell's reputation was sullied by accusations of cowardice, but this was never substantiated and he went on to command a division, and later a corps, at times.

15. Carman, *The Maryland Campaign*, vol. I, 401, 403, 409; OR 19, pt. 1, 53-5, 281; Carman, *The Maryland Campaign*, vol. II, 18, 172, 264, 272.

16. Carman, *The Maryland Campaign*, vol. II, 279-80, 281, 283; Walker, *History of the Second Army Corps*, 112-13.

17. Thomas L. Livermore, *Days and Events, 1860 – 1866* (Boston: Houghton Mifflin Company, 1920), 137-38.

18. Carman, *The Maryland Campaign*, vol. II, 288, 294; OR 19, pt. 1, 278.

19. OR 19, pt. 1, 192; Welsh, *Medical Histories of Union Generals*, 278; Mason, *Until Antietam*, 189, 192; Carman, *The Maryland Campaign* of 1862, vol. II, 295, 342-43. Ezra Carman noted that Richardson's division lost 1,145 men. Carman, *The Maryland Campaign* of 1862, vol. II, 351.

20. Hartwig, *To Antietam Creek*, Appendix B, Strength of Union and Confederate Forces. The brigade numbered about 1,339 at Antietam. Carman, *The Maryland Campaign*, vol. II, 573, 574

21. OR 19, pt. 1, 287; Carman, *The Maryland Campaign*, vol. II, 573, 574.

22. Charles A. Fuller, *Personal Recollections of the War of 1861* (Hamilton, NY: Edmonston Publishing, Inc, 1906), 56.

23. Carman, *The Maryland Campaign*, vol. II, 172, 263; Armstrong *Unfurl Those Colors*, 172-173. Carman says Richardson's division crossed at the same ford as Sedgwick, which he states was Pry's Ford. However, Armstrong suggests the ford was farther to the south.

24. Kennedy Hickman, "*American Civil War: Brigadier General John C. Caldwell*, ThoughtCo, Feb 11, 2020, thoughtco.com/brigadier-general-john-c-caldwell-2360391. A court of inquiry cleared Caldwell of wrongdoing—a charge leveled by Maj. Gen. George Sykes at Gettysburg.

25. OR 19, pt. 1, 288.

26. Thomas L. Livermore, *Days and Events*, 132; Fuller, *Personal Recollections*, 58.

27. OR 19, 284.

28. Fuller, *Personal Recollections*, 58.

29. William H. Osbourne, *The History of the 29th Regiment, Massachusetts Volunteer Infantry* (Boston, MA: Albert J. Wright, Printer, 1877), 187.

30. OR 19, pt. 1, 1047.

31. OR 19, pt. 1, 289; Fuller, *Personal Recollections*, 59; United States Army, *Medal of Honor Recipients, Civil War*. The citation identifies the flag as the 4th Alabama; however, the 4th Alabama was part of Law's brigade, Hood's division, which was on a different part of the field at Antietam. The flag was likely the 44th Alabama, part of R.H. Anderson's division which was in the vicinity of the sunken road where the flag was captured.

32. Livermore, *Days and Events*, 140.

33. Charles A. Hale, *The Story of My Personal Experience at Antietam*, John R. Brooke Papers, Historical Society of Pennsylvania; OR 19, pt. 1, 284-287, 288.

34. Carman, E., *The Maryland Campaign*, vol. II, 288; OR 19, pt. 1, 287, 1018, 1030.

35. *OR* 19, pt. 1, 289.

36. *OR* 19, pt. 1, 289, 291.

37. Livermore, *Days and Events*, 141.

38. Carman, *The Maryland Campaign,* vol. II, 290

39. James Longstreet, *Manassas to Appomattox: Memoirs of the Civil War in America* (Philadelphia, PA: J.B. Lippincott Co., 1895), 250-251.

40. *OR* 19, pt. 1, 284-28.

41. Carman, *The Maryland Campaign,* vol. II, 573-574; *OR* 19, pt. 1, 287.

42. Hartwig, *To Antietam Creek*, Appendix B, Strength of Union and Confederate Forces. The brigade probably numbered 1,400 at Antietam. R.L. Murray, *New Yorkers in the Civil War. Irish Brigade at Antietam* (Wolcott, NY: Benedum Books, 2006) vol. 6, 12, hereinafter: *Irish Brigade at Antietam*; Phillip Thomas Tucker, *God Help The Irish! – The History of the Irish Brigade* (Abilene, TX: McWhiney Foundation Press, 2007), 79. Some sources have reported the brigade's effective strength at 1,085 before the battle.

43. *OR* 19, pt. 1, 192.

44. Edwin C. Bearss, *Fields of Honor – Pivotal Battles of the Civil War* (Washington, DC: National Geographic Society, 2007), 108; Marion V. Armstrong, *Unfurl Those Colors*, 45. Ted Alexander, *The Battle of Antietam – The Bloodiest Day* (Charleston, SC: History Press, 2011), 35; David Power Conyngham, *The Irish Brigade and Its Campaigns* (New York: Fordham University Press, 1994), 33; Tucker, *God Help The Irish!*, 33, 37-42; "Buck 'n ball" usually consisted of a .69 cal. ball and three .32-ca. balls resembling buckshot.

46. Joseph McCormack, "Father William Corby," Irish Cultural Society of the Garden City Area, Apr. 2002, c7da7bf7-3797-4e70-8593-d038c30b3fa9.filesusr.com/ugd/5f59bb_8aa38c77764f4e3884006855e39624d0.pdf; Tucker, *God Help The Irish!*, 57.

47. Armstrong, *Unfurl Those Colors*, 81; Tucker, *God Help The Irish*, 56.

48. Armstrong, *Unfurl Those Colors,* 67; Alexander, *The Battle of Antietam – The Bloodiest Day*, 89.

49. Tucker, *God Help The Irish*, 60, 66-69.

50. Conyngham, *The Irish Brigade*, 56; Tucker, *God Help The Irish*, 70-71.

51. Armstrong, *Unfurl Those Colors*, 66.

52. Armstrong, *Unfurl Those Colors*, 121-22, 131.

53. *OR* 19, pt. 1, 293.

54. Harsh, *Taken at the Flood*, 396-97; Armstrong, *Unfurl Those Colors*, 208-18, 220; Carman, *The Maryland Campaign*, vol. II, 598.

55. *OR* 19, pt. 1, 277, 285 and 293; Joseph G. Bilby, *The Irish Brigade in the Civil War: The 69th New York and Other Irish Regiments of the Army of the Potomac* (New York: Da Capo Press, 1997), 53-54; W.L.D. O'Grady, "88th Regiment Infantry" in *New York at Gettysburg*, 3 volumes (Albany, NY: J.B. Lyon Co., 1900), vol. 2, 512.

56. Carman, *The Maryland Campaign,* vol. II, 263-64; Murray, *Irish Brigade at Antietam*, 14; Bilby, *The Irish Brigade in the Civil War*, 54-55.

57. *OR* 19, Pt. 1, 294-95; Tucker, *God Help The Irish*, 83; Conyngham, *The Irish Brigade and its Campaigns*, 305; Carman, *The Maryland Campaign*, vol. II, 264, 266-67.

58. Carman, *The Maryland Campaign*, vol. II, 268-69; *OR* 19, pt. 1, 298.

59. Carman, *The Maryland Campaign,* vol. II, 271-72; Osbourne, William H. *The History of the 29th Regiment, Massachusetts Volunteer Infantry* (Boston, MA: Albert J. Wright, Printer, 1877), 186-87.

60. Carman, *The Maryland Campaign,* vol. II, 279-80.

61. Tucker, *God Help The Irish*, 85, 89, 90; *OR* 19, pt. 1, 192, 296.

62. Hartwig, *To Antietam Creek*, Appendix B, Strength of Union and Confederate Forces. The brigade probably numbered about 1336 at Antietam. Carman, *The Maryland Campaign*, vol. II, 573-574.

63. *OR* 19, pt. 1, 192.

64. *OR* 5,19; *The Union Army.* 9 volumes (Wilmington, NC: Broadfoot Publishing Company, 1997) vol. I, 522, 384-85, vol. II, 89, 92, 98-99; Civil War Data Base accessed on June 6, 2020, http://www.civilwardata.com/active/hdsquery.dll?Officer?261&U

65. Josiah M. Favill, *The Diary of a Young Officer Serving with the Armies of the United States during the War of the Rebellion* (Chicago, IL: R.R. Donnelley & Sons, 1909), 182-83.

66. Carman, *The Maryland Campaign,* vol. I, 370; *OR* 19, pt. 1, 300.

67. *OR* 19, pt. 1, 301.

68. *OR* 19, pt. 1, 299, 301.

69. *OR* 19, pt. 1, 278.

70. *OR* 19, pt. 1, 299, 304; Carman, *The Maryland Campaign*, vol. II, 286; Irvin G. Myers, *We Might as Well Die Here: The 53rd Pennsylvania Veteran Volunteer Infantry* (Shippensburg, PA: White Mane Publishing, Co., 2004), 39-41; Bates, *History of Pennsylvania Reserves*, vol. II, 93.

71. Carman, *The Maryland Campaign*, vol. II, 290; *OR* 19, pt. 1, 299, 302, 303; *Utica Evening Telegraph*, March 16, 1863; Favill, *The Diary of a Young Officer*, 187.

72. *OR* 19, pt. 1, 299, 302, 303.

73. *OR* 19, pt. 1, 299-300.

74. Favill, *The Diary of a Young Officer*, 197.

75. Heitman, *Historical Register and Dictionary of the United States Army*, vol. 1, 872, 70; Warner, *Generals in Blue*, 430-31; "A Sedgwick Genealogy: Descendants of Deacon Benjamin Sedgwick," Hubert M. Sedgwick, comp. (New Haven, CT: New Haven Colony Historical Society, 1961), retrieved on September 1, 2020 at http://www.sedgwick.org/na/families/robert1613/B/2/9/2/B292-sedgwick-gen-john-article.html.

76. Carman, *The Maryland Campaign*, vol. II, 526-28; Hartwig, *To Antietam Creek*, 676-77 (note 1 and 2).

77. At the time of the Civil War, Wisconsin Avenue that runs through the modern Tenleytown in Washington,

D.C., was called the Rockville Road. "Map of the Defenses of Washington," 1865, Map Room, Library of Congress.

78. *OR* 19, pt. 2, 182; Hartwig, *To Antietam Creek*, 192, 284, 289-290; *OR* 19, pt. 1, 48; Carman, *The Maryland Campaign*, vol. II, 172.

79. *OR* 19, pt. 1, 48; Hartwig *To Antietam Creek*, 334; *OR* 51, pt. 1, 831.

80. Hartwig, *To Antietam Creek*, 492-93; *OR* 51, pt. 1, 834-35.

81. Hartwig, *To Antietam Creek,* 494-95, 507, 515; Chase Philbrick to Col. J.C. Stearnes and Gen. Harry Heth, July 26, 1893, Carman Correspondence, NYPL, Box 9.

82. Carman, *The Maryland Campaign*, vol. II, 171; John E. Reilly to Ezra Carman, March 4, 1905, NYPL; Armstrong, *Unfurl Those Colors*, 166.

83. McClellan directed Sumner to hold his 1st Division under Israel Richardson until replaced by Morell's division, V Corps. Richardson would not get underway for about a half hour; Eugene Sullivan to Ezra Carman, March 28, 1905, enclosing an unpublished MSS titled "Around the Camp Fire," NYPL, Carman Correspondence.

84. *OR* 19, pt. 1, 305-06, 315-316. Col. James Suiter of Gorman's brigade is the only commander in Sedgwick's division to report "crowding" in the East Woods.

85. Cope Map #8 (9:00 to 9:30 a.m.).

86. L. N. Chapin, *A Brief History of the Thirty-Fourth Regiment NYSV* (New York: n.p., 1903), 64.

87. Carman, *The Maryland Campaign*, vol. II, 180, 194.

88. *OR* 19, pt. 1, 305-308, 310-312, 319-322; Carman, Map #8 (9 to 9:30 a.m.), and #9 (10:30 a.m.).

89. *OR* 19, pt. 1, 305-308.

90. *OR* 19, pt. 1, 305-308, 314-315, 318-319; Joseph R. C. Ward, *History of the One-Hundred and Sixth Regiment Pennsylvania Volunteers, 1861-1865* (Philadelphia: Grant, Faires & Rogers, 1906), 90-95; Carman, Map #9 (10:30 a.m.).

91. *OR* 19, pt. 1, 192; Carman, *The Maryland Campaign*, vol. II, 575. This figure does not include the 25 casualties suffered by the division artillery, the 1st Rhode Island Light, Battery A (Tompkins) and the 1st United States, Battery I (Woodruff); Cope Map #10 (Noon).

92. Welsh, *Medical Histories of Union Generals*, 294-95.

93. Hartwig, *To Antietam Creek*, Appendix B, Strength of Union and Confederate Forces. The brigade probably numbered 1,691 at Antietam. Carman, *The Maryland Campaign*, vol. II, 575.

94. OR 19, pt. 1, 192.

95. Unless otherwise noted, the source for Gorman's biography comes from James A. Baker, "Lives of the Governors of Minnesota." *Collections of the Minnesota Historical Society XIII* (1908), 50-55; Heitman, *Historical Register and Dictionary of the United States Army*, vol. 1, 466.

96. *National Almanac and Annual Record for the Year 1864* (Philadelphia: George W. Childs, 1864), 141; Richard L. Gorman entry retrieved May 1, 2020 from http://www.1stminnesota.net/#/soldier/1029; James Gorman entry retrieved May 2, 2020 from http://civilwardata.com/active/hdsquery.dll?SoldierHistory?U&1321106; Carman, *The Maryland Campaign*, vol. II, 575.

97. Richard Moe, *The Last Full Measure: The Life and Death of the First Minnesota Volunteers* (New York: Henry Holt and Company, 1993), 177.

98. John E. Reilly to Ezra Carman, March 4, 1905 in Carman Correspondence, NYPL; OR 19, pt. 1, 315-316.

99. Chapin, *A Brief History of the Thirty-Fourth Regiment NYSV*, 64; Cope Map, # 8 (9:00 to 9:30 a.m.). Ed Walker of the 1st Minnesota vividly described the march toward the West Woods: "We passed a spot where Secesh had their line of battle and the dead lay in rows in a line as they fell. I never could have believed [it] had I not seen it. Here we passed fragments of regiments that had been in the fight in the morning, they cheered us as we passed. We now crossed the turnpike, had to climb two fences, this was the place they were last drove from, the fences are perfectly riddle with bullets. Our men lay thick here, it was a hard place to carry. After climbing the fences and crossing the road we came into a piece of woods and advancing through it we found Secesh waiting for us." Moe, *The Last Full Measure*, 180-81.

100. Carman, *The Maryland Campaign*, vol. II, 193; Armstrong, *Unfurl Those Colors*, 180.

101. BetteJo Hall-Caldwell, "Col. James A. Suiter, 34th NY Volunteer Infantry," retrieved July 28, 2020 at https://herkimer.nygenweb.net/herktown/colsuiter.html

102. OR 19, pt. 1, 315-316; Carman, *The Maryland Campaign*, vol. II, 197.

103. OR 19, pt. 1, 315-316.

104. OR 19, pt. 1, 315-316; Carman, *The Maryland Campaign*, vol. II, 180; Cope Map # 8, (9:00 to 9:30 a.m.)

105. Carman, *The Maryland Campaign*, vol. II, 200-01, 201 (note. 49); Cope Map #8, (9:00 to 9:20 a.m.); OR 19, pt. 1, 315-316; Philip Crewel to [friend] John, September 19, 1862. Sold at Heritage auctions; Chapin, *A Brief History of the Thirty-Fourth Regiment*, 118. Barton was discharged in Philadelphia on January 24, 1863 "by reason of such wounds" received at Antietam.

107. Thomas H. Eaton to Ezra Carman, March 28, 1905, NYPL. Eaton served in Company H of the 72nd Pennsylvania, (Howard's Brigade); Cope Map #8, (9:00 to 9:30 a.m.). See Howard's brigade's entry for additional information on the 72nd Pennsylvania.

108. Andrew E. Ford, *The Story of the Fifteenth Regiment: Massachusetts Volunteer Infantry in the Civil War, 1861-1864* (Clinton, MA: Press of W.J. Coulter, 1898), 195; OR 19, pt. 1, 312-314.

109. Ford, *The Story of the Fifteenth Regiment*, 195, 180; OR 19, pt. 1, 312-314.

110. Carman observed that the guns on Hauser's Ridge "gave time for McLaws to come up." One may argue that without these guns, the outcome of the day would have been much different. Carman, *The Maryland Campaign*,

vol. II, 218. Cope Map, #8 (9 to 9:30 a.m). Brockenbrough's, Raine's, Poague's, and D'Aquin's batteries were situated along the ridge. McCarthy's battery pulled in south of the Alfred Poffenberger barn, but only for a short time.

111. Information on Andrew's Sharpshooters is from Antietam on the Web and retrieved on June 17, 2020 at http://antietam.aotw.org/officers.php?unit_id=520&from=results; see also Senechal de la Roche, *"Our Aim Was Man": Andrew's Sharpshooters in the American Civil War* (Amherst: University of Massachusetts Press, 2016); Ford, *The Story of the Fifteenth Regiment: Massachusetts Volunteer Infantry*, 195.

112. Chase Philbrick to Col. J.C. Stearnes and General Heth, ?/26/1893, NYPL; OR 19, pt. 1, 312-14.

113. Paul Semmes' commanded the 10th and 53rd Georgia and the 15th and 32nd Virginia regiments. OR 19, pt. 1, 312-314; Lafayette McLaws to Henry Heth, December 13, 1894. NA-AS. Two days after the battle, Edwin Sumner described the events of the day to his wife. One observation he made was "The enemy fought like maniacs to give you an idea of it." Edwin Sumner to Hannah Wickersham Foster Sumner, September 22, 1862, Sumner Papers, Box 1, Folder 3, Library of Congress.

114. Sgt. Jonathan Stowe, 15th Massachusetts Infantry, 2nd Corps diary entry, Sept. 17, 1862, *Civil War Times Illustrated Collection*, USAMHI.

115. OR 19, pt. 1, 310-312.

116. Edward B. Robins to Ezra A. Carman, April 5, 1900, NYPL; Roland Bowen, *From Ball's Bluff to Gettysburg . . . and Beyond: The Civil War Letters of Private Roland E. Bowen, 15th Massachusetts Infantry*. Gregory Coco, ed. (Gettysburg: Thomas Publishers, 1994), 135.

117. This location is at the intersection of Hagerstown Pike and the current day Starke Avenue. John W. Kimball to Ezra A. Carman, February 17, 1900, Carman Correspondence, NYPL, Box 3, Folder 5; Edward B. Robins to Ezra A. Carman, April 5, 1900, Carman Correspondence, NYPL, Box 2, Folder 5; John W. Kimball to Ezra A. Carman, May 26, 1899, Carman Correspondence, NYPL, Box 3, Folder 5. Carman, however, states that Kimball only held this position for "few minutes" before retiring to the North Woods. By then the regiment had the "greatest loss sustained by any regiment on the field, and 52 1/2 per cent of those taken into action." Thomas Clemens, the editor of the Carman manuscript, points out that "The claim of greatest loss for a regiment is true in a numeric sense, but not as a percentage." Carman, *The Maryland Campaign*, vol. II, 212-213 (note 74).

118. OR 19, pt. 1, 316-17; Carman, *The Maryland Campaign*, vol. II, 211.

119. OR 19, pt. 1, 316-17.

120. Information about this unit from Antietam on the Web, retrieved June 17, 2020 at http://antietam.aotw.org/officers.php?unit_id=522&from=results that points to State of Minnesota, Board of Commissioners, *Minnesota in the Civil War and Indian Wars 1861-1865*, 2 volumes (St. Paul, MN: Pioneer Press Company, 1890-93), vol. 2, 132-134; OR 19, pt. 1, 317; William J. Colville to J.C. Stearns and Harry Heth, December 10, 1892, NA-AS.

121. Colville to Stearns and Heth, December 10, 1892; Carman, *The Maryland Campaign*, vol. II, 212, 218.

122. Colville to Stearns and Heth, December 10, 1892; OR 19, pt. 1, 314-15.

123. Colville to Stearns and Heth, December 10, 1892; Carman, *The Maryland Campaign*, vol. II, 301.

124. OR 19, pt. 1, 192.

125. Welsh, *Medical Histories of Union Generals*, 133-34; www.1stminnesota.net/#/soldier/1238 retrieved on July 27, 2020.

126. Hartwig, *To Antietam Creek*, Appendix B, Strength of Union and Confederate Forces. The brigade numbered about 1,800 at Antietam. Carman, *The Maryland Campaign*, vol. II, 575.

127. OR 19, pt. 1, 192. Thomas Clemens on Howard's losses writes: "Of Howard's Brigade our information is fragmentary and conflicting." Carman, *The Maryland Campaign*, vol. 2, 575. The OR is also inaccurate in its totals for the brigade as the chart figures per column for casualties totals 485 while the aggregate column lists 545. OR 19, pt. 1, 192.

128. California Military Department, California State Military History and Museums Program, essay by Gary Lash retrieved July 10, 2020, http://www.militarymuseum.org/69thPA.html; Bradley M. Gottfried, *Stopping Pickett: The History of the Philadelphia Brigade* (Shippensburg, PA: White Mane Publishing Co., 1999), 1-25.

129. Carman, *The Maryland Campaign*, vol. III, 235-36; https://www.battlefields.org/learn/biographies/oliver-o-howard. Retrieved August 11, 2020.

130. Isaac J. Wistar, *Autobiography of Isaac Jones Wistar, 1827-1905* (Philadelphia: Wistar Institute of Anatomy and Biology, 1937), 398-99.

131. OR 19, pt. 1, 318-319.

132. OR 19, pt. 1, 305-306; Ward, *History of the One-Hundred and Sixth Regiment Pennsylvania*, 105.

133. OR 19, pt. 1, 305-306, Carman, *The Maryland Campaign*, vol. II, 195.

134. OR 19, pt. 1, 305-306; Ward, *History of the One-Hundred and Sixth Regiment Pennsylvania*, 89; OR 19, pt. 1, 318-319.

135. Ward and Howard have nearly similar passages but here Ward states: "the left of the line reaching to the church" which is a different description than found in Howard. Ward, *History of the One-Hundred and Sixth Regiment Pennsylvania*, 89; Carman, *The Maryland Campaign*, vol. II, 196.

136. OR 19, pt. 1, 305-306.

137. OR 19, pt. 1, 305-306; Ward, *History of the One-Hundred and Sixth Regiment Pennsylvania*, 89.

138. Ward, *History of the One-Hundred and Sixth Regiment Pennsylvania*, 89-90; *OR* 19, pt. 1, 318-319. The description is of the topography of the field to the immediate right (east) of the Pike. The field there rises 20 to 30 feet as it meets the road. In an intriguing note written years later Joseph Ward of the 106th Pennsylvania asserted that "Sumner had previously sent orders twice to Howard to change front to the left, but General Howard never received them on account of one aide being killed and the other wounded." Ward, *History of the One-Hundred and Sixth Regiment Pennsylvania*, 94. By moving the brigade *forward*, Howard may have sealed the division's fate. If Howard had fully realized the emergency on his left, he might have brought his brigade around to face his attackers; instead his flank was fully exposed. Howard has also been faulted for not holding his brigade back to act as a reserve. Doing so "placed [Howard's brigade] in too great proximity to the other two [brigades], and thus, while intended to act as a reserve, subjected [it] to as deadly a fire as those it was intended to support." *OR* 19, pt. 1, 318-319. From a private's point of view, Sylvester Byrne of the 72nd Pennsylvania stated: "There was a time when Criticism of a commanding officer was a court martial offense, but it has been my opinion ever since that any non-commissioned officer of the 72nd could have handled the Brigade better than it was on Sept 17 1862." Sylvester Byrne to Ezra Carman, March 17, 1905, NYPL.

139. Sylvester Byrne of the 72nd Pennsylvania recalled the "left of the regiment extended down to, but did not reach the Church." Byrne's correspondence (and recollection) are "strengthened by my visit over the ground on the morning of September 18th (on burial detail). I made good use of my eyes and what I saw made a lasting impression in my memory." He also visited the field a number of times after the war. Byrne to Carman, March 15, 1905, March 17, 1905, May 22, 1905, NYPL; Cope Map #8, (9:00 to 9:30 a.m.)

140. John Lockhart to Carman, March 13, 1905, NYPL; Byrne to Carman, May 22, 1905; Thomas Eaton to Carman, April 1, 1905, NYPL. Eaton is quoting from his diary. Not all companies on the left of the 72nd were affected by the 34th's breaking. John Lockhart, serving as Captain of Company I, was in the next to last company on the left of the regiment. He wrote Carman, that "some of our troops were in our front. I am under the impression that some of the boys told me that it was the 34th N.Y. *As none of the troops came through our line,* I cannot say for certain." Italics added. Lockhart to Carman, March 13, 1905; individual first names and ranks from Civil War Veterans' Card File, 1861-1866, Pennsylvania State Archives at http://www.digitalarchives.state.pa.us.

141. Bates, *History of Pennsylvania Volunteers*, vol. 2, 701; Ward, *History of the One-Hundred and Sixth Regiment Pennsylvania*, 89-90.

142. Ward, *History of the One-Hundred and Sixth Regiment Pennsylvania*, 90; Bates, *History of Pennsylvania Volunteers*, vol. 2, 701.

143. *OR* 19, pt. 1, 305-306; Carman, *The Maryland Campaign*, vol. II, 196.

144. Ward, *History of the One-Hundred and Sixth Regiment Pennsylvania*, 90; Bates, *History of Pennsylvania Volunteers*, vol. 2, 701.

145. Ward, *History of the One-Hundred and Sixth Regiment Pennsylvania*, 91-92.

146. Ward, *History of the One-Hundred and Sixth Regiment Pennsylvania*, 90.

147. *OR* 19, pt. 1, 318-319.

148. Ward, *History of the One-Hundred and Sixth Regiment Pennsylvania*, 90-9; John E. Reilly to Ezra Carman, March 4, 1905, NYPL. ; "At that fence there was no other regiment or company formation but the 106 PV yet there were members of the 69th & 72d Regts with some officers. Those of the 69th under command of their officer formed a company. Those of the 72d were [halted] by our men and compelled by our officers to stay." Joseph Ward to Carman, July 20, 1905, NYPL, Carman Correspondence, Box 3, Folder 5; Ward, *History of the One-Hundred and Sixth Regiment Pennsylvania*, 90-91; individual first names and ranks from Civil War Veterans' Card File, 1861-1866, Pennsylvania State Archives at http://www.digitalarchives.state.pa.us.

149. Ward, *History of the One-Hundred and Sixth Regiment Pennsylvania*, 94; *OR* 19, 1, 318-19. After the stand at the fence, 106th then fell further back and to the right and formed between the D.R. Miller house and barn. After gathering regimental members scattered during the withdrawal, Howard ordered them to support artillery in the North Woods. Ward, *History of the One-Hundred and Sixth Regiment Pennsylvania*, 91; Bates, *History of Pennsylvania Volunteers*, vol. 2, 831.

150. Howard to Carman, January 23, 1905, NYPL. After Antietam, Howard took command of Sedgwick's division until the end of the year. He assumed command of the XI Corps prior to Chancellorsville and ended his Civil War service as commander of the Army of the Tennessee. Afterwards he headed the Freedmen's Bureau for four years during which time he founded Howard University. He served as West Point's Superintendent, and in 1893 received the Medal of Honor for his actions at Seven Pines. He died in October 1909 in Burlington, Vermont. Carman, *The Maryland Campaign*, vol. III, 235-36; David K. Thompson, "Oliver Otis Howard," in Essential Civil War Curriculum retrieved August 11, 2020 at https://www.essentialcivilwarcurriculum.com/oliver-otis-howard.html

151. Hartwig, *To Antietam Creek*, Appendix B, Strength of Union and Confederate Forces. The brigade probably numbered 1,946 at Antietam. Carman, *The Maryland Campaign*, vol. II, 575.

152. *OR* 19, pt. 1, 192-93.

153. Frederick Phisterer, *New York in the War of Rebellion*, 6 volumes (Albany: J.B. Lyon Co., 1912), 3, 2519; Dyer, *A Compendium of the War of the Rebellion*, vol. I, 276, 291,

1426.

154. *Cullum's Register* entry for Napoleon Dana at https://penelope.uchicago.edu/Thayer/E/Gazetteer/Places/America/United_States/Army/USMA/Cullums_Register/1139*.html. His classmates included John Pope, Abner Doubleday, D.H. Hill, George Sykes, R.H. Anderson, Lafayette McLaws, and James Longstreet; Napoleon J.T. Dana biographical essay at the First Minnesota website, http://www.1stminnesota.net/#/soldier/1237 and retrieved July 15, 2020.

155. OR 19, pt. 2, 182; D. Hartwig, *To Antietam Creek*, 192, 289, 334; OR 19, pt. 1, 48; Carman, *The Maryland Campaign*, vol. II, 370; OR 51, pt. 1, 831.

156. Eugene Sullivan to Ezra Carman, March 28, 1905, enclosing an unpublished MSS titled "Around the Camp Fire," NYPL; OR 19, pt. 1, 315-316.

157. OR 19, 1, 319-21; Carman Map # 7 (8:30 to 8:40 a.m.); John G. B. Adams, *Reminiscences of the Nineteenth Massachusetts Regiment* (Boston: Wright & Potter Printing Company, 1899), 44; OR 19, pt. 1, 323. The identity of the artillery targeting Sedgwick's division is not known. Stephen Lee's battalion of artillery is a possibility as are Carter's King William Artillery, Hardaway's Alabama, and Patterson's Georgia batteries. Carman Map, #6 (8:00 a.m.) and Carman Map, # 7 (8:30 to 8:40 a.m.).

158. The troops lying down may have been the 124th Pennsylvania (XII Corps); OR 19, pt. 1, 319-21; Tate, *General Edwin Vose Sumner*, 173-74; Cope Map, #7 (8:30 to 8:40 a.m.).

159. OR 19, pt. 1, 319-21.

160. Carman, *The Maryland Campaign*, vol. II, 59; Harsh, *Taken at the Flood*, 391-92.

161. OR 19, pt. 1, 319-21, 883; undated handwritten note, NYPL.

162. OR 19, pt. 1, 319-21.

163. Undated handwritten note, NYPL Carman Correspondence.

164. Fred C. Wexler, *The Tammany Regiment: A History of the Forty-Second New York Volunteer Infantry, 1861-1864* (Bloomington, IN: iUniverse, 2016), 145; OR 19 pt. 1, 321-23; Carman, *The Maryland Campaign*, vol. II, 195, 206.

165. Undated and unnamed newspaper account in the Massachusetts Historical Society, Hallowell Papers; OR 19 1, 321; Carman, *The Maryland Campaign*, vol. II, 204.

166. OR 19, 1, 321-322; Hall continued to command the brigade until December 15, 1862, Dyer, *A Compendium of the War of the Rebellion*, vol. I, 291.

167. Carman, *The Maryland Campaign*, vol. II, 210; Phisterer, *New York in the War of Rebellion*, 2519; Daniel A. O'Mara to Ezra Carman, February 28th, 1905.

168. OR 19, pt. 1, 514-15; Dwight Stinson unpublished NPS Report (1962), ANB Library; Sumner, "The Antietam Campaign," vol. 14, 11.

169. Carman Map #8 (9:00 to 9:30 a.m.); Carman, *The Maryland Campaign*, vol. II, 211 (note 70). Thomas Clemens, notes that "The direct quote from Francis Palfrey is found on p. 87 of his book *The Antietam and Fredericksburg* (New York: Charles Scribner's Sons, 1882). Robins, in his letter to Carman, cited a September 29, 1862, letter from Lt. Henry Patten which confirmed the firing to the rear, and said the noise prevented their hearing the order to retire."

170. Norwood Hallowell to Ezra Carman, February 24, 1905, NYPL, Carman Correspondence, Box 3 Folder 4; Carman, *The Maryland Campaign*, vol. II, 211n70; Undated account from an unidentified newspaper in the Norwood Penrose Hallowell Papers scrapbook states that Hallowell was wounded in the shoulder "with shattering of bones," Massachusetts Historical Society, Norwood Penrose Hallowell Papers, 1764-1914, Scrapbook Vol. 5, 1861-1885; bulk: 1861-1863. Retrieved on July 1, 2020 at http://www.masshist.org/collection-guides/digitized/fa0370/vol5#32; Hallowell to Carman, February 24, 1905; The John G. Palfrey collection of Oliver Wendell Holmes, Jr. Papers, 1715-1938, Family and Personal Scrapbook created by Oliver Wendell Holmes, Jr., 1861-1865, Harvard Law School Library.

171. Regimental surgeon Edward Revere, grandson of Paul Revere, was not as fortunate as Hallowell or Holmes. Tending to a wounded soldier on the field, he was killed instantly by a shot through his heart. His brother, Lt. Col. Paul Revere, Inspector General of II Corps, who was riding with Sumner that morning, survived with a gun shot wound to his arm—less than a year later he would be killed at Gettysburg. *The Boston Daily Advertiser*, July 14, 1863 in the Massachusetts Historical Society, Norwood Penrose Hallowell Papers, 1764-1914, Scrapbook Vol. 5, 1861-1885.

172. *The Boston Daily Advertiser*, July 14, 1863 in the Massachusetts Historical Society, Norwood Penrose Hallowell Papers, 1764-1914, Scrapbook Vol. 5, 1861-1885. Semmes' engagement with the 15th Massachusetts and the enfilading fire from the 82nd NY, both of Dana's command cost him dearly. "Nearly one half of the brigade were killed and wounded [and] three of the regimental commanders were wounded." Carman, *The Maryland Campaign*, vol. II, 199, 206-207. Jubal Early lagged behind Semmes and did not fully participate in the advance. Carman writes that Semmes' three regiments equaled 250 men. Carman, *The Maryland Campaign*, vol. II, 217.

173. Carman, *The Maryland Campaign*, vol. II, 211-219; OR 19, 1, 323. After Hincks and Devereaux were wounded, Weymouth took over the command and eventually filed the regiment's Official Report. It is difficult to determine how many times the ad hoc formation fell back. The highest number cited is four times from the Annual Report of the Massachusetts Adjutant General. *Annual Report of the Adjutant-General, of the Commonwealth of Massachusetts, with Reports from the Quartermaster-General, Surgeon-General, and Master of Ordnance, for the Year Ending December 31, 1862,* (Boston: Wright & Potter, 1863), 222-23.

174. *OR* 19, 1, 323; Carman, *The Maryland Campaign*, vol. II, 218-19.

175. William Colville to Ezra Carman, December 10, 1892, NA-AS; Cope Map #10 (Noon to 12:15 p. m.).

176. *OR* 19, 1, 305-306.

177. Dana sat on a military commission for a while but never took field command again. Following the war, he entered into business affairs and served as deputy commissioner of pensions for the federal government from 1895 to 1897. His wound, however, continued to bother him for the remainder of his life. Welsh, *Medical Histories of Union Generals*, 89-90.

178. Warner, *Generals in Blue*, 161-62; Stephen W. Sears, *Lincoln's Lieutenants: The High Command of the Army of the Potomac* (New York: Houghton Mifflin Harcourt, 2017), 227; Dyer, *A Compendium of the War of the Rebellion*, vol. I, 291.

179. Sears, *Lincoln's Lieutenants*, 393; Carman, *The Maryland Campaign*, vol. II, 567.

180. Walker, *History of the Second Corps*, 93-99; *OR* 19, pt. 1, 52; Carman, *The Maryland Campaign*, vol. I, 370, 403, 411.

181. *OR* 19, pt. 1, 323, 1,023; Carman, *The Maryland Campaign*, vol. II, 246. According to historian Ezra Carman and Gen. French, the right flank of Weber's brigade was hit by the small (40-man) 8th South Carolina of Joseph Kershaw's brigade, attempting to capture Tompkins' battery nearby. They opened fire on Weber's flank and according to French, opened a "sudden and terrible fire." Tompkins' guns warded off the attack. Historian Thomas Clemens did not believe this action actually occurred. Carman, *The Maryland Campaign*, vol. II, 247-48, 248 (note 13).

182. William P. Seville, *History of the First Regiment, Delaware Volunteers, From the Commencement of the "Three Months' Service" to the Final Muster-Out at the Close of the Rebellion* (Wilmington, DE: The Historical Society of Delaware, 1884), 47-48; Marion Armstrong, *Unfurl Those Colors*, 210, 212; Carman, *The Maryland Campaign*, vol. II, 247-49. The timing of the Confederate counterattack has been contested. Ezra Carman believed it came when Morris' brigade arrived and helped beat back the advance. Marion Armstrong posited it occurred after Weber's initial repulse.

183. *OR* 19, pt. 1, 324; Armstrong, *Unfurl Those Colors*, 215; Carman, *The Maryland Campaign*, vol. II, 251; Frederick L. Hitchcock, *War from the Inside or Personal Experiences, Impressions, and Reminiscences of One of the "Boys" in the War of the Rebellion* (Philadelphia: Press of J. B. Lippincott Company, 1904), 59.

184. Carman, *The Maryland Campaign*, vol. II, 280-81, 297; Armstrong, *Unfurl Those Colors*, 220, 241.

185. *OR* 19, pt. 1, 193.

186. Hartwig, *To Antietam Creek*, Appendix B, Strength of Union and Confederate Forces; Carman, *The Maryland Campaign*, vol. II, 576.

187. *OR* 19, pt. 1, 193.

188. William Kepler, *History of the Three Months' and Three Years' Service of the Fourth Regiment Ohio Volunteer Infantry in the War for the Union* (Cleveland, OH: Leader Printing Co., 1886), 79; David W. Mellot, "A Dear Bought Name: The 7th West Virginia Infantry's Assault on Bloody Lane," *Civil War Regiments*, vol. 5, no. 3 (1997), 130.

189. Warner, *Generals In Blue*, 267-58; Armstrong, *Unfurl Those Colors*, 64-65.

190. Frank J. Welcher, *The Union Army, 1861 – 1865: Organization and Operations* (Bloomington, IN: Indiana University Press, 1989), vol. I, 315; Armstrong, *Unfurl Those Colors*, 77.

191. Nancy Niblack Baxter, *The Gallant Fourteenth: The Story of an Indiana Civil War Regiment* (Carmel, IN: Guild Press of Indiana, Inc., 1999), 96.

192. Franklin Sawyer, *A Military History of the 8th Ohio Vol. Inf'y: Its Battles, Marches and Army Movements* (Cleveland, OH: Fairbanks & co.., 1881), 70-71; Armstrong, *Unfurl Those Colors*, 87-90.

193. Sawyer, *A Military History of the 8th Ohio*, 81; Thomas Galwey, *The Valiant Hours, Narrative of "Captain Brevet," An Irish-American in the Army of the Potomac* (Mechanicsburg, PA: Stackpole Books, 1961), 35; Frederick L. Hitchcock, *War from the Inside: The Story of the 132nd Regiment Pennsylvania Volunteer Infantry*, 46.

194. Hitchcock, *War from the Inside*, 46-47.

195. Carman, *The Maryland Campaign*, vol. I, 398-402; Armstrong, *Unfurl Those Colors*, 126.

196. *OR* 19, pt. 2, 307-8; Sawyer, *A Military History of the 8th Ohio*, 75.

197. Hitchcock, *War from the Inside*, 56; Galwey, *The Valiant Hours*, 42.

198. *OR* 19, pt. 1, 275, 323; Armstrong, *Unfurl Those Colors*, 167; Harsh, *Taken at the Flood*, 385.

199. *OR* 19, pt. 1, 323-24; Sawyer, *A Military History of the 8th Ohio*, 76-77; Armstrong, *Unfurl Those Colors*, 207.

200. Galwey, *The Valiant Hours*, 38-40; Carman, Vol. II, 243-44; Harsh, *Taken at the Flood*, 395.

201. Carman, *The Maryland Campaign*, vol. II, 246; Armstrong, *Unfurl Those Colors*, 212-13.

202. Carman, *The Maryland Campaign*, vol. II, 251.

203. *OR* 19, pt. 1, 327; Carman, *The Maryland Campaign*, vol. II, 255; Galway, *The Valiant Hours*, 40.

204. *OR* 19, pt. 1, 331; Baxter, *The Gallant Fourteenth*, 98-99; Armstrong, *Unfurl Those Colors*, 218-219; Hitchcock, *War From The Inside*, 59.

205. Carman, *The Maryland Campaign*, vol. II, 254, 260; *OR* 19, pt. 1, 327; Hitchcock, *War from the Inside*, 61-62.

206. Carman, *The Maryland Campaign*, vol. II, 263-64; Baxter, *The Gallant Fourteenth*, 100.

207. Armstrong, *Unfurl Those Colors*, 220, 241.

208. Sawyer, *A Military History of the 8th Ohio*, 81.

209. Baxter, *The Gallant Fourteenth*, 103.

210. Hartwig, *To Antietam Creek*, Appendix B, Strength of Union and Confederate Forces; Carman, *The Maryland Campaign*, vol. II, 576.

211. *OR* 19, pt. 1, 193.

212. *The Union Army*, vol. I, 128, 288, 452; Bates, *History of Pennsylvania Volunteers*, vol. 4, 204.

213. Roger D. Hunt, *Colonels in Blue: Union Army Colonels of the Civil War The New England States: Connecticut, Maine, Massachusetts, New Hampshire, Rhode Island, Vermont* (Atglen PA: Schiffer Military History Books, 2001), 32.

214. H. S. Stevens, *Souvenir of Excursion to Battlefields by the Society of the Fourteenth Connecticut Regiment and Union at Antietam, September 1891* (Washington, DC: Gibson Brothers, Printers, 1893), 49; Charles D. Page, *History of the Fourteenth Regiment, Connecticut Vol. Infantry* (Meriden, CT: The Horton Printing Co., 1906), 26-28; George H. Washburn, *Military History and Record of the 108th Regiment, N. Y. Vols., From 1862 to 1984* (Rochester, NY: Press of E. R. Andrews, 1894), 19.

215. Washburn, *Military History and Record of the 108th Regiment, N. Y. Vols.,* 24; Page, *History of the Fourteenth Regiment,* 34-36; OR 19, pt. 1, 333.

216. John D. Hemmingen, *Diary of John D. Hemmingen, Company E, 130th Pennsylvania,* September 17, 1862 entry, Michael Winey Collection, USAMHI.

217. Stevens, *Souvenir of Excursion to Battlefields,* 49-50; Page, *History of the Fourteenth Regiment,* 37; OR 19, pt. 1, 333.

218. Page, *History of the Fourteenth Regiment,* 37-38; Stevens, *Souvenir of Excursion to Battlefields,* 52.

219. Carman, *The Maryland Campaign,* vol. II, 251.

220. OR 19, pt. 1, 335, 336. Col. John Andrews of the 1st Delaware (Weber's brigade) had nothing good to say about Morris' men. He reported, "A charge was then ordered and attempted, but our second line, composed of new levies, instead of supporting our advance, fired into our rear." OR 19, pt. 1, 337.

221. OR 19, pt. 1, 193; The New York State Military History Museum Site accessed on April 8, 2020, https://dmna.ny.gov/historic/reghist/civil/infantry/108thInf/Porter_Letters/1862_09_20.pdf

222. OR 19, pt. 1, 18, 577; Civil War Data Base accessed on April 6, 2020 http://www.civilwardata.com/active/hdsquery.dll?SoldierHistory?U&587108; Hunt, *Colonels in Blue: New England States,* 32.

223. Carman, *The Maryland Campaign,* vol. II, 576.

224. OR 19, pt. 1, 193.

225. Warner, *Generals in Blue,* 545-6; Marion V. Armstrong Jr., *Unfurl Those Colors,* 150-1; Seville, *History of the First Regiment,* 45; OR 18, 386-7.

226. Seville, *History of the First Regiment,* 11-4, 24-6, 28-9, 37-40, 42, 43, 46.

227. *The Union Army,* vol. II, 51-2; L. Allison Wilmer, J.H. Harrett, George H. Vernon, State Commissioners, *History and Roster of Maryland Volunteers, War of 1861-5,* 2 volumes (Baltimore: Press of Guggenheimer, Weil & Co.: 1898), vol. I, 179; George R. Graham, "The Fifth Maryland Infantry at Antietam," NA–AS; https://mpv.052.myftpupload.com/civil-war-letters-2/by-state-regiment/union-civil-war-letters-

delaware/l10-3-62de/?fbclid=IwAR3G4GshGYoz-UejW59Rz9-9jXT8l0TntD42vctfR6DY85TYHn7cleN8H-I Accessed March 20, 2021.

228. Thomas G. Murphey, *Four Years in the War: The History of the First Regiment of Delaware Veteran Volunteers* (Philadelphia: J.S. Claxton, 1866), 76, 77; Armstrong, *Unfurl Those Colors,* 149; Graham, "The Fifth Maryland Infantry at Antietam;" Seville, *History of the First Regiment,* 46.

229. OR 19, pt. 1, 323; J.K. Polk Racine, "Reminiscence of Antietam," *Cecil Whig* (Elkton, MD), 24 September 1898, p. 6.

230. Carman, *The Maryland Campaign,* vol. II, 246-7. Although Carman writes that "the right of Weber's line was struck by the 8th South Carolina of Kershaw's Brigade," there is some doubt as to which Confederate troops were involved, see Carman, *The Maryland Campaign,* vol. II, 248 (note 13); Graham, "The Fifth Maryland Infantry at Antietam;" quoted in William B. Styple, ed., *Writing and Fighting the Civil War: Soldier Correspondence to the New York Sunday Mercury* (Kearney, NJ: Belle Grove Publishing Company, 2000), 128-130. The color bearer may have been Pvt. John D. Tuft, see "Local Affairs," *Cecil Whig* [Elkton, MD], 27 September 1862, p. 2; Wilmer, et al., *History and Roster of Maryland Volunteers,* vol. I, 217.

231. Graham, "The Fifth Maryland Infantry at Antietam;" OR 19, pt. 1, 337, 1037; Carman, *The Maryland Campaign,* vol. II, 241.

232. Graham, "The Fifth Maryland Infantry at Antietam," quoted in Styple, ed., *Writing and Fighting the Civil War,* 128-130; Clark, ed., *Histories of the Several Regiments and Battalions from North Carolina in the Great War 1861-'65,* 5 volumes (Raleigh, NC: State of North Carolina, 1901), vol. 1, 247; John B. Gordon, *Reminiscences of the Civil War* (New York: Charles Scribner's Sons, 1904), 87; Carman, *The Maryland Campaign,* vol. II, 248-9; Seville, *History of the First Regiment,* 48.

233. Graham, "The Fifth Maryland Infantry at Antietam;" Carman, *The Maryland Campaign,* vol. II, 248-9; Walter F. Beyer and Oscar F. Keydel, comp., *Deeds of Valor: How America's Heroes Won the Medal of Honor,* 2 volumes (Detroit, MI: The Perrien-Keydel Company: 1901), vol. I, 83-5; Seville, *History of the First Regiment,* 49.

234. OR 19, pt. 1, 332, 337; Carman, *The Maryland Campaign,* vol. II, 248, 252; "The Panic of the 5th Maryland," *Blue Hen's Chicken and Commonwealth* (Wilmington, DE), 1 October 1862, p. 2. Lt. Col. Sanford Perkins of the 14th Connecticut reported that the 5th Maryland "broke, which threw three companies of my right wing into confusion," see OR 19, pt. 1, 333; Morris and Perkins may have mistaken the troops that fell back through the 14th Connecticut since it was the 1st Delaware that was in front of the 14th Connecticut; Armstrong, *Unfurl Those Colors,* 216; J. K. Polk Racine,

"One of the Fiercest Battles Ever Waged by Mortal Men," *Cecil Whig* (Elkton, MD), 15 October 1898, p. 6.

235. Welsh, M.D, *Medical Histories of Union Generals*, 361-2; Warner, *Generals in Blue*, 546; quoted in Styple, ed., *Writing and Fighting the Civil War*, 128-130; OR 19, pt. 1, 336; Graham, "The Fifth Maryland Infantry at Antietam," *Cecil Whig* [Elkton, MD], 27 September 1862, p. 2.

236. Graham, "The Fifth Maryland Infantry at Antietam;" "Local Affairs,"; Seville, *History of the First Regiment*, 53-4; quoted in Styple, ed., *Writing and Fighting the Civil War*, 128-130.

## V Corps

1. McClellan, *McClellan's Own Story*, 139; Carman, *The Maryland Campaign*, vol. I, 133-34. Porter was no fan of Pope, and his dispatches to Ambrose Burnside contained a wealth of incriminating statements that would be used to help convict the V Corps commander of not doing all that he could to support Pope at Second Bull Run. OR 19, pt. 3, 700, 733; Carman, *The Maryland Campaign*, vol. I, 416-17.

2. Warner, *Generals in Blue*, 378-79; Carman, *The Maryland Campaign*, vol. I, 156-57; William H. Powell, *The Fifth Corps* (New York: G. P. Putnam's Sons, 1896), 6.

3. OR 19, pt. 2, 253-54, 255. Brig. Gen. Andrew Humphreys' division of rookies was delayed, according to Porter, "by exchanging unserviceable arms in five regiments and obtaining transportation and provision . . ." OR 19, pt. 1, 338.

4. OR 19, pt. 1, 338; OR 19, pt. 2, 296; Carman, *The Maryland Campaign*, vol. I, 403-06.

5. Carman, *The Maryland Campaign*, vol. I, 409-10. McClellan and Porter were initially joined by three other corps commanders (Joseph Hooker, Edwin Sumner, and Ambrose Burnside, Jacob Cox). They left the hill because of danger posed by Confederate artillery fire, but McClellan and Porter remained, and together made the decision not to initiate an attack on that day (September 15). Thomas Clemens has determined the Pry House was not McClellan's headquarters but a command post.

6. OR *Suppl.*, vol. 3, 466-67.

7. OR 19, pt. 1, 338. Porter's order to pull Sykes' men back across Antietam Creek even though they were meeting success was questioned after the war. Capt. Thomas Anderson recalled Buchanan receiving a request from the commander of the troops across the creek to charge an enemy battery. The note was sent to McClellan who was sitting on his horse with Sykes and Porter. Porter, according to Anderson, nixed the idea, telling McClellan, "Remember, general, I command the last reserve of the last army of the Republic." Porter refuted this claim after it was made. Thomas Anderson, "The Reserve at Antietam," *Century Magazine*, vol. 32, no. 5 (1886), 783; Fitz John Porter, "Memoranda on the Civil War: 'The Reserve at Antietam'," *Century Magazine*, vol. 33, no. 3 (1887), 472.

8. OR 51, pt. 1, 845; OR 19, pt. 1, 212, 339; Carman, *The Maryland Campaign*, vol. II, 387-88.

9. Carman, *The Maryland Campaign*, vol. II, 502.

10. Carman, *The Maryland Campaign*, vol. II, 393.

11. OR 19, pt. 1, 339; Carman, *The Maryland Campaign*, vol. II, 508.

12. OR 19, pt. 1, 339.

13. Warner, *Generals in Blue*, 378-80; Otto Eisenschiml, *The Celebrated Case of Fitz John Porter* (Indianapolis, IN: Bobbs-Merrill, 1950), 240-41.

14. Warner, *Generals in Blue*, 330-31.

15. OR *Suppl.*, vol. 3, 466-67; Carman, *The Maryland Campaign*, vol. I, 188; OR 51, pt. 1, 832; Gottfried, *The Maps of Antietam*, 22-23; Cope Map #7 (8:30-8:40 a.m.) and #8 (9:00-9:30 a.m.); OR 19, pt. 1,338; ; Carman, *The Maryland Campaign*, vol. II, 388. Morell's division does not appear on the Cope maps until the #8 map (9:00-9:30 a.m.).

16. Hartwig, *To Antietam Creek*, Appendix B, Strength of Union and Confederate Forces, but see OR 19, pt. 1, 346.

17. OR 19, pt. 1, 204. James Barnes gives a different tabulation at the end of his report, which states the brigade's loss as 92 killed, 131 wounded, and 103 missing, totaling 326 casualties, or 19.1%. OR 19, pt. 1, 348.

18. OR 11, pt. 2, 30. Hennessy, *Second Manassas Battlefield Map Study*, 459.

19. Warner, *Generals in Blue*, 20-21.

20. OR 19, pt. 2, 197; Mark A. Snell, "Baptism of Fire: The 118th ('Corn Exchange') Pennsylvania Infantry at the Battle of Shepherdstown," *Civil War Regiments: A Journal of the American Civil War*, vol. 6, no. 2, 123.

21. OR 19, pt. 1, 338; J. L. Smith, *History of the 118th Pennsylvania Volunteers Corn Exchange Regiment* (Philadelphia, PA: J. L. Smith, 1905), 30.

22. Hewett, et. al., OR *Supplement*, vol. 3, 466; Carman, *The Maryland Campaign*, vol. II, 263, 388, 391-92.

23. OR *Suppl.*, vol. 3, 466-67; OR 19 pt. 1, 339-40.

24. OR 19, pt. 1,340; Edwin C. Bennett, *Musket and Sword* (Boston, MA: Coburn Publishing Co., 1900), 97.

25. OR vol. 19, pt. 1, 346; Joseph Hayes, "Battle of Sheppardstown," Box 4, Joshua Lawrence Chamberlain Papers, LOC.

26. Hayes, "Battle of Sheppardstown;" OR 19, pt. 1, 346.

27. OR 19, pt. 1, 347, 352; J. Gregory Acken, ed., *Inside the Army of The Potomac: The Civil War Experience of Captain Francis Adams Donaldson* (Mechanicsburg, PA: Stackpole Books, 1998), 456.

28. Smith, *History of the 118th Pennsylvania Volunteers*, 60-61.

29. Smith, *History of the 118th Pennsylvania Volunteers*, 61-64.

30. OR 19, pt. 1, 348-49; Acken, ed., *Inside the Army of the Potomac*, 134.

31. OR 19, pt. 1, 204, 347.

32. Hartwig, *To Antietam Creek*, Appendix B, Strength of Union and Confederate Forces.

33. *OR* 19, pt. 1, 194.

34. Warner, p. 3, 190-91.

35. Dyer, *Compendium of the War of the Rebellion*, vol. I, 302; vol. III, 1019, 1251, 1260, 1283, 1410, 1595.

36. Hartwig, *To Antietam Creek*, Appendix B, Strength of Union and Confederate Forces.

37. *OR* 19, pt. 1, 194.

38. Dyer, *Compendium of the War of the Rebellion*, vol. I, 303; Antietam on the Web, https://antietam.aotw.org/officers.php?officer_id=902.

39. Dyer, *Compendium of the War of the Rebellion*, vol. III, 1226, 1288, 1410, 1411, 1420, 1601.

40. Timothy J. Reese, *Sykes' Regular Infantry Division 1861-1865* (Jefferson NC: McFarland, 1990), 17.

41. *OR* 11 pt 2, 225; *OR* 12 pt 3, 483; *OR* 51 pt 1, 791.

42. *OR* 19 pt 1, 40; *OR* 19 pt 2, 296.

43. *OR* 19 pt 1, 356.

44. *OR* 19 pt 1, 351.

45. The 1st battalion of the 12th U.S. maintained a skirmish line on the west bank of Antietam creek. *OR* 19, pt 1, 353.

46. *OR* 19, pt. 1, 351.

47. Carman, *The Maryland Campaign*, vol. II, 369. Dryer's command included his own 4th U.S. Infantry, two battalions of the 14th U.S. Infantry, and a battalion of the 2nd & 10th U.S. Infantry from Lovell's brigade. Capt. Blunt's 1st battalion of the 12th U.S. did not participate in Dryer's advance. William H. Powell "Memoranda on the Civil War: More Light on the Reserve at Antietam" *Century Magazine*, vol. 33, no. 5 (March 1887), 804; *OR* 19 pt 1, 351, 357.

48. *OR* 19 pt 1, 367.

49. *OR* 19 pt 1, 351.

50. Thomas A. McGrath, *Shepherdstown: Last Clash of the Antietam Campaign* (Lynchburg VA: Schroeder Publications, 2008), 94.

51. Hartwig, *To Antietam Creek*, Appendix B, Strength of Union and Confederate Forces. However, another analysis showed a total of 1,952 when numbers of officers and enlisted men present for duty taken from the August 1862 returns are adjusted for changes up until September 14. It also includes Companies A & D of the 8th U. S. that were attached to the 2-12th U.S. *Returns from Regular Army Infantry Regiments, June 1821–December 1916*. NARA microfilm publication M665.

52. Carman used casualty numbers from *OR* 19, pt. 1, 194. 32 of 39 casualties were in the 4th U. S. Infantry.

53. Reese, *Sykes' Regular Infantry*, 69.

54. *OR* 11, pt. 2, 358, 487.

55. Thomas H. Evans "The Enemy Sullenly Held on to the City," *Civil War Times Illustrated*, April, 1968, 32; Wilkins Papers, September 8, 1862; Reese, *Sykes' Regular Infantry*, 131.

56. *OR* 51, pt. 1, 826; Edward Cassedy, ed., *Dear Friends at Home: The Civil War Letters and Diaries of Sergeant Charles T. Bowen Twelfth United States Infantry First Battalion 1861-1864* (Baltimore: Butternut and Blue, 2001), 152.

57. *OR* 19, pt. 2, 296.

58. *OR* 19, pt. 1, 356.

59. Harsh, *Taken at the Flood*, 336.

60. The four horse batteries commanded by John Tidball, Peter Hains, Horatio Gibson, and James Robertson were armed with three-inch ordnance rifles.

61. *OR* 19, pt. 1, 358; Cassedy, ed., *Dear Friends*, 154.

62. Lovell's troops were the 2nd and 10th U.S. commanded by Capt. John Poland. This regiment served under the command of Capt. Dryer while fighting on the west side of Antietam Creek.

63. *OR* 19, pt. 1, 360.

64. Thomas Anderson "The Reserve at Antietam" *Century Magazine* 32, no.5 (1886), 783; Carman, *The Maryland Campaign*, vol. II, 368.

65. *OR* 19, pt. 1, 356.

66. Anderson "The Reserve," 783.

67. Anderson "The Reserve," 783.

68. Anderson "The Reserve," 783; Powell "Memoranda on the Civil War," 804.

69. Anderson "The Reserve," 783; Carman, *The Maryland Campaign*, vol. II, 384.

70. Anderson "The Reserve," 785; Powell "Memoranda on the Civil War," 804.

71. *OR* 19, pt. 1, 351.

72. Hartwig, *To Antietam Creek*, Appendix B, Strength of Union and Confederate Forces. However, another analysis showed a total of 1,387 when numbers of officers and enlisted men present for duty taken from the August 1862 returns are adjusted for changes up till September 14. *Returns from Regular Army Infantry Regiments, June 1821–December 1916*. NARA microfilm publication M665.

73. Carman used casualty numbers from *OR* 19, pt. 1, 194. 55 of 56 casualties were in the 2nd and 10th U. S. Infantry.

74. Poland's battalion was formed from nine companies of the 2nd U.S. and three companies of the 10th U.S. Of the 697 men assigned to Lovell's brigade, 226 of 697 or 32% were absent sick. One company of the 1st U.S. was attached to Boote's regiment the 6th U.S. August and September 1862. *Returns from Regular Army Infantry Regiments, June 1821–December 1916*.

75. The monthly returns for September reflect 726 men absent sick in the regiments of Lovell's brigade, approximately 32% of the total brigade strength.

76. *OR* 12, pt. 2, 497; Reese, *Sykes' Regulars*, 78.

77. *OR* 51, pt. 1, 815.

78. Reese, *Sykes' Regulars*, 123, 136.

79. The three batteries were Weeds, von Kleisers, and Tafts. Weed had four 3-inch ordnance rifles. Taft and von Kleiser each had four 20 pound Parrots. Duncan

Vance, "Lieut. D.M. Vance" *Urbana Union* (Urbana Ohio), October 1, 1862.

80. *OR* 19, pt. 1, 362. Buchanan's battalion was the 1-12th U.S. commanded by Capt. Matthew Blunt. The horse batteries belonged to Tidball, Robertson, Hains and Gibson. The artillery battery from Sykes' division was Randol's battery.

81. The Confederate infantry in the lane from the Holcombe Legion and 17th South Carolina. Garnett's brigade of Virginia infantry were further back in the cornfield below the crest of the hill. Poland encountered the Confederate batteries of Charles Squires' Washington Artillery (LA) and George Moody's battery (VA) of Stephen Lee's artillery battalion. *OR* 19, pt. 1, 363. Patrick Breen "Why the Union Army Did Not Win at Antietam," *National Tribune* April 18, 1895.

82. *OR* 19, pt. 1, 363.

83. *OR* 19, pt. 1, 363.

84. Breen, "Union Army."

85. *OR* 19, pt. 1, 362.

86. John Ames to mother Sep 21 1862, Ames Papers, USAMHI; McGrath *Shepherdstown*, 97.

87. *OR* 19, pt. 1, 361.

88. *OR* 19, pt. 1, 365.

89. Carman, *The Maryland Campaign*, vol. III, 3.

90. Burke who was born in Connecticut and was not awarded the Medal of Honor until 30 years after the battle, on April 21, 1892. Shortly after Antietam, the sergeant was appointed a second lieutenant in the 2nd U.S. He retired in 1899 as a brigadier general. Heitman *Historical Register and Dictionary of the United States Army*, vol. I, 263.

91. Hartwig, *To Antietam Creek*, Appendix B, Strength of Union and Confederate Forces. In Warren's Second Bull Run report, (*OR* 12, pt. 2, 502), he reports bringing 1,000 men into battle (490 in the 5th New York and 510 in the 10th New York). In Brian Pohanka's masterful history, he concludes the total losses for Warren's brigade was 449 (334 in the 5th New York and 115 in the 10th New York) leaving an approximate brigade strength of 551. However, some 220 recruits joined the 5th New York prior to Antietam, so another estimate of the brigade's strength is 771.

92. *OR* 19, pt. 1, 195.

93. Allan Nevins, ed., *A Diary of Battle The Personal Journals of Colonel Charles S. Wainright 1861-1865* (New York: Hartcourt, 1962), 36; Charles W. Cowtan, *Services of the Tenth New York Volunteers (National Zouaves)* (New York: Charles Ludwig, 1882), 53, 83.

94. Cowtan, *Tenth New York*, 82.

95. Brian Pohanka, *Vortex of Hell: A History of the 5th New York Volunteer Infantry* (Lynchburg VA: Schroeder Publications, 2012), 283, 365.

96. Pohanka, *Vortex of Hell*, 360.

97. Pohanka, *Vortex of Hell*, 368.

98. Pohanka, *Vortex of Hell*, 369.

99. *OR* 19, pt. 1, 351. Cowtan, *Tenth New York*, 146.

100. *OR* 19, pt. 1, 62, 339, 351, 367; Cope Map #12 (3 p.m.), #13 (4:20 p.m.), #14 (5:30 p.m.); Alfred Davenport, *Camp and Field Life of the Fifth New York Volunteer Infantry* (New York: Dick and Fitzgerald, 1879), 315.

101. Davenport, *Camp and Field*, 317; *OR* 19, pt. 1, 367.

102. Davenport, *Camp and Field*, 318; Cowtan, *Tenth New York*, 148.

103. McGrath, *Shepherdstown*, 124; *OR* 19, pt. 1, 352.

104. Pohanka, *Vortex of Hell*, 360.

## VI Corps

1. Mark A. Snell, *From First To Last: The Life of William B. Franklin* (Fordham University Press, New York, 2002), 8, 9, 24, 52-64, 109; Hartwig, *To Antietam Creek*, 20; Ezra A, Carman, *The Maryland Campaign*, vol. I, 148.

2. Snell, *From First To Last*, 124; Hartwig, *To Antietam Creek*, 20; Carman, *The Maryland Campaign*, vol. I, 140, 144, 705 (note 28); *OR* 19, pt. 2, 138-39.

3. William B. Franklin, "Notes on Crampton's Gap and Antietam," *Battles and Leaders of the Civil War*, vol. II, 591-596; Carman, *The Maryland Campaign*, vol. I, 168-197; Maurice G. D'Aoust, "'Little Mac' Did Not Dawdle," *Civil War Times*, October 2012, 36-37; Hartwig, *To Antietam Creek*, 287-89.

4. Hartwig, *To Antietam Creek*, 292, 441-442, 471-472; *OR* 19, pt. 1, 854; Snell, *From First To Last*, 176-184, 211; Carman, *The Maryland Campaign*, vol. I, 298. Bartlett was consulted about the point of attack because he had gained Slocum's and Franklin's respect on the Peninsula and he had personally inspected the ground on the right.

5. "Franklin, "Notes on Crampton's Gap and Antietam," vol. II, 591-596; Steven R Stotelmyer, *Too Useful To Sacrifice: Reconsidering George B. McClellan's Generalship in the Maryland Campaign from South Mountain to Antietam* (El Dorado Hills, CA: Savas Beatie, 2019), 83; Snell, *From First To Last*, 187-189; Hartwig, *To Antietam Creek*, 476-477.

6. Hartwig, *To Antietam Creek*, 641; Franklin, "Notes on Crampton's Gap and Antietam," vol. II, 596-597; Snell, *From First To Last*, 192; Carman, *The Maryland Campaign*, vol. II, 286, 305, 326, 330; Carman-Cope Map #14 (5:30 p.m.).

7. Carman, *The Maryland Campaign*, vol. II, 327, 345, 491, 501; Snell, *From First To Last*, 194-195; Franklin, "Notes on Crampton's Gap and Antietam," vol. II, 587.

8. Carman, *The Maryland Campaign*, vol. I, 311; Carman, *The Maryland Campaign of 1862*, vol. II, 601.

9. Snell, *From First To Last*, 202.

10. Dyer, *A Compendium of the War of the Rebellion*, vol. I, 308.

11. Warner, *Generals in Blue*, 451-52; Larry Tagg, *The Generals of Gettysburg: The Leaders of America's Greatest Battle* (Mason City, IA: Savas Publishing Company, 1998), 143.

12. *OR* 19, pt. 1, 378.

13. *OR* 19, pt. 1, 380; Carman, *The Maryland Campaign*, 305-06.

14. *OR* 19, pt. 1, 183, 380-81; Carman, *The Maryland Campaign*, 303-05.

15. *OR* 19, pt. 1, 195, 381-82.

16. Hartwig, *To Antietam Creek*, Appendix B, Strength of Union and Confederate Forces; Bradley M. Gottfried, *Kearny's Own: The History of the First New Jersey Brigade in the Civil War* (New Brunswick, NJ: The Rutgers University Press, 2005), 74.

17. *OR* 19, pt. 1, 195. These are the losses at Antietam. The brigade previously lost 172 men (38 killed and 134 wounded at Crampton's Gap on September 14. Carman, *The Maryland Campaign*, vol. I, 310.

18. Dyer, *A Compendium of the War of the Rebellion*, vol. III, 1356-58; Gottfried, *Kearny's Own*, 51-55, 63-67.

19. Warner, *Generals in Blue*, 508.

20. *OR* 19, pt. 1, 378, 380, 382; Gottfried, *Kearny's Own*, 69-70.

21. Gottfried, *The Maps of Antietam*, 78-79.

22. *OR* 19, pt. 1, 380.

23. *Elizabeth New Jersey Journal*, September 23, 1862; Gottfried, *Kearny's Own*, 71-72.

24. *OR* 19, pt. 1, 386, 387; *Newark Daily Advertiser*, September 20, 1862; *Paterson Guardian* (New Jersey), October 15, 1962.

25. *OR* 19, pt. 1, 386, 861, 870-71.

26. Timothy J. Reese, *Sealed with Their Lives: The Battle of Crampton's Gap* (Baltimore, MD: Butternut and Blue, 1998), 158-59; *OR* 19, pt. 1, 871; Gottfried, *Kearny's Own*, 72-73.

27. *OR* 19, pt. 1, 183.

28. Camille Baquet, *History of the First Brigade, New Jersey Volunteers from 1861 to 1865* (Trenton, NJ: MacCrellish & Quigley, State Printers, 1910), 47; *OR* 19, pt. 1, 383; Gottfried, *Kearny's Own*, 74.

29. Oscar Westlake to parents, September 21, 1862; John Kuhn Collection (private); Reuben Brooks to brother, September 28, 1862, Rutgers University Library; Baquet, *History of the First Brigade*, 54; Gottfried, *Kearny's Own*, 75.

30. *OR* 19, pt. 1, 195.

31. Hartwig, *To Antietam Creek*, Appendix B, Strength of Union and Confederate Forces.

32. Darrell L. Collins, *The Army of the Potomac: Order of Battle, 1861-1865, with Commanders, Strengths, Losses, and More.* (Jefferson, NC: McFarland & Company, 2013), 79.

33. *The Union Army*, vol. I, 42, vol. II, 59, 68-69; Carman, *The Maryland Campaign*, vol. III, 288; Dyer, *A Compendium of the War of the Rebellion*, vol. III, 1220, 1411, 1414, 1605.

34. *The Union Army*, vol. I, 432; Carman, *The Maryland Campaign*, vol. III, 288; Fox, *Regimental Losses in the American Civil War*, 229.

35. Carman, *The Maryland Campaign*, vol. III, 180; Henry P. Smith (ed.), *History of Broome County: With Illustrations and Biographical Sketches of Some of Its Prominent Men and Pioneers* (Syracuse, NY: D. Mason, 1885), 162, 168, 169.

36. *The Union Army*, vol. I, 432; Collins, *The Army of the Potomac. Order of Battle, 1861-1865*, 20, 32.

37. *Third Annual Report of the Bureau of Military Statistics of the State of New York*: Transmitted to the Legislature February 3, 1866 (Albany, NY: G. Wendell Printer, 1866) 130; C. B. Fairchild, *History of the 27th Regiment N. Y. Vols.: Being a Record of its More than Two Years of Service in the War for the Union, from May 21st, 1861, to May 31st, 1863* (Binghamton, NY: Carl & Matthews, Printers, 1888), 89. The marches north were difficult for the men. William Morse recorded in his diary on September 12 how the officers had "filled themselves with whiskey [and] led us off at an unreasonable rate and many of the boys fell out regardless of court-martial and quite a number fainted. The doctors had plenty to do and one of them said three marches were killing the men faster than the bullets ever would." William L. Caynor, *Without a Scratch: Diary of William Holmes Morse, Color Bearer of the 5th Maine Infantry* (Wilmington, NC: Broadfoot Publishing, 2007), 71.

38. *OR* 19, pt. 1, 388, 390, 391, 392, 393; Caynor, *Without a Scratch*, 73.

39. *OR* 19, pt. 1, 380; Carman, *The Maryland Campaign of 1862*, vol. I, 297, 298, 302.

40. George W. Bicknell. *History of the Fifth Regiment Maine Volunteers* (Portland, ME: H. L. Davis, 1871), 136-137; *OR* 19, pt. 1, 394.

41. Carman, *The Maryland Campaign*, vol. I, 301, 303; Bicknell, *History of the Fifth Regiment Maine Volunteers*. 138.

42. Carman, *The Maryland Campaign*, vol. I, 304; *OR* 19, pt. 1, 392.

43. Bicknell. *History of the Fifth Regiment Maine Volunteers*, 140; Carman, *The Maryland Campaign*, vol. I. 304; Fairchild, *History of the 27th Regiment N. Y. Vols*, 91.

44. Newton Martin Curtis, *From Bull Run to Chancellorsville. The Story of the Sixteenth New York Infantry, Together With Personal Reminiscences* (New York: G.P. Putnam's Sons, 1906), 169; Carman, *The Maryland Campaign*, vol. I., 308; *OR* 19, pt. 1, 389; Fairchild, *History of the 27th Regiment N. Y. Vols.*, 92.

45. Darrell L. Collins, *The Army of the Potomac*, 62. Losses of the brigade at Crampton's Gap were as follows: the 5th Maine had 32 casualties (4 killed, 28 wounded); the 16th New York had 61 casualties (20 killed, 41 wounded); the 27th New York had 33 casualties (6 killed, 27 wounded), and 96th Pennsylvania had 91 casualties (20 killed, 71 wounded).

46. Carman, *The Maryland Campaign*, vol. I, 326-327; Bicknell, *History of the Fifth Regiment Maine Volunteers*, 145-146; Fairchild, *History of the 27th Regiment N. Y. Vols.*, 95.

47. Carman, *The Maryland Campaign*, vol. I, 330-331; Darrell L. Collins, *The Army of the Potomac*, 68-69. Losses in the brigade at Antietam were: 5th Maine (5 wounded), 16th New York (2 wounded), 27th New York (0 casualties), and 96th Pennsylvania (1 killed, 1 wounded). Bicknell. *History of the Fifth Regiment Maine Volunteers*, 148.

48. Curtis, *From Bull Run to Chancellorsville*, 196-197.

49. Hartwig, *To Antietam Creek*, Appendix B, Strength of Union and Confederate Forces.

50. *OR* 19, pt. 1, 195; Darrell L. Collins, *The Army of the Potomac*, 79.

51. Dyer, *"A Compendium of the War of the Rebellion,* vol. III, 1412, 1416; Phisterer, *"New York in the War of the Rebellion,"* vol. II, 389, 397, 398.

52. Dyer, *"A Compendium of the War of the Rebellion,* vol. III, 1605; Bates, *History of Pennsylvania Volunteers,* vol. III, 335.

53. Carman, *The Maryland Campaign,* vol. III, 266; Cyrus B. Comstock, "Memoir of John Newton, 1823-1895," A Biographical Memoir Read before the National Academy, November 13, 1901, *National Academy of Sciences. Biographical Memories* (National Academy of Sciences. Washington D.C. 1902), vol. IV, 235.

54. *The Union Army*, vol. I, 43, vol. II, 61, 72, 73; Darrell L. Collins, *The Army of the Potomac*, 30, 42; *OR* 11, pt. 1. 457; Hartwig, *To Antietam Creek*, 36, 38, 40.

55. Carman, *The Maryland Campaign,* vol. I, 168, 169.

56. Hartwig, *To Antietam Creek*, 438.

57. Hartwig, *To Antietam Creek*, 442, 447; Ryan A. Conklin, *The 18th New York Infantry in the Civil War: A History and Roster.* (Jefferson, NC: McFarland & Co., 2016), 268.

58. Carman, *The Maryland Campaign,* vol. I, 302; Hartwig, *To Antietam Creek*. 442, 447; Conklin, *The 18th New York*, 268.

59. Carman, *The Maryland Campaign,* vol. I, 304; Hartwig, *To Antietam Creek*. 451; *OR* 19, pt. 1, 380, 396.

60. Carman, *The Maryland Campaign,* vol. I, 304- 05; *OR* 19, pt. 1, 380, 396-97.

61. *OR* 19, pt. 1, 396- 97, 398, 399; Conklin, *The 18th New York Infantry*, 278; Hartwig, *To Antietam Creek*, 465, 466.

62. *OR* 19, pt. 1, 396, 399, 400, 401.

63. *OR* 19, pt. 1, 195, 381, 398, 399, 401. Collins, *The Army of the Potomac*, 62. Losses in the brigade at Crampton's Gap were as follows: the 18th New York had 54 casualties (11 killed, 41 wounded, 2 missing); the 31st New York had 4 casualties (1 killed, 3 wounded); the 32nd NY had 51 casualties (11 killed, 40 wounded), and 95th Pennsylvania had 15 casualties (1 killed, 14 wounded).

64. *OR* 19, pt, 1. 376, 377; Carman, *The Maryland Campaign*, vol. II, 326, 327, 329.

65. *Third Annual Report of the Bureau of Military Statistics of the State of New York: Transmitted to the Legislature February 3, 1866* (Albany, NY: G. Wendell Printer, 1866) 222.

66. Collins, *The Army of the Potomac*, 69. Losses in the brigade at Antietam were: 18th New York (4 wounded), 31st New York (3 wounded), 32nd New York (4 wounded), and 95th Pennsylvania (1 killed, 9 wounded). *OR* 19, pt. 1, 70; *Third Annual Report of the Bureau of Military Statistics of the State of New York*, 229.

67. George B. McClellan, *Civil War Papers of George B. McClellan: Selected Correspondence, 1860-1865*, Stephen W. Sears, ed. (New York: Ticknor & Fields, 1989), 94, 97;

Sears, *Lincoln's Lieutenants*, 87; Stewart Sifakis, *Who Was Who in the Civil War* (New York: Facts on File, 1988), 608-09.

68. Kerry A. Trask, *Fire Within: A Civil War Narrative* (Kent, OH: Kent State University Press, 1995), 127; Robert S. Westbrook, *History of the 49th Pennsylvania Volunteers* (Altoona, PA: Altoona Times Print, 1897), 122-23.

69. *OR* 19, pt. 1, 374, 401, 406, 408; Carman, *The Maryland Campaign*, vol. 1, 305, 311, 441-42.

70. *OR* 19, pt. 1, 376-77, 402-03; Westbrook, *History of the 49th Pennsylvania Volunteers*, 124; Williams, *From the Cannon's Mouth*, 129. The Cope map of 1200 hrs shows the brigade in close connection with Cowan's and Frank's batteries, but Hancock's report states it also supported Cothran's, which was actually further to the left and supported by Gordon's brigade (Crawford's division, XII Corps). *OR* 19, pt. 1, 406.

71. *OR* 19, pt. 1 , 342.

72. *OR* 19, pt. 1, 195-96. Hartwig, *To Antietam Creek*, Appendix B, Strength of Union and Confederate Forces.

73. Warner, *Generals in Blue*, 202-03.

74. Dyer, *Compendium of the War of the Rebellion*, vol. I, 310; vol. III, 1220, 1420, 1590, 1615.

75. Carman, *The Maryland Campaign*, vol. I, 179, 309; vol. II, 305-06; *OR* 19, pt. 1, 406-07.

76. *OR* 19, pt. 1, 196. Hartwig, *To Antietam Creek*, Appendix B, Strength of Union and Confederate Forces.

77. Dyer, *Compendium of the War of the Rebellion*, vol. I, 310; vol. III, 1649-51.

78. Warner, *Generals in Blue*, 47.

79. *OR* 19, pt. 1, 407-08. Carman, *The Maryland Campaign*, vol. I, 305, 309, 311.

80. Carman, *The Maryland Campaign*, vol. II, 287, 325; *OR* 19, pt. 1, 408-09.

81. Hartwig, *To Antietam Creek*, Appendix B, Strength of Union and Confederate Forces. The brigade numbered about 1,684 at Antietam. Carman, *The Maryland Campaign*, vol. II, 578.

82. Carman, *The Maryland Campaign*, vol. II, 602. Carman did not supply a definition of "engaged" but it appears to mean "attacked" as the Sixth Corps reported 439 total casualties for Antietam, 342 which were from Irwin's brigade. *OR* 19, pt. 1, 196.

83. Dickson College Archives.

84. *OR* 19, pt. 1, 374-75; Thomas W. Hyde, *Following the Greek Cross Or, Memories of the Sixth Army Corps* (Boston: Houghton, Mifflin and Company, 1894), 94.

85. Carman, *The Maryland Campaign*, vol. II, 286, 320, 322; *OR* 19, pt. 1, 409; Hyde, *Following the Greek Cross*, 94. Hyde recalled, "seeing a body of the enemy about some barns on our left flank we charged them, tearing down the rail fences as we went. We drove them out losing a dozen men then dashed back again at the run and lay down on the left of the Germans who had lost heavily."

Carman believed the three regiments were aligned, *en echelon*, but not all believe this was the case.

86. *OR* 19, pt. 1, 409, 414, 416; Carman, *The Maryland Campaign*, vol. II, 322-23; George T. Stevens, *Three Years in the Sixth Corps: A Concise Narrative of Events in the Army of the Potomac from 1861 to the Close of the Rebellion, April, 1865* (New York: D. Van Nostrand, Publisher, 1870), 148-149; Frederick David Bidwell, *History of the Forty-Ninth New York Volunteers* (Albany, NY: J. B. Lyon Company, 1916), 20-21.

87. *OR* 19, pt. 1, 415-16; Bidwell, *History of the Forty-Ninth New York Volunteers*, 21. Capt. Nathan Babcock of the 77th New York reported that after "getting our new position, the enemy's shot and shell fell thick among us and quite a number of my men were wounded, but my men behaved nobly through the entire day, even amidst the most galling fire and shelling of the enemy." *OR* 19, pt. 1, 416.

88. Hyde, *Following the Greek Cross*, 97. Hyde recalled Vegesack responding, "Let them wave! They are our glory said the old Swede, and he kept riding back and forth behind the regiment revolver in hand to shoot skulkers, the most prominent feature on the field."

89. Hyde, *Following the Greek Cross*, 97; Carman, *The Maryland Champaign*, vol. II, 344-45. Captain Emory Upton's Official Report, completed on September 26, 1862 noted, "I rode to the left of Colonel Irwin's Brigade there I saw a rebel regiment drawn up in line of battle and that could be enfiladed from that position. I ordered forward four of Wolcott's guns."

90. *OR* 19, pt. 1, 412-13; Carman, *The Maryland Campaign*, vol. II, 345; Hyde, *Following the Greek Cross*, 99-100. Words exchanged vary from Hyde's and Irwin's after-battle reports and Hyde's book. The word "Barleycorn" appears in later publications based on Hyde's book published in 1894. The reference to John Barleycorn suggested Irwin had been drinking or was drunk when he ordered Hyde's regiment forward. If true, Hyde's accusation was a serious one, and Carman's inclusion of this accusation was unusual for him. No official inquiry was held, and Irwin resigned after being wounded in the leg in the spring of 1863. Irwin died in 1886 and was not able to challenge Hyde's "assertion." Hyde, *Following the Greek Cross*, 104-105; Hunt, *Brevet Brigadiers in Blue*, 309.

91. Hyde, *Following the Greek Cross*, 100-106. Carman, *The Maryland Campaign*, vol. II, 345-8; *OR* 19, pt. 1, 412-13. Irwin quickly realized the folly of his orders. He wrote in his report, "Finding the regiment so severely engaged, I was very anxious to support them, but my orders were positive not to advance my line. I rode rapidly forward, and requested the officer commanding the right regiment of the Second Brigade to support Major Hyde, which he declined to do without orders from General Brooks. I then returned to my own line to ask for a support from the rear, but in a few minutes, I had the extreme pleasure of seeing the shattered but brave remnant of the Seventh Maine in good order return to my lines. No words of mine can do justice to the firmness, intelligence, and heroic courage with which this regiment performed its dangerous task … Alone and surrounded by the enemy, they fought until nearly all their cartridges were expended. They then delivered one fierce parting volley, closed their ranks around their colors, and fell slowly back to the line of battle." *OR* 19, pt. 1, 410-11.

92. Maj. Hyde wrote in his after-battle report, "I drove the enemy from the trees and buildings. Colonel Irwin ordered me to clear, but for want of support was unable either to push on after his line was pierced or to hold the position that was gained." *OR* 19, pt. 1, 412-13.

93. *OR* 19, pt. 1, 411.

## IX Corps

1. Warner, *Generals in Blue*, 409, 486-7; *OR* 12, pt. 2, 257; Dyer, *A Compendium of the War of the Rebellion*, vol. I, 313-6; William Marvel, *Burnside* (Chapel Hill, NC: The North Carolina Press, 2000), 107; *OR* 19, pt. 1, 421.

2. Augustus Woodbury, *Major General Ambrose E. Burnside and the Ninth Army Corps: A Narrative of Campaigns in North Carolina, Maryland, Virginia, Ohio, Kentucky, Mississippi and Tennessee, During the War for the Preservation of the Republic* (Providence, RI: Sidney S. Rider & Brother, 1867), 104; Dyer, *A Compendium of the War of the Rebellion*, vol. I, 313, 317; Marvel, *Burnside*, 94; Jacob D. Cox, "Forcing Fox's Gap and Turner's Gap," in *Battles and Leaders of the Civil War*, vol. 2, 583-84; *OR* 19, pt. 1, 416; *OR* 12, pt. 2, 261-2; *OR* 12, pt. 3, 566, 568-9, 814-6; Charles F. Johnson, *The Long Roll* (East Aurora, NY: Roycrofters, 1911), 180.

3. Carman, *The Maryland Campaign*, vol. I, 317-9, 328-30; *OR* 19, pt. 1, 417, 435, 458-60. See *OR* 19, pt. 1, 187 for casualty returns (but see Cox's report, *OR* 19, pt. 1, 460, which tallies total casualties for the Kanawha Division of 528, considerably higher than the 356 reported in the official returns). Hartwig, *To Antietam Creek*, 368, Appendix C.

4. *OR* 19, pt. 1, 418, 423; *OR* 19, pt. 2, 296, 297, 308; Jacob D. Cox, *Military Reminiscences of the Civil War*, 2 vols. (New York: Scribner's Sons, 1900), vol. I, 383; Carman, *The Maryland Campaign*, vol. II, 402 (note 8); Hartwig, *To Antietam Creek*, 495-96.

5. Jacob Cox, "The Battle of Antietam," in *Battles and Leaders*, vol. 2, 634; Carman, *The Maryland Campaign*, vol. II, 425; *OR* 19, pt. 1, 31, 63, 419. For a fuller analysis of the timing controversy, see Maurice D'Aoust, "Unraveling the Myths of Burnside Bridge," *Civil War Times*, XLVI, Vol. 7 (September 2007), 50-57.

6. Cox, "The Battle of Antietam," 650; Carman, *The Maryland Campaign*, vol. II, 462; Scott, ed., *Forgotten Valor: The Memoirs, Journals & Civil War Letters of Orlando B. Willcox* (Kent, OH: The Kent State University Press, 1999), 366; *OR* 19, pt. 1, 445.

7. *OR* 19, pt. 1, 198; Carman, *The Maryland Campaign*, vol. II, 619.

8. Hazard Stevens, *The Life of Isaac Ingalls Stevens,* 2 volumes (Boston: Houghton, Mifflin and Company, 1900), vol. II, 485-6; Dyer, *A Compendium of the War of the Rebellion,* vol. I, 313-14; Samuel P. Bates, *Brief History of the One Hundredth Regiment (Roundheads)* (New Castle, PA: W. B. Thomas, 1884), 14; *OR 12,* pt. 3, 588.

9. Scott, ed., *Forgotten Valor,* 11, 234, 327; *OR 19,* pt. 1, 432; Michigan Adjutant-General's Dept, *Record of Service of Michigan Volunteers in the Civil War, 1861-1865,* and George H. Turner, comp. (Kalamazoo, MI: Ihling Bros. & Everard, 1900), vol. 1, 1.

10. *OR 19,* pt. 1, 432; Bates, *History of Pennsylvania Volunteers,* vol. III, 558; Allen D. Albert, ed., *History of the Forty-Fifth Regiment, Pennsylvania Volunteer Infantry Regiment, 1861-1865* (Williamsport, PA: Grit Publishing Company, 1912), 47.

11. *OR 19,* pt. 1, 427-33; Albert, *History of the Forth-Fifth Regiment,"* 229.

12. *OR 19,* pt. 1, 186, 432; Carman, *The Maryland Campaign,* vol. I, 406.

13. *OR 19,* pt. 1, 429-33.

14. Scott, *Forgotten Valor,* 366-7, 371; Carman, *The Maryland Campaign,* vol. II, 444, 446 (note 26).

15. *OR 19,* pt. 1, 196-97.

16. Hartwig, *To Antietam Creek,* Appendix B, Strength of Union and Confederate Forces. Carman, puts the brigade strength at Antietam as 1,395. Carman, *The Maryland Campaign,* vol. II, 579.

17. The 8th Michigan transferred from Christ's brigade to Welsh's brigade on September 16. *OR 19,* pt. 1, 177, 196; Carman, *The Maryland Campaign,* vol. III, 195.

18. Bates, *History of Pennsylvania Volunteers,* vol. III, 1277; James L. Bowen, *Massachusetts in the War, 1861-1865* (Springfield, MA: Clark W. Bryan & Co., 1889), 419; William Todd, *The Seventy-Ninth Highlanders, New York Volunteers in the War of Rebellion, 1861-1865* (Albany, NY: Brandow, Barton & Co., 1886), 1.

19. *OR 19,* pt. 1, 431-2; Turner, *Record of Service of Michigan Volunteers in the Civil War,* vol. 17, 1; "Elon G. Mills Diary, 1862-1864" 12 August 1862 entry, https://deepblue.lib.umich.edu/handle/2027.42/100349?show=full (accessed 29 March 2020).

20. *OR 19,* pt. 1, 427-8; Carman, *The Maryland Campaign,* vol. I, 333-4 (note 41).

21. *OR 19,* pt. 1, 428-9, 433-4, 437-8, 1020-1; "The Division of General Willcox in Sunday's Battle," *The Detroit Free Press,* September 20, 1862, p. 3; Scott, *Forgotten Valor,* 354; Gabriel Campbell to Ezra Carman, August 23, 1899, NYPL.

22. *OR 19,* pt. 1, 186, 427-9, 437-8; "Telegraph! Last Night's Report," *Buffalo Evening Post,* September 17, 1862, p. 3; Kurt Graham, "Death of a Brigade: Drayton's Brigade at Fox's Gap, September 14, 1862," http://www.angelfire.com/ga2/PhillipsLegion/deathofabrigade.html. The 17th Michigan would earn the name "Stonewall Regiment" for its actions at Fox's Gap,

including charges against several stone fences, see Turner, *Record of Service of Michigan Volunteers,* vol. 17, 2.

23. Carman, *The Maryland Campaign,* vol. I, 406; *OR 19,* pt. 1, 432.

24. *OR 19,* pt. 1, 429-31; Todd, *The Seventy-ninth Highlanders,* 243.

25. Carman, *The Maryland Campaign,* vol. II, 359, 441, 435; *OR 19,* pt. 1, 896-7.

26. *OR 19,* pt. 1, 196, 438; "Reunion of the 50th P.V." *The Bradford Star* [Towanda, PA], 15 September 1898, 2; Mills diary, 18 September 1862 entry; *OR 19,* pt. 1, 438-9. The ground in this area was not heavily wooded so perhaps Christ confused this action with the fighting three days earlier at Fox's Gap, where there were more trees.

27. Carman, *The Maryland Campaign,* vol. II, 444, 446 (note 26); *OR 19,* pt. 1, 432.

28. Hartwig, *To Antietam Creek,* Appendix B, Strength of Union and Confederate Forces. Carman puts the brigade's strength at Antietam as 1,623. Carman, *The Maryland Campaign,* vol. II, 579.

29. The 8th Michigan transferred from Christ's brigade to Welsh's brigade on September 16. *OR 19,* pt. 1, 177, 196. Also, see "Forty-Fifth Pennsylvania Infantry," *The National Tribune* [Washington, DC], 21 June 1906, 3 (citing Fox's Regimental Losses), which states that the 45th Pennsylvania lost 6 killed and mortally wounded at Antietam.

30. Albert, ed., *History of the Forty-Fifth Regiment, Pennsylvania Volunteer Infantry,* 13-33; Bates, *History of Pennsylvania Volunteers,* vol. I, 1057-9, vol. III, 553-9 Woodbury, *Major General Ambrose E.Burnside,* 104.

31. *OR 19,* pt. 1, 431-2. Albert, *History of the Forth-Fifth Regiment,* 47.

32. Albert, *History of the Forth-Fifth Regiment,* 51; *OR 19,* pt. 1, 439.

33. *OR 19,* pt. 1, 428-9, 433-4, 437-8, 441, 1020-1; "The Division of General Willcox in Sunday's Battle," *The Detroit Free Press,* September 20, 1862, 3; George Swinscoe to Ezra Carman, July 19, 1899, NYPL; Albert, *History of the Forth-Fifth Regiment,* 51-2.

34. Hartwig, *To Antietam Creek,* 356; *OR,* vol. 19, pt. 1, 440, 442, 461, 1020-1; Scott, ed., *Forgotten Valor,* 369.

35. *OR 19,* pt. 1, 429-31, 442; Todd, *The Seventy-ninth Highlanders,* 243.

36. *OR 19,* pt. 1, 441, 442; Carman, *The Maryland Campaign,* vol. II, 443-4, (note 24).

37. Carman, *The Maryland Campaign,* vol. II, 441; *OR 19,* pt. 1, 426, 896-7.

38. Carman, *The Maryland Campaign,* vol. II, 440, 441; Scott, ed., *Forgotten Valor,* 361.

39. Carman, *The Maryland Campaign,* vol. II, 444, 446 n. 26; *OR 19,* pt. 1, 432; Scott, ed., *Forgotten Valor,* 371.

40. http://www.arlingtoncemetery.net/ssturgis.htm (accessed on 7/4/2020); https://www.nps.gov/mana/learn/historyculture/order-of-battle.htm (accessed on 7/21/2020). After the Civil

War, Sturgis once again found himself in command of cavalry-- the 7th U.S. cavalry. Sturgis would have been at the Battle of the Little Big Horn, however, his recruiting assignment left his second in-command, George Armstrong Custer, in charge. Custer led the 7th U.S. cavalry to its fateful disaster at the battle, also known as Custer's Last Stand. Custer served on McClellan's staff at Antietam as a captain. The most notable act performed by Custer at the battle was knocking on Philip Pry's door and notifying the family that McClellan had selected their house for his headquarters. The Reserve Corps consisted of Brig. Gen. Abram Piatt's brigade containing the 63rd Indiana (four companies) and the 86th New York. These troops did not participate in the Maryland Campaign as they were assigned to the defense of Washington.

41. OR 19, pt. 1, 178; Committee of the Regimental Association, *History of the Thirty-Fifth Regiment Massachusetts Volunteers, 1862-1865. With a Roster* (Boston: Mills, Knight & Co, 1884), 24-26; Edward O. Lord, *History of the Ninth Regiment, New Hampshire Volunteers in the War of the Rebellion* (Concord, NH: Republican Press, 1895), 46-59.

42. OR 19, pt. 1, 443. The number of men lost at Fox's Gap reported by Sturgis was later revised to reflect a loss of 157. OR 19, pt. 1, 187. Maj. Gen. Jesse Reno was the acting IX Corps commander after Burnside was elevated to wing command.

43. Carman, *The Maryland Campaign*, vol. II, 582; OR 19, pt. 1, 178, 443-44.

44. OR 19, pt. 1, 444-45. The term to "see the elephant" meant the soldiers saw their first battle.

45. Hartwig, *To Antietam Creek*, Appendix B, Strength of Union and Confederate Forces; Carman, *The Maryland Campaign*, vol. II, 415; Lyman Jackson, *History of the Sixth New Hampshire in the War for the Union* (Concord, NH: Republican Press, 1891), 1, 2; Lord, ed., *History of the Ninth Regiment, New Hampshire Volunteers*, 70-71; Joseph Gould, *The Story of the Forty-Eighth: A Record of the Campaigns of the Forty-eighth Regiment Pennsylvania Veteran Volunteer Infantry During the Four Eventful Years of its Service in the War for the Preservation of the Union* (Philadelphia: [Forty-eight] Regimental Association, 1908), 21-3; OR 19, pt. 1, 186. The 2nd Maryland and the 6th New Hampshire each had 150 men, for a total strength of 300 men at Antietam. The 48th Pennsylvania a month after the battle of Antietam reported a strength of 467 men; the regiment lost 60 men during the battle. By adding these numbers, a possible strength of 527 men was available for the battle (barring sickness, desertion, etc.). The historian for the 9th New Hampshire estimated the strength of the regiment at 900 men prior to the battle of South Mountain. The regiment lost 29 men during the battle, leaving them with a possible strength of 870 men for Antietam.

46. OR 19, pt. 1, 197.

47. Wilmer, Jarrett, Vernon, and George, eds., *History and Roster of Maryland Volunteers*, 71-72; Jackson, *History of the Sixth New Hampshire*, 1-2; Lord, *History of the Ninth Regiment*, 6; Gould, *The Story of the Forty-Eighth*, 21.

48. Gould, *The Story of the Forty-Eighth*, 21-22.

49. Lord, *History of the Ninth Regiment, New Hampshire Volunteers*, 58.

50. Lord, *History of the Ninth Regiment, New Hampshire Volunteers*, 71-73.

51. Lord, *History of the Ninth Regiment, New Hampshire Volunteers*, 58, 71-73; Carman, *The Maryland Campaign of 1862*, vol. I, 338-39; OR 19, pt. 1 186; Gottfried, *Maps of Antietam*, 44, 46.

52. Carman, *The Maryland Campaign*, vol. I, 338-39, 342; Gottfried, *Maps of Antietam*, 44, 46; OR 19, pt.1, 443, 186.

53. Carman, *The Maryland Campaign*, vol. II, 414.

54. Carman, *The Maryland Campaign*, vol. II, 415; OR 19, pt. 1, 444; Jackson, *History of the Sixth New Hampshire in the War for the Union*, 103.

55. Carman, *The Maryland Campaign*, vol. II, 415; OR 19, pt. 1, 447, 444; Jackson, *History of the Sixth New Hampshire in the War for the Union*, 104.

56. Carman, *The Maryland Campaign*, vol. II, 415; OR 19, pt. 1, 447; John Michael Priest, ed., *Captain James Wren's Diary: From New Bern To Fredericksburg* (Shippensburg, PA: White Mane Publishing Company, 1990), 73.

57. Carman, *The Maryland Campaign*, vol. II, 420, 431; Jackson, *History of the Sixth New Hampshire in the War for the Union*, 106.

58. Carman, *The Maryland Campaign*, vol. II, 484-485.

59. Warner, *Generals in Blue*, 340-41.

60. Hartwig, *To Antietam Creek*, Appendix B, Strength of Union and Confederate Forces; Charles F. Walcott, *History of the Twenty-first Regiment, Massachusetts Volunteers, in the War for the Preservation of the Union, 1861-1865: With Statistics of the War and of Rebel Prisons* (Boston: Houghton, Mifflin and Company, 1882), 195; Committee, *History of the Thirty-Fifth Regiment Massachusetts Volunteers*, 26; Carman, *The Maryland Campaign*, vol. I, 417. The 21st Massachusetts had about 150 men for the battle of Antietam. The 35th Massachusetts historian estimated the regiment's strength prior to the battle of South Mountain at 800 men, with a loss of 63 men, this gives the regiment a possible effective force of 737 at Antietam. The twin 51's each had about 335 men for the battle of Antietam. Adding the possible effective force of the combined regiments gives at least 1,557 men available for the battle of Antietam.

61. OR 19, pt. 1, 187, 197. This number reflects the combined loss for the brigade at both the battle of South Mountain and Antietam.

62. Walcott, *History of the Twenty-first Regiment, Massachusetts Volunteers*, 1, 2, 5, 9, 17, 131, 186 359, 383; Dyer, *A Compendium of the War of the Rebellion*, vol. I, 191; Thomas H. Parker, *History of the 51st Regiment of P.V. and V.V., from its Organization, at Camp Curtin, Harrisburg, Pa., in 1861, to its being Mustered out of the United States Service at Alexandria, Va., July 27th, 1865* (Philadelphia: King &

Baird, Printers, 1869), 11, 13, 29, 212-213, 220-21, 259, 314, 531, 600.

63. Committee, *History of the Thirty-Fifth Regiment Massachusetts*, 2, 9, 10, 15, 19, 21, 22. The men enlisted for three years or for the duration of the war, the latter created confusion when the men wanted to return home after serving three years.

64. *Los Angeles Herald*, December 14, 1899.

65. Committee, *History of the Thirty-Fifth Regiment Massachusetts*, 22.

66. Committee, *History of the Thirty-Fifth Regiment Massachusetts*, 26, 27; Walcott, *History of the Twenty-first Regiment, Massachusetts Volunteers*, 188; *OR* 19, pt. 1, 448. The brigade had an estimated 1,650 men prior to Antietam, this number reflects the strength of the brigade at Antietam, added to the casualties sustained at the battle of South Mountain.

67. Walcott, *History of the Twenty-first Regiment, Massachusetts Volunteers*, 189, 190; Committee, *History of the Thirty-Fifth Regiment Massachusetts*, 27-29. The historian of the 21st Massachusetts was critical of Ferrero for selecting the 35th Massachusetts to perform this nighttime reconnaissance. The green troops lacked the proper training and the experience to perform such a difficult task correctly.

68. Parker, *History of the 51st Regiment of P.V. and V.V.*, 224-225; Gottfried, *The Maps of Antietam*, 52.

69. Walcott, *History of the Twenty-first Regiment, Massachusetts Volunteers*, 188; Committee, *History of the Thirty-Fifth Regiment Massachusetts*, 29, 30; Carman, *The Maryland Campaign*, vol. I, 342-43; Parker, *History of the 51st Regiment of P.V. and V.V.*, 225-226; *OR* 19, pt. 1, 448. Ferrero in his report stated, "The sudden fire produced temporary confusion in one of my new regiments [35th Massachusetts]"

70. Parker, *History of the 51st Regiment of P.V. and V.V.*, 226-27; Committee, *History of the Thirty-Fifth Regiment Massachusetts*, 30; *OR* 19, pt. 1, 187; Walcott, *History of the Twenty-first Regiment, Massachusetts Volunteers*, 189-90, 194-95. At the time, many believed it was the volley from Hood's men that struck down Reno. However, the 35th Massachusetts may have actually delivered the volley. Walcott, *History of the Twenty-first Regiment, Massachusetts Volunteers*, 194, 198, 199.

71. Walcott, *History of the Twenty-first Regiment, Massachusetts Volunteers*, 194, 198, 199; *OR* 19, pt. 1, 448

72. Walcott, *History of the Twenty-first Regiment, Massachusetts Volunteers*, 200; Gottfried, *The Maps of Antietam*, 210; William Potter letters, William Potter Family Collection; Parker, *History of the 51st Regiment of P.V. and V.V.*, 231-33.

73. William Potter letters; Gottfried, *The Maps of Antietam*, 212; Parker, *History of the 51st Regiment of P.V. and V.V.*, 233.

74. Walcott, *History of the Twenty-first Regiment, Massachusetts Volunteers*, 200-01.

75. Parker, *History of the 51st Regiment of P.V. and V.V.*, 233-35; Gottfried, *The Maps of Antietam*, 214; William Potter letters; Walcott, *History of the Twenty-first Regiment, Massachusetts Volunteers*, 203. Despite his men's success in crossing the bridge, Col. Potter was critical of the IX Corps' role.

76. Gottfried, *The Maps of Antietam*, 232; Parker, *History of the 51st Regiment of P.V. and V.V.*, 239; William Potter Letters; *History of the Twenty-first Regiment, Massachusetts Volunteers*, 202-203; *OR* 19, pt. 1, 448; Committee, *History of the Thirty-Fifth Regiment Massachusetts*, 47-50.

77. *OR* 19, pt. 1, 187, 197.

78. Dyer, *A Compendium of the War of the Rebellion*, vol. I, 354; Warner, *Generals in Blue*, 359-60.

79. Warner, *Generals in Blue*, 409-10; John W. Schildt, *The Ninth Corps at Antietam* (Chewsville, MD: n.p., 1988), 17-18.

80. Carman, *The Maryland Campaign*, vol. I, 192, 289, 339, 375; *OR* 19, pt. 1, 187, 450.

81. *OR* 19, pt. 1, 419; Carman, *The Maryland Campaign*, vol. II, 425, 581.

82. Cox, "Battle of Antietam," vol. II, 650-51; *OR* 19, pt. 1, 419; Cox, *Military Reminiscences*, 304-05.

83. Cope Map #12 (3:30 – 3:45 p.m.); Gottfried, *The Maps of Antietam*, 216; Carman, *The Maryland Campaign*, vol. II, 440.

84. *OR* 19, pt. 1, 197; Carman, *The Maryland Campaign*, vol. II, 462, 462 n. 53; T. H. Hawley to Ezra Carman, December 8, 1896; Seth D. Bingham to Ezra Carman, October 17, 1896; Harrison Fairchild to Ezra Carman, March 20, 1896, NYPL; Welsh, *Medical Histories of Union Generals*, 282-83.

85. Hartwig, *To Antietam Creek*, Appendix B, Strength of Union and Confederate Forces. Carman, puts the brigade's strength at Antietam as 943. Carman, *The Maryland Campaign*, vol. II, 581.

86. *OR* 19, pt. 1, 197; the 9th New York monument on the battlefield, which dates to 1897, lists 240 casualties, compared to 235 in the Official Records.

87. Carman, *The Maryland Campaign*, vol. III, 212; Matthew J. Graham, *The Ninth Regiment New York Volunteers (Hawkins' Zouaves): Being a History of the Regiment and Veteran Association from 1860 to 1900* (New York: E. P. Coby & Co.: 1900), 22-3, 36-9, 250; Phisterer, ed., *New York in the War of the Rebellion*, vol. IV, 3201-2. Carman noted that four companies of the 103rd New York were "left in North Carolina." Carman, *The Maryland Campaign*, vol. II, 581, but see *OR* 9, 414, and August 9 and August 23, 1862 letters of Capt. Henry Sand who claims there were three companies, instead of four. Henry Sand, *Crossing Antietam: The Civil War Letters of Captain Henry Augustus Sand, Company A, 103rd New York Volunteers*, Peter H. Sand and John F. McLaughlin, eds. (Jefferson, NC: McFarland & Company, Inc., 2016), 109, 120.

88. Graham, *The Ninth Regiment*, 243, 256-7; J.H.E. Whitney, *The Hawkins Zouaves: (Ninth N. Y. V.) Their*

*Battles and Marches* (New York: published by author, 1866), 127.

89. OR 19, pt. 1, 449-50; Whitney, *The Hawkins Zouaves*, 128-9; Graham, *The Ninth Regiment*, 263-5; Johnson, *The Long Roll*, 183; Frank Moore, ed., *The Rebellion Record : A Diary of American events, with Documents, Narratives, Illustrative Incidents, Poetry, etc. With an Introductory Address on the Causes of the Struggle, and the Great Issues before the Country, by Edward Everett*, 13 volumes (New York: G.P. Putnam's Sons, 1861-1863; Van Nostrand, 1864-1868), vol. V, 461-3.

90. Moore, *The Rebellion Record*, vol. V, 461; Carman, *The Maryland Campaign*, vol. I, 195; Graham, *The Ninth Regiment*, 268-9; Whitney, *The Hawkins Zouaves*, 129-30; OR 19, pt. 1, 450; Johnson, *The Long Roll*, 184.

91. OR 19, pt. 1, 450, 459; Carman, *The Maryland Campaign*, vol. I, 339-42; Clark, ed., *North Carolina Regiments*, vol. I, 245.

92. Graham, *The Ninth Regiment*, 272-3; OR 19, pt. 1, 450; Charles K. Crofut to Mira, September 28, 1862; Hartwig, *To Antietam Creek*, 372; David L. Thompson, "In the Ranks to the Antietam," in *Battles and Leaders of the Civil War*, vol. II, 558.

93. Graham, *The Ninth Regiment*, 273-4, 278, 282; Whitney, *The Hawkins Zouaves*, 132; Moore, *The Rebellion Record*, vol. V, 461.

94. OR 19, pt. 1, 450-1; Moore, *The Rebellion Record*, vol. V, 461; Carman, *The Maryland Campaign*, vol. II, 425-6. See notes 44 and 46 for a discussion of Union difficulties in locating a suitable ford downstream from the bridge.

95. Carman, *The Maryland Campaign*, vol. II, 426, 428-30; Curt Johnson and Richard C. Anderson, Jr., *Artillery Hell: The Employment of Artillery at Antietam* (College Station, TX: Texas A&M University Press, 1995), 23-4; David L. Thompson, "With Burnside at Antietam," in *Battles and Leaders*, vol. II, 661; Graham, *The Ninth Regiment*, 289-90.

96. Carman, *The Maryland Campaign*, vol. I, 428-9, 448-9; Johnson, *The Long Roll*, 191; Moore, *The Rebellion Record*, vol. V, 461; Whitney, *The Hawkins Zouaves*, 143.

97. Carman, *The Maryland Campaign*, vol. II, 449-51; Johnson, *The Long Roll*, 194; OR 19, pt. 1, 451; Graham, *The Ninth Regiment*, 296.

98. Thompson, "With Burnside at Antietam," vol. II, 661-2; Johnson, *The Long Roll*, 193; Sand, *Crossing Antietam*, 136-7; Graham, *The Ninth Regiment*, 296, 304; Moore, *The Rebellion Record*, vol. V, 462; OR 19, pt. 1, 451.

99. OR 19, pt. 1, 426; Carman, *The Maryland Campaign*, vol. II, 454-5; Though many believed Fairchild's brigade suffered the highest percentage of casualties of any Union brigade at Antietam, Brig. Gen. George Hartsuff's I Corps brigade, which fought in the Cornfield, appears to have suffered a higher percentage; Whitney, *The Hawkins Zouaves*, 150-3.

100. Hartwig, *To Antietam Creek*, Appendix B, Strength of Union and Confederate Forces; Carman, *The Maryland Campaign*, vol. II, 581.

101. OR 19, pt. 1, 197.

102. Leslie J. Gordon, "All Who Went into That Battle Were Heroes: Remembering the 16th Regiment Connecticut Volunteers at Antietam," in *The Antietam Campaign*, Gary W. Gallagher, ed. (Chapel Hill, NC: The University of North Carolina Press, 1999), 172.

103. John David Hoptak, "Brigadier General Edward Harland," *The 48th Pennsylvania Volunteer Infantry*, https://48thpennsylvania.blogspot.com/2009/11/brigadier-general-edward-harland.html. (accessed February 22, 2021).

104. Gordon, "All Who Went into That Battle Were Heroes," 173; W. A. Croffut and John Moses Morris, *The Military and Civil History of Connecticut During the War of 1861-65* (New York: Ledyard Bill, 1869), 261.

105. Carman, *The Maryland Campaign of 1862*, vol. I, 339; Walter J Yates, ed., *Souvenir of excursion to Antietam and dedication of Monuments of the 8th, 11th, 14th and 16th Regiments of Connecticut Volunteers* (New London, CT: n.p., 1894), 24; Jennie Porter Arnold, "At Antietam," *National Tribune*, October 18, 1888.

106. Wolcott Marsh to Anna, September 24, 1862, ANB Library; Bernard F. Blakeslee, *History of the Sixteenth Connecticut Volunteers* (Hartford, CT: The Case, Lockwood and Brainard Co., Printers, 1875), 10-11.

107. Lesley J. Gordon, "Bad Luck Regiment: The 16th Connecticut Infantry," *HistoryNet*, accessed on May 13, 2020, https://www.historynet.com/bad-luck-regiment-the-16th-connecticut-infantry.htm; Henry J. Spooner, "The Maryland Campaign with the Fourth Rhode Island," MOLLUS, *Personal Narratives of Events in the War of the Rebellion, Being Papers Read Before the Rhode Island Soldiers and Sailors Historical Society* (n.p; Published by the Society, 1903), vol. 9, 228.

108. Brig. Gen. David R. Jones, Brig. Gen. Robert Toombs' direct superior, was tasked with defending the Lower Bridge and the lower part of the battlefield. Coincidentally, Jones was the brother-in-law and dear friend of Col. Henry Kingsbury of the 11th CT. When Jones was told his men were responsible for mortally wounding Kingsbury, the once genial 'Neighbor' Jones was reportedly overcome with grief and guilt. These immense emotions further damaged Jones' already declining health and he suffered a fatal heart attack or stroke less than four months after the battle. Jones died on January 15, 1863 and his closest friends and family firmly believed that he died of a broken heart. Croffut and Morris, *The Military and Civil History of Connecticut*, 266.

109. Carman, *The Maryland Campaign*, vol. II, 426-430; George Merriman to May, September 24, 1862, copy at ANB Library.

110. OR 19, pt. 1, 453; *National Tribune*, October 18, 1881; Gordon, "Bad Luck Regiment; Carman, *The Maryland Campaign of 1862*, vol. II, 429, 457.

111. Carman, *The Maryland Campaign of 1862*, vol. II, 466-67; Jacob Bauer to wife, September 20, 1862, copy at ANB Library.

112. Yates, ed., *Souvenir of Excursion to Antietam and Dedication of Monuments of the 8th, 11th, 14th and 16th Regiments of Connecticut Volunteers*, 25; Henry Clay Hall to sister, October 5, 1862; Marsh to Anna, September 24, 1862; "Rodman's Brigade at Antietam, *National Tribune*, November 9, 1886; Carman, *The Maryland Campaign*, vol. II, 483.

113. Blakeslee, *History of the Sixteenth Connecticut Volunteers*, 17; OR 19, pt. 1, 197.

114. William Cochran, *General Jacob Dolson Cox: Early Life and Military Services* (Oberlin, OH: Bibliotheca Sacra Co., 1901), 4-7, 9, 13, 17-21, 23-28, 31-33.

115. Horton and Teverbaugh, *A History of the Eleventh Regiment -Ohio Infantry* (Dayton, Ohio, W.J. Shuey, 1866), 68-69.

116. Carman, *The Maryland Campaign* vol. I, 317; Jacob Cox, *Cox: Recollections of The Civil War*, vol.1, 231, 232.

117. Cox, *Cox: Recollections of the Civil War*, vol.1, 232.

118. Hartwig, *To Antietam Creek*, Appendix B, Strength of Union and Confederate Forces; https://48thpennsylvania.blogspot.com/2008/09/getting-to-know-eliakim-parker-scammon.html (accessed 06/10/2020); https://www.nps.gov/parkhistory/online_books/shubert/chap5.htm ( accessed on 6/30/2020). Scammon's dismissal for disobedience of orders was cited as, "Conduct to the Prejudice of Good Order and Military Discipline." During an expedition with U.S. engineers to the southwest, Scammon mismanaged an accounting book and $350 in public funds were unaccounted for.

6. Carman, *The Maryland Campaign*, vol. II, 472-473, 475-477, 486.

119. Hoptak, *The Battle of South Mountain*, 45. The average strength for the brigade has been estimated at 1,500 prior to South Mountain.

120. OR 19, pt. 1, 187, 198. This is the combined loss of the brigade at both the Battles of South Mountain and Antietam.

121. Joseph B. Foraker, James S. Robinson, and H.A. Axlinel, *Official Roster of the Soldiers of the State of Ohio in the War of the Rebellion, 1861-1865,* 5 volumes, (Akron, OH: The Werner Ptg. And Mfg. Co., 1886), vol. 2, 351; vol. 3, 69, 394; "30th Regiment Ohio Volunteer Infantry," *Ohio Civil War Central,* http://www.www.ohiocivilwarcentral.com/entry.php?rec=1246 (May 14, 2020); https://48thpennsylvania.blogspot.com/2008/09/getting-to-know-eliakim-parker-scammon.html (accessed 06/11/2020).

122. Carman, *The Maryland Campaign*, vol. 1, 343; Hoptak, *The Battle of South Mountain*, 178; OR 19, pt. 1, 463.

123. "Hugh Boyle Ewing," *Ohio Civil War Central,* <http://www.www.ohiocivilwarcentral.com/entry.php?rec=985>

124. Carman, *The Maryland Campaign*, vol. 1, 318; Cox, *Recollections of The Civil War*, vol. 1, 232, 233;

125. Cox, *Recollections of The Civil War*, vol. I, 233 Carman, *The Maryland Campaign of 1862*, vol.1, 317, 319.

126. Carman, *The Maryland Campaign*, vol. I, 323-325.

127. Carman, *The Maryland Campaign*, vol. I , 324-325; Gottfried, *The Maps of Antietam*, pg. 26, 28; Rutherford Birchard Hayes, *Diary and Letters of Rutherford Birchard Hayes: Nineteenth President of the United States 1822-1893,* Charles Richard Williams, ed., (Columbus,OH: Ohio State Archaeological and Historical Society, 1922), vol. 2, 354, 356. Hayes was transported to Middletown the following day. He wrote to his mother about his injury: "The arm is of course rendered useless and will be so for some weeks." Fortunately he also reported to his mother that he was "free from pain."

128. Cox, *Recollections of The Civil War*, vol. I, 233-236.

129. Cox, *Recollections of The Civil War*, vol. I, 236, 238; OR 19, pt. 1, 187. The brigade lost 62 men killed; 195 wounded; 8 missing.

130. OR 19, pt. 2, 463; Cox, *Recollections of The Civil War*, vol. I, 285; Gottfried, *The Maps of Antietam*, 214.

131. Cox, *Recollections of The Civil War*, vol. 1, 284; William H. Armstrong, *Major McKinley: William McKinley & the Civil War* (Kent, OH: The Kent State University Press, 2000), 38-39. Years after the war, some suggested that McKinley should be awarded the Medal of Honor for this action at Antietam. Once he learned of this attempt, a humble McKinley declined the honor. McKinley did not receive the Medal of Honor but he did receive a monument at Antietam after his assassination.

132. Gottfried, *The Maps of Antietam*, 226; Carman, *The Maryland Campaign*, vol. II, 440; Cox, *Recollections of The Civil War*, vol. I, 286.

133. Cox, *Recollections of The Civil War*, vol. I, 286. Though Cox and other veterans of Ewing's brigade insisted A.P. Hill's men were wearing Union uniforms, the Confederates claimed it was not so, but a small portion may have worn some form of blue uniform. The Union signal station on Red Hill observed Hill's arrival and threat he posed to the exposed left flank of the Union line. A message was sent to Burnside's headquarters warning him of this danger. Unfortunately, Burnside was not at his headquarters, as he had ridden forward to observe the advance of the line. Carman, *The Maryland Campaign*, vol. II, 468, 470; Gottfried, *The Maps of Antietam*, 226, 228.

134. OR 19, pt. 2, 470; Carman, *The Maryland Campaign*, vol. II, 470, 473; Gottfried, *The Maps of Antietam*, 230.

135. Gottfried, *The Maps of Antietam*, 230; OR 19, pt. 1, 198, 466. The brigade lost 182 (28k-134w-20m) at Antietam.

136. "30th Regiment Ohio Volunteer Infantry," *Ohio Civil War Central*, 2020, Ohio Civil War Central. http://www.www.ohiocivilwarcentral.com/entry.php?rec=1246 accessed June 11, 2020.

https://mountainaflame.blogspot.com/2010/12/artillery-on-mountain-federal.html.

137. Hartwig, *To Antietam Creek*, Appendix B, Strength of Union and Confederate Forces; Hoptak, *The Battle of South Mountain*, 54.

138. OR 19, pt. 1, 187,198. These numbers reflect the combined loss at both the Battle of South Mountain and the Battle of Antietam.

139. J.H. Horton and Solomon Teverbaugh, *A History of the Eleventh Regiment-Ohio Infantry* (Dayton, OH: W.J. Shuey, 1866), 20, 61, 64; *Official Roster of the Soldiers of the State of Ohio in the War of the Rebellion*, 1861-1866, three volumes (Cincinnati, OH: The Ohio Valley Pub. & MFG. CO.,1886), vol. III, 776, 377.

140. Horton and Teverbaugh, *A History of the Eleventh Regiment Ohio Infantry*, 68-69; Martin F. Schmitt, ed., *General George Crook: His Autobiography* (Norman, OK: University of Oklahoma Press, 1946), xi, 1, 40-41. George Crook was known as "three stars" to the American Indians due to his rank as a major general, a rank represented by three stars. Crook died in 1890 and was laid to rest in Arlington National Cemetery.

141. Hoptak, *The Battle of South Mountain*, 54, 56-60; Carman, *The Maryland Campaign*, vol. I, 329-330.

142. John Amrine, *The National Tribune*, March 10, 1910, 7.

143. Schmitt, ed., *General George Crook*, 97.

144. Schmitt, ed., *General George Crook*, 97; OR 19, pt. 1, 472; Carman, *The Maryland Campaign*, vol. II, 412.

145. OR 19, pt. 1, 472; OR, 51, pt. 1, 161-165.

146. John Amrine, *The National Tribune*, March 10, 1910, 7.

147. Carman, *The Maryland Campaign,* vol. II, 415,417; Crook, *The National Tribune*, March 10, 1910, 7; Jacob Cox, *Cox: Recollections of The Civil War*, vol. I, 282.

148. Carman, *The Maryland Campaign*, vol. II, 447, 486-487.

150. OR 19, pt. 1, 472.

151. OR 19, pt. 1, 187, 198.

## XII Corps

1. Fox, *Regimental Losses in the American Civil War*, 88.

2. Carman, *The Maryland Campaign*, vol. II, 583. McClellan noted its strength as 10,126, but this is total, and includes noncombatants.

3. OR 19, pt. 2, 297; Williams, *From the Cannon's Mouth*, 123.

4. Warner, *Generals in Blue*, 309; Carman, *The Maryland Campaign*, vol. II, 112; Thomas G. Clemens, "'Too Bad, Poor Fellows:' Joseph K. Mansfield and the XII Corps at Antietam," in *Corps Commanders in Blue: Union Major Generals in the Civil War*, Ethan S. Rafuse, ed. (Baton Rouge, LA: Louisiana State University Press, 2014), 65, 67, 71.

5. OR 19, pt. 1, 475; Williams, *From the Cannon's Mouth*, 125; Clemens, "Too Bad, Poor Fellows," 85. Mansfield's alignment put the two middle companies of each regiment side by side, with the other companies behind them, forming a column two companies wide and five ranks deep. Thomas Clemens believed Mansfield deployed his troops in this manner to exercise firm control over the large number of green troops in his command. Clemens, "Too Bad, Poor Fellows," 86.

6. Williams, *From the Cannon's Mouth*, 125-26; Carman, *The Maryland Campaign*, vol. II, 113. Mansfield's rationale was that new troops would run away if ordered to undertake this complex movement in the open. Carman, *The Maryland Campaign*, vol. II, 115.

7. OR 19, pt. 1, 492; Carman, *The Maryland Campaign*, vol. II, 161 (note 81); Gould, *First-Tenth-Twenty Ninth Maine*, 240-41; *OR Suppl.*, vol. 3, 562-64; John Mead Gould, *Joseph K. F. Mansfield, Brigadier General of the U. S. Army: A Narrative of Events Connected with his Mortal Wounding at Sharpsburg, Maryland* (Portland, ME: Stephen Berry, Printer, 1895), 3-32.

8. OR 19, pt. 1, 475.

9. Williams, *From the Cannon's Mouth*, 127.

10. OR 19, pt. 1, 476-77; Carman, *The Maryland Campaign*, vol. II, 601.

11. Warner, *Generals in Blue*, 559-560; Sifakis, *Who Was Who in the Civil War*, 716-17; Tagg, *The Generals of Gettysburg*, 146-47. Williams' rank in Mexico is disputed. Warner and Sifakis believed he was a "lieutenant colonel" but Tagg pegged him as simply a "lieutenant."

12. Williams, *From the Cannon's Mouth*, 119.

13. OR 19, vol. 1, 157, 478-80; Williams, *From the Cannon's Mouth*, 124.

14. Williams, *From the Cannon's Mouth*, 125-26; Carman, *The Maryland Campaign of 1862*, vol. II, 115; OR 19, pt. 1, 484; Alpheus Williams to Ezra Carman, May 16, 1877, NYPL. Only the 1st Division's 1st and 3rd Brigades were present during the Maryland Campaign. The Second Brigade did not form until October, 1862. Dyer, *A Compendium of the War of the Rebellion*, vol. I, 320-21.

15. OR 19, pt. 1, 484; Williams, *From the Cannon's Mouth*, 128; Carman, *The Maryland Campaign of 1862*, vol. II, 123.

16. Carman, *The Maryland Campaign of 1862*, vol. II, 166, 189, 230-31,302, 328; OR 19, vol. 1, 198-99.

17. Hartwig, *To Antietam Creek*, Appendix B, Strength of Union and Confederate Forces. The brigade may have actually fielded 2,525 at Antietam. OR 19, pt. 1, 477-78.

18. OR 19, pt. 2, 198.

19. Dyer, *A Compendium of the War of the Rebellion*, vol. III, 1008; Edwin Marvin, *Fifth Regiment Connecticut Volunteers. A History Compiled from Diaries and Official Reports* (Hartford, CT: Press of Wiley, Waterman & Eaton, 1889), 237, 240; Fox, *Regimental Losses in the American Civil War*, 88. Crawford's brigade also included the 5th Connecticut, but it was detached at Frederick, Maryland on September 14, 1862 to serve Provost Duty, and rejoined the brigade on December 11, 1862 at Sandy Hook, Maryland.

20. John W. Schildt, *The Twelfth Corps at Antietam* (Brunswick, MD: E. Graphics, 2012), 14-15; Charles W. Boyce, *A Brief History of the Twenty-Eighth Regiment New*

York Volunteers (Buffalo, NY: The Matthews-Northrup Co., 1896), 44; Warner, *Generals in Blue*, 99.

21. John M. Gould, *History of the First-Tenth-Twenty-Ninth Maine Regiment in Service of the United States from May 3, 1861 to June 21, 1866* (Portland, ME: Stephen Berry, 1871), 46; Williams, *From the Cannon's Mouth*, 125-26; OR 19, 2, 224.

22. Carman, *The Maryland Campaign*, vol. I, 175-76; Schildt, *The Twelfth Corps at Antietam*, 49.

23. Carman, *The Maryland Campaign*, vol. I, 370; Boyce, *A Brief History of the Twenty-Eighth Regiment New York Volunteers*, 46.

24. Regimental Committee, *History of the One Hundred and Twenty-Fifth Regiment Pennsylvania Volunteers 1862- 1863* (Philadelphia: J. B. Lippincott Company, 1906), 55.

25. Carman, *The Maryland Campaign*, vol. I, 403-04.

26. Carman, *The Maryland Campaign*, vol. II, 112; Regimental Committee, *History of the One Hundred and Twenty-Fifth Regiment Pennsylvania, 1862-1863*, 56.

27. Carman, *The Maryland Campaign*, vol. II, 24, 27, 43; Frederick Crouse, *"An Account of the Battle of Antietam."* ANB Library.

28. Miles Clayton Huyette, *The Maryland Campaign and the Battle of Antietam* (Buffalo, NY: By author, 1915), 27-28.

29. Joseph L. Harsh, *Taken at the Flood*, 369-72; OR 19, pt. 1, 475; Carman, *The Maryland Campaign of September 1862*, vol. II, 113-15.

30. Harsh, *Taken at the Flood*, 373-74; Regimental Committee, *History of the One Hundred and Twenty-Fifth Regiment Pennsylvania*, 1862-1863, 64.

31. OR 19, pt. 1, 491; Carman, *The Maryland Campaign*, vol. II, 116, 123-24.

32. OR, 19, pt. 1, 484, 487; Carman, *The Maryland Campaign*, vol. II, 115-16. A clearly frustrated Williams conferenced with the commanders of his three veteran regiments under a tree, telling them how they should deploy when ordered. Col. Knipe of the 46th Pennsylvania was to "double-quick in advance and cover the deployment of the new regiments, when the time came." Carman, *The Maryland Campaign*, vol. II, 113, 115; Alpheus Williams to Ezra Carman, May 16, 1877, NYPL.

33. Bates, *Pennsylvania Volunteers*, vol. IV, 90-91; Robert M. Green, *History of the One Hundred and Twenty-Fourth Regiment Pennsylvania Volunteers in the War of the Rebellion— 1862-1863* (Philadelphia: Ware Bros. Company, 1907), 30-32; Carman, *The Maryland Campaign of 1862*, vol. II, 123-25; OR 19, 1, 475,484, 491; Gould, *History of the First-Tenth-Twenty-Ninth Maine Regiment New York State Volunteers*, 236-37. Crawford reported the 124th Pennsylvania "was detached from my brigade by some superior order unknown to me, and sent in advance through the woods on our right to Miller's farm, to hold that position." Williams issued the "superior order" and brought them west toward the North Woods near Hagerstown Pike and told them to remain there until brigade's other regiments could be brought up. The 124th Pennsylvania was intended to shore up the I

Corps' line in this sector, but it was gone by the time the Pennsylvanians arrived. It was later joined by Col. William Goodrich's brigade of Greene's division. OR 19, pt. 1, 475, 484.

34. Carman, *The Maryland Campaign*, vol. II, 11.

35. Carman, *The Maryland Campaign*, vol. II, 120-23; OR, 19, pt. 1, 486-91; Bates, *Pennsylvania Volunteers*, vol. IV, 167.

36. Gould, *History of the First-Tenth-Twenty-Ninth Maine Regiment*, 238-39; Carman, *The Maryland Campaign*, vol. II, 122-23, 125; OR, 19, 1, 486-87, 489-90; *The Lewiston Falls Journal* (Maine), October 2, 1862.

37. Carman, *The Maryland Campaign*, vol. II, 161-62; Regimental Committee, *History of the One Hundred and Twenty-Fifth Regiment Pennsylvania Volunteers*, 67, 68-9; OR, 19, 1, 492.

38. OR, 19, 1, 492; Carman, *The Maryland Campaign*, vol. II, 178-82; Regimental Committee, *History of the One Hundred and Twenty-Fifth Regiment Pennsylvania Volunteers*, 71-72.

39. Bates, *Pennsylvania Volunteers*, vol. IV, 109; Regimental Committee, *History of the One Hundred and Twenty-Fifth Regiment Pennsylvania Volunteers*, 72-73; Mac Wyckoff, *A History of the 2nd South Carolina Infantry: 1861-65* (Fredericksburg, VA: Sergeant Kirkland's Museum and Historical Society, 1994), 45.

40. OR, 19, pt. 1, 486; Harsh, *Taken at the Flood*, 430-31.

41. OR, 19, pt. 1, 198.

42. Hartwig, *To Antietam Creek*, Appendix B, Strength of Union and Confederate Forces. The brigade may have numbered 2,210 at Antietam. OR 19, pt. 1, 498.

43. OR, 19, pt. 1, 199.

44. Dyer, *A Compendium of the War for the Rebellion*, vol. III, 1130, 1248, 1362, 1447, 1674; E. R. Brown, *The Twenty-Seventh Indiana Volunteer Infantry in the War of the Rebellion 1861 – 1865* (np: np, 1899), 225-26. The historian of the 13th New Jersey gave the rookie perspective of the veterans: "The battle-scarred veteran, clothed in scanty raiment, unencumbered with any of the 'indispensible' articles we had brought with us excited our pity and frequent disgust. We could not understand the cause of his cheerfulness as he gazed at our fine quarters and new clothes, nor the supreme satisfaction with which he inventoried everything we possessed, until he volunteered the information, in his laconic way.—'Well, boys, they're all very nice, but you'll wear the shine off, and be glad to do with less before you get through with this business.'" Samuel Toombs, *Reminiscences of the War: Comprising a Detailed Account of the Experiences of the Thirteenth Regiment New Jersey Volunteers in Camp, on the March, and in Battle* (Orange, NJ: journal Office, 1878), 13.

45. Warner, *Generals in Blue*, 177-78.

46. Toombs, *Reminiscences of the War* 14; Brown, *The Twenty-Seventh Indiana Volunteer Infantry*, 228-29. Joseph Cromwell related the story of how he dropped out of the ranks because of sunstroke, and when he awoke, he learned that Capt. Hugh Irish had applied ointment to his

bleeding feet., "I turned my head so he could not see the tears in my eyes. "Joseph E. Cromwell, *The Young Volunteer: The Everyday Experiences of a Soldier Boy in the Civil War* (New York: G. W. Dillingham Company, 1906), 79.

47. Brown, *The Twenty-Seventh Indiana Volunteer Infantry*, 233-34; Steven S. Raab, ed., *With the 3rd Wisconsin Badgers: The Living Experience of the Civil War Through the Journals of Van R. Willard* (Mechanicsburg, PA: Stackpole Books, 1999), 85-86; Lyman Richard Comey, *A Legacy of Valor: The Memoirs and Letters of Captain Henry Newton Comey, 2nd Massachusetts Infantry* (Knoxville, TN: The University of Tennessee Press, 2004), 74-75; Edwin E. Bryant, *History of the Third Regiment of Wisconsin Veteran Volunteer Infantry 1861 – 1865* (Madison, WI: Democrat Printing Co., 1891), 121; OR, 19, pt. 1, 479.

48. Brown, *The Twenty-Seventh Indiana Volunteer Infantry*, 238; Cromwell, *The Young Volunteers*, 108; Bryant, *History of the Third Regiment of Wisconsin Veteran Volunteer Infantry*, 122-23; Raab, ed., *With the 3rd Wisconsin Badgers*, 88; Comey, ed., *A Legacy of Valor*, 75.

49. Brown, *The Twenty-Seventh Indiana Volunteer Infantry*, 239.

50. OR, 19, pt. 1, 494-95, 498, 500; Carman, *The Maryland Campaign*, vol. II, 125-26.

51. Carman, *The Maryland Campaign*, vol. II, 126, 128, 130; Julian Wisner Hinkley, *A Narrative of Service with the Third Wisconsin* (Madison, WI: Wisconsin History Commission, 1912), 55.

52. OR, 19, pt. 1, 495.

53. Robert Gould Shaw, *Blue-Eyed Child of Fortune: The Civil War Letters of Colonel Robert Gould Shaw*, Russell Duncan and William S. McFeely, eds., (Athens, GA: The University of Georgia Press, 1992), 240.

54. OR, 19, pt. 1, 495, 500-01, 502, Joseph Edward Cromwell, The Young Volunteers, 135.

55. Carman, *The Maryland Campaign*, vol. II, 231, 302; OR, 19, pt. 1, 501, 502.

56. Carman, *The Maryland Campaign*, vol. II, 309.

57. OR, 19, pt. 1, 199.

58. Warner, *Generals In Blues*, 186-187.

59. Richard Eddy, *History of the Sixtieth New York State Volunteers*, (Philadelphia, PA: By the Author, 1864), 75-77; David & Jeanne Heidler, *Encyclopedia of the American Civil War: A Political, Social and Military History*, 2 volumes (Santa Barbara, CA: ABC-CLIO, Inc., 2000), vol. II, 880.

60. New York Monuments Commission, *In Memoriam George Sears Greene Brevet Major-General United States Volunteers, 1801-1899*, (Albany, NY: J.B. Lyon Company, State Printers, 1909), 66-68; OR 12, pt. 1, 552; OR 51, pt. 1, 720.

61. OR 12, pt. 2, 158-159; OR 19, pt. 1, 37-38.

62. Williams, *From the Cannon's Mouth*, 120; Thomas M. O'Brien & Oliver Diefendorf, *General Orders of the War Department, Embracing the Years / 1861, 1862 & 1863. Adapted Specifically for the Use of the Army and Navy of the United States*, 2 volumes (New York, NY: Derby & Miller, 1864), vol. 1, 389; *An Invitation to Battle*, Monocacy National Battlefield, https://www.nps.gov/mono/learn/historyculture/an-invitation-to-battle.htm (accessed May 27, 2020); OR 19, pt. 1, 157.

63. Williams, *From the Cannon's Mouth*, 123-124.

64. OR 19, pt. 1, 218, 475; John Richards Boyle, *Soldiers True: The Story of the One Hundred and Eleventh Regiment Pennsylvania Veteran Volunteers, and its Campaigns in the War for the Union 1861—1865* (New York, NY: Eaton & Mains, 1903), 57; Lawrence Wilson, *Itinerary of the Seventh Ohio Volunteer Infantry, 1861-1864* (New York & Washington: The Neale Publishing Company, 1907), 204.

65. OR 19, pt. 1, 475-76, 504-505; Gottfried, *The Maps of Antietam*, 182-83; Carman, *The Maryland Campaign*, vol. II, 583-84.

66. Gottfried, *The Maps of Antietam*, 160-63; Harsh, *Taken at the Flood*, 374-75; Carman, *The Maryland Campaign*, vol. II, 124; OR 19, pt. 1, 475-76, 505.

67. Carman, *The Maryland Campaign*, vol. II, 134-38; Gottfried, *The Maps of Antietam*, 160-65.

68. Carman, *The Maryland Campaign*, vol. II, 139-41; Gottfried, *The Maps of Antietam*, 166-69; OR 19, pt. 1, 505.

69. Carman, *The Maryland Campaign*, vol. II, 157-59; Gottfried, *The Maps of Antietam*, 166-69.

70. Gottfried, *The Maps of Antietam*, 180-81; OR vol. 19, pt. 1, 505.

71. OR 19, pt. 1, 843, 918-19; Gottfried, *The Maps of Antietam*, 180-81.

72. OR 19, pt. 1, 476, 505; Harsh, *Taken at the Flood*, 392-93; Carman, *The Maryland Campaign*, vol. II, 234; Gottfried, *The Maps of Antietam*, 182-83; Wilson, *Itinerary of the Seventh Ohio Volunteer Infantry*, 211.

73. Carman, *The Maryland Campaign*, vol. II, 306-21; OR 19, pt. 1, 505, 916, 920-21; Gottfried, *The Maps of Antietam*, 182-83.

74. OR 19, pt. 1, 199, 475-78, 504-05; New York Monuments Commission, *In Memoriam George Sears Greene*, 75-6.

75. Hartwig, *To Antietam Creek*, Appendix B, Strength of Union and Confederate Forces. The brigade may have numbered 1,191 at Antietam. Carman, *The Maryland Campaign*, vol. II, 135.

76. OR, 19, pt. 1, 199.

77. John M. McLaughlin, *A Memoir of Hector Tyndale* (Philadelphia, PA: n.p., 1882), 6.

78. McLaughlin, *A Memoir of Hector Tyndale*, 7.

79. McLaughlin, *A Memoir of Hector Tyndale*, 8.

80. Dyer, *A Compendium of the War of the Rebellion*, vol. I, 321; Bates, *Pennsylvania Volunteers*, vol. I, 428. See also, OR, 19, pt 1, 480-481 for the daily itinerary of the division.

81. William F. Fox, "Slocum and His Men: A History of the Twelfth and Twentieth Army Corps," in *Memoriam Henry Warner Slocum, 1826-1894* (Albany, New York: J.B. Lyon Company, Printers, 1904), 139.

82. J. Hume letter, ANB Library. Hume says he passed through on Tuesday, but all other accounts put members of the XII Corps passing through Turner's Gap on Monday.

83. See Carman, *The Maryland Campaign,* vol. II, 135 (note 39) for further discussion on regimental strength. Tyndale wrote years after the battle he took 1050 into the fight. Other authors state the 66th had 200 men and the other two Ohio regiments had about the same. McLaughlin, *A Memoir of Hector Tyndale,* 55; D. Cunningham and W. W. Miller, *Antietam: Report of The Ohio Antietam Battlefield Commission* (Springfield, OH: Springfield Publishing Company, State Printers, 1904), 45, 84. Cunningham and Miller, *Ohio Antietam,* 44.

85. Carman, *The Maryland Campaign,* vol. II, 127, (note 28) for a discussion on the order of regiments in the Cornfield.

86. Cunningham and Miller, *Ohio Antietam Battlefield Commission,* 45.

87. *OR,* 19, pt. 1, 506.

88. It was reported that the 30th Virginia lost 68% of their men. Carman, *The Maryland Campaign,* vol. II, 617.

89. W.H.H. Fithian letter, ANB Library.

90. Carman, *The Maryland Campaign,* vol. III, 299; "Antietam Medals of Honor," Antietam National Battlefield Library.

91. Hartwig, *To Antietam Creek,* Appendix B, Strength of Union and Confederate Forces. The brigade may have numbered only 536 at Antietam. Carman, *The Maryland Campaign,* vol. II, 135.

92. OR 19, pt 1, 199.

93. Carman, *The Maryland Campaign,* vol. III, 290.

94. Fox, "Slocum and His Men," 133-134. Prince remained in Libby Prison for about five months before being paroled.

95. Bates, *Pennsylvania Volunteers,* vol. III, 953-54.

96. Boyle, *Soldiers True,* 53; OR 19, pt 1, 480; OR 19, pt 1, 179.

97. William B. Matchett, *Maryland and the Glorious Third in the War for the Union: Reminiscences in the Life of Her* (Washington: TJ Brashears Printers, 1882), 21.

98. Boyle, *Soldiers True,* 57.

99. Carman, *The Maryland Campaign,* vol. II, 139.

100. OR 19, pt. 1, 511.

101. OR 19, pt. 1, 513.

102. Carman, *The Maryland Campaign,* vol II, 306 and 308.

103. Carman, *The Maryland Campaign,* vol II, 310-311.

104. OR 19, pt. 1, 511.

105. OR 19, pt. 1, 199; Boyle, *Soldiers True,* 59-60.

106. Hartwig, *To Antietam Creek,* Appendix B, Strength of Union and Confederate Forces. The brigade may have numbered only 777 at Antietam. Carman, *The Maryland Campaign,* vol. 2, 135.

107. OR 19, pt. 1, 199.

108. Dyer, *Compendium,* vol. 1, 322, 351; vol. 3, 1017, 1426-27, 1435; John David Hoptak, "Col. William Goodrich Profile," *Antietam on the Web;* OR 19, pt. 1, 504, 514, 516; Carman, *The Maryland Campaign,* vol. 2, 158.

109. OR 19, pt. 1, 475, 506, 515; Gottfried, *The Maps of Antietam,* 161, 165; Ezra Carman, "The 76th New York," NA-AS; Carman, *The Maryland Campaign,* vol. 2, 158.

110. Carman, *The Maryland Campaign,* vol. 2, 158; David Sparks, ed., *Inside Lincoln's Army, the Diary of General Marsena Rudolph Patrick, Provost Marshal General, Army of the Potomac* (New York: Thomas Yoseloff, 1964), 149; OR 19, pt. 1, 514; Lester Wilson to Ezra Carman, November 17, 1899, NYPL

111. Carman, *The Maryland Campaign,* vol. II, 159; OR 19, pt. 1, 514; George Ryan to Ezra Carman, December 8, 1897, NA-AS; Sparks, *Inside Lincoln's Army,* 149-50.

112. "The 76th New York;" OR 19, pt. 1, 514.

113. Carman, *The Maryland Campaign,* vol. 2, 142, 157. A veteran recalled a "general officer" telling the Marylanders to drive the 124th forward. William Fulton to Ezra Carman, December 21, 1899, NA-AS.

114. Carman, *The Maryland Campaign,* vol. 2, 226, 302; Fulton to Carman, December 21, 1899, NA-AS.

115. Carman, *The Maryland Campaign,* vol. 2, 310.

116. Carman, *The Maryland Campaign,* vol. II, 315-17; Charles Hopkins to Ezra Carman, January 15, 1900, NA-AS; OR 19, pt. 1, 199, 515.

## Pleasonton's Cavalry Division

1. Hartwig, *To Antietam Creek,* Appendix B, Strength of Union and Confederate Forces; The division may have numbered only 3,828 at Antietam. Carman, *The Maryland Campaign,* vol. II, 601.

2. Hartwig, *To Antietam Creek,* 155.

3. McClellan, *Civil War Papers,* 396; Worthington C. Ford, ed., *A Cycle of Adams Letters 1861-1862,* 2 volumes (New York: Kraus Reprint, 1969); Edward W. Emerson, *Life and Letters of Charles Russell Lowell* (Port Washington, NY: Kennikat Press, 1971), 229.

4. Stephen Z. Starr, *The Union Cavalry in the Civil War,* 3 volumes (Baton Rouge, LA: Louisiana State University Press, 1979), vol. 1, 240; Hartwig, *To Antietam Creek,* 155-56; Benjamin W. Crowninshield, "Cavalry in Virginia During the War of the Rebellion," *Journal of the Military Service Institution,* vol. 12 (May 1891), 26; Carman, *The Maryland Campaign,* vol. I, 165 (note 5).

5. OR 51, pt. 1, 781, 783.

6. Hartwig, *To Antietam Creek,* 155-56, 163-64; Carman, *The Maryland Campaign,* vol. I, 164, 165 (note 5); OR 51, pt. 1, 781, 783.

7. Hartwig, *To Antietam Creek,* 155; 814-15; Benjamin W. Crownishield, *A History of the First Massachusetts Cavalry Volunteers* (Boston: Houghton Mifflin & Co., 1891), 71-72; OR 19, pt. 2, 192.

8. OR 19, pt. 2, 201; OR 19, pt. 1, 208; Carman, *The Maryland Campaign,* vol. I, 166-67; Hartwig, *To Antietam Creek,* 173-74. The Confederates lost 30 men on

September 8; Farnsworth lost 13. Hartwig, *To Antietam Creek*, 174.

9. OR 19, pt. 1, 208-09; Carman, *The Maryland Campaign*, vol. I, 167-68; Hartwig, *To Antietam Creek*, 178.

10. OR 19, pt. 2, 192, 210.

11. OR 51, pt. 1, 802-3, 807; OR 19, pt. 1, 209; Carman, *The Maryland Campaign*, vol. I, 178; Hartwig, *To Antietam Creek*, 184; Laurence H. Freiheit, *Boots and Saddles: Cavalry During the Maryland Campaign of September 1862* (Iowa City, IA: Camp Pop Publishing, 2012), 180-82.

12. OR 19, pt. 1, 209; OR 19, pt. 1, pt. 1, 829; Hartwig, *To Antietam Creek*, 271.

13. Carman, *The Maryland Campaign*, vol. I, 195; OR 19, pt. 1, 826-27. Pleasonton did not report on this action in his campaign report.

14. OR 19, pt. 1, 209-10.

15. Cox, "Forcing Fox's Gap and Turner's Gap," vol. 2, 586; OR 19, pt. 1, 210-11; Gilbert G. Wood, et al. *History of the Sixth New York (Second Ira Harris Guard) Second Brigade, First Division, Cavalry Corps Army of the Potomac 1861-1865* (Worcester, MA: The Blanchard Press, 1908), 53-64. Pleasonton reported 16 casualties and predicted 80 losses among the Virginians. OR 19, pt. 1, 210-11.

16. Carman, *The Maryland Campaign*, vol. II, 358-59; OR 19, pt. 1, 210; Samuel Young to Ezra Carman, April 8, 1898, NA-AS.

17. Abner Hard, *History of the Eight Cavalry Regiment, Illinois Volunteers, During the Great Rebellion* (Aurora, IL: n.p, 1868), 185; John C. Tidball and Lawrence M. Kaplan, *Artillery Service in the War of the Rebellion, 1861-1865* (Yardley, PA: Westholme Publishing, 2001), 95; Carman, *The Maryland Campaign*, vol. II, 361-64.

18. OR 19, pt. 1, 211-12.

19. OR 19, pt. 1, 212.

## Longstreet's Wing

1. Carman, *The Maryland Campaign*, vol. I, 458-63.

2. Davis, *The Confederate General*, vol. IV, 91.

3. Moxley Sorrel, *Recollections of a Confederate Staff Officer*, Bell Irvin Wiley, ed. (Jackson, TN: McCowat-Mercer Press, Inc., 1958), 97.

4. Longstreet, *From Manassas to Appomattox*, 200-01; Carman, *The Maryland Campaign*, vol. I, 82, 94; Harsh, *Taken at the Flood*, 51.

5. Hartwig, *To Antietam Creek*, 110-11; James Longstreet, "The Invasion of Maryland," *Battles & Leaders of the Civil War*, vol. II, 663; Longstreet, *From Manassas to Appomattox*, 201-02; OR 19, pt. 2, 603; H. J. Eckenrode & Bryan Conrad, *James Longstreet: Lee's War Horse* (Chapel Hill, NC: University of North Carolina Press, 1986), 114-15.

6. OR 19, pt. 1, 145, 839; Carman, *The Maryland Campaign*, vol. I, 229-30; Longstreet, "The Invasion of Maryland," 665; Gary Gallagher, *Lee the Soldier* (Lincoln, NE: University of Nebraska Press, 1996), 8, 26. Longstreet claimed that when Lee gave him orders to march for Boonsboro the following day, he suggested a different approach: Withdraw Hill from the Boonsboro/Turner Gap sector and send him to Sharpsburg where Longstreet would meet him. He claimed "Sharpsburg was a strong defensive position from which we could strike the flank or rear of any force that might be sent to the relief of Harpers Ferry." The strategy sounds reasonable, but there is no indication that Longstreet ever visited Sharpsburg, let alone being aware of its "strong defensive position." Lee, according to Longstreet, vetoed the idea. Longstreet, "The Invasion of Maryland," 665.

7. OR 19, pt. 1, 839, 1020; Longstreet, *From Manassas to Appomattox*, 224; Longstreet, "The Invasion of Maryland," 666. Historian Joseph Harsh claimed Longstreet assumed operational control over the forces deployed at Turner's and Fox's Gap. While this makes sense, none of the references he cites specifically state such a change in command. Harsh, *Taken at the Flood*, 266.

8. Longstreet, *From Manassas to Appomattox*, 227; Carman, *The Maryland Campaign*, vol. I, 393-94; Carman, *The Maryland Campaign*, vol. II, 7, 11; OR 19, pt. 1, 886, 937; Harsh, *Taken at the Flood*, 304.

9. Sorrel, *Recollections of a Confederate Staff Officer*, 104; Carman, *The Maryland Campaign*, vol. II, 88 (note 62), 599.

10. Harsh, *Taken at the Flood*, 397.

11. OR 19, pt. 1, 915, 1,037; Marion V. Armstrong, *Opposing the Second Corps at Antietam: The Fight for the Confederate Left and Center on America's Bloodiest Day* (Tuscaloosa, AL: University of Alabama Press, 2016), 97; Carman, *The Maryland Campaign*, vol. II, 250, 284; Longstreet, *From Manassas to Appomattox*, 249-50.

12. Sorrel, *Recollections of a Confederate Staff Officer*, 105-06; Carman, *The Maryland Campaign*, vol. II, 276; Andrew Hero, Jr., to Ezra Carman, May 1, 1896, NYPL; Jeffry D. Wert, *General James Longstreet: The Confederacy's Most Controversial Soldier* (New York: Simon & Schuster, 1993), 198.

13. Carman, *The Maryland Campaign*, vol. II, 288.

14. OR 19, pt. 1, 840.

15. Carman, *The Maryland Campaign*, vol. II, 508, 611.

## McLaws' Division

1. John C. Oeffinger, ed., *A Soldier's General: The Civil War Letters of Major General Lafayette McLaws* (Chapel Hill and London: University of North Carolina Press, 2002), 6.

2. William C. Davis, ed., *The Confederate General*, 6 volumes (Harrisburg, PA: Publication of the National Historical Society, 1992), vol. IV, 129.

3. Davis, ed., *The Confederate General*, vol. IV, 129.

4. Oeffinger, *A Soldier's General*, 154; Harsh, *Taken at the Flood*, 34.

5. Helen Trimpi, "Lafayette McLaws' Aide-De-Camp: the Maryland Campaign Diary of Captain Henry Lord Page King," *Civil War Regiments*, vol. 6, No. 2 (1998), 30;

Carman, *The Maryland Campaign,* vol. I, 112, 116; *OR* 19, pt. 1, 852.

6. "John Thomas Parham Talks Before the A.P. Hill Camp of Confederate Veterans," September 6, 1894, George S. Bernard Collection of the O. Winston Link Museum, History Museum of Western Virginia, Historical Society of Western Virginia. https://hswv.pastperfectonline.com/archive/56C0EF56-C2A3-4F31-AC68-798584273832, Retrieved on January 3, 2020; *OR* 19, pt. 1, 852.

7. *OR* 19, pt. 1, 858; Carman, *The Maryland Campaign,* vol. I, 233.

8. Hartwig, *To Antietam Creek,* 268. The reporter wrote the "funeral" quote in the *Boston Evening Transcript,* September 19, 1862.

9. *OR* 19, pt. 1, 854.

10. *OR* 19, pt. 1, 854; Carman, *The Maryland Campaign,* vol. I, 311.

11. Carman, *The Maryland Campaign,* vol. I, 383.

12. *OR* 19, pt. 1, 855.

13. Carman, *The Maryland Campaign,* vol. I, 384, 385.

14. McLaws' letter to Isaac Pennypacker about Maj. Gen. William Franklin, https://digitalcommons.wofford.edu/littlejohnmclaws/9/ Retrieved on April 27, 2021.

15. "John Thomas Parham Talks before the A.P. Hill Camp of Confederate Veterans."

16. "John Thomas Parham Talks before the A.P. Hill Camp of Confederate Veterans;" Carman, *The Maryland Campaign,* vol. II, 184; Mac Wyckoff, *The Third South Carolina Infantry, 1861-1865* (Fredericksburg, VA: Sergeant Kirkland's Museum and Historical Society, Inc., 1948), 34.

17. Carman, *The Maryland Campaign,* vol. II, 185, 188.

18. Carman, *The Maryland Campaign,* vol. II, 185, 188; *OR* 19, pt. 1, 859.

19. *OR* 19, pt. 1, 858; Carman, *The Maryland Campaign,* vol. II, 198.

20. Albert Wymer Henley Diary, https://13thmississippi.com/2011/03/15/battles-sharpsburg/; Carman, *The Maryland Campaign,* vol. II, 197; Robert W. Shand, "Incidents in the Life of a Private Soldier in the War Waged by the United States Against the Confederate States, 1861-1865," University of South Carolina Library.

21. Carman, *The Maryland Campaign,* vol. II, 9.

22. Carman, *The Maryland Campaign,* vol. II, 197-203, 215, 9; Guy Everson and Edward Simpson, eds., *Far, Far From Home: The Wartime Letters of Dick and Tally Simpson, Third South Carolina Volunteers,* (New York, NY: Oxford University Press, 1994), 150.

23. *OR* 19, pt. 1, 865, 308, 869; D. Augustus Dickert, *History of Kershaw's Brigade, with Complete Roll of Companies, Biographical Sketches, Incidents, Anecdotes, Etc.* (Newberry, SC: Elbert H. Aull Company, 1899), 156; Carman, *The Maryland Campaign,* vol. II, 204; Shand, *Incidents in the Life of a Private Soldier,* 37.

24. *OR* 19, pt. 1, 872; Carman, *The Maryland Campaign,* vol. II, 207.

25. *OR* 19, pt. 1, 858; Carman, *The Maryland Campaign,* vol. II, 593, 602.

26. Davis, *"The Confederate General,"* vol. IV, 129; Carman, *The Maryland Campaign,* vol. II, 215.

27. Hartwig, *To Antietam Creek,* Appendix B, Strength of Union and Confederate Forces. The brigade's strength at Antietam was 935. But see *OR* 19, pt. 1, 860.

28. *OR* 19, pt. 1, 861, 862. The loss figures are for casualties at Antietam, including Read's artillery battery, with four killed and ten wounded. Kershaw's brigade also lost 213 on Maryland Heights (35k-178w-0m) during the effort to capture Harpers Ferry.

29. Mac Wyckoff, *The Third South Carolina Infantry,* 66.

30. Wyckoff, *The Third South Carolina Infantry,* 63, 64; Dickert, *History of Kershaw's Brigade,* 145.

31. Robert W. Shand, *Incidents in the Life of a Private Soldier,* 34.

32. *OR* 19, pt. 1, 852, 853.

33. Wyckoff, *The Third South Carolina Infantry,* 68.

34. *OR* 19, pt. 1, 864.

35. Simpson and Everson, eds., *Far, Far From Home,* 149.

36. Wyckoff, *The Third South Carolina Infantry,* 68.

37. Dickert, *History of Kershaw's Brigade,* 147; *OR* 19, pt. 1, 863.

38. Shand, *Incidents in the Life of a Private Soldier,* 35; *OR* 19, pt. 1, 864.

39. *OR* 19, pt. 1, 863.

40. Harsh, *Taken at the Flood,* 224; *OR* 19, pt. 1, 864.

41. Dickert, *History of Kershaw's Brigade,* 148; *OR* 19, pt. 1, 863. A Union soldier in the 126th New York recalled, "The woods were filled with rebels coming toward us and yelling like Indians."

42. *OR* 19, pt. 1, 863, 536; Wyckoff, *The Third South Carolina Infantry,* 71.

43. *OR* 19, pt. 1, 867.

44. *OR* 19, pt. 1, 854; Wyckoff, The Third South Carolina, 72.

45. Glen A. Swain, Sr., *The Bloody 7th – Regimental Roster Set* (Wilmington, North Carolina: Broadfoot Publishing Company, 2014), 1.

46. Dickert, *History of Kershaw's Brigade,* 149.

47. *OR* 19, pt. 1, 854; Dickert, *History of Kershaw's Brigade,* 149.

48. Shand, *Incidents of a Private Soldier,* 35; Wyckoff, *The Third South Carolina Infantry,* 73.

49. Shand, *Incidents of a Private Soldier,* 35

50. Carman, *The Maryland Campaign,* vol. I, 268, 268 (note 115).

51. *OR* 19, pt. 1, 865; Shand, *Incidents of a Private Soldier,* 35; Wyckoff, *The Third South Carolina Infantry,* 74.

52. *OR* 19, pt. 1, 858.

53. *OR* 19, pt. 1, 858.

54. Ezra A. Carman, *The Maryland Campaign,* vol. II, 226, 234; *OR* 19, pt. 1, 869; Wyckoff, *A History of the 2nd South Carolina Infantry,* 45. Kershaw's brigade was on the right

of McLaws' division during the West Woods fight because Cobb's brigade wandered off and took position on the Sunken Road.

55. *OR* 19, pt. 1, 868.

56. *OR* 19, pt. 1, 865. Maj. Franklin Gaillard took command after Kennedy was wounded in the foot during the attack on 125th Pennsylvania

57. *OR* 19, pt. 1, 865, 308; Dickert, *History of Kershaw's Brigade*, 156. Kershaw wrote in his report, "The colors of this (7th South Carolina) regiment, shot from the staff, formed the winding-sheet of the last man of the color company at the extreme point reached by our troops that day." Corporal Jacob G. Orth, 28th Pennsylvania, Tyndale's Brigade, Greene's division, received the Medal of Honor for capturing a battle flag, reportedly of the 7th South Carolina.

58. *OR* 19, pt. 1, 324.

59. Carman, *The Maryland Campaign*, vol. II, 226; *OR* 19, pt. 1, 869; Wyckoff, *The Third South Carolina Infantry*, 76. Wyckoff refers to a letter from Y.J. Pope dated March 20, 1895.

60. *OR* 19, pt. 1, 862; Shand, *Incidents of a Private Soldier*, 37; Carman, *The Maryland Campaign*, vol. II, 602. By the time the 2nd South Carolina withdrew through the West Woods, it was on its third commander and had lost its battle flag. After Col. Aiken was wounded, Maj. William Capers White briefly took command before he was killed by Tomkins' battery. Command of the regiment then fell to Capt. John Hard.

61. Arthur W. Bergeron, Jr., *Guide to Louisiana Confederate Military Units, 1861-1865* (Baton Rouge, LA: Louisiana State University Press, 1989), 4. The legion was a combined military unit of infantry, artillery and cavalry that was already antiquated by the Civil War. Soon after its organization, the Cobb Legion units were separated. The artillery became the Troup Artillery, and the cavalry remained Cobb's Legion of cavalry. The infantry component consisted of only seven companies, and was commanded by Howell Cobb's brother, Col. Thomas Reade Rootes Cobb.

62. Hartwig, *To Antietam Creek*, 680; *OR* 19, pt. 1, 860-862. Gen. McLaws' report gives very detailed participation and casualty rates for both Crampton's Gap and Antietam.

63. *OR* 19, pt. 1, 861, 862, 871; Carman, *The Maryland Campaign of September 1862,* vol. I, 312; Carman, *The Maryland Campaign of September 1862*, vol. II, 602. These figures are the brigade's casualties at Antietam, which seem low; however, the brigade's numerical integrity had suffered greatly at Crampton's Gap where Cobb lost 686 (52%) of the 1,310. According to the brigade's official report for the Antietam battle, by the time the brigade reached Sharpsburg, there were only 357 men in the line.

64. *Stewart Sifakis, Compendium of the Confederate Armies: South Carolina and Georgia* (New York: Facts on File,

1995), *215, 228, 280*; Harsh, *Taken at the Flood*, 34-37; Hartwig, *To Antietam Creek*, 455.

65. Ezra Warner, *Generals in Gray* (Baton Rouge, LA: Louisiana State University Press, 1959), 55; Hartwig, *To Antietam Creek*, 455, 456.

66. Carman, *The Maryland Campaign*, vol. I, 230-233; Harsh, *Taken at the Flood,* 178-180; *OR* 19, pt. 1, 852-854.

67. *OR* 19, pt. 1, 854, 870; Hartwig, *To Antietam Creek,* 455, 456. Semmes met with Cobb after he arrived, but did not specify which gap – Crampton's or Brownsville – he thought was the primary objective of the union assault. As senior officer, it was still incumbent upon Cobb to determine which gap on his own.

68. Reese, *Sealed With Their Lives*, 126; *OR* 19, pt. 1, 861, 870.

69. Carman, *The Maryland Campaign*, vol. I, 309. The order and placement of Cobb's regiments on either side of the mountain crest is one of considerable variation. No official report specifies the individual locations, and scholars have attempted to recreate the order via personal accounts. Most agree, however, that Cobb's Legion was the right anchor of the line and bore the brunt of the New Jersey brigade attack in front, flank and rear.

70. Reese, *Sealed With Their Lives*, 140-142, 302. Lt. Col. Lamar would die the next morning as a captive.

71. Hartwig, *To Antietam Creek*, 466, 467. This volley into the 15th NC likely came from the New Jersey Brigade coming up the Gapland Road after driving in the Confederate right.

72. Reese, *Sealed With Their Lives,* 159-165; Elizabeth Whitley Roberson, *In Care of Yellow River: The Complete Civil War Letters of Private Eli Pinson Landers to His Mother*, (Gretna, LA: Pelican Publishing Company, 1997), 97; Hartwig, *To Antietam Creek,* 468-470.

73. Hoptak, *The Battle of South Mountain*, 110, 116; Reese, *Sealed With Their Lives,* 169; *OR* 19, pt. 1, 854, 855, 861. The casualties were 58 killed, 186 wounded and 442 missing.

74. *OR* 19, pt. 1, 857, 871; Armstrong, *Opposing the Second Corps at Antietam*, 33-36; Reese, *Sealed With Their Lives,* 266. The author found no source offering a description of Cobb's whereabouts. One possible explanation is that he was tending to the arrangements for Col. John Basil Lamar, his volunteer aide-de-camp and brother-in-law, who died on the morning of the 15th from his wound received in Padgett's field. Lamar was temporarily buried in a borrowed burial crypt in Charles Town, (West) Virginia; *OR* 19, pt. 1, 871. The official report for the brigade's actions at Antietam was written by Lt. Col. MacRae.

75. *OR* 19, pt. 1, 872; Armstrong, *Opposing the Second Corps at Antietam*, 99; Carman, *The Maryland Campaign*, vol. II, 250, 251. Much of the punishment taken by Cobb's brigade came from Capt. John A. Tompkins' Battery A, 1st Rhode Island Light located just southeast of the Dunker Church plateau. Composed of six 10-lb Parrotts,

Tompkins was in a perfect position to enfilade the counterattacking Confederates.

76. OR 19, pt. 1, 872; Armstrong, *Opposing the Second Corps at Antietam,* 131; Carol Reardon and Tom Vossler, *A Field Guide to Antietam,* (Chapel Hill, NC: The University of North Carolina Press, 2016), 195-197; Gottfried, *The Maps of Antietam,* 198, 199; Carman, *The Maryland Campaign,* vol. II, 341; OR 19, pt. 1, 859. McLaws stated that Cobb's brigade lost 43 percent at Antietam.

77. OR 19, pt. 1, 860-862, 865, 884; Sifakis, *Compendium of the Confederate Armies,* 281, 282; Reese, *Sealed With Their Lives,* 267; Warner, *Generals in Gray,* 55.

78. Hartwig, *To Antietam Creek,* Appendix B, Strength of Union and Confederate Forces; OR 19, pt. 1, 860. The brigade may have numbered 786 at Antietam.

79. OR 19, pt. 1, 862.

80. Tagg, *The Generals of Gettysburg ,* 216-217.

81. OR 19, pt. 1, 857; Ronald H. Mosely, ed., *The Stilwell Letters: A Georgian in Longstreet's Corps, Army of Northern Virginia* (Macon, GA: Mercer University Press, 2002), 39-40.

82. OR 19, pt. 1, 876-77; Carman, *The Maryland Campaign,* vol. I, 301.

83. Carman, *The Maryland Campaign of 1862,* vol. I, 301-05. Carman noted that the 32nd Virginia "were more spectators than participants in the action . . . as they were not engaged."

84. Carman, *The Maryland Campaign,* vol. I, 431; OR 19, pt. 1, 861. Col. E. B. Montague of the 32nd Virginia reported "My infantry force was not engaged, though they were ready and anxious to take part in the conflict." OR 19, 1, 876-77.

85. OR 19, pt. 1, 857-62.

86. OR 19, pt. 1, 857; John Parham to Ezra A. Carman, October 5, 1899, NA-AS.

87. OR 19, 1, 857; "John Thomas Parham Talks Before the A.P. Hill Camp of Confederate Veterans," September 6, 1894, George S. Bernard Collection of the O. Winston Link Museum, History Museum of Western Virginia, Historical Society of Western Virginia. Object ID 2009.75.037. Retrieved on December 10, 2020 at https://hswv.pastperfectonline.com/archive/56C0EF56-C2A3-4F31-AC68-798584273832.

88. OR 19, pt. 1, 857; John Parham to Ezra A. Carman, October 5, 1899, NA-AS; Carman, *The Maryland Campaign,* vol. II, 185.

89. Carman, *The Maryland Campaign,* vol. II, 185-186, 198; Cope Map, #8, (9 to 9:30 a.m.).

90. OR 19, pt. 1, 877-79.

91. OR 19, pt. 1, 872-76, 877-79; Carman, *The Maryland Campaign,* vol. II, 199.

92. OR 19, pt. 1, 877-79; Carman, *The Maryland Campaign,* vol. II, 199; John Parham to Ezra A. Carman, October 18, 1899, NA-AS.

93. OR 19, 1, 877-79; Carman, *The Maryland Campaign,* vol. II, 199; John Parham of the 32nd Virginia estimated that more than half of its men were lost at this position.

John Parham to Ezra A. Carman, October 18, 1899, NA-AS.

94. OR 19, pt. 1, 877-79; Carman, *The Maryland Campaign,* vol. II, 215. Historian Joseph Harsh observed that "the chase after Sedgwick had become a jumble of units, and its progress became further disorganized by fences and the irregularities of the ground." Harsh, *Taken at the Flood,* 391.

95. Carman, *The Maryland Campaign,* vol. II, 217.

96. Carman, *The Maryland Campaign,* vol. II, 223.

97. Carman, *The Maryland Campaign,* vol. II, 223; OR 19, pt. 1, 877-79, 882; Callom Jones to Ezra A. Carman, October 13, 1899, NA-AS. Lt. Robert Knaggs, the regimental adjutant of the 7th Michigan was one that got away. After helping a wounded captain to the barn "where the wounded were being carried," Knaggs "thought I would see where the Johnnies were before stopping long." He didn't go far for he "found the Johnnies at the other corner" of the barn. "I had to run" but he soon found himself in a lane with "a stake and rider fence on both sides." He made good his escape "by running in and out of the corners of the fence." Jay C. Martin, *General Henry Baxter, 7th Michigan Volunteer Infantry: A Biography* (Jefferson, N.C.: McFarland Publishers, 2015), 78.

98. Carman, *The Maryland Campaign,* vol. II, 223-24; William Stores to Ezra A. Carman, December 30, 1899, NA-AS.

99. Carman, *The Maryland Campaign,* vol. II, 224. The exact location may have been the Alfred Poffenberger barn which was being used as a hospital. See Clemens, p. 342, note 68 citing a September 30, 1899 letter to Carman from Callom Jones, 15th Virginia, "who stated we 'had orders . . . to report to the brigade hospital where we stayed all the next day.'" OR 19, pt. 1, 872-878.

100. Carman, *The Maryland Campaign,* vol. II, 215; John W. Lynch, *The Dorman-Mashbourne Letters: With Brief Accounts of the 10th and 53rd Georgia Regiments, CSA* (Senoia, GA: Down South Publishing, 1995), 31-32.

101. OR 19, pt. 1, 860-861, 872-76, 881-83; Carman, *The Maryland Campaign,* vol. II, 215, 224. The losses by regiment are: 15th Virginia, 58%; 10th Georgia, 57%; 32nd Virginia, 45%; and the 53rd Georgia, 30%.

102. Hartwig, *To Antietam Creek,* Appendix B, Strength of Union and Confederate Forces. According to McLaws' official report, Barksdale's strength prior to Harpers Ferry was only 960. OR 19, pt. 1, 860.

103. OR 19, pt. 1, 860. Barksdale's losses at Harpers Ferry were 2 killed; 15 wounded; and none missing. Using McLaws' number of 960 at the beginning of the campaign and 17 losses at Harpers Ferry, 52 men must have fallen out or been lost on the march from Harpers Ferry to Antietam.

104. Mike M. Hubbert, "The Travels of the 13th Mississippi Regiment: Excerpts from the Diary of Mike M. Hubbert of Attala County (1861-1862)," *Journal of*

*Mississippi History,* vol. 45 (1983), 306; Harsh, *Taken at the Flood,* 36; OR 19, pt. 1, 1019.

105. James Dinkins, *1861-1865, By an Old Johnnie: Personal Recollections and Experiences in the Confederate Army,* (Cincinnati, OH: The Robert Clark Company, 1897), 53; Harsh, *Taken at the Flood,* 55.

106. *history.house.gov:* History, Art and Archives: United States House of Representatives, Historical Highlights: "The Most Infamous Floor Brawl in the History of the U.S. House of Representatives," Feb 6, 1858. In 1858, a brawl broke out over the status of Kansas involving over 30 Congressmen on the House floor. In the melee, two Republicans pulled the hairpiece off the head of the staunch States' Rights Democrat Barksdale, and the melee "dissolved into a chorus of laughter and jeers."

107. James W. McKee, "William Barksdale," *Mississippi Encyclopedia,* Center for Study of Southern Culture, July 10, 2017. National Park Service, Barksdale's Brigade, Antietam on the Web.

108. Henley Diary, 6 September 1862 entry; Trimpi, "Lafayette McLaws' Aide-De-Camp, 30.

109. Mike Hubbert; Maryland Civil War Trails Historical Marker, Landon House, *From Hospitality to Hospital,"* located in Urbana, Maryland. Although the plaque identifies the band as belonging to the 18th Mississippi Cavalry (vice infantry), that unit was not organized until later in the fall of 1862.

110. Carman, *The Maryland Campaign of September 1862,* vol. I, 212; Simpson, Everson and Simpson, *Far, Far From Home,* 149.

111. Henley diary, 10 September 1862 entry.

112. OR 19, pt. 1, 542.

113. OR 19, pt. 1, 853.

114. Lafayette McLaws to I.R. Pennypacker, May 20, 1888, Lafayette McLaws Papers, Littlejohn Collection, Wofford College; OR 19, pt. 1, 853; Wyckoff, *The Third South Carolina Infantry,* 42; Carman, *Maryland Campaign of 1862,* vol. I, 233.

115. Carman, *The Maryland Campaign of 1862,* vol. I, 233.

116. Dickert, *History of Kershaw's Brigade,* 148.

117. OR 19, pt. 1, 862.

118. OR 19, pt. 1, 863; Joseph Pierro, ed., *The Maryland Campaign of September 1862: Ezra A. Carman's Definitive Study of the Union and Confederate Armies at Antietam* (London: Routledge, 2008), 114.

119. Wayne Mahood, *Fight all Day, March All Night: A Medal of Honor Recipient's Story,* (Albany, NY: SUNY Press, Excelsoir Editions, 2012), 19.

120. OR 19, pt. 1, 862; James Dinkins, *Personal Recollections,* 54.

121. OR 19, pt. 1, 860, 861.

122. Pierro, *The Maryland Campaign,* 119; Dinkins, *Personal Recollections,* 54.

123. Dinkins, *Personal Recollections,* 54.

124. Robert W. Shand, *Incidents in the Life of a Private Soldier,* 34.

125. Dinkins, *Personal Recollections,* 56, 57.

126. Mike Hubbert quote on Maryland Civil War Trails Historical marker.

127. Henley diary, September 17, 1862 entry.

128. Dinkins, *Personal Recollections,* 59; Henley diary, September 17, 1862 entry.

129. Carman, *The Maryland Campaign,* vol. II, 197.

130. OR 19, pt. 1, 858; Carman, *The Maryland Campaign,* vol. II, 198.

131. Lt. Col. William Luse, commander of the 18th Mississippi, and Col. Benjamin Humphrey, commander of the 21st Mississippi, had not yet reached the field from their march from Harpers Ferry. Maj J.C. Campbell took command of the 18th Mississippi at Antietam and was killed. Capt John Sims commanded the 21st Mississippi. Both Luse and Humphreys caught up with their regiments in the afternoon of the 17th.

132. Carman, *Maryland Campaign, vol. II,* 200; Private Edward Buruss, "Memoirs," copy in the ANB Library.

133. OR 19, pt. 1, 320; T. Harry Williams, ed., "The Civil War Letters of William Cage," *Louisiana Historical Quarterly,* vol. XXXIX, number 1 (January, 1956), 122.

134. OR 19, pt. 1, 883, 318.

135. Pierro, *The Maryland Campaign,* 226. Armstrong, *Unfurl Those Colors,* 191; Carman, *Maryland Campaign of 1862,* vol. II, 214.

136. Carman, *Maryland Campaign,* vol. II, 214, 215.

137. Carman, *Maryland Campaign,* vol. II, 215.

138. OR 19, pt. 1, 860; Williams, ed., "Letters of William L. Cage. 122-23.

## Anderson's Division

1. Davis, *The Confederate General,* vol. I, 28-29; F. Ray Sibley, Jr., *The Confederate Order of Battle: The Army of Northern Virginia* (Shippensburg, PA: White Mane Publishing Company, 1996), 23, 27-28.

2. Ronald G. Giffin, *The 11th Alabama Volunteer Regiment in the Civil War* (Jefferson, NC: McFarland Press, 2008), 122-23.

3. Longstreet, *Manassas to Appomattox,* 205; Carman, *The Maryland Campaign,* vol. I, 116; Giffin, *The 11th Alabama Volunteer Regiment,* 123.

4. Gottfried, *The Maps of Antietam,* 98-99, 110-11; OR 19, vol. 1, 855.

5. *OR Supplement,* vol. 3, 568; C. Irvine Walker, *The Life of Lieutenant General Richard Heron Anderson* (Charleston, SC: Art Publishing Col, 1917), 100; William W. Chamberlaine, *Memoirs of the Civil War* (Washington, DC: Press of Byron S. Adams, 1912), 33; Carman, *The Maryland Campaign,* vol. II, 587. No one filed a report for the division, only one of the six brigades reported their actions, and only one of 26 regiments filed a report so reliance is placed on the scarcity of first-person accounts. Historian Robert K. Krick believed there was a "disintegration" of the division and illustrated the "haphazard way in which R.H. Anderson administered his division when he returned to its command." Robert

K. Krick, "It Appears as Though Mutual Extermination Would Put a Stop to the Awful Carnage: Confederates in Sharpsburg's Bloody Lane," in *The Antietam Campaign*, Gary Gallagher, ed. (Chapel Hill, NC: The University of North Carolina Press, 1999), 240.

6. Freeman, *Lee's Lieutenants*, vol. 2, 211-12; *OR* 19, pt. 1,023; Krick, "It Appears as Though Mutual Extermination Would Put a Stop to the Awful Carnage," 239-40.

7. Carman, *The Maryland Campaign*, vol. II, 259-60; John F. Jones to Ezra Carman, n.d., NA-AS; Ezra Carman on Pryor's Brigade, copy at ANB Library; Armstrong, *Opposing the Second Corps*, 103-04.

8. Hartwig, *To Antietam Creek*, Appendix B, Strength of Union and Confederate Forces. Carman, estimated that Wilcox's brigade numbered 640 at Antietam. Carman, *The Maryland Campaign*, vol. II, 259-71.

9. This figure is extrapolated from two accounts: Maj. Hilary Herbert stated his 8th Alabama had 120 on the morning of the battle and H. L. Stevenson believed his 10th Alabama contained "about 200 men." Maurice S. Fortin, ed., "Colonel Hilary A. Herbert's 'History of the Eighth Alabama Volunteer Regiment, C.S. A.' *Alabama Historical Quarterly*, vol. XXXIX (1977), 80; H. L. Stevenson Memoirs, Chicago Public Library; Carman, *The Maryland Campaign*, vol. 2, 587 (note 117).

10. Carman, *The Maryland Campaign*, vol. II, 602.

11. Steward Sifakis, *Compendium of the Confederate Armies: Alabama* (New York: Facts on File, 1992), 66-71; Warner, *Generals in Gray*, 337; Sibley, *The Confederate Order of Battle*, 23. Sibley, noted "It is highly unusual for one man to command both a division and a brigade." Sibley, *The Confederate Order of Battle*, 242, note 32.

12. Giffin, *The 11th Alabama Volunteer Regiment in the Civil War*, 123; Warner, *Generals in Gray*, 66-67. Wilcox spent several days at a Hagerstown hotel and then left for Martinsburg on September 14. He remained here in bed for five days and needed over a week for further recuperation before he could rejoin his brigade on September 22. Cadmus Wilcox Papers, LOC. Historian Robert K. Krick questioned why an officer from a different brigade in a different division, would be placed in charge of the brigade. Krick, "It Appears as Though Mutual Extermination," 241.

13. *OR* 19, vol. 1, 855; Fortin, "Herbert's 'History of the Eighth Alabama Volunteer Regiment," 75.

14. Fortin, ed., Fortin, "Herbert's 'History of the Eighth Alabama Volunteer Regiment," 76; James Edmonds Saunders, "Sketch of Wilcox's Brigade. By Gen. Cadmus Marcellus Wilcox," *Publications of the Alabama Historical Society*, vol. 3, 141; Vaughn M. Stewart, "Bailey G. McClellan and His Civil War." copy in the 10th Alabama folder, ANB Library.

15. Fortin, "Herbert's 'History of the Eighth Alabama Volunteer Regiment," 77-79; Carman, *The Maryland Campaign of 1862*, vol. II, 259, 269; Z. Abney to R. D. Parker, December 8 and 22, 1899, Chicago Public Library; Alexander Chisholm to Maj. J. M. Poule, September 5, 1891, Carman Papers, NYPL; John Hughes to Capt. R. D. Parker, February 25, 1900. Chicago Public Library; Armstrong, *Opposing the Second Corps*, 103-03, 115; Bailey George McClelen, *I Saw The Elephant*, Norman E. Rouke, ed., (Shippensburg, PA: Burd Street Press, 1995), 29-30.

16. Fortin, "Herbert's 'History of the Eighth Alabama Volunteer Regiment," 79-80; Hilary Herbert to Ezra Carman, January 15, 1902, NA-AS.

17. Carman, *The Maryland Campaign*, vol. II, 347; *OR* 19, pt. 1, 910; Fortin, "Herbert's 'History of the Eighth Alabama Volunteer Regiment," 80.

18. Fortin, ed., "Herbert's 'History of the Eighth Alabama Volunteer Regiment," 80, 83; Griffin, *The 11th Alabama Volunteer Regiment in the Civil War*, 126.

19. Warner, *Generals in Gray*, 66-67.

20. Hartwig, *To Antietam Creek*, Appendix B, Strength of Union and Confederate Forces. Carman estimated that Parham had 550 men in three regiments at Crampton's Gap. This figure comes from taking the average as 183 men per regiment. Carman, *The Maryland Campaign*, vol. I, 312. By Antietam, the brigade only numbered 84 men. Carman, *The Maryland Campaign*, vol. II, 602 (note 4).

21. Carman, *The Maryland Campaign*, vol. II, 602. Longstreet lists total brigade losses of 227 (8k-92w-127m). *OR* 19, pt. 1, 843. However, the army's report shows losses of only 76 (8k-68w), but does not include the considerable number captured at Crampton's Gap. *OR* 19, pt. 1, 812. The brigade lost heavily, 203 men (5k-74w-124m) at Crampton's Gap. Carman, *The Maryland Campaign*, vol. I, 312.

22. Sifaskis, *Compendium of the Confederate Armies: Virginia*, 174-75, 184-85, 190-91, 228-29; Davis, *The Confederate General*, vol. IV, 143. Some Orders of Battle include the 61st Virginia, but the regiment's organization was not completed until October of 1862 and it does not appear to have marched with the brigade into Maryland. Sifaskis, *Compendium of the Confederate Armies: Virginia*, 256-57.

23. Robert E. L. Krick, *Staff Officers in Gray* (Chapel Hill, NC: The University of North Carolina Press, 2003), 256; John Horn, *The Petersburg Regiment in the Civil War: A History of the 12th Virginia Infantry from John Brown's Hanging to Appomattox, 1859-1865* (El Dorado Hill, CA: Savas Beatie, 2019), 103. After recovering from his wound, Parham returned to his regiment and commanded it at Chancellorsville, Gettysburg and beyond. It appears he became a provost marshal at Richmond in October, 1864. He was back in command of his regiment by the end of January, 1865 but "died before war's close, a belatedly mortal wound." William Parham entry, https://antietam.aotw.org/officers.php?officer_id=709, "Antietam on the Web" site.

24. Horn, *The Petersburg Regiment*, 100-02; Philip Brown, *Reminiscences of the War of 1861-1865* (Richmond, VA: Whittet & Shepperson, Printers, 1917), 31.

419

25. George S. Bernard, *War Talks of Confederate Veterans* (Petersburg, VA: Fenn & Owen, Publishers, 1892), 23; Carman, *The Maryland Campaign*, vol. I, 233, 300-01, 306; Reese, *Sealed with Their Lives*, 72-75, 85; Gottfried, *Maps of Antietam*, 76-77; Brown, *Reminiscences of the War of 1861-1865*, 32. The location of the 41st Virginia is unclear. The regiment's historian thought Gen. Semmes may have positioned it at the top of the gap, which is unlikely. William D. Henderson, *41st Virginia Infantry* (Lynchburg, VA: H. E. Howard, 1986), 16.

26. Reese, *Sealed with their Lives*, 80; Carman, *The Maryland Campaign*, vol. I, 311-12.

27. OR 19, pt. 1, 382-83, 389; Gottfried, *Kearny's Own*, 70-72; Horn, *The Petersburg Regiment*, 106; Bernard, *War Talks of Confederate Veterans*, 28.

28. OR 19, pt. 1, 383; Gottfried, *The Maps of Antietam*, 82-83; Horn, *The Petersburg Regiment*, 108; Brown, *Reminiscences of the War of 1861-1865*, 32-33.

29. Carman, *The Maryland Campaign*, vol. I, 312; Horn, *The Petersburg Regiment*, 110.

30. Horn, *The Petersburg Regiment*, 114-15; Bernard, *War Talks of Confederate Veterans*, 23; Carman, *The Maryland Campaign*, vol. II, 257; Chamberlaine, *Memoirs of the Civil War*, 34.

31. Hartwig, *To Antietam Creek*, Appendix B, Strength of Union and Confederate Forces. By Antietam, the brigade numbered 649. Carman estimated 147 men in each regiment of Anderson's division. Carman, *The Maryland Campaign*, vol. II, 588 (note 117).

32. Carman, *The Maryland Campaign*, vol. II, 602.

33. Stewart Sifakis, *Compendium of the Confederate Armies: Mississippi* (New York: Facts on File, 1995), 70-71, 92-93, 99, 104-105; Davis, *The Confederate General*, vol. II, 119; Carman, *The Maryland Campaign*, vol. II, 545 (n. 60).

34. Warner, *Generals in Gray*, 86; Davis, *The Confederate General*, vol. v, 51.

35. Dobbins, ed., *Grandfather's Journal*, 102-03; Robert G. Evans, ed., *The Sixteenth Mississippi Infantry: Civil War Letters and Reminiscences* (Oxford, MS: The University of Mississippi Press, 2002), 113.

36. Ada Christine Lightsey, *The Veteran's Story* (Meridian, MS: The Meridian News, 1899), n.p.; Dobbins, ed., *Grandfather's Journal*, 103-04; Evans, ed., *The Sixteenth Mississippi Infantry*, 112.

37. Evans, *The Sixteenth Mississippi Infantry*, 114; James Kirkpatrick Diary, September 10, 1862 entry (Briscoe Center for American History, The University of Texas, Austin); *A Historical Sketch of the Quitman Guards, Company E. Sixteenth Mississippi Regiment, Harris' Brigade* (New Orleans, LA: Isaac T. Hinton, Printer, 1866), 33; Dobbins, ed., *Grandfather's Journal*, 104-05; Gottfried, *Maps of Antietam*, 99.

38. Kirkpatrick Diary, September 16, 1862 entry; Dobbins, ed., *Grandfather's Journal*, 105; Lightsey, *The Veteran's Story*, n.p.; Evans, *The Sixteenth Mississippi Infantry*, 115.

39. Carman, *The Maryland Campaign*, vol. II, 259, 271; OR 19, pt. 1, 884-85; *A Historical Sketch of the Quitman Guards*, 34.

40. Dobbins, ed., *Grandfather's Journal*, 105-06; Carman, *The Maryland Campaign*, vol. II, 280; James Shinn Memoirs, Southern Historical Collection, University of North Carolina. An officer in the 4th North Carolina (Anderson's brigade) believed the general stampede of Confederates was actually caused by Posey's brigade. "I think Featherston [Posey] was started to the right, but instead of getting there came up behind us, where he was not needed, for we could have held our position indefinitely. He sustained great loss in killed and wounded and I have always thought was the cause of the line breaking, for when he found he was not needed there he gave an order to fall back, which was mistaken for a general order and all that could walk went back with him, which caused a general break in the line." Carman, *The Maryland Campaign*, vol. II, 281.

41. Evans, *The Sixteenth Mississippi Infantry*, 119; Carman, *The Maryland Campaign*, vol. II, 602, 616.

42. Hartwig, *To Antietam Creek*, Appendix B, Strength of Union and Confederate Forces. Carman, estimated that Armistead's brigade numbered 735 at Antietam. He concluded that each of Anderson's regiments numbered about 147 men. Carman, *The Maryland Campaign*, vol. II, 588 (note 117).

43. Carman, *The Maryland Campaign*, vol. II, 602.

44. Stewart Sifakis, *Compendium of the Confederate Armies: Virginia* (New York: Facts on File, 1992), 179-80, 187-88, 225-26, 245-46, 251-52.

45. Warner, *Generals in Gray*, 11-12; Tagg, *The Generals of Gettysburg*, 243-44.

46. OR 19, pt. 2, 595.

47. Carman, *The Maryland Campaign*, vol. I, 233-23.

48. Carman, *The Maryland Campaign*, vol. II, 312, 314.

49. McGrath, *Shepherdstown*, 64; OR 19, pt. 1, 831-32.

50. McGrath, *Shepherdstown*, 65-66, 90, 211; OR 19, pt. 1, 367, 612, 832.

51. Hartwig, *To Antietam Creek*, Appendix B, Strength of Union and Confederate Forces; Zack C. Waters and James C. Edmonds, *A Small but Spartan Band* (Tuscaloosa, AL: The University of Alabama Press, 2010), 39. The brigade's strength at Antietam is extrapolated—the three Florida regiments probably numbered 570 men.

52. Carman, *The Maryland Campaign*, vol. II, 602.

53. Stewart Sifakis, *Compendium of the Confederate Armies: Florida and Arkansas* (New York: Facts on File, 1992), 16-17, 21-22, 24; Sifakis, *Compendium of the Confederate Armies: Alabama*, 74-75; Sifakis, *Compendium of the Confederate Armies: Virginia*, 163-64 Sibley, *The Confederate Order of Battle*, 5, 6, 17.

54. Davis, ed., *The Confederate General*, vol. V, 64-65; Freeman, *Lee's Lieutenants*, vol. 2, 141; Longstreet, *From Manassas to Appomattox*, 248.

55. Carman, *The Maryland Campaign*, vol. I, 233, 242; Gottfried, *The Maps of Antietam*, 98-99; Waters and

Edmonds, *A Small but Spartan Band*, 31-32; I. M. Auld to mother, September 22, 1862. Auld Letters, Putnam County Department of Archives and History, Palatka, Florida.

56. Dobbins, ed., *Grandfather's Journal*, 103; Auld to mother, September 22, 1862.

57. Carman, *The Maryland Campaign*, vol. II, 270; David Lang to E.A. Carman, n.d., David Lang Letterbooks, vol. 2, Florida State Archives, Tallahassee, FL; Waters and Edmonds, *A Small but Spartan Band*, 34; Krick, "It Appears as Though Mutual Extermination," 240.

58. Carman, *The Maryland Campaign*, vol. II, 259, 260, 262, 269; *OR* 19, pt. 1, 1,037.

59. *OR* 19, pt. 1, 1,048; Carman, *The Maryland Campaign*, vol. II, 270.

60. Carman, *The Maryland Campaign*, vol. II, 279, 280, 349; Gottfried, *The Maps of Antietam*, 198-99; *OR* 19, pt. 1, 1,025, 1,048. Hill described the advance of the 7th Maine (William Irwin's brigade; William Smith's division, VI Corps), which was sent forward toward the Piper farmstead.

61. Carman, *The Maryland Campaign*, vol. II, 602; Council A. Bryan, "Letter from the 5th Florida," *Florida Sentinel* (Tallahassee), October 7, 1862.

62. Freeman, *Lee's Lieutenants*, vol. 2, 265-66.

63. Hartwig, *To Antietam Creek*, Appendix B, Strength of Union and Confederate Forces; *Augusta Constitutionalist* (Georgia), October 3, 1862. Wright's brigade probably numbered 443 at Antietam, but Col. William Gibson of the 48th Georgia claimed that only 250 men went into battle at the Sunken Road. *OR Suppl.*, vol. 3, 569.

64. Carman, *The Maryland Campaign*, vol. II, 603.

65. Sifakis, *Compendium of the Confederate Armies: South Carolina and Georgia*, 185, 225-226, 261-62; Sifakis, *Compendium of the Confederate Armies: Alabama*, 114.

66. Davis, *The Confederate General*, vol. VI, 161.

67. *Augusta Daily Constitutionalist*, September 20, 1862.

68. Carman, *The Maryland Campaign of 1862*, vol. I, 233-34; *OR* 19, pt. 1, 853.

69. Captain Charles Andrews, "Diary of the 3rd Georgia Infantry Regiment, 1861 – 1865," 9, (copy in the Bradley Gottfried Collection); Carman, *The Maryland Campaign*, vol. II, 260.

70. *OR Suppl.*, vol. 3, 569; Carman, *The Maryland Campaign*, vol. 2, 260; *OR* 19, pt. 1, 1,051.

71. Carman, *The Maryland Campaign*, vol. II, 261-62; *OR Suppl.*, vol. 3, 569; *OR* 19, pt. 1, 327.

72. *OR Suppl.*, vol. 3, 569; Carman, *The Maryland Campaign*, vol. II, 262; ; Charles E. Boyd, *Devil's Den: A History of the 44th Alabama Volunteer Infantry Regiment, Confederate States Army* (Birmingham, AL: Banner Press, 1987), 20-21. A October 3, 1862 letter to an unknown hometown newspaper claimed the regiment only numbered 60 men during the fight.

73. *OR Suppl.*, vol. 3, 569; Carman, *The Maryland Campaign*, vol. II, 293; Chamberlaine, *Memoirs of the Civil War*, 34-35.

74. Clyde G. Wiggins, III, ed., *My Dear Friend: The Civil War Letters of Alva Benjamin Spencer, 3rd Georgia Regiment, Company C* (Macon, GA: Mercer University Press, 2007), 63-64.

## D.R. Jones' Division

1. Davis, ed., *The Confederate General*, vol. III, 200-01; Carman, *The Maryland Campaign*, vol. II, 593; W. H. Palmer to Ezra Carman, April 22, 1895, NA-AS.

2. *OR* 19, pt. 1, 885-86; Gottfried, *Maps of Antietam*, 62-71.

3. Gottfried, *Maps of Antietam*, 40-53.

4. *OR* 19, pt. 1, 886; Carman, *The Maryland Campaign*, vol. I, 393.

5. Palmer to Hotchkiss, April 22, 1895.

6. *OR* 19, pt. 1, 886-87.

7. *OR* 19, pt. 1, 887-88.

8. Davis, ed., *The Confederate General*, vol. III, 2001.

9. Hartwig, *To Antietam Creek*, Appendix B, Strength of Union and Confederate Forces. Carman estimated the brigade numbered about 638 men at Antietam. Carman, *The Maryland Campaign*, vol. II, 589-90.

10. Carman, *The Maryland Campaign*, vol. II, 603.

11. Harsh, *Sounding the Shallows*, 54, 104; Sifakis, *Compendium of the Confederate Armies: South Carolina and Georgia*, 181, 213, 216-17, 222-23; Warner, *Generals in Gray*, 25-26, 306-07. Toombs' argumentative behavior did not endear him to his superiors. He harped about not attempting to capture Washington after First Bull Run and had unkind words for army commander Joe Johnston and President Jefferson Davis. He challenged D.H. Hill to a duel after the North Carolinian accused him of cowardice during Second Manassas. He finally resigned his commission on March 4, 1863 because he was not promoted. Davis, ed., *The Confederate General*, vol. VI, 50-51. Toombs, upon request from division commander David Jones, commanded a demi-division of his brigade as well as those of G. T. Anderson and Thomas Drayton, from September 5 to 13. After this informal arrangement ended, Toombs still acted as if he was in command of three brigades rather than just his own. Harsh, *Sounding the Shallows*, 53-54.

12. Warner, *Generals in Gray*, 25-26.

13. *OR* 19, pt. 1, 885.

14. Carman, *The Maryland Campaign*, vol. I, 345, 383.

15. Carman, *The Maryland Campaign*, vol. I, 383-84.

16. *OR* 19, pt. 2, 888-89; Carman, *The Maryland Campaign*, vol. II, 588. Toombs claimed the hill he was to fall back on was about 400 yards south of the bridge. However, approximately 500 yards is a more accurate measurement.

17. *OR* 19, pt. 1, 890; *OR*, vol. 51, pt. 1, 162.

18. Carman, *The Maryland Campaign*, vol. II, 407; *OR* 19, pt. 1, 889.

19. Carman, *The Maryland Campaign*, vol. II, 407.

20. *OR* 51, pt. 1, 162.

21. Carman, *The Maryland Campaign*, vol. II, 409-12, 581; *OR* 19, pt. 1, 197; B. Keith Toney, "'Dying As Brave Men Should Die': The Attack and Defense of Burnside Bridge," *Civil War Regiments*, vol. 6, no. 2: 98.

22. Carman, *The Maryland Campaign*, vol. II, 414-16; *OR* 19, pt. 1, 197.

23. Kevin Pawlak, "Close and Concentrated: 9th Corps Artillery Conquers the Burnside Bridge," *Antietam Brigades (blog)*, February 2, 2019, http://antietambrigades.blogspot.com/2019/02/close-and-concentrated-9th-corps.html; Theodore T. Fogle, "Bloodletting at Burnside Bridge," *America's Civil War*, September 2015, 18.

24. Carman, *The Maryland Campaign*, vol. II, 416-23, 428; Fogle, "Bloodletting at Burnside Bridge;" *OR* 19, pt. 1, 163.

25. Carman, *The Maryland Campaign*, vol. II, 423; "The Twentieth Georgia Regiment," *Macon* (Georgia) *Telegraph*, October 25, 1862; Henry Benning, "Notes by General H. L. Benning on Battle of Sharpsburg," in *Southern Historical Society Papers*, vol. 16, (1888), 393.

26. Carman, *The Maryland Campaign*, vol. II, 423-24.

27. *OR* 19, pt. 1, 891.

28. Carman, *The Maryland Campaign*, vol. II, 460; *OR* 51, pt. 1, 164; Styple, ed., *Writing & Fighting from the Army of Northern Virginia*, 149.

29. Styple, ed., *Writing & Fighting*, 149, 152; Carman, *The Maryland Campaign*, vol. II, 470.

30. "Army Correspondence," *Southern Confederacy* (Atlanta, GA), October 4, 1862; Styple, ed., *Writing & Fighting*, 152; "A Reception to the Governor," *The Atlanta Constitution*, December 18, 1885; Carman, *The Maryland Campaign of September 1862*, vol. II, 472.

31. *OR*, vol. 51, pt. 1, 164.

32. Carman, *The Maryland Campaign of September 1862*, vol. II, 477-78; John W. Lokey, *My Experiences in the War Between the States* (Tishomingo, OK: John R. Lokey, 1959), 12.

33. Styple, ed., *Writing & Fighting*, 152; Carman, *The Maryland*, vol. II, 488.

34. *OR*, vol. 19, pt. 1, 887; "Army Correspondence," *Southern Confederacy* (Atlanta, GA), October 5, 1862; Jack D. Welsh, *Medical Histories of Confederate Generals* (Kent, OH: The Kent State University Press, 1995), 214-15; Pleasant A. Stovall, *Robert Toombs: Statesman, Speaker, Soldier, Sage* (New York: Cassell Publishing Company, 1892), 268; Krick, *Staff Officers in Gray*, 140, 288.

35. Hartwig, *To Antietam Creek*, Appendix B; J. Evans Edings, diary entry September 11, 1862; Edward Willis Papers, Manuscript Division, Library of Congress. Edings served as Assistant Adjutant General to Brig. Gen. Drayton.

36. J. Evans Edings, diary entry September 11, 1862. Drayton and his his five unit commanders did not file after action reports, so there is no official information regarding numbers and casualties for the brigade in the Maryland Campaign. Until recently, most histories of the campaign (including Ezra Carman's comprehensive manuscript) have omitted the inclusion of the Phillips Georgia Legion (Carman, *The Maryland Campaign*, vol. 2, 548, note 81). Edings' diary entries for September 11, 17, and 18 provide "Effective Strength" muster records of all five individual units in the brigade. I am greatly indebted to Kurt Graham for sharing this information.

37. Davis, ed., *The Confederate General*, vol. II, 76-77; Sifakis, *Compendium of the Confederate Armies: South Carolina and Georgia*, 88-89, 62-63, 263-64, 265; Stephen D. Lee, "Who Fired the First Gun at Sumter?" *Southern Historical Society Papers*, vol. 9 (1881), 501-02; Ashley Halsey, Jr., *Who Fired The First Shot and Other Untold Stories of the Civil War* (New York: Hawthorn Books Inc., 1963) 27-36; Ellsworth Elliot, Jr., *West Point In The Confederacy* (New York: G.A. Baker & Co., Inc., 1941), 328; *OR* 12, pt. 2, 579-80; *OR* 21, 1030. There is strong evidence that James gave the order to fire the first cannon at Fort Sumter in Charleston Harbor on April 12, 1861-- in effect starting the American Civil War.

38. *Savannah Republican*, September 20, 1862; *Athens* (Georgia) *Watchman*, October 1, 1862.

39. Rev. George G. Smith, "Reminiscences," Georgia Department of Archives and History, Morrow, Georgia, 53; Henry E. Young, Letter to Wife, September 22, 1862, ANB Library; Solomon A. Marsh, Letter to Wife, September 8, 1862, ANB Library; William DeSassure, "Private Army Correspondence," *The York Enquirer*, October 8, 1862; Wellington Alexander, *Writing & Fighting the Confederate War* (Kearny, NJ: Belle Grove Publishing Company, 2002), 99.

40. Marsh to Wife, September 8, 1862.

41. *OR* 19, Pt. 1, 885; Hartwig, *To Antietam Creek*, 339, 730 (note 40); *OR* 19, pt. 1, 908, 1020, 1032.

42. *OR* 19, pt. 1, 1032.

43. Kurt Graham, "Death of a Brigade," Society of the Descendants of Frederick Fox Newsletter, 1/9: 1-10.

44. Stotelmyer, *Too Useful To Sacrifice*, 71-72; Peter McGlashen, *Savannah Republican*, October 16, 1862; Graham, "Death of a Brigade," 1/9: 10; Edings diary entry, September 11, 18, 1862, Willis Papers, LOC. Casualties ranged from 85% of the overwhelmed 3rd South Carolina Battalion, 76% of the 50th Georgia, 60% of the 51st Georgia, 40% of the Phillips Legion, and 25% of the 15th South Carolina.

45. *OR* 19, pt. 1, 889

46. Carman, *The Maryland Campaign of September 1862*, vol. II, 407.

47. William O. Fleming, "The Fiftieth Georgia in the Battle of Sharpsburg," *Savannah Republican* (assumed), date unknown, M.J. Solomon's Scrapbook, Duke University Library, Durham, NC, 392. The Solomons, a Jewish family, lived in Savanah, Georgia, during the war owned an apothecary. The scrapbook contains newspaper clippings from the first year and a half of the war.

48. Fleming, "The Fiftieth Georgia in the Battle of Sharpsburg;" Carman, *The Maryland Campaign*, vol. II, 460.

49. DeSassure, "Private Army Correspondence," *The York (SC) Enquirer*, October 8, 1862; Carman, *The Maryland Campaign*, vol. II, 442-44, 447; OR 19, pt. 1, 886-87; Stotelmyer, *Too Useful To Sacrifice*, 178.

50. Carman, *The Maryland Campaign*, vol. II, 451-52; Henry E. Young, Letter to Wife, September 22, 1862, ANB Library; Fleming, "The Fiftieth Georgia in the Battle of Sharpsburg," *Savannah Republican* (assumed), date unknown, M.J. Solomon's Scrapbook, page 392; Jones, OR 19, pt. 1, 886-87.

51. Edings diary entries September 11, 17, 18, 1862; OR 21, 1029-30.

52. Hartwig, *To Antietam Creek*, Appendix B, Strength of Union and Confederate Forces. The brigade probably numbered 260 at Antietam. Carman, *The Maryland Campaign*, vol. II, 373, 588, 590.

53. Carman lists Garnett's losses as 274 (44k-211w-19m) for the campaign. This includes losses of 196 (35k-142w-19m) at South Mountain and 78 at Antietam. Carman, *The Maryland Campaign*, vol. I, 377; vol. II, 603.

54. Sikfakis, *Compendium of the Confederate Armies: Virginia*, 177-78, 193-94, 194-95, 212, 250-51; Sibley, Jr., *The Confederate Order of Battle: The Army of Northern Virginia*, 16, 24; Eppa Hunton, *Autobiography of Eppa Hunton* (Richmond, VA: The William Byrd Press, 1933), 79.

55. Davis, ed., *The Confederate General*, vol. II, 168-69.

56. William Nathaniel Wood, *Reminiscences of Big I* (Jackson, TN: McCowat-Mercer Press, Inc., 1956), 33; J. G. de Roulhac Hamilton, ed., *The Papers of Randolph Abbott Shotwell*, 2 volumes (Raleigh, NC: The North Carolina Historical Commission, 1929), vol. 1, 308-09.

57. William & Patricia Young, *56th Virginia Infantry* (Lynchburg, VA: H. E. Howard, 1991), 56-57; Wood, *Reminiscences of Big I*, 35.

58. OR 19, pt. 1, 894, 898; Wood, *Reminiscences of Big I*, 35; Carman, *The Maryland Campaign*, 356-57; Gottfried, *The Maps of Antietam*, 64-65. Ezra Carman posited that Longstreet's march to Boonsboro was so strenuous that as many as half the men fell from the ranks. Carman, *The Maryland Campaign*, vol. I, 245.

59. Carman, *The Maryland Campaign*, vol. I, 357-58, 358 (note 30), 360; OR 19, pt. 1, 894-95.

60. Henry T. Owen, "Incidents of the Battle of South Mountain," *Philadelphia Weekly Times*, July 23, 1880.

61. OR 19, pt. 1, 895, 1,021; Carman, *The Maryland Campaign*, vol. I, 377; Hunton, *Autobiography of Eppa Hunton*, 80.

62. Carman, *The Maryland Campaign*, vol. II, 389, 393.

63. OR 19, pt. 1, 896; Carman, *The Maryland Campaign*, vol. II, 383- 85; Wood, *Reminiscences of Big I*, 38.

64. OR 19, pt. 1, 896-97; Carman, *The Maryland Campaign*, vol. II, 488-69.

65. Carman, *The Maryland Campaign*, vol. II, 603.

66. Hartwig, *To Antietam Creek*, Appendix B, Strength of Union and Confederate Forces. The brigade numbered approximately 443 at Antietam. Carman, *The Maryland Campaign*, vol. II, 588.

67. Kemper's brigade lost 75 men (11k-57w-7m) at South Mountain and another 69 (10k-43w-16m) at Antietam for a total of 144 (21-100-23). Carman, *The Maryland Campaign*, vol. I, 378; vol. II, 603.

68. Sikfakis, *Compendium of the Confederate Armies: Virginia*, 155-56, 176-77, 183-84, 191-92, 204-05; Sibley, Jr., *The Confederate Order of Battle*, 1, 3, 5; Davis, *The Confederate General*, vol. III, 96.

69. Davis, *The Confederate General*, vol. IV, 5, 7.

70. Alexander Hunter, *Johnny Reb and Billy Yank* (New York: The Neale Publishing Company, 1905), 269-71; C. T. Loehr Statement, no date, Carman Papers, NYPL; Joseph T. Durkin, ed., *John Dooley, Confederate Soldier: His War Journal* (Notre Dame, IN: University of Notre Dame Press, 1963), 24; David Johnston, *The Story of a Confederate Boy in the Civil War* (Portland, OR: Glass & Prudhomme, Co., 1914), 131-32. David Johnston of the 7th Virginia exaggerated the number left behind to 20,000 and believed at least some of the men remained behind because of an aversion to invading the north. Johnston, *A Confederate Boy*, 132.

71. Hunter, *Johnny Reb and Billy Yank*, 278; Durkin, ed., *John Dooley, Confederate Soldier*, 34; Johnston, *A Confederate Boy*, 139; George Wise, *History of the Seventeenth Virginia Infantry, C.S.A.* (Baltimore, MD: Kelly, Piet & Company, 1870), 107-11; David E. Johnston, *Four Years a Soldier* (Princeton, WV: n.p., 1887), 192. George Wise put the starting time for the march back to Boonsboro on September 14 at 5:00 p.m., but David Johnston claimed it was 11:00 a.m. If the column arrived at Boonsboro by 2:30 p.m., it is more likely the column got an earlier start.

72. OR 19, pt. 1, 894, 904; Carman, *The Maryland Campaign*, vol. I, 356-57; Durkin, ed., *John Dooley, Confederate Soldier*, 35; Johnston, *A Confederate Boy*, 139-40; Gottfried, *The Maps of Antietam*, 64-65; Wm. H. Palmer to Ezra Carman, August 26, 1899, NA-AS.

73. Hunter, *Johnny Reb and Billy Yank*, 281; OR 19, pt. 1, 904; Carman, *The Maryland Campaign*, vol. I, 378. C. T. Loehr recalled, "we changed our position several times firing from behind fences and rocks until darkness set in, when we withdrew & fell back unmolested from the enemy to the Turnpike. . ." Loehr Statement.

74. OR 19, pt. 1, 905; Carman, *The Maryland Campaign*, vol. I, 389, 393; vol. II, 435-36, 451; Johnston, *A Confederate Boy*, 149-50; David Johnston to Ezra Carman, September 21, 1897, NA-AS; Hunter, *Johnny Reb and Billy Yank*, 283; Alexander Hunter, "A High Private's Sketch of Sharpsburg," *Southern Historical Society Papers*, vol. XI, no. 1 (January, 1883), 14. Regiments from Toombs' and Drayton's brigades were further to the south near the Lower Bridge, but they were not contiguous with the rest of Lee's army. David Johnston of the 7th Virginia claimed the two regiments, 7th and 24th Virginia formed

the extreme right flank of Lee's army until A.P. Hill's division arrived. David Johnston to Ezra Carman, September 23, 1897, NA-AS.

75. Hunter, *Johnny Reb and Billy Yank*, 288; Johnston, *A Confederate Boy*, 150; Hunter, "A High Private's Sketch of Sharpsburg," 18.

76. Hunter, "A High Private's Sketch of Sharpsburg," 18; Carman, *The Maryland Campaign*, vol. II, 453-56; *OR* 19, pt. 1, 905; Durkin, ed., *John Dooley, Confederate Soldier*, 46-47.

77. Carman, *The Maryland Campaign*, vol. II,456, 477, 603-04; Johnston, *A Confederate Boy*, 153; 30; Charles T. Loehr, *War History of the Old First Virginia Infantry Regiments, Army of Northern Virginia* (Richmond, VA: William Ellis Jones, 1884), 30.

78. Hartwig, *To Antietam Creek*, Appendix B, Strength of Union and Confederate Forces; *Charleston Courier*, October 1, 1862. James Walker wrote to Carman (July 18, 1898) estimating his strength to be 1,250, but Carman thought this number was too high. Carman, *The Maryland Campaign*, vol. 2, 378 (note 36). The brigade probably numbered 723 at Antietam.

79. In addition to the 216 men Walker's brigade lost at Antietam, it also sustained 32 (3k-29w) casualties at South Mountain for a total of 248 (29k-213w-6m). Carman, *The Maryland Campaign*, vol. I, 378; vol. II, 604; *OR* 19, pt. 1, 907-08.

80. Sifakis, *Compendium of the Confederate Armies: South Carolina and Georgia*, 51-52, 60-61, 67-68, 69-70, 72-73, 110.

81. Warner, *Generals in Gray*, 155; Krick, *Lee's Colonels*, 331.

82. James Hagood Memoirs, University of South Carolina Library, 74; *OR* 19, pt. 1, 885; James J. Baldwin, III, *The Eagle Struck: A Biography of Brigadier General Micah Jenkins and a History of the 5th South Carolina Volunteers and the Palmetto Sharpshooters* (Shippensburg, PA: Burd Street Press, 1996), 162-63; Richard Lewis, *Camp Life of a Confederate Boy of Bratton's Brigade, Longstreet's Corps, C.S.A.* (Charleston, SC: The News and Courier Book Presses, 1883), 31-32; Frank M. Mixson, *Reminiscences of a Private* (Columbia, SC: The State Company, 1910), 25- 26.

83. Baldwin, III, *The Eagle Struck*, 163; Mixson, *Reminiscences of a Private*, 27; Hagood Memoirs, 74, 79; Longstreet, *From Manassas to Appomattox*, 224-225.

84. Hagood Memoirs, 79-80; Carman, *The Maryland Campaign*, 362-63, 378; Baldwin, *The Eagle Struck*, 165-66; *OR* 19, pt. 1, 235, 905-6. Carman believed the 76th New York and 7th Indiana were the regiments attacking the stone wall in the darkness. They were later relieved by Col. William Christian's brigade. Carman, *The Maryland Campaign*, 363.

85. Carman, *The Maryland Campaign*, 389; Hagood Memoirs, 80; *OR* 19, pt. 1, 906, 907; Cope Maps (Daybreak through 1:00 p.m.)

86. Cope Map #12 (3:30 – 3:45 p.m.) and Map #13 (4:20 p.m.) Hagood Memoirs, 85; James Lide Coker, *History of*

*Company G, Ninth S. C. Regiment, Infantry and of Company E. Sixth Regiment, Infantry Army* (Greenwood, SC: The Attic Press, 1979), 111-12; *OR* 19, pt. 1, 907; Mixson, *Reminiscences of a Private*, 30-32; Baldwin, *The Eagle Struck*, 170-71. Hagood claimed he men "charged, with wild yells, upon the enemy's troops. The latter fled in dismay, and only stopped when the Confederates ceased the pursuit." Hagood Memoirs, 85-86. None of the other accounts mentioned this counterattack.

87. *OR* 19, pt. 1, 907; Cope Map #14 (5:30 p.m.).

88. *OR* 19, pt. 1, 907.

89. *OR* 19, pt. 1, 907-08; Carman, *The Maryland Campaign*, vol. II, 604.

90. Hartwig, *To Antietam Creek*, Appendix B, Strength of Union and Confederate Forces. Carman put Anderson's numbers at about 550, but this did not include the 140 men that Maj. F.H. Little commanded in his detached command. *OR* 19, pt. 1, 912.

91. In addition to the 87 men lost at Antietam, Anderson's brigade lost an additional seven (3w-4m) at Fox's Gap for a total of 94 (8k-80w-6m) casualties. Carman, *The Maryland Campaign*, vol. I, 377; vol. II, 604.

92. Sifakis, *Compendium of the Confederate Armies: South Carolina and Georgia*, 196-197, 200, 202-03, 206-07, 272-73; Evans, *Confederate Military History*, vol. 6, 391.

93. Warner, *Generals in Gray*, 6-7; Tagg, *Generals of Gettysburg*, 229-230.

94. W. H. Andrews, *Footprints of a Regiment: A Recollection of the 1st Georgia Regulars* (Atlanta, GA: Longstreet Press, 1992), 71; *OR* 19, pt. 1, 911; Styple, ed., *Writing & Fighting From the Army of Northern Virginia*, 147.

95. Andrews, *Footprints of a Regiment*, 73; Carman, *The Maryland Campaign*, vol. I, 332-33, 339-40, 377; *OR* 19, pt. 1, 377, 908-09.

96. Carman, *The Maryland Campaign*, vol. I, 389; *OR* 19, pt. 1, 909; Cope Map, #1 (Daybreak) and No. 7 (8:30 – 8:40 a.m.).

97. Carman, *The Maryland Campaign*, vol. II, 179-80, 201, 205-06; Andrews, *Footprints of a Regiment*, 78, 80; William H. Andrews to Ezra Carman, February 6, 1899, NA-AS; Warren Wilkinson and Steven E. Woodworth, *A Scythe of Fire: A Civil War Story of the Eighth Georgia Infantry Regiment* (New York: William Morrow, 2002), 185-86; Cope Map, No. 8 (9:00 – 9:30 a.m.), #9 (10:30 a.m.). According to Andrews' letter to Ezra Carman, Kershaw's men marched over Anderson's prone soldiers. W. H. Andrews to Ezra Carman, February 6, 1899 and undated letter, NA-AS.

98. Carman, *The Maryland Campaign*, vol. II, 206-07, 293-94; *OR* 19, pt. 1, 909-10; Cope Map, No. 11 (1:00 p.m.).

99. *OR* 19, pt. 1, 910; Carman, *The Maryland Campaign*, vol. II, 347; Cope Map, # 14 (5:30 p.m.).

100. Cope Map #1 (Daybreak), No. 8 (9:00 – 9:30 a.m.); H. D. D. Twiggs to Ezra Carman, December 28, 1898, NA-AS; Carman, *The Maryland Campaign*, vol. II, 359, 361.

101. Carman, *The Maryland Campaign*, vol. II, 361, 363, 368, 369, 435, 441, 444 (note 24); Cope Map #12 (3:30 to 3:45 p.m.

102. Cope Map Number 11 (1:00 p.m.); Carman, *The Maryland Campaign*, vol. II, 436; OR 19, pt. 1, 911-12.

103. Carman, *The Maryland Campaign*, vol. II, 460, 460 (note 51); OR 19, pt. 1, 912; Styple, ed., *Writing & Fighting From the Army of Northern Virginia*, 149.

104. Carman, *The Maryland Campaign*, vol. II, 604.

## Walker's Division

1. Warner, *Generals in Gray*, 319-320; OR 7, 20; Leonidas B. Giles, *Terry's Texas Rangers*, (Self Published, 1911, digitized by the Sloan Foundation, LOC, 2008), 15 & 25.

2. Warner, *Generals in Gray*, 320; OR vol. 9, 460, 475; OR 11, pt. 2, 487-88, 906-08, 915; OR 11, pt. 3, 565, 575, 579.

3. Carman, *The Maryland Campaign*, vol. I, 94; Davis, ed., *The Confederate General*, vol. VI, 88; Clark, ed., *North Carolina Regiments*, vol. II, 601; OR 19, pt. 1, 811; Calvin L. Collier, *They'll Do To Tie To!* (Little Rock, AR: Arkansas Civil War Centennial Commission, 1959), 81. Regarding the nature of Walker's wound and his return to service, the *Official Records* are mute. There is also no specific date that has been discovered about the date of "Walker's Division's" formation. It appears that because he was the senior officer available when his and Ransom's brigades were ordered north into Maryland, he became the division commander.

4. Harsh, *Taken at the Flood*, 134-35; *The Maryland Campaign*, vol. I, 95; OR 19, pt. 1, 912-13; *North Carolina in the Great War*, Vol. II, 601. There is some confusion in the historiography about the dates of these movements in Walker's account in the *Official Records* and the popular account he wrote for *Century Magazine*, later compiled into *Battles and Leaders*, twenty-four years later. In addition, Walker contends in the latter account that he was made privy to information at the time by Lee, who had yet to share with his wing commanders. See *Taken at the Flood*, 133-45

5. Hartwig, *To Antietam Creek*, 230-31; Clark, *North Carolina Regiments*, vol. II, 274; OR 19, pt. 1, 913. It is interesting to note that the history of the 24th North Carolina Infantry in *North Carolina Regiments*, vol. II, gets the date of this skirmish wrong, claiming it occurred on the first night the regiment was in Maryland as opposed to the third.

6. OR 19, pt. 1, 42-43.

7. Hartwig, *To Antietam Creek*, 232; Clark, *North Carolina Regiments*, vol. II, 601; OR 19, pt. 1, 913. It should be noted that the modern spelling of Hillsborough has dropped the "ugh" at the end.

8. OR 19, pt. 1, 913; Hartwig, *To Antietam Creek*, 526.

9. OR 19, pt. 1, 958; Hartwig, *To Antietam Creek*, 529-530; Carman, *The Maryland Campaign*, vol. I, 246-47

10. Carman, *The Maryland Campaign*, vol. I, 247; OR 19, pt. 1, 913; Hartwig, *To Antietam Creek*, 531-32.

11. Harsh, *Taken at the Flood*, 273-275.

12. OR 19, pt. 1, 914.

13. Clark, ed., *North Carolina Regiments*, vol. II, 275, 601; IV, 570-71; vol. III, 67; OR 19, pt. 1, 914.

14. OR 19, pt. 1, 914, 919.

15. Harsh, *Sounding the Shallows*, 19; OR 19, pt. 1, 914-915, 919-920.

16. Gottfried, *The Maps of Antietam*, 176-79; Clark, ed., *North Carolina Regiments*, Vol. V, 75; OR 19, pt. 1, 915, 920.

17. OR 19, pt. 1, 914-15, 918; Clark, *North Carolina Regiments*, vol. III, 68.

18. Gottfried, *The Maps of Antietam*, 182-183; OR 19, pt. 1, 843, 915-17.

19. Hartwig, *To Antietam Creek*, Appendix B, Strength of Union and Confederate Forces. The brigade probably numbered 2,164 at Antietam. Carman, *The Maryland Campaign*, vol. II, 591.

20. Carman, *The Maryland Campaign*, vol. II, 604.

21. Harsh, *Taken at the Flood*, 40-41.

22. Vannoy Manning File, ANB Library.

23. Vannoy Manning File, ANB Library. The regiment from Arkansas with 1,353 men mustered into service surrendered with 144 at the end of the war.

24. 48th North Carolina file, ANB Library.

25. Questions are always raised regarding S.O.191, such as who lost the copy, what happened to other copies, etc. It is said that Gen. Walker pinned his copy to the inside of his coat. Carman, *The Maryland Campaign*, vol. I, 283.

26. Carman, *The Maryland Campaign*, vol. I, 226.

27. John A. Sloan, *Reminiscences of the Guilford Grays, Co. B, 27th North Carolina Regiment* (Washington, D.C.: R.O. Polkinhorn Printers, 1883), 42; OR, 19 pt 1, 913.

28. Byrd Barnett Tribble, *Benjamin Cason Rawlings: First Virginia Volunteer for the South*. (Baltimore, MD: Butternut and Blue, 1996), 55.

29. Harsh, *Taken at the Flood*, 392.

30. Tribble, *Benjamin Cason Rawlings*, 57.

31. Tribble, *Benjamin Cason Rawlings*, 57; Carman, *The Maryland Campaign*, vol. II, 312; OR 19, 591, 618; Robert K. Krick, *30th Virginia Infantry* (Lynchburg, VA: H. E. Howard, Inc., 1983), 30.

32. Sloan, *Reminiscences of the Guilford Grays*, 44.

33. Sloan, *Reminiscences of the Guilford Grays*, 44-45. Carman, *The Maryland Campaign*, vol. II, 299.

34. Hartwig, *To Antietam Creek*, Appendix B, Strength of Union and Confederate Forces. The brigade numbered approximately 1,600 at Antietam. Vannoy Manning File, ANB Library. The strength figure is prior to the addition of the 46th North Carolina, with an estimated strength of 320. OR 19, pt. 1, 919.

36. Carman, *The Maryland Campaign*, vol. II, 604; OR 19, pt. 1, 811, 843. The Official Records lists 186 losses for Ransom's brigade, but there is a significant discrepancy between General Longstreet's official report of the casualties and the report made by the Medical Director of the Army of Northern Virginia. It is possible that

Longstreet's higher casualty numbers include the losses of the 46th North Carolina. This difference in casualties is further exacerbated by Joseph Harsh's, *Sounding the Shallows* (Table 24, page 201).

37. Clark, *North Carolina Regiments*, vol. II, 274, 291, 295, 303, 310, 591, 594-96. The 24th North Carolina was first known as the 14th North Carolina infantry prior to its reorganization in May 1862 when it was redesignated. Clark, *North Carolina Regiments*, vol. II, 269, 271. The casualties sustained by Ransom's brigade at Malvern Hill were 69 killed and 354 wounded for a total of 423. Clark, *North Carolina Regiments*, vol. II, 333.

38. Warner, *Generals in Gray*, 253-54; Clark, *North Carolina Regiments*, vol. II, 599. When Robert Ransom, Jr., was promoted to major general in the spring of 1863, he was transferred back to North Carolina. His older brother, Matt W. Ransom, was subsequently placed in command of Ransom's brigade and promoted to brigadier general on June 13, 1863. Matt Ransom commanded the brigade for the remainder of the war.

39. Clark, *North Carolina Regiments*, vol. II, 601-02. The colonel of the 26th North Carolina, Zebulon Vance, was elected governor of North Carolina and resigned his commission. Lt. Col. Harry Burgwyn, not yet 21 years old assumed command of the regiment. General Ransom made it known that "he wanted no boy Colonel in his brigade" and opposed Burgwyn's promotion to command the regiment. This did not sit well with the regiment and a request for transfer was issued and accepted. The opening in Ransom's brigade was not filled until spring 1863, when the 56th North Carolina was assigned to the command. The 26th North Carolina was eventually assigned Brig. Gen. James Johnston Pettigrew's brigade. Both Burgwyn and Pettigrew died during the Gettysburg Campaign.

40. Carman, *The Maryland Campaign*, vol. I, 94; Clark, *North Carolina Regiments*, vol. II, 601; OR 19, pt. 1, 811.

41. Hartwig, *To Antietam Creek*, 230-31; Clark, *North Carolina Regiments*, vol. II, 274; OR 19, pt. 1, 913. The history of the 24th North Carolina gets the date of this skirmish wrong, claiming that it occurred on the first night the regiment was in Maryland as opposed to the third. Clark, *North Carolina Regiments*, vol. II, 274

42. OR 19, pt. 1, 913; Hartwig, *To Antietam Creek*, 526.

43. Clark, *North Carolina Regiments*, vol. IV, 570-71; vol. II, 275, 601; vol. III, 67; OR 19, pt. 1, 914.

44. OR 19, pt. 1, 914, 919; Harsh, *Sounding the Shallows*, 19; OR 19, pt. 1, 914-15, 919-20; Gottfried, *The Maps of Antietam*, 178-79; Clark, *North Carolina Regiments*, vol. V, 75; OR 19, pt. 1, 920.

45. OR 19, pt. 1, 920; Carman, *Maryland Campaign*, vol. II, 229; Gottfried, *The Maps of Antietam*, 180-181; Clark, *North Carolina Regiments*, vol. II, 275; Judge Walter Clark, "Sharpsburg - Reminiscences of This Hard-Fought Battle," *The Wilmington* (NC) *Messenger*, October 7, 1894, page 2; NARA, Record Group 94, Antietam Studies 2-234 – 24 N.C., William Rose letter, NA-AS. The attack of the 24th North Carolina against Patrick's brigade was memorialized in the last stanza of a poem about the regiment by the wife of its colonel, Mary Bayard. Clark, *North Carolina Regiments*, vol. II, 276.

46. OR 19, pt. 1, 920; *The Maps of Antietam*, 180-181.

47. OR 19, pt. 1, 916, 920; Harsh, *Taken at the Flood*, 392-93; Gottfried, *The Maps of Antietam*, 182-83; Carman, *The Maryland Campaign*, vol. II, 308-13; Clark, *North Carolina Regiments*, vol. V, 77. The movements of Ransom's brigade at this point are difficult to determine as different sources use different times or misidentify the troops they were facing. It is apparent that the 2nd Massachusetts and 13th New Jersey attacked across the Miller pasture and suffered terribly from the fire of Ransom's brigade on the edge of the West Woods.

48. Carman, *The Maryland Campaign*, vol. II, 316-21; OR 19, pt. 1, 916, 920-21; Gottfried, *The Maps of Antietam*, 182-83.

49. OR 19, pt. 1, 916-17, 920-21; Clark, *North Carolina Regiments*, vol. III, 129.

50. Clark, *North Carolina Regiments*, vol. II, 276.

51. OR 19, pt. 1, 917. The heaviest losses occurred in the 24th and the 49th North Carolina. In both cases, these regiments were far more exposed than the rest of the brigade: the 24th North Carolina, when it moved northward beyond the West Woods shortly after the arrival of Ransom's brigade, and the 49th North Carolina when it spearheaded the Confederate counterattack near the Dunker Church around mid-day.

## Hood's Division

1. Ezra J. Warner, *Generals in Gray*, 142; "Cullum's List"; Grady McWhiney and Perry D. Jamieson, *Attack and Die – Civil War Military Tactics and the Southern Heritage*, (The University of Alabama Press, Tuscaloosa and London, 1982), 108.

2. Susannah J. Ural, *Hood's Texas Brigade* (Louisiana State University Press, Baton Rouge, 2017), 78. Former U.S. Senator Louis T. Wigfall was the first commander of the Texas Brigade and resigned his commission to take a seat in the Confederate Senate representing Texas.

3. John J. Hennessy, *Return to Bull Run – The Campaign and Battle of Second Manassas*, (New York: Simon and Schuster, 1993), 562.

4. Hennessy, *Return to Bull Run*, 289-98.

5. James V. Murfin, *The Gleam of Bayonets: The Battle of Antietam and the Maryland Campaign of September 1862* (New York: Thomas Yoseloff, 1965) 63, 90; Jerry W. Holsworth, "Uncommon Valor, Hood's Texas Brigade in the Maryland Campaign," *Blue & Gray Magazine*, August 1996, 9.

6. Ural, *Hood's Texas Brigade*, 116.

7. Harsh, *Taken at the Flood*, 190, 256; OR 19, pt. 1, 839 and 922; Ural, *Hood's Texas Brigade*, 117; Longstreet, "The Invasion of Maryland," vol. 2, 666; OR 19, pt. 1, 839, 922.

8. Carman, *The Maryland Campaign*, vol. I, 342, 389; Joe Owen, Philip McBride, and Joe Allport, *Texans at Antietam* (United Kingdom: Fonthill Media Limited, 2017), 33, 39; Stotelmyer, *Too Useful to Sacrifice*, 76.

9. *OR* 19, pt. 1, 937; Harsh, *Taken at the Flood*, 306; Carman, *The Maryland Campaign*, vol. I, 394.

10. Murfin, *The Gleam of Bayonets*, 210; Holsworth, "Uncommon Valor," 13.

11. *OR* 19, pt. 1, 923, 927-29; James I. Robertson, *Stonewall Jackson, The Man, The Soldier, The Legend* (New York: Macmillan Publishing, 1997), 613. Historians often refer to Miller's Cornfield as "The Cornfield" and known at Antietam as "America's Deadliest Square Mile." *Trail arms* was a command used for troops to grip their weapon near the muzzle with the butt of the weapon "trailing" a few inches above the ground to aid in reloading while charging forward.

12. *OR* 19, pt. 1, 923, 928, 938; Harsh, *Taken at the Flood*, 425.

13. Thomas W. Cutrer, ed., *Longstreet's Aide: The Civil War Letters of Major Thomas J. Goree* (Charlottesville, VA: University Press of Virginia, 1995), 100.

14. Hartwig, *To Antietam Creek*, Appendix B, Strength of Union and Confederate Forces. The brigade numbered about 854 at Antietam. *OR* 19, pt. 1, 929.

15. *OR* 19, pt. 1, 925.

16. Charles E. Brooks, "Popular Sovereignty in the Confederate Army: The Case of Colonel John Marshall and the Fourth Texas Infantry Regiment," in *The View from the Ground Experiences of Civil War Soldiers*, Aaron Sheehan – Dean, ed. (Lexington: University of Kentucky Press, 2007), 214.

17. Ural, *Hood's Texas Brigade*, 111.

18. James Lile Lemon, *Feed Them the Steel: Being The Wartime Recollections of Captain James Lile Lemon Co. A., 18th Georgia Infantry, CSA*, Mark H. Lemon, ed. (n.p.:n.p., 2013), 36.

19. Murfin, *Gleam of Bayonets*, 364.

20. Owen, *Texas at Antietam*, et al., 14; Holsworth, "Uncommon Valor," 7; Warner, *Generals in Grey*, 343.

21. *OR* 19, pt. 1, 145; Holsworth, "Uncommon Valor, Hood's Texas Brigade in the Maryland Campaign," 6, 11

22. Holsworth, "Uncommon Valor," 12; Owen et al., *Texas at Antietam*, 33, 39, 190.

23. Harsh, *Taken at the Flood*, 302; Holsworth, "Uncommon Valor," 12, 13; Owen et al, *Texas at Antietam*, 12; *OR* 19, pt. 1, 927.

24. *OR* 19, pt. 1, 927, 932; Holsworth, "Uncommon Valor," 14.

25. Owen et al., *Texas at Antietam*, 113.

26. Sears, *Landscape Turned Red*, 194; Holsworth, "Uncommon Valor," 16; Harsh, *Taken at the Flood*, 372-3. Gibbon's Brigade drew the nickname of the "Black Hat Brigade" for wearing the U.S. Army 1840s tall, black, Hardee hats usually pinned up on one side with a brass eagle insignia. They also wore white leggings and are more commonly known the "Iron Brigade," another sobriquet that they earned for their performance at the Battle of South Mountain. They were the only all-western brigade in the eastern theater. *OR* 19, pt. 1, 821; Cope Map #2 (6:00 – 6:30 a.m.).

27. *OR* 19, pt. 1, 923; Holsworth, "Uncommon Valor," 18; Harsh *Taken at the Flood*, 374; Lemon, *"Feed Them the Steel*, 34.

28. Dawes, *Service with the Sixth Wisconsin Volunteers*, 91; Ural, *Hood's Texas Brigade*, 124; Holsworth, "Uncommon Valor," 20.

29. *OR* 19, pt .1, 932-3; Holsworth, "Uncommon Valor," 52-3; P. A. Work, "The 1st Texas Regiment of the Texas Brigade of the Army of Northern Virginia at the Battles of Boonsboro Pass or Gap and Sharpsburg or Antietam, MD in September 1862," copy at the ANB Library; Houston *Tri-Weekly Telegraph*, October 15, 1862.

30. W.T. Hill, July 21, 1891 letter to Maj. John M. Gould, Gould Papers; *OR* 19, pt. 1, 936; Holsorth, "Uncommon Valor," 54.

31. Carman, *The Maryland Campaign*, vol. II, 109; Ural, *Hood's Texas Brigade*, 128; *OR* 19, pt. 1, 937.

32. Hartwig, *To Antietam Creek*, Appendix B, Strength of Union and Confederate Forces. The brigade probably fielded 1,146 at Antietam. Carman, *The Maryland Campaign*, vol. II, 109, 593.

33. *OR* 19, pt. 1, 925

34. Murfin, *The Gleam of Bayonets*, 364; Warner, *Generals in Gray*, 174-5.

35. Sears, *Landscape Turned Red*, 85, 95; *OR* 19, pt. 1, 145.

36. Carman, *The Maryland Campaign*, vol. II, 345, 347, 378; *OR* 19, pt. 1, 922; Robert K. Krick, *Lee's Colonels: A Biographical Register of the Field Officers of the Army of Northern Virginia* (Dayton, OH: Press of Morningside Bookshop, 1984), 219; Jeffrey D. Stocker, ed., *From Huntsville to Appomattox: R. T. Coles's History of the 4th Regiment, Alabama Volunteer Infantry, C.S.A., Army of Northern Virginia* (Knoxville, TN: University of Tennessee Press, 1996), 63-64; Steven H. Stubbs, *Duty, Honor, Valor: The Story of the Eleventh Mississippi Infantry Regiment* (Philadelphia, MS: Dancing Rabbit Press, Inc., 2000), 298-99; Andrew J. Baker to J. M. Gould, June 17, 1897, Gould Papers.

37. Harsh, *Taken at the Flood*, 306, 325; Carman, *The Maryland Campaign*, vol. II, 7; *OR* 19, pt. 1, 937.

38. Harsh, "Taken at the Flood," 358; Carman, *The Maryland Campaign*, vol. II, 31-35, 37, 40; *OR* 19, pt. 1, 937; Stocker, ed., *From Huntsville to Appomattox*, 65; Sears, *Landscape Turned Red*, 176; *National Tribune*, July 16, 1891. Not all of Law's brigade may have moved forward to the edge of the woods. Andrew Baker of the 11th Mississippi (Law's brigade) claimed his regiment remained behind Wofford's brigade in support. Baker to Gould, June 17, 1897, Gould Papers.

39. *OR* 19, pt. 1, 923; Carman, *The Maryland Campaign*, vol. II, 88, 90; Billy Ellis, *Tithes of Blood: A Confederate Soldier's Story* (Murfreesboro, TN: Southern Heritage

Press, 1997), 77; D.C. Love to John M. Gould, April 29, 1891, Gould Papers.

40. Carman, *The Maryland Campaign*, vol. II, 94-95; Love to Gould, April 29, 1891, Gould Papers; Steven R. Davis, "'. . . Like Leaves in an Autumn Wind': The 11th Mississippi Infantry in the Army of Northern Virginia," *Civil War Regiments*, vol. 2, no. 4 (1992), 288-89; Richard W. Iobst and Louis H. Manarin *The Bloody Sixth: The Sixth North Carolina Regiment Confederate States of America* (Raleigh, NC: North Carolina Confederate Centennial Commission, 1965), 95-96.

41. Carman, *The Maryland Campaign*, vol. II, 94-96, 98; Eberly, Jr., *Bouquets from the Cannon's Mouth*, 131. The Mississippians saw a Union officer on a white horse and opened fire, but were not able to hit Gen. Joseph Hooker.

42. Carman, *The Maryland Campaign*, vol. II, 97-99; *OR* 19, pt. 1, 938. James Johnston, an aide to Law recounted his experiences at Sharpsburg. Just after driving the Pennsylvania Reserves from the fence lining the Cornfield, he saw "right over the hill and right up the fence came fresh thousands of Yankees." Law ordered him to the rear to fetch reinforcements, so he returned to the position occupied by J.R. Jones' division on the west side of Hagerstown Pike earlier that morning. "To my astonishment, I found our men had gone and I saw a Brigade of Yankees in line not 150 yards in front of me." Johnston spurred his horse and got away, but could not return with reinforcements for Law. Stubbs, *Duty, Honor, Valor*: 308-09.

43. Harsh, *Taken at the Flood*, 375; Stocker, ed., *From Huntsville to Appomattox*, 68; *OR* 19, pt. 1, 938; *History of the First-Tenth-Twenty-ninth Main Regiment*, 240-42.

44. Carman, *The Maryland Campaign*, vol. II, 605, 616.

45. *OR* 19, pt. 1, 938.

## Evans' Independent Brigade

1. Hartwig, *To Antietam Creek*, Appendix B, Strength of Union and Confederate Forces. The brigade numbered approximately 550 at Antietam. Carman, *The Maryland Campaign*, vol. II, 592.

2. Carman, *The Maryland Campaign*, vol. II, 605.

3. Freeman, *Lee's Lieutenants*, vol. 2, 63; Sifakis, *Compendium of Confederate Armies: South Carolina and Georgia*, 91, 93, 98, 108; Davis, ed., *The Confederate General*, vol. II, 107-08. Evans and Hood had been feuding several days before the fight and Lee thought it best to split up the command to control further acrimony. Harsh, *Taken at the Flood*, 354-55.

4. *Charleston Daily Courier*, September 23, 1862.

5. *OR* 19, pt. 1, 939, 941, 945; DeWitt Boyd Stone, Jr., ed., *Wandering to Glory: Confederate Veterans Remember Evans' Brigade* (Columbia, SC: South Carolina University Press, 2002), 58; Carman, *The Maryland Campaign*, vol. 1, 354-55.

6. Stone, Jr., ed., *Wandering to Glory*, 60. *OR* 19, pt. 1, 941, 945, 948; Gottfried, *The Maps of Antietam*, 60; Civil War diary of Griffin Lewis Baldwin, ANB Library.

7. *OR* 19, pt. 1, 939, 942, 1021, 1035; Carman, *The Maryland Campaign*, vol. 1, 356; Stone, Jr., Ed. *Wandering to Glory*, 61. Lt. Dubose was captured by the enemy.

8. *OR* 19, pt. 1, 939, 942; Carman, *The Maryland Campaign*, vol. II, 373.

9. Carman, *The Maryland Campaign*, vol. II, 369-73, 380-81; *OR* 19, pt. 1, 357, 949.

10. *OR* 19, pt. 1, 945-46.

11. Carman, *The Maryland Campaign*, vol. II, 605; *OR* 19, pt. 1, 942; Freeman, *Lee's Lieutenants*, vol. 2, 270; Stone, Jr., Ed. *Wandering to Glory*, 69.

## Jackson's Wing

1. Davis, *The Confederate General*, vol. III, 150, 152.

2. Carman, *The Maryland Campaign*, vol. II, 598; Robertson, *Stonewall Jackson*, 609.

3. Davis, ed., *The Confederate General*, vol. III, 206-07; Robertson, *Stonewall Jackson*, 587-88. Jackson also placed Gen. William Starke under arrest because he would not obey an order to bring his brigade into Frederick so the men who had taken goods without paying for them could be identified. Starke refused to comply and he was placed under arrest. When Jackson learned it was his Stonewall Brigade at fault, he released Starke from arrest without apology or explanation. Robertson, *Stonewall Jackson*, 590. The only division commander not under arrest was Alexander Lawton and he feared he was next. Edward Porter Alexander, *Fighting for the Confederacy: The Personal Recollections of General Edward Porter Alexander*, Gary W. Gallagher, ed., (Chapel Hill, NC: University of North Carolina Press, 1989), 141.

4. John H. Worsham, *One of Jackson's Foot Cavalry: His Experience and What he Saw during the War 1861-1865* (New York: Neale Publishing Company, 1912),140; *OR* 19, pt. 1, 953. Jackson attended a church service while at Frederick and fell asleep midway through the minister's remarks, thus missing the blessing to President Abraham Lincoln. Henry Kyd Douglas, *I Rode with Stonewall: Being Chiefly the War Experience of the Youngest Member of Jackson's Staff from the John Brown Raid to the Hanging of Mrs. Surratt* (Chapel Hill, NC: University of North Carolina Press, 1940), 149-50. According to Ezra Carman, A.P. Hill's division crossed South Mountain at Turner's Gap and bivouacked a mile from Boonsboro. The other two divisions were behind, camping between Turner's Gap and Middletown. Carman, *The Maryland Campaign*, vol. I, 227.

5. *OR* 19, pt. 1, 953-54; Carman, *The Maryland Campaign*, vol. II, 16.

6. Carman, *The Maryland Campaign*, vol. II, 51, 53, 55; Cope Map #1 (Daybreak).

7. Sibley, *The Confederate Order of Battle*, 30, 32; *OR* 19, pt. 1, 955-56; Robertson, *Stonewall Jackson*, 613.

8. *OR* 19, pt. 1, 957; Carman, *The Maryland Campaign*, vol. II, 463-73.

9. Jackson reported slightly more casualties in his report: 2,438. *OR* 19, pt. 1, 958.

**Lawton's (Ewell's) Division**

1. Sibley, *The Confederate Order of Battle*, 10-11, 14, 21, 25, 235 (note 104).

2. Davis, *The Confederate General*, vol. IV, 27.

3. *OR* 19, pt. 1, 966-67; Carman, *The Maryland Campaign*, vol. I, 93, 250.

4. Carman, *The Maryland Campaign*, vol. II, 16; *OR* 19, pt. 1, 967.

5. Cope Map #1 (Daybreak); #2 (6:00 – 6:20 a.m.).

6. Cope Map #7 (8:30 – 8:40 a.m.); *OR* 19, pt. 1, 969; Carman, *The Maryland Campaign*, vol. II, 591-92, 598, 611.

7. Hartwig, *To Antietam Creek*, Appendix B, Strength of Union and Confederate Forces. The brigade probably fielded 1,150 at Antietam.Carman, *The Maryland Campaign*, vol. II, 593, 606; *OR* 10, pt. 1, 974.

8. Civil War Soldiers & Sailors System https://www.nps.gov/civilwar/soldiers-and-sailors-overview.htm; Harsh, *Taken At The Flood*, 85-89.

9. Pharris D. Johnson, ed., *Under The Southern Cross: Army Life with Gordon Bradwell* (Macon, GA: Mercer University Press 1999) 95; Annette Suarez, *Source Book On The Early History of Cuthbert & Randolph* (Atlanta: GA: Cherokee Publishing, 1982), 182 (courtesy Karan Pittman).

10. Harrison Wells letter, UNC University Libraries, The Southern Historical Collection, https://finding-aids.lib.unc.edu/05422/; Harsh, *Taken at the Flood*, 88-92.

11. Harsh, *Taken at the Flood;* 174; Wells letter.

12. Wells letter; Harsh, *Taken at the Flood*, 357; Hartwig, *To Antietam Creek*, 598, 613.

13. Hartwig, *To Antietam Creek*, 626; Wells; Carman, *Maryland Campaign*, vol. II, 55-56; Gregory White, *This Most Bloody & Cruel Drama: A History of the 31st Georgia Volunteer Infantry* (Baltimore: Blue & Gray Publishing Company, 1997) 48-49.

14. Carman, *The Maryland Campaign*, vol. II, 56, 554; Johnson, *Under The Southern Cross*, 89.

15. Carman, *The Maryland Campaign*, vol. II, 53, 55; Johnson, *Under The Southern Cross*, 89.

16. Johnson, *Under The Southern Cross,* 89-90; White, *This Most Bloody & Cruel Drama*, 49; Carman, *The Maryland Campaign*, vol. II, 57-62; *OR* 19, pt. 1, 968.

17. Carman, *The Maryland Campaign*, vol. II, 63-65.

18. Carman, *The Maryland Campaign*, vol. II, 63-65, 81-82; White, *History of the 31st Georgia*, 51; Johnson, *Under The Southern Cross*, 90. A journalist from Georgia on the field wrote, "Seeing he was mortally wounded, Douglas refused to be removed, preferring, as he said, to die upon the field." Styple, ed., *Writing & Fighting the Confederate War*, 106.

19. Carman, *The Maryland Campaign*, vol. II, 76-77; Johnson, *Under The Southern Cross*, 90; Dawes, *Service With The Sixth Wisconsin*, 90-91.

20. White, *History of the 31st Georgia*, 51, 53; Johnson, *Under The Southern Cross*, 91; *OR* 19, pt. 1, 974.

21. Harsh, *Taken At The Flood*, 447; White, *History of the 31st Georgia*, 54; Harsh, *Sounding The Shallows*, 214; Wells letter.

22. Hartwig, *To Antietam Creek*, Appendix B, Strength of Union and Confederate Forces. The brigade probably field 1,225 at Antietam. Carman, *The Maryland Campaign*, vol. II, 593.

23. Carman, *The Maryland Campaign*, vol. 2, 606.

24. Sikakis, *Compendium of the Confederate Armies: Virginia*, 185-86, 205-06, 217-18, 232, 239, 244, 151-53; Warner, *Generals in Gray*, 82.

25. Freeman, *Lee's Lieutenants*, vol. 2, xxviii, 259-60.

26. *OR* 19, pt. 1, 965-66; Charles C. Osborne, *Jubal: The Life and Times of General Jubal A. Early, CSA* (Chapel Hill, NC: Alqonguin Books, 1992), 119; Jubal Early, *General Jubal A. Early: Autobiographical Sketch and Narrative of the War Between the States* (Wilmington, NC: Broadfoot Publishing Company, 1989), 136-37.

27. Captain D. Buck, *With the Old Confeds: Actual Experiences of a Captain in the Line* (Baltimore, MD: H. E. Houck & Co., 1925), 63; Kevin C. Ruffner, *44th Virginia Infantry* (Lynchburg, VA: H. E. Howard, 1987), 24.

28. *OR* 19, pt. 1, 955, 967; Robertson, *Stonewall Jackson*, 611.

29. *OR* 19, pt. 1, 955, 968; Early, *General Jubal A. Early,* 141; Carman, *The Maryland Campaign*, vol. II, 92, 108.

30. Carman, *The Maryland Campaign*, vol. II, 152-53; *OR* 19, pt. 1, 969.

31. *OR* 19, pt. 1, 969; Carman, *The Maryland Campaign*, vol. II, 153, 155.

32. Early, *General Jubal A. Early*, 144; *OR,* 19, pt. 1, 969.

33. Carman, *The Maryland Campaign*, vol.II, 157.

34. *OR* 19, pt. 1, 970; Marion V. Armstrong, *Disaster in the West Woods* (Middletown, MD: Western Maryland Interpretive Association, 2002), 44; Carman, *The Maryland Campaign*, vol. II, 180.

35. Carman, *The Maryland Campaign*, vol. II, 181, 182, 188; *OR* 19, pt. 1, 971.

36. Carman, *The Maryland Campaign*, vol. II, 200, 203, 225.

37. Robert J. Driver, *58th Virginia Infantry* (Lynchburg, VA: H. E. Howard, 1990), 35; Richard B. Kleese, *49th Virginia Infantry* (Lynchburg, VA: H. E. Howard, 1990), 29.

38. McGrath, *Shepherdstown*, 119; *OR* 19, pt. 1, 149, 821, 956, 971.

39. Hartwig, *To Antietam Creek*, Appendix B, Strength of Union and Confederate Forces; Carman, *The Maryland Campaign*, vol. II, 53.

40. Carman, *The Maryland Campaign*, vol. II, 606.

41. Sifakis, *Compendium of Confederate Armies: Alabama*, 75-76; Sifakis, *Compendium of Confederate Armies: South Carolina and Georgia*, 208-09, 224; Stewart Sifakis, *Compendium of the*

*Confederate Armies: North Carolina* (New York: Facts on File, 1992), 78-79, 114-15; Davis, *The Confederate General*, vol. VI, 60-61, 86-87. Thomas Oates of the 15th Alabama claimed in his unit history that he recommended Walker for the post. William C. Oates, *The War Between the Union and the Confederacy and its Lost Opportunities* (Dayton, OH: Morningside Bookshop, 1985), 153.

42. James Cooker Nisbet, *Four Years on the Firing Line*, Bell Irvin Wiley, ed., (Wilmington, NC: Broadfoot Publishing Company, 1987), 100-01; Randall Allen and Keith S. Bohannon, *Campaigning with 'Old Stonewall: Confederate Captain Ujanirtus Allen's Letters to his Wife* (Baton Rouge, LA: Louisiana State University, 1998), 161-62.

43. *OR* 19, pt. 1, 965-66.

44. *OR* 19, pt. 1, 965-66, 976; Carman, *The Maryland Campaign*, 43, 53; Cope Map #1 (Daylight); James Nesbit to John Gould, April 21, 1891; John James to John Gould, April 25, 1891, Gould Papers.

45. *OR* 19, pt. 1, 976.

46. Cope Map #2 (6–6:20 a.m.); *OR* 19, pt. 1, 976; Carman, *The Maryland Campaign*, vol. II, 59-60.

47. *OR* 19, pt. 1, 977; Cope Map #4 (7:30 a.m); Nisbet, *Four Years on the Firing Line*, 103.

48. J. Gary Laine and Morris M. Penny, *Law's Alabama Brigade in the War Between the Union and the Confederacy* (Shippensburg, PA: White Mane Publishing Company, 1996), 24; William A. McClendon, *Recollections of War Times by an Old Veteran While Under Stonewall Jackson and Lieutenant General James Longstreet: How I Got in and How I got Out* (Mongtomery, AL: Paragon Press, 1909), 143-44.

49. Carman, *The Maryland Campaign*, vol. II, 91-92; Cope Maps #4 (7:20 a.m.), #5 (7:30 a.m.), #6 (8:00 a.m.), and #7 (8:30-8:40 a.m.); Nisbet, *Four Years on the Firing Line*, 105-06.

50. Carman, *The Maryland Campaign*, vol. II, 606. Walker reported casualties of 228. *OR* 19, pt. 1, 978.

51. Hartwig, *To Antietam Creek*, Appendix B, Strength of Union and Confederate Forces. The brigade probably fielded 550 men at Antietam. Carman, *The Maryland Campaign*, vol. II, 593.

52. Carman, *The Maryland Campaign*, vol. II, 606; Darrell L. Collins, *The Army of the Northern Virginia. Organization, Strength, Casualties, 1861-1865.* (Jefferson, NC: McFarland & Company, 2016), 154, 275; Harsh, *Sounding the Shallows.* 88, 89; *OR* 19, pt. 1, 978, 979. Hays states in his report that he carried no more than 550 men into the battle at Sharpsburg. This is may be an understatement as the Present for Duty Report of September 22 shows 936 present. However, straggling was excessive during the march to Sharpsburg. Hays also puts his casualties at 323.

53. Collins, *The Army of the Northern Virginia.* 4; Stewart Sifakis, *Compendium of the Confederate Armies: Louisiana* (New York: Facts on File, 1995), 75-84, 96-97; Bergeron, *Guide to Louisiana Confederate Military Units*, 83, 108, 150; Harsh. *Sounding the Shallows*, 65.

54. Carman, *The Maryland Campaign*, vol. III, 230; Harry W. Pfanz, *Gettysburg. Culp's Hill & Cemetery Hill.* (Chapel Hill: The University of North Carolina Press, 1993), 236.

55. Collins, *The Army of the Northern Virginia*, 263, 269.

56. *OR* 19, pt. 1, 965, 966; James Gannon, *Irish Rebels, Confederate Tigers: A History of the 6th Louisiana Volunteers* (Mason City, IA: Savas Publishing, 1998), 127.

57. James B. Sheeran, *Confederate Chaplain: A War Journal*, Joseph T. Durkin, ed. (Milwaukee, WI: The Bruce Publishing Company, 1960), 24.

58. *OR* 19, pt. 1, 966.

59. *OR* 19, pt. 1, 966; Gannon, *Irish Rebels, Confederate Tigers*, 129.

60. *OR* 19, pt. 1, 967; Terry L. Jones, *Lee's Tigers: The Louisiana Infantry in the Army of Northern Virginia* (Baton Rouge, LA: Louisiana State University, 1987), 128; Gannon, *Irish Rebels, Confederate Tigers*, 130.

61. Carman, *The Maryland Campaign*, vol. II, 38; *OR* 19, pt. 1, 967.

62. Carman, *The Maryland Campaign*, vol. II, 54, 63; *OR* 19, pt. 1, 968; Gannon, *Irish Rebels, Confederate Tigers*, 135; Diary of George Wren, September 17, 1862 entry, Woodruff Library, Emory University.

63. Carman, *The Maryland Campaign*, vol. II, 64, 65, 110; Jones; *Lee's Tigers*. 129, 130.

64. Cope Map #3 (6:45–7:00 a.m.); Carman, *The Maryland Campaign*, vol. II, 82-84, 89; Jones, *Lee's Tigers*, 130; Gannon. *Irish Rebels, Confederate Tigers*, 135-36; George Wren diary, September 17, 1862 entry.

65. Carman, *The Maryland Campaign*, vol. II, 82-84, 89; *OR* 19, pt. 1, 968.

66. Cope Map #5 (7:30 a.m.), #11 (1:00 p.m.); Carman, *The Maryland Campaign*, vol. II, 314, 339, 342; *OR* 19, pt. 1, 979; Gannon, *Irish Rebels, Confederate Tigers*, 139; George Wren diary, September 17, 1862 entry.

67. *OR* 19, pt. 1, 972, 979; George Wren diary, September 17, 1862 entry.

68. *OR* 19, pt. 1, 973.

69. *OR* 19, pt. 1, 973; Collins, *The Army of the Northern Virginia*, 155.

## A.P. Hill's Division

1. Martin Schenck, *Up Came Hill: The Story of the Light Division and its Leaders* (Harrisburg, PA: The Stackpole Company, 1958), 17-20.

2. Joseph T. Glatthaar, *General Lee's Army: From Victory to Collapse* (New York: Free Press, 2008), 341; Tagg, *The Generals of Gettysburg*, 301; Freeman, *Lee's Lieutenants*, vol. 2, xxiv; Warner, *Generals in Gray*, 134-35.

3. William W. Hassler, ed., *One of Lee's Best Men: The Civil War Letters of General William Dorsey Pender* (Chapel Hill, NC: The University of North Carolina Press, 1965), 171; Robertson, *General A. P. Hill*, 130-32; Clark, *North Carolina Regiments*, vol. 4, 165.

4. *OR*, 19, pt. 1, 980-81; Harsh, *Taken at the Flood*, 418.

5. William Kelsey McDaid, "Four Years of Arduous Service: The History of the Branch-Lane Brigade in the Civil War, Ph.D. Dissertation, Michigan State University, 1987, 117."

6. *OR*, 19, pt. 1, 981.

7. *OR*, 19, pt. 1, 982.

8. Hartwig, *To Antietam Creek*, Appendix B, Strength of Union and Confederate Forces. The brigade probably numbered about 1,000 at Antietam.

10. Sifakis, *Compendium of the Confederate Armies: North Carolina*, 93-94, 110, 124-125.

11. Michael C. Hardy, *General Lee's Immortals: The Battles and Campaigns of the Branch-Lane Brigade in the Army of Northern Virginia, 1861–1865* (El Dorado Hills, CA: Savas Beatie, 2018), 98.

12. Davis, *The Confederate General*, vol. I, 118-19; Warner, *Generals in Gray*, 31; Robertson, *A. P. Hill*, 60.

13. J. S. Harris, *Historical Sketches, Seventh Regiment North Carolina Troops* (Mooresville, NC: Mooresville Printing Co., 1893), 22; Hardy, *General Lee's Immortals*, 95-97; C. F. Mills Papers, Duke University; McDaid, *Four Years of Arduous Service*, 114-15.

14. Lawrence Branch to Nancy Branch, September 16, 1862, Branch Papers, North Carolina Division of Archives and History, Raleigh, North Carolina; Austin Jones, *The Capture of Harpers Ferry* (n.p.: n.d, 1922), 2; Michael C. Hardy, *The Thirty-Seventh North Carolina Troops* (Jefferson, NC: McFarland & Company, 2003), 97; McDaid, *Four Years of Arduous Service*, 122. The enemy may have left this sector unprotected because it was thought to be difficult for advancing troops to traverse. McDaid, *Four Years of Arduous Service*, 122.

15. *OR*, 19, pt. 1, 985-86; Clark, *North Carolina Regiments*, vol. 2, 33; James Lane to Ezra Carman, February 10, 1900, NA-AS; W. J. Montgomery to Ezra Carman, July 10, 1900, NA-AS; Hardy, *Thirty-Seventh North Carolina Troops*, 98.

16. Hardy, *General Lee's Immortals*, 102-04; Carman, *The Maryland Campaign*, vol. II, 470-72, 478-80.

17. Carman, *The Maryland Campaign*, vol. II, 478-79.

18. *Weekly State Journal*, October 1, 1862; James Lane to Ezra Carman, March 22, 1895, NA-AS; Clark, *North Carolina Regiments*, vol. 2, 554; Carman, *The Maryland Campaign*, vol. II, 479; W.G. Morris to Ezra Carman, June 1, 1896; Hardy, *General Lee's Immortals*, 106-07.

19. Hartwig, *To Antietam Creek*, Appendix B, Strength of Union and Confederate Forces; Hardy, *General Lee's Immortals*, 107.

20. *OR*, 19, pt. 1, 986; Hardy, *General Lee's Immortals*, 107.

21. Hancock, *Four Brothers in Gray*, 149-50; *OR*, 19, pt. 1, 986.

22. Hartwig, *To Antietam Creek*, Appendix B, Strength of Union and Confederate Forces. The brigade may have entered the battle of Antietam with fewer than 500 men.

23. Carman, *The Maryland Campaign*, vol. II, 607.

24. Sifakis, *Compendium of the Confederate Armies: South Carolina and Georgia*, 53-54, 56, 85, 86; Davis, *The Confederate General*, vol. III, 41-43; vol. IV, 122-23; Robertson, *General A. P. Hill*, 60.

25. J. F. J. Caldwell, *The History of a Brigade of South Carolinians, Known First as "Gregg's" and Subsequently as "McGowan's Brigade"* (Philadelphia: King & Baird Publishers, 1866), 40-41.

26. *OR* 19, pt. 1, 987; Andrew B. Wardlaw diary, September 15, 1862 entry (copy at the ANB Library).

27. Caldwell, *The History of a Brigade of South Carolinians*, 43, 44-45; *OR* 19, pt. 1, 987-88; Alexander C. Haskell to Ezra Carman, June 16, 1896, NA-AS.

28. Carman, *The Maryland Campaign*, vol. II, 2, 464-65; *OR* 19, pt. 1, 988, 999; Haskell to Carman, June 16, 1896.

29. *OR* 19, pt. 1, 996-97.

30. *OR* 19, pt. 1, 991-92; Caldwell, *The History of a Brigade of South Carolinians*, 46.

31. *OR* 19, pt. 1, 993-94.

32. Carman, *The Maryland Campaign*, vol. II, 473, 482, 484, 508, 607.

33. *OR* 19, pt. 1, 988-90; Caldwell, *The History of a Brigade of South Carolinians*, 50; Carman, *The Maryland Campaign*, vol. II, 607.

34. Hartwig, *To Antietam Creek*, Appendix B, Strength of Union and Confederate Forces. The brigade may have entered the battle of Antietam with fewer than 500 men.

35. Ezra Carman does not provide figures for the brigade because it saw such little action in the campaign. Carman, *The Maryland Campaign*, vol. II, 606. No report was filed for the brigade.

36. Sifakis, *Compendium of the Confederate Armies: Virginia*, 199, 227, 236, 249; Warner, *Generals in Gray*, 87.

37. *OR*, 19, pt. 1, 980, 1004; Gottfried, *Maps of Antietam*, 220; Carman, *The Maryland Campaign*, vol. II, 480; Homer D. Musselman, *47th Virginia Infantry* (Lynchburg, VA: H. E. Howard, 1991), 35; Wayland Fuller Dunaway, *Reminiscences of a Rebel* (New York: Neale Publishing Company, 1913), 47.

38. Carman, *The Maryland Campaign*, vol. III, 7.

39. Hartwig, *To Antietam Creek*, Appendix B, Strength of Union and Confederate Forces. Gen. Archer counted only 350 men in the ranks at Sharpsburg. *OR*, 19, pt. 1, 1000.

40. Carman, *The Maryland Campaign*, vol. II, 607.

41. Sifakis, *Compendium of the Confederate Armies: Tennessee* (Facts on File: New York, 1992), 88, 102, 113; Sifakis, *Compendium of the Confederate Armies: Alabama*, 61; Sifakis, *Compendium of the Confederate Armies: South Carolina and Georgia*, 220; Davis, *The Confederate General*, vol. I, 35, 37; vol. III, 73; vol. I, 37-38; Robertson, *General A. P. Hill*, 61.

42. *OR*, 19, pt. 1, 980, 1000, 1003; Randy Bishop, *The Tennessee Brigade: A History of the Volunteers of the Army of Northern Virginia* (Bloomington, IN: Authorhouse, 2005), 127-29; Mockbee, "The 14th Tennessee Infantry Regiment," *Civil War Regiments*, vol. 5, No. 1 (1995), 20; Felix Motlow, "Campaigns in Northern Virginia," *Confederate Veteran*, vol. XI, no. 10, 310; Joe Bennett

McBrien, *The Tennessee Brigade* (Chattanooga: Hudson Printing and Lithographing Company, 1977), 46-47.

43. Bishop, *The Tennessee Brigade*, 130; *OR*, 19, pt. 1, 1000; C. A. Porter Hopkins, ed., "The James J. Archer Letters." Part I. *Maryland Historical Magazine*, vol. 56, no. 2 (June, 1961), 140; G. W. Gleaton to Ezra Carman, February 10, 1900, NA-AS.

44. *OR*, 19, pt. 1, 1001, 1003; Carman, *The Maryland Campaign*, vol. 2, 472-73; Gottfried, *The Maps of Antietam*, 230; Hopkins, ed., "The James J. Archer Letters," 140-41; George Howard to Ezra Carman, August 12, 1898, NA-AS; Gleaton to Carman, February 10, 1900. According to Gleaton, Archer rode up to Col. Peter Turney of the 1st Tennessee and angrily asked who issued the order. Turney said he thought the order came from Archer.

45. Carman, *The Maryland Campaign*, vol. 2, 475-76, 485; Hopkins, ed., "The James J. Archer Letters, 141; Felix Motlow, "Campaigns in Northern Virginia," 310; *OR*, 19, pt. 1, 1001. Among the captured was Lt. Col. Theodore Jones, commander of the 30th Ohio.

46. Hopkins, ed., "The James J. Archer Letters," 141; *OR*, 19, pt. 1, 1001-02.

47. Hartwig, *To Antietam Creek*, Appendix B, Strength of Union and Confederate Forces. The brigade may have numbered under 800 at Antietam.

48. Carman, *The Maryland Campaign*, vol. II, 607. Gen. Pender does not provide information on the strength of his brigade nor the number of missing/captured.

49. Sifakis, *Compendium of the Confederate Armies: North Carolina*, 107, 116, 133, 138; Warner, *Generals in* Gray, 233; Davis, *The Confederate General*, vol. V, 10-11; Robertson, *General A. P. Hill*, 60-61. The 38th was mustered into service in January, 1862.

50. George H. Mills, *History of the 16th North Carolina Regiment* (n.p.: n.p., n.d.), 23-24; Hassler, ed., *One of Lee's Best Men*, 172-74; Clark, ed., *North Carolina Troops*, vol. I, 759.

51. Carman, *The Maryland Campaign*, vol. I, 250; *OR*, 19, pt. 1, 980, 1004.

52. Clark, ed., *North Carolina Troops*, vol. I, 760; Clark, ed., *North Carolina Troops*, vol. II, 685; *OR*, 19, pt. 1, 980, 1004; Carman, *The Maryland Campaign*, vol. I, 264

53. Clark, ed., *North Carolina Troops*, vol. II, 585, 686; Gottfried, *Maps of Antietam*, 220; *OR*, 19, pt. 1, 981, 1004.

54. *OR*, 19, pt. 1, 982, 1004; Clark, ed., *North Carolina Troops*, vol. I, 761.

55. Hartwig, *To Antietam Creek*, Appendix B, Strength of Union and Confederate Forces.

56. Minimal, as the brigade was left behind at Harpers Ferry.

57. Stewart Sifakis, *Compendium of the Confederate Armies: South Carolina and Georgia*, 212-213; Davis, *The Confederate General* vol. I, 27, vol. VI, 45.

58. Draughton Stith Haynes, *The Field Diary of a Confederate Soldier While Serving with the Army of Northern Virginia C. S. A.*, William Hynes, ed., (Darien, GA: The Ashantilly Press, 1963) 15-16).

59. *OR*, 19, pt. 1, 980; Gottfried, *The Maps of Antietam*, 102; Haynes, *The Field Diary of a Confederate Soldier*, 16-20; James M. Kimbrough, "My War History 1861- 1865," Chickamauga-Chattanooga National Military Park; John J. Fox, *Red Clay to Richmond: Trail of the 35th Georgia Infantry Regiment, C. S. A.* (Winchester, VA: Angle Valley Press, 2004), 119-20.

60. Jeffrey C. Lowe and Sam Hodges, *Letters to Amanda: The Civil War Letter of Marion Hill Fitzpatrick, Army of Northern Virginia* (Macon, GA: Mercer University Press, 1998), 27-28; *OR*, 19, pt. 1, 981; Haynes, *The Field Diary of a Confederate Soldier*, 20; *OR*, 19, pt. 1, 1006.

## J.R. Jones (Stonewall) Division

1. Sibley, *The Confederate Order of Battle*, 10, 13, 20, 24.

2. Davis, ed., *The Confederate General*, vol. III, 206-07.

3. *OR* 19, pt. 1, 952, 1006-07; Carman, *The Maryland Campaign*, vol. I, 93; Harlan R. Jessup, ed., *The Painful News I Have to Write: Letters and Diaries of Four Hite Brothers of Page County in the Service of the Confederacy* (Baltimore, MD: Butternut & Blue, 1998), 117; Cope Map #1 (Daybreak). Gen. Jones wrote in his report: I found the division at this time very much reduced in numbers by the recent severe battles and the long and wearisome marches." *OR* 19, pt. 1, 1007.

4. Thomas M. Rankin, *23rd Virginia Infantry* (Lynchburg, VA: H. E. Howard, Inc., 1985), 48.

5. Cope Map # 3 (6:45 – 7:00 a.m.), #4 (7:30 a.m.), Map #7 (8:30 – 8:40 a.m.); *OR* 19, pt. 1, 956, 1008; Robertson, *Stonewall Jackson*, 613; Carman, *The Maryland Campaign*, vol. II, 76-80.

6. John D. Chapla, *48th Virginia Infantry* (Lynchburg, VA: H. E. Howard, Inc., 1989), 40; Cope Map #8 (9:00 – 9:30 a.m.), Cope Map #11 (1:00 p.m.), Cope Map #13 (4:20 p.m.).

7. *OR* 19, pt. 1, 1009; Carman, *The Maryland Campaign*, vol. II, 609.

8. Hartwig, *To Antietam Creek*, Appendix B, Strength of Union and Confederate Forces. Col. Williams, who commanded the brigade at the end of the battle, believed there were "about 250 muskets" during the battle. *OR* 19, pt. 1, 1013.

9. Carman, *The Maryland Campaign*, vol. II, 609. The official battle reports list the total number of casualties as 79 (11 killed and 68 wounded). *OR* 19, pt. 1, 812.

10. Warner, *Generals in Gray*, 339-40; Robert Driver, "A. J. Grigsby," *Lexington (Virginia) News Gazette*, September 30, 2003.

11. *OR* 19, pt. 1, 954, 1011; George B. Baylor, *Bull Run To Bull Run: or Four Years in the Army of Northern Virginia* (Richmond, VA: B. F. Johnson Publishing Company, 1900), 73; James I. Robertson, Jr., *The Stonewall Brigade* (Baton Rouge, LA: Louisiana State University Press, 1963), 155.

12. John D. Chapla, *42nd Virginia Infantry* (Lynchburg, VA: H. E. Howard, Inc., 1983), 26; Worsham, *One of*

*Jackson's Foot Cavalry*, 141; Chapla, *48th Virginia Infantry*, 38.

13. *OR* 19, pt. 1, 954, 1012; Robertson, Jr., *The Stonewall Brigade*, 156; E. E. Stickley, "Battle of Sharpsburg," *Confederate Veteran*, vol. XXII (1914), 66; Carman, *The Maryland Campaign*, vol. II, 37, 67; Cope Map #1 (Daybreak).

14. Stickley, "Battle of Sharpsburg," 66; Carman, *The Maryland Campaign*, vol. II, 68. Stickley claimed the brigade was ordered forward against the irresistible enemy charge. "'Forward, charge bayonets, common time! March!' The command was obeyed cheerfully and with vigor, the men charging and firing as they went. But at a short distance they halted by the powerful battle lines in front. They met at reasonably close range and a battle royal was on."

15. Carman, *The Maryland Campaign*, vol. II, 75; Cope Map #3 (6:45 – 7:00 p.m.); J. M. Garnett to Ezra Carman, February 25, 1895, NA-AS. Grigsby's men probably brought on their own defeat for their skirmishers fired into the Iron Brigade, advancing across Hagerstown Pike, causing its second line, composed of the 19th Indiana and 7th Wisconsin to cross the road with Patrick's brigade to take on the Stonewall Division. Carman, *The Maryland Campaign*, vol. II, 75.

16. Cope Map # 7(8:30 – 8:40 a.m.) and #8 (9:00 – 9:30 a.m.).

17. Cope Map #11 (1:00 p.m.), #13 (4:20 p.m.); Lowell Reidenbaugh, *27th Virginia Infantry* (Lynchburg, VA: H. E. Howard, Inc., 1993), 71.

18. Driver, "A. J. Grigsby," *Lexington (Virginia) News Gazette*. More than 40 officers signed a petition asking for Grigsby's assignment. It read, "No bolder or more daring officer ever led troops into a fight or managed them better when actually engaged." Their pleas fell on deaf ears and Grigsby went off to Richmond for a meeting with President Jefferson Davis. The meeting descended into a shouting match and Grigsby left empty handed. He resigned his commission on November 19, 1862. Jackson performed poorly at the battle of Fredericksburg and was killed at Chancellorsville.

19. Hartwig, *To Antietam Creek*, Appendix B, Strength of Union and Confederate Forces. The brigade probably numbered approximately 200 at Antietam. Carman, *The Maryland Campaign*, vol. II, 609 (note 39).

20. Carman, *The Maryland Campaign*, vol. vol. II, 609.

21. Sifakis, *Compendium of the Confederate Armies: Virginia*, 153-54, 197-98, 229-30, 237-38; Sibley, *The Confederate Order of Battle*, 10, 13, 20, 24; Carman, *The Maryland Campaign*, vol. I, 106; vol. II, 256 (note 30).

22. Krick, *Lee's Colonels* 278; Chapla, *42nd Virginia Infantry*, 118.

23. "The 21st Virginia at the Battle of Sharpsburg," copy at ANB Library; Susan A. Riggs, *21st Virginia Infantry* (Lynchburg, VA: H. E. Howard, Inc., 1991), 22-23; Robert J. Driver, *1st Virginia Infantry Battalion* (Lynchburg, VA: H. E. Howard, Inc., 1996), 28; Worsham, *One of*

*Jackson's Foot Cavalry*, 138. John Worsham noted the brigade led the army's advance after crossing the Potomac River. Worsham, *One of Jackson's Foot Cavalry*, 137.

24. Chapla, *42nd Virginia Infantry*, 26; Worsham, *One of Jackson's Foot Cavalry*, 141; Chapla, *48th Virginia Infantry*, 38.

25. *OR* 19, pt. 1, 1007; Chapla, *42nd Virginia Infantry*, 26; Allen Wright, "The 42nd Virginia Infantry," 62, copy at ANB Library.

26. Chapla, *48th Virginia Infantry*, 39; Wright, "The 42nd Virginia Infantry," 63; Robert Withers to Ezra Carman, March 14, 1895, NA-AS.

27. Cope Map #1 (Daybreak); Wright, "The 42nd Virginia Infantry," 62; Worsham, *One of Jackson's Foot Cavalry*, 144; Carman, *The Maryland Campaign*, vol. II, 572; 62; Chapla, *48th Virginia Infantry*, 39.

28. Cope Map #2 (6:00–6:20 a.m.); Chapla, *48th Virginia Infantry*, 39; Chapla, *42nd Virginia Infantry*, 27; Worsham, *One of Jackson's Foot Cavalry*, 144; Driver, *1st Virginia Infantry Battalion*, 29; Wright, "The 42nd Virginia Infantry, 63.

29. Cope Map #3 (6:45–7:00 a.m.); Carman, *The Maryland Campaign*, vol. II, 75, 180; Chapla, *48th Virginia Infantry*, 39-40.

30. Chapla, *48th Virginia Infantry*, 40; Chapla, *42nd Virginia Infantry*, 27.

31. Hartwig, *To Antietam Creek*, Appendix B, Strength of Union and Confederate Forces. The brigade probably numbered approximately 550 at Antietam. Carman does not provide a strength estimate for the brigade. It appears the 47th Alabama contained 147 men during the battle, the 48th Alabama had 163, and the 23rd Virginia counted 120. The 37th Virginia's strength is unknown, but is estimated to be the same as the 23rd Virginia's. The 10th Virginia was left at Martinsburg and was not present during the battle of Sharpsburg. Laine and Morris, *Law's Alabama Brigade*, 35; http://antietam.aotw.org/officers.php?unit_id=617.

32. Carman, *The Maryland Campaign*, vol. II, 609. The official battle reports list the total number of casualties as 171 (28 killed and 143 wounded). *OR* 19, pt. 1, 813.

33. Sifakis, *Compendium of the Confederate Armies: Virginia*, 181-82, 202-03, 224-25; Sifakis, *Compendium of the Confederate Armies: Alabama*, 117-19.

34. Davis, *The Confederate General*, vol. VI, 25; John W. Wayland, *History of Rockingham County, Virginia* (Dayton, VA: Ruebush-Elkings, 1912), 138; Krick, *Lee's Colonels*, 334.

35. Carman does not mention Taliferro's brigade in his first volume of his seminal *The Maryland Campaign* book and the regiments making up the brigade are not listed in his order of battle. Carman, *The Maryland Campaign*, vol. I, 466.

36. Cope Map #1 (Daybreak), #3 (6:45 – 7:00 a.m.); Carman, *The Maryland Campaign*, vol. II, 67, 77-78;

Rankin, *23rd Virginia Infantry*, 50; Richard Jennings to Ezra Carman, December 15, 1897, NA-AS.

37. *OR* 19, pt. 1, 1017.

38. Cope Map #4 (7:20 a.m.), #9 (10:30 a.m.); Laine and Penny, *Law's Alabama Brigade*, 35; Carman, *The Maryland Campaign*, vol. II, 159, 609.

39. Thomas M. Rankin, *37th Virginia Infantry* (Lynchburg, VA: H. E. Howard, Inc., 1987), 56.

40. Hartwig, *To Antietam Creek*, Appendix B, Strength of Union and Confederate Forces. The brigade probably numbered approximately 650 at Antietam. Collins, *The Army of the Northern Virginia*, 278; Carman, *The Maryland Campaign of 1862*, Vol. II, 77. The official battle reports list the total number of casualties as 274 (70 killed and 204 wounded). *OR* 19, pt. 1, 813.

41. Harsh. *Sounding the Shallows*, 63; Sifakis, *Compendium of the Confederate Armies: Louisiana*, 62-65, 68-70, 85-86, 88-89, 98-99.

42. Ezra Carman, *The Maryland Campaign of 1862*, Vol. III, 290; Douglas S. Freeman, *Lee's Lieutenants: A Study in Command*. Abridged by Stephen W. Sears. (New York: Scribners, 1998), 308; Spencer C. Tucker, *American Civil War: The Definitive Encyclopedia and Document Collection*. 4 volumes (Santa Barbara, CA: ABC Clio, 2013), Vol. IV, 1858.

43. Collins, *The Army of the Northern Virginia*. 263, 268.

44. Carman, *The Maryland Campaign of 1862*, Vol. I, 228; *OR* 19, pt. 1, 1006, 1014; William C. Davis, ed., *The Confederate General*, vol. V, 199.

45. Carman, *The Maryland Campaign*, vol. I, 228; *OR* 19, pt. 1, 1006, 1014.

46. *OR* 19, pt. 1, 1007, 1016.

47. *OR* 19, pt. 1, 1016.

48. Cope Map #1 (daybreak); Carman, *The Maryland Campaign*, vol. II, 38, 67; *OR* 19, pt. 1, 1007, 1016.

49. *OR* 19, pt. 1, 1015, 1016-1017; Carman, *The Maryland Campaign*, vol. II, 38.

50. Carman, *The Maryland Campaign*, vol. II, 67-68, 76.

51. Cope Map #3 (6:45 – 7:00 a.m.); Carman, *The Maryland Campaign*, vol. II, 76-77; *OR* 19, pt. 1, 1016-1017.

52. Jones. *Lee's Tigers*, 131; Carman, *The Maryland Campaign*, vol. II, 77, 78; *OR* 19, pt. 1, 1008, 1017. According to Ezra Carman, Starke was mortally wounded when 160 yards north of the West Woods and 140 yards west of Hagerstown Pike. Carman, *The Maryland Campaign*, vol. II, 78.

53. *OR* 19, pt. 1, 1017; Carman, *The Maryland Campaign* vol. II, 79.

54. Carman, *The Maryland Campaign*, vol. II, 152-53; *OR* 19, pt. 1, 1015, 1017.

55. Carman, *The Maryland Campaign* vol. II, 79, 80, 561 (note 162); Terry L. Jones, *Lee's Tigers*. 131, 132; *OR* 19, pt. 1, 1017-18.

56. *OR* 19, pt. 1, 1015.

## D.H. Hill's Division

1. Warner, *Generals in Gray*, 136; Davis, *The Confederate General*, vol. III, 102-04.

2. *OR* 19, pt. 1, 1020; Daniel H. Hill, "The Battle of South Mountain or Boonsboro," *Battles & Leaders of the Civil War*, vol. II, 560; *OR* 19, pt. 1, 1019, 1022; Carman, *The Maryland Campaign*, vol. I, 230, 319; *OR Suppl.*, vol. 3, 582.

3. *OR* 19, pt. 1, 1019-20; Hill, "The Battle of South Mountain or Boonsboro," 560; Hal Bridges, *Lee's Maverick General: Daniel Harvey Hill* (New York: McGraw Hill, 1961), 100-01. Hill has been criticized for not riding up the mountain with his two brigades to reconnoiter the terrain and properly place them. Ezra Carman noted that Hill believed Stuart was overseeing the defense of the gaps and he was merely providing supporting infantry. This proved not to be the case as Stuart noted the "gap was no place for cavalry operations." Carman, *The Maryland Campaign*, vol. I, 320-21.

4. Carman, *The Maryland Campaign*, vol. I, 332, 340, 376-77; *OR* 19, pt. 1, 1020; Harsh, *Sounding the Shallows*, 181; *OR Suppl.*, vol. 3, 583. Although Hill was generally complimentary toward his troops, he noted in his report, "The artillerists of [A. S.] Cutts' battalion behaved gallantly, but their firing was the worst I ever witnessed." He amplified his criticism later by writing, the artillery fire was "as harmless as blank cartridge salutes in honor of a militia general . . . the enemy did not honor by so much as a dodge." Hill, "The Battle of South Mountain or Boonsboro," 573-74. Not all agreed with Hill's assessment of his effectiveness on September 14. Lee and Stuart apologist, William Allan, wrote: "Hill's troops were badly handled. The field was not understood, and the troops not promptly enough put into position." William Allan, *The Army of Northern Virginia in 1862* (Boston, MA: Houghton Mifflin and Co., 1892), 360. However, historian Thomas Clemens put the blame squarely on Jeb Stuart's shoulders. Carman, *The Maryland Campaign*, vol. I, 373 (note 63).

5. Carman, *The Maryland Campaign*, vol. I, 387-88; Carman, *The Maryland Campaign*, vol. II, 42.

6. *OR* 19, pt. 1, 1022; Carman, *The Maryland Campaign*, vol. II, 119, 133-34; William DeRosset to Henry Heth, February 22, 1894, NA-AS; Stephen Thruston to William DeRosset, July 28, 1896, NA-AS.

7. *OR* 19, pt. 1, 1036-38; Carman, *The Maryland Campaign*, vol. II, 239-41; Armstrong, *Unfurl Those Colors*, 228-30.

8. *OR* 19, pt. 1, 1024, 1038; Carman, *The Maryland Campaign*, vol. II, 288. Hill could be complementary about Confederate artillery. He watched as Capt. Thomas Carter's battery battered Col. Harrison Fairchild's brigade (Rodman's division, IX Corps) and noted in his report: "The firing was beautiful, and the Yankee columns (1,200 yards distant) were routed by this artillery fire alone, unaided by musketry. This is the only instance I have ever known of infantry being broken by artillery fire

at long range." He could not resist a dig in the next sentence, however: "It speaks badly for the courage of Burnside's men." *OR 19*, pt. 1, 1025.

9. *Richmond Times Dispatch*, December 20, 1896; Carman, *The Maryland Campaign*, vol. I, 504-05.

10. Hartwig, *To Antietam Creek*, Appendix B, Strength of Union and Confederate Forces. The brigade numbered approximately 1, 349 at Antietam. Carman, *The Maryland Campaign*, vol. II, 598.

11. Carman, *The Maryland Campaign*, vol. II, 607.

12. *Sifakis, Compendium of the Confederate Armies: North Carolina*, 79-80, 85-86; *Sifakis, Compendium of the Confederate Armies: South Carolina and Georgia*, 188-89, 256-57.

13. Davis, *The Confederate General*, vol. V, 89; Warner, *Generals in Gray*, 257.

14. *OR 19*, pt. 1, 1018-21, 103l; Carman, *The Maryland Campaign*, vol. I, 320. Rosser was initially deployed along the Loop Road.

15. Carman, *The Maryland Campaign*, vol. I, 332-33; *OR 19*, pt. 1, 1021, 1032.

16. Carman, *The Maryland Campaign*, vol. I, 340-41, 344; *OR 19*, pt. 1, 1021, 1032; Calvin Leach diary, September 14, 1862 entry, Southern Historical Collection, University of North Carolina, Chapel Hill, NC; William DeRosset to S. D. Thruston, July 12, 1886, copy at the ANB Library.

17. Henry W. Thomas, *History of the Doles-Cook Brigade of The Army of Northern Virginia* (Atlanta, GA: The Franklin Printing and Publishing Company, 1903), 68-69.

18. *OR 19*, pt. 1, 1022; Carman, *The Maryland Campaign*, vol. I, 387-88; Cope Map #1 (Daybreak); DeRosset to Thruston, July 12, 1886.

19. *OR 19*, pt. 1, 1032-33; Thomas, *History of the Doles-Cook Brigade*, 469.

20. Cope Map #3 (6:45–7:00 a.m.); #5 (7:30 a.m.); *OR 19*, pt. 1, 1033; Carman, *The Maryland Campaign*, vol. II, 81, 118-20; Thomas, *History of the Doles-Cook Brigade*, 69; Hamilton Brown to Ezra Carman, September 14, 1897, NA-AS; William Hurlbert to Ezra Carman, September 18, 1897, NA-AS. The historian of the 44th Georgia recalled, "Our brigade was considerably confused owing to the heat from these burning buildings, and at the time the regiments got 'mixed up,' and just in the midst of the confusion and before order was restored General Ripley was wounded." Thomas, *History of the Doles-Cook Brigade*, 470.

21. Carman, *The Maryland Campaign*, vol. II, 119-120; Cope Map # 6 (8:00 a.m.); Thomas, *History of the Doles-Cook Brigade*, 470; *The Countryman* (Georgia), October 6, 1862; John Key to Ezra Carman, September 29, 1897. Maj. Key claimed his men had not eaten in 40 hours prior to being thrown into battle.

22. Carman, *The Maryland Campaign*, vol. II, 120, 122-23.

23. Cope Map #7 (8:30–8:40 a.m.); Clark, ed., *North Carolina Regiments*, vol. I, 187-89; Carman, *The Maryland Campaign*, vol. II, 128, 138; Leach diary, September 17, 1862 entry. The Cope map shows the 44th Georgia leading the retreating column, followed by the 1st North Carolina and then the 44th Georgia. The 3rd North Carolina is shown in position behind Colquitt's men. An officer in the 3rd North Carolina recalled one of his men yelling to Colquitt's troops: "Come on, boys; we've no ammunition, but we will go with you!" Clark, ed., *North Carolina Regiments*, vol. I, 188-90. The last Cope Map #14 (5:30 p.m.) does not show any of D.H. Hill's brigades. However, the historian of the 44th Georgia wrote "About three o'clock p.m. the brigade was moved to the front and formed line of battle, and so remained until late in the afternoon."

24. Thomas, *History of the Doles-Cook Brigade*, 470.

25. *OR 19*, pt. 1, 1,026; Carman, *The Maryland Campaign*, vol. II, 119 (note 14), 142-43. Col. William DeRosset reported his 3rd North Carolina actually lost 343 of the 547 he brought into action. William DeRosset, "History of the Third North Carolina," *Wilmington (NC) Messenger*, September 8, 1895.

26. Hartwig, *To Antietam Creek*, Appendix B, Strength of Union and Confederate Forces. The brigade probably numbered approximately 850 at Antietam. Carman, *The Maryland Campaign*, vol. II, 596 (note 162). See Rodes report in *OR 19*, pt. 1, 1039. He probably began the campaign with 1,200 men. In addition to the 203 men lost at Antietam, the brigade lost an addition 422 (61k-157w-204m) for a total of 625 (111-289-225). Carman, *The Maryland Campaign*, vol. I, 376; vol. II, 607.

27. Harsh, *Sounding the Shallows*, 74; Sifakis, *Compendium of the Confederate Armies. Alabama*, 56, 62-63, 64-65, 72, 93-94. The remaining two companies of the 26th Alabama had been diverted to reinforce Ft. Donelson (Tennessee), where they surrendered and awaited parole.

28. Carman, *The Maryland Campaign*, vol. III, 281.

29. *OR 19*, pt. 1, 1019; Cullen Andrews Battle, *Third Alabama!: The Civil War Memoir of Brigadier General Cullen Andrews Battle, CSA*, Brandon H. Beck, ed. (Tuscaloosa, AL: University of Alabama Press, 2002), 34; Carman, *The Antietam Campaign*, vol. I,89-90.

30. Carman, *The Maryland Campaign*, vol. I, 89-90; *OR 19*, pt. 1, 1019.

31. *OR 19*, pt. 1, 1019.

32. Carman, *The Maryland Campaign*, vol. I, 348; Harlan Eugene Cross Jr., *Letters Home: Three Years Under General Lee in the 6th Alabama* (Fairfax, VA: History4All, Inc., 2013), 63; Robert E. Park, *Sketch of the Twelfth Alabama Infantry of Battle's Brigade, Rodes' Division, Early's Corps, of the Army of Northern Virginia.* (Richmond, VA: W.E. Jones, Book and Job Printer, 1906) 88; Hartwig, *To Antietam Creek*, 381; *OR 19*, pt. 1, 1033.

33. Hartwig, *To Antietam Creek*, 381-382; *OR 19*, pt. 1, 1033.

34. Hoptak, *The Battle of South Mountain*, 97; *OR 19*, pt. 1, 1034-35.

35. *OR 19*, pt. 1, 1020, 1034-35; D. Hartwig. *To Antietam Creek*, 379, 381-82.

36. Hartwig, *To Antietam Creek*, 381, 384.

37. Park, *Sketch of the Twelfth Alabama Infantry,* 89; Cross Jr. *Letters Home.* 64; Battle, *Third Alabama!* 56; Hartwig. *To Antietam Creek.* 383, 389; OR 19, pt. 1, 1035. Rodes was not satisfied with the performance of Evans' South Carolinians on his right, and characterized them as "stragglers" whose brigade had "been compelled to give way and had retired," thus leaving him in an exposed position.

38. Harsh, *Sounding the Shallows,* 16; OR 19, pt. 1, 1034, 1035-1036.

39. OR 19, pt. 1, 1021, 1036. Rodes reported that the brigade lost 61 killed, 157 wounded and 204 missing.

40. OR 19, pt. 1, 1036.

41. OR 19, pt. 1, 1036; Krick, "It Appeared As Though Mutual Extermination," 224.

42. OR 19, pt. 1, 1036; Krick, "It Appeared As Though Mutual Extermination," 224.

43. OR 19, pt. 1, 1037; Krick, "It Appeared As Though Mutual Extermination, 232.

44. Krick, "It Appeared As Though Mutual Extermination," 228.

45. OR 19, pt. 1, 1036, 1037; Krick, "It Appeared As Though Mutual Extermination," 224.

46. Battle, *Third Alabama,* 59.

47. OR 19, pt. 1, 943; 1037.

48. OR 19, pt. 1, 1023; Armstrong, *Opposing the Second Corps,* 90; Cross, *Letters Home,* 64.

49. Krick, "It Appeared As Though Mutual Extermination, 231; Carman, *The Maryland Campaign,* vol. II, 248; OR 19, pt. 1, 1037; Armstrong, *Opposing the Second Corps,* 91; 1st Delaware Monument, Antietam Battlefield.

50. Carman, *The Maryland Campaign,* vol. II, 250-251; OR 19, pt. 1, 1037.

51. Battle, *Third Alabama,* 59; Krick, "*It Appeared As Though Mutual Extermination,*" 231.

52. Krick, "It Appeared As Though Mutual Extermination," 232; Carman, *The Maryland Campaign,* vol. II, 265. This enfilading fire might have come from the 69th New York, on the right of the Irish Brigade (Richardson's division).

53. OR 19, pt. 1, 1037, 1038.

54. OR 19, pt. 1, 1038.

55. OR 19, pt. 1, 1038.

56. Carman, *The Maryland Campaign,* vol. II, 294; OR 19, pt. 1, 1024.

57. Battle, *Third Alabama,* 59; OR 19, pt. 1, 1038. Rodes reported losses at Sharpsburg of 50 killed, 132 wounded, and 21 missing.

58. Battle, *Third Alabama,* 59.

59. Hartwig, *To Antietam Creek,* Appendix B, Strength of Union and Confederate Forces; Carman, *The Maryland Campaign,* vol. II, 598; OR 19, pt. 1, 1041; E.M. Dugand to John A, Gould, April 1892; Thomas Ruffin, Jr. to Father, October 14, 1862, J. G. de Roulhac Hamilton, ed., *The Papers Of Thomas Ruffin* (Raleigh, NC: Edward & Broughton Printing Co., 1920), 262.; Clark, *North Carolina Regiments,* vol. 2, 627; Anselm Evans, *Confederate Military History,* 12 volumes (Atlanta GA: Confederate Publishing Company, 1899), vol. V, 111; Carman, *The Maryland Campaign,* vol. II, 596-97 (note 168). McRae states the brigade strength at "scarce 1,000 men." Dugand gives the strength of the 5th NC at "400 conscripts." Ruffin lists the strength of the 13th at 212 men. Montgomery lists the strength of the 12th at 92 men. This yields an effective strength for the three regiments of 704. As of this writing the author has been unable to obtain any documented numbers for the 20th and 23rd regiments. The *Confederate Military History* provides an average regimental strength during the Maryland Campaign of 150, "Owing to long field service and poor equipment." Therefore, an assumed combined strength of 300 men for the two regiments yields a brigade strength of 1,004 which agrees with McRae's numbers. Clemens lists an additional 115 officers which yields a total strength of 1,119. However, as of this writing, exact numbers remain unknown. The brigade counted only 672 men on September 18, 1862. Carman, *The Maryland Campaign,* vol. II, 133, 607. Carman lists the brigade strength on September 17 as 756.

60. Carman, *Maryland Campaign,* vol. II, 607. The brigade lost an additional 379 men at Fox's Gap for a total loss of 463.

61. Charles D. Walker, *Biographical Sketches of the Graduates and Eleves of the Virginia Military Institute* (Philadelphia, PA: J.B. Lippencott & Co., 1875), 227-36; Richard E. Clem, "Confederate General Finds Peace in a Battle," *The Washington Times,* August 12, 2006; Warner, *Generals in Gray,* 98-99. Virginian Samuel Garland's maternal great-grandmother was a sister of President James Madison, the fourth president of the United States.

62.https://www.nps.gov/civilwar/search-battle-units.htm; accessed May 4, 2020; Harsh, *Taken At The Flood,* 33-37.

63. Harsh, *Taken at the Flood,* 71; Clark, ed., *North Carolina Regiments,* vol. 2, 217.

64. Douglas, *I Rode With Stonewall,* 147-48; OR 19, pt. 2, 603-04; Lewis H. Steiner, *Report Of Lewis H. Steiner, M.D., Inspector of the Sanitary Commission* (Randolph, NY: Anson D.F., 1862), 21-22; Harsh, *Taken at the Flood,* 185-86.

65. OR 19, pt. 1, 1032.

66. Harsh, *Taken at the Flood,* 235-36; D.H. Hill to James Longstreet, Feb. 11, 1885, Longstreet Papers, University of North Carolina; Colquitt to Hill, July 4, 1885, Hill Personal Papers, North Carolina State Archives, Raleigh NC; George D. Gratten, "The Battle Of Boonsboro Gap Or South Mountain," *Southern Historical Society Papers,* vol. 39, No. 1 (April 1914), 36.

67. Dugand to Gould, April 1892; Harsh, *Sounding the Shadows,* 16; OR 19, pt. 1, 1039; D.H. Hill, "The Lost Dispatch- Letter from General D.H. Hill," *Southern Historical Society Papers,* January to December 1885, 422; Hill, "The Battle Of South Mountain, or Boonsboro," vol. 2, 561-62, OR 19, pt. 1, 1019.

68. Thomas Rosser to D.H. Hill, July 10, 1883, D.H. Hill Personal Papers.

69. Rosser to D.H. Hill, July 10, 1883; Duncan McRae to D.H. Hill, August 21, 1885, D.H. Hill Personal Papers; John Purifoy to Ezra Carman, July 15, 1899, NA-AS.

70. Gottfried, *The Maps Of Antietam*, 26-29.

71. Carman, *The Maryland Campaign*, vol. II, 325-26; Hill, "The Battle Of South Mountain," 563-64; Thomas Ruffin to D.H. Hill, August 4, 1885, D.H. Hill Personal Papers; Walker, *Biographical Sketches*, 235-36.

72. *OR* 19, pt. 1, 1040-41; Letter to D.H. Hill, August 21, 1885, D.H. Hill Personal Papers; Clark, ed, *North Carolina Regiments*, vol. II, 2, 220-21; Alfred Iverson to D.H. Hill, August 23, 1885, D.H. Hill Personal Papers.

73. John Calvin Gorman, "An Account of the late Battles," *Raleigh North Carolina Standard*, October 1, 1862; Thomas Ruffin, Jr., to Father, October 14, 1862, in *The Papers of Thomas Ruffin*, vol. III, 262-63.

74. *OR* 19, pt. 1, 1046; Thomas Rosser to D.H. Hill, July 10, 1883; Hill, "The Battle Of South Mountain, or Boonsboro," 566; Dugand to Gould, April 1892.

75. Clark, ed., *North Carolina Regiments*, vol. 2, 627; Hartwig, *To Antietam Creek*, 683.

76. Carman, *The Maryland Campaign*, vol. II, 132, 756; Antietam National Battlefield Historic Tablet No. 340 (Located South Side Cornfield Avenue).

77. *OR* 19, pt. 1043, 1023; Carman, *The Maryland Campaign*, vol. II, 134; Clark, ed., *North Carolina Regiments*, vol. 2, 223.

78. Carman, *The Maryland Campaign*, vol. II, 133, 136-46; *OR* 19, pt. 1, 1044; Antietam National Battlefield Historic Tablet No. 313 (Located Opposite Antietam National Cemetery).

79. McRae to Hill, August 21, 1885, D.H. Hill Personal Papers; *OR* 19, pt. 1, 1027, 1044; Carman, *The Maryland Campaign*, vol. II, 607.

80. Clark, ed., *North Carolina Regiments*, vol. 2, 627; Iverson to Hill, August 23, 1885, D.H. Hill Personal Papers, (italics by author); Ruffin, *The Papers of Thomas Ruffin*, 263; *OR* 19, pt. 1, 1027, 1029, 1045.

81. Carman, *The Maryland Campaign*, vol. III, 259.

82. Hartwig, *To Antietam Creek*, Appendix B, Strength of Union and Confederate Forces. The brigade probably numbered approximately 1,174 at Antietam. Carman, *The Maryland Campaign*, vol. II, 598. Carman lists the loss for Anderson's brigade at South Mountain as 90.

83. Carman, *The Maryland Campaign*, vol. II, 607.

84. Daniel Hill and James Irwin, ed., "Gen. George Burgwyn Anderson," *The Land We Love*," vol. 3, no. 2 (1867), 95.

85. Hill, "Gen. George Burgwyn Anderson," 95. Harsh, *Sounding the Shallows*, 104. Harsh lists G.B. Anderson's brigade as having only been involved in one campaign before the Maryland Campaign and Antietam was the first major engagement for the 14th N.C.

86. Hill, "Gen. George Burgwyn Anderson," 96-97.

87. Hill, "Gen. George Burgwyn Anderson," 97.

88. G, "An Account of the late Battles," *The North Carolina Standard*, Wednesday October 1, 1862.

89. George Gorman, ed. "Capt. John Calvin Gorman: 2nd North Carolina, Memoirs of a Rebel, "*Military Images*, Nov./Dec. 1981, 4.

90. *OR*, 19 pt. 1, 1049.

91. Carman, *The Maryland Campaign*, vol. I, 376.

92. *OR*, 19 pt 1, 1050.

93. G, *Account of the late Battles*. Due to the nature of the terrain, it is difficult to say the exact length of Anderson's line in the road. The men used the terrain to their advantage, so this was not the typical shoulder-to-shoulder battle line familiar to students of the Civil War.

94. Capt. E.A. Osborne, "The Fourth N. C. Regiment: Col. E.A. Osborne's Sketch of It." *Daily Charlotte Observer*, May 31, 1896.

95. G, "An Account of the late Battles."

96. Carman, *The Maryland Campaign*, vol. II, 262-263.

97. Carman, *The Maryland Campaign*, vol. II, 278-282. One can imagine the confusion in the lane. Following the battle there was strong discussion on who broke from the road first, Rodes' brigade or Anderson's brigade. Other participants joined in the discussion to support their argument or friends. Who actually broke first might be a question that will ever be fully answered.

98. *OR* 19 pt. 1, 1048, Carman, *The Maryland Campaign*, vol. II, 607-08.

99. Hill, "Gen. George Burgwyn Anderson," 99. Lt. Col. Robert Anderson was killed in action May 5, 1864.

100. Hartwig, *To Antietam Creek*, 680; Carman, *The Maryland Campaign*, vol. II, 596, 597; *OR* 19, pt. 1, 1052-54. Colquitt does not give any strength or casualty figures in his official report despite being heavily engaged at both South Mountain and Antietam. Carman gives Colquitt's total on the field at South Mountain as 1,250, however, more than a hundred additional men were on picket and camp guard duty in Boonsboro. Netting the 109 casualties from Turner's Gap and the men not engaged, Colquitt actually fielded over 1,300 men at Antietam, which was more than he had at South Mountain.

101. *OR* 19, pt. 1, 1026; Carman, *The Maryland Campaign*, vol. I, 376; vol. II, 608. Colquitt lost 109 at South Mountain and 722 at Antietam.

102. Sifakis, *Compendium of the Confederate Armies: South Carolina and Georgia*, 193, 194, 227, 234, 236; James Madison Folsom, *Heroes and Martyrs of Georgia: Georgia's Record in the Revolution of 1861* (Baltimore, MD: Butternut and Blue, 1995), 51.

103. Warner, *Generals in Gray*, 58.

104. Hartwig, *To Antietam Creek*, 100; Folsom, *Heroes and Martyrs*, 52.

105. Hartwig, *To Antietam Creek*, 123, 298, 300; *OR* 19, pt. 1, 1019, 1052. Johnson and Anderson, Jr., *Artillery Hell*, 45. The artillery was Capt. John Lane's Georgia battery of six guns from Cutts' battalion.

106. Grattan, "The Battle of Boonsboro Gap or South Mountain," 34. Although Stuart declined to leave any cavalry for screening Colquitt's front, there remained two companies on hand until nightfall of September 13. *OR,* 19, pt. 1, 1052.

107. Harsh, *Taken at the Flood,* 236, 237; Grattan, "*Battle of Boonsboro Gap,*" 35, 36; Hartwig, *To Antietam Creek,* 290. Reno's fourth division under Brig. Gen. Isaac Rodman had mistakenly returned to Frederick.

108. *OR* 19, pt. 1, 1053. Other than the positions of the 23rd and 28th, Colquitt does not give the regimental alignment south of the National Road. Hartwig, *To Antietam Creek,* 310; Carman, *The Maryland Campaign,* vol. I, 363, 364; vol. 2, 126, 127. Carman describes the skirmish battalion as five companies (Co. A from each regiment) who were regularly drilled as skirmishers. When fighting as a brigade, this battalion was deployed with each company covering the front of its own regiment, returning to their place on the right of its regiment when the engagement became general. It was convenient and effective, and Arnold's battalion was noted for its efficiency.

109. *OR* 19, pt. 1, 1053; Carman, *The Maryland Campaign,* vol. I, 330.

110. Hoptak, *The Battle of South Mountain,* 127, 128; Tully Graybill to wife, Sept. 26, 1862, quoted in Hartwig, *To Antietam Creek,* 426; Carman, *The Maryland Campaign,* vol. I, 376.

111. Harsh, *Taken at the Flood,* 294, 296. Gen. Lee was under the impression that Union cavalry was in possession of the area around Sharpsburg where he decided to consolidate his forces, so Rodes and Colquitt were ordered to march straight through to Sharpsburg to secure the town. Finding no cavalry, Rodes (who was in charge of the two brigades) ordered Colquitt on to the Potomac River to secure the Shepherdstown Ford. The farm near where Colquitt was placed on September 16 was the William Roulette Farm, and the sunken farm lane was soon to be known as Bloody Lane. Carman, *The Maryland Campaign,* vol. II, 31, 127.

112. R.V. Cobb to Ezra Carman, 23 February 1892, NA-AS; *OR,* 19, pt. 1, 1053; Carman, *The Maryland Campaign,* vol. II, 127 (note 28). The battle order of Colquitt's brigade has never been solidified. The only certainty is that the 13th Alabama was on the left and the 6th Georgia was on the right. Carman's order is (L-R) 13th Alabama, 28th, 23rd, 27th and 6th Georgia.

113. Carman, *The Maryland Campaign,* vol. II, 131, 132, 138. Garland was killed at South Mountain, so Col. Duncan McRae of the 5th North Carolina was in command of the brigade. Ben Miliken to E. A. Carman, December 20, 1897, NA-AS.

114. *OR* 19, pt. 1, 1037; Carman, *The Maryland Campaign,* vol. II, 297, 299, 376, 380.

115. *OR* 19, pt. 1, 1054; Carman, *The Maryland Campaign,* vol. II, 608, 616; Folsom, *Heroes and Martyrs,* 25.

116. Warner, *Generals in Gray,* 58.

## Stuart's Cavalry Division

1. Warner, *Generals in Gray,* 296; Davis, *The Confederate General,* vol. VI, 19.

2. Hartwig, *To Antietam Creek,* 88-89, 103.

3. OR 19, pt. 1, 814, 828; Carman, *The Maryland Campaign,* vol. I, 91-92.

4. Heros von Borke, *Memoirs of the Confederate War for Independence,* 2 volumes (Edinburgh, Scotland: W. Blackwood, 1866), vol. II, 131; OR 19, pt. 1, 815, 822, 825; Carman, *The Maryland Campaign,* vol. I, 92, 167-68, note 13); Harsh, *Taken at the Flood,* 205, 208, 230-31, 275-76. Historians, such as Joseph Harsh believed Lee would have made different decisions had Stuart conveyed for intelligence in a timely manner.

5. Freiheit, *Boots and Saddles,* 168-69; Harsh, *Taken at the Flood,* 166.

6. OR 19, pt. 2, 603-4, 817-18; Carman, *The Maryland Campaign,* vol. I, 187-196, 261; Freiheit, *Boots and Saddles,* 419, 215-31; Harsh, *Taken at the Flood,* 205.

7. OR 19, pt. 2, 819, 826-27; Harsh, *Taken at the Flood,* 231; Carman, *The Maryland Campaign,* vol. II. 569.

8. Carman, *The Maryland Campaign,* vol. II. 335-37; Freiheit, *Boots and Saddles,* 383; OR 19, pt. 1, 824; Cope Map, #1 (daybreak), #11 (1 p.m.).

9. OR 19, pt. 1, 814-20; Carman, *The Maryland Campaign,* vol. I, 192-95; Carman, *The Maryland Campaign,* vol. II, 30-31, 41, 151, 152.

10. Harsh, *Taken at the Flood,* 114-15; OR 19, pt. 1, 816.

11. Freiheit, *Boots and Saddles,* 457.

12. Freiheit, *Boots and Saddles,* 94.

13. Harsh, *Sounding the Shallows,* 88, 89. Brig. Gen. Beverly Robertson's cavalry brigade also served during the Second Bull Run and Maryland Campaigns, although still technically part of the Army of the Valley District. Temporarily under the command of Col. Thomas Munford, this brigade would become the 3rd Cavalry Brigade, A.N.V. in October 1862, under the command of W.H.F. "Rooney" Lee.

14. Carman, *The Maryland Campaign,* vol. III, 227; Freeman, *Lee's Lieutenants,* 36, 85.

15. Sifakis, *Compendium of the Confederate Armies: North Carolina,* 60; Sifakis, *Compendium of the Confederate Armies: South Carolina and Georgia,* 40-41, 165-66; Sifakis, *Compendium of the Confederate Armies: Virginia,* 114-15, 118; Sifakis, *Compendium of the Confederate Armies: Mississippi,* 60; Robert S. Seigler, *South Carolina's Military Organizations,* 4 volumes (Charleston, SC: The History Press, Charleston. 2008), vol. II, 287-296.

16. Harsh, *Sounding the Shallows,* 74, 76, 89.

17. Carman, *The Maryland Campaign,* vol. I, 86; Freiheit, *Boots and Saddles,* 118; OR 19, pt. 1, 822; Edward G. Longacre, *Gentleman and Soldier: A Biography of Wade Hampton III,* (Nashville, TN: Rutledge Hill Press, 2003), 92.

18. Carman, *The Maryland Campaign,* vol. I, 92; Chris J. Hartley, *Stuart's Tarheels: James B. Gordon and His North*

*Carolina Cavalry* (Baltimore, MD: Butternut and Blue Press, 1996), 124; Longacre, *Gentleman and Soldier*, 93; *OR* 19, pt. 1, 822.

19. Freiheit, *Boots and Saddles*, 168; Chris J. Hartley, *Stuart's Tarheels*, 126-27.

20. Carman, *The Maryland Campaign*, vol. I, 167-68; Freiheit, *Boots and Saddles*, 168; Longacre, *Gentleman and Soldier*, 93; *OR* 19, pt. 1, 822.

21. Freiheit, *Boots and Saddles*, 201-05; Longacre, *Gentleman and Soldier*, 95; Carman, *The Maryland Campaign*, vol. I, 187.

22. Carman, *The Maryland Campaign*, vol. I, 187, 193; Freiheit, *Boots and Saddles*, 215-18; *OR* 19, pt. 1, 823.

23. Carman, *The Maryland Campaign*, vol. I, 194; Freiheit, *Boots and Saddles*, 215-22; *OR* 19, pt. 1, 823-24.

24. Freiheit, *Boots and Saddles*, 222.

25. Carman, *The Maryland Campaign*, vol. I, 196; Freiheit, *Boots and Saddles*, 224-29.

26. Carman, *The Maryland Campaign*, vol. I, 196-197; Freiheit, *Boots and Saddles*, 230-31, 239.

27. Carman, *The Maryland Campaign*, vol. I, 261; Freiheit, *Boots and Saddles*, 319; *OR* 19, pt. 1, 824.

28. Carman, *The Maryland Campaign*, vol. I, 261; Freiheit, *Boots and Saddles*, 319-20.

29. Carman, *The Maryland Campaign*, vol. II, 335-37; Freiheit, *Boots and Saddles*, 383; *OR* 19, pt. 1, 824.

30. Harsh, *Sounding the Shallows*, 215-216; Carman, *The Maryland Campaign*, vol. III, 15-16; Freiheit, *Boots and Saddles*, 393, 394, 398, 399; *OR* 19, pt. 1, 821, 824.

31. Donald A. Hopkins, *The Little Jeff: The Jeff Davis Legion, Cavalry Arm of Northern Virginia* (Shippensburg, PA: White Mane Publishing, 1999), 102; Sifakis, *Compendium of the Confederate Armies: South Carolina and Georgia*, 167-68; Sifakis, *Compendium of the Confederate Armies: Virginia*, 118; Ted Alexander, ed., *Southern Revenge! Civil War History of Chambersburg, Pennsylvania* (Shippensburg, PA: White Mane, 1989), 49-62.

32. Hartwig, *To Antietam Creek*, Appendix B, Strength of Union and Confederate Forces.

33. Estimated.

34. Sifakis, *Compendium of the Confederate Armies: Virginia*, 101-3, 105-7, 107-9, 109-11, 116-18; Sibley, *The Confederate Order of Battle*, 2, 8, 19, 26.

35. Davis, *The Confederate General*, vol. IV, 36, 38.

36. *OR* 19, pt. 1, 814-20; Robert L. Beale, *History of the Ninth Virginia Cavalry in the War Between the States* (Richmond, VA: B. F. Johnson Publishing Company, 1899), 37; Carman, *The Maryland Campaign*, vol. I, 91-2, 187, 321, 345, 386, 396; George W. Beale, *A Lieutenant of Cavalry in Lee's Army* (Boston: The Gorham Press, 1899), 43. George Beale of the 9th Virginia Cavalry described the village of Hamburg as "rude and scattering" and noted the "manufacture of brandy seemed to be the chief employment of the villagers, and at the early hour of our passage through the place, both the men and women gave proof that they were free imbibers of the product of their stills, and it was not easy to find a sober inhabitant of either sex. George W. Beale, "The Cavalry Fight at Boonsboro' Graphically Described," *Southern Historical Society Papers*, vol. 25 (1897), 276.

37. Carman, *The Maryland Campaign*, vol. I, 194-95, 321; Thomas Rosser to Antietam National Battlefield Board, May 12, 1897, NA-AS. When McClellan heard Fitz Lee was in Westminster, heading for Gettysburg, he sent Col. Andrew McReynolds' brigade thundering in that direction. *OR* 19, pt. 2, 271; Carman, *The Maryland Campaign*, vol. I, 192.

38. George Beale, "The Cavalry Fight at Boonsboro," 277; *Richmond Dispatch*, July 16, 1897; Beale, *History of the Ninth Virginia Cavalry*, 40; H. B. McClellan, *The Life and Campaigns of Major-General J. E. B. Stuart, Commander of the Cavalry of the Army of Northern Virginia* (Secaucus, NJ: Blue & Gray Press, 1993), 124-25; Carman, *The Maryland Campaign*, vol. I, 396-401, 398 (note 38); Hard, *History of the Eight Illinois Cavalry Regiment*, 331-32; *OR* 19, pt. 1, 210; Fitzhugh Lee to Ezra Carman, February 11, 1896, NA-AS.

39. Beale, *A Lieutenant of Cavalry in Lee's Army*, 48; Carman, *The Maryland Campaign*, vol. I, 390, 394-95, vol. II, 30-31, 41, 151, 152; Beale, "The Cavalry Fight at Boonsboro," 280; Hartwig, *To Antietam Creek*, 615.

40. Carman, *The Maryland Campaign*, vol. II, 337, vol. I. 386.

41. Hartwig, *To Antietam Creek*, Appendix B, Strength of Union and Confederate Forces.

42. Estimated.

43. Sifakis, *Compendium of the Confederate Armies: Virginia*, 104-05, 113-14.

44. *OR* 19, pt. 2, 595; Freeman, *Lee's Lieutenants*, vol. 2, 169, 169 (note 13); W. W. Blackford, *War Years with Jeb Stuart* (New York: Charles Scribners' Sons, 1945), 229; Bruce S. Allardice, *More Generals in Gray* (Baton Rouge, LA: Louisiana State University, 1995), 171.

45. *OR* 19, pt. 1, 814-15, 828; Carman, *The Maryland Campaign*, vol. I, 86. The brigade also included the 6th Virginia Cavalry but it had been left at Centreville to collect arms and supplies. *OR* 19, pt. 1, 825.

46. *OR* 19, pt. 1, 815, 825; Carman, *The Maryland Campaign*, vol. I, 167. Munford lost 15 men.

47. Carman, *The Maryland Campaign*, vol. I, 176-79; *OR* 19, pt. 1, 825. Ezra Carman reported that Farnsworth continued his pursuit of the 12th Virginia the following day and caught up with it outside of Barnesville, driving it through the town and capturing its flag and 27 prisoners. Neither Stuart nor Munford mention this action. Carman, *The Maryland Campaign*, vol. I, 166-67; *OR* 19, pt. 1, 815, 825.

48. *OR* 19, pt. 1, 825; Carman, *The Maryland Campaign*, vol. I, 195; Hartwig, *To Antietam Creek*, 443.

49. Carman, *The Maryland Campaign*, vol. I, 196; *OR* 19, pt. 1, 450, 824; Hard, *Eight Illinois Cavalry*, 176; W. N. Pickerill, *History of the Third Indiana Cavalry* (Indianapolis, IN: Aetna Printing Company, 1906), 25-9.

50. Carman, *The Maryland Campaign*, vol. I, 300-02; *OR* 19, pt. 1, 826-27. When the reinforcements arrived, Gen. Cobb wisely asked Munford to position them. *OR* 19, pt. 1, 826-27.

51. *OR* 19, pt. 1, 827.

52. Carman, *The Maryland Campaign*, vol. I, 382, 391 (note 20), 395 (note 31); Carman, *The Maryland Campaign*, vol. II, 429, 436-37, 437 (note 10); *OR* 19, pt. 2, 609; Cope Map #1 (Daybreak).

53. Carman, *The Maryland Campaign*, vol. II, 41-42, 152.

54. Allardice, *More Generals in Gray*, 171-72. Munford made no secret of his dislike of Jeb Stuart and this may have blocked his promotion.

# BIBLIOGRAPHY

## Archival Sources

### Antietam National Battlefield Library
Ezra Carman, "Pryor's Brigade."
 "Civil War Diary of Griffin Lewis Baldwin."
Jacob Bauer to wife, September 20, 1862
J. T. Baynes to Lizzie, September 25, 1862
Edward Bragg to wife, September 21, 1862
W. Burlingame, "Personal Reminiscences of the Civil War."
Edward Buruss, "Memoirs."
George Cramer to wife, September 4, 1862
Frederick Crouse, "An Account of the Battle of Antietam."
William DeRosset to S. D. Thruston, July 12, 1886
Prince A. Dunton to Byron Milliken, September 24, 1862
W.H.H. Fithian letter
Henry Clay Hall to sister, October 5, 1862
Matthew Hurlenger Diary
Solomon A. Marsh, Letter to Wife, September 8, 1862
Wolcott Marsh to Anna, September 24, 1862
Francis W. Pee Account
George Merriman to May, September 24, 1862
11th Pennsylvania Infantry Morning Reports
James Miles Smith to "Dear Friends," September 20, 1862
Vaughn M. Stewart, "Bailey G. McClellan and His Civil War."
Dwight Stinson unpublished NPS Report (1962)
"The 21st Virginia at the Battle of Sharpsburg."
Andrew B. Wardlaw diary
P. A. Work, "The 1st Texas Regiment of the Texas Brigade of the Army of Northern Virginia at the Battles of Boonsboro Pass or Gap and Sharpsburg or Antietam, MD in September 1862."
Allen Wright, "The 42nd Virginia Infantry."
Henry E. Young, Letter to Wife, September 22, 1862

### Antietam Studies, National Archives
William H. Andrews to Ezra Carman, February 6, 1899 and an undated letter
Hamilton Brown to Ezra Carman, September 14, 1897
Ezra Carman, "The 76th New York."
R.V. Cobb to Ezra Carman, 23 February 1892
William Colville to Ezra Carman, December 10, 1892
William DeRosset to Henry Heth, February 22, 1894
James B. Dorr to Ezra Carman, December 6, 1899
J. M. Garnett to Ezra Carman, February 25, 1895
G.W. Gleaton to Ezra Carman, February 10, 1900
George R. Graham, "The Fifth Maryland Infantry at Antietam."
Alexander Haskell to Ezra Carman, June 16, 1896
John Hendrickson to Ezra Carman, December 6, 1894
Hilary Herbert to Ezra Carman, January 15, 1902
Charles Hopkins to Ezra Carman, January 15, 1900
George Howard to Ezra Carman, August 12, 1898

William Hurlbert to Ezra Carman, September 18, 1897
Richard Jennings to Ezra Carman, December 15, 1897
David Johnston to Ezra Carman, September 21, 1897 and September 23, 1897
Callom Jones to Ezra A. Carman, October 13, 1899
James Lane to Ezra Carman, March 22, 1895 & February 10, 1900
John Key to Ezra Carman, September 29, 1897
Fitzhugh Lee to Ezra Carman, February 11, 1896
Lafayette McLaws to Henry Heth, December 13, 1894
Ben Miliken to E. A. Carman, 20 December 1897
W.G. Morris to Ezra Carman, June 1, 1896 & July 10, 1900
Wm. H. Palmer to Ezra Carman, April 22, 1895 & August 26, 1899
John Parham to Ezra A. Carman, October 5 & October 18, 1899
John Purifoy to Ezra Carman, July 15, 1899
W. L. Rogers to Ezra Carman, January 19, 1893
William Rose to Ezra Carman, April 12, 1900
Alfred Sellers to Ezra Carman, September 30, 1897
Henry Shaefer to Ezra Carman, Dec. 20, 1894
William Stores to Ezra A. Carman, December 30, 1899
Stephen Thruston to William DeRosset, July 28, 1896
H. D. D. Twiggs to Ezra Carman, December 28, 1898
Robert Withers to Ezra Carman, March 14, 1895
Samuel Young to Ezra Carman, April 8, 1898

**Carman Papers, New York Public Library**
Seth D. Bingham to Ezra Carman, October 17, 1896
Sylvester Byrne to Ezra Carman, March 15, 1905 & March 17, 1905
Gabriel Campbell to Ezra Carman, August 23, 1899
Thomas H. Eaton to Ezra Carman, March 28, 1905 & April 1, 1905
Harrison Fairchild to Ezra Carman, March 20, 1896
William Fulton to Ezra Carman, December 21, 1899
Norwood Hallowell to Ezra Carman, February 24, 1905
Andrew Hero, Jr., to Ezra Carman, May 1, 1896
John F. Jones to Ezra Carman, n.d.
John W. Kimball to Ezra A. Carman, May 26, 1899 & February 17, 1900
John Lockhart to Carman, March 13, 1905
C. T. Loehr Statement, no date
Chase Philbrick to Col. J.C. Stearnes and Gen. Harry Heth, July 26, 1893
John E. Reilly to Ezra Carman, March 4, 1905
Edward B. Robins to Ezra A. Carman, April 5, 1900
George Ryan to Ezra Carman, December 8, 1897
Eugene Sullivan to Ezra Carman, March 28, 1905
George Swinscoe to Ezra Carman, July 19, 1899
Alpheus Williams to Ezra Carman, May 16, 1877
Lester Wilson to Ezra Carman, November 17, 1899

**Chicago Public Library**
Z. Abney to R. D. Parker, December 8 and 22, 1899
John Hughes to Capt. R. D. Parker, February 25, 1900
H. L. Stevenson Memoirs.

**Chickamauga-Chattanooga National Military Park Library (Fort Oglethorpe, GA)**
James M. Kimbrough, "My War History 1861- 1865."

**Duke University Library (Durham, NC)**
C. F. Mills Papers
M.J. Solomon's Scrapbook

**Georgia Department of Archives and History (Morrow, Georgia)**
Rev. George G. Smith, "Reminiscences."

**Gould Papers (Darmouth Univerity, Hanover, NH)**
Andrew J. Baker to J. M. Gould, June 17, 1897
John Bryson to John M. Gould, October 18, 1893
S. E. Chandler to J.M. Gould, April 15,1893
Alexander Chisholm to Maj. J. M. Poule, September 5, 1891
David P. Craig to John M. Gould, Jan. 15, 1892
Capt. Jacob Davis to John Gould, October 31, 1892
John Delaney to Battlefield Board, March 27, 1891
E.M. Dugand to John Gould, April 1892
Lt. William Gifford to John Gould, March 7, 1893
W.T. Hill to Maj. John M. Gould, July 21, 1891
Frank Holsinger to John M. Gould, February 29, 1892
Wm. H. Humphrey to John M. Gould, March 23, 1893
George A. Hussey to John M. Gould, May 21, 1892
John James to John Gould, April 25, 1891
D. C. Love to John M. Gould, April 29, 1891
James Nesbit to John Gould, April 21, 1891
Capt. E. R. Shurly to John Gould, undated letter
John Vautier to John Gould, December 5, 1892

**Harvard Law School Library (Boston, MA)**
Oliver Wendell Holmes, Jr. Papers, 1715-1938, The John G. Palfrey Collection

**Historical Society of Pennsylvania (Philadelphia)**
Hale, Charles A. *The Story of My Personal Experience at Antietam*, John R. Brooke Papers

**John Kuhn Collection**
Oscar Westlake to parents, September 21, 1862

**Library of Congress**
J. Evans Edings Diary. Edward Willis Papers
Joseph Hayes, "Battle of Sheppardstown," Joshua Lawrence Chamberlain Papers
"Map of the Defenses of Washington, 1865," Map Division
Edwin Sumner Papers
Cadmus Wilcox Papers

**National Archives**
"Returns from Regular Army Infantry Regiments, June 1821–December 1916."

**New York State Library (Albany, NY)**
John Bryson, "Manuscript History of the 30th New York Infantry Regiment."
William Prince Letters

**North Carolina Division of Archives and History (Raleigh, North Carolina)**
Branch Papers

**Putnam County Department of Archives and History (Palatka, Florida)**
Auld Letters

**Rutgers University Library (New Brunswick, NJ)**
Reuben Brooks Letters

**Wofford College Library**
Lafayette McLaws to I.R. Pennypacker, May 20, 1888, Lafayette McLaws Papers, Littlejohn Collection

**Woodruff Library, Emory University (Atlanta, GA)**
Diary of George Wren

**University of Michigan (William Clements Library, Ann Arbor, MI)**
Capt. John D. Wilkins, 3rd U.S. Infantry, Papers, 1862-1865. Schoff Civil War Collection

**University of North Carolina (Chapel Hill, NC)**
D.H. Hill Personal Papers
Calvin Leach Diary
James Longstreet Papers

**University of South Carolina Library (Columbia, SC)**
Robert W. Shand, "Incidents in the Life of a Private Soldier in the War Waged by the United States Against the Confederate States, 1861-1865."
James Hagood Memoirs

**University of Texas (Austin, TX)**
James Kirkpatrick Diary, Briscoe Center for American History

**U.S. Army Military History Institute (Carlisle, PA)**
Ames Papers
Samuel R. Beardsley Papers
John D. Hemmingen Diary
Phelps Papers
Jonathan Stowe Diary
Samuel Waters Memoir

## Newspapers

*Athens (GA) Watchman*, October 1, 1862
*Augusta (GA) Constitutionalist*, October 3, 1862
*Boston Evening Transcript*, September 19, 1862
*Brooklyn Eagle*, April 25, 1898
*Cape Ann Light and Gloucester (MA) Telegraph*, September 27, 1862
*Charleston (WV) Courier*, September 23, 1862 & October 1, 1862
*Cherry Valley (NY) Gazette*, October 1, 1862
*Cincinnati Daily Commercial*, September 22, 1862
*Columbia Democrat* (Bloomington, Pennsylvania), September 27, 1862
*Elizabeth New Jersey Journal*, September 23, 1862

*Houston Tri-Weekly Telegraph*, October 15, 1862

*Los Angeles Herald*, 14 December, 1899

*National Tribune*, July 16, 1891

*Newark Daily Advertiser*, September 20, 1862

*Paterson (NY) Guardian*, October 15, 1962

*Richmond Times Dispatch*, December 20, 1896 & July 16, 1897

*Savannah (GA) Republican*, September 20, 1862

*The Boston Daily Advertiser*, July 14, 1863

*The Countryman (GA)*, October 6, 1862

*The Lewiston Falls Journal* (Maine), October 2, 1862

*Weekly State Journal (WV)*, October 1, 1862

## Newspaper Articles

"A Reception to the Governor," *The Atlanta Constitution*, December 18, 1885.

"Army Correspondence," *Southern Confederacy* (Atlanta, GA), October 4, 1862 & October 5, 1862.

Bryan, Council A. "Letter from the 5th Florida," *Florida Sentinel* (Tallahassee), October 7, 1862.

Clark, Walter "Sharpsburg - Reminiscences of This Hard-Fought Battle," *The Wilmington (NC) Messenger*, October 7, 1894.

Clem, Richard E. "Confederate General Finds Peace in a Battle," *The Washington Times*, August 12, 2006.

DeRosset, William. "History of the Third North Carolina," *Wilmington (NC) Messenger*, September 8, 1895.

DeSassure, William. "Private Army Correspondence," *The York (SC) Enquirer*, October 8, 1862.

Driver, Robert. "A. J. Grigsby," *Lexington (VA) News Gazette*, September 30, 2003.

Fleming, William O. "The Fiftieth Georgia in the Battle of Sharpsburg," *Savannah Republican* (assumed), date unknown.

"From the Maine 16th—Antietam," *Lewiston (ME) Daily Evening Journal*, October 16, 1862.

G, "An Account of the late Battles." *The North Carolina Standard*: Wednesday October 1, 1862.

Gorman, John Calvin. "An Account of the late Battles," *Raleigh North Carolina Standard*, October 1, 1862.

Howard, Oliver. "Personal Reminiscences of the War of the Rebellion," *National Tribune*, April 3, 1884.

Osborne, E.A. "The Fourth N. C. Regiment: Col. E.A. Osborne's Sketch Of It." *Daily Charlotte (NC) Observer*, May 31, 1896.

Owen, Henry T. "Incidents of the Battle of South Mountain," *Philadelphia Weekly Times*, July 23, 1880.

Racine, J. K. Polk. "One of the Fiercest Battles Ever Waged by Mortal Men," *Cecil Whig* [Elkton, MD], 15 October 1898.

_____. "Reminiscence of Antietam," *Cecil Whig* [Elkton, MD], 24 September 1898.

"Peter McGlashen Communication," *Savannah (GA) Republican*, October 16, 1862.

"Reunion of the 50th P.V." *The Bradford Star* [Towanda, PA], 15 September 15, 1898.

"Rodman's Brigade at Antietam, *National Tribune*, November 9, 1886.

"Telegraph! Last Night's Report," *Buffalo Evening Post*, September 17, 1862.

"The Division of General Willcox in Sunday's Battle," *The Detroit Free Press*, 20 September 1862.

"The Division of General Willcox in Sunday's Battle," *The Detroit Free Press*, 20 September 1862.

"The Panic of the 5th Maryland," *Blue Hen's Chicken and Commonwealth* [Wilmington, DE], 1 October 1862.

"The Twentieth Georgia Regiment," *Macon (Georgia) Telegraph*, October 25, 1862.

## Books

*A Historical Sketch of the Quitman Guards, Company E. Sixteenth Mississippi Regiment, Harris' Brigade*. New Orleans, LA: Isaac T. Hinton, Printer, 1866.

Acken, J. Gregory ed. *Inside the Army of The Potomac: The Civil War Experience of Captain Francis Adams Donaldson*. Mechanicsburg, PA: Stackpole Books, 1998.

Adams, John G. B. *Reminiscences of the Nineteenth Massachusetts Regiment*. Boston: Wright & Potter Printing

Company, 1899.

Albert, Allen D. ed. *History of the Forty-Fifth Regiment, Pennsylvania Volunteer Infantry Regiment, 1861-1865*. Williamsport, PA: Grit Publishing Company, 1912.

Alexander, Edward Porter. *Fighting for the Confederacy: The Personal Recollections of General Edward Porter Alexander*, Gary W. Gallagher, ed. Chapel Hill, NC: University of North Carolina Press, 1989.

Alexander, Ted, ed. *Southern Revenge! Civil War History of Chambersburg, Pennsylvania*. Shippensburg, PA: White Mane, 1989.

_____. *The Battle of Antietam – The Bloodiest Day*. Charleston, SC: History Press, 2011.

Allan, William. *The Army of Northern Virginia in 1862* (Boston, MA: Houghton Mifflin and Co., 189**2**.

Allardice, Bruce S. *More Generals in Gray*. Baton Rouge, LA: Louisiana State University, 1995.

Allen, Randall and Keith S. Bohannon. *Campaigning with 'Old Stonewall: Confederate Captain Ujanirtus Allen's Letters to his Wife*. Baton Rouge, LA: Louisiana State University, 1998.

Andrews, W. H. *Footprints of a Regiment: A Recollection of the 1st Georgia Regulars*. Atlanta, GA: Longstreet Press, 1992.

*Annual Report of the Massachusetts Adjutant General. Annual Report of the Adjutant-General, of the Commonwealth of Massachusetts, with Reports from the Quartermaster-General, Surgeon-General, and Master of Ordnance, for the Year Ending December 31, 1862*. Boston: Wright & Potter, 1863.

Armstrong, Marion V. *Disaster in the West Woods: General Edwin Sumner and the II Corps*. Middletown, MD: Western Maryland Interpretive Association, 2002.

_____. *Unfurl Those Colors! McClellan, Sumner, & the Second Corps in the Antietam Campaign*. Tuscaloosa, AL: University of Alabama Press, 2008.

_____. *Opposing the Second Corps at Antietam: The Fight for the Confederate Left and Center on America's Bloodiest Day*. Tuscaloosa, AL: University of Alabama Press, 2016.

Armstrong, William H. *Major McKinley: William McKinley & the Civil War*. Kent, OH: The Kent State University Press, 2000.

Ayoub, Michael N. *The Campfire Chronicles: The Words and Deeds of the 88th Pennsylvania 1861-1865* . n.p.: Xlibris Corporation, 2010.

Baldwin, James J. *The Eagle Struck: A Biography of Brigadier General Micah Jenkins and a History of the 5th South Carolina Volunteers and the Palmetto Sharpshooters*. Shippensburg, PA: Burd Street Press, 1996.

Battle, Cullen Andrews. *Third Alabama!: The Civil War Memoir of Brigadier General Cullen Andrews Battle, CSA*, Brandon H. Beck, ed. Tuscaloosa, AL: University of Alabama Press, 2002.

Baquet, Camille. *History of the First Brigade, New Jersey Volunteers from 1861 to 1865*. Trenton, NJ: MacCrellish & Quigley, State Printers, 1910.

Bates, Samuel P. *History of Pennsylvania Volunteers 1861-65*. Five volumes. Harrisburg, PA: B. Singerly, Printer, 1869.

_____. *Brief History of the One Hundredth Regiment (Roundheads)*. New Castle, PA: W. B. Thomas, 1884.

Baxter, Nancy Niblack *The Gallant Fourteenth: The Story of an Indiana Civil War Regiment*. Carmel, IN: Guild Press of Indiana, Inc., 1999.

Baylor, George B. *Bull Run To Bull Run: or Four Years in the Army of Northern Virginia*. Richmond, VA: B. F. Johnson Publishing Company, 1900.

Beale, George W. *A Lieutenant of Cavalry in Lee's Army*. Boston: The Gorham Press, 1899.

Beale, R.L.T. *History of the Ninth Virginia Cavalry in the War Between the States*. Richmond, VA: B.F. Johnson Publishing Co., 1899.

Bearss, Edwin C. *Fields of Honor – Pivotal Battles of the Civil War*. Washington, DC: National Geographic Society, 2007.

Beaudot, William J. K. and Lance J. Herdegen, eds. *An Irishman in the Iron Brigade: The Civil War Memoirs of James P. Sullivan, Sergt., Company K, 6th Wisconsin Volunteers*. New York: Fordham University Press, 1993.

Bennett, Edwin C. *Musket and Sword*. Boston, MA: Coburn Publishing Co., 1900.

Bergeron, Arthur W. Jr. *Guide to Louisiana Confederate Military Units, 1861-1865*. Baton Rouge, LA: Louisiana State University Press, 1989.

Bernard, George S. *War Talks of Confederate Veterans*. Petersburg, VA: Fenn & Owen, Publishers, 1892.

Beyer, Walter F. and Oscar F. Keydel, compilers. *Deeds of Valor: How America's Heroes Won the Medal of Honor*.

Two volumes. Detroit, MI: The Perrien-Keydel Company, 1901.

Bicknell. George W. *History of the Fifth Regiment Maine Volunteers*. Portland, ME: H. L. Davis, 1871.

Bidwell, Frederick David. *History of the Forty-Ninth New York Volunteers*. Albany, NY: J. B. Lyon Company, 1916.

Bilby, Joseph G. *The Irish Brigade in the Civil War: The 69th New York and Other Irish Regiments of the Army of the Potomac*. New York: Da Capo Press, 1997.

Bishop, Randy. *The Tennessee Brigade: A History of the Volunteers of the Army of Northern Virginia*. Bloomington, IN: Authorhouse, 2005.

Blackford, W. W. *War Years with Jeb Stuart*. New York: Charles Scribners' Sons, 1945.

Blakeslee, Bernard F. *History of the Sixteenth Connecticut Volunteers*. Hartford, CT: The Case, Lockwood and Brainard Co., Printers, 1875.

Board of Commissioners, *Minnesota in the Civil War and Indian Wars 1861-1865*. Two volumes. St. Paul: Pioneer Press Company, 1890-93.

Bowen, James L. *Massachusetts in the War, 1861-1865*. Springfield, MA: Clark W. Bryan & Co., 1889.

Bowen, Roland. *From Ball's Bluff to Gettysburg . . . and Beyond: The Civil War Letters of Private Roland E. Bowen, 15th Massachusetts Infantry*. Gregory Coco, ed. Gettysburg, PA: Thomas Publishers, 1994.

Boyce, Charles W. *A Brief History of the Twenty-Eighth Regiment New York Volunteers*. Buffalo, NY: Thet Matthews-Northrup Co., 1896.

Boyle, John Richards. *Soldiers True: The Story of the One Hundred and Eleventh Regiment Pennsylvania Veteran Volunteers, and its Campaigns in the War for the Union 1861—1865*. New York, NY: Eaton & Mains, 1903.

Bridges, Hal. *Lee's Maverick General: Daniel Harvey Hill*. New York: McGraw Hill, 1961.

Brown, E. R. *The Twenty-Seventh Indiana Volunteer Infantry in the War of the Rebellion 1861 – 1865*. np: np, 1899.

Boyd, Charles E. *Devil's Den: A History of the 44th Alabama Volunteer Infantry Regiment, Confederate States Army*. Birmingham, AL: Banner Press, 1987.

Brown, Philip. *Reminiscences of the War of 1861-1865*. Richmond, VA: Whittet & Shepperson, Printers, 1917.

Bryant, Edwin E. *History of the Third Regiment of Wisconsin Veteran Volunteer Infantry 1861 – 1865*. Madison, WI: Democrat Printing Co., 1891.

Buck, Captain D. *With the Old Confeds: Actual Experiences of a Captain in the Line*. Baltimore, MD: H. E. Houck & Co., 1925.

Caldwell, J. F. J. *The History of a Brigade of South Carolinians, Known First as "Gregg's" and Subsequently as "McGowan's Brigade."* Philadelphia: King & Baird Publishers, 1866.

Carman, Ezra. *The Maryland Campaign of September 1862*, Thomas Clemens, ed., Three volumes. El Dorado Hills: Savas Beatie, 2010, 2012.

Cassedy, Edward, ed., *Dear Friends at Home: The Civil War Letters and Diaries of Sergeant Charles T. Bowen Twelfth United States Infantry First Battalion 1861-1864*. Baltimore: Butternut and Blue, 2001.

Caynor, William L. *Without a Scratch: Diary of William Holmes Morse, Color Bearer of the 5th Maine Infantry*. Wilmington, NC: Broadfoot Publishing, 2007.

Chamberlaine, William W. *Memoirs of the Civil War*. Washington, DC: Press of Byron S. Adams, 1912.

Chapin, L. N. *A Brief History of the Thirty-Fourth Regiment NYSV*. New York: n.p., 1903.

Chapla, John D. *48th Virginia Infantry*. Lynchburg, VA: H. E. Howard, Inc., 1989.

_____. *42nd Virginia Infantry*. Lynchburg, VA: H. E. Howard, Inc., 1983.

Clark, Walter ed. *Histories of the Several Regiments and Battalions from North Carolina in the Great War 1861-'65*, Five volumes. Raleigh, NC: State of North Carolina, 1901.

Cochran, William *General Jacob Dolson Cox: Early Life and Military Services*. Oberlin, OH: Bibliotheca Sacra Co., 1901.

Coker, James Lide. *History of Company G, Ninth S. C. Regiment, Infantry and of Company E. Sixth Regiment, Infantry Army*. Greenwood, SC: The Attic Press, 1979.

Conklin, Ryan A. *The 18th New York Infantry in the Civil War: A History and Roster*. Jefferson, NC: McFarland & Co., 2016.

Conyngham, David Power. *The Irish Brigade and Its Campaigns*. New York: Fordham University Press, 1994.

Collier, Calvin L. *They'll Do To Tie To!* Little Rock, AR: Arkansas Civil War Centennial Commission, 1959.

Collins, Darrell L. *The Army of the Potomac. Order of Battle, 1861-1865, with Commanders, Strengths, Losses, and More.*

Jefferson, NC: McFarland & Company, 2013.

_____. *The Army of the Northern Virginia. Organization, Strength, Casualties, 1861-1865*. Jefferson, NC: McFarland & Company, 2016.

Cook, Benjamin F. *History of the Twelfth Massachusetts Volunteers (Webster Regiment)*. Boston, MA: Twelfth (Webster) Regiment Association, 1882.

Comey, Lyman Richard. *A Legacy of Valor: The Memoirs and Letters of Captain Henry Newton Comey, 2nd Massachusetts Infantry*. Knoxville, TN: The University of Tennessee Press, 2004.

Cromwell, Joseph E. *The Young Volunteer: The Everyday Experiences of a Soldier Boy in the Civil War*. New York: G. W. Dillingham Company, 1906.

Committee of the Regimental Association. *History of the Thirty-Fifth Regiment Massachusetts Volunteers, 1862-1865. With a Roster*. Boston: Mills, Knight & Co, 1884.

Cowtan, Charles W. *Services of the Tenth New York Volunteers (National Zouaves)*. New York: Charles Ludwig, 1882.

Cox, Jacob D. *Military Reminiscences of the Civil War*, Two vols. New York: Scribner's Sons, 1900.

Craig, George E. *In Memoriam: Maj. Gen. George L. Hartsuff*. Norwood, MA: Charles G. Wheelock, 1875.

Croffut, W. A. and John Moses Morris. *The Military and Civil History of Connecticut During the War of 1861-65*. New York: Ledyard Bill, 1869.

Cross, Harlan Eugene, Jr. *Letters Home: Three Years Under General Lee in the 6th Alabama*. Fairfax, Virginia. History4All, Inc. 2013.

Crownishield, Benjamin W. *A History of the First Massachusetts Cavalry Volunteers*. Boston: Houghton Mifflin & Co., 1891.

Cullum, George. *Biographical Register of the Officers and Graduates of the U.S. Military Academy at West Point, NY*. Boston: Houghton Mifflin, 1891.

Cunningham, D. and W. W. Miller, W.W. *Antietam: Report of The Ohio Antietam Battlefield Commission*. Springfield, OH: Springfield Publishing Company, State Printers, 1904.

Curtis, Newton Martin. *From Bull Run to Chancellorsville. The Story of the Sixteenth New York Infantry, Together With Personal Reminiscences*. New York. G.P. Putnam's Sons, 1906.

Cutrer, Thomas W., ed. *Longstreet's Aide: The Civil War Letters of Major Thomas J. Goree*. Charlottesville, VA: University Press of Virginia, 1995.

McDaid, William Kelsey. *Four Years of Arduous Service: The History of the Branch-Lane Brigade in the Civil War*. Ph.D. Dissertation, Michigan State University, 1987.

Davenport, Alfred. *Camp and Field Life of the Fifth New York Volunteer Infantry*. New York: Dick and Fitzgerald, 1879.

Davis, William C., ed. *The Confederate General*. Six volumes. Harrisburg, PA: Publication of the National Historical Society, 1992.

Dawes, Rufus R. *Service with the Sixth Wisconsin Volunteers*. Marietta, Ohio: E. P. Alderman & Sons, 1890.

de la Roche, Senechal. *"Our Aim Was Man": Andrew's Sharpshooters in the American Civil War*. Amherst: University of Massachusetts Press, 2016.

Dickert, D. Augustus. *History of Kershaw's Brigade, with Complete Roll of Companies, Biographical Sketches, Incidents, Anecdotes, Etc*. Newberry, SC: Elbert H. Aull Company, 1899.

Dinkins, James. *1861-1865, By an Old Johnnie: Personal Recollections and Experiences in the Confederate Army*. Cincinnati, OH: The Robert Clark Company, 1897.

Douglas, Henry Kyd. *I Rode with Stonewall: Being Chiefly the War Experience of the Youngest Member of Jackson's Staff from the John Brown Raid to the Hanging of Mrs. Surratt*. Chapel Hill, NC: University of North Carolina Press, 1940.

Driver, Robert J. *58th Virginia Infantry*. Lynchburg, VA: H. E. Howard, 1990.

_____. *1st Virginia Infantry Battalion*. Lynchburg, VA: H. E. Howard, Inc., 1996.

Dunaway, Wayland Fuller. *Reminiscences of a Rebel*. New York: Neale Publishing Company, 1913.

Dunn, Craig L. *Iron Men, Iron Will: The Nineteenth Indiana Regiment of the Iron Brigade*. Indianapolis, IN: Guild Press, 1995.

Durkin, Joseph T. ed. *John Dooley, Confederate Soldier: His War Journal*. Notre Dame, IN: University of Notre Dame Press, 1963.

Dyer, Frederick H. *A Compendium of the War of the Rebellion*, Three volumes. New York: Thomas Yoseloff, 1959.

Early, Jubal. *General Jubal A. Early: Autobiographical Sketch and Narrative of the War Between the States*. Wilmington, NC: Broadfoot Publishing Company, 1989.

Eberly, Robert, Jr. *Bouquets From The Cannon's Mouth*. Shippensburg, PA: White Mane Publishing, 2005.

Eckenrode, H. J. and Bryan Conrad, *James Longstreet: Lee's War Horse*. Chapel Hill, NC: University of North Carolina Press, 1986.

Eddy, Richard. *History of the Sixtieth New York State Volunteers*. Philadelphia, PA: By the Author, 1864.

Eicher, John H. and David J. Eicher. *Civil War High Commands*. Stanford, CA: Stanford University Press, 2001.

Eisenschiml, Otto. *The Celebrated Case of Fitz John Porter*. Indianapolis, IN: Bobbs-Merrill, 1950.

Elliot, Ellsworth, Jr. *West Point In The Confederacy*. New York: G.A. Baker & Co., Inc., 1941.

Ellis, Billy. *Tithes of Blood: A Confederate Soldier's Story*. Murfreesboro, TN: Southern Heritage Press, 1997.

Emerson, Edward W. *Life and Letters of Charles Russell Lowell*. Port Washington, NY: Kennikat Press, 1971.

Ent, Uzal. *The Pennsylvania Reserves in the Civil War A Comprehensive History*. Jefferson, NC: McFarland & Company, 2012.

Evans, Anselm. *Confederate Military History*. 12 volumes. Atlanta GA: Confederate Publishing Company, 1899.

Evans, Robert G., , ed. *The Sixteenth Mississippi Infantry: Civil War Letters and Reminiscences*. Oxford, MS: The University of Mississippi Press, 2002.

Everson, Guy and Edward Simpson, eds. *Far, Far From Home: The Wartime Letters of Dick and Tally Simpson, Third South Carolina Volunteers*. New York, NY: Oxford University Press, 1994.

Fairchild, C. B. *History of the 27th Regiment N. Y. Vols.: Being a Record of its More than Two Years of Service in the War for the Union, from May 21st, 1861, to May 31st, 1863*. Binghamton, NY: Carl & Matthews, Printers, 1888.

Favill, Josiah M. *The Diary of a Young Officer Serving with the Armies of the United States during the War of the Rebellion*. Chicago, IL: R.R. Donnelley & Sons, 1909.

Folsom, James Madison. *Heroes and Martyrs of Georgia: Georgia's Record in the Revolution of 1861*. Baltimore, MD: Butternut and Blue, 1995.

Ford, Andrew E. *The Story of the Fifteenth Regiment: Massachusetts Volunteer Infantry in the Civil War, 1861-1864*. Clinton, MA: Press of W.J. Coulter, 1898.

Ford, Worthington C., ed. *A Cycle of Adams Letters 1861-1862*. Two volumes. New York; Kraus, 1969.

Fox, William F. *Regimental Losses in the Civil War*. Dayton, OH: Morningside Press reprint, 1985.

Fox, John J. *Red Clay to Richmond: Trail of the 35th Georgia Infantry Regiment, C. S. A.* Winchester, VA: Angle Valley Press, 2004.

Freeman. Douglas. *Lee's Lieutenants: A Study in Command*. 3 volumes. New York: Charles Scribners Sons, 1943.

_____. *Lee's Lieutenants: A Study in Command*. Abridged by Stephen W. Sears. New York: Scribners, 1998.

Freiheit, Laurence H. *Boots and Saddles: Cavalry During the Maryland Campaign of September 1862*. Iowa City, IA: Camp Pope Publishing, 2012.

Fuller, Charles A. *Personal Recollections of the War of 1861*. Hamilton, NY: Edmonston Publishing, Inc, 1906.

Gaff, Alan D. *On Many A Bloody Field: Four Years in the Iron Brigade*. Bloomington, IN: Indiana University Press, 1996.

Gallagher, Gary. *Lee the Soldier*. Lincoln, NE: University of Nebraska Press, 1996.

Galwey, Thomas. *The Valiant Hours, Narrative of "Captain Brevet," An Irish-American in the Army of the Potomac*. Mechanicsburg, PA: Stackpole Books, 1961.

Gannon, James. *Irish Rebels, Confederate Tigers: A History of the 6th Louisiana Volunteers*. Mason City: IA: Savas Publishing, 1998.

Gates, Theodore B. *The "Ulster Guard" [20 th N. Y. State Militia] and the War of the Rebellion*. New York: Benj. H. Tyrrel, 1879.

Gibbon, John. *Personal Recollections of the Civil War*. Dayton, OH: Morningside Bookshop, 1988.

Gibbs, Joseph. *Three Years In The Bloody Eleventh*. University Park: PA The Pennsylvania State University Press, 2002.

Giles, Leonidas B. *Terry's Texas Rangers*. Self Published, 1911, digitized by the Sloan Foundation, LoC, 2008.

Glatthaar, Joseph T. *General Lee's Army: From Victory to Collapse*. New York: Free Press, 2008.

Glover, Edwin A. *Bucktailed Wildcats: A Regiment of Civil War Volunteers*. New York: T. Yoseloff, 1960.

Green, Robert M. *History of the One Hundred and Twenty-fourth Regiment Pennsylvania Volunteers in the War of the Rebellion—1862-1863*. Philadelphia: Ware Bros. Company, 1907.

Gordon, John B. *Reminiscences of the Civil War*. New York: Charles Scribner's Sons, 1904.

Gottfried, Bradley M. *Stopping Pickett: The History of the Philadelphia Brigade*. Shippensburg, PA: White Mane Publishing Co., 1999.

_____.*Kearny's Own: The History of the First New Jersey Brigade in the Civil War*. New Brunswick, NJ: The Rutgers University Press, 2005.

Gould, John M. *History of the First-Tenth-Twenty-Nineth Maine Regiment in Service of the United States from May 3, 1861 to June 21, 1866*. Portland, ME: Stephen Berry, 1871.

Gould, John Mead. *Joseph K. F. Mansfield, Brigadier General of the U. S. Army: A Narrative of Events Connected with his Mortal Wounding at Sharpsburg, Maryland*. Portland, ME: Stephen Berry, Printer, 1895.

Gould, Joseph, *The Story of the Forty-Eighth: A Record of the Campaigns of the Forty-eighth Regiment Pennsylvania Veteran Volunteer Infantry During the Four Eventful Years of its Service in the War for the Preservation of the Union*. Philadelphia: [Forty-eight] Regimental Association, 1908.

Graham, Matthew J. *The Ninth Regiment New York Volunteers (Hawkins' Zouaves): Being a History of the Regiment and Veteran Association from 1860 to 1900*. New York: E. P. Coby & Co.: 1900.

Giffin, Ronald G. *The 11th Alabama Volunteer Regiment in the Civil War*. Jefferson, NC: McFarland Press, 2008.

Hall, Isaac. *History of the Ninety-Seventh Regiment New York Volunteers*. Utica, NY: L.C. Childs & Son, 1896.

Halsey, Ashley, Jr. *Who Fired The First Shot and Other Untold Stories of the Civil War*. New York: Hawthorn Books Inc., 1963.

Hamilton, J. G. de Roulhac, ed. *The Papers of Randolph Abbott Shotwell*. Two volumes. Raleigh, NC: The North Carolina Historical Commission, 1929.

____. *The Papers Of Thomas Ruffin*. Edward & Broughton Printing Co., NC, 1920.

Hancock, M. A. *Four Brothers in Gray*. Sparta, NC: Imaging Specialists, 2013.

Hard, Abner. *History of the Eight Cavalry Regiment, Illinois Volunteers, During the Great Rebellion*. Aurora, IL: n.p, 1868.

Hardin, Martin *History of the Twelfth Regiment, Pennsylvania Volunteer Reserve Volunteeer Corps*. New York: By Author, 1890.

Hardy, Michael C. *The Thirty-Seventh North Carolina Troops*. Jefferson, NC: McFarland & Company, 2003.

____. *General Lee's Immortals: The Battles and Campaigns of the Branch-Lane Brigade in the Army of Northern Virginia, 1861 – 1865*. El Dorado Hills, CA: Savas Beatie, 2018.

Harris, J. S. *Historical Sketches, Seventh Regiment North Carolina Troops*. Mooresville, NC: Mooresville Printing Co., 1893.

Harsh, Joseph L. *Taken at the Flood: Robert E. Lee & Confederate Strategy in the Maryland Campaign of 1862*. Kent, OH: The Kent State University Press, 1999.

_____. *Sounding the Shallows: A Confederate Compendium for The Maryland Campaign*. Kent, OH: The Kent State University Press, 2000.

Hartley, Chris J. *Stuart's Tarheels: James B. Gordon and His North Carolina Cavalry*. Butternut and Blue Press, Baltimore, Md. 1996.

Hartwig, D. Scott. *To Antietam Creek: The Maryland Campaign of September 1862*. Baltimore, MD: The Johns Hopkins University Press, 2012.

Hassler, William W. ed. *One of Lee's Best Men: The Civil War Letters of General William Dorsey Pender*. Chapel Hill, NC: The University of North Carolina Press, 1965.

Hayes, Rutherford Birchard. *Diary and Letters of Rutherford Birchard Hayes: Nineteenth President of the United States, 1822-1893*. Charles Richard Williams, ed. Ohio State Archaeological and Historical Society, 1922.

Haynes, Draughton Stith. *The Field Diary of a Confederate Soldier While Serving with the Army of Northern Virginia C. S. A.* William Hynes, ed. Darien, GA: The Ashantilly Press, 1963.

Hebert, Walter H. *Fighting Joe Hooker*. Indianapolis, IN: The Bobbs-Merrill Company, 1944.

Heidler, David & Jeanne Heidler. *Encyclopedia of the American Civil War: A Political, Social and Military History*. Two volumes. Santa Barbara, CA: ABC-CLIO, Inc., 2000.

Heitman, Francis B. *Historical Register and Dictionary of the United States Army, From Its Organization September 29,*

*1789, to March 2, 1903.* Two volumes. Washington, D.C.: Government Printing Office, 1903.

Henderson, William D. *41st Virginia Infantry.* Lynchburg, VA: H. E. Howard, 1986.

Hennessy, John. *Second Manassas Battlefield Map Study.* Lynchburg, VA: H. E. Howard, Inc., 1985.

_____. *Return to Bull Run – The Campaign and Battle of Second Manassas.* New York: Simon and Schuster, 1993.

Herdegen, Lance J. *The Iron Brigade in the Civil War and Memory: The Black Hats from Bull Run to Appomattox and Thereafter.* El Dorado Hills, CA: Savas Beatie, 2012.

Hewett, Janet B., Noah Andre Trudeau, and Bryce A. Suderow, eds., *Supplement to the Official Records of the Union and Confederate Armies.* 100 vols. Wilmington, NC: Broadfoot Publishing Company, 1994.

Hinkley, Julian Wisner. *A Narrative of Service with the Third Wisconsin.* Madison, WI: Wisconsin History Commission, 1912.

Hitchcock, Frederick L. *War from the Inside or Personal Experiences, Impressions, and Reminiscences of One of the "Boys" in the War of the Rebellion.* Philadelphia: Press of J. B. Lippincott Company, 1904.

Hopkins. Donald A. *The Little Jeff: The Jeff Davis Legion, Cavalry Arm of Northern Virginia.* Shippensburg, PA: White Mane Publishing, 1999.

Hoptak, John David. *The Battle of South Mountain.* Charleston, SC: The History Press, 2011.

Horn, John. *The Petersburg Regiment in the Civil War: A History of the 12th Virginia Infantry from John Brown's Hanging to Appomattox, 1859-1865.* El Dorado Hill, CA: Savas Beatie, 2019.

Horton J.H. and Solomon Teverbaugh. *A History of the Eleventh Regiment -Ohio Infantry.* Dayton, OH: W.J. Shuey, 1866.

Hough, Franklin. *History of Duryee's Brigade During the Campaign in Virginia Under General Pope and in Maryland Under General McClellan in the Summer and Autumn of 1862.* Albany, NY: J. Munsell, 1864.

Hunt, Roger D. *Colonels in Blue Union Army Colonels of the Civil War The New England States: Connecticut, Maine, Massachusetts, New Hampshire, Rhode Island, Vermont.* Atglen PA: Schiffer Military History Books, 2001.

Hunter, Alexander. *Johnny Reb and Billy Yank.* New York: The Neale Publishing Company, 1905.

Hunt, Roger D. and Jack R. Brown. *Brevet Brigadiers in* Blue. Gaithersburg, MD: Olde Soldier Books, 1990.

Hunton, Eppa. *Autobiography of Eppa Hunton.* Richmond, VA: The William Byrd Press, 1933.

Huyette, Miles Clayton. *The Maryland Campaign and the Battle of Antietam.* Buffalo, NY: By author, 1915.

Hyde, Thomas W. *Following the Greek Cross Or, Memories of the Sixth Army Corps.* Boston: Houghton, Mifflin and Company, 1894.

Iobst, Richard W., and Louis H. Manarin *The Bloody Sixth: The Sixth North Carolina Regiment Confederate States of America.* Raleigh, NC: North Carolina Confederate Centennial Commission, 1965.

Jackson, Lyman. *History of the Sixth New Hampshire in the War for the Union.* Concord, NH: Republican Press, 1891.

Jessup, Harlan R., ed. *The Painful News I Have to Write: Letters and Diaries of Four Hite Brothers of Page County in the Service of the Confederacy.* Baltimore, MD: Butternut & Blue, 1998.

Jones, Austin. *The Capture of Harpers Ferry.* n.p.: n.d, 1922.

Jones. Terry L. *Lee's Tigers. The Louisiana Infantry in the Army of Northern Virginia.* Baton Rouge, LA: Louisiana State University, 1987.

Johnson, Charles F. *The Long Roll.* East Aurora, NY: Roycrofters, 1911.

Johnson, Curt and Richard C. Anderson, Jr. *Artillery Hell: The Employment of Artillery at Antietam.* College Station, TX: Texas A&M University Press, 1995.

Johnson, Pharris D., ed. *Under The Southern Cross: Army Life with Gordon Bradwell.* Macon, GA: Mercer University Press 1999.

Johnston, David E. *Four Years a Soldier.* Princeton, WV: n.p., 1887.

_____. *The Story of a Confederate Boy in the Civil War.* Portland, OR: Glass & Prudhomme, Co., 1914.

Kauffman, Doug. *Tobias's Story: The Life and Civil War Career of Tobias B. Kaufman.* Bloomington, IN: Xlibris, 2012.

Kepler, William. *History of the Three Months' and Three Years' Service of the Fourth Regiment Ohio Volunteer Infantry in the War for the Union.* Cleveland, OH: Leader Printing Co., 1886.

Kimball, George. *A Corporal's Story: Civil War Recollections of the Twelfth Massachusetts.* Alan D. Gaff and Donald H. Gaff, eds. Norman, OK: University of Oklahoma Press, 2014.

Kleese, Richard B. *49th Virginia Infantry.* Lynchburg, VA: H. E. Howard, 1990.

451

Krick, Robert E. L. *Staff Officers in Gray.* Chapel Hill, NC: The University of North Carolina Press, 2003.

Krick, Robert K., *30th Virginia Infantry: The Virginia Regimental Histories Series.* Lynchburg, VA: H. E. Howard, Inc., 1983.

_____. *Lee's Colonels: A Biographical Register of the Field Officers of the Army of Northern Virginia.* Dayton, OH: Press of Morningside Bookshop, 1984.

Laine, J. Gary and Morris M. Penny. *Law's Alabama Brigade in the War Between the Union and the Confederacy.* Shippensburg, PA: White Mane Publishing Company, 1996.

Lemon, James Lile. *Feed Them the Steel: Being The Wartime Recollections of Captain James Lile Lemon Co. A., 18th Georgia Infantry, CSA,* Mark H. Lemon, ed. n.p.:n.p., 2013.

Lewis, Richard. *Camp Life of a Confederate Boy of Bratton's Brigade, Longstreet's Corps, C.S. A.* Charleston, SC: The News and Courier Book Presses, 1883.

Lightsey, Ada Christine. *The Veteran's Story.* Meridian, MS: The Meridian News, 1899.

Livermore, Thomas L. *Days and Events, 1860 – 1866.* Boston: Houghton Mifflin Company, 1920.

Loehr, Charles T. *War History of the Old First Virginia Infantry Regiments, Army of Northern Virginia.* Richmond, VA: William Ellis Jones, 1884.

Lokey, John W. *My Experiences in the War Between the States.* Tishomingo, OK: John R. Lokey, 1959.

Lord, Edward O. *History of the Ninth Regiment, New Hampshire Volunteers in the War of the Rebellion .* Concord, NH: Republican Press, 1895.

Longacre, Edward G. *Gentleman and Soldier: A Biography of Wade Hampton III.* Nashville, TN: Rutledge Hill Press, 2003.

Longstreet, J., *Manassas to Appomattox: Memoirs of the Civil War in America.* Philadelphia, PA: J.B. Lippincott Co., 1895.

Lowe, Jeffrey C. and Sam Hodges, *Letters to Amanda: The Civil War Letter of Marion Hill Fitzpatrick, Army of Northern Virginia.* Macon, GA: Mercer University Press, 1998.

Lynch, John W. *The Dorman-Mashbourne Letters: With Brief Accounts of the 10th and 53rd Georgia Regiments, CSA.* Senoia, GA: Down South Publishing, 1995.

McBrien, Joe Bennett. *The Tennessee Brigade.* Chattanooga: Hudson Printing and Lithographing Company, 1977.

McClelen, Bailey George. *I Saw The Elephant.* Norman E. Rouke, ed. Shippensburg, PA: Burd Street Press, 1995.

McClellan, George B. *McClellan's Own Story.* New York: Charles I. Webster and Co., 1887.

_____. *Civil War Papers of George B. McClellan: Selected Correspondence, 1860-1865.* Stephen W. Sears, ed. New York: Ticknor & Fields, 1989.

McClellan, H. B. *The Life and Campaigns of Major-General J. E. B. Stuart, Commander of the Cavalry of the Army of Northern Virginia.* Secaucus, NJ: Blue & Gray Press, 1993.

McClendon, William A. *Recollections of War Times by an Old Veteran While Under Stonewall Jackson and Lieutenant General James Longstreet: How I Got in and How I got Out.* Mongtomery, AL: Paragon Press, 1909.

McGrath, Thomas A. *Shepherdstown: Last Clash of the Antietam Campaign.* Lynchburg VA: Schroeder Publications, 2008), 94.

McLaughlin, John M., *A Memoir of Hector Tyndale.* Philadelphia, PA: n.p., 1882.

McPherson, James M. *Crossroads of Freedom: Antietam, The Battle That Changed the Course of the Civil War.* New York, NY: Oxford University Press, 2002.

McWhiney, Grady, and Perry D. Jamieson. *Attack and Die – Civil War Military Tactics and the Southern Heritage.* The University of Alabama Press, Tuscaloosa and London, 1982.

Mahood, Wayne. *Fight all Day, March All Night: A Medal of Honor Recipient's Story.* Albany, NY: SUNY Press, Excelsoir Editions, 2012.

Martin, Jay C. *General Henry Baxter, 7th Michigan Volunteer Infantry: A Biography.* Jefferson, N.C.: McFarland Publishers, 2015.

Marvel, William. *Burnside.* Chapel Hill, NC: The North Carolina Press, 2000.

Marvin, Edwin. *Fifth Regiment Connecticut Volunteers: A History Compiled from Diaries and Official Reports* (Hartford, CT: Press of Wiley, Waterman & Eaton, 1889.

Mason, Jack C. *Until Antietam: The Life and Letters of Major General Israel B. Richardson, U. S. Army.* Carbondale,

IL: Southern Illinois University Press, 2009.

Matchett, William B. *Maryland and the Glorious Third in the War for the Union: Reminiscences in the Life of Her.* Washington: TJ Brashears Printers, 1882.

Michigan Adjutant-General's Dept, and George H. Turner. *Record of Service of Michigan Volunteers in the Civil War, 1861-1865.* Kalamazoo, MI: Ihling Bros. & Everard, 1900.

Mills, J. Harrison. *Chronicles of the Twenty-First Regiment New York State Volunteers Embracing the Full History of the Regiment.* Buffalo, NY: The 21st Reg't Veteran Association of Buffalo, 1887.

Mills, George H. *History of the 16th North Carolina Regiment.* n.p.: n.p., n.d.

Mixson, Frank M. *Reminiscences of a Private.* Columbia, SC: The State Company, 1910.

Moe, Richard. *The Last Full Measure: The Life and Death of the First Minnesota Volunteers.* New York: Henry Holt and Company, 1993.

Moore, Frank, ed. *The Rebellion Record :A Diary of American events, with Documents, Narratives, Illustrative Incidents, Poetry, etc. With an Introductory Address on the Causes of the Struggle, and the Great Issues before the Country, by Edward Everett,* 13 volumes. New York: G.P. Putnam's Sons, 1861-1863; Van Nostrand, 1864-1868.

Mosely, Ronald H., ed. *The Stilwell Letters: A Georgian in Longstreet's Corps, Army of Northern Virginia.* Macon, GA: Mercer University Press, 2002.

Murfin, James V. *The Gleam of Bayonets: The Battle of Antietam and the Maryland Campaign of September 1862.* New York: Thomas Yoseloff, 1965.

Murphey, Thomas G. *Four Years in the War: The History of the First Regiment of Delaware Veteran Volunteers.* Philadelphia: J.S. Claxton, 1866.

Musselman, Homer D. *47th Virginia Infantry.* Lynchburg, VA: H. E. Howard, 1991.

Myers, Irvin G. *We Might as Well Die Here: The 53rd Pennsylvania Veteran Volunteer Infantry.* Shippensburg, PA: White Mane Publishing Company, 2004

Murray, R. L. *New Yorkers in the Civil War A Historic Journal.* Wolcott, New York: Benedum Books, 2004.

*National Almanac and Annual Record for the Year 1864.* Philadelphia: George W. Childs, 1864.

New York Monuments Commission, *In Memoriam George Sears Greene Brevet Major-General United States Volunteers, 1801-1899.* Albany, NY: J.B. Lyon Company, State Printers, 1909.

Nevins, Allan, ed. *A Diary of Battle The Personal Journals of Colonel Charles S. Wainwright 1861-1865.* New York: Hartcourt, 1962.

Nisbet, James Cooker. *Four Years on the Firing Line.* Bell Irvin Wiley, ed. Wilmington, NC: Broadfoot Publishing Company, 1987.

Nolan, Alan T. *The Iron Brigade: A Military History.* Bloomington, IN: Indiana University Press, 1961.

O'Brien, Thomas M. & Oliver Diefendorf. *General Orders of the War Department, Embracing the Years 1861, 1862 & 1863. Adapted Specifically for the Use of the Army and Navy of the United States,* Two volumes. New York, NY: Derby & Miller, 1864.

Oates, William C. *The War Between the Union and the Confederacy and its Lost Opportunities.* Dayton, OH: Morningside Bookshop, 1985.

Oeffinger, John C., ed. *A Soldier's General: The Civil War Letters of Major General Lafayette McLaws.* Chapel Hill and London, University of North Carolina Press, 2002.

Osborne, Charles C. *Jubal: The Life and Times of General Jubal A. Early, CSA.* Chapel Hill, NC: Alqonguin Books, 1992.

Osbourne, William H. *The History of the 29th Regiment, Massachusetts Volunteer Infantry.* Boston, MA: Albert J. Wright, Printer, 1877.

Owen, Joe Philip McBride, and Joe Allport. *Texans at Antietam.* United Kingdom: Fonthill Media Limited, 2017.

Page, Charles D. *History of the Fourteenth Regiment, Connecticut Vol. Infantry.* Meriden, CT: The Horton Printing Co., 1906.

Palfrey, Francis W. *The Antietam and Fredericksburg.* NY: Charles Scribner's Sons, 1882.

Park, Robert E. *Sketch of the Twelfth Alabama Infantry of Battle's Brigade, Rodes' Division, Early's Corps, of the Army of Northern Virginia.* W.E. Jones, Book and Job Printer. Richmond. 1906.

Parker, Thomas H. *History of the 51st Regiment of P.V. and V.V., from its Organization, at Camp Curtin, Harrisburg, Pa., in 1861, to its being Mustered out of the United States Service at Alexandria, Va., July 27th, 1865.* Philadelphia:

King & Baird, Printers, 1869.

Pfanz, Harry W. *Gettysburg: Culp's Hill & Cemetery Hill.* The University of North Carolina Press, Chapel Hill, 1993.

Phisterer, Frederick. *New York in the War of Rebellion.* 6 volumes. Albany: J.B. Lyon Co., 1912.

Pickerill, W. N. *History of the Third Indiana Cavalry.* Indianapolis, IN: Aetna Printing Company, 1906.

Pierro, Joseph, ed. *The Maryland Campaign of September 1862: Ezra A. Carman's Definitive Study of the Union and Confederate Armies at Antietam.* London: Routledge, 2008.

Pohanka, Brian. *Vortex of Hell History of the 5th New York Volunteer Infantry.* Lynchburg VA: Schroeder Publications, 2012.

Powell, William. H. *The Fifth Corps.* New York: G. P. Putnam's Sons, 1896.

Priest, John Michael, ed. *Captain James Wren's Diary: From New Bern To Fredericksburg.* Shippensburg, PA: White Mane Publishing Company, 1990.

Raab, Steven S. ed. *With the 3rd Wisconsin Badgers: The Living Experience of the Civil War Through the Journals of Van R. Willard.* Mechanicsburg, PA: Stackpole Books, 1999.

Rankin, Thomas M. *23rd Virginia Infantry.* Lynchburg, VA: H. E. Howard, Inc., 1985.

_____. *37th Virginia Infantry.* Lynchburg, VA: H. E. Howard, Inc., 1987.

Raus, Jr. Edmund J., *Banners South A Northern Community at War.* The Kent State University Press, Kent Ohio, 2005.

Reardon, Carol and Tom Vossler. *A Field Guide to Antietam.* Chapel Hill, NC: The University of North Carolina Press, 2016.

Reed, Thomas. *The Original Iron Brigade.* Madison, NJ: Fairleigh Dickinson University Press, 2011.

Reese, Timothy. *Sykes Regular Infantry Division 1861-1865.* Jefferson NC: McFarland, 1990.

_____. *Sealed with Their Lives: The Battle of Crampton's Gap.* Baltimore, MD: Butternut and Blue, 1998.

Regimental Committee. *History of the One Hundred and Twenty-Fifth Regiment Pennsylvania Volunteers 1862- 1863.* Philadelphia: J. B. Lippincott Company, 1906.

Reidenbaugh, Lowell. *27th Virginia Infantry.* Lynchburg, VA: H. E. Howard, Inc., 1993.

Riggs, Susan A. *21st Virginia Infantry.* Lynchburg, VA: H. E. Howard, Inc., 1991.

Roberson, Elizabeth Whitley. *In Care of Yellow River: The Complete Civil War Letters of Private Eli Pinson Landers to His Mother.* Gretna, LA: Pelican Publishing Company, 1997.

Robertson, James I., Jr. *General A. P. Hill: The Story of a Confederate Warrior.* New York: Random House, 1987.

_____. *Stonewall Jackson, The Man, The Soldier, The Legend.* New York: Macmillan Publishing, 1997.

_____. *The Stonewall Brigade.* Baton Rouge, LA: Louisiana State University Press, 1963.

Ruffner, Kevin C. *44thVirginia Infantry.* Lynchburg, VA: H. E. Howard, 1987.

Sand, Henry. *Crossing Antietam: The Civil War Letters of Captain Henry Augustus Sand, Company A, 103rd New York Volunteers.* Peter H. Sand and John F. McLaughlin, eds. Jefferson, NC: McFarland & Company, Inc., 2016.

Sawyer, Franklin. *A Military History of the 8th Ohio Vol. Inf'y: Its Battles, Marches and Army Movements.* Cleveland, OH: Fairbanks & co.., 1881.

Schenck, Martin. *Up Came Hill: The Story of the Light Division and its Leaders.* Harrisburg, PA: The Stackpole Company, 1958.

Schildt, John W. *The Ninth Corps at Antietam.* Chewsville, MD: n.p., 1988.

_____. *The Twelfth Corps at Antietam.* Brunswick, MD: E. Graphics, 2012.

Schmitt, ed. Martin F. *General George Crook: His Autobiography.* Norman, OK: University of Oklahoma Press, 1946.

Scott, Robert Garth, ed. *Forgotten Valor: The Memoirs, Journals & Civil War Letters of Orlando B. Willcox.* Kent, OH: The Kent State University Press, 1999.

Sears, Stephen W. *Lincoln's Lieutenants: The High Command of the Army of the Potomac.* New York: Houghton, Mifflin Harcourt, 2017.

Seigler, Robert S. *South Carolina's Military Organizations,* 4 volumes. Charleston, SC: The History Press, 2008.

Seville, William P. *History of the First Regiment, Delaware Volunteers, From the Commencement of the "Three Months' Service" to the Final Muster-Out at the Close of the Rebellion.* Wilmington, DE: The Historical Society of Delaware, 1884.

Shaw, Albert D. *A Full Report of the First Re-union and Banquet of the Thirty-Fifth N. Y. Vols.* Times Printing and

Publishing House Watertown N.Y. 1888: Reprint Higginson Book Company Salem Massachusetts 1998.

Sheeran, James B. *Confederate Chaplain: A War Journal*, Joseph T. Durkin, ed. Milwaukee, WI: The Bruce Publishing Company, 1960.

Shaw, Robert Gould. *Blue-Eyed Child of Fortune: The Civil War Letters of Colonel Robert Gould Shaw*. Russell Duncan and William S. McFeely, eds. Athens, GA: The University of Georgia Press, 1992.

Sibley, Jr., F. Ray. *The Confederate Order of Battle: The Army of Northern Virginia*. Shippensburg, PA: White Mane Publishing Company, 1996.

Sifakis, Stewart. *Who Was Who in the Civil War*. New York: Facts on File, 1988.

_____. *Compendium of the Confederate Armies: Alabama*. New York: Facts on File. 1992.

_____. *Compendium of the Confederate Armies: Florida and Arkansas*. New York: Facts on File. 1992.

_____. *Compendium of the Confederate Armies: North Carolina*. New York: Facts on File. 1992.

_____. *Compendium of the Confederate Armies: Virginia*. New York: Facts on File. 1992.

_____. *Compendium of the Confederate Armies: Mississippi*. New York: Facts on File. 1995.

_____. *Compendium of the Confederate Armies: Louisiana*. New York: Facts on File, 1995.

Sloan, John A. *Reminiscences of the Guilford Grays, Co. B, 27th North Carolina Regiment*. Washington, D.C.: R.O. Polkinhorn Printers, 1883.

Small, A. R. *The Sixteenth Maine Regiment in the War of the Rebellion*. Portland, ME: B. Thurston & Company, 1886.

Smith, A. P. *History of the Seventy-Sixth Regiment New York Volunteers: What it Endured and Accomplished*. Cortland, NY: Jacob Miller, Binder, 1866.

Smith, Henry P. ed. *History of Broome County: With Illustrations and Biographical Sketches of Some of Its Prominent Men and Pioneers*. Syracuse, N.Y., D. Mason. 1885.

Smith, J. L. *History of the 118th Pennsylvania Volunteers Corn Exchange Regiment*. Philadelphia, PA: J. L. Smith, 1905.

Snell, Mark A. *From First To Last: The Life of William B. Franklin*. Fordham University Press, New York, 2002.

Sorrel, Moxley. *Recollections of a Confederate Staff Officer*. Bell Irvin Wiley, ed. Jackson, TN: McCowat-Mercer Press, Inc., 1958.

Sparks, David ed. *Inside Lincoln's Army, the Diary of General Marsena Rudolph Patrick, Provost Marshal General, Army of the Potomac*. New York: Thomas Yoseloff, 1964.

Starr, Stephen Z. *The Union Cavalry in the Civil War*. Three volumes. Baton Rouge, LA: Louisiana State University Press, 1979.

Steiner, Lewis H. *Report Of Lewis H. Steiner, M.D., Inspector of the Sanitary Commission*. Randolph, NY: Anson D.F., 1862.

Stevens, George T. *Three Years in the Sixth Corps: A Concise Narrative of Events in the Army of the Potomac from 1861 to the Close of the Rebellion, April, 1865*. New York: D. Van Nostrand, Publisher, 1870.

Stevens, H. S. *Souvenir of Excursion to Battlefields by the Society of the Fourteenth Connecticut Regiment and Union at Antietam, September 1891*. Washington, DC: Gibson Brothers, Printers, 1893.

Stevens, Hazard. *The Life of Isaac Ingalls Stevens*. Two volumes. Boston: Houghton, Mifflin and Company, 1900.

Stocker, Jeffrey D., ed. *From Huntsville to Appomattox: R. T. Coles's History of the 4th Regiment, Alabama Volunteer Infantry, C.S.A., Army of Northern Virginia*. Knoxville, TN: University of Tennessee Press, 1996.

Stone, DeWitt Boyd Jr., ed. *Wandering to Glory: Confederate Veterans Remember Evans' Brigade*. Columbia, SC: South Carolina University Press, 2002.

Stotelmyer, Steven R. *Too Useful To Sacrifice – Reconsidering George B. McClellan's Generalship in the Maryland Campaign from South Mountain to Antietam*. El Dorado Hills, CA: Savas Beatie, 2019.

Stovall, Pleasant A. *Robert Toombs: Statesman, Speaker, Soldier, Sage*. New York: Cassell Publishing Company, 1892.

Stubbs, Steven H. *Duty, Honor, Valor: The Story of the Eleventh Mississippi Infantry Regiment*. Philadelphia, MS: Dancing Rabbit Press, Inc., 2000.

Suarez, Annette. *Source Book On The Early History of Cuthbert & Randolph*. Atlanta: GA: Cherokee Publishing, 1982.

Swain, Glen A. Sr. *The Bloody 7th – Regimental Roster Set*. Wilmington, North Carolina: Broadfoot Publishing

Company, 2014.

Styple, William B. ed. *Writing and Fighting the Civil War: Soldier Correspondence to the New York Sunday Mercury.* Kearney, NJ: Belle Grove Publishing Company, 2000.

Sypher, J. R. *History of the Pennsylvania Reserve Corps.* Lancaster, PA: Elias Barr & Co, 1865.

Tagg, Larry. *The Generals of Gettysburg: The Leaders of America's Greatest Battle.* Mason City, IA: Savas Publishing Company, 1998.

Tate, Thomas K. *General Edwin Vose Sumner, USA.* New York: McFarland & Company, 2013,

Taylor, Paul. *Glory Was Not Their Companion The Twenty-Sixth New York Volunteer Infantry in the Civil War.* Jefferson, NC: McFarland & Company, Inc., 2005.

Tenney, William J. *The Military and Naval History of the Rebellion in the United States.* New York, NY: D. Appleton & Co., 1865.

Tevis, C. V. and D. R. Marquis. *History of the Fighting Fourteenth.* Brooklyn: Brooklyn Eagle, 1911.

*The Union Army.* Nine volumes. Wilmington, NC: Broadfoot Publishing Company, 1997.

*Third Annual Report of the Bureau of Military Statistics of the State of New York.* Transmitted to the Legislature February 3, 1866. Albany, NY: G. Wendell Printer, 1866.

Thomas, Henry W. *History of the Doles-Cook Brigade of Northern Virginia . . .* Atlanta, GA: The Franklin Printing and Publishing Company, 1903.

Thomas, Mary Warner and Richard A. Sauers, eds. *The Civil War Letters of First Lieutenant James B. Thomas, Adjutant 107th Pennsylvania Volunteers.* Baltimore, MD: Butternut & Blue, 1995.

Thomas, M. O'Brien & Oliver Diefendorf. *General Orders of the War Department, Embracing the Years / 1861, 1862 & 1863. Adapted Specifically for the use of the Army and Navy of the United States.* New York, NY: Derby & Miller, 1864.

Thomson, Howard and William H. Rauch, *History of the "Bucktails:" Kane Rifle Regiment of the PA Reserve Corps (13th Pennsylvania Reserves, 42nd of the Line).* Philadelphia, PA: Electric Printing Co., 1906.

Thomson, Orville. *From Philippi to Appomattox: Narrative of the Service of the Seventh Indiana Infantry in the War for the Union.* Baltimore, MD: Butternut & Blue, 1993.

Tidball, John C. and Lawrence M. Kaplan. *Artillery Service in the War of the Rebellion,* 1861-1865. Yardley, PA: Westholme Publishing, 2001.

Todd, William. *The Seventy-ninth Highlanders, New York Volunteers in the War of Rebellion, 1861-1865.* Albany, NY: Brandow, Barton & Co., 1886.

Toombs, Samuel. *Reminiscences of the War: Comprising a Detailed Account of the Experiences of the Thirteenth Regiment New Jersey Volunteers in Camp, on the March, and in Battle.* Orange, NJ: Journal Office, 1878.

Trask, Kerry A. *Fire Within: A Civil War Narrative.* Kent, OH: Kent State University Press, 1995.

Tribble, Byrd Barnett. *Benjamin Cason Rawlings: First Virginia Volunteer for the South.* Baltimore, MD: Butternut and Blue, 1996.

Tucker, Phillip Thomas. *"God Help The Irish!" – The History of the Irish Brigade.* Abilene, TX: McWhiney Foundation Press, 2007.

Tucker, Spencer C. *American Civil War: The Definitive Encyclopedia and Document Collection.* 4 volumes. Santa Barbara, CA: ABC Clio, 2013.

United States War Department: *The War of the Rebellion: A Compilation of the Official Records of the Union and Confederate Armies,* 128 volumes. Washington: U.S. Government Printing Office, 1880-1901.

Ural, Susannah J. *Hood's Texas Brigade.* Louisiana State University Press, Baton Rouge, 2017.

Vautier, John D. *History of the 88th Pennsylvania Volunteers in the War for the Union 1861-1865.* Philadelphia: J.B. Lippincott Company, 1894.

Waitt, Ernest L. *History of the Nineteenth Regiment Massachusetts Volunteer Infantry 1861 -1865.* Salem, MA: The Salem Press, 1906.

Walcott, Charles F. *History of the Twenty-first Regiment, Massachusetts Volunteers, in the War for the Preservation of the Union, 1861-1865: With Statistics of the War and of Rebel Prisons.* Boston: Houghton, Mifflin and Company, 1882.

Walker, Charles D. *Biographical Sketches of the Graduates and Eleves of the Virginia Military Institute.* Philadelphia, PA, J.B. Lippencott & Co., 1875.

Walker, C. Irvine. *The Life of Lieutenant General Richard Heron Anderson*. Charleston, SC: Art Publishing Col, 1917.

Walker, Francis A. *History of the Second Army Corps in the Army of the Potomac*. New York: Charles Scribner's Sons, 1886.

Ward, Joseph R. C. *History of the One-Hundred and Sixth Regiment Pennsylvania Volunteers, 1861-1865*. Philadelphia: Grant, Faires & Rogers, 1906.

Warner, Ezra. *Generals in Gray*. Baton Rouge, LA: Louisiana State University Press, 1959.

_____. *Generals in Blue: Lives of the Union Commanders*. Baton Rouge, LA: Louisiana State University Press, 1991.

Washburn, George H. *Military History and Record of the 108th Regiment, N. Y. Vols., From 1862 to 1984*. Rochester, NY: Press of E. R. Andrews,1894.

Waters, Zack C. and James C. Edmonds. *A Small but Spartan Band*. Tuscaloosa, AL: The University of Alabama Press, 2010.

Wayland, John W. *History of Rockingham County, Virginia*. Dayton, VA: Ruebush-Elkings, 1912.

Welsh, Jack D. *Medical Histories of Confederate Generals*. Kent, OH: The Kent State University Press, 1995.

_____. *Medical Histories of Union Generals*. Kent: OH: Kent State University Press, 1996.

Welcher, Frank J. *The Union Army, 1861 – 1865: Organization and Operations*. Bloomington, IN: Indiana University Press, 1989.

Wert, Jeffry D. *General James Longstreet: The Confederacy's Most Controversial Soldier*. New York: Simon & Schuster, 1993.

Westbrook, Robert S. *History of the 49th Pennsylvania Volunteers*. Altoona, PA: Altoona Times Print, 1897.

Wexler, Fred C. The Tammany Regiment: A History of the Forty-Second New York Volunteer Infantry, 1861-1864. Bloomington, IN: iUniverse, 2016.

White, Gregory. *This Most Bloody & Cruel Drama: A History of the 31st Georgia Volunteer Infantry*. Baltimore: Blue & Gray Publishing Company, 1997.

Whitney, J.H.E. *The Hawkins Zouaves: (Ninth N. Y. V.) Their Battles and Marches*. New York: Published by author, 1866.

Wiggins, III, Clyde G., ed. *My Dear Friend: The Civil War Letters of Alva Benjamin Spencer, 3rd Georgia Regiment, Company C*. Macon, GA: Mercer University Press, 2007.

Wilkinson, Warren and Steven E. Woodworth, *A Scythe of Fire: A Civil War Story of the Eighth Georgia Infantry Regiment*. New York: William Morrow, 2002.

Williams, Alpheus S. *From the Cannon's Mouth: The Civil War Letters of General Alpheus S. Williams*, Milo M. Quaife, ed. Lincoln, NB: University of Nebraska Press, 1995.

Wilmer, L. Allison, J.H. Harrett, George H. Vernon, State Commissioners. *History and Roster of Maryland Volunteers, War of 1861-5*, Two volumes. Baltimore: Press of Guggenheimer, Weil & Co, 1898.

Wilson, Lawrence. *Itinerary of the Seventh Ohio Volunteer Infantry, 1861-1864*. New York & Washington: The Neale Publishing Company, 1907.

Wise, George. *History of the Seventeenth Virginia Infantry, C.S.A.* Baltimore, MD: Kelly, Piet & Company, 1870.

Wistar, Isaac J. *Autobiography of Isaac Jones Wistar, 1827-1905*. Philadelphia: Wistar Institute of Anatomy and Biology, 1937.

Wood, Gilbert G. et al. *History of the Sixth New York (Second Ira Harris Guard) Second Brigade, First Division, Cavalry Corps Army of the Potomac 1861-1865*. Worcester, MA: The Blanchard Press, 1908.

Wood, William Nathaniel. *Reminiscences of Big I*. Jackson, TN: McCowat-Mercer Press, Inc., 1956.

Woodbury, Augustus. *Major General Ambrose E. Burnside and the Ninth army Corps: a Narrative of Campaigns in North Carolina, Maryland, Virginia, Ohio, Kentucky, Mississippi and Tennessee, During the War for the Preservation of the Republic*. Providence, RI: Sidney S. Rider & Brother, 1867.

Woodward, E.M. *Our Campaigns: The Marches, Bivouacs, Battles, Incidents of Camp Life, and History of our Regiment during its three Years Term of Service*. Philadelphia, PA: John E. Potter, Publisher, 1865.

Worsham, John H. *One of Jackson's Foot Cavalry: His Experience and What he Saw during the War 1861-1865*. New York: Neale Publishing Company, 1912.

Wyckoff, Mac *A History of the 2nd South Carolina Infantry: 1861-65*. Fredericksburg, VA: Sergeant Kirkland's Museum and Historical Society, 1994.

_____. *The Third South Carolina Infantry, 1861-1865*. Fredericksburg, VA: Sergeant Kirkland's Museum and

Historical Society, Inc., 1998.

Yates, ed., Walter J. *Souvenir of Excursion to Antietam and Dedication of Monuments of the 8th, 11th, 14th and 16th Regiments of Connecticut Volunteers.* New London, CT: n.p., 1894.

Young, William and Patricia. *56th Virginia Infantry.* Lynchburg, VA: H. E. Howard, 1991.

## Articles and Essays

Amrine, John. *The National Tribune*, March 10, 1910.

Anderson, Thomas. "The Reserve at Antietam." *Century Magazine*, vol. 32, no. 5 (1886), 783.

Arnold, Jennie Porter. "At Antietam." *National Tribune*, October 18, 1888.

Baker, James A. "Lives of the Governors of Minnesota." *Collections of the Minnesota Historical Society*, vol. XIII (1908), 50-55.

Barnes, Edward L. "The 95th New York." *National Tribune*, January 7, 1886.

Beale, George W. "The Cavalry Fight at Boonsboro' Graphically Described." *Southern Historical Society Papers*, vol. 25 (1897), 276-80.

Benning, Henry "Notes by General H. L. Benning on Battle of Sharpsburg." in *Southern Historical Society Papers*, vol. 16, (1888), 393-95.

Breen, Patrick. "Why the Union Army Did Not Win at Antietam." *National Tribune* April 18, 1895.

Brooks, Charles E. "Popular Sovereignty in the Confederate Army: The Case of Colonel John Marshall and the Fourth Texas Infantry Regiment." In *The view from the Ground Experiences of Civil War Soldiers*, edited by Aaron Sheehan - Dean. Lexington: University of Kentucky Press, 2007.

Casey, James, ed. "The Ordeal of Adoniram Judson Warner, His Minutes of South Mountain and Antietam." *Civil War History*, vol. XXVII, no. 3 (1982), 213-36.

Clemens, Tom. "'Black Hats'" Off to the Original 'Iron Brigade." *Columbiad*, vol. 1, Number 1, (Spring, 1997), 46-58.

_____. "'Too Bad, Poor Fellows:' Joseph K. Mansfield and the XII Corps at Antietam." in *Corps Commanders in Blue: Union Major Generals in the Civil War.* Ethan S. Rafuse, ed. Baton Rouge, LA: Louisiana State University Press, 2014.

Comstock, Cyrus B. "Memoir of John Newton, 1823-1895." A Biographical Memoir Read before the National Academy, November 13, 1901. *National Academy of Sciences. Biographical Memories* (National Academy of Sciences. Washington D.C. 1902), Vol. IV, 233- 40.

Cox, Jacob D. "The Battle of Antietam." in *Battles and Leaders*, vol. 2, 630-60.

Cox, Jacob D. "Forcing Fox's Gap and Turner's Gap." in *Battles and Leaders of the Civil War*, vol. 2, 583-90.

Crowninshield, Benjamin W. "Cavalry in Virginia During the War of the Rebellion." *Journal of the Military Service Institution*, vol. 12 (May 1891), 527-51.

D'Aoust, Maurice. "Unraveling the Myths of Burnside Bridge." *Civil War Times*, XLVI, Vol. 7 (September 2007), 50-57.

_____. "'Little Mac' did not Dawdle," *Civil War Times*, October 2012, 36-37.

Davis, Steven R. "'. . . Like Leaves in an Autumn Wind': The 11th Mississippi Infantry in the Army of Northern Virginia." *Civil War Regiments*, vol. 2, no. 4 (1992), 269-312.

Evans, Thomas H. "The Enemy Sullenly Held on to the City." *Civil War Times Illustrated*, April, 1968, 32.

Fogle, Theodore T. "Bloodletting at Burnside Bridge." *America's Civil War*, September 2015, 18.

Fortin, Maurice S. ed. "Colonel Hilary A. Herbert's 'History of the Eighth Alabama Volunteer Regiment, C.S.A.'" *Alabama Historical Quarterly*, vol. XXXIX (1977), 5-321.

Fox, William F. "Slocum and His Men: A History of the Twelfth and Twentieth Army Corps." in *In Memoriam Henry Warner Slocum, 1826-1894.* Albany, New York, J.B. Lyon Company, Printers, 1904.

Franklin, William B. "Notes on Crampton's Gap and Antietam." *Battles and Leaders of the Civil War*, vol. 2, 591-597.

Gordon, Leslie J. "All Who Went into That Battle Were Heroes: Remembering the 16th Regiment Connecticut Volunteers at Antietam." in *The Antietam Campaign*, Gary W. Gallagher, ed. Chapel Hill, NC: The University of North Carolina Press, 1999, 169-91.

Gorman, George, ed. "Capt. John Calvin Gorman: 2nd North Carolina, Memoirs of a Rebel." *Military Images*,

Nov/Dec 1981, 4-5.

Graham, Kurt. "Death of a Brigade." Society of the Descendants of Frederick Fox Newsletter, 1/9: 1-10.

Gratten, George D. "The Battle Of Boonsboro Gap Or South Mountain." *Southern Historical Society Papers*, vol. 39, No. 1 (April 1914), 39-44.

Hill, Daniel and James Irwin, ed. "Gen. George Burgwyn Anderson." *The Land We Love*. vol. 3, no. 2 (1867), 93-100.

Hill, D.H. "The Lost Dispatch- Letter from General D.H. Hill." *Southern Historical Society Papers*, vol. XIII, (1885), 420-23.

Hill, Daniel H. "The Battle of South Mountain or Boonsboro." *Battles & Leaders of the Civil War*, vol. 2, 557-81.

Holsworth, Jerry W. "Uncommon Valor, Hood's Texas Brigade in the Maryland Campaign." *Blue & Gray Magazine*, August 1996, 6- 55.

Hopkins, C. A. Porter, ed., "The James J. Archer Letters." *Maryland Historical Magazine*, vol. 56, no. 2 (June, 1961), 125-149.

Hubbert, Mike M. "The Travels of the 13th Mississippi Regiment: Excerpts from the Diary of Mike M. Hubbert of Attala County (1861-1862)." *Journal of Mississippi History* vol. 45 (1983), 306.

Hunter, Alexander. "A High Private's Sketch of Sharpsburg." *Southern Historical Society Papers*, vol. XI, no. 1 (January, 1883), 10-21.

Lee, Stephen D. "Who Fired the First Gun at Sumter?" *Southern Historical Society Papers*, vol. 9 (1881), 501-02.

Longstreet, James. "The Invasion of Maryland." *Battles & Leaders of the Civil War*, vol. 2, 663-74.

Krick, Robert K. "It Appears as Though Mutual Extermination Would Put a Stop to the Awful Carnage: Confederates in Sharpsburg's Bloody Lane." in *The Antietam Campaign*, Gary Gallagher, ed. Chapel Hill, NC: The University of North Carolina Press, 1999), 223-258.

Mellot, David W. "A Dear Bought Name: The 7th West Virginia Infantry's Assault on Bloody Lane." *Civil War Regiments*, vol. 5, no. 3 (1997), 124-50.

Mockbee, Robert T. "The 14th Tennessee Infantry Regiment." *Civil War Regiments,* vol. 5, No. 1 (1995), 1-44.

Motlow, Felix. "Campaigns in Northern Virginia." *Confederate Veteran*, vol. XI, no. 10, 310.

Nolan, Alan T. and Marc Storch, "The Iron Brigade Earns its Name." *Blue and Gray Magazine*, vol. XXI, Issue 6 (2004), 6-50.

O'Grady, W.L.D. "88th Regiment Infantry." in *New York at Gettysburg*, Three volumes. Albany, NY: J.B. Lyon Co., 1900, 510-516.

Porter, Fitz John. "Memoranda on the Civil War: 'The Reserve at Antietam.'" *Century Magazine*, vol. 33, no. 3 (1887).

Powell, William H. "Memoranda on the Civil War: More Light on the Reserve at Antietam." *Century Magazine* 33, no. 5 (March 1887), 804.

Saunders, James Edmonds. "Sketch of Wilcox's Brigade. By Gen. Cadmus Marcellus Wilcox." *Publications of the Alabama Historical Society*, vol. 3, 141.

Snell, Mark A. "Baptism of Fire: The 118th ('Corn Exchange') Pennsylvania Infantry at the Battle of Shepherdstown." *Civil War Regiments: A Journal of the American Civil War*, vol. 6, no. 2 (1998), 119-42.

Spooner, Henry J. "The Maryland Campaign with the Fourth Rhode Island." MOLLUS, *Personal Narratives of Events in the War of the Rebellion, Being Papers Read Before the Rhode Island Soldiers and Sailors Historical Society* (n.p; Published by the Society, 1903), vol. 9, 211-35.

Stickley, E. E. "Battle of Sharpsburg." *Confederate Veteran*, vol. XXII (1914), 66-67.

Sumner, Samuel S. "The Antietam Campaign." *Papers of the Historical Society of Massachusetts*. Wilmington, NC: Broadfoot Publishing Company, 1990.

Thompson, David L. "With Burnside at Antietam," in *Battles and Leaders*, vol. 2, 660-62.

_____. "In the Ranks to the Antietam," in *Battles and Leaders of the Civil War*, vol. II, 556-58.

Toney, Keith. "'Dying As Brave Men Should Die': The Attack and Defense of Burnside Bridge." *Civil War Regiments*, vol. 6, no. 2: 89-118.

Trimpi, Helen. "Lafayette McLaws' Aide-De-Camp: the Maryland Campaign Diary of Captain Henry Lord Page King." *Civil War Regiments*, vol. 6, No. 2 (1998), 23-57.

Williams, T. Harry, ed. "The Civil War Letters of William Cage." *Louisiana Historical Quarterly*, vol. XXXIX, number 1 (January, 1956), 122.

**Internet**

**13th Mississippi Infantry Regiment Website**
https://13thmississippi.com/2011/03/15/battles-sharpsburg (Albert Wymer Henley diary)
**48th Pennsylvania Volunteer Infantry Website**
https://48thpennsylvania.blogspot.com/2008/09/getting-to-know-eliakim-parker-scammon.html (Eliakim Scammon)
https://48thpennsylvania.blogspot.com/2009/11/brigadier-general-edward-harland.html (Edward Harland)
**American Battlefield Trust**
https://www.battlefields.org/learn/biographies/oliver-o-howard (Oliver O. Howard)
**Antietam Brigades (Kevin Pawlak)**
http://antietambrigades.blogspot.com/2019/02/close-and-concentrated-9th-corps.html ("Close and Concentrated: 9th Corps Artillery Conquers the Burnside Bridge")
**Antietam on the Web**
http://antietam.aotw.org/officers.php?unit_id=520&from=results (Andrew's Sharpshooters)
http://antietam.aotw.org/officers.php?unit_id=617 (23rd Virginia Infantry)
https://antietam.aotw.org/officers.php?unit_id=8 (Barkdale's Brigade)
https://antietam.aotw.org/officers.php?officer_id=709 (William Parham)
**Arlington Cemetery**
http://www.arlingtoncemetery.net/ssturgis.htm   (Daniel Sturgis)
**California Military Department, California State Military History and Museums Program**
http://www.militarymuseum.org/69thPA.html (69 th Pennsylvania Infantry)
**Civil War Data Base**
http://www.civilwardata.com/active/hdsquery.dll?SoldierHistory?U&587108
**First Minnesota Volunteer Infantry Regiment Website**
http://www.1stminnesota.net/#/soldier/1029  (Richard L. Gorman entry)
http://www.1stminnesota.net/#/soldier/1238 (Willis A. Gorman entry)
**Gordon, Lesley J. "Bad Luck Regiment: The 16th Connecticut Infantry."**
https://www.historynet.com/bad-luck-regiment-the-16th-connecticut-infantry.htm;
**Graham, Kurt. "Death of a Brigade: Drayton's Brigade at Fox's Gap, September 14, 1862.**
http://www.angelfire.com/ga2/PhillipsLegion/deathofabrigade.html.
**Hall-Caldwell, BetteJo. "Col. James A. Suiter, 34th NY Volunteer Infantry."**
https://herkimer.nygenweb.net/herktown/colsuiter.html
**Hickman, Kennedy. "***American Civil War: Brigadier General John C. Caldwell***, ThoughtCo.**
thoughtco.com/brigadier-general-john-c-caldwell-2360391
**Historical Data Systems, Inc.**
http://civilwardata.com/active/product.html (Index)
http://www.civilwardata.com/active/hdsquery.dll?SoldierHistory?U&1443356 (William Christian entry)
http://www.civilwardata.com/active/hdsquery.dll?Officer?261&U (John Brooke entry)
http://civilwardata.com/active/hdsquery.dll?SoldierHistory?U&1321106 (Richard Gorman entry)

**Massachusetts Historical Society**
http://www.masshist.org/collection-guides/digitized/fa0370/vol5#32 (Norwood Penrose Hallowell Papers, 1764-1914, Scrapbook Vol. 5, 1861-1885)
**McCormack, Joseph. "Father William Corby."**
 c7da7bf7-3797-4e70-8593-d038c30b3fa9.filesusr.com/ugd/5f59bb_8aa38c77764f4e3884006855e39624d0.pdf
**Mississippi Encyclopedia, Center for Study of Southern Culture**
https://mississippiencyclopedia.org/entries/william-barksdale/ (William Barksdale)
**Moses, Rachel. "'[A]s He Lived for Others, So Did He Die:' The Life of Israel B. Richardson."**

https://www.civilwarmed.org/richardson/
**National Park Service, Manassas Site**
https://www.nps.gov/mana/learn/historyculture/order-of-battle.htm (Second Bull Run Order of Battle)
**National Park Service, Monocacy Site**
https://www.nps.gov/mono/learn/historyculture/an-invitation-to-battle.htm (Special Orders Number 191)
**New York State Military Museum and Veterans Research Center**
https://dmna.ny.gov/historic/reghist/civil/infantry/108thInf/Porter_Letters/1862_09_20.pdf (108th New York Infantry Regiment)
**O. Wilson Link Museum (History Museum of Western Virginia)**
https://hswv.pastperfectonline.com/archive/56C0EF56-C2A3-4F31-AC68-798584273832 (John Parham Talks Before the A.P. Hill Camp of Confederate Veterans, September 6, 1894)
**Ohio Civil War Central**
http://www.www.ohiocivilwarcentral.com/entry.php?rec=1246 (30th Regiment Ohio Volunteer Infantry)
http://www.www.ohiocivilwarcentral.com/entry.php?rec=985 (Hugh Boyle Ewing**)**
**Pennsylvania State Archives**
http://www.digitalarchives.state.pa.us (Civil War Veterans' Card File, 1861-1866)
**Sedgwick, Hubert M. comp. "A Sedgwick Genealogy: Descendants of Deacon Benjamin Sedgwick**
http://www.sedgwick.org/na/families/robert1613/B/2/9/2/B292-sedgwick-gen-john-article.html
**Tim Ware Website**
https://mountainaflame.blogspot.com/2010/12/artillery-on-mountain-federal.html (Artillery on the Mountain: Federal)
**United States House of Representatives**
https://history.house.gov/Historical-Highlights/1851-1900/The-most-infamous-floor-brawl-in-the-history-of-the-U-S--House-of-Representatives/#:~:text=This%20Frank%20Leslie's%20Illustrated%20sketch,night%20of%20February%205%2D6. ("The Most Infamous Floor Brawl in the History of the U.S. House of Representatives,")
**University of Michigan (Bentley Library)**
https://deepblue.lib.umich.edu/handle/2027.42/100349?show=full (Elon G. Mills Diary)
**University of North Carolina (Southern Historical Collection)**
https://finding-aids.lib.unc.edu/05422 (Harrison Wells letter)
**Wofford University—"Digital Commons"**
https://digitalcommons.wofford.edu/littlejohnmclaws/9/ (Letter: Lafayette McLaws to Isaac R. Pennypacker, August 30, 1889)

# INDEX

Cooperstown, NY, 111

Coppens, George, 253

Corby, William, 77

Corning, Joseph, 144

Cost, John, 59

Cothran, George, 198, 199, 403 (note 70)

Couch, Darius, and his division, 127, 128, 129, 130, 145, 146, 213, 377, 382

Coulter, Richard, 45, 51, 52, 53, 54, 311

Cowan, Andrew, 141, 403 (note 70)

Cowtan, Charles, 124, 126

Cox, Jacob, and his corps/division, 147, 148, 150, 178, 179, 180; South Mountain, 152, 155, 156, 171, 181, 185, 350, 352, 361, 365, 369; Antietam, 149, 157, 172, , 182, 183, 186, 187, 265, 380, 399 (note 5)

Crampton's Gap, 128; Confederates, 214, 220, 221, 227, 228, 229, 230, 231, 232, 237, 240, 243, 246, 247, 253, 373, 274, 376, 382, 383, 416 (notes 62, 63), 419 (note 20); Union, 129, 130, 131, 132, 134, 135, 136, 137, 138, 140, 142, 143, 169, 225, 403 (note 63),

Crawford, Samuel, and his brigade, 61, 190, 191, 192, 193, 194, 195, 196, 198, 301, 354, 410 (note 19), 411 (note 33)

Crewel, Philip, 87

Crook, George, and his brigade, 148, 149, 157, 159, 161, 175, 178, 179, 180, 182, 184, 185, 186, 187, 188

Cross, Edward, 73, 74, 75, 76

Cross Keys, Battle of, 317

Crouse, Frederick, 194

Crowder, John, 310, 312

Crutchfield, Stapleton, 306

Cumming, Alfred, 241, 242, 243, 244, 245, 249, 253, 278

Cumming, John, 260, 261

Curtin, Andrew, 26, 65, 127, 160

Cutts, A.S. and his battalion, 36, 355, 356, 434 (note 4), 437 (note 105)

Dana, Napoleon, and his brigade, 70, 83, 84, 85, 86, 87, 88, 91, 93, 94, 95, 96, 233, 397 (note 177)

Daniel, Junius, and his brigade, 280

Darby, George, 63

Davies, Thomas, 134, 137

Davis, Benjamin, 234, 376, 377

Davis, Jefferson, 248, 257, 263, 307, 323, 334, 337, 342, 352, 364, 421 (note 11), 433 (note 18)

Davis, Walter, 113

Davis, William, 222

Dawes, Rufus, 33, 40, 42, 43, 296, 312, 385 (note 38)

Delaney, John, 48

Delaware Units: *Infantry: 1st*, 98, 104, 105, 106, 107, 108, 230, 358, 398 (note 219); *2nd*, 75, 80, 81; *3rd*, 95, 209

Dennison, William, 178, 179

DeRosset, William, 353, 435 (note 25)

DeSaussure, William, 264, 265

Devereux, Arthur, 96

Dickert, D. Augustus, 223, 224, 225

Dingle, J.H., 296

Dinkins, James, 235, 237, 238

District of Columbia Units: *Infantry, 2nd*, 114

Dix, John 105

Doles, George, 353, 354,

Donaldson, Francis, 113

Dooley, John, 272, 273

Douglass, Marcellus, and his brigade, 295, 306, 307, 308, 309; Harpers Ferry, 307, 308, 313; takes position at Antietam, 42, 310, 317, 318, 321, 341; fights Doubleday's troops, 43, 312, 347; fights Ricketts' troops, 45, 48, 49,

Hayes, Joseph, 113

Haynes, Draughton, 336

Hays, Harry, and his brigade, 307, 308, 319, 320, 321, 430 (note 52); Harpers Ferry, 313, 317, preliminary movements, 306, 311, 341; Cornfield, 45, 51, 54, 55, 318; withdrawal, 319, 322

Head, George, 123

Heintzelman, Samuel, 127, 134,

Hemmingen, John, 103

Henagan, John, 224,

Henley, Albert, 221, 235, 236, 238

Herbert, Hilary, 242, 243, 244, 419 (note 9)

Hickman, Charles, 92

Higgins, Jacob, 194, 196

Higginson, H., 212

Hill, A.F., 56

Hill, A.P., and his division, 150, 271, 305, 313, 322, 323, 324, 327, 330, 331, 332, 335, 336, 424 (note 74), 428 (note 4); Harpers Ferry, 282, 306, 308, 328, 329, 334; Antietam, 125, 149, 151, 157, 159, 168, 170, 174, 176, 183, 187, 258, 261, 262, 267, 276, 280, 326, 337, 409 (note 133); Shepherdstown, 111, 113, 116, 123, 307, 316, 333, 337, 383

Hill, Archibald, 63, 64, 65

Hill, Ashbel, 300

Hill, D.H., and his division, 26, 115, 218, 227, 257, 270, 322, 349, 350, 351, 360, 421 (note 11); preliminary movements, 277, 279, 355, 375; to the South Mountain fight, 217, 291, 365, 368; Fox's Gap, 153, 155, 156, 175, 179, 264, 265, 294, 352, 362; Frosttown Plateau/Gap, 36, 302, 303, 356, 357; Turner's Gap, 214, 369, 378, 434 (notes 3, 4, 8); to Antietam, 128, 221, 292, 363, 373, 414 (note 6); Cornfield/East Woods, 27, 28, 68, 198, 200, 297, 319, 354, 364, 435 (note 23); Sunken Road, 73, 78, 97, 100, 143, 241, 253, 358, 367; post Sunken Road action, 75, 76, 145, 146, 230, 254, 278, 359

Hill, Henry, 146

Hildt, George, 183

Hilton, M., 304

Hinck, Edward, 93, 96, 396 (note 173)

Hirst, Benjamin, 102

Hitchcock, Frederick, 99, 100, 101

Hobson, Edwin, 358, 359

Hoffman Farm, 59, 198

Hofmann, William, and his brigade, 29, 30, 35

Holmes, Oliver, 95, 396 (note 170)

Holmes, Theophilus, 280

Holmes, William, 168, 260, 261

Holmesburg, PA, 39

Holsinger, Frank, 64

Hood, John, and his division, 61, 216, 221, 277, 278, 291, 291, 292, 293, 294, 298, 302, 303, 306, 310, 317, 333, 347, 391 (note 188), 428 (note 3); South Mountain, 59, 166, 217, 258, 295, 353, 407 (note 70); preliminary actions at Antietam, 16, 60, 370; advance, 33, 37, 38, 43, 45, 56, 64, 124, 153, 296, 300, 312, 319, 322, 348; Cornfield fight, 27, 30, 57, 68, 218, 299, 308; retreat, 65, 199, 202, 301, 363

Hooker, Joseph, and his corps, 26, 27, 28, 33, 45, 55, 56, 66, 384 (notes 1, 7, 8), 428 (note 41);preliminary actions, 52, 62, 69, 99; South Mountain, 29, 31, 34, 41, 58, 59, 152, 155, 294; preparation for battle of Antietam, 32, 53, 70, 84, 189, 190, 194, 201, 370, 399 (note 5);Antietam, 37, 38, 49, 57, 60, 61, 64, 67, 68, 195, 196, 198, 207, 292, 296, 299, 300, 311

Hope, James, 84

Hopkinson, Oliver, 107

Houghton, William, 101

Howard, Oliver, and his brigade, 70, 83, 89, 90, 142; preliminary actions, 84, 86; defeat, 88, 91, 92, 93, 94, 95, 394 (notes 127, 135), 395 (notes 138, 149, 150); aftermath, 85, 96

Howe, Church, 86

Hubbert, Mike, 235, 248

Hudson, Henry, 85, 88, 96

Hunt, Charles, 94

Hyattstown, MD, 83, 117, 134, 212, 373, 375,

Hyde, Thomas, 145, 146, 403 (note 85), 404 (notes 88, 90, 91, 92)

Illinois Units: *Infantry: 23rd,* 77; *Cavalry: 8th,* 211, 212, 213, 376, 379, 381, 382

Indiana Units: *Infantry: 7th,* 33, 34, 35, 424 (note 84); *14th,* 98, 99, 100, 101, 102, *19th,* 37, 38, 39, 41, 43, 44, 338, 339, 341, 343, 347, 348, 354, 369, 370, 433 (note 15), *27*th, 197, 198, 371

Ingham, James, 154

Irish, Hugh, 199, 411 (note 46)

Irwin, William, and his brigade, 98, 129, 136, 140, 141, 143, 144, 145, 146, 403 (note 82), 404 (notes 89, 90, 92)

Iverson, Alfred, 304, 362, 364, 371

Jackson, J., 43

Jackson, Conrad, 66

Jackson, Lyman, 186

Jackson, Samuel, 57, 68, 390 (note 191)

Jackson, Thomas, and his wing, 40, 44, 62, 99, 131, 189, 218, 248, 256, 268, 283, 305, 306, 307, 317, 337, 340, 342, 345, 346, 349, 389 (note 176), 390 (note 187), 433 (note 18); Union orders about, 128; To Frederick, 213, 216, 323, 359, 372, 428 (notes 3, 4); To Harpers Ferry, 217, 223, 236, 308, 313, 325, 343, 373, 381; Harpers Ferry, 220, 225, 237, 281, 282, 320, 338, 360, 368, 374; To Antietam/pre-fight, 27, 221, 232, 285, 288, 292, 295, 310, 314, 324, 335, 341, 350; Antietam, 226, 252, 289, 293, 315, 316, 321, 339, 380; after Antietam, 309, 322

James, George, 263, 265

Jardine, Edward, 171, 174

Jefferson, MD, 128, 130, 135, 137, 140, 143, 169, 171, 214, 231, 281, 373. 382

Jenkins, Micah, and his brigade, 257, 258, 270, 274; South Mountain, 217, 269, 379; Antietam, 156, 172, 260, 265, 266, 267, 273, 304

Jennings, R.P., 345

Johnson, Bradley, 338, 342,

Johnson, Charles, 172, 173

Jones, Austin, 325

Jones, Collom, 234, 417 (note 99)

Jones, D.R , and his division, 217, 257, 263, 271, 274, 276, 298, 408 (note, 108); to South Mountain, 277, 291; South Mountain, 36, 218, 269, 352; Antietam, 149, 176, 216, 258, 266, , 270, 279, 304, 306, 328

Jones, Henry, 177

Jones, J.R., and his division, 27, 305, 306, 337, 338, 342, 343, 432 (note 3); Harpers Ferry, 346, 347; Antietam, 29, 37, 43, 195, 210, 296, 308, 311, 314, 315, 339, 341, 345, 348, 428 (note 42)

Jones, Robert, 254, 255

Jones, Samuel, 276

Jones, Theodore, 184, 432 (note 45)

Jones, Watters, 311

Johnston, Albert, 250

Johnston, David, 272, 273, 423 (notes 70, 71, 74)

Johnston, James, 428 (note 42)

Johnston, Joseph, 248, 372, 421 (note 11)

Kearny, Phil, 127, 132, 246

Kearse, Francis, 266, 267

Keedysville, MD, I Corps, 26, 47, 50, 53, 59, 63, 67; II Corps, 69, 72, 78, 81, 84, 97, 99, 102, 105; V Corps, 111; VI Corps, 129, 136, 139, 142; XII Corps, 192, 194, 198; Pleasonton's division, 214, 215; Confederates, 220, 270, 303, 357, 370, 376, 379

Kelly, Henry, 113

Kelly, Patrick, 79

Kemper, James, and his brigade, 257, 258, 271, 423 (note 67); South Mountain, 29, 31, 34, 36, 217, 269, 270, 272, 275; Antietam, 173, 177, 261, 262, 265, 267, 273, 274, 276

Kennedy, John, 224, 226, 416 (note 56)

170, 174, 193, 271; Maryland Campaign, 65, 73, 108, 213, 272

Line Farm, 64 190, 201, 204, 207

Little, F.H., 279 , 424 (note 90)

Lockhart, John, 91, 395 (note 140)

Long Bridge, 130, 132, 134, 137, 143, 150, 204

Longstreet, James, and his wing, 52, 115, 128, 216, 217, 240, 258, 263, 271, 283, 291, 305, 323; initial actions during Maryland Campaign, , 219, 220, 236, 302, 310, 360, 373, 376, 378, 380; march to South Mountain, 36, 155, 257, 259, 264, 275, 277, 292, 298, 423 (note 58); South Mountain, 50, 269, 270, 350; activities prior to Antietam, 118, 303, 414 (notes 6, 7); Antietam, 129, 144, 153, 218, 241, 278, 285, 293, 316, , 358; rallies troops at Antietam,  75, 76, , 286

Louisiana Units: *Infantry: 1st Batt.,* 301; *1st,* 346, 348; *2nd,* 346, 347, 348; *5th,* 319, 320; *6th,* 319, 320; *7th,* 319, 320, 346; *8th,* 319, 321; *9th,* 319, 322, 346, 348; *10th,* 346; *15th,* 346, 347, 348*; Artillery: Moody's,* 154, 199, 270, 275, 401 (note 81)*; Miller's,* 76, 218; *Squires',* 154, 401 (note 81)

Loudoun Heights, 237, 281, 282, 284, 287, 288, 306, 335,

Love, D.C., 299

Lovell, Charles, and his brigade, 110, 112, 116, 118, 119, 120, 121, 122, 123, 125, 153, 154, 337, 400 (notes 47, 62, 74, 75)

Lowe, John, 309, 312

Lower Bridge, 116, 125, 126, 161, 164, 358; deployments, 148, 169, 172, 173, 259, 265, 266, 275, 276, 282, 292, 374, 380, 383, 408 (note 108), 423 (note 74); attack on, 151, 153, 159, 166,  168, 170, 175, 179, 182, 186, 260, 273; capture/crossing, 110, 11, 156, 187, 218

Luse, Richard, 235, 418 (note 131)

Lyle, Peter, 45, 50, 51, 54

Lynch, James, 91

Lyman, Chauncey, 63

Lynchburg, VA, 283, 355, 359

MacThomson, James, 47, 48, 387 (note 104)

MacRae, William, 230, 416 (note 74)

Magilton, Albert, and his brigade, 62, , 389 (note 176), 390 (note 183); South Mountain, 56, 58, 63, 67, 302, 303; Antietam, 57, 59, 64, 65, 68, 195, 300

Magruder, J.B.. 291

Mahone, William, and his brigade. 130, 132, 135, 228, 231, 240, 245, 246, 253, 355, 373, 382

Maine Units: *Infantry: 3rd,* 90; *5th,* 134, 235, 136, 138, 402 (notes 45, 46); *6th,* 141; *7th,* 129, 141, 143, 144, 145, 146, 244, 278, 421 (note 60); *10th,* 190, 193, 195, 197, 301, 319, *11th,* 73; *16th,* 52*; Cavalry: 1st,* 211, 213

Malvern Hill, Battle of, Confederate actions, 231, 235, 245, 250, 276, 280, 287, 291, 298, 321, 337, 340, 346, 349, 355, 426 (note 37); Union actions, 57, 77, 114, 134, 137, 141, 142, 211

Manassas Junction, VA, 62, 66, 317

Manning, Van, and his brigade, 280,  283, , 287; Harpers Ferry, 284; Antietam, 81, 98, 144, 202, 203, 205, 208, 218, 230, 282, , 285, 286, 289

Mansfield, Joseph, and his corps, 189, 197, 198, 207, 209; preliminary actions; 27, 70, 90, 125, 190, 192, 194, 195, 198, 201, 204, 410 (notes 5, 6); in the fight at Antietam, 65, 300, 301

Marsh, Solomon, 263, 264

Marsh, Walcott, 175

Marshall, John, 125

Martin, "Howdy", 295

Martin, William, 376, 377

Martin, Willis, 310

Martinsburg, VA, 277, 279, 346, 377, 419 (note 12); Confederate plans/approach, 290, 305, 306, 322, 338, 344; Confederates enter, 307, 320, 325, 332, 336, 340, 347, 348, 380, 433 (note 31)

Maryland Heights, 129, 306, 335; McLaws' division, 219, 220, 223, 224, 225, 227, 229, 231, 232, 236, 237, 415 (note 28); Anderson's division, 240, 242, 245, 249; Walker's division, 281, 282

Maryland Units: *Infantry: 2nd,* 158, 159, 160, 161, 162, 163, 260, 387 (note 95), 406 (note 45); *3rd,* 206, 207, 208; *5th,* 103, 104, 105, 106, 107, 108, 358, 398 (note 234); *Purnell Legion,* 192, 203, 209, 210, 211, 289, 315*; Artillery: Wolcott's,* 145, 404 (note 88)

Massachusetts Units: *Infantry: 2nd,* 192, 197, 198, 199, 200, 203, 282, 288, 426 (note 47); *9th,* 114; *12th,* 53, 54, 55, 321, 388 (note 132); *13th,* 53, 54, 321; *15th,* 83, 85, 86, 87, 88, 92, 95, 222, 233, 316, 396 (note 172); *18th,* 112, 113, *19th,* 70, 88, 89, 93, 94, 96, 234; *20th,* 93, 94, 95, *21st,* 164, 165, 166, 167, 168, 406 (note 60); *22nd,* 113, *28th,* 151, 153, 154; *29th,* 72, 76, 77, 78, 79, 80, 241; *32nd,* 114; *35th,* 158, 164, 165, 166, 168, 187, 262, 406 (note 60), 407 (notes 67, 69, 70); *Cavalry: 1st,* 211, 212, 213, 215, 287, 372, 376, 378; *Cook's,* 152, 155, 156

Matthews, Ezra, 50, 300, 318

McCall, George, 65, 66, 390 (notes 187, 188)

McCalmont, John, 65

McClelen, Bailey, 243

McClellan, George, 28, 35, 62, 65, 77, 109, 111, 127, 191, 385; background, 121, 214, 140, 141, 147, 193, 256, 389 (note 176); 390 (note 187); given command/early activities, 47, 80, 97, 117, 151, 158, 164, 178, 180, 201, 211, 212, 410 (note 1); march to Frederick, 26, 213, 373, 381, 382; Frederick to South Mountain, 128, 217, 240, 255, 439 (note 37); South Mountain, 41, 57, 137, 246; to the banks of Antietam Creek, 50, 83, 102, 115, 118, 148, 198; activities prior to the battle of Antietam, 27, 59, 69, 70, 99, 100, 103, 169, 189; Antietam, 60, 110, 116, 120, 129, 136, 149, 157, 176, 214, 215, 393 (note 83), 399 (note 5), 399 (note 7); post-Antietam, 73, 406 (note 40)

McCorkle, W.H., 329

McCrimmon, Robert, 261

McDaniel, Henry, 261,

McDowell, Battle of, 345

McDowell, Irwin, 30, 35, 44, 46, 62, 140, 336

McElroy, Kennon, 235

McGee, Dennis, 60

McGlashen, Peter, 265

McGill, James, 203, 208, 211, 289

McGowan, Samuel, 328, 330,

McIntosh, David, 177, 258, 261, 280, 324 326, 328

McKeen, Henry, 73, 74

McKibbin, David, 119, 120

McKibbin, Robert, 118

McKinley, William, 182, 409 (note 131)

McLaws, Lafayette, 216, 217, 218, 231, 383, 396 (note 154), 416 (notes 54, 62), 417 (notes 76, 102, 103); before Harpers Ferry, 219, 220, 223, 227, 235, 373, 375; Harpers Ferry, 224, 225, 239, 240, 242, 245, 249, 281, 282, 306; South Mountain, 128, 129, 140, 228, 229, 243, 246, 376, 377; Antietam, 70. 86, 196, 202, 210, 221, 222, 226, 232, 233, 238, 251, 288, 308, 316, 339, 342, 393 (note 110)

McLemore, O.K., 298,

McLoughlin, George, 122

McMaster, F.W., 156, 303, 304

McMichael, Richards, 81

McNeil, Hugh, 58, 60, 295

McRae, Duncan, 364, 436 (note 59); South Mountain; 361, 362, 365, 366; Antietam, 106, 199, 202, 297, 301, 351, 363, 364

McReynolds, Andrew, 213, 439 (note 37)

Meade, George, and his division, 26, 55, 62, 65, 66, 389 (note 173), 390 (note 183); South Mountain, 31, 34, 45, 47, 52, 58, 59, 63, 67, 302, 356; preliminary actions at Antietam, 27, 53, 56, 295, 310, 370; Antietam, 38, 57, 60, 64, 68, 70, 190, 195, 198, 296, 297, 300, 351, 353

Meagher, Thomas, and his brigade, 76, 77, 102, 152; to the Sunken Road, 71, 72, 78, 101, 253; the Sunken Road, 74, 79, 81, 145, 244, 249, 255, 436 (note 52); after the battle, 80

Means, Robert, 63, 390 (note 178)

Means, S.C., 381

Mechanicsville, Battle of, 57, 62, 66, 319, 324, 331, 336, 346

Mechanicsville, MD, 47, 50

Medill, William, 376

Mell, Benjamin, 228

Mercerville, PA, 49

Merriman, George, 176, 408 (note 109)

482

Trinity College, 30

Turner, Ike, 297

Turner's Gap

Turney, Peter, 331, 332, 333, 432 (note 44)

Twiggs, Hansford, 156, 279

Tyler, Lyndford, 92

Tyndale, Hector, and his brigade, 190, 201, 202, 203, 204, 205, 206, 207, 208, 285, 371, 413 (note 83), 416 (note 57)

U.S. Units: *Infantry: 1st,* 120, 400 (note 74); *2nd,* 122, 400 (note 74), 401 (note 90); *3rd,* 115, 117, 118, 1119, 120; *4th,* 32, 116, 117, 118, 120, 121, 122, 371, 400 (notes 47, 52); *6th,* 120, 121, 123, 400 (note 74); *10th,* 120, 121, 122, 123, 400 (notes 47, 62, 73, 74); *1-11th,* 120, 121, 123, 143; *12th,* 117, 127, 327, 400 (notes 45, 47); *1-12th,* 118, 401 (note 80); *2-12th,* 117, 119, 400 (note 51); *14th,* 117, 119, 400 (note 47); *1-14th,* 119, *2-14th,* 117, 119; *17th,* 120, 123; *1-17th,* 120; *Sharpshooters, 2nd,* 30, 32, 33, 43, 348, 385 (note 27); *Cavalry: 1st,* 69, 83, 212, 372, 373, 375, *2nd,* 211, 301; *5th, 6th,* 213, 214, 381, 382, *Artillery: Benjamin's* 148, 150, 151, 160, 180; *Campbell's,* 40, 41, 42, 234, 296, 348; *Chapin's,* 381; *Clark's,* 159, 169, 171, 172, 173; *Graham's,* 73, 82, 118; *Muhlenberg's,* 163; *Randol's,* 116, 125, 401 (note 80); *Ransom's,* 65, 199, 297, 300, 341, 354, 371, *Thomas,'* 144, *Tidball's,* 214, 215, 279, 400 (note 60), 401 (note 80), *Van Reed's,* 116, 118, *Weed's,* 116, 279, 400 (note 79); *Williston's,* 145, *Woodruff's,* 83

Upper Bridge, 380; crossing by I Corps, 27, 42, 45, 48, 53, 56, 59, 67, 370; crossing by II Corps, 70, 72, 73, 97; crossing by VI Corps, 139; crossing by XII Corps, 189, 192, 204, 207

Upton, Emery, 145, 404 (note 89)

Upton Hill, VA, 31, 34

Urbana, MD, 69, 97, 115, 125, 132, 134, 236, 373, 375, 378, 381, 418 (note 109)

Utica, NY, 150, 77

Vance, Duncan, 121

Vance, Zebulon, 426 (note 39)

Vautier, John, 50, 51

Vegesack, Ernest, 145, 404 (note 88)

Vermont Units: *Infantry: 2nd,* 142; *3rd,* 140; *4th,* 140; *5th,* 142; *6th,* 142

Virginia Units: *Infantry: 1st,* 257, 259, 271, 272, 273; *1st Virginia Battalion,* 342; *2nd,* 132, 135, 246, 251, 340, 381; *3rd,* 252, 253, *4th,* 317, 340; *5th,* 340, 341; *6th,* 135, 138, 245, 246, 247, 256, 278; *7th,* 173, 271, 272, 331, 340, 380, 381, 423 (notes 70, 74); *8th,* 268, 269, 270, *9th,* 250, 251; *10th,* 344, 345, 433 (note 31); *11th,* 271, 272, 273, 359; *12th,* 132, 135, 245, 246, 247; *13th,* 88, 96, 234, 313, 314, 317, 323; *14th,* 250; *15th,* 231, 233, 234, 417 (notes 99, 101); *16th,* 132, 245, 246; *17th,* 271, 272, 273; *18th,* 268, 270; *19th,* 32, 268, 269, 270; *21st,* 306, 362, 343, 344; *22nd Batt.,* 330; *23rd,* 344, 345, 433 (note 31); *24th,* 271, 272, 273, 274, 423 (note 74); *25th,* 313, 315; *27th,* 340; *28th,* 268, 269, 270; *31st,* 313, 315; *32nd,* 231, 232, 233, 234, 294 (note 113), 417 (notes 83, 93, 101); *33rd,* 337, 340; *40th,* 330, 331; *41st,* 231, 245, 246, 420 (note 25); *42nd,* 342, 344; *47th,* 330, 331; *48th,* 342, 343, 344, *49th,* 308, 313, 314, 315, *55th,* 330; *56th,* 268, 269, 270; *57th,* 250; *58th,* 3113, 316 *60th,* 346; *Cavalry: 1st,* 372, 377, 378, 380; *2nd,* 380, 381, 382, 383; *3rd,* 377, 379; *4th,* 377, 379; *5th,* 361, 377, 378, 379, 380; *6th,* 439 (note 45); *7th,* 212, 383; *8th Batt.,* 375; *9th,* 60, 212, 277, 378, 379, 380, 439 (note 43); *10th,* 374, 375, 377; *12th,* 212, 213, 214, 380, 381, 382, 383, 439 (note 47) *17th Batt.* 380, 381; *Artillery: Branch's,* 287; *Chew's,* 135, 373, 376, 381, *French's,* 284; *Hart's,* 375, 376; *Pegram's,* 328; *Poague's,* 42, 340, 341

Wadsworth, James, 30, 31, 35, 387 (note 94)

Wainwright, Charles, 124

Wainwright, William, 29, 33, 34, 35

Waldhauer, David, 375

Walker, Francis, 69

Walker, James, and his brigade, 306, 307, 308, 317, 430 (note 41); Harpers Ferry, 3113; initial action at Antietam, 45, 48, 49, 56, 61, 293, 295, 311, 318, 424 (notes 78, 79); retreat, 51, 319, 322

Walker, John, and his division, 216, 217, 218, 280, 282, 283, 284, 287, 290, 425 (notes 3, 4, 25); Harpers Ferry, 220, 223, 225, 237, 281; Antietam, 192, 210, 251, 285, 288, 306, 339, 353

Walker, Joseph, and his brigade, 257, 274, 275; South Mountain, 34, 379; Antietam, 154, 156, 157, 258, 276

Walker, Richard, 253

Wallace, William, 86

Walton, James, 118

# CONTRIBUTORS

**Claire Affinito:** Claire serves as an education intern at Antietam National Battlefield and has volunteered and worked at the park since 2018. She graduated from Shepherd University in 2019 with a bachelor's degree in history and in 2020 with a second bachelor's degree in Secondary Social Studies Education. Claire is currently enrolled in the history graduate program at Boston University.

**Brian S. Baracz:** Brian has been a park ranger at Antietam National Battlefield since 2000. He grew up in Cleveland, Ohio and currently lives in Frederick, Maryland. Brian received his degree in History from UMBC.

**Matthew Borders:** Matt is a Park Ranger at Monocacy National Battlefield with a BA from Michigan State University and MS from Eastern Michigan University. He has worked for the American Battlefield Protection Program and Antietam National Battlefield. Matt is a Certified Antietam Battlefield Guide. He received the *Save Historic Antietam Foundation's* Dr. Joseph Harsh Award and has written two books on Union soldiers during the Maryland Campaign.

**Mac Bryan:** Mac graduated from Shepherd College (Business Administration) and started his professional career at the News Division of the American Broadcasting Company. He retired as the Chief Financial Officer of a national trade association. Following retirement, Mac renewed his study of American history focusing on the Civil War, primarily, the Battle of Antietam. Mac is currently a volunteer and Ambassador at Antietam and a Certified Antietam Battlefield Guide.

**James M. Buchanan:** Jim received his BA and MA (History) from University of Maryland, and an MA in teaching from Antioch University. He was also a teacher in the D.C. Public Schools and Emerson College Preparatory School. He served as Associate editor of the Documentary History of the Supreme Court, 1789-1800; Program Director, National Institute for Citizen Education in the Law; Education Specialist, Federal Judicial Center; and is a volunteer and Certified Antietam Guide.

**Lucas I. Cade:** Lucas Cade is a lifelong student of history. Earning a Bachelors degree in History and Education from Troy State University and a Masters degree in Economic Development from the University of Southern Mississippi, he has combined history and business for his entire career. A Certified Battlefield Guide at Antietam National Battlefield, Mr. Cade lives in Hagerstown, Maryland.

**Jason Campbell:** Jason graduated from Hagerstown Community College and Hood College. He worked in retail for 16-years and became a park volunteer at Antietam National Battlefield. The latter experience was followed by becoming a Certified Antietam Battlefield Guide and then a seasonal park ranger for the National Park Service. He is currently a permanent park ranger working in Washington D.C. on the National Mall and Memorial Parks.

**Thomas G. Clemens:** After earning a doctorate from George Mason University, where he studied under Dr. Joseph L. Harsh, Tom taught for years at Hagerstown Community College, retiring as *Professor Emeritus*. He edited and annotated Ezra A. Carman's narrative of the *Maryland Campaign of September 1862,* which has received several awards. Tom is the founding member and current president of Save Historic Antietam Foundation Inc., a non-profit battlefield preservation organization, and an Antietam Battlefield Guide.

**Bradley M. Gottfried:** After receiving his Ph.D. in Zoology from Miami University in 1976, Brad went on to a successful 40-year career in higher education, retiring in 2017 as the president of the College of Southern Maryland. He has written 14 books on the Civil War, including the *Maps of Antietam* and the *Brigades of Gettysburg* and became a Certified Antietam Certified Guide in 2019.

**Robert Gottschalk:** Bob's interest in the Civil War spans 60 years. A native of Philadelphia, he graduated from West Chester University (History) and was a temporary ranger at Antietam during the 125th anniversary year. Bob continued providing interpretive programs at Antietam and a variety of other historic sites. He has been working on a compilation of the armies between July 1862 and January 1863 for the past 13 years. Bob currently lives near Indianapolis.

**Laura Marfut:** Laura is a retired U.S. Army colonel with master degrees in International Relations and Education, and a Master of Strategic Studies from the U.S. Army War College. She became a certified Antietam Battlefield Guide in 2019 and added Harpers Ferry and South Mountain credentials the following year. She volunteers for Hospice of Washington County and as an Antietam Battlefield Ambassador. She and her husband Ed live in Hagerstown, Maryland.

**Sharon A. Murray:** Sharon A. Murray is a native Idahoan with degrees in History and Mining Engineering from the University of Idaho. She volunteers at Antietam National Battlefield in multiple capacities, as a Battlefield Ambassador, a photographer, a cannoneer and in cleaning and repainting the parks historic cast iron tablets. She has been a Certified Battlefield Guide since 2014. She is currently writing a biography of Colonel Benjamin Franklin "Grimes" Davis.

**Kevin R. Pawlak:** Kevin Pawlak is a Historic Site Manager for the Prince William County Office of Historic Preservation. He has been an Antietam Battlefield Guide since 2012. Kevin graduated as a History major from Shepherd University. He is the author of five books and several articles on the American Civil War, including *To Hazard All: A Guide to the Maryland Campaign, 1862*.

**Martin Pritchett:** Born in Southern Kansas, Martin is a member of the Oklahoma Shawnee tribe. He grew up in a military family that took him from the Midwest to Europe. A veteran of 23 years in the United States Coast Guard and Texas General Land Office specializing in coastal search and rescue, environmental protection response, and maritime port safety. After seven years as an Antietam Battlefield Ambassador, Martin became a Certified Antietam Battlefield Guide.

**Gary W. Rohrer:** Gary was born and raised in Washington County, Maryland, where his family goes back at least 225 years. His study of the Civil War and passion for the 1862 Maryland Campaign spans more than 55 years. Gary is a NPS Certified Antietam, South Mountain and Harpers Ferry Battlefield Guide. He holds a BSCE from the University of Maryland and an MBA from Frostburg State University, and is a US Navy veteran.

**James A Rosebrock:** Jim is a retired Army officer and Department of Justice employee. He is a National Park Service Certified Battlefield Guide at Antietam National Battlefield and served as Chief Guide from 2011 - 2018. Jim has two Civil War-related blogs and is currently writing the companion book to *Brigades of Antietam* which will cover the Union and Confederate artillery during the Maryland Campaign.

**William Sagle:** An Antietam Battlefield guide for eleven years and the 2016 recipient of the O.T. Reilly award for outstanding performance, William began conducting programs at the battlefield in 1981. His grasp of tactics and weaponry was noticed and encouraged by NPS Rangers and developed into unique viewpoints on the battle. As a guide, William conducted tours for groups ranging from military professionals to those of a more casual interest in the specifics of Antietam.

**J. O. Smith:** A native of Miami, Florida, J.O. Smith has been a volunteer at Antietam National Battlefield since 2017 and a certified battlefield guide since 2018. He has a master's degree in history from the University of Georgia and undergraduate and law degrees from Duke University. He is an attorney and lives with his family near Annapolis, Maryland.

**Joseph Stahl:** In retirement, Joe became a volunteer and NPS Licensed Battlefield Guide at Antietam and Harpers Ferry. He grew up in St. Louis where he received BS and MS degrees from Missouri University of Science and Technology and an MBA from Washington University in St. Louis. Joe has coauthored 3 books and more than two dozen articles.

**Steven R. Stotelmyer:** After growing up in Hagerstown, Maryland, Steve served in the US Navy and then earned a Bachelor of Science degree from Frostburg State College and a Master of Arts from Hood College. He has worked as a teacher, surveyor and civil engineer. Steve is the author of *The Bivouacs of the Dead* and *Too Useful To Sacrifice*. Steve is a NPS Volunteer and a Certified Antietam Battlefield and South Mountain Tour Guide.

www.ingramcontent.com/pod-product-compliance
Lightning Source LLC
Chambersburg PA
CBHW062018090426
42811CB00005B/892